DTMF	Dual-tone multiple frequency		IA5	International alphabet number five
DVA	Distance vector algorithm		IANA	Internet Assigned Numbers Authority
DVB	Digital video broadcast		ICMP	Internet control message protocol
DVB-S/T	DVB-satellite/terrestrial		IDCT	Inverse DCT
DVD	Digital versatile disk		IDEA	International data encryption algorithm
DVMRP	Distance vector MRP		IDFT	Inverse DFT
			IDSL	ISDN-DSL
EBCDIC	Extended binary coded decimal interchange code		IEE	Institution of Electrical Engineers
ECB	Electronic code book/Event control block		IEEE	Institute of Electrical and Electronics Engineers
ED	End delimiter		IETF	Internet Engineering Task Force
EF	Expedited forwarding		IGE	International gateway exchange
EGP	Exterior gateway protocol		IGMP	Internet group management protocol
EIA	Electrical Industries Association		IGP	Interior gateway protocol
EOM	End of message		INIC	Internet Network Information Center
EOS	End of stream		IP	Internet protocol
ES	End system		IS	Intermediate system/Integrated services
			ISDN	Integrated services digital network
FCS	Frame check sequence		ISI	Intersymbol interference
FDD	Frequency division duplex		ISO	International Standards Organization
FDDI	Fiber distributed data interface		ISP	Internet service provider
FDM	Frequency-division multiplexing		ITU-T	International Telecommunications Union – Telecommunications (Sector)
FIFO	First-in, first-out			
FM	Frequency modulation		IWU	Interworking unit
FN	Fiber node		IXC	Interexchange carrier
FQDN	Fully-qualified DN			
FRA	Frame relay adapter		JPEG	Joint photographic experts group
FSK	Frequency-shift keying			
FTP	File transfer protocol		LAN	Local area network
FTTB	Fiber-to-the-building		LAPB	Link access procedure, balanced
FTTH	Fiber-to-the-home		LAPM	Link access procedure modems
FTTK/C	Fiber-to-the-kurb/curb		LCN	Logical channel number
FTTcab	Fiber-to-the-cabinet		LE	LAN emulation
			LEC	LE client
GA	Grand Alliance		LECS	LE configuration server
GB	Guard-band		LED	Light-emitting doide
GEO	Geostationary/geosynchronous earth orbit		LEP	LE protocol
GIF	Graphics interchange format		LES	LE server
GLP	Gateway location protocol		LGN	Logical group number
GOB	Group of blocks		LL	Link layer
GOP	Group of pictures		LLC	Logical link control
GSTN	General switched telephone network		LMDS	Local MDS
GW	Gateway		LNB/C	Low noise block/converter
			LPC	Linear predictive coding
HDB3	High density bipolar 3		LS	Link state
HDLC	High-level data link contol		LWE	Lower window edge
HDSL	High-speed DSL		LXC	Local exchange carrier
HDTV	High-definition television		LZ	Lempel–Ziv
HE	Headend		LZW	Lempel–Ziv–Welsh
HEC	Header checksum			
HFC	Hybrid fiber coax		MA	Multiple access
HTML	HyperText markup language		MAC	Medium access control
HTTP	HyperText transfer protocol		MAN	Metropolitan area network
HTTPD	HTTP daemon			

Continued on inside back cover

multimedia communications

Pearson Education

We work with leading authors to develop the strongest educational materials in Multimedia Communications, bringing cutting edge thinking and best learning practice to a global market.

Under a range of well-known imprints, including Addison Wesley, we craft high quality print and electronic publications which help readers to understand and apply their content, whether studying or at work.

To find out about the complete range of our publishing please visit us on the World Wide Web at:

www.pearsoneduc.com

multimedia communications

Applications, Networks, Protocols and Standards

fred halsall

ADDISON-WESLEY

An imprint of **Pearson Education**

Harlow, England · London · New York · Reading, Massachusetts · San Francisco · Toronto · Don Mills, Ontario · Sydney
Tokyo · Singapore · Hong Kong · Seoul · Taipei · Cape Town · Madrid · Mexico City · Amsterdam · Munich · Paris · Milan

Pearson Education Limited
Edinburgh Gate
Harlow
Essex CM20 2JE
England

and Associated Companies throughout the World.

Visit us on the World Wide Web at:
www.pearsoneduc.com

First published 2001

© Pearson Education Limited 2001

ISBN 0-201-39818-4

British Library Cataloguing-in-Publication Data
A catalogue record for this book can be obtained from the British Library.

Library of Congress Cataloging-in-Publication Data
A catalog record for this book can be obtained from the Library of Congress.

10 9 8 7 6 5 4 3 2 1
05 04 03 02 01 00

Typeset by 30 in New Baskerville 10/12pt
Printed and bound in the United States of America

short contents

contents

preface

Objectives

Multimedia communications embraces a range of applications and networking infrastructures. The term multimedia is used to indicate that the information/data relating to an application may be composed of a number of different types of media which are integrated together in some way. The different media types are text, images, speech, audio and video and some example applications are video telephony (speech and video), multimedia electronic mail (text, images and audio for example), interactive television (text, audio and video), electronic commerce (text, images, audio and video), Web TV (text, audio and video) and many others.

In practice, there are a number of different types of network that are used to provide the networking infrastructure. These include not only networks that were designed from the outset to provide multimedia communication services – normally referred to as broadband multiservice networks – but also networks that were designed initially to provide just a single type of service and it is as a result of advances in various technologies that these can now support a range of other (multimedia) services. For example, public (and private) switched telephone networks (PSTNs) were designed initially to provide a basic telephony service but they are now used to support a range of more advanced multimedia applications involving all of the different media types. Similarly, computer networks such as the Internet, which were designed initially to provide general data communication services such as electronic mail and file transfers, can now support a much richer set of multimedia applications.

In terms of the different types of media, text and images are generated and represented in a digital form. Speech, audio and video, however, are generated in the form of continuously varying – normally referred to as analog - signals. Hence in order to integrate all of the different media types together, it is necessary to first convert the various analog signals into a digital form. The integrated digital information stream can then be stored within a computer and transmitted over a network in a unified way. In addition, unlike text and images which are created in the form of a single block of digital information, since speech, audio and video are continuously varying signals, the digitization process can produce large volumes of information which carries on increasing with time. Hence in most multimedia applications, in order to reduce the volume of information to be transferred, a range of compression algorithms are applied to the different media types prior to integrating them together.

In addition to the compression algorithms that have been used for many years with text and images, there is now available a wide range of algorithms for the compression of speech, audio and video. Until recently, however, because of the relatively low levels of compression that could be achieved, multimedia applications involving speech, audio and video – video telephony and video conferencing for example – required a high-capacity transmission channel to transmit the integrated source information. The rapid advances that have taken place in the field of compression over the past few years, however, mean that the capacity of the transmission channel required has reduced to the point that most types of communication network can now support a range of multimedia applications.

In addition, it is as a result of the same advances in compression algorithms, coupled with the development of the associated integrated circuits, that most television broadcasts are now in a digital form. A major issue in relation to analog television has always been the high level of transmission capacity that is required to broadcast the composite television signal containing the integrated audio and video signals. The move to (compressed) digital means that a transmission channel that was once used to broadcast a single (analog) television program can now be used to broadcast multiple (digital) programs. Moreover, the use of digital transmission means that other digital services can use the same channels so enabling multimedia applications such as interactive television and electronic commerce to be supported.

As we can conclude from this brief overview, the subject of multimedia communications involves a wide range of different subject areas. These include how the different media types are represented in their digital form, the range of compression algorithms that are used with these media types, the communication requirements of the different types of multimedia applications, the operation of the different types of communication networks that are used, the communication protocols associated with these networks and how they have been extended to meet the more demanding requirements of multimedia applications.

In addition, as with all applications that involve the use of a communication network, it is imperative that the two (or more) items of equipment that are attached to the network to provide the service, operate and interpret the transmitted information in the same way. This can only be achieved by the adoption of international standards for all applications and for all of the different types of network. Also their adoption by all the manufacturers of the related equipment. Hence an understanding of the range of standards that have been developed for use with all aspects of multimedia communications is also an important subject area. This book addresses all of these subject areas to a depth that enables the reader to build up a thorough understanding of the technical issues associated with mulimedia communications.

Intended readership

The book has been written primarily as a course textbook for both university and college students studying courses relating to the technical issues associated with multimedia communications. Typically, the students will be studying in a computer science, computer systems, computer engineering or electronic engineering department/school. In addition, it is suitable for computer professionals and engineers who wish to build up a working knowledge of this rapidly evolving subject. At one extreme this requires the reader to understand the techniques that are used to transmit a digital bitstream over the different types of transmission media such as copper wire, coaxial cable, radio and optical fiber. At the other extreme it requires an understanding of the software that is used in the different types of equipment – multimedia PCs and workstations, set-top boxes etc. – that are used to support multimedia applications. The first is the domain of the electronics engineer and the second the computer scientist. The book, however, is suitable for use with courses for both types of student since care has been taken to ensure that the level of detail required in each subject area is understandable by both categories of reader.

In order to achieve this goal, a chapter has been included which describes how the different types of media are represented and, associated with this, how analog signals are converted into a digital form. Also the principle of operation of television broadcasting and computer displays. In addition, a chapter that covers the basic techniques that are used to achieve the reliable transfer of a block/stream of digital information over a transmission channel. These include the essential theory that determines the rate at which data can be transmitted over a cannel. Also, the different methods that are used to detect the presence of transmission errors – bit corruptions – in a received block/stream of information and the procedures that are followed when this occurs. The latter form what is called a communications protocol. Hence this chapter also includes an introduction to the subject of protocols to give the reader who has no previous knowledge of this subject the necessary foundation for the later chapters that describe the operation of the different types of network that support multimedia applications.

9.1 Intended usage

To the instructor

As we can see from the list of contents of the book, the book covers a wide range of subject areas each of which is to a depth that makes it interesting and academically challenging. As a result, the book can be used with many different courses relating to multimedia applications and networks. Ideally, in order to obtain a comprehensive understanding of the subject, a set of courses should be involved which collectively cover the total contents of the book from principles through to details of compression algorithms, applications, networks and protocols. Alternatively, one or two courses could be involved covering a subset of these subject areas. For example, a course may cover the subject areas of multimedia applications, multimedia information representation and the different types of compression algorithms that are used. Another may cover the basics of digital communications and an overview of the operation of the different types of network that are used. Alternatively, a pair of courses covering the detail operation of the Internet and its protocols and the World Wide Web.

As indicated earlier, all of the subject areas are covered to a depth that enables the reader to build up an in-depth technical understanding of the subject of multimedia communications. Hence because of the technical nature of the subject, to help the reader to understand each topic within an area, either a worked example or a relatively detailed diagram is used to illustrate the concepts involved. This is considered to be one of the main advantages of the book owing to the technical detail associated with many of the topics covered. Also, both the examples and diagrams are seen as being particularly useful for instructors as they can be used directly for lectures. To facilitate this, therefore, both the worked examples and all the diagrams are available to instructors in their electronic form so reducing considerably the time required to prepare a set of lectures for a course. These can be downloaded from **www.booksites.net/halsall**. In addition, each chapter has a comprehensive set of exercises which have been structured to help the student to revise the topics covered in each chapter in a systemmatic way. Any errors that are found in the text or figures can be reported to me using the email address **halsall@pearsoned-ema.com**.

To the student

The book has been structured to be used for self-study. Worked examples are included in most chapters and, to aid understanding of all the topics that are covered, associated with each topic is a relatively detailed diagram which illustrates the concepts involved. These you should find particularly useful since they facilitate understanding the many technical details associated with many of the techniques that are used. In addition, the comprehensive set of exercises at the end of each chapter have been structured to help you to test your knowledge and understanding of each of the topics covered in a chapter in a systematic way.

acknowledgments

I should like to take this opportunity to thank various people for their help during the period I was preparing the manuscript. Firstly my postgraduate students and research assistants for their help with obtaining numerous papers and documents relating to multimedia and, in particular, Dr Jurek Wechta for guiding the group and generally keeping the ship afloat in my absence. Also my secretary Irene Dendle for her help in preparing the manuscript and fielding the day-to-day queries relating to my taught masters program. Finally my wife Rhiannon for her unwavering support, patience, and understanding while I was writing the book. It is to her that I dedicate the book.

Fred Halsall
September 2000

A Companion Web Site accompanies

MULTIMEDIA COMMUNICATIONS

by Fred Halsall

Visit the *Multimedia Communications* Companion Web Site at
www.booksites.net/halsall
to find valuable teaching and learning material including:

For Students:
- Study material designed to help you improve student results
- Chapter-by-chapter summaries
- Web links for key multimedia and data communications web sites organised by chapter
- Recommended key readings

For Lecturers:
- A secure, password protected site with teaching material
- Downloadable worked examples and diagrams for use in lectures and seminars
- Chapter summaries
- Case notes, points to stress, and teaching tips highlighted for each chapter

Also: This is a regularly maintained and updated site.

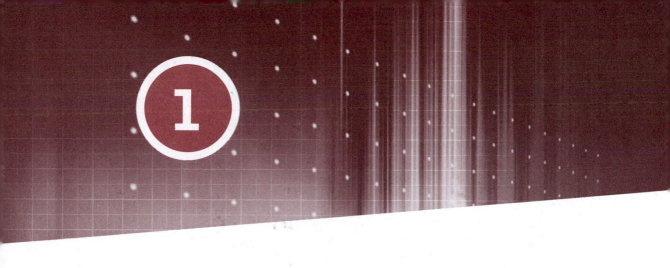

multimedia communications

1.1 Introduction

Within the context of this book, multimedia communications embraces a range of applications and networking infrastructures. The term "**multimedia**" is used to indicate that the information/data being transferred over the network may be composed of one or more of the following media types:

- **text:** this includes both unformatted text, comprising strings of characters from a limited character set, and formatted text strings as used for the structuring, access, and presentation of electronic documents;
- **images:** these include computer-generated images, comprising lines, curves, and circles, and digitized images of documents and pictures;
- **audio:** this includes both low-fidelity speech, as used in telephony, and high-fidelity stereophonic music as used with compact discs;
- **video:** this includes short sequences of moving images (also known as video clips) and complete movies/films.

The applications may involve either person-to-person communications or person-to-system communications. In general, two people communicate with each other through suitable **terminal equipment (TE)** while a person interacts with a system using either a **multimedia personal computer** (**PC**) or **workstation**. Typically, these are located either in the home or on a desktop in an office and the system is a **server** containing a collection of files or documents each comprising digitized text, images, audio, and video information either singly or integrated together in some way. Alternatively, the server may contain a library of digitized movies/videos and the user interacts with the server by means of a suitable selection device that is connected to the **set-top box** (**STB**) associated with a television.

In practice, there are a number of different types of network that are used to provide the networking infrastructure. These include not only networks that were designed from the outset to provide multimedia communication services but also networks that were designed initially to provide just a single type of service and it is as a result of advances in various technologies that these can now provide a range of other services. For example, **public switched telephone networks** (**PSTNs**) – also known as **general switched telephone networks** (**GSTNs**) – were designed initially to provide a basic switched telephone service but, as a result of advances in digital signal processing hardware and associated software, they now provide a range of more advanced services involving text, images, and video. Similarly, data networks that were designed initially to support basic data applications such as electronic mail and file transfers, now support a much richer set of applications that involve images, audio, and video.

In this chapter we shall present an overview of, firstly, how the different media types are represented, secondly, the different types of network that are used to provide multimedia communication services, and thirdly, a selection of the applications that these networks support. Finally, we describe the meaning of a range of terms that are associated with multimedia communications.

1.2 Multimedia information representation

Applications involving text and images comprise **blocks** of digital data. In the case of text, for example, a typical unit is a block of characters with each character represented by a fixed number of **binary digits** (**bits**) known as a **codeword**. Similarly, a digitized image comprises a two-dimensional block of what are called **picture elements** with each element represented by a fixed number of bits. Also, since a typical application involving text and images comprises a short request for some information – a file, for example – and the file contents being returned, the duration of the overall transaction is relatively short.

In applications involving audio and video, however, the audio and video signals vary continuously with time as the amplitude of the speech, audio, or video signal varies. This type of signal is known as an **analog signal** and, typically, the duration of applications that involve audio and/or video can be relatively long. A typical telephone conversation, for example, can last for several minutes while a movie (comprising audio and video) can last for a number of hours.

In applications that involve just a single type of media, the basic form of representation of the particular media type is often used. Similarly, in applications that involve either text-and-images or audio-and-video their basic form is often used since the two media types in these applications have the same form of representation. However, in applications that involve the different media types integrated together in some way, it becomes necessary to represent all four media types in a digital form. In the case of text and images, this is their standard form of representation. For audio and video, however, because their basic forms of representation are analog signals, these must be converted into a corresponding digital form before they can be integrated with the two other media types.

As we shall describe in the next chapter, the digitization of an audio signal produces a digital signal which, because the amplitude of the signal varies continuously with time, is of a relatively high bit rate. This is measured in **bits per second** (**bps**) and, in the case of a speech signal, for example, a typical bit rate is 64 kbps. Moreover, because applications involving audio can be of a long duration, this bit rate must be sustained over an equally long time period. The same applies to the digitization of a video signal except that much higher bit rates and longer time durations are involved. In general, however, as we shall expand upon in the next section, the communication networks that are used to support applications that involve audio and video cannot support the very high bit rates that are required for representing these media types in a digital form. As a result, a technique known as **compression** is first applied to the digitized signals in order to reduce the resulting bit rate to a level which the various networks can support. Compression is also applied to text and images in order to reduce the time delay between a request being made for some information and the information becoming available on, say, the screen of a computer. We shall describe a selection of the compression algorithms that are used with text and images in Chapter 3 and those used with audio and video in Chapter 4.

1.3 Multimedia networks

There are five basic types of communication network that are used to provide multimedia communication services:

- telephone networks,
- data networks,
- broadcast television networks,
- integrated services digital networks,
- broadband multiservice networks.

As the names imply, the first three network types were initially designed to provide just a single type of service: telephony, data communications, and broadcast television respectively. The last two network types, however, were designed from the outset to provide multiple services. We shall describe the essential features of each type of network separately and, in the case of the first three network types, the technological developments that have enabled them to provide additional services.

1.3.1 Telephone networks

Public switched telephone networks have been in existence for many years and have gone through many changes during this time. They were designed to provide a basic switched telephone service which, with the advent of the other network types, has become known as a **plain old telephone service** or **POTS**. The term "switched" is used to indicate that a subscriber can make a call to any other telephone that is connected to the total network. Initially, such networks spanned just a single country but later the telephone networks of different countries were interconnected so that they now provide an international switched service. The main components of the network are shown in diagrammatic form in Figure 1.1(a).

As we can see, telephones located in the home or in a small business are connected directly to their nearest **local exchange/end office**. Those located in a medium or large office/site are connected to a private switching office known as a **private branch exchange** or **PBX**. The PBX provides a (free) switched service between any two telephones that are connected to it. In addition, the PBX is connected to its nearest local (public) exchange which enables the telephones that are connected to the PBX also to make calls through a PSTN. More recently, **cellular phone networks** have been introduced which provide a similar service to mobile subscribers by means of handsets that are linked to the cellular phone network infrastructure by radio. The switches used in a cellular phone network are known as **mobile switching centers** (**MSCs**) and these, like a PBX, are also connected to a switching office in a PSTN which enables both sets of subscribers to make calls to one another. Finally, international calls are routed to and switched by **international gateway exchanges** (**IGEs**).

As we indicated earlier, a speech signal is an analog signal since it varies continuously with time according to the amplitude and frequency variations of the sound resulting from the speech. A microphone is used to convert this into an analog electrical signal. Because of this, telephone networks operate in what is called a **circuit mode** which means that, for each call, a separate circuit is set up through the network – of the necessary capacity – for the duration of the call. The **access circuits** that link the telephone handsets to a PSTN or PBX were designed, therefore, to carry the two-way analog signals associated with a call. Hence, although within a PSTN all the switches and the transmission circuits that interconnect them now operate in a **digital mode**,

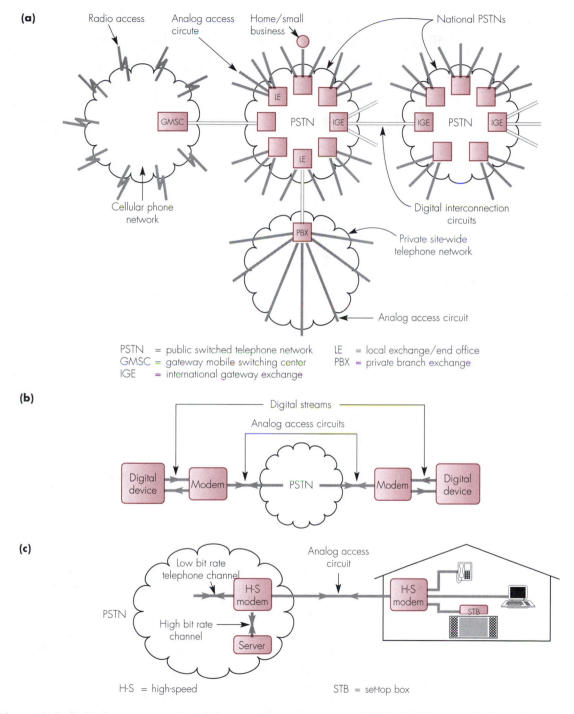

Figure 1.1 Telephone networks: (a) network components; (b) digital transmission using modems; (c) multiple services via an H-S modem.

to carry a digital signal – a stream of binary 1s and 0s – over the analog access circuits requires a device known as a **modem**. The general scheme is shown in Figure 1.1(b).

Essentially, at the sending side, the modem converts the digital signal output by the source digital device into an analog signal that is compatible with a normal speech signal. This is routed through the network in the same way as a speech signal and, at the receiving side, the modem converts the analog signal back again into its digital form before relaying this to the destination digital device. Modems also have the necessary circuits to set up and terminate a call. Hence by using a pair of modems – one at each subscriber access point – a PSTN can also be used to provide a switched digital service. The early modems supported only a very low bit rate service of 300 bps but, as a result of advances in digital signal processing circuits, modems are now available that support bit rates of up to 56 kbps. As we shall expand upon in Chapter 4, this is sufficient to support, not only applications that comprise text and images integrated together, but also services that comprise speech and low-resolution video.

In addition, continuing advances in digital signal processing techniques mean that modems are now available for use with the same access circuits that provide a high bit rate channel which is in addition to the speech channel used for telephony. Typically, the bit rate of this second channel is such that it can support high-resolution audio and video and hence they are used to provide access to servers that support a range of entertainment-related applications. The general scheme is shown in Figure 1.1(c) and, as we shall see in Chapter 4, such applications require bit rates in excess of 1.5 Mbps. This illustrates the technological advances that have been made in this area since the early modems were introduced in the early 1960s and, as we can deduce from this, a PSTN can now support not only speech applications but also a wide range of other multimedia communication applications.

1.3.2 Data networks

Data networks were designed to provide basic data communication services such as **electronic mail** (**email**) and general file transfers. The user equipment connected to these networks, therefore, is a computer such as a PC, a workstation, or an email/file server. The two most widely deployed networks of this type are the **X.25 network** and the **Internet**. Because of its operational mode, however, the X.25 network is restricted to relatively low bit rate data applications and hence is unsuitable for most multimedia applications.

The Internet is made up of a vast collection of interconnected networks all of which operate using the same set of **communication protocols**. A communication protocol is an agreed set of rules that are adhered to by all communicating parties for the exchange of information. The rules define not only the sequence of messages that are exchanged between the communicating parties but also the syntax of these messages. Hence by using the same set of communication protocols, all the computers that are connected to the Internet can communicate freely with each other irrespective of their type or manufacturer. This is also the origin of the term "**open systems interconnection**". Figure 1.2 shows a selection of the different types of interconnected network.

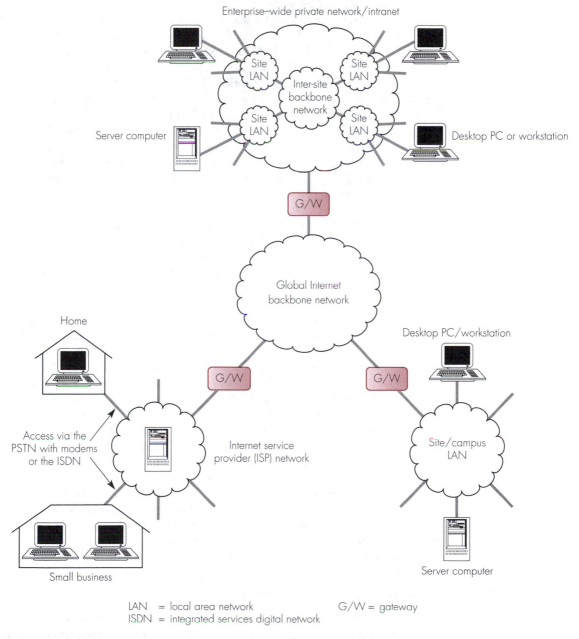

Figure 1.2 A selection of the network types connected to the Internet.

As we can see, in the case of a user at home or in a small business, access to the Internet is through an intermediate **Internet service provider (ISP) network**. Normally, since this type of user wants access to the Internet intermittently, the user devices are connected to the ISP network either through a PSTN with modems or through an **integrated services digital network (ISDN)** which, as we shall explain in Section 1.3.4, provides access at a higher bit rate. Alternatively, business users obtain access either through a **site/campus network** if the business comprises only a single site or, if it comprises multiple sites, through an **enterprise-wide private network**. The same approach is used by most colleges and universities. In the case of a single site/campus, the network is known as a (private) **local area network** or **LAN**. For an enterprise-wide network comprising multiple sites the sites are interconnected together using an **inter-site backbone network** to provide a set of enterprise-wide communication services. In addition, providing the communication protocols used by all the computers connected to the network are the same as those defined for use with the Internet, then all the users also have access to the range of services provided by the Internet. The enterprise network is then known as an **intranet** since all internal services are provided using the same set of communication protocols as those defined for the Internet. The different types of network are all connected to the **Internet backbone network** through an interworking unit called a **gateway** which, because it is responsible for routing and relaying all messages to and from the connected network, is also known as a **router**.

All data networks operate in what is called a **packet mode**. Essentially, a **packet** is a container for a block of data and, at its head, is the address of the intended recipient computer which is used to route the packet through the network. This mode of operation was chosen since the format of the data associated with data applications is normally in the form of discrete blocks of text or binary data with varying time intervals between each block. More recently, however, multimedia PCs have become available that support a range of other applications. For example, with the addition of a microphone and a pair of speakers – together with a sound card and associated software to digitize the speech – PCs are now used to support telephony and other speech-related applications. Similarly, with the addition of a video camera and associated hardware and software, a range of other applications involving video can be supported. Also, since their introduction, higher bit rate transmission circuits and routing nodes have become available and, as we shall expand upon in Chapters 3 and 4, more efficient algorithms to represent speech, audio, and video in a digital form. Collectively, therefore, this means that packet-mode networks – and the Internet in particular – now support not only general data communication applications but also a range of other multimedia communication applications involving speech, audio, and video.

1.3.3 Broadcast television networks

Broadcast television networks were designed to support the diffusion of analog television (and radio) programs throughout wide geographical areas. In the case of a large town or city, the broadcast medium is normally a **cable**

distribution network while for larger areas, a **satellite network** or sometimes a **terrestrial broadcast network** is used. Since their introduction, digital television services have become available with these networks which, together with a low bit rate return channel for interaction purposes, provide a range of additional services such as games playing and home shopping. The general architecture of a cable distribution network and a satellite/terrestrial broadcast network are shown in Figure 1.3(a) and (b) respectively.

As we can see in Figure 1.3(a), the set-top box attached to the cable distribution network provides not only control of the television channels that are received but also access to other services. For example, when a **cable modem**

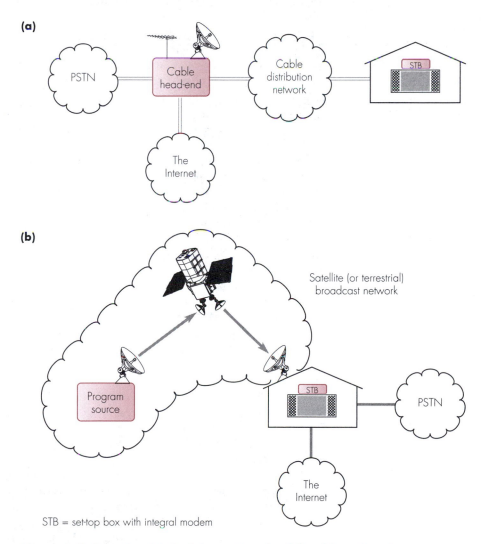

STB = set-top box with integral modem

Figure 1.3 Broadcast television networks: (a) cable networks; (b) satellite/terrestrial broadcast networks.

is integrated into the STB this provides both a low bit rate channel and a high bit rate channel from the subscriber back to the **cable head-end**. Typically, the low bit rate channel is used to connect the subscriber to a PSTN and the high bit rate channel to connect the subscriber to the Internet. Hence in addition to providing basic broadcast radio and television services, cable distribution networks also provide access to the range of multimedia communication services that are available with both a PSTN and the Internet. Similarly, as we can see in Figure 1.3(b), in the case of satellite and terrestrial broadcast networks, when a high-speed PSTN modem is integrated into the STB this provides the subscriber with an interaction channel so enhancing the range of services these networks support. This is the origin of the term "**interactive television**".

1.3.4 Integrated services digital networks

Integrated services digital networks started to be deployed in the early 1980s and were originally designed to provide PSTN users with the capability of having additional services. This was achieved firstly, by converting the access circuits that connect user equipment to the network – a telephone for example – into an all-digital form and secondly, by providing two separate communication channels over these circuits. These allow users either to have two different telephone calls in progress simultaneously or two different calls such as a telephone call and a data call. With an ISDN, therefore, the access circuit is known as a **digital subscriber line** (**DSL**).

The subscriber telephone can be either a digital phone or a conventional analog one. In the case of a digital phone, the electronics that are needed to convert the analog voice and call setup signals into a digital form are integrated into the phone handset. With an analog phone, the same electronics are located in the network termination equipment so making the digital mode of operation of the network transparent to the subscriber phone.

As we shall describe in Section 2.5.1, the digitization of a telephone-quality analog speech signal produces a constant bit rate binary stream – normally referred to as a **bitstream** – of 64 kbps. Hence, the basic DSL of the ISDN – known as the **basic rate access** or **BRA** – supports two 64 kbps channels. These can either be used independently (as they were intended) or as a single combined 128 kbps channel. Because of the design of an ISDN, however, since the two channels were intended for two different calls, this requires two separate circuits to be set up through the switching network independently. Hence to synchronize the two separate 64 kbps bitstreams into a single 128 kbps stream requires an additional box of electronics to perform, what is known as, the **aggregation** function.

In addition, a single higher bit rate channel of either 1.5 or 2 Mbps is supported. This is known as the **primary rate access** or **PRA**. Also, a more flexible way of obtaining a switched 128 kbps service has been introduced by many network operators. Indeed, the service provided has been enhanced and now supports a single switched channel of $p \times 64$ kbps where $p = 1, 2, 3... 30$. The various services provided are summarized in Figure 1.4 and, as we can deduce

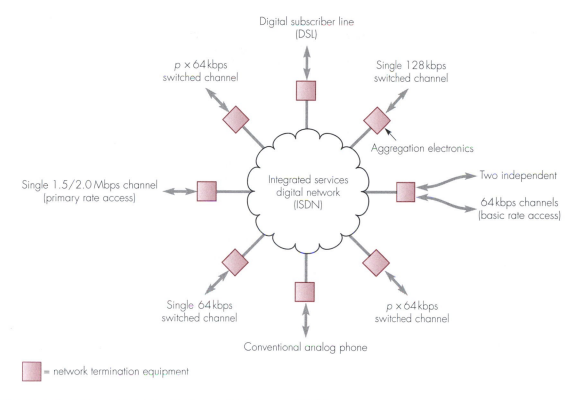

Figure 1.4 Alternative services provided by an ISDN.

from this, an ISDN can support a range of multimedia applications. It should be noted, however, that because of the relatively high cost of digitizing the access circuits, in general the cost of the services associated with an ISDN are higher than the equivalent service provided by a PSTN.

1.3.5 Broadband multiservice networks

Broadband multiservice networks were designed in the mid-1980s for use as public switched networks to support a wide range of multimedia communication applications. The term "**broadband**" was used to indicate that the circuits associated with a call could have bit rates in excess of the maximum bit rate of 2 Mbps – 30×64 kbps – provided by an ISDN. As such, they were designed to be an enhanced ISDN and hence were called **broadband integrated services digital networks** or **B-ISDN**. Also, for the same reason, an ISDN is sometimes referred to as **narrowband ISDN** or **N-ISDN**.

At the time the B-ISDN was first conceived, the technology associated with the digitization of a video signal was such that, in general, an ISDN could not support services that included video. Since that time, however, considerable advances have been made in the field of compression with the effect that not only can an ISDN now support multimedia communication applications that include video, but also so can the other three types of network that we have described. The combined effect, therefore, has been to slow down considerably the deployment of B-ISDN. However, a number of the basic design features associated with the B-ISDN have been used as the basis of other broadband multiservice networks.

For example, by definition, multiservice networks implies that the network must support multiple services. In practice, however, as we shall expand upon in the next section, different multimedia applications require different bit rates, the rate being determined by the types of media that are involved. Hence the switching and transmission methods that are used within these networks must be more flexible than those used in networks such as a PSTN or ISDN which were initially designed to provide a single type of service. To achieve this flexibility, all the different media types associated with a particular multimedia application are first converted in the source equipment into a digital form. These are then integrated together and the resulting binary stream is divided into multiple fixed-sized packets known as **cells**. In practice, this type of information stream provides a much more flexible way of both transmitting and switching the multimedia information associated with the different types of application.

For example, in terms of transmission, the cells relating to the different applications can be integrated together more flexibly. Also, the use of fixed-sized cells means that the switching of cells can be carried out much faster than if variable-length packets were used. Since the different multimedia applications generate cell streams of different rates, this mode of operation means that the rate of transfer of cells through the network also varies and hence this mode of transmission is known as the **asynchronous transfer mode** or **ATM**. Broadband multiservice networks, therefore, are also known as **ATM networks** or sometimes **cell-switching networks**. For example, there are **ATM local area networks (ATM LANs)** that span a single site and **ATM metropolitan area networks (ATM MANs)** that span a large town or city. An example of a broadband multiservice network is shown in Figure 1.5 and, as we can see, the ATM MAN is being used as a high-speed backbone network to interconnect a number of LANs distributed around a large town or city. Note also that although two of the LANs are ATM LANs, the other two are simply higher-speed versions of older data-only LANs. This is typical of ATM networks in general which must often interwork with older (legacy) networks.

1.4 Multimedia applications

There are many and varied applications that involve multiple media types. In general, however, they can be placed into one of three categories:

- interpersonal communications,
- interactive applications over the Internet,
- entertainment applications.

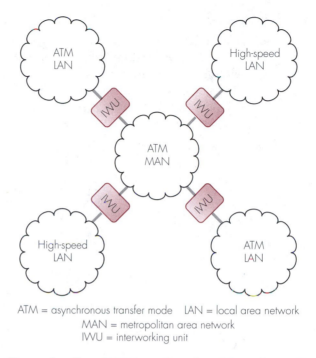

ATM = asynchronous transfer mode   LAN = local area network
MAN = metropolitan area network
IWU = interworking unit

Figure 1.5 Example of an ATM broadband multiservice network.

We shall discuss some examples from each category in the following sections. As we described in Section 1.1, however, in many instances the networks that are used to support these applications were initially designed to provide a service that involved just a single type of medium and it is as a result of advances in various related technologies that they are now used to support multimedia applications. Hence, in addition to these new services, the same networks are still used to support the basic application for which they were designed. Indeed, in some instances, the particular application supported has been enhanced. Thus, although from an applications perspective multimedia communications implies that two or more media types are involved, we shall also include selected examples of applications that these networks were designed to support even though only a single type of medium is involved.

1.4.1 Interpersonal communications

Interpersonal communications may involve speech, image, text, or video. In some cases just a single type of medium is involved while in others two or more media types are integrated together. We shall discuss some examples from each category separately.

Speech only

Traditionally, interpersonal communications involving speech – telephony – have been provided using telephones that are connected either to a public switched telephone network (PSTN/ISDN/cellular phone network) or a PBX. The general scheme is shown in Figure 1.6.

Alternatively, by using a multimedia PC equipped with a microphone and speakers, the user can take part in telephone calls through the PC. This

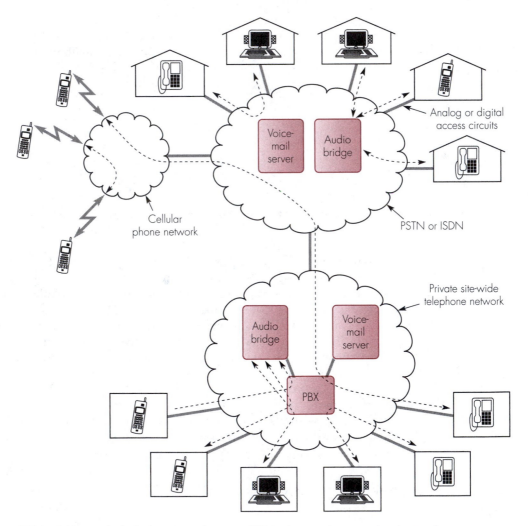

PSTN = Public switched telephone network
PBX = Private branch exchange

ISDN = Integrated services digital networrk

Figure 1.6 Speech-only interpersonal communications: public and private switched telephone networks.

requires a telephone interface card and associated software and is known as **computer telephony integration** or **CTI**. The added advantages of using a PC instead of a conventional telephone are many. For example, the user can create his or her own private directory of numbers and initiate a call simply by selecting the desired number on the PC screen. More generally, providing the access circuit to the network has sufficient capacity – normally referred to as the circuit's **bandwidth** – it is possible to integrate telephony with all the other networked services provided by the PC.

In addition to telephony, many public and private networks support additional services. Two examples are voice-mail and teleconferencing. **Voice-mail**, for example, is used in the event of the called party being unavailable. A spoken message can then be left in the **voice mailbox** of the called party. This is located in a central repository known as the **voice-mail server**. The message can be read by the owner of the mailbox the next time he or she contacts the server.

Teleconferencing calls involve multiple interconnected telephones/PCs. Each person can hear and talk to all of the others involved in the call. This type of call is known variously as a **conference call** or, since it involves a telephone network, a **teleconferencing call** or sometimes an **audioconferencing call**. It requires a central unit known as an **audio bridge** which provides the necessary support to set up a conference call automatically.

The Internet is also used to support telephony. Initially, because the Internet was designed to support computer-to-computer communications, just (multimedia) PC-to-PC telephony was supported. This was subsequently extended so that a standard telephone could also be used. See Figure 1.7.

In the case of a PC-to-PC telephone call, the standard addresses that are used to identify individual computers connected to the Internet are used in the same way as for a data transfer application. However, because the Internet operates in a packet mode, both PCs must have the necessary hardware and software to convert the speech signal from the microphone into packets on input and back again prior to output to the speakers. Telephony over the Internet is also known, therefore, as **packet voice** or, because the network protocol associated with the Internet is called the Internet protocol (IP), **voice over IP** (**VoIP**).

When a PC connected to the Internet needs to make a call to a telephone that is connected to a PSTN/ISDN, because these both operate in a circuit mode, an interworking unit known as a **telephony gateway** must be used. The PC user first sends a request to make a (telephone) call to a preallocated telephony gateway using the latter's Internet address. Then, assuming the user is registered to use this service, the gateway requests from the source PC the telephone number of the called party. On receipt of this, the source gateway initiates a session (call) with the telephony gateway nearest to the called party using the Internet address of the gateway. The called gateway then initiates a call to the recipient telephone using its telephone number and the standard call setup procedure of the PSTN/ISDN. Assuming the called party answers,

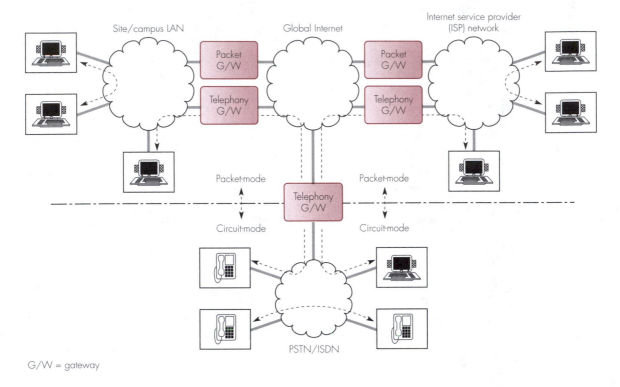

G/W = gateway

Figure 1.7 Telephony over the Internet.

the called gateway then signals back to the PC user – through the source gateway – that the call can commence. A similar procedure is followed to clear the call on completion.

Image only

An alternative form of interpersonal communications over a PSTN or an ISDN is by the exchange of electronic images of documents. This type of service is known as **facsimile** – or simply **fax** – and is illustrated in Figure 1.8. Normally, this type of communication involves the use of a pair of fax machines, one at each network termination point. To send a document, the caller keys in the (telephone) number of the intended recipient and a circuit is set up through the network in the same way as for a telephone call. The two fax machines communicate with each other to establish operational parameters after which the sending machine starts to scan and digitize each page of the document in turn. Both fax machines have an integral modem within them and, as each page is scanned, its digitized image is simultaneously transmitted over the network and, as this is received at the called side, a printed version of the document is produced. Finally, after the last page of the document has been sent and received, the connection through the network is cleared by the calling machine in the normal way.

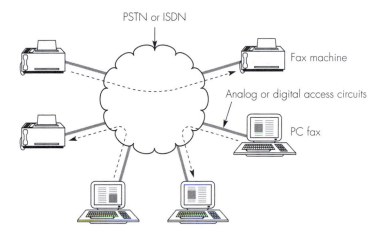

Figure 1.8 Image-only interpersonal communications: facsimile (fax) examples.

It is also possible to use a PC instead of a normal fax machine to send an electronic version of a document that is stored directly within the PC's memory. This mode of operation is known as **PC fax**. Essentially, the digital image of each page of the document is sent in the same way as the scanned image produced by a conventional fax machine. As with telephony, this requires a telephone interface card and associated software. The latter operates in exactly the same way as that in a fax machine and hence the terminal at the called side can be either a fax machine or another similar PC. In addition, with PC fax it is possible to send the digitized document over other network types such as an enterprise network. In this case, a LAN interface card and associated software are used. This mode of operation is particularly useful when working with paper-based documents such as invoices, and so on.

Text only

An example of interpersonal communications involving just text is electronic mail (email). The user terminal is normally a PC or a workstation and, as we described earlier in Section 1.3.2, the most widespread network used is the Internet. Various operational scenarios are shown in Figure 1.9(a).

In the case of a user at home, access to the Internet is through a PSTN/ISDN and an intermediate Internet service provider (ISP) network. Alternatively, business users obtain access either through an enterprise network or a site/campus network. Associated with each network is a set of one or more server computers. Each is known as an **email server** and, collectively, these contain a **mailbox** for each user connected to that network. A user can both create and deposit mail into his or her mailbox and read mail from it. Both the email servers and the internetwork gateway operate using the standard Internet communication protocols.

(a)

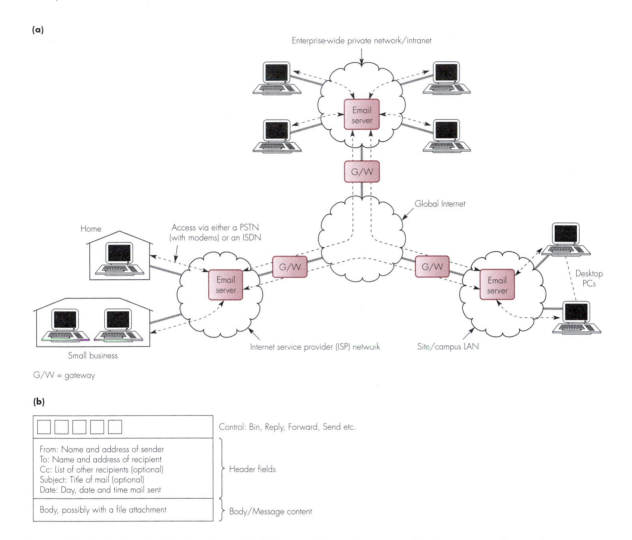

(b)

Figure 1.9 Text-only electronic mail: (a) email transfer examples; (b) example email message format.

The format of a typical text-only email message is shown in Figure 1.9(b) and, as we can see, at the head is the unique Internet-wide name of both the sender and recipient of the mail. In addition, a copy of the mail can be sent to multiple recipients each of whom is listed in the cc part of the mail header, the acronym "cc" being the abbreviation for "carbon copy" which was the original means of making (paper) copies of documents. Normally, the contents of text-only mail comprise unformatted text, typically strings of ASCII characters.

Text and images

An example of an application that involves both text and images integrated together is **computer-supported cooperative working** (**CSCW**). The network used is an enterprise network, a LAN, or the Internet and the general scheme is illustrated in Figure 1.10. Typically, a distributed group of people – each in his or her place of work – are all working on the same project. The user terminal is either a PC or a workstation and a window on each person's display is used as a shared workspace. This is known as a **shared whiteboard** and, normally, the display comprises text and images integrated together. The software associated with CSCW comprises a central program – known as the **whiteboard program** – and a linked set of support programs, one in each PC/workstation. The latter is made up of two parts: a change-notification part and an update-control part. Whenever a member of the group updates the contents of his or her whiteboard, the **change-notification** part sends details of the changes to the whiteboard program. This relays the changes to the **update-control** in each of the other PCs/workstations and these in turn proceed to update the contents of their copy of the whiteboard.

Speech and video

An example application that uses speech and video integrated together is **video telephony** which is now supported by all the network types. Figure 1.11(a) shows the general scheme.

In the case of the home, the terminals used are normally dedicated to providing the videophone service, while in an office, a single multimedia

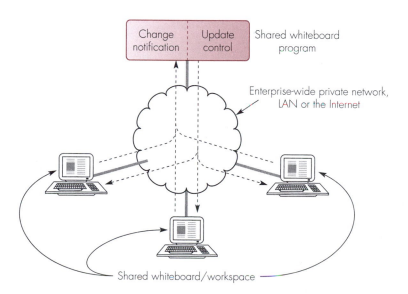

Figure 1.10 Text-and-image computer-supported cooperative working (CSCW).

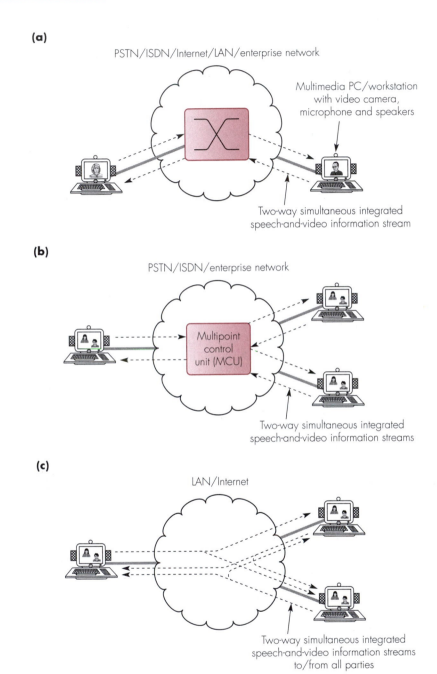

(a)

PSTN/ISDN/Internet/LAN/enterprise network

Multimedia PC/workstation
with video camera,
microphone and speakers

Two-way simultaneous integrated
speech-and-video information stream

(b)

PSTN/ISDN/enterprise network

Multipoint
control
unit (MCU)

Two-way simultaneous integrated
speech-and-video information streams

(c)

LAN/Internet

Two-way simultaneous integrated
speech-and-video information streams
to/from all parties

**Figure 1.11 Speech-and-video interpersonal communications:
(a) two-party video telephone call; (b) videoconferencing using an
MCU; (c) videoconferencing using a broadcast network.**

PC/workstation is used to provide the videophone service together with a range of other services. In both cases, the terminals/PCs incorporate a video camera in addition to the microphone and speaker used for telephony. With a dedicated terminal, a separate screen is used for the display whilst with a multimedia PC or workstation, the (moving) image of the called party is displayed in a window of the PC/workstation screen. The network must provide a two-way communication channel between the two parties of sufficient bandwidth to support the integrated speech-and-video generated by each terminal/PC.

The integration of video with speech means that the bandwidth of the access circuits required to support this type of service is higher than that required for speech only. Moreover, as with telephony, a call may involve not just two persons – and hence terminals/PCs – but several people each located in their own office. This type of call is then known as a **desktop videoconferencing call** and is now widely used in large corporations involving multiple geographically distributed sites in order to minimize travel between the various locations. As we indicated earlier, large corporations of this type have an enterprise-wide network to link the sites together and, in order to support videoconferencing, there is a central unit called a **multipoint control unit (MCU)** – or sometimes a **videoconferencing server** – associated with this network. An example is shown in Figure 1.11(b).

In principle, a separate window on the screen of each participant's PC/workstation should be used to display the video image of all the other participants. In practice, however, this would require multiple integrated speech-and-video communication channels, one for each participant, being sent to each of the other participants. Normally, this would require more bandwidth than is available. Hence instead, the integrated speech-and-video information stream from each participant is sent to the MCU which then selects just a single information stream to send to each participant. For example, with a voice-activated MCU, whenever the MCU detects a participant speaking, it relays the information stream from that participant to all the other participants. In this way, only a single two-way communication channel between each location and the MCU is required thereby reducing considerably the communication bandwidth needed.

Alternatively, some networks such as LANs and the Internet support what is called **multicasting**. This means that all transmissions from any of the PCs/workstations belonging to a predefined **multicast group** are received by all the other members of the group. Thus with networks that support multicasting, it is possible to hold a conferencing session without an MCU. The principle is shown in Figure 1.11(c) and, as we can deduce from this, this is only feasible when only a limited number of participants are involved owing to the high load it places on the network.

While the application just described involves only a single person at each location, there are other applications that involve groups of people at one or more of the locations. Two examples are shown in Figure 1.12. In part (a) a person at one location is communicating with a group of people at another location. This is the case, for example, with the transmission of a live lecture or seminar. Typically, the information stream transferred from the lecturer to the (remote) class would be integrated speech-and-video together with electronic copies of transparencies and other documents used in the lecture. In the reverse direction, the information may comprise just speech – for questions – or integrated speech-and-video to enable the lecturer to both see and hear the members of the class at the remote location. In terms of communications requirements, these are similar to those for a two-party videophone call. Alternatively, if the lecture is being relayed to multiple locations, either a separate communications channel is required to each remote site or an MCU

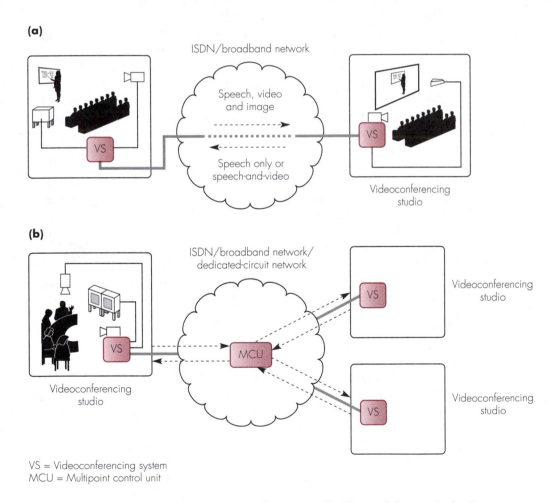

(a)

(b)

VS = Videoconferencing system
MCU = Multipoint control unit

Figure 1.12 Speech-and-video interpersonal communications: (a) remote lecture; (b) multiparty (group) videoconferencing.

is used at the lecturer's site. As we can see, because of the relatively high bandwidth that is involved, the network is either an ISDN that supports multiple 64 kbps channels or a broadband multiservice network if one is available.

In the example in Figure 1.12(b), there is a group of people at each location. This type of application has been in use for many years and was the first example of videoconferencing. Normally, since a group of people are present at each location, specially equipped rooms called **videoconferencing studios** are used which contain all the necessary audio and video equipment. This comprises one or more video cameras, a large-screen display, and associated audio equipment, all of which is connected to a unit called a **videoconferencing system**. A conference can involve just two locations or, more usually, multiple locations as shown in the figure. In the case of the latter, an MCU is normally used to minimize the bandwidth demands on the access circuits to the network. In the figure, the MCU is shown as a central facility within the network and hence only a single two-way communications channel is required for each access circuit of the network. This is the type of arrangement with a telecommunications-provider conference, for example. Alternatively, if a private network is being used, the MCU is normally located at one of the sites. The communication requirements at that site are then more demanding since it must support multiple input channels – one from each of the other sites – and a single output channel, the stream from which must be broadcast to all of the other sites.

Multimedia

The example discussed earlier concerning Internet-based electronic mail – email – assumed the information content of each email message consisted of text only. In addition, however, mail containing other media types such as images, audio, and video are also used. Three examples of electronic mail consisting of media types other than text are voice-mail, video-mail, and multimedia mail.

Voice-mail is similar in principle to that described earlier in relation to telephone networks. With Internet-based voice-mail, however, there is a voice-mail server associated with each network. This is in addition to the email server shown earlier in Figure 1.9(a). The user first enters a voice message addressed to the intended recipient and the local voice-mail server then relays this to the server associated with the intended recipient's network. The stored voice message is then played out the next time the recipient accesses his or her voice-mailbox. The same mode of operation is used for video-mail except in this case the mail message comprises an integrated speech-and-video sequence.

Multimedia mail is an extension of text-only mail inasmuch as the basic content of the mail comprises textual information. With multimedia mail, however, the textual information is annotated with a digitized image, a speech message, or a video message, as shown in Figure 1.13. In the case of speech-and-video, the annotations can be sent either directly to the mailbox

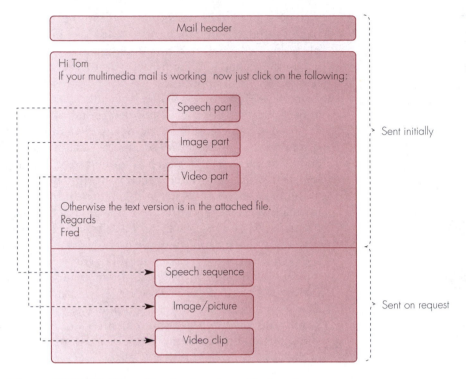

Figure 1.13 Multimedia electronic mail structure.

of the intended recipient together with the original textual message – and hence stored and played out in the normal way – or they may have to be requested specifically by the recipient when the textual message is being read. In this way, the recipient can always receive the basic text-only message but the multimedia annotations can be received only if the terminal being used by the recipient supports voice and/or video.

1.4.2 Interactive applications over the Internet

In addition to a range of interpersonal communication applications, the Internet is also used to support a range of interactive applications, the most widely used being for interactions with a **World Wide Web** (**WWW**) or simply **Web**, server. This comprises a linked set of multimedia information servers that are geographically distributed around the Internet. The total information stored on all the servers is equivalent to a vast library of documents. The general principle is illustrated in Figure 1.14(a).

Each document comprises a linked set of **pages** and the linkages between the pages are known as **hyperlinks**. These are pointers – also known as **references** – either to other pages of the same document or to any other document within the total Web. In this way, a reader of a document has the

(a)

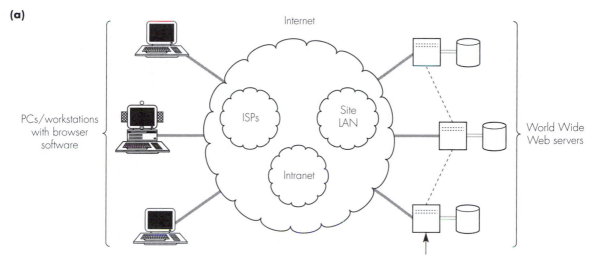

PCs/workstations with browser software

Internet

ISPs

Site LAN

Intranet

World Wide Web servers

Multimedia information servers (some with transaction capabilities) connected to a site LAN, an intranet, or an ISP network

(b)

Home page

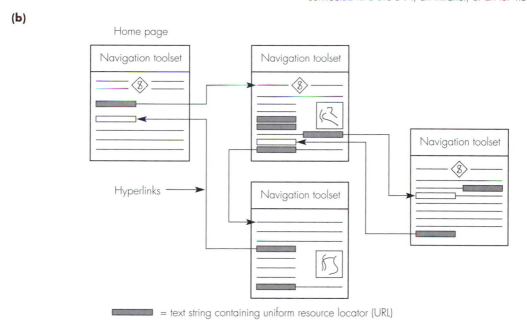

Navigation toolset

Hyperlinks

Navigation toolset

Navigation toolset

Navigation toolset

▬▬▬ = text string containing uniform resource locator (URL)

Figure 1.14 Interactions with a World Wide Web server: (a) schematic; (b) hypertext linkages between the pages of a set of documents.

option, at well-defined points throughout the pages that make up a document, to jump either to a different page of the same document or to a different document. Also, to return subsequently to a specific point on a page at a later time. The optional linkage points within documents are defined by the creator of the document and are known as **anchors** since it is to these that the necessary linkage information is attached. Documents comprising only text are created using what is called **hypertext,** while those comprising multimedia information are created using what is known as **hypermedia**. The general structure of this type of document is shown in Figure 1.14(b).

There is no central authority for the introduction of new documents into the Web. Anyone can create a new document at a particular server site – providing the server has been allocated an Internet address – and make hyperlink references from it to any other document on the Web. Each document has a unique address – known as a **uniform resource locator** or **URL** – which identifies both the location of the server on the Internet where the first page of the document is stored and also the file reference on that server. The first page of a document is known as the **home page** and all the hyperlinks on this and the other pages have similar URLs associated with them. As we can deduce from this, the physical location of a page is transparent to the user and, in theory, can be located anywhere on the Web.

A standard format is used for writing documents. This is known as the **Hypertext Markup Language** (**HTML**) and it is also used for writing client software to explore the total contents of the Web, that is, the contents of the linked information on all the Web servers. The client function is called a **browser** and there are a number of user-friendly browsers available to explore the contents of the Web. These allow a user to create a directory of previously visited servers and to open up a dialog with a particular server at the click of the mouse. Once a desired document has been located, the user simply clicks on an anchor point within a page of the document to activate the linkage information stored at that point. It is also possible to return to the previous anchor at any time. With a hypertext document, the anchor is usually an underlined word or phrase while with a hypermedia document it is normally an icon of an appropriate shape; for example, a loudspeaker for a sound annotation or a video camera for a video clip. It is of course the presence of sound and video annotations that brings a document to life and adds value over a simple printed page.

In some applications the client simply wishes to browse through the information stored at a particular site. Examples include browsing through sales literature, product information, application notes periodicals, newspapers, and so on. In general, there is no charge for accessing this information. However, access to books, journals, and similar documents may be by subscription only.

In applications such as **homeshopping**, **homebanking**, and so on – more generally known as **teleshopping** and **telebanking** – a client may wish not only to browse through the information at a site but also to initiate an additional **transaction**. Here the server must provide additional transaction processing support for, say, ordering and purchasing. Since this will often involve a financial transaction, more rigorous security procedures are required for access and authentication purposes.

1.4.3 Entertainment applications

Entertainment applications can be one of two types:

- movie/video-on-demand,
- interactive television.

We shall discuss each application separately.

Movie/video-on-demand

This category of application is similar in principle to that described in the previous section except that, in general, the video and audio associated with entertainment applications must be of a much higher quality/resolution since wide-screen televisions and stereophonic sound are often used. As we shall describe in Section 4.3.3, a digitized movie/video – with sound – requires a minimum channel bit rate (bandwidth) of 1.5 Mbps. Hence the network used to support this type of application must be either a PSTN with a high bit rate modem – as we showed earlier in Figure 1.1(c) – or a cable network of the type we showed in Figure 1.3(a). As we saw earlier in Section 1.3.1, in the case of a PSTN, the high bit rate channel provided by the modem is used only over the access circuit and provides additional services to the other switched services that the PSTN supports. The general operational scheme in both cases is shown in Figure 1.15(a).

As we can see, the information stored on the server is a collection of digitized movies/videos. Normally the subscriber terminal comprises a conventional television with a selection device for interaction purposes. The user interactions are relayed to the server through a set-top box which also contains the high bit rate modem. By means of a suitable menu, the subscriber is able to browse through the set of movies/videos available and initiate the showing of a selected movie. This type of application is known as **movie-on-demand** (**MOD**) or sometimes **video-on-demand** (**VOD**). In addition to selecting a movie, the subscriber can control the showing of the movie by using similar controls to those used on a conventional video cassette recorder (VCR), that is, pause, fast-forward, and so on.

A key feature of MOD is that a subscriber can initiate the showing of a movie selected from a large library of movies at any time of the day or night. Hence, as we can deduce from Figure 1.15(b), this means that the server must be capable of playing out simultaneously a large number of video streams equal to the number of subscribers currently watching a movie. This requires the information flow from the server to be extremely high since it must support not just the transmission of a possibly large number of different movies, but also multiple copies of each movie. Technically this is very challenging and costly since, in general, the cost of the server is directly related to the aggregate information flow rate from it.

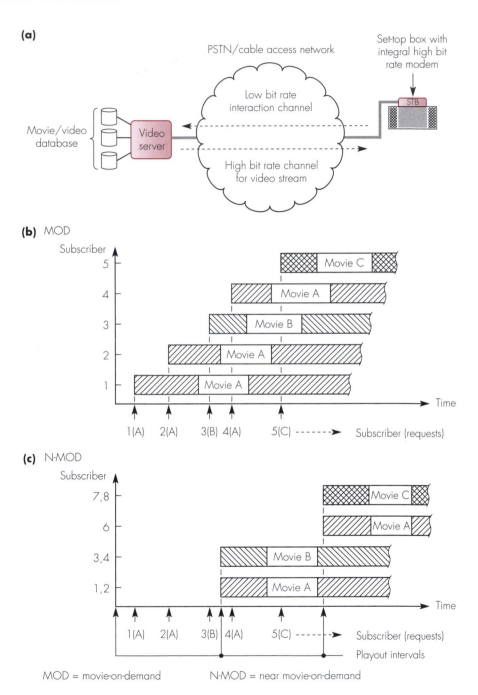

Figure 1.15 Interactions with a video server: (a) networking schematic; (b) movie-on-demand; (c) near movie-on-demand.

In practice, if the server is supporting a large number of subscribers, then it is common for several subscribers to request the same movie within a relatively short time interval between each request. An alternative mode of operation is also used, therefore, in which requests for a particular movie are not played out immediately but instead are queued until the start of the next playout time of that movie as shown in Figure 1.15(c). In this way, all requests for the same movie which are made during the period up to the next playout time are satisfied simultaneously by the server outputting a single video stream. This mode of operation, is known as **near movie-on-demand** or **N-MOD**. Clearly, however, the viewer is unable to control the playout of the movie.

Similar applications are also used within a business environment, except that the stored information in the server is typically training and general educational material, company news, and so on, and thus the number of stored videos is normally much less as is the number of simultaneous users. This means that the video servers required are less sophisticated than those used in public MOD/N-MOD systems. Also, the stored video streams/programs are often in a different format. The format used is the same as that used with **CD-ROMs** since the received video stream can then be displayed directly on the screen of a multimedia PC or workstation. The communication requirements of the private network, however, are the same as those identified for use with a public network.

Interactive television

Broadcast television networks include cable, satellite, and terrestrial networks. The basic service provided by these networks is, of course, the diffusion of both analog and digital television (and radio) programs. In addition, however, as we saw earlier in Section 1.3.3, the set-top box (STB) associated with these networks also has a modem within it. In the case of a cable network, as we show in Figure 1.16(a), the STB provides both a low bit rate connection to the PSTN and a high bit rate connection to the Internet. Hence by connecting appropriate terminal equipment to the STB – a keyboard, telephone, and so on – the subscriber is able to gain access to all the services provided through the PSTN and the Internet. In addition, through the connection to the PSTN, the subscriber is able to actively respond to the information being broadcast. This is the origin of the term "interactive television" and typical uses of the return channel are for voting, participation in games, home shopping and so on. As we see in Figure 1.16(b), a similar set of services are available through satellite and terrestrial broadcast networks, except that the STB associated with these networks requires a high-speed modem to provide the connections to the PSTN and the Internet.

(a)

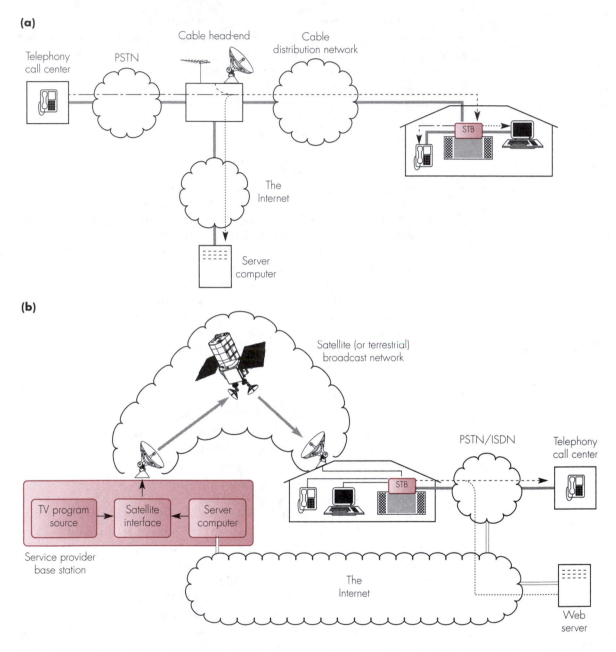

Figure 1.16 Interactive television: (a) cable distribution network; (b) satellite/terrestrial broadcast network.

1.5 Application and networking terminology

Before we leave this chapter it will be helpful if we first review some of the terminology used in relation to the different media types and also the terminology and operational characteristics of the different types of communication channels provided by the various networks we have identified. A selection of the terms that are used are shown in Figure 1.17. We shall describe each term separately as well as its origin and interrelationship with the other terms.

1.5.1 Media types

As we identified in Section 1.4 when we described the different multimedia applications, the information flow associated with the different applications can be either continuous or block-mode. In the case of **continuous media**, this means that the information stream is generated by the source continuously in a time-dependent way. In general, therefore, continuous media is

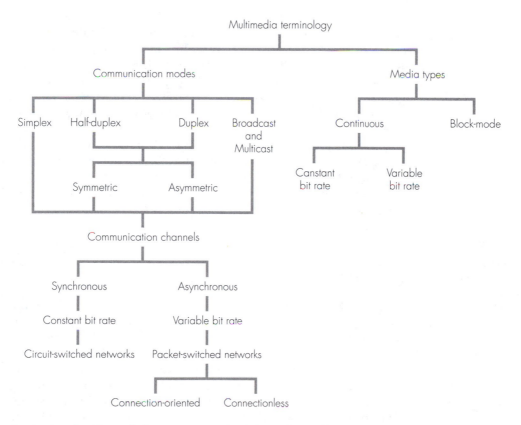

Figure 1.17 A selection of the terms used with multimedia.

passed directly to the destination as it is generated and, at the destination, the information stream is played out directly as it is received. This mode of operation is called **streaming** and, since continuous media is generated in a time-dependent way, it is also known as **real-time media**. With continuous media, therefore, the bit rate of the communications channel that is used must be compatible with the rate the source media is being generated. Two examples of media types that generate continuous streams of information in real time are audio and video.

In terms of the bit rate at which the source information stream is generated, this may be at either a **constant bit rate** (**CBR**) or a **variable bit rate** (**VBR**). With audio, for example, the digitized audio stream is generated at a constant bit rate which is determined by the frequency the audio waveform is sampled and the number of bits that are used to digitize each sample. In the case of video, however, as we shall expand upon in Section 2.6.1, although the individual pictures/frames that make up the video are generated at a constant rate, after compression, the amount of information associated with each frame varies. In general, therefore, the information stream associated with compressed video is generated at fixed time intervals but the resulting bit rate is variable.

In the case of **block-mode media**, the source information comprises a single block of information that is created in a time-independent way. For example, a block of text representing an email or computer program, a two-dimensional matrix of pixel values that represents an image, and so on. Normally, therefore, block-mode media is created in a time-independent way and is often stored at the source in, say, a file. Then, when it is requested, the block of information is transferred across the network to the destination where it is again stored and subsequently output/displayed at a time determined by the requesting application program. This mode of operation is known as **downloading** and, as we can deduce with block-mode media, the bit rate of the communications channel need not be constant but must be such that, when a block is requested, the delay between the request being made and the contents of the block being output at the destination is within an acceptable time interval. This is known as the **round-trip delay** (**RTD**) and, for human–computer interactions, ideally, this should be no more than a few seconds.

1.5.2 Communication modes

In terms of the communication channels that are provided by the various network types, as we show in Figure 1.18, the transfer of the information streams associated with an application can take place in one of five modes:

■ **simplex:** this means the information associated with the application flows in one direction only. An example is the transmission of photographic images from a deep-space probe at predetermined times since this involves just a unidirectional flow of information from the probe to an earth station;

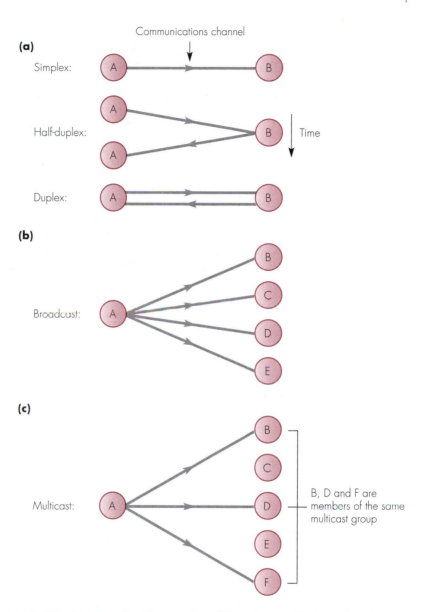

Figure 1.18 Communication modes: (a) unicast; (b) broadcast; (c) multicast.

- **half-duplex:** this means that information flows in both directions but alternately. This mode is also known as **two-way alternate** and an example is a user making a request for some information from a remote server and the latter returning the requested information;

- **duplex:** this means that information flows in both directions simultaneously. It is also known as **two-way simultaneous** and an example is the two-way flow of digitized speech and video associated with a video telephony application;

- **broadcast:** this means that the information output by a single source node is received by all the other nodes – computers, and so on – that are connected to the same network. An example is the broadcast of a television program over a cable network as all the television receivers that are connected to the network receive the same set of programs;

- **Multicast**: this is similar to a broadcast except that the information output by the source is received by only a specific subset of the nodes that are connected to the network. The latter form what is called a **multicast group** and an example application is videoconferencing which involves a predefined group of terminals/computers connected to a network exchanging integrated speech and video streams.

In the case of half-duplex and duplex communications, the bit rate associated with the flow of information in each direction can be either equal or different; if the flows are equal, the information flow is said to be **symmetric** and if the flows are different, **asymmetric**. For example, a video telephone call involves the exchange of an integrated digitized speech and video stream in both directions simultaneously and hence a symmetric duplex communications channel is required. Alternatively, in an application involving a browser (program) and a Web server, a low bit rate channel from the browser to the Web server is required for request and control purposes and a higher bit rate channel from the server to the subscriber for the transfer of, say, the requested file. Hence for this type of application, an asymmetric half-duplex communications channel is sufficient.

1.5.3 Network types

In the same way that there are two types of information stream associated with the different media types – continuous and block-mode – so there are two types of communications channel associated with the various network types, one that operates in a time-dependent way known as **circuit-mode** and the other in a time-varying way known as **packet-mode**. The first is known as a **synchronous communications channel** since it provides a constant bit rate service at a specified rate. The second is known as an **asynchronous communications channel** since it provides a variable bit rate service, the actual rate being determined by the (variable) transfer rate of packets across the network.

Circuit-mode

A circuit-mode network is shown in Figure 1.19 and, as we can see, it comprises an interconnected set of **switching offices/exchanges** to which the subscriber terminals/computers are connected. This type of network is known as a **circuit-switched network** and, prior to sending any information, the source must first set up a connection through the network. Each subscriber terminal/computer has a unique network-wide number/address associated with it and, to make a call, the source first enters the number/address of the intended communication partner. The local switching office/exchange then uses this to set up a connection through the network to the switching office/exchange to which the destination is connected and, assuming the destination is free and ready to receive a call, a message is returned to the source indicating that it can now start to transfer/exchange information. Finally, after all the information has been transferred/exchanged, either the source or the destination requests for the connection to be cleared. The bit rate associated with the connection is fixed and, in general, is determined by the bit rate that is used over the access circuits that connect the source and destination terminal/computer to the network.

The messages associated with the setting up and clearing of a connection are known as **signaling messages**. As we can deduce from the above, with a circuit-switched network there is a time delay while a connection is being established. This is known as the **call/connection setup delay** and two examples of networks that operate in this way are a PSTN and an ISDN. With

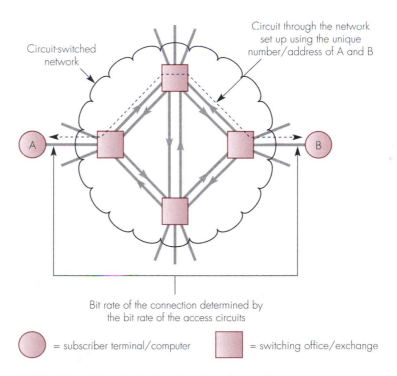

Figure 1.19 Circuit-switched network schematic.

a PSTN, the call setup delay can range from a fraction of a second for a local call through to several seconds for an international call. With an ISDN, however, the delay ranges from tens of milliseconds through to several hundred milliseconds.

Packet-mode

As we see in Figure 1.20, there are two types of packet-mode network: **connection-oriented** (**CO**) and **connectionless** (**CL**). The principle of operation of a connection-oriented network is shown in Figure 1.20(a) and, as we can see, it comprises an interconnected set of **packet-switching exchanges** (**PSEs**). This type of network is known as a **packet-switched network** and, as with a circuit-switched network, each terminal/computer that is connected to the network has a unique network-wide number/address associated with it. With a connection-oriented network, as the name implies, prior to sending any information, a connection is first set up through the network using the addresses of the source and destination terminals. However, in a packet-switched network, the connection/circuit that is set up utilizes only a variable portion of the bandwidth of each link and hence the connection is known as a **virtual connection** or, more usually, a **virtual circuit** (**VC**).

To set up a VC, the source terminal/computer sends a *call request* control packet to its local PSE which contains, in addition to the address of the source and destination terminal/computer, a short identifier known as a **virtual circuit identifier** (**VCI**) Each PSE maintains a table that specifies the outgoing link that should be used to reach each network address and, on receipt of the *call request* packet, the PSE uses the destination address within the packet to determine the outgoing link to be used. The next free identifier (VCI) for this link is then selected and two entries are made in a **routing table**. The first specifies the incoming link/VCI and the corresponding outgoing link/VCI and the second, in order to route packets in the reverse direction, the inverse of these, as we show in the example in the figure. The *call request* packet is then forwarded on the selected outgoing link and the same procedure is followed at each PSE along the route until the destination terminal/computer is reached.

Collectively, the VCIs that are used on the various links form the virtual circuit and, at the destination, assuming the call is accepted, a *call accepted* packet is returned to the source over the same route/virtual circuit. The information transfer phase can then start but, since a VC is now in place, only the VCI is needed in the packet header instead of the full network-wide address. Each PSE first uses the incoming link/VCI to determine the outgoing link/VCI from the routing table. The existing VCI in the packet header is then replaced with that obtained from the routing table and the packet is forwarded on the identified outgoing link. The same procedure is followed to return information in the reverse direction and, when all information has been transferred/exchanged, the VC is cleared and the appropriate VCIs are released by passing a *call clear* packet along the VC.

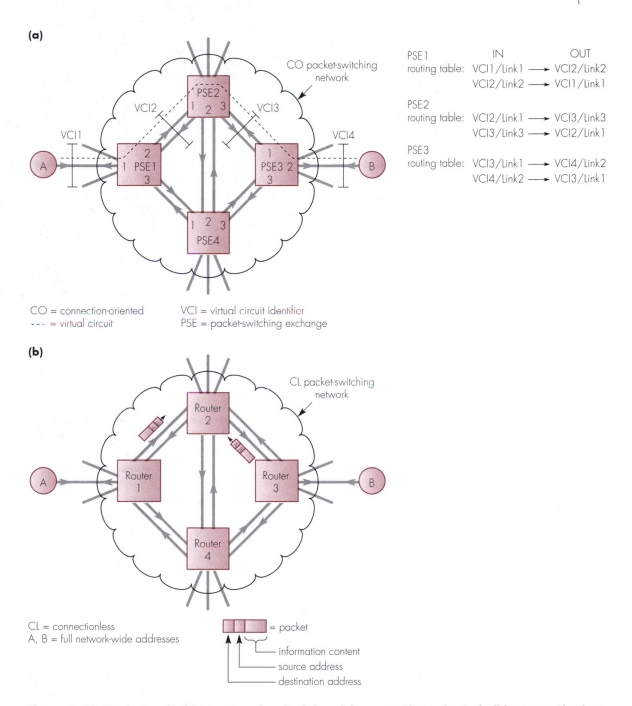

Figure 1.20 Packet-switching network principles: (a) connection-oriented; (b) connectionless.

In contrast, with a connectionless network, the establishment of a connection is not required and the two communicating terminals/computers can communicate and exchange information as and when they wish. In order to do this, however, as we show in Figure 1.20(b), each packet must carry the full source and destination addresses in its header in order for each PSE to route the packet onto the appropriate outgoing link. In a connectionless network, therefore, the term **router** is normally used rather than packet-switching exchange.

In both network types, as each packet is received by a PSE/router on an incoming link, it is stored in its entirety in a memory buffer. A check is then made to determine if any transmission/bit errors are present in the packet header – that is, the signal that is used to represent a binary 0 is corrupted and is interpreted by the receiver as a binary 1 and vice versa – and, if an error is detected, the packet is simply discarded. The service offered by a packet-switched network is said, therefore, to be a **best-effort service**. If no errors are detected then the addresses/VCIs carried in the packet header are read to determine the outgoing link that should be used and the packet is placed in a queue ready for forwarding on the selected outgoing link. All packets are transmitted at the maximum link bit rate. However, with this mode of operation, it is possible for a sequence of packets to be received on a number of incoming links all of which need forwarding on the same outgoing link. Hence a packet may experience an additional delay while it is in the output queue for a link waiting to be transmitted. Clearly, this delay will be variable since it depends on the number of packets that are currently present in the queue when a new packet arrives for forwarding. This mode of operation is known as (packet) **store-and-forward** and, as we can see, there is a packet store-and-forward delay in each PSE/router. The sum of the store-and-forward delays in each PSE/router contributes to the overall transfer delay of the packet across the network. The mean of this delay is known as the **mean packet transfer delay** and the variation about the mean the **delay variation** or **jitter**.

An example of a packet-switched network that operates in the connectionless mode is the Internet, which we shall describe in some detail in Chapter 9. Two examples of networks that operate in the connection-oriented mode are the international X.25 packet-switching network and ATM networks. As we explained in Section 1.3.2, the X.25 network is used primarily for the transfer of files containing text and binary data between large computers. Because of the packet format that is used, the routing of packets is relatively slow with the effect that the X.25 network is unsuitable for most multimedia applications. In contrast, as we described in Section 1.3.5, ATM networks have been designed from the outset to support all types of multimedia applications. This is achieved by using high bit rate interconnecting links and, once a virtual circuit has been set up, a very small fixed-sized packet of 53 bytes is used to transfer the information associated with the call. Each small packet is known as a **cell** and includes a short 5-byte header which enables cells to be switched at the very high link bit rates that are used. It is for this reason that ATM networks are also known as **fast packet-switching networks** or sometimes **cell-switching networks**. We shall describe the operation of ATM networks in Chapter 10.

1.5.4 Multipoint conferencing

As we described in Section 1.4.1, multipoint conferencing features in many interpersonal applications including audio- and videoconferencing, data sharing, and computer-supported cooperative working. Essentially, these involve the exchange of information between three or more terminals/computers. In practice, because of the different modes of operation of the two network types – circuit-switched and packet-switched – multipoint conferencing is implemented in one of two ways: centralized and decentralized.

The **centralized mode** is used with circuit-switched networks such as a PSTN or an ISDN and, as we show in Figure 1.21(a), with this mode a centralized conference server is used. Prior to sending any information, each terminal/computer to be involved in the conference must first set up a connection to the server. Each terminal/computer then sends its own media stream – comprising, say, audio, video, and data integrated together in some way – to the server using the established connection. The server, in turn, then distributes either the media stream received from a selected terminal/computer or a mix of the media streams received from several terminals/computers back to all the other terminals/computers that are involved in the conference.

The **decentralized mode** is used with packet-switched networks that support multicast communications. Examples include local area networks, intranets, and the Internet. In this mode, as we show in Figure 1.21(b), the output of each terminal/computer is received by all the other members of the conference/multicast group. Hence a conference server is not normally used and instead it is the responsibility of each terminal/computer to manage the information streams that it receives from the other members.

In addition, a third mode known as the **hybrid mode** can be used. This is shown in Figure 1.21(c) and, as we can see, it is used when the various terminals/computers that make up the conference are attached to different network types. In the example shown, the conference comprises four terminals/computers, two attached to a circuit-switched network and two to a packet-switched network that supports multicasting. As in the centralized mode, a conference server is used and the output of each terminal/computer is sent to the server either over individual circuits – terminals A and B – or using multicasting – terminals C and D. However, in this mode, as in the centralized mode, it is the server that determines the output stream(s) to be sent to each terminal.

As we explained in Section 1.4.1, there are four types of conferencing:

■   data conferencing: this involves data only and examples include data sharing and computer-supported cooperative working;

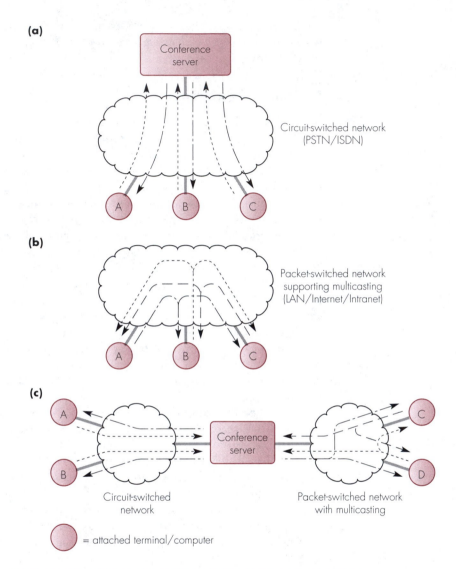

Figure 1.21 Multipoint conferencing modes of operation: (a) centralized; (b) decentralized; (c) hybrid.

- audioconferencing: this involves audio (speech) only;
- videoconferencing: this involves speech and video synchronized and integrated together;
- multimedia conferencing: this involves speech, video, and data integrated together.

With data conferencing, the information flow between the various parties is relatively infrequent. Normally, therefore, the conference server is a general-purpose computer with the conference function implemented in software. With the other three types of conferencing, however, the information flows demand the use of special purpose units. In the case of audioconferencing, the unit is called an **audio bridge** and typical units support from six through to 48 conference participants. With video and multimedia conferencing, the unit is called a multipoint control unit (MCU) and, because of the volume and rate of the information being exchanged, normally, the centralized mode of working is used with both network types.

An MCU consists of two parts: the first is known as the **multipoint controller** (**MC**) part and is concerned with the establishment of connections to each of the conference participants and with the negotiation of an agreed set of operational parameters – screen resolution, refresh rate, and so on. The second part is known as the **multipoint processor** (**MP**) and is concerned with the distribution of the information streams generated during the conference. The latter include such functions as the mixing of the various media streams into an integrated stream, voice-activated switching and continuous presence.

When using an audio bridge, a call is scheduled for a particular date, time, and duration and everyone who is to take part in the call is assigned a user ID and password. At the appropriate time, all participants call in and, after they have been verified to join the conference, they can hear and speak to the other participants. In a similar way, when using an MCU, a call is scheduled as for an audio bridge and, once the conference starts, each participant can hear, see, and share data with the other participants. With an MCU, however, in addition to the participants calling in – known as the **dial-in mode** – in some instances, the MCU calls the participants – the **dial-out mode** – which, in general, provides better security.

In the **voice-activated switching mode**, the face of the participant is displayed in a window on the screen of the participant's terminal/computer and, in a second window, is the face of the (remote) participant who is currently talking. When another participant starts to talk, the face of the new speaker replaces the face of the current remote participant. In the event of two (or more) participants starting to talk at the same time, the MCU normally selects the person who speaks the loudest. In the **continuous-presence mode**, however, the remote window is divided into a number of smaller windows, each of which displays the face of the last set of participants who spoke or who are currently speaking. With both modes the speech from all participants is normally mixed into a single stream and hence each participant can always hear what is said by all the other participants.

1.5.5 Network QoS

The operational parameters associated with a communications channel through a network are known as the **network Quality of Service** (**QoS**) **parameters** and collectively they determine the suitability of the channel

in relation to its use for a particular application. In practice, the QoS parameters associated with a circuit-switched network are different from
those associated with a packet-switched network and hence we shall discuss
each separately.

Circuit-switched network

The QoS parameters associated with a constant bit rate channel that is set up
through a circuit-switched network include:

- the bit rate,
- the mean bit error rate,
- the transmission delay.

The mean **bit error rate** (**BER**) of a channel is the probability of a bit
being corrupted during its transmission across the channel in a defined time
interval. Hence, for a constant bit rate channel, this equates to the probability
of a bit being corrupted in a defined number of bits. A mean BER of 10^{-3},
therefore, means that, on average, for every 1000 bits that are transmitted, 1 of
these bits will be corrupted. In some applications, providing the occurrence of
bit errors is relatively infrequent, their presence is acceptable while in other
applications it is imperative that no residual bit errors are present in the
received information. For example, if the application involves speech, then an
occasional bit error will go unnoticed but in an application involving the transfer of, say, financial information, it is essential that the received information
contains no errors. Hence with such applications, prior to transmission the
source information is normally divided into blocks the maximum size of which
is determined by the mean BER of the communications channel.

For example, if the mean BER is 10^{-3}, then the number of bits in a block
must be considerably less than 1000 otherwise, on average, every block will
contain an error and will be discarded. Normally, however, bit errors occur
randomly and hence, even with a block size of, say, 100 bits, blocks may still
contain an error but the probability of this occurring is considerably less. In
general, if the BER probability is P and the number of bits in a block is N,
then, assuming random errors, the probability of a block containing a bit
error, P_B, is given by:

$$P_B = 1 - (1 - P)^N$$

which approximates to $N \times P$ if $N \times P$ is less than 1.

In practice, most networks – both circuit-switched and packet-switched –
provide an **unreliable service** which is also known as a **best-try** or **best-effort**
service. This means that any blocks containing bit errors will be discarded
either within the network – packet-switched networks – or in the network
interface at the destination – both packet-switched and circuit-switched networks. Hence if the application dictates that only error-free blocks are

Example 1.1

Derive the maximum block size that should be used over a channel which has a mean BER probability of 10^{-4} if the probability of a block containing an error – and hence being discarded – is to be 10^{-1}.

Answer:

$$P_{\text{B}} = 1 - (1 - P)^N$$

Hence $0.1 = 1 - (1 - 10^{-4})^N$ and $N = 950$ bits

Alternatively, $P_{\text{B}} = N \times P$

Hence $0.1 = N \times 10^{-4}$ and $N = 1000$ bits

acceptable, it is necessary for the sending terminal/computer to divide the source information into blocks of a defined maximum size and for the destination to detect when a block is missing. When this occurs the destination must request that the source send another copy of the missing block. The service offered is then said to be a **reliable service**. Clearly, this will introduce a delay so the retransmission procedure should be invoked relatively infrequently, which dictates a small block size. This, however, leads to high overheads since each block must contain the additional information that is associated with the retransmission procedure. Normally, therefore, the choice of block size is a compromise between the increased delay resulting from a large block size – and hence retransmissions – and the loss of transmission bandwidth resulting from the high overheads of using a smaller block size.

The **transmission delay** associated with a channel is determined not only by the bit rate that is used but also delays that occur in the terminal/computer network interfaces (known as codec delays), plus the propagation delay of the digital signals as they pass from the source to the destination across the network. This is determined by the physical separation of the two communicating devices and the velocity of propagation of a signal across the transmission medium. In free space, for example, the latter is equal to the speed of light $(3 \times 10^8 \text{ ms}^{-1})$ while it is a fraction of this in physical media, a typical value being $2 \times 10^8 \text{ ms}^{-1}$.

Notice that the propagation delay in each case is independent of the bit rate of the communications channel and, assuming the codec delay remains constant, is the same whether the bit rate is 1 kbps, 1 Mbps, or 1 Gbps.

Packet-switched network

The QoS parameters associated with a packet-switched network include:

- the maximum packet size,
- the mean packet transfer rate,

Example 1.2

Determine the propagation delay associated with the following communication channels:

(i)   a connection through a private telephone network of 1 km,

(ii) a connection through a PSTN of 200 km,

(iii) a connection over a satellite channel of 50 000 km.

Assume that the velocity of propagation of a signal in the case of (i) and (ii) is 2×10^8 ms^{-1} and in the case of (iii) 3×10^8 ms^{-1}.

Answer:

Propagation delay T_p = physical separation/velocity of propagation

(i) $T_p = \dfrac{10^3}{2 \times 10^8} = 5 \times 10^{-6}$ s

(ii) $T_p = \dfrac{200 \times 10^3}{2 \times 10^8} = 10^{-3}$ s

(iii) $T_p = \dfrac{5 \times 10^7}{3 \times 10^8} = 1.67 \times 10^{-1}$ s

■ the mean packet error rate,
■ the mean packet transfer delay,
■ the worst-case jitter,
■ the transmission delay.

In a packet-switched network, although the rate at which packets are transferred across the network is influenced strongly by the bit rate of the interconnecting links, because of the variable store-and-forward delays in each PSE/router, the actual rate of transfer of packets across the network is also variable. Hence the **mean packet transfer rate** is a measure of the average number of packets that are transferred across the network per second and, coupled with the packet size being used, determines the equivalent mean bit rate of the channel.

The **mean packet error rate** or **PER** is the probability of a received packet containing one or more bit errors. It is the same, therefore, as the block error rate associated with a circuit-switched network which we derived in the previous section. Hence it is related to both the maximum packet size and the worst-case BER of the transmission links that interconnect the PSEs/routers that make up the network.

We defined the meaning of the term "mean packet transfer delay" in Section 1.5.3 when we described the operation of packet-mode networks. It is the summation of the mean store-and-forward delay that a packet experiences in each PSE/router that it encounters along a route and the term "jitter" is the worst-case variation in this delay. As we just explained, the transmission delay is the same whether the network operates in a packet mode or a circuit mode and includes the codec delay in each of the two communicating computers and the signal propagation delay.

1.5.6 Application QoS

The network QoS parameters define what the particular network being used provides rather than what the application requires. The application itself, however, also has QoS parameters associated with it. In an application involving images, for example, the parameters may include a minimum image resolution and size, while in an application involving video, the digitization format and refresh rate may be defined. The application QoS parameters that relate to the network include:

- the required bit rate or mean packet transfer rate,
- the maximum startup delay,
- the maximum end-to-end delay,
- the maximum delay variation/jitter,
- the maximum round-trip delay.

For applications involving the transfer of a constant bit rate stream, the important parameters are the required bit rate/mean packet transfer rate, the end-to-end delay, and, equally important, the delay variation/jitter since this can cause problems in the destination decoder if the rate of arrival of the bitstream is variable. For interactive applications, however, the **startup delay** defines the amount of time that elapses between an application making a request to start a session and the confirmation being received from the application at the destination – a server, for example – that it is prepared to accept the request. Hence this includes, in addition to the time required to establish a network connection – if this is required – the delay introduced in both the source and the destination computers while negotiating that the session can take place. As we saw earlier in Section 1.5.1, the round-trip delay is important since, for human–computer interaction to be successful, the delay between a request for some information being made and the start of the information being received/displayed should be as short as possible and, ideally, should be less than a few seconds.

As we can see from the above, for applications that involve the transfer of a constant bit rate stream, a circuit-switched network would appear to be most appropriate since, firstly, the call setup delay is often not important and secondly, the channel provides a constant bit rate service of a known rate.

Conversely, for interactive applications, a connectionless packet-switched network would appear to be most appropriate since with this there is no network call setup delay and any variations in the packet transfer delay are not important.

An example application that illustrates the benefits of a packet-switched network over a circuit-switched network is the transfer of a large file of data from a server computer connected to the Internet to a client PC/workstation in a home. As we showed earlier in Figures 1.2 and 1.18, access to the Internet from home can be by means of a PSTN (with a modem), an ISDN connection, or a cable modem. In the case of a PSTN and an ISDN, these operate in a circuit-switched mode and provide a constant bit rate channel of in the order of 28.8 kbps (PSTN with modem) and 64/128 kbps (ISDN). In contrast, cable modems operate in a packet mode and, as we shall see later in Section 11.2.1, the modems in each of the homes in a cable region time-share the use of a single high bit rate channel/circuit. A typical bit rate of the shared channel is 27 Mbps and the number of concurrent users of the channel may be several hundred. Hence, assuming 270 concurrent users, each user would get a mean data rate of 100 kbps.

With this type of application, however, the main parameter of interest is not the mean data/bit rate but the time to transmit the complete file. With a PSTN and an ISDN, this is directly related to the channel bit rate and the size of the file. With a cable modem, however, although they time-share the use of the 27 Mbps channel, when they gain access to it, the file transfer takes place at the full rate. Hence assuming the file size is 100 Mbits, the minimum time to transmit the file using the different Internet access modes is:

PSTN and 28.8 kbps modem:	57.8 minutes
ISDN at 64 kbps:	26 minutes
ISDN at 128 kbps:	13 minutes
cable modem at 27 Mbps:	3.7 seconds

In the case of a cable modem, if other transfer requests occur during the time the file is being transmitted, then the completion time of each transfer request will increase as they share the use of the channel. Nevertheless, with this type of application, the probability of multiple users requesting a transfer in this short window of time is relatively low.

In many instances, however, this does not mean that the alternative network types cannot be used. For interactive applications, for example, the call setup delay with an ISDN or an ATM network – and a PSTN for local calls – is very fast and, for many applications, quite acceptable. Similarly, for constant bit rate applications, providing the equivalent mean bit rate provided by the network is greater than the input bit rate and the maximum jitter is less than a defined value, then a packet-switched network can be used. To overcome the effect of jitter a technique known as **buffering** is used, the general principles of which are shown in Figure 1.22.

As we show in the figure, the effect of jitter is overcome by retaining a defined number of packets in a memory buffer at the destination before play-out of the information bitstream is started. The memory buffer operates

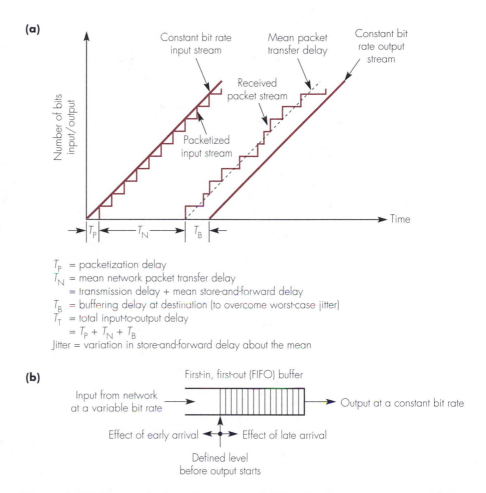

(a)

T_P = packetization delay
T_N = mean network packet transfer delay
    = transmission delay + mean store-and-forward delay
T_B = buffering delay at destination (to overcome worst-case jitter)
T_T = total input-to-output delay
    = $T_P + T_N + T_B$
Jitter = variation in store-and-forward delay about the mean

(b)

Figure 1.22 Transmission of a constant bit rate stream over a packet-switched network: (a) timing schematic; (b) FIFO buffer operation.

using a first-in, first-out (FIFO) discipline and the number of packets retained in the buffer before output starts is determined by the worst-case jitter and the bit rate of the information stream. However, as we show in part (a) of the figure, when using a packet-switched network for this type of application, an additional delay is incurred at the source as the information bitstream is converted into packets. This is known as the **packetization delay** and adds to the transmission delay of the channel. Hence in order to minimize the overall input-to-output delay, the packet size used for an application is made as small as possible but of sufficient size to overcome the effect of the worst-case jitter.

In order to simplify the process of determining whether a particular network can meet the QoS requirements of an application, a number of standard application **service classes** have been defined. Associated with each service class is a

Example 1.3

A packet-switched network with a worst-case jitter of 10 ms is to be used for a number of applications each of which involve a constant bit rate information stream. Determine the minimum amount of memory that is required at the destination and a suitable packet size for each of the following input bit rates. It can be assumed that the mean packet transfer rate of the network exceeds the equivalent input bit rate in each case.

(i)   64 kbps

(ii) 256 kbps

(iii) 1.5 Mbps.

Answer:

(i)   At 64 kbps, 10 ms = 640 bits
      Hence choose a packet size of, say, 800 bits with a FIFO buffer of 1600 bits – 2 packets – and start playout of the bitstream after the first packet has been received.

(ii) At 256 kbps, 10 ms = 2560 bits
      Hence choose a packet size of, say, 2800 bits with a FIFO buffer of 4800 bits.

(iii) At 1.5 Mbps, 10 ms = 15000 bits
      Hence choose a packet size of, say, 16 000 bits with a FIFO buffer of 32 000 bits.

Notice that if the computed packet size exceeds the network maximum packet size, then the equivalent number of packets must be sent before playout starts. For example, if the maximum network packet size was 8000 bits, then for case (iii) above playout would not start until two packets have been received and the FIFO buffer should hold four packets.

specific set of QoS parameters and a network can either meet this set of parameters or not. Also, for networks that support a number of different service classes – the Internet for example – in order to ensure the QoS parameters associated with each class are met, the packets relating to each class are given a different **priority**. It is then possible to treat the packets relating to each class differently.

For example, as we shall see in Chapter 9, in the Internet, packets relating to multimedia applications involving real-time streams are given a higher priority than the packets relating to applications such as email. Typically, packets containing real-time streams such as audio and video are also more sensitive to delay and jitter than the packets containing textual information. Hence during periods of network congestion, the packets containing real-time streams are transmitted first. Packets containing video are more sensitive to packet loss than packets containing audio and hence are given a higher priority.

Summary

In this chapter we have discussed:

- the different types of media that are used in multimedia applications,
- the different types of communication networks that are used to support these applications,
- a selection of the different types of application.

Media types

The different types of media that are used in multimedia applications are summarized in Figure 1.23. In some applications only a single type of medium is involved while in others multiple media types are used. As we described in Section 1.2, the basic form of representation of both text and images consists of a block of binary codewords. Each codeword consists of a fixed number of binary digits and represents, for example, a single character (text) or a single picture element (image). In contrast, the basic form of

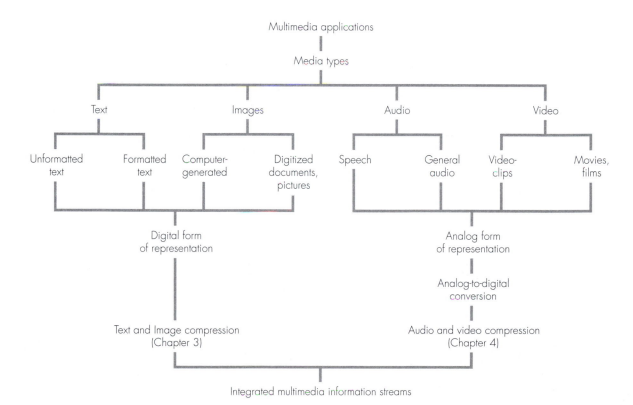

Figure 1.23 Alternative types of media used in multimedia applications.

representation of both audio and most video signals is in the form of an analog signal whose amplitude and frequency varies continuously with time. Hence in applications that involve audio and video integrated with text and/or images, it is necessary first to convert the audio and video signals into a digital form. We shall describe the digital form of representation of all four media types in more detail in the next chapter.

In practice, the bandwidth associated with the basic form of representation of the different media types is greater than the bandwidth of the communication networks that are used to support multimedia applications. Hence in most applications, a technique known as compression is applied to the source information prior to it being transferred over the network. We shall describe a selection of the different compression algorithms that are used with text and images in Chapter 3 and a selection of those used with audio and video in Chapter 4.

Network types

The different types of communication networks that are used to support multimedia applications are summarized in Figure 1.24 and a selection of the applications that each network type supports are shown in Figure 1.25.

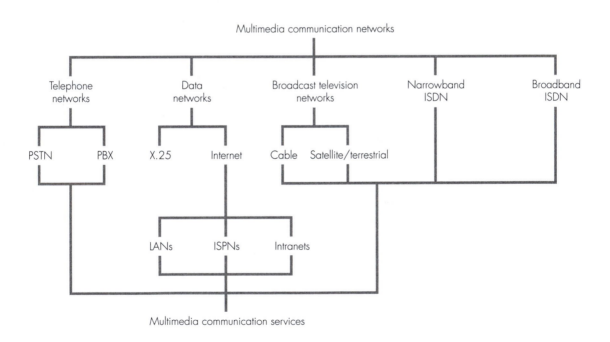

Figure 1.24 Multimedia communication networks.

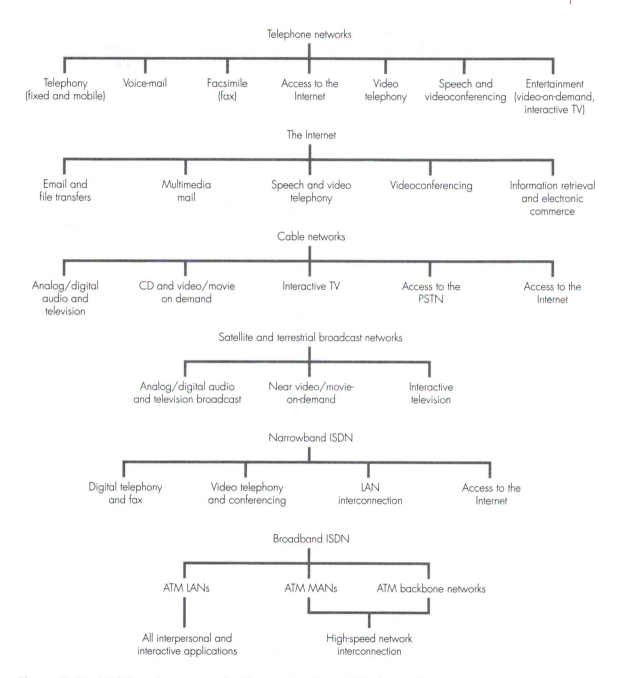

Figure 1.25 Multimedia communication networks and their services.

In the case of telephone networks, these were designed initially to provide a switched telephone service both nationally/internationally (a PSTN) and at a single site (a PBX). Also, with the advent of the first modems, they provided a low bit rate switched data service. Later, as a result of advances in modem technology and related compression algorithms, the transfer of digitized documents (facsimile) was supported. These developments have continued and the PSTN now supports a wide range of applications that involve all four media types either singly or integrated together in some way.

Similarly, with data networks – and in particular the Internet. Although designed initially to support applications that involve only text and images, the advances in compression algorithms means that the Internet now supports a similar range of multimedia applications. The applications associated with broadcast television networks have been enhanced by the same advances in modem technology and compression algorithms.

The last two network types – narrowband and broadband ISDN – were both designed from the outset to provide an enhanced set of services to those provided by a PSTN. A narrowband ISDN, for example, has a range of digital access alternatives which, collectively, support a wide range of multimedia applications. Broadband ISDN was designed from the start to support multimedia applications that involve all four media types. In practice, however, because of the wider set of (multimedia) applications that the other networks can now support, broadband ISDN is not as yet widely deployed. Nevertheless, the basic transmission and switching technology associated with it – known as the asynchronous transfer mode (ATM) and cell switching respectively – has been used in high-speed LANs and for high-speed network interconnection.

We shall discuss in some detail the operation of these various network types in Chapters 7–11 and the communication protocols and other application-related issues that are associated with them in Chapters 12–14.

Multimedia applications

We have chosen to place all multimedia applications into one of three categories:

- interpersonal communications,
- interactive applications over the Internet,
- entertainment applications.

There are a number of applications in each category each of which involves various media types. A selection of the applications, together with the type of media involved, are summarized in Table 1.1. Note that each type of application can be supported by a number of different network types. For example, video telephony is supported by a PSTN, the Internet, and both narrowband and broadband ISDN.

Table 1.1 Multimedia applications summary.

Category	Media	Application descriptions
Interpersonal communications	Speech	Telephony, voice-mail, teleconferencing
	Image	Facsimile
	Text	Electronic mail
	Text and images	Computer-supported cooperative working (CSCW)
	Speech and video	Video telephony, video mail, videoconferencing
	Text, image audio and video	Multimedia electronic mail, multiparty video games etc.
Interactive applications over the Internet	Text, image, audio and video	Information retrieval (news, weather, books magazines, video games, product literature etc.)
		Electronic commerce
Entertainment services	Audio and video	Audio/CD-on-demand
		Movie/video-on-demand
		Near movie/video-on-demand
		Analog and digital television broadcasts
		Interactive television

Exercises

Section 1.2

1.1 (a) State the basic form of representation of:
(i) text,
(ii) an image,
(iii) audio,
(iv) video.
State the form of representation that is used when all are integrated together and give your reason.

1.2 State the meaning of the term "bits per second" in relation to digitized audio and video. What is the meaning of the term "compression" and why is compression used?

Section 1.3

1.3 With the aid of a diagram, explain the meaning of the following terms relating to a switched telephone network:
(i) POTS,
(ii) local exchange/end office,
(iii) PBX,
(iv) mobile switching center,
(v) international gateway exchange.

1.4 Explain why a pair of modems is required to transmit a digital signal over a PSTN. With the aid of a diagram, show the location of the two modems when two digital devices communicate over a PSTN and the types of signal – analog or digital – that are used over each part of the access circuit.

1.5 Show in the form of a diagram how a high-speed modem provides a range of additional services to basic telephony and data services. State a typical access bit rate that is used.

1.6 With the aid of a diagram, describe how the following gain access to the Internet:
(i) a user at home or in a small business,
(ii) a distributed community of users around a single site or campus,
(iii) a distributed set of users all attatched to the same enterprise-wide private network. Why is the latter sometimes called an intranet?

1.7 Explain why most data networks operate in a packet mode. Hence explain why services involving audio and video are supported.

1.8 State the aim of all broadcast television networks.
With the aid of diagrams, explain how additional services are provided with
(i) a cable distribution network and
(ii) a satellite/terrestrial broadcast network.

1.9 With aid of a diagram, explain the meaning of the following terms relating to ISDN:
(i) digital subscriber line,
(ii) basic rate access,
(iii) aggregation,
(iv) primary rate access,
(v) p × 64.

1.10 Explain the meaning of the term "broadband" in relation to a B-ISDN and why the deployment of such networks has been delayed.

1.11 Explain the meaning of the following terms relating to a B-ISDN:
(i) a cell,
(ii) ATM,
(iii) cell switching.

Section 1.4

1.12 In relation to speech-only interpersonal communications involving both public (PSTN/

ISDN) and private (PBX) networks, with the aid of a diagram explain how voice-mail and teleconferencing are supported. Include in your descriptions the role of a voice-mail server and an audio bridge.

1.13 With the aid of a diagram, explain the function of a telephony gateway in relation to Internet telephony. Hence state the origin of the term "voice over IP" (VoIP).

1.14 Describe the principal operation of a fax machine and why modems are required. What is the meaning of the term "PC fax"?

1.15 Show in the form of a diagram the networks and essential items of equipment that are used to send an email message from a PC user at home to
(i) a PC attached to a site/campus LAN,
(ii) a PC attached to a site/campus LAN,
(iii) a PC attached to an enterprise-wide private network/intranet.

1.16 With the aid of a diagram, explain the basic principles behind computer-supported cooperative working (CSCW). Include in your explanation the role of the following:
(i) shared whiteboard,
(ii) whiteboard program,
(iii) change-notification,
(iv) update control.

1.17 Use a schematic diagram to illustrate each of the following:
(i) a two-party video phone call,
(ii) a videoconferencing call using an MCU,
(iii) a videoconferencing call using a broadcast network. Show on your diagrams the bandwith requirements of the access circuits in each case.

1.18 Explain the role of an MCU in relation to a videoconferencing session involving multiple geographically distributed videoconferencing studios.
Quantify the bandwidth implications of locating the MCU at one of the sites.

1.19 With multimedia electronic mail, when a message in a number of different formats is sent –

for example, speech-with-video, speech-only and text – normally the first version in output first. Why is this?

1.20 Use a schematic diagram to explain the meaning of the following terms relating to interactive applications over the inernet:
   (i)   a Web server,
   (ii) a browser,
   (iii) the World Wide Web.

1.21 In relation to a document stored on a Web server, explain the meaning of the following terms:
   (i)   Web page,
   (ii) home page,
   (iii) hyperlink,
   (iv) URL,
   (v) HTML.

1.22 With the aid of a diagram, explain the principle of operation of movie/video-on-demand. Identify the bandwidth requirements associated with this type of application.

1.23 What is the limiting factor associated with movie/video-on-demand? Explain how this effect is reduced with near movie-on-demand.

1.24 Explain the meaning of the term "interactive television" and, with the aid of diagrams, how this is using either a cable distribution network or a satellite/terrestrial broadcast network. Explain how Internet access is obtained with each network type.

Section 1.5

1.25 What is the meaning of the following terms relating to the different types of media used in multimedia communications:
   (i)   block-mode media,
   (ii) continuous media,
   (iii) streaming,
   (iv) constant bit rate,
   (v) variable bit rate?

1.26 With the aid of diagrams, explain the meaning of the following operational modes of a communication channel:
   (i)   simplex,
   (ii) half-duplex,
   (iii) duplex,
   (iv) broadcast
   (v) multicast,
   (vi) asymmetric and symmetric.

1.27 With the aid of a diagram explain the principle of operation of a circuit-mode network. Include in your explanation the need for signaling (messages) and the overheads of the connection setup delay associated with this.

1.28 With the aid of diagrams, explain the principle of operation of a CO packet-mode network. Include in your explanation the need for a virtual connection/circuit, a virtual circuit identifier, and a routing table.

1.29 In relation to a CL packet-mode network, explain the meaning of the following terms:
   (i)   best effort service,
   (ii) store-and-forward display,
   (iii) mean packet transfer delay,
   (iv) jitter.

1.30 With the aid of diagrams, explain the following operational modes of multipoint conferencing:
   (i)   centralized,
   (ii) decentralized,
   (iii) hybrid.

1.31 Identify the application domain and explain the operation of the following types of conference server:
   (i)   general purpose,
   (ii) audio bridge,
   (iii) multipoint control unit,

1.32 In relation to conference servers, explain the meaning of the following terms:
   (i)   multipoint controller,
   (ii) multipoint processor,
   (iii) dial-in mode,

     (iv) dial-out mode,
     (v)   voice activated switching,
     (vi) continuous presence.

1.33   Identify and explain the meaning of the key QoS parameters associated with the following network types:
     (i)   circuit-switched,
     (ii)   packet-switched.

1.34   Define the BER probability of a transmission line/channel. How does this influence the maximum block size to be used with the line/channel?

1.35   Define the transmission delay of a transmission line/channel. First identify the individual sources of delay that contribute to this.

1.36   Identify and explain the meaning of the key parameters associated with application QoS.

1.37   With the aid of a diagram explain the meaning of the following terms relating to packet-switched network:

     (i)   packetization delay,
     (ii) mean packet transfer delay,
     (iii) jitter.

Hence describe how the effects on a constant bit rate stream of packetization delay and jitter can be overcome by buffering.

1.38   A Web page of 10 Mbytes is being retrieved from a Web server. Assuming negligible delays within the server and trunk network, quantify the time to transfer the page over the following types of access circuit:
     (i)   a PSTN modem operating at 28.8 kbps,
     (ii)   an aggregated basic rate access line of 128 kbps,
     (iii) a primary rate ISDN access line of 1.5 Mbps,
     (iv) a high-speed modem operating at 6 Mbps,
     (v)   a cable modem operating at 27 Mbps.

1.39   Discuss the term "application service classes". Include in your dicussion how packets belonging to different classes are treated within the network.

Multimedia information representation

2.1 Introduction

All types of multimedia information are stored and processed within a computer in a digital form. In the case of textual information consisting of strings of characters entered at a keyboard, for example, each character is represented by a unique combination of a fixed number of bits – known as a **codeword** – and hence the complete text by a string of such codewords. Similarly, computer-generated graphical images are made up of a mix of lines, circles, squares, and so on, each represented in a digital form. A line, for example, is represented by means of the start and end coordinates of the line relative to the complete image, each coordinate being defined in the form of a pair of digital values.

In contrast, devices such as microphones and many video cameras produce electrical signals whose amplitude varies continuously with time, the amplitude of the signal at any point in time indicating the magnitude of the sound-wave/image-intensity at that instant. As we indicated in Section 1.2, a signal whose amplitude varies continuously with time is known as an **analog signal**. In order to store and process such signals – and hence types of media – within a computer, it is necessary first to convert any time-varying analog signals into a digital form. In addition, the signals used to operate devices such as loudspeakers – for speech and audio – and computer monitors – for the display of digitized images for example – are also analog signals. Thus digital values representing such media types must be converted back again into a corresponding time-varying analog form on output from the computer.

The conversion of an analog signal into a digital form is carried out using an electrical circuit known as a **signal encoder**. This, as we will expand upon in the next section, operates by first **sampling** the amplitude of the analog signal at repetitive time intervals and then converting the amplitude of each sample into a corresponding digital value. Similarly, the conversion of the stored digitized samples relating to a particular media type into their corresponding time-varying analog form is performed by an electrical circuit known as a **signal decoder**.

In this way, all the media types associated with the various multimedia applications discussed in the last chapter are stored and processed within a computer in an all-digital form. This means that the different media types can be readily integrated together and, equally important, the resulting integrated bitstream can be transmitted over a single all-digital communications network. This chapter is concerned with the way the different media types are represented in their digital form and, where appropriate, the conversion operations that are used. Before discussing this, however, it will be helpful if we first gain an understanding of the general principles relating to how analog signals are converted into their digital form and vice versa.

2.2 Digitization principles

2.2.1 Analog signals

The general properties relating to any time-varying analog signal are shown in Figure 2.1. As we can see in part (a) of the figure, the amplitude of such signals varies continuously with time. In addition, a mathematical technique known as **Fourier analysis** can be used to show that any time-varying analog signal is made up of a possibly infinite number of single-frequency sinusoidal signals whose amplitude and phase vary continuously with time relative to each other. As an example, the highest and lowest frequency components of the signal shown in Figure 2.1(a) may be those shown in Figure 2.1(b).

The range of frequencies of the sinusoidal components that make up a signal is called the **signal bandwidth** and two examples are shown in part (c) of the figure. These relate to an audio signal, the first a speech signal and the second a music signal produced by, say, an orchestra. In terms of speech, humans produce sounds – which are converted into electrical signals by a

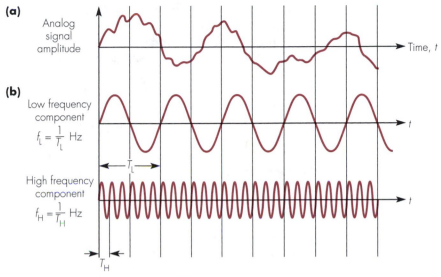

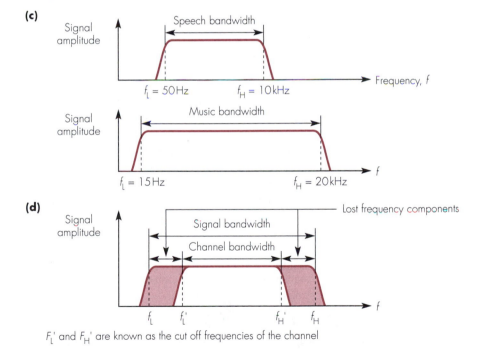

Figure 2.1 Signal properties: (a) time-varying analog signal; (b) sinusoidial frequency components; (c) signal bandwidth examples; (d) effect of a limited bandwidth transmission channel.

microphone – that are made up of a range of sinusoidal signals varying in frequency between 50 Hz and 10 kHz. In the case of a music signal, however, the range of signals is wider and varies between 15 Hz and 20 kHz, this being comparable with the limits of the sensitivity of the ear.

Ideally, when an analog signal is being transmitted through a network, the bandwidth of the transmission channel – that is, the range of frequencies the channel will pass – should be equal to or greater than the bandwidth of the signal. If the bandwidth of the channel is less than this, then some of the low and/or high frequency components will be lost thereby degrading the quality of the received signal. This type of transmission channel is called a **bandlimiting channel** and its effect is shown in Figure 2.1 (d).

2.2.2 Encoder design

As indicated in Section 2.1, the conversion of a time-varying analog signal – of which an audio signal is an example – into a digital form is carried out using an electronic circuit known as a (signal) encoder. The principles of an encoder are shown in Figure 2.2 and, as we can see in part (a), it consists of two main circuits: a **bandlimiting filter** and an **analog-to-digital converter** (**ADC**), the latter comprising a sample-and-hold and a quantizer. A typical **waveform set** for a signal encoder is shown in part (b) of the figure. The role of the bandlimiting filter, as we shall see below, is to remove selected higher-frequency components from the source signal (A). The output of the filter (B) is then fed to the **sample-and-hold** circuit which, as its name implies, is used to sample the amplitude of the filtered signal at regular time intervals (C) and to hold the sample amplitude constant between samples (D). This, in turn, is fed to the **quantizer** circuit which converts each sample amplitude into a binary value known as a codeword (E).

The most significant bit of each codeword indicates the polarity (sign) of the sample, positive or negative relative to the zero level. Normally, a binary 0 indicates a positive value and a binary 1 a negative value. Also, as we can deduce from the time-related set of waveforms shown in Figure 2.2(b), to represent the amplitude of a time-varying analog signal precisely, requires firstly, the signal to be sampled at a rate which is higher than the maximum rate of change of the signal amplitude and secondly, the number of different quantization levels used to be as large as possible. We shall consider each of these requirements separately.

Sampling rate

In relation to the sampling rate, the **Nyquist sampling theorem** states that: in order to obtain an accurate representation of a time-varying analog signal, its amplitude must be sampled at a minimum rate that is equal to or greater than twice the highest sinusoidal frequency component that is present in the signal. This is known as the **Nyquist rate** and is normally represented as either Hz or, more correctly, **samples per second** (**sps**). Sampling a signal at a rate

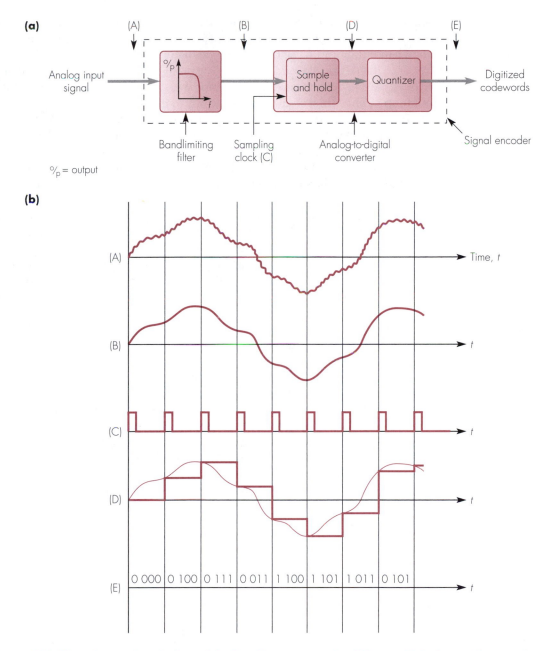

Figure 2.2 Signal encoder design: (a) circuit components; (b) associated waveform set.

which is lower than the Nyquist rate results in additional frequency components being generated that are not present in the original signal which, in turn, cause the original signal to become **distorted**.

The distortion caused by sampling a signal at a rate lower than the Nyquist rate is best illustrated by considering the effect of undersampling a single-frequency sinusoidal signal as shown in Figure 2.3.

In this example, the original signal is assumed to be a 6 kHz sinewave which is sampled at a rate of 8 ksps. Clearly this is lower than the Nyquist rate of 12 ksps (2 × 6 kHz) and, as we can see, results in a lower-frequency 2 kHz signal being created in place of the original 6 kHz signal. Because of this, such signals are called **alias signals** since they replace the corresponding original signals.

In general, this means that all frequency components present in the original signal that are higher in frequency than half the sampling frequency being used (in Hz), will generate related lower-frequency alias signals which will simply add to those making up the original source signal thereby causing it to become distorted. However, by first passing the source signal through a bandlimiting filter which is designed to pass only those frequency components up to that determined by the Nyquist rate, any higher-frequency components in the signal which are higher than this are removed before the signal is sampled. Because of this function the bandlimiting filter is also known as an **antialiasing filter**.

In practice, as we indicated earlier, the transmission channel used/available often has a lower bandwidth than that of the source signal. In such cases, in order to avoid distortion, it is the bandwidth – and hence frequency range – of the transmission channel that determines the sampling rate used rather than the bandwidth of the source signal. Since in such cases the source signal may have higher frequency components than those dictated by the Nyquist rate of the transmission channel, it is necessary first to pass the source signal through a bandlimiting filter which is designed to pass only those sinusoidal frequency components which are within the bandwidth of the transmission channel. In this way, the generation of any alias signals caused by **undersampling** the source signal is avoided.

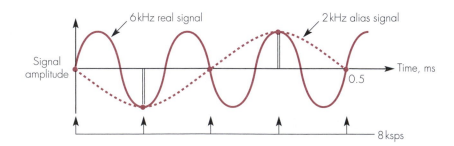

Figure 2.3 Alias signal generation due to undersampling.

Example 2.1

Determine the rate of the sampler and the bandwidth of the bandlimiting filter in an encoder which is to be used for the digitization of an analog signal which has a bandwidth from 15 Hz through to 10 kHz assuming the digitized signal:

(i) is to be stored within the memory of a computer,

(ii) is to be transmitted over a channel which has a bandwidth from 200 Hz through to 3.4 kHz.

Answer:

The Nyquist sampling rate must be at least twice the highest frequency component of the signal or transmission channel. Hence:

(i) The sampling rate must be at least 2 × 10 kHz = 20 kHz or 20 ksps and the bandwidth of the bandlimiting filter is from 0 Hz through to 10 kHz.

(ii) The sampling rate must be at least 2 × 3.4 kHz = 6.8 kHz or 6.8 ksps and the bandwidth of the bandlimiting filter is from 0 Hz through to 3.4 kHz.

In practice, it should be noted that, because of imperfections in filters, some higher frequency components above the filter cut-off frequency may be passed and hence the sampling rate is normally higher than the two derived values. In the case of (ii), for example, it is common to assume that frequency components of up to 4 kHz may be passed by the bandlimiting filter and hence a sampling rate of 8 ksps is normally used.

Quantization intervals

To represent in a digital form the amplitudes of the set of analog samples shown earlier in Figure 2.2 precisely, would require an infinite number of binary digits since, when a finite number of digits is used, each sample can only be represented by a corresponding number of discrete levels. The effect of using a finite number of bits can be seen by considering the example shown in Figure 2.4. In this example we use just three bits to represent each sample including a sign bit. This results in four positive and four negative quantization intervals, the two magnitude bits being determined by the particular quantization interval the analog input signal is in at the time of each sample.

As we can deduce from part (a) of the figure, if V_{max} is the maximum positive and negative signal amplitude and n is the number of binary bits used, then the magnitude of each **quantization interval**, q, is given by

$$q = \frac{2V_{max}}{2^n}$$

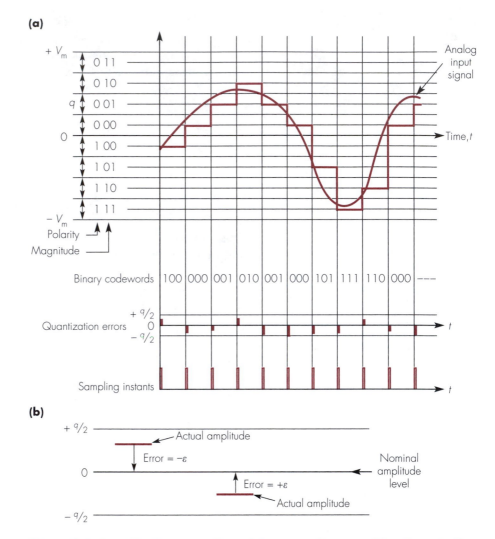

Figure 2.4 Quantization procedure: (a) source of errors; (b) noise polarity.

Also, as we can see, a signal anywhere within a quantization interval will be represented by the same binary codeword. This means that each codeword corresponds to a nominal amplitude level which is at the center of the corresponding quantization interval. Hence the actual signal level may differ from this by up to plus or minus $q/2$.

The difference between the actual signal amplitude and the corresponding nominal amplitude is called the **quantization error** and, for the example shown in Figure 2.4, the quantization error values are shown expanded in part (b) of the figure. Normally, the error values will vary randomly from sample to sample and hence the quantization error is also known as **quantization noise**, the term "noise" being used in electrical circuits to refer to a signal whose amplitude varies randomly with time.

Another related factor which influences the choice of the number of quantization intervals used for a particular signal is its smallest amplitude relative to its peak amplitude. With high-fidelity music, for example, it is important to be able to hear very quiet passages without any distortion created by quantization noise. The ratio of the peak amplitude of a signal to its minimum amplitude is known as the **dynamic range** of the signal, **D**. Normally it is quantified using a logarithmic scale known as **decibels** or **dB**:

$$D = 20 \log_{10} (V_{max} / V_{max}) \, \text{dB}$$

Hence when determining the quantization interval – and thus number of bits to be used – it is necessary to ensure that the level of quantization noise relative to the smallest signal amplitude is acceptable.

Example 2.2

An analog signal has a dynamic range of 40 dB. Determine the magnitude of the quantization noise relative to the minimum signal amplitude if the quantizer uses (i) 6 bits and (ii) 10 bits:

Answer:

$$D = 20 \log_{10} \frac{V_{max}}{V_{min}} \, \text{dB} \quad \text{Quantization noise} = \pm \frac{q}{2} = \pm \frac{V_{max}}{2^n}$$

Hence $40 = 20 \log_{10} \dfrac{V_{max}}{V_{min}}$

and $V_{min} = \dfrac{V_{max}}{100}$

(i) $n = 6$ bits

Hence $\dfrac{q}{2} = \pm \dfrac{V_{max}}{2^6} = \pm \dfrac{V_{max}}{64}$

(ii) $n = 10$ bits

Hence $\dfrac{q}{2} = \pm \dfrac{V_{max}}{2^{10}} = \pm \dfrac{V_{max}}{1024}$

As we can see from these values, with 6 bits the quantization noise is greater than V_{min} and hence is unacceptable. With 10 bits, however, the quantization noise is an order of magnitude less than V_{min} and hence will have a much reduced effect.

2.2.3 Decoder design

As indicated in Section 2.1, although analog signals are stored, processed and transmitted in a digital form, normally, prior to their output, they must be converted back again into their analog form; loudspeakers, for example, are driven by an analog current signal. The electronic circuit that performs this conversion operation is known as a (signal) decoder, the principles of which are shown in Figure 2.5.

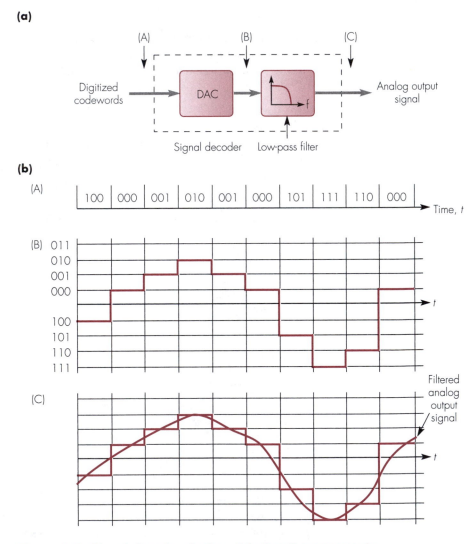

Figure 2.5 Signal decoder design: (a) circuit components; (b) associated waveform set.

First, each digital codeword (A) is converted into an equivalent analog sample using a circuit called a **digital-to-analog converter** or **DAC**. This produces the signal shown in (B), the amplitude of each level being determined by the corresponding codeword. Since this is a time-varying signal, as indicated earlier, Fourier analysis can be used to show that this type of signal comprises not just the sinusoidal frequency components that make up the original (filtered) analog signal, but also an infinite number of additional higher-frequency components. In order to reproduce the original signal, the output of the DAC is passed through a **low-pass filter** which, as its name implies, only passes those frequency components that made up the original filtered signal (C). Normally, the high-frequency cut-off of the low-pass filter is made the same as that used in the bandlimiting filter of the encoder. Because of its function, the low-pass filter is also known as a **recovery** or **reconstruction filter**.

Finally, since in most multimedia applications involving audio and video the communications channel is two-way simultaneous, the terminal equipment must support both input and output simultaneously. Hence the audio/video signal encoders and decoders in each terminal equipment are often combined into a single unit called an **audio/video encoder-decoder** or simply an **audio/video codec**.

2.3 Text

Essentially, there are three types of text that are used to produce pages of documents:

- **unformatted text:** this is also known as **plaintext** and enables pages to be created which comprise strings of fixed-sized characters from a limited character set;
- **formatted text:** this is also known as **richtext** and enables pages and complete documents to be created which comprise of strings of characters of different styles, size, and shape with tables, graphics, and images inserted at appropriate points;
- **hypertext:** this enables an integrated set of documents (each comprising formatted text) to be created which have defined linkages between them.

We shall discuss the three types separately.

2.3.1 Unformatted text

Figure 2.6 illustrates two examples of character sets that are widely used to create pages consisting of unformatted text strings.

The table shown in part (a) tabulates the set of characters that are available in the **ASCII character set**, the term "ASCII" being an abbreviation for the **American Standard Code for Information Interchange**. This is one of the

(a)

Bit positions 7				0	0	0	0	1	1	1	1
6				0	0	1	1	0	0	1	1
5				0	1	0	1	0	1	0	1
4	3	2	1								
0	0	0	0	NUL	DLE	SP	0	@	P	\	p
0	0	0	1	SOH	DC1	!	1	A	Q	a	q
0	0	1	0	STX	DC2	"	2	B	R	b	r
0	0	1	1	ETX	DC3	#	3	C	S	c	s
0	1	0	0	EOT	DC4	$	4	D	T	d	t
0	1	0	1	ENQ	NAK	%	5	E	U	e	u
0	1	1	0	ACK	SYN	&	6	F	V	f	v
0	1	1	1	BEL	ETB	'	7	G	W	g	w
1	0	0	0	BS	CAN	(	8	H	X	h	x
1	0	0	1	HT	EM	)	9	I	Y	i	y
1	0	1	0	LF	SUB	*	:	J	Z	j	z
1	0	1	1	VT	ESC	+	;	K	[	k	{
1	1	0	0	FF	FS	,	<	L	\	l	|
1	1	0	1	CR	GS	-	=	M	]	m	}
1	1	1	0	SO	RS	.	>	N	^	n	~
1	1	1	1	SI	US	/	?	O	—	o	DEL

(b)

Bit positions 7				0	0	0	0	1	1	1	1
6				0	0	1	1	0	0	1	1
5				0	1	0	1	0	1	0	1
4	3	2	1								
0	0	0	0					@	P		
0	0	0	1					A	Q		
0	0	1	0					B	R		
0	0	1	1					C	S		
0	1	0	0					D	T		
0	1	0	1					E	U		
0	1	1	0					F	V		
0	1	1	1					G	W		
1	0	0	0					H	X		
1	0	0	1					I	Y		
1	0	1	0					J	Z		
1	0	1	1					K	[		
1	1	0	0					L	\		
1	1	0	1					M	]		
1	1	1	0					N	^		
1	1	1	1					O	—		

Figure 2.6 Two example character sets to produce unformatted text: (a) the basic ASCII character set; (b) supplementary set of mosaic characters.

most widely used character sets and the table includes the binary codewords used to represent each character. As we can see, each character is represented by a unique 7-bit binary codeword. The use of 7 bits means that there are 128 (2^7) alternative characters and the codeword used to identify each character is obtained by combining the corresponding column (bits 7–5) and row (bits 4–1) bits together. Bit 7 is the most significant bit and hence the codeword for uppercase M, for example, is 1001101.

In addition to all the normal alphabetic, numeric and punctuation characters – collectively referred to as **printable characters** – the total ASCII character set also includes a number of **control characters**. These include:

- format control characters: BS (backspace), LF linefeed), CR (carriage return), SP (space), DEL (delete), ESC (escape), and FF (form feed);
- information separators: FS (file separator) and RS (record separator);
- transmission control characters: SOH (start-of-heading), STX (start-of-text), ETX (end-of-text), ACK (acknowledge), NAK (negative acknowledge), SYN (synchronous idle), and DLE (data link escape).

The latter, as we shall describe later in Section 6.4.3, are sometimes used to control the transmission of blocks of characters which are made up of the other characters in the set.

The character set tabulated in Figure 2.6(b) is a supplementary version of that shown in part (a). Here the characters in columns 010/011 and 110/111 are replaced with the set of **mosaic characters** shown. These are then used, together with the various uppercase characters illustrated, to create relatively simple graphical images.

An example application of this particular character set is in **Videotex** and **Teletext** which are general broadcast information services available through a standard television set and used in a number of countries. Some examples of typical Teletext/Videotex symbols are shown in Figure 2.7. As we can see, although in practice the total page is made up of a matrix of symbols and characters which all have the same size (in terms of their height and width), some simple graphical symbols and text of larger sizes can be constructed by the use of groups of the basic symbols.

2.3.2 Formatted text

An example of formatted text is that produced by most word processing packages. It is also used extensively in the publishing sector for the preparation of papers, books, magazines, journals, and so on. It enables documents to be created that consist of characters of different styles and of variable size and shape, each of which can be plain, bold, or italicized. In addition, a variety of document formatting options are supported to enable an author to structure a document into chapters, sections and paragraphs, each with different headings and with tables, graphics, and pictures inserted at appropriate points.

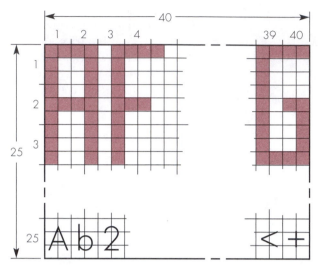

Note: Grid only included as a template.

Figure 2.7 Example Videotex/Teletext characters.

To achieve each of these features, the author of the document enters a specific command which, typically, results in a defined format-control character sequence – normally a reserved format-control character followed by a pair of other alphabetic or numeric characters – being inserted at the beginning of the particular character string, table, graphic or picture. In this way, each page of the document comprises the string of characters that make up the textual part of the page – plus, where appropriate, the associated tables, graphics, or pictures – with the corresponding format-control character sequences interspersed at appropriate points. An example formatted text string is as shown in part (a) of Figure 2.8 and the printed version of this string is shown in part(b).

As we can deduce from the above, in order to print a document consisting of formatted text, the printer must first be set up – that is, the microprocessor within the printer must be programmed – to detect and interpret the format-control character sequences in the defined way and to convert the following text, table, graphic, or picture into a line-by-line form ready for printing. In addition, to help the author visualize the layout of each page prior to printing, commands such as *print preview* are often provided which cause the page to be displayed on the computer screen in a similar way to how it will appear when it is printed. This is the origin of the term **WYSIWYG**, an acronym for what-you-see-is-what-you-get.

(a)

```
<B><FONT SIZE=4><P>Formatted Text</P>
</B></FONT>
<P>This is an example of formatted text, it includes:</P>
<FONT SIZE=2>
</FONT><I><P>Italics,</I> <B>Bold</B> and <U>Underlining</P>
</U>
<FONT FACE="French Script MT"><P>Different Fonts</FONT> and <FONT
SIZE=4>Font Sizes</P>
```

(b)

Formatted text
This is an example of formatted text, it includes:
Italics, **Bold** and <u>Underlining</u>
Different fonts and Font Sizes

Figure 2.8 Formatted text: (a) an example formatted text string; (b) printed version of the string.

2.3.3 Hypertext

As we saw earlier in Section 1.4.2 hypertext is a type of formatted text that enables a related set of documents – normally referred to as **pages** – to be created which have defined linkage points – referred to as **hyperlinks** – between each other. For example, most universities describe their structure and the courses and support services they offer, in a booklet known as a prospectus. Like most such booklets, this is organized in a hierarchical way and, in order for a reader to find out information about a particular course, and the facilities offered by the university, typically, the reader would start at the index and use this to access details about the various departments, the courses each offers, and so on, by switching between the different sections of the booklet.

In a similar way, as we show in Figure 2.9, hypertext can be used to create an electronic version of such documents with the index, descriptions of departments, courses on offer, library, and other facilities all written in hypertext as pages with various defined hyperlinks between them to enable a person to browse through its contents in a user-friendly way. Typically, the linked set of pages that make up the prospectus would all be stored in a single server computer. However, should a particular department choose to provide a more in-depth description of the courses and facilities it offers – for example, the contents of courses, current research projects, staff profiles, or publications – these can also be implemented as a linked set of pages on a different computer and, providing all the computers at the site are connected to the same network (and use the same set of communication protocols), additional hyperlinks between the two sets of pages can be introduced.

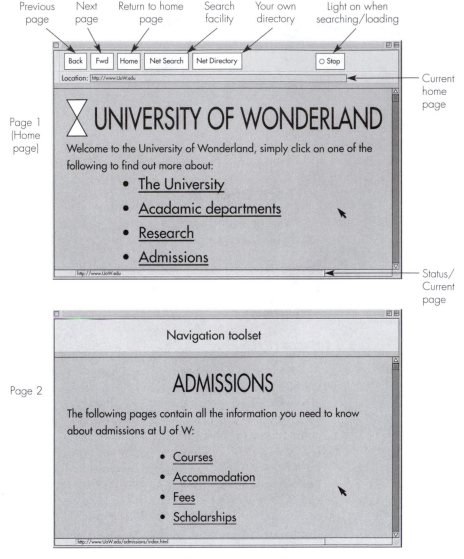

Figure 2.9 Example of an electronic document written in hypertext.

The linked set of pages that are stored in a particular server are accessed and viewed using a client program known as a **browser**. This can be running in either the same computer on which the server software is running or, more usually, in a separate remote computer.

Associated with each set of linked pages is a page known as the **home page**. Normally, this comprises a form of index to the set of pages linked to it, each of which has a hyperlink entry-point associated with it. Typically, hyperlinks take the form of an underlined text string and the user initiates the access and display of a particular page by pointing and clicking the mouse on the appropriate string/link.

Associated with each link, in addition to the textual name of the link and the related format-control information for its display, is a unique network-wide name known as a **uniform resource locator** or **URL**. This comprises a number of logical parts – including the unique name of the host computer where the page is stored and also the name of the file containing the page – which collectively enables the browser program to locate and read each requested page. Hence to access the home page of a particular server, the user first enters its URL – in response to a prompt by the browser program – and, in turn, the browser uses this, first to locate the server computer on which the particular page is stored and then to request the page contents from the server. The page contents are stored in a specific formatted text and, on receipt of the contents, the browser displays these on the client computer screen using the included format control commands. In this way, after accessing the home page associated with a site, a user is able to access and browse through the contents of the linked set of pages in the order he or she chooses.

An example of a hypertext language is **HTML** which stands for **HyperText Markup Language**. We shall discuss HTML in detail in section 15.3 and restrict oursleves here to its essential features in order to gain an understanding of the form of representation of a typical hypertext page. HTML is an example of a more general set of what are known as **mark-up languages**. These are used to describe how the contents of a document are to be presented on a printer or a display, the term "mark-up" being that used by a copy editor when the printing of documents was carried out manually. Other mark-up languages include **Postscript** (known as a (printed) page description language), **SGML** (the acronym for **Standard Generalized Mark-up Language** on which HTML is based), **Tex**, and **Latex**. In general, the output of these languages is similar to that produced by many word-processing systems but, unlike word processors, they are concerned only with the formatting of a document in preparation for its printing or display.

As the name implies, HTML is concerned solely with hypertext and has been designed specifically for use with the World Wide Web and, in particular, for the creation of Web pages. It is concerned primarily with the formatting of pages – to enable a browser program running on a remote computer to display a retrieved page on its local screen – and for the specification of hyperlinks – to enable a user to browse interactively through the contents of a set of pages linked together by means of hyperlinks.

The page formatting commands – known as **directives** in HTML and each sandwiched between a pair of **tags** (<>) – include commands to start a new paragraph (<P>), start and end boldface (<B>text</B>), present in the form of a bulleted list (<HL>list</HL>), include an image (<IMG SRC=" an image">), and so on. Other media types such as sound and video clips can also be included, giving rise to the term **hypermedia**. Indeed, the terms "hypermedia" and "hypertext" are often used interchangeably when referring to pages created in HTML.

The specification of a hyperlink is made by specifying both the URL of where the required page is located, together with the textual name of the link. For example, the specification of a hyperlink to a page containing 'Further details' would have the form <A HREF="URL">Further details </A>. Hence, as we can see, a hypertext string is similar to a formatted text string, except that at the linkage points within a page additional text strings are found that define the URL of the linked page.

2.4 Images

Within the context of this book, images include computer-generated images – more generally referred to as **computer graphics** or simply **graphics** – and digitized images of both documents and pictures. Although ultimately all three types of image are displayed (and printed) in the form of a two-dimensional matrix of individual picture elements – known as **pixels** or sometimes **pels** – each type is represented differently within the computer memory or, more generally, in a computer file. Also, each type of image is created differently and hence it is helpful for us to consider each separately.

2.4.1 Graphics

There is a range of software packages and programs available for the creation of computer graphics. These provide easy-to-use tools to create graphics that are composed of all kinds of visual objects including lines, arcs, squares, rectangles, circles, ovals, diamonds, stars, and so on, as well as any form of hand-drawn (normally referred to as **freeform**) objects. Typically, these are produced by drawing the desired shape on the screen by means of a combination of a cursor symbol on the screen – a pencil or paint brush for example – and the mouse. Facilities are also provided to edit these objects – for example to change their shape, size, or color – and to introduce complete predrawn images, either previously created by the author of the graphic or selected from a gallery of images that come with the package. The latter is often referred to as **clip-art** and the better packages provide many hundreds of such images. Textual information can also be included in a graphic, together with precreated tables and graphs and digitized pictures and photographs which have been previously obtained. Objects can overlap each other with a selected object nearer to the front than another. In addition, you can add fill or add shadows to objects in order to give the complete image a three-dimensional (3-D) effect.

A computer's display screen can be considered as being made up of a two-dimensional matrix of individual picture elements – pixels – each of which can have a range of colors associated with it. For example, **VGA (video graphics array)** is a common type of display and, as we show in Figure 2.10(a), consists of a matrix of 640 horizontal pixels by 480 vertical pixels with, for example, 8 bits per pixel which allows each pixel to have one of 256 different colors.

All objects – including freeform objects – are made up of a series of lines that are connected to each other and, what may appear as a curved line, in practice is a series of very short lines each made up of a string of pixels which, in the limit, have the resolution of a pair of adjacent pixels on the screen. Some examples are shown in Figure 2.10(b)

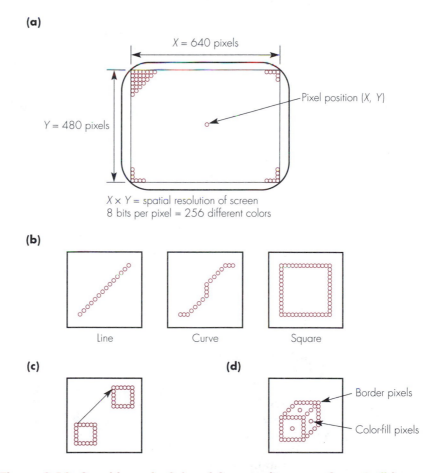

Figure 2.10 Graphics principles: (a) example screen format; (b) some simple object examples; (c) effect of changing position attribute; (d) solid objects.

Each object has a number of **attributes** associated with it. These include its shape – a line, a circle, a square, and so on – its size in terms of the pixel positions of its border coordinates, the color of the border, its shadow, and so on. In this way, editing an object involves simply changing selected attributes associated with the object. For example, as we show in Figure 2.10(c), we can move a square to a different location on the screen by simply changing its border coordinates and leaving the remaining attributes unchanged.

An object shape is said to be either open or closed. In the case of an open object, the start of the first line and the end of the last line that make up the object's border are not connected – that is, they do not start and end on the same pixel – whilst with a closed object they are connected. In the case of a closed object, the pixels enclosed by its border can all be assigned the same color – known as the **color-fill** – to create solid objects as shown in Figure 2.10(d). This operation is also known as **rendering**. In this way, all objects are drawn on the screen by the user simply specifying the name of the object and its attributes – including its color-fill and shadow effect if required – and a set of more basic lower-level commands are then used to determine both the pixel locations that are involved and the color that should be assigned to each pixel.

As we can deduce from the above, the representation of a complete graphic is analogous to the structure of a program written in a high-level programming language. For instance, a program consists of a main body together with a number of procedures/functions, each of which has a set of parameters associated with it and performs a specific function. In the same way, a graphic consists of the set of commands (each with attributes) that are necessary to draw the different objects that make up the graphic. Also, in the same way that the procedures/functions in a program can be a mix of those created by the writer of the program and those available as library procedures/functions, so the objects associated with a graphic can be either those created by the author or those selected from the set of standard objects or the clip-art gallery. And in the same way that a procedure/function in a program may, in turn, call a number of lower-level functions, so the commands associated with objects use the lower-level commands to display the objects on the screen. Finally, in the same way that the main body of a program is concerned with invoking the various procedures/functions in the order necessary to implement a particular computational task, so the main body of a graphic representation is concerned with invoking the different object commands in the correct sequence to create the desired graphic taking into account any overlapping objects.

We can conclude that there are two forms of representation of a computer graphic: a high-level version (similar to the source code of a high-level program) and the actual pixel-image of the graphic (similar to the byte-string corresponding to the low-level machine code of the program and known more generally as the **bit-map format**). A graphic can be transferred over a network in either form. In general, however, the high-level language form is much more compact and requires less memory to store the image and less bandwidth for its transmission. In order to use the high-level language form, however, the destination must of course be able to interpret the various high-level commands. So instead the bit-map form is often used and, to help with this, there are a number of standardized forms of representation such as **GIF** (**graphical interchange format**) and **TIFF** (**tagged image file format**). There are also software packages such as **SRGP** (**simple raster graphics package**) which convert the high-level language form into a pixel-image form. We shall discuss a selection of these in the next chapter.

2.4.2 Digitized documents

An example of a digitized document is that produced by the scanner associated with a **facsimile (fax) machine**, the principles of which are shown in Figure 2.11.

The scanner associated with a fax machine operates by scanning each complete page from left to right to produce a sequence of scan lines that start

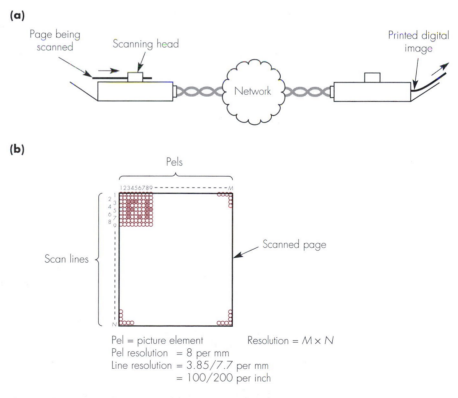

(a)

(b)

Pel = picture element   Resolution = $M \times N$
Pel resolution = 8 per mm
Line resolution = 3.85/7.7 per mm
              = 100/200 per inch

Figure 2.11 Facsimile machine principles: (a) schematic; (b) digitization format.

at the top of the page and end at the bottom. The vertical resolution of the scanning procedure is either 3.85 or 7.7 lines per millimeter which is equivalent to approximately 100 or 200 lines per inch. As each line is scanned, the output of the scanner is digitized to a resolution of approximately 8 picture elements – known as **pels** with fax machines – per millimeter.

Fax machines use just a single binary digit to represent each pel, a 0 for a white pel and a 1 for a black pel. Hence the digital representation of a scanned page is as shown in Figure 2.11(b) which, for a typical page, produces a stream of about two million bits. The printer part of a fax machine then reproduces the original image by printing out the received stream of bits to a similar resolution. In general, the use of a single binary digit per pel means that fax machines are best suited to scanning bitonal (black-and-white) images such as printed documents comprising mainly textual information.

2.4.3 Digitized pictures

In the case of scanners which are used for digitizing continuous-tone monochromatic images – such as a printed picture or scene – normally, more than a single bit is used to digitize each picture element. For example, good quality black-and-white pictures can be obtained by using 8 bits per picture element. This yields 256 different levels of gray per element – varying between white and black – which gives a substantially improved picture quality over a facsimile image when reproduced. In the case of color images, in order to understand the digitization format used, it is necessary first to obtain an understanding of the principles of how color is produced and how the picture tubes used in computer monitors (on which the images are eventually displayed) operate.

Color principles

It has been known for many years that the human eye sees just a single color when a particular set of three primary colors are mixed and displayed simultaneously. In fact, a whole spectrum of colors – known as a **color gamut** – can be produced by using different proportions of the three primary colors red (R), green (G), and blue (B). This principle is shown in Figure 2.12 together with some examples of colors that can be produced.

The mixing technique used in part (a) is known as **additive color mixing** which, since black is produced when all three primary colors are zero, is particularly useful for producing a color image on a black surface as is the case in display applications. It is also possible to perform the complementary **subtractive color mixing** operation to produce a similar range of colors. This is shown in part(b) of the figure and, as we can see, with subtractive mixing white is produced when the three chosen primary colors cyan (C), magenta (M), and yellow (Y) are all zero. Hence this choice of colors is particularly useful for producing a color image on a white surface as is the case in printing applications.

(a)

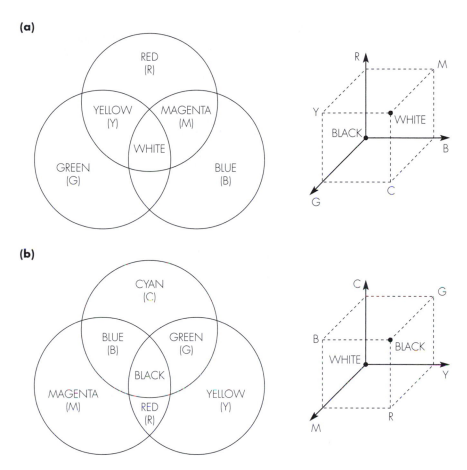

(b)

Figure 2.12 Color derivation principles: (a) additive color mixing; (b) subtractive color mixing.

The same principle is used in the picture tubes associated with color television sets with the three primary colors R, G, and B. Also, in most computer monitors since, in general, those used with personal computers use the same picture tubes as are used in television sets. Hence, in order to be compatible with the computer monitors on which digital pictures are normally viewed, the digitization process used yields a color image that can be directly displayed on the screen of either a television set or a computer monitor. The general principles associated with the process are shown in Figure 2.13.

Raster-scan principles

The picture tubes used in most television sets operate using what is known as a **raster-scan**. This involves a finely-focussed electron beam – the raster – being scanned over the complete screen. Each complete scan comprises a number of discrete horizontal lines the first of which starts at the top left

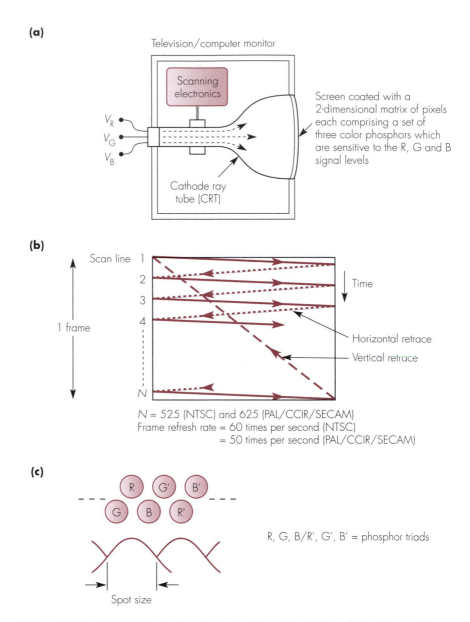

Figure 2.13 Television/computer monitor principles: (a) schematic; (b) raster-scan principles; (c) pixel format on each scan line.

corner of the screen and the last of which ends at the bottom right corner. At this point the beam is deflected back again to the top left corner and the scanning operation repeats in the same way. This type of scanning is called **progressive scanning** and is shown in diagrammatic form in Figure 2.13(b).

Each complete set of horizontal scan lines is called a **frame** and, as we can see, each frame is made up of N individual scan lines where N is either 525 (North and South America and most of Asia) or 625 (Europe and a number of other countries). The inside of the display screen of the picture tube is coated with a light-sensitive phosphor that emits light when energized by the electron beam. The amount of light emitted – its brightness – is determined by the power in the electron beam at that instant. During each horizontal (line) and vertical (frame) retrace period the electron beam is turned off and, to create an image on the screen, the level of power in the beam is changed as each line is scanned.

In the case of black-and-white picture tubes just a single electron beam is used with a white-sensitive phosphor. Color tubes use three separate, closely-located beams and a two-dimensional matrix of pixels. Each pixel comprises a set of three related color-sensitive phosphors, one each for the red, green, and blue signals. The set of three phosphors associated with each pixel is called a **phosphor triad** and a typical arrangement of the triads on each scan line is as shown in Figure 2.13(c). As we can deduce from this, although in theory each pixel represents an idealized rectangular area which is independent of its neighboring pixels, in practice each pixel has the shape of a **spot** which merges with its neighbors. A typical spot size is 0.025 inches (0.635 mm) and, when viewed from a sufficient distance, a continuous color image is seen.

Television picture tubes were designed, of course, to display moving images. The persistence of the light/color produced by the phosphor, therefore, is designed to decay very quickly and hence it is necessary to continuously **refresh** the screen. In the case of a moving image, the light signals associated with each frame change to reflect the motion that has taken place during the time required to scan the preceding frame, while for a static/still image, the same set of light signals are used for each frame. The **frame refresh rate** must be high enough to ensure the eye is not aware the display is continuously being refreshed. A low refresh rate leads to what is called **flicker** which is caused by the previous image fading from the eye retina before the following image is displayed. To avoid this, a refresh rate of at least 50 times per second is required. In practice, the frame refresh rate used is determined by the frequency of the mains electricity supply which is either 60 Hz in North and South America and most of Asia and 50 Hz in Europe and a number of other countries.

Most current picture tubes operate in an analog mode, that is, the amplitude of each of the three color signals is continuously varying as each line is scanned. In the case of digital television – and digitized pictures stored within the memory of a computer – the color signals are in a digital form and comprise a string of pixels with a fixed number of pixels per scan line. Hence in order to display a stored image, the pixels that make up each line are read from memory in time-synchronism with the scanning process and converted into a continuously varying analog form by means of a digital-to-analog converter.

Since in practice the area of the computer memory that holds the string of pixels that make up the image – the pixel image – must be accessed continuously as each line is scanned, normally a separate block of memory known as the **video RAM** – RAM being the acronym for **random access memory** – is used to store the pixel image. In this way, the graphics program needs only to write into the video RAM whenever either selected pixels or the total image changes. An example architecture showing the various steps involved is given in Figure 2.14

Typically, the graphics program is used to create the high-level version of the image interactively (using either the keyboard or a mouse) and the **display controller** part of the program interprets sequences of display commands and converts them into displayed objects by writing the appropriate pixel values into the video RAM. The latter is also known, therefore, as the **frame/display/refresh buffer**. Normally the **video controller** is a hardware subsystem that reads the pixel values stored in the video RAM in time-synchronism with the scanning process and, for each set of pixel values, converts these into the equivalent set of red, green, and blue analog signals for output to the display.

Pixel depth

The number of bits per pixel is known as the **pixel depth** and determines the range of different colors that can be produced. Examples are 12 bits – 4 bits per primary color yielding 4096 different colors – and 24 bits – 8 bits per

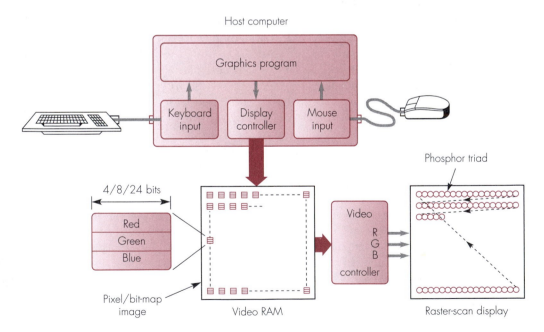

Figure 2.14 Raster-scan display architecture.

primary color yielding in excess of 16 million (2^{24}) colors. In practice, however, the eye cannot discriminate between such a range of colors and so in some instances a selected subset of this range is used. The selected colors in the subset are then stored in a table and each pixel value is used as an address to a location within the table which contains the corresponding three color values. The table is known as the **color look-up table** or **CLUT**. For example, if each pixel is 8 bits and the CLUT contains 24 bit entries, this will provide a subset of 256 (2^8) different colors selected from a palette of 16 million (2^{24}) colors. In this way, the amount of memory required to store an image can be reduced significantly.

Aspect ratio

Both the number of pixels per scanned line and the number of lines per frame vary, the actual numbers used being determined by what is known as the **aspect ratio** of the display screen. This is the ratio of the screen width to the screen height. The aspect ratio of current television tubes is 4/3 with older tubes – on which PC monitors are based – and 16/9 with the widescreen television tubes.

In the United States, the standard for color television has been defined by the **National Television Standards Committee** (**NTSC**) while in Europe three color standards exist **PAL** (UK), **CCIR** (Germany), and **SECAM** (France). As we indicated earlier, the NTSC standard uses 525 scan lines per frame while the three European standards all use 625 scan lines. In neither case, however, are all lines displayed on the screen since some are used to carry control and other information. In practice, therefore, the number of visible lines per frame – which is equal to the vertical resolution in terms of pixels – is 480 with an NTSC monitor and 576 with the other three standards. Thus in order to avoid distortion on a screen which has a 4/3 aspect ratio – for example when displaying a square of, say, ($N \times N$) pixels – it is necessary to have 640 pixels ($480 \times 4/3$) per line with an NTSC monitor and 768 ($576 \times 4/3$) pixels per line with a European monitor. This produces a lattice structure that is said to produce **square pixels** and is shown in diagrammatic form in Figure 2.15. Some example screen resolutions associated with the more common computer monitors based on television picture tubes – together with the amount of memory required to store the corresponding image – are shown in Table 2.1

As we can deduce from the table, the memory requirements to store a single digital image can be high and vary between 307.2 kbytes for an image displayed on a **VGA** (**video graphics array**) screen with 8 bits per pixel through to approximately 2.36 Mbytes for a **SVGA** (**Super VGA**) screen with 24 bits per pixel. It should be noted that the more expensive computer monitors are not based on television picture tubes and hence are not constrained by the 4/3 aspect ratio. An example is $1280 \times 1024 \times 24$ which may have a refresh rate as high as 75 frames per second to produce a sharper image.

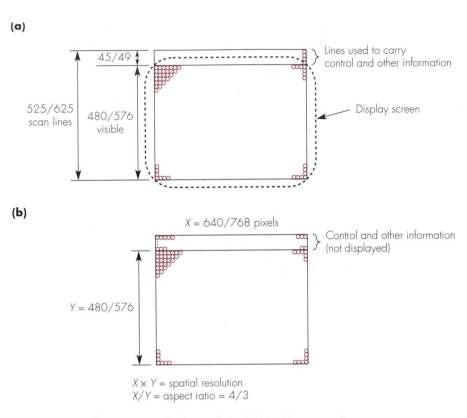

Figure 2.15 Screen resolutions: (a) visible lines per frame; (b) digitization spatial resolution.

Table 2.1 Example display resolutions and memory requirements.

Standard	Resolution	Number of colors	Memory required per frame (bytes)
VGA	640 × 480 × 8	256	307.2 kB
XGA	640 × 480 × 16	64 K	614.4 kB
	1024 × 768 × 8	256	786.432 kB
SVGA	800 × 600 × 16	64 k	960 kB
	1024 × 768 × 8	256	786.432 kB
	1024 × 768 × 24	16 M	2359.296 kB

Example 2.3

Derive the time to transmit the following digitized images at both 64 kbps and 1.5 Mbps:

- a $640 \times 480 \times 8$ VGA-compatible image,
- a $1024 \times 768 \times 24$ SVGA-compatible image.

Answer:

The size of each image in bits is:

$$VGA = 640 \times 480 \times 8 = 2.457600 \text{ Mbits}$$
$$SVGA = 1024 \times 768 \times 24 = 18.874368 \text{ Mbits}$$

Hence the time to transmit each image is:

$$\text{At 64 kbps: VGA} = \frac{2.4576 \times 10^6}{64 \times 10^3} = 38.4 \text{ s}$$

$$SVGA = \frac{18.874368 \times 10^6}{64 \times 10^3} = 294.912 \text{ s}$$

$$\text{At 1.5 Mbps: VGA} = \frac{2.4576 \times 10^6}{1.5 \times 10^6} = 1.6384 \text{ s}$$

$$SVGA = \frac{18.874368 \times 10^6}{1.5 \times 10^6} = 12.5829 \text{ s}$$

As we can see, the times to transmit a signal image at 64 kbps are such that interactive access would not be feasible, nor at 1.5 Mbps with the higher-resolution SVGA image.

Digital cameras and scanners

A typical arrangement that is used to capture and store a digital image produced by a scanner or a digital camera – either a still-image camera or a video camera – is shown in Figure 2.16(a). In the figure it is assumed that the captured image is transferred to the computer directly as it is produced. Alternatively, in the case of digital cameras, a set of digitized images can be stored within the camera itself and then downloaded into the computer at a later time.

An image is captured within the camera/scanner using a solid-state device called an **image sensor**. This is a silicon chip which, in digital cameras, consists of a two-dimensional grid of light-sensitive cells called **photosites**. When the camera shutter is activated, each photosite stores the level of intensity of the light that falls on it. A widely-used image sensor is a **charge-coupled**

(a)

(b)

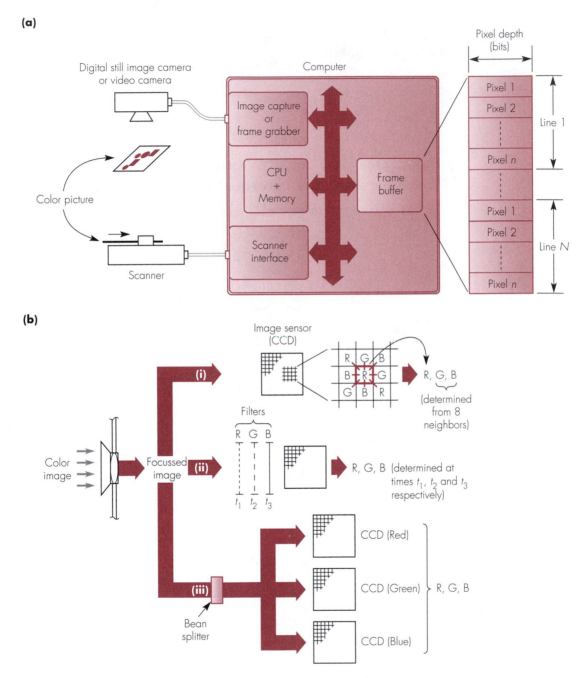

Figure 2.16 Color image capture: (a) schematic; (b) RGB signal generation alternatives.

device (**CCD**). This comprises an array of photosites on its surface and operates by converting the level of light intensity that falls on each photosite into an equivalent electrical charge. The level of charge – and hence light intensity – stored at each photosite position is then read out and converted into a digital value using an ADC. A similar technique is used in scanners except the image sensor comprises just a single row of photosites. These are exposed in time-sequence with the scanning operation and each row of stored charges are read out and digitized before the next scan occurs.

For color images, the color associated with each photosite – and hence pixel position – is obtained in a number of ways. These include the three methods shown in Figure 2.16(b).

(i) In this method, the surface of each photosite is coated with either a red, green, or blue filter so that its charge is determined only by the level of red, green, or blue light that falls on it. The coatings are arranged in a 3×3 grid structure as shown in the figure. The color associated with each photosite/pixel is then determined by the output of the photosite – R, G, or B – together with each of its 8 immediate neighbors. The levels of the two other colors in each pixel are then estimated by an interpolation procedure involving all nine values. This method is used with most consumer-quality cameras.

(ii) This method involves the use of three separate exposures of a single image sensor, the first through a red filter, the second a green filter, and the third a blue filter. The color associated with each pixel position is then determined by the charge obtained with each of the three filters – R, G, and B. Since three separate exposures are required for each image, this approach cannot be used with video cameras. It is used primarily with high-resolution still-image cameras in locations such as photographic studios where the camera can be attached to a tripod.

(iii) This method uses three separate image sensors, one with all the photosites coated with a red filter, the second coated with a green filter, and the third coated with a blue filter. A single exposure is used with the incoming light split into three beams each of which exposes a separate image sensor. This method is used in professional-quality high-resolution still and moving image cameras since, in general, they are more costly owing to the use of three separate sensors and associated signal processing circuits.

Once each image/frame has been captured and stored on the image sensor(s), the charge stored at each photosite location is read and digitized. Using a CCD, the set of charges on the matrix of photosites are read a single row at a time. First the set of charges on the first row of photosites are transferred to what is called the **readout register**. Each of the photosites in a row is coupled to the corresponding photosites in the two adjoining rows and, as each row is transferred to the readout register, the set of charges on each of the other rows in the matrix move down to the next row of photosite positions. Once in the readout register, the charge on each photosite position is shifted out, amplified and digitized using an ADC. This procedure then repeats until the set of charges on all rows have been read out and digitized.

For a low-resolution image of 640×480 pixels and a pixel depth of 24 bits – 8 bits each for the R, G, and B signals – the amount of memory required to store each image is 921 600 bytes. If this is output directly to the computer, then the bit-map can be loaded straight into the frame buffer ready to be displayed. If it is to be stored within the camera, however, then multiple images of this size need to be stored prior to them being output to a computer. The set of images are stored in an integrated circuit memory that is either on a removable card or fixed within the camera. In the first case, the card is simply removed and inserted into the PCMCIA slot of a computer and in the second case the contents of the memory are downloaded to the computer by means of a cable link. Once within the computer, software can be used to insert the digital image(s) into a document, send it by email, and so on. Alternatively, photo-editing software can be used to manipulate a stored image; for example, to change its size or color

There are a number of file formats used to store a set of images. One of the most popular is a version of the tagged image file format (TIFF) called **TIFF for electronic photography** (**TIFF/EP**). This allows many different types of image data to be stored in the image file including data (such as the date and time and various camera settings) associated with each image.

2.5 Audio

Essentially, we are concerned with two types of audio signal: speech signals as used in a variety of interpersonal applications including telephony and video telephony, and music-quality audio as used in applications such as CD-on-demand and broadcast television. In general, audio can be produced either naturally by means of a microphone or electronically using some form of synthesizer. In the case of a synthesizer, the audio is created in a digital form and hence can be readily stored within the computer memory. A microphone, however, generates a time-varying analog signal and in order to store such signals in the memory of a computer, and to transmit them over a digital network, they must first be converted into a digital form using an audio signal encoder. Also, since loudspeakers operate using an analog signal, on output of all digitized audio signals the stream of digitized values must be converted back again into its analog form using an audio signal decoder.

We discussed the general principles behind the design of a signal encoder and decoder earlier in the chapter in Section 2.2 and here we will simply apply these principles to explain the digitization of both speech and music produced by a microphone. We shall then discuss the format of synthesized audio in a separate section.

The bandwidth of a typical speech signal is from 50 Hz through to 10 kHz and that of a music signal from 15 Hz through to 20 kHz. Hence the sampling rate used for the two signals must be in excess of their Nyquist rate which is 20 ksps (2 × 10 kHz) for speech and 40 ksps (2 × 20 kHz) for music. The number of bits per sample must be chosen so that the quantization noise generated by the sampling process is at an acceptable level relative to the minimum signal level. In the case of speech, assuming linear (equal) quantization intervals, tests have shown that this dictates the use of a minimum of 12 bits per sample and for music 16 bits. In addition, since in most applications involving music stereophonic (stereo) sound is utilized (and hence two such signals must be digitized) this results in a bit rate double that of a monaural (mono) signal.

Example 2.4

Assuming the bandwidth of a speech signal is from 50 Hz through to 10 kHz and that of a music signal is from 15 Hz through to 20 kHz, derive the bit rate that is generated by the digitization procedure in each case assuming the Nyquist sampling rate is used with 12 bits per sample for the speech signal and 16 bits per sample for the music signal. Derive the memory required to store a 10 minute passage of stereophonic music.

Answer:

(i) Bit rates: Nyquist sampling rate = $2 f_{max}$
    Speech: Nyquist rate = 2 × 10 kHz = 20 kHz or 20 ksps
    Hence with 12 bits per sample, bit rate generated
    = 20 k × 12 = 240 kbps
    Music: Nyquist rate = 2 × 20 kHz = 40 kHz or 40 ksps
    Hence bit rate generated = 40 k × 16 = 640 kbps (mono)
    or   2 × 640 k = 1280 kbps (stereo)

(ii) Memory required: Memory required = bit rate (bps) × time (s)/8 bytes
    Hence at 1280 kbps and 600 s,

$$\text{Memory required} = \frac{1280 \times 10^3 \times 600}{8} = 96 \text{ Mbytes}$$

In practice, both the sampling rate used and the number of bits per sample are often less than these values. In the case of speech, for example, the bandwidth of the network used in many interpersonal applications is often much less than the bandwidth of the source signal thus dictating a lower sampling rate with fewer bits per sample. Similarly, with music, the sampling rate is often lowered in order to reduce the amount of memory that is required to store a particular passage of music. A practical example of the digitization parameters used in each case is now presented.

2.5.1 PCM speech

As we described in Chapter 1, most interpersonal applications involving speech use for communication purposes a public switched telephone network (PSTN). Because this has been in existence for many years the operating parameters associated with it were defined some time ago. Initially, a PSTN operated with analog signals throughout, the source speech signal being transmitted and switched (routed) unchanged in its original analog form. Progressively, however, the older analog transmission circuits were replaced by digital circuits. This was carried out over a number of years and, because of the need to interwork between the earlier analog and newer digital equipments during the transition period, the design of the digital equipment was based on the operating parameters of the earlier analog network. The bandwidth of a speech circuit in this network was limited to 200 Hz through to 3.4 kHz. Also, although the Nyquist rate is 6.8 kHz, the poor quality of the bandlimiting filters used meant that a sampling rate of 8 kHz was required to avoid aliasing. In order to minimize the resulting bit rate, 7 bits per sample were selected for use in North America and Japan and 8 bits per sample in Europe (both including a sign bit) which, in turn, yields bit rates of 56 kbps and 64 kbps respectively. More modern systems have moved to using 8 bits per sample in each case, giving a much improved performance over early 7 bit systems. The digitization procedure is known as **pulse code modulation** or **PCM** and the international standard relating to this is defined in **ITU-T Recommendation G.711**. Figure 2.17 (a) shows the circuits that make up a PCM encoder and decoder.

As we can see, both the encoder and decoder, in addition to the circuits shown earlier in Figs. 2.2(a) and 2.5(a), consist of two additional circuits: a **compressor** (encoder) and an **expander** (decoder). The role of these circuits can best be described by reconsidering the quantization operation described earlier. This used equal – also known as linear – quantization intervals which means that, irrespective of the magnitude of the input signal, the same level of quantization noise is produced. The effect of this is that the noise level is the same for both low amplitude (quiet) signals and high amplitude (loud) signals. The ear, however, is more sensitive to noise on quiet signals than it is on loud signals. Hence to reduce the effect of quantization noise with just 8 bits per sample, in a PCM system the quantization intervals are made non-linear (unequal) with narrower intervals used for smaller amplitude signals than for larger signals. This is achieved by means of the compressor circuit and, at the destination, the reverse operation is performed by the expander circuit. The overall operation is known as **companding**. The input/output relationship of both circuits is shown in Figure 2.17(b) and (c) respectively; that shown in part (b) is known as the **compression characteristic** and that in part (c) the **expansion characteristic**. For clarity, just 5 bits per sample are used.

(a)

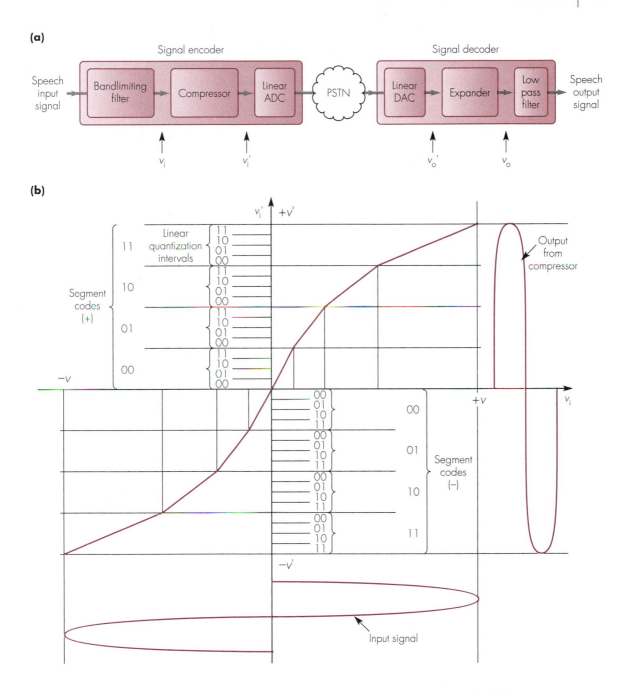

Figure 2.17 PCM principles: (a) signal encoding and decoding schematic; (b) compressor characteristic; (c) expander characteristic.

(c)

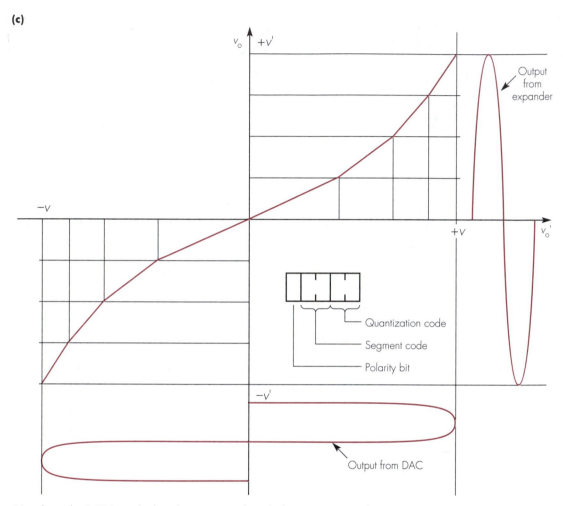

Note that in the G.711 standard a 3-bit segment code and 4-bit quantization code are used.

Figure 2.17 Continued

Prior to the input signal being sampled and converted into a digital form by the ADC, it is passed through the compressor circuit which effectively compresses the amplitude of the input signal. The level of compression – and hence the quantization intervals – increases as the amplitude of the input signal increases. The resulting compressed signal is then passed to the ADC which, in turn, performs a linear quantization on the compressed signal. Similarly, at the destination, each received codeword is first fed into a linear DAC. The analog output from the DAC is then passed to the expander circuit which performs the reverse operation of the compressor circuit. More modern systems perform both the compressor and expander operations digitally but the same principles apply.

In practice, for historical reasons, there are two different compression-expansion characteristics in use: μ-**law**, which is used in North America and Japan, and **A-law** which is used in Europe and some other countries. Hence, as we can deduce from Figure 2.17(a), it is necessary to carry out a conversion operation when communicating between the two systems. In both cases, however, the use of companding gives a perceived level of performance with 8 bits that is comparable with the performance obtained with 12 bits and uniform quantization intervals.

2.5.2 CD-quality audio

The discs used in CD players and CD-ROMs are digital storage devices for stereophonic music and more general multimedia information streams. There is a standard associated with these devices which is known as the **CD-digital audio** (**CD-DA**) standard. As indicated earlier, music has an audible bandwidth of from 15 Hz through to 20 kHz and hence the minimum sampling rate is 40 ksps. In the standard, however, the actual rate used is higher than this rate firstly, to allow for imperfections in the bandlimiting filter used and secondly, so that the resulting bit rate is then compatible with one of the higher transmission channel bit rates available with public networks.

One of the sampling rates used is 44.1 ksps which means the signal is sampled at 23 microsecond intervals. Since the bandwidth of a recording channel on a CD is large, a high number of bits per sample can be used. The standard defines 16 bits per sample which, as indicated earlier, tests have shown to be the minimum required with music to avoid the effect of quantization noise. With this number of bits, linear quantization can be used which yields 65 536 equal quantization intervals. The recording of stereophonic music requires two separate channels and hence the total bit rate required is double that for mono. Hence:

$$\text{Bit rate per channel} = \text{sampling rate} \times \text{bits per sample}$$
$$= 44.1 \times 10^3 \times 16 = 705.6 \text{ kbps}$$

and,   Total bit rate $= 2 \times 705.6 = 1.411 \text{ Mbps}$

This is also the bit rate used with CD-ROMs which are widely used for the distribution of multimedia titles. Within a computer, however, in order to reduce the access delay, multiples of this rate are used.

As we can deduce from Example 2.5, it is not feasible to interactively access a 30s portion of a multimedia title over a 64 kbps channel. And with a 1.5 Mbps channel the time is still too high for interactive purposes.

2.5.3 Synthesized audio

Once digitized, any form of audio can be stored within a computer. However, as we can see from the results obtained in the next example, the amount of

Example 2.5

Assuming the CD-DA standard is being used, derive:

(i) the storage capacity of a CD-ROM to store a 60 minute multimedia title,

(ii) the time to transmit a 30 second portion of the title using a transmission channel of bit rate:

■ 64 kbps
■ 1.5 Mbps.

Answer:

(i) The CD-DA digitization procedure yields a bit rate of 1.411 Mbps. Hence storage capacity for 60 minutes

$$= 1.411 \times 60 \times 60 \text{ Mbits}$$
$$= 5079.6 \text{ Mbits or } 634.95 \text{ Mbytes}$$

(ii) One 30 second portion of the title $= 1.411 \times 30 = 42.33$ Mbits
Hence time to transmit this data:

At 64 kbps $\quad = \dfrac{42.33 \times 10^6}{64 \times 10^3} = 661.4 \text{ s} \qquad$ (about 11 minutes)

At 1.5 Mbps $\quad = \dfrac{42.33 \times 10^6}{1.5 \times 10^6} = 28.22 \text{ s}$

memory required to store a digitized audio waveform can be very large, even for relatively short passages. It is for this reason that synthesized audio is often used in multimedia applications since the amount of memory required can be between two and three orders of magnitude less than that required to store the equivalent digitized waveform version. In addition, it is much easier to edit synthesized audio and to mix several passages together. The main components that make up an audio synthesizer are shown in Figure 2.18.

The three main components are the computer (with various application programs), the keyboard (based on that of a piano), and the set of sound generators. Essentially, the computer takes input commands from the keyboard and outputs these to the sound generators which, in turn, produce the corresponding sound waveform – via DACs – to drive the speakers.

Pressing a key on the keyboard of a synthesizer has a similar effect to pressing a key on the keyboard of a computer inasmuch as, for each key that is pressed, a different codeword – known as a message with a synthesizer keyboard – is generated and read by the computer program. Essentially, the messages indicate such things as which key on the keyboard has been pressed and the pressure applied. The control panel contains a range of different

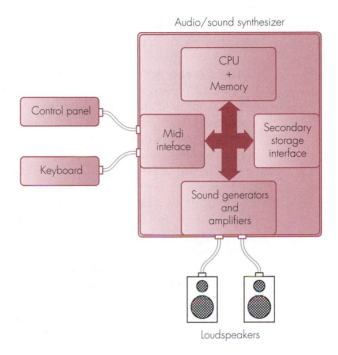

Figure 2.18 Audio/sound synthesizer schematic.

switches and sliders that collectively allow the user to indicate to the computer program additional information such as the volume of the generated output and selected sound effects to be associated with each key.

The secondary storage interface allows the sequence of messages – including those associated with the control panel – relating to a particular piece of audio to be saved on secondary storage such as a floppy disk. In addition, there are programs to allow the user to edit a previously entered passage and, if required, to mix several stored passages together. The sequencer program associated with the synthesizer then ensures that the resulting integrated sequence of messages are synchronized and output to the sound generators to create the merged passage.

As well as a (piano) keyboard, there is a range of other possible inputs from instruments such as an electric guitar, all of which generate messages similar to those produced by the keyboard. Hence in order to discriminate between the inputs from the different possible sources, a standardized set of messages have been defined for both input and for output to the corresponding set of sound generators. These are defined in a standard known as the **Music Instrument Digital Interface** (**MIDI**). As the name implies, this does not just define the format of the standardized set of messages used by a synthesizer, but also the type of connectors, cables, and electrical signals that are used to connect any type of device to the synthesizer.

The format of a MIDI message consists of a *status byte*, which defines the particular event that has caused the message to be generated, followed by a number of *data bytes* which collectively define a set of parameters associated with the event. An example of an event is a key being pressed on the keyboard and typical parameters would then be the identity of the key, the pressure applied, and so on. As we indicated earlier, there can be a variety of instrument types used for input and output. Thus it is also necessary to identify the type of instrument that generated the event so that when the corresponding message is output to the sound generators, the appropriate type of sound is produced. Thus the different types of device have a MIDI code associated with them; a piano, for example, has a code of 0 and a violin a code of 40. In addition, some codes have been assigned for specific special effects such as the sound from a cannon and the applause from an audience.

As we can deduce from the above, a passage of audio produced by a synthesizer consists of a very compact sequence of messages – each comprising a string of bytes – which can either be played out by the sequencer program directly – and hence heard by the composer – or saved in a file on a floppy disk. Typically, in many interactive applications involving, say, multimedia pages comprising text and a passage of music, a synthesizer is first used to create the passage of music which is then saved in a file. The author of the pages then links the file contents to the text at the point where the music is to be played. Clearly, since the music is in the form of a sequence of MIDI messages, it is necessary to have a **sound card** in the client computer to interpret the sequence of messages and generate the appropriate sounds. The sound generators use either **FM synthesis** techniques or samples of sound produced by real instruments. The latter is known as **wavelet synthesis**.

2.6 Video

Video features in a range of multimedia applications:

- entertainment: broadcast television and VCR/DVD recordings;
- interpersonal: video telephony and videoconferencing;
- interactive: windows containing short video clips.

The quality of the video required, however, varies considerably from one type of application to another. For example, for video telephony, a small window on the screen of a PC is acceptable while for a movie, a large screen format is preferable. In practice, therefore, there is not just a single standard associated with video but rather a set of standards, each targeted at a particular application domain. Before describing a selection of these we must first acquire an understanding of the basic principles associated with broadcast television on which all the standards are based.

2.6.1 Broadcast television

We considered the basic principles of color television picture tubes earlier in Section 2.4.3 when the topic of digitized pictures was discussed. As you may recall, a color picture/image is produced from varying mixtures of the three primary colors red, green and blue. The screen of the picture tube is coated with a set of three different phosphors – one for each color – each of which is activated by a separate electron beam. The three electron beams are scanned in unison across the screen from left to right with a resolution of either 525 lines (NTSC) or 625 lines (PAL/CCIR/SECAM). The total screen contents are then refreshed at a rate of either 60 or 50 frames per second respectively, the rate being determined by the frequency of the mains electricity supply used in the different countries.

The computer monitors used with most personal computers use the same picture tubes as those in broadcast television receivers and hence operate in a similar way. The three digitized color signals that make up a stored picture/image are read from the computer memory in time-synchronism with the scanning operation of the display tube and, after each complete scan of the display, the procedure repeats so producing a flicker-free color image on the screen. In principle, broadcast television could operate in a similar way, but in practice it operates slightly differently both in terms of the scanning sequence used and in the choice of color signals. We shall look at each separately.

Scanning sequence

Although it is necessary to use a minimum refresh rate of 50 times per second to avoid flicker, to produce smooth motion, a refresh rate of 25 times per second is sufficient. Hence in order to minimize the amount of transmission bandwidth that is required to broadcast the television signal, this characteristic of the eye is exploited by transmitting the image/picture associated with each frame in two halves. Each is known as a **field**, the first comprising only the odd scan lines and the second the even scan lines. The two fields are then integrated together in the television receiver using a technique known as **interlaced scanning**, the principles of which are shown in Figure 2.19.

As we can see, in a 525-line system each field comprises 262.5 lines – 240 visible – while in a 625-line system each field comprises 312.5 lines – 288 visible, the remainder being used for other purposes. Each field is refreshed alternately at 60/50 fields per second and hence the resulting frame refresh rate is only 30/25 frames per second. As discussed, the higher field rate tricks the eye into thinking the frame rate is double what it is in practice. In this way, a refresh rate equivalent to 60/50 frames per second is achieved but with only half the transmission bandwidth.

Color signals

For historical reasons, the received signals associated with a color television broadcast had to be such that they could be used by an existing (unmodified) monochrome (black-and-white) television set to produce the same picture in high-quality monochrome. In addition, a color television had to be able to

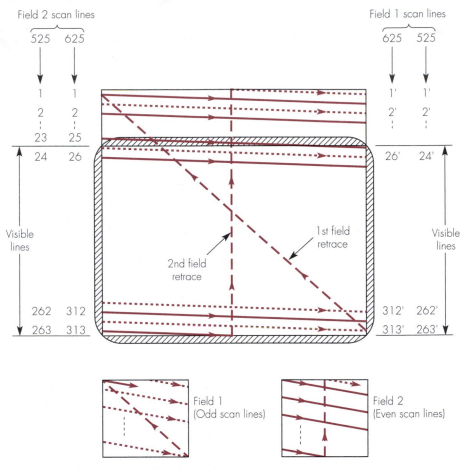

525-line systems : 262.5 each field, 240 visible
625-line systems : 312.5 each field, 288 visible

Figure 2.19 Interlaced scanning principles.

produce black-and-white pictures from monochrome broadcasts. For these reasons a different set of color signals from R, G, and B were selected for color television broadcasts.

The three main properties of a color source that the eye makes use of are:

■ **brightness:** this represents the amount of energy that stimulates the eye and varies on a gray scale from black (lowest) through to white (highest). It is thus independent of the color of the source;

■ **hue:** this represents the actual color of the source, each color has a different frequency/wavelength and the eye determines the color from this;

■ **saturation:** this represents the strength or vividness of the color, a pastel color has a lower level of saturation than a color such as red. Also, a saturated color such as red has no white light in it.

The term **luminance** is used to refer to the brightness of a source, and the hue and saturation, because they are concerned with its color, are referred to as its **chrominance** characteristics.

As we saw in Section 2.4.3, a range of colors can be produced by mixing the three primary colors R, G, and B. In a similar way, a range of colors can be produced on a television display screen by varying the magnitude of the three electrical signals that energize the red, green, and blue phosphors. For example, if the magnitude of the three signals are in the proportion

$$0.299R + 0.587G + 0.114B$$

then the color white is produced on the display screen. Hence, since the luminance of a source is only a function of the amount of white light it contains, for any color source its luminance can be determined by summing together the three primary components that make up the color in this proportion. That is,

$$Y_s = 0.299 \ R_s + 0.587 \ G_s + 0.144 \ B_s$$

where Y_s is the amplitude of the luminance signal and R_s, G_s, and B_s are the magnitudes of the three color component signals that make up the source. Thus, since the luminance signal is a measure of the amount of white light it contains, it is the same as the signal used by a monochrome television. Two other signals, the **blue chrominance** (C_b), and the **red chrominance** (C_r), – are then used to represent the coloration – hue and saturation – of the source. These are obtained from the two **color difference** signals:

$$C_b = B_s - Y_s \quad \text{and} \quad C_r = R_s - Y_s$$

which, since the Y signal has been subtracted in both cases, contain no brightness information. Also, since Y is a function of all three colors, then G can be readily computed from these two signals. In this way, the combination of the three signals Y, C_b, and C_r contains all the information that is needed to describe a color signal while at the same time being compatible with monochrome televisions which use the luminance signal only.

Chrominance components

In practice, although all color television systems use this same basic principle to represent the coloration of a source, there are some small differences between the two systems in terms of the magnitude used for the two chrominance signals. These arise from the constraint that the bandwidth of the transmission channel for color broadcasts must be the same as that used for monochrome. As a result, in order to fit the Y, C_b, and C_r signals in the same bandwidth, the three signals must be combined together for transmission. The resulting signal is then known as the **composite video signal**. As a result of doing this, however, if the two color difference signals are transmitted at their original magnitudes, the amplitude of the luminance signal can become greater than that of the equivalent monochrome signal. This leads to a degradation in the quality of the monochrome picture and hence is unacceptable.

To overcome this effect, the magnitude of the two color difference signals are both scaled down. In addition, since they both have different levels of luminance associated with them, the scaling factor used for each signal is different. In practice, the two color difference signals are referred to by different symbols in each system. In the PAL system, for example, C_b and C_r are referred to as U and V respectively and the scaling factors used for the three signals are:

$$\text{PAL:} \quad Y = 0.299\,R + 0.587\,G + 0.114\,B$$
$$U = 0.493\,(B - Y)$$
$$V = 0.877\,(R - Y)$$

In the case of the NTSC system, the two color difference signals are combined to form two different signals referred to as I and Q. The scaling factors used are:

$$\text{NTSC:} \quad Y = 0.299\,R + 0.587\,G + 0.114\,B$$
$$I = 0.74\,(R - Y) - 0.27\,(B - Y)$$
$$Q = 0.48\,(R - Y) + 0.41\,(B - Y)$$

Example 2.6

Derive the scaling factors used for both the U and V (as used in PAL) and I and Q (as used in NTSC) color difference signals in terms of the three R, G, B color signals.

Answer:

PAL:
$$Y = 0.299\,R + 0.587\,G + 0.114\,B$$
$$U = 0.493\,(B - Y) \quad \text{and} \quad V = 0.877\,(R - Y)$$

Hence
$$U = 0.493\,B - 0.493\,(0.299\,R + 0.587\,G + 0.114\,B)$$
$$= -0.147\,R - 0.289\,G + 0.437\,B$$

and
$$V = 0.877\,R - 0.877\,(0.299\,R + 0.587\,G + 0.114\,B)$$
$$= 0.615\,R - 0.515\,G - 0.100\,B$$

NTSC:
$$I = 0.74\,(R - Y) - 0.27\,(B - Y)$$
$$= 0.74\,R - 0.27\,B - 0.47\,Y$$
$$= 0.599\,R - 0.276\,G - 0.324\,B$$
$$Q = 0.48\,(R - Y) + 0.41\,(B - Y)$$
$$= 0.48\,R + 0.41\,B - 0.89\,Y$$
$$= 0.212\,R - 0.528\,G + 0.311\,B$$

Signal bandwidth

As we saw in the last section, the bandwidth of the transmission channel used for color broadcasts must be the same as that used for a monochrome broadcast. As a result, for transmission, the two chrominance signals must occupy the same bandwidth as that of the luminance signal. The baseband spectrum of a color television signal in both the NTSC and PAL systems is shown in parts (a) and (b) of Figure 2.20 respectively.

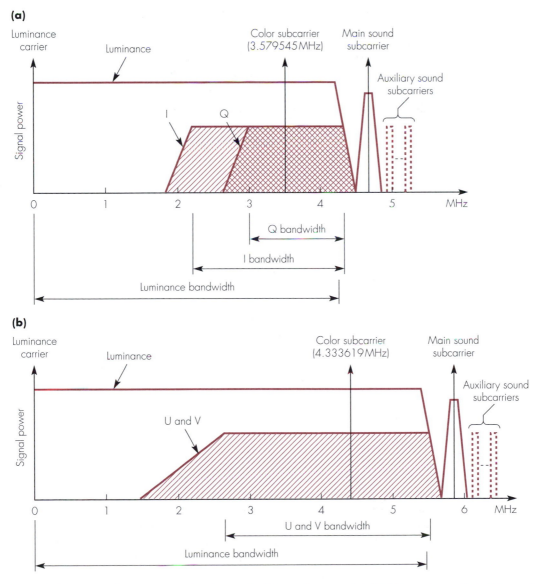

Figure 2.20 Baseband spectrum of color television signals: (a) NTSC system; (b) PAL system.

In practice, most of the energy associated with the luminance signal is in the lower frequency signals and hence the lower part of its frequency spectrum. Hence in order to minimize the level of interference between the luminance and two chrominance signals, firstly, the latter are transmitted in the upper part of the luminance frequency spectrum using two separate subcarriers and secondly, to restrict the bandwidth used to the upper part of the spectrum, a smaller bandwidth is used for both chrominance signals. In addition, both of the two chrominance subcarriers have the same frequency but they are 90 degrees out of phase with each other. Each is modulated independently in both amplitude and phase by the related chrominance signal. Using this technique, the two signals can use the same portion of the luminance frequency spectrum.

In the NTSC system the eye is more responsive to the I signal than the Q signal. Hence to maximize the use of the available bandwidth while at the same time minimizing the level of interference with the luminance signal, the I signal has a modulated bandwidth of about 2 MHz and the Q signal a bandwidth of about 1 MHz. With the PAL system, the larger luminance bandwidth – about 5.5 MHz relative to 4.2 MHz – allows both the U and V chrominance signals to have the same modulated bandwidth which is about 3 MHz. As we show in the figure, the audio/sound signal is transmitted using one or more separate subcarriers which are all just outside of the luminance signal bandwidth. Typically, the main audio subcarrier is for mono sound and the auxiliary subcarriers are used for stereo sound. When these are added to the baseband video signal, the composite signal is called the **complex baseband signal**.

2.6.2 Digital video

In the previous section we described the underlying principles of broadcast television and, in particular, the origin of the three component signals that are used. In most multimedia applications the video signals need to be in a digital form since it then becomes possible to store them in the memory of a computer and to readily edit and integrate them with other media types. In addition, although for transmission reasons the three component signals have to be combined for analog television broadcasts, with digital television it is more usual to digitize the three component signals separately prior to their transmission. Again, this is done to enable editing and other operations to be readily performed.

Since the three component signals are treated separately in digital television, in principle it is possible simply to digitize the three RGB signals that make up the picture. The disadvantage of this approach is that the same resolution – in terms of sampling rate and bits per sample – must be used for all three signals. Studies on the visual perception of the eye have shown that the resolution of the eye is less sensitive for color than it is for luminance. This means that the two chrominance signals can tolerate a reduced resolution relative to that used for the luminance signal. Hence a significant saving in terms of the resulting bit rate – and hence transmission bandwidth – can be achieved by using the luminance and two color difference signals instead of the RGB signals directly.

Digitization of video signals has been carried out in television studios for many years in order, for example, to perform conversions from one video format into another. In order to standardize this process – and hence make the exchange of television programmes internationally easier – the international body for television standards, the **International Telecommunications Union – Radiocommunications Branch (ITU-R)** – formerly known as the **Consultative Committee for International Radiocommunications (CCIR)** – defined a standard for the digitization of video pictures known as **Recommendation CCIR-601**. In addition, a number of variants of this standard have been defined for use in other application domains such as digital television broadcasting, video telephony, and videoconferencing. Collectively these are known as **digitization formats** and, in practice, they all exploit the fact that the two chrominance signals can tolerate a reduced resolution relative to that used for the luminance signal. We shall now describe a selection of these.

4:2:2 format

This is the original digitization format used in Recommendation CCIR-601 for use in television studios. The three component (analog) video signals from a source in the studio can have bandwidths of up to 6 MHz for the luminance signal and less than half this for the two chrominance signals. To digitize these signals, as we described in Section 2.2, it is necessary to use band-limiting filters of 6 MHz for the luminance signal and 3 MHz for the two chrominance signals with a minimum sampling rate of 12 MHz (12 Msps) and 6 MHz respectively.

In the standard, however, a line sampling rate of 13.5 MHz for luminance and 6.75 MHz for the two chrominance signals was selected, both of which are independent of the particular scanning standard – NTSC, PAL and so on – being used. The 13.5 MHz rate was chosen since it is the nearest frequency to 12 MHz which results in a whole number of samples per line for both 525- and 625-line systems. The number of samples per line chosen is 702 and can be derived as follows:

In a 525-line system, the total line sweep time is 63.56 microseconds but, during this time, the beam(s) is (are) turned off – set to the black level – for retrace for 11.56 microseconds which yields an active line sweep time of 52 microseconds. Similarly, in a 625-line system, the total line sweep time is 64 microseconds with a blanking time of 12 microseconds which also yields an active line sweep time of 52 microseconds. Hence in both cases, a sampling rate of 13.5 MHz yields:

$$52 \times 10^{-6} \times 13.5 \times 10^6 = 702 \text{ samples per line}$$

In practice, the number of samples per line is increased to 720 by taking a slightly longer active line time which results in a small number of black samples

at the beginning and end of each line for reference purposes. The corresponding number of samples for each of the two chrominance signals is then set at
half this value; that is, 360 samples per active line. This results in $4Y$ samples for
every $2C_b$ and $2C_r$ samples which is the origin of the term 4:2:2, the term 4:4:4
normally indicating the digitization is based on the R, G, B signals.

The number of bits per sample was chosen to be 8 for all three signals
which corresponds to 256 quantization intervals. In addition, the vertical resolution for all three signals was also chosen to be the same, the precise
number being determined by the scanning system in use; that is, 480 lines
with a 525-line system and 576 lines with a 625-line system, the numbers 480
and 576 being the number of active (visible) lines in the respective system.
Also, since the 4:2:2 format is intended for use in television studios, non-
interlaced scanning is used at a frame refresh rate of either 60 Hz for a
525-line system or 50 Hz for a 625-line system.

Since each line is sampled at a constant rate (13.5 and 6.75 MHz) with a
fixed number of samples per line (720 and 360), the samples for each line
are in a fixed position which repeats from frame to frame. The samples are
then said to be **orthogonal** and the sample method **orthogonal sampling**.
Since each system (525 and 625) has a fixed number of (active) lines per
frame, the sampling positions for each of the three signals relative to a rectangular grid are as shown in Figure 2.21.

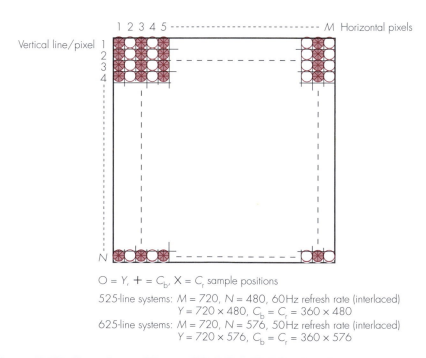

$O = Y$, $+ = C_b$, $X = C_r$ sample positions

525-line systems: $M = 720$, $N = 480$, 60 Hz refresh rate (interlaced)
$Y = 720 \times 480$, $C_b = C_r = 360 \times 480$
625-line systems: $M = 720$, $N = 576$, 50 Hz refresh rate (interlaced)
$Y = 720 \times 576$, $C_b = C_r = 360 \times 576$

Figure 2.21 Sample positions with 4:2:2 digitization format.

Example 2.7

Derive the bit rate and the memory requirements to store each frame that result from the digitization of both a 525-line and a 625-line system assuming a 4:2:2 format. Also find the total memory required to store a 1.5 hour movie/video.

Answer:

525-line system: The number of samples per line is 720 and the number of visible lines is 480. Hence the resolution of the luminance (Y) and two chrominance (C_b and C_r) signals are:

$$Y = 720 \times 480$$
$$C_b = C_r = 360 \times 480$$

Bit rate: Line sampling rate is fixed at 13.5 MHz for Y and 6.75 MHz for both C_b and C_r, all with 8 bits per sample.

Hence: Bit rate $= 13.5 \times 10^6 \times 8 + 2\,(6.75 \times 10^6 \times 8) = 216\,\text{Mbps}$

Memory required: Memory required per line $= 720 \times 8 + 2\,(360 \times 8)$
$$= 11\,520 \text{ bits or } 1440 \text{ bytes}$$

Hence memory per frame, each of 480 lines $= 480 \times 11\,520$
$$= 5.5296 \text{ Mbits or } 691.2 \text{ kbytes}$$

and memory to store 1.5 hours assuming 60 frames per second:
$$= 691.2 \times 60 \times 1.5 \times 3600 \text{ kbytes}$$
$$= 223.9488 \text{ Gbytes}$$

625-line system: Resolution: $Y = 720 \times 576$
$$C_b = C_r = 360 \times 576$$

Bit rate $= 13.5 \times 10^6 \times 8 + 2\,(6.75 \times 10^6 \times 8) = 216\,\text{Mbps}$

Memory per frame $= 576 \times 11\,520 = 6.635\,55$ Mbits or 829.44 kbytes

and memory to store 1.5 hours assuming 50 frames per second:
$$= 829.44 \times 50 \times 1.5 \times 3600 \text{ kbytes}$$
$$= 223.9488 \text{ Gbytes}$$

It should be noted that, in practice, the bit rate figures are less than the computed values since they include samples during the retrace times when the beam is switched off. Nevertheless, as we can deduce from the computed values, both the bit rate and the memory requirements are very large for both systems and it is for this reason that the various lower resolution formats have been defined.

4:2:0 format

This format is a derivative of the 4:2:2 format and is used in digital video broadcast applications. It has been found to give good picture quality and is derived by using the same set of chrominance samples for two consecutive lines. Since it is intended for broadcast applications, interlaced scanning is used and the absence of chrominance samples in alternative lines is the origin of the term 4:2:0. The position of the three sample instants per frame are as shown in Figure 2.22.

As we can see from the figure, this yields the same luminance resolution as the 4:2:2 format but half the chrominance resolution:

$$\text{525-line system:} \qquad Y = 720 \times 480$$
$$C_b = C_r = 360 \times 240$$

$$\text{625-line system:} \qquad Y = 720 \times 576$$
$$C_b = C_r = 360 \times 288$$

The bit rate in both systems with this format is:

$$13.5 \times 10^6 \times 8 + 2\,(3.375 \times 10^6 \times 8) = 162 \text{ Mbps}$$

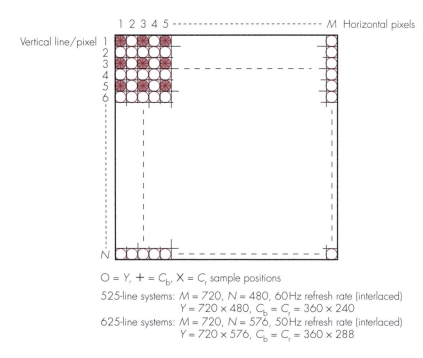

$O = Y, + = C_b, X = C_r$ sample positions
525-line systems: $M = 720, N = 480$, 60Hz refresh rate (interlaced)
$Y = 720 \times 480, C_b = C_r = 360 \times 240$
625-line systems: $M = 720, N = 576$, 50Hz refresh rate (interlaced)
$Y = 720 \times 576, C_b = C_r = 360 \times 288$

Figure 2.22 Sample positions in 4:2:0 digitization format.

It should be noted, however, that, as we pointed out in Example 2.7, this is the worst-case bit rate since it includes samples during the retrace times when the beam is switched off. Also, to avoid flicker effects with the chrominance signals, the receiver uses the same chrominance values from the sampled lines for the missing lines. With large-screen televisions, flicker effects are often reduced further by the receiver storing the incoming digitized signals of each field in a memory buffer. A refresh rate of double the normal rate – 100/120 Hz – is then used with the stored set of signals used for the second field.

HDTV formats

There are a number of alternative digitization formats associated with high-definition television (HDTV). The resolution of those which relate to the older 4/3 aspect ratio tubes can be up to 1440×1152 pixels and the resolution of those which relate to the newer 16/9 wide-screen tubes can be up to 1920×1152 pixels. In both cases, the number of visible lines per frame is 1080 which produces a square-pixel lattice structure with both tube types. Both use either the 4:2:2 digitization format for studio applications or the 4:2:0 format for broadcast applications. The corresponding frame refresh rate is either 50/60 Hz with the 4:2:2 format or 25/30 Hz with the 4:2:0 format. Hence in the case of the 1440×1152 resolution, the resulting worst-case bit rates are four times the values derived in the previous two sections and proportionally higher for the wide-screen format.

SIF

The **source intermediate format** (**SIF**) has been found to give a picture quality comparable with that obtained with video cassette recorders (VCRs). It uses half the spatial resolution in both horizontal and vertical directions as that used in the 4:2:0 format – a technique known as **subsampling** – and, in addition, uses half the refresh rate – also known as **temporal resolution**. This means that the frame refresh rate is 30 Hz for a 525-line system and 25 Hz for a 625-line system. Since the SIF is intended for storage applications, progressive (non-interlaced) scanning is used. The digitization format is known, therefore, as 4:1:1. The positions of the three sampling instants per frame are as shown in Figure 2.23.

As we can deduce from the figure, this yields resolutions of:

$$525\text{-line system:} \qquad Y = 360 \times 240$$
$$C_b = C_r = 180 \times 120$$

$$625\text{-line system:} \qquad Y = 360 \times 288$$
$$C_b = C_r = 180 \times 144$$

The worst-case bit rate in both systems with this format is:

$$6.75 \times 10^6 \times 8 + 2(1.6875 \times 10^6 \times 8) = 81 \text{ Mbps}$$

At the receiver, the missing samples are estimated by interpolating between each pair of values that are sent.

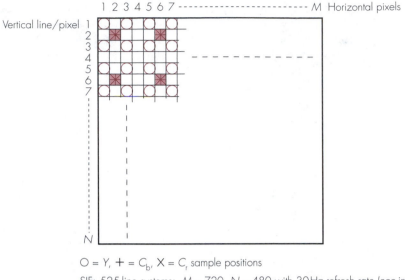

O = Y, + = C_b, X = C_r sample positions

SIF: 525-line systems: M = 720, N = 480 with 30 Hz refresh rate (non-interlaced)
Y = 360 × 240, C_b = C_r = 180 × 120

625-line systems: M = 720, N = 576 with 25 Hz refresh rate (non-interlaced)
Y = 360 × 288, C_b = C_r = 180 × 144

CIF: M = 720, N = 576 with 30 Hz refresh rate (non-interlaced)
Y = 360 × 288, C_b = C_r = 180 × 144

Figure 2.23 Sample positions for SIF and CIF.

CIF

The **common intermediate format** (**CIF**) has been defined for use in videoconferencing applications. It is derived from the SIF and uses a combination of the spatial resolution used for the SIF in the 625-line system and the temporal resolution used in the 525-line system. This yields a spatial resolution of:

$$Y = 360 \times 288$$
$$C_b = C_r = 180 \times 144$$

with a temporal resolution of 30 Hz using progressive scanning. The positions of the sampling instants per frame are the same as for SIF and hence the digitization format is 4:1:1. Similarly, the worst-case bit rate is the same and hence is 81 Mbps. As we can deduce from this, to convert to the CIF, a 525-line system needs a line-rate conversion and a 625-line system a frame-rate conversion.

In addition to the basic CIF, a number of higher-resolution derivatives of the CIF have been defined. As we described earlier in Section 1.4.1, there are a number of different types of videoconferencing applications including those that involve a linked set of desktop PCs and those that involve a linked set of videoconferencing studios. In general, therefore, because most desktop applications use switched circuits, a typical bit rate used is a single 64 kbps ISDN channel. For linking videoconferencing studios, however, dedicated circuits are normally used that comprise multiple 64 kbps channels. Hence because the bit rate of these circuits is much higher – typically four or sixteen 64 kbps channels – then a higher-resolution version of the basic CIF can be used to improve the quality of the video. Two examples are:

$$4\text{CIF:} \quad Y = 720 \times 576$$
$$C_b = C_r = 360 \times 288$$
$$16\text{CIF:} \quad Y = 1440 \times 1152$$
$$C_b = C_r = 720 \times 576$$

QCIF

The **quarter CIF (QCIF)** format has been defined for use in video telephony applications. It is derived from the CIF and uses half the spatial resolution of CIF in both horizontal and vertical directions and the temporal resolution is divided by either 2 or 4. This yields a spatial resolution of:

$$Y = 180 \times 144$$
$$C_b = C_r = 90 \times 72$$

with a temporal resolution of either 15 or 7.5 Hz. The worst-case bit rate with this format is:

$$3.375 \times 10^6 \times 8 + 2 \, (0.843\,75 \times 10^6 \times 8) = 40.5 \, \text{Mbps}$$

The positions of the three sampling instants per frame are as shown in Figure 2.24 and, as we can see, it has the same 4:1:1 digitization format as CIF.

As we described in Section 1.4.1, a typical video telephony application involves a single switched 64 kbps channel and the QCIF is intended for use with such channels. In addition, there are lower-resolution versions of the QCIF which are intended for use in applications that use lower bit rate channels such as that provided by a modem and the PSTN. These lower-resolution versions are known as **sub-QCIF** or **S-QCIF** and an example is:

$$Y = 128 \times 96$$
$$C_b = C_r = 64 \times 48$$

It should be noted, however, that although the sampling matrix appears sparse, in practice, only a small screen (or a small window of a larger screen) is normally used for video telephony and hence the total set of samples may occupy all the pixel positions on the screen or window.

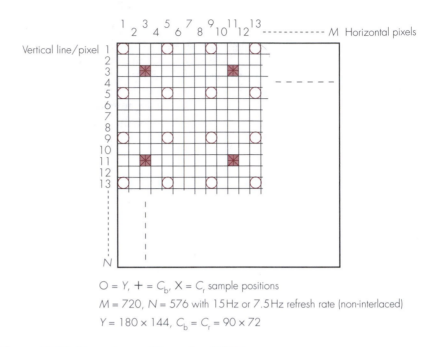

$O = Y, + = C_b, X = C_r$ sample positions

$M = 720, N = 576$ with 15 Hz or 7.5 Hz refresh rate (non-interlaced)

$Y = 180 \times 144, C_b = C_r = 90 \times 72$

Figure 2.24 Sample positions for QCIF.

2.6.3 PC video

All the digitization formats described in Section 2.6.2 are intended for use with standard television receivers. However, as we discussed in Chapter 1, a number of multimedia applications that involve live video, use a window on the screen of a PC monitor for display purposes. Examples include desktop video telephony and videoconferencing, and also **video-in-a-window**.

As we discussed under the subheading "Aspect ratio" in Section 2.4.3, in order to avoid distortion on a PC screen – for example when displaying a square of $N \times N$ pixels – it is necessary to use a horizontal resolution of 640 ($480 \times 4/3$) pixels per line with a 525-line PC monitor and 768 ($576 \times 4/3$) pixels per line with a 625-line PC monitor. Hence for multimedia applications that involve mixing live video with other information on a PC screen, the line sampling rate is normally modified in order to obtain the required horizontal resolution.

To achieve the necessary resolution with a 525-line monitor, the line sampling rate is reduced from 13.5 MHz to 12.2727 MHz while for a 625-line monitor, the line sampling rate must be increased from 13.5 MHz to 14.75 MHz. In the case of desktop video telephony and videoconferencing, the video signals from the camera are sampled at this rate prior to transmission and hence can be displayed directly on a PC screen. In the case of a digital television broadcast a conversion is necessary before the video is displayed. The various digitization formats for use with PC video are as shown in Table 2.2. It should be remembered that all PC monitors use progressive (non-interlaced) scanning rather than interlaced scanning.

Table 2.2 PC video digitization formats.

Digitization format	System	Spatial resolution	Temporal resolution
4:2:0	525-line	$Y = 640 \times 480$ $C_b = C_r = 320 \times 240$	60 Hz
	625-line	$Y = 768 \times 576$ $C_b = C_r = 384 \times 288$	50 Hz
SIF	525-line	$Y = 320 \times 240$ $C_b = C_r = 160 \times 240$	30 Hz
	625-line	$Y = 384 \times 288$ $C_b = C_r = 192 \times 144$	25 Hz
CIF		$Y = 384 \times 288$ $C_b = C_r = 192 \times 144$	30 Hz
QCIF		$Y = 192 \times 144$ $C_b = C_r = 96 \times 72$	15/7.5 Hz

2.6.4 Video content

In the preceding section we described the various digitization formats that have been defined for use in different application domains of digital video. In terms of the actual video content, therefore, this depends on the particular application. For example, in entertainment applications, the content will be either a broadcast television program or, in a video-on-demand application, a digitized movie that is accessed from a suitable server. Similarly, in interpersonal applications such as video telephony and videoconferencing, the video source will be derived from a video camera and the digitized sequence of pixels relating to each frame are transmitted across the network. As the pixels are received at the destination, they are displayed directly on either a television screen or a computer monitor.

In addition, in many interactive applications that involve video, the short video clips associated with the application are obtained by plugging a video camera into a **video capture board** within the computer that is preparing the (interactive) page contents. Normally, the computer stores the digitized video produced by such boards into a file ready for linking to the other page contents.

In other applications the video may be generated by a computer program rather than a video camera. This type of video content is normally referred to as **computer animation** or sometimes, because of the way it is generated,

animated graphics. A range of special programming languages is available for creating computer animation. Hence in the same way that a graphical image produced by a graphics program can be represented in the form of either a high-level program or a pixel image, so a computer animation can be represented in the form of either an animation program or a digital video. As before, the form used depends on the application. In general the digital video form of representation of an animation requires considerably more memory and transmission bandwidth than the corresponding high-level program form.

The negative side of a high-level program form is that the low-level animation primitives that the program uses – move object, rotate object, object fill, and so on – have to be executed very fast in order to produce smooth motion on the display. Hence it is now common to have an additional (**3-D**) **graphics accelerator** processor to carry out these functions. Typically, the (host) processor simply passes the sequence of low-level primitives to the accelerator processor at the appropriate rate. The accelerator then, in turn, executes each set of primitives to produce the corresponding pixel image in the video RAM at the desired refresh rate.

Summary

In this chapter we have described the different ways that the range of media types associated with the various multimedia applications we identified in Chapter 1 are represented in their digital form. These included various types of text, images, digitized documents and pictures, audio – both speech and music – and video. In the case of audio and video, the conversion operations that are used to convert them from their source analog form into their corresponding digital form were also described. In practice, with these basic forms of representation, the amount of bandwidth that is required to transfer the total quantity of information associated with a particular application is considerably larger than that which is available with many of the communication networks used for these applications.

For example, the bandwidth available for digital television – in terms of bits per second – is in the order of 40 Mbps with cable and terrestrial broadcast systems and 60 Mbps with a satellite channel. Clearly, these are both still considerably less than the bit rate requirement of 162 Mbps that is generated using the 4:2:0 digitization format. Similarly, the bit rate available with a connection through the all-digital ISDN is between 64 kbps and 2 Mbps and hence again the bandwidth requirements for videoconferencing – 81 Mbps with the CIF – and video telephony – 40.5 Mbps with the QCIF – are both far in excess of these two values. Hence in order to provide such services over the related networks, it is necessary to reduce the bandwidth requirements of the source signals considerably. In addition, when using public networks such as a

PSTN or an ISDN in which call charges are based on the duration of a call, considerable cost savings can be made if the amount of data to be transmitted is reduced. For example, if the amount of data is reduced by a factor of two, then the cost of the call will be halved.

In most multimedia applications, therefore, a technique known as compression is first applied to the source information prior to its transmission. This is done either to reduce the volume of data to be transmitted – for example with text, fax, and images – or to reduce the bandwidth that is required for its transmission – for example with speech, audio, and video. In the next chapter we describe a range of compression algorithms that have been developed to reduce the volume of the data associated with text, fax, and images and, in Chapter 4, a range of compression algorithms associated with audio and video.

Exercises

Section 2.1

2.1 Explain the meaning of the following terms:
   (i) codeword,
   (ii) analog signal,
   (iii) signal encoder,
   (iv) signal decoder.

Section 2.2

2.2 With the aid of a set of signal waveforms, show the principles of how a time-varying analog signal is made up of a range of sinusoidal frequency components of differing amplitude and phase relative to one another.

2.3 Define the term "signal bandwidth". Hence show in graphical form the bandwidth of a speech signal and a music signal. Clearly show the dimensions of the horizontal and vertical axes.

2.4 Define the meaning of the term "channel bandwidth" in relation to a transmission channel. Hence with the aid of a diagram, explain the meaning of the term "bandlimiting channel".

2.5 Use a diagram to identify the main circuit components associated with a signal encoder. Hence by means of an associated set of signal waveforms, explain the meaning of the terms:
   (i) bandlimiting filter,
   (ii) ADC,
   (iii) sample-and-hold,
   (iv) quantizer.

2.6 Explain the meaning of the following terms relating to the sampling of an analog signal:
   (i) Nyquist sampling theorem,
   (ii) Nyquist rate.

2.7 Show by means of a diagram how sampling of an analog signal at a rate lower than the Nyquist rate can generate additional lower-frequency alias signals to those present in the original waveform. How can this be avoided?

2.8 Define the meaning of the term "quantization interval" and how this influences the accuracy of the sampling process of an analog signal. Hence with the aid of a diagram, explain the meaning of the terms "quantization error" and "quantization noise".

2.9 State the meaning of the term "dynamic range" as applied to an analog signal and show how this is expressed in decibels. How does this influence the number of bits to be used for the quantizer part of an ADC?

2.10 With the aid of a diagram and an associated waveform set, explain the function of the following components that make up a signal decoder:
   (i) DAC,
   (ii) low-pass filter.

Why is the latter also known as a recovery/reconstruction filter?

Section 2.3

2.11 State the meaning of the following types of text:
  (i) unformatted/plaintext,
  (ii) formatted/richtext,
  (iii) hypertext.

2.12 By means of examples, show how the 7-bit ASCII character set can be extended to create additional characters and symbols. State one of the uses of an extended character set.

2.13 How is formatted text different from unformatted text? Hence describe the meaning of the term "text" and "document formatting commands". What is the origin of the acronym WYSIWYG?

2.14 Describe the terms "hypertext", "pages/documents", and "hyperlinks".

2.15 With the aid of diagrams where appropriate, describe the meaning of the following terms relating to HTML and the World Wide Web:
  (i) browser,
  (ii) home page,
  (iii) URL,
  (iv) page formatting commands.

Section 2.4

2.16 Explain the meaning of the following terms relating to graphical images:
  (i) visual object,
  (ii) freeform object,
  (iii) clip-art,
  (iv) 3-D objects.

2.17 With the aid of diagrams, explain the meaning of the following terms relating to graphical images:
  (i) pixels,
  (ii) video graphics array,
  (iii) image object,
  (iv) object attributes,
  (v) open and closed object shapes,
  (vi) rendering,
  (vii) bit-map format.

2.18 With the aid of a diagram, explain the meaning of the following terms relating to facsimile machines:
  (i) scanning,
  (ii) pels,
  (iii) digitization resolution.

2.19 What is the difference between a bitonal image and a continuous-tone image?

2.20 With the aid of diagrams where appropriate, explain the meaning of the terms:
  (i) color gamut,
  (ii) additive color mixing,
  (iii) subtractive color mixing.

  Give an application of both color mixing methods.

2.21 With the aid of diagrams, describe the raster-scan operation associated with TV/computer monitors. Include in your description the meaning of the terms:
  (i) line scan,
  (ii) horizontal and vertical retrace,
  (iii) phosphor triad,
  (iv) frame refresh rate,
  (v) flicker,
  (vi) pixel depth,
  (vii) video RAM,
  (viii) video controller.

2.22 Define the aspect ratio of a display screen. Give two examples for current widely used screen sizes.

2.23 What is the number of scan lines per frame associated with each of the following TV monitors:
  (i) NTSC,
  (ii) PAL?

  In practice, the number of visible lines per frame are less than these values. State what these are for each type of monitor. In each case, derive the number of pixels per scan line that are used to obtain square pixels assuming a 4/3 aspect ratio.

2.24 Most high resolution computer monitors are not based on television picture tubes. What is the amount of memory that is required to

store an image with each of the following display sizes:
(i) 1024×768,
(ii) 1280×1024?

Derive the time to transmit an image with each type of display assuming a bit rate of
(i) 56 kbps,
(ii) 1.5 Mbps.

2.25 With the aid of a diagram, explain how a digital image produced by a scanner or digital camera is captured and stored within the memory of a computer.

2.26 With the aid of a diagram, explain how a color image is captured within a camera or scanner using each of the following methods:
(i) single image sensor,
(ii) a single image sensor with filters,
(iii) three separate image sensors. Include in your explanations the terms "photosites" and "CCDs" and the role of the readout register.

Section 2.5

2.27 With the aid of a diagram, explain the principle of operation of a PCM speech codec. Include in your diagram the operation of the compressor in the encoder and the expander in the decoder. Use for example purposes 5 bits per sample.

2.28 Identify the main features of the MIDI standard and its associated messages.

Section 2.6

2.29 With the aid of a diagram, explain the principles of interlaced of scanning as used in most TV broadcast applications. Include in your explanation the meaning of the terms "field", "odd scan lines", and "even scan lines". Show the number of scan lines per field with
(i) a 525-line system and
(ii) a 625-line system. Why do computer monitors not use interlaced scanning?

2.30 State and explain the three main properties of a color source that the eye makes of. Hence

explain the meaning of the terms "luminance", "chrominance", and "color difference" and how the magnitude of each primary color present in the source is derived from these.

2.31 Why is the chrominance signal transmitted in the form of two color different signals? Identify the color difference signals associated with the NTSC and PAL systems.

2.32 State the meaning of the term "composite video signal" and, with the aid of a diagram, describe how the two color difference signals are transmitted within the same frequency band as that used for the luminance signal.

2.33 Explain why, for digital TV transmission, the three digitized signals used are the luminance and two color difference signals rather than the RGB signals. Why are a number of different digitization formats used?

2.34 With the aid of diagrams, describe the following digitization formats:
(i) 4:2:2,
(ii) 4:2:0,
(iii) SIF,
(iv) CIF,
(v) QCIF,
(vi) S-QCIF.

For each format, state the temporal resolution and the sampling rate used for the luminance and the two color difference signals. Give an example application of each format.

2.35 Derive the bit rate that results from the digitization of a 525-line and a 625-line system using the 4:2:0 digitization format and interlaced scanning. Hence derive the amount of memory required to store a 2-hour movie/ video.

2.36 Explain why modifications to the received (broadcast) TV signal have to be made if the signal is to be displayed in a window of a computer monitor. Hence assuming the SIF format, derive the spatial resolution required with
(i) a 525-line and
(ii) a 625-line system.

Text and image compression

3.1 Introduction

In the previous chapter we described the way the different types of media used in multimedia applications – text, fax, images, speech, audio, and video – are represented in a digital form. We derived the memory and bandwidth requirements for each type and, as we concluded in Section 2.7, in most cases, the bandwidths derived were greater than those that are available with the communication networks over which the related services are provided. In addition, when using a public network in which call charges are based on the duration of a call, considerable cost savings can be made if the volume of information to be transmitted is reduced.

In almost all multimedia applications, therefore, a technique known as **compression** is first applied to the source information prior to its transmission. This is done either to reduce the volume of information to be transmitted – text, fax, and images – or to reduce the bandwidth that is required for its transmission – speech, audio, and video. In this chapter we shall consider a selection of the compression algorithms which are used with text, fax, and images and, in Chapter 4, we shall describe a selection of the compression algorithms that are used with audio and video.

3.2 Compression principles

Before we describe some of the compression algorithms in widespread use, it will be helpful if we first build up an understanding of the principles on which they are based. We shall discuss the under the headings:

- source encoders and destination decoders,
- lossless and lossy compression,
- entropy encoding,
- source encoding.

3.2.1 Source encoders and destination decoders

As have just indicated, prior to transmitting the source information relating to a particular multimedia application, a compression algorithm is applied to it. This implies that in order for the destination to reproduce the original source information – or, in some instances, a nearly exact copy of it – a matching decompression algorithm must be applied to it. The application of the compression algorithm is the main function carried out by the **source encoder** and the decompression algorithm is carried out by the **destination decoder**.

In applications which involve two computers communicating with each other, the time required to perform the compression and decompression algorithms is not always critical. So both algorithms are normally implemented in software within the two computers. The general scheme is shown in part (a) of Figure 3.1 and an example application which uses this approach is the compression of text and/or image files. In other applications, however, the time required to perform the compression and decompression algorithms in software is not acceptable and instead the two algorithms must be performed by special processors in separate units as shown in part (b) of the figure. Example applications which use this approach are those which involve speech, audio, and video.

3.2.2 Lossless and lossy compression

Compression algorithms can be classified as being either lossless or lossy. In the case of a **lossless compression algorithm** the aim is to reduce the amount of source information to be transmitted in such a way that, when the compressed information is decompressed, there is no loss of information. Lossless compression is said, therefore, to be **reversible**. An example application of lossless compression is for the transfer over a network of a text file since, in such applications, it is normally imperative that no part of the source information is lost during either the compression or decompression operations.

In contrast, the aim of **lossy compression algorithms**, is normally not to reproduce an exact copy of the source information after decompression but

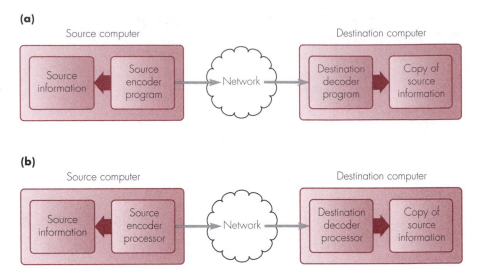

Figure 3.1 Source encoder/destination decoder alternatives: (a) software only; (b) special processors/hardware.

rather a version of it which is perceived by the recipient as a true copy. In general, with such algorithms the higher the level of compression being applied to the source information the more approximate the received version becomes. Example applications of lossy compression are for the transfer of digitized images and audio and video streams. In such cases, the sensitivity of the human eye or ear is such that any fine details that may be missing from the original source signal after decompression are not detectable.

3.2.3 Entropy encoding

Entropy encoding is lossless and independent of the type of information that is being compressed. It is concerned solely with how the information is represented. We shall describe two examples which are in widespread use in compression algorithms in order to illustrate the principles involved. In some applications they are used separately while in others they are used together.

Run-length encoding

Typical applications of this type of encoding are when the source information comprises long substrings of the same character or binary digit. Instead of transmitting the source string in the form of independent codewords or bits, it is transmitted in the form of a different set of codewords which indicate not only the particular character or bit being transmitted but also an indication of the number of characters/bits in the substring. Then, providing the destination knows the set of codewords being used, it simply interprets each codeword received and outputs the appropriate number of characters or bits.

For example, in an application that involves the transmission of long strings of binary bits that comprise a limited number of substrings, each substring can be assigned a separate codeword. The total bit string is then transmitted in the form of a string of codewords selected from the codeword set. An example application which uses this technique is for the transmission of the binary strings produced by the scanner in a facsimile machine. In many instances – for example when scanning typed documents – the scanner produces long substrings of either binary 0s or 1s. Instead of transmitting these directly, they are sent in the form of a string of codewords, each indicating both the bit – 0 or 1 – and the number of bits in the substring. For example, if the output of the scanner was:

00000001111111110000011...

this could be represented as: 0,7 1,10 0,5 1,2 ... . Alternatively, since only the two binary digits 0 and 1 are involved, if we ensure the first substring always comprises binary 0s, then the string could be represented as 7, 10, 5, 2 ... . To send this in a digital form, the individual decimal digits would be sent in their binary form and, assuming a fixed number of bits per codeword, the number of bits per codeword would be determined by the largest possible substring. We shall describe an application that uses this approach in Section 3.4.3 when we describe the compression of digitized documents.

Statistical encoding

Many applications use a set of codewords to transmit the source information. For example, as we described earlier in Section 2.3.1, a set of ASCII codewords are often used for the transmission of strings of characters. Normally, all the codewords in the set comprise a fixed number of binary bits, for example 7 bits in the case of ASCII. In many applications, however, the symbols – and hence codewords – that are present in the source information do not occur with the same frequency of occurrence; that is, with equal probability. For example, in a string of text, the character A may occur more frequently than, say, the character P which occurs more frequently than the character Z, and so on. Statistical encoding exploits this property by using a set of variable-length codewords with the shortest codewords used to represent the most frequently occurring symbols.

In practice, the use of variable-length codewords is not quite as straightforward as it first appears. Clearly, as with run-length encoding, the destination must know the set of codewords being used by the source. With variable-length codewords, however, in order for the decoding operation to be carried out correctly, it is necessary to ensure that a shorter codeword in the set does not form the start of a longer codeword otherwise the decoder will interpret the string on the wrong codeword boundaries. A codeword set that avoids this happening is said to possess the **prefix property** and an example of an encoding scheme that generates codewords that have this property is the **Huffman encoding algorithm** which we shall describe in Section 3.3.1.

The theoretical minimum average number of bits that are required to transmit a particular source stream is known as the **entropy** of the source and can be computed using a formula attributed to Shannon:

$$\text{Entropy, } H = -\sum_{i=1}^{n} P_i \log_2 P_i$$

where n is the number of different symbols in the source stream and P_i is the probability of occurrence of symbol i. Hence the efficiency of a particular encoding scheme is often computed as a ratio of the entropy of the source to the average number of bits per codeword that are required with the scheme. The latter is computed using the formula:

$$\text{Average number of bits per codeword} = \sum_{i=1}^{n} N_i P_i$$

Example 3.1

A statistical encoding algorithm is being considered for the transmission of a large number of long text files over a public network. Analysis of the file contents has shown that each file comprises only the six different characters M, F, Y, N, 0, and 1 each of which occurs with a relative frequency of occurrence of 0.25, 0.25, 0.125, 0.125, 0.125, and 0.125 respectively. If the encoding algorithm under consideration uses the following set of codewords:

M = 10, F = 11, Y = 010, N = 011, 0 = 000, 1 = 001

compute:

(i)   the average number of bits per codeword with the algorithm,

(ii) the entropy of the source,

(iii) the minimum number of bits required assuming fixed-length codewords.

Answer:

(i)   Average number of bits per codeword

$$= \sum_{i=1}^{6} N_i P_i = (2(2 \times 0.25) + 4(3 \times 0.125))$$

$$= 2 \times 0.5 + 4 \times 0.375 = 2.5$$

3.1 Continued

(ii) Entropy of source

$$= \sum_{i=1}^{6} P_i \log_2 P_i = -(2(0.25\log_2 0.25) + 4(0.125\log_2 0.125))$$

$$= 1 + 1.5 = 2.5$$

(iii) Since there are 6 different characters, using fixed-length code-words would require a minimum of 3 bits (8 combinations).

3.2.4 Source encoding

Source encoding exploits a particular property of the source information in order to produce an alternative form of representation that is either a compressed version of the original form or is more amenable to the application of compression. Again, we shall describe two examples in widespread use in order to illustrate the principles involved.

Differential encoding

Differential encoding is used extensively in applications where the amplitude of a value or signal covers a large range but the difference in amplitude between successive values/signals is relatively small. To exploit this property of the source information, instead of using a set of relatively large codewords to represent the amplitude of each value/signal, a set of smaller codewords can be used each of which indicates only the difference in amplitude between the current value/signal being encoded and the immediately preceding value/signal. For example, if the digitization of an analog signal requires, say, 12 bits to obtain the required dynamic range but the maximum difference in amplitude between successive samples of the signal requires only 3 bits, then by using only the difference values a saving of 75% on transmission bandwidth can be obtained.

In practice, differential encoding can be either lossless or lossy and depends on the number of bits used to encode the difference values. If the number of bits used is sufficient to cater for the maximum difference value then it is lossless. If this is not the case, then on those occasions when the difference value exceeds the maximum number of bits being used, temporary loss of information will result.

Transform encoding

As the name implies, transform encoding involves transforming the source information from one form into another, the other form lending itself more readily to the application of compression. In general, there is no loss of information associated with the transformation operation and this technique is used in a number of applications involving both images and video. For example, as we saw in Section 2.4.3, the digitization of a continuous-tone monochromatic image produces a two-dimensional matrix of pixel values each of which represents the level of gray in a particular position of the image. As we go from one position in the matrix to the next, the magnitude of each pixel value may vary. Hence, as we scan across a set of pixel locations, the rate of change in magnitude will vary from zero, if all the pixel values remain the same, to a low rate of change if, say, one half is different from the next half, through to a high rate of change if each pixel magnitude changes from one location to the next. Some examples are shown in Figure 3.2(a).

The rate of change in magnitude as one traverses the matrix gives rise to a term known as **spatial frequency** and, for any particular image, there will be a mix of different spatial frequencies whose amplitudes are determined by the related changes in magnitude of the pixels. This is true, of course, if we scan the matrix in either the horizontal or the vertical direction and this, in turn, gives rise to the terms **horizontal** and **vertical frequency components** of the image. In practice, the human eye is less sensitive to the higher spatial frequency components associated with an image than the lower frequency components. Moreover, if the amplitude of the higher frequency components falls below a certain amplitude threshold, they will not be detected by the eye. Hence in terms of compression, if we can transform the original spatial form of representation into an equivalent representation involving spatial frequency components, then we can more readily identify and eliminate those higher frequency components which the eye cannot detect thereby reducing the volume of information to be transmitted without degrading the perceived quality of the original image.

The transformation of a two-dimensional matrix of pixel values into an equivalent matrix of spatial frequency components can be carried out using a mathematical technique known as the **discrete cosine transform (DCT)**. The transformation operation itself is lossless – apart from some small rounding errors in the mathematics – but, once the equivalent matrix of spatial frequency components – known as coefficients – has been derived, then any frequency components in the matrix whose amplitude is less than a defined threshold can be dropped. It is only at this point that the operation becomes lossy. The basic principle behind the DCT is as shown in Figure 3.2(b) and we shall describe it in more detail in Section 3.4.5 when we discuss the topic of image compression.

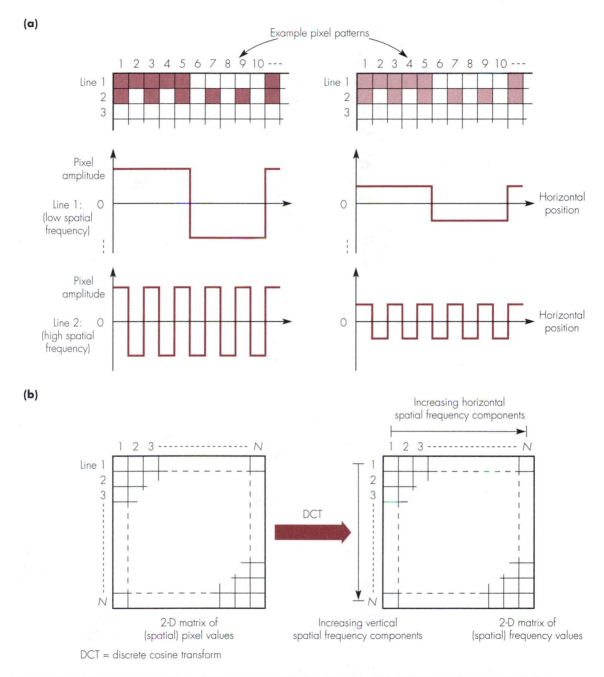

DCT = discrete cosine transform

Figure 3.2 Transform coding: (a) example pixel patterns; (b) DCT transform principles.

3.3 Text compression

As we saw in Section 2.3, the three different types of text – unformatted, formatted, and hypertext – are all represented as strings of characters selected from a defined set. The strings comprise alphanumeric characters which are interspersed with additional control characters. The different types of text use and interpret the latter in different ways. As we can deduce from this, any compression algorithm associated with text must be lossless since the loss of just a single character could modify the meaning of a complete string. In general, therefore, we are restricted to the use of entropy encoding and, in practice, statistical encoding methods.

Essentially, there are two types of statistical encoding methods which are used with text: one which uses single characters as the basis of deriving an optimum set of codewords and the other which uses variable-length strings of characters. Two examples of the former are the Huffman and arithmetic coding algorithms and an example of the latter is the **Lempel-Ziv (LZ) algorithm**. We shall describe the principles of each of these algorithms in this section.

There are two types of coding used for text. The first is intended for applications in which the text to be compressed has known characteristics in terms of the characters used and their relative frequencies of occurrence. Using this information, instead of using fixed-length codewords, an optimum set of variable-length codewords is derived with the shortest codewords used to represent the most frequently occurring characters. The resulting set of codewords are then used for all subsequent transfers involving this particular type of text. This approach is known as **static coding**.

The second type is intended for more general applications in which the type of text being transferred may vary from one transfer to another. In this case the optimum set of codewords is also likely to vary from one transfer to another. To allow for this possibility, the codeword set that is used to transfer a particular text string is derived as the transfer takes place. This is done by building up knowledge of both the characters that are present in the text and their relative frequency of occurrence dynamically as the characters are being transmitted. Hence the codewords used change as a transfer takes place, but in such a way that the receiver is able to dynamically compute the same set of codewords that are being used at each point during a transfer. This approach is known as **dynamic** or **adaptive coding** and, since each uses a different algorithm to derive the codeword set, we shall describe each separately.

3.3.1 Static Huffman coding

With static Huffman coding the character string to be transmitted is first analyzed and the character types and their relative frequency determined. The coding operation involves creating an unbalanced tree with some branches (and hence codewords, in practice) shorter than others. The degree of imbalance is a function of the relative frequency of occurrence of the characters: the larger the spread, the more unbalanced is the tree. The resulting tree is known as the **Huffman code tree**.

A Huffman (code) tree is a **binary tree** with branches assigned the value 0 or 1. The base of the tree, normally the geometric top in practice, is known as the **root node** and the point at which a branch divides, a **branch node**. The termination point of a branch is known as a **leaf node** to which the symbols being encoded are assigned. An example of a Huffman code tree is shown in Figure 3.3(a). This corresponds to the string of characters AAAABBCD.

As each branch divides, a binary value of 0 or 1 is assigned to each new branch: a binary 0 for the left branch and a binary 1 for the right branch. The codewords used for each character (shown in the leaf nodes) are determined by tracing the path *from* the root node out to each leaf and forming a

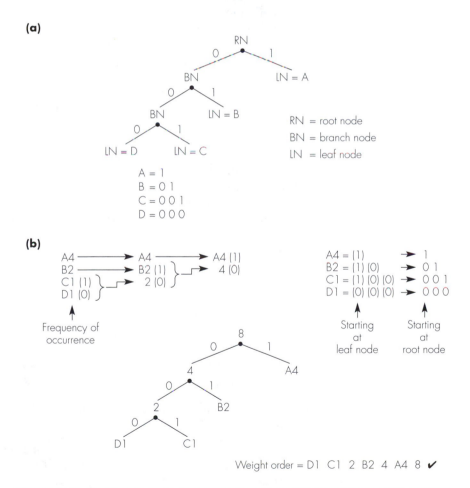

Figure 3.3 Huffman code tree construction: (a) final tree with codes; (b) tree derivation.

string of the binary values associated with each branch traced. We can deduce from the set of codes associated with this tree that it would take

$$4 \times 1 + 2 \times 2 + 1 \times 3 + 1 \times 3 = 14 \text{ bits}$$

to transmit the complete string AAAABBCD.

To illustrate how the Huffman code tree in Figure 3.3(a) is determined, we must add information concerning the frequency of occurrence of each character. Figure 3.3(b) shows the characters listed in a column in decreasing (weight) order. We derive the tree as follows.

The first two leaf nodes at the base of the list – C1 and D1 – are assigned to the (1) and (0) branches respectively of a branch node. The two leaf nodes are then replaced by a branch node whose weight is the sum of the weights of the two leaf nodes; that is, two. A new column is then formed containing the new branch node combined with the remaining nodes from the first column, again arranged in their correct weight order. This procedure is repeated until only two nodes remain.

To derive the resulting codewords for each character, we start with the character in the first column and then proceed to list the branch numbers – 0 or 1 – as they are encountered. Thus for character A the first (and only) branch number is (1) in the last column while for C the first is (1) then (0) at branch node 2 and finally (0) at branch node 4. The actual codewords, however, start at the root and not the leaf node hence they are the reverse of these bit sequences. The Huffman tree can then be readily constructed from the set of codewords.

We check that this is the optimum tree – and hence set of codewords – by listing the resulting weights of all the leaf and branch nodes in the tree starting with the smallest weight and proceeding from left to right and from bottom to top. The codewords are optimum if the resulting list increments in weight order.

Example 3.2

A series of messages is to be transferred between two computers over a PSTN. The messages comprise just the characters A through H. Analysis has shown that the probability (relative frequency of occurrence) of each character is as follows:

A and B = 0.25,   C and D = 0.14,   E, F, G, and H = 0.055

(a) Use Shannon's formula to derive the minimum average number of bits per character.

(b) Use Huffman coding to derive a codeword set and prove this is the minimum set by constructing the corresponding Huffman code tree.

3.2 Continued

(c) Derive the average number of bits per character for your codeword set and compare this with:
(i)   the entropy of the messages (Shannon's value),
(ii) fixed-length binary codewords,
(iii) 7-bit ASCII codewords.

Answer:

(a) Shannon's formula states:

$$\text{Entropy, } H = -\sum_{i=1}^{8} P_i \log_2 P_i \text{ bits per codeword}$$

Therefore:

$$H = -(2(0.25 \log_2 0.25) + 2(0.14 \log_2 0.14) + 4(0.055 \log_2 0.055))$$
$$= 1 + 0.794 + 0.921 = 2.175 \text{ bits per codeword}$$

(b) The derivation of the codeword set using Huffman coding is shown in Figure 3.4(a). The characters are first listed in weight order and the two characters at the bottom of the list are assigned to the (1) and (0) branches. Note that in this case, however, when the two nodes are combined, the weight of the resulting branch node (0.11) is greater than the weight of the two characters E and F (0.055). Hence the branch node is inserted into the second list higher than both of these. The same procedure then repeats until there are only two entries in the list remaining.

The Huffman code tree corresponding to the derived set of codewords is given in Figure 3.4(b) and, as we can see, this is the optimum tree since all leaf and branch nodes increment in numerical order.

(c) Average number of bits per codeword using Huffman coding is:

$$2 (2 \times 0.25) + 2(3 \times 0.14) + 4(4 \times 0.055) = 2.72 \text{ bits per codeword}$$

which is 99.8% of the Shannon value.

Using fixed-length binary codewords:

There are 8 characters – A through H – and hence 3 bits per codeword is sufficient which is 90.7% of the Huffman value.

Using 7-bit ASCII codewords:

7 bits per codeword
which is 38.86% of the Huffman value.

(a)

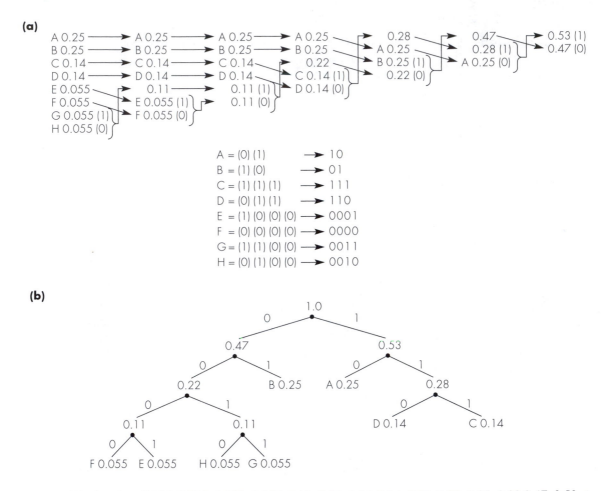

A = (0) (1)   → 10
B = (1) (0)   → 01
C = (1) (1) (1) → 111
D = (0) (1) (1) → 110
E = (1) (0) (0) (0) → 0001
F = (0) (0) (0) (0) → 0000
G = (1) (1) (0) (0) → 0011
H = (0) (1) (0) (0) → 0010

(b)

Weight order = 0.055 0.055 0.055 0.055 0.11 0.11 0.14 0.14 0.22 0.25 0.25 0.28 0.47 0.53 ✔

Figure 3.4 Huffman encoding example: (a) codeword generation; (b) Huffman code tree.

Since each character in its encoded form has a variable number of bits, the received bitstream must be interpreted (decoded) in a bit-oriented way rather than on fixed 7/8 bit boundaries. Because of the order in which bits are assigned during the encoding procedure, however, Huffman codewords have the unique property that a shorter codeword will never form the start of a longer codeword. If, say, 011 is a valid codeword, then there cannot be any longer codewords starting with this sequence. We can confirm this by considering the codes derived in the earlier examples in Figures 3.3 and 3.4.

This property, known as the **prefix property**, means that the received bitstream can be decoded simply by carrying out a recursive search bit by bit until each valid codeword is found. A flowchart of a suitable decoding algorithm is given in Figure 3.5(a). The algorithm assumes a table of codewords is available at the receiver and this also holds the corresponding ASCII codeword. The received bit stream is held in the variable BITSTREAM and the variable CODEWORD is used to hold the bits in each codeword while it is being constructed. As we can deduce from the flowchart, once a codeword is identified the corresponding ASCII codeword is written into the variable RECEIVE_BUFFER. The procedure repeats until all the bits in the received string have been processed. An example of a decoded string corresponding to the codeword set derived in Figure 3.3 is given in Figure 3.5(b).

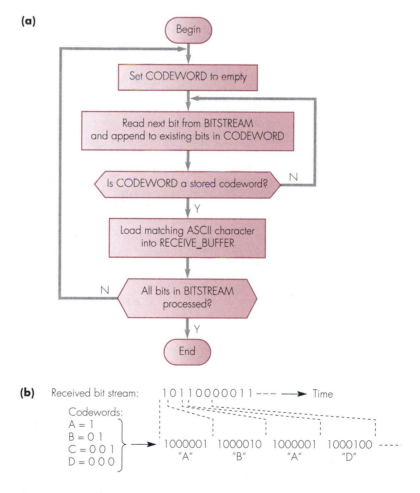

Figure 3.5 Decoding of a received bitstream assuming codewords derived in Figure 3.3: (a) decoding algorithm; (b) example.

As the Huffman code tree (and hence codewords) varies for different sets of characters being transmitted, for the receiver to perform the decoding operation it must know the codewords relating to the data being transmitted. This can be done in two ways. Either the codewords relating to the next set of data are sent before the data is transmitted, or the receiver knows in advance what codewords are being used.

The first approach leads to a form of adaptive compression since the codewords can be changed to suit the type of data being transmitted. The disadvantage is the overhead of having to send the new set of codewords (and corresponding characters) whenever a new type of data is to be sent. An alternative is for the receiver to have one or more different sets of codewords and for the sender to indicate to the receiver (through an agreed message) which codeword set to use for the next set of data.

For example, since a common requirement is to send text files generated by a word processor (and hence containing normal textual information), detailed statistical analyses have been carried out into the frequency of occurrence of the characters in the English alphabet in normal written text. This information has been used to construct the Huffman code tree for the alphabet. If this type of data is being sent, the transmitter and receiver automatically use this set of codewords. Other common data sets have been analyzed in a similar way and, for further examples, you may wish to consult the bibliography at the end of the book.

3.3.2 Dynamic Huffman coding

The basic Huffman coding method requires both the transmitter and the receiver to know the table of codewords relating to the data being transmitted. With dynamic Huffman coding, however, the transmitter (encoder) and receiver (decoder) build the Huffman tree – and hence codeword table – dynamically as the characters are being transmitted/received.

With this method, if the character to be transmitted is currently present in the tree its codeword is determined and sent in the normal way. If the character is not present – that is, it is its first occurrence – the character is transmitted in its uncompressed form. The encoder updates its Huffman tree either by incrementing the frequency of occurrence of the transmitted character or by introducing the new character into the tree.

Each transmitted codeword is encoded in such a way that the receiver, in addition to being able to determine the character that is received, can also carry out the same modifications to its own copy of the tree so that it can interpret the next codeword received according to the new updated tree structure.

To describe the details of the method, assume that the data (file) to be transmitted starts with the following character string:

This is simple ...

The steps taken by the transmitter are shown in Figure 3.6(a–g).

Both transmitter and receiver start with a tree that comprises the root node and a single **empty leaf node** – a leaf node with a zero frequency of occurrence – assigned to its 0-branch. There is always just one empty leaf node in the tree and its position – and codeword – varies as the tree is being constructed. It is represented in Figure 3.6 as e0.

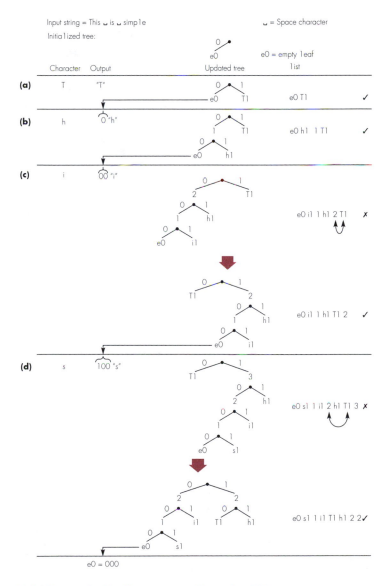

Figure 3.6 Dynamic Huffman encoding algorithm.

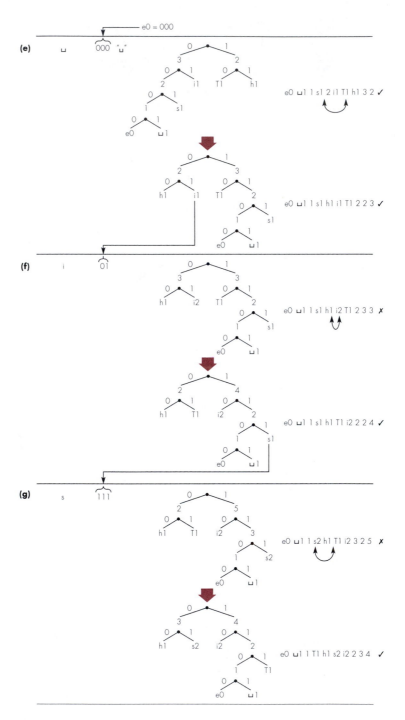

Figure 3.6 Continued

The encoder then starts by reading the first character **T** and, since the tree is empty, it sends this in its uncompressed – say, ASCII – form. This is shown as "T" in the figure. The character is then assigned to the 1-branch of the root and, since this is the first occurrence of this character, it is shown as T1 in the tree. On reception, since the decoder's tree is also empty, it interprets the received bit string as an uncompressed character and proceeds to assign the character to its tree in the same way (Figure 3.6(a)).

For each subsequent character, the encoder first checks whether the character is already present in the tree. If it is, then the encoder sends the current codeword for the character in the normal way, the codeword being determined by the position of the character in the tree. If it is not present, then the encoder sends the current codeword for the empty leaf – again determined by its position in the tree – followed by the uncompressed codeword for the character. Since the decoder has the same tree as the encoder, it can readily deduce from the received bit string whether it is the current codeword of a (compressed) character or that of the empty leaf followed by the character in its uncompressed form.

The encoder and decoder proceed to update their copy of the tree based on the last character that has been transmitted/received. If it is a new character, the existing empty leaf node in the tree is replaced with a new branch node, the empty leaf being assigned to the 0-branch and the character to the 1-branch (Figure 3.6(b)).

If the character is already present in the tree, then the frequency of occurrence of the leaf node is incremented by unity. On doing this, the position of the leaf node may not now be in the optimum position in the tree. Hence each time the tree is updated – either by adding a new character or by incrementing the frequency of occurrence of an existing character – both the encoder and decoder check, and if necessary modify, the current position of all the characters in the tree.

To ensure that both the encoder and decoder do this in a consistent way, they first list the weights of the leaf and branch nodes in the updated tree from left to right and from bottom to top starting at the empty leaf. If they are all in weight order, all is well and the tree is left unchanged. If there is a node out of order, the structure of the tree is modified by exchanging the position of this node with the other node in the tree – together with its branch and leaf nodes – to produce an incremented weight order. The first occurrence is in Figure 3.6(c) and other examples are in parts (d)–(g).

The steps followed when a character to be transmitted has previously been sent are shown in Figure 3.6(f). At this point, the character to be transmitted is **i** and when the encoder searches the tree, it determines that **i** is already present and transmits its existing codeword – 01. The encoder then increments the character's weight – frequency of occurrence – by unity to i2 and updates the position of the modified node as before. Another example is shown in Figure 3.6(g) when the character **s** is to be transmitted.

We can deduce from this example that the savings in transmission bandwidth start only when characters begin to repeat themselves. In practice, the savings with text files can be significant, and dynamic Huffman coding is now used in a number of communication applications that involve the transmission of text.

3.3.3 Arithmetic coding

As we can deduce from Examples 3.1 and 3.2, Huffman coding achieves the Shannon value only if the character/symbol probabilities are all integer powers of ½. Clearly, in many instances, this is not the case and hence the set of codewords produced are rarely optimum. In contrast, the codewords produced using arithmetic coding always achieve the Shannon value. Arithmetic coding, however, is more complicated than Huffman coding and so we shall limit our discussion of it to the basic static coding mode of operation.

To illustrate how the coding operation takes place, consider the transmission of a message comprising a string of characters with probabilities of:

$$\mathbf{e} = 0.3, \quad \mathbf{n} = 0.3, \quad \mathbf{t} = 0.2, \quad \mathbf{w} = 0.1, \quad . = 0.1$$

At the end of each character string making up a message, a known character is sent which, in this example, is a period **.** . When this is decoded at the receiving side, the decoder interprets this as the end of the string/message.

Unlike Huffman coding which was a separate codeword for each character, arithmetic coding yields a single codeword for each encoded string of characters. The first step is to divide the numeric range from 0 to 1 into a number of different characters present in the message to be sent – including the termination character – and the size of each segment by the probability of the related character. Hence the assignments for our set of five characters may be as shown in Figure 3.7(a).

As we can see, since there are only five different characters, there are five segments, the width of each segment being determined by the probability of the related character. For example, the character **e** has a probability of 0.3 and hence is assigned the range from 0.0 to 0.3, the character **n** – which also has a probability of 0.3 – the range from 0.3 to 0.6, and so on. Note, however, that an assignment in the range, say, 0.8 to 0.9, means that the probability in the cumulative range is from 0.8 to 0.8999... . Once this has been done, we are ready to start the encoding process. An example is shown in Figure 3.7(b) and, in this example, we assume the character string/message to be encoded is the single word **went.** .

The first character to be encoded **w** is in the range 0.8 to 0.9. Hence, as we shall see, the final (numeric) codeword is a number in the range 0.8 to 0.8999 ... since each subsequent character in the string subdivides the range 0.8 to 0.9 into progressively smaller segments each determined by the probabilities of the characters in the string.

(a)

Example character set and their probabilities:

e = 0.3, **n** = 0.3, **t** = 0.2, **w** = 0.1, **.** = 0.1

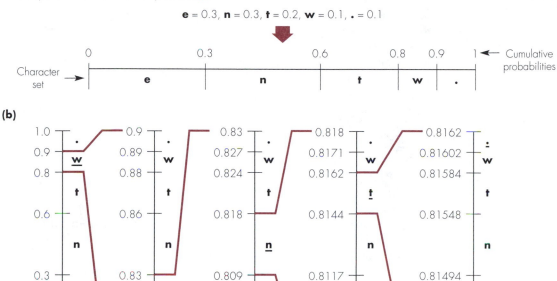

(b)

Encoded version of the character string **went.** is a single codeword in the range 0.816 02 ≤ codeword < 0.8162

Figure 3.7 Arithmetic coding principles: (a) example character set and their range assignments; (b) encoding of the string went..

As we can see in the example, since **w** is the first character in the string, the range 0.8 to 0.9 is itself subdivided into five further segments, the width of each segment again determined by the probabilities of the five characters. Hence the segment for the character **e**, for example, is from 0.8 to 0.83 (0.8 + 0.3 × 0.1), the character **n** from 0.83 to 0.86 (0.83 + 0.3 × 0.1), and so on.

The next character in the string is **e** and hence its range (0.8 to 0.83) is again subdivided into five segments. With the new assignments, therefore, the character **e** has a range from 0.8 to 0.809 (0.8 + 0.3 × 0.03), the character **n** from 0.809 to 0.818 (0.809 + 0.3 × 0.03), and so on. This procedure continues until the termination character **.** is encoded. At this point, the segment range of **.** is from 0.816 02 to 0.8162 and hence the codeword for the complete string is any number within the range:

$$0.816\,02 \leq \text{codeword} > 0.8162$$

In the static mode, the decoder knows the set of characters that are present in the encoded messages it receives as well as the segment to which each character has been assigned and its related range. Hence with this as a start point, the decoder can follow the same procedure as that followed by the encoder to determine the character string relating to each received codeword. For example, if the received codeword is, say, 0.8161, then the decoder can readily determine from this that the first character is **w** since it is the only character within the range 0.8 to 0.9. It then expands this interval as before and determines that the second character must be **e** since 0.8161 is within the range 0.8 to 0.83. This procedure then repeats until it decodes the known termination character **.** at which point it has recreated the, say, ASCII string relating to **went.** and passes this on for processing.

As we can deduce from this simple example, the number of decimal digits in the final codeword increases linearly with the number of characters in the string to be encoded. Hence the maximum number of characters in a string is determined by the precision with which floating-point numbers are represented in the source and destination computers. As a result, a complete message may be first fragmented into multiple smaller strings. Each string is then encoded separately and the resulting set of codewords sent as a block of (binary) floating-point numbers each in a known format. Alternatively, **binary arithmetic coding** can be used but, as we indicated earlier, this is outside the scope of the book. Further details relating to arithmetic coding can be found in the bibliography for this chapter at the end of the book.

3.3.4 Lempel–Ziv coding

The Lempel–Ziv (LZ) compression algorithm, instead of using single characters as the basis of the coding operation, uses strings of characters. For example, for the compression of text, a table containing all the possible character strings – for example words – that occur in the text to be transferred is held by both the encoder and decoder. As each word occurs in the text, instead of sending the word as a set of individual – say, ASCII – codewords, the encoder sends only the index of where the word is stored in the table and, on receipt of each index, the decoder uses this to access the corresponding word/string of characters from the table and proceeds to reconstruct the text into its original form. Thus the table is used as a dictionary and the LZ algorithm is known as a **dictionary-based** compression algorithm.

Most word-processing packages have a dictionary associated with them which is used for both spell checking and for the compression of text. Typically, they contain in the region of 25 000 words and hence 15 bits – which has 32 768 combinations – are required to encode the index. To send the word "multimedia" with such a dictionary would require just 15 bits instead of 70 bits with 7-bit ASCII codewords. This results in a compression ratio of 4.7:1. Clearly, shorter words will have a lower compression ratio and longer words a higher ratio.

Example 3.3

The LZ algorithm is to be used to compress a text file prior to its transmission. If the average number of characters per word is 6, and the dictionary used contains 4096 words, derive the average compression ratio that is achieved relative to using 7-bit ASCII codewords.

Answer:

In general, a dictionary with an index of n bits can contain up to 2^n entries. Now $4096 = 2^{12}$ and hence an index of 12 bits is required.

Using 7-bit ASCII codewords and an average of 6 characters per word requires 42 bits.

Hence compression ratio = $42/12 = 3.5{:}1$.

As with the other static coding methods, the basic requirement with the LZ algorithm is that a copy of the dictionary is held by both the encoder and the decoder. Although this is acceptable for the transmission of text which has been created using a standard word-processing package, it can be relatively inefficient if the text to be transmitted comprises only a small subset of the words stored in the dictionary. Hence a variation of the LZ algorithm has been developed which allows the dictionary to be built up dynamically by the encoder and decoder as the compressed text is being transferred. In this way, the size of the dictionary is often a better match to the number of different words in the text being transmitted than if a standard dictionary was used.

3.3.5 Lempel–Ziv–Welsh coding

The principle of the Lempel–Ziv–Welsh (LZW) coding algorithm is for the encoder and decoder to build the contents of the dictionary dynamically as the text is being transferred. Initially, the dictionary held by both the encoder and decoder contains only the character set – for example ASCII – that has been used to create the text. The remaining entries in the dictionary are then built up dynamically by both the encoder and decoder and contain the words that occur in the text. For example, if the character set comprises 128 characters and the dictionary is limited to, say, 4096 entries, then the first 128 entries would contain the single characters that make up the character set and the remaining 3968 entries would each contain strings of two or more characters that make up the words in the text being transferred. As we can see, the more frequently the words stored in the dictionary occur in the text, the higher the level of compression.

In order to describe how the dictionary is built up, let us assume that the text to be compressed starts with the string:

This is simple as it is ...

Since the idea is for the dictionary to contain only words, then only strings of characters that consist of alphanumeric characters are stored in the dictionary and all the other characters in the set are interpreted as word delimiters.

Initially, the dictionary held by both the encoder and decoder contains only the individual characters from the character set being used; for example, the 128 characters in the ASCII character set. Hence the first word in the example text is sent by the encoder using the index of each of the four characters T, h, i, and s. At this point, when the encoder reads the next character from the string – the first space (SP) character – it determines that this is not an alphanumeric character. It therefore transmits the character using its index as before but, in addition, interprets it as terminating the first word and hence stores the preceding four characters in the next available (free) location in the dictionary. Similarly the decoder, on receipt of the first five indices/codewords, reads the character stored at each index and commences to reconstruct the text. When it determines that the fifth character is a space character, it interprets this as a word delimiter and proceeds to store the word *This* in its dictionary.

The same procedure is followed by both the encoder and decoder for transferring the other words except the encoder, prior to sending each word in the form of single characters, first checks to determine if the word is currently stored in its dictionary and, if it is, it sends only the index for the word. Similarly the decoder, since it also has the word stored in its dictionary, uses the index to access the string of characters that make up the word. So with the example text string, after the space character following the second occurrence of the word *is*, the contents of the dictionary held by both the encoder and the decoder will be as shown in Figure 3.8(a). As we can see, since this is the second occurrence of the word *is*, it is transferred using only the index of where it is stored in the dictionary (129).

As we can deduce from this example, a key issue in determining the level of compression that is achieved, is the number of entries in the dictionary since this, in turn, determines the number of bits that are required for the index. With a static dictionary, the number of entries is fixed and, for the example we identified earlier, a dictionary containing 25 000 words requires 15 bits to encode the index. When building the dictionary dynamically, however, the question arises as to how many entries should be provided for the dictionary. Clearly, if too few entries are provided then the dictionary will contain only a subset of the words that occur in the text while if too many are provided, then it will contain empty spaces which, in turn, makes the index unnecessarily long. In order to optimize the number of bits used for the index, at the commencement of each transfer the number of entries is set to a relatively low value but, should the available space become full, then the number of entries is allowed to increase incrementally.

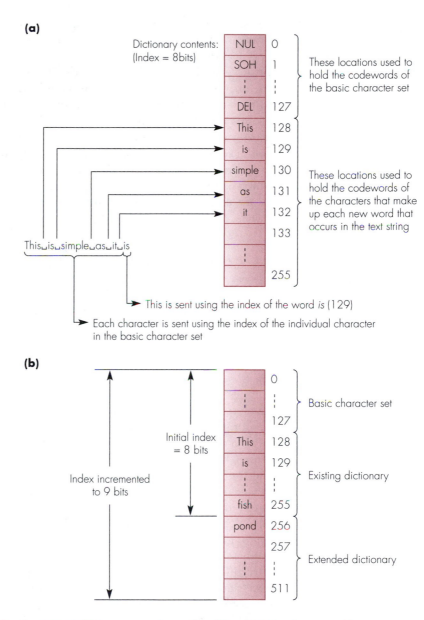

Figure 3.8 LZW compression algorithm: (a) basic operation; (b) dynamically extending the number of entries in the dictionary.

For example, in an application that uses 128 characters in the basic character set, then both the encoder and decoder would start with, say, 256 entries in the dictionary. This requires an index/codeword length of 8 bits and the dictionary would provide space for the 128 characters in the character set and a further 128 locations for words that occur in the text. Should this number of locations become insufficient, on detecting this, both the encoder and decoder would double the size of their dictionary to 512 locations. Clearly, this necessitates an index length of 9 bits and so from this point, the encoder uses 9-bit codewords. However, since the decoder has also doubled the size of its own directory, it expects 9-bit codewords from this point. In this way, the number of entries in the dictionary more accurately reflects the number of different words in the text being transferred and hence optimizes the number of bits used for each index/codeword.

The procedure is shown in diagrammatic form in Figure 3.8(b). In this example it is assumed that the last entry in the existing table at location 255 is the word *fish* and the next word in the text that is not currently in the dictionary is *pond*.

3.4 Image compression

Recall from Section 2.4 how images can be of two basic types: computer-generated (also known as graphical) images and digitized images (of both documents and pictures). Although both types are displayed (and printed) in the form of a two-dimensional matrix of individual picture elements, normally a graphical image is represented differently in the computer file system. Typically, this is in the form of a program (written in a particular graphics programming language) and, since this type of representation requires considerably less memory (and hence transmission bandwidth) than the corresponding matrix of picture elements, whenever possible, graphics are transferred across a network in this form. In the case of digitized documents and pictures, however, once digitized, the only form of representation is as a two-dimensional matrix of picture elements.

In terms of compression, when transferring graphical images which are represented in their program form, a lossless compression algorithm must be used similar, for example, to those in the last section. However, when the created image/graphic is to be transferred across the network in its bit-map form, then this is normally compressed prior to its transfer. There are a number of different compression algorithms and associated file formats in use and we shall describe two of these in the next two sections.

To transfer digitized images a different type of compression algorithm must normally be employed and, in practice, two different schemes are used. The first is based on a combination of run-length and statistical encoding. Hence it is lossless and is used for the transfer of the digitized documents generated by scanners such as those used in facsimile machines. The second is based on a combination of transform, differential, and run-length encoding and has been developed for the compression of both bitonal and color digitized pictures. Since there is an international standard associated with both schemes, we shall limit our discussion to these two schemes.

3.4.1 Graphics interchange format

The **graphics interchange format** (**GIF**) is used extensively with the Internet for the representation and compression of graphical images. Although color images comprising 24-bit pixels are supported – 8 bits each for R, G, and B – GIF reduces the number of possible colors that are present by choosing the 256 colors from the original set of 2^{24} colors that match most closely those used in the original image. The resulting table of colors therefore consists of 256 entries, each of which contains a 24-bit color value. Hence instead of sending each pixel as a 24-bit value, only the 8-bit index to the table entry that contains the closest match color to the original is sent. This results in a compression ratio of 3:1. The table of colors can relate either to the whole image – in which case it is referred to as the **global color table** – or to a portion of the image, when it is referred to as a **local color table**. The contents of the table are sent across the network – together with the compressed image data and other information such as the screen size and aspect ratio – in a standardized format. The principles of the scheme are shown in Figure 3.9(a).

As we show in Figure 3.9(b), the LZW coding algorithm can be used to obtain further levels of compression. We described this earlier in Section 3.3.5 when we discussed text compression and, in the case of image compression, this works by extending the basic color table dynamically as the compressed image data is being encoded and decoded. As with text compression, the occurrence of common strings of pixel values – such as long strings of the same color – are detected and these are entered into the color table after the 256 selected colors. However in this application, since each entry in the color table comprises 24 bits, in order to save memory, to represent each string of pixel values just the corresponding string of 8-bit indices to the basic color table are used. If we limit each entry in the table to 24 bits, then this will allow common strings comprising three pixel values to be stored in each location of the extended table. Normally, since the basic table contains 256 entries, an initial table size of 512 entries is selected which allows for up to 256 common strings to be stored. As with text compression, however, should more strings be found, then the number of entries in the table is allowed to increase incrementally by extending the length of the index by 1 bit.

GIF also allows an image to be stored and subsequently transferred over the network in an interlaced mode. This can be useful when transferring images over either low bit rate channels or the Internet which provides a variable transmission rate. With this mode, the compressed image data is organized so that the decompressed image is built up in a progressive way as the data arrives. To achieve this, the compressed data is divided into four groups as shown in Figure 3.10 and, as we can see, the first contains 1/8 of the total compressed image data, the second a further 1/8, the third a further 1/4, and the last the remaining 1/2.

(a)

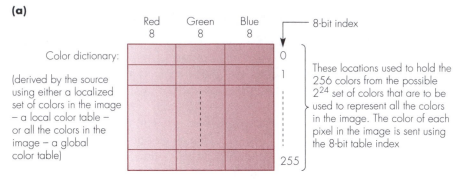

Red   Green   Blue
8   8   8
8-bit index

Color dictionary:

(derived by the source using either a localized set of colors in the image – a local color table – or all the colors in the image – a global color table)

0
1
255

These locations used to hold the 256 colors from the possible 2^{24} set of colors that are to be used to represent all the colors in the image. The color of each pixel in the image is sent using the 8-bit table index

The color dictionary, screen size, and aspect ratio are sent with the set of indexes for the image.

(b)

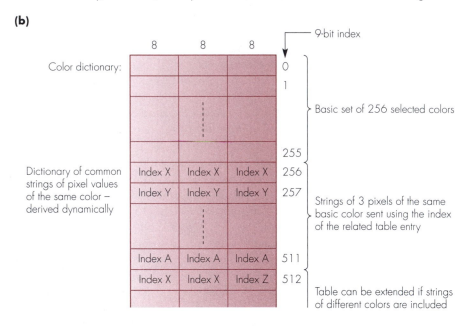

8   8   8
9-bit index

Color dictionary:

0
1

Basic set of 256 selected colors

255

Dictionary of common strings of pixel values of the same color – derived dynamically

Index X	Index X	Index X	256
Index Y	Index Y	Index Y	257
Index A	Index A	Index A	511
Index X	Index X	Index Z	512

Strings of 3 pixels of the same basic color sent using the index of the related table entry

Table can be extended if strings of different colors are included

Figure 3.9 GIF compression principles: (a) basic operational mode; (b) dynamic mode using LZW coding.

3.4.2 Tagged image file format

The **tagged image file format** (**TIFF**) is also used extensively. It supports pixel resolutions of up to 48 bits – 16 bits each for R, G, and B – and is intended for the transfer of both images and digitized documents. The image data, therefore, can be stored – and hence transferred over the network – in a number of different formats. The particular format being used is indicated by a code number and these range from the uncompressed format (code number 1) through to LZW-compressed which is code number 5. Code numbers 2, 3, and 4 are intended for use with digitized documents. These use the same

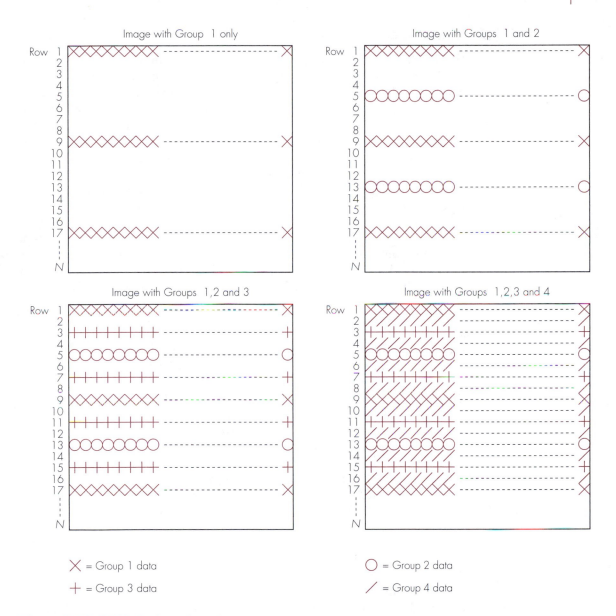

Figure 3.10 GIF interlaced mode.

compression algorithms that are used in facsimile machines which we discuss in the next section.

The LZW compression algorithm that is used is the same as that used with GIF. It starts with a basic color table containing 256 colors and the table can be extended to contain up to 4096 entries containing common strings of pixels in the image being transferred. Again, a standard format is used for the transfer of both the color table and the compressed image data.

3.4.3 Digitized documents

We described the principle of operation of the scanners used in facsimile machines to digitize bitonal images (such as a printed document) in Section 2.4.3. The digital representation of a scanned page was shown in Figure 2.11(b) and, even though only a single binary bit is used to represent each picture element, with the resolutions used, this produces an uncompressed bit stream of the order of 2 Mbits. In most cases this must be transferred using modems and the public switched telephone network. The relatively low bit rates available with modems means that it would be both costly and time consuming to transfer a total document comprising many pages in this basic form.

With most documents, many scanned lines consist only of long strings of white picture elements – pels – while others comprise a mix of long strings of white and long strings of black pels. Since facsimile machines are normally used with public carrier networks, the ITU-T has produced standards relating to them. These are T2 (Group 1), T3 (Group 2), T4 (Group 3), and T6 (Group 4). The first two are earlier standards and are now rarely used. The last two, however, both operate digitally; Group 3 with modems for use with an analog PSTN, and Group 4 all-digital for use with digital networks such as the ISDN. Both use data compression, and compression ratios in excess of 10:1 are common with most document pages. The time taken to transmit a page is reduced to less than a minute with Group 3 machines and, because of the added benefit of a higher transmission rate (64 kbps), to less than a few seconds with a Group 4 machine.

As part of the standardization process, extensive analyses of typical scanned document pages were made. Tables of codewords were produced based on the relative frequency of occurrence of the number of contiguous white and black pels found in a scanned line. The resulting codewords are fixed and grouped into two separate tables: the **termination-codes table** and the **make-up codes table**. The codewords in each table are shown in Figure 3.11.

Codewords in the termination-codes table are for white or black run-lengths of from 0 to 63 pels in steps of 1 pel; the make-up codes table contains codewords for white or black run-lengths that are multiples of 64 pels. A technique known as **overscanning** is used which means that all lines start with a minimum of one white pel. In this way, the receiver knows the first codeword always relates to white pels and then alternates between black and white. Since the scheme uses two sets of codewords (termination and make-up) they are known as **modified Huffman codes**. As an example, a run-length of 12 white pels is coded directly as 001000. Similarly, a run-length of 12 black pels is coded directly as 0000111. A run-length of 140 black pels, however, is encoded as 000011001000 + 0000111; that is, 128 + 12 pels. Run-lengths exceeding 2560 pels are encoded using more than one make-up code plus one termination code.

There is no error-correction protocol with Group 3. From the list of codewords, we can deduce that if one or more bits is corrupted during its

(a)

White run-length	Code-word	Black run-length	Code-word
0	00110101	0	0000110111
1	000111	1	010
2	0111	2	11
3	1000	3	10
4	1011	4	011
5	1100	5	0011
6	1110	6	0010
7	1111	7	00011
8	10011	8	000101
9	10100	9	000100
10	00111	10	0000100
11	01000	11	0000101
12	001000	12	0000111
13	000011	13	00000100
14	110100	14	00000111
15	110101	15	000011000
16	101010	16	0000010111
17	101011	17	0000011000
18	0100111	18	0000001000
19	0001100	19	00001100111
20	0001000	20	00001101000
21	0010111	21	00001101100
22	0000011	22	00000110111
23	0000100	23	00000101000
24	0101000	24	00000010111
25	0101011	25	00000011000
26	0010011	26	000011001010
27	0100100	27	000011001011
28	0011000	28	000011001100
29	00000010	29	000011001101
30	00000011	30	000001101000
31	00011010	31	000001101001
32	00011011	32	000001101010
33	0010010	33	000001101011
34	00010011	34	000011010010
35	00010100	35	000011010011
36	00010101	36	000011010100
37	00010110	37	000011010101
38	00010111	38	000011010110
39	00101000	39	000011010111
40	00101001	40	000001101100
41	00101010	41	000001101101
42	00101011	42	000011011010
43	00101100	43	000011011011
44	00101101	44	000001010100
45	00000100	45	000001010101
46	00000101	46	000001010110
47	00001010	47	000001010111
48	00001011	48	000001100100
49	01010010	49	000001100101
50	01010011	50	000001010010
51	01010100	51	000001010011
52	01010101	52	000000100100
53	00100100	53	000000110111
54	00100101	54	000000111000
55	01011000	55	000000100111
56	01011001	56	000000101000
57	01011010	57	000001011000
58	01011011	58	000001011001
59	01001010	59	000000101011
60	01001011	60	000000101100
61	00110010	61	000001011010
62	00110011	62	000001100110
63	00110100	63	000001100111

(b)

White run-length	Code-word	Black run-length	Code-word
64	11011	64	0000001111
128	10010	128	000011001000
192	010111	192	000011001001
256	0110111	256	000001011011
320	00110110	320	000000110011
384	00110111	384	000000110100
448	01100100	448	000000110101
512	01100101	512	0000001101100
576	01101000	576	0000001101101
640	01100111	640	0000001001010
704	011001100	704	0000001001011
768	011001101	768	0000001001100
832	011010010	832	0000001001101
896	011010011	896	0000001110010
960	011010100	960	0000001110011
1024	011010101	1024	0000001110100
1088	011010110	1088	0000001110101
1152	011010111	1152	0000001110110
1216	011011000	1216	0000001110111
1280	011011001	1280	0000001010010
1344	011011010	1344	0000001010011
1408	011011011	1408	0000001010100
1472	010011000	1472	0000001010101
1536	010011001	1536	0000001011010
1600	010011010	1600	0000001011011
1664	011000	1664	0000001100100
1728	010011011	1728	0000001100101
1792	00000001000	1792	00000001000
1856	00000001100	1856	00000001100
1920	00000001101	1920	00000001101
1984	000000010010	1984	000000010010
2048	000000010011	2048	000000010011
2112	000000010100	2112	000000010100
2176	000000010101	2176	000000010101
2240	000000010110	2240	000000010110
2304	000000010111	2304	000000010111
2368	000000011100	2368	000000011100
2432	000000011101	2432	000000011101
2496	000000011110	2496	000000011110
2560	000000011111	2560	000000011111
EOL	00000000001	EOL	00000000001

Figure 3.11 ITU–T Group 3 and 4 facsimile conversion codes: (a) termination-codes, (b) make-up codes.

transmission through the network, the receiver will start to interpret subsequent codewords on the wrong bit boundaries. The receiver thus becomes unsynchronized and cannot decode the received bit string. To enable the receiver to regain synchronism, each scanned line is terminated with a known **end-of-line** (**EOL**) **code**. In this way, if the receiver fails to decode a valid codeword after the maximum number of bits in a codeword have been scanned (parsed), it starts to search for the EOL pattern. If it fails to decode an EOL after a preset number of lines, it aborts the reception process and informs the sending machine. A single EOL precedes the codewords for each scanned page and a string of six consecutive EOLs indicates the end of each page.

Because each scanned line is encoded independently, the T4 coding scheme is known as a **one-dimensional coding** scheme. As we can conclude, it works satisfactorily providing the scanned image contains significant areas of white or black pels which occur, for example, where documents consist of letters and line drawings. Documents containing photographic images, however, are not satisfactory as the different shades of black and white are represented by varying densities of black and white pels. This, in turn, results in a large number of very short black or white run-lengths which, with the T4 coding scheme, can lead to a **negative compression ratio**; that is, more bits are needed to send the scanned document in its compressed form than are needed in its uncompressed form.

For this reason the alternative T6 coding scheme has been defined. It is an optional feature in Group 3 facsimile machines but is compulsory in Group 4 machines. When supported in Group 3 machines, the EOL code at the end of each (compressed) line has an additional tag bit added. If this is a binary 1 then the next line has been encoded using the T4 coding scheme, if it is a 0 then the T6 coding scheme has been used. The latter is known as **modified-modified READ** (**MMR**) **coding**. It is also known as **two-dimensional** or **2D coding** since it identifies black and white run-lengths by comparing adjacent scan lines. READ stands for **relative element address designate**, and it is "modified" since it is a modified version of an earlier (modified) coding scheme.

MMR coding exploits the fact that most scanned lines differ from the previous line by only a few pels. For example, if a line contains a black-run then the next line will normally contain the same run plus or minus up to three pels. With MMR coding the run-lengths associated with a line are identified by comparing the line contents, known as the **coding line** (**CL**), relative to the immediately preceding line, known as the **reference line** (**RL**). We always assume the first reference line to be an (imaginary) all-white line and the first line proper is encoded relative to this. The encoded line then becomes the reference line for the following line, and so on. To ensure that the complete page is scanned, the scanner head always starts to the left of the page, so each line always starts with an imaginary white pel.

We identify the run lengths associated with a coding line as one of three possibilities or **modes** relative to the reference line. Examples of the three modes are shown in Figure 3.12. The three modes are identified by the position of the next run-length in the reference line $(b_1 b_2)$ relative to the start

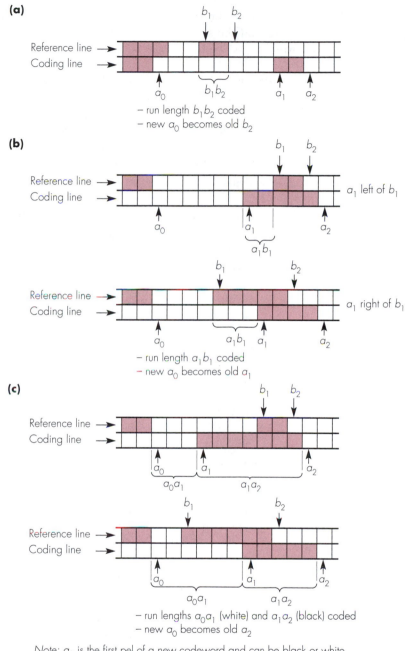

(a)

- run length $b_1 b_2$ coded
- new a_0 becomes old b_2

(b)

a_1 left of b_1

a_1 right of b_1

- run length $a_1 b_1$ coded
- new a_0 becomes old a_1

(c)

- run lengths $a_0 a_1$ (white) and $a_1 a_2$ (black) coded
- new a_0 becomes old a_2

Note: a_0 is the first pel of a new codeword and can be black or white
a_1 is the first pel to the right of a_0 with a different color
b_1 is the first pel on the reference line to the right of a_0 with a different color
b_2 is the first pel on the reference line to the right of b_1 with a different color

**Figure 3.12 Some example run-length possibilities: (a) pass mode;
(b) vertical mode; (c) horizontal mode.**

and end of the next pair of run-lengths in the coding line (a_0a_1 and a_1a_2). Note that the same procedure is used to encode the runs of both black and white pels. The three possibilities are:

1   **Pass mode:** This is the case when the run-length in the reference line (b_1b_2) is to the left of the next run-length in the coding line (a_1a_2), that is, b_2 is to the left of a_1. An example is given in Figure 3.12(a) and, for this mode, the run-length b_1b_2 is coded using the codewords given in Figure 3.11. Note that if the next pel on the coding line, a_1, is directly below b_2 then this is not pass mode.

2   **Vertical mode:** This is the case when the run-length in the reference line (b_1b_2) overlaps the next run-length in the coding line (a_1a_2) by a maximum of plus or minus 3 pels. Two examples are given in Figure 3.12(b) and, for this mode, just the difference run-length a_1b_1 is coded. Most codewords are in this category.

3   **Horizontal mode:** This is the case when the run-length in the reference line (b_1b_2) overlaps the run-length (a_1a_2) by more than plus or minus 3 pels. Two examples are given in Figure 3.12(c) and, for this mode, the two run-lengths a_0a_1 and a_1a_2 are coded using the codewords in Figure 3.11.

A flowchart of the coding procedure is shown in Figure 3.13. Note that the first a_0 is set to an imaginary white pel *before* the first pel of the line and hence the first a_0a_1 run-length will be $a_0a_1 - 1$. If during the coding of a line a_1, a_2, b_1, or b_2 are not detected, then they are set to an imaginary pel positioned immediately after the last pel on the respective line.

Once the first/next position of a_0 has been determined, the positions of a_1, a_2, b_1, and b_2 for the next codeword are located. The mode is then determined by computing the position of b_2 relative to a_1. If it is to the left, this indicates pass mode. If it is not to the left, then the magnitude of a_1b_1 is used to determine whether the mode is vertical or horizontal. The codeword for the identified mode is then computed and the start of the next codeword position, a_0, updated to the appropriate position. This procedure repeats alternately between white and black runs until the end of the line is reached. This is an imaginary pel positioned immediately after the last pel of the line and is assumed to have a different color from the last pel. The current coding line then becomes the new reference line and the next scanned line the new coding line.

Since the coded run-lengths relate to one of the three modes, additional codewords are used either to indicate to which mode the following codeword(s) relate – pass or horizontal – or to specify the length of the codeword directly – vertical. The additional codewords are given in a third table known as the **two-dimensional code table**. Its contents are as shown in Table 3.1. The final entry in the table, known as the **extension mode**, is a unique codeword that aborts the encoding operation prematurely before the end of the page. This is provided to allow a portion of a page to be sent in its uncompressed form or possibly with a different coding scheme.

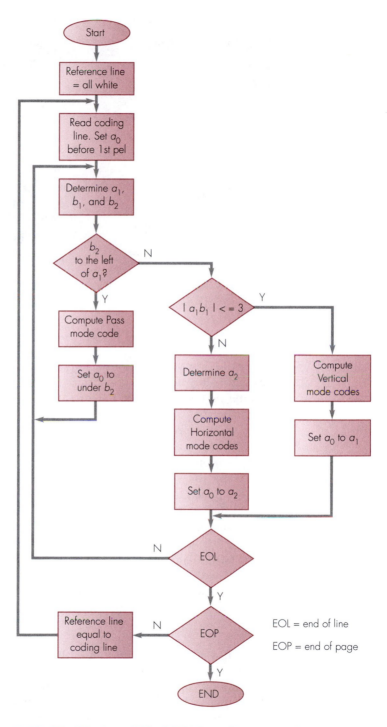

Figure 3.13 Modified-modified READ coding procedure.

Table 3.1 Two-dimensional code table contents.

Mode	Run-length to be encoded	Abbreviation	Codeword
Pass	$b_1 b_2$	P	$0001 + b_1 b_2$
Horizontal	$a_0 a_1, a_1 a_2$	H	$001 + a_0 a_1 + a_1 a_2$
Vertical	$a_1 b_1 = 0$	V(0)	1
	$a_1 b_1 = -1$	$V_R(1)$	011
	$a_1 b_1 = -2$	$V_R(2)$	000011
	$a_1 b_1 = -3$	$V_R(3)$	0000011
	$a_1 b_1 = +1$	$V_L(1)$	010
	$a_1 b_1 = +2$	$V_L(2)$	000010
	$a_1 b_1 = +3$	$V_L(3)$	0000010
Extension			0000001000

3.4.4 Digitized pictures

We described the digitization of both continuous-tone monochromatic pictures and color pictures in Section 2.4.3. We also calculated the amount of computer memory required to store and display these pictures on a number of popular types of display and tabulated these in Table 2.1. The amount of memory ranged from (approximately) 307 kbytes through to 2.4 Mbytes and, as we concluded, all would result in unacceptably long delays in most interactive applications that involve low bit rate networks.

In order to reduce the time to transmit digitized pictures, compression is normally applied to the two-dimensional array of pixel values that represents a digitized picture before it is transmitted over the network. The most widely-adopted standard relating to the compression of digitized pictures has been developed by an international standards body known as the **Joint Photographic Experts Group (JPEG)**. JPEG also forms the basis of most video compression algorithms and hence we shall limit our discussion of the compression of digitized pictures to describing the main principles of the JPEG standard.

3.4.5 JPEG

As we can deduce from the name, the JPEG standard was developed by a team of experts, each of whom had an in-depth knowledge of the compression of digitized pictures. They were working on behalf of the ISO, the ITU, and the IEC and JPEG is defined in the international standard **IS 10918**. In practice, the standard defines a range of different compression modes, each of which is intended for use in a particular application domain. We shall restrict our discussion here to the **lossy sequential mode** – also known as the **baseline mode** – since it is this which is intended for the compression of both monochromatic and color digitized pictures/images as used in multimedia communication applications. There are five main stages associated with this mode: image/block preparation, forward DCT, quantization, entropy encoding, and frame building. These are shown in Figure 3.14 and we shall discuss the role of each separately.

Image/block preparation

As we described in Section 2.4.3, in its pixel form, the source image/picture is made up of one or more 2-D matrices of values. In the case of a continuous-tone monochrome image, just a single 2-D matrix is required to store the set of 8-bit gray-level values that represent the image. Similarly, for a color image, if a CLUT is used just a single matrix of values is required.

Alternatively, if the image is represented in an *R, G, B* format three matrices are required, one each for the *R, G,* and *B* quantized values. Also, as we saw in Section 2.6.1 when we discussed the representation of a video signal, for color images the alternative form of representation known as Y, C_b, C_r can optionally be used. This is done to exploit the fact that the two chrominance signals, C_b and C_r, require half the bandwidth of the luminance signal, Y. This in turn allows the two matrices that contain the digitized chrominance components to be smaller in size than the Y matrix so producing a reduced form

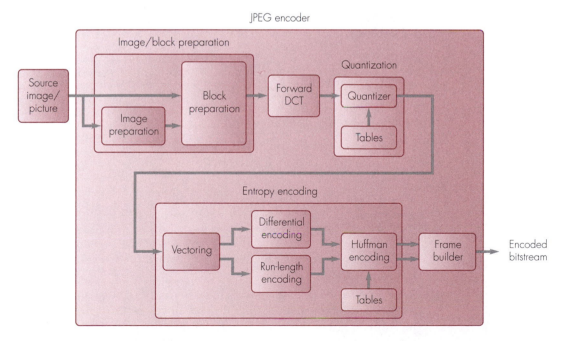

Figure 3.14 JPEG encoder schematic.

of representation over the equivalent *R, G, B* form of representation. For example, in the 4:2:0 format, groups of four neighboring chrominance values are averaged to produce a single value in the reduced matrix so reducing the size of the C_b and C_r matrices by a factor of four. The four alternative forms of representation are shown in Figure 3.15(a).

Once the source image format has been selected and prepared, the set of values in each matrix are compressed separately using the DCT. Before performing the DCT on each matrix, however, a second step known as **block preparation** is carried out. This is necessary since to compute the transformed value for each position in a matrix requires the values in all the locations of the matrix to be processed. It would be too time consuming to compute the DCT of the total matrix in a single step so each matrix is first divided into a set of smaller 8×8 submatrices. Each is known as a **block** and, as we can see in part (b) of the figure, these are then fed sequentially to the DCT which transforms each block separately.

Forward DCT

We described the principles of the DCT earlier in Section 3.2.4. Normally, each pixel value is quantized using 8 bits which produces a value in the range 0 to 255 for the intensity/luminance values – *R, G, B,* or *Y* – and a value in the range –128 to +127 for the two chrominance values – C_b and C_r. In order to compute the (forward) DCT, however, all the values are first centered around zero by subtracting 128 from each intensity/luminance value. Then, if the input 2-D matrix is represented by: $P[x, y]$ and the transformed matrix by $F[i, j]$, the DCT of each 8×8 block of values is computed using the expression:

$$F[i, j] = \frac{1}{4} C(i) C(j) \sum_{x=0}^{7} \sum_{y=0}^{7} P[x, y] \cos \frac{(2x + 1) i\pi}{16} \cos \frac{(2y + 1) j\pi}{16}$$

where $C(i)$ and $C(j) = 1/\sqrt{2}$ for $i, j = 0$

$\qquad\qquad\qquad\quad = 1$ for all other values of i and j

and $x, y, i,$ and j all vary from 0 through 7.

You can find further details relating to the DCT in the bibliography for this chapter at the end of the book. However, we can deduce a number of points by considering the expression above:

■ All 64 values in the input matrix, $P[x, y]$ contribute to each entry in the transformed matrix, $F[i, j]$.

■ For $i = j = 0$, the two cosine terms (and hence horizontal and vertical frequency coefficients) are both 0. Also, since $\cos(0)=1$, the value in location $F[0,0]$ of the transformed matrix is simply a function of the summation of all the values in the input matrix. Essentially, it is the mean of all 64 values in the matrix and is known as the **DC coefficient**.

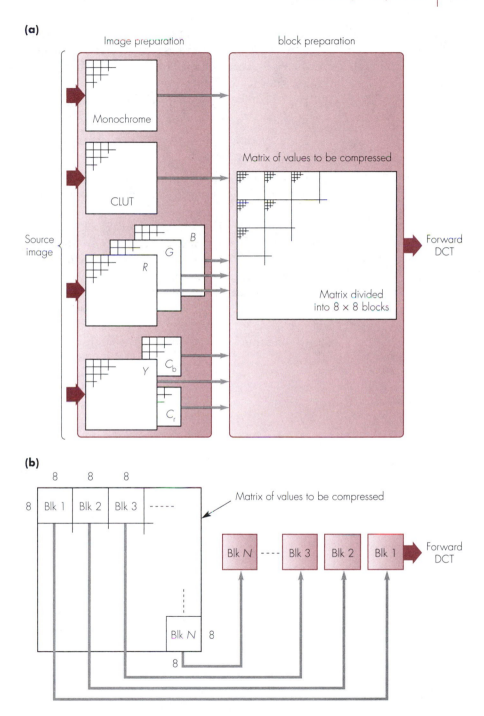

Figure 3.15 Image/block preparation: (a) image preparation; (b) block preparation.

- Since the values in all the other locations of the transformed matrix have a frequency coefficient associated with them – either horizontal ($x = 1$–7 for $y = 0$), vertical ($x = 0$ for $y = 1$–7) or both ($x = 1$–7 for $y = 1$-7) – they are known as **AC coefficients**.

- For $j = 0$, only horizontal frequency coefficients are present which increase in frequency for $i = 1$–7.

- For $i = 0$, only vertical frequency coefficients are present which increase in frequency for $j = 1$–7.

- In all other locations in the transformed matrix, both horizontal and vertical frequency coefficients are present to varying degrees.

The above points are summarized in Figure 3.16. In order to gain a qualitative understanding of the likely values present in a transformed block, consider a typical image comprising, say, 640×480 pixels. Assuming a block size of 8×8 pixels, the image will comprise 80×60 or 4800 blocks each of which, for a screen width of, say, 16 inches (400 mm), will occupy a square of only 0.2×0.2 inches (5×5 mm). Hence those regions of a picture that contain a single color will generate a set of transformed blocks all of which will have firstly, the same (or very similar) DC coefficient and secondly, only a few AC

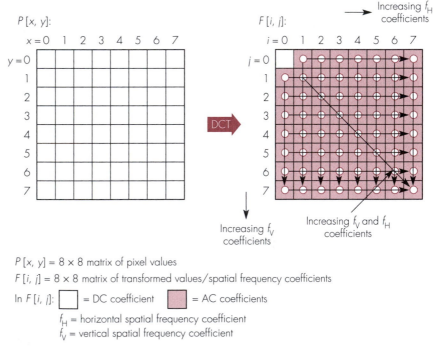

$P[x, y] = 8 \times 8$ matrix of pixel values

$F[i, j] = 8 \times 8$ matrix of transformed values/spatial frequency coefficients

In $F[i, j]$: ⬜ = DC coefficient 🟪 = AC coefficients

f_H = horizontal spatial frequency coefficient
f_V = vertical spatial frequency coefficient

Figure 3.16 DCT computation features.

coefficients within them. Thus it is only those areas of a picture which contain color transitions that will generate a set of transformed blocks with different DC coefficients and a larger number of AC coefficients within them. It is these features that are exploited in the quantization and entropy encoding phases of the compression algorithm.

Quantization

In theory, providing the forward DCT is computed to a high precision using, say, floating point arithmetic, there is very little loss of information during the DCT phase. Although in practice small losses occur owing to the use of fixed point arithmetic, the main source of information loss occurs during the quantization and entropy encoding stages where the compression takes place.

As we identified earlier in Section 3.2.4 when we first discussed transform encoding, the human eye responds primarily to the DC coefficient and the lower spatial frequency coefficients. Thus if the magnitude of a higher frequency coefficient is below a certain threshold, the eye will not detect it. This property is exploited in the quantization phase by dropping – in practice, setting to zero – those spatial frequency coefficients in the transformed matrix whose amplitudes are less than a defined threshold value. It should be noted, however, that although the eye is less sensitive to these frequency coefficients, once dropped, the same coefficients cannot be retrieved during the decoding procedure.

In addition to determining whether a particular spatial frequency coefficient is above a defined threshold, the quantization process aims to reduce the size of the DC and AC coefficients so that less bandwidth is required for their transmission. Instead of simply comparing each coefficient with the corresponding threshold value, a division operation is performed using the defined threshold value as the divisor. If the resulting (rounded) quotient is zero, the coefficient is less than the threshold value while if it is non-zero, this indicates the number of times the coefficient is greater than the threshold rather than its absolute value. For example, if the divisor is set to 16, then this will save 4 bits over the use of the absolute value. Clearly, this saving is at the expense of the precision used for the absolute values since in the decoder, these are determined by simply multiplying the received values by the corresponding threshold value.

As discussed, the sensitivity of the eye varies with spatial frequency, which implies that the amplitude threshold below which the eye will detect a particular spatial frequency also varies. In practice, therefore, the threshold values used vary for each of the 64 DCT coefficients. These are held in a two-dimensional matrix known as the **quantization table** with the threshold value to be used with a particular DCT coefficient in the corresponding position in the matrix.

Clearly, as we can see from the above, the choice of threshold values is important and, in practice, is a compromise between the level of compression that is required and the resulting amount of information loss that is accept-

Example 3.4

Assuming a quantization threshold value of 16, derive the resulting quantization error for each of the following DCT coefficients:

127, 72, 64, 56, −56, −64, −72, −128

Answer:

Coefficient	Quantized value	Rounded value	Dequantized value	Error
127	127/16 = 7.9375	8	8 × 16 = 128	−1
72	4.5	5	80	+8
64	4	4	64	0
56	3.5	4	64	+8
−56	−3.5	−4	−64	−8
−64	−4	−4	−64	0
−72	−4.5	−5	−80	−8
−128	−8	−8	−128	0

As we can deduce from these figures, the maximum quantization error is plus or minus 50% of the threshold value used.

able. Although the JPEG standard includes two default quantization table values – one for use with the luminance coefficients and the other for use with the two sets of chrominance coefficients – it also allows for customized tables to be used and sent with the compressed image. An example set of threshold values is given in the quantization table shown in Figure 3.17 together with a set of DCT coefficients and their corresponding quantized values. We can conclude a number of points from the values shown in the tables:

■ The computation of the quantized coefficients involves rounding the quotients to the nearest integer value.

■ The threshold values used, in general, increase in magnitude with increasing spatial frequency.

■ The DC coefficient in the transformed matrix is largest.

■ Many of the higher-frequency coefficients are zero.

It is the last two points that are exploited during the following entropy encoding stage.

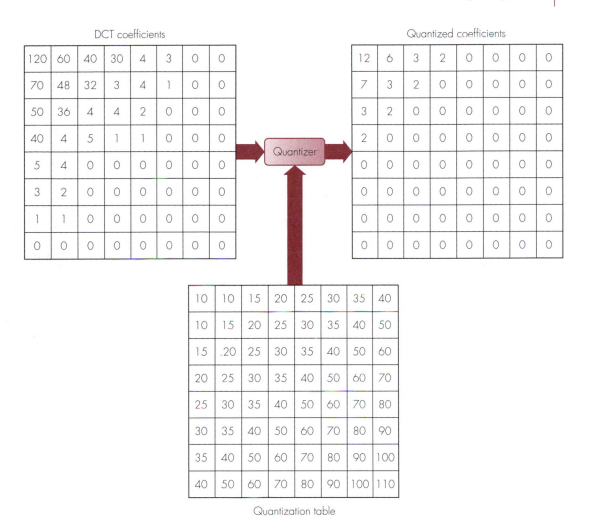

Figure 3.17 Example computation of a set of quantized DCT coefficients.

Entropy encoding

As we saw earlier in Figure 3.14, the entropy encoding stage comprises four steps: vectoring, differential encoding, run-length encoding, and Huffman encoding. We shall describe the role of each step separately.

Vectoring The various entropy encoding algorithms we described earlier in Section 3.2.3 operate on a one-dimensional string of values, that is, a vector. As we have just seen, however, the output of the quantization stage is a 2-D matrix of values. Hence before we can apply any entropy encoding to the set of values in the matrix, we must first represent the values in the form of a single-dimension vector. This operation is known as **vectoring**.

As we saw in Figure 3.17, the output of a typical quantization is a 2-D matrix of values/coefficients which are mainly zeros except for a number of non-zero values in the top left-hand corner of the matrix. Clearly, if we simply scanned the matrix using a line-by-line approach, then the resulting (1×64) vector would contain a mix of non-zero and zero values. In general, however, this type of information structure does not lend itself to compression. In order to exploit the presence of the large number of zeros in the quantized matrix, a **zig-zag scan** of the matrix is used as shown in Figure 3.18.

As we can deduce from the figure, with this type of scan, the DC coefficient and lower-frequency AC coefficients – both horizontal and vertical – are scanned first. Also, all the higher-frequency coefficients are in a sequential order so making this form of representation more suitable for compression. As we saw earlier in Figure 3.14, two different encoding schemes are applied in parallel to the values in the vector. The first is differential encoding, which is applied to the DC coefficient only, and the second is run-length encoding, which is applied to the remaining values in the vector containing the AC coefficients.

Differential encoding The first element in each transformed block is the DC coefficient which is a measure of the average color/luminance/chrominance associated with the corresponding 8×8 block of pixel values. Hence it is the largest coefficient and, because of its importance, its resolution is kept as high as possible during the quantization phase. Because of the small physical area covered by each block, the DC coefficient varies only slowly from one block to the next.

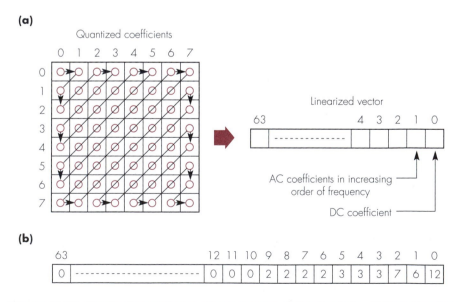

Figure 3.18 Vectoring using a zig-zag scan: (a) principle; (b) vector for example shown in Figure 3.17.

As we described in Section 3.2.4, the most efficient type of compression with this form of information structure is differential encoding since this encodes only the difference between each pair of values in a string rather than their absolute values. Hence in this application, only the difference in magnitude of the DC coefficient in a quantized block relative to the value in the preceding block is encoded. In this way, the number of bits required to encode the relatively large magnitudes of the DC coefficients is reduced.

For example, if the sequence of DC coefficients in consecutive quantized blocks – one per block – was:

$$12, 13, 11, 11, 10, \dots$$

the corresponding difference values would be:

$$12, 1, -2, 0, -1, \dots$$

the first difference value always being encoded relative to zero. The difference values are then encoded in the form (*SSS*, *value*) where the *SSS* field indicates the number of bits needed to encode the *value* and the value field the actual bits that represent the value. The rules used to encode each value are summarized in Figure 3.19(a).

As we can see, the number of bits required to encode each value is determined by its magnitude. A positive value is then encoded using the unsigned binary form and a negative value by the complement of this. Note also that a value of zero is encoded using a single 0 bit in the *SSS* field.

Example 3.5

Determine the encoded version of the following difference values which relate to the encoded DC coefficients from consecutive DCT blocks:

$$12, 1, -2, 0, -1$$

Answer:

Value	SSS	Value
12	4	1100
1	1	1
-2	2	01
0	0	
-1	1	0

(a)

Difference value	Number of bits needed (SSS)	Encoded value
0	0	
−1, 1	1	1 = 1 , −1 = 0
−3, −2, 2, 3	2	2 = 10 , −2 = 01
		3 = 11 , −3 = 00
−7..−4, 4.. 7	3	4 = 100 , −4 = 011
		5 = 101 , −5 = 010
		6 = 110 , −6 = 001
		7 = 111 , −7 = 000
−15...−8, 8...15	4	8 = 1000 , −8 = 0111
		⋮

(b)

Number of bits needed (SSS)	Huffman codeword
0	010
1	011
2	100
3	00
4	101
5	110
6	1110
7	11110
⋮	
11	111111110

Figure 3.19 Variable-length coding: (a) coding categories; (b) default Huffman codewords.

Run-length encoding The remaining 63 values in the vector are the AC coefficients and, because of the zig-zag scan, the vector contains long strings of zeros within it. To exploit this feature, the AC coefficients are encoded in the form of a string of pairs of values. Each pair is made up of (*skip, value*) where skip is the number of zeros in the run and *value* the next non-zero coefficient. Hence the 63 values in the vector shown earlier in Figure 3.18 would be encoded as:

$$(0,6)\,(0,7)\,(0,3)\,(0,3)\,(0,3)\,(0,2)\,(0,2)\,(0,2)\,(0,2)\,(0,0)$$

Note that the final pair (0,0) indicates the end of the string for this block and that all the remaining coefficients in the block are zero. Also, that the *value* field is encoded in the form *SSS/value*.

Example 3.6

Derive the binary form of the following run-length encoded AC coefficients:

$$(0,6)\,(0,7)\,(3,3)\,(0,-1)\,(0,0)$$

Answer:

AC coefficients	Skip	SSS/Value	
0,6	0	3	110
0,7	0	3	111
3,3	3	2	11
0,–1	0	1	0
0,0	0	0	

Huffman encoding As we saw in Section 3.4.3 when we described the encoding of digitized documents, significant levels of compression can be obtained by replacing long strings of binary digits by a string of much shorter codewords, the length of each codeword being a function of its relative frequency of occurrence. Normally, a table of codewords is used with the set of codewords precomputed using the Huffman coding algorithm. The same approach is used to encode the output of both the differential and run-length encoders.

For the differential-encoded DC coefficients in the block, the bits in the *SSS* field are not sent in their unsigned binary form as shown in Example 3.5 but in a Huffman-encoded form. This is done so that the bits in the *SSS* field have the prefix property – which we described earlier in Section 3.3.1 – and this enables the decoder to determine unambiguously the first *SSS* field from the received encoded bitstream.

Example 3.7

Determine the Huffman-encoded version of the following difference values which relate to the encoded DCT coefficients from consecutive DCT blocks.

$$12, 1, -2, 0, -1$$

Use for example purposes, the default Huffman codewords defined earlier in Figure 3.19(b).

▶

3.7 Continued

Answer:

Value	SSS	Huffman-encoded SSS	Encoded value	Encoded bitstream
12	4	101	1100	1011100
1	1	011	1	0111
−2	2	100	01	10001
0	0	010		010
−1	1	011	0	0110

As we can deduce from the set of Huffman-encoded *SSS* fields, they illustrate that, providing the decoder uses the same set of codewords, it can readily determine the *SSS* field from the received (encoded) bitstream by searching the bitstream bit-by-bit – starting from the leftmost bit – until it reaches a valid codeword. The number of bits in the corresponding *SSS* value is then read from the table in Figure 3.19(b) and this is used to determine the number of following bits in the bitstream that contain the related *value.*

For each of the run-length encoded AC coefficients in the block, the bits that make up the *skip* and *SSS* fields are treated as a single (composite) symbol and this is then encoded using either the default table of Huffman codewords shown in Table 3.2 or a table of codewords that is sent with the encoded bitstream. Again, this is done so that the string of encoded composite symbols all have the prefix property so that the decoder can interpret the received bitstream on the correct coefficient boundaries. To enable the decoder to discriminate between the *skip* and *SSS* fields, each combination of the two fields is encoded separately and the composite symbol is then replaced by the equivalent Huffman codeword.

As we can deduce from Example 3.8, to decode the received bitstream the receiver first searches the bitstream – starting at the leftmost bit – for a valid codeword and, on finding this (100), determines the corresponding *skip* (0) and *SSS* (3) fields from the Huffman table. The *SSS* field is then used to determine the number of bits in the run-length value field and, after reading and decoding these, the process repeats until the EOB codeword is received indicating that the remaining coefficients are all zero. Because of the use of variable-length codewords in the various parts of the entropy encoding stage, this is also known as the **variable-length coding (VLC) stage**.

Table 3.2 Default Huffman codewords for encoding AC coefficients.

Skip/SSS	Codeword	Skip/SSS	Codeword	Skip/SSS	Codeword
0/0	1010 (= EOB)	3/8	1111111110010100	7/6	1111111110110010
0/1	00	3/9	1111111110010101	7/7	1111111110110011
0/2	01	3/10	1111111110010110	7/8	1111111110110100
0/3	100	4/1	111011	7/9	1111111110110101
0/4	1011	4/2	1111111000	7/10	1111111110110110
0/5	11010	4/3	1111111110010111	8/1	11111010
0/6	111000	4/4	1111111110011000	8/2	1111111111000000
0/7	1111000	4/5	1111111110011001	8/3	1111111101110111
0/8	1111110110	4/6	1111111110011010	8/4	1111111110111000
0/9	1111111110000010	4/7	1111111110011011	8/5	1111111110111001
0/10	1111111110000011	4/8	1111111110011100	8/6	1111111110111010
1/1	1100	4/9	1111111110011101	8/7	1111111110111011
1/2	111001	4/10	1111111110011110	8/8	1111111110111100
1/3	1111001	5/1	1111010	8/9	1111111110111101
1/4	111110110	5/2	1111111001	8/10	1111111011110
1/5	1111111010	5/3	1111111110011111	9/1	111111000
1/6	111111110000101	5/4	1111111110100000	9/2	1111111110111111
1/7	1111111110000101	5/5	1111111110100001	9/3	1111111111000000
1/8	1111111110000110	5/6	1111111110100010	9/4	1111111111000001
1/9	1111111110000111	5/7	1111111110100011	9/5	1111111111000010
1/10	1111111110001000	5/8	1111111110100100	9/6	1111111111000011
2/1	11011	5/9	1111111110100101	9/7	1111111111000100
2/2	11111000	5/10	1111111110100110	9/8	1111111111000101
2/3	1111110111	6/1	1111011	9/9	1111111111000110
2/4	1111111110001001	6/2	11111111000	9/10	1111111111000111
2/5	1111111110001010	6/3	1111111110100111	10/1	111111001
2/6	1111111110001011	6/4	1111111110101000	10/2	1111111111001000
2/7	1111111110001100	6/5	1111111110101001	10/3	1111111111001001
2/8	1111111110001101	6/6	1111111110101010	10/4	1111111111001011
2/9	1111111110001110	6/7	1111111110101011	10/5	1111111111001011
2/10	1111111110001111	6/8	1111111110101100	10/6	1111111111001100
3/1	111010	6/9	1111111110101101	10/7	1111111111001101
3/2	111110111	6/10	1111111110101110	10/8	1111111111001110
3/3	11111110111	7/1	11111001	10/9	1111111111001111
3/4	1111111110010000	7/2	11111111001	10/10	1111111111010000
3/5	1111111110010001	7/3	1111111110101111	11/1	111111010
3/6	1111111110010010	7/4	1111111110110000	11/2	1111111111010001
3/7	1111111110010011	7/5	1111111110110001	11/3	1111111111010010

Table 3.2 Continued

Skip/SSS	Codeword	Skip/SSS	Codeword	Skip/SSS	Codeword
11/4	1111111111010011	13/6	1111111111100111	15/7	1111111111111011
11/5	1111111111010100	13/7	1111111111101000	15/8	1111111111111100
11/6	1111111111010101	13/8	1111111111101001	15/9	1111111111111101
11/7	1111111111010110	13/9	1111111111101010	15/10	1111111111111110
11/8	1111111111010111	13/10	1111111111101011		
11/9	1111111111011000	14/1	111111110110		
11/10	1111111111011001	14/2	1111111111101100		
12/1	111111010	14/3	1111111111101101		
12/2	1111111111011010	14/4	1111111111101110		
12/3	1111111111011011	14/5	1111111111101111		
12/4	1111111111011100	14/6	1111111111110000		
12/5	1111111111011101	14/7	1111111111110001		
12/6	1111111111101110	14/8	1111111111110010		
12/7	1111111111011111	14/9	1111111111110011		
12/8	1111111111000000	14/10	1111111111110100		
12/9	1111111111100001	15/0	111111110111		
12/10	1111111111100010	15/1	1111111111110101		
13/1	11111111010	15/2	1111111111110110		
13/2	1111111111100011	15/3	1111111111110111		
13/3	1111111111100100	15/4	1111111111111000		
13/4	1111111111100101	15/5	1111111111111001		
13/5	1111111111100110	15/6	1111111111111010		

EOB = end of block

Example 3.8

Derive the composite binary symbols for the following set of run-length encoded AC coefficients:

$$(0,6)\,(0,7)\,(3,3)\,(0,-1)\,(0,0)$$

Assuming the *skip* and *SSS* fields are both encoded as a composite symbol, use the Huffman codewords shown in Table 3.2 to derive the Huffman-encoded bitstream for this set of symbols.

3.8 Continued

Answer:

The *skip* and *SSS* fields for this set of AC coefficients were derived earlier in Example 3.6. Hence:

AC coefficient	Composite symbol skip	SSS	Huffman codeword	Run-length value
0,6	0	3	100	6 = 110
0,7	0	3	100	7 = 111
3,3	3	2	111110111	2 = 10
0, −1	0	1	00	1 = 0
0,0	0	0	1010	

The Huffman-encoded bitstream is then derived by adding the run-length encoded value to each of the Huffman codewords:

100110   100111   11111011110   000   1010

In this example, the number of bits required to transmit the set of AC coefficients for the 8×8 block of pixels is 29 and, assuming 6 bits for the DC coefficient, the total for the block is 35 bits. Hence assuming each pixel value is 8 bits, the resulting compression ratio for this block is 512/35 or, approximately, 14.6:1.

Frame building

Typically, the bitstream output by a JPEG encoder – corresponding to, say, the compressed version of a printed picture – is stored in the memory of a computer ready for either integrating with other media if necessary or accessing from a remote computer. As we can see from the above, in order for the decoder in the remote computer to be able to interpret all the different fields and tables that make up the bitstream, it is necessary to delimit each field and set of table values in a defined way. The JPEG standard, therefore, also includes a definition of the structure of the total bitstream relating to a particular image/picture. This is known as a *frame* and its outline structure is shown in Figure 3.20.

The role of the **frame builder** shown earlier in Figure 3.14 is to encapsulate all the information relating to an encoded image/picture in this format and, as we can see, the structure of a frame is hierarchical. At the top level, the complete frame-plus-header is encapsulated between a *start-of-frame* and an *end-of-frame* delimiter which allows the receiver to determine the start and

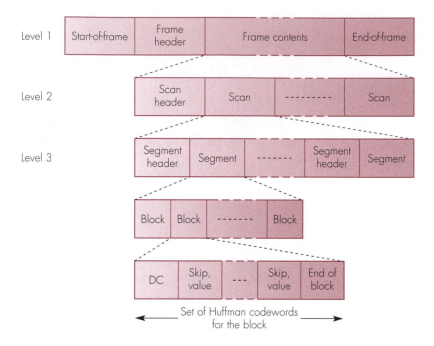

Figure 3.20 JPEG encoder output bitstream format.

end of all the information relating to a complete image/picture. The *frame header* contains a number of fields that include:

- the overall width and height of the image in pixels;
- the number and type of components that are used to represent the image (CLUT, R/G/B, $Y/C_b/C_r$);
- the digitization format used (4:2:2, 4:2:0 etc.).

At the second level, a frame consists of a number of components each of which is known as a *scan*. These are also preceded by a header which contains fields that include:

- the identity of the components (R/G/B etc.);
- the number of bits used to digitize each component;
- the quantization table of values that have been used to encode each component.

Typically, each scan/component comprises one or more *segments* each of which can contain a group of (8×8) blocks preceded by a header. This contains the Huffman table of values that have been used to encode each block in the segment should the default tables not be used. In this way, each segment can be decoded independently of the others which overcomes the possibility of bit errors propagating and affecting other segments. Hence each complete frame contains all the information necessary to enable the JPEG decoder to identify each field in a received frame and then perform the corresponding decoding operation.

JPEG decoding

As we can see in Figure 3.21, a JPEG decoder is made up of a number of stages which are simply the corresponding decoder sections of those used in the encoder. Hence the time to carry out the decoding function is similar to that used to perform the encoding.

On receipt of the encoded bitstream the **frame decoder** first identifies the control information and tables within the various headers. It then loads the contents of each table into the related table and passes the control information to the **image builder**. It then starts to pass the compressed bitstream to the Huffman decoder which carries out the corresponding decompression operation using either the default or the preloaded table of codewords. The two decompressed streams containing the DC and AC coefficients of each block are then passed to the differential and run-length decoders respectively. The resulting matrix of values is then dequantized using either the default or the preloaded values in the quantization table.

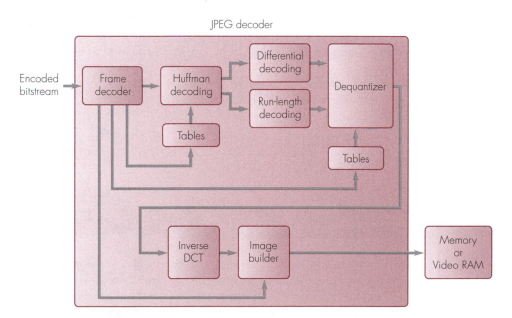

Figure 3.21 JPEG decoder schematic.

Each resulting block of 8×8 spatial frequency coefficients is passed in turn to the **inverse DCT** which transforms them back into their spatial form using the expression:

$$P[x, y] = \frac{1}{4} \sum_{i=0}^{7} \sum_{j=0}^{7} C(i)\, C(j)\, F[i, j] \cos \frac{(2x+1)\, i\, \pi}{16} \cos \frac{(2y+1)\, j\, \pi}{16}$$

where $C(i)$ and $C(j) = 1/\sqrt{2}$ for $i, j = 0$
$= 1$ for all other values of i and j.

The image builder then reconstructs the original image from these blocks using the control information passed to it by the frame decoder. Although the JPEG standard is relatively complicated owing to the number of encoding/decoding stages associated with it, compression ratios in excess of 20:1 can be obtained while still retaining a good quality output image/picture. This level of compression, however, applies to pictures whose content is relatively simple – that is, have relatively few color transitions – and, for more complicated pictures, compression ratios nearer to 10:1 are more common. These figures, however, assume each pixel location has three planes associated with it – R/G/B or $Y/C_b/C_r$ – and hence if a CLUT is used, then both figures can be multiplied by a factor of 3. Nevertheless, even with a compression ratio of 10:1, the amount of memory required with the various types of display tabulated in Table 2.1 is reduced to a range of from 30 kbytes through to 240 kbytes. More importantly, the time delay incurred in accessing these images is reduced by a factor of 10.

Finally, as with the GIF, it is also possible to encode and rebuild the image in a progressive way by first sending an outline of the image and then progressively adding more detail to it. This can be achieved in the following ways:

■ **progressive mode:** in this mode, first the DC and low-frequency coefficients of each block are sent and then the higher-frequency coefficients;

■ **hierarchial mode:** in this mode, the total image is first sent using a low resolution – for example 320×240 – then at a higher resolution such as 640×480.

Summary

In this chapter we have described a selection of the compression algorithms that are used for the compression of text and images. In general, compression is applied to both media types in order to reduce the time taken to transfer the source information over a network. This is done either to reduce the cost of the network connection or, in interactive applications, to reduce the response time to a request for the source information.

The basic techniques associated with all compression algorithms were first identified and described. These were classified as being either entropy encoding algorithms or source encoding. Entropy encoding exploits how the source information is represented and we described two examples: run-length encoding and statistical encoding.

Run-length encoding is used when the source information contains long strings of the same symbol such as a character, a bit, or a byte. Instead of sending the source information in the form of independent codewords, it is sent by simply indicating the particular symbol in each string together with an indication of the number of symbols in the string.

Statistical encoding exploits the fact that not all symbols in the source information occur with equal probability. Hence, instead of encoding all the symbols with fixed-length codewords, variable-length codewords are used with the shortest ones used to encode those symbols that occur most frequently.

In contrast, source encoding exploits a particular property of the source information in order to produce an alternative form of representation that is either a compressed version of the original form or is more amenable to the application of compression. Two examples were described: differential encoding and transform encoding.

Differential encoding is used when the amplitude of the values that make up the source information cover a large range but the difference between successive values is relatively small. Instead of using a set of relatively large codewords to represent the actual amplitude of each value, a set of smaller codewords is used, each of which indicates only the difference in amplitude between the current value being encoded and the immediately preceding value.

As the name implies, transform encoding involves transforming the source information into an alternative form of representation that lends itself more readily to the application of compression. The example that we described was the discrete cosine transform (DCT). This is used for image compression and transforms the matrix of pixel values that represent the image into a matrix of spatial frequency components which, in turn, lends itself more readily to the application of compression.

In terms of text compression, when the compressed source information is decompressed by the receiver, there is normally no loss of information. The compression algorithms that have this property are known as lossless and we described a number of such algorithms. These included both static and dynamic Huffman coding, arithmetic coding, and the LZW coding algorithm. The two Huffman algorithms and arithmetic coding are based on the relative frequency of occurrence of single characters in the source information and the LZW algorithm strings of characters.

In terms of image compression, we described a number of the algorithms that are used for the compression of graphical images, digitized documents, and digitized pictures. For use with graphical images we described the GIF and TIFF standards, for digitized documents two modified Huffman coding algorithms, and for digitized pictures the JPEG algorithm. All the algorithms that were described are part of international standards which, in addition to the compression algorithm, also define the format of the compressed information when it is being stored or transferred across a network.

Exercises

Section 3.2

3.1 Explain the meaning of the following terms relating to compression:
  (i) source encoders and destination decoders,
  (ii) lossless and lossy compression,
  (iii) entropy encoding,
  (iv) source encoding.

3.2 Explain the meaning of the following terms relating to statistical encoding:
  (i) run-length encoding,
  (ii) statistical encoding.

3.3 Explain the meaning of the following terms relating to statistical encoding:
  (i) prefix property,
  (ii) entropy,
  (iii) Shannon's formula,
  (iv) coding efficiency.

3.4 Explain the meaning of the following terms relating to source encoding:
  (i) differential encoding,
  (ii) transform encoding

3.5 With the aid of diagrams, explain in a qualitative way the meaning of the following terms relating to transform encoding:
  (i) spatial frequency,
  (ii) horizontal and vertical frequency components,
  (iii) discrete cosine transform (DCT).

Section 3.3

3.6 Explain the meaning of the following terms relating to text compression algorithms:
  (i) static coding,
  (ii) dynamic/adaptive coding.

3.7 With the aid of an example, describe the rules that are followed to construct the Huffman code tree for a transmitted character set.

3.8 Messages comprising seven different characters, A through G, are to be transmitted over a data link. Analysis has shown that the relative frequency of occurrence of each character is:

  A 0.10, B 0.25, C 0.05, D 0.32, E 0.01, F 0.07, G 0.2

  (i) Derive the entropy of the messages.
  (ii) Use static Huffman coding to derive a suitable set of codewords.
  (iii) Derive the average number of bits per codeword for your codeword set to transmit a message and compare this with both the fixed-length binary and ASCII codewords.

3.9 (i) State the prefix property of Huffman codes and hence show that your codeword set derived in Exercise 3.8 satisfied this.
  (ii) Derive a flowchart for an algorithm to decode a received bit string encoded using your codeword set.
  (iii) Give an example of the decoding operation assuming the received bit string comprises a mix of the seven characters.

3.10 The following character string is to be transmitted using Huffman coding:

  ABACADABACADABACABAB

  (i) Derive the Huffman code tree.
  (ii) Determine the savings in transmission bandwidth over normal ASCII and binary coding.

3.11 With reference to the example shown in Figure 3.6 relating to dynamic Huffman coding:
  (i) Write down the actual transmitted bit pattern corresponding to the character string:

  "This is"

assuming ASCII coding is being used.
  (ii) Deduce the extensions to the existing Huffman tree if the next word transmitted is "the".

3.12 Assuming the character set and associate probability assignments given in Figure 3.7, derive the codeword value for the character string *newt*. Assuming this is recieved by the destination, explain how the decoder determines the original string from the received codeword value.

3.13 Explain the principle of operation of the LZ compression algorithm. Hence assuming a dictionary of 16 000 words and an average word length of 5 bits, derive the average compression ratio that is achieved relative to using 7-bit ASCII codewords.

3.14 Explain the principle of operation of the LZW compression algorithm and how this is different from the LZ algorithm.

3.15 Assume the contents of a file that consists of 256 different words – each composed of alphanumeric characters from the basic ASCII character set – is to be sent over a network using the LZW algorithm. If the file contents start with the string:

> *This is easy as it is easy ...*

show the entries in the dictionary of the encoder up to this point and the string of codewords that are sent. Also show how the receiver builds up its own dictionary and determines the original file contents from this.

3.16 Assume the same message as in Exercise 3.15 but with the number of different words much larger and unknown. How can the algorithm be changed to accommodate this?

Section 3.4

3.17 Explain the basic mode of operation of GIF. Include in your explanation the size of the color table used, how each pixel value is sent, and how the receiver knows the image parameters used by this source.

3.18 In relation to GIF, explain how the LZW coding algorithm can be applied to the (compressed) image data. Include in your explanation how compression is achieved and how the receiver interprets the compressed information.

3.19 With the aid of a diagram, describe the interlaced mode of operation of GIF. Include the potential applications of this mode and how the receiver knows it is being used.

3.20 Describe the principles of TIFF and its application domains.

3.21 Explain the meaning of the following terms relating to facsimile machines:
(i) termination codes,
(ii) make-up codes,
(iii) overscanning,
(iv) the EOL code and its uses.

3.22 Discriminate between a one-dimensional coding scheme and a two-dimensional (MMR) scheme.

3.23 Given a scanned line of pels, assuming a one-dimensional coding scheme, deduce an algorithm
(i) to determine the transmitted codewords, and
(ii) to decode the received string of codewords. Use the Huffman tables in Fig. 3.11 as a guide.

3.24 With the aid of pel patterns, assuming an MMR coding scheme, explain the meaning of the following terms:
(i) pass mode,
(ii) vertical mode,
(iii) horizontal mode. Hence with the aid of the code table given in Table 3.1, deduce an algorithm to perform the encoding operation.

3.25 With the aid of a diagram, identify the five main stages associated with the baseline mode of operation of JPEG and give a brief description of the role of each stage.

3.26 With the aid of a diagram, explain how the individual 8×8 blocks of pixel values are derived by the image and block preparation stage for each of the following source image forms:
(i) monochrome/CLUT,
(ii) RGB,
(iii) Y, C_b, C_r.

In relation to the Y, C_b, C_r format, show the order in which the blocks are output.

3.27 With the aid of a diagram, explain the meaning of the following terms relating to the DCT algorithm:
 (i)   DC coefficient,
 (ii) horizontal and vertical spatial frequency coefficients.

 Hence by considering a typical image of 1024×768 pixels displayed on a 17 inch (432 mm) screen, explain where the savings in bandwidth arise with JPEG.

3.28 State the characteristic of the eye that is exploited in the quantization phase of the JPEG algorithm. Hence assuming the set of DC coefficients and threshold values shown in Figure 3.17, explain how the set of quantization coefficients are derived.

3.29 Use a range of DCT coefficients and a selected quantization threshold to derive how the maximum quantization error is determined by the choice of threshold value.

3.30 State the characteristics of the values in the quantized coefficient matrix that are exploited during the entropy encoding stage. Why is vectoring using a zig-zag scan applied to the matrix?

3.31 Explain why differential encoding is used for the compression of the DC coefficients in successive blocks. By means of an example set of coefficients, estimate the savings in bandwidth that are achieved.

3.32 Using the set of coding categories listed in Figure 3.19(a), determine the encoded version of the following string of DC coefficients.

 16, 15, 16, 14, 12, ...

3.33 Describe how the 63 quantized AC coefficients in a vector are encoded using run-length encoding. Hence derive the encoded form of the following vector of quantized AC coefficients:

 6, 7, 0, 0, 0, 3, −1, 0, 0, ..., 0.

3.34 Describe how the differential-encoded DC coefficients from a string of successive blocks are set using Huffman encoding. Hence assuming the default Huffman codewords shown in Figure 3.19(b), derive the encoded bitstream for the set of differential encoded DC coefficients you derived in Exercise 3.32.

3.35 Describe how the set of run-length encoded AC coefficients for a block are sent using Huffman encoding. Hence assuming the set of default Huffman codewords listed in Table 3.2, derive the Huffman-encoded bitstream for the set of run-length encoded coefficients you derived in Exercise 3.33. How is the end of the set of encoded coefficients for a block determined?

3.36 All the information relating to a compressed image/picture generated by the various stages in the JPEG encoder is encapsulated within a single frame in such a way that the decoder can identify the individual fields that are present. Show the structure of a frame in a diagram and describe the role of the main fields in each of the headers that are used.

3.37 With the aid of Figure 3.21, explain how the various parts of the encoded frame identified in Exercise 3.36 are used to recreate the original image.

 Identify the two alternate ways that can be used to recreate an image in a progressive way.

Audio and video compression

4.1 Introduction

As we described in Chapter 2, unlike text and images, both audio and most video signals are continuously varying analog signals. Hence, as we saw in Section 2.2, after digitization, both comprise a continuous stream of digital values, each value representing the amplitude of a sample of the particular analog signal taken at repetitive time intervals. As a result, the compression algorithms associated with digitized audio and video are different from those we described in the last chapter. In this chapter, therefore, we shall describe a selection of these algorithms, first those relating to audio and then those relating to video.

4.2 Audio compression

We discussed the digitization of audio signals in Section 2.5 and, as we saw, the digitization process is known as **pulse code modulation** or **PCM**. This involves sampling the (analog) audio signal/waveform at a minimum rate which is twice that of the maximum frequency component that makes up the signal. Alternatively, if the (frequency) bandwidth of the communications channel to be used is less than that of the signal, then the sampling rate is determined by the bandwidth of the communications channel. The latter is then known as a **bandlimited signal**.

In the case of a speech signal, the maximum frequency component is 10 kHz and hence the minimum sampling rate is 20 ksps. For general audio, music for example, the figures are 20 kHz and 40 ksps respectively. The number of bits per sample also varies and, typically, is 12 bits for speech and 16 bits for general audio. In addition, for a stereophonic signal, two signals must be digitized. As we saw in Example 2.4, this produces a bit rate of 240 kbps for a speech signal and 1.28 Mbps for a stereophonic music/general audio signal, the latter being the rate used with compact discs.

In practice, however, in most multimedia applications involving audio, the bandwidth of the communication channels that are available dictate rates that are less than these. This can be achieved in one of two ways: either the audio signal is sampled at a lower rate (and, if necessary, with fewer bits per sample) or a compression algorithm is used. Although the first approach is relatively simple to implement, using a lower sampling rate has the disadvantage that the quality of the decoded signal is reduced owing to the loss of the higher-frequency components from the original signal. Also, the use of fewer bits per sample results in the introduction of higher levels of quantization noise. Normally, therefore, a compression algorithm is used since, as we shall see, this achieves a comparable perceptual quality (as perceived by the ear) to that obtained with a higher sampling rate but with a reduced bandwidth requirement. In this section we consider a selection of the compression algorithms that are widely used for audio in a range of multimedia applications.

4.2.1 Differential pulse code modulation

Differential pulse code modulation (**DPCM**) is a derivative of standard PCM and exploits the fact that, for most audio signals, the range of the differences in amplitude between successive samples of the audio waveform is less than the range of the actual sample amplitudes. Hence if only the digitized difference signal is used to encode the waveform then fewer bits are required than for a comparable PCM signal with the same sampling rate. A DPCM encoder and decoder are shown in Figure 4.1(a) and a simplified timing diagram for the encoder is shown in Figure 4.1(b).

Essentially, the previous digitized sample of the analog input signal is held in the register (R) – a temporary storage facility – and the difference signal (DPCM) is computed by subtracting the current contents of the register (R_o) from the new digitized sample output by the ADC (PCM). The value in the register is then updated by adding to the current register contents the computed difference signal output by the subtractor prior to its transmission. The decoder operates by simply adding the received difference signal (DPCM) to the previously computed signal held in the register (PCM). Typical savings with DPCM, are limited to just 1 bit which, for a standard PCM voice signal, for example, reduces the bit rate requirement from 64 kbps to 56 kbps.

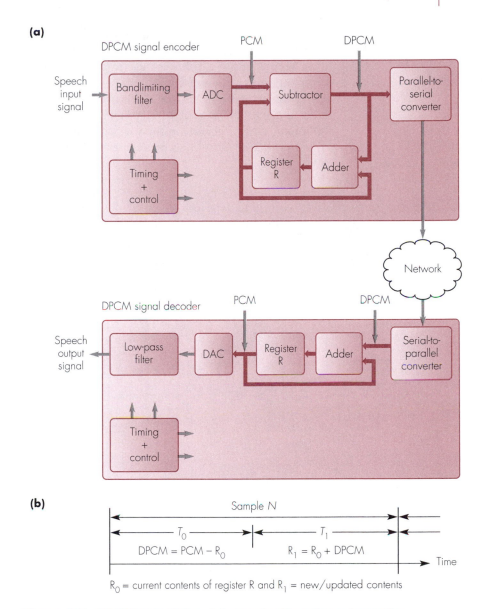

(a)

(b)

R_0 = current contents of register R and R_1 = new/updated contents

Figure 4.1 DPCM principles: (a) encoder/decoder schematic; (b) encoder timing.

As we can deduce from the circuit shown in Figure 4.1(a), the output of the ADC is used directly and hence the accuracy of each computed difference signal – also known as the **residual** (signal) – is determined by the accuracy of the previous signal/value held in the register. As we saw in Section 2.2, all ADC operations produce quantization errors and hence a string of, say, positive errors, will have a cumulative effect on the accuracy of the value that is held in the register. This means, therefore, that with a basic DPCM scheme, the previous value held in the register is only an approximation. Hence more sophisticated techniques have been developed for estimating – also known as predicting – a more accurate version of the previous signal. To achieve this, these predict the previous signal by using not only the estimate of the current signal but also varying proportions of a number of the immediately preceding estimated signals. The proportions used are determined by what are known as **predictor coefficients** and the principle is shown in Figure 4.2.

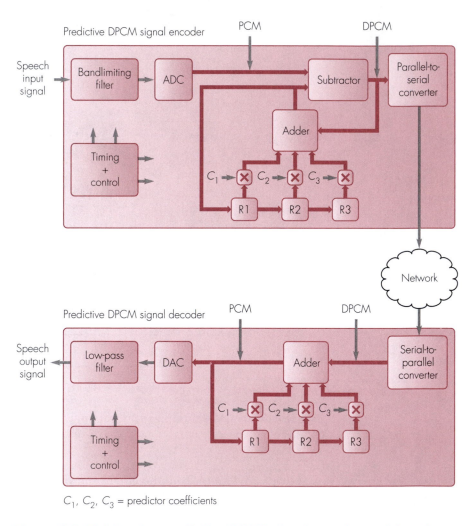

C_1, C_2, C_3 = predictor coefficients

Figure 4.2 Third-order predictive DPCM signal encoder and decoder schematic.

In this example, the difference signal is computed by subtracting varying proportions of the last three predicted values from the current digitized value output by the ADC. For example, if the three predictor coefficients have the values $C_1 = 0.5$ and $C_2 = C_3 = 0.25$, then the contents of register R1 would be shifted right by 1 bit (thereby multiplying its contents by 0.5) and registers R2 and R3 by 2 bits (multiplying their contents by 0.25). The three shifted values are then added together and the resulting sum subtracted from the current digitized value output by the ADC (PCM). The current contents of register R1 are then transferred to register R2 and that of register R2 to register R3. The new predicted value is then loaded into register R1 ready for the next sample to be processed. The decoder operates in a similar way by adding the same proportions of the last three computed PCM signals to the received DPCM signal. By using this approach, a similar performance level to standard PCM is obtained by using only 6 bits for the difference signal which produces a bit rate of 32 kbps.

4.2.2 Adaptive differential PCM

Additional savings in bandwidth – or improved quality – can be obtained by varying the number of bits used for the difference signal depending on its amplitude; that is, using fewer bits to encode (and hence transmit) smaller difference values than for larger values. This is the principle of **adaptive differential PCM** (**ADPCM**) and an international standard for this is defined in **ITU-T Recommendation G.721**. This is based on the same principle as DPCM except an eight-order predictor is used and the number of bits used to quantize each difference value is varied. This can be either 6 bits – producing 32 kbps – to obtain a better quality output than with third-order DPCM, or 5 bits – producing 16 kbps – if lower bandwidth is more important.

A second ADPCM standard, which is a derivative of G.721, is defined in **ITU-T Recommendation G.722**. This provides better sound quality than the G.721 standard at the expense of added complexity. To achieve this, it uses an added technique known as **subband coding**. The input speech bandwidth is extended to be from 50 Hz through to 7 kHz – compared with 3.4 kHz for a standard PCM system – and hence the wider bandwidth produces a higher-fidelity speech signal. This is particularly important in conferencing applications, for example, in order to enable the members of the conference to discriminate between the different voices of the members present. The general principle of the scheme is shown in Figure 4.3.

To allow for the higher signal bandwidth, prior to sampling the audio input signal, it is first passed through two filters: one which passes only signal frequencies in the range 50 Hz through to 3.5 kHz, and the other only frequencies in the range 3.5 kHz through to 7 kHz. By doing this, the input (speech) signal is effectively divided into two separate equal-bandwidth signals, the first known as the **lower subband signal** and the second the **upper subband signal**. Each is then sampled and encoded independently using

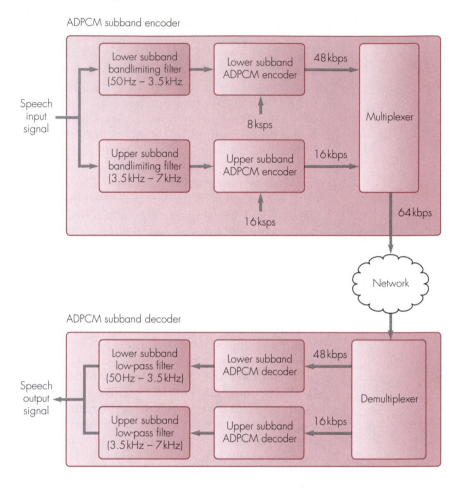

Figure 4.3 ADPCM subband encoder and decoder schematic.

ADPCM, the sampling rate of the upper subband signal being 16 ksps to allow for the presence of the higher frequency components in this subband.

The use of two subbands has the advantage that different bit rates can be used for each. In general, the frequency components that are present in the lower subband signal have a higher perceptual importance than those in the higher subband. The operating bit rate can be 64, 56, or 48 kbps. With a bit rate of 64 kbps, for example, the lower subband is ADPCM encoded at 48 kbps and the upper subband at 16 kbps. The two bitstreams are then multiplexed (merged) together – to produce the transmitted (64 kbps) signal – in such a way that the decoder in the receiver is able to divide them back again into two separate streams for decoding.

A third standard based on ADPCM is also available. This is defined in **ITU-T Recommendation G.726**. This also uses subband coding but with a speech bandwidth of 3.4 kHz. The operating bit rate can be 40, 32, 24, or 16 kbps.

4.2.3 Adaptive predictive coding

Even higher levels of compression – but at higher levels of complexity – can be obtained by also making the predictor coefficients adaptive. This is the principle of **adaptive predictive coding** (**APC**) and with this, the predictor coefficients continuously change.

In practice, the optimum set of predictor coefficients continuously vary since they are a function of the characteristics of the audio signal being digitized; for example, the actual frequency components that make up the signal at a particular instant of time.

To exploit this property, the input speech signal is divided into fixed time segments and, for each segment, the currently prevailing characteristics are determined. The optimum set of coefficients are then computed and these are used to predict more accurately the previous signal. This type of compression can reduce the bandwidth requirements to 8 kbps while still obtaining an acceptable perceived quality.

4.2.4 Linear predictive coding

All the algorithms we have considered so far are based on sampling the time-varying speech waveform and then either sending the quantized samples directly (PCM) or sending the quantized difference signal (DPCM and its derivatives). With the advent of inexpensive digital signal processing circuits, an alternative approach has become possible which involves the source simply analyzing the audio waveform to determine a selection of the perceptual features it contains. These are then quantized and sent and the destination uses them, together with a sound synthesizer, to regenerate a sound that is perceptually comparable with the source audio signal. This is the basis of the **linear predictive coding** (**LPC**) technique and, although with this the generated sound – normally speech – can often sound synthetic, very high levels of compression (and hence low bit rates) can be achieved.

Clearly, the key to this approach is to identify the set of perceptual features to be used and, in terms of speech, the three features which determine the perception of a signal by the ear are its:

- pitch: this is closely related to the frequency of the signal and is important because the ear is more sensitive to frequencies in the range 2–5 kHz than to frequencies that are higher or lower than these;
- period: this is the duration of the signal;
- loudness: this is determined by the amount of energy in the signal.

In addition, the origins of the sound are important. These are known as **vocal tract excitation parameters** and classified as:

- voiced sounds: these are generated through the vocal chords and examples include the sounds relating to the letters m, v, and l;

■ unvoiced sounds: with these the vocal chords are open and examples include the sounds relating to the letters f and s.

Once these have been obtained from the source waveform, it is possible to use them, together with a suitable model of the vocal tract, to generate a synthesized version of the original speech signal. The basic features of an LPC encoder/decoder are shown in Figure 4.4.

The input speech waveform is first sampled and quantized at a defined rate. A block of digitized samples – known as a segment – is then analyzed to determine the various perceptual parameters of the speech that it contains. The speech signal generated by the vocal tract model in the decoder is a function of the present output of the speech synthesizer – as determined by the current set of model coefficients – plus a linear combination of the previous set of model coefficients. Hence the vocal tract model used is adaptive

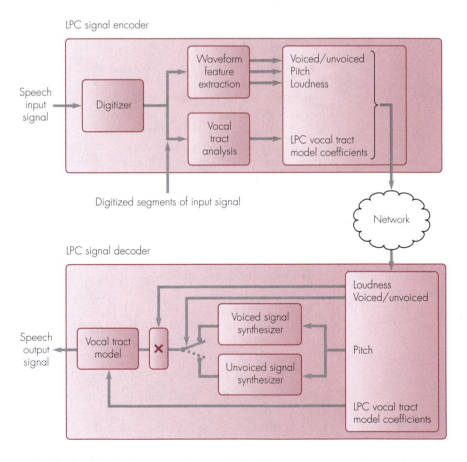

Figure 4.4 Linear predictive coding (LPC) signal encoder and decoder schematic.

and, as can be seen, the encoder determines and sends a new set of coefficients for each quantized segment.

As we can see from the above, the output of the encoder is a string of frames, one for each segment. Each frame contains fields for pitch and loudness – the period is determined by the sampling rate being used – a notification of whether the signal is voiced or unvoiced, and a new set of computed model coefficients. Some LPC encoders use up to ten sets of previous model coefficients to predict the output sound (**LPC-10**) and use bit rates as low as 2.4 kbps or even 1.2 kbps. As indicated, however, the generated sound at these rates is often very synthetic and hence LPC coders are used primarily in military applications in which bandwidth is all-important.

4.2.5 Code-excited LPC

The synthesizers used in most LPC decoders are based on a very basic model of the vocal tract. A more sophisticated version of this, known as a **code-excited linear prediction (CELP) model**, is also used and, in practice, is just one example of a family of vocal tract models known as **enhanced excitation (LPC) models**. These are also intended primarily for applications in which the amount of bandwidth available is limited but the perceived quality of the speech must be of an acceptable standard for use in various multimedia applications.

In the CELP model, instead of treating each digitized segment independently for encoding purposes, just a limited set of segments is used, each known as a **waveform template**. A precomputed set of templates are held by the encoder and decoder in what is known as a **template codebook**. Each of the individual digitized samples that make up a particular template in the codebook are differentially encoded. Each codeword that is sent selects a particular template from the codebook whose difference values best match those quantized by the encoder. In this way, there is continuity from one set of samples to another and, as a result, an improvement in sound quality is obtained.

There are now four international standards available that are based on this principle. These are **ITU-T Recommendations G.728, 729, 729(A), and 723.1** all of which give a good perceived quality at low bit rates.

All coders of this type have a delay associated with them which is incurred while each block of digitized samples is analyzed by the encoder and the speech is reconstructed at the decoder. The combined delay value is known as the coder's **processing delay**. In addition, before the speech samples can be analyzed, it is necessary to buffer – store in memory – the block of samples. The time to accumulate the block of samples is known as the **algorithmic delay** and, in some CELP coders, this is extended to include samples from the next successive block, a technique known as **lookahead**. These delays occur in the coders, of course, and hence are in addition to the end-to-end transmission delay over the network. Nevertheless, the combined delay value of a coder is an important parameter as it often determines the suitability of the coder for a specific application. For example, in a conventional telephony application, a low-delay coder is required since a large delay can impede the flow of a conversation. In contrast, in an interactive application that involves the output of speech stored in a file, for example, a delay of several seconds before the speech starts to be output is often acceptable and hence the coder's delay is less important. Other parameters of the coder that are considered are the **complexity** of the coding algorithm and the **perceived quality** of the output speech and, in general, a compromise has to be reached between a coder's speech quality and its delay/complexity.

The delay associated with a basic PCM coder is very small as it is equal to the time interval between two successive samples of the input waveform. Hence at the basic PCM sampling rate of 8 ksps the delay is equal to 0.125 ms. This same delay also applies, of course, to ADPCM coders. In contrast, the four CELP-based standards have delay values in excess of these as multiple samples are involved. These are summarized in Table 4.1 which also includes the bit rate(s) associated with each standard and the principal application for which each has been developed. The use of the extension .1 with G.723.1 is used to discriminate this standard from the earlier G.723 standard which has now been integrated with G.721 into the G.726 standard.

Table 4.1 Summary of CELP-based standards.

Standard	Bit rate	Total coder delay	Example application domain
G.728	16 kbps	0.625 ms	Low bit rate telephony
G.729	8 kbps	25 ms	Telephony in cellular (radio) networks
G.729(A)	8 kbps	25 ms	Digital simultaneous voice and data (DSVD)
G.723.1	5.3/6.3 kbps	67.5 ms	Video and Internet telephony

4.2.6 Perceptual coding

Both LPC and CELP are used primarily for telephony applications and hence the compression of a speech signal. Perceptual encoders, however, have been designed for the compression of general audio such as that associated with a digital television broadcast. They also use a model but, in this case, it is known as a **psychoacoustic model** since its role is to exploit a number of the limitations of the human ear.

Using this approach, sampled segments of the source audio waveform are analyzed – as with CELP-based coders – but only those features that are perceptible to the ear are transmitted. For example, although the human ear is sensitive to signals in the range 15 Hz through to 20 kHz, the level of sensitivity to each signal is non-linear; that is, the ear is more sensitive to some signals than others. Also, when multiple signals are present – as is the case with general audio – a strong signal may reduce the level of sensitivity of the ear to other signals which are near to it in frequency, an effect known as **frequency masking**. In addition, when the ear hears a loud sound, it takes a short but finite time before it can hear a quieter sound, an effect known as **temporal masking**. A psychoacoustic model is used to identify those signals that are influenced by both these effects. These are then eliminated from the transmitted signals and, in so doing, this reduces the amount of information to be transmitted.

Sensitivity of the ear

We defined the dynamic range of a signal in Section 2.2.2. It is the ratio of the maximum amplitude of the signal to the minimum amplitude and is measured in decibels (dB). In the case of the ear, its dynamic range is the ratio of the loudest sound it can hear to the quietest sound and is in the region of 96 dB. As we have just seen, however, the sensitivity of the ear varies with the frequency of the signal and, assuming just a single-frequency signal is present at any one time, the perception threshold of the ear – that is, its minimum level of sensitivity – as a function of frequency is shown in Figure 4.5(a).

As we can see, the ear is most sensitive to signals in the range 2–5 kHz and hence signals within this band are the quietest the ear is sensitive to. The vertical axis, therefore, indicates the amplitude level of all the other signal frequencies relative to this level – measured in dB – that are required for them to be heard. Hence in the figure, although the two signals A and B have the same relative amplitude, signal A would be heard – that is, it is above the hearing threshold – while signal B would not.

Frequency masking

When an audio sound consists of multiple frequency signals is present, the sensitivity of the ear changes and varies with the relative amplitude of the signals. For example, the curve shown in Figure 4.5(b) shows how the sensitivity of the ear changes in the vicinity of a loud signal. In this example, signal B is larger in amplitude than signal A and, as we can see, this causes the basic sensitivity curve of the ear to be distorted in the region of signal B. As a result, signal A will no longer be heard even though on its own, it is above the hearing threshold of the ear for a signal of that frequency. This is the origin of the term frequency masking and, in practice, the masking effect also varies with frequency as we show in Figure 4.6.

The various curves show the masking effect of a selection of different frequency signals – 1, 4, and 8 kHz – and, as we can see, the width of the masking curves – that is, the range of frequencies that are affected – increase with increasing frequency. The width of each curve at a particular signal level is known as the **critical bandwidth** for that frequency and experiments have shown that, for frequencies less than 500 Hz, the critical bandwidth remains constant at about 100 Hz. For frequencies greater than 500 Hz, however, the critical bandwidth increases (approximately) linearly in multiples of 100 Hz. For example, for a signal of 1 kHz (2 × 500 Hz), the critical bandwidth is

(a)

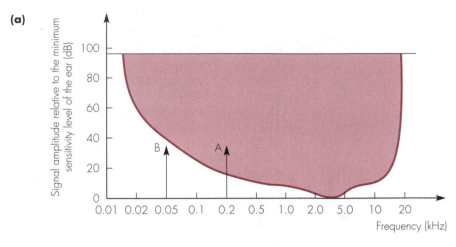

(b)

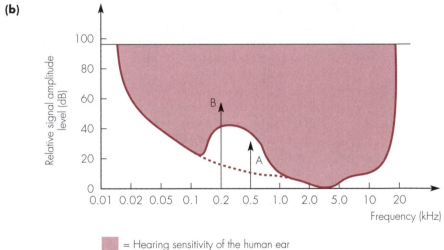

▨ = Hearing sensitivity of the human ear

Figure 4.5 Perceptual properties of the human ear: (a) sensitivity as a function of frequency; (b) frequency masking.

about 200 (2 × 100) Hz while at 5 kHz (10 × 500 Hz) it is about 1000 (10 × 100) Hz. Hence if the magnitude of the frequency components that make up an audio sound can be determined, it becomes possible to determine those frequencies that will be masked (and hence inaudible) and do not therefore need to be transmitted.

Temporal masking

As indicated earlier, after the ear hears a loud sound, it takes a further short time before it can hear a quieter sound. This is known as temporal masking and the general effect is shown in Figure 4.7. As we can see, after the loud

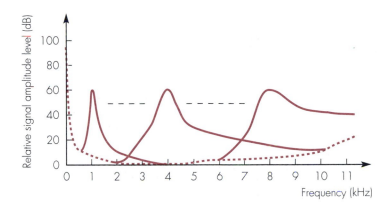

Figure 4.6 Variation with frequency of effect of frequency masking.

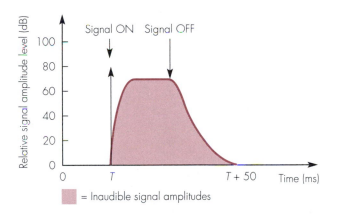

Figure 4.7 Temporal masking caused by a loud signal.

sound ceases it takes a short period of time (in the order of tens of milliseconds) for the signal amplitude to decay. During this time, signals whose amplitudes are less than the decay envelope will not be heard and hence need not be transmitted. Clearly, however, in order to exploit this phenomenon, it is necessary to process the input audio waveform over a time period that is comparable with that associated with temporal masking.

4.2.7 MPEG audio coders

In practice, perceptual coding is used in a range of different audio compression applications. For example, as we shall describe later in Section 4.3.4, the **Motion Pictures Expert Group** (**MPEG**) was formed by the ISO to formulate a set of standards relating to a range of multimedia applications that involve the use of video with sound. The coders associated with the audio compression part of these standards are known as **MPEG audio coders** and a number of these use perceptual coding.

All the signal processing operations associated with a perceptual coder are carried out digitally and a schematic diagram of a basic encoder and decoder is shown in Figure 4.8(a).

The time-varying audio input signal is first sampled and quantized using PCM, the sampling rate and number of bits per sample being determined by the specific application. The bandwidth that is available for transmission is divided into a number of **frequency subbands** using a bank of **analysis filters** which, because of their role, are also known as **critical-band filters**. Each frequency subband is of equal width and, essentially, the bank of filters maps each set of 32 (time-related) PCM samples into an equivalent set of 32 frequency samples, one per subband. Hence each is known as a **subband sample** and indicates the magnitude of each of the 32 frequency components that are present in a segment of the audio input signal of a time duration equal to 32 PCM samples. For example, assuming 32 subbands and a sampling rate of 32 ksps – that is, a maximum signal frequency of 16 kHz – each subband has a bandwidth of 500 Hz.

In a basic encoder, the time duration of each sampled segment of the audio input signal is equal to the time to accumulate 12 successive sets of 32 PCM – and hence subband – samples; that is, a time duration equal to 384 (12 x 32) PCM samples.

In addition to filtering the input samples into separate frequency subbands, the analysis filter bank also determines the maximum amplitude of the 12 subband samples in each subband. Each is known as the **scaling factor** for the subband and these are passed both to the psychoacoustic model and, together with the set of frequency samples in each subband, to the corresponding quantizer block.

The processing associated with both frequency and temporal masking is carried out by the psychoacoustic model which is performed concurrently with the filtering and analysis operations. The 12 sets of 32 PCM samples are first transformed into an equivalent set of frequency components using a mathematical technique known as the **discrete Fourier transform** (**DFT**). Then, using the known hearing thresholds and masking properties of each subband, the model determines the various masking effects of this set of signals. The output of the model is a set of what are known as **signal-to-mask ratios** (**SMRs**) and indicate those frequency components whose amplitude is below the related audible threshold. In addition, the set of scaling factors are used to determine the quantization accuracy – and hence bit allocations – to be used for each of the audible components. This is done so that those frequency components that are in regions of highest sensitivity can be quantized with more accuracy (bits) – and hence less quantization noise – than those in regions where the ear is less sensitive. In a basic encoder, all the frequency components in a sampled segment are encoded and these are carried in a frame the format of which is shown in Figure 4.8(b).

(a)

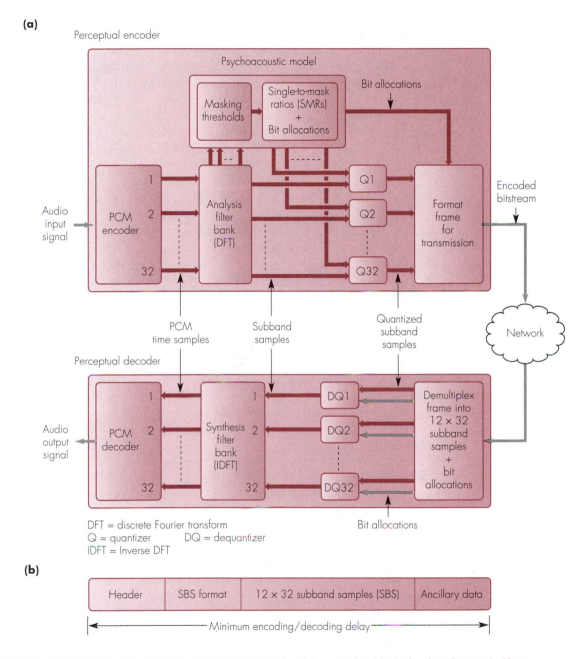

DFT = discrete Fourier transform
Q = quantizer   DQ = dequantizer
IDFT = Inverse DFT

(b)

Header	SBS format	12 × 32 subband samples (SBS)	Ancillary data

← Minimum encoding/decoding delay →

Figure 4.8 MPEG perceptual coder schematic: (a) encoder/decoder implementation schematic (b) example frame format.

The *header* contains information such as the sampling frequency that has been used. The quantization is performed in two stages using a form of companding. The peak amplitude level in each subband – the scaling factor – is first quantized using 6 bits – giving 1 of 64 levels – and a further 4 bits are then used to quantize the 12 frequency components in the subband relative to this level. Collectively this is known as the *subband sample (SBS) format* and, in this way, all the information necessary for decoding is carried within each frame. In the decoder, after the magnitude of each set of 32 subband samples have been determined by the dequantizers, these are passed to the **synthesis filter** bank. The latter then produces the corresponding set of PCM samples which are decoded to produce the time-varying analog output segment. The *ancillary data* field at the end of a frame is optional and is used, for example, to carry additional coded samples associated with, say, the surround-sound that is present with some digital video broadcasts.

The use in the encoder of different scaling factors for each subband means that the frequency components in the different subbands have varying levels of quantization noise associated with them. As we described in Section 2.2.2, this means that the frequency components in the different subbands have varying signal-to-noise ratios. The bank of synthesis filters in the decoder, however, limits the level of quantization noise in each subband to the same band of frequencies as the set of frequency components in that subband. As a result, the effect of quantization noise is reduced since the signal-to-noise ratio in each subband is increased by the larger amplitude of the signal frequency components in each subband masking the reduced level of quantization noise that is present.

As we can deduce from the figure, the psychoacoustic model is not required in the decoder and, as a consequence, it is less complex than the encoder. This is a particularly desirable feature in audio and video broadcast applications, for example, in which the cost of the decoder is an important factor. Also, it means that different psychoacoustic models can be used or, if bandwidth is plentiful, none at all.

An international standard based on this approach is defined in **ISO Recommendation 11172-3**. There are three levels of processing associated with this known as layers 1, 2, and 3. Layer 1 is the basic mode and the other two have increasing levels of processing associated with them which, in turn, produce a corresponding increase in the level of compression for the same perceived audio quality. For example, layer 1 does not include temporal masking but this is present in layers 2 and 3.

As we have already indicated, in terms of applications, MPEG audio is used primarily for the compression of general audio and, in particular, for the audio associated with various digital video applications. The performance of the three layers and examples of their corresponding application domains are summarized in Table 4.2. As we can see, the encoders associated with each of the three layers obtain increasing levels of compression and perceptual quality. The encoder and decoder delay figures are determined by the PCM sampling rate used and the corresponding frame size. For example, with layer 1, the sampling rates used are:

- 32 ksps for use with broadcast communications equipment,
- 44.1 ksps for use with CD-quality audio equipment,
- 48 ksps for use with professional sound equipment.

These produce corresponding frame durations of 12, 8.7, and 8 milliseconds with 384 samples per frame. The actual input-to-output delay, however, can be as much as two to three times these values owing to additional processing delays in the encoder and decoder. Layer 2 is identical to a standard known as **MUSICAM** and indeed was based on this. The format of each layer 2 frame is similar to that of layer 1 except that each frame contains three sets of 384 samples and hence is of a time duration equal to 1152 samples.

The bit rate figures shown in Table 4.2 are all for a single audio channel. In practice, four alternative forms of audio have been identified for multimedia applications: monophonic, dual monophonic, two-channel (also known as disjoint) stereo, and single-channel joint stereo. The latter is the digitized version of the composite stereo sound signal and hence exploits the redundancy that is present between the two channels. So the bandwidth required for audio may be the figures shown in the table – for monophonic and joint stereo – or double the values shown – for dual monophonic and two-channel stereo. Since the three layers require increasing levels of complexity (and hence cost) to achieve a particular perceived quality, the choice of layer and bit rate is often a compromise between the desired perceived quality and the available bit rate.

Table 4.2 Summary of MPEG layer 1, 2 and 3 perceptual encoders

Layer	Application	Compressed bit rate	Quality	Example input-to-output delay
1	Digital audio cassette	32 – 448 kbps	Hi-fi quality at 192 kbps per channel	20ms
2	Digital audio and digital video broadcasting	32 – 192 kbps	Near CD-quality at 128 kbps per channel	40ms
3	CD-quality audio over low bit rate channels	64 kbps	CD-quality at 64 kbps per channel	60ms

4.2.8 Dolby audio coders

The psychoacoustic models associated with the various MPEG coders control the quantization accuracy of each subband sample by computing and allocating the number of bits to be used to quantize each sample. Since the quantization accuracy that is used for each sample in a subband may vary from one set of subband samples to the next, the bit allocation information that is used to quantize the samples in each subband is sent with the actual quantized samples. This information is then used by the decoder to dequantize the set of subband samples in the frame. This mode of operation of a perceptual coder is known, therefore, as the **forward adaptive bit allocation mode** and, for comparison purposes, a simplified schematic diagram showing this operational mode is given in Figure 4.9(a). As we indicated at the end of the last section, it has the advantage that the psychoacoustic model is required only in the encoder. It has the disadvantage, however, that a significant portion of each encoded frame contains bit allocation information which, in turn, leads to a relatively inefficient use of the available bit rate.

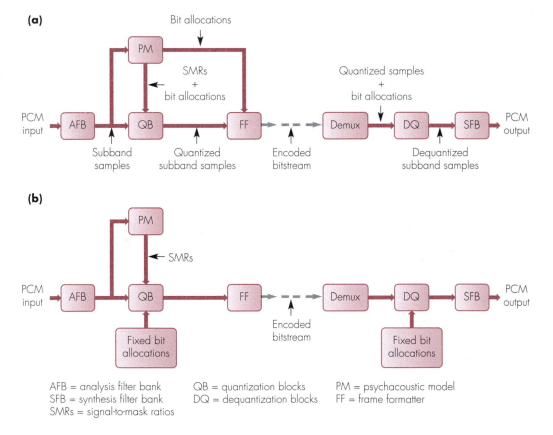

Figure 4.9 Perceptual coder schematics: (a) forward adaptive bit allocation (MPEG); (b) fixed bit allocation (Dolby AC-1).

A variation of this approach is to use a fixed bit allocation strategy for each subband which is then used by both the encoder and decoder. The principle of operation of this mode is shown in Figure 4.9(b). Typically, the bit allocations that are selected for each subband are determined by the known sensitivity characteristics of the ear and the use of fixed allocations means that this information need not be sent in the frame. This approach is used in a standard known as **Dolby AC-1**, the acronym "AC" meaning **acoustic coder**. It was designed for use in satellites to relay FM radio programs and the sound associated with television programs. It uses a low-complexity psychoacoustic model with 40 subbands at a sampling rate of 32 ksps and proportionately more at 44.1 and 48 ksps. A typical compressed bit rate is 512 kbps for two-channel stereo.

A second variation, which allows the bit allocations per subband to be adaptive while at the same time minimizing the overheads in the encoder bit-stream, is for the decoder also to contain a copy of the psychoacoustic model. This is then used by the decoder to compute the same – or very similar – bit allocations that the psychoacoustic model in the encoder has used to quantize each set of subband samples. Clearly, however, in order for the psychoacoustic model in the decoder to carry out its own computation of the bit allocations, it is necessary for it to have a copy of the subband samples. Hence with this operational mode, instead of each frame containing bit allocation information – in addition to the set of quantized samples – it contains the encoded frequency coefficients that are present in the sampled waveform segment. This is known as the **encoded spectral envelope** and this mode of operation, the **backward adaptive bit allocation mode**. Figure 4.10(a) illustrates the principle of operation of both the encoder and decoder.

This approach is used in the **Dolby AC-2** standard which is utilized in many applications including the compression associated with the audio of a number of PC sound cards. Typically, these produce audio of hi-fi quality at a bit rate of 256 kbps. For broadcast applications, however, it has the disadvantage that, since the same psychoacoustic model is required in the decoder, the model in the encoder cannot be modified without changing all decoders.

To meet this requirement, a third variation has been developed that uses both backward and forward bit allocation principles. This is known as the **hybrid backward/forward adaptive bit allocation mode** and is illustrated in Figure 4.10(b).

As we can deduce from part (a) of the figure, with the backward bit allocation method on its own, since the psychoacoustic model uses the encoded spectral envelope, the quantization accuracy of the subband samples is affected by the quantization noise introduced by the spectral encoder. Hence in the hybrid scheme, although a backward adaptive bit allocation scheme is used as in AC-2 – using PM_B – an additional psychoacoustic model – PM_F – is used to compute the difference between the bit allocations computed by PM_B and those that are computed by PM_F using the forward-adaptive bit allocation scheme. This information is then used by PM_B to improve the quantization

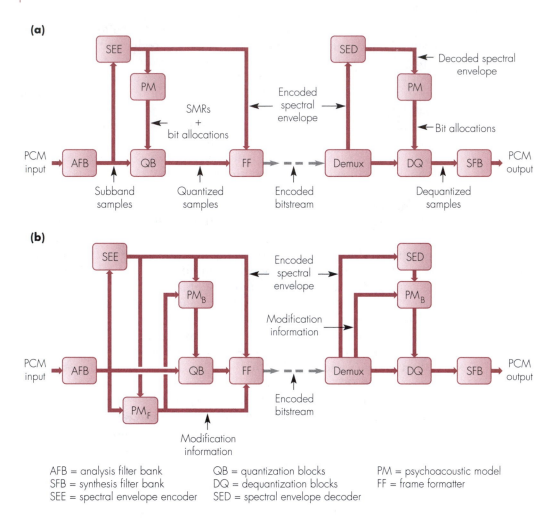

(a)

PCM input → AFB → QB → FF ⤍ Demux → DQ → SFB → PCM output

Subband samples
Quantized samples
Encoded bitstream
Dequantized samples

SEE, PM, SMRs + bit allocations, Encoded spectral envelope, Decoded spectral envelope, SED, PM, Bit allocations

(b)

PCM input → AFB → QB → FF ⤍ Demux → DQ → SFB → PCM output

SEE, PM_B, Encoded spectral envelope, Modification information, SED, PM_B, PM_F, Modification information, Encoded bitstream

AFB = analysis filter bank   QB = quantization blocks   PM = psychoacoustic model
SFB = synthesis filter bank   DQ = dequantization blocks   FF = frame formatter
SEE = spectral envelope encoder SED = spectral envelope decoder

Figure 4.10 Perceptual coder schematic: (a) backward adaptive bit allocation (Dolby AC-2); (b) hybrid backward/forward adaptive bit allocation (Dolby AC-s).

accuracy of the set of subband samples. The modification information is also sent in the encoded frame and is used by the PMB in the decoder to improve the dequantization accuracy. In addition, should it be required to modify the operational parameters of the PMB in the encoder and decoder(s), then this information can be sent also with the computed difference information. As we can see from the figure, the PMF must compute two sets of quantization information for each set of subband samples and hence is relatively complex. However, since this is not required in the decoder, this is not an issue.

The hybrid approach is used in the **Dolby AC-3** standard which has been defined for use in a similar range of applications as the MPEG audio standards including the audio associated with **advanced television** (**ATV**). This is the HDTV standard in North America and, in this application, the acoustic quality of both the MPEG and Dolby audio coders were found to be comparable. The sampling rate can be 32, 44.1, or 48 ksps depending on the bandwidth of the source audio signal. Each encoded block contains 512 subband samples. However, in order to obtain continuity from one block to the next, the last 256 subband samples in the previous block are repeated to become the first 256 samples in the next block and hence each block contains only 256 new samples. Assuming a PCM sampling rate of 32 ksps, although each block of samples is of 8 ms duration – 256/32 – the duration of each encoder block is 16 ms. The audio signal bandwidth at this sampling rate is 15 kHz and hence each subband has a bandwidth of 62.5 Hz, that is, 15 k/256. The (stereo) bit rate is, typically, 192 kbps.

4.3 Video compression

As we described in Chapter 1, video (with sound) features in a number of multimedia applications:

- interpersonal: video telephony and videoconferencing;
- interactive: access to stored video in various forms;
- entertainment: digital television and movie/video-on-demand.

However, as we described in Section 2.6.2, the quality of the video used in these applications varies and is determined by the digitization format and frame refresh rate used. As you may recall, the digitization format defines the sampling rate that is used for the luminance, Y, and two chrominance, C_b and C_r, signals and their relative position in each frame. We derived a number of (worst-case) bit rates that are generated with different digitization formats and these ranged from in the order of 10 Mbps for the sub-quarter common intermediate format (SQCIF), as used for video telephony, to 162 Mbps for the 4:2:0 format as used for digital television broadcasts.

In practice, therefore, as we described in Chapter 1, the bit rate requirements resulting from all the digitization formats defined in Section 2.6.2 are substantially larger than the bit rates of the transmission channels that are available with the networks associated with these applications. It is for this reason that compression is used in all applications that involve video. However, there is not just a single standard associated with video but rather a range of standards, each targeted at a particular application domain. The majority are all now international standards and we shall describe a number of these in this section. Prior to doing this, however, we shall first describe the basic principles on which the standards are based.

4.3.1 Video compression principles

In the context of compression, since video is simply a sequence of digitized pictures, video is also referred to as **moving pictures** and the terms "frame" and "picture" are used interchangeably. In general, we shall use the term frame except where a particular standard uses the term picture.

In principle, one approach to compressing a video source is to apply the JPEG algorithm described earlier in Section 3.4.5 to each frame independently. This approach is known as **moving JPEG** or **MJPEG**. As we concluded at the end of that section, however, typical compression ratios obtainable with JPEG are between 10:1 and 20:1, neither of which is large enough on its own to produce the compression ratios needed.

In practice, in addition to the spatial redundancy present in each frame, considerable redundancy is often present between a set of frames since, in general, only a small portion of each frame is involved with any motion that is taking place. Examples include the movement of a person's lips or eyes in a video telephony application and a person or vehicle moving across the screen in a movie. In the case of the latter, since a typical scene in a movie has a minimum duration of about 3 seconds, assuming a frame refresh rate of 60 frames per second, each scene is composed of a minimum of 180 frames. Hence by sending only information relating to those segments of each frame that have movement associated with them, considerable additional savings in bandwidth can be made by exploiting the temporal differences that exist between many of the frames.

The technique that is used to exploit the high correlation between successive frames is to predict the content of many of the frames. As we shall describe, this is based on a combination of a preceding – and in some instances a succeeding – frame. Instead of sending the source video as a set of individually-compressed frames, just a selection is sent in this form and, for the remaining frames, only the differences between the actual frame contents and the predicted frame contents are sent. The accuracy of the prediction operation is determined by how well any movement between successive frames is estimated. This operation is known as **motion estimation** and, since the estimation process is not exact, additional information must also be sent to indicate any small differences between the predicted and actual positions of the moving segments involved. The latter is known as **motion compensation** and we shall discuss each issue separately.

Frame types

As we can see from the above, there are two basic types of compressed frame: those that are encoded independently and those that are predicted. The first are known as **intracoded frames** or **I-frames**. In practice, there are two types of predicted frames: **predictive** or **P-frames** and **bidirectional** or **B-frames** and because of the way they are derived, the latter are also known as **intercoded** or **interpolation frames**. A typical sequence of frames involving just I- and P-frames is shown in Figure 4.11(a) and a sequence involving all three frame types is shown in part (b) of the figure.

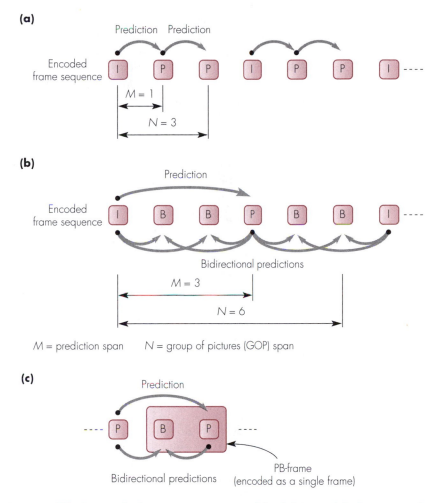

Figure 4.11 Example frame sequences with: (a) I- and P-frames only; (b) I-, P- and B-frames; (c) PB-frames.

I-frames are encoded without reference to any other frames. Each frame is treated as a separate (digitized) picture and the Y, C_b and C_r matrices are encoded independently using the JPEG algorithm (DCT, quantization, entropy encoding – described earlier in Section 3.4.5) except that the quantization threshold values that are used are the same for all DCT coefficients. Hence the level of compression obtained with I-frames is relatively small. In principle, therefore, it would appear to be best if these were limited to, say, the first frame relating to a new scene in a movie. In practice, however, the compression algorithm is independent of the contents of frames and hence has no knowledge of the start and end of scenes. Also, I-frames must be present in the output stream at regular intervals in order to allow for the possibility of the contents of an encoded I-frame being corrupted during transmission. Clearly, if an I-frame was corrupted then, in the case of a movie, since the predicted frames are based on the contents of an I-frame, a complete scene would be lost which, of course, would be totally unacceptable. Normally, therefore, I-frames are inserted into the output stream relatively frequently. The number of frames/pictures between successive I-frames is known as a **group of pictures** or **GOP**. It is given the symbol N and typical values for N are from 3 through to 12.

As we can deduce from Figure 4.11(a), the encoding of a P-frame is relative to the contents of either a preceding I-frame or a preceding P-frame. As indicated, P-frames are encoded using a combination of motion estimation and motion compensation and hence significantly higher levels of compression can be obtained with them. In practice, however, the number of P-frames between each successive pair of I-frames is limited since any errors present in the first P-frame will be propagated to the next. The number of frames between a P-frame and the immediately preceding I- or P-frame is called the **prediction span**. It is given the symbol M and typical values range from 1, as in Figure 4.11(a), through to 3, as in Figure 4.11(b).

As we shall describe shortly, motion estimation involves comparing small segments of two consecutive frames for differences and, should a difference be detected, a search is carried out to determine to which neighbouring segment the original segment has moved. In order to minimize the time for each search, the search region is limited to just a few neighbouring segments. In applications such as video telephony, the amount of movement between consecutive frames is relatively small and hence this approach works well. In those applications that may involve very fast moving objects, however, it is possible for a segment to have moved outside of the search region. To allow for this possibility, in applications such as movies, in addition to P-frames, a second type of prediction frame is used. These are the B-frames and, as we can see in Figure 4.11(b), their contents are predicted using search regions in both past and future frames. In addition to allowing for occasional fast moving objects, this also provides better motion estimation when, for example, an object moves in front of or behind another object.

As we can deduce from the two example frame sequences shown in Figure 4.11, for P-frames their contents are encoded by considering the contents of the current (uncoded) frame relative to the contents of the immediately preceding (uncoded) frame. In the case of B-frames, however, three (uncoded) frame contents are involved: the immediately preceding I- or P-frame, the current frame being encoded, and the immediately succeeding I- or P-frame. This results in an increase in the encoding (and decoding) delay which is equal to the time to wait for the next I- or P-frame in the sequence. In practice, however, B-frames provide the highest level of compression and, because they are not involved in the coding of other frames, they do not propagate errors.

To perform the decoding operation, the received (compressed) information relating to I-frames can be decoded immediately it is received in order to recreate the original frame. With P-frames, the received information is first decoded and the resulting information is then used, together with the decoded contents of the preceding I- or P-frame, to derive the decoded frame contents. In the case of B-frames, the received information is first decoded and the resulting information is then used, together with both the immediately preceding I- or P-frame contents and the immediately succeeding P- or I-frame contents, to derive the decoded frame contents. Hence in order to minimize the time required to decode each B-frame, the order of encoding (and transmission) of the (encoded) frames is changed so that both the preceding and succeeding I- or P-frames are available when the B-frame is received. For example, if the uncoded frame sequence is:

IBBPBBPBBI...

then the reordered sequence would be:

IPBBPBBIBBPBB.

Hence, with B-frames, the decoded contents of both the immediately preceding I- or P-frame and the immediately succeeding P- or I-frame are available when the B-frame is received.

A fourth type of frame known as a PB-frame has also been defined. This does not refer to a new frame type as such but rather the way two neighbouring P- and B-frames are encoded as if they were a single frame. The general principle is as shown in Figure 4.11(c) and, as we shall expand upon in Section 4.3.3, this is done in order to increase the frame rate without significantly increasing the resulting bit rate required.

Finally, although only used in a specific type of application, a fifth type of frame known as a **D-frame** has been defined for use in movie/video-on-demand applications. As we described in Section 1.4.3, with this type of application, a user (at home) can select and watch a particular movie/video which is stored in a remote server connected to a network. The selection operation is performed by means of a set-top box and, as with a VCR, the user may wish to rewind or fast-forward through the movie. Clearly, this requires the compressed video to be decompressed at much higher speeds. Hence to support this function, the encoded video stream also contains D-frames which are inserted at regular intervals throughout the stream. These are highly compressed frames and are ignored during the decoding of P- and B-frames. As you may recall from our earlier discussion of the DCT compression algorithm in Section 3.4.5, the DC coefficient associated with each 8×8 block of pixels – both for the luminance and the two chrominance signals – is the mean of all the values in the related block. Hence by using only the encoded DC coefficients of each block of pixels in the periodically inserted D-frames, a low-resolution sequence of frames is provided each of which can be decoded at the higher speeds that are expected with the rewind and fast-forward operations.

Motion estimation and compensation

As we showed earlier in Figure 4.11, the encoded contents of both P- and B-frames are predicted by estimating any motion that has taken place between the frame being encoded and the preceding I- or P-frame and, in the case of B-frames, the succeeding P- or I-frame. The various steps that are involved in encoding each P-frame are shown in Figure 4.12.

As we show in Figure 4.12(a), the digitized contents of the Y matrix associated with each frame are first divided into a two-dimensional matrix of

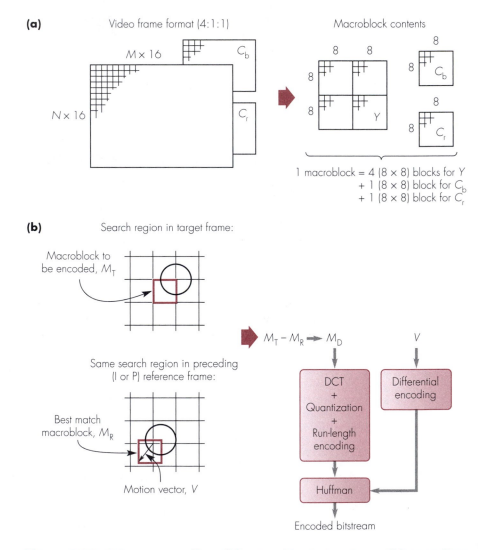

Figure 4.12 P-frame encoding: (a) macroblock structure; (b) encoding procedure.

16 ×16 pixels known as a **macroblock**. In the example, the 4:1:1 digitization format is assumed and hence the related C_b and C_r matrices in the macro-block are both 8×8 pixels. For identification purposes, each macroblock has an **address** associated with it and, since the block size used for the DCT oper-ation is also 8×8 pixels, a macroblock comprises four DCT blocks for luminance and one each for the two chrominance signals.

To encode a P-frame, the contents of each macroblock in the frame – known as the **target frame** – are compared on a pixel-by-pixel basis with the contents of the corresponding macroblock in the preceding -I or P-frame. The latter is known as the **reference frame**. If a close match is found, then only the address of the macroblock is encoded. If a match is not found, the search is extended to cover an area around the macroblock in the reference frame. Typically, this comprises a number of macroblocks as shown in Figure 4.12(b).

In practice, the various standards do not specify either the extent of the search area or a specific search strategy and instead specify only how the results of the search are to be encoded. Normally, only the contents of the Y matrix are used in the search and a match is said to be found if the mean of the absolute errors in all the pixel positions in the difference macroblock is less than a given threshold. Hence, using a particular strategy, all the possible macroblocks in the selected search area in the reference frame are searched for a match and, if a close match is found, two parameters are encoded. The first is known as the **motion vector** and indicates the (x,y) offset of the macro-block being encoded and the location of the block of pixels in the reference frame which produces the (close) match. The search – and hence offset – can be either on macroblock boundaries or, as in the figure, on pixel boundaries. The motion vector is then said to be **single-pixel resolution**. The second para-meter is known as the **prediction error** and comprises three matrices (one each for Y, C_b and C_r) each of which contains the difference values (in all the pixel locations) between those in the target macroblock and the set of pixels in the search area that produced the close match.

Since the physical area of coverage of a macroblock is small, the motion vectors can be relatively large values. Also, most moving objects are normally much larger than a single macroblock. Hence, when an object moves, multi-ple macroblocks are affected in a similar way. The motion vectors, therefore, are encoded using differential encoding (DE) and the resulting codewords are then Huffman encoded. The three difference matrices, however, are encoded using the same steps as for I-frames: DCT, quantization, entropy encoding. Finally, if a match cannot be found – for example if the moving object has moved out of the extended search area – the macroblock is encoded independently in the same way as the macroblocks in an I-frame.

To encode a B-frame, any motion is estimated with reference to both the immediately preceding I- or P-frame and the immediately succeeding P- or I-frame. The general scheme is shown in Figure 4.13. The motion vector and difference matrices are computed using first the preceding frame as the

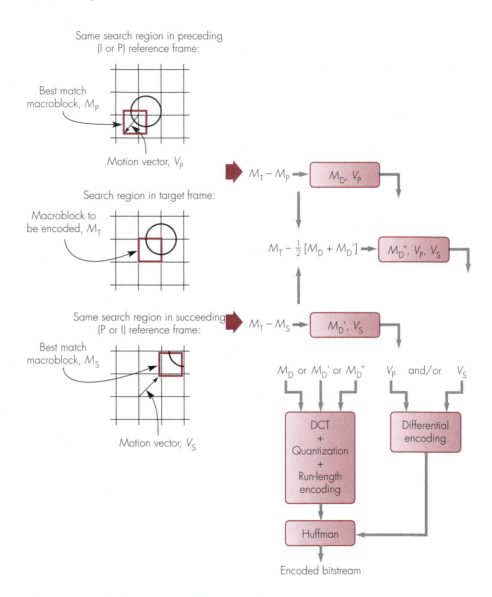

Figure 4.13 B-frame encoding procedure.

reference and then the succeeding frame as the reference. A third motion vector and set of difference matrices are then computed using the target and the mean of the two other predicted sets of values. The set with the lowest set of difference matrices is then chosen and these are encoded in the same way as for P-frames. The motion vector is then said to be to a resolution of a fraction of a pixel; for example, **half-pixel resolution**.

Implementation issues

A schematic diagram showing the essential units associated with the encoding of I-, P-, and B-frames is given in parts (a), (b) and (c) of Figure 4.14 respectively and an example format of the encoded bitstream output by the encoder is given in part (d) of the figure.

As we can deduce from part (a) of the figure, the encoding procedure used for the macroblocks that make up an I-frame is the same as that used in the JPEG standard to encode each 8×8 block of pixels. This was described earlier in Section 3.4.5 and, as we can see, the procedure involves each macroblock being encoded using the three steps: forward DCT, quantization, and entropy encoding. Hence assuming four blocks for luminance and two for chrominance, each macroblock would require six 8×8 pixel blocks to be encoded.

In the case of P-frames, the encoding of each macroblock is dependent on the output of the motion estimation unit which, in turn, depends on the contents of the macroblock being encoded and the contents of the macroblock in the search area of the reference frame that produces the closest match to that being encoded. There are three possibilities:

(1) If the two contents are the same, only the address of the macroblock in the reference frame is encoded.

(2) If the two contents are very close, both the motion vector and the difference matrices associated with the macroblock in the reference frame are encoded.

(3) If no close match is found, then the target macroblock is encoded in the same way as a macroblock in an I-frame.

As we can see in Figure 4.14(b), in order to carry out its role, the motion estimation unit containing the search logic, utilizes a copy of the (uncoded) reference frame. This is obtained by taking the computed difference values – between the frame currently being compressed (the target frame) and the current reference frame – and decompressing them using the dequantize (DQ) plus inverse DCT (IDCT) blocks. After the complete target frame has been compressed, the related set of difference values are used to update the current reference frame contents ready to encode the next (target) frame. The same procedure is followed for encoding B-frames except both the preceding (reference) frame and the succeeding frame to the target frame are involved.

As we can see from the above, for each macroblock, it is necessary to identify the type of encoding that has been used. This is the role of the **formatter** and a typical format that is used to encode the macroblocks in each frame is shown in part (d) of the figure. The *type* field indicates the type of frame being encoded – I-, P-, or B- – and the *address* identifies the location of the macroblock in the frame. The *quantization value* is the threshold value

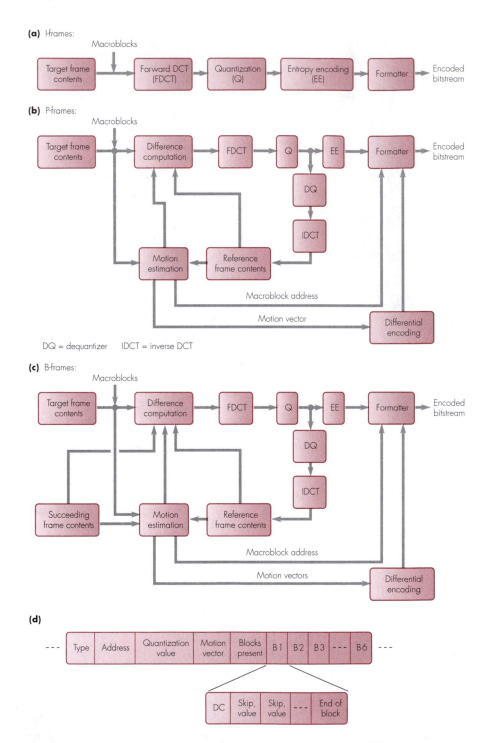

Figure 4.14 Implementation schematics: (a) I-frames; (b) P-frames; (c) B-frames; (d) example macroblock encoded bitstream format.

that has been used to quantize all the DCT coefficients in the macroblock and *motion vector* is the encoded vector if one is present. The *blocks present* indicates which of the six 8×8 pixel blocks that make up the macroblock are present – if any – and, for those present, the JPEG-encoded DCT coefficients for each block. As we can deduce from this, the amount of information output by the encoder varies and depends on the complexity of the source video. Hence a basic video encoder of the type shown in Figure 4.14 generates an encoded bitstream that has a variable bit rate.

The decoding of the received bitstream is simpler (and hence faster) than the encoding operation since the time-consuming motion estimation processing is not required. As the encoded bitstream is received and decoded, each new frame is assembled a macroblock at a time. Decoding the macroblocks of an I-frame is the same as decoding the blocks in a JPEG-encoded image. To decode a P-frame, the decoder retains a copy of the immediately preceding (decoded) I- or P- frame in a buffer and uses this, together with the received encoded information relating to each macroblock, to build the Y, C_b, and C_r matrices for the new frame in a second buffer. With uncoded macroblocks, the macroblock's address is used to locate the corresponding macroblock in the previous frame and its contents are then transferred into the second buffer unchanged. With fully-encoded macroblocks, these are decoded directly and the contents transferred to the buffer. With macroblocks containing a motion vector and a set of difference matrices, then these are used, together with the related set of matrices in the first buffer, to determine the new values for the macroblock in the second buffer. The decoding of B-frames is similar except three buffers are used: one containing the decoded contents of the preceding I- or P-frame, the second the decoded contents of the succeeding P- or I-frame, and the third to hold the frame being assembled.

Performance

The compression ratio for I-frames – and hence all intracoded frames – is similar to that obtained with JPEG and, for video frames, typically is in the region of 10:1 through 20:1 depending on the complexity of the frame contents. The compression ratio of both P- and B- frames is higher and depends on the search method used. However, typical figures are in the region of 20:1 through 30:1 for P-frames and 30:1 through 50:1 for B-frames.

4.3.2 H.261

The H.261 video compression standard has been defined by the ITU-T for the provision of video telephony and videoconferencing services over an integrated services digital network (ISDN). Hence, as we described earlier in Section 1.3.4, it is assumed that the network offers transmission channels of multiples of 64 kbps. The standard is also known, therefore, as $p \times 64$ where p can be 1 through 30. The digitization format used is either the common intermediate format (CIF) or the quarter CIF (QCIF). Normally, the CIF is used for videoconferencing and the QCIF for video telephony, both of which we described in Section 2.6.2. However, because each frame is divided into macroblocks of 16×16 pixels for compression, the horizontal resolution is reduced from 360 to 352 pixels to produce an integral number of 22 macro-blocks. Hence, since both formats use subsampling of the two chrominance signals at half the rate used for the luminance signal, the spatial resolution of each format is:

$$\text{CIF: } Y = 352 \times 288, \quad C_b = C_r = 176 \times 144$$
$$\text{QCIF: } Y = 176 \times 144, \quad C_b = C_r = 88 \times 72$$

Progressive (non-interlaced) scanning is used with a frame refresh rate of 30 fps for the CIF and either 15 or 7.5 fps for the QCIF.

Just I- and P- frames are used in H.261 with three P-frames between each pair of I-frames. The encoding of each of the six 8×8 pixel blocks that make up each macroblock in both I- and P-frames – 4 blocks for Y and one each for C_b and C_r – is carried out using the procedures described in the last section. The format of each encoded macroblock is shown in outline in Figure 4.15(a) and the format of each complete frame is shown in part (b) of the figure.

As we described in the last section, each macroblock has an *address* associated with it for identification purposes and the *type* field indicates whether the macroblock has been encoded independently – intracoded – or with reference to a macroblock in a preceding frame – intercoded. The *quantization value* is the threshold value that has been used to quantize all the DCT coefficients in the macroblock and *motion vector* is the encoded vector if one is present. The *coded block pattern* indicates which of the six 8×8 pixel blocks that make up the macroblock are present – if any – and, for those present, the JPEG-encoded DCT coefficients are given in each block.

The start of each new (encoded) video frame/picture is indicated by the *picture start code*. This is followed by a *temporal reference* field which is a time-stamp to enable the decoder to synchronize each video block with an associated audio block containing the same time stamp. The *picture type* field indicates whether the frame is an I- or P-frame. Although the encoding operation is carried out on individual macroblocks, a larger data structure known as a *group of (macro) blocks (GOB)* is also defined. As we show in Figure 4.15(c), this is a matrix of 11×3 macroblocks, the size of which has been chosen so that both the CIF and QCIF comprise an integral number of GOBs – 12 in the case of the CIF (2×6) and 3 in the case of the QCIF (1×3) which allows interworking between the two formats. At the head of each GOB is a unique *start code* which is chosen so that no valid sequence of variable-length codewords from the table of codewords used in the entropy encoding stage can produce the same code. In the event of a transmission error affecting a GOB, the decoder simply searches the received bitstream for this code which signals the start of the next GOB. For this reason the *start code* is also known as a

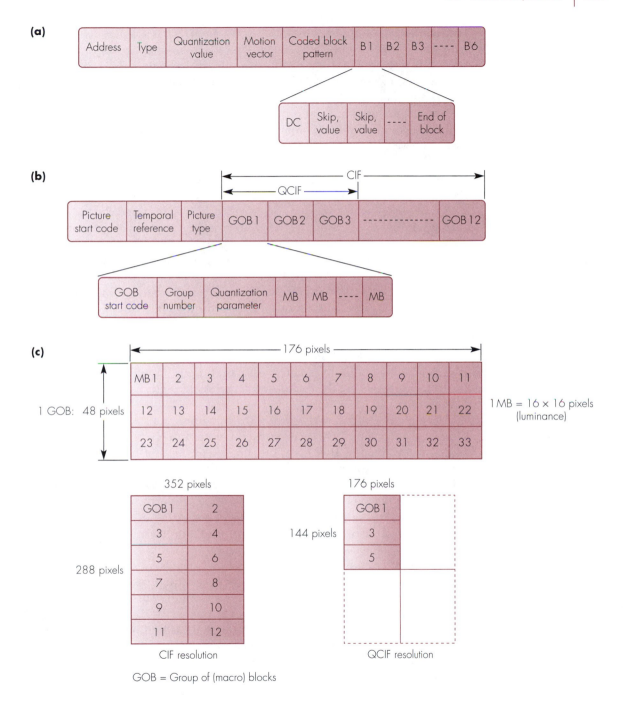

Figure 4.15 H.261 encoding formats: (a) macroblock format; (b) frame/picture format; (c) GOB structure.

resynchronization marker. In addition, each GOB has a *group number* associated with it which allows for a string of GOBs to be missing from a particular frame. This may be necessary, for example, if the amount of (compressed) information to be transmitted is temporarily greater than the bandwidth of the transmission channel.

As we indicated at the end of our earlier discussion on motion estimation, the amount of information produced during the compression operation varies. However, since the transmission bandwidth that is available with the target applications of the H.261 standard is fixed – 64 kbps or multiples of this – in order to optimize the use of this bandwidth, it is necessary to convert the variable bit rate produced by the basic encoder into a constant bit rate. This is achieved by first passing the encoded bitstream output by the encoder through a **first-in, first-out (FIFO) buffer** prior to it being transmitted and then providing a feedback path from this to the quantizer unit within the encoder. The general scheme is shown in Figure 4.16(a) and the role of the FIFO buffer is shown in Figure 4.16(b).

As you may recall from our earlier discussion of the JPEG standard in Section 3.4.5, the output bit rate produced by the encoder is determined by the quantization threshold values that are used; the higher the threshold, the lower the accuracy and hence the lower is the output bit rate. Hence, since the same compression technique is used for macroblocks in video encoders, it is possible to obtain a constant output bit rate from the encoder by dynamically varying the quantization threshold used. This is the role of the FIFO buffer.

As the name implies, the order of the output from a FIFO buffer is the same as that on input. However, since the output rate from the buffer is constant – determined by the (constant) bit rate of the transmission channel – if the input rate temporarily exceeds the output rate then the buffer will start to fill. Conversely, if the input rate falls below the output rate then the buffer contents will decrease. In order to exploit this property, two threshold levels are defined: the *low threshold* and the *high threshold*. The amount of information in the buffer is continuously monitored and, should the contents fall below the *low threshold*, then the quantization threshold is reduced – thereby increasing the output rate from the encoder. Conversely, should the contents increase beyond the *high threshold*, then the quantization threshold is increased in order to reduce the output rate from the encoder.

Normally, the control procedure operates at the GOB level rather than at the macroblock level. Hence, should the high threshold be reached, first the quantization value associated with the GOB is increased and, if this is not sufficient, GOBs are dropped until the overload subsides. Of course, any adjustments to the quantization threshold values that are made must be made also to those used in the matching dequantizer. In addition, the standard also allows complete frames to be missing in order to match the frame rate to the level of transmission bandwidth that is available.

(a)

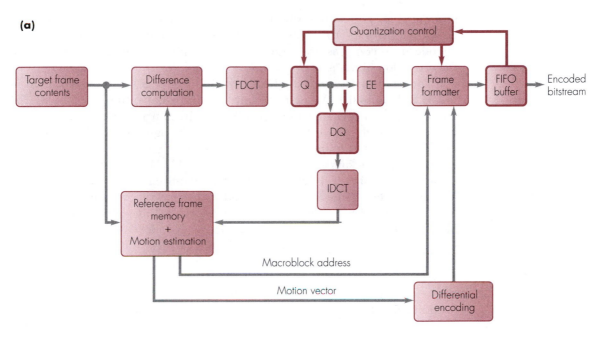

Macroblock address

Motion vector

(b)

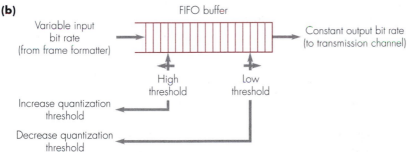

Figure 4.16 H.261 video encoder principles: (a) implementation schematic; (b) FIFO buffer operation.

4.3.3 H.263

The H.263 video compression standard has been defined by the ITU-T for use in a range of video applications over wireless and public switched telephone networks (PSTNs). The applications include video telephony, videoconferencing, security surveillance, interactive games playing, and so on, all of which require the output of the video encoder to be transmitted across the network connection in real time as it is output by the encoder. As we described in Section 1.3.1, the access circuit to the PSTN operates in an analog mode and to transmit a digital signal over these circuits, requires a modem. Typical maximum bit rates over switched connections range from 28.8 kbps through to 56 kbps and hence the requirement of the video encoder is to compress the video associated with these applications down to these very low bit rates.

The basic structure of the H.263 video encoder is based on that used in the H.261 standard. At bit rates lower than 64 kbps, however, the H.261 encoder gives a relatively poor picture quality. Since it uses only I- and P-frames, at low bit rates it has to revert to using a high quantization threshold and a relatively low frame rate. The high quantization threshold leads to what are known as **blocking artifacts** which are caused by the macroblocks encoded using high thresholds differing from those quantized using lower thresholds. The use of a low frame rate can also lead to very jerky movements. In order to minimize these effects, the H.263 standard has a number of advanced coding options compared with those used in an H.261 encoder. We shall limit our discussion of H.263 to an overview of a collection of these options.

Digitization formats

We described the various digitization formats associated with digital video in Section 2.6.2. In the case of the H.263 standard, the two mandatory formats are the QCIF and the sub-QCIF (S-QCIF). As with H.261, however, because each frame is divided into macroblocks of 16×16 pixels for compression, the horizontal resolution is reduced from 180 to 176 pixels to produce an integral number of (11) macroblocks. Hence, since subsampling of the two chrominance signals is used, the two alternative spatial resolutions are:

$$QCIF: \quad Y = 176 \times 144, \quad C_b = C_r = 88 \times 72$$
$$S\text{-}QCIF: \quad Y = 128 \times 96, \quad C_b = C_r = 64 \times 68$$

Progressive scanning is used with a frame refresh rate of either 15 or 7.5 fps.

In practice, the support of both formats is mandatory only for the decoder, and the encoder need support only one of them. As you may recall from Section 4.3.1, the motion estimation unit is not required in the decoder and hence is less expensive to implement than the encoder. The additional cost of having two alternative decoders is, therefore only small. However, by having a choice for the encoder, this means that either a simple – and hence low-cost – encoder design based on the S-QCIF can be used for applications such as games playing, or a more sophisticated design based on the QCIF can be used for applications such as videoconferencing. The decoder can be the same in both cases as it supports both formats.

Frame types

In order to obtain the higher levels of compression that are needed, the H.263 standard uses I-, P-, and B-frames. Also, in order to use as high a frame rate as possible, optionally, neighboring pairs of P- and B-frames can be encoded as a single entity. As we described in Section 4.3.1, the resulting encoded frame is known as a PB-frame and, because of the much reduced encoding overheads that are required, its use enables a higher frame rate to be used with a given transmission channel.

As we showed earlier in Figure 4.11(c), a PB-frame comprises a B-frame and the immediately succeeding P-frame. The encoded information for the corresponding macroblock in both these frames is interleaved, with the information for the P-frame preceding that of the B-frame. Hence at the decoder, as the encoded information is received, the macroblock for the P-frame is reconstructed first using the received information relating to the P-macroblock and the retained contents of the preceding P-frame. The contents of the reconstructed P-macroblock are then used, together with the received encoded information relating to the macroblock in the corresponding B-frame and the retained contents of the preceding P-frame, to bidirectionally predict the decoded contents of the B-macroblock. Then, when the decoding of both frames is complete, the B-frame is decoded first followed by the P-frame.

Unrestricted motion vectors

As we showed earlier in Figures 4.12 and 4.13, the motion vectors associated with predicted macroblocks are normally restricted to a defined area in the reference frame around the location in the target frame of the macroblock being encoded. In addition, the search area is restricted to the edge of the frame. This means that should a small portion of a potential close-match macroblock fall outside of the frame boundary, then the target macroblock is automatically encoded as for an I-frame. This occurs even though the portion of the macroblock within the frame area is a close match.

To overcome this limitation, in the unrestricted motion vector mode, for those pixels of a potential close-match macroblock that fall outside of the frame boundary, the edge pixels themselves are used instead and, should the resulting macroblock produce a close match, then the motion vector, if necessary, is allowed to point outside of the frame area. In practice, with the small digitized frame formats that are used with the H.263 standard, this has been found to give a significant improvement in the level of compression obtained.

Error resilience

As we indicated earlier, the target network for the H.263 standard is a wireless network or a PSTN. With this type of network there is a relatively high probability that transmission (bit) errors will be present in the bitstream received by the decoder. Normally, such errors are characterized by periods when a string of error-free frames is received followed by a short burst of errors which, typically, corrupt a string of macroblocks within a frame. In practice, it is not possible to identify the specific macroblocks that are corrupted but rather that the related group of (macro)blocks (GOB) contains one or more macroblocks that are in error. Also, as we can deduce from the frame sequences we showed earlier in Figure 4.11, because the contents of many frames are predicted from information in other frames, it is highly probable that the same GOB in each of the following frames that are derived from the GOB in error will contain errors. This means that when an error in a GOB occurs, the error will persist for a number of frames, hence making the error more apparent to the viewers.

As we explained in Section 4.3.2, when an error in a GOB is detected, the decoder skips the remaining macroblocks in the affected GOB and searches for the unique resynchronization marker (start code) at the head of the next GOB. It then recommences decoding from the start of this GOB. In order to mask the error from the viewer, an **error concealment scheme** is incorporated into the decoder. For example, a common approach is to use the contents of the corresponding GOB from the preceding (decoded) frame.

In addition, since a PSTN provides only a relatively low bit rate transmission channel, to conserve bandwidth, intracoded (I) frames are inserted at relatively infrequent intervals. Hence in applications such as video telephony in which the video and audio are being transmitted in real time, the lack of I-frames has the effect that errors within a GOB may propagate to other regions of the frame due to the resulting errors in the motion estimation vectors and motion compensation information. With digitization formats such as the QCIF (which has only three GOBs per frame) the resulting effect can be very annoying to the viewer. A typical effect is shown in diagrammatic form in Figure 4.17(a) and, as we can see, although the initial error occurs in one GOB position, it rapidly spreads to other neighbouring GOBs. It is for this reason that schemes are included in the standard that aim at minimizing the effects of errors on neighbouring GOBs. The schemes include **error tracking**, **independent segment decoding**, and **reference picture selection**. We shall discuss the principle of operation of each of these schemes separately.

Error tracking With real-time applications such as video telephony, a two-way communications channel is required for the exchange of the compressed audio and video information generated by the codec in each terminal. This means that there is always a return channel from the receiving terminal back to the sending terminal and this is used in all three schemes by the decoder in order to inform the related encoder that an error in a GOB has been detected. Typically, errors are detected in a number of ways including:

- one or more out-of-range motion vectors,
- one or more invalid variable-length codewords,
- one or more out-of-range DCT coefficients,
- an excessive number of coefficients within a macroblock.

In the error tracking scheme, the encoder retains what is known as error prediction information for all the GOBs in each of the most recently transmitted frames; that is, the likely spatial and temporal effects on the macroblocks in

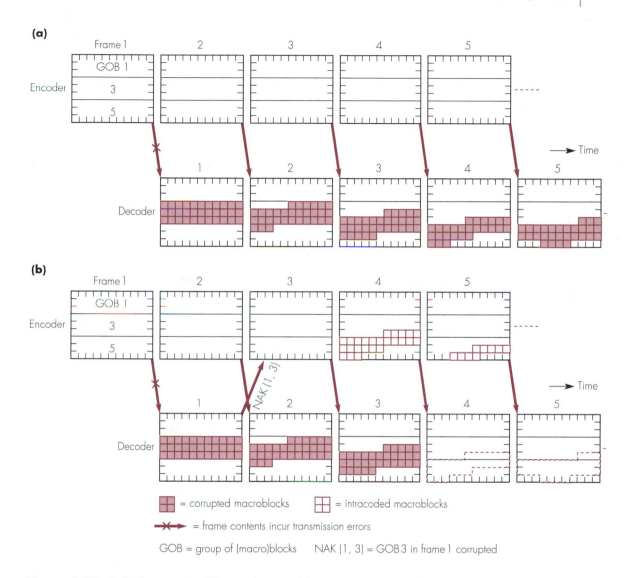

Figure 4.17 H.263 error tracking scheme: (a) example error propagation; (b) same example with error tracking applied.

the following frames that will result if a specific GOB in a frame is corrupted. When an error is detected, the return channel is used by the decoder to send a negative acknowledgment (NAK) message back to the encoder in the source codec containing both the frame number and the location of the GOB in the frame that is in error. The encoder then uses the error prediction information relating to this GOB to identify the macroblocks in those GOBs in later frames that are likely to be affected. It then proceeds to transmit the macroblocks in these frames in their intracoded form. The principle of the scheme is shown in Figure 4.17(b).

The example frame sequence shows in diagrammatic form how the corrupted macroblocks shown in part(a) of the figure are predicted and, for each affected frame, the predicted macroblocks are sent in their intracoded form. Hence in the example, on receipt of NAK(1,3), it is assumed that the encoder has predicted and retained error prediction information relating to frame 1. Since the next frame to be encoded is frame 4, the affected macroblocks are intracoded rather than predicted. Similarly for the affected macroblocks in frame 5.

Independent segment decoding The aim of this scheme is not to overcome errors that occur within a GOB but rather to prevent these errors from affecting neighboring GOBs in succeeding frames. To achieve this, each GOB is treated as a separate subvideo which is independent of the other GOBs in the frame. This means, therefore, that motion estimation and compensation is limited to the boundary pixels of a GOB rather than a frame. The operation of the scheme is shown in parts (a) and (b) of Figure 4.18.

As we can see from part (a), although when an error in a GOB occurs the same GOB in each successive frame is affected – until a new intracoded GOB is sent by the encoder – neighbouring GOBs are not affected. Clearly, however, a limitation of this scheme is that the efficiency of the motion estimation and compensation in the vertical direction is reduced significantly owing to the search area being limited to a single GOB. Thus, the scheme is not normally used on its own but in conjunction with either the error tracking scheme – as we show in Figure 4.18(b) – or, more usually, with the reference picture selection scheme described below.

Reference picture selection This scheme is similar to the error tracking scheme inasmuch as it endeavors to stop errors propagating by the decoder returning acknowledgment messages when an error in a GOB is detected. The scheme can be operated in two different modes as we show in parts(a) and (b) of Figure 4.19.

The mode of operation we show in part (a) is known as the *NAK mode* and, in this mode, only GOBs in error are signaled by the decoder returning a NAK message. As we showed earlier in Figure 4.11, normally intercoded (P or B) frames are encoded using an intracoded (I) frame as the initial reference frame. However, as we showed in Figure 4.14, during the encoding of intercoded frames a copy of the (decoded) preceding frame is retained by the encoder. With this scheme, therefore, the encoder can select any of these previously decoded frames as the reference. Hence in the example shown in Figure 4.19(a), when the NAK relating to frame 2 is received, the encoder selects (the decoded) GOB 3 of frame 1 as the reference to encode GOB 3 of the next frame – frame 5 in this example.

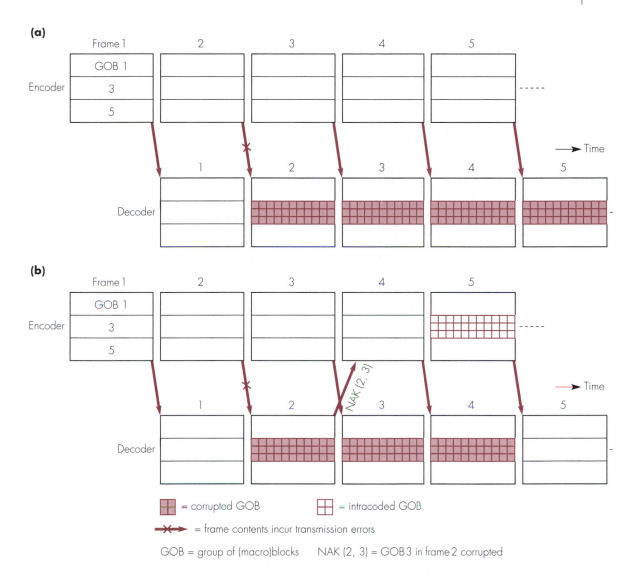

= corrupted GOB   = intracoded GOB

= frame contents incur transmission errors

GOB = group of (macro)blocks   NAK (2, 3) = GOB 3 in frame 2 corrupted

Figure 4.18 Independent segment decoding: (a) effect of a GOB being corrupted; (b) when used with error tracking.

As we can see in the figure, with this scheme the GOB in error will propagate for a number of frames, the number being determined by the round-trip delay of the communications channel; that is, the time delay between the NAK being sent by the decoder and an intercoded frame derived from the initial I-frame being received.

The alternative mode of operation is known as the *ACK mode* since, as we show in Figure 4.19(b), with this mode all frames received without errors are

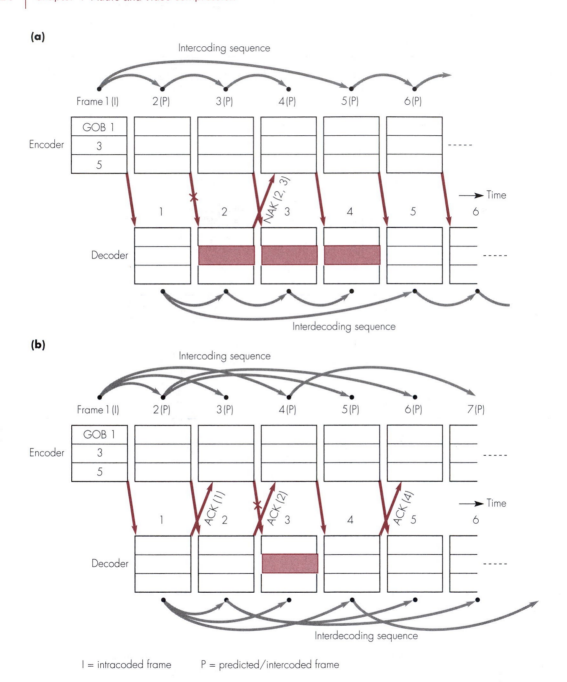

I = intracoded frame   P = predicted/intercoded frame

Figure 4.19 Reference picture selection with independent segment decoding: (a) NAK mode; (b) ACK mode.

acknowledged by the decoder returning an ACK message. Only frames that have been acknowledged are used as reference frames. Hence, in the example, the lack of an ACK for frame 3 means that frame 2 must be used to encode frame 6 in addition to frame 5. At this point the ACK for frame 4 is received and hence the encoder then uses this to encode frame 7. The effect of using a reference frame which is distant (in time) from the frame being encoded is to reduce the encoding efficiency for the frame. Thus the ACK mode performs best when the round-trip delay of the communications channel is short and, ideally, less than the time the encoder takes to encode each frame.

4.3.4 MPEG

The **Motion Pictures Expert Group** (**MPEG**) was formed by the ISO to formulate a set of standards relating to a range of multimedia applications that involve the use of video with sound. The outcome is a set of three standards which relate to either the recording or the transmission of integrated audio and video streams. Each is targeted at a particular application domain and describes how the audio and video are compressed and integrated together. The three standards, which use different video resolutions, are:

■ **MPEG-1:** This is defined in a series of documents which are all subsets of **ISO Recommendation 11172**. The video resolution is based on the source intermediate digitization format (SIF) with a resolution of up to 352×288 pixels. The standard is intended for the storage of VHS-quality audio and video on CD-ROM at bit rates up to 1.5 Mbps. Normally, however, higher bit rates of multiples of this are more common in order to provide faster access to the stored material.

■ **MPEG-2:** This is defined in a series of documents which are all subsets of **ISO Recommendation 13818**. It is intended for the recording and transmission of studio-quality audio and video. The standard covers four levels of video resolution:
– Low: based on the SIF digitization format with a resolution of up to 352×288 pixels. It is compatible with the MPEG-1 standard and produces VHS-quality video. The audio is of CD quality and the target bit rate is up to 4 Mbps;
– Main: based on the 4:2:0 digitization format with a resolution of up to 720×576 pixels. This produces studio-quality digital video and the audio allows for multiple CD-quality audio channels. The target bit rate is up to 15 Mbps or 20 Mbps with the 4:2:2 digitization format;
– High 1440: based on the 4:2:0 digitization format with a resolution of 1440×1152 pixels. It is intended for high-definition television (HDTV) at bit rates up to 60 Mbps or 80 Mbps with the 4:2:2 format.
– High: based on the 4:2:0 digitization format with a resolution of 1920×1152 pixels. It is intended for wide-screen HDTV at a bit rate of up to 80 Mbps or 100 Mbps with the 4:2:2 format.

■ **MPEG-4:** Initially, this standard was concerned with a similar range of applications to those of H.263, each running over very low bit rate channels ranging from 4.8 to 64 kbps. Later its scope was expanded to embrace a wide range of interactive multimedia applications over the Internet and the various types of entertainment networks.

Unlike these three standards which are concerned with the compression of the multimedia information associated with an application, the **MPEG-7** standard is concerned with describing the structure and features of the content of the (compressed) multimedia information produced by the different standards. The resulting descriptions are then used in **search engines** to locate particular items of material that have a defined feature.

The MPEG-3 standard was to be focussed on HDTV but was not developed separately as the work was subsequently incorporated into MPEG-2. Hence we shall restrict our discussion to MPEG-1, the main and high levels of MPEG-2, and selected features of the MPEG-4 standard. MPEG-7 is outside of the scope of the book.

The first three MPEG standards are in three parts: video, audio, and system. The video and audio parts are concerned with the way each is compressed and how the resulting bitstreams are formatted. The system part is concerned with how the two streams are integrated together to produce a synchronized output stream. We shall discuss just the video compression part of the MPEG-1/2 standards in this chapter and the system parts in the next chapter.

4.3.5 MPEG-1

The MPEG-1 (and MPEG-2) video standard uses a similar video compression technique as H.261. As indicated, the digitization format used with MPEG-1 is the source intermediate format (SIF) which we described in Section 2.6.2. However, as with the H.261 standard, because each frame is divided into macroblocks of 16×16 pixels for compression, the horizontal resolution is reduced from 360 to 352 pixels to produce an integral number of (22) macroblocks. Hence, since the two chrominance signals are subsampled at half the rate of the luminance signal, the spatial resolutions for the two types of video source are:

NTSC: $Y = 352 \times 240$, $C_b = C_r = 176 \times 120$
PAL: $Y = 352 \times 288$, $C_b = C_r = 176 \times 144$

Also, since the application domain of MPEG-1 is for the storage of video (with audio), progressive scanning is used with a refresh rate of 30 Hz (for NTSC) and 25 Hz (for PAL).

The standard allows the use of I-frames only, I- and P-frames only, or I-, P- and B-frames, the latter being the most common. No D-frames are supported in any of the MPEG standards and hence, in the case of MPEG-1, I-frames must be used for the various random-access functions associated with VCRs. The accepted maximum random-access time is 0.5 seconds and so this is the main factor – along with video quality – that influences the maximum separation of I-frames in the frame sequence used. Two example sequences are:

IBBPBBPBBI...   and   IBBPBBPBBPBBI...

the first being the original sequence proposed for use with PAL (which has a slower frame refresh rate) and the second for use with NTSC. The second standard is now used with both systems and is illustrated in Figure 4.20.

Example 4.1

An MPEG-1 system uses the frame sequence shown in Figure 4.20.

(i) Define the terms M and N and hence determine their values for the sequence shown in the figure.

(ii) Derive a suitable reordered sequence that ensures firstly, only two frames must be stored in the decoder, and secondly, the required I- and/or P-frames are available to decode each P- and B-frame as they are received.

Answer:

(i) As we described earlier in Section 4.3.1 under the subheading of "Frame types", M is the distance (in frames) between a P-frame and the immediately preceding I- or P- frame, and N is the number of frames between two successive I-frames. The latter is known as a group of pictures or GOP. Hence for the frame sequence shown in Figure 4.20, $M = 3$ and $N = 12$.

(ii) A suitable reordered frame sequence that meets the defined requirements is:

IPBBPBBPBBIBBPBB ...

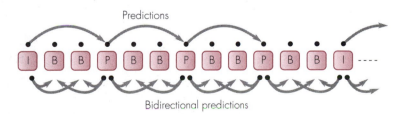

Predictions

Bidirectional predictions

Figure 4.20 MPEG-1 example frame sequence.

The compression algorithm used in MPEG-1 is based on the H.261 standard. Hence each macroblock is made up of 16×16 pixels in the Y plane and 8×8 pixels in the C_b and C_r planes. However, there are two main differences. The first is that time-stamps (temporal references) can be inserted within a frame to enable the decoder to resynchronize more quickly in the event of one or more corrupted or missing macroblocks. The number of macroblocks between two time-stamps is known as a *slice* and a slice can comprise from 1 through to the maximum number of macroblocks in a frame. Typically, a slice is made equal to 22 which is the number of macroblocks in a line.

The second difference arises because of the introduction of B-frames which increases the time interval between I and P frames. To allow for the resulting increase in the separation of moving objects with P-frames, the search window in the reference frame is increased. Also, to improve the accuracy of the motion vectors, a finer resolution is used. Typical compression ratios vary from about 10:1 for I-frames, 20:1 for P-frames and 50:1 for B-frames.

As with the H.261 standard, the compressed bitstream produced by the video encoder is hierarchical and is shown in Figure 4.21(a). At the top level, the complete compressed video is known as a **sequence** which, in turn, con-

---

Example 4.2

A digitized video is to be compressed using the MPEG-1 standard. Assuming a frame sequence of:

> IBBPBBPBBPBBI...

and average compression ratios of 10:1 (I), 20:1 (P) and 50:1 (B), derive the average bit rate that is generated by the encoder for both the NTSC and PAL digitization formats.

Answer:

> Frame sequence = IBBPBBPBBPBBI...
>
> Hence: 1/12 of frames are I-frames, 3/12 are P-frames, and 8/12 are B-frames.

and   Average compression ratio $= (1 \times 0.1 + 3 \times 0.05 + 8 \times 0.02)/12$

$$= 0.0342 \text{ or } 29.24{:}1$$

NTSC frame size:

> Without compression $= 352 \times 240 \times 8 + 2\,(176 \times 120 \times 8)$
>
> $\qquad\qquad\qquad = 1.013760 \text{ Mbits per frame}$
>
> With compression $= 1.01376 \times 1/29.24$
>
> $\qquad\qquad\qquad = 34.670 \text{ kbits per frame}$

Hence bit rate generated at 30 fps = 1.040 Mbps

4.2 Continued

PAL frame size:

$$\text{Without compression} = 352 \times 288 \times 8 + 2\,(176 \times 144 \times 8)$$
$$= 1.216512\,\text{Mbits per frame}$$

$$\text{With compression} \quad = 1.216512 \times 1/29.24$$
$$= 41.604\,\text{kbits per frame}$$

Hence bit rate generated at 25 fps = 1.040 Mbps

Normally, allowing for packetization and multiplexing overheads, a bandwidth of 1.2 Mbps is allocated for the video. Hence, assuming a maximum bit rate of 1.5 Mbps, this leaves 300 kbps for the compressed audio stream.

sists of a string of **groups of pictures** (**GOPs**) each comprising a string of I, P or B pictures/frames in the defined sequence. Each picture/frame is made up of **N slices**, each of which comprises multiple macroblocks, and so on down to an 8×8 pixel block. Hence in order for the decoder to decompress the received bitstream, each data structure must be clearly identified within the bitstream. The format of the bitstream is shown in Figure 4.21(b).

The start of a sequence is indicated by a *sequence start code*. This is followed by three parameters, each of which applies to the complete video sequence. The *video parameters* specify the screen size and aspect ratio, the *bitstream parameters* indicate the bit rate and the size of the memory/frame buffers that are required, and the *quantization parameters* contain the contents of the quantization tables that are to be used for the various frame/picture types. These are followed by the encoded video stream which, as we can see, is in the form of a string of GOPs.

Each GOP (IBBP...) is separated by a *(GOP) start code* which is followed by a *time-stamp* for synchronization purposes and a *parameters* field which defines the particular sequence of frame types that are used in each GOP. This is then followed by the string of encoded pictures/frames in each GOP. Each is separated by a *picture start code* and is followed by a *type* field (I, P or B), *buffer parameters*, which indicate how full the memory buffer should be before the decoding operation should start, and *encode parameters* which indicate the resolution used for the motion vectors. This is followed by a string of slices, each comprising a string of macroblocks. Each slice is separated by a *slice start code* which is followed by a *vertical position* field, which defines the scan line the slice relates to, and a *quantization parameter* that indicates the scaling factor that applies to this slice. This is then followed by a string of macroblocks each of which is encoded in the same way as for H.261, the basic principles of which we described earlier in Section 4.3.1. As we can deduce from this, a slice is similar to the GOB used in the H.261 standard.

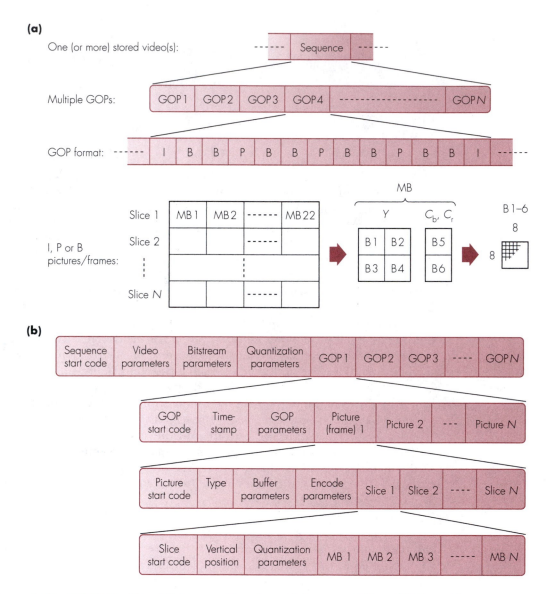

(a)

One (or more) stored video(s):

Sequence

Multiple GOPs:

GOP 1 | GOP 2 | GOP 3 | GOP 4 | ------------------- | GOP N

GOP format: | I | B | B | P | B | B | P | B | B | P | B | B | I

I, P or B pictures/frames:

MB

Slice 1 | MB 1 | MB 2 | ------ | MB 22

Y | Cb, Cr

B1 | B2 | B5
B3 | B4 | B6

B 1–6

(b)

Sequence start code | Video parameters | Bitstream parameters | Quantization parameters | GOP 1 | GOP 2 | GOP 3 | ---- | GOP N

GOP start code | Time-stamp | GOP parameters | Picture (frame) 1 | Picture 2 | --- | Picture N

Picture start code | Type | Buffer parameters | Encode parameters | Slice 1 | Slice 2 | ---- | Slice N

Slice start code | Vertical position | Quantization parameters | MB 1 | MB 2 | MB 3 | ----- | MB N

Figure 4.21 MPEG-1 video bitstream structure: (a) composition; (b) format.

4.3.6 MPEG-2

As we indicated in Section 4.3.4, MPEG-2 supports four levels – low, main, high 1440 and high – each targeted at a particular application domain. In addition, there are five **profiles** associated with each level: simple, main, spatial resolution, quantization accuracy, and high. These have been defined so that the four levels and five profiles collectively form a two-dimensional table which acts as a framework for all standards activities associated with MPEG-2. In this way the development of both the existing standards and any new standards can take place relative to one another. For example, at a particular level, the decoders used with a given profile will be able to decode all the lower profiles that have been defined for that level, hence making interworking between older and newer equipments possible. As indicated earlier, since the low level of MPEG-2 is compatible with MPEG-1, we shall restrict our discussion of MPEG-2 to the **main profile at the main level** (**MP@ML**) and the two high levels relating to HDTV.

MP@ML

The target application of the MP@ML standard is for digital television broadcasting. Hence interlaced scanning is used – which we described in Section 2.6.1 – with a resulting frame refresh rate of either 30 Hz (NTSC) or 25 Hz (PAL). The 4:2:0 digitization format is used with a resolution of either 720×480 pixels at 30 Hz or 720×576 pixels at 25 Hz. The output bit rate from the system multiplexer can range from 4 Mbps through to 15 Mbps, the actual rate used being determined by the bandwidth available with the broadcast channel.

The video coding scheme is similar to that used in MPEG-1 the main difference resulting from the use of interlaced – instead of progressive – scanning. The use of interlaced scanning means that each frame is made up of two (interlaced) fields and, as we show in Figure 4.22(a), alternative lines are present in each field. Hence for I-frames, the question arises as to how the DCT blocks are derived from each macroblock. As we show in parts (b) and (c) of the figure, two alternatives are possible depending on whether the DCT blocks are derived from the lines in a field – **field mode** – or the lines in a frame – **frame mode**.

As described in Section 2.6.1, for a frame refresh rate – temporal resolution – of 30/25 Hz, the corresponding field refresh rate is 60/50 Hz. The choice of field or frame mode is thus determined by the amount of motion present in the video. If a large amount of motion is present, then it is better to perform the DCT encoding operation on the lines in a field – part (b) – since this will produce a higher compression ratio owing to the shorter time interval between successive fields. Alternatively, if there is little movement, the frame mode can be used since the longer time interval between successive (complete) frames is less important. Hence in this case, the macroblocks/DCT blocks are derived from the lines in each complete frame – part (c). In fact, the standard allows either mode to be used, the choice being determined by the type of video; for example, a live sporting event is likely to be encoded using the field mode and a studio-based program the frame mode.

In relation to the motion estimation associated with the encoding of macroblocks in P- and B-frames, three different modes are possible: field, frame, and mixed. In the field mode, the motion vector for each macroblock

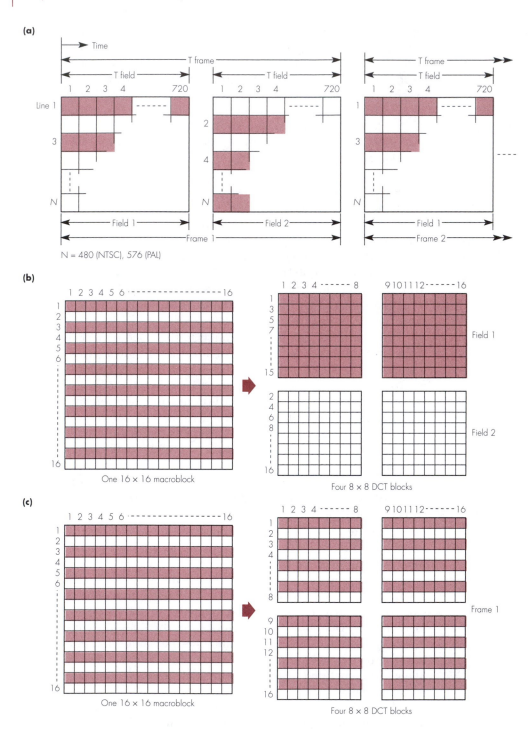

Figure 4.22 MPEG-2 DCT block derivation with I-frames: (a) effect of interlaced scanning; (b) field mode; (c) frame mode.

is computed using the search window around the corresponding macroblock in the immediately preceding (I or P) field for both P- and B-frames and, for B-frames, the immediately succeeding (P or I) field. The motion vectors, therefore, relate to the amount of movement that has taken place in the time to scan one field. In the frame mode, a macroblock in an odd field is encoded relative to that in the preceding/succeeding odd field(s) and similarly for the macroblocks in even fields. In this case, therefore, the motion vectors relate to the amount of movement that has taken place in the time to scan two fields; that is, the time to scan a complete frame. In the mixed mode, the motion vectors for both field and frame modes are computed and the one with the smallest (mean) values is selected.

HDTV

There are three standards associated with HDTV: **advanced television** (**ATV**) in North America, **digital video broadcast** (**DVB**) in Europe, and **multiple sub-Nyquist sampling encoding** (**MUSE**) in Japan and the rest of Asia. All three standards, in addition to defining the digitization format and audio and video compression schemes used, also define how the resulting digital bitstreams are transmitted over the different types of broadcast network.

In addition to these standards, as with normal digital television, there is an **ITU-R HDTV specification** concerned with the standards used in television studios for the production of HDTV programs and also for the international exchange of programs. This defines a 16/9 aspect ratio with 1920 samples per line and 1152 (1080 visible) lines per frame. Currently, interlaced scanning is used with the 4:2:0 digitization format. In the future, however, it is expected that progressive scanning will be introduced with the 4:2:2 format.

The ATV standard, which was formulated by an alliance of a large number of television manufacturers, is also known as the **Grand Alliance** (or simply **GA**) **standard**. It includes the ITU-R HDTV specification and a second, lower-resolution format. This also uses a 16/9 aspect ratio but with a resolution of 1280×720. The video compression algorithm in both cases is based on the main profile at the high level (MP@HL) of MPEG-2 and the audio compression standard is based on Dolby AC-3.

The DVB HDTV standard is based on the 4/3 aspect ratio and defines a resolution of 1440 samples per line and 1152 (1080 visible) lines per frame. As we can see, this is exactly twice the resolution of the low-definition PAL digitization format of 720×576. The video compression algorithm is based on what is known as the **SSP@H1440 – spatially-scaleable profile at high 1440** – of MPEG-2 which is very similar to that used with MP@HL. The audio compression standard is MPEG Audio layer 2.

The MUSE standard is based on a 16/9 aspect ratio with a digitization format of 1920 samples per line and 1035 lines per frame. The video compression algorithm is similar to that used in MP@HL.

4.3.7 MPEG-4

The main application domain of the MPEG-4 standard is in relation to the audio and video associated with interactive multimedia applications over the Internet and the various types of entertainment networks. The standard contains features to enable a user not only to passively access a video sequence (or complete video) – using, for example, start/stop/pause commands – but also to access and manipulate the individual elements that make up each scene within the sequence/video. If the accessed video is a computer-generated cartoon, for example, the user may be given the capability – by the creator of the video – to reposition, delete, or alter the movement of the individual characters within a scene. In addition, because of its high coding efficiency with scenes such as those associated with video telephony, the standard is also used for this type of application running over low bit rate networks such as wireless and PSTNs. For such applications, therefore, it is an alternative to the H.263 standard.

Scene composition

The main difference between MPEG-4 and the other standards we have considered is that MPEG-4 has a number of what are called **content-based functionalities**. Before being compressed each scene is defined in the form of a background and one or more foreground **audio-visual objects** (**AVOs**). Each AVO is in turn defined in the form of one or more **video objects** and/or **audio objects**; for example, a stationary car in a scene may be defined using just a single video object while a person who is talking may be defined using both an audio and a video object. In a similar way, each video and audio object may itself be defined as being made up of a number of subobjects. For example, if a person's eyes and mouth are the only things that move, in order to exploit this, the person's face may be defined in the form of three subobjects: one for the head and the other two for the eyes and mouth. Once this has been done, the encoding of the background and each AVO is carried out separately and, in the case of AVOs consisting of both audio and video objects, each has additional timing information relating to it to enable the receiver to synchronize the various objects and subobjects together before they are decoded.

Each audio and video object has a separate **object descriptor** associated with it which allows the object – providing the creator of the audio and/or video has provided the facility – to be manipulated by the viewer prior to it being decoded and played out. The language used to describe and modify objects is called the **binary format for scenes** (**BIFS**). This has commands to delete an object and, in the case of a video object, change its shape, appearance – color for example – and, if appropriate, animate the object in real time. Audio objects have a similar set of commands, to change its volume for example. It is also possible to have multiple versions of an AVO, the first containing the base-level compressed audio and video streams and the others various levels of enhancement detail. This type of compression is called scaling and allows the encoded contents of an AVO to be played out at a rate and resolution that matches those of the interactive terminal being used.

At a higher level, the composition of a scene in terms of the AVOs it contains is defined in a separate **scene descriptor**. This defines the way the various AVOs are related to each other in the context of the complete scene; for example, the position of each AVO on the display screen and the composition of each AVO in terms of the objects and subobjects it comprises.

A simple example illustrating how a frame/scene is defined in the form of a number of AVOs using content-based image coding is shown in Figure 4.23. As we can see, each video frame is segmented into a number of **video object planes** (**VOPs**) each of which corresponds to an AVO of interest. Hence in our simple example, the frame is shown as consisting of three VOPs: VOP 0 to represent the person approaching the car, VOP 1 the remainder of the car parked outside the house, and VOP 2 the remainder of the background. Each VOP is encoded separately based on its shape, motion, and texture.

As we show in the figure, each VOP is encapsulated within a rectangle which, in practice, is chosen so that it completely covers the related AVO using the minimum number of macroblocks. The spatial coordinates of the VOP are then relative to the coordinates of the top-left macroblock. The motion and texture of each VOP are encoded using a procedure similar, for example, to one of those we described earlier in the chapter. The resulting

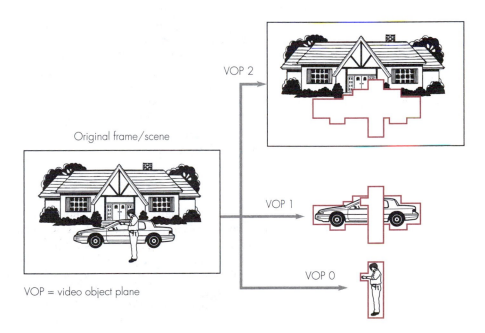

Figure 4.23 Content-based video coding principles showing how a frame/scene is defined in the form of multiple video object planes.

bitstreams are then multiplexed together for transmission together with the related object and scene descriptor information. Similarly, at the receiver, the received bitstream is first demultiplexed and the individual streams decoded. The decompressed information, together with the object and scene descriptions, are then used to create the video frame that is played out on the terminal. Typically, the latter is a multimedia PC or TV set and the audio relating to each scene is played out in time synchronism with the video.

Audio and video compression

The audio associated with an AVO is compressed using one of the algorithms we described earlier in the chapter and depends on the available bit rate of the transmission channel and the sound quality required. Examples range from G.723.1 (CELP) for interactive multimedia applications over the Internet and video telephony over wireless networks and PSTNs, through to Dolby AC-3 or MPEG Layer 2 for interactive TV applications over entertainment networks.

An overview of the structure of the encoder associated with the audio and video of a frame/scene is shown in part (a) of Figure 4.24 and the essential features of each VOP encoder are shown in part (b). As we can see, first each VOP is identified and defined and is then encoded separately. In practice, the segmentation of a video frame into various objects – from which each VOP is derived – is a difficult image-processing task. In principle, it involves identifying regions of a frame that have similar properties such as color, texture, or brightness. Each of the resulting object shapes is then bounded by a rectangle (which contains the minimum number of macroblocks) to form the related VOP. Each is then encoded based on its shape, motion, and texture. Thus any VOP which has no motion associated with it will produce a minimum of compressed information. Also, since the VOP(s) which move often occupy only a small portion of the scene/frame, the bit rate of the multiplexed videostream is much lower than that obtained with the other standards. For applications that support interactions with a particular VOP, a number of advanced coding algorithms are available to perform the shape coding function.

Transmission format

As we show in Figure 4.25, all the information relating to a frame/scene encoded in MPEG-4 is transmitted over a network in the form of a **transport stream** (**TS**), consisting of a multiplexed stream of **packetized elementary streams** (**PESs**). As indicated earlier, it is intended that MPEG-4 should be used with applications relating to many different types of network including the Internet, a PSTN, a wireless network, or an entertainment network – cable/satellite/terrestrial. However, as we shall expand upon in Section 5.5.2 in the next chapter, a standard 188-byte packet format has been defined for use in the various types of digital TV broadcast networks. In most cases, the MPEG-4 transport stream uses this same packet format since this helps interworking with the encoded bitstreams associated with the MPEG-1/2 standards.

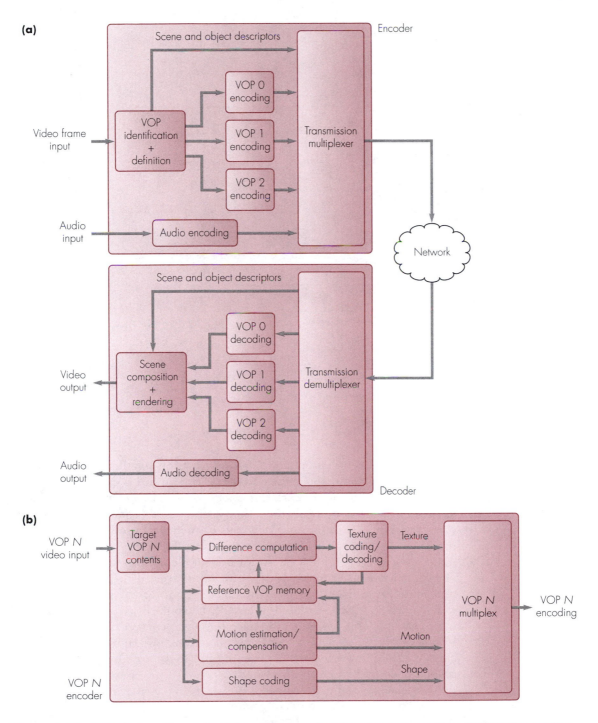

Figure 4.24 MPEG-4 coding principles: (a) encoder/decoder schematics; (b) VOP encoder schematic.

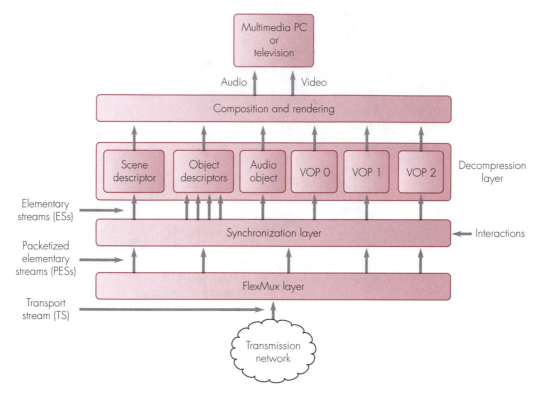

Figure 4.25 MPEG-4 decoder schematic.

The compressed audio and video information relating to each AVO in the scene is called an **elementary stream** (**ES**) and this is carried in the payload field of a PES packet. Each PES packet contains a *type* field in the packet header and this is used by the **FlexMux layer** to identify and route the PES to the related synchronization block in the **synchronization layer**. The compressed audio and video associated with each AVO is carried in a separate ES. Associated with each object descriptor is an **elementary stream descriptor** (**ESD**) which is used by the synchronization layer to route each ES to its related decoder. Each PES also contains timing information in the form of time-stamps and these are used to ensure the compressed information relating to each AVO is passed to the decoder at the correct time instants. The stream of object descriptor blocks and the scene descriptor block are both carried in separate elementary streams and these are also passed to their related decoder blocks in time synchronism with the compression information associated with the individual AVOs.

The output from the decoders associated with each AVO making up a frame, together with the related object scene descriptor information, is then passed to the **composition and rendering block**. As the name implies, the latter takes the decompressed data relating to each AVO and, together with the scene descriptor information, uses this to compose each frame ready for output to the display screen. The audio relating to each frame/scene is then played out in time synchronism with the video.

Error resilience techniques

As with the H.263 standard, a number of techniques are included in the MPEG-4 standard which make the encoding scheme more resilient to transmission errors. As we indicated earlier, these are important with transmission channels such as those associated with wireless networks and PSTNs. They include:

■ the use of fixed-length video packets as the base-level data structure instead of GOBs;

■ a new variable-length coding (VLC) scheme based on reversible VLCs.

We shall discuss the principles of each technique separately.

Video packets As we explained earlier in Sections 4.3.2 and 4.3.3 in the discussions relating to the error resilience techniques used in the H.261 and H.263 standards, resynchronization markers are inserted by the encoder at the start of each GOB to enable the decoder, on detecting an error in a GOB, to locate the end of the affected GOB and the start of the next GOB from where decoding recommences. A similar technique is used in the MPEG-1 and MPEG-2 standards at the slice level. In each case, however, when an error in a GOB/slice occurs, the complete set of macroblocks in the GOB/slice is discarded as there is no way of identifying the specific macroblocks that are corrupted.

In practice, the amount of compressed information in each GOB varies and depends on the level of activity/motion taking place in the related part of the frame. Thus, as we show in Figure 4.26(a), the number of bits in each GOB varies. In the figure, for example, it is assumed that the QCIF format is being used and that most of the activity is occurring in GOB 3 which, therefore, is much longer than the other two GOBs. Should a transmission error in a frame occur, it is highly probable that GOB 3 will be affected. This, of course, is the one we would prefer not to be affected. To overcome this effect, in MPEG-4 the compressed bitstream is divided into groups each comprising, not an equal number of macroblocks, but rather an equal number of bits. The resulting group of (compressed) bits is known as a **video packet** and, as with GOBs, these are separated by resynchronization markers.

The effect of using fixed-length video packets for the transmission of the compressed bitstream shown in Figure 4.26(a) is shown in part(b) of the figure and, as we can see, the effect is to have multiple resynchronization markers in those areas of the frame where most activity is taking place. With

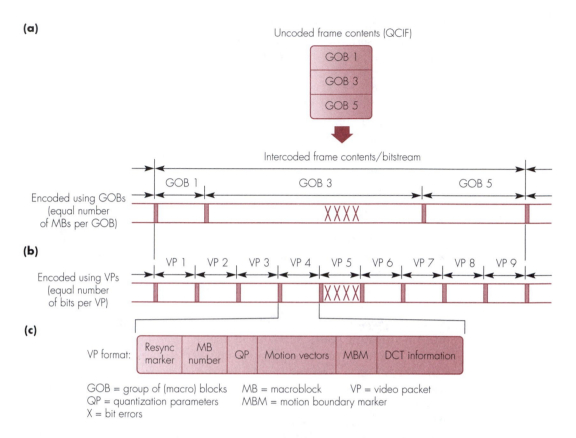

Figure 4.26 MPEG-4 encoding: (a) conventional GOB approach; (b) using fixed-length video packets; (c) video packet format.

this scheme, therefore, when an error occurs, only a reduced set of macroblocks are affected leaving the macroblocks in the remaining packets unaffected. In the standard, the suggested spacing of the resynchronization markers is determined by the link bit rate of the transmission channel; for example, for a bit rate of 24 kbps, the suggested spacing – and hence length of each video packet – is 512 bits.

The format of each video packet is shown in Figure 4.26(c) and, as we can see, it is similar to that of a GOB – which we showed earlier in Figure 4.15 (b) – except that after the resynchronization marker (GOB start code), the GOB number is replaced by the number of the first macroblock – relative to the complete frame – in the packet. In addition, in order to make the contents of each packet independent of the contents of other packets, the motion vectors are limited to the boundaries of the macroblocks that are in the packet.

A further refinement, as we show in the figure, is to separate the motion vectors for each macroblock in the packet from the DCT information. Normally, as we saw earlier in Figure 4.14(d), for each macroblock the encoded motion vector and DCT information are located together. As a result, the motion vectors and DCT information in a GOB are distributed throughout the complete GOB with the effect that, when an error in a GOB occurs, the complete GOB must be discarded. However, by separating these two fields by a unique bit pattern – known as the **motion boundary marker** (**MBM**) – it is then possible to identify separately each set of values and, if only one set is corrupted, the other set can be used.

An additional level of resilience is achieved by (optionally) including in the header of each packet a copy of the picture/frame-level parameters. These include the spatial dimensions of the picture/frame, the type of coding used (intra or inter), and temporal reference information (time-stamps). Clearly, if this is corrupted, then the decoder must discard the total frame contents. Hence by replicating this information in the header of each packet – or a selected number of packets – the decoder can use a voting system to determine if errors in the frame header were present and, if errors are detected, utilize the alternative information from the head of a packet instead. In order to indicate to the decoder that frame-level information is present in the header of a packet, the encoder sets a bit in the header field known as the **header extension code** (**HEC**) **bit**.

Reversible VLCs

As we showed earlier in Figure 4.14 and described in the associated text, after compression, the resulting motion vectors and DCT information are entropy encoded prior to transmission using a table of variable-length codewords (VLCs). When using conventional Huffman VLCs of the type we described in Section 3.4.5, any bit errors that occur will cause the decoder to lose synchronization and, typically, discard the remaining codewords until it finds the next motion boundary or resynchronization marker. In order to minimize this effect, MPEG-4 uses what are known as **reversible VLCs** (**RVLCs**). Unlike conventional VLCs which have the prefix property, RVLCs can be decoded when read either from left-to-right or right-to-left. This means that the list of codewords making up the compressed bitstream can be identified whether the bitstream is decoded in either the forward or the reverse direction.

A simple way of producing a set of RVLCs is to first choose a set of VLCs each of which has a constant **Hamming weight**; that is, each codeword has the same number of binary 1s. The associated set of RVLCs is then produced by adding a fixed-length prefix and suffix to each of the corresponding VLCs. To illustrate this, a list of RVLCs and their derivation is shown in Figure 4.27(a). In this (simple) example, each VLC in the set has a Hamming weight of 1 and the fixed-length prefix and suffix is a single binary 1. Hence each RVLC in the resulting set of RVLCs has three binary 1s in it. As we can

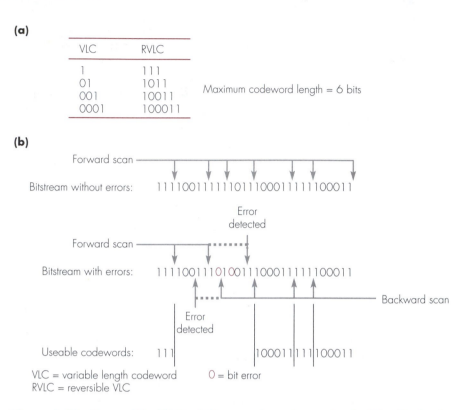

Figure 4.27 Reversible VLCs: (a) example codeword set; (b) effect of transmission errors on decoding procedure.

deduce from the set of codewords, they do not have the prefix property but, when decoding a string of codewords, each can be readily identified by counting the number of binary 1s and, on receipt of each third 1, the end of a codeword is signaled. Moreover, this applies whether the bitstream is scanned in the forward or the reverse direction.

To exploit this property, the decoder first scans the received bitstream in the forward direction in the normal way identifying valid codewords as it proceeds. If an invalid (corrupted) codeword is detected, it terminates the search but, instead of discarding the remaining bits, it simply skips to the next motion boundary or resynchronization marker and proceeds to scan the bitstream in the reverse direction until it encounters an invalid codeword in this direction. The general principle is shown in Figure 4.27(b) and, as we can see, when an error is present, the two scans locate the error at different points in the bitstream resulting in an overlap region. The usable codewords are then determined by ensuring that, for each direction, the position pointer of the last correctly decoded codeword is less than the corresponding error detection pointer in the opposite direction.

Summary

In this chapter we have described the underlying principles associated with both audio and video compression. In addition, we have presented an overview of a number of international standards that have been defined for use in a range of multimedia applications.

The standards relating to audio compression are divided into algorithms for the compression of speech – as used in a range of interpersonal communication applications – and algorithms for the compression of general audio. The latter are used primarily in entertainment applications.

The standards relating to speech compression are summarized in Table 4.3. They are all ITU-T Recommendations except for LPC-10 which is a military standard. They all relate to interpersonal applications (including telephony, video telephony, and videoconferencing) and each has been defined for use with a particular networking infrastructure.

Table 4.3 Summary of Speech compression standards and their applications.

Standard	Compression Technique	Compressed bit rate (kbps)	Speech Quality	Example applications
G.711	PCM + companding	64	Good	PSTN/ISDN telephony
G.721	Adaptive differential PCM (ADPCM)	32 16	Good Fair	Telephony at reduced bit rates
G.722	ADPCM with subband coding	64 56/48	Excellent Good	Audio conferencing
G.726	ADPCM with subband coding	40/32 24/16	Good Fair	General telephony at reduced bit rates
LPC–10	Linear predictive coding (LPC)	2.4/1.2	Poor	Telephony in military Networks
G.728	Code-excited LPC (CELP)	16	Good	Low delay/low bit rate Telephony
G.729	CELP	8	Good	Telephony in cellular (radio) networks
G.729(A)	CELP	8	Good	Simultaneous telephony and data (fax)
G.723.1	CELP	6.3 5.3	Good Fair	Video and Internet Telephony

The general audio compression standards are summarized in Table 4.4. As we can see, the majority are intended for use in various entertainment applications.

A summary of the various video compression standards that were described is given in Table 4.5 and, as we can see, these have been defined for use in a range of multimedia applications. The two ITU-T standards – H.261 and H.263 – are intended for use with various types of network including PSTNs, ISDNs, LANs, intranets, and the Internet. Example applications include video telephony, videoconferencing, and security surveillance. The three MPEG standards – MPEG-1, 2, and 4 – are intended for use in various entertainment applications including the storage of video on CD-ROMs, digital video broadcasting, and more general interactive multimedia applications. The MPEG-7 standard is concerned with a means of defining the structure and content of the (compressed) information produced by the other standards.

Table 4.4 Summary of compression standards for general audio.

Standard		Compressed bit rate (kbps)	Quality	Example applications
MPEG Audio	Layer 1	32 – 448	Hi-fi quality at 192 kbps	Digital audio cassettes
	Layer 2	32 – 192	Near CD at 128 kbps	Digital audio and digital video broadcasting
	Layer 3	64	CD quality	CD-quality over low bit rate channels
Dolby audio coders	AC-1	512 kbps	Hi-fi quality	Radio and television satellite relays
	AC-2	256 kbps	Hi-fi quality	PC sound cards
	AC-3	192 kbps	Near CD quality	Digital video broadcasting

Table 4.5 Summary of video compression standards.

Standard	Digitization format	Compressed bit rate	Example applications
H.261	CIF/QCIF	× 64 kbps	Video telephony/conferencing over × 64 kbps channels (p = 1-30) and LANs
H.263	S-QCIF/QCIF	<64 kbps	Video telephony/conferencing and security surveillance over low bit rate channels

Table 4.5 Continued

Standard	Digitization format	Compressed bit rate	Example applications
MPEG-1/ISO11172	SIF	<1.5Mbps	Storage of VHS-quality video on CD-ROMs
MPEG-2/ISO 13818			
Low	SIF	<4Mbps	Recording of VHS-quality video
Main	4:2:0	<15Mbps	Digital video broadcasting
	4:2:2	<20Mbps	
High 1440	4:2:0	<60Mbps	High definition television (4/3 aspect ratio)
	4:2:2	<80Mbps	
High	4:2:0	<80Mbps	High definition television (16/9 aspect ratio)
	4:2:2	<100Mbps	
MPEG-4	Various	5kbps-tens Mbps	Versatile multimedia coding standard
MPEG-7	–	–	Structure and content descriptions of compressed multimedia information -search engines

Exercises

Section 4.2

4.1 With the aid of a schematic diagram, explain the operation of a basic DPCM signal encoder and decoder. Include in your explanation the source of errors that can arise.

4.2 Explain how the performance of a basic DPCM scheme can be improved by utilizing a more accurate version of the previous signal. Hence with the aid of a schematic diagram of the signal encoder and decoder, explain the principle of operation of a third-order DPCM scheme.

4.3 Explain how a basic ADPCM scheme obtains improved performance over a DPCM scheme. Give examples of the performance of a G.721-complaint codec.

4.4 With the aid of a schematic diagram of the signal encoder and decoder, explain how better sound quality – for the same bit rate – can be obtained using a subband coding ADPCM. Give examples of the bit rates used for the lower and higher subbands and state an application of this type of codec.

4.5 State the principle of operation of a G.726-compliant codec and give some example operating bit rates that are used.

4.6 Explain briefly how higher levels of compression can be obtained by making the predictor coefficients associated with ADPCM adaptive.

4.7 Explain the principles on which LPC codes are based. Hence, with the aid of a schematic diagram of an LPC encoder and decoder, identify the perception parameters and associated vocal tract excitation parameters that are used. Explain how these are used by the decoder to generate the output speech signal. State the meaning of LPC-10.

4.8 Explain the main difference between an LPC codec and a CELP codec. Include in your explanation the meaning of the terms "waveform template" and "template codebook".

4.9 Explain the meaning of the following terms relating to speech coders:
(i) processing delay,
(ii) algorithmic delay,
(iii) lookahead,
(iv) coder delay.

State the latter for a G.711 (PCM) and a G.723.1 (CELP) coder and hence explain how the coder delay often determines the suitability of a coder for a specific application.

4.10 Explain the principles on which perceptual coders are based and how they differ from an LPC and CELP coder.

4.11 With the aid of a graph, show how the sensitivity of the human ear varies with frequency. Explain clearly the dimensions of the y-axis of your graph and, by showing two equal-amplitude signals on your graph, explain how one may be heard and the other not.

4.12 With the aid of a graph showing the sensitivity of the human ear, explain the meaning of the term "frequency masking". Illustrate on your graph the masking effect of a loud signal on neighboring signals.

4.13 With the aid of a diagram showing the sensitivity of the human ear, illustrate how the effect of frequency masking varies with frequency. Hence explain the term "critical bandwidth" and identify how this also varies with frequency. Deduce how this effect can be exploited.

4.14 With the aid of a graph, explain the meaning of the term "temporal masking". What are the implications of exploiting this effect?

4.15 In relation to the schematic diagram shown in Figure 4.8 of an MPEG perceptual decoder, explain the operation of/meaning of the following:
(i) PCM encoder,
(ii) frequency subbands,
(iii) subband simple,
(iv) sampled segment duration,
(v) subband scaling factor,
(vi) psychoacoustic model,
(vii) quantizer,
(viii) frame formatter.

4.16 In relation to the schematic diagram shown in Figure 4.8 of an MPEG perceptual decoder, explain the operation/meaning of the following:
(i) frame demultiplexer,
(ii) dequantizer,
(iii) synthesis filter bank,
(iv) PCM decoder.

What are the implications of not requiring a psychoacoustic model in the decoder?

4.17 In relation to MPEG perceptual coders, explain the three levels of processing used and an application and typical bit rate of each.

4.18 With the aid of schematic diagrams, explain the difference between the forward adaptive bit allocation mode as used with an MPEG perceptual coder and the fixed bit allocation mode as used with a Dolby AC-1 coder.

4.19 With the aid of schematic diagrams, explain the operation of the following two types of perceptual coder:
(i) backward adaptive bit allocation (Dolby AC-2)
(ii) hybrid backward/forward adaptive bit allocation (Dolby AC-3).

State typical operational parameters with each coder type and an example application of each.

Section 4.3

4.20 Explain the meaning of the following terms relating to video compression:
  (i)   moving pictures,
  (ii) MJPEG,
  (iii) motion estimation and compensation.
  Include in your explanation why the latter is used.

4.21 With the aid of example frame sequences, explain the meaning of the following types of compressed frame and the reasons for their use:
  (i)   I-frames,
  (ii) P-frames,
  (iii) B-frames.

4.22 Explain why I-frames are inserted into the compressed output stream relatively frequently. Hence explain the terms "group of pictures" (GOP) and "prediction span".

4.23 Assuming the uncoded frame sequence is:

  ...IBBPBBPBBBBI...

  explain the implications of transmitting the compressed frames in this sequence. Hence derive a recorded sequence that overcomes any deficiencies.

4.24 With the aid of a frame sequence diagram, explain the meaning of the term "PB-frame" and why such frames are sometimes used.

4.25 Explain the application of D-frames and the compression technique that is used with them.

4.26 In relation to the encoding procedure of I-, P-, and B-frames, explain the meaning and use of the following terms:
  (i)   macroblock,
  (ii)   macroblock address,
  (iii) target frame,
  (iv)   preceding reference frame,
  (v)   succeeding reference frame,
  (vi)   motion vector,
  (vii) prediction error.

4.27 With the aid of a diagram, explain how the motion vector and prediction error are computed for a P-frame. Use for example purposes single-pixel resolution.

4.28 With the aid of diagrams, explain how the motion vectors(s) and prediction error are computed for a B-frame. Include in your explanation the meaning of the term "half-pixel resolution".

4.29 State and explain the encoding procedure used with
  (i)   the motion vector and
  (ii) the prediction error.

4.30 In relation to the block schematic diagrams shown in Figure 4.14, explain
  (i)   the encoding of an I-frame,
  (ii) the derivation of the contents of the reference frame used when encoding P- and B-frames,
  (iii) the role of the frame formatter including the meaning of each of the fields shown in part (d) of the figure.

4.31 State the following relating to the CIF and QCIF formats of the H.261 encoding standard:
  (i)   the horizontal and vertical resolution in pixels
  (ii) the number of macroblocks per frame
  (iii) the number of GOBs per frame and their identity.

4.32 In relation to the macroblock and frame/picture formats shown in Figure 4.15, explain the role of the following fields:
  (i)   quantization value,
  (ii) coded block pattern,
  (iii) temporal reference,
  (iv) start code/resyncronization marker.

4.33 With the aid of Figure 4.16, explain the role and operation of the quantization control block. Include in your explanation the use of the FIFO buffer and the associated high and low threshold levels.

4.34 Describe the following relating to the H.263 video compression standard assuming the QCIF:
  (i)   the number of pixels per frame,
  (ii) the number of GOBs per frame,
  (iii) the encoding of a PB frame,
  (iv) unrestricted motion vectors.

4.35 With reference to the frame sequence diagram shown in Figure 4.17(a), explain how
  (i)   the corruption of one or more macroblocks within a GOB may corrupt the whole GOB

(ii) errors within a GOB may propagate to other neighbouring GOBs.

4.36 With the aid of the frame sequence diagram shown in Figure 4.17(b), explain the operation of the error tracking scheme. Include in your explanation:
(i) how errors are detected,
(ii) error prediction information and its use,
(iii) NAK messages and their content.

4.37 With the aid of the frame sequence diagram shown in Figure 4.18(b), explain the operation of the independent segment decoding scheme. Include in your explanation:
(i) how errors in a GOB do not propagate to neighbouring GOBs,
(ii) how error tracking can be used to improve error concealment.

4.38 With the aid of the sequence diagrams in Figures 4.19(a) and (b), explain the operation of the reference picture selection scheme. Include:
(i) how the propagation of errors in a GOB is overcome in the NAK mode
(ii) how the choice of reference frame is made in the ACK mode.

4.39 For the MPEG-1 frame sequence shown in Figure 4.20, derive a suitable recorded sequence of frames that results in minimum delays in the decoder.

4.40 State how the compression algorithm used with MPEG-1 differs from that used in the H.261 standard.

4.41 Assuming the frame sequence shown in Figure 4.21(a) and average ratios of 12:1 (I), 20:1 (P), and 40:1 (B), derive the average bit rate generated by an MPEG-1 encoder for both the NTSC and PAL digitization formats.

4.42 Explain the meaning of the following terms relating to the video bitstream structure shown in Figure 4.21:
(i) sequence,
(ii) GOP,
(iii) slice,
(iv) time-stamp,
(v) buffer and encode parameters.

4.43 With the aid of a diagram, explain the difference between interlaced and progressive scanning.

4.44 With the aid of the examples shown in Figure 4.22, explain how the DCT blocks are derived from each macroblock in an I-frame
(i) in the field mode and
(ii) in the frame mode.
State an application for each mode.

4.45 With the aid of a diagram, explain the meaning of the following terms relating to MPEG-4 video compression standard:
(i) content-based functionality,
(ii) audio and video objects,
(iii) video object plain.

4.46 With the aid of the diagrams shown in Figure 4.24, explain the meaning of the terms:
(i) scene and object descriptions,
(ii) scene composition and rendering,
(iii) texture, motion, and shape encoding.

4.47 In relation to the schematic diagram of an MPEG-4 decoder shown in Figure 4.25, explain the role of the following:
(i) transport stream,
(ii) flexmux layer,
(iii) PES,
(iv) synchronization layer,
(v) ES,
(vi) decomposition layer,
(vii) composition and rendering layer.

4.48 With the aid of the diagrams shown in Figure 4.26, explain:
(i) the advantages of using fixed-length video packets instead of GOBs with low bit rate wireless and PSTNs
(ii) the separation of the motion vectors and DCT information in each video packet by motion boundary marker
(iii) the replication of picture/frame-level parameters in the header of each video packet.

4.49 With the aid of the diagrams shown in Figure 4.27, explain:
(i) how reversible variable-length codewords (RVLCs) reduce the effects of transmission errors
(ii) the derivation of RVLCs
(iii) forward and reverse scans and their use.

Standards for multimedia communications

5.1 Introduction

In Chapter 1 we identified the different types of communication networks that are used to provide multimedia services. We also described a range of multimedia applications that use these networks and, although these are many and varied, we showed that they can be classified into one of three categories: interpersonal communications, interactive applications over the Internet, and entertainment applications.

In Chapter 2 we described the way the different types of media that are used in multimedia applications – text, images, speech, audio, and video – are represented in a digital form and we concluded that a number of the network types used can only support multimedia applications as a result of the technological advances that have taken place in the field of compression. Hence in Chapters 3 and 4 we described a selection of the different algorithms and standards that are used for the compression of the different media types.

In general, however, most of the multimedia applications we described in Chapter 1 involve not just a single type of medium but rather a number of media types that are integrated together in some way. For example, an interpersonal application such as videoconferencing – and most entertainment applications – involve speech and video integrated together while a typical interactive application over the Internet involves text and images integrated together. Hence in addition to the standards that we described for the compression of the different types of media, a range of application-level standards have been defined that are concerned with how the integrated information streams associated with the various applications are structured. And since the different types of network that are used to support multimedia applications operate in different ways, there is often a range of standards associated with a particular application, each intended for use with a specific type of network.

Standards are necessary because it is essential that the two or more items of equipment that are used for the application interpret the integrated information stream in the same way. They are also necessary at the networking level. For instance, with all types of network there is a finite probability that the information bitstream received from the network will contain bit/transmission errors and hence it is necessary also to ensure that both communicating parties utilize the same standards for detecting the presence of bit errors in the received information stream and, in some instances, requesting that another (hopefully error-free) copy of the information is sent. This is just one aspect of what is called a **communications protocol**. Other aspects include the initiation and clearing of a communications session between the two communicating applications and, in some instances, the setting up and clearing of a connection through the particular network being used.

In this chapter we present an overview of the standards that have been defined for use with multimedia communications. In practice, these are many and varied and relate both to the operation of the various networks that are used and also to the hardware and software in the computers (and other types of terminal equipment) that are connected to these networks to provide their users with access to multimedia communication services. A common framework known as a **reference model** is used for defining the various standards. We shall describe the structure of this in the next section and a selection of the standards that have been defined for use with specific multimedia applications in the following sections.

5.2 Reference models

Although the range of multimedia applications (and the different network types that are used to support them) are numerous and varied, the standards associated with the three types of application mentioned in the introduction have a common structure, as we show in Figure 5.1.

As we can see, standards are required at both the application level and the networking level, the latter including those for interfacing equipment to the network – network interface standards – and those relating to the

(a)

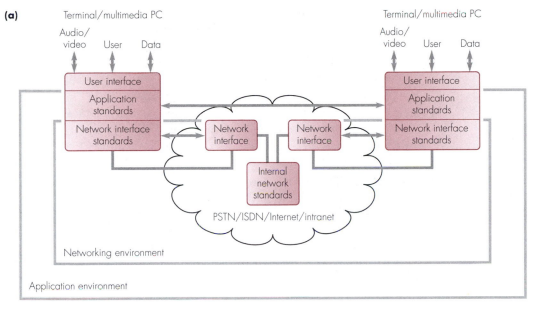

(b)

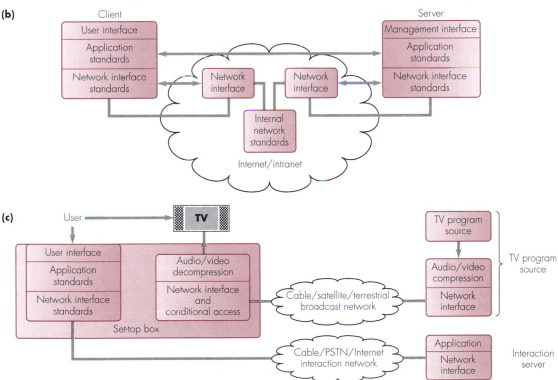

(c)

Figure 5.1 Standards requirements for multimedia applications: (a) interpersonal; (b) interactions over the Internet; (c) entertainment.

internal operation of the networks – internal networking standards. The functionality of each set of standards is as follows:

- **application standards:** these provide users, through an appropriate interface, with access to a range of multimedia communication applications;
- **network interface standards:** as we explained in section 1.5.3, different types of network operate in different modes – circuit-switched or packet-switched, connection-oriented or connectionless – and hence each network type has a different set of standards for interfacing to it;
- **internal network standards:** these are concerned with the internal operation of the network and again differ from one type of network to another.

As we show in the figure, the last two standards are concerned solely with networking issues and are said to be within the **networking environment**. Also, in the case of network interface standards, since these operate over the access circuit to the network, they are said to have only **local significance**. Application standards, however, are network-independent and relate to communications between the two (or more) terminals/computers involved in the application. Normally, the latter are referred to as **end systems** and these communications are said to have **end-to-end significance**. The application standards build on the set of networking standards to create what is known as the **application environment**.

In practice, associated with each standard is the set of procedures that are to be used to perform the particular function. Examples include, the content and structure of the source information stream associated with an application, how the information stream is formatted prior to its transmission over the network, the way transmission errors are detected, the procedure that is to be followed to obtain another copy of a corrupted block of information, and so on. Clearly, for each function, both communicating parties must adhere to the same set of procedures and collectively these form the communications protocol relating to that function.

The communication subsystem that is required in each end system associated with an application is a complex piece of hardware and software. Early implementations of the software for such subsystems were often based on a single, complex, unstructured program – normally written in an assembly language – with many interactions between the different parts. As a result, the software was difficult to test and often very difficult to modify. To overcome these deficiencies, later implementations were based on a **layered architecture**. This means that the complete communication subsystem is broken down into a number of protocol layers each of which performs a well-defined function.

The actual protocol layers that are used for each type of application differ and are influenced strongly by the type of equipment that is used to provide the application. In the case of interpersonal applications, for example, the user equipment can be either a terminal that is dedicated to providing this type of application or a multimedia PC/workstation that can be used to support both interpersonal and interactive applications. With a multimedia PC/workstation, the protocol layers that are normally used are based on what is called the **TCP/IP reference model** and hence we shall use this in order to identify and describe the function of the different protocol layers present. In general, the protocols that are used with a dedicated terminal are a subset of these.

5.2.1 TCP/IP reference model

As we indicated in the introduction, a reference model is simply a common framework for defining the specific set of protocols to be used with a particular application/network combination. The resulting set of protocols are then known as the **protocol stack** for that application/network combination. In the case of the TCP/IP reference model, the name is derived from two of the protocols – rather than layer functions – that form the core of the protocol stack used with the Internet. More recently, however, the choice of layer functions that were used for the TCP/IP protocol stack have been used in a more general way for other multimedia applications. This has been achieved by making the network interface layers applicable to different types of network rather than just the Internet. The general structure of the modified model in relation to the original model is shown in Figure 5.2(a) and part (b) shows its application in relation to the various standards we identified in Figure 5.1. We shall describe the role of each layer in the modified model separately.

Physical layer

The physical layer is concerned with how the binary information stream associated with an application is transmitted over the access circuit to the network interface. As we shall expand upon in Chapter 6, the signals that are used to represent each binary 1 and 0 in the stream vary for different types of access circuit. Hence depending on the choice of access circuit, it is also necessary to select a specific way of representing each binary 1 and 0 as well as the physical dimensions of the plug and socket to be used to connect the terminal/computer (end system) to the access circuit termination. Typically, this is in the home or office and again a number of alternatives are possible.

Link layer

Although selected applications such as telephony over a PSTN or an ISDN generate a constant bit rate stream that is transmitted transparently over the total network, most multimedia applications involve multiple media types integrated together in some way. Hence, as we shall expand upon in the following sections, the more usual form of representing the source information stream is in the form of a contiguous stream of blocks with each block containing the integrated media stream associated with the application. Also, as

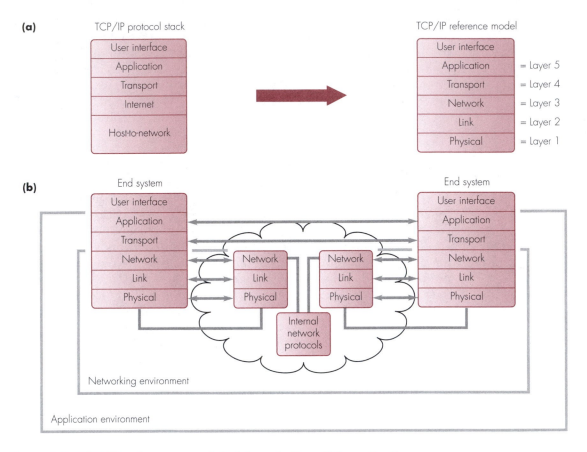

Figure 5.2 TCP/IP reference model: (a) evolution; (b) application.

we described earlier in Section 1.5.3, in a packet-switched network, as each packet is received by a packet-switching exchange, it is checked for the presence of transmission errors. It is the role of the link layer to indicate the start and end of each block within the source bitstream and, in a packet-switched network, to add error check bits to the information bitstream for error detection – and in some instances error correction – purposes.

Network layer

The network layer is concerned with how the source information stream gets from one end system to another across the total network. With a connection-oriented network, this involves the setting up of a network connection, the exchange of the information relating to the call/session, and the subsequent clearing of the connection. In the case of a connectionless network, it involves formatting the source information into packets, each with the unique network-wide address of the two (source and destination) communicating end systems at its head. As we can see from this, there are a number of different network layer protocols, each concerned with a particular type of network. Also, as with the link and physical layers, the network protocol is not concerned with the content of the information stream being transferred/exchanged but simply how it is transferred.

Transport layer

It is the role of the transport layer to mask the differences between the service offered by the various network types from the application layer and instead, to provide the application with a network-independent information interchange service. In addition, since there can be multiple applications running in the same end system concurrently, the transport layer is also responsible for directing each information flow to and from the related application.

As we indicated in Section 1.5.5, all of the networks that are used for multimedia applications provide a best-effort service. This means that with a circuit-switched network, bit errors may be present in the constant bit rate information stream after its passage through the network and, with a packet-switched network, some packets may be missing from the received stream as those which incur bit errors will have been discarded by the network. For applications such as telephony, this is acceptable. For other applications, however, it is essential that only error-free information is received by the destination application. Hence there are two types of service provided by the transport layer, the first known as an **unreliable transport service** and the second a **reliable transport service**. Thus for a particular application, the appropriate service – and hence protocol – is chosen.

Application layer

The application layer provides the user, through a suitable interface, with access to a range of multimedia communication services. Examples include email, Web access, telephony, videoconferencing, and so on. Associated with each application is a specific application protocol which provides the user with the corresponding service. Typically, therefore, the application layer in an end system contains a selection of application protocols, each providing a particular service. In the case of interpersonal communications, these include application protocols for email, telephony, and videoconferencing while in interactive applications, they include application protocols for access to remote information servers and servers containing stored videos/movies.

5.2.2 Protocol basics

Each layer performs a well-defined function in the context of the overall communication subsystem. The protocol to be used at each layer is chosen to meet the needs of a particular application/network combination. The two communicating protocols within each layer operate according to a defined set of rules in order to implement the desired function of the layer. Normally, this is achieved by adding appropriate **protocol control information (PCI)** to the head of the information being transferred. The complete block – information plus PCI – is known as a **protocol data unit (PDU)** and this is then sent to the corresponding protocol in the remote system. The two procotols are said to operate at the same **peer layer** within the protocol stack.

In practice, although the two protocols communicate by exchanging protocol control information at a peer level, as we show in Figure 5.3(a), the actual PDUs containing the PCI are transferred using the services provided by the protocol layer immediately below it in the protocol stack. Each layer provides a defined set of services to the layer immediately above it. The selected protocol at that layer then implements these services by communicating with the peer protocol in the remote system according to the defined protocol. Hence as we show in part (b) of the figure, as the information to be transferred is passed down from one layer to the next, the protocol at each layer adds its own PCI at the head of what it receives and, once the link layer protocol has added its own PCI – including the error check bits at the tail – it is this that is encoded and transmitted over the network to the remote system. Conversely, as the received information stream is passed up from one layer to the next in the remote system, each layer protocol reads and removes its own PCI from the head and, after interpreting this according to the defined protocol for that layer, passes the remaining information up to the protocol layer immediately above it.

5.3 Standards relating to interpersonal communications

As we described in Section 1.4.1, interpersonal communications such as telephony, video telephony, data conferencing, and videoconferencing are provided both by circuit-mode networks such as a PSTN or an ISDN and packet-mode networks such as a LAN, an intranet, or the Internet. Most of the standards relating to these applications have been defined by the ITU-T and there are separate standards relating to both types of network. Before describing these standards, it will be helpful if we first identify the use of the different constituent parts that they contain.

To do this, consider an application involving two design engineers working jointly on a project and having a meeting relating to the project over a network. Typically, each will be using a multimedia PC or workstation and an example communication session may comprise multiple phases along the following lines.

First, the session may start with a telephone conversation and, during this, the design/image on each engineer's screen – normally referred to as **user data** – is sent to the other party. They then decide to bring in a third person who is working (remotely) on the project and, since one of the engineers has not met this person, they convert to a videoconferencing call and, during this phase, all three members start to discuss the design jointly.

(a)

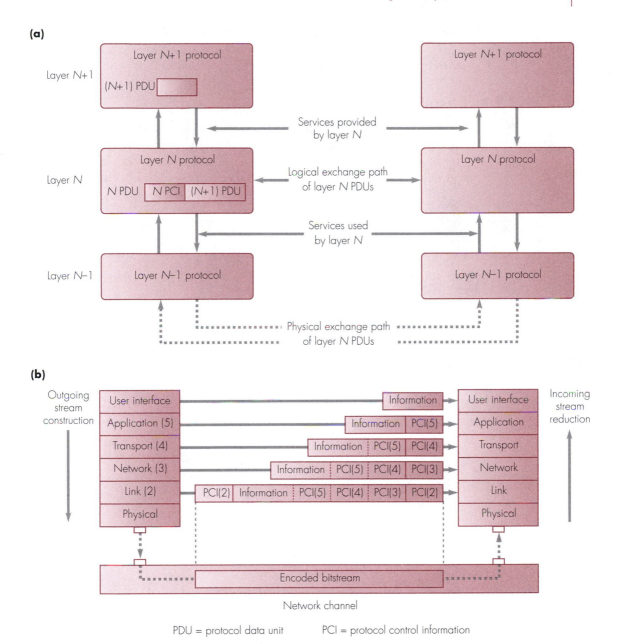

PDU = protocol data unit   PCI = protocol control information

Figure 5.3 Protocol basics: (a) layer interactions and terminology; (b) end-to-end transfer.

As we can deduce from this example, the content of the information stream being transferred varies. It starts with speech only, then speech with user data, then speech with video, and finally speech, video, and user data. In the case of an ISDN, each media type is allocated a fixed portion of the channel bandwidth and hence each can be used as and when required. With a PSTN and most packet-switched networks, the appropriate amount of bandwidth is allocated on-demand as the session progresses.

5.3.1 Circuit-mode networks

The functionality of the various standards that are used in end systems connected to a circuit-mode network is shown in Figure 5.4.

As we explained earlier in Section 1.5.3, with networks such as a PSTN (plus modem) and an ISDN, once a connection through the network has

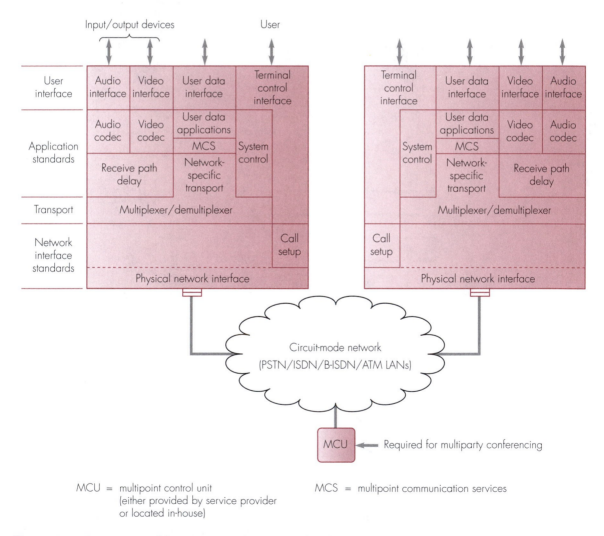

Figure 5.4 Structure of interpersonal communication standards for circuit-mode networks.

been set up, the connection provides a constant bit rate channel over which the user can transfer any type of digital information. Hence in relation to the TCP/IP reference model we described in Section 5.2.1, the network interface standards relate primarily to the physical connection to the network termination and with the procedures followed to set up and clear/tear-down a connection. The basic transport layer function is provided by the multiplexer/demultiplexer. Essentially, the multiplexer merges the source information from the three application streams – audio, video, and user data – and the system control application into a single stream for transmission over the constant bit rate channel provided by the connection and, on receipt of the merged stream, the demultiplexer routes the constituent streams to the corresponding application.

The system control application is concerned with negotiating and agreeing on the operational parameters to be used with the call/session. These are based on the **capabilities** of the end systems involved in the call and enable, for example, a simple terminal to communicate with a more sophisticated terminal/computer. With a PSTN, the system control function includes the management of the available transmission bandwidth during a call. Both of these functions are achieved by the two system control application protocols exchanging appropriate messages – protocol data units – over the network connection. In the case of a two-party call, this involves the applications in the two end systems communicating directly with each other while with a multiparty conference call, it involves each end system communicating with a multipoint control unit (MCU) as we explained in Section 1.5.4.

The audio and video codecs each use a particular compression algorithm which is appropriate for the application and within the bandwidth limits provided by the network. Also, in order to synchronize the audio and video streams – to achieve **lip-sync** for example – a delay is often introduced at the receiver into one of the streams. As we explained in the previous section, the user data application is concerned with the transfer of data such as a digitized image or the contents of a file. Normally, therefore, the data is sent in the form of individual blocks/packets and the application uses an appropriate reliable transport protocol to overcome lost/corrupted packets. In addition, if the user data is to be shared between the various members of a conference, the application uses the services provided by a protocol known as a **multipoint communications service (MCS)**. A copy of this is present in each end system and this, in turn, relays a copy of all transmitted data to the other members of the conference via the MCU.

The actual standards that have been defined for use with the different types of circuit-mode network – including a B-ISDN and local area networks that provide a guaranteed bandwidth such as an ATM LAN – are summarized in Table 5.1. The standard/recommendation at the head of each column is a system-level standard and embraces a number of additional standards for the various component functions such as audio and video compression, and so on. We shall describe the main features of each standard separately.

Table 5.1 Summary of the standards used with the different types of circuit-mode network.

Standard	H.320	H.324	H.321	H.310	H.322
Network	ISDN	PSTN	B-ISDN (ATM)	B-ISDN (ATM)	Guaranteed bandwidth LANs
Audio codec	G.711* G.722 G.728	G723.1* G.729	G.711* G.722 G.728	G.711* G.722 G.728 MPEG-1*	G.711* G.722 G.728
Video codec	H.261	H.261* H.263*	H.261	H.261* MPEG-2*	H.261
User data application	T.120	T.120	T.120	T.120	T.120
Multiplexer/ demultiplexer	H.221	H.223	H.221	H.221 H.222	H.221
System control	H.242	H.245	H.242	H.245	H.242
Call setup (signaling)	Q.931	V.25	Q.931	Q.2931	Q.931

* = mandatory

H.320

The H.320 standard is intended for use in end systems that support a range of multimedia applications over an ISDN. Hence, as we described in Section 1.3.4, the usable bandwidth of a connection is $p \times 64$ kbps where p can be 1 through 30. For video telephony, for example, p is either 1 or 2 while for videoconferencing p is 2 or greater.

Audio The choice of audio/speech compression standard can be selected from one of three ITU-T recommendations: G.711, G.722, and G.728. The choice is determined primarily by the amount of transmission bandwidth available for the audio. For example, as we described in Section 2.5.1, G.711 relates to standard PCM and requires 64 kbps of bandwidth. Alternatively, as we described in Section 4.2.2, the G.722 standard gives an improved performance with the same bit rate but at the expense of added complexity in the codec. Clearly, however, since both standards require 64 kbps, they can only be used in multimedia applications when multiple 64 kbps channels are being used. If only a single 64 kbps channel is available, then the G.728 standard described in Section 4.2.5 must be used and, although the perceptual quality of the speech is inferior to standard PCM, the bit rate required is only 16 kbps. This leaves 48 kbps for the other media types which is typical of many video telephony applications. In general, the other two standards are selected primarily for videoconferencing applications as these need the higher quality speech to discriminate between the voices of the different members of the conference.

Video The video compression standard is H.261 and, as we described in Section 4.3.2, a constant output bit rate from the encoder (of the allocated rate) is obtained by varying the quantization threshold that is used dynamically. The video resolution can be either quarter-screen (QCIF) or full-screen (CIF), the actual resolution used being negotiated at the start of the conference.

User data The user data applications are based on the **T.120 standard** which, in practice, consists of a set of recommendations. As we show in Table 5.1, the same standard is used with all the different types of circuit-mode network. There is a set of application-specific recommendations that support the sharing of various media types:

- T.124: sharing of text for what is known as text chat,
- T.126: still-image and whiteboard sharing,
- T.127: sharing of file contents(text and binary),
- T.128: sharing of text documents and spreadsheets,

and a series of communications-related recommendations:

- T.122: multipoint control unit (MCU) procedures,
- T.125: multipoint communication services (MCS) procedures,
- T.123: a series of network-specific transport protocols all of which provide a reliable transport service.

The standard also includes extensions to allow the use of non-standard protocols to be negotiated.

System control/call setup The call setup (signaling) procedure associated with an ISDN is defined in **Recommendation Q.931** and, as we shall expand upon in Section 7.4.1, this involves the exchange of messages over a separate 16 kbps channel known as the **signaling channel**. Also, with an ISDN the bandwidth associated with the audio, video, and data streams are negotiated and fixed at the start of a conference. Hence the system control standard – **Recommendation H.242** – is concerned primarily with the negotiation of the bandwidth/bit rate to be used for each stream. Once an end system has set up a connection to the MCU, the system control within the end system informs the multipoint controller part of the MCU of its capabilities. These include the video format (QCIF or CIF) and compression standards it supports, the audio compression standards, the T.120 user data applications, and the proposed bit rate of each channel. The MCU then negotiates and agrees a minimum set of capabilities so that all members of the conference can participate.

Multiplexing The multiplexer/demultiplexer layer is defined in **Recommendation H.221** and describes how the audio, video, and data streams are multiplexed together for transmission over the network. Normally, the fixed portions of the available bandwidth are allocated using a technique known as **time division multiplexing (TDM)** which we will describe in more detail in Section 7.2.3. Hence the role of H.221 is to ensure that each input stream is placed into its allocated position in the output bitstream and, at the receiver, to pass each stream to the appropriate application.

H.324

The H.324 standard is intended for use in end systems that support a range of interpersonal communication applications over low bit rate switched networks such as a PSTN. In general, therefore, the network interface is a modem which, in the case of a PSTN, provides a bit rate of up to 56 kbps. Normally, as we shall expand upon in Section 7.2.2, the modem contains auto dial and auto answer facilities for the establishment of a call/network connection using the standard dialing, ringing, and answering procedure.

Video and audio The video compression standard can be either H.261 or the H.263 standard which we described in Section 4.3.3 of the last chapter. As we explained, the H.263 standard uses the same compression technique as H.261 but contains a number of more advanced coding features in order to operate over lower bit rate channels such as those provided by a PSTN. The audio compression standard is either G.723.1 or G.729, both of which we described in Section 4.2.5. The G.723.1 standard is the most common and, as we explained, operates at a bit rate of either 5.3 or 6.3 kbps. Also, although there is an algorithmic (codec) delay associated with both codecs, this is normally less than the video codec delay. Hence in order to obtain lip-sync, a delay has to be added to the audio stream at the receiver. The actual delay is measured at the sending side and, as part of the H.245 system control protocol, a message containing the required delay is sent to the receiver.

User data The user data application standard is T.120 and basically this contains the same set of protocols as are used in an H.320-compliant terminal except for the network-specific transport protocol, T.123. The H.223 multiplexing standard, however, is different. Because of the relatively low – and possibly variable – bit rate that is available, the audio, video, and user data streams are not allocated fixed portions of the available bandwidth but rather these are negotiated using the H.245 system control protocol. This occurs both prior to a call commencing and as the call is in progress and, at any point in time, each stream may be present or not. For example, when a large file is to be transferred, it is possible to temporarily suspend the video stream until the file contents have been sent.

Multiplexing The total channel bandwidth is divided into a number of separate **logical channels** each of which is identified by means of a **logical channel number (LCN)**. The first – LCN0 – is used to carry the control stream and each of the remaining channels carries a separate media stream. The allocation of LCNs is controlled by the transmitter and, when it wishes to open a new channel, it sends an H.245 control message which includes the media type and the type of codec being used. The role of the multiplexer is then to merge those streams that are currently present into the available bandwidth. This is achieved by using what is known as a **bit-oriented protocol,** the principles of which are shown in Figure 5.5

We shall describe the bit-oriented mode of transmission in more detail in Section 6.5.3. Essentially, however, the transmitted bitstream is treated as a string of bytes and, as we show in the figure, this is divided into a number of separate information fields. Each field comprises a variable number of bytes and is separated by one or more **flag bytes**. These have the bit pattern 01111110 and a technique known as **zero bit insertion and deletion** is used to ensure that this pattern cannot be present in the information field. At the start of each information field is a header (byte) and the combined header plus information field is known as a **multiplex protocol data unit** or **M-PDU**. The header byte includes a **multiplex code** which specifies a particular mix of media and control logical channels, and, since each M-PDU may contain a different code, a different mix of logical channels.

As we show in Figure 5.5, the multiplex code is 4 bits in length and forms the index to a table known as the **multiplex table**. A copy of the table is held by both the transmitter and receiver and each entry in the table specifies a particular sequence of logical channels and the number of bytes in each channel. Hence the transmitter can readily change the usage of the available bandwidth (by the various sources) very quickly by simply changing the multiplex code in the header byte. Although in theory there can be a large number of different mixes of logical channels, at any point in time, the table contains just 16 entries. For a particular application, this is normally sufficient but, as part of the system control function, a new set of entries can be sent by the transmitter should this be required.

Adaptation In order to allow for the possibility of transmission errors being present in the received byte stream associated with each logical channel, additional bytes are added by the transmitter for error detection purposes to enable the receiver to detect the presence of errors and, if necessary, to request another copy of the affected bytes. This function is also part of the H.223 standard and is known as the **adaptation layer**. In general, the different types of media – audio, video, and user data – require different levels of

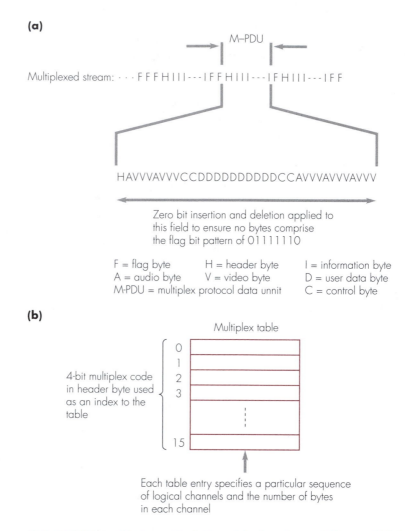

Figure 5.5 H.223 multiplex principles: (a) structure of the multiplexed byte stream; (b) multiplex table usage.

protection against transmission errors. Hence the adaptation layer supports three different schemes – AL1, 2, and 3 – each of which provides a different error-handling capability. The user then selects the most appropriate scheme to meet the requirements of the application. For example, AL1 is intended for use with user data applications since it has features to support the retransmission of any corrupted blocks of data. AL2 is intended for use with the audio and video streams as it supports error detection but retransmission is optional. AL3 is intended for use with video applications that require a higher level of protection. It again supports error detection and also the retransmission of corrupted blocks.

Multipoint conferencing The H.324 standard also supports multipoint conferencing via an MCU. However, since the modems associated with each end system may be operating at different bit rates, during the establishment of the conference the MCU negotiates an agreed minimum bit rate with all the participants by the exchange of system control messages. In addition, interworking between an H.324 terminal and an H.320 terminal is supported either by a device known as an **H.324/H.320 gateway** or an MCU and **dual-mode terminals** which support both interfaces. In the case of a gateway, this communicates with an H.324 terminal using the H.223 multiplex standard and with an H.320 terminal using the H.221 standard. The role of the gateway is then to convert the content of the audio, data, and control streams into/from the appropriate format. This procedure is known as **transcoding** and, in the case of the audio stream, this must be carried out in real time as the audio stream is relayed by the gateway. In practice, this requires a significant amount of processing as it converts from one audio format into another. In the case of the video stream, the processing required is, in general, too great and normally, therefore, the video stream is not transcoded and instead the H.261/QCIF combination is negotiated prior to the conference commencing.

System control The H.245 system control standard is concerned with the overall control of the end system and, as we can see from the above, this involves many functions. These include the exchange of messages for the negotiation of capabilities, the opening and closing of logical channels, the transmission of the contents of the multiplex table, and the choice of adaptation layers. All the messages are defined in a standard syntax known as **Abstract Syntax Notation One (ASN.1)** and an associated encoding scheme is used to ensure that the exchanged messages are interpreted in an unambiguous way by all types of end system. We describe these in more detail in Section 13.2. Because of their importance, a separate error control scheme is applied to all system control messages before they are multiplexed with the three application media streams.

H.321/H.310

Both the H.321 and the H.310 standards are intended for use with terminals that provide a range of multimedia applications over a B-ISDN which, as we explained in Section 1.3.5, is also known as an ATM network.

The H.321 standard relates to the provision of interpersonal communication applications over a B-ISDN and, in practice, is an adaptation of the H.320 standard that is used with an ISDN. Hence, as we can see from Table 5.1, all the standards associated with H.321 are the same as those used with H.320. This simplifies the interworking across both types of network and the only difference is that the network interface layers associated with H.321 relate to interfacing the end system to a B-ISDN rather than an ISDN.

The H.310 standard is intended for use with end systems that support not only interpersonal applications but also interactive and entertainment applications. Hence, as we can see from Table 5.1, the audio and video standards include the H.321 set which are intended for interpersonal communications and also additional standards – MPEG-1 audio and MPEG-2 video plus their associated multiplex standard H.222 – for use in interactive and entertainment applications. Also, in order to support the wider range of applications, the more comprehensive system control standard H.245 is used. We shall defer the description of the standards associated with interactive and entertainment applications until Sections 5.4 and 5.5 respectively.

H.322

The H.322 standard is intended for use with end systems that support interpersonal communication applications over a local area network (LAN) that provides communication channels of a guaranteed bandwidth. Examples include ATM LANs, the operation of which we shall explain in Section 10.5. In general, the communication channels associated with these networks are able to support multiples of 64 kbps and hence, as we can see from Table 5.1, the same set of standards are used with H.322 as are used with an H.320 end system in order to simplify interworking across both types of network.

5.3.2 Packet-switched networks

Two alternative sets of protocols have been defined for providing interpersonal communication services over packet-switched networks, one defined by the ITU in Recommendation H.323 and the other by the IETF. In this section we shall discuss both standards.

H.323

As we described earlier in Section 1.3.2, normally, the access network used with both an intranet and the Internet is a campus/site LAN. Hence the H.323 standard pertaining to packet-switched networks relates primarily to how interpersonal communications are achieved between end systems that are attached either to the same LAN or to different LANs that are interconnected together in some way. Unlike the H.322 standard which relates to LANs that offer a guaranteed bandwidth/QoS, the H.323 standard is intended for use with LANs that provide a non-guaranteed QoS which, in practice, as we shall expand upon in Section 8.2, applies to the majority of LANs.

As we show in Figure 5.6, the standard comprises components for the packetization and synchronization of the audio and video streams, an admission control procedure for end systems to join a conference, multipoint conference control, and interworking with terminals that are connected to the different types of circuit-switched networks. The standard is independent of the underlying transport and network interface protocols and hence can be used with any type of LAN. It is assumed, however, that the transport layer provides both an unreliable (best-effort) service and a reliable service which, in practice, is the case for most LANs. With an end system connected to a

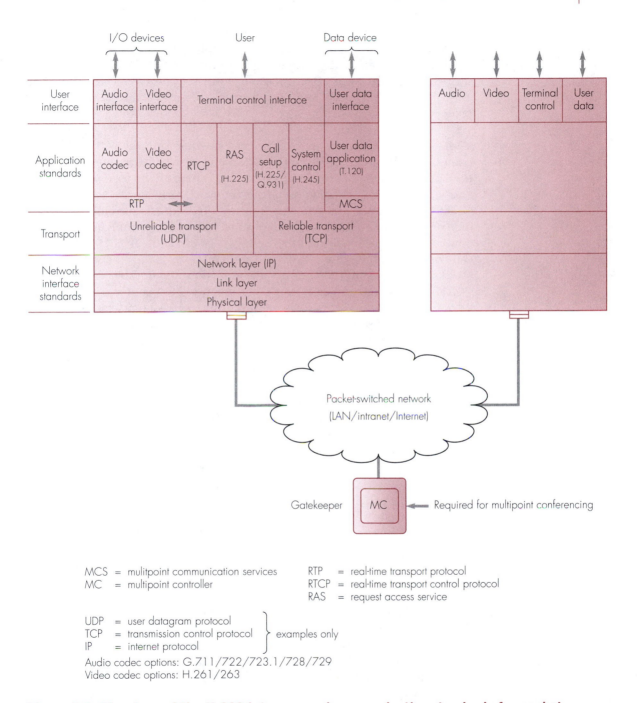

Figure 5.6 Structure of the H.323 interpersonal communication standards for packet-switched networks.

LAN and communicating over an intranet or the Internet, for example, the network layer protocol is the **internet protocol (IP)**, the unreliable transport service is provided by the **user datagram protocol (UDP)**, and the reliable transport service by the **transmission control protocol (TCP)**. We shall describe the operation of the IP protocol in Chapter 9 and both transport protocols in Chapter 12.

Audio and video coding In order to simplify interworking with terminals/ computers that are attached to the different types of circuit-mode networks, the H.323 standard allows a variety of coding options to be used for the audio and video streams. The audio codec standard, for example, can be either G.711 or G.728 in order to simplify interworking with H.320-compliant terminals or G.723.1 or G.729 for interworking with H.324-compliant terminals. Similarly, the video codec standard can be either H.261 or H.263. Prior to a call commencing, however, an agreed coding standard must be negotiated to avoid the necessity of transcoding the audio and video streams.

The output streams of both the audio and video codecs are formatted into packets for transfer over the network using the **real-time transport protocol (RTP)**. As we shall explain in Section 12.5.1, this is used for the transfer of real-time information and, at the head of each RTP packet is a format specification which defines how the packet contents/payload are structured. There are standardized formats for the information streams produced by all the different audio and video codecs. In addition, as part of the **real-time transport control protocol (RTCP)**, the sending end system sends information to enable the receiving end system to synchronize the audio and video streams. Other information transferred as part of the RTCP includes the transmitted packet rate, the packet transmission delay (sender to receiver), the percentage of packets lost/corrupted, and the interarrival jitter (receiver to sender). This information can then be used to optimize the number and size of receiver buffers and to determine if the retransmission of lost packets is feasible. For example, if the transmission delay is below a defined threshold – for example if all the end systems are attached to the same LAN – it may be feasible to request the retransmission of corrupted packets. Conversely, if the delay is greater than the threshold then retransmissions are not possible.

Call setup As we shall expand upon in Chapter 8, LANs that do not provide a guaranteed QoS have no procedures to limit the number of calls/sessions that are using the LAN concurrently. Although this is acceptable with applications such as text-based file transfers which require only short bursts of bandwidth, with applications that involve audio and video, this approach is often not acceptable since the potentially large bandwidth that would be required to support many concurrent calls/sessions could exceed the total bandwidth available with the LAN. In order to limit the number of concurrent calls that involve multimedia, a device called an **H.323 gatekeeper** can (optionally) be used.

Essentially, during the setting up of a multimedia conferencing call, each end system involved in the conference must first obtain permission from the gatekeeper. Then, depending on the current level of usage of the LAN, the gatekeeper decides whether the call can take place. If an increase in the allocated bandwidth is required during a call, then again prior permission must be obtained from the gatekeeper. In addition, as we described in Section 1.5.4, since with a LAN the use of an MCU is optional, if an MCU is not being used, then the functions of the multipoint controller (MC) part of the MCU relating to the setting up of a multipoint call are often incorporated into the gatekeeper. The messages that are exchanged to set up a call are shown in Figure 5.7.

As we show in the figure, the setting up of a call is carried out in two stages. First the end system initiating the call obtains permission from the gatekeeper to set up a call by sending an *access request (ARQ)* message to the gatekeeper (1) and the gatekeeper responding with either an *access confirm (ACF)* or an *access reject (ARJ)* message (2). Assuming permission is received, for a two-party call the initiating terminal then sends a *setup* request message directly to the called end system (3). The latter first acknowledges receipt of the setup request by returning a *call proceeding* message directly to the initiating end system (4) and then proceeds to obtain permission from the

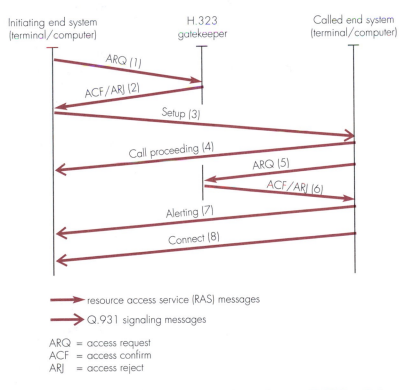

Figure 5.7 Two-party call setup procedure using an H.323 gatekeeper.

gatekeeper to take part in the call by means of the exchange of *ARQ* (5) and *ACF* (6) messages. Assuming permission is granted, the called end system sends an *alerting* message directly to the initiating end system (7) which is equivalent to the ringing tone heard when setting up a telephone call over a PSTN. Finally, if the user accepts the call, then the called end system returns a *connect* message directly to the initiating end system (8).

The messages exchanged with the gatekeeper concerned with the two end systems obtaining permission to set up a call are part of the **resource access service (RAS) protocol** and the example messages concerned with call setup which are exchanged directly by the two end systems are part of the Q.931 signaling protocol. In practice, both the RAS and Q.931 protocols are part of recommendation H.225. A similar procedure is followed for a multiparty conference call except all the messages are exchanged via the gatekeeper since this also contains the multipoint controller part of an MCU.

Once a call has been set up, the exchange of system control messages using the H.245 control protocol can then start. These include the negotiation of capabilities and the opening of logical channels for the audio, video, and user data streams. As we shall expand upon in Section 12.2, associated with both the UDP and the TCP protocols is a **port number**. This is carried in the header of the protocol data unit (PDU) associated with each protocol and is used to identify the application protocol to which the PDU contents relate. Also, as we shall expand upon in Section 12.2, in the header of the PDUs associated with the IP is the identity of the protocol (UDP or TCP) that created the packet to be transferred. Hence, as we show in Figure 5.8, on receipt of each packet from the network, the IP uses the **protocol identifier** to route the packet contents to either the UDP or the TCP. The latter then uses

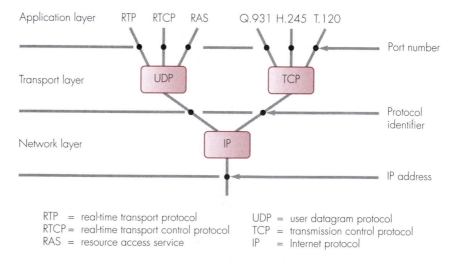

RTP = real-time transport protocol
RTCP = real-time transport control protocol
RAS = resource access service

UDP = user datagram protocol
TCP = transmission control protocol
IP = Internet protocol

Figure 5.8 H.323 multiplexing/demultiplexing.

the port number at the head of the packet to relay the packet contents – the application protocol data unit – to the appropriate application protocol. Thus the multiplexing and demultiplexing operations associated with H.323 are carried out by the IP/UDP/TCP combination.

Interworking In addition to the operation of the end systems, the H.323 standard also defines how interworking with end systems that are attached to a circuit-mode network is achieved. This is through a device known as an **H.323 gateway** and the general scheme is shown in Figure 5.9.

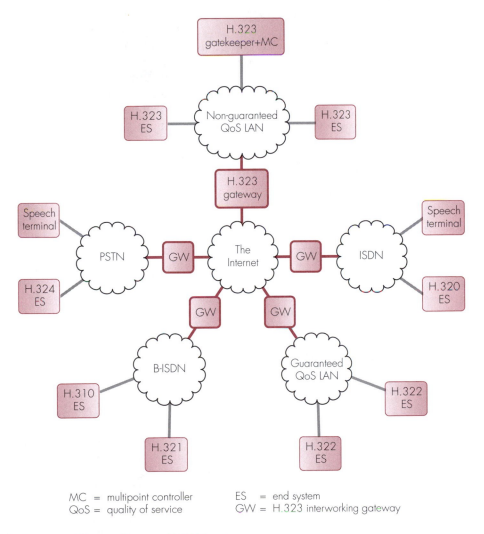

MC = multipoint controller   ES = end system
QoS = quality of service   GW = H.323 interworking gateway

Figure 5.9 Interworking using an H.323 gateway.

The role of a gateway is to provide translations between the different procedures (and related control messages) associated with each network type. Hence translations are necessary for the procedures and messages associated with call setup and clearing (signaling), system control, and the two different multiplexing techniques. Also, if the two (or more) communicating end systems are using different audio and video codec standards, then transcoding between the two different coding techniques must be carried out. In order to minimize the amount of transcoding required in the gateway, the same audio and video codec standards are used whenever possible. Hence, as we saw earlier in Table 5.1, to make interworking easier, selected audio and video codec standards are made mandatory, which means that the end system must always be able to operate with these codecs. Thus in the case of interworking with an H.320-end system connected to an ISDN, both end systems should operate using G.711 audio and H.261/QCIF video. Similarly, in the case of interworking with an H.324-terminal connected to a PSTN, both terminals should operate using G.723.1 and either H.261 or H.263 video. If a common standard is not supported – determined during the capability exchange procedure – then the gateway must perform the appropriate transcoding procedures. However, as we show in Figure 5.9, a gateway can have multiple interfaces and, in practice, can support multiple calls simultaneously. Hence if transcoding is necessary, this restricts the number of simultaneous calls. Also, as with a gatekeeper, in some instances the gateway incorporates the MCU functions since this minimizes the amount of traffic on the LAN itself.

A second function associated with a gateway relates to address translation. This is necessary when interworking between end systems that are attached to different networks because each uses a different addressing scheme. For example, in the case of a LAN that uses the TCP/IP protocol set, the address of an end system is an IP address while with a PSTN or an ISDN the address is a conventional telephone number, all of which have a different format. Also, in the case of a LAN, end systems (computers in practice) are often referred to by a symbolic name rather than by their IP address. So to simplify interworking, all the end systems on a LAN are given an alias PSTN and/or ISDN number which can be used by a caller from outside that is connected to either a PSTN or an ISDN. Similarly, all the end systems that are external to the LAN can be allocated an alias IP address or symbolic name. The gatekeeper then performs the necessary translations between the different address types during the call setup procedure.

IETF

The early IETF standards relating to interpersonal communications over the Internet were concerned with providing a basic two-party telephony service between two IP hosts. Later, this was expanded to provide a more versatile facility supporting both multiparty conferencing and broadcast services. The membership of a conference or broadcast can vary as it progresses and the audio, video, and data involved can be integrated together in a dynamic way. To support these functions the IETF has developed a range of protocols which, in general, complement those associated with H.323.

In terms of the protocols used within a host/end system attached to the Internet, the main difference is the use of a different signaling protocol set from that used with H.323. These are the **session initiation protocol (SIP)** and the related **session description protocol (SDP)**. Essentially, these replace the RAS, call setup, and system control protocols shown in Figure 5.6.

SIP provides services for user location, call establishment, and call participation management. It is a simple request-response – also known as transaction – type of protocol and is defined in RFC 2543. The user of a host – which wants to set up a telephony call for example – sends a request message to the user of the called host which then responds by returning a suitable response message. Both the request and the response are made through an application program known as a user agent (UA) which maps the request and its response into the standard message format used by SIP.

On receipt of a request, the UA in the calling host formats a SIP message and this is transferred to the UA in the called host, normally using UDP. On receipt of the request, appropriate actions are initiated by the UA which then proceeds to map the response into the standard SIP format. The response is then returned to the UA in the client using the service provided by UDP.

Examples of SIP request messages – also known as *commands* or *methods* – are:

- *options*: this is sent to solicit the capabilities supported by a host;
- *invite*: this is sent to invite the user of a host to join in a call/session;
- *bye*: this is sent when the user of a host intends to leave a call/session.

Each message (PDU) consists of a header and a body. For example, the header of an *invite* request message contains fields such as *to* for the address of the called user and *from* for the address of the caller. Normally, the message body contains the individual media streams relating to the call.

An important feature of SIP is the location service it supports. Normally, users are identified by a symbolic name similar to an email address which, as we shall see in Section 14.2, is converted into an actual IP address and port number by a server called the **domain name server (DNS)**. When the required user host is attached to a different domain, then multiple servers are involved in performing the name-to-address resolution service. In addition, as with the H.323 standard, gateways are used to enable a user attached to the Internet to set up a call/session involving a user attached to another network such as a PSTN. An associated gateway location protocol (GLP) is then used to enable a SIP server to locate the gateway associated with a different network. We shall discuss the user location service of SIP and the operation of a SIP gateway in Section 14.6.1.

The SDP protocol is closely related to SIP. When a user is invited to join in a call/session, for example, the *invite* message includes SDP fields which define the individual media streams the caller can support, their format and the address and port numbers associated with each stream. Also, for broadcast calls/sessions – a lecture given over the Internet for example – the start and stop times of the lecture and contact details of the lecturer. The response contains a list of the media streams that the called party can support. All the fields relating to SDP are represented in a textual form. The contact details of the lecturer, for example, are symbolic names and IP addresses are in dotted-decimal. SDP, therefore, is a form of description language. Again, we shall discuss this further in Chapter 14, Section 14.6.2.

5.3.3 Electronic mail

From a user perspective, electronic mail (email) is probably the most popular interpersonal communications facility. As we explained earlier in Section 1.4.1, since an email message is delivered to the recipient's mailbox in a matter of seconds, email is much faster than postal mail and, since it does not require the recipient to be available to receive the message, it is often more convenient than a telephone call. Further advantages are that it is very straightforward to send the same message to groups of people and, with multimedia extensions, a mail message can contain various types of media including speech and video.

Internet mail

The two basic components associated with a text-based email system that uses the Internet – email clients and email servers – are shown in Figure 5.10.

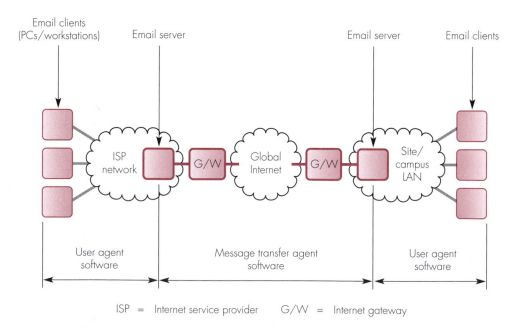

Figure 5.10 Email over the Internet.

Normally, an email client is a desktop PC which runs a program known as the **user agent (UA)**. As its name implies, this provides the user interface to the email system and acts as an agent to create new (mail) messages, initiate the sending of a message, read a received message from the user's mailbox, reply to a received message, forward a received message to another user, and to delete unwanted messages from the user's mailbox.

The email server is a server computer that maintains an IN and OUT mailbox for all the users/clients that are registered with it. The IN mailbox is used to store mail messages that have been received for the user and the OUT mailbox messages that have either been sent or are awaiting delivery. In addition, the server has software both to interact with the user agent software in each client and also to manage the transfer of mail messages over the Internet. The software associated with the latter function is known as the **message transfer agent (MTA)** and is concerned with the sending and receiving of messages to/from email servers that are also connected directly to the Internet over previously established TCP logical connections.

The protocol stack used to support email over the Internet is shown in Figure 5.11. Normally, the protocol stack associated with the access network – the internet service provider (ISP) network, and the site/campus LAN shown in the figure – is based on PC network protocols such as Novell Netware. A copy of the user agent software is run in each client (the UA client) and this communicates with a similar piece of software in the email server (the UA server) in order to log in to the server and to deposit and retrieve mail into/from the mailbox of the client. The set of mailboxes in the email server are contained in a database known as the **message store (MS)**. In addition, a copy of the user's (IN and OUT) mailbox is often held in the client machine. The UA client periodically retrieves any received mail from the message store and transfers this to its own local mailbox ready for reading by the user. An example protocol associated with the user agent function is the **post office protocol, version 3, (POP3)** which is defined in **RFC 1939**.

The standard structure of (ASCII) text-based mail associated with the Internet is defined in **RFC 822** and we showed an example of this earlier in Figure 1.9(b). Essentially, an email message comprises a header and a message body. The structure of the header is defined in **RFC 821**. It comprises several fields which include the email address of the sender and the intended recipient(s). The body part contains the actual message contents.

As we described in the previous section, the (reliable) transport protocol and the network protocol associated with the Internet are the TCP and IP respectively. Because the equivalent protocols associated with the various types of access network are different from these, the email server normally has two interfaces: one for communicating with the set of registered clients over the access network and the other for communicating with other email servers that are also connected directly to the Internet.

The application protocol associated with the transfer of messages between the MTA in two servers is the **simple mail transfer protocol (SMTP)**.

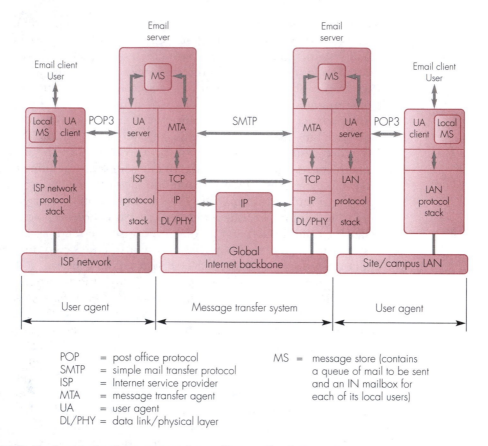

POP   = post office protocol
SMTP   = simple mail transfer protocol
ISP   = Internet service provider
MTA   = message transfer agent
UA   = user agent
DL/PHY = data link/physical layer

MS = message store (contains a queue of mail to be sent and an IN mailbox for each of its local users)

Figure 5.11 Protocol stack to support email over the Internet.

This is also defined in RFC 821 and we shall explain its operation in Section 14.3. Essentially, an email message is transferred by the MTA in the sending server by it first establishing a TCP connection to the MTA in the recipient server. The email address of both the sender and the intended recipient in the header of the message are in the form of symbolic names. Hence the sending MTA requests another application protocol known as the **domain name server (DNS)** for the related Internet address of the recipient server. It then uses this, together with its own Internet address, to create an Internet packet – also known as a **datagram**. As we shall expand upon in Section 9.6, the routing of packets over the Internet is carried out by the IP and hence the Internet address is known also as the **IP address**. Each Internet packet, therefore, contains the IP address of both the sending and recipient servers at its head and the email message as its contents. The IP address of the recipient server is used to route the packet over the Internet and, on receipt, the MTA in the server deposits the message contained in the packet into the recipient's mailbox.

MIME

The RFC 822 standard was defined for use with email messages that are written in English and are made up of just ASCII characters. As the Internet expanded, however, so the need to send messages in different languages evolved. And with the advent of multimedia PCs and workstations, so the need to send messages that contain other media types – audio, images, and video – arose. As a result, extensions to the basic format defined in RFC 822 were added. These are defined in **RFC 2045** and are known as **multipurpose Internet mail extensions** or **MIME**. By retaining the same basic format, existing mail programs and protocols can still be used.

In order to retain compatibility with RFC 822, with MIME additional encoding rules are given in the message header which define the type and structure of the message contents. Examples include image/JPEG and video/MPEG. It is also possible to define multipart messages with each part being of a different type and, if required, output in parallel. An example use of this is for a message which contains a video clip and an associated sound track which need to be output simultaneously. The first field in a MIME message header, however, is the *MIME-Version* and, if this is not present, then the message is assumed to consist of just ASCII text. More details about MIME are given in Section 14.3.2.

Email gateways

The structure we showed earlier in Figure 5.11 assumed that both email servers were connected to the Internet and hence could communicate directly using the SMTP/TCP/IP protocol stack. With many companies and large enterprises, however, often this is not the case and instead a different email system is used. Nevertheless, in addition to sending and receiving mail to/from other employees within the company/enterprise, many of these employees may also require to send and receive mail to/from people whose computers/PCs are connected either to a different company/enterprise network or to the Internet. In practice, there are two problems associated with doing this: first the format of the mail messages is often different and second the application protocols are also different. To overcome these problems, a device known as an **email gateway** is used, the general arrangement being shown in Figure 5.12.

As we show in the figure, the gateway has a number of interfaces, one for connecting to the local email server at the site and the others for connecting to those networks (including the Internet) with which the employees at the site wish to communicate. To transfer a message that is addressed to an outside network, the email server first transfers the message to a message buffer in the email gateway using the protocol stack associated with the company/enterprise network. The email address in the header of the message is then read by an application-level program to determine the network over which the mail should be forwarded. Assuming the external network is the Internet, the program proceeds to reformat the message into the RFC 822 format and then forwards this using the TCP/IP protocol stack as

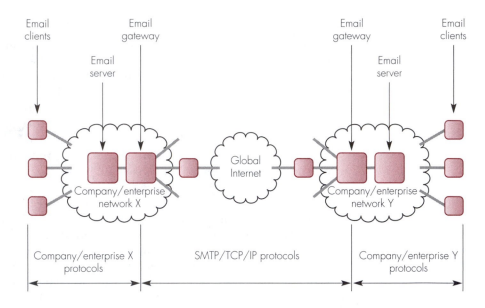

Figure 5.12 Email across dissimilar networks using an email gateway.

described previously. A similar procedure is followed in the reverse direction except the message format has to be changed from RFC 822 to the format used by the company network.

As we can see from the above, the translation procedure can be a time consuming process, especially when a number of different networks are involved and the message contents comprise more than just text. It is for this reason that, increasingly, companies are converting their networks to work using the SMTP/TCP/IP protocols. In the case of a large multisite company, the complete enterprise network is then known as an intranet. This has the advantage of not only removing the need for email gateways, but also enabling employees of the company to access and browse the World Wide Web directly and for selected servers – containing product literature for example – to be accessed from people outside the company.

5.4 Standards relating to interactive applications over the Internet

As we explained in Section 1.4.2, in the context of multimedia communications, most interactive applications over the Internet are concerned with interactions with a World Wide Web server. Hence in this section we shall identify a selection of the standards that have been defined for use with this type of interactive application. We shall identify and explain the role of these standards by considering various application scenarios.

5.4.1 Information browsing

The most basic type of interaction using the Web is for information browsing since with this, the Web user wishes only to browse through information that has been made available on a particular Web server at a site. Typically, as we explained in section 1.4.2, the information comprises an integrated set of one or more Web pages. Each page in the set contains linkages to other pages which can be located either on the same server or on any other server that is connected to the Internet. Typically, the Web pages are written in the HyperText Markup Language (HTML) and contain all the information necessary both to display the contents of a page – text, images, and so on – on the screen of the user/client machine and also to locate the other pages that have linkages with the page. The general arrangement used for information browsing is as shown in Figure 5.13.

A page is accessed and its contents displayed by means of a program known as a **browser** which runs in the user/client machine. The browser locates and fetches each requested page and, by interpreting the formatting commands that the page contains, the page contents are displayed. In addition, by the user clicking the mouse on a linkage point within the displayed page, the page that is linked to that point is accessed by the browser and displayed in the same way. There are a number of browser programs available, some popular examples being Netscape Navigator, NSCA Mosaic, and Microsoft Internet Explorer.

A page can contain two types of text – plaintext and underlined text (hypertext) – tables, images, and sometimes other media such as a sound track or a video clip. In the case of underlined text, in addition to the text,

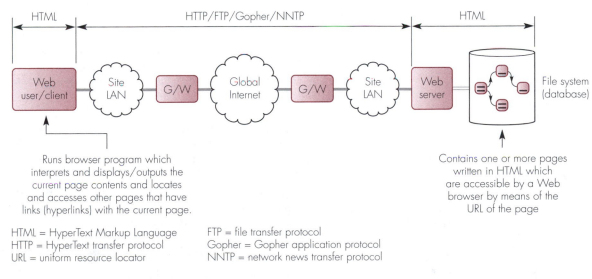

Runs browser program which interprets and displays/outputs the current page contents and locates and accesses other pages that have links (hyperlinks) with the current page.

Contains one or more pages written in HTML which are accessible by a Web browser by means of the URL of the page

HTML = HyperText Markup Language
HTTP = HyperText transfer protocol
URL = uniform resource locator

FTP = file transfer protocol
Gopher = Gopher application protocol
NNTP = network news transfer protocol

Figure 5.13 Information browsing.

this contains all the information that is necessary for the browser to access the contents of the linked page. This is known as a **hyperlink** and the linkage comprises the name of the application protocol (also known as the **scheme**) that is to be used – normally the **hypertext transfer protocol (HTTP)** – and the symbolic Internet name of the server machine (also known as the **domain**) in which the page is stored. Normally, this contains the top-level page for the site, which in turn contains hyperlinks to all the next-level pages. Alternatively, if a specific page is required, it is also possible to specify the (local) directory and name of the file that contains the required page. Collectively, these fields form what is called the **uniform resource locator (URL)** for the page. Two examples are:

http://www.microsoft.com
http://www.mpeg.org/index.html

Notice that all the characters can be either upper or lower case.

In the case of images (and other media types), the media type is in the form of a **tag (IMG)** with a parameter that indicates the name of the field where the image is stored. These are written in the page text at the point where the image is to be displayed and, when the browser interprets the tag, it reads the (compressed) image from the file. The file name also includes the image format and, by using a corresponding decompression algorithm, the browser displays the (decompressed) image at the appropriate point on the screen. Example formats include GIF and JPEG which we described in Sections 3.4.1 and 3.4.5 respectively. In the case of audio and video, these are output either in a similar way (if the browser contains the appropriate decompression code) or the contents of the file containing the audio/video are passed by the browser to a separate program for output known as a **helper application** or **external viewer**.

Each page is accessed and transferred over a TCP connection using the HTTP application-level protocol. Each HTTP interaction comprises a request from the browser written in the form of an ASCII string and a response from the server written in the RFC 822 format with MIME extensions, both of which we described earlier in Section 5.3.3. In order to allow for the possibility that the linked set of pages may be distributed over a number of different servers, a separate TCP connection is established between the client and server for each interaction and, once the response has been received, the TCP connection is cleared. HTTP is known, therefore, as a **stateless protocol** and we shall describe it in more detail in Section 15.2.2.

In addition to using HTTP to access pages written in HTML, a browser can also access other information using a number of the older application protocols. These allow access to the contents of:

■   a file on the client machine on which the browser is running,
■   a remote file using the **file transfer protocol (FTP)**,

- a Gopher (text-only) file using the **gopher protocol**,
- a news article from a UseNet server using the **network news transfer protocol (NNTP)**.

A summary of the protocols that we have identified is presented in Figure 5.14. In the figure it is assumed that all pages are written in HTML and that the browser, in addition to HTTP, supports all the other application protocols we have just listed. Also, that it has various support facilities to decompress the contents of image, audio, and video files that may be included in a page.

5.4.2 Electronic commerce

When browsing the Web for information, the flow of information is unidirectional from the server to the client machine. As we explained in Section 1.4.2, however, some applications also involve the transfer of information in the

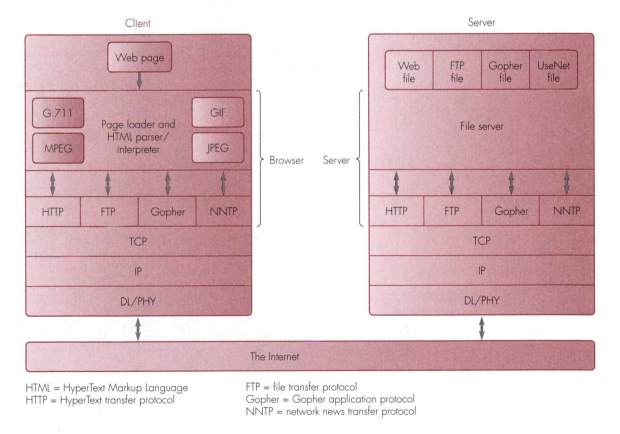

HTML = HyperText Markup Language
HTTP = HyperText transfer protocol

FTP = file transfer protocol
Gopher = Gopher application protocol
NNTP = network news transfer protocol

Figure 5.14 Protocol stack to support information browsing.

reverse direction from the client to a server; for example, after browsing the information at a site, to send details of your credit card in order to purchase, say, a book or theater ticket. This is just one example of what is known more generally as **electronic commerce** or **e-commerce** and there is a range of standards associated with this type of application.

In order to meet this requirement, it is possible to include what is known as a **form** into an HTML page. In the same way that a printed order form contains blank spaces for you to enter your name and other information and to make selections, so a typical HTML form is written to have a similar appearance. The user then uses the mouse and keyboard to enter the requested information and, when all the information has been entered and the appropriate selections made, typically, the user clicks on a symbolic **submit** button to initiate the sending of the entered information back to the server machine.

In addition to having a standardized way for a user of a client machine to enter and initiate the sending of information (forms/submit), there is also a standard for use at the server for processing the received information. This is known as the **common gateway interface (CGI)** and, in addition to accepting and processing the input from forms, the CGI may also initiate the output of other (unsolicited) pages that contain related information. The general arrangement that is used to support e-commerce is shown in Figure 5.15 and we shall present further details of forms and CGI in Section 15.3.6.

As we shall see, a second function associated with CGI is that of **network security**. Clearly, when information such as credit card details is sent over a network, it is essential that it is received only by the intended recipient. Hence there are standards for achieving this and, as we shall expand upon in Section 15.6, they are based on either a **private** or **public key encryption** scheme. At the application level, it is also necessary to authenticate that a par-

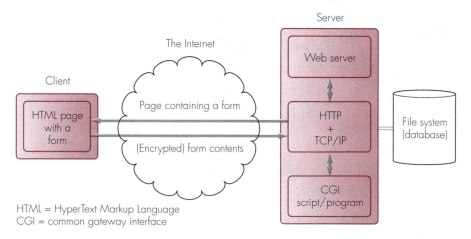

HTML = HyperText Markup Language
CGI = common gateway interface

Figure 5.15 Electronic commerce.

ticular transaction was initiated by the owner of the credit card and not an impostor. Again there are associated standards which we shall also discuss in Section 15.6.

5.4.3 Intermediate systems

The discussion in the previous two sections assumed that both the client and server machines were connected directly to the Internet. In some instances, however, this is not the case and communication between the client and server is achieved through a networking device known as an **intermediate system**.

For example, as we explained in the last section, many enterprise networks now use the same set of protocols as are used with the Internet, the enterprise network then being known as an intranet. This is done both to simplify access to the Web from the various sites that make up the enterprise network and also to enable (external) Web users to access information that is stored on a server connected to the enterprise network. Normally, however, for security reasons access to a server that is connected to an intranet is not provided directly but rather through an intermediate system known as a **firewall** or **security gateway**.

As we show in Figure 5.16(a), the gateway controls the flow of information both to and from the intranet. To do this, the gateway intercepts all incoming requests from the Internet for access to the enterprise server and also all responses from the server that need to be forwarded over the Internet. Each Internet packet contains the IP address of both the source of the packet and the intended recipient/destination. Hence in the most basic type of gateway, the gateway simply maintains a separate list of all source and destination IP addresses that are allowed to pass both into and out from the intranet and any packets that have addresses different from these are discarded. This approach is known as **packet filtering** and is often used when the intranet itself comprises a large number of interconnected sites. In practice, however, it is not too difficult for a hacker to break this system and hence an alternative approach that performs the filtering operation at the application layer rather than the IP layer is also used. With this approach, the gateway behaves like the enterprise server to all incoming requests and only if the gateway is satisfied that a request is from a legitimate user is it relayed to the real server. Similarly, all responses from the real server are sent via the gateway. The same controls are applied to internal requests from a client connected to the intranet for an external server.

A second type of intermediate system is required when a browser supports only the HTTP application protocol. To access information that requires a different application protocol from HTTP it is necessary to use what is known as a **proxy server**. As we show in Figure 5.16(b), all requests for information are passed to the proxy server using the HTTP, but a proxy server can also communicate with other servers using application protocols

(a)

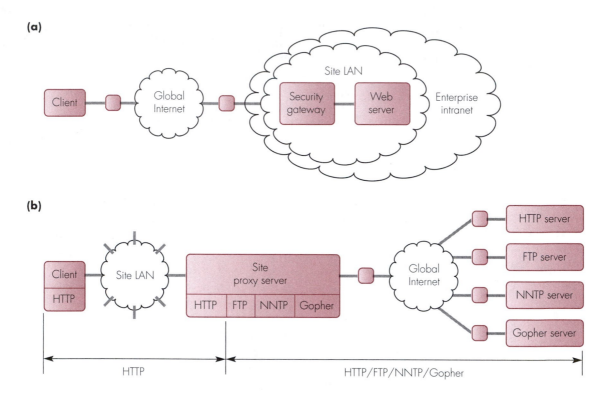

(b)

Figure 5.16 Intermediate systems: (a) security gateway; (b) proxy server.

such as FTP, NNTP, and Gopher. Hence if the information requested requires a different application protocol from HTTP, the proxy server makes the request on behalf of the client using the appropriate protocol. Similarly, on receipt of the requested information, this is passed to the client using HTTP. As we show in the figure, a proxy server can support a number of clients and, in some instances, performs other functions such as those associated with a security gateway.

5.4.4 Java and JavaScript

A disadvantage of using only HTML to write Web pages is that it is then relatively difficult to incorporate new features into pages – such as a new decoder – since this would necessitate modifications to the browser code. To overcome this constraint, it is possible to implement portions of the code for a page as self-contained subprograms – known as **applets** – which are independent of the HTML interpreter. Then, in the same way that an image is accessed and displayed when its tag is interpreted (by the HTML interpreter), so an applet is identified by a tag and, when this is interpreted, the applet code is loaded and run.

The advantage of using applets is that since each applet is a self-contained program, by implementing those parts of a page that contain code that is likely to change in the form of applets (for example media decoders), then any changes that do occur can be incorporated into the server rather than the browser. For example, if the browser contained only a particular type of image decoder and pages became available that contained images that were encoded using a different coder, then without applets the browser code would need to be modified. By using applets, however, the new decoder could be written as an applet – located either on the same server as the current page or on a different server – and, by simply specifying the applet with an applet tag within the page, so the applet for the new decoder would be loaded and run without any modifications to the browser itself. It is also possible to include applets for sound and video. The sound/video can then be output either when the applet is loaded or under control of the user at the click of the mouse.

An example of a programming language that is used to produce applets that are downloaded from a server is **Java**. This is based on C++ but, in order to obtain portability, there are no input/output statements associated with Java. A program written in Java is compiled to run on any machine. The compiled program is known as an applet and, in order for the applet to be run on a variety of different types of (client) machine, the applet code produced by the compiler is for what is called a **virtual machine**. The compiled/applet code is known as **bytecode** and, to run the applet, the browser, in addition to an HTML interpreter, must also contain an interpreter of the Java bytecode. The general scheme is shown in Figure 5.17.

In addition to downloading applets into pages written in HTML, it is also possible to implement a browser simply as a collection of applets. In this case, at startup, the browser comprises just a Java loader/interpreter and everything else is then implemented in the form of applets which are loaded on demand. Hence to access a page written in HTML, the HTML loader/interpreter would be loaded first and, if the accessed page contains an image, then the corresponding image decoder would be loaded and so on. Again, the advantage of this approach is that new versions of the various software components can be introduced more readily.

It is also possible to embed Java code into an HTML page directly. The language used to do this is called **JavaScript**. We shall return to the subject of Java and JavaScript in Section 15.5.

5.5 Standards for entertainment applications

We identified the two types of entertainment applications in Section 1.4.3 under the headings of movie/video-on-demand and interactive television. The standards relating to both types of application are concerned with the way the audio and video are integrated together prior to transmission – the transmission format – and the operational characteristics of the different

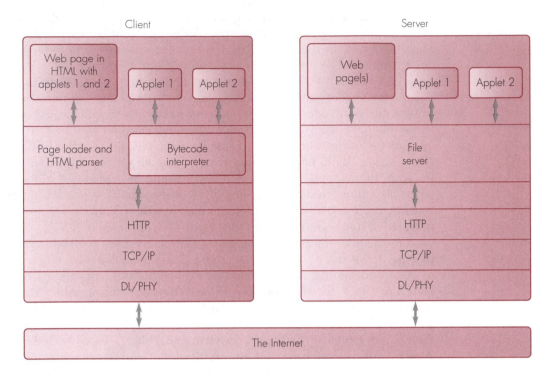

Figure 5.17 Protocol stack to support the browsing of pages containing Java applets.

types of distribution network that are used. We shall discuss the standards relating to both types of application separately.

5.5.1 Movie/video-on-demand

As we showed in Figure 1.15, movie/video-on-demand involves a movie/video being accessed from a server and transmitted over either the access network of a PSTN or a cable TV network. In both cases, the server is managed by the particular network operator and the subscriber interacts with the server to request a specific movie/video.

Transmission format

As we explained in Section 4.3.4, the standard relating to the storage of a VHS-quality video on a server is MPEG-1. The bit rate associated with MPEG-1 is 1.5 Mbps and this must support the video and audio streams associated with the movie/video.

The audio compression standards adopted for all the MPEG standards are defined in **ISO Recommendation 11172-3**. They are based on perceptual/subband coding which we described in Section 4.2.6. As you may recall, there are three alternative standards – known as layers – and typical performance figures for each were given in Table 4.2. The figures shown in the table are for a single audio channel. Also, as we concluded at the end of Section 4.2.7, because the complexity and cost of the encoder – for a particular perceived quality – increases with the level of compression obtained, the choice of compression standard is a compromise between the bandwidth available and the desired perceived quality. As we indicated at the end of Example 4.2, the amount of bandwidth available for the audio associated with MPEG-1 is limited to 300 kbps. Hence a typical choice of audio is either layer-1 compression with single-channel joint-stereo at 256 kbps or layer-2 compression with dual-channel stereo at 128 kbps per channel. The format of the layer-1 audio stream was shown earlier in Figure 4.8(b).

We described the MPEG-1 video compression standard in Section 4.3.5 and the frame structure used for the video was shown in Figure 4.21. The digitization format used is the source intermediate format (SIF) with a resolution of either 352×240 pixels at 30 fps (NTSC) or 352×288 at 25 fps (PAL). The audio and video streams produced by the related encoders are then multiplexed together for storage on the server – a CD-ROM, DVD or hard disk – and subsequent transmission over the distribution network. The essential components that make up an MPEG-1 encoder and decoder are illustrated in Figure 5.18(a) and the format of the output bitstream from the encoder is given in part (b) of the figure

As we can see, in addition to the encoded video and audio streams, it is also possible to store related private (user) data. The output streams produced by both the video and audio encoders are known as **elementary streams (ESs)**. Prior to multiplexing the two streams together, however, since they are both encoded independently, timing information is added to both streams to enable the decoder to output both in synchronism. This is carried out by first dividing each (audio and video) ES into a sequence of discrete packets. Each is known as a **packetized ES** or **PES** and, at its head, is a *type* field that indicates whether the packet contents are audio, video, or private data. There is also a *time-stamp* which indicates the time the audio/video contained within the PES should be output. The time-stamps are generated using a 90 kHz **system time clock** (**STC**) which has a resolution of 33 bits. The header also indicates the amount of data – audio, video, or private – in the PES. Typically, the content of a PES is 2048 bytes.

The stream of PESs from both sources – and private data if present – are multiplexed together into a data structure known as a **pack**. At its head are two headers: a *pack header* and a *system header*. The first contains timing and output bit rate information. The timing information is a **system clock reference (SCR)** and is used by the decoder to synchronize its own system time clock at regular intervals to that of the encoder. The system header contains information such as the buffer size requirements and the number and type of elementary streams that are present.

On receipt of the pack bitstream, the demultiplexer passes the system clock reference to the local system time clock for synchronization and then routes each PES to the appropriate (audio/video) depacketizer. The latter

(a)

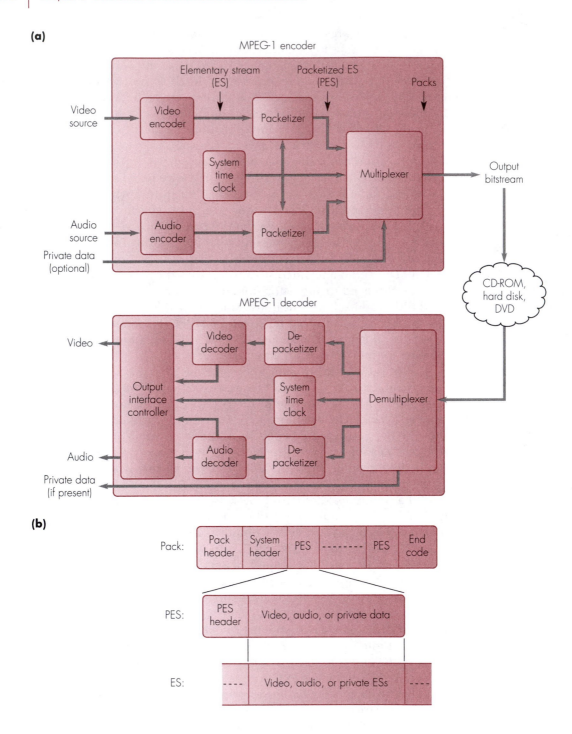

Figure 5.18 MPEG-1: (a) encoder/decoder; (b) output bitstream format.

then rebuilds the original ESs from the related PES contents and these are passed to the corresponding decoder. The timing information relating to each video/audio packet/frame is extracted from the ES and passed, together with the decompressed contents of the ES, to the **output interface controller**. The latter is responsible for outputting the synchronized audio and video in the desired (analog) format and hence includes digital-to-analog converters.

Distribution network

As we indicated at the beginning of this section, movie/video-on-demand to the home can be provided in one of two ways: over an existing twisted-pair line owned by a telephone company or a cable distribution network owned by a cable TV company. In addition, near movie/video-on-demand can be provided by a satellite company, normally by means of pay-per-view. In this case, however, a normal (higher bit rate) broadcast channel is used and hence we shall discuss this under the heading of interactive television.

As we shall see in Section 11.5, high bit rate modems for use with twisted-pair telephone lines provide a forward channel from the local exchange/switching office to subscriber premises of in excess of 1.5 Mbps together with a lower bit rate return channel for interaction purposes. Both these channels are in addition to the existing (analog) channel used for telephony and such modems are used not only to support movie/video-on-demand but also other interactive applications such as fast-access to the Internet.

The technology used in high bit rate modems is known as **asymmetric digital subscriber line** (**ADSL**) and we shall discuss it further in Section 11.5.1. Essentially, however, as we see in Figure 5.19(a), at the customer premises the conventional telephone socket outlet is replaced by an **ADSL subscriber unit** which, in addition to a telephone socket, provides a connection to a television set-top box. The subscriber is able to interact with the server and receive the requested movie/video over the forward channel. Typically, the technology supports a maximum length of twisted-pair cable of 2.5 miles/4 km.

With the telephone network a separate twisted-pair wire goes to each home and hence the facility is available to all subscribers. As we show in the figure, on the network side, the twisted-pair wires from multiple subscribers in an area are terminated in a piece of equipment called an **ADSL network termination unit**. This is located either in the local exchange/switching office or, more usually, in a kurb-side unit. The outputs from a number of such units are then multiplexed/demultiplexed together for transmission purposes back to the local exchange using optical fiber cable, the overall distribution network being known as **fiber-to-the-kurb** (**FTTK**). In addition, although much more expensive because of the need to lay new access cables, it is also possible to take the fiber cable directly to the home. The network is then known as **fiber-to-the-home** (**FTTH**) and clearly, this solution removes the necessity for having (ADSL) modems.

In the case of cable TV networks, a typical distribution network architecture is as shown in Figure 5.19(b). These support, in addition to the multiple TV channels broadcast from the cable TV company local office to all

(a)

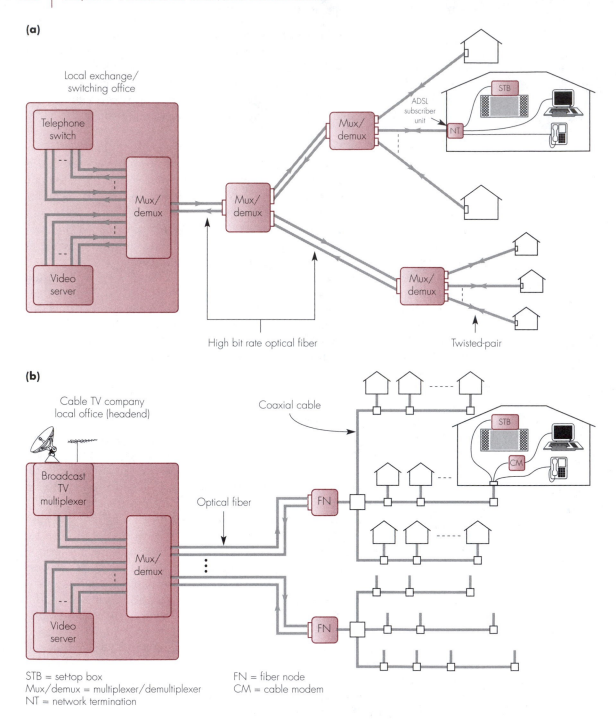

Figure 5.19 Movie/video-on-demand: (a) telephony company architecture; (b) cable TV company architecture.

subscribers, an additional duplex channel that is accessible by each subscriber. The unit used to provide this facility is known as a **cable modem** and this can be used to support a range of applications including movie/video-on-demand, fast Internet access, and so on.

As we show in the figure, the distribution network within a localized area consists of coaxial cable. This passes all the homes within that area and, in the case of broadcast TV programs, these are all multiplexed together onto the one cable and are accessible to all subscribers. Normally, however, each channel is encrypted so that only those registered subscribers with the appropriate decoder can decrypt and view the channels. In the case of the services supported by the cable modem, each subscriber can select the appropriate application separately. Also, because of the high bit rates involved, optical fiber is normally used to link each cable segment to the cable TV company local office. This type of distribution network is known as a **hybrid-fiber-coax** (**HFC**) network.

5.5.2 Interactive television

As we showed earlier in Figure 1.16, the digitized TV programs associated with interactive television can be provided by a cable, satellite, or terrestrial broadcast network. In the case of interactive television, however, the quality of the (broadcast) TV signal is better than that used for video-on-demand.

Transmission format

The video compression standard is based on MPEG-2 which we described earlier in Section 4.3.6. For screens with a 4/3 aspect ratio, the 4:2:0 digitization format is used with a resolution of either 720×480 pixels at 30 fps (NTSC), 720×576 at 25 fps (PAL) or 1440×1152 at 25 fps (European HDTV). For screens with a 16/9 aspect ratio, the same 4:2:0 digitization format is used but with a resolution of 1280×720 pixels (ATV/GA).

The audio compression standard is either MPEG layer 2 (PAL) or Dolby AC-3 (NTSC and ATV/GA). In both cases, up to five full-bandwidth channels – left, right, center, and two surround-sound channels – can be present and also one or more lower-bandwidth channels for commentaries and voice-overs such as translations.

The format of both the audio and video elementary and packetized streams and the encoding of a single television program are similar to those used for MPEG-1. However, since in broadcast applications multiple TV programs are multiplexed together for transmission over the distribution network, an additional format is defined for this purpose. The output stream produced by a single program encoder is known as a **program stream** (**PS**) and the output stream containing multiple programs the **transport stream** (**TS**). The general arrangement is shown in Figure 5.20.

As we can see in Figure 5.20(a), if the digitized TV program is to be stored – rather than broadcast – then the program stream is used directly. If it is to be multiplexed with other programs, then the output streams from the set of program encoders are fed to a second multiplexer known as the **transport stream multiplexer** and it is the output of this that is fed to either a

(a)

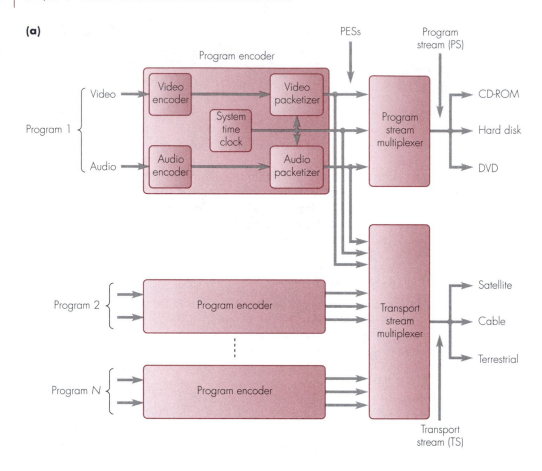

(b)

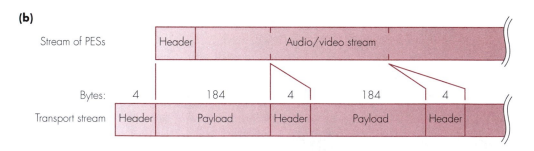

Figure 5.20 TV program multiplexing: (a) PS and TS generation; (b) TS format.

satellite, cable, or terrestrial transmitter. The format of this stream is shown in part (b) of the figure and, as we can see, is divided into a string of 188-byte packets, each comprising a 44-byte header and a 184-byte contents field known as the **payload.**

The header contains a number of fields which include a *synchronization byte,* to enable the receiver(s) to interpret the packet header and its contents on the correct byte boundaries, a *packet identifier (PID)*, to enable the receiver to relate the TS packet payload to the correct PES during its reassembly, an *adaptation flag* (bit) and a *payload flag* (bit). Typically, the length of the PES output by the video and audio packetizers is 2048 bytes and hence these must be fragmented/segmented into multiple 184-byte segments for transmission. Since this does not divide equally into 2048, then the payload of the last TS packet may not be full. If this is the case, then the adaptation flag in the header of this packet is set and the first byte in the payload field indicates the number of bytes in what is known as the *adaptation field*. This comprises, in addition to *stuffing bytes* to fill the payload, a time-stamp indicating when the TS packet was created. This is known as the *program clock reference* and has the same role as the SCR used in an MPEG-1 output stream. Because of the presence of the adaptation field, the payload may not contain any PES data and, if this is the case, the payload flag in the header is set to inform the receiver of this.

In addition to fragments of PES packets, the payload of TS packets is also used to carry system-level tables. These are the **program allocation table (PAT)**, the **program map table (PMT)**, the **conditional access table (CAT)**, and also one or more **private tables**. The presence of a system-level table – instead of a PES fragment – is indicated by a PID of zero in the TS packet header. Since a possibly large number of different program streams – each comprising multiple PES packets – can be present in the transport stream, collectively the system tables are used to inform the receiver about the program streams that are currently present. For example, the PAT contains a field that defines the link between the PID carried in each TS packet header and the corresponding television program. Similarly, the PMT indicates the PID of the elementary streams that make up each program. And, if the program has conditional access – for example, pay-per-view – it indicates the code required to unscramble the related program TS packet contents. A CAT is sent to the receiver whenever a program is present in the TS which has conditional access. The CAT contains the necessary access control data used by the set-top box to allow or inhibit access to the program. Finally, the private tables are intended for service providers and include tables such as a program guide (to allow a subscriber to see the programs currently available), the set of channel frequencies that are being used for the current set of programs, and time-and-date information for the set-top box.

Summary

In this chapter we have identified and presented an overview of the standards that have been defined for use with multimedia communications. We showed that these are many and varied and relate both to the operation of the various networks that are used and also to the hardware and software in the computers (and other types of terminal equipment) that are attached to these networks to provide their users with access to multimedia communication services. A summary of the specific multimedia applications that we described is given in Figure 5.21.

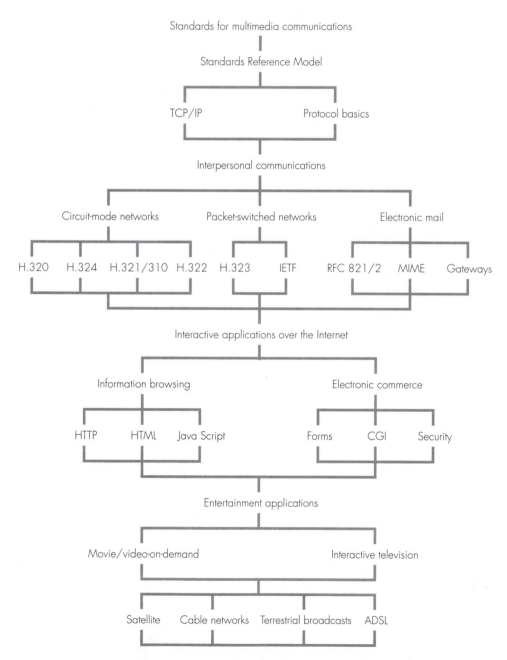

Figure 5.21 Summary of standards identified/discussed in Chapter 5.

Exercises

Section 5.2

5.1 List the reasons why standards are necessary for networked applications involving dissimilar computer/end systems.

5.2 With the aid of the diagrams shown in Figure 5.1, explain the meaning of the following terms relating to standards for multimedia applications:
(i) application standards,
(ii) network interface standards,
(iii) internal network standards,
(iv) networking environment,
(v) local significance,
(vi) end-to-end significance,
(vii) application environment.

5.3 With the aid of the diagrams shown in Figure 5.2, describe the role of each of the five layers that make up the TCP/IP reference model.

5.4 With the aid of a diagram, explain the meaning and role of the following:
(i) peer layer communication,
(ii) protocol data unit (PDU),
(iii) protocol control information,
(iv) outgoing stream construction,
(v) incoming stream reduction.

Section 5.3

5.5 In relation to the set of standards for circuit-mode networks shown in Figure 5.4, explain the role of the following component parts:
(i) call setup,
(ii) multiplexer/demultiplexer,
(iii) system control,
(iv) MCS/MCU,
(v) receive path delay.

5.6 In relation to the set of standards that are used with the different types of circuit-mode network identified in Table 5.1, discuss the following issues:
(i) the choice of audio codec,
(ii) the choice of video codec,

(iii) the role of the user data application protocols,
(iv) the role of the system control and call setup protocols.

5.7 With the aid of the diagrams shown in Figure 5.5, explain the operation of the H.223 multiplexer as used with a PSTN. Include in your explanation:
(i) the structure and content of the information field,
(ii) the structure and role of the multiplex table.

5.8 In relation to the set of standards relating to H.323 shown in Figure 5.6, explain the following:
(i) the role of the gatekeeper during the setting up of a call,
(ii) the role of the gateway during interworking with end systems attached to a circuit-mode network.

5.9 In relation to the set of standards defined by the IETF for interpersonal communications over the Internet, explain the roles of the following:
(i) the session initiation protocol and the related session description protocol,
(ii) the gateway location protocol.

5.10 List the advantages of email over postal mail.

5.11 With the aid of the schematic diagrams shown in Figures 5.10 and 5.11, explain the role of the following when sending an email message:
(i) the user agent,
(ii) an email server including the message store,
(iii) the POP3 protocol,
(iv) the message transfer agent and the SMTP,
(v) the domain name server,
(vi) MIME.

5.12 With the aid of the schematic diagram shown in Figure 5.12, explain how email is sent across the Internet via an email gateway.

Section 5.4

5.13 With the aid of the schematic diagrams shown in Figures 5.13 and 5.14, explain the role of the following when browsing the Web:
   (i)   the browser,
   (ii)   HTML,
   (iii) URL,
   (iv)   HTTP,
   (v)   helper application,
   (vi)   FTP, Gopher, and NNTP.

5.14 With the aid of a diagram, identify and explain the role of the following relating to e-commerce over the Internet:
   (i)   forms,
   (ii)   submit button,
   (iii) CGI scripts,
   (iv)   encryption.

5.15 With the aid of the schematic diagrams shown in Figure 5.16 (a) and (b), explain the role of the following types of intermediate system:
   (i)   a security gateway,
   (ii)   a proxy server,
   (iii) a cache server.

5.16 With the aid of Figure 5.17, explain how a Java applet can be downloaded and run in a browser. Include in your explanation the meaning and use of:
   (i)   bytecode,
   (ii)   bytecode interpreter.

Section 5.5

5.17 With the aid of the schematic diagrams shown in Figure 5.18, explain the use/meaning of the following relating to movie/video-on-demand:
   (i)   elementary stream,

   (ii)   packetized ES,
   (iii) system time clock,
   (iv)   pack,
   (v)   pack header,
   (vi)   system clock reference,
   (vii) output interface controller.

5.18 With the aid of a diagram, describe the essential parts of a twisted-pair access network that has been upgraded to support movie/video-on-demand and high-speed access to the Internet. Include in your description the meaning and use of:
   (i)   ADSL,
   (ii)   ADSL subscriber unit,
   (iii) ADSL network termination unit.

5.19 With the aid of a diagram, describe the essential parts of a cable distribution network that has been upgraded to support digital TV and other high-speed services. Include in your description the meaning and use of:
   (i)   hybrid-fiber-coax network,
   (ii)   fiber node,
   (iii) cable modem.

5.20 With the aid of Figure 5.20(a), explain the use/meaning of the following relating to interactive television:
   (i)   program stream,
   (ii)   transport stream multiplexer
   (iii) transport stream format,
   (iv)   synchronization byte,
   (v)   program clock reference,
   (vi)   system-level tables.

Digital communications basics

6.1 Introduction

As we showed in Figure 5.1 in the last chapter, associated with all the networks that are used to support multimedia applications is a standard network interface to which all the end systems/terminal equipments that are attached to the network must adhere. Hence in each end system is a **network interface card** (**NIC**) – consisting of hardware controlled by associated software – that performs the related network interface functions. In the following chapters we describe the interface associated with the different types of network that we identified in Figure 5.1 and also we present an insight into the operation both of the networks and, where appropriate, the internal (network) protocols that are used.

In the last chapter we also identified a selection of the application standards relating to multimedia and found that, in general, the integrated information stream generated by the various applications is a series of blocks of binary data of varying size. In some instances, the application involves a dialog using these blocks while in others it involves the transfer of a stream of blocks. In terms of the network interface, however, the information relating to the different applications that is to be transferred over the network is treated simply as a string of one or more blocks containing what is referred to as (network) user data.

Although the various networks that are used operate in different ways, the physical and link layers of both the network interface standards and the internal network standards have a number of common features associated with them. So before we describe the operation of the various networks and their interfaces, we shall discuss in this chapter the basic principles associated with digital communications which are common for all networks.

The access lines (and the internal transmission lines used within the various networks) all use bit-serial transmission. In general, therefore, the signal output by the NIC simply varies between two voltage levels ($+V$ and $-V$ for example) at a rate determined by the transmitted bit rate. This mode of transmission is known as **baseband transmission** and is illustrated in Figure 6.1(a). Thus with networks that provide a digital interface, such as a LAN and an ISDN, baseband transmission is also used over the access lines to the network. With networks such as a PSTN, however, analog transmission is used over the access lines since, as we shall expand upon in Section 7.2.1, the presence of a transformer in the speech path means a DC signal – for example a long string of binary 0s or 1s – will not be discernible. As we saw in Section 2.5.1, the bandwidth used over these lines is that of a bandlimited speech signal and is from 200 Hz through to 3400 Hz. Hence as we show in Figure 6.1(b), prior to transmitting the baseband signal output by the NIC, it is necessary first to convert this signal into an analog signal within the same bandwidth that is used for speech. This is done, for example, by modulating – also known as mixing or multiplying – a single-frequency audio signal/tone – chosen from within the bandwidth used for a speech signal and known as the **carrier signal** – by the binary signal to be transmitted. This mode of transmission is known as **modulated transmission** and the unit that performs the modulation and demodulation functions is a modem.

We shall describe modems and this mode of transmission further in Section 7.2.2. It should be noted, however, that even though modulated transmission is sometimes used over the access lines to the network – and also within the various types of broadcast entertainment networks – normally, the output from the NIC within each end system is a baseband signal.

When transmitting any type of electrical signal over a transmission line, the signal is **attenuated** (decreased in amplitude) and **distorted** (misshapen) by the transmission medium. Also, present with all types of transmission medium is an electrical signal known as **noise**. The amplitude of the noise signal varies randomly with time and adds itself to the electrical signal being transmitted over the line. The combined effect is that at some stage, the receiver is unable to determine from the attenuated received signal with noise whether the transmitted signal was a binary 1 or 0. An example showing the combined effect of attenuation, distortion, and noise on a baseband signal is shown in Figure 6.2.

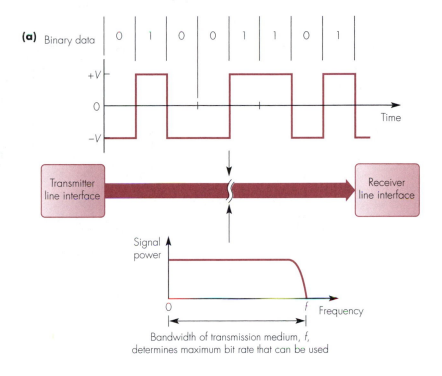

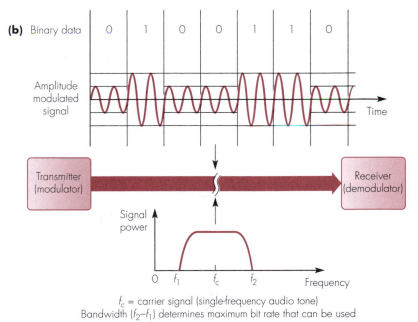

Figure 6.1 Modes of transmission: (a) baseband transmission; (b) modulated transmission.

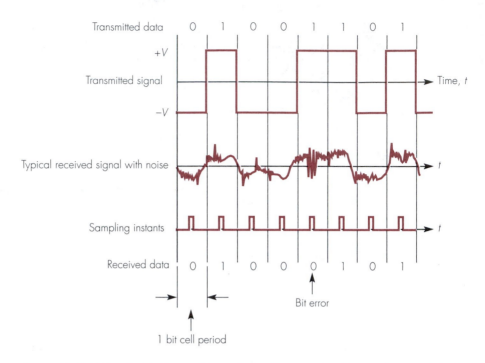

Figure 6.2 Effect of attenuation, distortion, and noise on transmitted signal.

In practice, the level of signal impairment is determined by:

■ the type of transmission medium,
■ the length of the transmission medium,
■ the bandwidth of the medium,
■ the bit rate of the data being transmitted.

We shall discuss the characteristics of the different types of transmission media in Section 6.2.

As we show in Figure 6.2, the received signal is at its peak amplitude in the center of each **bit cell period**. Hence in order for the receiving electronics to determine the signal level (and hence bit) present on the line during each bit cell period, it endeavors to sample the received signal at the center of each bit cell. When the receiver is doing this, it is said to be in **bit synchronism** with the incoming bitstream. However, although the receiver knows the nominal bit rate being used by the transmitter to transmit the bitstream, the receiver electronics operates quite independently of the transmitter with the effect that the receiver clock used to sample the signal will be slightly different from that used at the transmitter. In practice, therefore, sampling the signal present on the line at the correct time instant is a non-trivial task.

Achieving bit synchronism is only the initial step in achieving the reliable transfer of information over a transmission line. Most of the bit synchronization methods that are used take a variable number of bits before bit synchronism is achieved. Hence in order to interpret the received bitstream on the correct character/byte boundaries, the receiver electronics must also be able to determine the start of each new character/byte and, where appropriate, the start and end of each block of characters/bytes. Again, when the receiver is doing this, it is said to be in **character/byte synchronism** and **block/frame synchronism** respectively. In practice, there are two alternative types of baseband transmission – asynchronous and synchronous – and each uses different methods to achieve the three levels of synchronization. We describe the methods used with asynchronous transmission in Section 6.4 and those used with synchronous transmission in Section 6.5.

As we showed in Figure 6.2, if the amplitude of the received signal falls below the noise signal level, then the received signal may be incorrectly interpreted and, if it is, a transmission/bit error will result. To allow for this possibility, additional bits are added to each transmitted block to enable the receiver to determine – to high probability – when transmission errors are present in a received block. We describe a selection of the methods that are used to detect the presence of transmission errors in Section 6.6.

In some applications, the loss of occasional blocks of information from the received bitstream can be tolerated and hence blocks that are found to contain transmission errors are simply discarded. In other applications, however, the loss of a block is unacceptable and it then becomes necessary for the receiver to request another copy of those blocks that contain errors. This involves the receiver sending what are called error control messages back to the transmitter. This is done in one of two ways and depends on whether the network interface offers a best-effort service or a reliable service. If the service offered is best-effort, both the network and link layers simply discard blocks in error and the error recovery procedure is carried out as part of the transport protocol in the two communicating end systems. If a reliable network service is offered, then the error recovery is part of the link protocol. We discuss link protocols in Section 6.7 and a practical example in Section 6.8. We shall defer the discussion of transport protocols until Chapter 12.

6.2 Transmission media

The transmission of an electrical signal requires a transmission medium which, normally, takes the form of a transmission line. In some cases, this consists of a pair of conductors or wires. Common alternatives are a beam of light guided by a glass fiber and electromagnetic waves propagating through free space. The type of transmission medium is important, since the various types of media have different bandwidths associated with them which, in turn, determines the maximum bit rate that can be used. We discuss the more common types of transmission media in the following subsections.

6.2.1 Two-wire open lines

A two-wire open line is the simplest transmission medium. Each wire is insulated from the other and both are open to free space. This type of line is adequate for connecting equipment that is up to 50 m apart using moderate bit rates (less than, say, 19.2 kbps). The signal, typically a voltage or current level relative to some ground reference, is applied to one wire while the ground reference is applied to the other.

Although a two-wire open line can be used to connect two computers (data terminal equipments or DTEs) directly, it is used mainly for connecting a DTE to local data circuit-terminating equipment (DCE) – for example a modem. Such connections usually utilize multiple lines, the most common arrangement being a separate insulated wire for each signal and a single wire for the common ground reference. The complete set of wires is then either enclosed in a single protected **multicore cable** or molded into a **flat ribbon cable** as shown in Figure 6.3(a).

With this type of line, care must be taken to avoid cross-coupling of electrical signals between adjacent wires in the same cable. This is known as **crosstalk** and is caused by **capacitive coupling** between the two wires. In addition, the open structure makes it susceptible to the pick-up of spurious **noise signals** from other electrical signal sources caused by **electromagnetic radiation**. The main problem with such signals is that they may be picked up in just one wire – for example the signal wire – creating an additional difference signal between the two wires. Since the receiver normally operates using the difference signal between the two wires, this can give rise to an erroneous interpretation of the combined (signal plus noise) received signal. These factors all contribute to the limited lengths of line and bit rates that can be used reliably.

6.2.2 Twisted-pair lines

We can achieve much better immunity to spurious noise signals by employing a twisted-pair line in which a pair of wires are twisted together. The proximity of the signal and ground reference wires means that any interference signal is picked up by both wires reducing its effect on the difference signal. Furthermore, if multiple twisted pairs are enclosed within the same cable, the twisting of each pair within the cable reduces crosstalk. A schematic of a twisted-pair line is shown in Figure 6.3(b).

Twisted-pair lines are suitable, with appropriate line driver and receiver circuits that exploit the potential advantages gained by using such a geometry, for bit rates in order of 1 Mbps over short distances (less than 100 m) and lower bit rates over longer distances. More sophisticated driver and receiver circuits enable bit rates of tens of Mbps to be achieved over similar distances. Such lines, known as **unshielded twisted pairs** (**UTPs**), are used extensively in telephone networks and (with special integrated circuits) in many local area networks. With **shielded twisted pairs** (**STPs**), a protective screen or shield is used to reduce further the effects of interference signals. This is shown in Figure 6.3(c) and is now preferred to UTP in networking applications.

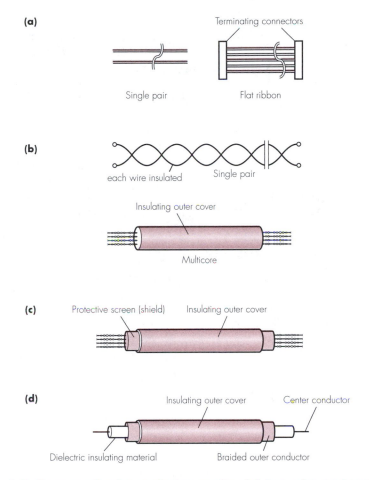

(a)

Terminating connectors

Single pair   Flat ribbon

(b)

each wire insulated   Single pair

Insulating outer cover

Multicore

(c)

Protective screen (shield)   Insulating outer cover

(d)

Insulating outer cover   Center conductor

Dielectric insulating material   Braided outer conductor

Figure 6.3 Copper wire transmission media: (a) two-wire and multiwire open lines; (b) unshielded twisted pair; (c) shielded twisted pair; (d) coaxial cable.

6.2.3 Coaxial cable

The main limiting factors of a twisted-pair line are its capacity and a phenomenon known as the **skin effect**. As the bit rate (and hence frequency) of the transmitted signal increases, the current flowing in the wires tends to flow only on the outer surface of the wire, thus using less of the available cross-section. This increases the electrical resistance of the wires for higher-frequency signals, leading to higher attenuation. In addition, at higher frequencies, more signal power is lost as a result of radiation effects. Hence, for applications that demand a high bit rate over long distances, coaxial cable is often used as the transmission medium.

Coaxial cable minimizes both these effects. Figure 6.3(d) shows the signal and ground reference wires as a solid center conductor running concentrically (coaxially) inside a solid (or braided) outer circular conductor. Ideally the space between the two conductors should be filled with air, but in practice it is normally filled with a dielectric insulating material with a solid or honeycomb structure.

The center conductor is effectively shielded from external interference signals by the outer conductor. Also only minimal losses occur as a result of electromagnetic radiation and the skin effect because of the presence of the outer conductor. Coaxial cable can be used with either baseband or modulated transmission, but typically 10 Mbps over several hundred meters – or higher with modulation – is perfectly feasible. As we shall see in Section 11.2, coaxial cable is used extensively in cable television (CATV) networks.

6.2.4 Optical fiber

While the geometry of coaxial cable significantly reduces the various limiting effects, the maximum signal frequency, and hence the bit rate that can be transmitted using a solid (normally copper) conductor, although very high, is limited. This is also the case for twisted-pair cable. **Optical fiber cable** differs from both these transmission media in that it carries the transmitted bitstream in the form of a fluctuating beam of light in a glass fiber, rather than as an electrical signal on a wire. Light waves have a much wider bandwidth than electrical waves, enabling optical fiber cable to achieve transmission rates of hundreds of Mbps. It is used extensively in the core transmission network of PSTNs and LANs and also CATV networks.

Light waves are also immune to electromagnetic interference and crosstalk. Hence optical fiber cable is extremely useful for the transmission of lower bit rate signals in electrically noisy environments, in steel plants, for example, which employ much high-voltage and current-switching equipments. It is also being used increasingly where security is important, since it is difficult physically to tap.

An optical fiber cable consists of a single glass fiber for each signal to be transmitted, contained within the cable's protective coating which also shields the fiber from any external light sources. See Figure 6.4(a). The light signal is generated by an optical transmitter, which performs the conversion from a normal electrical signal as used in a DTE. An optical receiver is used to perform the reverse function at the receiving end. Typically, the transmitter uses a **light-emitting diode** (**LED**) or **laser diode** (**LD**) to perform the conversion operation while the receiver uses a light-sensitive **photodiode** or **photo transistor**.

The fiber itself consists of two parts: an optical core and an optical cladding with a lower refractive index. Light propagates along the optical fiber core in one of three ways depending on the type and width of core material used. These transmission modes are shown in Figure 6.4(b).

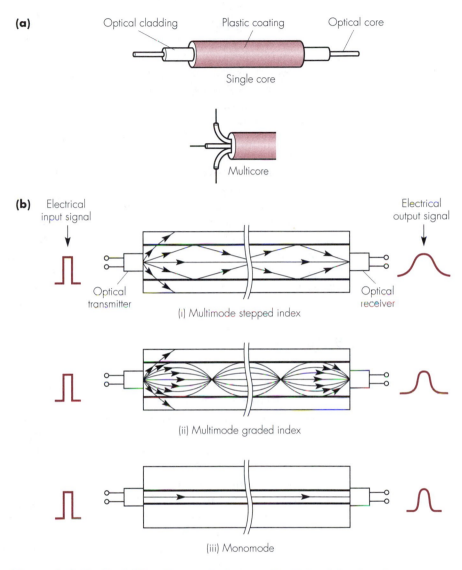

Figure 6.4 Optical fiber transmission media: (a) cable structures; (b) transmission modes.

In a **multimode stepped index fiber** the cladding and core material each has a different but uniform refractive index. All the light emitted by the diode at an angle less than the critical angle is reflected at the cladding interface and propagates along the core by means of multiple (internal) reflections. Depending on the angle at which it is emitted by the diode, the light will take a variable amount of time to propagate along the cable. Therefore the received signal has a wider pulse width than the input signal with a corresponding decrease in the maximum permissible bit rate. This effect is known as **dispersion** and means this type of cable is used primarily for modest bit rates with relatively inexpensive LEDs compared to laser diodes.

Dispersion can be reduced by using a core material that has a variable (rather than constant) refractive index. As we show in Figure 6.4(b), in a **multi-mode graded index fiber** light is refracted by an increasing amount as it moves away from the core. This has the effect of narrowing the pulse width of the received signal compared with stepped index fiber, allowing a corresponding increase in maximum bit rate.

Further improvements can be obtained by reducing the core diameter to that of a single wavelength (3–10μm) so that all the emitted light propagates along a single (dispersionless) path. Consequently, the received signal is of a comparable width to the input signal and is called **monomode fiber**. It is normally used with LDs and can operate at hundreds of Mbps.

Alternatively, multiple high bit rate transmission channels can be derived from the same fiber by using different portions of the optical bandwidth for each channel. This mode of operation is known as **wave-division multiplexing** (**WDM**) and, when using this, bit rates in excess of tens of Gbps can be achieved.

6.2.5 Satellites

All the transmission media we have discussed so far have used a physical line to carry the transmitted information. However, data can also be transmitted using electromagnetic (radio) waves through free space as in **satellite** systems. A collimated **microwave beam**, onto which the data is modulated, is transmitted to the satellite from the ground. This beam is received and retransmitted (relayed) to the predetermined destination(s) using an on-board circuit known as a **transponder**. A single satellite has many transponders, each covering a particular band of frequencies. A typical satellite channel has an extremely high bandwidth (500 MHz) and can provide many hundreds of high bit rate data links using a technique known as **time division multiplexing** (**TDM**). We shall describe this in Section 7.2.3 but, essentially, the total available capacity of the channel is divided into a number of subchannels, each of which can support a high bit rate link.

Satellites used for communication purposes are normally **geostationary**, which means that the satellite orbits the earth once every 24 hours in synchronism with the earth's rotation and hence appears stationary from the ground. The orbit of the satellite is chosen so that it provides a line-of-sight communication path to the transmitting station(s) and receiving station(s). The degree of the collimation of the microwave beam retransmitted by the satellite can be either coarse, so that the signal can be picked up over a wide geographical area, or finely focussed, so that it can be picked up only over a limited area. In the second case the signal power is higher allowing smaller-diameter receivers called **antennas** or **dishes** to be used. Satellites are widely used for data transmission applications ranging from interconnecting different national computer communication networks to providing high bit rate paths to link communication networks in different parts of the same country. They are also used in entertainment applications for the broadcast of TV programs.

A typical satellite system used for TV broadcast applications is shown in Figure 6.5(a). Only a unidirectional transmission path is used with the up and down channels operating at different frequencies. For data communication applications, however, a more common configuration involves a central hub ground station that communicates with a number of ground stations distributed around the country. Each ground station has a small antenna associated with it – typically 1 meter in diameter – which, in addition to receiving the signal transmitted by the hub station, allows the station to transmit back to the hub. Such ground stations are known as **very small aperture terminals** or **VSATs**. Typically, as we show in Figure 6.5(b), the computer associated with each VSAT communicates with a central computer connected to the hub. Normally, the central site broadcasts to all VSATs at a high bit rate of 0.5–2 Mbps while in the reverse direction each VSAT transmits at a lower bit rate of up to 64 kbps.

To communicate with a particular VSAT, the central site broadcasts the message with the identity of the intended VSAT at the head of the message. For applications that require VSAT-to-VSAT communication, all messages are first sent to the central site – via the satellite – which then broadcasts them to the intended recipients. With the next generation of higher-powered satellites it will be possible for the routing to be carried out on board the satellite without passing through a central site. Direct VSAT-to-VSAT communication is then possible.

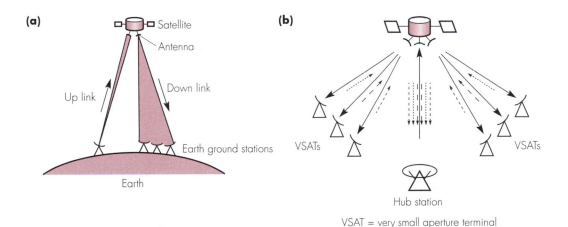

(a) Satellite, Antenna, Up link, Down link, Earth ground stations, Earth

(b) VSATs, VSATs, Hub station, VSAT = very small aperture terminal

Figure 6.5 Satellite systems: (a) broadcast television; (b) data communications.

6.2.6 Terrestrial microwave

Terrestrial microwave links are widely used to provide communication links when it is impractical or too expensive to install physical transmission media, for example across a river or perhaps a swamp or desert. As the collimated microwave beam travels through the earth's atmosphere, it can be disturbed by such factors as manufactured structures and adverse weather conditions. With a satellite link, on the other hand, the beam travels mainly through free space and is therefore less prone to such effects. Nevertheless, line-of-sight microwave communication through the earth's atmosphere can be used reliably for the transmission of relatively high bit rates over distances in excess of 50 km.

6.2.7 Radio

Radio transmission using lower-frequency radio waves (c.f. microwaves) is also used for the transmission of digital information in place of fixed-wire links over distances up to several kilometers.

Modulated transmission is used and example applications include mobile telephony and more general mobile data applications. A radio transmitter – known as a **base station** – is located at a fixed-wire termination point as shown in Figure 6.6(a). This provides a cordless link to the fixed-wire termination point for any handset/terminal that is within the (radio) field of coverage of the base station.

Multiple base stations must be used for applications such as mobile telephony that require a wider coverage area or a higher density of users. The coverage area of each base station is restricted – by limiting its power output – so that it provides only sufficient channels to support the total number of calls in that area. Wider coverage is achieved by arranging multiple base stations in a cell structure as shown in Figure 6.6(b). In practice, the size of each cell varies and is determined by such factors as the handset/terminal density and local terrain.

Each base station operates using a different band of frequencies from its neighbors. However, since the field of coverage of each base station is limited, it is possible to reuse its frequency band in other parts of the network. All the base stations within a region are connected by fixed-wire lines to a mobile switching center (MSC) which, in turn, is connected both to MSCs in other regions and the fixed telephone network. In this way, a handset can make and receive calls both to other handsets and also to telephones that are connected to the fixed network.

A similar arrangement can be utilized within a building to provide cordless links to computer-based equipment within each office. In such cases one or more base stations are located on each floor of the building and connected to the fixed network. Each base station provides cordless links to the fixed network for all the computers in its field of coverage. This avoids rewiring whenever a new computer is installed or moved, but at the cost of providing a radio unit to convert the data into and from a radio signal. The usable data rate is often much lower than that achieved with fixed wiring.

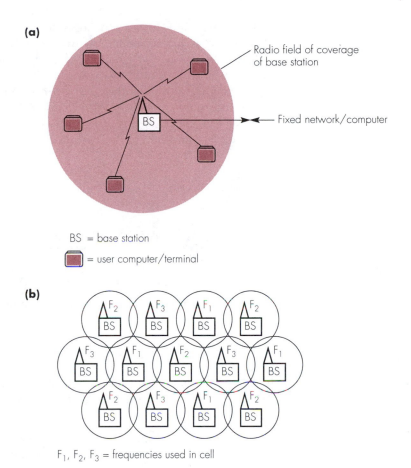

Figure 6.6 Ground-based radio transmission: (a) single cell; (b) multiple cells.

6.2.8 Signal propagation delay

As we saw in Section 1.5.5, there is always a short but finite time delay for a signal (electrical, optical, or radio) to propagate (travel) from one end of a transmission medium to the other. This is known as the **propagation delay**, T_p, of the medium. At best, signals propagate (radiate) through the medium at the speed of light $(3 \times 10^8 \, \text{ms}^{-1})$. The speed of propagation for twisted-pair wire or coaxial cable is a fraction of this figure. Typically, it is in the region of $2 \times 10^8 \, \text{ms}^{-1}$, that is, a signal will take $0.5 \times 10^{-8} \, \text{s}$ to travel 1 m through the medium. Although this may seem insignificant, in some situations the resulting delay is important.

As we explain later in Section 6.7.1, in many instances, on receipt of each block of data/information, an acknowledgment of correct (or otherwise) receipt is returned to the sender. An important parameter of a transmission link, therefore, is the **round-trip delay** associated with the link, that is, the time delay between the first bit of a block being transmitted by the sender and the last bit of its associated acknowledgement being received. Clearly, this is a function not only of the time taken to transmit the frame at the link bit rate – known as the transmission delay, T_x – but also of the propagation delay of the link, T_p. The relative weighting of the two times varies for different types of link and hence the two times are often expressed as a ratio a such that:

$$a = \frac{T_p}{T_x}$$

where
$$T_p = \frac{\text{physical separation } S \text{ in meters}}{\text{velocity of propagation } V \text{ in meters per second}}$$

and
$$T_x = \frac{\text{number of bits to be transmitted } N}{\text{link bit rate } R \text{ in bits per second}}$$

Example 6.1

A 1000-bit block of data is to be transmitted between two computers. Determine the ratio of the propagation delay to the transmission delay, a, for the following types of data link:

(i) 100 m of twisted-pair wire and a transmission rate of 10 kbps,
(ii) 10 km of coaxial cable and a transmission rate of 1 Mbps,
(iii) 50 000 km of free space (satellite link) and a transmission rate of 10 Mbps.

Assume that the velocity of propagation of an electrical signal within each type of cable is $2 \times 10^8\,\mathrm{ms^{-1}}$, and that of free space $3 \times 10^8\,\mathrm{ms^{-1}}$.

Answer:

(i) $T_p = \dfrac{S}{V} = \dfrac{100}{2 \times 10^8} = 5 \times 10^{-7}\,\mathrm{s}$

$T_x = \dfrac{N}{R} = \dfrac{1000}{10 \times 10^3} = 0.1\,\mathrm{s}$

$a = \dfrac{T_p}{T_x} = \dfrac{5 \times 10^{-7}}{0.1} = 5 \times 10^{-6}$

6.1 Continued

(ii) $T_p = \dfrac{S}{V} = \dfrac{10 \times 10^3}{2 \times 10^8} = 5 \times 10^{-5}\,\text{s}$

$T_x = \dfrac{N}{R} = \dfrac{1000}{1 \times 10^6} = 1 \times 10^{-3}\,\text{s}$

$a = \dfrac{T_p}{T_x} = \dfrac{5 \times 10^{-5}}{1 \times 10^{-3}} = 5 \times 10^{-2}$

(iii) $T_p = \dfrac{S}{V} = \dfrac{5 \times 10^{-7}}{3 \times 10^8} = 1.67 \times 10^{-1}\,\text{s}$

$T_x = \dfrac{N}{R} = \dfrac{1000}{10 \times 10^6} = 1 \times 10^{-4}\,\text{s}$

$a = \dfrac{T_p}{T_x} = \dfrac{1.67 \times 10^{-1}}{1 \times 10^{-4}} = 1.67 \times 10^3$

We can conclude from this example:

- If a is less than 1, then the round-trip delay is determined primarily by the transmission delay.
- If a is equal to 1, then both delays have equal effect.
- If a is greater than 1, then the propagation delay dominates.

Furthermore, in case (c) it is interesting to note that, providing blocks are transmitted contiguously, there will be:

$$10 \times 10^6 \times 1.67 \times 10^{-1} = 1.67 \times 10^6\,\text{bits}$$

in transit between the two end systems at any one time, that is, the sending system will have transmitted 1.67×10^6 bits before the first bit arrives at the receiving system. Such links are said, therefore, to have a large **bandwidth/delay product**, where bandwidth relates to the bit rate of the link and delay the propagation delay of the link. We shall discuss these implications further in Section 6.7.1.

6.3 Sources of signal impairment

A selection of the various attenuation and distortion effects that can degrade a signal during transmission are shown in Figure 6.7. Any signal carried on a transmission medium is affected by attenuation, limited bandwidth, delay distortion, and noise. Although all are present and produce a combined effect, we shall consider the source of each impairment separately.

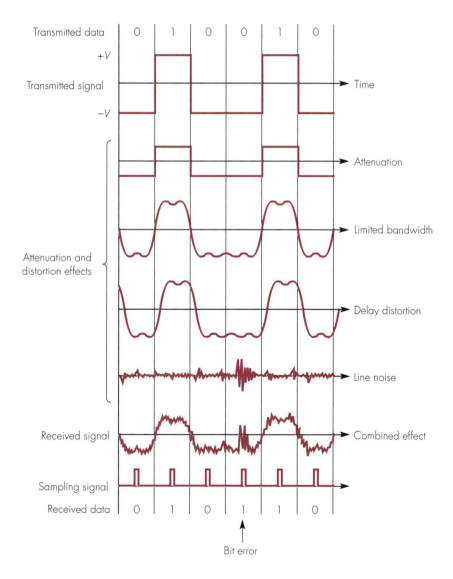

Figure 6.7 Sources of signal impairment.

6.3.1 Attenuation

As a signal propagates along a transmission medium (line) its amplitude decreases. This is known as **signal attenuation**. Normally, to allow for attenuation, a limit is set on the length of the cable that can be used to ensure that the receiver circuitry can reliably detect and interpret the received attenuated signal. If the cable is longer, one or more **amplifiers** – also known as **repeaters** – are inserted at intervals along the cable to restore the received signal to its original level.

Because there is a small but finite *capacitance* between the two wires making up a transmission line, signal attenuation increases as a function of frequency. Hence, since a signal comprises a range of frequencies, the signal is also distorted. To overcome this effect, the amplifiers are designed to amplify different frequency signals by varying amounts. Alternatively, devices known as **equalizers** are used to equalize the attenuation across a defined band of frequencies.

We measure both attenuation and amplification – also known as **gain** – in **decibels** (**dB**). If we denote the transmitted signal power level by P_1 and the received power by P_2, then

$$\text{Attenuation} = 10 \log_{10} \frac{P_1}{P_2} \text{ dB}$$

and

$$\text{Amplification} = 10 \log_{10} \frac{P_2}{P_1} \text{ dB}$$

Since both P_1 and P_2 have the same unit of **watts**, then decibels are dimensionless and simply a measure of the relative magnitude of the two power levels. The use of logarithms means that the overall attenuation/ amplification of a multisection transmission channel can be determined simply by summing together the attenuation/amplification of the individual sections.

More generally, as we shall expand upon in Section 6.5.1, when we transmit binary information over a limited-bandwidth channel such as PSTN, we can often use more than two signal levels. This means that each signal element can represent more than a single binary digit. In general, if the number of signal levels is M, the number of bits per signal element m, is given by:

$$m = \log_2 M$$

For example, if four signal levels are used to transmit a data bitstream, then each signal element can be used to transmit two binary digits.

The rate of change of the signal is known as the **signaling rate** (R_s) and is measured in **baud**. It is related to the data bit rate, R, by the following expression:

$$R = R_s \log_2 M$$

Example 6.2

A transmission channel between two communicating DTEs is made up of three sections. The first introduces an attenuation of 16 dB, the second an amplification of 20 dB, and the third an attenuation of 10 dB. Assuming a mean transmitted power level of 400 mW, determine the mean output power level of the channel.

Answer:

Either:

For first section, $\quad 16 = 10 \log_{10} \dfrac{400}{P_2} \quad$ Hence $P_2 = 10.0475$ mW

For second section, $\quad 20 = 10 \log_{10} \dfrac{P_2}{10.0475} \quad$ Hence $P_2 = 1004.75$ mW

For third section, $\quad 10 = 10 \log_{10} \dfrac{1004.75}{P_2} \quad$ Hence $P_2 = 100.475$ mW

That is, the mean output power level = 100.475 mW

Or:

Overall attenuation of channel = $(16 - 20) + 10 = 6$ dB

Hence $\quad 6 = 10 \log_{10} \dfrac{400}{P_2}$ and $P_2 = 100.475$ mW

6.3.2 Limited bandwidth

Any communications channel/transmission medium – twisted-pair wire, coaxial cable, radio, and so on – has a defined bandwidth associated with it which specifies the band of sinusoidal frequency components that will be transmitted by the channel unattenuated. Hence when transmitting data over a channel, we need to quantify the effect the bandwidth of the channel will have on the transmitted data signal.

We can use a mathematical technique known as **Fourier analysis** to show that any periodic signal – that is, a signal which repeats itself at equal time intervals (known as the period) – is made up of an infinite series of sinusoidal frequency components. The period of the signal determines the **fundamental frequency** component: the reciprocal of the period in seconds yields the frequency in **cycles per second** (**Hz**). The other components have frequencies which are multiples of this and these are known as the **harmonics** of the fundamental.

In terms of data transmission, the signals of interest are binary sequences and, although in practice a transmitted binary message may be made up of randomly varying sequences, for analysis purposes we shall consider selected periodic sequences such as 101010..., 110110..., 11101110..., and so on. In the first example, the sequence 10 repeats with a period of two bit-cell intervals, in the second, the sequence 110 with a period of three intervals, and so on. We can deduce from this that the sequence 101010... has the shortest period and will yield the highest fundamental frequency component. This means that other sequences will yield frequencies less than this and hence, for analysis purposes, the sequence with the shortest period is often referred to as the **worst-case sequence**.

For transmission purposes there are two basic binary signal types: **unipolar** and **bipolar**. An example of each is shown in Figure 6.8(a). With a unipolar signal, the signal amplitude varies between a positive voltage level – say, $+V$ – and 0 volts. We call such signals **return-to-zero (RZ)** signals. With a bipolar signal, the signal amplitude varies between a positive and a negative voltage level – say $+V$ and $-V$. These signals are **non-return-to-zero (NRZ)** signals. A unipolar signal has a mean signal level of $V/2$ while a bipolar signal has a mean of zero. The amplitude variation of a unipolar signal is V while for a bipolar signal it is $2V$. These differences yield slightly different Fourier series which, for the two signal types, are as follows:

$$\text{Unipolar} \quad v(t) = \frac{V}{2} + \frac{2V}{\pi}\left\{\cos\omega_0 t - \frac{1}{3}\cos 3\omega_0 t + \frac{1}{5}\cos 5\omega_0 t - \ldots\right\}$$

$$\text{Bipolar} \quad v(t) = \frac{4V}{\pi}\left\{\cos\omega_0 t - \frac{1}{3}\cos 3\omega_0 t + \frac{1}{5}\cos 5\omega_0 t - \ldots\right\}$$

where: $v(t)$ is the voltage signal representation as a function of time,
ω_0 is the fundamental frequency component in radians per second,
$f_0 = \omega_0/2\pi$ is the fundamental frequency in Hz,
$T = 1/f_0$ is the period of the fundamental frequency in seconds.

We can deduce from these expressions that any periodic binary sequence is made up of an infinite series of sinusoidal signals including the fundamental frequency component, f_0, a third harmonic component, $3f_0$, a fifth harmonic, $5f_0$, and so on.

Note that for binary sequences only the odd harmonic components are present and that their amplitude diminishes with increasing frequency. To illustrate the effect of this, the fundamental together with the third and fifth harmonics of a bipolar signal are shown in diagrammatic form in Figure 6.8(b).

Since a communications channel has a limited bandwidth, as we can deduce from the above, when a binary data signal is transmitted over a channel, only those frequency components that are within the channel bandwidth will be received. The effect of this on the example binary signal 101010... is

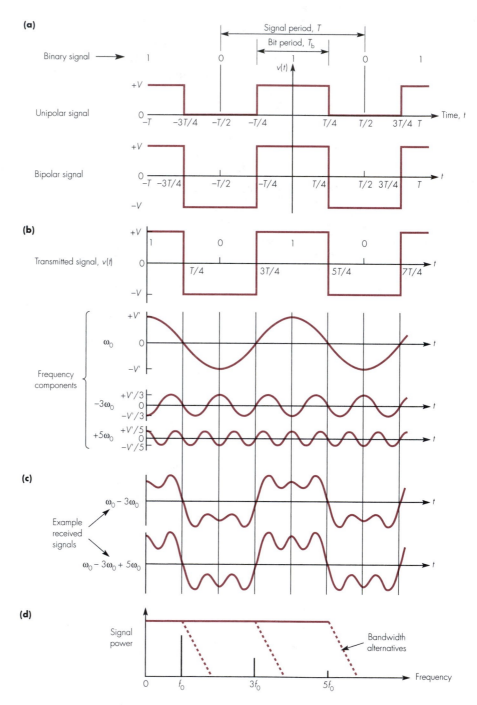

Figure 6.8 Effect of limited bandwidth: (a) alternative binary signals; (b) frequency components of a periodic binary sequence; (c) examples of received signals; (d) bandwidth representations.

shown in Figure 6.8(c). As we can see, the larger the channel bandwidth, the more higher-frequency components are received and hence the closer is the received signal to the original (transmitted) signal.

As the bandwidth of a channel is measured in Hz, normally, it is shown as a function of frequency as illustrated in Figure 6.8(d). In the figure, there are three alternative bandwidths: the first allows sinusoidal signals of frequencies up to f_0 to pass unattenuated, the second up to $3f_0$, and the third up to $5f_0$. In practice, however, when only a two-level (binary) signal is being transmitted, the receiver simply samples the received signal at the center of each bit-cell interval. This means that the receiver need only discriminate between the binary 1 and 0 levels at the sampling instant and the exact shape of the signal outside these instances is less important. As we discussed earlier, the sequence 101010... generates the highest-frequency components while a sequence of all 1s or all 0s is equivalent to a zero frequency of the appropriate amplitude. Hence a channel with a bandwidth from 0 Hz to a frequency (in Hz) equal to half the bit rate (in bps) – that is, a channel that passes only frequency components up to the fundamental frequency of the binary sequence 101010 – can often give a satisfactory performance.

Example 6.3

A binary signal of rate 500 bps is to be transmitted over a communications channel. Derive the minimum bandwidth required assuming (i) the fundamental frequency only, (ii) the fundamental and third harmonic, and (iii) the fundamental, third, and fifth harmonics are to be received.

Answer:

The worst-case sequence 101010... at 500 bps has a fundamental frequency component of 250 Hz. Hence the third harmonic is 750 Hz and the fifth harmonic 1250 Hz. The bandwidth required in each case is as follows:

(i) 0–250 Hz; (ii) 0–750 Hz; (iii) 0–1250 Hz.

As we mentioned earlier, it is also possible to transmit more than one bit with each change in signal amplitude thereby increasing the data bit rate. Nevertheless, the bandwidth of the channel always limits the maximum data rate that can be obtained. A formula derived by **Nyquist** for determining the maximum information transfer rate of a noiseless transmission channel, C, is given by the expression:

$$C = 2W \log_2 M$$

where W is the bandwidth of the channel in Hz and M is the number of levels per signaling element. In practice, as we shall see in Sections 6.4 and 6.5, additional bits are added for transmission control purposes and hence the useful data rate is often less than the transmitted bit rate. So when we transmit information over a communications channel, three rates are involved – the signaling rate, the bit rate, and the data rate – all of which may be the same or different.

Example 6.4

Data is to be transmitted over the access line to a PSTN using a transmission scheme with eight levels per signaling element. If the bandwidth of the PSTN is 3000 Hz, deduce the Nyquist maximum data transfer rate.

Answer:

$$C = 2W \log_2 M$$
$$= 2 \times 3000 \times \log_2 8$$
$$= 2 \times 3000 \times 3$$
$$= 18\,000 \, \text{bps}$$

In practice the data transfer rate will be less than this because of other effects such as noise.

6.3.3 Delay distortion

The rate of propagation of a sinusoidal signal along a transmission line varies with the frequency of the signal. Consequently, when we transmit a digital signal the various frequency components making up the signal arrive at the receiver with varying delays, resulting in **delay distortion** of the received signal. The amount of distortion increases as the bit rate of the transmitted data increases for the following reason: as the bit rate increases, so some of the frequency components associated with each bit transition are delayed and start to interfere with the frequency components associated with a later bit. Delay distortion is also known as **intersymbol interference**; its effect is to vary the bit transition instants of the received signal. Since the received signal is normally sampled at the nominal center of each bit cell, this can lead to incorrect interpretation of the received signal as the bit rate increases.

We can best observe the level of intersymbol interference associated with a transmission channel by means of an **eye diagram**, an example of which is shown in Figure 6.9. This diagram is obtained by displaying the signal received from the channel on an oscilloscope which is triggered by the transitions in the signal. Hence, assuming the received signal contains random

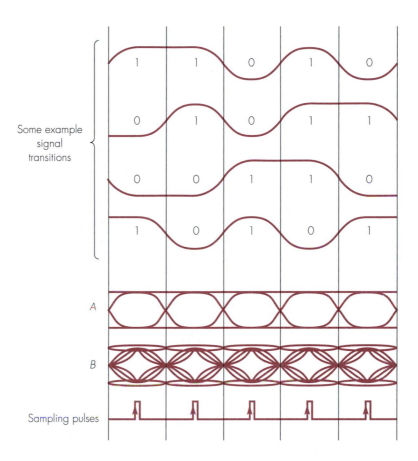

Figure 6.9 Examples of (binary) eye diagrams resulting from intersymbol interference: A, ideal; B, typical.

binary 1 and 0 signal transitions, the oscilloscope will display all the possible signals superimposed on one another. Two examples are shown in the figure. In the absence of intersymbol interference the signal will be of the form shown as *A*, while with interference the signal will be of the form shown as *B*. We can deduce that the higher the level of interference, the smaller the central section – known as the **eye** – becomes.

6.3.4 Noise

In the absence of a signal, a transmission line or channel ideally has zero electrical signal present. In practice, however, there are random perturbations on the line even when no signal is being transmitted. These are caused by what is known as **thermal noise**, which is present in all types of transmission media. It is called **line noise** and, in the limit, as a transmitted signal becomes attenuated, its level is reduced to that of the line (background) noise. An important parameter associated with the received signal, therefore, is the ratio of the average power in the received signal, S, to the power in the noise level, N. The ratio S/N is called the **signal-to-noise ratio** (**SNR**) and is normally expressed in decibels, that is:

$$\text{SNR} = 10 \log_{10} \frac{S}{N} \text{ dB}$$

Clearly, a high SNR means a high power signal relative to the prevailing noise level, resulting in a good-quality signal. Conversely, a low SNR means a low-quality signal. The theoretical maximum information (data) rate of a transmission medium is related to the SNR and we can determine this rate using a formula attributed to Shannon and Hartley. This is known as the **Shannon–Hartley law**, which states:

$$C = W \log_2 \left(1 + \frac{S}{N}\right) \text{ bps}$$

where C is the information (data) rate in bps, W is the bandwidth of the line/channel in Hz, S is the average signal power in watts, and N is the random noise power in watts.

Example 6.5

Assuming that a circuit through a PSTN has a bandwidth of 3000 Hz and a typical signal-to-noise power ratio of 20 dB, determine the maximum theoretical information (data) rate that can be achieved.

Answer:

$$\text{SNR} = 10 \log_{10} \left(\frac{S}{N}\right)$$

Therefore: $\qquad 20 = 10 \log_{10} \left(\dfrac{S}{N}\right)$

Hence: $\qquad \dfrac{S}{N} = 100$

Now: $\qquad C = W \log_2 \left(1 + \dfrac{S}{N}\right)$

Therefore: $\qquad C = 3000 \times \log_2 (1 + 100)$

$$= 19\,963 \text{ bps}$$

As we have explained, thermal noise is present in a line even when nothing is being transmitted. In addition, there are other noise signals present that are caused by electrical activity external to the transmission line. We identified one source of this, crosstalk, in Section 6.2.1 when we discussed open-wire and twisted pair transmission lines. Crosstalk is caused by unwanted electrical coupling between adjacent lines. This coupling results in a signal that is being transmitted in one line being picked up by adjacent lines as a small but finite (noise) signal.

There are several types of crosstalk but in most cases the most limiting impairment is **near-end crosstalk** or **NEXT**. This is also known as **self-crosstalk** since it is caused by the strong signal output by a transmitter circuit being coupled (and hence interfering) with the much weaker signal at the input to the local receiver circuit. As we showed in Figure 6.2, the received signal is normally significantly attenuated and distorted and hence the amplitude of the coupled signal from the transmit section can be comparable with the amplitude of the received signal.

Special integrated circuits known as **adaptive NEXT cancelers** are now used to overcome this type of impairment. A typical arrangement is shown in Figure 6.10. The canceler circuit adaptively forms an attenuated replica of the crosstalk signal that is coupled into the receive line from the local transmitter and this is subtracted from the received signal. Such circuits are now used in many applications involving UTP cable, for example, to transmit data at high bit rates.

6.4 Asynchronous transmission

With asynchronous transmission, each character or byte that makes up a block/message is treated independently for transmission purposes. Hence it can be used both for the transfer of, say, single characters that are entered at a keyboard, or for the transfer of blocks of characters/bytes across a low bit rate transmission line/channel.

Within end systems, all information is transferred between the various circuits and subsystems in a word or byte parallel mode. Consequently, since all transfers that are external to the system are carried out bit-serially, the transmission control circuit on the network interface card (NIC) must perform the following functions:

■ parallel-to-serial conversion of each character or byte in preparation for its transmission on the line;

■ serial-to-parallel conversion of each received character or byte in preparation for its storage and processing in the receiving end system;

■ a means for the receiver to achieve bit, character, and frame synchronization;

■ the generation of suitable error check digits for error detection and the detection of such errors at the receiver should they occur.

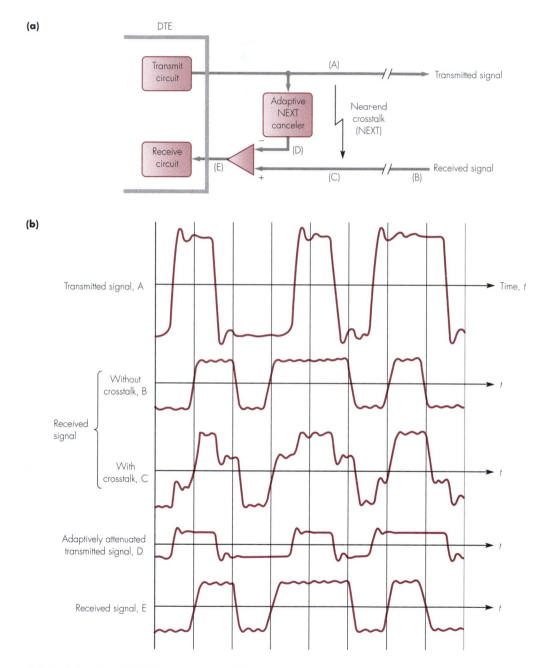

Figure 6.10 Adaptive NEXT cancelers: (a) circuit schematic; (b) example waveforms.

As we show in Figure 6.11(a), parallel-to-serial conversion is performed by a **parallel-in, serial-out (PISO) shift register**. This, as its name implies, allows a complete character or byte to be loaded in parallel and then shifted out bit-serially. Similarly, serial-to-parallel conversion is performed by a **serial-in, parallel-out (SIPO) shift register** which executes the reverse function.

To achieve bit and character synchronization, we must set the receiving transmission control circuit (which is normally programmable) to operate with the same characteristics as the transmitter in terms of the number of bits per character and the bit rate being used.

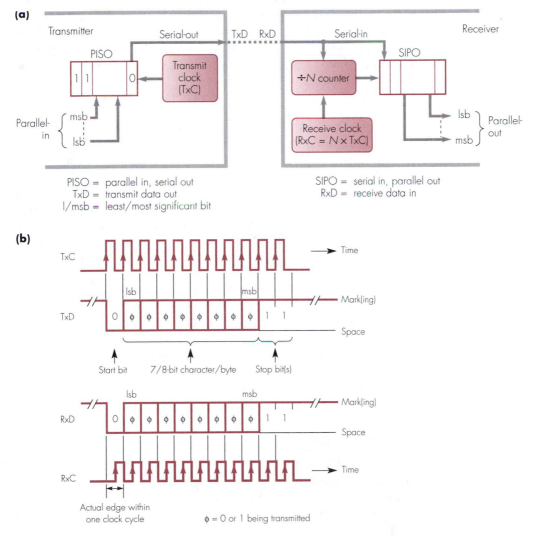

Figure 6.11 Asynchronous transmission: (a) principle of operation; (b) timing principles.

6.4.1 Bit synchronization

In asynchronous transmission, the receiver clock (which is used to sample and shift the incoming signal into the SIPO shift register) runs asynchronously with respect to the incoming signal. In order for the reception process to work reliably, we must devise a scheme whereby the local (asynchronous) receiver clock samples (and hence shifts into the SIPO shift register) the incoming signal as near to the center of the bit cell as possible.

To achieve this, each character/byte to be transmitted is encapsulated between a *start bit* and one or two *stop bits*. As we show in Figure 6.11(b), the start bit is a binary 0 (and known as a *space*) and the stop bit a binary 1 (and known as a *mark*). When transmitting a block comprising a string of characters/bytes, the start bit of each character/byte immediately follows the stop bit(s) of the previous character/byte. When transmitting random characters, however, the line stays at the stop/1 level until the next character is to be transmitted. Hence between blocks (or after each character), the line is said to be *marking* (time).

The use of a start and stop bit per character/byte of different polarities means that, irrespective of the binary contents of each character/byte, there is a guaranteed $1 \rightarrow 0$ transition at the start of each new character/byte. A local receiver clock of N times the transmitted bit rate ($N = 16$ is common) is used and each new bit is shifted into the SIPO shift register after N cycles of this clock. The first $1 \rightarrow 0$ transition associated with the start bit of each character is used to start the counting process. Each bit (including the start bit) is sampled at (approximately) the center of each bit cell. After the first transition is detected, the signal (the start bit) is sampled after $N/2$ clock cycles and then subsequently after N clock cycles for each bit in the character and also the stop bit(s). Three examples of different clock rate ratios are shown in Figure 6.12.

Remembering that the receiver clock (RxC) is running asynchronously with respect to the incoming signal (RxD), the relative positions of the two signals can be anywhere within a single cycle of the receiver clock. Those shown in the figure are just arbitrary positions. Nevertheless, we can deduce from these examples that the higher the clock rate ratio, the nearer the sampling instant will be to the nominal bit cell center. Because of this mode of operation, the maximum bit rate normally used with asynchronous transmission is 19.2 kbps.

6.4.2 Character synchronization

As we indicated in Section 6.4 above, the receiving transmission control circuit is programmed to operate with the same number of bits per character and the same number of stop bits as the transmitter. After the start bit has been detected and received, the receiver achieves character synchronization simply by counting the programmed number of bits. It then transfers the received character/byte into a local **buffer register** and signals to the control-

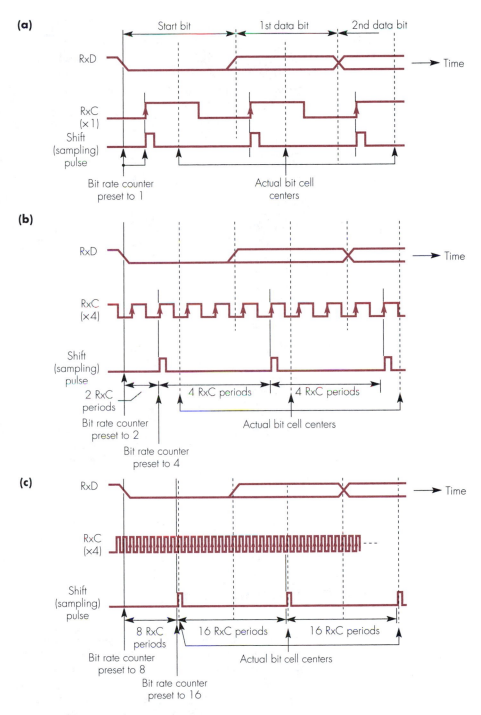

Figure 6.12 Examples of three different receiver clock rate ratios: (a) ×1; (b) ×4; (c) ×16.

Example 6.6

A block of data is to be transmitted across a serial data link. If a clock of 19.2 kHz is available at the receiver, deduce the suitable clock rate ratios and estimate the worst-case deviations from the nominal bit cell centers, expressed as a percentage of a bit period, for each of the following data transmission rates:

(i)   1200 bps

(ii)   2400 bps

(iii) 9600 bps

Answer:

It can readily be deduced from Figure 6.12 that the worst-case deviation from the nominal bit cell centers is approximately plus or minus one half of one cycle of the receiver clock.

Hence:

(i)   At 1200 bps, the maximum RxC ratio can be ×16. The maximum deviation is thus ± 3.125%.

(ii)   At 2400 bps, the maximum RxC ratio can be ×8. The maximum deviation is thus ± 6.25%.

(iii) At 9600 bps, the maximum RxC ratio can be ×2. The maximum deviation is thus ± 25%.

Clearly, the last case is unacceptable. With a low-quality line, especially one with excessive delay distortion, even the second may be unreliable. It is for this reason that a ×16 clock rate ratio is used whenever possible.

ling device (a microprocessor, for example) on the NIC that a new character/byte has been received. It then awaits the next line signal transition that indicates a new start bit (and hence character) is being received.

6.4.3 Frame synchronization

When messages comprising blocks of characters or bytes – normally referred to as **information frames** – are being transmitted, in addition to bit and character synchronization, the receiver must be able to determine the start and end of each frame. This is known as frame synchronization.

The simplest method of transmitting blocks of printable characters is to encapsulate the complete block between two special (nonprintable) transmission control characters: STX (start-of-text) which indicates the start of a new frame after an idle period, and ETX (end-of-text) which indicates the end of the frame. As the frame contents consist only of printable characters, the receiver can interpret the receipt of an STX character as signaling the start of a new frame and an ETX character as signaling the end of the frame. This is shown in Figure 6.13(a).

Although the scheme shown is satisfactory for the transmission of blocks of printable characters, when transmitting blocks that comprise strings of bytes (for example, the contents of a file containing compressed speech or video), the use of a single ETX character to indicate the end of a frame is not sufficient. In the case of a string of bytes, one of the bytes might be the same as an ETX character, which would cause the receiver to terminate the reception process abnormally.

To overcome this problem, when transmitting this type of data the two transmission control characters STX and ETX are each preceded by a third

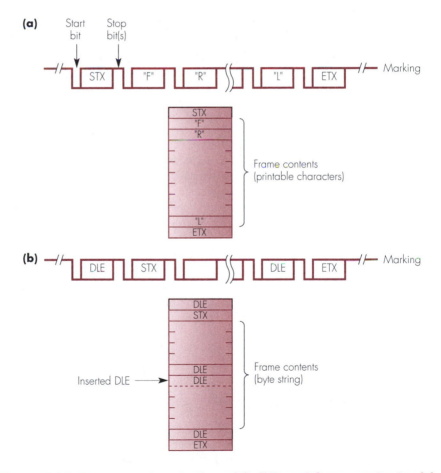

Figure 6.13 Frame synchronization with different frame contents: (a) printable characters; (b) string of bytes.

transmission control character known as **data link escape** (**DLE**). The modified format of a frame is then as shown in Figure 6.13(b).

Remember that the transmitter knows the number of bytes in each frame to be transmitted. After transmitting the start-of-frame sequence (DLE-STX), the transmitter inspects each byte in the frame prior to transmission to determine if it is the same as the DLE character pattern. If it is, irrespective of the next byte, a second DLE character (byte) is transmitted before the next byte. This procedure is repeated until the appropriate number of bytes in the frame have been transmitted. The transmitter then signals the end of the frame by transmitting the unique DLE-STX sequence.

This procedure is known as **character** or **byte stuffing**. On receipt of each byte after the DLE-STX start-of-frame sequence, the receiver determines whether it is a DLE character (byte). If it is, the receiver then processes the next byte to determine whether that is another DLE or an ETX. If it is a DLE, the receiver discards it and awaits the next byte. If it is an ETX, this can reliably be taken as being the end of the frame.

6.5 Synchronous transmission

The use of an additional start bit and one or more stop bits per character or byte means that asynchronous transmission is relatively inefficient in its use of transmission capacity, especially when transmitting messages that comprise large blocks of characters or bytes. Also, the bit (clock) synchronization method used with asynchronous transmission becomes less reliable as the bit rate increases. This results, firstly, from the fact that the detection of the first start bit transition is only approximate and, secondly, although the receiver clock operates at N times the nominal transmit clock rate, because of tolerances there are small differences between the two which can cause the sampling instant to drift during the reception of a character or byte. We normally use synchronous transmission to overcome these problems. As with asynchronous transmission, however, we must adopt a suitable method to enable the receiver to achieve bit (clock) character (byte) and frame (block) synchronization. In practice, there are two synchronous transmission control schemes: character-oriented and bit-oriented. We shall discuss each separately but, since they both use the same bit synchronization methods, we shall discuss these methods first.

6.5.1 Bit synchronization

Although we often use the presence of a start bit and stop bit(s) with each character to discriminate between asynchronous and synchronization transmission, the fundamental difference between the two methods is that with asynchronous transmission the receiver clock runs asynchronously (unsynchronized) with respect to the incoming (received) signal, whereas with synchronous transmission the receiver clock operates in synchronism with the received signal.

As we have just indicated, start and stop bits are not used with synchronous transmission. Instead each frame is transmitted as a contiguous stream of binary digits. The receiver then obtains (and maintains) bit synchronization in one of two ways. Either the clock (timing) information is embedded into the transmitted signal and subsequently extracted by the receiver, or the receiver has a local clock (as with asynchronous transmission) but this time it is kept in synchronism with the received signal by a device known as a **digital phase-lock-loop** (**DPLL**). As we shall see, the DPLL exploits the $1 \rightarrow 0$ or $0 \rightarrow 1$ bit transitions in the received signal to maintain bit (clock) synchronism over an acceptably long period. Hybrid schemes that exploit both methods are also used. The principles of operation of both schemes are shown in Figure 6.14.

Clock encoding and extraction

The alternative methods of embedding timing (clock) information into a transmitted bitstream are shown in Figure 6.15. The scheme shown in part (a) is called **Manchester encoding** and that in part (b) **differential Manchester encoding**.

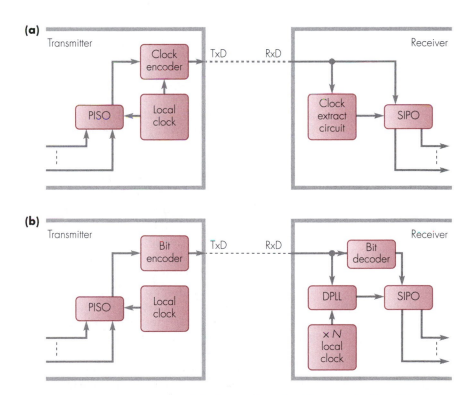

Figure 6.14 Alternative bit/clock synchronization methods with synchronuous transmission: (a) clock encoding; (b) digital phase-lock-loop (DPLL).

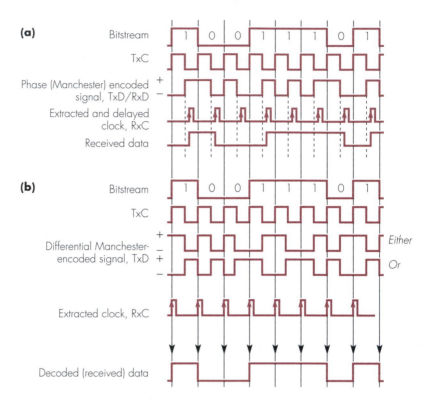

Figure 6.15 Synchronous transmission clock encoding methods: (a) Manchester; (b) differential Manchester.

As we can see, with Manchester encoding each bit is encoded as either a low-high signal (binary 1) or a high-low signal (binary 0), both occupying a single bit-cell period. Also, there is always a transition (high-low or low-high) at the center of each bit cell. It is this that is used by the clock extraction circuit to produce a clock pulse which is then delayed to the center of the second half of the bit cell. At this point the received (encoded) signal is either high (for binary 1) or low (for binary 0) and hence the correct bit is sampled and shifted into the SIPO shift register.

The scheme shown in Figure 6.15(b) is differential Manchester encoding. This differs from Manchester encoding in that although there is still a transition at the center of each bit cell, a transition at the start of the bit cell occurs only if the next bit to be encoded is a 0. This has the effect that the encoded output signal may take on one of two forms depending on the assumed start level (high or low). As we can see, however, one is simply an inverted version of the other and this is the origin of the term "differential". As we show later in Figure 7.12(c), and explain in the accompanying text, a differential driver circuit produces a pair of differential signals and the differential receiver operates by determining the difference between these two signals. For example, if the two signals each vary between +*V* and −*V*, then the difference would be +2*V* and −2*V*. The extracted clock is generated at the start of each bit cell. At this point the received (encoded) signal either changes – for example, from +2*V* to −2*V* or −2*V* to +2*V* in which case a binary 0 is shifted into the SIPO – or remains at the same level, in which case a binary 1 is shifted into the SIPO.

The two Manchester encoding schemes are **balanced codes** which means there is no mean (DC) value associated with them. This is so since a string of binary 1s (or 0s) will always have transitions associated with them rather than a constant (DC) level. This is an important feature since it means that the received signal can be **AC coupled** to the receiver electronics using a transformer. The receiver electronics can then operate using its own power supply since this is effectively isolated from the power supply of the transmitter.

Digital phase-lock-loop

An alternative approach to encoding the clock in the transmitted bit stream is to utilize a stable clock source at the receiver which is kept in time synchronism with the incoming bit stream. However, as there are no start and stop bits with a synchronous transmission scheme, we must encode the information in such a way that there are always sufficient bit transitions ($1 \rightarrow 0$ or $0 \rightarrow 1$) in the transmitted waveform to enable the receiver clock to be resynchronized at frequent intervals. One approach is to pass the data to be transmitted through a **scrambler** which randomizes the transmitted bitstream so removing contiguous strings of 1s or 0s. Alternatively, the data may be encoded in such a way that suitable transitions will always be present.

The bit pattern to be transmitted is first differentially encoded as shown in Figure 6.16(a). We refer to the resulting encoded signal as a **non-return-to-zero-inverted** (**NRZI**) waveform. With NRZI encoding the signal level (1 or 0) does not change for the transmission of a binary 1, whereas a binary 0 causes a change. This means that there will always be bit transitions in the incoming signal of an NRZI waveform, providing there are no contiguous streams of binary 1s. On the surface, this may seem no different from the normal NRZ waveform but, as we shall describe in Section 6.5.3, if a bit-oriented scheme with zero bit insertion is used, an active line will always have a binary 0 in the transmitted bitstream at least every five bit cells. Consequently, the resulting waveform will contain a guaranteed number of transitions, since long strings of 0s cause a transition every bit cell. This enables the receiver to adjust its clock so that it is in synchronism with the incoming bitstream.

The circuit used to maintain bit synchronism is known as a digital phase-lock-loop and is shown in Figure 6.16(b). A crystal-controlled oscillator (clock source), which can hold its frequency sufficiently constant to require only very small adjustments at irregular intervals, is connected to the DPLL. Typically, the frequency of the clock is 32 times the bit rate used on the data

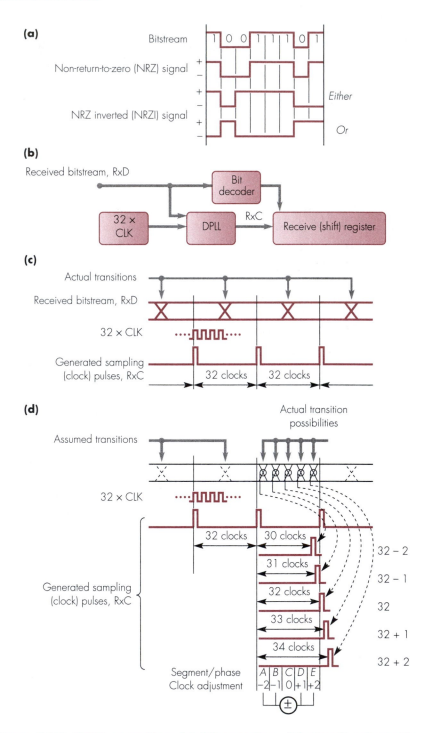

Figure 6.16 DPLL operation: (a) bit encoding; (b) circuit schematic; (c) in phase; (d) clock adjustment rules.

link and is used by the DPLL to derive the timing interval between successive samples of the received bitstream.

Assuming the incoming bitstream and the local clock are in synchronism, the state (1 or 0) of the incoming signal on the line will be sampled (and hence clocked into the SIPO shift register) at the center of each bit cell with exactly 32 clock periods between each sample. This is shown in Figure 6.16(c).

Now assume that the incoming bitstream and local clock drift out of synchronism because of small variations in the latter. The sampling instant is adjusted in discrete increments as shown in Figure 6.16(d). If there are no transitions on the line, the DPLL simply generates a sampling pulse every 32 clock periods after the previous one. Whenever a transition ($1 \rightarrow 0$ or $0 \rightarrow 1$) is detected, the time interval between the previously generated sampling pulse and the next is determined according to the position of the transition relative to where the DPLL thought it should occur. To achieve this, each bit period is divided into five segments, shown as A, B, C, D, and E in the figure. For example, a transition occurring during segment A indicates that the last sampling pulse was too close to the next transition and hence late. The time period to the next pulse is therefore shortened to 30 clock periods. Similarly, a transition occurring in segment E indicates that the previous sampling pulse was too early relative to the transition. The time period to the next pulse is therefore lengthened to 34 clock periods. Transitions in segments B and D are clearly nearer to the assumed transition and hence the relative adjustments are less (-1 and $+1$ respectively). Finally a transition in segment C is deemed to be close enough to the assumed transition to warrant no adjustment.

In this way, successive adjustments keep the generated sampling pulses close to the center of each bit cell. In practice, the widths of each segment (in terms of clock periods) are not equal. The outer segments (A and E) being further away from the nominal center, are made longer than the three inner segments. For the circuit shown, a typical division might be $A = E = 10$, $B = D = 5$, and $C = 2$. We can readily deduce that in the worst case the DPLL requires 10 bit transitions to converge to the nominal bit center of a waveform: 5 bit periods of coarse adjustments (± 2) and 5 bit periods of fine adjustments (± 1). Hence when using a DPLL, it is usual before transmitting the first frame on a line, or following an idle period between frames, to transmit a number of characters/bytes to provide a minimum of 10 bit transitions. Two characters/bytes each composed of all 0s, for example, provide 16 transitions with NRZI encoding. This ensures that the DPLL generates sampling pulses at the nominal center of each bit cell by the time the opening character or byte of a frame is received. We must stress, however, that once in synchronism (lock) only minor adjustments normally take place during the reception of a frame.

We can deduce from Figure 6.16(a), that with NRZI encoding the maximum rate at which the encoded signal changes polarity is one half that of Manchester encoding. If the bit period is T, with NRZI encoding the maximum rate is $1/T$, whereas with Manchester encoding it is $2/T$. The maximum rate is known as the **modulation rate**. As we described in Section 6.3.2, the highest fundamental frequency component of each scheme is $1/T$ and $2/T$ respectively. This means that, for the same data rate, Manchester encoding requires twice the transmission bandwidth of an NRZI encoded signal, that is, the higher the modulation rate, the wider is the required bandwidth.

The effect of this is that Manchester and differential Manchester encoding are both used extensively in applications such as LANs. As we shall expand upon in Chapter 8, LANs operate in a single office or building and hence use relatively short cable runs. This means that even though they operate at high bit rates – for example 10 Mbps and higher – the attenuation and bandwidth of the transmission medium are not generally a problem. In contrast, as we shall expand upon in Chapter 7, in networks such as an ISDN twisted-pair cable is often used with relatively high bit rates and over distances of several kilometers. Hence encoding schemes such as NRZI are used with each bit represented by a full-width pulse. We shall describe a number of examples of each scheme in later chapters.

6.5.2 Character-oriented

As we indicated at the beginning of Section 6.5, there are two types of synchronous transmission control scheme: character-oriented and bit-oriented. Both use the same bit synchronization methods. The major difference between the two schemes is the method used to achieve character and frame synchronization.

Character-oriented transmission is used primarily for the transmission of blocks of characters, such as files of ASCII characters. Since there are no start or stop bits with synchronous transmission, an alternative way of achieving character synchroniztion must be used. To achieve this the transmitter adds two or more transmission control characters, known as **synchronous idle** or **SYN** characters, before each block of characters. These control characters have two functions. Firstly, they allow the receiver to obtain (or maintain) bit synchronization. Secondly, once this has been done, they allow the receiver to start to interpret the received bitstream on the correct character boundaries – **character synchronization**. The general scheme is shown in Figure 6.17.

Part (a) shows that frame synchronization (with character-oriented synchronous transmission) is achieved in just the same way as for asynchronous transmission by encapsulating the block of characters – the frame contents – between an STX-ETX pair of transmission control characters. The SYN control characters used to enable the receiver to achieve character synchronization precede the STX start-of-frame character. Once the receiver has obtained bit synchronization it enters what is known as the **hunt mode**. This is shown in Figure 6.17(b).

When the receiver enters the hunt mode, it starts to interpret the received bitstream in a window of eight bits as each new bit is received. In this way, as each bit is received, it checks whether the last eight bits were equal to the known SYN character. If they are not, it receives the next bit and repeats

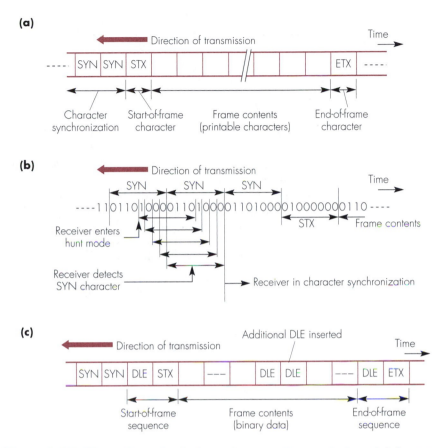

Figure 6.17 Character-oriented synchronous transmission: (a) frame format; (b) character synchronization; (c) data transparency (character stuffing).

the check. If they are, then this indicates it has found the correct character boundary and hence the following characters are then read after each subsequent eight bits have been received.

Once in character synchronization (and hence reading each character on the correct bit boundary), the receiver starts to process each subsequently received character in search of the STX character indicating the start of the frame. On receipt of the STX character, the receiver proceeds to receive the frame contents and terminates this process when it detects the ETX character. On a point-to-point link, the transmitter normally then reverts to sending SYN characters to allow the receiver to maintain synchronism. Alternatively, the above procedure must be repeated each time a new frame is transmitted.

Finally, as we can see in Figure 6.17(c), when binary data is being transmitted, data transparency is achieved in the same way as described previously by preceding the STX and ETX characters by a DLE (data link escape) character and inserting (stuffing) an additional DLE character whenever it detects a DLE in the frame contents. In this case, therefore, the SYN characters precede the first DLE character.

6.5.3 Bit-oriented

The need for a pair of characters at the start and end of each frame for frame synchronization, coupled with the additional DLE characters to achieve data transparency, means that a character-oriented transmission control scheme is relatively inefficient for the transmission of binary data. Moreover, the format of the transmission control characters varies for different character sets, so the scheme can be used only with a single type of character set, even though the frame contents may be pure binary data. To overcome these problems, a more universal scheme known as **bit-oriented transmission** is now the preferred control scheme as it can be used for the transmission of frames comprising either printable characters or binary data. The main features of the scheme are shown in Figure 6.18(a). It differs mainly in the way the start and end of each frame is signaled.

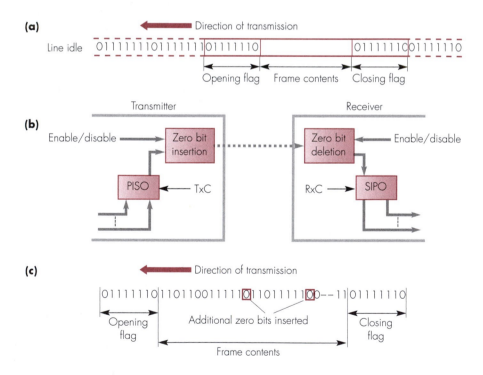

Figure 6.18 Bit-oriented synchronous transmission: (a) framing structure; (b) zero bit insertion circuit location; (c) example transmitted frame contents.

The start and end of a frame are both signaled by the same unique 8-bit pattern 01111110, known as the **flag byte** or **flag pattern**. We use the term "bit-oriented" because the received bitstream is searched by the receiver on a bit-by-bit basis for both the start-of-frame flag and, during reception of the frame contents, for the end-of-frame flag. Thus in principle the frame contents need not necessarily comprise multiples of 8 bits.

To enable the receiver to obtain and maintain bit synchronism, the transmitter sends a string of **idle bytes** (each comprising 01111111) preceding the start-of-frame flag. Recall that with NRZI encoding the 0 in the idle byte enables the DPLL at the receiver to obtain and maintain clock synchronization. On receipt of the opening flag, the received frame contents are read and interpreted on 8-bit (byte) boundaries until the closing flag is detected. The reception process is then terminated.

To achieve data transparency with this scheme, we must ensure that the flag pattern is not present in the frame contents. We do this by using a technique known as **zero bit insertion** or **bit stuffing**. The circuit that performs this function is located at the output of the PISO register, as shown in Figure 6.18(b). It is enabled by the transmitter only during transmission of the frame contents. When enabled, the circuit detects whenever it has transmitted a sequence of five contiguous binary 1 digits, then automatically inserts an additional binary 0 digit. In this way, the flag pattern 01111110 can never be present in the frame contents between the opening and closing flags.

A similar circuit at the receiver located prior to the input of the SIPO shift receiver performs the reverse function. Whenever a zero is detected after five contiguous 1 digits, the circuit automatically removes (deletes) it from the frame contents. Normally the frame also contains additional error detection digits preceding the closing flag which are subjected to the same bit stuffing operation as the frame contents. An example stuffed bit pattern is shown in Figure 6.18(c).

6.6 Error detection methods

As we indicated in Section 6.1, when transmitting a bitstream over a transmission line/channel a scheme is normally incorporated into the transmission control circuit of the NIC to enable the presence of bit/transmission errors in a received block to be detected. In general, this is done by the transmitter computing a set of (additional) bits based on the contents of the block of bits to be transmitted. These are known as error detection bits and are transmitted together with the original bits in the block. The receiver then uses the complete set of received bits to determine (to a high probability) whether the block contains any errors.

The two factors that determine the type of error detection scheme used are the **bit error rate** (**BER**) probability of the line and the type of errors, that is whether the errors occur as random single-bit errors or as groups of contiguous strings of bit errors. The latter are referred to as **burst errors**. The BER is the probability P of a single bit being corrupted in a defined time interval. Thus a BER of 10^{-3} means that, on average, 1 bit in 10^{-3} will be corrupted during a defined time period.

If we are transmitting single characters using asynchronous transmission (say 8 bits per character plus 1 start and 1 stop bit), the probability of a character being corrupted is $1 - (1 - P)^{10}$ which, if we assume a BER of 10^{-3}, is approximately 10^{-2}. Alternatively, if we are transmitting blocks of say 125 bytes using synchronous transmission, then the probability of a block (frame) containing an error is approximately 1. This means that on average every block will contain an error. Clearly, therefore, this length of frame is too long for this type of line and must be reduced to obtain an acceptable throughput.

The type of errors present is important since, as we shall see, the different types of error detection scheme detect different types of error. Also, the number of bits used in some schemes determines the burst lengths that are detected. The three most widely used schemes are parity, block sum check, and cyclic redundancy check. We shall consider each separately.

6.6.1 Parity

The most common method used for detecting bit errors with asynchronous and character-oriented synchronous transmission is the **parity bit method**. With this scheme the transmitter adds an additional bit – the parity bit – to each transmitted character prior to transmission. The parity bit used is a function of the bits that make up the character being transmitted. On receipt of each character, the receiver then performs the same function on the received character and compares the result with the received parity bit. If they are equal, no error is assumed, but if they are different, then a transmission error is assumed.

To compute the parity bit for a character, the number of 1 bits in the code for the character are added together (modulo 2) and the parity bit is then chosen so that the total number of 1 bits (including the parity bit itself) is either even – **even parity** – or odd – **odd parity**. The principles of the scheme are shown in Figure 6.19.

The circuitry used to compute the parity bit for each character comprises a set of **exclusive-OR (XOR)** gates connected as shown in Figure 6.19(c). The XOR gate is also known as a **modulo-2 adder** since, as shown by the **truth table** in part (b) of the figure, the output of the exclusive-OR operation between two binary digits is the same as the addition of the two digits without a carry bit. The least significant pair of bits are first XORed together and the output of this gate is then XORed with the next (more significant) bit, and so on. The output of the final gate is the required parity bit which is loaded into the transmit PISO register prior to transmission of the character. Similarly, on receipt, the recomputed parity bit is compared with the received parity bit. If it is different, this indicates that a transmission error has been detected.

(a)

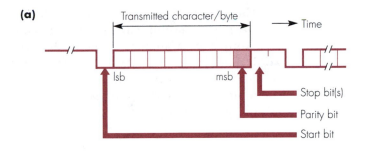

(b)

(c)

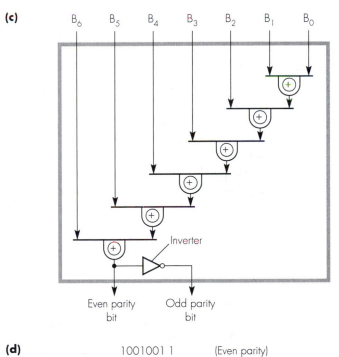

(d)   1001001 1   (Even parity)
                         1001001 0   (Odd parity)

Figure 6.19 Parity bit method: (a) position in character; (b) XOR gate truth table and symbol; (c) parity bit generation circuit; (d) two examples.

The term used in coding theory to describe the combined message unit, comprising the useful data bits and the additional error detection bits, is codeword. The minimum number of bit positions in which two valid codewords differ is known as the **Hamming distance** of the code. As an example, consider a coding scheme that has seven data bits and a single parity bit per codeword. If we assume even parity is being used, consecutive codewords in this scheme will be:

$$0000000\ 0$$
$$0000001\ 1$$
$$0000010\ 1$$
$$0000011\ 0$$

We can deduce from this list that such a scheme has a Hamming distance of 2 since each valid codeword differs in at least two bit positions. This means that the scheme does not detect 2-bit errors since the resulting (corrupted) bit pattern will be a different but valid codeword. It does, however, detect all single-bit errors (and all odd numbers of bit errors) since, if a single bit in a codeword is corrupted, an invalid codeword will result.

6.6.2 Block sum check

When blocks of characters (or bytes) are being transmitted, there is an increased probability that a character (and hence the block) will contain a bit error. The probability of a block containing an error is known as the **block error rate**. When blocks of characters (frames) are being transmitted, we can achieve an extension to the error detecting capabilities obtained from a single parity bit per character (byte) by using an additional set of parity bits computed from the complete block of characters (bytes) in the frame. With this method, each character (byte) in the frame is assigned a parity bit as before (**transverse** or **row parity**). In addition, an extra bit is computed for each bit position (**longitudinal** or **column parity**) in the complete frame. The resulting set of parity bits for each column is referred to as the **block (sum) check character** since each bit making up the character is the modulo-2 sum of all the bits in the corresponding column. The example in Figure 6.20(a) uses odd parity for the row parity bits and even parity for the column parity bits, and assumes that the frame contains printable characters only.

We can deduce from this example that although two bit errors in a character will escape the row parity check, they will be detected by the corresponding column parity check. This is true, of course, only if no two bit errors occur in the same column at the same time. Clearly, the probability of this occurring is much less than the probability of two bit errors in a single character occurring. The use of a block sum check significantly improves the error detection properties of the scheme.

(a)

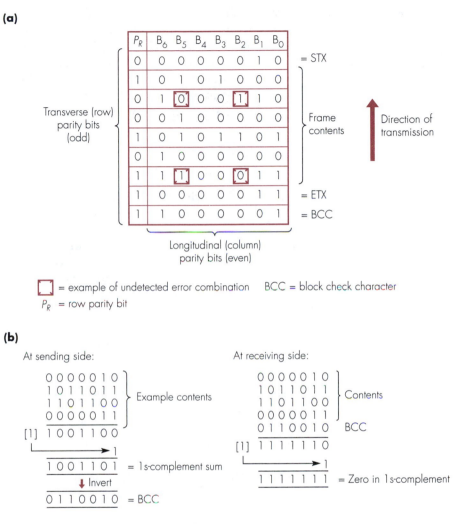

Figure 6.20 Block sum check method: (a) row and column parity bits; (b) 1s complement sum.

(b)

At sending side:

```
0 0 0 0 0 1 0
1 0 1 1 0 1 1     Example contents
1 1 0 1 1 0 0
0 0 0 0 0 1 1
[1] 1 0 0 1 1 0 0
```

```
1 0 0 1 1 0 1  = 1s-complement sum
   ↓ Invert
0 1 1 0 0 1 0  = BCC
```

At receiving side:

```
0 0 0 0 0 1 0
1 0 1 1 0 1 1     Contents
1 1 0 1 1 0 0
0 0 0 0 0 1 1
0 1 1 0 0 1 0  BCC
[1] 1 1 1 1 1 1 0
```

```
1 1 1 1 1 1 1  = Zero in 1s-complement
```

A variation of the scheme is to use the 1s-complement sum as the basis of the block sum check instead of the modulo-2 sum. The principle of the scheme is shown in Figure 6.20(b).

In this scheme, the characters (or bytes) in the block to be transmitted are treated as unsigned binary numbers. These are first added together using 1s-complement arithmetic. All the bits in the resulting sum are then inverted and this is used as the block check character (BCC). At the receiver, the 1s-complement sum of all the characters in the block – including the block check character – is computed and, if no errors are present, the result should be zero. Remember that with 1s-complement arithmetic, end-around-carry is used, that is, any carry out from the most significant bit position is added to the existing binary sum. Also, zero in 1s-complement arithmetic is represented by either all binary 0s or all binary 1s.

As we shall see in later chapters, since the 1s-complement sum is readily computed, it is used as the error-detection method in a number of applications which require the error detection operation to be performed in software only.

6.6.3 Cyclic redundancy check

The previous two schemes are best suited to applications in which random single-bit errors are present. When bursts of errors are present, however, we must use a more rigorous method. An error burst begins and ends with an erroneous bit, although the bits in between may or may not be corrupted. Thus, an error burst is defined as the number of bits between two successive erroneous bits including the incorrect two bits. Furthermore, when determining the length of an error burst, the last erroneous bit in a burst and the first erroneous bit in the following burst must be separated by B or more correct bits, where B is the length of the error burst. An example of two different error burst lengths is shown in Figure 6.21. Notice that the first and third bit errors could not be used to define a single 11-bit error burst since an error occurs within the next 11 bits.

The most reliable detection scheme against error bursts is based on the use of **polynomial codes**. Polynomial codes are used with frame (or block) transmission schemes. A single set of check digits is generated (computed) for each frame transmitted, based on the contents of the frame, and is appended by the transmitter to the tail of the frame. The receiver then performs a similar computation on the complete frame plus check digits. If no

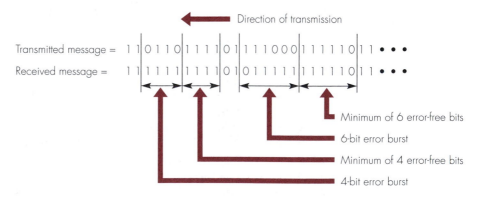

Figure 6.21 Error burst examples.

errors have been induced, a known result should always be obtained; if a different answer is found, this indicates an error.

The number of check digits per frame is selected to suit the type of transmission errors anticipated, although 16 and 32 bits are the most common. The computed check digits are referred to as the **frame check sequence** (**FCS**) or the **cyclic redundancy check** (**CRC**) digits.

The underlying mathematical theory of polynomial codes is beyond the scope of this book but, essentially, the method exploits the following property of binary numbers if modulo-2 arithmetic is used. Let:

$M(x)$ be a k-bit number (the message to be transmitted)

$G(x)$ be an $(n + 1)$-bit number (the divisor or generator)

$R(x)$ be an n-bit number such that $k > n$ (the remainder)

Then if:

$$\frac{M(x) \times 2^n}{G(x)} = Q(x) + \frac{R(x)}{G(x)} \text{ , where } Q(x) \text{ is the quotient,}$$

$$\frac{M(x) \times 2^n + R(x)}{G(x)} = Q(x), \text{ assuming modulo -2 arithmetic.}$$

We can readily confirm this result by substituting the expression for $M(x) \times 2^n / G(x)$ into the second equation, giving:

$$\frac{M(x) \times 2^n + R(x)}{G(x)} = Q(x) + \frac{R(x)}{G(x)} + \frac{R(x)}{G(x)}$$

which is equal to $Q(x)$ since any number added to itself modulo 2 will result in zero, that is, the remainder is zero.

To exploit this, the complete frame contents, $M(x)$, together with an appended set of zeros equal in number to the number of FCS digits to be generated (which is equivalent to multiplying the message by 2^n, where n is the number of FCS digits) are divided modulo 2 by a second binary number, $G(x)$, the **generator polynomial** containing one more digit than the FCS. The division operation is equivalent to performing the exclusive-OR operation bit by bit in parallel as each bit in the frame is processed. The remainder $R(x)$ is then the FCS which is transmitted at the tail of the information digits. Similarly, on receipt, the received bitstream including the FCS digits is again divided by the same generator polynomial – that is, $(M(x) \times 2^n + R(x))/G(x)$ – and, if no errors are present, the remainder is all zeros. If an error is present, however, the remainder is nonzero.

Example 6.7

A series of 8-bit message blocks (frames) is to be transmitted across a data link using a CRC for error detection. A generator polynomial of 11001 is to be used. Use an example to illustrate the following:

(a) the FCS generation process,

(b) the FCS checking process.

Answer:

Generation of the FCS for the message 11100110 is shown in Figure 6.22(a). Firstly, four zeros are appended to the message, which is equivalent to multiplying the message by 2^4, since the FCS will be four bits. This is then divided (modulo 2) by the generator polynomial (binary number). The modulo-2 division operation is equivalent to performing the exclusive-OR operation bit by bit in parallel as each bit in the dividend is processed. Also, with modulo-2 arithmetic, we can perform a division into each partial remainder, providing the two numbers are of the same length, that is, the most significant bits are both 1s. We do not consider the relative magnitude of both numbers. The resulting 4-bit remainder (0110) is the FCS, which is then appended at the tail of the original message when it is transmitted. The quotient is not used.

At the receiver, the complete received bit sequence is divided by the same generator polynomial as used at the transmitter. Two examples are shown in Figure 6.22(b). In the first, no errors are assumed to be present, so that the remainder is zero – the quotient is again not used. In the second, however, an error burst of four bits at the tail of the transmitted bit sequence is assumed. Consequently, the resulting remainder is nonzero, indicating that a transmission error has occurred.

The choice of generator polynomial is important since it determines the types of error that are detected. Assume the transmitted frame, $T(x)$ is:

$$110101100110$$

and the error pattern, $E(x)$ is:

$$00000000\ 1001$$

that is, a 1 in a bit position indicates an error. Hence, with modulo-2 arithmetic:

$$\text{Received frame} = T(x) + E(x)$$

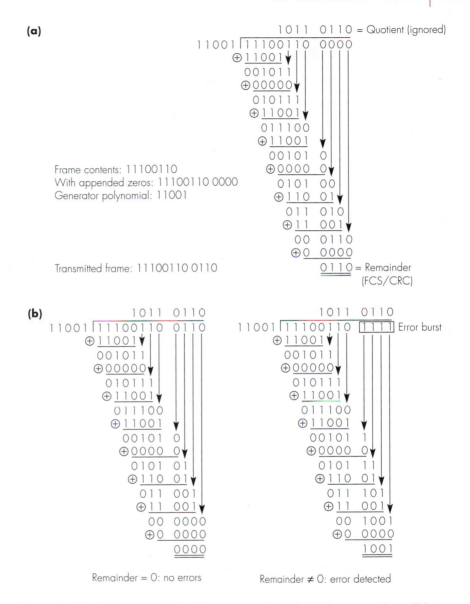

(a)

Frame contents: 11100110
With appended zeros: 11100110 0000
Generator polynomial: 11001

Transmitted frame: 11100110 0110

(b)

Remainder = 0: no errors   Remainder ≠ 0: error detected

Figure 6.22 CRC error detection example: (a) FCS generation; (b) two error detection examples.

Now:

$$\frac{T(x) + E(x)}{G(x)} = \frac{T(x)}{G(x)} + \frac{E(x)}{G(x)}$$

but $T(x)/G(x)$ produces no remainder. Hence an error is detected only if $E(x)/G(x)$ produces a remainder.

For example, all $G(x)$ have at least three terms (1 bits) and $E(x)/G(x)$ will yield a remainder for all single-bit and all double-bit errors with modulo-2 arithmetic and hence be detected. Conversely, an error burst of the same length as $G(x)$ may be a multiple of $G(x)$ and hence yield no remainder and go undetected.

In summary, a generator polynomial of R bits will detect:

- all single-bit errors,
- all double-bit errors,
- all odd number of bit errors,
- all error bursts $0 < R$,
- most error bursts $\geq R$.

The standard way of representing a generator polynomial is to show those positions that are binary 1 as powers of X. Examples of CRCs used in practice are thus:

$$
\begin{aligned}
\text{CRC-6} \quad &= X^{16} + X^{15} + X^2 + 1 \\
\text{CRC-CCITT} \quad &= X^{16} + X^{12} + X^5 + 1 \\
\text{CRC-32} \quad &= X^{32} + X^{26} + X^{23} + X^{16} + X^{12} + X^{11} + X^{10} + X^8 + X^7 \\
&\quad + X^5 + X^4 + X^2 + X + 1
\end{aligned}
$$

Hence CRC-16 is equivalent in binary form to:

$$1\ 1000\ 0000\ 0000\ 0101$$

With such a generator polynomial, 16 zeros would be appended to the frame contents before generation of the FCS. The latter would then be the 16-bit remainder. CRC-16 will detect all error bursts of less than 16 bits and most error bursts greater than or equal to 16 bits. CRC-16 and CRC-CCITT are both used extensively with networks such as an ISDN, while CRC-32 is used in most LANs. Also, although the requirement to perform multiple (modulo-2) divisions may appear to be relatively complicated, as we show in Appendix B, it can be done readily in hardware (and software) and, in practice, this is integrated into the transmission control circuit.

6.7 Protocol basics

In Section 6.6 we described the different methods that are used to detect the presence of transmission errors. Also, as we explained in Section 6.1, in most cases any blocks/frames that are received containing errors are simply discarded by the link layer. It is then left to the transport layer in each of the two communicating end systems to detect any missing blocks and, if necessary, to request that another copy of these is retransmitted. However, in a small number of cases the error recovery procedure is performed in the link layer; for example, in the link layer associated with a PSTN. In this section we describe the basic principles associated with the error control procedure that is used and we then use this to explain how a protocol is specified.

6.7.1 Error control

The transmission control circuit associated with most network interfaces performs both the transmission control and error detection functions we explained in Sections 6.5 and 6.6. The link layer protocol then builds on these basic functions to provide the required link layer service. Typically, the receiving link protocol checks the received frame for possible transmission errors and then returns a short control message/frame either to acknowledge its correct receipt or to request that another copy of the frame is sent. This type of error control is known as **automatic repeat request** (**ARQ**) and the aim of all ARQ schemes is to provide a *reliable* link layer service. In this context, "reliable" means that the two peer link layer protocols will communicate with each other in order to deliver a sequence of blocks that is submitted to the sending link layer protocol. Thus

- the blocks will be delivered by the receiving link layer protocol in the same sequence as they were submitted and with no duplicate copies of any of the blocks;
- to a high probability, each block will be free of any bit errors.

The most basic type of ARQ scheme is **idle RQ** and so we shall start by explaining this. We then identify the limitations of idle RQ and explain how these are overcome in the **continuous RQ** scheme. In practice, there are two types of continuous RQ: selective repeat and go-back-N, both of which we describe. We then return to the idle RQ scheme to explain how the error control part of a protocol is specified.

6.7.2 Idle RQ

In order to discriminate between the sender (source) and receiver (destination) of data frames – more generally referred to as information or **I-frames** – the terms **primary** (**P**) and **secondary** (**S**) are used respectively. The idle RQ protocol operates in a half-duplex mode since the primary, after sending an I-frame, waits until it receives a response from the secondary as to whether the frame was correctly received or not. The primary then either sends the next frame, if the previous frame was correctly received, or retransmits a copy of the previous frame if it was not.

The secondary informs the primary of a correctly received frame by returning a (positive) **acknowledgment** or **ACK-frame**. Similarly, if the secondary receives an I-frame containing errors, then it returns a **negative acknowledgment** or **NAK-frame**. Three example frame sequences illustrating various aspects of this basic procedure are shown in Figure 6.23. The following points should be noted when interpreting the sequences:

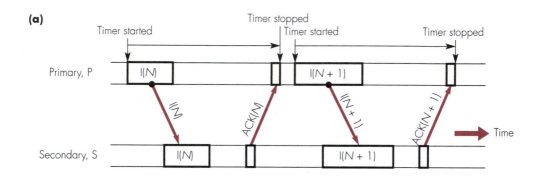

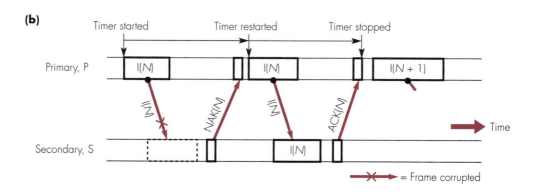

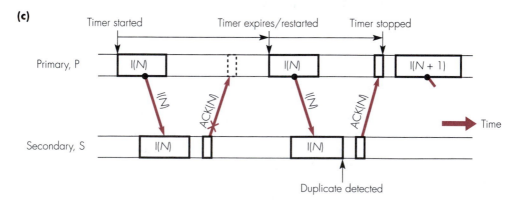

Figure 6.23 Idle RQ error control scheme: (a) error free; (b) corrupted I-frame; (c) corrupted ACK-frame.

- P can have only one I-frame outstanding (awaiting an ACKNAK-frame) at a time.

- When P initiates the transmission of an I-frame it starts a timer.

- On receipt of an error-free I-frame, S returns an ACK-frame to P and, on receipt of this, P stops the timer for this frame and proceeds to send the next frame – part (a).

- On receipt of an I-frame containing transmission errors, S discards the frame and returns a NAK-frame to P which then sends another copy of the frame and restarts the timer – part (b).

- If P does not receive an ACK- (or NAK-) frame within the timeout interval, P retransmits the I-frame currently waiting acknowledgment – part (c). However, since in this example it is an ACK-frame that is corrupted, S detects that the next frame it receives is a duplicate copy of the previous error-free frame it received rather than a new frame. Hence S discards the duplicate and, to enable P to resynchronize, returns a second ACK-frame for it. This procedure repeats until either an error-free copy of the frame is received or a defined number of retries is reached in which case the network layer in P would be informed of this.

As we show in the figure, in order for S to determine when a duplicate is received, each frame transmitted by P contains a unique identifier known as the **send sequence number N(S)** (N, $N + 1$, and so on) within it. Also, S retains a record of the sequence number contained within the last I-frame it received without errors and, if the two are the same, this indicates a duplicate. The sequence number in each ACK- and NAK-frame is known as the **receive sequence number N(R)** and, since P must wait for an ACK- or NAK-frame after sending each I-frame, the scheme is known also as **send-and-wait** or sometimes **stop-and-wait**.

Link utilization

Before considering the error procedures associated with the two types of continuous RQ scheme, we shall first quantify the efficiency of utilization of the available link capacity with the idle RQ scheme. The efficiency of utilization U is a ratio of two times, each measured from the point in time the transmitter starts to send a frame. It is defined as:

$$U = \frac{T_{ix}}{T_t}$$

where T_{ix} is the time for the transmitter to transmit a frame and T_t equals T_{ix} plus any time the transmitter spends waiting for an acknowledgment.

To quantify the link utilization with idle RQ, a frame sequence diagram with the various component times identified is given in Figure 6.24. In practice, in most cases for which the idle RQ protocol is adequate, the time to

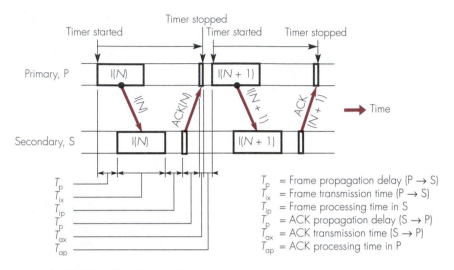

Figure 6.24 Idle RQ link utilization.

process an I-frame T_{ip} and its associated ACK-frame T_{ap} are both short compared with their transmission times T_{ix} and T_{ax}. Also, since an ACK-frame is much shorter than an I-frame, T_{ax} is negligible compared with T_{ix}. Hence the minimum total time before the next frame can be transmitted is often approximated to $T_{ix} + 2T_p$ where T_p is the signal propagation delay of the link. An approximate expression for U is thus:

$$U = \frac{T_{ix}}{T_{ix} + 2T_p}$$

or:

$$U = \frac{1}{1 + 2T_p/T_{ix}}$$

As we described earlier in Section 6.2.8, the ratio T_p/T_{ix} is often given the symbol a and hence:

$$U = \frac{1}{1 + 2a}$$

In Example 6.1 we saw that a can range from a small fraction for low bit rate links of modest length to a large integer value for long links and high bit rates. For these two extremes, U varies between a small fraction and near unity (100%).

Example 6.8

A series of 1000-bit frames is to be transmitted using an idle RQ proto-col. Determine the link utilization for the following types of data link assuming a transmission bit rate of (a) 1 kbps and (b) 1 Mbps. Assume that the velocity of propagation of the first two links is $2 \times 10^8 \text{ ms}^{-1}$ and that of the third link $3 \times 10^8 \text{ ms}^{-1}$. Also the bit error rate is negligible.

(i)   a twisted-pair cable 1 km in length,

(ii) a leased line 200 km in length,

(iii) a satellite link of 50 000 km.

Answer:

The time taken to transmit a frame T_{ix} is given by:

$$T_{ix} = \frac{\text{Number of bits in frame, } N}{\text{Bit rate, } R, \text{ in bps}}$$

At 1 kbps:

$$T_{ix} = \frac{1000}{10^3} = 1 \text{ s}$$

At 1 Mbps:

$$T_{ix} = \frac{1000}{10^6} = 10^{-3} \text{ s}$$

$$T_p = \frac{S}{V} \quad \text{and} \quad U = \frac{1}{1 + 2a}$$

(i) $T_p = \dfrac{10^3}{2 \times 10^8} = 5 \times 10^{-6} \text{ s}$

    (a) $a = \dfrac{5 \times 10^{-6}}{1} = 5 \times 10^{-6}$ and hence $(1 + 2a) \cong 1$ and $U = 1$

    (b) $a = \dfrac{5 \times 10^{-6}}{10^{-3}} = 5 \times 10^{-3}$ and hence $(1 + 2a) \cong 1$ and $U = 1$

(ii) $T_p = \dfrac{200 \times 10^3}{2 \times 10^8} = 1 \times 10^{-3} \text{ s}$

    (a) $a = \dfrac{1 \times 10^{-3}}{1} = 1 \times 10^{-3}$ and hence $(1 + 2a) \cong 1$ and $U = 1$

    (b) $a = \dfrac{1 \times 10^{-3}}{10^{-3}} = 1$ and hence $(1 + 2a) > 1$ and $U = \dfrac{1}{1 + 2} = 0.33$

▶

6.8 Continued

(iii) $T_p = \dfrac{50 \times 10^6}{3 \times 10^8} = 0.167\,\text{s}$

(a) $a = \dfrac{0.167}{1} = 0.167$ and hence $(1 + 2a) > 1$ and $U = \dfrac{1}{1 + 0.334} = 0.75$

(b) $a = \dfrac{0.167}{10^{-3}} = 167$ and hence $(1 + 2a) > 1$ and $U = \dfrac{1}{1 + 334} = 0.003$

The results are summarized in Figure 6.25 from which we can make some interesting observations. Firstly, for relatively short links for which a is less than 1, the link utilization is (to a good approximation) 100% and is independent of the bit rate. This means that an idle RQ protocol is perfectly adequate for short links and modest bit rates. Examples are networks based on modems and an analog PSTN. Secondly, for longer terrestrial links, the link utilization is high for low bit rates (and hence low values of a) but falls off significantly as the bit rate (and hence a) increases. Thirdly, the link utilization is poor for satellite links, even at low bit rates. We can conclude that an idle RQ protocol is unsuitable for such applications and also for those that involve high bit rate terrestrial links which include all of the networks that are used for multimedia.

6.7.3 Continuous RQ

With a continuous RQ error control scheme, link utilization is much improved at the expense of increased buffer storage requirements. As we shall see, a duplex link is required for its implementation. An example illustrating the transmission of a sequence of I-frames and their returned ACK-frames is shown in Figure 6.26. You should note the following points when interpreting the operation of the scheme:

- P sends I-frames continuously without waiting for an ACK-frame to be returned.
- Since more than one I-frame is awaiting acknowledgment, P retains a copy of each I-frame transmitted in a **retransmission list** that operates on a FIFO queue discipline.
- S returns an ACK-frame for each correctly received I-frame.
- Each I-frame contains a unique identifier which is returned in the corresponding ACK-frame.
- On receipt of an ACK-frame, the corresponding I-frame is removed from the retransmission list by P.

(a)

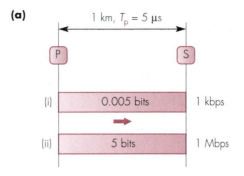

(b)

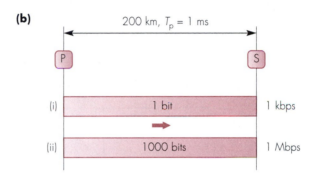

(c)

Figure 6.25 Effect of propagation delay as a function of data transmission rate; parts correspond to Example 6.8.

- Frames received free of errors are placed in the **link receive** list to await processing.
- On receipt of the next in-sequence I-frame expected, S delivers the information content within the frame to the upper network layer immediately it has processed the frame.

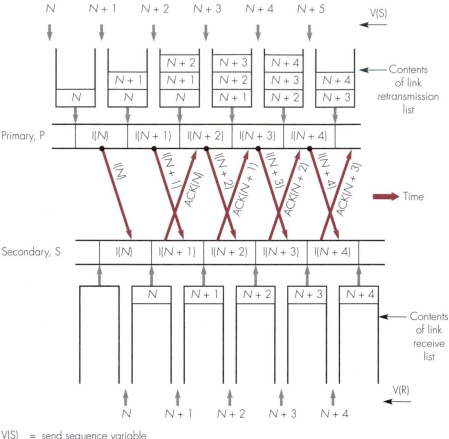

V(S) = send sequence variable
V(R) = receive sequence variable

Figure 6.26 Continuous RQ frame sequence without transmission errors.

To implement the scheme, P must retain a send sequence variable V(S), which indicates the send sequence number N(S) to be allocated to the next I-frame to be transmitted. Also, S must maintain a receive sequence variable V(R), which indicates the next in-sequence I-frame it is waiting for.

The frame sequence shown in Figure 6.26 assumes that no transmission errors occur. When an error does occur, one of two retransmission strategies may be followed:

■ S detects and requests the retransmission of just those frames in the sequence that are corrupted – selective repeat.

■ S detects the receipt of an out-of-sequence I-frame and requests P to retransmit all outstanding unacknowledged I-frames from the last correctly received, and hence acknowledged, I-frame – go-back-N.

Note that with both continuous RQ schemes, corrupted frames are discarded and retransmission requests are triggered only after the next error-free frame is received. Hence, as with the idle RQ scheme, a timeout is applied to each frame transmitted to overcome the possibility of a corrupted frame being the last in a sequence of new frames.

Selective repeat

Two example frame sequence diagrams that illustrate the operation of the selective repeat retransmission control scheme are shown in Figure 6.27. The sequence shown in part(a) shows the effect of a corrupted I-frame being received by S. The following points should be noted when interpreting the sequence:

- An ACK-frame acknowledges all frames in the retransmission list up to and including the I-frame with the sequence number the ACK contains.
- Assume I-frame $N+1$ is corrupted.
- S returns an ACK-frame for I-frame N.
- When S receives I-frame $N+2$ it detects I-frame $N+1$ is missing from $V(R)$ and hence returns a NAK-frame containing the identifier of the missing I-frame $N+1$.
- On receipt of NAK $N+1$, P interprets this as S is still awaiting I-frame $N+1$ and hence retransmits it.
- When P retransmits I-frame $N+1$ it enters the **retransmission state**.
- When P is in the retransmission state, it suspends sending any new frames and sets a timeout for the receipt of ACK $N+1$.
- If the timeout expires, another copy of I-frame $(N+1)$ is sent.
- On receipt of ACK $N+1$ P leaves the retransmission state and resumes sending new frames.
- When S returns a NAK-frame it enters the retransmission state.
- When S is in the retransmission state, the return of ACK-frames is suspended.
- On receipt of I-frame $N+1$, S leaves the retransmission state and resumes returning ACK-frames.
- ACK $N+1$ acknowledges all frames up to and including frame $N+4$.
- A timer is used with each NAK-frame to ensure that if it is corrupted (and hence NAK $N+1$ is not received), it is retransmitted.

The sequence shown in Figure 6.27(b) shows the effect of a corrupted ACK-frame. The following points should be noted:

- Assume ACK N is corrupted.
- On receipt of ACK-frame $N+1$, P detects that I-frame N is still awaiting acknowledgment and hence retransmits it.

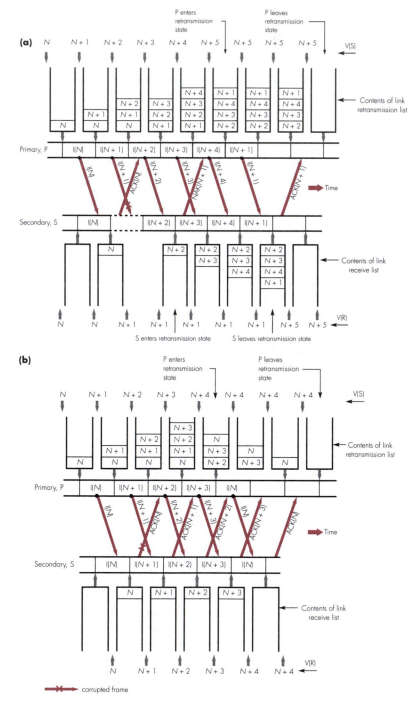

Figure 6.27 Selective repeat: (a) effect of corrupted I-frame; (b) effect of corrupted ACK-frame.

■ On receipt of the retransmitted I-frame N, S determines from its received sequence variable that this has already been received correctly and is therefore a duplicate.

■ S discards the frame but returns an ACK-frame to ensure P removes the frame from the retransmission list.

Go-back-N

Two example frame sequence diagrams that illustrate the operation of the go-back-N retransmission control scheme are shown in Figure 6.28. The sequence shown in part(a) shows the effect of a corrupted I-frame being received by S. The following points should be noted:

■ Assume I-frame $N+1$ is corrupted.

■ S receives I-frame $N+2$ out of sequence.

■ On receipt of I-frame $N+2$, S returns NAK $N+1$ informing P to go back and start to retransmit from I-frame $N+1$.

■ On receipt of NAK $N+1$, P enters the retransmission state. When in this state, it suspends sending new frames and commences to retransmit the frames waiting acknowledgment in the retransmission list.

■ S discards frames until it receives I-frame $N+1$.

■ On receipt of I-frame $N+1$, S resumes accepting frames and returning acknowledgments.

■ A timeout is applied to NAK-frames by S and a second NAK is returned if the correct in-sequence I-frame is not received in the timeout interval.

The frame sequence shown in Figure 6.28(b) shows the effect of a corrupted ACK-frame. Note that:

■ S receives each transmitted I-frame correctly.

■ Assume ACK-frames N and $N+1$ are both corrupted.

■ On receipt of ACK-frame $N+2$, P detects that there are two outstanding I-frames in the retransmission list (N and $N+1$).

■ Since it is an ACK-frame rather than a NAK-frame, P assumes that the two ACK-frames for I-frames N and $N+1$ have both been corrupted and hence accepts ACK-frame $N+2$ as an acknowledgment for the outstanding frames.

In order to discriminate between the NAK-frames used in the two schemes, in the selective repeat scheme a NAK is known as a **selective reject** and in the go-back-N scheme a **reject**.

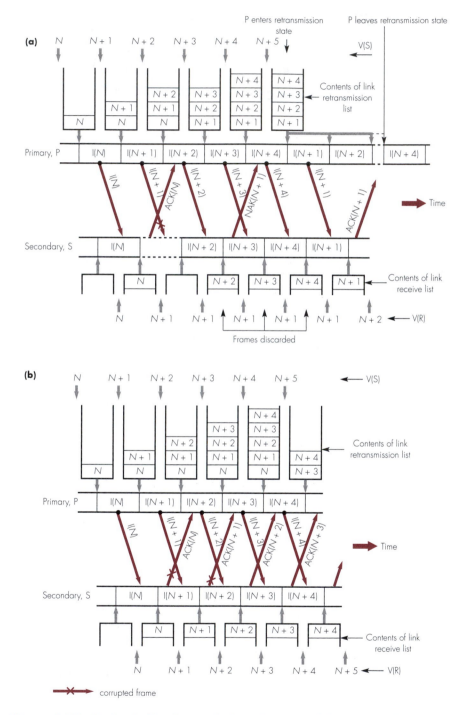

Figure 6.28 Go-back-N retransmission strategy: (a) corrupted I-frame; (b) corrupted ACK-frame.

6.7.4 Flow control

Error control is only one component of a data link protocol. Another important and related component is flow control. As the name implies, it is concerned with controlling the rate of transmission of frames on a link so that the receiver always has sufficient buffer storage resources to accept them prior to processing.

To control the flow of frames across a link, a mechanism known as a **sliding window** is used. The approach is similar to the idle RQ control scheme in that it essentially sets a limit on the number of I-frames that P may send before receiving an acknowledgment. P monitors the number of outstanding (unacknowledged) I-frames currently held in the retransmission list. If the destination side of the link is unable to pass on the frames sent to it, S stops returning acknowledgment frames, the retransmission list at P builds up and this in turn can be interpreted as a signal for P to stop transmitting further frames until acknowledgments start to flow again.

To implement this scheme, a maximum limit is set on the number of I-frames that can be awaiting acknowledgment and hence are outstanding in the retransmission list. This limit is the **send window**, K for the link. If this is set to 1, the retransmission control scheme reverts to idle RQ with a consequent drop in transmission efficiency. The limit is normally selected so that, providing the destination is able to pass on or absorb all frames it receives, the send window does not impair the flow of I-frames across the link. Factors such as the maximum frame size, available buffer storage, link propagation delay, and transmission bit rate must all be considered when selecting the send window.

The operation of the scheme is shown in Figure 6.29. As each I-frame is transmitted, the **upper window edge** (**UWE**) is incremented by unity. Similarly, as each I-frame is acknowledged, the **lower window edge** (**LWE**) is incremented by unity. The acceptance of any new message blocks, and hence the flow of I-frames, is stopped if the difference between UWE and LWE becomes equal to the send window K. Assuming error-free transmission, K is a fixed window that moves (slides) over the complete set of frames being transmitted. The technique is thus known as "sliding window".

The maximum number of frame buffers required at S is known as the **receive window**. We can deduce from the earlier frame sequence diagrams that with the idle RQ and go-back-N schemes only one buffer is required. With selective repeat, however, K frames are required to ensure frames are delivered in the correct sequence.

6.7.5 Sequence numbers

Until now, we have assumed that the sequence number inserted into each frame by P is simply the previous sequence number plus one and that the range of numbers available is infinite. Defining a maximum limit on the number of I-frames being transferred across a link not only limits the size of the link retransmission and receive lists, but also makes it possible to limit the

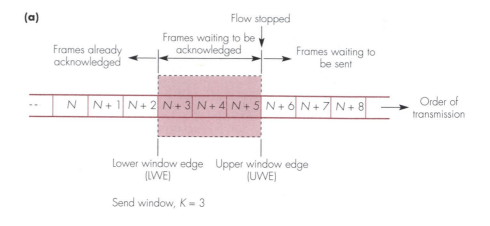

Send window, $K = 3$

(b)

Protocol	Send window	Receive window
Idle RQ	1	1
Selective repeat	K	K
Go-back-N	K	1

Figure 6.29 Flow control principle: (a) sliding window example; (b) send and receive window limits.

range of sequence numbers required to identify each transmitted frame uniquely. The number of identifiers is a function of both the retransmission control scheme and the size of the send and receive windows.

For example, with an idle RQ control scheme, the send and receive windows are both 1 and hence only two identifiers are required to allow S to determine whether a particular I-frame received is a new frame or a duplicate. Typically, the two identifiers are 0 and 1; the send sequence variable is incremented modulo 2 by P.

With a go-back-N control scheme and a send window of K, the number of identifiers must be at least $K+1$. We can deduce this by considering the case when P sends a full window of K frames but all the ACK-frames relating to them are corrupted. If only K identifiers were used, S would not be able to determine whether the next frame received is a new frame – as it expects – or a duplicate of a previous frame.

With a selective repeat scheme and a send and receive window of K, the number of identifiers must not be less than $2K$. Again, we can deduce this by considering the case when P sends a full window of K frames and all subsequent acknowledgments are corrupted. S must be able to determine whether any of the next K frames are new frames. The only way of ensuring that S can deduce this is to assign a completely new set of K identifiers to the next window of I-frames transmitted, which requires at least $2K$ identifiers. The limits for each scheme are summarized in Figure 6.30(a).

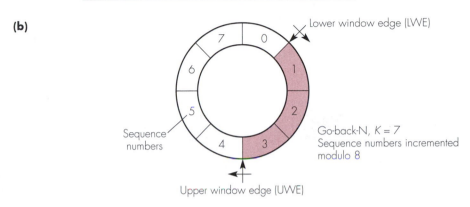

(a)

Protocol	Maximum number of frame identifiers
Idle RQ	2
Selective repeat	$2K + 1$
Go-back-N	$K + 1$

(b)

Lower window edge (LWE)

Sequence numbers

Go-back-N, $K = 7$
Sequence numbers incremented
modulo 8

Upper window edge (UWE)

Figure 6.30 Sequence numbers: (a) maximum number for each protocol; (b) example assuming eight sequence numbers.

In practice, since the identifier of a frame is in binary form, a set number of binary digits must be reserved for its use. For example, with a send window of, say, 7 and a go-back-N control scheme, three binary digits are required for the send and receive sequence numbers yielding eight possible identifiers: 0 through 7. The send and receive sequence variables are then incremented modulo 8 by P and S respectively. This is illustrated in Figure 6.30(b).

6.7.6 Layered architecture

The frame sequence diagrams that we showed earlier provide a qualitative description of the error control (and flow control) components of a link layer protocol that is based on an idle RQ scheme – Figure 6.23 – and a continuous RQ scheme – Figures 6.26–28. In practice, however, it is not possible to describe fully the operation of all aspects of a protocol using just this method. Normally, therefore, the operation of a protocol is specified in a more formal way and, in order to gain an insight into how this is done, we shall specify the error control component of the idle RQ error control scheme.

Before we do this, we revisit the subject of layering which we first introduced in Section 5.2.2. As we showed in Figure 5.3(a), this involves decoupling each protocol layer one from another and defining a formal interface between them. Assuming an idle RQ scheme, a suitable layered architecture for the link layer is as shown in Figure 6.31. As we have described, the service provided to the network layer in the source is to transfer in a reliable way a series of blocks of information to the network layer in the destination. Also, depending on the BER probability of the line, a maximum block size will be specified that ensures a good percentage of I-frames transmitted will be free of errors.

As we show in Figure 6.31, in order to decouple the network and link layers in each system, we introduce a queue between them. Each queue is simply a data structure that implements a first-in, first-out (FIFO) queuing discipline. Elements are added to the tail of the queue and are removed from the head.

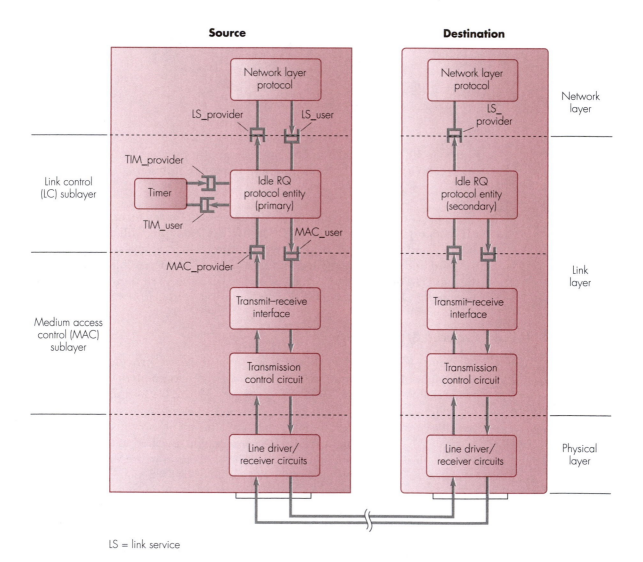

LS = link service

Figure 6.31 Example layered architecture showing the layer and sublayer interfaces associated with the idle RQ protocol.

Normally, the user service primitive(s) associated with a layer is(are) passed between layers using a data structure known as an **event control block** (**ECB**). This has the primitive type in the first field and an array containing the user data in a second field. For example, whenever the network layer protocol wishes to send a message block – the contents of a data structure – it first obtains a free ECB, sets the primitive type field to L_DATA.request, writes the address pointer of the data structure in the user data field, and inserts the ECB at the tail of the link layer (LS_user) input queue ready for reading by the idle RQ primary.

When the idle RQ protocol software is next run, it detects the presence of an entry (ECB) in the LS_user queue, reads the entry from the head of the queue, and proceeds to create an I-frame containing the send sequence number and the contents of the user data field. It then initiates the transmission of the frame to the secondary protocol using the services provided by the transmission control circuit. Normally, as we show in the figure, associated with the latter is a piece of low-level software which, in practice, is part of the **basic input-output software** (**BIOS**) of the computer. Assuming bit-oriented transmission, as the frame contents are being output, the transmission control circuit generates the CRC for the frame and adds the start and end flags. As we can deduce from this, therefore, the link layer comprises two sublayers: the **link control** (**LC**) – which is concerned with the implementation of the error and flow control procedures that are being used and is independent of the type of transmission control mode – and the **medium access control** (**MAC**) **sublayer** – which is concerned with the transmission of preformatted blocks using a particular transmission control mode which may vary for different networks. The physical layer comprises suitable bit/clock encoding circuits, line driver and receiver circuits, and the plug and socket pin definitions.

At the destination, assuming the received frame is error free, the MAC sublayer passes the frame contents to the LC sublayer using a MAC_DATA.indication primitive in an ECB and the MAC_provider queue. The LC sublayer then uses the send sequence number at the head of the frame to confirm it is not a duplicate and passes the frame contents – the message block – up to the network layer in an ECB using the LS_provider output queue with the primitive type set to L_DATA.indication. It then creates and returns an ACK-frame to P using a MAC_DATA.request primitive in an ECB and the MAC_user queue.

When the destination network layer protocol is next run, it detects and reads the ECB from the LS_provider queue and proceeds to process the contents of the message block it contains according to the defined network layer protocol. At the sending side, assuming the ACK-frame is received free of errors, the MAC sublayer passes the frame to the LC sublayer primary which frees the memory buffer containing the acknowledged I-frame and checks the LS_user input queue for another waiting ECB. If there is one, the procedure is repeated until all queued blocks have been transferred. Note that the LS_user queue and the retransmission list are quite separate. The first is used to hold new message blocks waiting to be transmitted and the second to hold frames – containing blocks – that have already been sent and are waiting to be acknowledged.

We can conclude that the adoption of a layered architecture means that each layer performs its own well-defined function in relation to the overall communications task. Each layer provides a defined service to the layer immediately above it. The service primitives associated with the service are each implemented by the layer protocol communicating with a peer layer protocol in the remote system. Associated with the protocol are protocol data units (PDUs) – for example, I-frame, ACK-frame, and so on in the case of the link layer – and these are physically transferred using the services provided by the layer immediately below it.

6.7.7 Protocol specification

Irrespective of the specification method that is used, we model a protocol as a **finite state machine** or **automaton**. This means that the protocol – or, more accurately, the **protocol entity** – can be in just one of a finite number of defined **states** at any instant. For example, it might be idle waiting for a message to send, or waiting to receive an acknowledgment. Transitions between states take place as a result of an incoming event, for example, a message becomes ready to send, or an ACK-frame is received. As a result of an incoming event, an associated **outgoing event** is normally generated, for example, on receipt of a message, format and send the created I-frame on the link, or on receipt of a NAK-frame, retransmit the waiting I-frame.

Some incoming events may lead to a number of possible outgoing events. The particular outgoing event selected is determined by the computed state of one or more **predicates** (boolean variables). As an example, predicate P1 may be true if the N(R) in a received ACK-frame is the same as the N(S) in the I-frame waiting to be acknowledged. Hence, if P1 is true, then free the memory buffer in which the I-frame is being held; if it is false, initiate retransmission of the frame.

An incoming event, in addition to generating an outgoing event (and possibly a change of state), may also have one or more associated **local** or **specific actions**. Examples include *start a timer* and *increment the send sequence variable*.

We shall now expand upon all of these aspects of the specification of a protocol by considering the specification of the error control procedure associated with the idle RQ protocol. To simplify the description, we shall consider only a unidirectional flow of I-frames – from the source to the destination. In most applications, however, a two-way flow is needed and both sides require a primary and a secondary.

All finite state machines – and hence protocol entities – operate in an atomic way. This means that once an incoming event has started to be processed, all processing functions associated with the event, including the generation of any outgoing event(s), local (specific) actions, and a possible change in state, are all carried out in their entirety (that is, in an indivisible way) before another incoming event is accepted.

To ensure this happens, the various incoming (and outgoing) event interfaces are decoupled from the protocol entity itself by means of queues. As we showed earlier in Figure 6.31, there is an additional pair of queues between the protocol entity and the transmit–receive procedure that controls the particular transmission control circuit being used. Similarly, there is a pair of queues between the protocol entity and the timer procedure. Normally, the latter is run at regular (tick) intervals by means of an **interrupt** and, if a timer is currently running, its current value is decremented by the tick value. If the value goes to zero, a **timer expired** message is returned to the protocol entity via the appropriate queue.

The role of the transmit–receive procedure is simply to transmit a preformatted frame passed to it or to receive a frame from the link and queue the frame for processing by the protocol entity. This procedure may also be run as a result of an interrupt, but this time from the transmission control circuit. Also, although in principle only a single input and output queue is necessary to interface the primary and secondary to their respective network layers, in practice a pair of queues is necessary at each interface in order to handle the duplex flows of primitives.

To simplify the specification procedure, we give each of the various incoming events, outgoing events, predicates, specific actions, and states associated with each protocol entity an abbreviated name. Prior to specifying the protocol, the various abbreviated names are listed and all subsequent references are made using these names. For the error control component of the idle RQ protocol, the list of abbreviated names for the primary is as shown in Figure 6.32.

Since each protocol entity is essentially a sequential system, we must retain information that may vary as different incoming events are received. This information is held in a number of **state variables**. Examples, for the primary, are the send sequence variable $V(S)$ – Vs in the specification – which holds the sequence number to be allocated to the next I-frame to be transmitted, the PresentState variable which holds the present state of the protocol entity, RetxCount which is a count of the number of erroneous frames received. Typically, if either RetxCount or ErrorCount reaches its maximum limit then the frame is discarded, an error message is sent to the network layer above and the protocol (entity) reinitializes.

The three most common methods that are used for specifying a communication protocol are **state transition diagrams**, **extended event–state tables**, and high-level structured programs. In many instances, we define a protocol as a combination of these coupled with time sequence diagrams to illustrate the user service primitives associated with the protocol.

The formal specification of the primary is shown in Figure 6.33. In part (a) a state transition diagram is used, in part (b) an extended event–state table, and in part (c) structured pseudocode.

Incoming events

Name	Interface	Meaning
LDATAreq	LS_user	L_DATA.request service primitive received
ACKRCVD	MAC_provider	ACK-frame received from S
TEXP	TIM_provider	Wait-ACK timer expires
NAKRCVD	MAC_provider	NAK-frame received from S

States

Name	Meaning
IDLE	Idle, no message transfer in progress
WTACK	Waiting an acknowledgment

Outgoing events

Name	Interface	Meaning
TxFrame	MAC_user	Format and transmit an I-frame
RetxFrame	MAC_user	Retransmit I-frame waiting acknowledgment
LERRORind	LS_provider	Error message: frame discarded for reason specified

Predicates

Name	Meaning
P0	N(S) in waiting I-frame = N(R) in ACK-frame
P1	CRC in ACK/NAK-frame correct

Specific actions

[1] = Start_timer using TIM_user queue
[2] = Increment Vs
[3] = Stop_timer using TIM_user queue
[4] = Increment RetxCount
[5] = Increment ErrorCount
[6] = Reset RetxCount to zero

State variables

Vs	= Send sequence variable
PresentState	= Present state of protocol entity
ErrorCount	= Number of erroneous frames received
RetxCount	= Number of retransmissions for this frame

Figure 6.32 Abbreviated names used in the specification of the idle RQ primary.

(a)

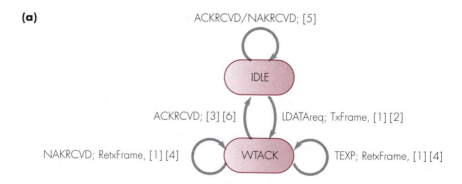

Figure 6.33 Specification of idle RQ primary in the form of: (a) a state transition diagram; (b) an extended event–state table; (c) pseudocode.

(b)

Incoming event / Present state	LDATAreq	ACKRCVD	TEXP	NAKRCVD
IDLE	1	0	0	0
WTACK	4	2	3	3

0 = [5], IDLE (error condition)

1 = TxFrame, [1] [2], WTACK

2 = P0 and P1: [3] [6], IDLE

      P0 and NOT P1: RetxFrame, [1] [4], WTACK

      NOT P0 and NOT P1: [5], IDLE

3 = RetxFrame, [1] [4], WTACK

4 = NoAction, WTACK

(c)

```
program    IdleRQ_Primary;
const      MaxErrCount;
           MaxRetxCount;
type       Events  = (LDATAreq, ACKRCVD, TEXP, NAKRCVD);
           States  = (IDLE, WTACK);
var        EventStateTable = array [Events, States] of 0..4;
           PresentState : States;
           Vs, ErrorCount, RetxCount : integer;
           EventType : Events;
procedure  Initialize;        } Initializes state variables and contents of EventStateTable
procedure  TxFrame;
procedure  RetxFrame;         } Outgoing event procedures
procedure  LERRORind;
procedure  Start_timer;
procedure  Stop_timer;        } Specific action procedures
function   P0 : boolean;
function   P1 : boolean;      } Predicate functions

begin      Initialize;
           repeat  Wait receipt of an incoming event
                   EventType := type of event
                   case EventStateTable [EventType, PresentState] of
                       0 : beginErrorCount := ErrorCount + 1; PresentState = IDLE;
                               if(ErrorCount = MaxErrCount) thenLERRORind end;
                       1 : beginTxFrame; Start_timer; Vs := Vs + 1; PresentState := WTACK end;
                       2 : beginif(P0 and P1) then begin Stop_timer; RetxCount := 0; PresentState := IDLE end;
                               else if (P0 and NOTP1) then begin RetxFrame; Start_timer;
                                                             RetxCount := RetxCount + 1;
                                                             PresentState := WTACK end;
                               else if (NOTP0 and NOTP1) then begin PresentState := IDLE; ErrorCount := ErrorCount + 1
                                                             if (ErrorCount = MaxErrorCount) then begin LERRORind; Initialize; end;
                           end;
                       3 : begin RetxFrame; Start_timer; RetxCount := RetxCount + 1; PresentState := WTACK;
                               if (RetxCount = MaxRetxCount) then begin LERRORind; Initialize; end;
                           end;
                       4 : begin NoAction end;
                   until Forever;
end.
```

Figure 6.33 Continued.

Using the state transition diagram method, the possible states of the protocol entity are shown in ovals with the particular states written within them. **Directional arrows** (also known as **arcs**) indicate the possible transitions between the states, with the incoming event causing the transition and any resulting outgoing event and specific actions, written alongside. If, for example, an L_DATA.request (LDATAreq) is received from LS_user interface, then the frame is formatted and output to the MAC_user interface (TxFrame), a timer is started for the frame [1], the send sequence variable incremented [2], and the WTACK state entered. Similarly, if an ACK-frame is received with an N(R) equal to the N(S) in the waiting frame and the CRC is correct, then the timer is stopped [3] and the transitions can be interpreted in a similar way.

Although state transition diagrams are useful for showing the correct operation of a protocol, because of space limitations it is not always practicable to show all possible incoming event possibilities including error conditions. Hence most state transition diagrams are incomplete specifications. Moreover, with all but the simplest of protocols, we need many such diagrams to define even the correct operation of a protocol. It is for these reasons that we use the extended event–state table and the structured program code methods.

Using the extended event–state table method – as we see in part (b) of the figure – we can show all the possible incoming events and protocol (present) states in the form of a table. For each state, the table entry defines the outgoing event, any specific action(s), and the new state for all possible incoming events. Also, if predicates are involved, the alternative set of action(s). Clearly, the extended event–state table is a far more rigorous method since it allows for all possible incoming-event, present-state combinations. A basic event–state table has only one possible action and next-state for each incoming-event/present-state combination. It is the presence of predicates – and hence possible alternative actions/next states – that gives rise to the use of the term "extended" event–state table.

When we are interpreting the actions to be followed if predicates are involved, we must note that these are shown in order. Hence the action to be followed if the primary is in the WTACK state and an ACK-frame is received (ACKRCVD), is first to determine if P0 and P1 are both true. If they are, then carry out specific action [3] and [6] and enter the IDLE state. Else, determine if {P0 and NOTP1} is true, and so on. If neither condition is true then an error is suspected and the actions are shown.

A feature of the extended event–state table is that it lends itself more readily to implementation in program code than a state transition diagram. We can see this by considering the pseudocode specification of the idle RQ primary in Figure 6.33(c). In the figure this is shown as a program but in practice it is implemented in the form of a procedure or function so it can be included with the other protocol layers in a single program. However, this does not affect the basic operation of the program shown.

When each program (layer) is first run, the Initialize procedure is invoked. This performs such functions as initializing all state variables to their initial values and the contents of the EventStateTable array to those in the extended event–state table. The program then enters an infinite loop waiting for an incoming event to arrive at one of its input queues.

The incoming event which causes the program to run is first assigned to EventType. The current contents of PresentState and EventType are then used as indices to the EventStateTable array to determine the integer – 0, 1, 2, 3, or 4 – that defines the processing actions associated with that event. For example, if the accessed integer is 2, this results in the predicate functions P0 and P1 being invoked and, depending on their computed state (true or false), the invocation of the appropriate outgoing event procedure, coupled with any specific action procedures(s) as defined in the specification; for example, starting or resetting the timer, and updating PresentState.

We have simplified the pseudocode to highlight the structure of each program and hence the implementation methodology. No code is shown for the various outgoing event procedures nor for the predicate functions. In practice, these must be implemented in an unambiguous way using the necessary steps listed in the specification.

6.7.8 User service primitives

As we explained in the last section, to initiate the transfer of a block of information across the transmission line/link, the source network layer uses an ECB with a L_DATA.request primitive and the block of information within it. Similarly, the destination link layer (protocol), on receipt of an error-free I-frame containing the block of information, also uses an ECB to pass the block to the network layer with a L_DATA.indication primitive within it.

Example 6.9

Use the frame sequence diagram shown earlier in Figure 6.23 and the list of abbreviated names given in Figure 6.34(a) to specify the operation of the idle RQ secondary using (i) a state transition diagram, (ii) an extended event–state table, (iii) pseudocode.

Answer:

The specification of the idle RQ secondary in each form is given in Figure 6.34(b), (c), and (d) respectively. Note that just two state variables are needed for the secondary: the receive sequence variable – shown as V_r in the specification – which holds the sequence number of the last correctly received I-frame, and ErrorCount which keeps a record of the number of erroneous I-frames received. Again, if ErrorCount reaches a defined maximum limit an error message – LERRORind – is output to the network layer in an ECB.

(a) **Incoming events**

Name	Interface	Meaning
IRCVD	MAC_provider	I-frame received from P

States

Name	Meaning
WTIFM	Waiting a new I-frame from P

Outgoing events

Name	Interface	Meaning
LDATAind	LS_provider	Pass contents of received I-frame to user AP with an L_DATA.indication primitive
TxACK(X)	MAC_user	Format and transmit an ACK-frame with N(R) = X
TxNAK(X)	MAC_user	Format and transmit a NAK-frame with N(R) = X
LERRORind	LS_provider	Issue error message for reason specified

Predicates

Name	Meaning
P0	N(S) in I-frame = Vr
P1	CRC in I-frame correct
P2	N(S) in I-frame = Vr − 1

Specific actions

[1] = Increment Vr
[2] = Increment ErrorCount

State variables

Vr = Receive sequence variable
ErrorCount = Number of erroneous frames received

(b)

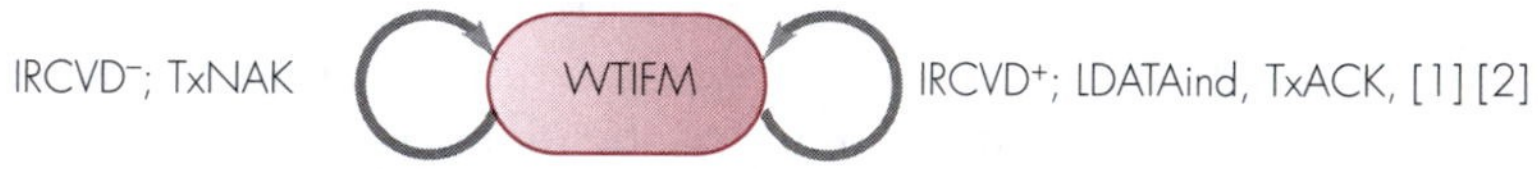

IRCVD⁻; TxNAK   (WTIFM)   IRCVD⁺; LDATAind, TxACK, [1] [2]

(c)

Incoming event / Present state	IRCVD
WTIFM	1

1 = NOT P1: TxNAK, [2]
P1 and P2: TxACK
P0 and P1: LDATAind, TxACK, [1]

Figure 6.34 Specification of idle RQ secondary: (a) abbreviated names; (b) state transition diagram; (c) extended event–state table; (d) pseudocode.

```
(d)   program   IdleRQ_Secondary;
      const.    MaxErrorCount;
      type      Events = IRCVD;
                States = WTIFM;
      var       EventStateTable = array [Events, States] of 1;
                EventType : Events;
                PresentState : States;
                Vr, X, ErrorCount : integer;
      procedure Initialize;          } Initializes state variables and contents of EventStateTable
      procedure LDATAind;            ⌉
      procedure TxACK(X);            │
      procedure TxNAK(X);            } Outgoing event procedures
      procedure LERRORind;           ⌋
      function  P0 : boolean;        ⌉
      function  P1 : boolean;        } Predicate functions
      function  P2 : boolean;        ⌋

      begin     Initialize;
                repeat Wait receipt of incoming event; EventType := type of event;
                       case EventStateTable[EventType, PresentState] of
                          1 : X := N(S) from I-frame;
                              if (NOTP1) then TxNAK(X);
                              else if(P1 and P2) then TxACK(X);
                              else if(P0 and P1) then begin LDATAind; TxACK(X); Vr := Vr + 1; end;
                              else begin ErrorCount := ErrorCount + 1; if (ErrorCount = MaxErrorCount) then
                                         begin LERRORind; Initialize; end;
                                 end;
                until Forever;
      end.
```

Figure 6.34 Continued.

For the error and flow control schemes we have outlined in the previous sections to function correctly, we have assumed that both communicating link protocols have been initialized so that they are ready to exchange information. For example, both sides of the link must start with the same send and receive sequence variables before any information frames are transmitted. In general, this is known as the initialization or **link setup** phase and, after all data has been exchanged across a link, there is a **link disconnection** phase. Since the link setup and disconnection phases are not concerned with the actual transfer of user data, they are collectively referred to as **link management**. The two link management functions are also initiated by the network layer (protocol) using an ECB and the set of primitives that we show in Figure 6.35(a). Since the primitives shown are in the same sequence as they are issued, this form of representing the various user service primitives associated with a protocol is known as a **time sequence diagram**. Note that to avoid the diagram becoming too cluttered, we have left off the two error indication primitives.

On receipt of an **L_CONNECT.request** primitive, the link protocol entity at the source initializes all state variables and then creates a **link SETUP** frame (PDU). This is sent to the correspondent (peer) link protocol entity in the destination using the selected transmission mode. On receipt of the SETUP frame, the destination initializes its own state variables and proceeds by sending an **L_CONNECT.indication** primitive to the correspondent LS_user and an acknowledgment frame back to the source.

(a)

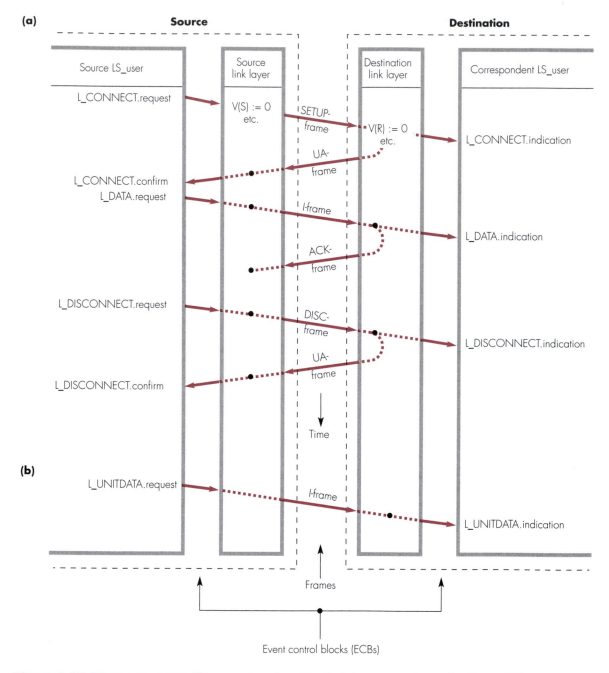

Figure 6.35 Time sequence diagram showing the link layer service primitives: (a) connection-oriented (reliable) mode; (b) connectionless (best-effort) mode.

Since this acknowledgment does not relate to an I-frame, it does not contain a sequence number. It is known, therefore, as an **unnumbered acknowledgment** or **UA-frame**. On receipt of this UA-frame, the source protocol entity issues the **L_CONNECT.confirm** primitive to the LS_user and the link is now ready for the transfer of data using the L_DATA service. Finally, after all data has been transferred, the setup link is released using the L_DISCONNECT service, which is also a confirmed service. The corresponding frame, known as a **disconnect** or **DISC frame**, is acknowledged using a UA-frame.

This mode of operation of the link layer is known as the connection-oriented mode and, as we have explained, it provides a reliable service. As we indicated at the start of Section 6.7, however, in many applications this mode of operation is not used and instead the simpler best-effort service is used in which the link layer protocol at the destination simply discards any frames received with errors. The two user service primitives associated with this mode are shown in Figure 6.35(b).

Since it is not necessary to set up a logical connection prior to sending blocks of information, this mode of operation is known as the connectionless mode and, in order to discriminate between the data transfer service associated with the two modes, as we show in the figure, the two service primitives used are **L_UNITDATA.request** and **L_UNITDATA.indication**. Also, since in the connectionless mode no retransmissions are used, no sequence numbers are required. Note, however, that the differences between the two modes occur only at the link control sublayer as both modes use the same medium access control sublayer.

6.8 The HDLC protocol

To conclude this chapter, we describe selected aspects of a practical example of a link layer protocol known as the **high-level data link control** (**HDLC**) protocol. This is an international standard that has been defined for use with a number of different network configurations and types. These include duplex point-to-point links as used over the access circuits associated with an ISDN, and half-duplex multidrop/broadcast links as used in some LANs. Hence there is the original HDLC protocol and a number of variants of it, each of which uses slightly different fields in the frame header and also a different MAC sublayer. Examples include the **link access procedure D-channel** (**LAPD**) which is used with an ISDN and the **logical link control** (**LLC**) which is used with LANs.

In HDLC, the frames sent by the primary to the secondary are known as **commands**, and those from the secondary to the primary as **responses**. Also, when the LC sublayer is operating in a connection-oriented (reliable) mode, all error and flow control frames are known as **supervisory frames** and the various frames that are used to set up and disconnect a logical link **unnumbered frames**. A standard format is used for all frames, however, and this is shown in Figure 6.36(a).

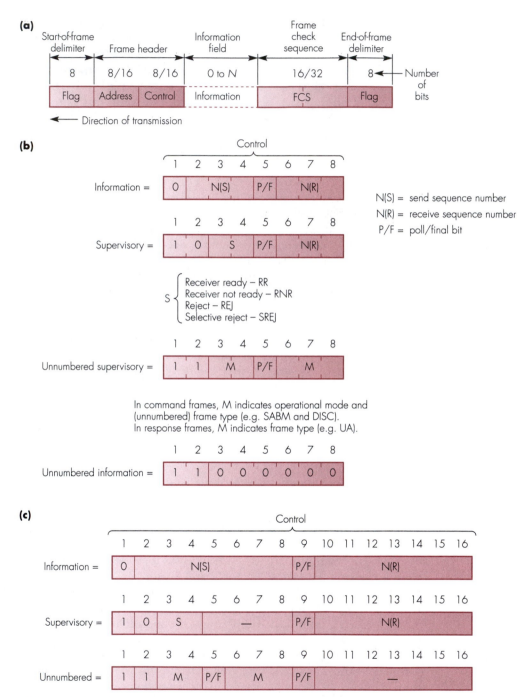

Note: With the indicated direction of transmission, all control field types are transmitted bit 8/16 first.

Figure 6.36 HDLC frame format and types: (a) standard/extended format; (b) standard control field bit definitions; (c) extended control field bit definitions.

As we can see, HDLC is based on a bit-oriented transmission control scheme with flags to indicate the start and end of each frame together with zero bit insertion and deletion to ensure the flag pattern (01111110) does not occur within the bitstream between the flags. The frame check sequence (FCS) is a 16-bit CRC that is computed using the generator polynomial:

$$x^{16} + x^{12} + x^5 + 1$$

The CRC is first generated using the procedure we described in Section 6.6.2 but an additional step is taken to make the check more robust. This involves adding sixteen 1s to the tail of the dividend (instead of zeros) and inverting the remainder. This has the effect that the remainder computed by the receiver is not all zeros but the bit pattern 0001 1101 0000 1111.

The various control field bit definitions are shown in Figure 6.36(b). The S-field in supervisory frames and the M-field in unnumbered frames are used to define the specific frame type. The send and receive sequence numbers – N(S) and N(R) – are used in conjunction with the error and flow control procedures.

The **P/F bit** is known as the **poll/final bit**. A frame of any type is called a **command frame** if it is sent by the primary station and a **response frame** if it is sent by a secondary station. The P/F bit is called the poll bit when used in a command frame and, if set, indicates that the receiver must acknowledge this frame. The receiver acknowledges this frame by returning an appropriate response frame with the P/F bit set; it is then known as the final bit.

The use of 3 bits for each of N(S) and N(R) means that sequence numbers can range from 0 through 7. This, in turn, means that a maximum send window of 7 can be selected. Although this is large enough for many applications, those involving very long links (satellite links, for example) or very high bit rates, require a larger send window if a high link utilization is to be achieved. The extended format uses 7 bits (0 through 127), thereby increasing the maximum send window to 127. This is shown in Figure 6.36(c).

The address field identifies the secondary station that sent the frame, and is not needed with point-to-point links. However, with multipoint links, the address field can be either eight bits – normal mode – or multiples of eight bits – extended mode. In the latter case, bit 1 of the least significant address octet(s) is(are) set to 0 and bit 1 is set to 1 in the last octet. The remaining bits form the address. In both modes, an address of all 1s is used as an all-stations broadcast address.

Unnumbered frames are used both to set up a logical link between the primary and secondary and to inform the secondary of the mode of operation to be used. For example, the set asynchronous balanced mode (SABM) command frame – indicated by the M-bits in the control field – is used to set up a logical link in both directions when a duplex point-to-point link is being used. Other examples are the DISC-frame (which is used to disconnect the link) and the UA-frame, which is a response frame and is sent to acknowledge receipt of the other (command) frames in this class. Also, when operating in the connectionless (best-effort) mode, no acknowledgment information is required. Hence all information is transmitted in **unnumbered information** (**UI**) frames with the control field set to 11000000.

The four supervisory frames are used to implement a continuous RQ error control scheme and have the following functions:

- receiver ready (RR): this has the same function as the ACK-frame in Figures 6.27 and 6.28;
- reject (REJ): this has the same function as the NAK-frame in the go-back-N scheme;
- selective reject (SREJ): this has the same function as the NAK-frame in the selective repeat scheme;
- receiver not ready (RNR): this can be used by the secondary to ask the primary to suspend sending any new I-frames.

Each RR (ACK) frame contains a receive sequence number – N(R) – which acknowledges correct receipt of all I-frames awaiting acknowledgment up to and including that with a N(S) equal to N(R) – 1. This is slightly different from what we used earlier in the frame sequence diagrams in Figures 6.27 and 6.28 in which N(R) acknowledged I-frames up to N(S). This is because in HDLC the receive sequence variable V(R) is incremented before the ACK-frame is returned rather than after as we used in the earlier figures. An example frame sequence diagram showing the use of the RR (ACK) and REJ (NAK) frames and the P/F bit is given in Figure 6.37. The example relates to a go-back-N error control scheme and, for clarity, just a unidirectional flow of I-frames which means the link is operating in the **normal response mode** (**NRM**).

When interpreting the figure, remember that each I-frame contains an N(S) and an N(R), the latter acknowledging frames flowing in the reverse direction and known as a **piggyback acknowledgment**. Hence, since in this example there are no I-frames flowing in the reverse direction, the N(R) field in the I-frames is always 0. Also, since an I-frame is a command, when the P-bit is set, this means that S must acknowledge the frame immediately using a RR (ACK) frame with the appropriate N(R) within it and, since it is being returned in response to a command (P = 1), with the F-bit set to 1.

The example also shows the use of REJ (NAK) frames. When S detects that I-frame I(2,0/P = 1) is out of sequence, it returns an REJ (1/F = 1). P then retransmits frames I(1,0) and I(2,0) with the P-bit again set to 1 in frame I(2,0). The receiver acknowledges correct receipt of each frame with the F-bit set to 1 in the last RR-frame. If selective retransmission is being used, then frame I(2,0/P = 1) will be accepted and an SREJ-frame returned to request that frame I(1,0) is retransmitted.

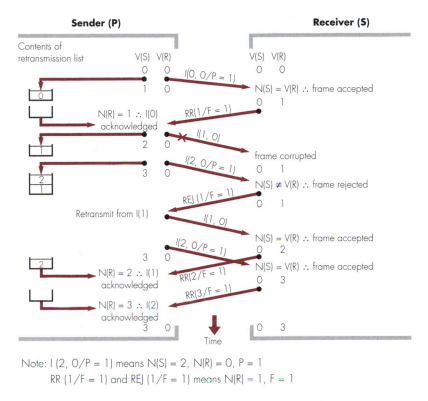

Note: I (2, 0/P = 1) means N(S) = 2, N(R) = 0, P = 1
RR (1/F = 1) and REJ (1/F = 1) means N(R) = 1, F = 1

Figure 6.37 HDLC normal response mode: example frame sequence diagram with single primary and secondary (i.e. no piggyback acknowledgments).

An example showing the use of piggyback acknowledgments is given in Figure 6.38. As we can see, in this example there is a flow of I-frames in both directions simultaneously and hence each side contains a primary and a secondary shown as combined P/S in the figure. For clarity, no transmission errors are shown.

As each I-frame is received, the N(S) and N(R) contained in the header are both read. N(S) is first compared with the receiver's V(R). If they are equal, the frame is in the correct sequence and is accepted; if they are not equal, the frame is discarded and an REJ or SREJ-frame returned. N(R) is examined and used to acknowledge any outstanding frames in the retransmission list. Finally, as no further I-frames are awaiting transmission, an RR-frame is used to acknowledge the outstanding unacknowledged frames in each retransmission list.

Flow control is particularly important when two-way simultaneous working is used; that is, the link is being operated in the **asynchronous balanced mode (ABM)**. As we can see in the example shown in Figure 6.38, the send and receive sequence variables – and hence numbers – are incremented

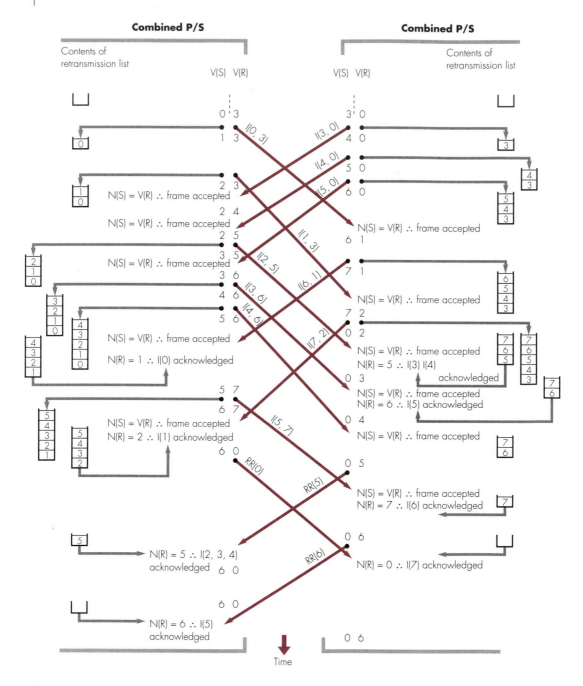

Figure 6.38 HDLC asynchronous balanced mode: piggyback acknowledgment procedure.

modulo 8 so the maximum send window K that can be used is 7. Thus a maximum of 7 I-frames can be awaiting acknowledgment in the retransmission list at any time. Each side of the link maintains a separate variable known as the retransmission count (RetxCount) which is initialized to zero when the logical link is set up. It is incremented each time an I-frame is transmitted, and hence each time a frame is placed in the retransmission list, and is decremented whenever a positive acknowledgment is received, and hence each time a frame is removed from the retransmission list. The primary stops sending I-frames when the retransmission count reaches K and does not resume until a positive acknowledgment is received either as a separate RR supervisory frame or piggybacked in an I-frame flowing in the reverse direction. We can conclude that transmission of I-frames is stopped when:

$$V(S) = \text{last } N(R) \text{ received} + K$$

Note that the window mechanism controls the flow of I-frames in only one direction and that supervisory and unnumbered frames are not affected by the mechanism. Hence, these frames can still be transmitted when the window is operating. An example with $K = 3$ is shown in Figure 6.39; for clarity, only the flow of I-frames in one direction is affected.

The use of a window mechanism means that the sequence numbers in all incoming frames must lie within certain boundaries. On receipt of each frame the secondary must check to establish that this is the case and, if not, take corrective action. Therefore each received $N(S)$ and $N(R)$ must satisfy the following conditions:

(1) $V(R)$ is less than or equal to $N(S)$ which is less than $V(R) + K$.
(2) $V(S)$ is greater than $N(R)$ which is greater than or equal to $V(S) -$ RetxCount.

If $N(S)$ equals $V(R)$, then all is well and the frame is accepted. If $N(S)$ is not equal to $V(R)$ but is still within the range, then a frame has simply been corrupted and a REJ (go-back-N) or a SREJ (selective repeat) frame is returned, indicating to the primary that a sequence error has occurred and from which frame to start retransmission.

If $N(S)$ or $N(R)$ is outside the range, then the sequence numbers at both ends of the link have become unsynchronized and the link must be reinitialized (set up). This is accomplished when the secondary, on detecting an out-of-range sequence number, discards the received frame and returns a **frame reject** (**FRMR**) – ABM – or a **command reject** (**CMDR**) – NRM – frame to the primary. The primary discards all waiting frames and proceeds to set up the link again by sending an SABM/SNRM and waiting for a UA response. On receipt of this response, both sides of the link reset their sequence and window variables enabling the flow of I-frames to be resumed. In fact, this is only one reason why a link may be reset; another is the receipt of an unnumbered frame, such as a UA, during the data transfer phase which indicates

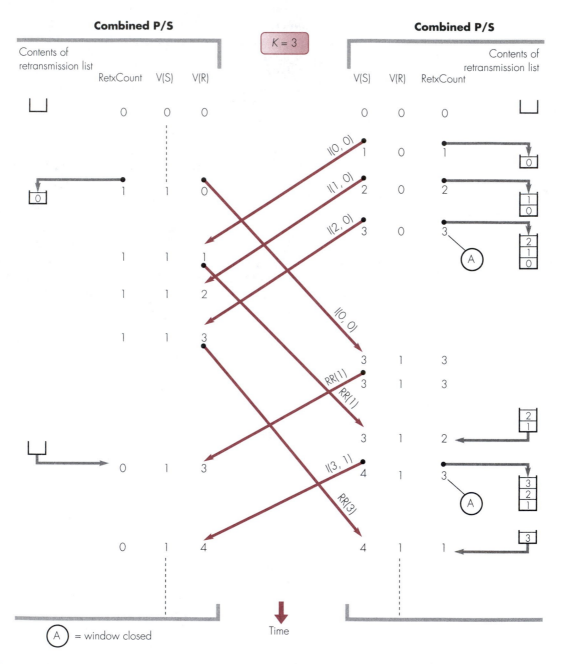

Figure 6.39 HDLC window flow control procedure.

that the primary and secondary have become unsynchronized.

The flow control procedure just outlined is controlled by the primary side of the link controlling the flow of I-frames according to the send window. In addition, it may be necessary for the secondary to stop the flow of I-frames as a result of some event occurring at its side of the link. For example, with a go-back-N retransmission strategy the receive window is 1 and it is reasonably straightforward to ensure that there are sufficient memory buffers available at the receiver. However, if selective retransmission is used, it is possible for the secondary to run out of free buffers to store any new frames. Hence, when the secondary approaches a point at which all its buffers are likely to become full, it returns an RNR supervisory frame to the primary to instruct it to stop sending I-frames. Acknowledgment frames are not affected, of course. When the number of full buffers drops below another preset limit, the secondary returns an RR-frame to the primary with a N(R) indicating from which frame to restart transmission.

A summary of the various service primitives and frame types (protocol data units) associated with HDLC is given in Figure 6.40(a). In practice, there are more unnumbered frames associated with HDLC than shown in the figure but, as mentioned earlier, the aim is simply to highlight selected aspects of HDLC operation. To reinforce understanding further, a (simplified) state transition diagram for HDLC is given in Figure 6.40(b). The first entry alongside each arc is the incoming event causing the transition (if any); the second entry is the resulting action. Note that a state transition diagram shows only the correct operation of the protocol entity; normally it is accompanied by a more complete definition in the form of an extended event–state table and/or pseudocode.

Summary

In this chapter we have discussed a range of topics relating to digital communications and these are summarized in Figure 6.41. As we have explained, the topics relate primarily to the way blocks of information/data are transmitted over a transmission line/channel reliably; that is, the received blocks are free of transmission/bit errors, are in the same sequence as they were submitted, and contain no duplicates. In the following chapters we shall show how many of the schemes we have described are utilized in the various types of network used to support multimedia applications.

(a)

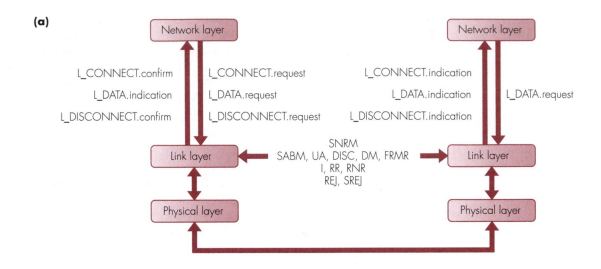

(b)

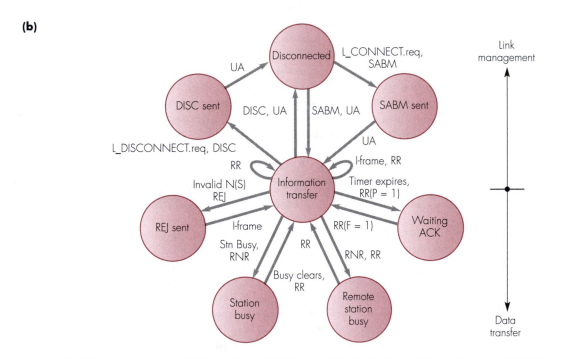

Figure 6.40 HDLC summary: (a) service primitives; (b) state transition diagram (ABM).

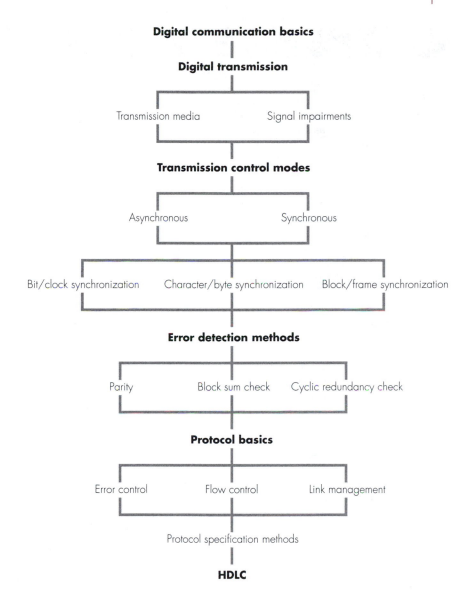

Figure 6.41 Summary of topics discussed relating to digital communications.

Exercises

Section 6.1

6.1 With the aid of the diagrams shown in Figure 6.1(a) and (b), explain the basic principles of the following transmission modes:
(i) baseband,
(ii) modulated.

6.2 With the aid of the waveform set shown in Figure 6.2, explain why the receiver samples the incoming signal as near to the center of each bit cell period as possible and, in some instances, bit errors occur.

Section 6.2

6.3 Explain why twisted-pair cable is preferred to non-twisted pair cable. What are the added benefits of using shielded twisted-pair cable?

6.4 With the aid of diagrams, explain the differences between the following transmission modes used with optical fiber:
(i) multimode stepped index,
(ii) multimode graded index,
(iii) monomode,
(iv) wave-division multiplexing.

6.5 State the meaning of the following relating to satellite systems:
(i) microwave beam,
(ii) transponder,
(iii) geostationary.

6.6 With the aid of diagrams, explain the operation of a satellite system that is used in
(i) TV broadcast applications and
(ii) data communication applications.

6.7 The maximum distance between two terrestrial microwave dishes, d, is given by the expression:

$$d = 7.14 \sqrt{Kh}$$

where h is the height of the dishes above ground and K is a factor that allows for the curvature of the earth. Assuming $K = 4/3$, determine d for selected values of h.

6.8 With reference to Figure 6.6(b), determine the frequency assignments for a cellular system assuming a 7-cell repeat pattern. Explain the advantages of this over the 3-cell repeat pattern shown in the figure.

6.9 Explain the terms "signal propagation delay" and "transmission delay". Assuming the velocity of propagation of an electrical signal is equal to the speed of light, determine the ratio of the signal propagation delay to the transmission delay, a, for the following types of data link and 1000 bits of data:
(i) 100 m of UTP wire and a transmission rate of 1 Mbps,
(ii) 2.5 km of coaxial cable and a transmission rate of 10 Mbps,
(iii) a satellite link and a transmission rate of 512 kbps.

Section 6.3

6.10 With the aid of sketches, explain the effect on a transmitted binary signal of the following:
(i) attenuation,
(ii) limited bandwidth,
(iii) delay distortion,
(iv) line and system noise.

6.11 Assuming 8 signal levels are used to transmit a data bitstream of 10 kbps, derive
(i) the number of bits per original element, and
(ii) the signaling rate in baud.

6.12 Explain why the binary sequence 101010 ... is referred to as the worst-case sequence when deriving the minimum bandwidth requirements of a transmission line/channel.

6.13 Derive the minimum channel bandwidth required to transmit at the following bit rates assuming (a) the fundamental frequency only and (b) the fundamental and third harmonic of the worst-case signal are to be received:
(i) 500 bps,
(ii) 2000 bps,
(iii) 1 Mbps.

6.14 A modem to be used with a PSTN uses four levels per signaling element. Assuming a noiseless channel and a bandwidth of 3000 Hz, derive the Nyquist maximum information transfer rate in bps.

6.15 With the aid of a diagram and associated waveform set, explain the meaning of the term "adaptive NEXT canceler" and how such circuits can improve the data transmission rate of a line.

Section 6.4

6.16 Explain the difference between asynchronous and synchronous transmission.

Assuming asynchronous transmission, one start bit, two stop bits, one parity bit, and two bits per signaling element, derive the useful information transfer rate in bps for each of the following signaling (baud) rates:
(i)   300,
(ii)   600,
(iii) 1200,
(iv)   4800.

6.17 With the aid of a diagram, explain the clock (bit) and character synchronization methods used with an asynchronous transmission control scheme. Use for example purposes a receiver clock rate ratio of ×1 and ×4 of the transmitter clock.

6.18 With the aid of the diagrams shown in Figure 6.13, explain how frame synchronization is achieved with an asynchronous transmission control scheme assuming the data being transmitted is
(i)   printable characters,
(ii)   binary bytes.

Section 6.5

6.19 With the aid of the diagrams shown in Figure 6.14 relating to bit/clock synchronization with synchronous transmission, explain how synchronization is achieved using
(i)   clock encoding,
(ii)   DPLL.

6.20 With the aid of the waveform sets shown in Figure 6.15, explain
(i)   the Manchester and
(ii)   the differential Manchester clock encoding methods.
Why do both methods yield balanced codes?

6.21 (i)   Explain under what circumstances data encoding and a DPLL circuit may be used to achieve clock synchronization. Also, with the aid of a diagram, explain the operation of the DPLL circuit.
(ii) Assuming the receiver is initially out of synchronism, derive the minimum number of bit transitions required for a DPLL circuit to converge to the nominal bit center of a transmitted waveform. How may this be achieved in practice?

6.22 Assuming a synchronous transmission control scheme, explain how character and frame synchronization are achieved:
(i)   with character-oriented transmission,
(ii)   with bit-oriented transmission.

6.23 Explain what is meant by the term "data transparency" and how it may be achieved using:
(i)   character stuffing,
(ii)   zero bit insertion.

Section 6.6

6.24 Explain the operation of the parity bit method of error detection and how it can be extended to cover blocks of characters.

Draw a circuit to compute the parity bit for a character and explain the difference between the terms "odd" and "even" parity.

6.25 With the aid of examples, define the following terms:
(i)   single-bit error,
(ii)   double-bit error,
(iii) error burst.

Produce a sketch showing the contents of a frame to illustrate the type of transmission errors that are not detected by a block sum check.

6.26 (a) Explain the principle of operation of a CRC error detection method. By means of an example, show how:
   (i) the error detection bits are generated,
   (ii) the received frame is checked for transmission errors. Use the generator polynomial.

$$x^4 + x^3 + 1$$

   (b) Use an example to show how an error pattern equal to the generator polynomial used in (a) will not be detected. List other error patterns that would not be detected with this polynomial.

6.27 In an engine management system, the sixteen binary messages 0000 through 1111 are to be transmitted over a data link. Each message is to be protected by a 3-bit CRC generated using the polynomial:

$$x^3 + x^2 + 1$$

   (i) Derive the 3 check bits for each of the three messages:

   0000   0001   0010

   (ii) State the meaning of the term "Hamming distance" and derive this for your code
   (iii) Show how a single-bit error and a double-bit error in a transmitted codeword are detected at the receiver assuming the transmitted message is 1111
   (iv) Give an example of a invalid received codeword that will not be detected.

Section 6.7

6.28 With the aid of frame sequence diagrams and assuming an idle RQ error control procedure with explicit retransmission, describe the following:
   (i) the factors influencing the minimum time delay between the transmission of two consecutive information frames
   (ii) how the loss of a corrupted information frame is overcome
   (iii) how the loss of a corrupted acknowledgment frame is overcome.

6.29 A series of information frames with a mean length of 100 bits is to be transmitted across the following data links using an idle RQ protocol. If the velocity of propagation of the links is 2×10^8 ms^{-1}, determine the link efficiency (utilization) for each type of link.
   (i) a 10 km link with a BER of 10^{-4} and a data transmission rate of 9600 bps
   (ii) a 500 m link with a BER of 10^{-6} and a data transmission rate of 10 Mbps.

6.30 With the aid of frame sequence diagrams, describe the difference between an idle RQ and a continuous RQ error control procedure. For clarity, assume that no frames are corrupted during transmission.

6.31 With the aid of frame sequence diagrams, describe how the following are overcome with a selective repeat error control scheme:
   (i) a corrupted information frame,
   (ii) a corrupted ACK frame.

6.32 Repeat Exercise 6.31 for a go-back-N scheme.

6.33 Discriminate between the send window and receive window for a link and how they are related with:
   (i) a selective repeat retransmission scheme,
   (ii) a go-back-N control scheme.

6.34 With the aid of frame sequence diagrams, illustrate the effect of a send window flow control limit being reached. Assume a send window of 2 and a go-back-N error control procedure.

6.35 Assuming a send window of K, deduce the minimum range of sequence numbers (frame identifiers) required with each of the following error control schemes:
   (i) idle RQ,
   (ii) selective repeat,
   (iii) go-back-N.

   Clearly identify the condition when the maximum number of identifiers is in use.

6.36 With the aid of Figure 6.31, explain the meaning of the following terms:
   (i) layered architecture,
   (ii) interlayer queues,

(iii) local event,
(iv) user services,
(v) used services.

6.37 Using the abbreviated names listed in Figure 6.32, show how the idle RQ primary can be specified in the form of:
(i) a state transition diagram,
(ii) an extended event–state table,
(iii) a high-level pseudocode program.

6.38 With the aid of a time sequence diagram, show a typical set of link layer service primitives assuming the link layer provides
(i) a reliable service and
(ii) a best-effort service.

Section 6.8

6.39 In relation to the IIDLC frame format shown in Figure 6.36, explain the meaning and use of the following terms:

(i) supervisory frames,
(ii) unnumbered frames,
(iii) poll/final bit,
(iv) command and response frames,
(v) extended control field bit definitions,
(vi) piggyback acknowledgment,
(vii) unnumbered information frame.

6.40 With the aid of the frame sequence diagram shown in Figure 6.37, explain how a corrupted I-frame is overcome in the normal response mode. Include in your explanation the use of the P/F bit.

6.41 With the aid of the frame sequence diagram shown in Figure 6.38, explain how the piggyback acknowledgment procedure works in the asynchronous balanced mode.

6.42 With the aid of the frame sequence diagram shown in Figure 6.39, describe the window flow control procedure used with the UDLC protocol.

Circuit-switched networks

7.1 Introduction

Although in Chapter 1 we discussed the operation and applications of a PSTN and an ISDN separately, in practice, as we shall expand upon later, both network types utilize the same core transmission and switching network to provide the related services and the only difference between the two networks is the way subscribers gain access to the core network. In this chapter, therefore, we shall discuss the operation of both a PSTN and an ISDN under the general heading of public circuit-switched networks.

All public circuit-switched networks consist of three hierarchical subnetworks:

- a relatively large number of **local access and switching networks**: these connect subscribers within a localized area to their nearest local exchange (LE) or end office (EO) and are concerned with the transmission and switching of calls within their own area;

- one or more **interexchange trunk/carrier networks**: these are national networks concerned with the transmission and switching of calls between different regional and national exchanges/offices;

- an interconnected set of **international networks**: associated with each national network is an international gateway exchange (IGE) and collectively these are concerned with the transmission and switching of calls internationally between the different national networks.

This general architecture is shown in Figure 7.1.

In some countries, the total national network is owned and managed by a single operator. In most countries, however, the various parts of the network are privately owned and managed by a number of operators. In some cases, the total local access and switching network is owned by a single operator and the various interexchange trunk networks are each owned by different operators. In others, there is one set of operators that own and run different parts of the local access network – known as **local exchange carriers (LXCs)** – and a different set of operators that run their own interexchange trunk networks – **interexchange carriers (IXCs)**. Nevertheless, the same basic architecture that we show in Figure 7.1 can be used to explain the principle of operation of this type of network. In practice, the overall network consists of three interrelated systems: transmission, switching, and signaling and hence we shall describe their operation under these headings.

Transmission system

Each subscriber within a localized area is connected to an LE/EO in that area by a dedicated circuit which, in the case of most homes, is a twisted-pair wire cable. This is known as the **customer line** or, more generally, the **subscriber line** (**SL**) as it is used exclusively by that subscriber. In the case of a PSTN, analog transmission is used over each subscriber line and hence, as we described in Section 2.5.1, all the signals relating to a call are analog signals within a bandwidth of 200 Hz through to 3.4 kHz. With an ISDN, digital transmission is used over the subscriber line which is then known as a **digital subscriber line** (**DSL**) since all the signals relating to a call are digital.

In the case of a customer premises which contains a PBX, as we explained earlier in Section 1.2, multiple calls can be in progress concurrently. Hence a digital subscriber line is used with a bit rate sufficient to support multiple simultaneous calls. Typical bit rates are 1.5 Mbps or 2 Mbps – or multiples of these – the first supporting 24 calls and the second 30 calls. A similar set of transmission circuits is used to interconnect the various exchanges within the network except, since the number of simultaneous calls can be much larger, optical fiber cables are used which operate at very high bit rates and hence can support many thousands of simultaneous calls.

As we explained in Section 1.3.1, in addition to telephony, a PSTN also provides a number of digital services including fax, access to the Internet, and high-speed access to various entertainment servers. In order to do this, modems are used to convert the digital signals associated with these applications into and from the analog signals used over the subscriber line. In the case of fax and Internet access, since these involve a switched connection similar to that used for telephony, low bit rate modems of up to 56 kbps are used. In the case of entertainment applications that do not utilize the switching network, however, modems supporting in excess of 1.5 Mbps are used.

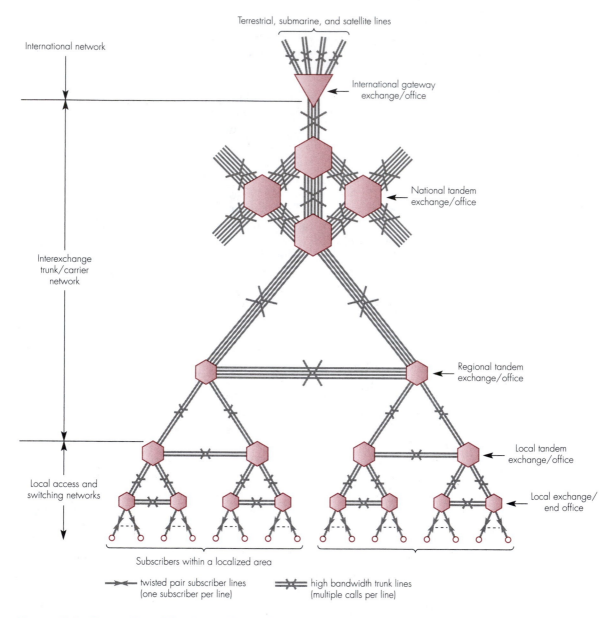

International network

Terrestrial, submarine, and satellite lines

International gateway
exchange/office

National tandem
exchange/office

Interexchange
trunk/carrier
network

Regional tandem
exchange/office

Local tandem
exchange/office

Local access and
switching networks

Local exchange/
end office

Subscribers within a localized area

twisted pair subscriber lines
(one subscriber per line)

high bandwidth trunk lines
(multiple calls per line)

Figure 7.1 General architecture of a national circuit-switched network.

Switching system

Each LE/EO within a local area has sufficient switching capacity to support a defined number of simultaneous calls/connections. In some instances, the calls are between two subscribers that are connected to the same LE/EO while in others they are between two subscribers connected to different exchanges.

In the first case, as we can see from Figure 7.1, a connection can be set up directly by the LE/EO without any other exchanges being involved. In all other cases, however, additional exchanges are involved, the number determined by the location of the LE/EO to which the called subscriber is connected.

- If the LE/EO is within the same local area, the connection involves just the two interconnected LEs/EOs.
- If the LE/EO is in a neighboring local area, the connection is through a local tandem exchange/office.
- If the LE/EO is in a different region, the connection is through either a pair of neighboring regional tandem exchanges/offices or, one or more additional higher-level national tandem exchanges/offices.
- If the LE/EO is in a different country, the connection is through the complete set of exchanges in each country including the two international gateway exchanges involved.

As we can deduce from the interconnection structure illustrated in Figure 7.1, within the total switching network, there are a number of alternative paths/routes between any two exchanges. The additional lines are provided both to increase capacity and to improve the resilience of the total network to exchange and/or line failures.

Signaling system

As we saw earlier in Section 1.2, both PSTNs and ISDNs operate in a circuit-switched mode. This means that, prior to a call taking place, a connection through the network between the two subscribers must be set up and, on completion of the call, the connection closed down. The setting up and closure of connections is carried out by the transfer of a defined set of control messages – known as **signaling messages** – between the calling and called subscriber and their LE/EO and also between the various exchanges that are involved.

The signaling messages used over the subscriber line are different from those used within the core transmission and switching (trunk) network. In the case of an analog subscriber line, the signaling messages are analog signals such as single-frequency audio tones. With a digital line, the signaling messages are also digital and, because an ISDN can support two (or more) calls simultaneously, the signaling messages are allocated a dedicated portion of the bandwidth/bit rate of the line. Within the trunk network, however, the signaling messages relating to both types of network are digital and use a common format and signaling protocol.

Thus, as we have stated, public circuit-switched networks comprise three interrelated systems: transmission systems, switching systems, and signaling systems. Hence in the remainder of this chapter we shall describe the underlying principles associated with each of these systems. In addition, since modems play an important role in the provision of multimedia communication services with public circuit-switched networks, we shall also discuss the principle of operation of the different types of low bit rate modem. We shall defer discussion of high bit rate modems until Chapter 11 where we discuss the different types of entertainment networks.

7.2 Transmission systems

As we explained in the last section, the transmission system comprises two parts: that used in the local access network and that used in the trunk network. The type of transmission used in the local access network can be either analog (PSTN) or digital (ISDN). Also, although all-digital transmission (and switching) is used in the trunk network, for historical reasons, there are two different types of digital transmission system used: one called the **plesiochronous digital hierarchy** (**PDH**) and the other the **synchronous digital hierarchy** (**SDH**), the latter also known as the **synchronous optical network** or **SONET**. We shall discuss the operation of each type of system separately.

7.2.1 Analog subscriber lines

As we mentioned in the introduction to the chapter, each subscriber line comprises a single twisted-pair wire that connects the subscriber network termination to a **line termination unit** (**LTU**) in the LE/EO. In practice, each subscriber line is made up of multiple cable sections with a combined length of up to about 5 miles (8 km) depending on the telecommunications operating company (teleco). In order to enable new customers to be added and faults on individual lines to be located, each subscriber line within a localized area is terminated at a **junction box**. Normally, this is located within a few hundred yards/meters of the customer premises within that area and, inside the box, the individual wire pair from each subscriber premises is joined to a second pair within a larger cable containing multiple pairs.

In addition, for cable lengths greater than a mile (1.5 km), the individual pairs within these cables are joined to a third set of pairs within an even larger cable. This is done in a road-side cabinet known as a **cross-connect**. Typically, the cable from a junction box to a cross-connect contains in the order of 50 pairs and that from a cross-connect to the LE/EO several hundred pairs.

Telephone basics

The various components that are present in a telephone are shown in Figure 7.2(a).

A d.c. voltage of 48 V is permanently applied to the subscriber line by the LTU and, when the handset is lifted, contacts in the *cradle switch unit* close which causes a current to flow from the LTU to the handset. This flow of current is detected by the LTU and, as a result, it applies a pair of low-frequency tones – collectively known as *dial-tone* – to the line. On hearing this,

(a)

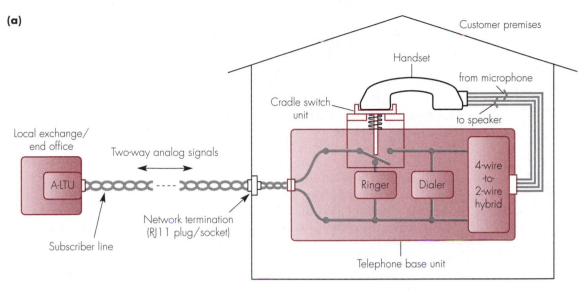

A-LTU = analog (subscriber) line termination unit

(b)

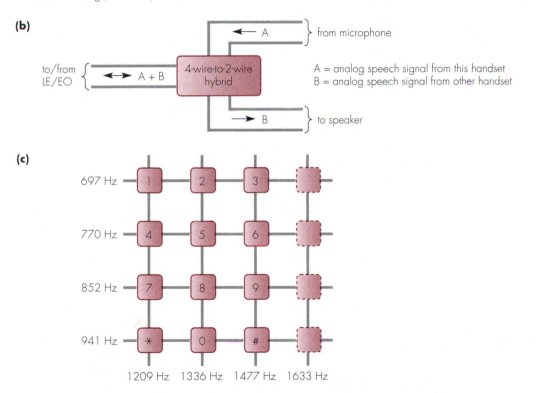

Figure 7.2 Analog subscriber line principles: (a) telephone components; (b) 4-wire-to-2-wire hybrid; (c) dual-tone multifrequency keypad.

the subscriber proceeds to enter the number of the called party using the telephone keypad which is connected to the *dialer*.

As we show in Figure 7.2(c), when each key on the keypad is pressed, a pair of (single-frequency) tones is applied to the line by the dialer; for example, pressing the digit 5 causes two tones to be applied, one of frequency 770 Hz and the other 1336 Hz. This type of dialing is known as **dual-tone multifrequency (DTMF) keying**. At the exchange end, a bank of filters – each of which detects just one of the tones – is used to determine the string of dialed digits that have been entered by the subscriber. The called number is then passed to the exchange *control processor* which proceeds to initiate the setting up of a connection through the switching network to the called party.

The *ringer circuit* is connected across the subscriber line before the *cradle switch unit* and, to alert the called subscriber of an incoming call, the LTU of the called party applies a series of short bursts of a pair of low frequency (*ringing*) *tones* to the line. The lifting of the handset by the called subscriber causes a current to flow as before and, in response, the LTU removes the ringing tone. Both subscribers are aware of this, and the conversation then starts.

As we indicated earlier, all transmission and switching within the trunk network is performed digitally. Hence as the analog speech signal from the calling subscriber is received, it is immediately sampled and converted into a (PCM) digital signal as we described in Section 2.5.1. Similarly, the received digital signal from the called subscriber is converted back into an analog form for onward transmission over the subscriber line. However, since the subscriber line comprises only a single pair of wires, this means that the same pair of wires must be used to transfer the two analog speech signals associated with the call. Hence in order for each subscriber not to hear their own voice when speaking, a unit known as a 4-wire- to 2-wire-hybrid is present in each telephone, the principle of which is shown in Figure 7.2(b).

Essentially, the output from the microphone in the handset (A) is passed to the subscriber line for onward transmission to the other party but, simultaneously, within the hybrid the same signal is subtracted from the combined signal received from the line (A + B). This means that only the signal received from the other party (B) is fed to the speaker in the handset. In practice, the hybrid is a transformer and, since a transformer will not pass a DC signal, it is the presence of the transformer that dictates the use of an analog signal. In addition, imperfections in the hybrid transformer often result in an attenuated version of the received signal – that is, from the distant subscriber – being coupled into the line from the microphone. Hence this signal is returned to the distant subscriber handset as if it was from the local subscriber but with a delay equal to twice the signal propagation delay time between the two subscribers. This is known as the **echo signal** and, providing it is received within less than 24 ms, it is not discernible to the remote subscriber. Above this value it is necessary to introduce a circuit known as an echo canceler to remove the echo signal.

Finally, the connection is closed down when either subscriber replaces the handset, the loss of current flow to the handset being detected by the related LTU which, in turn, initiates the clearing of the network connection.

Remote concentrator units

The distance between the subscriber premises and the LE/EO is limited by the attenuation that occurs in the subscriber line. Hence in order to provide a connection to subscribers that are beyond the maximum allowable distance, a device known as a **remote concentrator unit** (**RCU**) is used. The general layout of the access network is then as shown in Figure 7.3.

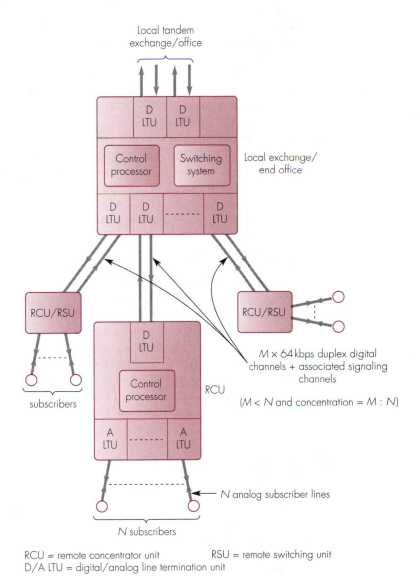

RCU = remote concentrator unit   RSU = remote switching unit
D/A LTU = digital/analog line termination unit

Figure 7.3 Access network structure with remote concentrator/ switching units.

Each subscriber line connected to an RCU is terminated by an LTU which performs a similar set of functions to those carried out by an A-LTU within an LE/EO. However, although the subscriber line used to connect each subscriber to the RCU operates using analog transmission, the circuit that connects the RCU to the LE/EO operates in a digital mode. As we indicated earlier, the two speech signals associated with a call are digitized to produce a corresponding pair of 64 kbps (PCM – pulse code modulation) digital signals. Hence, in theory, the digital circuits that are used to link the RCU to the LE/EO must each operate at a bit rate that supports $N \times 64$ kbps where N is the number of subscriber lines connected to the RCU. Normally, however, the number of calls that take place concurrently, M, is much less than N. Hence in order to reduce the bit rate of the digital circuit, the bit rate is made equal to $M \times 64$ kbps rather than $N \times 64$ kbps. This is the origin of the term **concentration** and is expressed as $N{:}M$, a typical figure being 8:1. Also, because RCUs effectively replace multiple (twister-pair) subscriber lines, they are known as **pair-gain systems**.

In addition to the digitized speech signals associated with each (active) call, the signaling information (dialed digits) associated with a call must also be passed to the LE/EO in a digital form. Normally, therefore, as we shall expand upon in Section 7.2.3, a portion of the bandwidth of the digital line is used to exchange the signaling messages associated with all of the currently active calls. As we show in the figure, this bandwidth is used to produce a channel known as the **signaling channel**.

To perform the various signaling functions associated with each call – off-hook detection, dial-digit collection, ringing, and so on – an RCU has a separate control processor within it that communicates with the control processor within the LE/EO to set up and release connections. Hence by adding some additional processing functions, it is also possible to allow the processor within an RCU to set up calls between any two subscribers that are connected directly to it rather than through the LE/EO. The RCU is then known as a **remote switching unit** (**RSU**) and, as we can deduce from Figure 7.3, the effect of using RCUs and RSUs is that each LE/EO can then operate with all-digital transmission and switching similar in principle to the various tandem exchanges used in the trunk network.

7.2.2 PSTN modems

As we explained in Section 6.1, in order to transmit a digital signal over an analog subscriber line, modulated transmission must be used; that is, the electrical signal that represents the binary bitstream output by the source equipment must first be converted into an analog signal that is compatible with a (telephony) speech signal. As we saw in Section 2.5.1, the range of signal frequencies that a public circuit-switched network passes is from 200 Hz through to 3400 Hz. This means that an analog subscriber line will not pass the low-frequency signals that could occur if, for example, the bitstream to be transmitted is made up of a very long string of binary 1s or 0s. For this reason, it is not possible simply to apply two voltage levels to the telephone line, since zero output will be obtained for both levels if the binary stream is all 1s or all 0s. Instead, we must convert the binary data into a form compatible with a speech signal at the sending end of the line and reconvert this signal back into its binary form at the receiver. The circuit that performs the first operation is known as a **modulator**, and the circuit performing the reverse function a **demodulator**. Since the two communicating devices normally both send and receive data, the combined device is known as a **modem**.

Using modems, data can be transmitted through the network either by setting up a switched path through the network as with a normal telephone call, or by leasing a **dedicated** (or **leased**) **line** from the network operator. Since leased lines bypass the normal switching equipment (exchange) in the network and are set up on a permanent or long-term basis, they are economically justifiable only for applications having a high utilization factor. An added advantage of a leased line is that its operating characteristics can be more accurately quantified than for a short-term switched circuit, making it feasible to operate at higher bit rates. Figure 7.4 shows the two alternative operating modes.

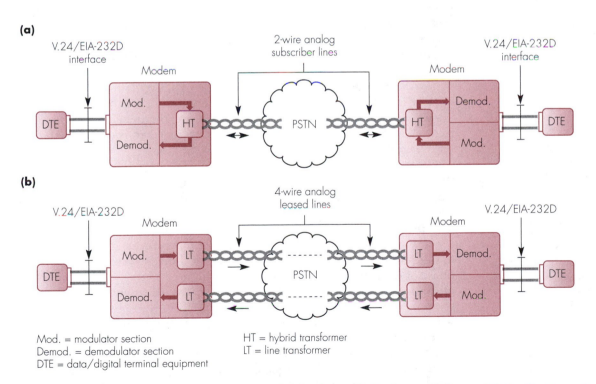

Mod. = modulator section
Demod. = demodulator section
DTE = data/digital terminal equipment

HT = hybrid transformer
LT = line transformer

Figure 7.4 Modem operating alternatives: (a) 2-wire switched connections; (b) 4-wire leased circuits.

As we can see, in the case of a switched connection, the two analog signals that carry the transmitted and received bitstreams must share the use of the single twisted-pair subscriber line. Hence, as in a telephone, a hybrid transformer is used. In the case of a leased circuit, however, normally a 4-wire – two pairs – line is used. We shall explain the principle of operation of the modem and the terminal interface to the modem separately.

Modem principles

Three basic types of modulation are used: amplitude, frequency, and phase. Since binary data is to be transmitted, in the simplest modems just two signal levels are used. The signal then switches (shifts) between these two levels as the binary signal changes (keys) between a binary 1 and 0. The three basic modulation types are known, therefore, as **amplitude shift keying (ASK)**, **frequency shift keying** (**FSK**) and **phase shift keying** (**PSK**) respectively. The essential components that make up the modulator and demodulator sections of a modem are shown in Figure 7.5(a) and example waveforms relating to the three modulation types in Figure 7.5(b).

With ASK, the amplitude of a single-frequency audio tone is keyed between two levels at a rate determined by the bit rate of the transmitted binary signal. The single-frequency audio tone is known as the **carrier signal** (since it effectively carries the binary signal as it passes through the network) and its frequency is chosen to be within the band of frequencies that are allowed over the access circuit. The amount of bandwidth required to transmit the binary signal is then determined by its bit rate: the higher the bit rate, the larger the required bandwidth.

With FSK, the amplitude of the carrier signal remains fixed and its frequency is keyed between two different frequency levels by the transmitted binary signal. The difference between these two frequencies is known as the frequency shift and the amount of bandwidth required is determined by the bit rate and the frequency shift.

With PSK, the amplitude and frequency of the carrier remains fixed and transitions in the binary signal being transmitted cause the phase of the carrier to change. As we can see in the figure, two types of PSK are used. The first uses two fixed carrier signals with a 180° phase difference between them to represent a binary 0 and 1. Since one signal is simply the inverse of the other, it is known as **phase-coherent PSK**. The disadvantage of this scheme is that a reference carrier signal is required at the receiver against which the phase of the received signal is compared. In practice, this requires more complex demodulation circuitry than the alternative **differential PSK**. With this scheme, phase shifts occur at each bit transition irrespective of whether a string of binary 1 or 0 signals is being transmitted; a phase shift of 90° relative to the current signal indicates a binary 0 is the next bit while a phase shift of 270° indicates a binary 1. As a result, the demodulation circuitry need determine only the magnitude of each phase shift rather than its absolute value. In practice, PSK is the most efficient modulation scheme in terms of the amount of bandwidth it requires and hence is the one used in modems that provide a bit rate in excess of 4.8 kbps.

(a)

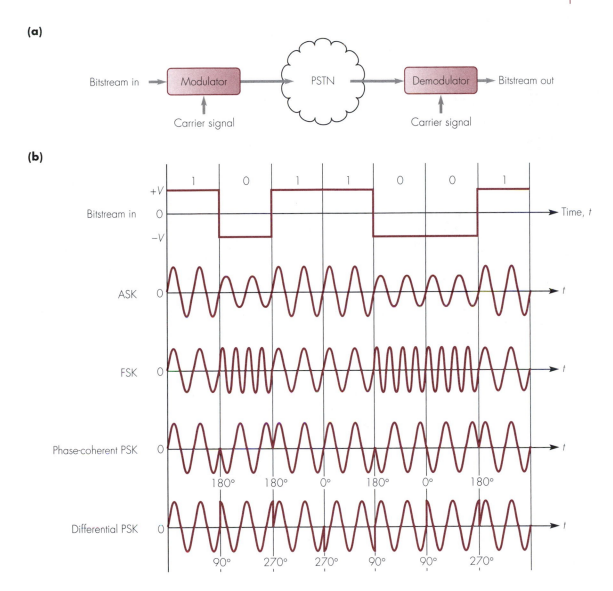

Figure 7.5 Modem principles: (a) modulator/demodulator schematic; (b) waveforms of basic modulation methods.

Multilevel modulation

As we can deduce from Figure 7.5, with the basic modulation methods just two different signal changes are used – in either amplitude, frequency, or phase – to represent the binary bitstream being transmitted. This means, therefore, that the maximum rate of change of the transmitted signal – that is, the baud rate – is equal to the bit rate of the input bitstream. Since the bandwidth of the access circuit is fixed, however, in order to obtain higher bit rates multiple signal levels are used. Hence instead of the transmitted signal changing at the same rate as the input bitstream, it changes at a lower rate.

For example, with PSK, if four phase changes are used – 0°, 90°, 180°, 270° – this enables each phase change to represent a pair of bits from the input bitstream, as we show in Figure 7.6(a). Because this scheme uses four phases, it is known as **quadrature PSK (QPSK)** or 4-PSK. Higher bit rates are achieved using larger numbers of phase changes. In practice, however, there is a limit to how many different phases can be used, as the reducing phase differences make it progressively more prone to the noise and phase impairments introduced during transmission. In order to minimize the number of phase changes required, two separate carriers are used, each of which is separately modulated.

As we show in Figure 7.6(b), the two carriers have the same frequency but there is a 90° phase difference between them. They are known, therefore, as the **in-phase carrier (I)** and the **quadrature carrier (Q)**. The two modulated carriers are transmitted concurrently and, as we show in the figure, with just a single phase change per carrier – 0° and 180° – there are four combinations of the two modulated signals which means that each combination can represent 2 bits from the input bitstream. This type of modulation is known as **quadrature amplitude modulation (QAM)** and, because there are four combinations, **4-QAM**.

In order to increase the bit rate further, a combination of ASK and PSK is used. This means that as well as the I and Q carriers changing in phase, their amplitude also changes. The complete phase diagram showing all the possible combinations of amplitude and phase is known as the **constellation diagram** and an example is shown in Figure 7.6(c). As we can see, this uses 16 combinations of two amplitude and two phase changes per carrier and is known therefore as **16-QAM**.

As we can see from the above, there are many combinations of the different modulation schemes. Hence for each application, it is essential that both modems utilize the same bit rate and modulation method. For this reason the ITU-T has defined a set of international standards for modems. These are known as the **V-series** set of standards and a selection of these is given in Figure 7.7. In this way, a person who buys a modem that adheres to, say, the V.29 standard, can readily use it to communicate with a V.29-compatible modem from a possibly different manufacturer.

As we can see, some of the standards relate to modems to be used with leased circuits and others with switched circuits/connections. Also most of the modems can operate at more than one rate. Hence once a connection has been set up and prior to transmitting any user information, the two communicating modems go through a **training phase** to determine the highest of the available bit rates that can be supported by the connection. This is done by one modem sending a standard bitstream and the other measuring the

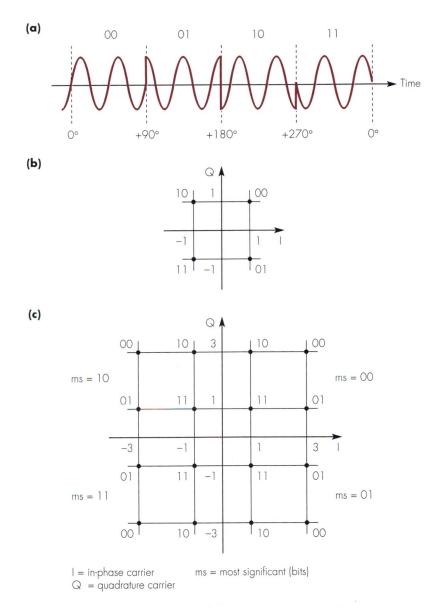

Figure 7.6 Multilevel modulation: (a) 4-PSK using a single carrier; (b) 4-QAM and (c) 16-QAM using two carriers, one at 90° (Q) out of phase with the other (I).

BER of the received stream. Normally, the lowest available bit rate is selected first and the rate is then increased progressively until the measured BER reaches a defined threshold. Typically this is in the region of 10^{-5} and 10^{-6} and, once this has been reached, both modems agree to operate at this rate.

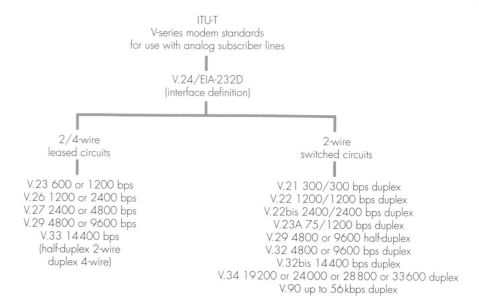

Figure 7.7 A selection of ITU-T V-series modem standards.

The choice of operating bit rate – and hence baud rate – is transparent to the user and the only observable effect of a lower bit rate is a slower response time in an interactive application, for example, or an inferior speech/video quality in an interpersonal application. Also, it should be remembered that the analog signal output by the modulator is converted into an equivalent digital signal for transmission and switching within the trunk network in just the same way that an analog speech signal is converted. Indeed, whether the source is speech or data is transparent to the network.

V.24/EIA-232D interface standard

As we showed earlier in Figure 7.4, a standard interface is used for connecting the serial part of a data terminal equipment (DTE) – a computer for example – to a PSTN modem. This is defined in ITU-T Recommendation **V.24** which is the same as the EIA standard **EIA-232D**, the latter being the latest version of the earlier RS-232A, B, and C standards. In the standards documents the modem is referred to as the **data circuit-terminating equipment** (**DCE**) and a diagram indicating the position of the interface in relation to two communicating DTEs/DCEs is shown in Figure 7.8(a).

The connector used between a DTE and a modem is a 25-pin connector of the type shown in Figure 7.8(b). It is defined in standard ISO 2110 and is known as a **DB25 connector**. Also shown is the total set of signals associated with the interface together with their names and pin assignments. In most cases, however, only a subset of the signals are required.

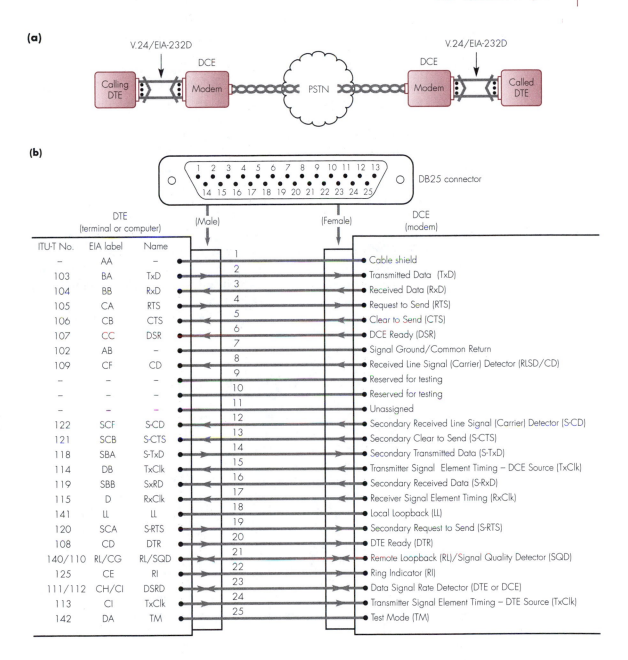

Figure 7.8 V.24/EIA-232D interface standards: (a) interface function; (b) connector, pin, and signal definitions.

The transmit data (TxD) and receive data (RxD) lines are used by the DTE to transmit and receive data respectively. The other lines collectively perform the timing and control functions associated with the setting-up and clearing of a switched connection through the PSTN and with performing selected test operations. The second (secondary) set of lines allows two data transfers to take place simultaneously over the one interface.

The timing control signals are concerned with the transmission (TxClk) and reception (RxClk) of the data on the corresponding data line. As we explained in Sections 6.4.1 and 6.5.1, data is transmitted using either an asynchronous or a synchronous transmission mode. In the asynchronous mode, the transmit and receive clocks are both generated by an independent clock source and fed directly to the corresponding pins of the DTE. In this mode, only the transmit and receive data lines are connected to the modem. In the synchronous mode, however, data is transmitted and received in synchronism with the corresponding clock signal and these are normally generated by the modem. The latter is then known as a **synchronous modem** and, when the signaling (baud) rate is less than the data bit rate – that is, multiple signal levels are being used – the transmit and receive clocks generated by the modem operate at the appropriate fraction of the line signaling rate.

We can best see the function and sequence of the various call-control lines by considering the setting-up and clearing of a call. Figure 7.9 shows how a connection (call) is first set up, some data is exchanged between the two DTEs in a half-duplex (two-way alternate) mode and the call is then cleared. We assume that the calling DTE is a user at a personal computer and its modem has automatic dialing facilities. Typically the called DTE is a server computer and its modem has automatic answering facilities. Such facilities are defined in **Recommendation V.25**. When a DTE is ready to make or receive data transfer requests, it sets the data terminal ready (DTR) line on and the local modem responds by setting the DCE ready (DSR) line on.

A connection is established by the calling DTE sending the telephone number of the modem (line) associated with the called DTE. On receipt of the ringing tone from its local switching office/telephone exchange, the called modem sets the ring indicator (RI) line to on and the called DTE responds by setting the request-to-send (RTS) line on. In response, the called modem sends a carrier signal – the data tone for a binary 1 – to the calling modem to indicate that the call has been accepted by the called DTE and, after a short delay to allow the calling modem to prepare to receive data, the called modem sets the clear-to-send (CTS) line on to inform the called DTE that it can start sending data. On detecting the carrier signal, the calling modem sets the carrier detect (CD) line on. The connection is now established and the data transfer phase can begin.

Typically, the called DTE (computer) starts by sending a short invitation-to-send message over the setup connection. When this has been sent, it prepares to receive the response from the calling DTE by setting the RTS line

(a)

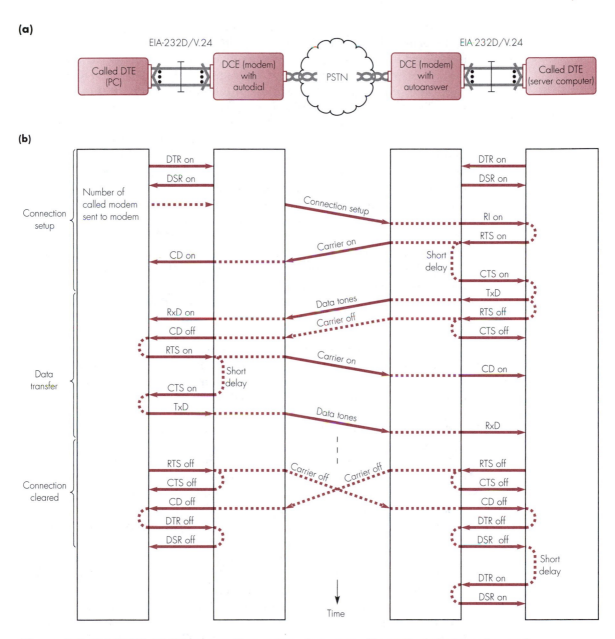

(b)

Figure 7.9 V.24/EIA-232D connection setup, two-way alternate data transfer and connection clearing sequences.

off and, on detecting this, the called modem stops sending the carrier signal and sets the CTS line off. At the calling side, the removal of the carrier signal is detected by the calling modem and, in response, it sets the CD line off. In order to send its response message, the calling DTE (PC) sets the RTS line on and, on receipt of the CTS signal from the modem, starts to send the message. This procedure then repeats as messages are exchanged between the two DTEs. Finally, after the complete transaction has taken place, the call is cleared. This is accomplished by both DTEs setting their RTS lines off which, in turn, causes the two modems to switch their carriers off. This is detected by both modems and they set their CD lines off. Both DTEs then set their DTR lines off and their modems respond by setting the DSR lines off thereby clearing the call. Typically, the called DTE (the server computer) then prepares to receive a new call by resetting its DTR line on after a short delay.

We have described the use of a half-duplex switched connection to illustrate the meaning and use of some of the control lines available with the standard. In practice, however, the time taken to change from the receive to the transmit mode in the half-duplex mode – known as the **turnaround time** – is not insignificant. It is preferable to operate in the duplex mode whenever possible, even when half-duplex working is required. In the duplex mode, both RTS lines are permanently left on and both modems maintain the CTS line on and a carrier signal to the remote modem.

When two DTEs are communicating and a fault develops, it is often difficult to ascertain the cause of the fault – the local modem, the remote modem, the communications line, or the remote DTE. To help identify the cause of faults, the interface contains three control lines: the local and remote loopback (LL and RL) and the test mode (TM). Their function is shown in Figure 7.10(a): in (i) a local loopback test is used and in (ii) a remote loopback.

The DTE (modem) always sets its DSR line on when it is ready to transmit or receive data. To perform a test on its local modem, the DTE sets the LL line on and, in response, the modem internally connects the output from the modulator circuit back to the input of the demodulator circuit. It then sets the TM line on and, when the DTE detects this, it transmits a known test (data) pattern on its TxD line and simultaneously reads the data from its RxD line. If the received data is the same as the test data, then the DTE assumes the local modem is working satisfactorily. If it is not – or no signal is present at all – then the local modem is assumed faulty.

If the local modem is deemed to be working correctly, then the DTE proceeds to test the remote modem by this time setting the RL control line on. On detecting the RL line going on, the local modem sends a predefined command to the remote modem which, in turn, performs a remote loopback as shown. The remote modem then sets its TM line on to inform the remote DTE it is involved in a test – and hence cannot transmit data – and returns an acknowledgment command back to the modem originating the test. The modem, on receipt of this, sets its TM line on and, on detecting this, the local DTE starts to transmit the test data pattern. Again, if this data is received

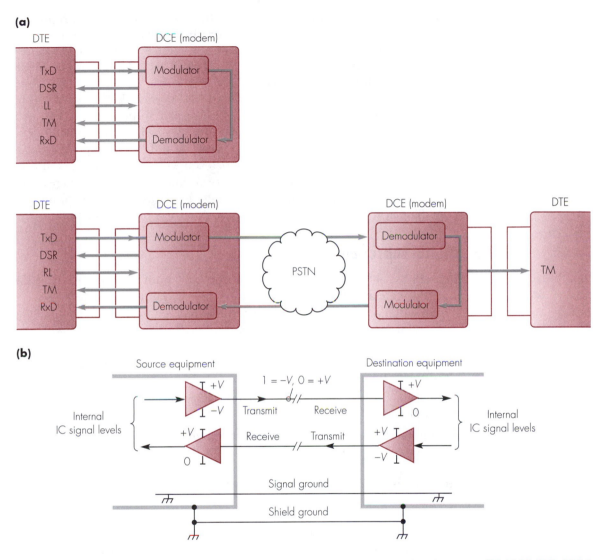

Figure 7.10 V.24/EIA-232D interface: (a) local and remote loopback tests; (b) V.28/RS.232A signal levels.

correctly, then both modems are assumed to be working correctly and the fault lies with the remote DTE. Alternatively, if the received data is badly corrupted then the remote modem is assumed to be faulty or, if no signal is received at all, then the PSTN line is assumed faulty.

The V.24/EIA-232D interface uses either a flat-ribbon or a multiple-wire cable which includes a single ground reference wire. However, because of the short distances – less than a few centimeters – between neighboring integrated circuits within a DTE computer, the signal levels used to represent binary data are very low power and, as a result, cannot be used directly for transferring signals outside of the computer. Hence, as we show in Figure 7.10(b), associated with each signal line of the V.24/EI-232D interface is a matching **line driver** and **line receiver** circuit.

The electrical signal levels are defined in standards **V.28/RS.232A**. The signals used on the lines are symmetric with respect to the ground reference signal and are at least $3V$: $+3V$ for a binary 0 and $-3V$ for a binary 1. In practice, the actual voltage levels used are determined by the supply voltages applied to the interface circuits, $\pm12V$ or even $\pm15V$ not being uncommon. The transmit line driver circuits convert the low-level signal voltages used within the equipment to the higher voltage levels used on the connecting lines. Similarly, the line receiver circuits perform the reverse function.

7.2.3 Digital subscriber lines

In an ISDN, all the signals associated with a call – both the two speech signals and the associated signaling messages – are transmitted over the subscriber line in a digital form. Also, as we saw in Figure 1.4 and in the accompanying text, an ISDN has a number of different subscriber line interfaces:

- a basic rate interface (BRI) that provides two independent 64 kbps duplex channels;
- a primary rate interface (PRI) that provides either 23 or 30 64 kbps duplex channels;
- a primary rate interface that provides a single duplex channel of $p \times 64$ kbps where p can be 1–23 or 1–30.

We shall discuss each interface separately.

Basic rate interface

As we explained in Section 1.3.4, the basic rate interface – and the associated **network termination unit** (**NTU**) – allows for two calls of 64 kbps duplex to be in progress concurrently. Hence, since the two calls can be set up independently – that is, the second call can be set up while the first is in progress – an additional duplex channel of 16 kbps is used for the exchange of the signaling messages relating to the two calls. This arrangement is known as **out-of-band signaling**. Each 64 kbps user channel is known as a **bearer** or **B-channel** and the 16 kbps signaling channel the **D-channel**. Hence the combined bit rate associated with this interface is 2B + D or 144 kbps duplex. Two examples of an NTU associated with an ISDN BRI are shown in Figure 7.11.

As we show in Figure 7.11(a), in the first example the NTU has two digital ports and two analog ports associated with it. The two analog ports are provided to enable the subscriber to utilize existing analog equipment such

(a)

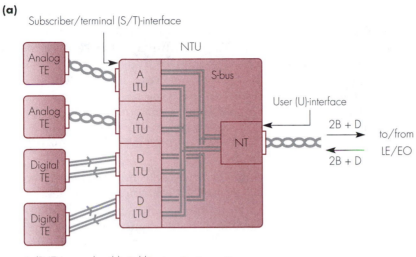

Subscriber/terminal (S/T)-interface

NTU

A/D LTU = analog/digital line termination unit

(b)

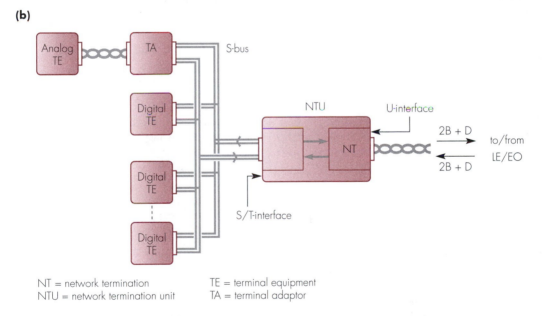

NT = network termination
NTU = network termination unit

TE = terminal equipment
TA = terminal adaptor

Figure 7.11 ISDN network termination alternatives: (a) 4-port NTU; (b) S-bus NTU.

as an analog phone, a fax machine, or a PC with modems. The two digital ports are provided to enable newer digital equipment with an ISDN interface to be used. In the case of the two analog ports, the conversion of the analog signals into and from their digital form is performed within the NTU. This means that the subscriber can use any mix of the four ports with any two active at one time.

As we show in Figure 7.11(b), a second mode of working is also used which allows from one up to eight devices to (time) share the use of the two B-channels. This mode of working is defined in **ITU-T Recommendation I.430**. In this mode the NTU has a single port associated with it to which is connected a duplex bus known as the subscriber or **S-bus**. The various terminal equipments (TEs) then gain access to the bus – and hence B-channels – using a defined interface and associated protocol. In the case of an existing analog TE, a device known as a **terminal adaptor** (**TA**) must be used to convert the analog signals associated with the TE into and from the digital signals used over the S-bus.

The S-bus must support the duplex flow of two (64 kbps) B-channels and the 16 kbps D-channel together with the contention resolution logic for time-sharing the use of the D-channel. To achieve this, the bitstream in each direction is divided into a stream of 48-bit frames each of which contains 16 bits for each of the two B-channels and 4 bits for the shared D-channel multiplexed in the order 8B1, 1D, 8B2, 1D, 8B1, 1D, 8B2, 1D. The remaining 12 bits are then used for various functions including:

- the start-of-frame synchronization pattern,
- contention resolution of the shared D-channel,
- the activation and deactivation of the interface of each TE,
- DC balancing.

The duration of each 48-bit frame is 250 microseconds which yields a bit rate of 192 kbps in each direction. As we show in Figure 7.12, an 8-pin connector is used to connect each user TE to the NTU. This is defined in the **ISO 8877** standard and is known as a **RJ45**. The relatively high bit rate and physical separations associated with the S-bus mean that **differential line driver and receiver circuits** must be used. As we show in the figure, this requires a separate pair of wires for each of the transmit and receive signals. This type of signal is defined in standards **V.11/RS-422A**.

A differential transmitter produces twin signals of equal and opposite polarity for every binary 1 or 0 signal to be transmitted. As the differential receiver is sensitive only to the difference between the two signals on its two inputs, noise picked up by both wires will not affect receiver operation. Differential receivers, therefore, are said to have good **common-mode rejection** properties. A derivative of the RS-422A, the **RS-423A/V.10**, can be used to accept single-ended (**unbalanced**) voltages output by an EIA-232D interface with a differential receiver.

An important parameter of any transmission line is its **characteristic impedance** (Z_0) because a receiver absorbs all of the received signal power only if the line is terminated by a resistor equal to Z_0. If this is not the case, **signal reflections** occur which further distort the received signal. Normally, therefore, lines are terminated by a resistor equal to Z_0, with values from 50 to 200 ohms being common.

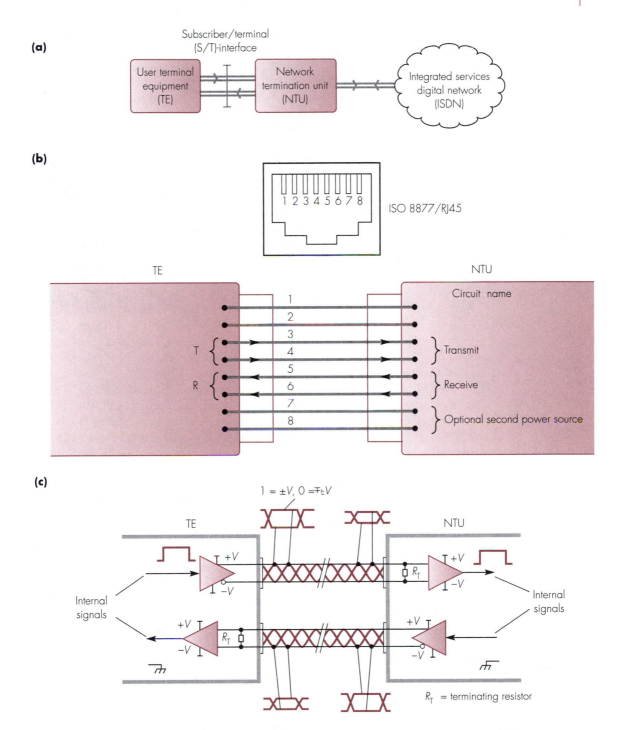

Figure 7.12 ISDN subscriber/terminal (S/T)-interface: (a) interface location; (b) socket, pin, and signal definitions; (c) signal levels.

The line code used over the S-bus is known as **alternate space inversion** (**ASI**) the principle of which is shown in Figure 7.13(a). As we can see, this is a 3-level code: +V, 0, and −V. The 0 level is used to indicate the transmission of a binary 1 and either +V or −V a binary 0: for every 0 bit transmitted, the line signal changes polarity from the last 0-bit level; that is, either from +V to −V or vice versa. This type of line signal is called **pseudoternary**.

At the start of each 48-bit frame is the 2-bit frame synchronization pattern of +V, −V. The line signal then changes according to the transmitted bit-stream with the first 0-bit encoded as −V. As we can deduce from the figure, however, the line signal will not be balanced if, overall, the number of 0 bits is odd. Hence, since each TE is connected to the bus by means of a transformer, the polarity of the various DC balancing bits present in each frame is chosen so that the mean DC level of the line is always zero.

Although the bus can have up to 4–8 TEs connected to it, only two can be active at any point in time. A scheme is required, therefore, to enable all the TEs to contend for access to the two B-channels in a controlled way. However, since the two calls must be set up by means of the D-channel (which is shared by all the TEs) the contention occurs for use of the D-channel. To resolve any possible contention, the NTU reflects the four D-bits present in the (48-bit) frame it is currently receiving (from the one or more TEs) back in the frame it is currently transmitting out in the reverse direction. The four reflected bits are known as the **echo** or **E-bits**.

When no TE is using the D-channel, the four D-bits are set to the 0 signal level. Hence prior to sending a request message to set up a call, the TE first reads the four E-bits from the frame currently being transmitted out by the NTU and only if they are all at the 0 level does it proceed to start to send the request message in the four D-channel bits in the next frame. In addition, to allow for the possibility of one or more other TEs starting to send a request message at the same time, each TE that is trying to send a message monitors the (reflected) E-bits in the frame currently being received to check that these are the same as the D-bits that it has just transmitted. If they are the same, then it continues to send the remaining bits in the message; if they are different, then it stops transmitting and tries again later. The principle of the scheme is shown in Figure 7.13(b) and, as we can see, because of the line code used, the winner of a contention will always be the TE whose message contains a 0 bit when the other(s) contains a 1 bit. Also, in the event of both B-channels being in use when a (successful) new request is made, then a busy response message will be returned to the requesting TE. If the call can be accepted, however, then an acceptance message will be returned and the signaling procedure continues.

The interface between the NTU and the subscriber line is known as the **U-interface** and this is defined in **ITU-T Recommendation G.961**. As we showed earlier in Figure 7.11, as with an analog subscriber line, a single pair of wires is used to connect the subscriber NTU to the LE/EO. This means, therefore, that both the transmitted and received digital bitstream of 144 kbps (2B + D)

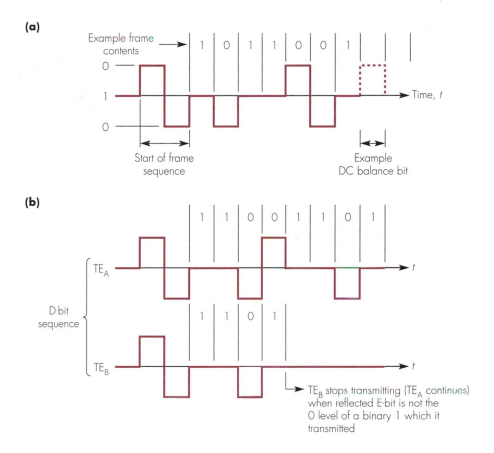

Figure 7.13 ISDN basic rate access S-bus line code principles: (a) alternate space inversion (ASI) line code; (b) example of contention resolution.

must be transmitted over the same pair of wires simultaneously. Hence in order for the receiver part of the NTU to receive only the incoming digital bit-stream, an electronic version of the hybrid transformer used with an analog line is incorporated into the NTU, as we show in Figure 7.14(a).

As we can see, in addition to the hybrid, the network termination includes a circuit known as an **adaptive echo canceler**. In practice, the hybrids present at each end of a subscriber line – there is also one in the line termination unit at the LE/EO – are not perfect and, as a result, an attenuated version of the transmitted signal (A) is echoed back from the remote hybrid and hence is passed to the receiver part of the NTU together with the wanted received signal (B). Essentially, the adaptive echo canceler circuit estimates the magnitude of the attenuated version of its own transmitted signal – that is, the echo signal – and subtracts this from the combined signal output by the hybrid.

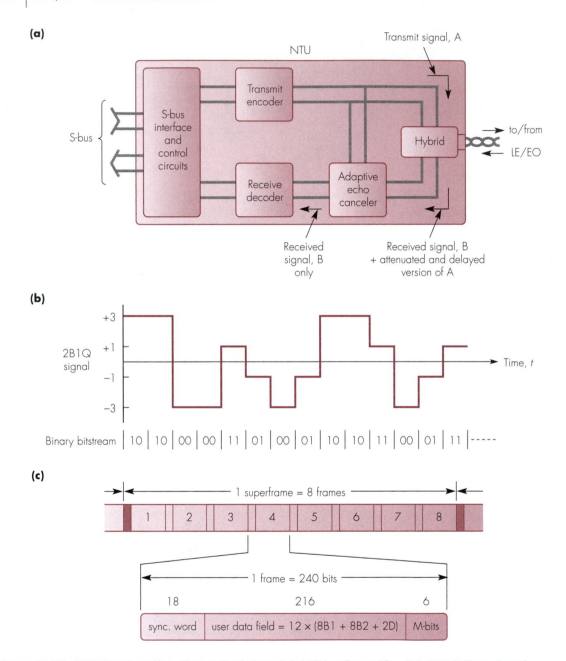

Figure 7.14 ISDN subscriber line principles: (a) NTU schematic; (b) 2B1Q line signal example; (c) frame and superframe format.

In order for the distance from the LE/EO to the subscriber NTU to be as large as possible, the line code used over the subscriber line is a 4-level code known as **two binary, one quaternary** (**2B1Q**), the principles of which are shown in Figure 7.14(b). As we can deduce from the example bitstream shown in the figure, with this code the maximum rate of change of the line signal – the baud rate – is one half of the bit rate. As a result, the bandwidth required for this code is one half that required for a 2-level bipolar code.

The total 2B + D bitstream is divided into a sequence of frames of 240 bits the format of which is shown in Figure 7.14(c). As we can see, each frame consists of:

- an initial 18-bit *synchronization word* comprising the quaternary symbol sequence of +3 +3 −3 −3 +3 +3 −3 −3 … to enable the receiver to determine the start of each frame;

- the *user data* field comprising a set of 12 groups of 18 bits, 8 bits for each of the two B-channels and 2 bits for the D-channel (multiplexed in the order 8B1, 8B2, 2D);

- a 6-bit field that relates to a separate M-channel that is used for maintenance messages and for other purposes.

A further structure known as a **superframe** which comprises eight frames is then defined by inverting the symbols in the synchronization word of the first frame. The resulting 48 M-bits are then used to carry a number of fields including a 12-bit CRC that is used to monitor the quality of the line.

Primary rate interface

In the case of a **primary rate interface** (**PRI**), only a single TE can be connected to the NTU. As we explained in the introduction, however, the TE can be a PBX, for example, which, in turn, supports multiple terminals each operating at 64 kbps or a reduced number of terminals operating at a higher bit rate. To provide this flexibility, the transmitted bitstream contains a single

---

Example 7.1

Deduce the bit rate and baud rate of the subscriber line of an ISDN basic rate access circuit assuming the 2B1Q line code and the frame format shown in Figure 7.14(c).

Answer:

Each 240-bit frame comprises $12 \times 8 = 96$ bits per B-channel. Hence, since this is equivalent to a bit rate of 64kbps, the total bit rate is $64 \times 240/96 = 160$ kbps.

Since there are 2 bits per signal element, the signaling rate = 80 kbauds.

D-channel which is used by the TE to set up the required call(s). The number of 64 kbps channels present in the bitstream is either 23 or 30 depending on the type of interface being used. These correspond to the 1.544 Mbps interface and 2.048 Mbps interface respectively. Since each operates in a different way, we shall discuss them separately.

1.544 Mbps interface The line code used with this interface is known as **alternate mark inversion** (**AMI**) with **bipolar and eight zeros substitution** (**B8ZS**). The principle of both coding schemes is shown in Figure 7.15(a).

As we can see, AMI is a 3-level code: $+V$, 0, and $-V$. The 0 level is used to indicate the transmission of a binary 0 and either $+V$ or $-V$ a binary 1: for every 1 bit transmitted, the line signal changes polarity from the last 1 bit level; that is, either from $+V$ to $-V$ or vice versa. Normally, as we explained in Section 6.5.1, a DPLL is used to obtain clock/bit synchronization. The disadvantage of AMI on its own, therefore, is that a long string of binary 0s will have no associated signal transitions. Consequently, the DPLL may lose bit synchronization whenever a string of 0s is present.

To overcome this limitation, the additional B8ZS coding scheme is used. As we can see, when B8ZS is used with AMI, the line code is the same as that with AMI on its own except that when a string of eight 0 bits is detected in the string these are encoded as 000VB0VB prior to transmission, where V is a violation (same polarity) transition and B a normal (opposite polarity) transition. With B8ZS present, therefore, the maximum string of 0 bits that can be present is seven, which is acceptable for the DPLL. We note also that both AMI and the combined scheme produce differential signals which allows longer cable lengths to be used with transformers at each end.

The transmitted bitstream is divided into a sequence of 193-bit frames the format of which is shown in Figure 7.15(b). As we can see, each frame comprises a single **framing** or **F-bit** followed by 24 8-bit time slots. The duration of each frame is 125 microseconds and hence each of the 8-bit time slots forms a 64 kbps channel. Also, 193 bits every 125 microseconds produces a bit rate of 1.544 Mbps. Normally, one of the time slots – and hence 64 kbps channels – is used as a signaling (D) channel and the messages carried over this relate to the setting up and closing down of the calls carried over the remaining 23(B) channels. The 23 time slots are used either singularly or in groups to provide the required bit rate.

In order for the receiver to detect the start of each frame using a single bit, a group of 24 frames – known as a **multiframe** – is defined. The F-bits from frames 4, 8, 12, 16, 20, and 24 are set to the bit sequence 0, 0, 1, 0, 1, 1 respectively and this is then known as the **frame alignment signal** (**FAS**). Six of the remaining 18 F-bits are then used for a 6-bit CRC which is used to monitor the quality of the line.

(a)

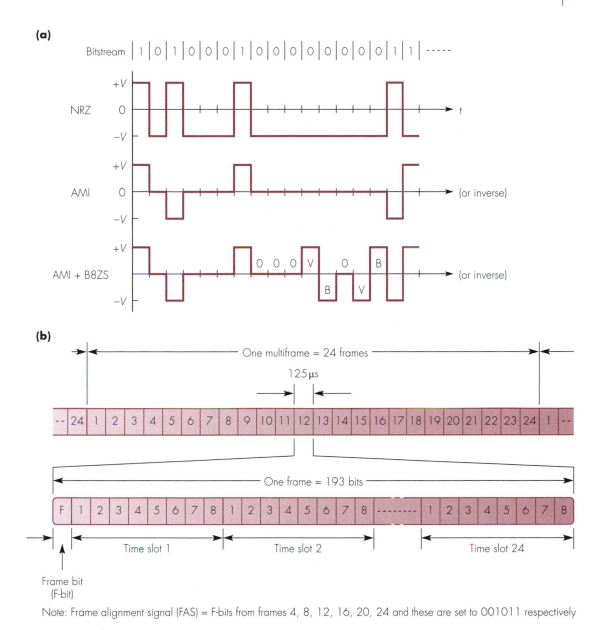

Figure 7.15 ISDN 1.544 Mbps primary rate interface principles: (a) line code; (b) frame and multiframe structure.

2.048 Mbps interface The principles of the line code and the framing structure used with the 2.048 Mbps interface are shown in parts (a) and (b) of Figure 7.16 respectively. As we can see, the line code is also AMI but the additional coding scheme used to obtain signal transitions when strings of 0 bits are being transmitted is the **high density bipolar 3** (**HDB3**) scheme.

This operates by replacing any string of four 0 bits by three 0 bits followed by a bit encoding violation; that is, a transition which is of the same polarity as the previous transition. Hence, as we can see, the first string of four 0 bits is replaced by 000V. With this basic rule, however, the presence of a long string of 0 bits would lead to a mean DC level being introduced into the signal as each set of four 0 bits is encoded in the same way. To overcome this, when transmitting a bitstream that contains a long string of 0 bits, after the first four 0 bits have been encoded, each successive set is changed to B00V. As we can see, this produces a signal of alternating polarity which removes the DC level that would have been present so allowing transformers to be used.

As we can see in Figure 7.16(b), the transmitted bitstream is divided into a sequence of 256-bit frames of duration 125 microseconds. Hence each time slot produces a 64 kbps channel and the bit rate of the bitstream is 2.048 Mbps. Time slot 0 is used for frame alignment and other maintenance functions. To achieve frame alignment, the contents of time slot 0 in alternate frames is as shown in the figure. The remaining bits – shown as x in the figure – are then used to carry a 4-bit CRC for line quality monitoring and other functions. Normally, time slot 16 is used as a signaling (D) channel and the remaining 30 time slots (1–15 and 17–31) are used either singly or in groups to provide the required bit rate. Note that the establishment of a superframe – comprising 16 frames – is optional and is done, for example, to obtain an added level of line quality monitoring. To achieve this, an additional frame alignment word is present in time slot 16 of frame 0.

7.2.4 Plesiochronous digital hierarchy

As we saw earlier in Section 7.1, within the trunk network digital transmission (and switching) is used throughout. For historical reasons, there are two types of transmission system used, one based on what is known as the plesiochronous (nearly synchronous) digital hierarchy (PDH) and the other on a synchronous digital hierarchy (SDH). We shall explain the principles of the PDH in this section and those of the SDH in the next section.

As we saw in Figure 7.1, a national circuit-switched network is made up of a hierarchy of digital transmission and switching systems. And as we explained in the previous two sections, in terms of transmission systems, multiplexing starts within the access network where, typically, the 64 kbps channels derived from the 24/32 time slots are multiplexed together. At higher levels in the hierarchy, however, the transmission systems must support progressively larger numbers of channels/simultaneous calls. Hence this

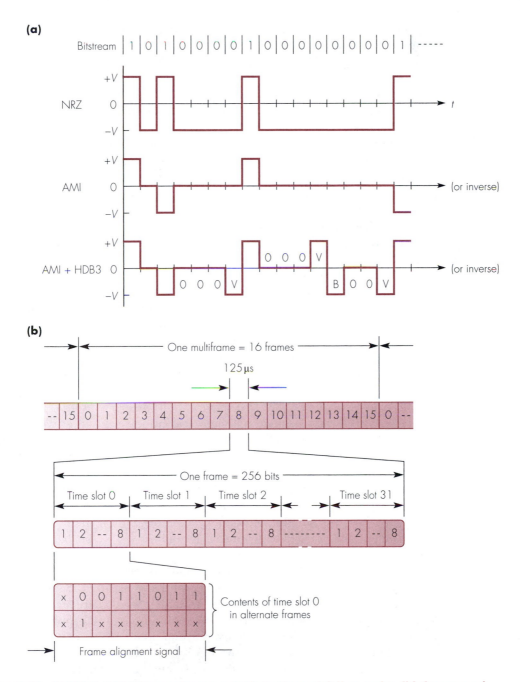

Figure 7.16 ISDN 2.048 Mbps primary rate interface: (a) line code; (b) frame and multiframe structure.

also is carried out in a hierarchical way by progressively multiplexing together multiple lower-level multiplexed streams.

The early multiplexers used in the trunk network operated in an analog mode and the newer digital multiplexers were introduced in an incremental way as these were upgraded. As a result, although all the replacement digital multiplexers operate at nominally the same bit rates, small variations in the timing circuits used in each multiplexer mean that, in practice, there are small differences in their actual bit rates. Hence when multiplexing together two or more lower-order multiplexed streams, steps have to be taken to compensate for the small differences in the timing of each stream. To overcome such differences, an output (multiplexed) bit rate that is slightly higher than the sum of the combined input bit rates is used. Any bits in the output bitstream that are not used are filled with what are called **justification bits**. The resulting set of higher-order multiplexed rates form the plesiochronous digital hierarchy.

The two alternative primary rate access circuits we described in the last section – 1.544 and 2.048 Mbps – form what is called the **primary multiplex group** of a related PDH. In the case of the 1.544 Mbps multiplex this is called a **DS1** or **T1** circuit and in the 2.048 Mbps multiplex an **E1 circuit**. Each is at the lowest level of the related hierarchy and hence all of the higher-level multiplexed groups contain multiples of either 24 or 32 64 kbps channels. The bit rate and derivation of the two sets of multiplexed groups are summarized in parts (a) and (b) of Figure 7.17.

As we explained in the last section, both primary multiplex groups are derived using what is called **byte interleaving** since the multiplexed stream comprises an 8-bit byte from each channel. This is done since a PCM sample of a speech signal is 8 bits and hence it is convenient electronically to multiplex together the complete set of 8-bit samples from each channel. In contrast, when multiplexing a number of primary-rate groups together, since each bitstream is independent of the others and arrives at the multiplexer bit serially, the various higher-level multiplex groups are formed using **bit interleaving**; that is, as each bit from each group arrives – 1 bit per group – they are transmitted out immediately in the output bitstream.

In the same way that additional bits (to the user data bits) are required in each primary multiplex group for framing and maintenance purposes, so additional bits are present in the various higher-level bitstreams for framing – to enable the corresponding receiving multiplexer to interpret the received bitstream on the correct multiplexed group boundaries – and maintenance. Hence the bit rates of all the higher-level multiplexed streams shown in Figure 7.17 contain additional bits for framing and maintenance purposes. For example, an E2 circuit contains the bitstreams from four 2.048 Mbps E1 circuits. Hence, since $4 \times 2.048 = 8.192$ Mbps and the actual bit rate is 8.448 Mbps, 0.256 Mbps are used. The various bit rates shown in the figure are often abbreviated to 1.5, 3, 6, 44, 274, 565 and 2, 8, 34, 140, 565 respectively.

(a)

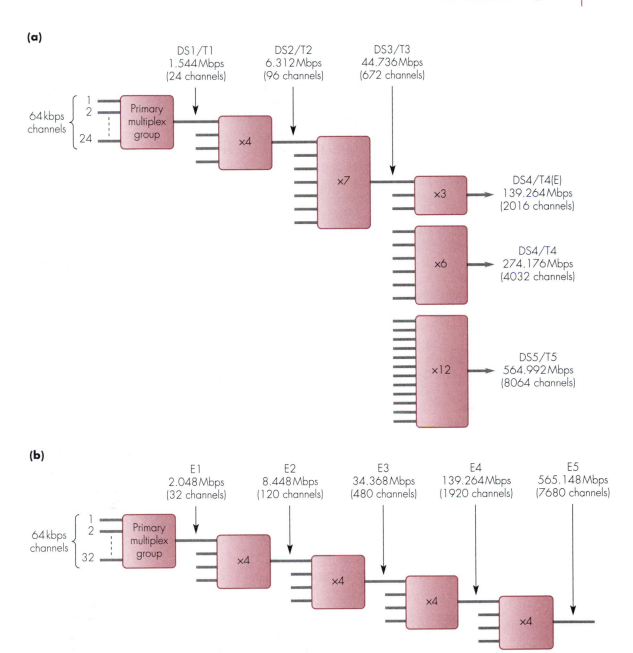

Figure 7.17 Plesiochronous digital hierarchies: (a) 1.544 Mbps derived multiplex hierarchy (b) 2.048 Mbps derived multiplex hierarchy.

Although the use of justification bits at each level in the hierarchy does not in itself pose a problem, their presence means that we cannot identify precisely the start of a lower-level multiplex bitstream within a higher-order stream. The effect of this is best seen by considering a typical operational requirement. Assume three switching centers/exchanges located in different towns/cities are interconnected by 140 Mbps (PDH) trunk circuits as shown in Figure 7.18(a). A business customer, with sites located somewhere between them, makes a request to link the sites together with, say, 2 Mbps leased circuits to create a private network. This is shown in schematic form in Figure 7.18(b). Because it is not possible to identify a lower bit rate channel from the higher-order bitstream, the operator must fully demultiplex the 140 Mbps stream down to the 2 Mbps level before this can be allocated to the customer. This stream must then be remultiplexed back into the 140 Mbps stream for onward transmission. This type of demultiplexing/multiplexing operation is performed by a device called a **drop-and-insert** or **add-drop multiplexer** (**ADM**) and, as we can deduce from Figure 7.18(c), the equipment required to meet this relatively simple request is very complicated.

Although it is not shown in the figure, at each switching office/exchange the allocated 2 Mbps leased circuit must be similarly identified and the switch bypassed in order to form a direct link between the customer sites. Hence when leased circuits are provided for customers in this way, careful records must be kept of the circuits and equipment being used for each customer so that if a fault is reported, appropriate remedial action can be taken. In practice, the provision of only basic performance monitoring within the frame formats of the PDH means that normally, it is the customer who has to alert the provider of the occurrence of faults.

To overcome these limitations, the more flexible synchronous digital hierarchy (SDH) is now used for all new installations. As we shall explain below, in addition to providing a more flexible transmission network which can be readily reconfigured to meet ever changing and expanding requirements, SDH equipment can be configured remotely and has a richer set of maintenance and error reporting functions.

7.2.5 Synchronous digital hierarchy

SDH was developed by Bellcore in the United States under the title of **synchronous optical network** (**SONET**). All SDH equipment is synchronized to a single master clock. The basic transmission rate defined in the SDH is 155.52 Mbps – abbreviated to 155 Mbps – and is known as a **synchronous transport module level 1** signal or simply **STM-1**. Higher rates of **STM-4** (622 Mbps) and **STM-16** (2.4 Gbps) are also defined. In the SONET hierarchy the term **synchronous transport signal** (**STS**) or sometimes **optical signal** (**OC**) is used to define the equivalent of an STM signal. In SONET the lower rate of 51.84 Mbps forms the first level signal – **STS-1/OC-1**. An STM-1 signal is produced by multiplexing three such signals together and hence is equivalent to an STS-3/OC-3 signal.

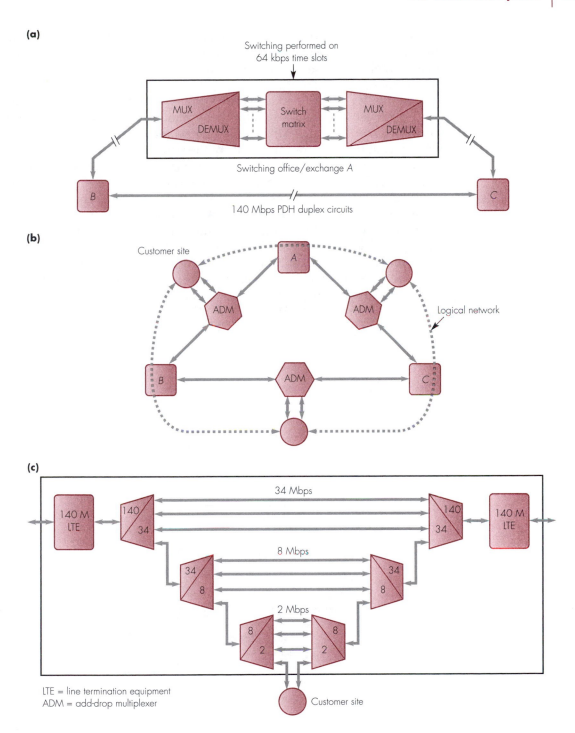

(a)

Switching performed on
64 kbps time slots

MUX
DEMUX

Switch
matrix

MUX
DEMUX

Switching office/exchange A

B

C

140 Mbps PDH duplex circuits

(b)

Customer site

A

ADM

ADM

Logical network

B

ADM

C

(c)

34 Mbps

140 M
LTE

140
34

140
34

140 M
LTE

8 Mbps

34
8

34
8

2 Mbps

8
2

8
2

LTE = line termination equipment
ADM = add-drop multiplexer

Customer site

Figure 7.18 Private network provision with a PDH transmission network: (a) existing network; (b) modified network; (c) ADM principles.

As with the PDH, the STM-1 signal consists of a repetitive set of frames which repeat with a period of 125 microseconds. The information content of each frame can be used to carry multiple 1.5/2/6/34/45 or 140 Mbps PDH streams.

Each of these streams is carried in a different **container** which also contains additional **stuffing bits** to allow for variations in actual rate. To this is added some control information known as the **path overhead** which allows such things as the bit error rate (BER) of the associated container to be monitored on an end-to-end basis by network management. The container and its path overhead collectively form a **virtual container** (**VC**) and an STM-1 frame can contain multiple VCs either of the same type or of different types. Some example multiplexing alternatives are shown in Figure 7.19. Note that the first digit of the lowest level container – and hence VC – is a 1 and the second digit indicates whether it contains a 1.5 Mbps PDH signal (1) or 2 Mbps (2).

The higher-order transmission rates are produced by multiplexing multiple STM-1 (STS-3/OC-3) signals together. For example, an STM-16 (STS-48/OC-48) signal is produced by multiplexing either 16 STM-1 (STS-3/OC-3) signals or 4 STM-4 (STS-12/OC-12) signals. To provide the necessary flexibility for each higher-order signal, in addition to the overheads

SONET	SDH	Bit rate (Mbps)
STS-1/OC-1		51.84
STS-3/OC-3	STM-1	155.52
STS-9/OC-9		466.56
STS-12/OC-12	STM-4	622.08
STS-18/OC-18		933.12
STS-24/OC-24		1244.16
STS-36/OC-36		1866.24
STS-48/OC-48	STM-16	2488.32

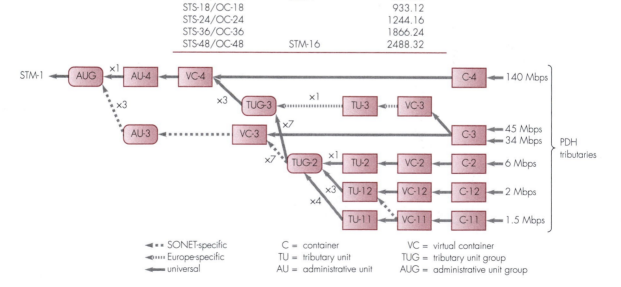

Figure 7.19 SDH/SONET multiplexing hierarchy and terminology.

at the head of each lower-level STM frame, a pointer is used to indicate the position of the lower-level STM frame within the higher-order frame.

We can best describe the structure of an SDH/SONET frame in relation to a complete synchronous transmission system since each frame contains management information relating to each constituent part. These parts include **sections**, **lines** and **paths** and their interrelationships are shown in Figure 7.20(a).

A section is a single length of transmission cable and both ends of the cable are terminated with a **section termination equipment** (**STE**). An example of an STE is a repeater which regenerates the optical/electrical signals

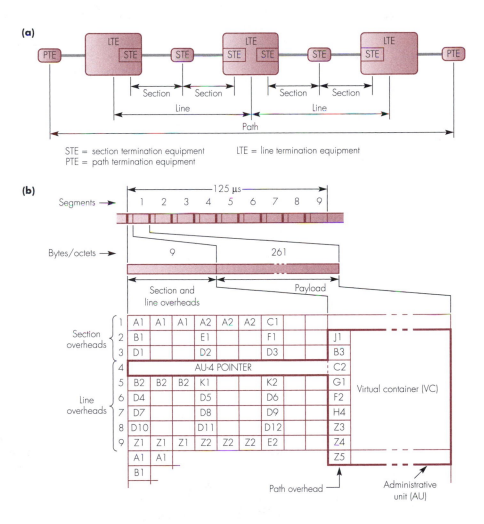

Figure 7.20 SDH/SONET detail: (a) managed entities; (b) frame format; (c) example VC mapping.

(c)

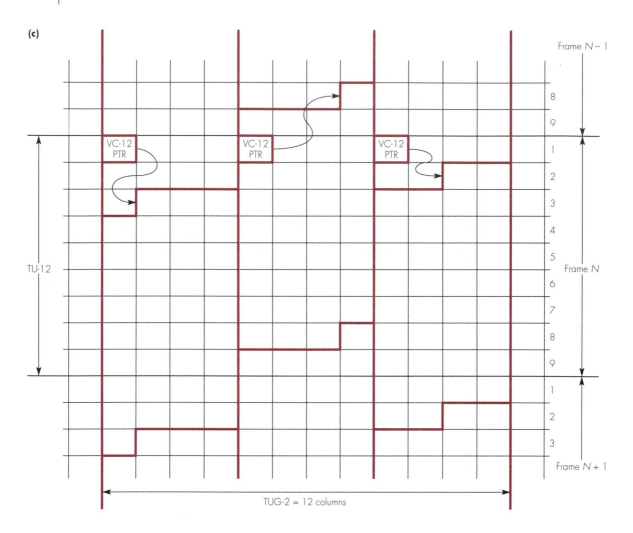

Figure 7.20 Continued.

being transmitted on this section of cable. A line extends across multiple cable sections and is terminated by a **line termination equipment** (**LTE**). Examples of LTEs are multiplexers and switching nodes. A path is an end-to-end transmission path through the complete transmission system. Each end of the path is terminated by a **path termination equipment** (**PTE**).

The structure of an STM-1 (STS-3/OC/3) frame is shown in Figure 7.20(b). As we can see, each frame comprises 2430 bytes/octets and repeats every 125 microseconds producing a bit rate of 155.52 Mbps. A frame comprises nine 270-byte **segments** each of which has a 9-byte header associated with it and a 261-byte **payload**. The header bytes are known as **overheads**. Normally, the segments making up a frame are shown with the segments one on top of the other since specific bytes in each header relate to one another.

The **section overhead** bytes relate to the management of a specific section. As we can see in Figure 7.20(b), some bytes are replicated for error protection purposes. The use of each byte is as follows:

A1–A2   Always the first bytes transmitted; used for framing.

B1   An 8-bit parity check used to monitor bit errors on the section.

C1   Identifies a specific STM-1 frame in a higher-order (STM-n) frame.

D1–D3   Form a data communication channel for network management messages relating to the section.

E1   Used for orderwire channels which are voice channels used by maintenance personnel.

F1   User channels, available for the management of customer premises equipment.

The **line overhead** bytes relate to the management of a complete line. The use of each byte is as follows:

B2   An 8-bit parity check used to monitor bit errors on the line.

D4–D12   Form a data communication channel for network management messages relating to the line.

E2   Orderwire channels relating to the complete line.

K1–K2   Form a signaling channel for automatic protection switching of the complete line.

Z1–Z2   Reserved for national use.

The columns in the payload field can be assigned in various ways to carry lower bit rate signals. To transport lower-level PDH streams – known as **tributaries** – the payload capacity in each container is allocated in integral numbers of columns. Each container has a column of path overhead bytes assigned to it and collectively these form the VC.

The identity of each byte given in Figure 7.20(b) and their uses are as follows:

J1   This byte verifies the VC path connection.

B3   8-bit parity for monitoring the bit error rate of the path.

C2   Indicates the composition of the VC payload.

G1   Used by the receiver to return the status of the received signal back to the transmitter.

F2   Provides a user data communication channel.

H4   Indicates whether the payload is part of a multiframe.

Z3–Z5   Available for national use.

A pointer is placed at the head of each VC and is used to indicate the start of the VC relative to the start of each frame. Note that if the container contains a PDH tributary, then the pointer value may change from frame to frame owing to possible timing differences. Different combinations of VCs can be used to fill up the payload area of a frame with smaller VCs being carried within larger ones. The VC and its pointer are known as a **tributary unit** (**TU**) if it carries a lower-order tributary or a **tributary unit group** (**TUG**) if it carries a number of lower-order tributaries. The largest VC in an STM-1 frame is known as an **administrative unit** (**AU**) and, as we show in Figure 7.20(b), the pointer to the start of this is written into the first octet position of the line overhead.

The example given in Figure 7.20(c) shows how three VC-12s can be carried within a TUG-2 frame. Each VC-12 comprises four columns of the STM-1 payload area and hence the TUG-2 comprises 12 columns. The VC-12 and its pointer forms a TU-12. The pointer always occupies the first byte position but, if the timing of the VC-12 contents relative to the STM-1 frame varies, then the position of the VC-12 is allowed to slip to accommodate this with the value in the pointer changing so that it always points to the first byte in the VC. A VC-12 will accommodate $4 \times 9 = 36$ bytes. Hence, since a VC-12 comprises 33 bytes – 32 bytes for the E1 frame plus 1 byte for the pointer – the remaining bytes are filled with what is referred to as **fixed stuff**.

In order to carry other signals which do not have a container defined to accept them, two or more TUs can be combined together using a technique known as **concatenation**. For example, five TU-2s can be concatenated to carry a single 32 Mbps signal. Four such signals can then be carried in a VC-4 instead of three if a standard C-3 container has been used. This technique is also used for the transport of ATM traffic.

All SDH equipment has software associated with it known as a **network management** (**NM**) **agent** and the communication channels in the overhead bytes are used by this to report any malfunctions of sections, lines, or paths to a central network management station. They are also used for the latter to download commands to change the allocation of the payload field associated with each STM-1 frame. For example, SDH ADMs can be configured – and reconfigured – remotely to provide any desired bandwidth mix without the need for demultiplexing. The general principle is shown in Figure 7.21. Redundant (standby) links are used between each pair of SDH multiplexers and these can be brought into service using commands received from a remote network management station.

7.3 Switching systems

As we showed earlier in Figure 7.1 and explained in the accompanying text, the total switching system comprises a hierarchical set of exchanges of varying switching capacity: local exchanges/end offices, regional tandem exchanges, and national tandem exchanges. Also, as we explained in Section 7.2.1, although within the local access network some analog transmission is

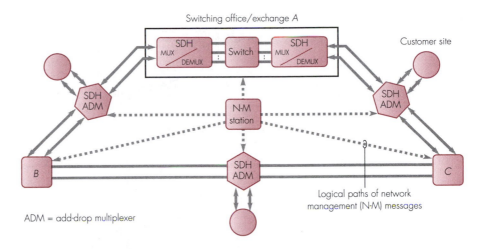

Figure 7.21 Service provision with SDH equipment using network management.

still in use, the use of remote concentrators and multiplexers means that all levels of exchange involve the switching of $125\,\mu/64\,$kbps time slots/channels from one incoming (PCM) line to another. Hence all switching exchanges operate in a similar way and the major difference between them is the volume of traffic that is switched. We shall restrict our discussion here to the basic principles on which all digital switching exchanges are based.

As we have just indicated, the basic requirement of a digital switching exchange is to switch the contents of each set of time slots in each of its incoming lines to any time slot position in any of its outgoing lines. Normally, the time slots in each input and output line are allocated independently and hence most connections involve a different time slot position in the input and output lines. As a result, a digital switch involves two different types of switching function: one to perform the switching between the input and output lines involved – **space switching** – and the other to perform the switching between the two time slot positions involved – **time-slot interchange** or **time switching**. We shall explain the principles of each first and then how they are combined to form a digital switching unit.

7.3.1 Time switching

The principle of operation of a time switch is shown in Figure 7.22. Assuming each PCM frame comprises N time slots/channels, the role of the time switch is to switch the contents of each time slot position read from the input line – an 8-bit byte/octet – and output it to a different time slot position in the output line. Hence, as we can deduce from the figure, since the contents of each time slot position in the input line needs to be switched to a later time

(a)

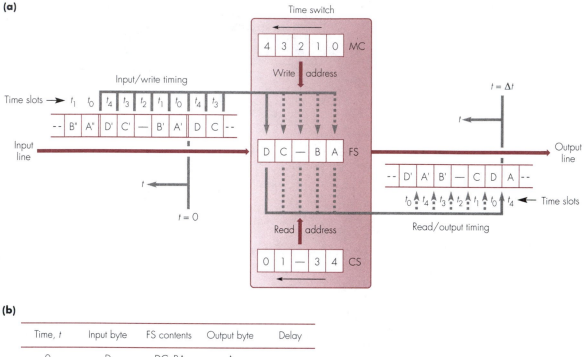

(b)

Time, t	Input byte	FS contents	Output byte	Delay
0	D	DC–BA	A	
t_0	A'	DC–BA'	D	
t_1	B'	DC–B'A'	C	
t_2	–	DC–B'A'	–	
t_3	C'	DC'–B'A'	B'	2ST
t_4	D'	D'C'–B'A'	A'	4ST
t_0	A"	D'C'–B'A"	D'	1ST
t_1	B"	D'C'–B"A"	C'	3ST

MC = modulo-N counter   FS = frame store   CS = connection store
Δt = switching delay = $T_{write} + T_{read}$ ST = slot time

Figure 7.22 Time switch principles: (a) switching schematic; (b) timing.

slot position in the output line, it is necessary to store the byte read from each time slot in a memory containing the same number of locations as there are time slots in the PCM frame. The memory is known, therefore, as the **frame store (FS)**.

As we show in the figure, because both the input and output (PCM) lines operate bit-serially, on input there is a serial-to-parallel conversion and on output a parallel-to-serial conversion. This means, therefore, that the contents of each of the time slots from the input line are written into the frame store after the last bit of the time slot has been received; that is, at the end of the time slot period. Conversely, the contents from each location in the frame store awaiting output are read at the start of the appropriate time slot period. As we can deduce from this, there is a time delay associated with a time switch which varies between 1 slot time, if the byte is to be output in the immediately following time slot, and $N-1$ slot times if it is to be output N time slots later; both times being in addition to the basic write/read cycle time of the frame store, Δt.

The addresses used to write into the frame store are obtained from a modulo-N counter that increments from $0-(N-1)$ in time synchronism with the arrival of each byte. Hence in the example, since $N = 5$, the counter increments from 0–4 and then repeats and, for each count value, the contents of the time slot just arrived are written into the frame store at the address currently held in the counter.

A second store (also containing N locations) called the **connection store** (**CS**) is then used to hold the set of addresses – and hence time slot positions – that are to be used for reading from the frame store and hence the order in which the current set of bytes in the frame store are to be transmitted out. So in the example, since time slot 0 in the output line is to contain the contents of time slot 4 from the input line, then the address 4 is present in the connection store at location 0. Again, the contents of the frame store are read in time synchronism with the start of each time slot period.

7.3.2 Space switching

A basic space switch comprises an array of M input and M output lines and an associated set of crosspoint switches. The signal present on each of the input lines is switched to a different output line by activating the appropriate

---

Example 7.2

A simple time switch is to be used to switch the time slot positions associated with (i) a 24-channel and (ii) a 32-channel PCM line. Derive the size of the frame store, address counter, and connection store in each case.

Answer:

(i) 24-channels:
   Frame store   = 24 locations each of 8 bits
   Address counter   = Modulo-24 counter (00000–10111 then repeat)
   Connection store = 24 locations each of 5 bits (00000–10111 used)

(ii) 32-channels:
   Frame store   = 32 locations each of 8 bits
   Address counter   = Modulo-32 counter (00000–11111 then repeat)
   Connection store = 32 locations each of 5 bits (00000–11111 used)

crosspoint switch. The set of crosspoints to be activated are held in a connection store and an example is shown in Figure 7.23(a). As we can see, in this example there are four input and four output lines and hence the connection store contains the output line – and thus crosspoint switch to be activated – for each of the four input lines. The crosspoints remain activated for the duration of the call.

In the case of a PCM space switch, the contents of each of the N time slots from each of the M input lines may need to be switched to a different output line. Hence each position in the connection store shown in Figure 7.23(a) has N entries, one for each time slot position. The crosspoints are activated in time synchronism with the arrival of each new set of time slots on the M input lines. A simple example is shown in Figure 7.23(b).

As we can see, in this example the switch comprises four input and four output lines as before but the signal present on each input line is a 4-channel PCM signal. Hence in this case, each entry in the connection store contains a set of four values which collectively indicate the crosspoints that are activated during each of the four time slot positions. The entries in the connection store for each time slot position are determined by first noting the time slot contents on a particular output line and then tracing back through the switch to determine the input line on which this arrives. The corresponding entry in the connection store is then set to the output line number which, in turn, indicates the crosspoint to be activated during this slot time. For example, for time slot position t_2, output line 1 contains contents C. Hence, tracing back through the switch, we find that this arrives on input line 0 and hence the connection store entry for this line is 1.

Example 7.3

A 7-input, 7-output line space switch is to be used to switch the contents of each set of time slot positions associated with (i) a 24-channel and (ii) a 32-channel PCM system. Derive the size of the connection store and the number of bits required for each entry in the store for both systems.

Answer:

(i) 24-channels:
Connection store has $7 \times 24 = 168$ locations
Each entry must have 3 bits: entries 000–110 to indicate the output line number (0–6) and hence the crosspoint position to be activated. Entry 111 is then used to indicate no crosspoint is to be activated; that is, the time slot is not in use.

(ii) 32-channels:
Connection store has $7 \times 32 = 224$ locations
Each entry must have 3 bits as for (i).

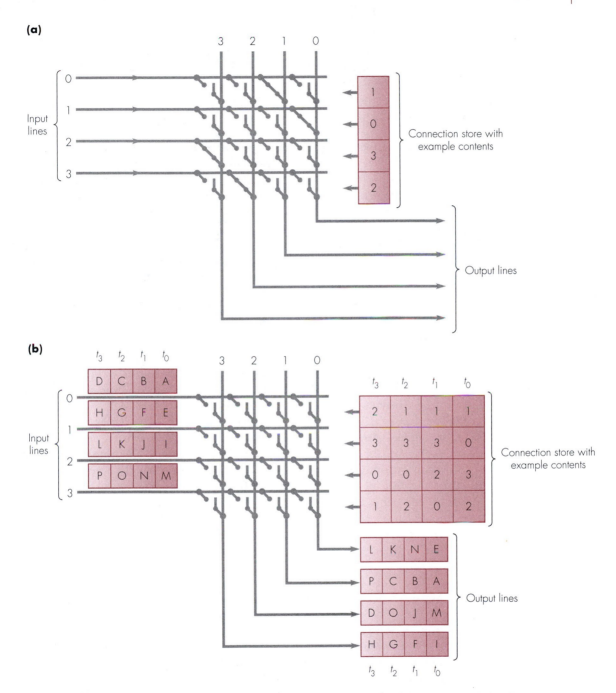

Figure 7.23 Space switch principle of operation: (a) basic space switch; (b) PCM space switch.

As we can deduce from the contents of the two sets of time slots associated with the input and output lines shown in Figure 7.23(a), a space switch simply changes the line on which each is transmitted and hence there is no delay associated with a space switch.

7.3.3 Digital switching units

As we explained earlier in Section 7.3, the requirement of a digital switching exchange is to be able to switch the contents of each time slot position in each of the input lines to a possibly different time slot position in a different output line. Therefore the overall switching operation involves a combination of both time and space switching, a simple example of which is shown in Figure 7.24(a).

As we can see, associated with each input line is a time switch which performs the time slot switching operation as defined by the contents of the related connection store. The single space switch then switches the rearranged set of time slots from one input line to the other.

With this simple configuration, since there are only two input/output lines there is always a time slot available in the required output line. As more lines are added, however, this is not necessarily the case. Although in terms of transmission, the time slots in each line can be allocated in a random way – during the call setup/signaling procedure – as existing calls terminate and new calls start, it is required also to ensure that the switching unit has the required capacity to switch the resulting number of calls. Hence for all but the smallest switches, switching units comprising multiple stages are used. As an example, a three-stage **time-space-time switch** is shown in Figure 7.24(b).

As we can see, each input line is passed through a separate time switch and each output line is preceded by a second time switch. The two sets of input and output time switches are then interconnected by a space switch which performs the required line switching operation. To perform the switching function, it is necessary to choose a time slot which is free in both the connection store of the input time switch and the frame store of the required output time switch. An example is shown in the figure which involves the switching of time slot 1 in input line 0 to time slot 8 in output line 2. To do this, the intermediate time slot chosen is 5.

As we can deduce from the figure, this carries out the switching operation in one direction only. However, since a duplex connection is required, a separate connection path in the reverse direction must also be established from input line 2 to output line 0. Hence, during the setting up of a new call/connection, the time slots to be used for the forward and reverse directions are reserved at the same time. Normally, to simplify the control of the switching network, the two time slots associated with each input/output line have a fixed separation between them; for example, 12 in the case of a 24-channel system and 16 in a 32-channel system. The same intermediate time slot is then used in both directions. In the example in Figure 7.24(b), the time slot separation is 12 and the intermediate time slot is 5 in both directions.

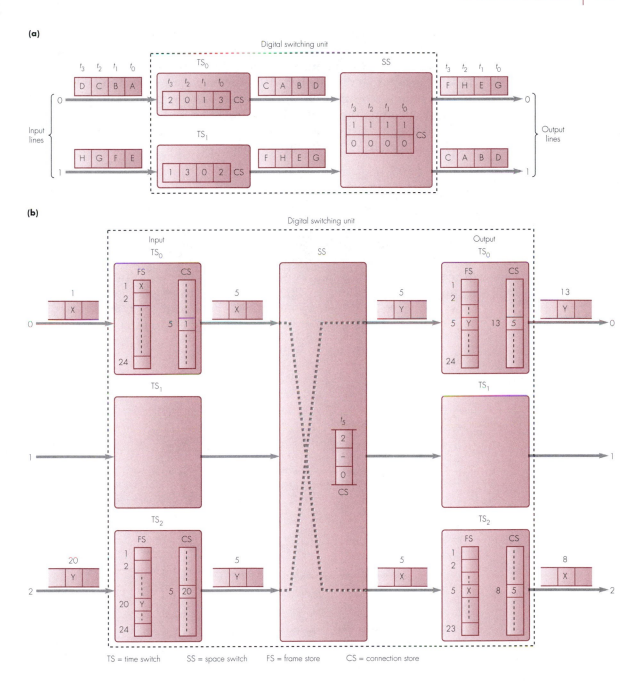

Figure 7.24 Digital switching units: (a) time-space switch; (b) time-space-time switch.

We can see from this example that since there is only a single space switch, a key factor in obtaining a free path through the switching network is the availability of a free intermediate time slot. In practice, traffic analysis can be used to show that the number of intermediate time slots must be twice the number of time slots in each input/output frame minus 1. This is achieved either by operating the space switch at twice the time slot arrival rate of the input lines or by having more than one space switch; for example, a large switch may operate with three intermediate space switches.

7.4 Signaling systems

The signaling operations associated with the setting up and clearing – also known as closing or tearing down – of a connection between two subscriber equipments involves two separate signaling systems: the first which operates over the local access networks associated with the two subscribers and the second which operates over the core trunk network. The two systems are shown in Figure 7.25(a) and, although they are interrelated, since each operates differently we shall describe the essential features of each separately.

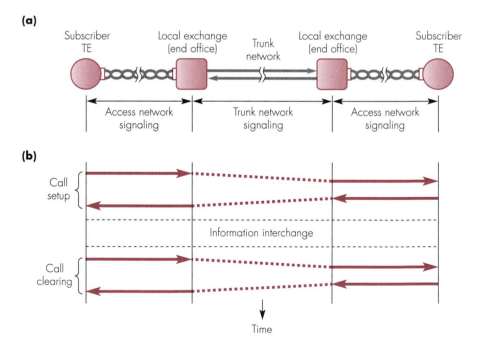

Figure 7.25 Signaling system components: (a) access and core trunk network components; (b) access network components.

7.4.1 Access network signaling

The basic operations associated with the setting up and closing down of a connection over the access network are shown in diagrammatic form in Figure 7.25(b). The steps involved are:

■ call setup: this includes the dialing, ringing, and answer stages;

■ interformation interchange: this is concerned with the exchange of information – speech/data – between the two subscribers;

■ call clearing: this results in the disconnection/release of the connection and can be initiated by either subscriber.

In practice, these basic operations are carried out differently over the various types of access network. These include both analog (PSTN) and digital (ISDN) access networks, the latter including the signaling operations that are required between an RCU/RSU/PBX and a local exchange/end office. We shall explain each separately.

Analog access circuits

We explained the basic features of an analog access circuit in the text associated with Figure 7.2. As you may recall, most signaling operations involve the transmission of one or more single-frequency audio tones. A selection of these is shown in Figure 7.26(a) and an example of their use in the setting up and clearing of a call/connection is given in Figure 7.26(b).

As we can see, in this example the call is successful and a connection would be set up. If the called subscriber line was busy, however, then the busy tone would be returned to the calling subscriber who would then replace the handset.

In the case of a modem, the same call setup and clearing sequences are followed by the incorporation of appropriate circuits within the modem. In addition, some modems – for example the V.32 – use an error detection and correction protocol during the information interchange phase in order to achieve a more reliable transfer of information. This is known as **link access procedure for modems** (**LAPM**) and these modems transmit the source information in frames using bit-oriented synchronous transmission and an HDLC-based error correcting protocol the principles of which we explained in the last chapter. The applicability of LAPM is shown in Figure 7.27(a).

Each modem comprises two functional units: a **user** (DTE) **interface part** (**UIP**) and an **error correcting part** (**ECP**). The LAPM protocol is associated with the latter while the UIP is concerned with the transfer of single characters/bytes across the local V.24 interface and with the interpretation of any flow control signals across this interface.

The UIP communicates with the ECP using a defined set of service primitives, as shown in the time sequence diagram in Figure 7.27(b). The different HDLC frame types used by the LAPM protocol entity to implement the various services are also shown.

(a)

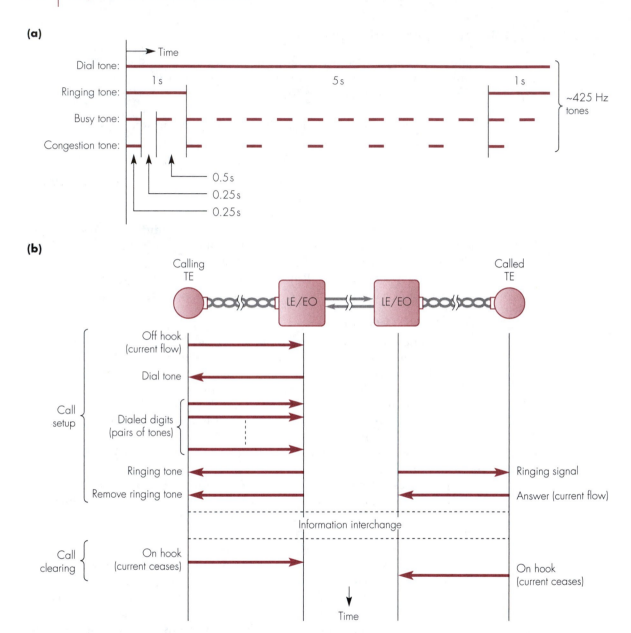

(b)

Figure 7.26 Analog access signaling: (a) a selection of the signals used; (b) sequence of signals exchanged to set up and clear a call.

(a)

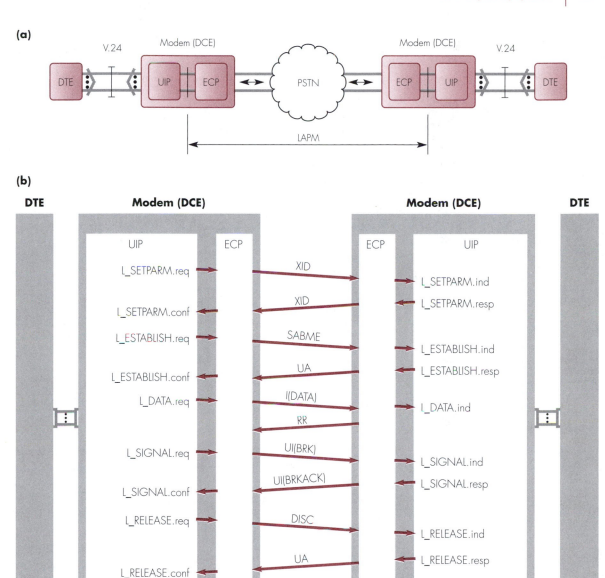

(b)

UIP = user interface part
DTE = data terminal equipment

ECP = error control part
DCE = data circuit-terminating equipment

Figure 7.27 LAPM: (a) operational scope; (b) user service primitives and corresponding frame types.

Before establishing a (logical) link, the originating and responding ECPs must agree on the operational parameters to be used with the protocol. These parameters include the maximum number of octets in I-frames, the acknowledgment timer setting, the maximum number of retransmission attempts, and the window size. Default values are associated with each of these, but if they are not used, the originating UIP must issue an L_SET-PARM.request primitive with the desired operational parameter values. The values are negotiated when the two ECPs exchange two special unnumbered frames – known as **exchange identification** (**XID**) – one as a command and the other as a response.

Once the operational parameters have been agreed, a link can then be set up when the UIP issues an L_ESTABLISH.request primitive. This, in turn, results in an SABM (normal) or SABME (extended) supervisory frame being sent by the ECP. The receiving ECP then issues an L_ESTABLISH.indication primitive to its local UIP and, on receipt of the response primitive, the receiving ECP returns a UA-frame. On receipt of this frame, the originating ECP issues a confirm primitive and the (logical) link is now set up. Data transfer can then be initiated using the L_DATA service.

Typically, the UIP first assembles a block of data, comprising characters or bytes received over the V.24 interface, then passes the complete block to the ECP using an L_DATA.request primitive. The ECP packs the data into the information field of an I-frame as a string of octets and transfers this using the normal error correcting procedure of the HDLC protocol. The receiving ECP then passes the (possibly error corrected) block of data to its local UIP which transfers it a character (byte) at a time bit-serially across the local V.24 interface.

If a flow control (break) condition is detected during the data transfer phase – for example, an X-OFF character is received or the DTR line becomes inactive – then the UIP stops outputting data to the local DTE and immediately issues an L_SIGNAL.request primitive to its local ECP. The local ECP then informs the distant ECP to (temporarily) stop sending any more data by sending a BRK (break) message in an unnumbered information (UI) frame. Recall that this, as the name implies, does not contain sequence numbers since it bypasses any error/flow control mechanisms. The receiving ECP then issues an L_SIGNAL.indication primitive to its local UIP and acknowledges receipt of the break message by returning a BRKACK message in another UI-frame. The UIP then initiates the same flow control signal across its own V.24 interface.

Finally, after all data has been transferred, the link is cleared when the originating UIP issues an L_RELEASE.request primitive. Again this is a confirmed service and the associated LAPM frames are DISC and UA.

ISDN digital access circuits

As we explained in Section 7.2.3, there are two alternative physical interfaces to an ISDN: basic rate and primary rate, the latter being either 1.544 Mbps or 2.048 Mbps. The basic rate interface provides a separate 16 kbps D-channel for signaling – in addition to the two 64 kbps user B-channels – and the two alternative primary rate interfaces include a 64 kbps signaling channel. Since both interfaces are digital, the setting up and clearing of calls/connections is carried out by the exchange of (signaling) messages over the respective D-channel. This mode of operation is called **channel associated signaling (CAS)**.

The signaling system associated with an ISDN digital access circuit is known as **digital subscriber signaling number one (DSS1)** and its composition is shown in Figure 7.28. Since the signaling messages must be received free of any transmission (bit) errors, a reliable data link protocol known as **link access procedure D-channel (LAPD)** is used to control their transfer over the interface. This is based on the HDLC protocol and is defined in **ITU-T Recommendation Q.921**. The format of the actual signaling messages and the protocol that is used to control their transfer is defined in **ITU-T Recommendation Q.931**. We shall describe the basic features of both protocols separately.

Q.921 (LAPD) Two types of service have been defined for use with LAPD. A time sequence diagram showing the two sets of service primitives is shown in Figure 7.29. As we can see, both an unacknowledged (connectionless) and an acknowledged (connection-oriented) service are supported. The connection-oriented service is used to transfer call setup messages between an item of user equipment — a telephone or a DTE – and the local exchange. The associated protocol incorporates error control The connectionless service is used for the transfer of management-related messages and the associated protocol uses a best-effort unacknowledged approach.

As we explained earlier in Section 7.2.3, multiple items of terminal equipment can time-share the use of the access circuit. However, all the layer 3 signaling messages are sent to a specific terminal equipment using the address field in the header of each LAPD frame the general structure of which is shown in Figure 7.30.

Two octets are used for the address field. These consist of two subaddresses: a **service access point identifier (SAPI)** and a **terminal endpoint identifier (TEI)**. Essentially, the SAPI identifies the class of service to which

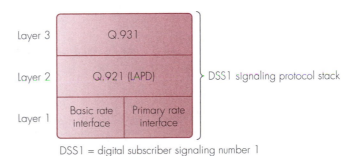

DSS1 = digital subscriber signaling number 1

Figure 7.28 ISDN digital access signaling protocol set.

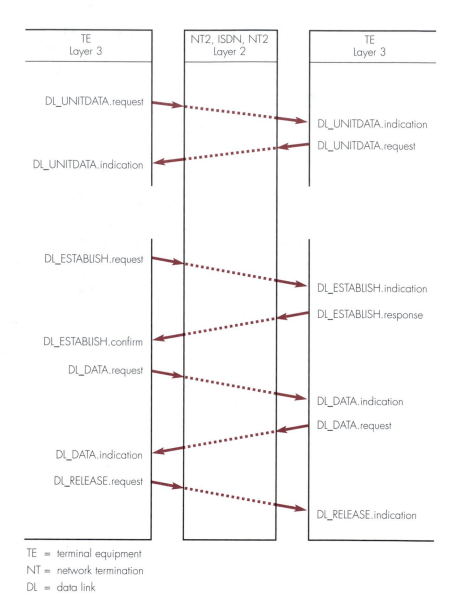

TE = terminal equipment
NT = network termination
DL = data link

Figure 7.29 LAPD user service primitives: (a) connectionless; (b) connection-oriented.

the terminal relates – speech, video, and so on – and the TEI uniquely identifies the terminal within that class. There is also a broadcast address – all binary 1s – that allows a message to be sent to all terminals in a class. This can be used, for example, to allow all telephones to receive an incoming call setup request message.

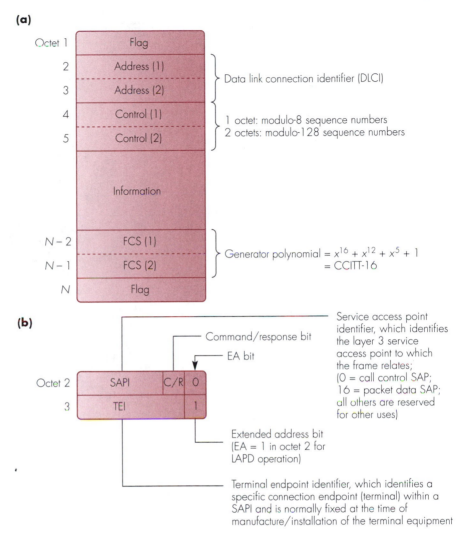

(a)

Octet 1	Flag
2	Address (1)
3	Address (2)
4	Control (1)
5	Control (2)
	Information
N − 2	FCS (1)
N − 1	FCS (2)
N	Flag

Data link connection identifier (DLCI)

1 octet: modulo-8 sequence numbers
2 octets: modulo-128 sequence numbers

Generator polynomial $= x^{16} + x^{12} + x^5 + 1$
$=$ CCITT-16

(b)

Command/response bit
EA bit

| Octet 2 | SAPI | C/R | 0 |
| 3 | TEI | | 1 |

Service access point
identifier, which identifies
the layer 3 service
access point to which
the frame relates;
(0 = call control SAP;
16 = packet data SAP;
all others are reserved
for other uses)

Extended address bit
(EA = 1 in octet 2 for
LAPD operation)

Terminal endpoint identifier, which identifies a
specific connection endpoint (terminal) within a
SAPI and is normally fixed at the time of
manufacture/installation of the terminal equipment

Figure 7.30 LAPD: (a) frame format; (b) address field usage.

The various control field formats – octets 4 and 5 – associated with LAPD are summarized in Figure 7.31, which also shows which frames can be sent as command frames and which as response frames.

In LAPD, as with LAPM, the additional unnumbered information (UI) frame is used. LAPD uses this with the connectionless service. Since there is no error control associated with this service (best-effort), all information is sent with a single control field with neither an N(S) nor an N(R). Such frames do have an FCS field however and, should this fail, the frame is simply discarded. Normally with this service the higher (user) layer must then detect the discarded frame – for example, by the lack of a suitable response (also in a UI-frame) – and make another attempt.

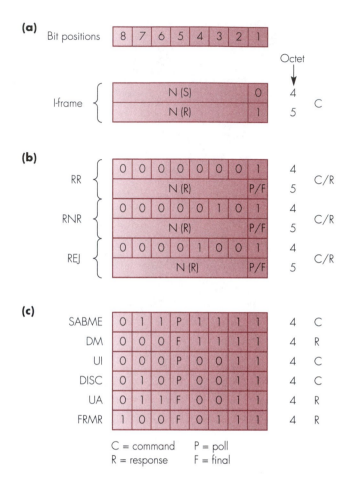

Figure 7.31 LAPD control field bit definitions: (a) information; (b) supervisory; (c) unnumbered.

Q.931 The Q.931 protocol is concerned with the sequence of the signaling messages (packets) that are exchanged over the D-channel to set up a call. An abbreviated list of the message types used is as follows:

- call establishment:
  - ALERTing
  - CALL PROCeeding
  - CONnect ACKnowledge
  - SETUP
  - Others;

- information transfer:
  - USER INFOrmation
  - Others;
- call clearing:
  - DISConnect
  - RELEASE
  - RELease COMPlete
  - Others.

Some of these messages have local significance (TE/LE) while others have end-to-end significance (TE/TE). However, all the messages are transferred across the interface in layer 2 (LAPD) I-frames. An example illustrating the use of some of these messages in setting up a conventional telephone call is shown in Figure 7.32(a).

During the setting up of a conventional telephone call over a PSTN, it is assumed that the called telephone operates in a standard way and hence the call setup phase involves only the setting up of a connection through the network. With an ISDN, however, since it was designed to support a range of services, it is necessary not only to set up a connection but also to establish an agreed set of operational parameters for the call between the two TEs. To do this, the call SETUP message, in addition to the address/number of the called TE – required to set up a network connection – also includes the proposed operational parameters for the call. The general format of all layer 3 messages is shown in Figure 7.32(b).

In addition to signaling messages, the ISDN D-channel can also be used for other purposes such as a low bit rate packet-switched facility. The *protocol discriminator* field is used to specify the protocol to which the message relates which, for ISDN signaling messages, is DSS1. The *call reference* field indicates the type of call involved and the *message type* the type of message the packet contains such as SETUP, CONNECT, and so on . The *message parameters* field contains other information relating to this message type such as the address/number of the called TE and the proposed operational parameters for the call.

PCM circuits

As we showed earlier in Figure 7.3 and explained in the accompanying text, in many instances remote concentrator units (RCUs) are used in the access network to terminate analog subscriber lines and relay the equivalent digital signals to the LE/EO. In practice, the circuit that links the RCU to the LE/EO is a PCM circuit similar to that used for the primary rate access to an ISDN. As we showed earlier in Figures. 7.15 and 7.16, there are two alternative PCM multiplexing structures in use, one comprising 24 channels and the other 32 channels. Also, in addition to each set of 24/32 time slots being multiplexed into a frame, a multiframe structure is established comprising 24/16 frames respectively.

(a)

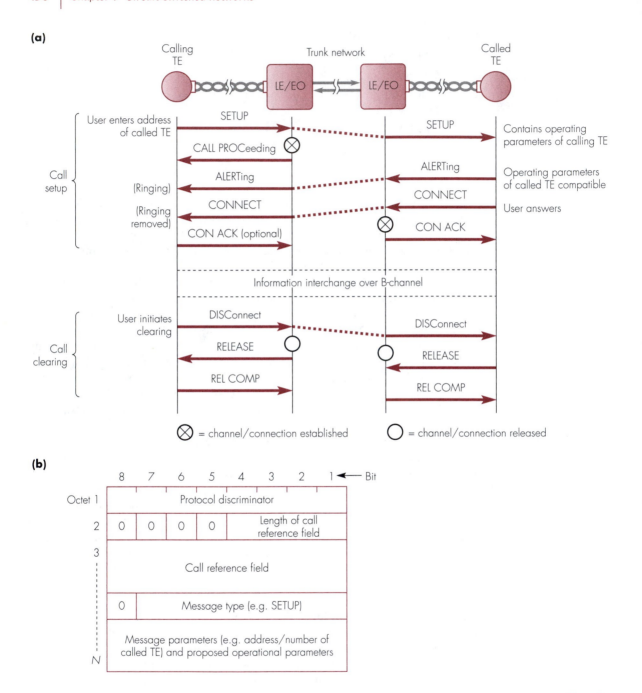

(b)

Figure 7.32 ISDN layer 3 signaling: (a) example message sequence to set up a conventional telephone call; (b) message format.

The RCU converts the analog speech signal relating to each active call into a 64 kbps PCM signal and uses a preassigned time slot in the PCM circuit to relay this to the LE/EO. Similarly, each PCM signal received from the preassigned time slot in the return direction is converted back into an analog signal by the RCU and relayed over the analog access circuit to the related subscriber TE. Hence as part of the call setup phase, on receipt of each new call request the RCU first determines the availability of a free time slot in the PCM circuit. Then, assuming one is available, the RCU proceeds to use selected bits in each multiframe associated with the time slot both to inform the LE/EO of the time slot number and also to relay the subsequent signaling information associated with the call.

The bits used for signaling in a 1.544 Mbps 24-channel PCM circuit are identified in Figure 7.33(a). As we can see, the least significant (eighth) bit from each time slot in frames 6 and 12 of each multiframe is used for the transfer of the signaling information associated with the corresponding time slot/channel. Therefore each time slot in every sixth frame contains seven information bits rather than eight. Although this is acceptable for speech, for data and other multimedia applications it is normal to operate all the channels at 56 kbps with this type of circuit.

The bits used in a 2.048 Mbps 32-channel PCM circuit are identified in part (b) of the figure. As we can see, with this type of circuit, except for frame 0, time slot 16 in each of the remaining 15 frames in a multiframe is used for the transfer of the signaling information associated with each of the 30 time slots/channels that are used for application information. As the names imply, this type of signaling is known as **channel associated signaling (CAS)**.

Example 7.4

Assuming channel associated signaling is being used, derive the bit rate of the signaling channel associated with each of the time slots in (i) a 24-channel PCM circuit and (ii) a 32-channel circuit.

Answer:

(i) As we can deduce from Figure 7.33(a), for each time slot, 1 bit in every sixth frame is used for signaling. Hence, since each frame is of 125 μs duration, we have 1 bit every $6 \times 125 = 750$ μs.
Thus the signaling rate per channel = $1/750 \times 10^{-6} = 1.333$ kbps.

(ii) As we can deduce from Figure 7.33(b), for each time slot, 4 bits every 16 frames are used for signaling. Hence we have 4 bits every $16 \times 125 = 2000$ μs.
Thus the signaling rate per channel = $4/2 \times 10^{-3} = 3$ kbps.

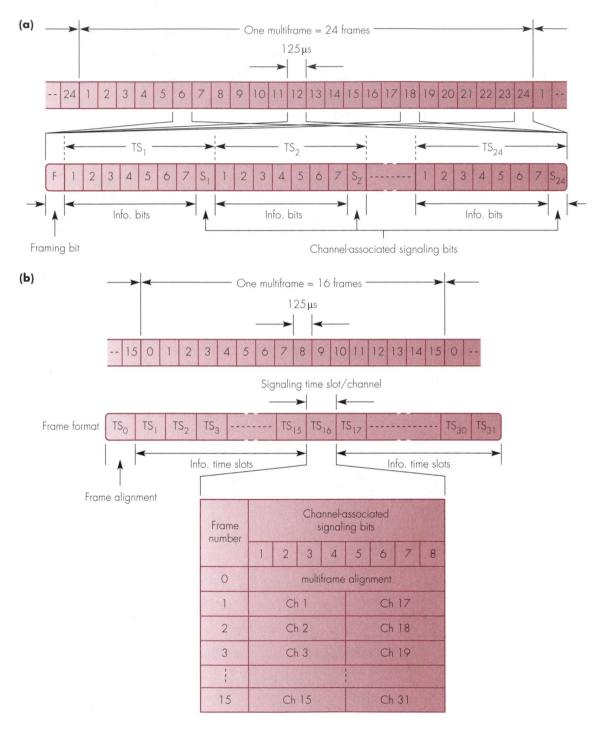

Figure 7.33 Signaling in PCM circuits: (a) 24-channel system; (b) 32-channel system.

An example set of signals/signaling messages associated with the setting up and clearing of a call/connection through an RCU is shown in Figure 7.34. The example relates to a conventional speech-only call and hence can be compared with the example we described earlier in Figure 7.26(b). It is assumed that the signaling messages are all transferred using the signaling channel associated with the assigned PCM time slot. Also, although not shown, the digitized speech signals associated with the call are transferred over the assigned PCM time slot. A similar set of signals/signaling messages is used if the intermediate device is a PBX or an RSU rather than an RCU. In the case of a PBX and RSU, however, local calls are processed directly and the procedure shown in Figure 7.34 is only invoked for calls external to their local switching domain.

7.4.2 Trunk network signaling

In early networks, channel associated signaling over PCM circuits was also used within the core trunk network. As the range of services supported by the network increased, so a more flexible form of signaling was introduced. For example, with a basic telephony service, a standard phone number is used which includes a country (if required), area, and local part. Then, when all calls use only these numbers, each exchange in the switching hierarchy can readily select one of a number of preallocated routes through the switching network using the various parts of the dialed number/address. With the advent of services based on non-standard numbers such as free-phone and local-charge, however, the number dialed does not contain these same parts. Hence before such calls/connections can be set up, the LE/EO must first obtain the standard number giving the location where the related service is being provided. However, since these types of number are introduced and changed quite frequently, it is not feasible for every LE/EO to have this information. Normally, therefore, this type of information is held only at a small number of locations within the network. On receipt of a call request involving, say, a free-phone number, prior to setting up the connection, the LE/EO sends an appropriate address-resolution signaling message to one of these locations and this responds with the standard number where the service is being provided.

As we can deduce from this, although the use of a small number of locations for this type of information means its management is made much easier, as a consequence, a faster and more flexible way of transferring signaling information is required. The solution adopted is to provide a separate network for the transmission and routing of signaling messages from that used for the actual call information interchange. This (signaling) network is then used to route and transfer all the signaling messages relating to all calls. This mode of working is known as **common channel signaling** (**CCS**) and the protocol stack that is associated with the signaling network, the **common channel signaling system number 7** or simply **SS7**. We shall restrict our discussion of network signaling to descriptions of the basic features of SS7.

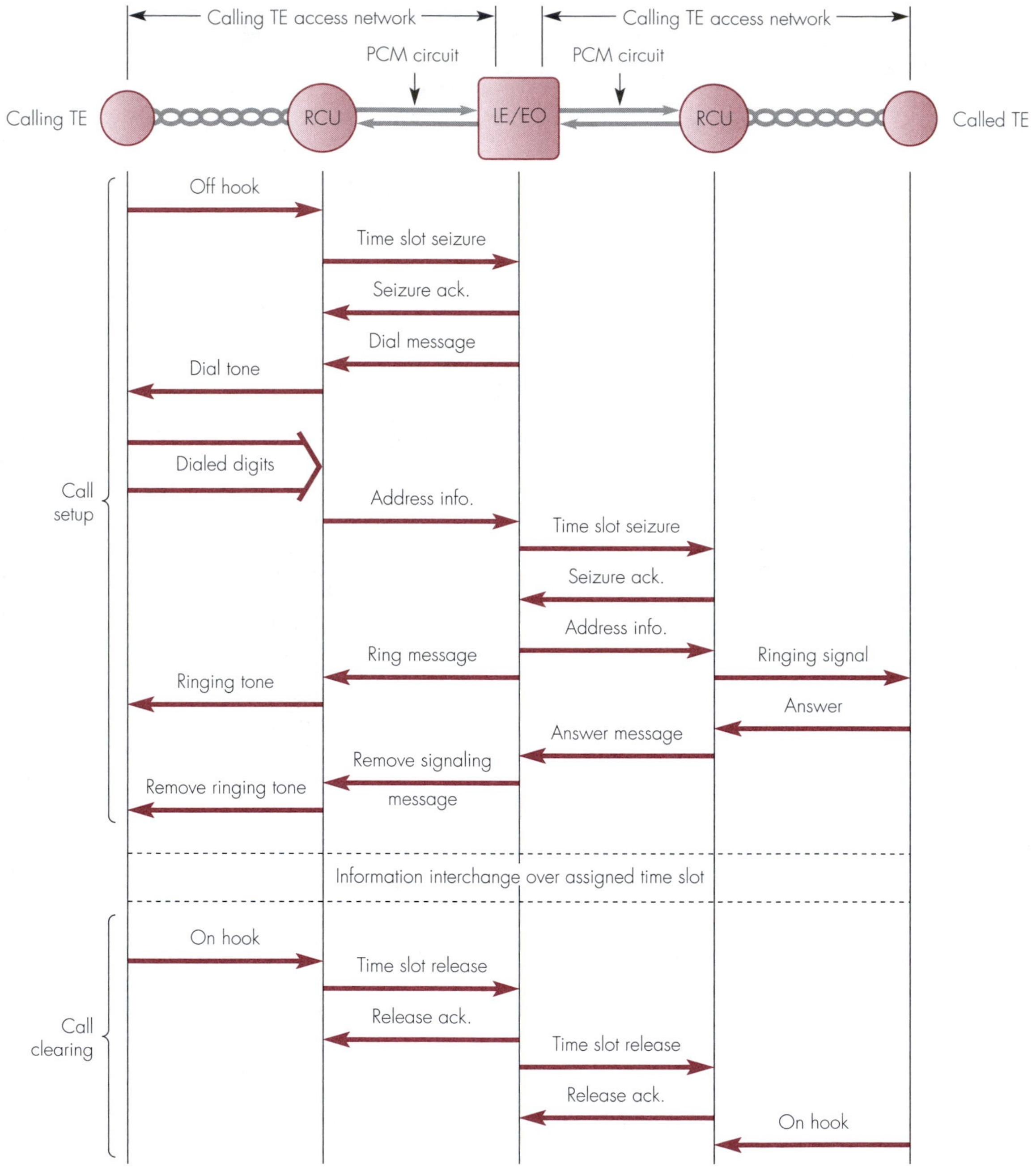

Figure 7.34 Analog access signaling through an RCU and PCM circuit.

SS7: components and terminology

Figure 7.35 shows a selection of the components and terminology associated with SS7 and, as we show in the figure, within each switching exchange/office is a collection of application protocols known as *parts* or *application service elements*. These include the **user part** (**UP**), the **address resolution part** (**ARP**), and the **operations**, **maintenance**, **and administration part** (**OMAP**). Each performs a separate function by exchanging signaling messages with a peer part in another system using the services provided by the **message transfer part** (**MTP**).

Each LE/EO contains one or more user parts, an ARP, and an OMAP. The role of the various user parts is, given a standard number/address, to set up a transmission path through the switching unit to the destination indicated in the number using one of the alternative paths/lines available. Examples of user parts include:

- TUP: the telephone (PSTN) user part,
- DUP: the data user part,
- ISUP: the ISDN user part.

As the name implies, the role of the ARP is, given a non-standard number/address (such as a free-phone number), to obtain the standard number where the related service is being provided.

The same signaling network is also used for the transfer of operational, maintenance, and administrative information relating to the total network. The OMAP in each exchange, therefore, is responsible for reporting fault conditions, receiving operational information, and so on to and from the nearest operations and management node.

In order to gain an understanding of the interactions between the various UPs and the ARP in each LE/EO, we shall consider the setting up of a connection using both a standard and a non-standard number. In the case of a standard number, the called number/address received from the subscriber TE – using CAS for example – is passed to the appropriate UP by the **local signaling interface** (**LSI**). The UP then proceeds to reserve a time slot/channel in a line to the destination LE/EO – using the international (if appropriate) and area parts of the number and the contents of a routing table held by each exchange – and relays the number in a signaling message to the next exchange along the selected path using the services provided by the message transfer part (MTP). This procedure then repeats until the signaling message is received by the UP in the destination LE/EO. Then, assuming the called TE is free and is prepared to accept the call, the UP returns an accept message over the signaling network and the information interchange then proceeds.

In the case of a call involving a non-standard number, prior to setting up a connection through the switching network, the UP passes the entered number to the ARP and this proceeds to send an address-resolution request (signaling) message to one of the higher-level tandem exchanges/offices in

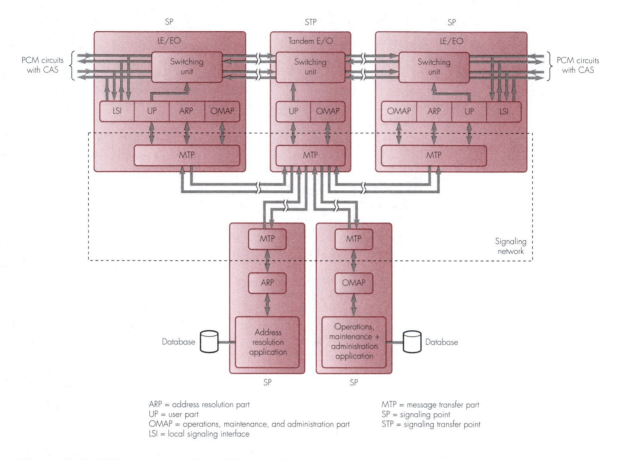

ARP = address resolution part
UP = user part
OMAP = operations, maintenance, and administration part
LSI = local signaling interface

MTP = message transfer part
SP = signaling point
STP = signaling transfer point

Figure 7.35 SS7 components and terminology.

the switching hierarchy using the MTP and the signaling network. Routing information relating to the ARP (and OMAP) signaling messages is held only in the higher-level exchanges. In the header of the messages relating to these parts is the identity of the required service, ARP, or OMAP, and also that of the initiating exchange. On receipt of such messages, the MTP in the higher-level tandem exchanges uses this to route the message to the network node providing this service using a previously assigned route. The address resolution application in this node then obtains the standard number of where the related service is being provided from a database and returns this in a message to the ARP in the LE/EO that originated the request, again using the signaling network. On receipt of the response message, the ARP in the LE/EO passes the standard number to the UP that initiated the request and the UP then proceeds to set up a network connection as previously described.

As we show in Figure 7.35, all LE/EOs and service nodes are known as **signaling points** (**SPs**) as they simply initiate and receive signaling messages.

The higher-level tandem exchanges/offices that can also route signaling messages are known as signaling transfer points (STPs). Hence, since only STPs can route signaling messages, the management of the related routing tables is much simpler. Also, although the signaling links are shown separate from the links that are used for the information relating to calls, normally, both share the same physical lines that interconnect the various exchanges shown earlier in Figure 7.1.

SS7: protocol architecture

A selection of the protocols associated with the SS7 protocol stack is shown in Figure 7.36(a). As we can see, the lowest three protocol layers make up the MTP and collectively they provide a basic reliable message transfer service through the signaling network. The function of each protocol is:

- **signaling data link**: this is the physical layer interface to the transmission channel(s) being used;
- **signaling link**: this is a connection-oriented (reliable) data link control protocol based on HDLC that incorporates error and flow control;
- **signaling network**: this is a connectionless protocol that provides message routing across the signaling network.

The format of the protocol data units associated with the signaling link and signaling network protocols is shown in Figure 7.36(b).

As we have just indicated, the signaling link protocol is based on HDLC and the *forward* and *backward sequence number* fields in the header of each I-frame are used for error and flow control purposes using a go-back-N error control scheme and a window flow control method. The *length indicator* is used to indicate the number of octets/bytes in the information field and the *frame check sequence* field is used to detect the presence of transmission errors.

The *service information octet* (*SIO*) and *signaling information field* (*SIF*) in the protocol control field of the signaling network protocol enable the application data to be routed through the signaling network to the destination node and, once there, to the intended application part. The SIO consists of two fields:

- *service indicator*: this specifies the application part to which the data in the message relates – TUP, DUP, ISUP, ARP, and so on;
- *subservice field*: this specifies the type of network (national/international) over which the message unit is traversing.

The SIF consists of three subfields:

- the *destination point code* is used by the signal network protocol in STPs to route the message unit to its intended destination exchange/node;

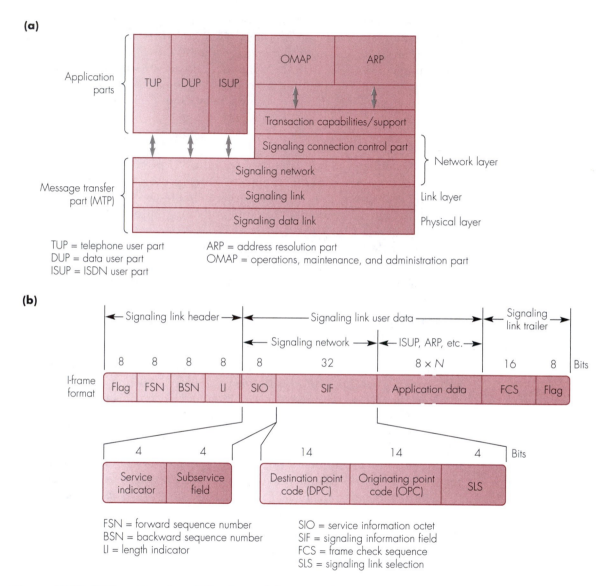

(a)

Application parts: TUP, DUP, ISUP

OMAP, ARP

Transaction capabilities/support

Signaling connection control part

Message transfer part (MTP):
Signaling network — Network layer
Signaling link — Link layer
Signaling data link — Physical layer

TUP = telephone user part
DUP = data user part
ISUP = ISDN user part

ARP = address resolution part
OMAP = operations, maintenance, and administration part

(b)

Signaling link header — Signaling link user data — Signaling link trailer

Signaling network — ISUP, ARP, etc.

Bits	8	8	8	8	8	32	8 × N	16	8
I-frame format	Flag	FSN	BSN	LI	SIO	SIF	Application data	FCS	Flag

Bits	4	4	14	14	4
	Service indicator	Subservice field	Destination point code (DPC)	Originating point code (OPC)	SLS

FSN = forward sequence number
BSN = backward sequence number
LI = length indicator

SIO = service information octet
SIF = signaling information field
FCS = frame check sequence
SLS = signaling link selection

Figure 7.36 SS7 protocol architecture: (a) protocol components; (b) format of MTP message units.

- the *originating point code* is used to route the reply message to the originating exchange/node;

- the *signaling link selection* field is used to indicate the link being used when a choice is available, the aim being to share the signaling traffic over those available.

Example application part message sequence

In order to describe a typical application part message sequence, a selection of the messages involved in the setting up and clearing of a channel is shown in Figure 7.37. The messages used in the figure relate to the ISDN user part and include:

■ *Initial address message (IAM)*: this is sent by the ISUP in the calling LE/EO to initiate the setting up of a call in the forward direction. Hence it contains the ISDN number/address of the calling and called party within it and also other information;

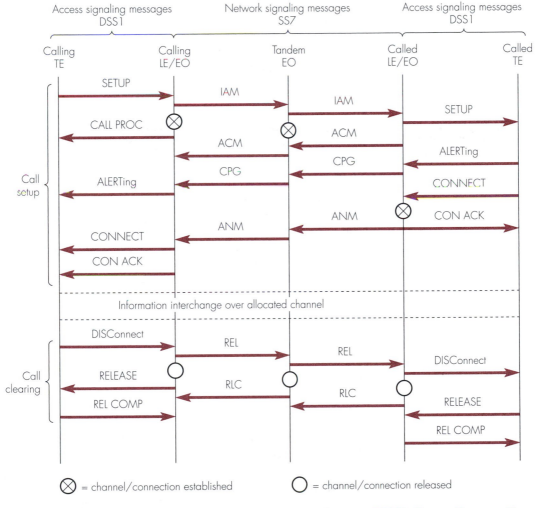

Figure 7.37 Network signaling message sequence to set up an ISDN channel/connection using SS7.

- *Address complete message (ACM)*: this is sent by the ISUP in the called LE/EO to indicate to the calling ISUP that all the address information required for routing (and hence establishing) the call to the called party has been received;

- *Call progress (CPG)*: this is sent by the called ISUP to indicate to the calling ISUP that an event has occurred that should be relayed to the calling TE;

- *Answer message (ANM)*: this is sent by the called ISUP to the calling ISUP to indicate the call has been answered and that charging should commence;

- *Release (REL)*: this can be sent in either direction to release the connection and to inform the other ISUP that this has been done;

- *Release complete (RLC)*: this is sent in response to the release message.

The example builds on the ISDN D-channel message interchange sequence associated with the DSS1 access protocol that we showed earlier in Figure 7.32(a).

Summary

In this chapter we have described the basic operational characteristics of public circuit-switched networks. We explained how the networks consist of three interrelated systems: transmission, switching, and signaling. Also, how the basic core switching network associated with these networks supports the services offered by both a PSTN and an ISDN and that the only difference between the two networks is the way subscribers gain access to the core network.

A summary of the topics discussed in relation to the two types of access network is given in Figure 7.38(a). As we can see, in the case of a PSTN, these utilize analog transmission within the access network to link the TEs of subscribers to the nearest network termination point and we described the operation of both the signaling system used and the operational characteristics of low bit rate modems. In the case of an ISDN, these utilize digital transmission and we described both the transmission and signaling schemes used with the basic rate interface (2B + D) and the two types of primary rate interface (23B + D and 30B + D).

The core transmission and switching network operates digitally and a summary of the topics we discussed is given in Figure 7.38(b). In terms of transmission, the interexchange lines utilize a mix of the older PDH and newer SDH/SONET multiplexing hierarchies to multiplex several thousands of channels/calls over these lines and we explained the operational characteristics of both systems. In terms of switching, we explained the basic principles of time switching and space switching and how these are combined to form a digital switching unit.

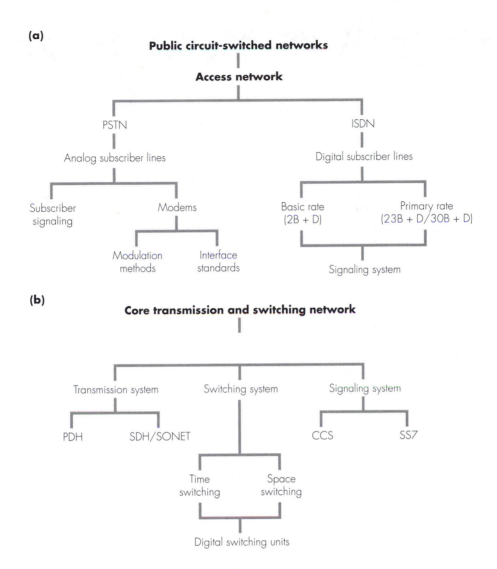

Figure 7.38 Public circuit-switched network summary: (a) access network; (b) core transmission and switching network.

The signaling system in the core network utilizes a separate network to transfer all the signaling messages between the trunk switching exchanges and the various supervisory nodes used for such functions as address resolution and network management. The network is known as the signaling network and this mode of operation common channel signaling (CCS). The protocol stack used in each exchange/node to control the transfer of signaling messages over the signaling network is known as SS7, the basic principles of which we also described.

Exercises

Section 7.1

7.1 With the aid of Figure 7.1, describe the role of the following:
(i) the local access and signaling networks,
(ii) the interexchange trunk/carrier networks,
(iii) international network.

7.2 Explain the meaning of the following terms relating to the total transmission system:
(i) analog subscriber line,
(ii) digital subscriber line,
(iii) low bit rate modems,
(iv) high bit rate access lines,
(v) interexchange trunk lines.

7.3 With the aid of examples, identify the switching exchanges involved in providing the following types of call between two subscribers connected to:
(i) the same LE/EO,
(ii) different LE/EOs within the same region,
(iii) different regions,
(iv) different countries.
Why are alternative lines/paths present?

7.4 State the role of the signaling system
(i) over the access lines,
(ii) over the interexchange trunk lines.

Section 7.2

7.5 Explain the meaning of the following terms relating to the analog access network of a PSTN:
(i) junction box,
(ii) cross-connect,
(iii) maximum cable length.

7.6 With the aid of the diagrams in Figure 7.2, explain the roles of the following:
(i) cradle switch unit,
(ii) ringer circuit,
(iii) dialer,
(iv) 4-wire to 2-wire hybrid,
(v) dual-tone multifrequency keypad,

(vi) echo signal,
(vii) echo canceler.

7.7 With the aid of Figure 7.3, explain the role of a remote concentrator unit in the access network of a PSTN. Include in your explanation the meaning of the terms "concentration" and "pair-gain". How is a remote switching unit different from a remote concentrator unit?

7.8 With the aid of Figure 7.4, explain the following modem operating modes:
(i) 2-wire switched connections,
(ii) 4-wire leased circuits.
What is the advantage of the latter and when is it used?

7.9 With the aid of the schematic diagram and waveform sets shown in Figure 7.5, explain the principle of operation of the three basic types of modulation used in modems. Include the role of the carrier signal and the difference between phase-coherent PSK and differential PSK.

7.10 With the aid of the diagrams shown in Figure 7.6, explain the operation of the following multilevel modulation schemes:
(i) single-carrier 4-PSK,
(ii) two-carrier 4-QAM,
(iii) two-carrier 16-QAM.

7.11 Assuming an input bit rate of 56 kbps, derive the line signaling rate in baud for each of the three modulation schemes identified in Exercise 7.9.

7.12 Explain the meaning of the term "training phase" and how the bit rate for a connection is established.

7.13 Identify the subset of lines from the V.24/EIA-232D interface that are used to carry out the setting up of a connection through the PSTN and the exchange of some data. With the aid of the time sequence diagram in Figure 7.9, explain how these are used.

7.14 With the aid of the two modem connections shown in Figure 7.10(a), explain how
   (i) a local loopback test and
   (ii) a remote loopback test is carried out.

7.15 Explain why line driver and receiver circuits must be used to connect a modem to the serial port of a computer. Describe the operation of such circuits.

7.16 With the aid of the two diagrams shown in Figure 7.11, explain the operation of the following ISDN network terminal alternatives:
   (i) a 4-port NTU,
   (ii) an S-bus NTU.
   Include in your explanation the meaning of the term "out-of-band" and how the use of the two B-channels is shared between the attached terminal equipments.

7.17 With the aid of the schematic diagrams shown in Figure 7.12, describe the operation of a differential line driver and receiver circuit and why these are used. Include the meaning of the term "common mode rejection" and "characteristic impedance".

7.18 In relation to the line signals shown in Figure 7.13, explain how
   (i) the DC balancing bits associated with each transmitted frame ensure the mean DC level of the line is always zero and
   (ii) contentions for use of the shared signaling channel are resolved.

7.19 With the aid of Figure 7.14(a), explain how the NTU supports duplex transmission over a single twisted-pair. Include in your explanation the operation of the adaptive echo canceler.

7.20 Explain why a 4-level code is used over the twisted-pair access line from an NTU. Also explain how the code works.

7.21 With the aid of the frame structure shown in Figure 7.14(c), explain the framing structure used over the access line. Include the use of the synchronization word.

7.22 With the aid of the waveform set and frame format details relating to the 1.544 Mbps primary rate interface shown in Figure 7.15, explain
   (i) the AMI line code and why this is supplemented with the B8ZS code,
   (ii) the frame structure used and why a superframe is defined for use with this.

7.23 With the aid of the waveform set and frame format details relating to the 2.048 Mbps primary rate interface shown in Figure 7.16, explain
   (i) the operation of the HDB3 line code,
   (ii) the frame structure, including how the start of each frame is determined.

7.24 Explain the meaning of the following terms relating to the plesichronous digital hierarchies:
   (i) justification bits,
   (ii) primary multiplex,
   (iii) DS1/T1 and E1,
   (iv) byte interleaving,
   (v) bit interleaving.

7.25 With the aid of the schematic diagrams shown in Figure 7.18, explain how a portion of a higher bit rate stream in a PDH can be derived and used using an add-drop-multiplexer. Identify the disadvantages of this approach.

7.26 In relation to the SDH/SONET, explain the meaning of the terms:
   (i) container,
   (ii) virtual container,
   (iii) path,
   (iv) line,
   (v) section,
   (vi) fixed stuff,
   (vii) concatenation.

7.27 With the aid of Figure 7.21, explain how a lower bit rate portion of a higher bit rate stream is derived using a SDH/SONET add-drop multiplexer.

Section 7.3

7.28 Discriminate between the following terms relating to switching systems: "space switching" and "time switching".

7.29 With the aid of Figure 7.22(a), explain the role of:
  (i)   the frame store,
  (ii) the modulo-N/address counter,
  (iii) the connection store.

  What is the maximum delay for a 24-channel system?

7.30 With the aid of the space switch diagrams shown in Figure 7.23, explain why the connection store requires four sets of entries. What would be the entry in the connection store if a time slot in one of the input lines was not in use?

7.31 Repeat Example 7.3 but this time assume an 8-input, 8-output space switch.

7.32 With the aid of the time-space-time switch shown in Figure 7.24(b), assume that time slot 5 in input line 1 is to be switched to time slot 10 in output line 2. Assuming an intermediate time slot is available, derive the contents of each connection store (CS) to do this.

7.33 Explain how duplex connections are set up through the T-S-T switch shown in Figure 7.24(b). State the number of intermediate time slots that should be provided with this switch to ensure non-blocking.

Section 7.4

7.34 With the aid of a diagram, discriminate between access networking signaling and core network signaling.

7.35 In relation to the diagrams shown in Figure 7.26 relating to analog access signaling:
  (i)   state the use of the congestion tone signal,
  (ii) state how the exchange determines a wrongly keyed number and its response to this.

7.36 With the aid of the time sequence diagram shown in Figure 7.27(b), explain how
  (i)   error correction and
  (ii) flow control are achieved during the information transfer phase.

7.37 With the aid of the signaling protocol set identified in Figure 7.28, explain the role of:
  (i)   LAPD (Q.921),
  (ii) Q.931.

7.38 In relation to the LAPD/Q921 protocol, state the roles of the service access point identifier and terminal endpoint identifier in the frame header. Explain the uses of the various control fields.

7.39 In relation to the Q.931 protocol:
  (i)   give examples of the information present in the SETUP message,
  (ii) explain the role of the protocol discriminator field in the message header.

7.40 Explain the meaning of the term "channel associated signaling" and give an example of its use.

7.41 With the aid of the diagrams shown in Figure 7.33, explain how the signaling messages relating to a specific time slot are assembled in
  (i)   a 24-channel system,
  (ii) a 32-channel system.

  State the bit rate of the signaling channel in each case.

7.42 In relation to the signaling messages shown in Figure 7.34, state the affect of the RCU being a PBX or RSU.

7.43 Explain the meaning of the term "common channel signaling" and how it is different from channel associated signaling.

7.44 With the aid of Figure 7.35, explain the meaning/use of the following SS7 components ad terminology:
  (i)   UP,
  (ii)   ARP,
  (iii) OMAP,
  (iv)   LSI,
  (v)   MTP,
  (vi)   SP,
  (vii) STP.

7.45 With the aid of Figure 7.35, explain how a connection is established using
  (i)   a standard, and
  (ii) a non-standard number.

7.46 With the aid of Figure 7.36(a), explain the role of the following protocols:
(i) signaling data link,
(ii) signaling link,
(iii) signaling network.

Hence, with the aid of the message format shown in Figure 7.36(b), describe the role of the following fields:

(i) FSN and BSN,
(ii) SID and SIF.

7.47 With the aid of Figures 7.26 and 7.37, produce a diagram that shows the exchange of the SS7 network signaling messages to set up a standard telephone channel/connection initiated using analog access signaling.

Enterprise networks

8.1 Introduction

When a person is at home, all calls relating to interpersonal and interactive applications must be made using a PSTN, an ISDN, or a cable distribution network. The calls are then charged at a rate determined by the call duration and the distance involved. In the case of a person in a business or large enterprise, however, the majority of the calls made are to other members of the same business/enterprise and only a small percentage are to people outside of the enterprise. Hence for all but the smallest businesses, in order to reduce call charges, most enterprises install their own private networks to handle those calls that are internal to the enterprise. Normally, the network comprises both a private branch exchange (PBX) and a local area network (LAN) and, collectively, these support all the interpersonal and interactive communications within the enterprise.

For an enterprise that occupies just a single site/establishment – for example, a small to medium-sized company, a hospital complex, a university campus – the PBX and LAN at the establishment handle all internal calls and only those calls that are external to the site are made using an appropriate public network such as a PSTN, an ISDN, or an Internet service provider

(ISP) network. For an enterprise that operates over multiple sites, however, when there is a significant proportion of intersite calls, an alternative solution is to extend the private facilities associated with each site to embrace all sites. This involves linking the sites together using high bit rate transmission lines that are leased from a (national) network provider. The resulting network is then known as a multisite **enterprise network** or, if the sites are located in different countries around the world, a **global enterprise network**.

Normally, leased lines are charged for on an annual rather than a per-call basis and hence this approach is only justified when the annual (public) call charges to other sites exceeds the cost of leasing the lines. An added benefit of creating a private network, however, is that it is often easier to offer more sophisticated services since the utilization of the bandwidth of the intersite leased lines is under the control of the enterprise network manager. Also, because the total network is private – apart from the transmission lines, of course – a private network is considered to be more secure than a public one.

As we explained in the last chapter, a PBX operates in a similar way to a local exchange/end office in a public network with the terminal equipment connected to the PBX using either analog or digital lines. In this chapter, we shall focus on the operation of the different types of LAN and the various approaches that are used to create multisite enterprise networks.

8.2 LANs

As we have just indicated, LANs are used to interconnect distributed communities of end systems – often referred to as **stations** in the context of LANs – including multimedia PCs, workstations, servers, and so on. Typically, these are distributed around an office, a single building, or a localized group of buildings, all of which belong to a single enterprise.

The early LANs – many of which are still in existence – operate using a shared, high bit rate, transmission medium to which all the stations are attached and the information frames relating to all calls are transmitted. To ensure the transmission bandwidth is shared fairly between all of the attached stations, a number of different medium access control (MAC) methods are used. These include **carrier-sense multiple-access with collision detection (CSMA/CD)** and **token ring**, both of which have a defined maximum number of attached stations and length of transmission medium associated with them. As we shall see, in practice the maximum distance is relatively small and hence most LANs of this type comprise multiple (LAN) **segments** that are interconnected together using either **repeaters** or devices known as **bridges** and a high bit rate (site-wide) **backbone subnetwork**. We explain the operation of Ethernet/IEEE802.3 LANs – which are based on the CSMA/CD MAC method – in Section 8.3 and token ring LANs in Section 8.4. The operation of bridges is explained in Section 8.5 and, as an example of a backbone network, the **fiber distributed interface (FDDI)** in Section 8.6.

More recently, higher bit rate versions of the older LAN types – now known as **legacy LANs** – have become available. To obtain the higher network throughputs that are required with multimedia applications, the central **hubs** associated with the earlier LANs have been upgraded to operate at much higher bit rates. Also, as we shall explain, the older hubs operate in a half-duplex mode and support only a single frame transfer at a time. Hence the newer hubs operate in a duplex mode and allow the frames relating to multiple calls to be transmitted concurrently. Examples include **fast Ethernet** hubs and **Ethernet switching** hubs, both of which we describe in Section 8.7.

In terms of the link layer protocol associated with LANs, the various LAN types all use a standard LC sublayer and there is a different MAC sublayer for each of the LAN types. We describe the structure and the user services offered by each sublayer in Section 8.8.

In multisite enterprise networks, the LANs associated with the different sites are interconnected together using various methods determined by the volume of intersite traffic involved. If this is relatively low, then switched ISDN connections can be used; if it is high, then high bit rate (digital) leased lines are used. Normally, these are leased from the operator of a national public circuit-switched network and are the same as those we described in Section 7.2.3. In both cases, however, a **gateway** is connected to the LAN at each site and this manages all intersite frame transfers. We explain the operation of some of the different types of technology that are used to interconnect the LANs at different sites in Section 8.9.

8.3 Ethernet/IEEE802.3

Ethernet networks – and the more recent derivative IEEE802.3 – are used extensively in technical and office environments. As we shall see, Ethernet has gone through many phases of development since its first introduction but, in general, the same basic mode of operation is still used. All frame transmissions between all the stations that are attached to the LAN take place over a shared 10 Mbps bus and the CSMA/CD MAC method is then used to share the use of the bus in an equitable way. We shall explain the principle of operation of this type of MAC method first and then other selected aspects in the following subsections.

CSMA/CD

Since all the stations are attached directly to the same cable/bus, it is said to operate in a **multiple access (MA) mode**. To transmit a block of data, the source station first encapsulates the data in a frame with the address of the destination station and its own address in the frame header and an FCS field at the tail of the frame. The bus operates in the **broadcast mode** which means that every frame transmitted is received by all the other stations that are attached to the bus. Hence as each of the other stations receives the frame, it first checks the frame is free of errors using the FCS and, if it is, it compares the destination address in the header with its own address. If they are different, the station simply discards the frame; if they are the same, the frame contents are passed up to the LC sublayer for processing together with the address of the source station.

With this mode of operation, two (or more) stations may attempt to transmit a frame over the bus at the same time. Because of the broadcast mode, this will result in the contents of the two (or more) frames being corrupted and a **collision** is said to have occurred. Hence in order to reduce the possibility of a collision, prior to sending a frame the source station first determines whether a signal/frame is currently being transmitted on the bus. If a signal – known as the **carrier** – is **sensed** (**CS**), the station defers its own transmission until the current frame transmission is complete and only then does it attempt to send its own frame. Even so, in the event of two (or more) stations waiting to send a frame, both will start to transmit their frame simultaneously on detecting that the transmission of the current frame is complete. When this happens, however, it is necessary for the two (or more) stations involved, to detect a collision has occurred before each has finished transmitting its own frame. In practice, because of the possibly large signal propagation delay of the bus and the high transmission bit rate used (10 Mbps), this is not as straightforward as it might seem.

A station detects that a collision has occurred by simultaneously monitoring the signal that is present on the cable all the time it is transmitting a frame. Then, if the transmitted and monitored signals are different, a collision is assumed to have occurred – **collision detected** (**CD**). As we show in Figure 8.1, however, a station can experience a collision not just at the start of a frame but after it has transmitted a number of bits. The worst-case time delay – and hence maximum number of bits that have been transmitted – before detecting that a collision has taken place is known as the **collision window** and occurs when the two colliding stations are attached to opposite extremities of the bus, as we show in the figure.

In the figure, station A has determined that no transmission is in progress and hence starts to transmit a frame – part (i). As we explained in Section 6.2.8, irrespective of the bit rate being used, the first bit of the frame will take a small but finite time to propagate over the transmission medium determined by the length of the cable, l, and the signal propagation velocity, v. The maximum length of cable is set at 2.5 km. Hence, assuming a v of 2×10^8 ms^{-1}, the worst-case signal propagation delay time, T_p, going from one end of the cable to the other, is given by:

$$T_p = l/v = 2.5 \times 10^3 / 2 \times 10^8 = 12.5 \text{ microseconds}$$

Now assume that, just prior to the first bit of the frame arriving at its interface, station B determines the transmission medium is free and starts to transmit a frame – part (ii).

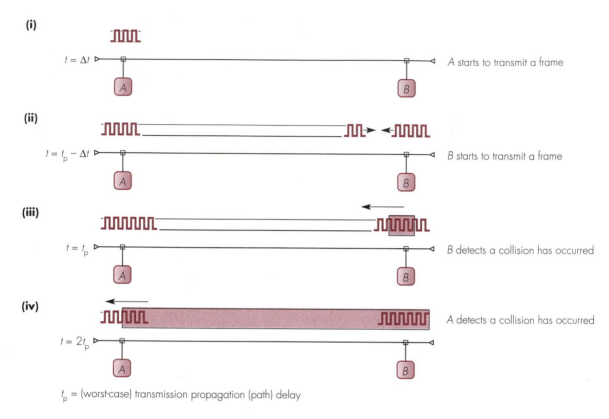

(i)

$t = \Delta t$ A   B   A starts to transmit a frame

(ii)

$t = t_p - \Delta t$ A   B   B starts to transmit a frame

(iii)

$t = t_p$ A   B   B detects a collision has occurred

(iv)

$t = 2t_p$ A   B   A detects a collision has occurred

t_p = (worst-case) transmission propagation (path) delay

Figure 8.1 CSMA/CD worst-case collision detection.

As we show, after B has transmitted just a few bits, the two signals collide – part (iii) – and the collision signal then continues to propagate back to station A – part (iv). Hence the worst-case time before station A detects that a collision has occurred, $2T_p$, is 25 microseconds. In addition, as we shall expand upon later, in order to transmit the signal over this length of cable, the cable is made up of five 500 m *segments*, all interconnected together by means of four devices called **repeaters**. Each repeater introduces a delay of a few microseconds in order to synchronize to each new frame. Hence the total worst-case time is set at 50 microseconds or, assuming a bit rate of 10 Mbps, after A has transmitted:

$$10 \times 10^6 \times 50 \times 10^{-6} = 500 \text{ bits}$$

A safety margin of 12 bits is then added to this and the minimum frame size is set at 512 bits or 64 bytes/octets. This is called the **slot time** (in bits) and ensures that station A will have detected a collision before it has transmitted its smallest frame. Also, to ensure that the collision signal persists for sufficient time for it to be detected by *A*, on detecting the collision, *B* continues to send a random bit pattern for a short period. This is known as the **jam sequence** and is equal to 32 bits.

After detecting a collision, the two (or more) stations involved then wait for a further random time interval before trying to retransmit their corrupted frames. As we shall explain later, the maximum frame size including a four-byte CRC is set at 1518 bytes and hence a collision will occur if two (or more) stations create a frame to send during the time another station is currently transmitting a maximum sized frame. This is equal to a time interval of:

$$1518 \times 8/10 \times 10^6 = 1.2144 \text{ milliseconds}$$

Clearly, the probability of this occurring increases with the level of traffic (number of frames) being generated and the maximum throughput of the LAN occurs when this limit is reached. Hence if a second collision should occur when a station is trying to send a frame, this is taken as a sign that the cable is currently overloaded. To avoid further loading the cable, therefore, the time interval between trying to retransmit a frame is increased exponentially after each new attempt is made using a process known as **truncated binary exponential backoff**. The actual time is a function of the slot time. The number of slot times before the *N*th retransmission attempt is chosen as a uniformly distributed random integer *R* in the range $0 \leq R < 2^K$, where $K = \min (N, \text{backoff limit})$. In the standard, the **backoff limit** is set to 10.

Wiring configurations

There are a number of different types of cable that can be used with Ethernet. These include:

- 10Base2: thin-wire (0.25 inch diameter) coaxial cable with a maximum segment length of 200 m;
- 10Base5: thick-wire (0.5 inch diameter) coaxial cable with a maximum segment length of 500 m.
- 10BaseT: hub (star) topology with twisted-pair drop cables of up to 100 m;
- 10BaseF: hub (star) topology with optical fiber drop cables of up to 1.5 km.

Although different types of cable are used, they all operate using the same CSMA/CD MAC method.

At the time the first Ethernet installations were carried out, the only transmission medium available that could operate at 10 Mbps was coaxial cable. Initially, thick-wire coaxial cable was installed since this can be used in relatively long lengths of up to 500 m before the transmitted/broadcast signal needs to be repeated. As we explained in Section 6.3.1, this involves the attenuated signal received at the extremity of the cable segment being amplified and restored to its original form before it is retransmitted out onto the next cable segment. Up to five cable segments – and hence four repeaters – can be used in this way. Hence the maximum length of cable the signal propagates is 2.5 km plus 4 repeaters which is the origin of the slot-time figure used in the standard.

The disadvantage of thick-wire coax is that it is relatively difficult to bend and hence install. To overcome this, thin-wire coax was used but, because of the increased (electrical) resistance associated with it, the maximum length of cable for each segment is reduced to 200 m.

More recently, as we explained in Section 6.2.2, with the arrival of inexpensive adaptive crosstalk canceler circuits to overcome near-end crosstalk (NEXT), it is possible to obtain bit rates of tens of Mbps over twisted-pair cable of up to 100 m in length. Also, it was found that, in a vast majority of offices, the maximum length of cable used for telephony to reach each desktop from the wiring closet was less than 100 m. Hence unshielded twisted-pair (UTP) cable – as used for telephony – has rapidly become the standard for use with Ethernet. The configuration used for each segment is shown in Figure 8.2(a).

Since the cable forms a physical bus, both thick and thin wire coaxial cable installations involve the cable passing near to each attached station. As we can see in the figure, however, with twisted-pair cable a star configuration is used with the hub located in the wiring closet and each station connected to it by means of twisted-pair drop cables. Normally, category three (CAT3) UTP cable is used as for telephony. Each cable contains four separate twisted-pairs. In the case of Ethernet, just two pairs are used: one pair for transmissions from the station to the hub and the second pair for transmissions in the reverse direction.

To emulate the broadcast mode of working associated with CSMA/CD, as we show in Figure 8.2(b), the repeater electronics within the hub repeats and broadcasts out the signal received from each of the input pairs onto all of the other output pairs. Hence the signal output by any of the stations is received by all the other stations and, as a result, the carrier sense function simply involves the MAC unit within each station determining whether a signal is currently being received on its input pair. Similarly, the collision detection function involves the station determining if signal arrives on its input pair while it is transmitting a frame on the output pair.

Because of their mode of operation, this type of hub is called a **repeater hub** and typical numbers of attached stations – and hence sockets – are from 8 through to 16. Above this number multiple hubs are stacked together and are connected by repeaters or, as we shall explain in Section 8.5, bridges. In the case of repeaters, the maximum length of cable between any two stations – including the 100 m drop cables – must not exceed 1.5 km. To achieve this coverage/distance, however, normally it is necessary to use a central hub to which each twisted-pair hub is connected by means of optical fiber cables.

(a)

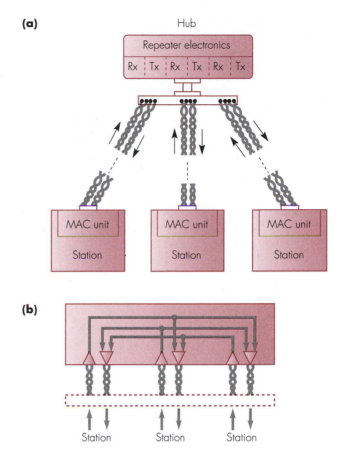

Figure 8.2 Hub configuration principles: (a) topology; (b) repeater schematic.

Frame format and operational parameters

The format of a frame and the operational parameters of a CSMA/CD network are shown in Figure 8.3. The *preamble* field is sent at the head of all frames. Its function is to allow the receiving electronics in each MAC unit and repeater to achieve bit synchronization before the actual frame contents are received. The preamble pattern is a sequence of seven bytes, each equal to the binary pattern 10101010. All frames are transmitted on the cable using Manchester encoding. Hence, as we explained in Section 6.5.1, the preamble results in a periodic waveform being received by the receiver electronics in each DTE which acts as a reference clock. The *start-of-frame delimiter* (*SFD*) is the single byte 10101011 which immediately follows the preamble and signals the start of a valid frame to the receiver.

(a)

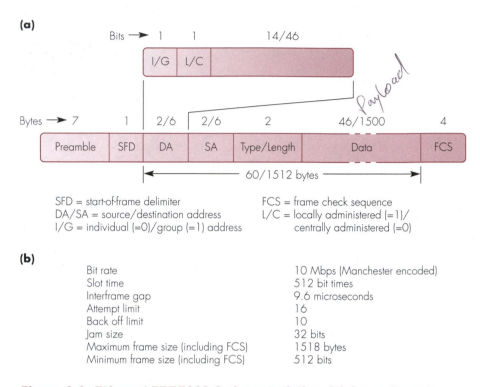

SFD = start-of-frame delimiter
DA/SA = source/destination address
I/G = individual (=0)/group (=1) address

FCS = frame check sequence
L/C = locally administered (=1)/
centrally administered (=0)

(b)

Bit rate	10 Mbps (Manchester encoded)
Slot time	512 bit times
Interframe gap	9.6 microseconds
Attempt limit	16
Back off limit	10
Jam size	32 bits
Maximum frame size (including FCS)	1518 bytes
Minimum frame size (including FCS)	512 bits

Figure 8.3 Ethernet/IEEE802.3 characteristics: (a) frame format; (b) operational parameters.

The *destination* and *source addresses* – also known as **MAC addresses** because they are used by the MAC sublayer – specify the identity of the hardware interface of both the intended destination station(s) and the originating station, respectively. Each address field can be either 16 or 48 bits, but for any particular LAN installation the size must be the same for all stations. The first bit in the destination address field specifies whether the address is an **individual address (=0)** or a **group address (=1)**. If an individual address is specified, the transmitted frame is intended for a single destination. If a group address is specified, the frame is intended either for a logically related group of stations (group address) or for all other stations connected to the network (**broadcast** or **global address**). In the latter case, the address field is set to all binary 1s and, for a group address, the address specifies a previously agreed group of stations. The type of grouping is specified in the second bit and can be locally administered (=1) or centrally administered (=0). Group addresses are used for multicasting and the MAC unit/circuit associated with each station in the multicast group is then programmed to read all frames with this group address at its head.

With the original Ethernet standard, the two-byte *type* field immediately follows the address fields and indicates the network layer protocol that created the information in the data field. With the more recent IEEE802.3 format, the next two bytes are used as a *length indicator* which indicates the number of bytes in the data field. If this value is less than the minimum number required for a valid frame (minimum frame size), a sequence of bytes is added, known as **padding**. The maximum size of the data field – normally referred to as the **maximum transmission unit** (**MTU**) – is 1500 bytes. Finally, the *frame check sequence* (*FCS*) field contains a four-byte (32-bit) CRC value that is used for error detection. Note that with the original Ethernet standard, the end of a frame is detected when signal transitions end.

Frame transmission and reception

The frame transmission sequence is summariized in Figure 8.4(a). When a frame is to be transmitted, the frame contents are first encapsulated by the MAC unit into the format shown in Figure 8.3(a). To avoid contention with other transmissions on the medium, the MAC unit first monitors the carrier sense signal and, if necessary, defers to any passing frame. After a short additional delay (known as the **interframe gap**) to allow the passing frame to be received and processed by the addressed station(s), transmission of the frame is initiated.

As the bitstream is transmitted, the transmitter simultaneously monitors the received signal to detect whether a collision has occurred. Assuming a collision has not been detected, the complete frame is transmitted and, after the FCS field has been sent, the MAC unit awaits the arrival of a new frame, either from the cable or from the LC sublayer within the station. If a collision is detected, the transmitter immediately turns on the collision detect signal and enforces the collision by transmitting the jam sequence to ensure that the collision is detected by all other stations involved in the collision. After the jam sequence has been sent, the MAC unit terminates the transmission of the frame and schedules a retransmission attempt after a short randomly-computed interval.

Figure 8.4(b) summarizes the frame reception sequence. The MAC unit first detects the presence of an incoming signal and switches on the carrier sense signal to inhibit any new transmissions from this station. The incoming preamble is used to achieve bit synchronization and, when the start-of-frame delimiter has been detected, with an IEEE802.3 LAN, the length indicator is read and used to determine the number of bytes that follow. The frame contents including the destination and source addresses are then received and loaded into a frame buffer to await further processing. The received FCS field is first compared with the computed FCS and, if they are equal, the frame content is further checked to ensure it contains an integral number of bytes and that it is neither too short nor too long. If any of these checks fail then the frame is discarded. If all checks pass, then the destination address is read from the head of the frame and, if the frame is intended for this station – that is, the address of the station is the same as that in the frame or, if it is a group address, the station is a member of the specified group – the frame contents are passed to the LC sublayer for processing.

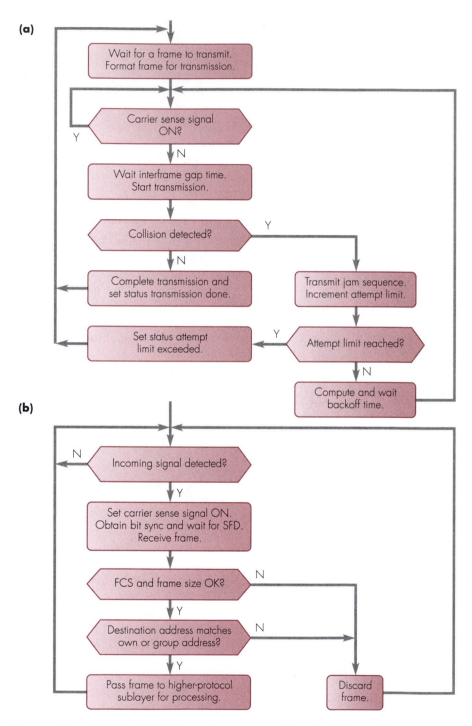

(a)

(b)

Figure 8.4 CSMA/CD MAC sublayer operation: (a) transmit; (b) receive.

8.4 Token ring

Token ring networks are also used in technical and office environments and, in addition, in industrial environments. As we can deduce from the previous section, with an Ethernet LAN the time to transmit a frame is nondeterministic since, during heavy load conditions when collisions are likely to be frequent, the transmission of a frame may be delayed and, in the limit, unsuccessful. Although in an office environment this is to a degree acceptable, in industrial environments such as manufacturing and process control, it is unacceptable. Hence although token ring LANs also use a high bit rate shared/broadcast transmission medium, in order to provide a deterministic service, they utilize a completely different MAC method.

Also, because the type of information – and hence frame contents – to be transmitted in an industrial application may have different levels of importance, frames can be assigned different priorities. The MAC method, therefore, also contains a priority control algorithm to ensure higher priority frames – for example those containing alarm messages – are transmitted before lower priority frames. We shall discuss this and other issues separately.

Control token

In a token ring LAN, all the stations are connected together by a set of unidirectional links in the form of a ring and all frame transmissions between any of the stations take place over it by circulating the frame around the ring. In its basic form, only one frame transfer can be in progress over the ring at a time. When the ring is first initialized, a single control token (frame) is generated and, in the absence of any frames to transmit, this continuously circulates around the ring. Then, when a station generates a frame to send, the steps taken by the MAC unit within each station are as illustrated in Figure 8.5.

Whenever a station wishes to send a frame, it first waits for the token. On receipt of the token, it initiates transmission of the frame, which includes the address of the intended recipient at its head. The frame is repeated (that is, each bit is received and then retransmitted) by all the stations in the ring until it circulates back to the initiating station, where it is removed. In addition to repeating the frame, each station reads and stores the frame contents. The intended recipient – indicated by the destination address in the frame header – retains a copy of the frame and indicates that it has done this by setting the response bits at the tail of the frame.

A station releases the token in one of two ways depending on the bit rate (speed) of the ring. With slower rings (4 Mbps), the token is released only after the response bits have been received. With higher speed rings (16 Mbps), it is released immediately after transmitting the last bit of the frame. This is known as **early** (**token**) **release** and, as we shall explain later, this is done to improve the level of utilization of the ring.

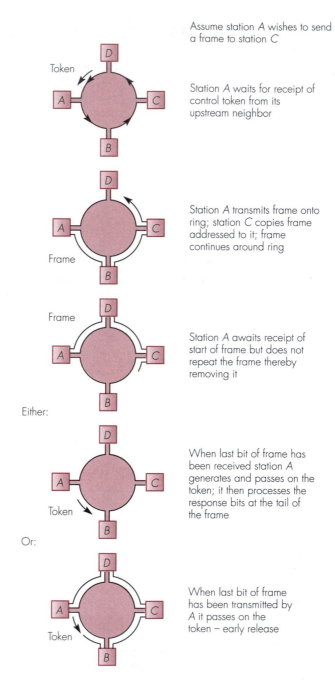

Assume station A wishes to send a frame to station C

Station A waits for receipt of control token from its upstream neighbor

Station A transmits frame onto ring; station C copies frame addressed to it; frame continues around ring

Station A awaits receipt of start of frame but does not repeat the frame thereby removing it

Either:

When last bit of frame has been received station A generates and passes on the token; it then processes the response bits at the tail of the frame

Or:

When last bit of frame has been transmitted by A it passes on the token – early release

Figure 8.5 Token ring network: principle of operation.

Wiring configurations

A small token ring network is shown in Figure 8.6(a). As we can see, in this configuration is a single hub – also known as a **concentrator** and located in, say, the wiring closet of an office – to which all the stations are attached by a cable containing two twisted-pairs, one for each direction of transmission. Within the hub, associated with each station is a **station coupling unit** (**SCU**) and, as we show in the figure, these are interconnected so that all the stations are interconnected together to form a unidirectional ring.

An SCU is shown in Figure 8.6(b) and, as we can see, it contains a set of relays and additional electronics to drive and receive signals to and from the cable. The relays are so arranged that whenever a station is switched off, the SCU is in the *bypassed state* and a continuous transmission path through the SCU is maintained. The insertion of a station into the ring is initiated when the station is switched on. A separate pair of wires in the drop cable is used to pass power from the station to the SCU and, when activated, the relays change position so that the station becomes inserted.

When the SCU is in the *inserted state*, all signals from the ring are routed through the MAC unit of the station. The receive/transmit electronics in the MAC unit then either simply read and relay (repeat) the received signal to the transmit side, if this station is not the originator of the frame, or remove the received signal from the ring, if it initiated the transmission.

The use of two pairs of relays connected in this way means that the MAC unit can detect certain open-circuit and short-circuit faults in either the transmit or the receive pair of signal wires. Also, in the bypassed state, the MAC unit can conduct self-test functions, since any data output on the transmit pair is looped back on the receive pair. Each station is connected to the SCU by a shielded twisted-pair (STP) cable containing three twisted-pair wires; one for transmission, the second for reception, and the third to supply power to the SCU.

As we show in Figure 8.6(c), larger configurations are formed by interconnecting multiple nodes/concentrators together by means of either an STP or optical fiber trunk cable. In this case, associated with each hub is a second relay unit known as a **trunk coupling unit** (**TCU**). This has the same function as an SCU except that the power to activate the relays – and hence insert the TCU and its attached stations into the ring – is from the power supply of the hub/concentrator. In this way, should a hub fail, the remainder of the ring will continue functioning.

Ring interface

The MAC unit in each station performs such functions as frame encapsulation and de-encapsulation, FCS generation and error detection, and the implementation of the MAC control algorithm. Associated with the ring is a single master station known as the **active ring monitor** that supplies the master clock for the ring. All stations are capable of performing this function and the active monitor is selected using a bidding process involving all the stations that are currently inserted into the ring.

(a)

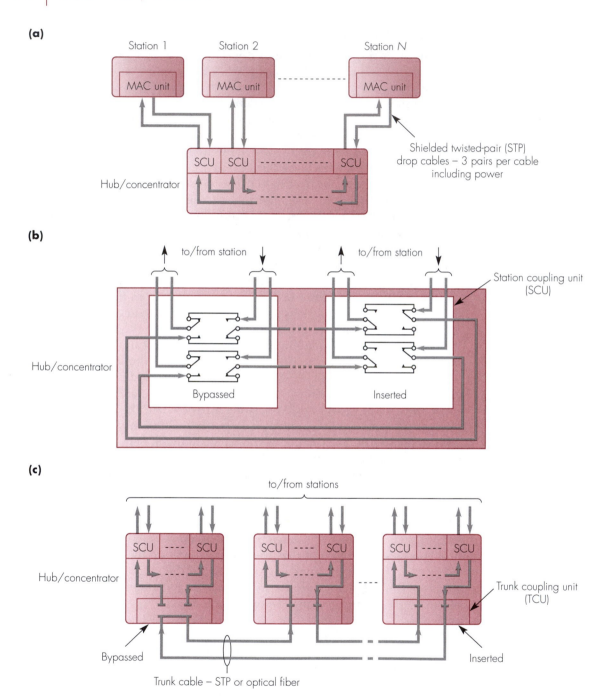

Figure 8.6 Token ring wiring configurations: (a) single hub; (b) station coupling unit; (c) multiple hubs/concentrators.

Each circulating bitstream is differential Manchester encoded by the active ring monitor and all other inserted stations in the ring frequency and phase lock their own clock using a DPLL and the incoming bitstream as we explained in Section 6.5.1. Hence there is only a small fraction of a bit delay in each ring interface as the repeater retransmits each bit as it is being received. In addition, when the station is the active ring monitor, it ensures the ring has a **minimum latency time**. This is the time, measured in bit times at the ring data transmission rate, taken for a signal to propagate once around the ring. The ring latency time includes the signal propagation delay through the ring transmission medium together with the sum of the delays through each MAC unit. For the control token to circulate continuously around the ring when none of the stations requires to use the ring (that is, all stations are simply in the repeat mode), the ring must have a minimum latency time of at least the number of bits in the token sequence to ensure that the token is not corrupted.

The token is 24 bits long, so when a station is the active ring monitor, its MAC unit provides a fixed 24-bit buffer, which effectively becomes part of the ring to ensure its correct operation under all conditions. Although the mean line signaling rate around the ring is controlled by a single master clock in the active monitor, the use of a separate DPLL circuit in each MAC unit means that the actual signaling rate may vary slightly around the ring. The worst-case variation is when the maximum number of stations (250) are all active, which is equivalent to plus or minus three bits. Unless the latency of the ring remains constant, however, bits will be corrupted as the latency decreases, or additional bits will be added as the latency increases. To maintain a constant ring latency, an additional **elastic (variable) buffer** with a length of six bits is added to the fixed 24-bit buffer. The resulting 30-bit buffer is initialized to 27 bits. If the received signal at the master MAC unit is faster than the master oscillator, the buffer is expanded by a single bit. Alternatively, if the received signal is slower, the buffer is reduced by a single bit. In this way the ring always comprises sufficient bits to allow the token to circulate continuously around the ring in the quiescent (idle) state.

Frame formats

In addition to the control token and information frames, additional frames are used for various ring management functions including the selection of an active ring monitor. Collectively, these are known as MAC frames.

Two basic formats are used in token rings: one for the control token and the other for normal frames. The control token is the means by which the right to transmit (as opposed to the normal process of repeating) is passed from one station to another, whereas a normal frame is used by a station to send either data or MAC information around the ring. The format of the two types of frame are given in Figure 8.7 together with the bit sequence used for each field.

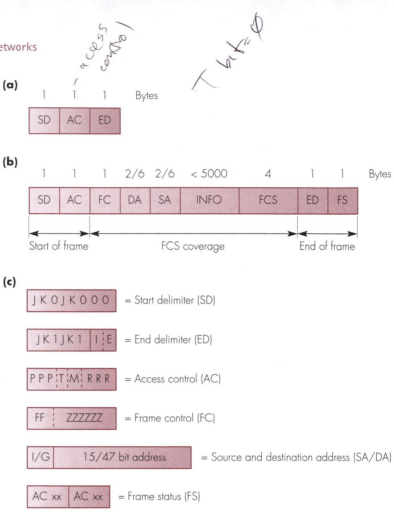

Figure 8.7 Token ring network frame formats and field descriptions: (a) token format; (b) frame format; (c) field descriptions.

The *start delimiter* (*SD*) and *end delimiter* (*ED*) fields are special bit sequences used to achieve data transparency. They exploit the symbol encoding method used on the cable medium: all information bits transmitted on the medium are differential Manchester encoded, except for selected bits in the SD and ED fields. In contrast, the J and K symbols depart from the normal encoding rules, being used instead to represent constant levels for the complete bit cell period. The J symbol has the same polarity as the preceding symbol, whereas a K symbol has the opposite polarity to the preceding symbol. In this way the receiver can reliably detect the start and end of each transmitted token or frame irrespective of its contents or length. Note, however, that only the first six symbols (JK1JK1 in Figure 8.7(c)) are used to indicate a valid end of frame. The other two bits, I and E, have other functions:

■ In a token, both the I- and E-bits are 0.

■ In a normal frame, the I-bit is used to indicate whether the frame is the first (or an intermediate) frame in a sequence (I = 1) or the last (or only) frame (I = 0).

■ The E-bit is used for error detection. It is set to 0 by the originating station but, if any station detects an error while receiving or repeating the frame (for example, FCS error), it sets the E-bit to 1 to signal to the originating station that an error has been detected.

The *access control* (*AC*) field comprises the priority bits, the token and monitor bits, and the reservation bits. As its name implies, the AC field is used to control access to the ring. When it is part of the token, the priority bits (P) indicate the priority of the token and hence which frames a station may transmit on receipt of the token. The token bit (T) discriminates between a token and an ordinary frame (0 indicates a token, 1 a frame). The monitor bit (M) is used by the active monitor to prevent a frame from circulating around the ring continuously. Finally, the reservation bits (R) allow stations holding high-priority frames to request (in either repeated frames or tokens) that the next token to be issued is of the requisite priority.

The *frame control* (*FC*) field defines the type of the frame (MAC or information) and certain control functions. If the frame type bits (F) indicate a MAC frame, all stations on the ring interpret and, if necessary, act on the control bits (Z). If it is an I-frame, the control bits are interpreted only by the stations identified in the destination address field. Both the *source* and *destination addresses* (*SA* and *DA*) are standard 16/48 bit MAC addresses.

The *information* (*INFO*) field is used to carry either user data or additional control information when included in a MAC frame. Although no maximum length is specified for the information field, it is limited in practice by the maximum time which a station is allowed to transmit a frame when holding the control token. A typical maximum length is 5000 bytes.

The *frame check sequence* (*FCS*) field is derived from a 32-bit CRC. Finally, the *frame status* (*FS*) field is made up of two fields: the address-recognized bits (A) and the frame-copied bits (C). Both the A- and C-bits are set to 0 by the station originating the frame. If the frame is recognized by one or more stations on the ring, the station(s) sets the A-bits to 1. Also, if it copies the frame, it sets the C-bits to 1. In this way, the originating station can determine whether the addressed station(s) is non-existent or switched off, is active but did not copy the frame, or is active and copied the frame.

Frame transmission

On receipt of a service request to transmit a block of data (which includes the destination address and the priority of the data as a parameter), the data is first encapsulated by the MAC unit into the standard format shown in Figure 8.7. The MAC unit awaits the reception of a token with a priority less than or equal to the priority of the assembled frame. Clearly, in a system that employs multiple priorities, a procedure must be followed to ensure that all stations have an opportunity to transmit frames in the correct order of priority. This procedure works as follows.

After formatting a frame and prior to receiving an appropriate token (that is, one with a priority less than or equal to the priority of the waiting frame), each time a frame or a token with a higher priority is repeated at the ring interface, the MAC unit reads the value of the reservation bits contained within the AC field. If these are equal to or higher than the priority of the waiting frame, the reservation bits are simply repeated unchanged. If they are lower, the MAC unit replaces the current value with the priority of the waiting frame. Then, assuming there are no other higher priority frames awaiting transmission on the ring, the token is passed on by the current owner (user) with this priority. On receipt of the token, the waiting MAC unit detects that the priority of the token is equal to the priority of the frame it has waiting to be transmitted. It therefore accepts the token by changing the token bit in the AC field to 1, prior to repeating this bit, which effectively converts the token to a start-of-frame sequence for a normal frame. The MAC unit then stops repeating the incoming signal and follows the converted start-of-frame sequence with the preformatted frame contents. While the frame contents are being transmitted, the FCS is computed and subsequently appended after the frame contents, before transmitting the end-of-frame sequence.

Once transmission of the waiting frame(s) has been started, the MAC unit stops repeating, thus removing the transmitted frame(s) after it has circulated the ring. In addition, the MAC unit notes the state of the A- and C-bits in the FS field at the tail of the frame(s) to determine whether the frame(s) has (have) been copied or ignored. It then generates a new token and forwards this on the ring to allow another waiting station to gain access to the ring. More than one frame may be sent on receipt of a usable token providing, firstly, that the priority of the other waiting frame(s) is greater than or equal to the priority of the token and, secondly, that the total time taken to transmit the other frame(s) is within a defined limit known as the **token holding time**. The default setting for the latter is 10 ms. The frame transmission operation is illustrated in Figure 8.8(a).

Frame reception

In addition to repeating the incoming signal/bitstream, the MAC unit within each active station on the ring detects the start of each frame by recognizing the special start-of-frame bit sequence. It then determines whether the frame should simply be repeated or copied. If the F-bits indicate that it is a MAC frame, the frame is copied and the C-bits are interpreted and, if necessary, acted upon. However, if the frame is a normal data-carrying frame and the DA matches either the station's individual address or relevant group address, the frame contents are copied into a frame buffer and passed on to the LC sublayer for further processing. In either case, the A- and C-bits in the frame status field at the tail of the frame are set accordingly prior to being repeated. The reception operation is shown in Figure 8.8(b).

(a)

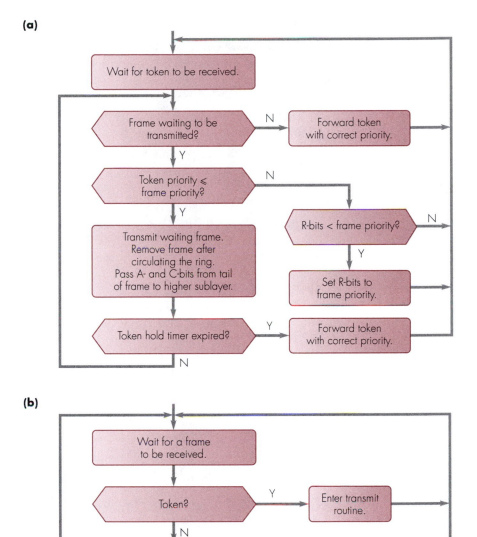

Figure 8.8 Token ring MAC sublayer operation: (a) transmit; (b) receive.

Priority operation

The priority assigned to a token by a MAC unit after it has completed transmitting any waiting frame(s) is determined by a mechanism that endeavors to ensure both of the following:

(1) Frames with a higher priority than the current ring service priority are always transmitted on the ring first.

(2) All stations holding frames with the same priority have equal access rights to the ring.

This is accomplished by using both the P- and the R-bits in the AC field of each frame coupled with a mechanism that ensures a station that raises the service priority level of the ring returns the ring to its original level after the higher priority frames have been transmitted.

To implement this scheme, each MAC unit maintains two sets of values. The first set comprises three variables Pm, Pr, and Rr. Pm specifies the highest priority value contained within any of the frames currently waiting transmission at the station. Pr and Rr are known as **priority registers** and contain, respectively, the priority and reservation values held within the AC field of the most recently repeated token or frame. The second set of values comprises two stacks known as the Sr and Sx stacks which are used as follows.

All frames transmitted by a station, on receiving a usable token, are assigned a priority value in the AC field equal to the present ring service priority Pr, and a reservation value of zero. After all waiting frames at or greater than the current ring priority have been transmitted, or until the transmission of another frame cannot be completed before the token holding time expires, the MAC unit generates a new token with:

(1) P = Pr   and R = the greater of Rr and Pm

if the station does not have any more waiting frames with a priority (as contained in register Pm) equal to or greater than the current ring service priority (as contained in register Pr), or does not have a reservation request (as contained in register Rr) greater than the current priority.

(2) P = the greater of Rr and Pm   and R = 0

if the station has another waiting frame(s) with a priority (as contained in Pm) greater than the current priority Pr, or if the current contents of Rr are greater than the current priority.

Since in the latter case the station effectively raises the service priority level of the ring, it becomes what is known as a **stacking station** and, as such, stores the value of the old ring service priority (Pr) on stack Sr and the new ring service priority (P) on stack Sx. These values are saved, as it is the responsibility of the station that becomes the stacking station to lower the ring service priority level when there are no frames ready to transmit, at any point on the ring, with a priority equal to or greater than the P stacked on Sx. Also, a stack is used rather than a single register because a stacking station may need to raise the service priority of the ring more than once before the service priority is returned to a lower priority level. The different values assigned to the P- and R-bits of the token and the actions performed on the two stacks are summarized in Figure 8.9(a).

Having become a stacking station, the MAC unit claims every token that it receives with a priority equal to that stacked on Sx to examine the

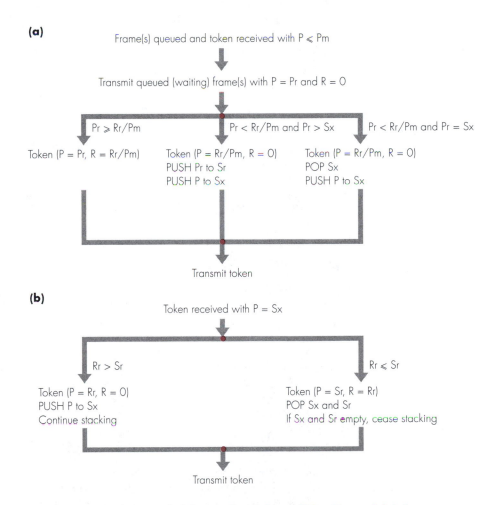

Figure 8.9 Token generation and stack modifications: (a) token generation [Note: Sx = 0 if stack empty]; (b) stack modification.

value in the R-bits of the AC field to determine if the service priority of the ring should be raised, maintained, or lowered. The new token is then transmitted with:

(1) P = Rr   and R = 0

if the value contained in the R-bits (the current contents of register Rr) is greater than Sr. The new ring service priority (P) is stacked (PUSHed) on to Sx and the station continues its role as a stacking station.

(2) P = Sr   and R = Rr (unchanged)

if the value contained in the R-bits is less than or equal to Sr. Both values currently on the top of stacks Sx and Sr are POPped from the stack and, if both stacks are then empty, the station discontinues its role as a stacking station. These two operations are summarized in Figure 8.9(b).

Example 8.1

A token ring network has been configured to operate with four priority classes: 0, 2, 4, and 8, with 8 the highest priority. After a period of inactivity when no transmissions occur on successive rotations of the token, four stations generate frames to send as follows:

Station 1	1 frame of priority 2
Station 7	1 frame of priority 2
Station 15	1 frame of priority 4
Station 17	1 frame of priority 4

Assuming the order of stations on the ring is in increasing numerical order and that station 1 receives the token first with a zero priority and reservation field, derive and show in table form the transmissions made by each station for the next eight rotations of the token. Include in your table the values in the priority and reservation fields both as each new token is generated and as each frame circulates around the ring. Also include the actions taken by the stacking station.

Answer:

The transmissions made by each station for the next eight rotations of the token are shown in Figure 8.10.

On the first rotation of the token, station 1 seizes the token and initiates the transmission of its waiting frame. Also on this rotation the reservation field in the frame is raised by station 7 to 2 and then by station 15 to 4.

8.1 Continued

On the second rotation, station 1 reads the reservation field from the frame and determines it must release the token with a priority of 4. Since it is raising the ring priority, it must become a stacking station and saves the current ring priority (0) on stack St and the new priority (4) on Sx. The token then rotates and is seized by station 15. Also on this rotation station 17 raises the reservation field from 0 to 4.

On the third rotation, station 15 releases the token with a priority and reservation field of 4. Station 17 therefore seizes the token and initiates the transmission of its waiting frame.

On the fourth rotation, station 7 updates the reservation field from 0 to 2 and this causes the token to be released by station 17 with the same priority (4) but a reservation value of 2.

On the fifth rotation, since station 1 is a stacking station, it detects Rr is greater than Sr and hence lowers the priority of the token/ring from 4 to 2 and saves the lower priority on the stack. Station 7 is therefore able to transmit its waiting frame.

On the sixth rotation, station 7 releases the token with the same priority since no reservations have been made.

On the seventh rotation, station 1 detects the reservation field in the token is less than the priority field and hence reduces the priority to 0 and thereby ceases to be a stacking station. The token has thus returned to its initial state and continues rotating until further frames are generated.

Ring management

We have been primarily concerned with the transmission of frames and tokens during normal operation of the ring. However, the ring must be set up before normal operation can take place. If a station wishes to join an already operational ring, the station must first go through an initialization procedure to ensure that it does not interfere with the correct functioning of the established ring. In addition, during normal operation it is necessary for each active station on the ring to monitor continuously its correct operation and, if a fault develops, to take corrective action to try to re-establish a correctly functioning ring. Collectively, these functions are known as **ring management**. A list of the various MAC frame types associated with these functions is given in Table 8.1 and a summary of the role of each function follows.

Initialization: When a station wishes to become part of the ring after being either switched on or reset, it enters an initialization sequence to ensure that no other stations in the ring are using the same address and to inform its immediate downstream neighbor that it has (re)entered the ring.

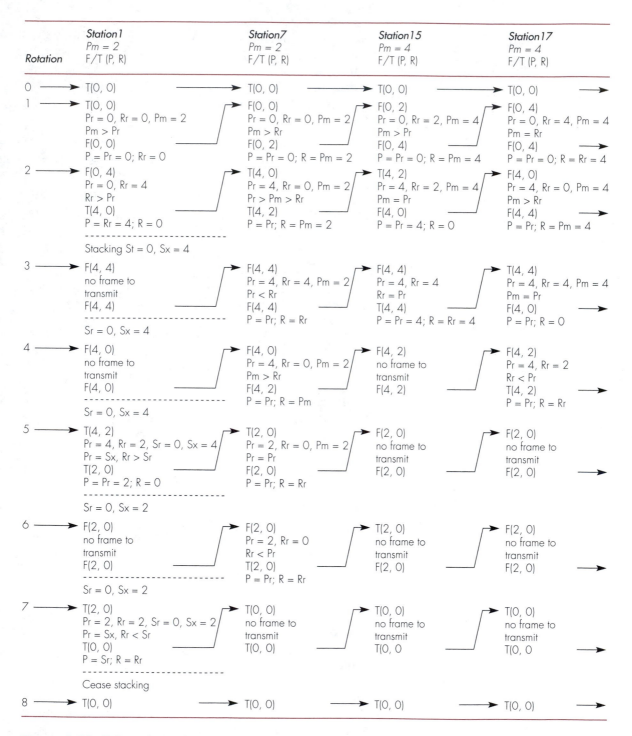

Figure 8.10 Token ring priority example.

Table 8.1 Token ring management: MAC frame types.

Frame type	Function
Duplicate address test (DAT)	Used during the initialization procedure to enable a station to determine that no other stations in the ring are using its own address
Standby monitor present (SMP)	Used in the initialization procedure to enable a station to determine the address of its upstream neighbor (successor) in the ring
Active monitor present (AMP)	These types of frames are transmitted at regular intervals by the currently active monitor and each station monitors their passage
Claim token (CT)	Used in the procedure to determine a new active monitor if the current one fails
Purge (PRG)	Used by a new active monitor to initialize all stations into the idle state
Beacon (BCN)	Used in the beaconing procedure

Standby monitor: Upon completion of the initialization sequence, the station can start to transmit and receive normal frames and tokens. In addition, the station enters the standby monitor state to monitor continuously the correct operation of the ring. It does this by monitoring the passage of tokens and special active monitor present (AMP) MAC frames – which are periodically transmitted by the currently active monitor – as they are repeated at the ring interface.

Active monitor: If the station is successful in its bid to become the new active monitor, it first inserts its latency buffer into the ring and enables its own clock. It then initiates the transmission of a purge (PRG) MAC frame to ensure that there are no other tokens or frames on the ring before it initiates the transmission of a new token.

Beaconing: If a serious failure such as a broken cable arises in the ring, a procedure known as beaconing informs each station on the ring that the token-passing protocol has been suspended (until the affected failure domain has been located and repaired). The failure domain consists of the following:

- the station that reports the failure, which is referred to as the **beaconing station**;
- the station upstream of the beaconing station;
- the ring medium between them.

We can see that the MAC procedures used with a token ring network are quite complicated, certainly compared with a CSMA/CD bus, for example. Remember, however, that most of the procedures are implemented in special integrated circuits within the MAC unit, so their operation is transparent to the user. Moreover, many of these ring management procedures are invoked only when faults develop and so the overheads associated with them are, on the whole, modest.

8.5 Bridges

There are two types of bridge, the ones that are used with Ethernet LANs, known as **transparent bridges**, and the others with token ring **LANs**, known as **source routing bridges**. Before we explain their operation, however, it will be helpful first to review the operation of repeaters since bridges were designed to overcome the limitations that occur when using repeaters.

Repeaters are used to ensure that the electrical signal transmitted by the line drivers within the MAC unit propagate throughout the network. For each LAN segment, in order to limit the signal attenuation to an acceptable level, there is a defined maximum limit set on the physical length of the segment and on the number of (end) stations that may be attached to it. When interconnecting segments, a repeater is used to limit the electrical drive requirements of the line driver circuit to that of a single segment. In this way, the presence of multiple segments (and hence repeaters) in a transmission path is transparent to the source station. The repeater, after achieving clock synchronization, simply regenerates all signals received on one segment and forwards (repeats) them onto the next segment. This form of interconnection is shown in Figure 8.11(a) and, as we can deduce from the figure, all frame transmissions from any station attached to a segment will propagate throughout the total LAN and hence be received by all the other attached stations. This means, therefore, that in terms of available bandwidth, the network behaves like a single segment.

In early LAN installations, because most traffic was text-based email and occasional file transfers, this mode of operation gave an acceptable performance in terms of network access and transfer delays. With the arrival of diskless nodes/stations, however, all disk accesses to the server are via the network and hence the demands on the network bandwidth are substantially higher. In most cases, the server and the set of diskless nodes it serves are all attached to the same LAN segment. Hence there is no necessity for the frames associated with such transfers to be transmitted beyond the segment on which they are generated. Bridges were introduced, therefore, to inhibit the forwarding of such frame transfers and only to forward those frames that are intended for a different segment.

Thus, the function of a bridge is similar to a repeater in that it is used for interconnecting LAN segments. However, when bridges are used, all frames

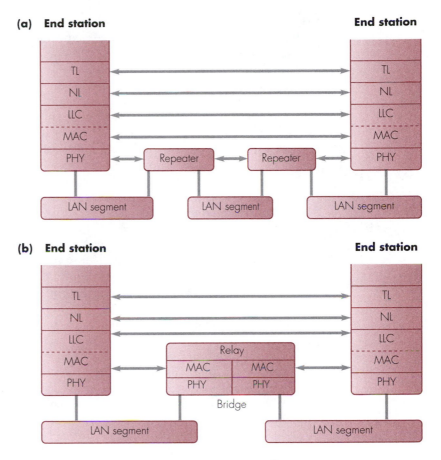

Figure 8.11 LAN interconnection: (a) repeaters; (b) bridges.

received from a segment are buffered (stored) and error checked before they are repeated (forwarded). Moreover, only frames that are free of errors and are addressed to stations on a different segment from the one on which they were received are forwarded. Consequently, all transmissions between stations connected to the same LAN segment are not forwarded and hence do not load the rest of the network. A bridge thus operates at the MAC sublayer in the context of our reference model. This is shown in Figure 8.11(b) and the resulting LAN is then referred to as a **bridged LAN**.

8.5.1 Transparent bridges

With a transparent bridge, as with a repeater, the presence of one (or more) bridges in a route between two communicating stations is transparent to the two stations. All routing decisions are made exclusively by the bridge(s). Moreover, a transparent bridge automatically initializes and configures itself (in terms of its routing information) in a dynamic way after it has been put into service. A schematic of a bridge is shown in Figure 8.12(a) and a simple bridged LAN in Figure 8.12(b).

A LAN segment is physically connected to a bridge through a **bridge port**. A basic bridge has just two ports whereas a **multiport bridge** has a number of connected ports (and hence segments). In practice, each bridge port comprises the MAC integrated circuit chipset associated with the particular type of LAN segment – CSMA/CD, Ethernet – together with some associated port management software. The software is responsible for initializing the chipset at start-up – chipsets are all programmable devices – and for buffer management. Normally, the available memory is logically divided into a number of fixed-size units known as buffers. Buffer management involves passing a free buffer (pointer) to the chipset for onward transmission (forwarding).

Every bridge operates in the **promiscuous mode** which means it receives and buffers all frames received on each of its ports. When a frame has been received at a port and put into the assigned buffer by the MAC chipset, the port management software prepares the chipset for a new frame and then passes the pointer of the memory buffer containing the received frame to the **bridge protocol entity** for processing. Since two (or more) frames may arrive concurrently at the ports and two or more frames may need to be forwarded from the same output port, the passing of memory pointers between the port management software and the bridge protocol entity software is carried out via a set of queues.

As we shall describe later, each port may be in a number of alternative states and processing of received frames is carried out according to a defined protocol. The function of the bridge protocol entity software is to implement the particular bridge protocol being used.

Frame forwarding (filtering)

A bridge maintains a **forwarding database** (also known as a **routing directory**) that indicates, for each port, the outgoing port (if any) to be used for forwarding each frame received at that port. If a frame is received at a port that is addressed to a station on the segment (and hence port) on which it was received, the frame is discarded; otherwise it is forwarded via the port specified in the forwarding database. The normal routing decision involves a simple look-up operation: the destination address in each received frame is first read and then used to access the corresponding port number from the forwarding database. If this is the same as the port on which it was received, the frame is discarded, else it is queued for forward transmission on the segment associated with the accessed port. This process is also known as **frame filtering**.

Bridge learning

A problem with transparent bridges is the creation of the forwarding database. One approach is for the contents of the forwarding database to be created in advance and held in a fixed memory, such as programmable

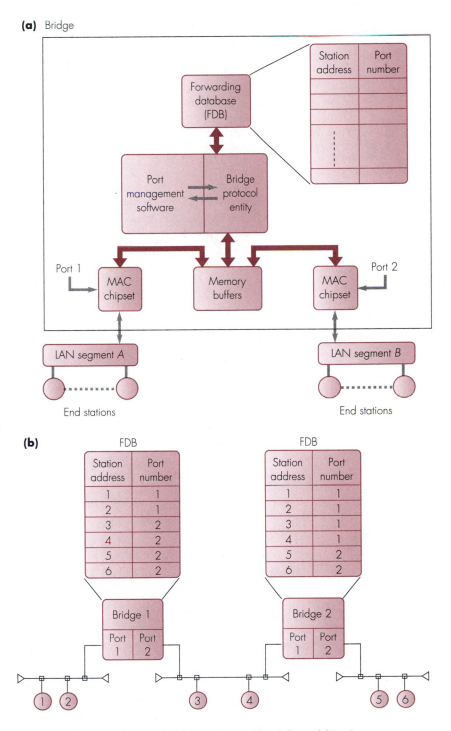

Figure 8.12 Transparent bridge schematic: (a) architecture; (b) application example.

read-only memory (PROM). The disadvantage is that the contents of the forwarding database in all bridges have to be changed whenever the network topology is changed – a new segment added, for example – or when a user changed the point of attachment (and hence segment) of his or her station. To avoid this, in most bridged LANs the contents of the forwarding database are not statically set up but rather are dynamically created and maintained during normal operation of the bridge. This is accomplished using a combination of a learning process and a dialog with other bridges to ascertain the topology of the overall installed LAN. An overview of the learning process is as follows.

When a bridge first comes into service, its forwarding database is initialized to empty. Whenever a frame is received, the *source address* within it is read and the incoming port number on which the frame was received is entered into the forwarding database. In addition, since the forwarding port is not known at this time, a copy of the frame is forwarded on all the other output ports of the bridge. As these frames propagate through the network, this procedure is repeated by each bridge. Firstly, the incoming port number is entered in the forwarding database against the source (station) address and a copy of the frame is forwarded on all the other output ports of the bridge. This action is referred to as **flooding** since it ensures that a copy of each frame transmitted is received on all segments in the total LAN. During the learning phase this procedure is repeated for each frame received by the bridge. In this way, all bridges in the LAN rapidly build up the contents of their forwarding databases.

This procedure works satisfactorily as long as stations are not allowed to migrate around the network (change their point of attachment) and the overall LAN topology is a simple tree structure (that is, there are no duplicate paths (routes) between any two segments). Such a tree structure is known as a **spanning tree**. Since in many networks, especially large networks, both these possibilities may occur, the basic learning operation is refined as follows.

The MAC address associated with a station is fixed at the time of its manufacture. If a user changes the point of attachment to the network of his or her PC/workstation, the contents of the forwarding database in each bridge must be periodically updated to reflect such changes. To accomplish this, an **inactivity timer** is associated with each entry in the database. Whenever a frame is received from a station within the predefined time interval, the timer expires and the entry is removed. Whenever a frame is received from a station for which the entry has been removed, the learning procedure is again followed to update the entry in each bridge with the (possibly new) port number. In this way the forwarding database in a bridge is continuously updated to reflect the current LAN topology and the addresses of the stations that are currently attached to the segments it interconnects. The inactivity timer also limits the size of the database since it contains only those stations that are currently active. This is important since the size of the database influences the speed of the forwarding operation.

The learning process works only if the total bridged LAN has a simple (spanning) tree topology. This means that there is only a single path between any two segments in the network. However, this condition may not always be met since additional bridges may be used to link two segments, for example, to improve reliability, or perhaps by mistake when a LAN is being updated.

Multiple paths between two segments cannot exist with the basic learning algorithm we have outlined since the flooding operation during the learning phase would cause entries in the forwarding database to be continuously overwritten. We can see this by considering the simple LAN topology shown in Figure 8.13. Clearly, if station 10 transmits a frame on segment 1 during the learning phase, then bridges B1 and B2 will both create an entry in their forwarding database – station 10/port 1 – and forward a copy of the frame onto segment 2. Each of these frames will in turn be received by the other bridge, and an entry will be made of station 10/port 2 and a copy of the frame output at port 1. In turn, each of these will be received by the other bridge, resulting in their corresponding entry for port 1 being updated. The frame will thus continuously circulate in a loop with the entries for each port being continuously updated.

Consequently, for topologies which offer multiple paths between stations, we need an additional algorithm to select just a single bridge for forwarding frames between any two segments. As we shall explain, this is done by setting

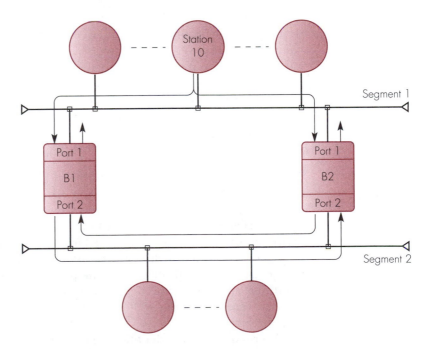

Figure 8.13 Effect of dual paths on learning algorithm.

selected bridge ports into the non-forwarding state and, in the topology in Figure 8.13, port 2 of bridge 2 would be selected. The resulting logical or **active topology** behaves as a single spanning tree and the algorithm is known as the **spanning tree algorithm**. Note that although the algorithm selects only a single port/bridge for connecting two segments – making redundant any alternative bridges that may have been introduced to improve reliability, for example – the algorithm is run at regular intervals and will dynamically select a set of bridges from those currently operational.

Spanning tree algorithm

With the spanning tree algorithm, all the bridges regularly exchange special frames (messages), known as **bridge protocol data units** (**BPDUs**). Each bridge has a priority value and a unique identifier. For the total bridged LAN, a single bridge is dynamically chosen by the spanning tree algorithm to be the **root bridge**. This is the bridge with the highest priority and the smallest identifier. It is determined/confirmed at regular intervals.

All the bridges in a LAN have a unique MAC group address which is used for sending all BPDUs between bridges. Also, the path cost associated with each bridge port is determined by the bit rate – known as the **designated cost** – of the segment to which it is attached; the higher the bit rate, the smaller the designated cost. All bridges know the designated cost of the segments to which they are attached.

When a bridge is first brought into service, it assumes it is the root bridge. A bridge that believes it is the root (all initially), initiates the transmission of a **configuration BPDU** on all of its ports (and hence the segments connected to it) at regular time intervals known as the **hello time**.

Each configuration BPDU contains a number of fields including:

- the identifier of the bridge which the bridge transmitting the BPDU believes to be the root (itself initially);
- the path cost to the root from the bridge port on which the BPDU was received (zero initially);
- the identifier of the bridge transmitting the BPDU;
- the identifier of the bridge port from which the BPDU was transmitted.

On receipt of a configuration BPDU, each bridge connected to the segment on which it was transmitted can determine, by comparing the identifier contained within it with its own identifier, firstly, whether the bridge has a higher priority or, if the priorities are equal, whether its own identifier is less than the identifier from the received frame. If this is the case, the receiving bridge will carry on assuming it is the root and simply discard the received frame.

Alternatively, if the identifier from the received BPDU indicates that it is not the root, the bridge proceeds by adding the path cost associated with the port on which the BPDU was received to that already within the frame. It then creates a new configuration BPDU containing this information, together with its own identifiers (bridge and port), and forwards a copy on all its other ports. This procedure is repeated by all bridges in the LAN. In this way the configuration BPDUs flood away from the root bridge to the extremities of the network and, at the same time, the path cost associated with each port of all the other bridges back to the root is computed. Thus, in addition to a single root bridge being established, all the other bridges will have determined the path cost associated with each of their ports. This is known as the **root path cost** (**RPC**) and the port that has the smallest RPC is then selected as the **root port** of the bridge. If two ports have the same RPC, the one with the lowest port number is chosen.

Once the root bridge and the root ports for the remaining bridges have been determined, the basis of the spanning tree has been established. The next step is to ensure that there are no loops/connections between the branches of the tree. This is done by selecting only a single bridge (port) to forward frames from each segment. This is known as the **designated bridge**. Its selection is based on the least path cost to the root bridge from the segment under consideration. If two bridge ports connected to a segment have the same path cost, the bridge with the smaller identifier is chosen. The bridge port connecting the segment to its designated bridge is known as the **designated port**. In the case of the root bridge, this is always the designated bridge for all the segments to which it is connected. Hence all its ports are designated ports.

When establishing the designated bridge port to be used with a segment, note that once a bridge port has been selected as a root port, it will not take part in the arbitration procedure to become a designated port. The choice of designated port is thus between the non-root ports connected to the segment under consideration.

The exchange of the configuration BPDUs between the two (or more) bridges involved will allow the two (or more) bridges to make a joint decision as to the port to be selected.

After the root bridge and the root and designated ports of all other bridges have been established, the state of the bridge ports can be set either to **forwarding** or to **blocking**. Initially, since all ports of the root bridge are designated ports, they are set to the forwarding state. For all the other bridges, only the root and designated ports are set to the forwarding state; the others are set to the blocking state. This establishes an active topology equivalent to a spanning tree. This procedure is then repeated at regular intervals (determined by the hello timer) to confirm the active topology or, in the event of a bridge failure, to reestablish a new topology.

Example 8.2

To illustrate how the various elements of the spanning tree algorithm work, consider the bridged LAN shown in Figure 8.14(a). The unique identifier of each bridge is shown inside the box representing the bridge together with the port numbers in the inner boxes connecting the bridge to each segment. Typically, the additional bridges on each segment are added to improve reliability in the event of a bridge failure. Also, assume that the LAN is just being brought into service, all bridges have equal priority, and all segments have the same designated cost (bit rate) associated with them. Determine the active (spanning tree) topology.

Answer:

(i)   First the exchange of configuration BPDUs will establish bridge B1 as the root bridge since this has the lowest identifier.

(ii) After the exchange of configuration BPDUs, the root path cost (RPC) of each port will have been computed. These are shown in Figure 8.14(b).

(iii) The root port (RP) for each bridge is then chosen as the port with the lowest RPC. For example, in the case of bridge B3, port 1 has an RPC of 1 and port 2 an RPC of 2, so port 1 is chosen. In the case of B2, both ports have the same RPC and hence port 1 is chosen since this has the smaller identifier. The selected RPs are also shown in the figure.

(iv) B1 is the root bridge so all its ports have a designated port cost (DPC) of 0. Hence they are the designated ports for segments S1, S2, and S3.

(v)   For S4, port 1 of B5 is an RP and hence is not involved in selecting the designated port. The two other ports connected to S4 both have a DPC of 1. Hence port 2 of B3 is selected as the designated port because it has a lower identifier than B4.

(vi) For S5, the only port connected to it is port 2 of B5 and hence this is selected.

(vii) Finally, for S6 both ports have a DPC of 1, so port 2 of B4 is selected rather than port 2 of B6.

The DPCs are shown in Figure 8.14(c) and the resulting active topology is thus as shown in Figure 8.14(d). Note that the DPC of a port is always equal to the RPC of the root port of the bridge.

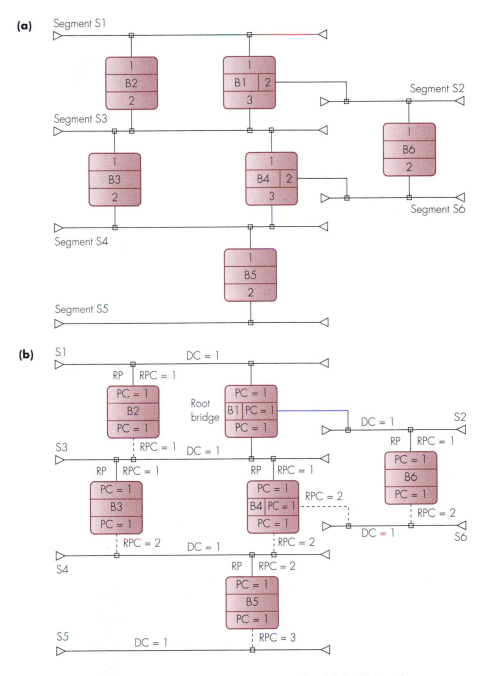

Figure 8.14 Active topology derivation example: (a) LAN topology; (b) root port selection; (c) designated port selection; (d) active topology.

(c)

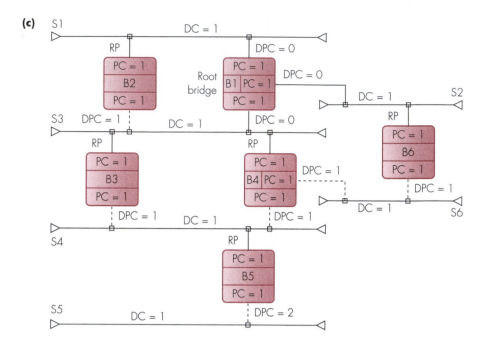

(d)

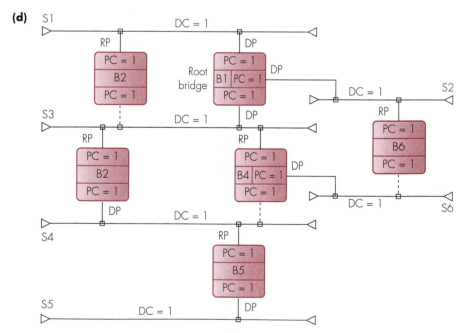

Figure 8.14 Continued.

8.5.2 Source routing bridges

Although we can use **source routing bridges** with any type of LAN segment, we use them primarily for the interconnection of token ring LAN segments. A typical network based on source routing bridges is shown in Figure 8.15(a).

The major difference between a LAN based on source routing bridges and one based on spanning tree bridges is that with the latter the bridges collectively perform the routing operation in a way that is transparent to the end stations. Conversely, with source routing, the end stations perform the routing function.

(a)

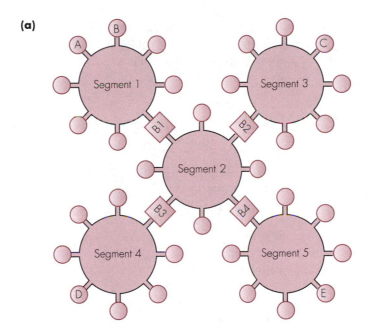

(b)   Routing table held by A: Destination B = Segment 1 (same segment)
                                                       C = Segment 1, B1, Segment 2, B2, Segment 3
                                                       |
                                                       |
                                                      E = Segment 1, B1, Segment 2, B4, Segment 5

          Routing table held by B: Destination A = Segment 1 (same segment)
                                                       |
                                                      |
                                                      D = Segment 1, B1, Segment 2, B3, Segment 4

          Routing table held by E: Destination A = Segment 5, B4, Segment 2, B1, Segment 1
                                                       |
                                                      |
                                                      C = Segment 5, B4, Segment 2, B2, Segment 3

Figure 8.15 **An example source routing bridged LAN: (a) topology; (b) routing table entries.**

With source routing, a station ascertains the route to be followed by a frame to each destination before any frames are transmitted. This information is inserted at the head of the frame and is used by each bridge to determine whether a received frame is to be forwarded on another segment or not. The routing information comprises a sequence of segment-bridge, segment-bridge identifiers. Routing tables for selected stations in the example network are shown in Figure 8.15(b).

On receipt of each frame, a bridge needs only to search the routing field at the head of the frame for its own identifier. Only if it is present and followed by the identifier of a segment connected to one of its output ports does it forward the frame on the specified LAN segment. Otherwise it is not forwarded. In either event, the frame is repeated at the ring interface by the bridge and, if forwarded, the address-recognized (A) and frame-copied (C) bits in the frame status (FS) field at the tail of the frame are set to indicate to the source station (bridge) that is has been received (forwarded) by the destination station (bridge).

Routing algorithm

The routing information field contained within each frame immediately follows the source address field at the head of the normal information frame. The modified frame format is thus as shown in Figure 8.16(a).

Since a routing information field is not always required – for example, if the source and destination stations are on the same segment – the first bit of the *source address* – the individual/group (I/G) address bit – is used to indicate whether routing information is present in the frame (1) or not (0). This can be done since the source address in a frame must always be an individual address, so the I/G bit is not needed for this purpose.

If routing information is present, its format is as shown in Figure 8.16(b). The *routing information* field consists of a *routing control* field and one or more *route designator* fields. The routing control field itself comprises three subfields: *frame type, maximum frame size,* and *routing field length.* In addition to normal information frames, two other frame types are associated with the routing algorithm. The frame type indicates the type of the frame.

Source routing bridges can be used for the interconnection of different types of LAN segments in addition to token rings. Since there is a different maximum frame size associated with each segment type, the *maximum frame size* field determines the largest frame size that can be used when transmitting a frame between any two stations connected to the LAN.

Prior to transmitting a route finding frame, a station sets the maximum frame size field to the (known) largest frame size that can be used in the total LAN. Before a bridge forwards the frame on a segment, the bridge checks this field with the (known) maximum frame size of the new segment. If the latter is smaller, the bridge reduces the frame size field to the lower value. In this way, the source station, on receipt of the corresponding route reply frame, can use this information when preparing frames for transmission to that destination.

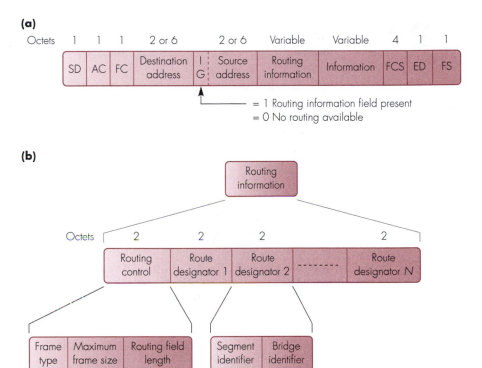

Figure 8.16 Token ring frame format: (a) position of routing information field; (b) structure of routing information field.

Since the number of segments (and bridges) traversed by a frame when going from a source to a destination may vary, the routing field length indicates the number of route designators present in the rest of the routing information field. Each route designator comprises a pair of segment and bridge identifiers.

The two additional frame types associated with the route finding algorithm are the **single-route broadcast frame** and the **all-routes broadcast frame**. To find a route, a station first creates and transmits a single-route broadcast frame with a zero routing field length and the maximum frame size set to the known largest value for the total LAN. As with spanning tree bridges, source routing bridges operate in the promiscuous mode and hence receive and buffer all frames at each of their ports. On receipt of a single-route broadcast frame, a bridge simply broadcasts a copy of the frame on each of the segments connected to its other ports. Since this procedure is repeated by each bridge in the LAN, a copy of the frame propagates throughout the LAN and is thus received by the intended destination station irrespective of the segment on which it is attached.

As we indicated earlier in Figure 8.13, if there are redundant bridges (and hence loops) in the LAN topology, multiple copies of the frame will propagate around the LAN. To prevent this, before any route finding frames are sent, the bridge ports are configured to give a spanning tree active topology. On the surface, this may appear to be the same procedure used with transparent bridges. With source routing bridges, however, the resulting spanning tree active topology is used only for routing the initial single-route broadcast frames. This ensures that only a single copy of the frame propagates through the network. The spanning tree active topology is not used for routing either normal information frames or the all-routes broadcast frame.

On receipt of a single-route broadcast frame, the required destination station returns an all-routes broadcast frame to the originating station. Unlike the single-route broadcast, this frame is not constrained to follow the spanning tree active topology at each intermediate bridge. Instead, on receipt of such frames, the bridge simply adds a new route designator field (comprising the segment identifier on which the frame was received and its own bridge identifier), increments the routing field length, and then broadcasts a copy of the frame on each of its other port segments.

In this way, one or more copies of the frame will be received by the originating source station via all the possible routes between the two stations. By examining the route designators in their routing control fields, the source station can select the best route for transmitting a frame to that destination. This route is then entered into its routing table and is subsequently used when transmitting any frames to that station.

Since the all-routes broadcast frame is not constrained to follow the spanning tree active topology, on receipt of such frames additional steps must be taken by each bridge to ensure that no frames are simply circulating in loops. Before transmitting a copy of the all-routes broadcast frame on an output segment, each bridge first searches the existing routing information in the frame to determine if the segment identifiers associated with the incoming and outgoing ports are already present together with its own bridge identifier. If they are, a copy of the frame has already been along the route, so this copy of the frame is not transmitted on the segment.

Note that it is not necessary to perform the route finding operation for each frame transmitted. Once a route to an intended destination has been determined and entered (cached) into the routing table of a station, this will be used for the transmission of all subsequent frames to that destination. Moreover, since most stations transmit the majority of their frames to a limited number of destinations, the number of route finding frames is relatively small compared with normal information frames for modest sized LANs.

Example 8.3

Assume the bridged LAN shown in Figure 8.17(a) is to operate using source routing. Also assume that all bridges have equal priority and all rings have the same designated cost (bit rate). Derive the following when station *A* wishes to send a frame to station *B*:

(i)   the active spanning tree for the LAN,

(ii) all the paths followed by the single-root broadcast frame(s),

(iii) all the paths followed by the all-routes broadcast frame(s),

(iv) the route (path) selected by *A*.

Answer:

(i)   (a)   Bridge B1 has the lowest identifier and is selected as the route.

      (b)   The root ports for each bridge are then derived as shown.

      (c)   The designated ports for each segment can now be derived and these are as shown.

      (d)   The active topology is as shown in Figure 8.17(b).

(ii) Paths of single-route broadcast frames:

$$R1{\rightarrow}B1{\rightarrow}R2{\rightarrow}B2{\rightarrow}R3$$
$$R2{\rightarrow}B3{\rightarrow}R5{\rightarrow}B6{\rightarrow}R6$$
$$R1{\rightarrow}B4{\rightarrow}R4{\rightarrow}B5$$

(iii) Paths of all-routes broadcast frames:

$$R6{\rightarrow}B6{\rightarrow}R5{\rightarrow}B3{\rightarrow}R2{\rightarrow}B2{\rightarrow}R3$$
$$B2{\rightarrow}B1{\rightarrow}R1$$
$$B1{\rightarrow}B4{\rightarrow}R4{\rightarrow}B5{\rightarrow}R5{\rightarrow}B3$$

(iv) Since each ring has the same bit rate, the route (path) selected is either:

$$R1{\rightarrow}B1{\rightarrow}R2{\rightarrow}B3{\rightarrow}R5{\rightarrow}B6{\rightarrow}R6$$

      or

$$R1{\rightarrow}B4{\rightarrow}R4{\rightarrow}B5{\rightarrow}R5{\rightarrow}B6{\rightarrow}R6$$

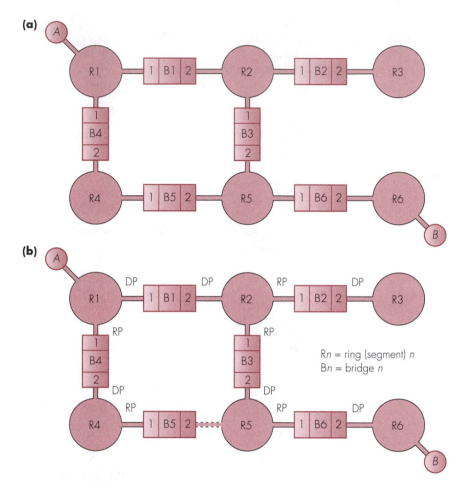

Figure 8.17 Source routing example: (a) topology; (b) spanning tree.

8.6 FDDI

As we explained in Section 8.2, in addition to bridges being introduced as a means of avoiding the traffic that is local to a segment from unnecessarily loading the entire LAN, backbone subnetworks were introduced to ensure the traffic that was forwarded between segments incurred only minimal delays. As an example, a small (but typical) establishmentwide LAN that includes bridges and backbone subnetworks is given in Figure 8.18.

Normally no end systems (workstations, servers, and so on) are connected to a backbone and they are used solely for intersegment traffic. For

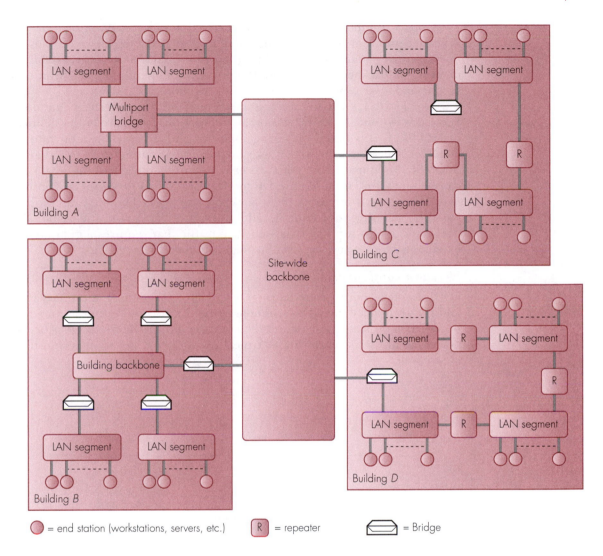

Figure 8.18 Typical establishmentwide LAN.

interconnecting only a small number of segments in a single building, backbones of the same type as the interconnected segments (CSMA/CD, or token ring) are used. They are known as **building backbones**.

As the number of interconnected segments increases, there comes a point at which the transmission bandwidth required by the backbone to meet the intersegment traffic starts to exceed that available with the basic LAN types. To overcome this problem, backbones based on newer high-speed LAN types are used. An example is the **fiber distributed data interface** (**FDDI**) **LAN**. This is an optical fiber-based ring network that supports a bit rate of

100 Mbps. It can be used for the interconnection of segments spread over a wider geographical area than a single building, such as a university campus or manufacturing plant. The resulting network is then known as an **establishment** or **site backbone**. We explain the principle of operation of FDDI in this section and some other high-speed LANs in Sections 8.7 and 8.8.

The FDDI LAN standard was developed by the American National Standards Institute (ANSI). It is now an international standard and is defined in ISO 9314. It is based on a ring topology and operates at a bit rate of 100 Mbps. Because of its role, it uses dual counter-rotating rings to enhance reliability. Multimode fiber connects each station together and the total ring can be up to 100 km in length. Up to 500 stations can be connected in the ring and hence it forms an ideal backbone network. The MAC method is based on a control token and, in addition to normal data traffic, optionally the ring can also support delay-sensitive traffic that requires a guaranteed maximum access delay; for example, digitized speech and video.

Network configuration

FDDI uses two counter-rotating rings to enhance reliability: the **primary ring** and the **secondary ring**. The secondary ring can be used either as an additional transmission path or purely as a back-up in the event of a break occurring in the primary ring. A typical network configuration is shown in Figure 8.19.

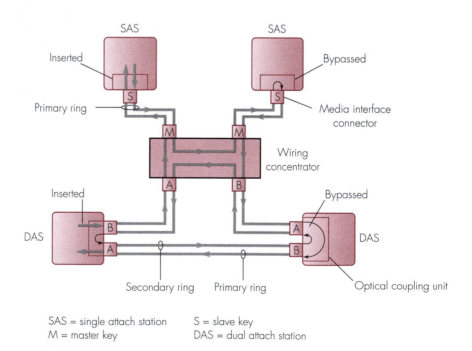

Figure 8.19 FDDI networking components.

As we can see, there are two types of station: a **dual attach station** (**DAS**) which is connected to both rings and a **single attach station** (**SAS**) which is attached only to the primary ring. In practice, most user stations are attached to the ring via **wiring concentrators** since then only a single pair of fibers is needed and the connection cost is lower.

If the LAN is being used as a backbone, then most attached stations are bridges. The protocol used to reconfigure the LAN into a single ring in the event of a ring failure is the same as the beaconing procedure associated with a token ring LAN. As we explained in Section 8.4, if a serious failure such as a broken cable arises in the ring, beacon MAC frames are issued by the station that detects the failure. Essentially, these are used to inform all other stations in the ring that the token-passing protocol has been suspended until the affected failure domain has been located and repaired. The failure domain consists of the station that detects the failure, its immediate upstream neighbor, and the ring segment in between them. The failure has deemed to be repaired when the station that issues the beacon frames starts to receive them after rotating around the ring; that is, on receipt of a beacon frame with its own MAC address at the head of the frame.

An example of a failure domain is shown in Figure 8.20(a) and a redundant ring configuration in Figure 8.20(b). In this example we assume a break has occurred in the ring segment between stations F and G. Hence G is the beaconing station and F its upstream neighbor. When a redundant ring is being used, the TCU not only supports the functions we explained in Section 8.4, but also the means to bypass a faulty ring segment or station. As an example, we show in Figure 8.20(c) how the faulty ring segment (failure domain) we identified in Figure 8.20(a) is bypassed.

Essentially, once the failure domain has been located and reported, the relays in the TCU of F and G are activated to (hopefully) re-establish a continuous ring. If isolating the suspected faulty segment does not remove the fault, the next step is to initiate the isolation of station G completely, as shown in Figure 8.20(d). Note from these illustrations that the redundant ring does not have a direct path to the MAC unit and simply provides a means of bypassing a section of the ring. The order of the stations in a re-established ring is the same as that in the original ring.

The basic fiber cable is **dual core** with **polarized duplex** (two-position) connectors at each end. This means that each end of the cable has a different physical key so that it can be connected into a matching socket only. This prevents the transmit and receive fibers from becoming inadvertently interchanged and bringing down the total network. As a further precaution, we use different connectors to connect each station type – SAS and DAS. In common with the basic token ring, we use special coupling units to isolate (bypass) a station when its power is lost. With FDDI, these are either active or passive fiber devices.

Although the topology is logically a ring, physically it is normally implemented in the form of a hub/tree structure. An example is shown in Figure 8.21(a). To ensure that changes to the wiring are carried out in a

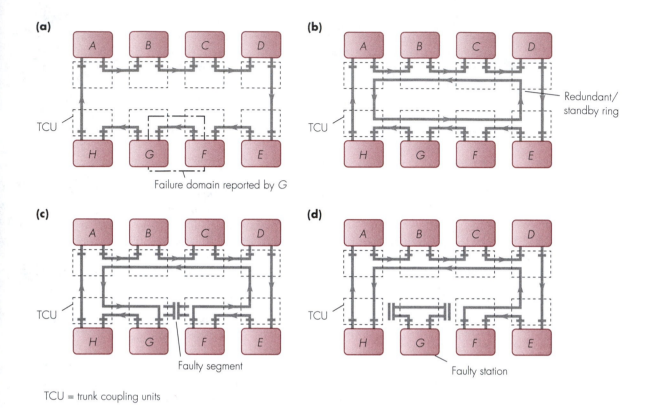

(a)

(b)

(c)

(d)

Failure domain reported by G

Redundant/standby ring

Faulty segment

Faulty station

TCU = trunk coupling units

Figure 8.20 Ring fault detection and isolation: (a) failure detection; (b) redundant ring configuration; (c) segment isolation; (d) station isolation.

controlled way, a combination of **patch panels** and **wiring concentrators** are used. Typically, these are located in the wiring closet associated with either a floor (if a local FDDI ring is being used) or a building (if the ring is a backbone). In the latter case, the patch panels are interconnected as shown in Figure 8.21(b) to create a tree structure to connect each station – high-speed servers or bridges – to the ring.

Each patch panel has a number of possible attachment points associated with it. In the absence of a connection at a particular point, the ring is maintained using short **patch cables**, each with the same type of connector. Adding a new station or concentrator simply involves removing a patch cable and replacing it with a corresponding drop cable. This approach is known as **structured wiring**.

Physical interface

The physical interface to the fiber cable is shown in Figure 8.22. In a basic token ring network, at any instant, there is a single active ring monitor which,

(a)

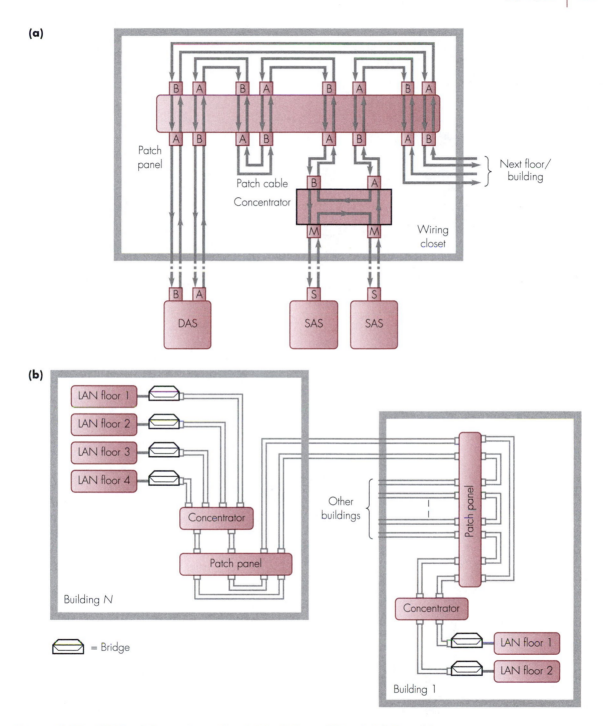

Figure 8.21 FDDI wiring schematic: (a) building; (b) establishment.

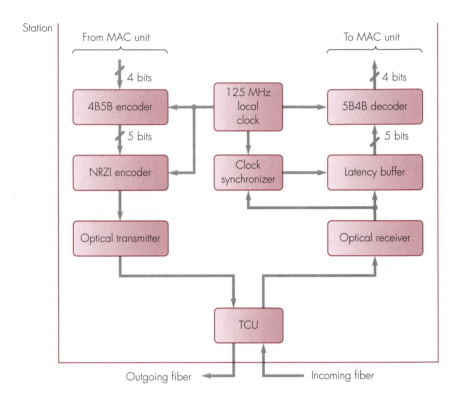

Figure 8.22 FDDI physical interface schematic.

among other things, supplies the master clock for the ring. Each circulating bitstream is encoded by the active ring monitor using differential Manchester encoding. All the other stations in the ring then frequency and phase lock to the clock extracted from this bitstream. However, such an approach is not suitable at the bit rates of an FDDI ring since this would require a signaling rate of 200 Mbaud. Instead, each ring interface has its own local clock. Outgoing data is transmitted using this clock while incoming data is received using a clock that is frequency and phase locked to the transitions in the incoming bitstream. As we shall see, all data is encoded prior to transmission so that there is a guaranteed transition in the bitstream at least every two bit cell periods, ensuring that each received bit is sampled (clocked) very near to the nominal bit cell center.

All data to be transmitted is first encoded, prior to transmission, using a **4 of 5 group code**. This means that for each 4 bits of data to be transmitted, a corresponding 5-bit codeword or symbol is generated by what is known as a **4B5B encoder**. The 5-bit symbols corresponding to each of the sixteen possible 4-bit data groups are shown in Figure 8.23(a). As we can see, there is a maximum of two consecutive zero bits in each symbol. The symbols are then shifted

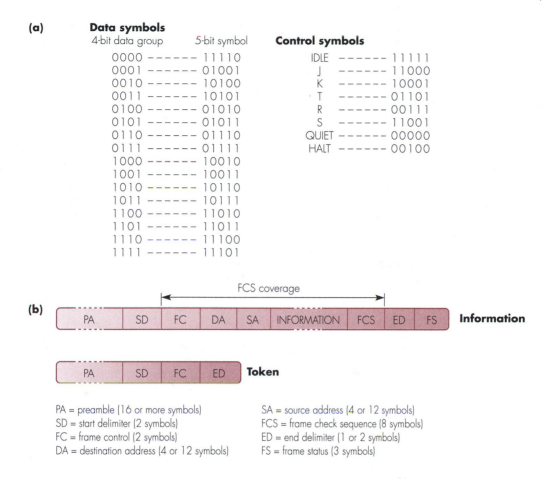

Figure 8.23 FDDI line coding and framing detail: (a) 4B5B codes; (b) frame formats.

out through a further NRZI encoder which produces a signal transition whenever a 1 bit is being transmitted and no transition when a 0 bit is transmitted. In this way, there is a guaranteed signal transition at least every two bits.

The use of 5 bits to represent each of the sixteen 4-bit data groups means that there are a further sixteen unused combinations of the 5 bits. Some of these combinations (symbols) are used for other (link) control functions, such as indicating the start and end of each transmitted frame or token. A list of the link control symbols is shown in Figure 8.23(a) and part (b) shows the format used for frames and tokens. In general, the meaning and use of each field is the same as with the basic token ring but, because symbols are used rather than bits, there are some differences in the structure of each field.

The *preamble* (*PA*) field consists of 16 or more IDLE symbols which, since they each consist of five 1 bits, cause the line signal to change at the maximum frequency. The line signal transitions are used for establishing (and maintaining) clock synchronization at the receiver. The *start delimiter* (*SD*) field consists of two control symbols (J and K) which enable the receiver to interpret the following frame contents on the correct symbol boundaries. The *FC, DA,* and *SA* fields have the same meaning as before, but the (decoded) information field in the data frames can be up to 4500 octets with FDDI. The *end delimiter* (*ED*) field contains one or two control symbols (*T*). Finally, the frame status (*FS*) field, although it has a similar function to the FS field in the basic ring, consists of three symbols that are combinations of the two control symbols R and S.

The local clock used in the physical interface is 125 MHz which, because of 4B5B encoding, yields a data rate of 100 Mbps and a signaling rate of 125 Mbaud. Since all transmissions are encoded into 5-bit symbols, each 5-bit symbol must first be buffered at the receiver before it can be decoded. However, the use of two symbols (J and K) for the SD field to establish correct symbol boundaries means that a 10-bit buffer is used at the receiver. This is known as the **latency** (or elastic) **buffer** since it introduces 10 bits of delay – latency – into the ring. At 125 Mbaud, this is equivalent to a delay of 0.08 µs

---

Example 8.4

Assuming a signal propagation delay in the fiber of 5 µs per 1 km, derive the latency of the following FDDI ring configurations in both time and bits assuming a usable bit rate of 100 Mbps.

(i)   2 km ring with 20 stations,

(ii) 20 km ring with 200 stations,

(iii) 100 km ring with 500 stations.

Answer:

Ring latency, T_1 = Signal propagation delay, T_p + N × station latency, T_s where N is the number of stations.

(i) $T_1 = 2 \times 5 + 20 \times 1$

$= 30 \,µs$ or 3000 bits

(ii) $T_1 = 20 \times 5 + 200 \times 1$

$= 300 \,µs$ or 30000 bits

(iii) $T_1 = 100 \times 5 + 500 \times 1$

$= 1000 \,µs$ or 100000 bits

Note that the above values assume that the primary ring only is in use. If a fault occurred, the three signal propagation delay values would each be doubled. Also, for dual attach stations, the station latency would be doubled.

but, allowing for additional gate and register transfer delays, this is normally rounded up to 1 µs per ring interface.

Frame transmission and reception

The short latency time (and hence number of bits in circulation) of the basic token ring means that a station, after initiating the transmission of an information frame, can wait until the FS field at the tail of the frame has been received before transmitting a new token without any noticeable loss in ring utilization. However, from Example 8.4 we can deduce that with an FDDI ring the loss in ring utilization will be significant if this mode of operation is adopted. With an FDDI ring, therefore, the early token release method is utilized; that is, a new token is transmitted immediately after the station has transmitted the FS symbol at the tail of a frame. The station then follows the token with IDLE symbols until it receives the SD symbols indicating the start of a new frame or token. The basic scheme is shown in Figure 8.24.

As we can see, as with the basic token ring, the source station removes a frame after it has circulated the ring. However, because of the long latency of an FDDI ring, more than one frame may be circulating around the ring at one time. Although not shown in Figure 8.24, the ring interface must repeat the SD, FC, and DA fields (symbols) of any received frames before it can determine if its own address is in the SA field. This can result in one or more frame fragments – comprising SD, FC, and DA fields – circulating around the ring. This means that a station, on receipt of the token, starts to transmit a waiting frame and concurrently receives and discards any frame fragments that may be circulating around the ring.

Timed token rotation protocol

Unlike the transmission control method used with the basic token ring – which is based on the use of the priority and reservation bits in the access control field of token and information frames – an FDDI ring uses a scheme that is based on a timed token rotation protocol that is controlled by a preset parameter known as the **target token rotation time** (**TTRT**).

For each rotation of the token, each station computes the time that has expired since it last received the token. This is known as the **token rotation time** (**TRT**) and includes the time taken by a station to transmit any waiting frames plus the time taken by all other stations in the ring to transmit any waiting frames for this rotation of the token. Clearly, if the ring is lightly loaded then the TRT is short but, as the loading of the ring increases, so the TRT measured by each station increases also. The TRT is thus a measure of the total ring loading.

The timed token rotation protocol ensures access to the ring is shared fairly between all stations by allowing a station to send any waiting frames only if its measured TRT is less than the preset TTRT for the ring. Hence, when a station has frames waiting to send, on receipt of the token it computes the difference between the TTRT and its current TRT. This is known as the **token hold time** (**THT**) since it determines for how long the station may transmit

Assume station A has a frame waiting to send to station C and station B has a frame waiting to send to station D

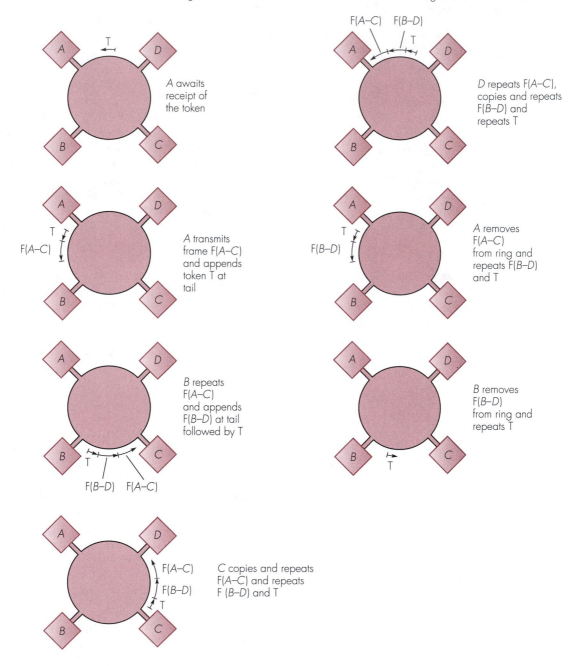

Figure 8.24 FDDI transmission example.

waiting frames before releasing the token. If the THT is positive, then the station can transmit for up to this interval. If it is negative, then the station must forego transmitting any waiting frames for this rotation of the token. A positive THT is thus known as an **early token** while a negative THT is known as a **late token**.

Example 8.5

The timed token rotation protocol is to be used to control access to a four-station FDDI ring network. All frames to be transmitted are of the same length and the TTRT to be used is equivalent to the transmission of four frames plus any ring latency. After an idle period when no frames are ready to send, all four stations receive a block of frames to send. Assuming the time for the token to rotate around the ring in the idle state is equal to the time to transmit the token, T_t, plus the ring latency T_1, derive and show in table form the number of frames each station can transmit for the next four rotations of the token.

Answer:

The number of frames that each station can transmit on the first four rotations of the token are shown in diagrammatic form in Figure 8.25. They are derived as follows.

After the idle period, the TRT of all stations will be $T_t + T_1$ since no frames have been transmitted. Once frames become ready to send, on receipt of the token station 1 computes a THT of 4 and hence transmits (XMIT) four waiting frames before passing on the token. However, since station 1 has sent four frames, none of the other stations is able to send any frames for this rotation of the token. This is so since their TRT is now greater than 4 in each case and hence their corresponding computed THT is negative.

On the second rotation of the token, the TRT of station 1 has incremented to 4 plus the ring latency, hence it is not able to send any waiting frames. This means that the TRT of station 2 is less than the TTRT and the computed THT is again 4 hence it can send four waiting frames. Again this will block stations 3 and 4 from sending any waiting frames on this rotation of the token.

On the third rotation of the token, the THT of stations 1 and 2 are both 4 plus the ring latency and hence neither can send frames. The TRT of station 3, however, is this time less than the TTRT and the computed THT is 4 hence it can transmit four waiting frames. Again station four is blocked.

Finally, on the fourth rotation of the token, stations 1, 2, and 3 are still all blocked and station 4 can transmit four frames. This simple example shows that the available transmission capacity is shared in an equitable way between all four stations.

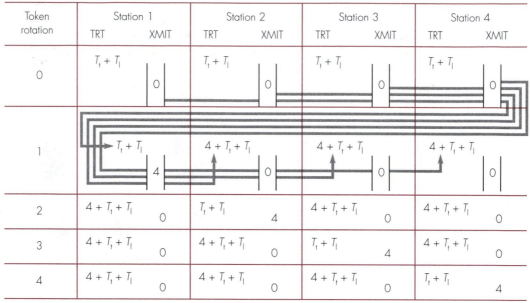

TRT = token rotation time
XMIT = number of frames transmitted on this rotation of the token
TTRT = target token rotation time

T_t = time to transmit the token
T_l = ring latency
TTRT = $4 + T_t + T_l$

Figure 8.25 FDDI timed token rotation protocol example.

Performance

There are two important performance measures associated with shared-medium networks: the **maximum obtainable throughput** and the **maximum access delay**. Both are strongly influenced by the MAC algorithm used to share the available transmission capacity between the attached stations. As we have just seen, in the case of an FDDI ring this is based on the use of a control token and the timed token rotation protocol. The important parameter associated with the protocol is the TTRT and, since this must be preset to the same value in all stations, it is important to quantify its effect on both the obtainable throughput and the access delay.

Although the nominal throughput of an FDDI ring is 100 Mbps, because of the ring latency and access control mechanism, the maximum obtainable throughput is less than this. Maximum obtained throughput (and access delay) implies that there are always frames waiting to be sent on receipt of the token at each ring interface. Under such conditions, we can compute the obtainable maximum throughput by considering the operating scenario in Example 8.5. In this, on receipt of the token, the first station transmits a set of frames up to the point when the TTRT expires before passing on the token. All the other stations in the ring are blocked from transmitting any frames during this rotation of the token. It is not until the token is passed to the next station in the ring on the following rotation that the second transmission burst of frames occurs.

As we can deduce from this, the transmission time lost during successive rotations of the token is made up of two parts: the time lost while the set of frames transmitted by the first station rotate around the ring – the ring latency – and the time taken for the token to be passed to the next station on the ring. We can express the maximum utilization of the nominal ring capacity, U_{max}, as follows:

$$U_{max} = \frac{TTRT - T_1}{(TTRT - T_1) + T_1 + T_t + (T_1 / n)} = \frac{n(TTRT - T_1)}{n(TTRT - T_1) + (n+1)T_1 + T_t}$$

where TTRT is the target token rotation time, T_1 is the ring latency, T_t is the time to transmit the token, and n is the number of stations in the ring.

In practice, the TTRT is very much greater than T_t. Hence the maximum utilization can be approximated to:

$$U_{max} = \frac{n(TTRT - T_1)}{nTTRT + T_1} \quad \text{or approximately,} \quad \frac{TTRT - T_1}{TTRT}$$

We can conclude that, to achieve a high level of ring utilization, we must select a TTRT which is significantly greater than the total ring latency. In addition, the selected TTRT must allow at least one frame of the maximum size to be present on the ring. The maximum size frame is 4500 bytes which requires 0.36 ms to transmit at 100 Mbps. The maximum ring latency was derived in Example 8.4 and, allowing for the secondary ring to be in use and the 500 stations to be all dual-attach stations, this is approximately 2 ms. Therefore the minimum TTRT allowable is 2.36 ms which, allowing for a safety margin, is set to 4 ms in the standard.

The access delay is defined as the time delay between the arrival of a frame at the ring interface of the source station and its delivery by the ring interface at the destination station. Thus access delay includes any time spent waiting in the ring interface queue at the source until a usable token – that is, an early token – arrives. It is meaningful only if the offered load is less than the maximum obtainable throughput of the ring, otherwise the interface queues continuously build up and the access delay gets progressively larger.

Providing the offered load is less than the maximum obtainable throughput, the maximum (worst case) access delay can also be deduced from Example 8.5. Recall that all stations simultaneously receive a set of frames at their ring interface queues such that they will each utilize the full TTRT quota for each rotation of the token. Assuming that station 1 is the first station able to transmit frames, the maximum access delay will be experienced by the last station on the ring – that is, station 4 – since this will receive a usable token only at the start of the fourth rotation of the token. Also, if the four frames in its ring interface queue are all addressed to station 3, then a further delay equal to the ring latency will be experienced while they are all transmitted around the ring to this station. The general expression used to compute the maximum access delay of an FDDI ring, A_{max}, is given by:

$$A_{max} = (n-1) \; (\text{TTRT} - T_1) + nT_1 + T_1$$
$$= (n-1) \; \text{TTRT} + 2T_1$$

where A_{max} is the worst-case time to receive a usable token and the other terms have the same meaning as before.

Clearly, since the ring latency is fixed for a particular ring configuration, the larger the ring TTRT, the larger the maximum access delay. As Example 8.6 shows, for all but the largest networks, the maximum obtainable throughput of an FDDI ring can be obtained with a TTRT equal to the minimum value of 4 ms. Hence although in the standard the maximum TTRT can be as high as 165 ms, it is common to operate the ring with a TTRT significantly less than this.

Example 8.6

Derive the maximum obtainable throughput and the maximum access delay for the following three ring configurations. Assume a TTRT of 4 ms has been chosen for each configuration.

(i)   2 km ring with 20 stations,

(ii) 20 km ring with 200 stations,

(iii) 100 km ring with 500 stations.

Answer:

The three ring configurations are the same as those used in Example 8.4 and hence the same computed ring latency times will be used here. Now:

Maximum available thoughput, $U_{max} = \dfrac{n(\text{TTRT} - T_1)}{n\text{TTRT} + T_1}$

Maximum access delay, $A_{max} = (n-1) \; \text{TTRT} + 2T_1$

(i)   From Example 8.4, $T_1 = 0.03$ ms. Hence:

$$U_{max} = \frac{20(4 - 0.03)}{20 \times 4 + 0.03} = 0.99$$

and

$$A_{max} = 19 \times 4 + 0.06 = 76.06 \text{ ms}$$

8.6 Continued

(ii) From Example 8.4, $T_1 = 0.3$ ms. Hence:

$$U_{max} = \frac{200\ (4 - 0.3)}{200 \times 4 + 0.3} = 0.92$$

and

$$A_{max} = 199 \times 4 + 0.6 = 796.6\ ms$$

(iii) From Example 8.4, $T_1 = 1$ ms. Hence:

$$U_{max} = \frac{500\ (4 - 1)}{500 \times 4 + 1} = 0.75$$

and

$$A_{max} = 499 \times 4 + 2 = 1.998\ s$$

8.7 High-speed LANs

As the application of LANs has become more diverse, so the demands on them in terms of information/data throughput have increased. As we have just described, by using a combination of bridges and a high bit rate backbone, the throughput of the total LAN is determined by the maximum throughput of each LAN segment. As we explained in Sections 8.3 and 8.4, the maximum throughput of the two basic LAN types is only a fraction of the bit rate that is used. Hence in order to meet the higher throughput requirements of the newer multimedia applications, a number of high-speed LAN types have been developed. These include variations of the basic Ethernet LAN and, since this is by far the most widely installed type of LAN, we shall restrict our discussion to three variations of Ethernet: (shared) **Fast Ethernet**, **Switched Fast Ethernet**, and **Gigabit Ethernet**.

8.7.1 Fast Ethernet

The aim of Fast Ethernet was to use the same shared, half-duplex transmission mode as Ethernet but to obtain a ×10 increase in operational bit rate over 10BaseT while at the same time retaining the same wiring systems, MAC method, and frame format. As we explained in Section 8.3, when using hubs with unshielded twisted-pair (UTP) cable, the maximum length of drop cable from the hub to a station is limited to 100 m by the driver/receiver electronics. Assuming just a single hub, this means that the maximum distance between any two stations is 200 m and the worst-case path length for collision detection purposes is 400 m plus the repeater delay in the hub. Clearly, therefore, a higher bit rate can be used while still retaining the same CSMA/CD MAC method and minimum frame size of 512 bits. In the standard, the bit rate is set at 100 Mbps over existing UTP cable. Hence the standard is also known as **100BaseT**.

Line code

The major technological hurdle to overcome with Fast Ethernet was how to achieve a bit rate of 100 Mbps over 100 m of UTP cable. Category 3 UTP cable – as used for telephony, and the most widely installed – contains four separate twisted-pair wires. To reduce the bit rate used on each pair, all four pairs are used to achieve the required bit rate of 100 Mbps in each direction.

With the CSMA/CD access control method, in the absence of contention for the medium, all transmissions are half-duplex, that is, either station-to-hub or hub-to-station. In a 10BaseT installation, just two of the four wire pairs are used for data transfers, one in each direction. Collisions are detected when the transmitting station (or hub) detects a signal on the receive pair while it is transmitting on the transmit pair. Since the collision detect function must also be performed in 100BaseT, the same two pairs are used for this function. The remaining two pairs are operated in a bidirectional mode, as shown in Figure 8.26(a).

The figure shows that data transfers in each direction utilize three pairs – pairs 1, 3, and 4 for transmissions between a station and the hub and pairs 2, 3, and 4 for transmissions between the hub and a station. Transmissions on pairs 1 and 2 are then used for collision detection and carrier sense purposes as with 10BaseT. This means that the bit rate on each pair of wires need only be 100/3 = 33.33 Mbps.

If we use Manchester encoding, a bit rate of 33.33 Mbps requires a baud rate of 33.33 Mbaud which exceeds the 30Mbaud limit set for use with such cables, as above this, unacceptably high levels of crosstalk are obtained. To reduce the baud rate, a 3-level (**ternary**) **code** is used instead of straight (2-level) binary coding. The code used is known as **8B6T** which means that, prior to transmission, each set of 8 binary bits is first converted into 6 ternary (3-level) symbols. From the example shown in Figure 8.26(b), we can deduce that this yields a symbol rate of:

$$\frac{100 \times 6/8}{3} = 25 \text{ Mbaud}$$

which is well within the set limit.

The three signal levels used are $+V, 0, -V$ which are represented simply as $+, 0, -$. The codewords are selected such that the line is DC balanced, that is, the mean line signal is zero. This maximizes the receiver's discrimination of the three signal levels since these are then always relative to a constant 0 (DC) level. To achieve this, we exploit the inherent redundancy present in the use of 6 ternary symbols. The 6 ternary symbols means that there are 729 (3^6)

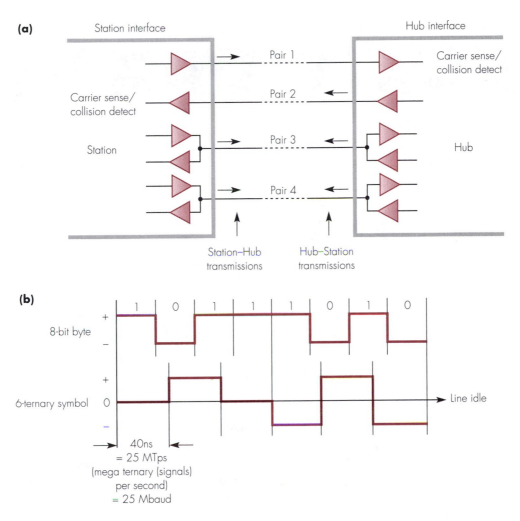

Figure 8.26 100 Base T: (a) use of wire pairs; (b) 8B6T encoding.

possible codewords. Since only 256 codewords are required to represent the complete set of 8-bit byte combinations, the codes used are selected, firstly, to achieve DC balance and secondly, to ensure all codewords have at least two signal transitions within them. This is done so that the receiver DPLL maintains clock synchronization.

To satisfy the first condition, we choose only those codewords with a combined weight of 0 or +1 and 267 codes meet this condition. To satisfy the second condition, we eliminate those codes with fewer than two transitions – five codes – and also those starting or ending with four consecutive zeros – six codes. This leaves the required 256 codewords, the first 128 of which are listed in Table 8.2.

Table 8.2 First 128 codewords of 8B6T codeword set.

Data byte	Codeword	Data byte	Codeword	Data byte	Codeword	Data byte	Codeword
00	− + 0 0 − +	20	− + + − 0 0	40	− 0 0 + 0 +	60	0 + + 0 − 0
01	0 − + − + 0	21	+ 0 0 + − −	41	0 − 0 0 + +	61	+ 0 + − 0 0
02	0 − + 0 − +	22	− + 0 − + +	42	0 − 0 + 0 +	62	+ 0 + 0 − 0
03	0 − + + 0 −	23	+ − 0 − + +	43	0 − 0 + + 0	63	+ 0 + 0 0 −
04	− + 0 + 0 −	24	+ − 0 + 0 0	44	− 0 0 + + 0	64	0 + + 0 0 −
05	+ 0 − − + 0	25	− + 0 + 0 0	45	0 0 − 0 + +	65	+ + 0 − 0 0
06	+ 0 − 0 − +	26	+ 0 0 − 0 0	46	0 0 − + 0 +	66	+ + 0 0 − 0
07	+ 0 − + 0 −	27	− + + + − −	47	0 0 − + + 0	67	+ + 0 0 0 −
08	− + 0 0 + −	28	0 + + − 0 −	48	0 0 + 0 0 0	68	0 + + − + −
09	0 − + + − 0	29	+ 0 + 0 − −	49	+ + − 0 0 0	69	+ 0 + + − −
0A	0 − + 0 + −	2A	+ 0 + − 0 −	4A	+ − + 0 0 0	6A	+ 0 + − + −
0B	0 − + − 0 +	2B	+ 0 + − − 0	4B	− + + 0 0 0	6B	+ 0 + − − +
0C	− + 0 − 0 +	2C	0 + + − − 0	4C	0 + − 0 0 0	6C	0 + + − − +
0D	+ 0 − + − 0	2D	+ + 0 0 − −	4D	+ 0 − 0 0 0	6D	+ + 0 + − −
0E	+ 0 − 0 + −	2E	+ + 0 − 0 −	4E	0 − + 0 0 0	6E	+ + 0 − + −
0F	+ 0 − − 0 +	2F	+ + 0 − − 0	4F	− 0 + 0 0 0	6F	+ + 0 − − +
10	0 − − + 0 +	30	+ − 0 0 − +	50	+ − − + 0 +	70	0 0 0 + + −
11	− 0 − 0 + +	31	0 + − − + 0	51	− + − 0 + +	71	0 0 0 + − +
12	− 0 − + 0 +	32	0 + − 0 − +	52	− + − + 0 +	72	0 0 0 − + +
13	− 0 − + + 0	33	0 + − + 0 −	53	− + − + + 0	73	0 0 0 + 0 0
14	0 − − + + 0	34	+ − 0 + 0 −	54	+ − − + + 0	74	0 0 0 + 0 −
15	− − 0 0 + +	35	− 0 + − + 0	55	− − + 0 + +	75	0 0 0 + − 0
16	− − 0 + 0 +	36	− 0 + 0 − +	56	− − + + 0 +	76	0 0 0 − 0 +
17	− − 0 + + 0	37	− 0 + + 0 −	57	− − + + + 0	77	0 0 0 − + 0
18	− + 0 − + 0	38	+ − 0 0 + −	58	− − 0 + + +	78	+ + + − − 0
19	+ − 0 − + 0	39	0 + − + − 0	59	− 0 − + + +	79	+ + + − 0 −
1A	− + + − + 0	3A	0 + − 0 + −	5A	0 − − + + +	7A	+ + + 0 − −
1B	+ 0 0 − + 0	3B	0 + − − 0 +	5B	0 − − 0 + +	7B	0 + + 0 − −
1C	+ 0 0 + − 0	3C	+ − 0 − 0 +	5C	+ − − 0 + +	7C	− 0 0 − + +
1D	− + + + − 0	3D	− 0 + + − 0	5D	− 0 0 0 + +	7D	− 0 0 + 0 0
1E	+ − 0 + − 0	3E	− 0 + 0 + −	5E	0 + + + − −	7E	+ − − − + +
1F	− + 0 + − 0	3F	− 0 + − 0 +	5F	0 + + − 0 0	7F	+ − − + 0 0

DC balance

As we have just indicated, all the codewords selected have a combined weight of either 0 or +1. For example, the codeword $+--+00$ has a combined weight of 0 while the codeword $0+++--$ has a weight of +1. Clearly, if a string of codewords each of weight +1 is transmitted, then the mean signal level at the receiver will move away rapidly from the zero level, causing the signal to be misinterpreted. This is known as **DC wander** and is caused by the use of transformers at each end of the line. The presence of transformers means there is no path for direct current (DC).

To overcome this, whenever a string of codewords with a weight of +1 is to be sent, the symbols in alternate codewords are inverted prior to transmission. For example, if a string comprising the codeword $0+++--$ is to be sent, then the actual codewords transmitted will be $0++--$, $0---++$, $0+++--$, $0---++$, and so on, yielding a mean signal level of 0. At the receiver, the same rules are applied and the alternative codewords will be reinverted into their original form prior to decoding. The procedure used for transmission is shown in the state transition diagram in Figure 8.27(a).

To reduce the latency during the decoding process, the 6 ternary symbols corresponding to each encoded byte are transmitted on the appropriate three wire pairs in the sequence shown in Figure 8.27(b). This means that the sequence of symbols received on each pair can be decoded independently. Also, the frame can be processed immediately after the last symbol is received.

End-of-frame sequence

The transmission procedure adopted enables further error checking to be added to the basic CRC. We can deduce from the state transition diagram in Figure 8.27(a) that the running sum of the weights is always either 0 or +1. At the end of each frame transmission – that is, after the four CRC bytes have been transmitted – one of two different **end-of-stream** (**EOS**) codes is transmitted on each of the three pairs. The code selected effectively forms a checksum for that pair. The principle of the scheme is shown in Figure 8.27(c).

In this figure, we assume the last of the four CRC bytes (CRC-4) is on pair 3. The next codeword transmitted on pair 4 is determined by whether the running sum of the weights on that pair – referred to as the checksum – is 0 or +1. The EOS function is complete at the end of this codeword and the length of the other two EOS codes are reduced by two or one times the latency, that is, 4T or 2T. This means the receiver can detect reliably the end of a frame since all signals should cease within a short time of one another. This allows for very small variations in propagation delay on each pair of wires.

Collision detection

An example station–hub transmission without contention is shown in Figure 8.28(a). Recall that a station detects a collision by detecting a signal on pair 2 while it is transmitting and, similarly, the hub detects a collision by the

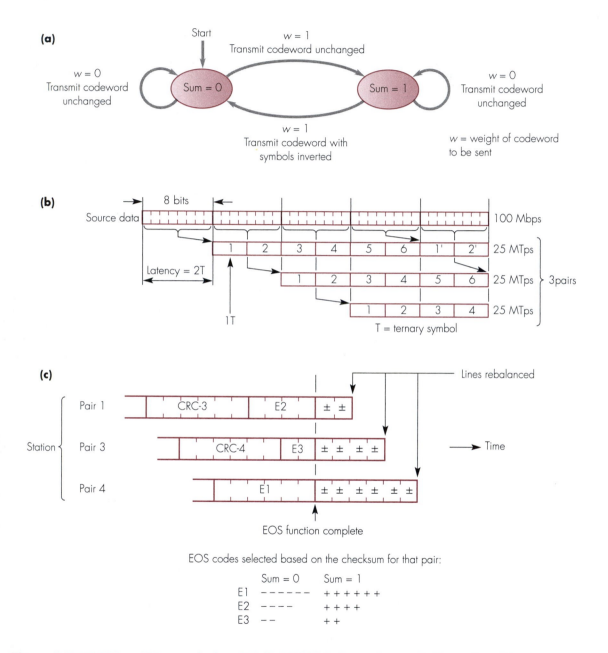

Figure 8.27 100BaseT transmission detail: (a) DC balance transmission rules; (b) 8B6T encoding sequence; (c) end of stream encoding.

presence of a signal on pair 1. However, as Figure 8.28(a) shows, the strong (unattenuated) signals transmitted on pairs 1, 3, and 4 from the station side each induce a signal into the collision detect – pair 2 – wire. This is near-end crosstalk (NEXT) and, in the limit, is interpreted by the station as a (collision) signal being received from the hub. The same applies for transmissions in the reverse direction from hub to station.

To minimize any uncertainty the preamble at the start of each frame is encoded as a string of 2-level (as opposed to 3-level) symbols, that is, only positive and negative signal levels are present in each encoded symbol. This increases the signal-level amplitude variations which, in turn, helps the station/hub to discriminate between an induced NEXT signal and the preamble of a colliding frame.

(a)

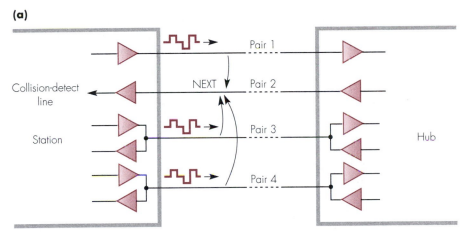

NEXT = near-end crosstalk

(b)

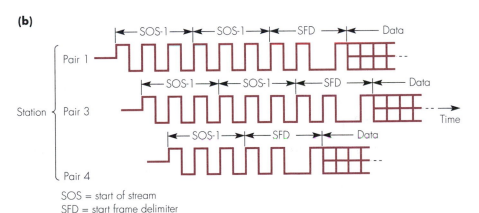

SOS = start of stream
SFD = start frame delimiter

Figure 8.28 Start-of-frame detail: (a) effect of NEXT; (b) preamble sequence.

The preamble pattern on each pair is known as the **start of stream** (**SOS**) and is made up of two 2-level codewords, SOS-1 and SFD. The complete pattern transmitted on each of the three pairs is shown in Figure 8.28(b) and, as we can see, the SFD codeword on each pair is staggered by sending only a single SOS-1 on pair 4. This means that the first byte of the frame is transmitted on pair 4, the next on pair 1, the next on pair 3, and so on. An acceptable start of frame requires all three SFD codes to be detected, and the staggering of them means that it takes at least four symbol errors to cause an undetectable start-of-frame error.

On detecting a collision, a station transmits the jam sequence and then stops transmitting. At this point, the station must be able to determine when the other station(s) involved in the collision cease transmitting in order to start the retry process. In practice, this is relatively easy since, in the nontransmitting (idle) state with 8B6T encoding, a zero signal level is present on the three data wires. This means that there is no induced NEXT signal in the collision detect wire which, in turn, enables the completion of the jam sequence from the hub side to be readily determined. Also, to improve the utilization of the cable, the interframe gap time is reduced from 9.6 µs to 960 ns.

100BaseX

In addition to the 100BaseT standard, a second Fast Ethernet standard is available, which is known as **100BaseX**. Unlike 100BaseT which was designed for use with existing category 3 UTP cable, 100BaseX was designed for use with the higher quality category 5 cable now being used in most new installations. In addition, it is intended for use with STP and optical fiber cables. The use of various types of transmission media is the origin of the "X" in the name.

Each different type of transmission medium requires a different physical sublayer. The first to be developed is that for use with multimode optical fiber cable as used in FDDI networks. Recall from the last section, the FDDI LAN is intended primarily as a backbone subnetwork since, unlike 100BaseT, it can span a distance up to several kilometers. Transmissions over an FDDI network use a bit encoding scheme known as 4B5B (sometimes written as 4B/5B) and this has also been adopted for use with 100BaseX, this version being known as **100BaseFX**.

The cable comprises two fibers, one of which is used for transmissions between the station and hub and the other for transmissions between the hub and the station. As with 10BaseT, collisions are detected if a (colliding) signal is present on the receive fiber during the time the station is transmitting a frame. However, because of the additional cost of both the electrical-to-optical conversion circuits and the associated optical plugs and sockets that are required per port, the cost of the MAC unit associated with the NIC is higher than that used with 100BaseT. Hence the most popular type of Fast Ethernet is 100BaseT and 100BaseFX is used primarily when longer drop cables are required.

8.7.2 Switched Fast Ethernet

As we explained at the start of Section 8.7.1, Fast Ethernet uses the same shared, half-duplex transmission mode as Ethernet. Hence in applications that involve access to, say, large enterprise Web servers, even though the server can handle multiple transfers concurrently, the overall access time and throughput experienced by the various stations using the server is limited by the shared access circuit connecting the server (station) to the hub.

In order to allow multiple access/transfers to be in progress concurrently, two developments have been made: the first, the introduction of a switched hub architecture, and the second, duplex working over the circuits that connect the stations to the hub. The resulting type of hub is known as a **Fast Ethernet switch**.

Switch architecture

The general architecture of a switching hub is shown in Figure 8.29. As we can see, each station is connected to the hub by means of a pair of (duplex) lines which, typically, are implemented as dual UTP (or STP) cables or dual multimode fiber cables. Recall from the last section, each UTP (and STP) cable contains four separate twisted pairs. In the case of 100BaseT, three pairs are used to transmit the 100 Mbps bitstream – in a half-duplex mode – and

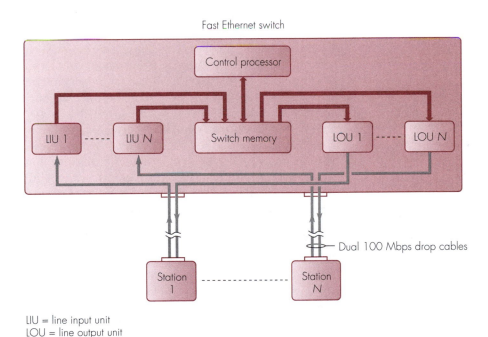

LIU = line input unit
LOU = line output unit

Figure 8.29 Fast Ethernet switch schematic.

the fourth pair is used to perform the carrier sense and collision detection functions. With a switching hub, however, CSMA/CD is not used and instead all stations can transmit and receive frames concurrently. Hence, as with 100BaseT, three pairs in each cable are used collectively to transmit frames (at 100 Mbps) in each direction.

In the case of dual multimode fiber cables, each fiber is used to transmit at 100 Mbps over several kilometers, one in each direction of transmission. Since the 4B5B coding scheme is used, the line signaling rate is 125 Mbaud. In addition, an active signal is maintained on each fiber continuously by transmitting an idle symbol during the idle period between frames. This ensures the receiver DPLL can maintain clock synchronism between successive frame transmissions.

Because each station can transmit frames simultaneously, a frame may be received at multiple input ports of the hub – and hence require processing – simultaneously. Similarly, two or more frames may require the same output line simultaneously. Hence associated with each input and output line is a memory buffer that can hold several frames waiting to be either processed (input) or transmitted (output). The frames – memory pointers to the start of the frame in practice – are stored in a FIFO queue. The control processor then reads the pointer to the frame at the head of each input queue in turn, obtains the destination MAC address from its head, and transfers the frame pointer to the tail of the required output queue to await transmission.

In order to retain the same connectionless mode of operation of the other LAN types, when the switch is first brought into service – and subsequently at periodic intervals – the control processor enters a learning state. This is similar to that used in transparent bridges which we described in Section 8.5.1. Hence when in the learning state, the switch simply initiates the onward transmission of a copy of each frame received from an input line onto all output lines. Prior to doing this, however, the control processor reads the source address from the head of the frame and keeps a record of this, together with the input port number on which the frame was received, in a routing table. The contents of the routing table are then subsequently used to route each received frame to a specific output port. As we can deduce from this, there is a store-and-forward delay associated with a switch. Also, as with a bridge, the FCS at the tail of each frame is used to check for the presence of transmission errors prior to the frame being forwarded and corrupted frames are discarded.

Flow control

As we can see from the above, under heavy load conditions it is possible for all the frame buffers within the switch to become full. At this point, therefore, the control processor must discard any new frame(s). Alternatively, an optional feature associated with switched hubs is to incorporate flow control into the switch. When using flow control, should the control processor find that the level of memory in use reaches a defined threshold, it initiates the transmission of what is called a **Pause** frame on all of its input ports.

On receipt of a Pause frame, the attached station must then stop sending any further frames to the switch until either a defined time has expired or it receives a notification from the switch that the overload condition has passed. Having sent a Pause frame, the control processor monitors the level of memory in use and, when this falls below a second level, it sends out a **Continue** frame on all input ports to inform the attached stations that they can now resume sending new frames.

Network configurations

An example (small) network configuration that includes a Fast Ethernet switching hub is shown in Figure 8.30. As we can see, in order to obtain a high level of throughput, the two servers are connected directly to the switch by means of duplex 100 Mbps lines. All the end-user stations then gain access to the servers through either a 10BaseT or a 100BaseT hub. As we explained in the last section, both these types of hub operate in the half-duplex repeating mode. Hence the duplex uplink port connecting each hub to the switch has bridging circuitry within the hub to temporarily buffer all frame transfers to and from the switch and to perform the CSMA/CD MAC protocol associated with the shared medium hub ports.

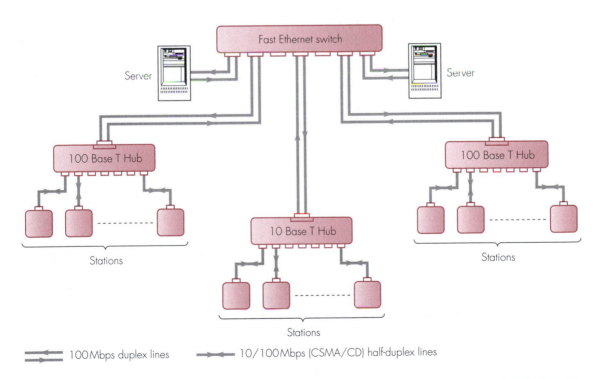

Figure 8.30 Example network configuration with a Fast Ethernet switch and 10/100BaseT hubs.

8.7.3 Gigabit Ethernet

As the name implies, the drop cables associated with Gigabit Ethernet hubs operate at 1000 Mbps (1 Gbps). They have been introduced to meet the throughput demands of an increasing number of servers that hold files containing multimedia information; examples include web pages comprising very high resolution graphics, motion video, and general audio. The hub can be either a simple repeater hub – that is, one that has no memory associated with it – or a switched hub.

An example application of a repeater hub is to distribute the output of a powerful supercomputer (performing, say, 3D scientific visualizations) to a localized set of workstations. The main issue when operating in the repeater mode is to ensure that the round-trip delay between any two stations – the slot time – exceeds the time required to transmit the smaller allowable frame of 512 bits. The time to transmit a 512-bit frame at 1 Gbps is 0.512 microseconds whereas the slot time is in the order of 2 microseconds. To overcome this, a technique known as **carrier extension** is used. This, as the name implies, ensures that a known signal is present on the line for the duration of the slot time and therefore a collision can still be detected. Alternatively, a technique called **frame bursting** can be used which allows multiple short frames to be transmitted one after the other up to the slot time.

In the case of a switched hub, these are used to perform a similar role to the Fast Ethernet switch we showed in Figure 8.30. As we can deduce from the figure, if all the attached hubs are 100BaseT – or Fast Ethernet switches – then the switch providing the backbone function must also be able to handle the increased load generated by the various hubs. Normally, however, the lines connecting each 100BaseT hub/switch to the Gigabit Ethernet hub operate at 100 Mbps and only the servers that are connected directly to the Gigabit hub operate at the full speed of 1 Gbps. However, since in this case both hubs operate in the duplex mode, the slot time is not an issue.

In terms of cabling, repeating hubs can use either category 5 UTP cable with a drop cable length of up to 100 m (1000BaseT) or STP cable providing the length of the drop cable is limited to 25 m (1000BaseCX). In the case of a switched hub used as a backbone, however, optical fiber cable is used that supports drop cable lengths of up to 200 m – using multimode fiber (1000BaseSX) – or up to 10 km if monomode fiber (1000BaseLX) is used. In the case of multimode fiber, an 8B/10B coding scheme is used; that is, each 8-bit group is encoded into a 10-bit symbol. Hence, since the line bit rate is 1 Gbps, the line signaling rate is 1.25 Gbaud. Apart from this, the internal architecture of the hubs is similar to those used in Fast Ethernet hubs and switches.

8.8 LAN protocols

As we have learnt, there is a range of different types of LAN each of which uses a different MAC method, transmission mode, and transmission medium. In the context of our reference model, however, these differences only manifest themselves at the MAC sublayer (of the link layer) and the physical layer. The link control sublayer – known as the **logical link control (LLC) sublayer** in the context of LANs – then offers a standard link layer service to the network layer above it.

Apart from FDDI, which is defined in ISO9314, the various protocol standards associated with LANs are all part of the **IEEE 802 series**. The framework used for defining the various standards is shown in Figure 8.31(a) and a selection of the protocols which we have described in the previous sections are listed in Figure 8.31(b).

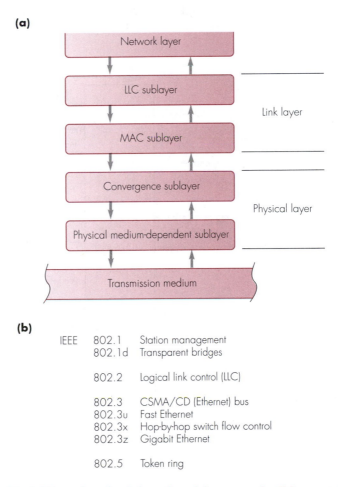

(a)

Network layer

LLC sublayer

MAC sublayer

Link layer

Convergence sublayer

Physical medium-dependent sublayer

Physical layer

Transmission medium

(b)

IEEE		
	802.1	Station management
	802.1d	Transparent bridges
	802.2	Logical link control (LLC)
	802.3	CSMA/CD (Ethernet) bus
	802.3u	Fast Ethernet
	802.3x	Hop-by-hop switch flow control
	802.3z	Gigabit Ethernet
	802.5	Token ring

Figure 8.31 LAN protocols: (a) protocol framework; (b) examples.

8.8.1 Physical layer

To cater for the different types of media and transmission bit rates, the physical layer has been divided into two sublayers: the **physical medium-dependent (PMD) sublayer** and the (physical) **convergence sublayer (CS)**. To facilitate the use of different media types, a **media-independent interface (MMI)** has been defined for use between the convergence and PMD sublayers. The role of the convergence sublayer is then to make the use of different media types and bit rates transparent to the MAC sublayer.

The set of signals associated with both interfaces vary slightly for the different types of Ethernet (802.3) and token ring (802.5). As an example, the set of signals associated with the different types of Ethernet are shown in Figure 8.32.

As we explained in Section 8.7.1, at bit rates in excess of 10 Mbps it is not possible to use clock encoding – for example Manchester – because the resulting high line signal transition (baud) rate would violate the limit set for use over UTP cable. Instead, bit encoding and a DPLL are used and, to

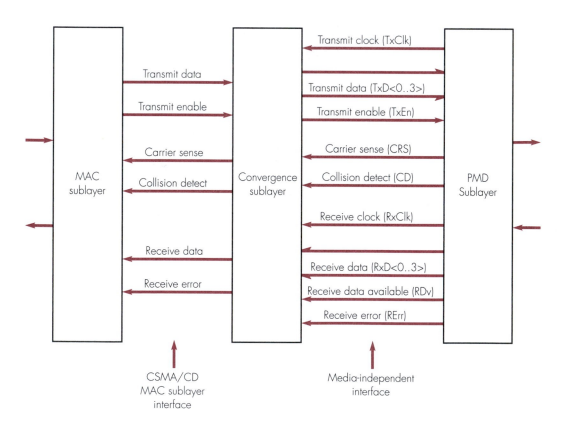

Figure 8.32 Fast Ethernet media-independent interface.

ensure the transmitted signal has sufficient transitions within it, the encoding schemes use one or more groups of 4 bits in each transmitted symbol. For example, one 4-bit group when 4B5B coding is used (100BaseSX), and two 4-bit groups when 8B/10B coding is used (1000BaseSX). Hence, all transfers over the MII are in 4-bit nibbles. The other control lines are concerned with the reliable transfer of these nibbles over the interface. The major functions of the convergence sublayer, therefore, are to convert the transmit and receive serial bitstream at the MAC sublayer interface into and from 4-bit nibbles for transfer across the MII, and, when half-duplex transmission is being used, to relay the carrier sense and collision detect signals generated by the PMD sublayer to the MAC sublayer.

8.8.2 MAC sublayer

Irrespective of the mode of operation of the MAC sublayer, a standard set of user service primitives is defined for use by the LLC sublayer. These are:

MA_UNITDATA.request

MA_UNITDATA.indication

MA_UNITDATA.confirm

A time sequence diagram illustrating their use is shown in Figure 8.33. For a CSMA/CD LAN, the confirm primitive indicates that the block of data associated with the request has been successfully (or not) transmitted – part (a) – while for a token ring LAN it indicates that the request has been successfully (or not) delivered, part (b).

Each service primitive has parameters associated with it. The MA_UNITDATA.request primitive includes: the required destination address (this may be an individual, group, or broadcast address), a service data unit (containing the data to be transferred – that is, the LLC PDU), and the required class of service associated with the PDU. This is used with token ring networks, for example, when a prioritized MAC protocol is being used.

The MA_UNITDATA.confirm primitive includes a parameter that specifies the success or failure of the associated MA_UNITDATA.request primitive. However, as we show in Figure 8.33, the confirm primitive is not generated as a result of a response from the remote LLC sublayer but rather by the local MAC entity. If the parameter indicates success, this simply shows that the MAC protocol entity (layer) was successful in transmitting the service data unit onto the network medium. If unsuccessful, the parameter indicates why the transmission attempt failed. As an example, if the network is a CSMA/CD bus, "excessive collisions" may be a typical failure parameter.

8.8.3 LLC sublayer

The LLC protocol is based on the high-level data link control (HDLC) protocol which we described earlier in Section 6.8. It therefore supports both a

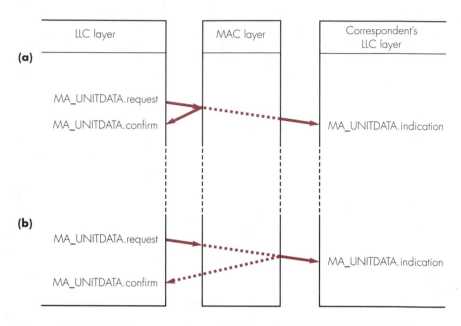

Figure 8.33 MAC user service primitives: (a) CSMA/CD; (b) token ring.

connectionless (best-effort) and a connection-oriented (reliable) mode. In almost all LAN networks, however, only the connectionless mode is used. Hence, since this operational mode adds only minimal functionality, when the older Ethernet MAC standard is being used – see the discussion on frame formats in section 8.3 – the LLC sublayer is often not present. Instead, the network layer – for example the Internet protocol (IP) – uses the services provided by the MAC sublayer directly.

When the newer IEEE 802.3 MAC standard is being used, the LLC sublayer is present. However, since it operates in the connectionless mode, the only user service primitive is L_DATA.request and all data is transferred in an unnumbered information (UI) frame. The interactions between the LLC and MAC sublayers are as shown in Figure 8.34.

The L_DATA.request primitive has parameters associated with it. These are: a specification of the source (local) and destination (remote) addresses and the user data (service data unit). The latter is the network layer protocol data unit (NPDU). The source and destination addresses are each a concatenation of the MAC sublayer address of the station and an additional service access point (SAP) address. In theory, this can be used for interlayer routing purposes within the protocol stack of the station. In applications such as the Internet, however, this feature is not used and both the destination SAP (DSAP) and the source SAP (SSAP) are set to AA (hex). In addition, two further fields are added. Collectively, the two fields form what is called the **subnet**

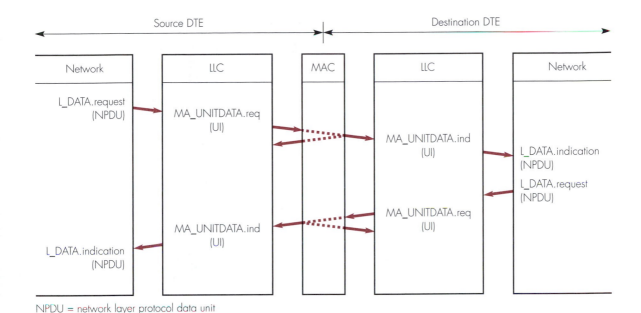

NPDU = network layer protocol data unit

Figure 8.34 LLC/MAC sublayer interactions.

access protocol (**SNAP**) header. The first is a 3-byte field known as the *organisation* (*org*) *code* – which, with the Internet, all three bytes are set to zero – and a two-byte *type* field. This is the same as that used in the original Ethernet standard and indicates the network layer protocol that created the NPDU.

A more detailed illustration of the interactions between the LLC and MAC sublayers is shown in Figure 8.35. The LLC sublayer reads the destination and source LLC service access point addresses (DSAP and SSAP) – from the two address parameters in the event control block (ECB) associated with the L_DATA.request service primitive – and inserts these at the head of an LLC PDU. It then adds an 8-bit *control* (*CTL*) field – set to 03 (hex) to indicate it is an unnumbered information (UI) frame – the 3-byte org code, the type field, followed by the network layer protocol data unit in the user data field. The resulting LLC PDU is then passed to the MAC sublayer as the user data parameter of an MA_UNITDATA.request primitive in a MAC ECB. Other parameters include the MAC sublayer destination and source addresses (DA and SA), the desired service class, and the number of bytes (length indicator) in the user data field. Typically, the service class is used by the MAC sublayer protocol entity to determine the priority to be associated with the frame if a token network is being used.

On receipt of the request, the MAC protocol entity creates a frame ready for transmission on the link. In the case of a CSMA/CD bus network, it creates

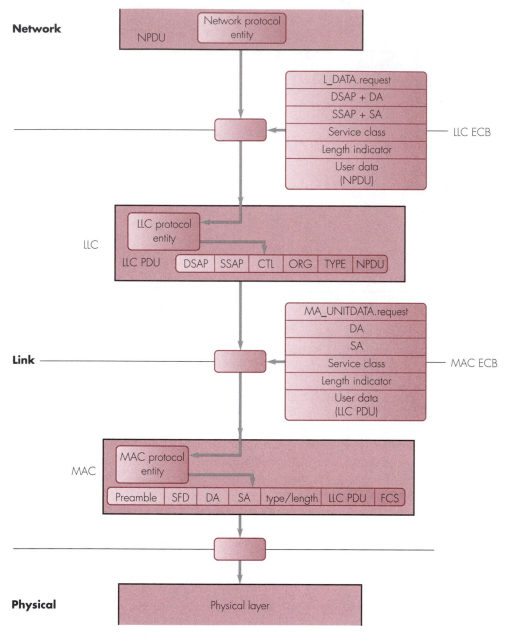

ECB = event control block

Figure 8.35 Interlayer primitives and parameters.

a frame containing the preamble and SFD fields, the DA and SA fields, an I-field, and the computed FCS field. The complete frame is then transmitted bit serially onto the cable medium using the appropriate MAC method.

A similar procedure is followed in the NIC of the destination station except that the corresponding fields in each PDU are read and interpreted by each layer. The user data field in each PDU is then passed up to the layer/sub-layer immediately above together with the appropriate address parameters.

8.8.4 Network layer

The most popular protocol stack used within LANs is **Novell NetWare**. Hence it is common for all the stations connected to a site LAN to communicate using this stack. The network layer protocol associated with this is a connectionless protocol known as the **internet packet exchange** (**IPX**) protocol and, as its name implies, it can route and relay packets over the total LAN. There is no LLC sublayer associated with the stack and hence the IPX protocol communicates directly with the MAC sublayer.

The protocol stack used within the Internet is TCP/IP and the network layer protocol associated with this stack is a connectionless protocol known as the Internet protocol (IP). Hence, as we showed earlier in Figure 5.11, it is common for server machines such as email servers that need to communicate across the Internet, to support both protocol stacks, IPX to communicate with client stations over the site LAN and IP to communicate with other servers over the Internet. Since both IPX and IP are connectionless protocols, they use a single packet to transfer all information over the related network with the full network address of both the source and destination stations in the packet header. We shall defer further discussion of network layer protocols until Chapter 9 when we discuss the operation of the Internet.

8.9 Multisite LAN interconnection technologies

As we saw in the introduction to Section 8.2, in multisite enterprise networks, the LANs associated with the different sites are interconnected together to form an enterprisewide network. As we shall explain, various technologies are available to do this and the choice of technology is determined by the volume of intersite traffic. If this is low, then a low bit rate – up to 56 kbps – leased line with modems is used or, if this is not sufficient, one or more leased 64 kbps ISDN channels. Alternatively, if the volume of traffic is high, then high bit rate leased lines are used, typical bit rates being 1.5 or 2 Mbps or multiples of these. In addition, a number of high bit rate switched services have become available from some telecom providers.

The aim of an enterprise network is to provide an integrated structure so that all communications across the total enterprise ARE transparent to the site/location of the employee's PCs/workstations and the various enterprisewide servers. Hence providing a physical link between sites is only the first step in connecting the LANs at the various sites together. Associated with each LAN is a gateway that provides the additional higher-level protocol support needed to ensure that the physical location of the application-level services is transparent to the end users.

In this section, we first describe the operation of the typical intersite gateways in Section 8.9.1. The first is based on remote bridges and the second on IP/IPX routers. We then describe two examples of switched services: switched ISDN (in Section 8.9.2) and frame relay in Section 8.9.3. A typical enterprise network architecture based on high bit rate leased circuits is then described in Section 8.9.4.

8.9.1 Intersite gateways

The simplest way of providing a transparent connection between sites is to use a **remote bridge** as the intersite gateway. Normally, such bridges are connected directly to the LAN backbone on one port and to the intersite line/network termination on the other. A similar bridge is then used at each site. An example network architecture is shown in Figure 8.36.

As we explained in Section 8.3, the 48-bit MAC address used in LANs to route frames are built into the MAC chipset at the time of its manufacture and each contains a unique address. In practice, therefore, it is possible to treat the interconnected set of site LANs as a single LAN and use just the MAC addresses at the head of each frame for routing.

As we have just explained, various schemes are used to set up connections between sites. Irrespective of the scheme used, however, there is a separate connection set up between each site and hence each pair of LANs. Thus even though each remote bridge has only two physical ports, logically, they behave like multiport bridges with a separate link to each of the other remote bridges. Normally, the spanning tree algorithm we described in Section 8.5.1 spans only a single site/LAN and the remote bridge at the site does not take part in the derivation of the active spanning tree. It does, however, perform the basic learning and forwarding/filtering functions. Hence after the learning phase, it can route all subsequent frames over their appropriate intersite link.

As we show in Figure 8.36, an alternative (and more flexible) way of providing a transparent connection between sites is to use an IP/IPX router as the gateway. Routers are used when either the site LANs are of different types and/or the intersite communications facility is itself a network and requires routing. In both these cases, MAC addresses cannot be used for routing purposes as they only have local significance to a particular site. Hence routing must be carried out at the network layer using either IP or IPX.

As we explained earlier in Section 8.8.4, both IP (as used with the Internet) and IPX (as used with Novell NetWare) are connectionless protocols and all information is transferred over the intersite communications facility in self-contained packets. At the head of each packet is the (enterprisewide) network address of both the source station and the destination

Intersite communications facility

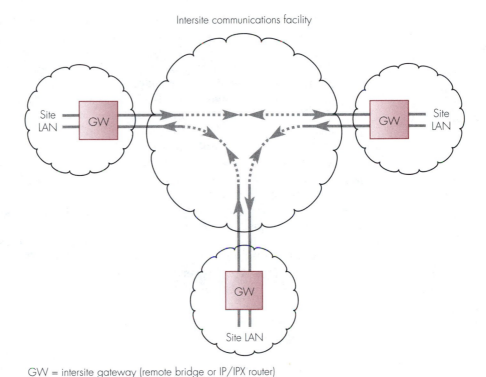

GW = intersite gateway (remote bridge or IP/IPX router)

Figure 8.36 Example enterprise network architecture.

station. As we shall expand upon in the next chapter when we discuss the operation of the Internet, each network address comprises a network identifier, which identifies uniquely each site network (LAN) within the context of the total enterprise, and a station identifier which identifies each station at that site. All routing over the intersite network is then carried out using these network addresses. It is for this reason that, when the IP protocol is used, the enterprise network is known also as an intranet. We shall defer further discussion of how the routing is carried out until Section 9.6 when we describe the operation of the IP protocol in some detail.

8.9.2 ISDN switched connections

As we explained in Section 7.2.3, a basic rate interface to an ISDN offers two, separately-switched 64 kbps digital channels. Also, with an ISDN, the connection setup time of a channel is only a fraction of a second. Hence for small enterprises, one solution is to set up (and close down) a channel on demand. For medium-sized enterprises, although the same approach is often acceptable, multiple 64 kbps channels are required to meet the intersite bandwidth requirements. As we explained in Section 7.2.3, to meet this type of requirement a service known as **ISDN multirate** is available from some telecom providers that allows the user to request the bandwidth of a call to be any multiple of 64 kbps. The service is also known as switched $p \times 64$ where p can be up to either 23 or 30 depending on the provider. In order to use the multiple channels as a single high bit rate channel, however, it is necessary to use a device called an **inverse multiplexer**. The general scheme is shown in Figure 8.37(a).

We introduced the concept of multiplexing in Section 7.2.3 as a means of transmitting multiple low bit rate – 64 kbps – digitized voice signals over a single high bit rate line. In contrast, inverse multiplexing is used to derive a single high bit rate channel using multiple lower bit rate channels. For example, an inverse multiplexer can be used to derive a single 384 kbps channel from six independent 64 kbps channels.

At the sending side, the inverse multiplexer first sets up the appropriate number of 64 kbps channels to the required destination. It then proceeds to segment the high bit rate digital stream output by the user equipment – for example a remote bridge – ready for transmission over the multiple low bit rate channels. At the receiving side, once the multiple channels have been set up, the inverse multiplexer accepts the bitstreams received from these channels and reassembles them back into a single high bit rate channel for onward transmission to the receiving terminal equipment.

Hence the function of the inverse multiplexers, in addition to call setup, is to make the segmentation and reassembly operations transparent to the user equipment. In practice, because each channel is set up independently, they may all traverse the ISDN trunk network across different routes/paths. This results in small time differences in the signals received from each channel. To compensate for this, the inverse multiplexer at the receiving side must perform delay compensation and resynchronization of the reassembled bitstream. The general scheme is shown in Figure 8.37(b).

To obtain a similar service to that provided by switched $p \times 64$, inverse multiplexers are avaliable that enable the user terminal equipment to set up and clear multiple 64 kbps circuits on demand. The technique is known as **bonding** and the principles of the scheme are shown in Figure 8.37(c).

In order to set up the high bit rate channel – in response to a user request – the inverse multiplexer at the calling side requests a single 64 kbps channel to be set up to the remote site. Once this is in place, the inverse multiplexer at the called side sends back a list of available local (extension) numbers. The calling multiplexer sets up the required number of additional channels – one at a time – and the two user equipments can then exchange data. During the call, a user terminal equipment can request that the aggregated bandwidth available is either increased or decreased by setting up or clearing channels dynamically. For example, if the terminal equipments are remote bridges then the aggregate bandwidth can be regulated to match the data traffic being exchanged at any point in time. An international standard has now been defined in **ITU-T recommendation H.221**, which is concerned with the operation of this type of equipment.

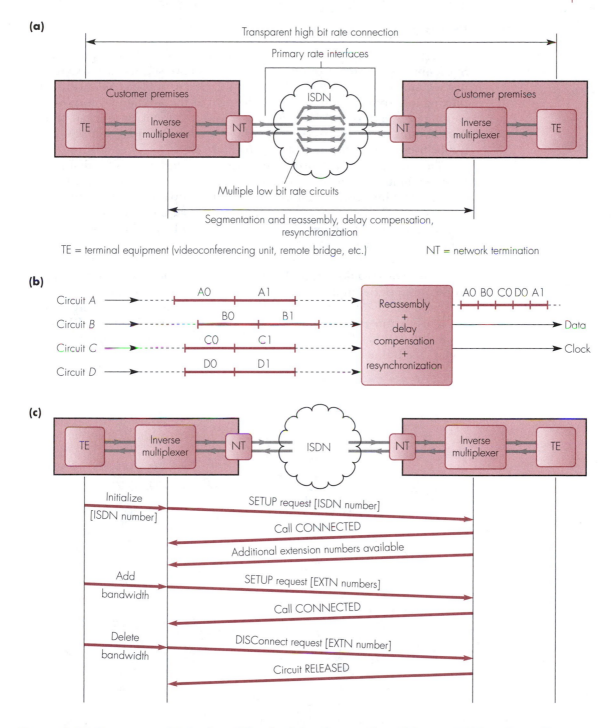

Figure 8.37 Inverse multiplexing: (a) principle of operation; (b) reassembly schematic; (c) bonding protocol.

8.9.3. Frame relay

Frame relay was initially defined as a service provided through an ISDN. Subsequently a number of telecom providers have set up networks to offer just a frame relay service. As the name implies, with frame relay, the multiplexing and routing of frames is performed at the link layer. Moreover, the routing of frames is very straightforward so the channel bit rate can be high, typical rates being up to 34 or 45 Mbps. A schematic diagram of a typical public frame relay network is shown in Figure 8.38.

The customer first informs the service provider of the sites that need to be interconnected. The provider then creates a set of permanent virtual connections that interconnect all the sites by setting up appropriate routing table entries in each frame relay node. The provider then informs the network manager at each site of the identifier that should be put into the header of a frame to reach each of the other sites.

All frames are multiplexed together onto the link connecting the **customer interface equipment** (**CIE**) to its nearest node. Logically, this appears to the customer equipment like a set of point-to-point connections between itself and all the other sites, each identified by the corresponding identifier.

The identifier is known as the **data link connection identifier** (**DLCI**) and is put into the header of each frame. It is then used by the network to route (relay) the frame to its intended destination.

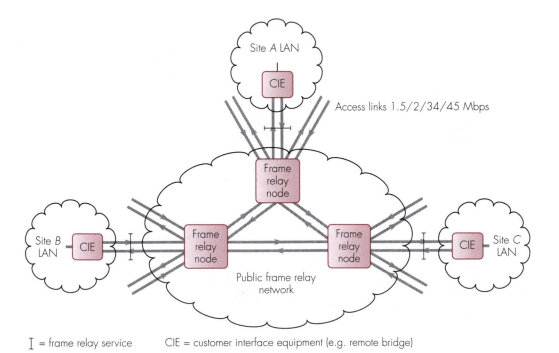

Figure 8.38 Public frame-relay network schematic.

The format of each frame is based on that used in the HDLC protocol and is shown in Figure 8.39(a). It comprises a 2-byte (extended) address header with no control field owing to the lack of any error control. In addition to the DLCI, the header contains the **forward explicit congestion notification (FECN) bit**, the **backward explicit congestion notification (BECN) bit** and the **discard eligibility (DE) bit**. These are used for controlling congestion within the network.

The DLCI, like the VCI in packet-switched networks, has only local significance on a specific network link and therefore changes as a frame traverses the links associated with a virtual path. When the virtual path is first set up, an entry is made in the routing table of each frame relay node along the route of the incoming link/DLCI and the corresponding outgoing link/DLCI to reach the intended destination of the frame. An example set of entries is shown in Figure 8.39(b) and the related routing of each frame is illustrated in Figure 8.39(c).

When a frame is received, the frame handler within each node simply reads the DLCI from within the frame and combines this with the incoming link number to determine the corresponding outgoing link and DLCI. The new DLCI is written into the frame header and the frame is queued for forwarding on the appropriate link. The order of relayed frames is thus preserved and their routing is very fast.

Since multiple frame transfers can be in progress concurrently over each link within the network, during periods of heavy traffic an outgoing link may become temporarily overloaded resulting in its queue starting to build up. This is known as **congestion** and the additional congestion control bits in each frame can be used to alleviate this condition.

Whenever the frame handler relays a frame to a link output queue, it checks the size of the queue. If this exceeds a defined limit, the frame handler signals this condition to the two end users involved in the transfer. This is done in the forward direction by setting the FECN bit in the frame header. In the backward direction, it is done by setting the BECN bit in the header of all frames which are received on this link. If the condition persists, the frame handler also returns a special frame called a **consolidated link layer management (CLLM)** frame to all CIEs that have routes (paths) involving the affected link. Such frames are simply relayed by each intermediate frame relay node in the normal way.

When the frame handler in a CIE receives an indication of network congestion, it temporarily reduces its frame forwarding rate until there are no further indications of congestion. If the overload increases, however, the frame relay node must start to discard frames. In an attempt to achieve fairness, the DE bit in the frame header is used since this is set by the frame handler in each CIE whenever the rate of entry of frames into the network exceeds the peak rate agreed at subscription time.

To minimize the possibility of wrongly delivered frames, the CRC at the tail of each frame is used to detect bit errors in the frame header (and information) fields. Then, if an error is detected, the frame is discarded. With the

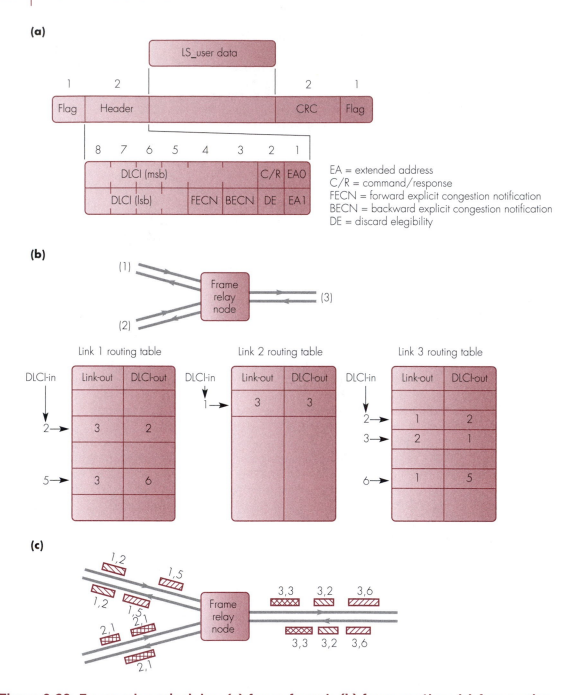

Figure 8.39 Frame relay principles: (a) frame format; (b) frame routing; (c) frame relay schematic.

frame relay service, error recovery is left to the higher protocol layers in the end-user stations. The cost of the service is based on the actual number of frames transferred.

8.9.4 High bit rate leased lines

A typical large multisite enterprise network based on high bit rate leased lines is illustrated in Figure 8.40. As we explained in Section 8.1, in addition to LAN (data) traffic, the network must also support intersite telephony traffic. Typically, the leased lines are either DS1/T1 (1.5 Mbps) or E1 (2 Mbps) or higher such as DS3 (44 Mbps) and E3 (34 Mbps). The multiple 64 kbps channels these contain are divided between telephony – for PBX interconnection – and data – for LAN interconnection – on a semipermanent basis using network management within each site multiplexer.

In the case of telephony, although a 64 kbps channel is used by the PBX for each call, it is now common to use each 64 kbps channel of the intersite leased circuit for more than one call. As we explained earlier in Section 4.2, there is now a range of compression algorithms/circuits available that provide good quality voice communication using 32, 16, or 8 kbps. This means that 2, 4, or 8 calls can be multiplexed into a single 64 kbps channel giving a substantial saving in the number of channels required between sites. The technique used to do this is known as **subrate multiplexing** and is particularly worthwhile over costly international leased lines.

In the case of data traffic, a common approach is to use a (private) **frame relay adapter** (**FRA**). These operate in a similar way to the frame relay nodes in a public frame relay network. The traffic between each pair of sites is allocated a portion of the bandwidth – number of 64 kbps channels – of the related leased line by network management. A set of DLCIs are then assigned to each path/route and these are loaded by network management into the routing tables of the interconnected set of FRAs. A related DLCI for each path is also passed to the remote bridge (or router) at each site and, once the set of MAC addresses associated with each path have been learnt by the bridge, it writes the appropriate DLCI in the header of each frame prior to passing the frame to its local FRA. The role of the FRA is then to relay each frame received from the remote bridge using the preassigned entries in its routing table and the corresponding set of aggregated channels.

Although not shown, there is a single network management station for the total network and all the devices shown in the figure have network management (agent) software within them. Normally, the management station is connected to one of the site multiplexers and a single 64 kbps channel of the intersite leased circuits is then used to transfer management-related messages to/from the management station and all the other network devices. The messages include configuration information to all devices – routing table entries, bandwidth allocations, and so on – and fault reports from the devices. In this way, should a fault develop or a reconfiguration be necessary, this can be done from a central site in a secure way.

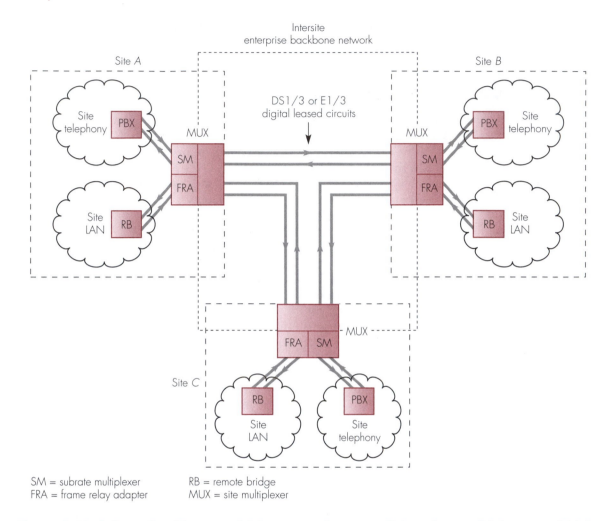

SM = subrate multiplexer   RB = remote bridge
FRA = frame relay adapter   MUX = site multiplexer

Figure 8.40 Schematic of large multisite enterprise network based on multiplexers and high bit rate leased circuits.

Finally, although most private networks are run and managed by the enterprise to which they belong, a number of telecom providers now offer the option for an equivalent private network to be set up within the provider's network. This is then known as a **virtual private network (VPN)**. These offer the same set of services to the private network but are managed and operated by the telecom provider. In general, VPNs are more expensive than private networks but they have the advantage that the enterprise need not then be involved in the recruitment of staff who are not concerned with the core business of the enterprise.

Summary

A summary of the various topics discussed in this chapter is given in Figure 8.41.

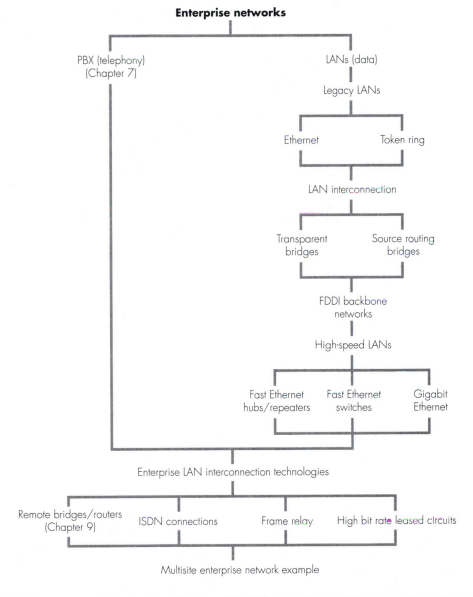

Enterprise networks

PBX (telephony)
(Chapter 7)

LANs (data)

Legacy LANs

Ethernet   Token ring

LAN interconnection

Transparent
bridges

Source routing
bridges

FDDI backbone
networks

High-speed LANs

Fast Ethernet
hubs/repeaters

Fast Ethernet
switches

Gigabit
Ethernet

Enterprise LAN interconnection technologies

Remote bridges/routers
(Chapter 9)

ISDN connections   Frame relay   High bit rate leased circuits

Multisite enterprise network example

Figure 8.41 Summary of the topics discussed in this chapter relating to enterprise networks.

Exercises

Section 8.1

8.1 What is the meaning of the term "enterprise network"? Describe the factors that determine when such networks are created.

Section 8.3

8.2 Explain the meaning of the following terms relating to the CSMA/CD medium access control method:
(i) multiple access,
(ii) broadcast mode,
(iii) collision,
(iv) carrier sense.

8.3 With the aid of Figure 8.1, explain the meaning of the term "slot time" and how this is derived. State how the slot time determines the maximum throughput of the LAN.

8.4 State the use of a jam sequence with the CSMA/CD MAC method and explain why a truncated binary exponential process is used.

8.5 Explain the origin of the hub configuration as is now used for Ethernet LANs. Also, with the aid of a diagram, explain how the broadcast mode of operation is achieved.

8.6 Two UTP hubs to which user stations are attached are each connected to a third hub by optical fiber cable in order to gain access to a server that is attached to the third hub. Derive the maximum length of optical fiber cable that can be used.

8.7 With the aid of the frame format shown in Figure 8.3(a), explain:
(i) the clock encoding method used and how the start of a new frame is detected,
(ii) how each station that receives a frame determines from the destination address whether the frame contents are intended for it,
(iii) the use of the type/length field.

8.8 Explain the meaning and use of:
(i) an interface gap,
(ii) a backoff limit,
(iii) an attempt limit.

Hence, with the aid of flow diagrams, describe the transmit and receive procedures followed by the CSMA/CD MAC sublayer.

Section 8.4

8.9 With the aid of Figure 8.5, explain how the transmission of frames over the ring is controlled using a token. Include in your explanation the two alternatives that are used by a station to release the token.

8.10 With the aid of the two wiring configurations used with a token ring shown in Figure 8.6, explain the meaning/use of the following:
(i) hub/concentrator,
(ii) station coupling unit,
(iii) trunk coupling unit.

8.11 Explain the meaning/use of the following relating to a token ring:
(i) active ring monitor,
(ii) minimum ring latency,
(iii) elastic buffer.

8.12 With the aid of the diagrams in Figure 8.7, explain:
(i) how the start and end of a frame is detected,
(ii) the role of the token, monitor, priority, and reservation bits in the access control field,
(iii) the role of the A and C bits in the frame status field.

8.13 With the aid of flow diagrams, explain the transmission and reception procedures of a frame with a token ring LAN. Include the meaning/use of the token hold timer.

8.14 Assume the same operating conditions as used in Example 8.1. After a period of inactivity, stations 1, 2, and 3 generates a frame to send. If the priority of the frames is 2, 0, and 2 respectively, derive and show in table form the transmissions made by each station for five further rotations of the token.

Section 8.5

8.15 How is a bridge different from a repeater? What are the advantages and disadvantages of each?

8.16 With the aid of the bridge architecture shown in Figure 8.12(a), explain the operation of a bridge including the meaning of the terms:
(i)   promiscuous mode,
(ii) forwarding database,
(iii) bridge learning.

8.17 With the aid of Figure 8.12(b), explain how the entries in the two forwarding databases would be built up assuming the following message exchanges: 1 to/from 3, 1 to/from 5, 2 to/from 4, 2 to/from 6.

8.18 With the aid of the LAN topology shown in Figure 8.13, explain why the learning process described in your solution to Exercise 8.16 would not work. Hence state how the topology needs to be changed.

8.19 In relation to the spanning tree algorithm, explain the meaning of the terms:
(i)   spanning tree,
(ii) root bridge,
(iii) designated cost,
(iv) root path cost,
(v)   root port,
(vi) designated port.

8.20 Assume the same bridged LAN topology as shown in Figure 8.14. Determine the active (spanning tree) topology for the following conditions:
(i)   bridge B1 fails
(ii) all bridges are in service but segments S1, 2, 4, and 5 have three times the designated cost of segments S3 and 6 (that is, they have a higher bit rate)
(iii) the same designated costs as in (ii) but bridge B5 has a higher priority than the other bridges.

8.21 With the aid of the LAN topology shown in Figure 8.15, state the routing entry held by station A to reach station D. Hence describe how a frame sent by A is routed to D. Include in your description the structure of the routing information carried in the frame header.

8.22 In relation to the route discovery algorithm used with a source routing bridged LAN, explain the meaning/use of
(i)   a single-route broadcast frame,
(ii) an all-routes broadcast frame.

Hence, with the aid of the LAN topology shown in Figure 8.17, explain how the indicated designation of each port is derived.

Section 8.6

8.23 With the aid of the LAN topology shown in Figure 8.18, explain the meaning/use of:
(i)   multiport bridge,
(ii) a building backbone,
(iii) a site-wide backbone.

8.24 With the aid of Figure 8.19, explain the meaning/use of the following relating to an FDDI backbone:
(i)   primary and secondary rings,
(ii) single attach and dual attach stations,
(iii) optical coupling unit,
(iv) patch panel wiring concentrator,
(v)   polarized duplex connectors.

8.25 State why 4B/5B encoding is used in FDDI LANs rather than differential Manchester encoding.

8.26 With the aid of the interface schematic shown in Figure 8.22, explain the meaning/use of:
(i)   the latency buffer,
(ii) 4B5B encoder/decoder,
(iii) clock synchronizer.

8.27 In relation to the timed token rotation protocol used with FDDI, explain the meaning of the terms:
(i)   TTRT,
(ii) TRT,
(iii) THT,
(iv) early/late token.

8.28 Define the terms (i) maximum obtainable throughput and (ii) the maximum access delay of a shared-medium network. Hence with the aid of the example shown in Figure 8.25, stating clearly any assumptions you make, derive an approximate formula for each in terms of the TTRT and ring latency, T_l.

Section 8.7

8.29 Derive the slot time in bits for a Fast Ethernet hub operating with drop cables of up to 100 m and a bit rate of 100 Mbps. State the implications of your answer in relation to that of a 10BaseT hub.

8.30 With the aid of the wiring configuration of a 100BaseT hub shown in Figure 8.26(a), explain how the carrier sense and collision detection functions associated with CSMA/CD are carried out.

8.31 State why the 8B6T encoding scheme is used for transmissions over each twisted-pair wire with 100BaseT. Also explain why a DC balancing scheme is required.

8.32 With the aid of the diagrams shown in Figures 8.27 and 8.28, explain:
(i) how DC balance is maintained,
(ii) the latency associated with the 8B6T encoding sequence,
(iii) how additional error detection is obtained by sending one of two different end-of-stream codes,
(iv) how the start-of-stream code used gives a more reliable collision detection.

8.33 What is the difference between a repeater hub and a switching hub? With the aid of Figure 8.29, explain the operation of a Fast Ethernet switch. Include in your explanation how duplex working is achieved.

8.34 With the aid of the network schematic shown in Figure 8.30, explain how a Fast Ethernet switch can be used to provide faster access to site servers for stations attached to 10/100BaseT hubs.

8.35 In relation to a Gigabit Ethernet repeater hub, explain how the shorter slot time is overcome using
(i) carrier extension,
(ii) frame bursting.

8.36 Produce a diagram of a network configuration similar to that shown in Figure 8.30 that shows how a Gigabit Ethernet switch can be used to interconnect several 100BastT hubs/switches to a server. Show clearly the bit rate used on each interconnecting line.

Section 8.8

8.37 With the aid of the protocol framework shown in Figure 8.31, explain the role of the following sublayer protocols:
(i) PMD,
(ii) convergence,
(iii) MAC, (iv) LLC.

8.38 With the aid of the interlayer parameters shown in Figure 8.35, explain the meaning/use of:
(i) the DSAP and SSAP,
(ii) SNP including the ORG and type fields,
(iii) CTL.

Section 8.9

8.39 With the aid of the diagram of an enterprise network shown in Figure 8.36, explain how intersite communications are carried out using the following types of intersite gateway:
(i) remote bridge,
(ii) IP/IPX router.

8.40 With the aid of the diagrams shown in Figure 8.37, state the role and describe the operation of an inverse multiplexer. Include in your description the principles of the delay compensation and resynchronization procedures.

8.41 With the aid of the network schematic shown in Figure 8.38, explain how a public frame relay network can be used to create an enterprise network. Hence use the frame format and routing principles shown in Figure 8.39 to explain how frames are relayed/routed between all the network sites. Include in your explanation the role of the following fields in each frame header:

(i) DLCI,

(ii) FECN, BECN and DE bits.

Explain the use of a CCLM frame and the actions carried out if a frame is corrupted.

8.42 With the aid of the network schematic shown in Figure 8.40, explain how both telephony (via a PBX) and data (via a remote bridge or router) are extended to cover an entire enterprise. Include in your explanation the role and operation of:

(i) a subrate multiplexer,

(ii) a frame relay adapter.

Can the latter also be used for telephony?

9

The Internet

9.1 Introduction

As we saw in Chapter 1, the Internet is a global network that supports a variety of interpersonal and interactive multimedia applications. A user gains access to these applications by means of an end system – normally referred to as a host – which, typically, is a multimedia PC, a network computer, or a workstation. As we showed in Figure 1.2, the Internet comprises a large number of different access networks which are interconnected together by means of a global internetwork. Associated with each access network – ISP network, intranet, enterprise network, site/campus LAN, and so on – is a **gateway** and the global internetwork consists of an interconnected set of regional, national, and international, networks all of which are interconnected together using high bit rate leased lines and devices known as **routing gateways** or simply **routers**.

The Internet operates in a packet-switched mode and Figure 9.1 shows the protocol stack associated with it. In the figure, we assume the network interface card in all hosts that are attached to an access network communicate with other hosts using the TCP/IP protocol stack. As we showed in Figure 5.11 (and explained in the accompanying text) this is not always the

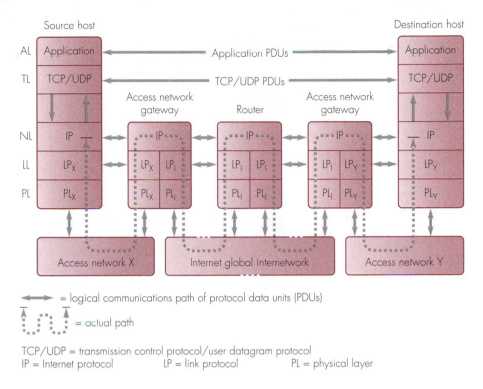

Figure 9.1 Internet networking components and protocols.

case. Nevertheless, any end system (host) that communicates directly over the Internet – the email server in Figure 5.11 for example – does so using the TCP/IP protocol stack.

In general, the various access networks have different operational parameters associated with them in terms of their bit rate, frame format, maximum frame size, and type of addresses that are used. For example, in the case of a site/campus LAN, as we saw in the last chapter, a token ring LAN uses a different bit rate, frame format, and maximum frame size from an Ethernet LAN. This means, therefore, that since bridges can only be used to interconnect LAN segments of the same type, they cannot be used to perform the network interconnection function. Hence instead, the routing and forwarding operations associated with a gateway are performed at the network layer. In the TCP/IP protocol stack the network layer protocol is the **Internet protocol** (**IP**) and, as we show in Figure 9.1, in order to transfer packets of information from one host to another, it is the IP in the two hosts, together with the IP in each Internet gateway and router involved, that perform the routing and other harmonization functions necessary.

The IP in each host (that communicates directly over the Internet) has a unique Internet-wide address assigned to it. This is known as the host's

Internet address or, more usually, its **IP address**. Each IP address has two parts: a **network identifier** (**netid**) and a **host identifier** (**hostid**). The allocation of netids is centrally managed by the **Internet Network Information Center** (**InterNIC**) and each access network has a unique netid assigned to it. For example, each campus/site LAN is assigned a single netid. The IP address of a host attached to an access network then contains the unique netid of the access network and a unique hostid. As with netids, hostids are centrally allocated but this time by the local administrator of the access network to which the host is attached.

The IP provides a connectionless best-effort service to the transport layer above it which, as we show in the figure, is either the transmission control protocol (TCP) or the user datagram protocol (UDP). Hence when either protocol has a block of information to transfer, it simply passes the block to its local IP together with the IP address of the intended recipient. The (source) IP first adds the destination and source IP addresses to the head of the block, together with an indication of the source protocol (TCP or UDP), to form what is known as an **IP datagram**. The IP then forwards the datagram to its local gateway. At this point the datagram is often referred to as a **packet** and hence the two terms are used interchangeably.

Each access gateway is attached to an internetwork router and, at regular intervals, the IP in these routers exchange routing information. When this is complete, each router has built up a **routing table** which enables it to route a packet/datagram to any of the other networks/netids that make up the Internet. Hence, on receipt of a packet, the router simply reads the destination netid from the packet header and uses the contents of its routing table to forward the packet on the path/route through the global internetwork first to the destination internetwork router and, from there, to the destination access gateway. Assuming the size of the packet is equal to or less than the maximum frame size of the destination access network, on receipt of the packet, the destination gateway reads the hostid part of the destination IP address and forwards the packet to the local host identified by the hostid part. The IP in the host then strips off the header from the packet and passes the block of information contained within it – known as the **payload** – to the peer transport layer protocol indicated in the packet header.

If the size of the packet is greater than the maximum frame size – that is, the **maximum transmission unit** (**MTU**) – of the destination access network, the IP in the destination gateway proceeds to divide the block of information contained in the packet into a number of smaller blocks each known as a **fragment**. Each fragment is then forwarded to the IP in the destination host in a separate packet the length of which is determined by the MTU of the access network. The destination IP then reassembles the fragments of information from each received packet to form the original submitted block of information and passes this to the peer transport layer protocol indicated in the packet header.

As we shall see in the following sections, the above is just a summary of the operation of the IP and, in practice, in order to perform the various functions we have just described, the IP uses a number of what are known as **adjunct protocols.** These are identified in Figure 9.2 and a summary of the role of each protocol is as follows:

■ **The address resolution protocol (ARP)** and the **reverse ARP (RARP)** are used by the IP in hosts that are attached to a broadcast LAN (such as an Ethernet or token ring) in order to determine the physical (MAC) address of a host or gateway given its IP address (ARP) and, in the case of the RARP, the reverse function.

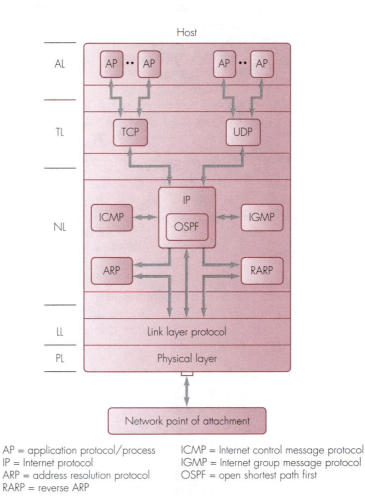

AP = application protocol/process
IP = Internet protocol
ARP = address resolution protocol
RARP = reverse ARP

ICMP = Internet control message protocol
IGMP = Internet group message protocol
OSPF = open shortest path first

Figure 9.2 IP adjunct protocols.

- **The open shortest path first** (**OSPF**) protocol is an example of a routing protocol used in the global internetwork. Such protocols are present in each internetwork router and are utilized to build up the contents of the routing table that is used to route packets across the global internetwork.

- The **Internet control message protocol** (**ICMP**) is used by the IP in a host or gateway to exchange error and other control messages with the IP in another host or gateway.

- The **Internet group management protocol** (**IGMP**) is used with multicasting to enable a host to send a copy of a datagram to the other hosts that are part of the same multicast group.

In this chapter we explain the operation of the different parts of the IP and each of the adjunct protocols in some detail. Also, we describe the structure of the Internet global internetwork in more detail as this influences the overall routing strategy and routing protocols that are used. Currently, the most widely used version of the IP is version 4 and hence most of the chapter is devoted to this. In a longer time span, however, this will be replaced by version 6. Hence we describe the main features of this too and how it differs and interoperates with version 4. We shall defer discussion of the two transport layer protocols until Chapter 12 when we describe application protocols and related issues.

9.2 IP datagrams

As we indicated in the introduction, the IP is a connectionless protocol and all user information is transferred in the payload part of what is known as a datagram. The header of each datagram contains a number of fields the format of which are shown in Figure 9.3.

The *version* field contains the version of the IP used to create the datagram and ensures that all systems – gateways, routers, and hosts – that process the datagram/packet during its transfer across the Internet to the destination host interpret the various fields correctly. The current version number is 4 and hence the IP is referred to as **IP version 4** or simply **IPv4**.

The header can be of variable length and the *intermediate header length* (*IHL*) field specifies the actual length of the header in multiples of 32-bit words. The minimum length (without options) is 5. If the datagram contains options, these are in multiples of 32 bits with any unused bytes filled with **padding** bytes. Also, since the IHL field is 4 bits, the maximum permissible length is 15.

The *type of service (TOS)* field allows an application protocol/process to specify the relative priority (precedence) of the application data and the pre-ferred attributes associated with the path to be followed. It is used by each gateway and router during the transmission and routing of the packet to transmit packets of higher priority first and to select a line/route that has the specified attributes should a choice be available. For example, if a route with

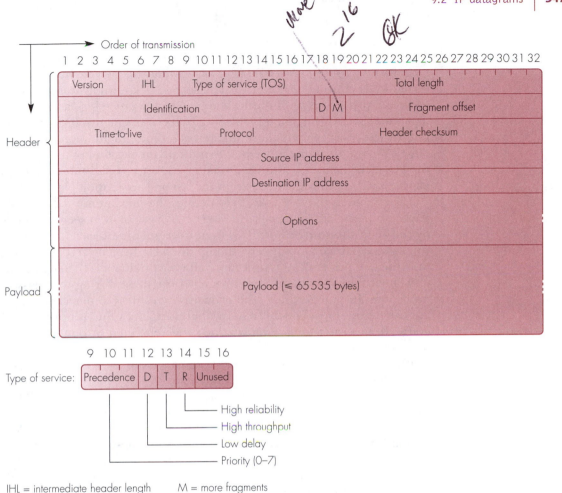

Figure 9.3 IP datagram/packet format and header fields.

a minimum delay is specified then, given a choice of routes, the line with the smallest delay associated with it should be chosen. We shall discuss the use of the TOS field further in Section 9.8.

The *total length* field defines the total length of the initial datagram including the header and payload parts. This is a 16-bit field and hence the maximum length is 65 535 (64K − 1) bytes and, as we explain in the next section, should the contents of the initial datagram need to be transferred in multiple (smaller) packets, then the value in *total length* is used by the destination host to reassemble the payload contained within each smaller packet – known as a fragment – into the original payload. In addition, each smaller packet contains the same value in the *identification* field to enable the destination host to relate each received packet fragment to the same original datagram.

The next three bits are known as *flag bits* of which two are currently used. The first is known as the *don't fragment* or *D-bit*. It is set by a source host and is examined by routers. A set D-bit indicates that the packet should be transferred in its entirety or not at all. The second is known as *more fragments* or *M-bit* and this also is used during the reassembly procedure associated with data transfers involving multiple smaller packets/fragments. It is set to 1 in all but the last packet/fragment in which it is set to 0. In addition, the *fragment offset* is used by the same procedure to indicate the position of the first byte of the fragment contained within a smaller packet in relation to the original packet payload. All fragments except the last one are in multiples of 8 bytes.

The value in the *time-to-live* field defines the maximum time for which a packet can be in transit across the Internet. The value is in seconds and is set by the IP in the source host. It is then decremented by each gateway and router by a defined amount and, should the value become zero, the packet is discarded. In principle, this procedure allows a destination IP to wait a known maximum time for an outstanding packet fragment during the reassembly procedure. In practice, it is used primarily by routers to detect packets that are caught in loops. For this reason, therefore, the value is normally a hop count. In this case, the *hop count* value is decremented by one by each gateway/router visited and, should the value become zero, the packet is discarded. We shall identify how looping can occur in Section 9.6 when we discuss the subject of routing.

The value in the *protocol* field is used to enable the destination IP to pass the payload within each received packet to the same (peer) protocol that sent the data. As we showed in Figure 9.2, this can be an internal network layer protocol such as the ICMP, or a higher-layer protocol such as TCP or UDP.

The *header checksum* applies just to the header part of the datagram and is a safeguard against corrupted packets being routed to incorrect destinations. It is computed by treating each block of 16 bits as an integer and adding them all together using 1s complement arithmetic. As we showed in the example in Figure 6.20(b), the checksum is then the complement (inverse) of the 1s complement sum.

The *source address* and *destination address* are the Internetwide IP addresses of the source and destination host respectively.

Finally, the *options* field is used in selected datagrams to carry additional information relating to:

- *security:* the payload may be encrypted for example, or be made accessible only to a specified user group. The *security* field then contains fields to enable the destination to decrypt the payload and authenticate the sender;

- *source routing:* if known, the actual path/route to be followed through the Internet may be specified in this field as a list of gateway/router addresses;

- *loose source routing:* this can be used to specify preferred routers in a path;

- *route recording:* this field is used by each gateway/router visited during the passage of a packet through the Internet to record its address. The resulting list of addresses can then be used, for example, in the source routing field of subsequent packets;
- *stream identification:* this, together with the source and destination addresses in the datagram header, enables each gateway/router along the path followed by the packet to identify the stream/flow to which the packet belongs and, if necessary, give the packet precedence over other packets. Examples include streams containing samples of speech or compressed video;
- *time-stamp:* if present, this is used by each gateway/router along the path followed by the packet to record the time it processed the packet.

9.3 Fragmentation and reassembly

As we explained in Section 9.1, if the size of a packet is greater than the MTU of the destination access network – or an intermediate network in the global internetwork – the IP in the destination gateway – or intermediate router – divides the information received in the packet into a number of smaller blocks known as fragments. Each fragment is then forwarded to the IP in the destination host in a separate packet the length of which is determined by the MTU of the access/intermediate network. The IP in the destination host then reassembles the fragments of information from each received packet to form the original submitted block of information. It then passes this to the peer transport layer protocol indicated in the protocol field of the packet header.

To see how the various fields in each packet header are used to perform this function, consider the transport protocol in a host that is attached to a token ring LAN transferring a block of 7000 bytes – including the transport protocol header – over the Internet to the transport protocol in a host that is attached to an Ethernet LAN. Let us assume that the MTU associated with the token ring LAN is 4000 bytes and that of the Ethernet LAN 1500 bytes. Also that the header of each IP datagram requires 20 bytes. The steps taken to transfer the complete block of 7000 bytes are shown in Figure 9.4(a).

Since the header of each datagram requires 20 bytes, the maximum usable data in each token ring frame is 4000 – 20 = 3980 bytes. Similarly, that in each Ethernet frame is 1500 – 20 = 1480 bytes. However, all fragments of user data (except the last one) must be in multiples of 8 bytes. So we shall have to limit the maximum user data in each packet transferred over the token ring to 3976 bytes. In the case of the Ethernet, 1480 is divisible by 8 and so this value can be used unchanged.

To transfer the block of 7000 bytes over the token ring LAN requires two datagrams, one with 3976 bytes of user data and the second 7000 – 3976 = 3024 bytes. The values for the various fields associated with the fragmentation and reassembly procedures in each datagram header are given in Figure 9.4(b).

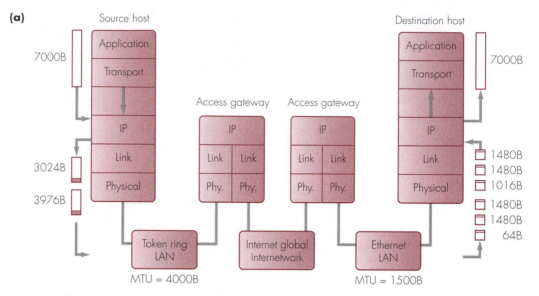

(a)

Note: All values shown are the amounts of user data in each packet/frame in bytes

(b) *Token ring LAN:*

	(i)	(ii)
Identification	20	20
Total length	7000	7000
Fragment offset	0	497
(User data)	3976	3024
M-bit	1	0

(c) *Ethernet LAN:*

	(i)	(ii)	(iii)	(iv)	(v)	(vi)
Identification	20	20	20	20	20	20
Total length	7000	7000	7000	7000	7000	7000
Fragment offset	0	185	370	497	682	867
(User data)	1480	1480	1016	1480	1480	64
M-bit	1	1	1	1	1	0

Figure 9.4 Fragmentation and reassembly example: (a) Internet schematic; (b) packet header fields for token ring LAN; (c) Ethernet LAN.

The value in the *identification* field is the same in all fragments and is used by the destination IP to relate each fragment to the same original block of information. In the example, we assume a value of 20 has been allocated by the IP in the source host.

The *total length* is the number of bytes in the initial datagram including the 20-byte header. However, since we have subtracted 20 from the maximum user data value associated with each LAN, we have shown this as 7000. Note that this is the same in all the datagram fragments and hence the destination IP can readily determine when all fragments have been received. The *fragment offset* then indicates the position of the user data in each fragment – in multiples of 8 bytes – relative to the start of the initial datagram. Finally, the *more fragments* (*M*) *bit* is 1 in each fragment and 0 in the final fragment.

We assume that the two datagrams/packets created by the source IP are transferred over the global internetwork unchanged and, on reaching the access gateway attached to the Ethernet LAN, the smaller maximum user data value of 1480 bytes means that both packets must be further fragmented. As we show in Figure 9.4(c), both packets must be fragmented into three smaller packets. The first into two maximum sized packets of 1480 bytes and a further packet containing $3976 - 2(1480) = 1016$ bytes, and the second containing two maximum sized packets and a further packet containing $3024 - 2(1480) = 64$ bytes. The IP in the destination host then reassembles the user data in each of the six packets it receives into the original 7000-byte block of information and delivers this to the peer transport protocol.

As we explained, the *time-to-live* field in each packet header – and fragment header – is present to avoid packets endlessly looping around the Internet (normally as a result of routing table inconsistencies) and also to set a maximum limit on the time a host needs to wait for a delayed/corrupted/discarded datagram fragment. Hence although the use of fragmentation would appear to be relatively straightforward, there are drawbacks associated with its use. For example, as we shall explain in Section 12.3.2, with the TCP transport protocol, if an acknowledgment of correct receipt of a submitted block is not received within a defined maximum time limit, the source TCP will retransmit the complete block. Thus, as we can deduce from the example in Figure 9.4, it only needs one of the six datagram fragments to be delayed or discarded to trigger the retransmission of the complete 7000-byte block. As a result, therefore, most TCP implementations avoid the possibility of fragmentation occurring by limiting the maximum submitted block size – including transport protocol header – to 1048 bytes or, in some instances, 556 bytes. Alternatively, as we shall expand upon in Section 9.7, it is possible for the source IP, prior to sending any transport protocol (user) data, to determine the MTU of the path to be followed through the Internet. Then, if this is smaller than the submitted user data, the source IP fragments the data using this MTU. In this way, no further fragmentation should be necessary during the transfer of the packets through the global internetwork.

9.4 IP addresses

Each host, gateway, and router has a unique Internetwide IP address assigned to it that comprises a netid and a hostid part. Hence in the case of gateways and routers that interconnect two (or more) networks together, each gateway/router port – also referred to as an interface – has a different netid associated with it. In order to give the Internet Network Information Center some flexibility when assigning netids, one of three different address formats can be used. Each format is known by an **address class** and, as we show in Figure 9.5, classes A, B, and C are all different types of unicast addresses.

Each of these classes is intended for use with a different size of network. For example, at one extreme a large national network and at the other a small site LAN. The class to which an address belongs can be determined from the position of the first zero bit in the first four bits. The remaining bits then specify the netid and hostid parts with the boundary separating the two parts located on byte boundaries to simplify decoding.

Class A addresses have 7 bits for the netid and 24 bits for the hostid; class B addresses have 14 bits for the netid and 16 bits for the hostid; and class C addresses have 21 bits for the netid and 8 bits for the hostid. Class A addresses are intended for use with networks that have a large number of attached hosts (up to 2^{24}) while class C addresses allow for a large number of networks each with a small number of attached hosts (up to 256). An example of a class A network is a large national network and an example of a class C network is a small site LAN.

Netids and hostids comprising either all 0s or all 1s have special meaning:

■ An address with a hostid of all 0s is used to refer to the network in the netid part rather than a host.

■ An address with a netid of all 0s implies the same network as the source network/netid.

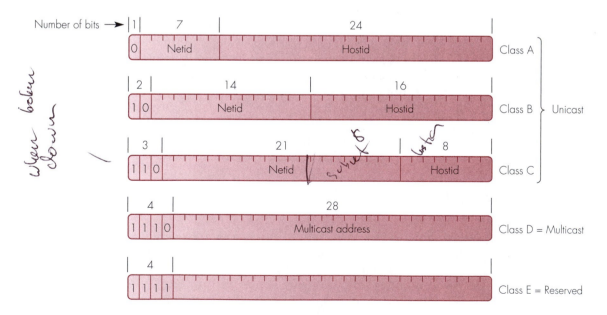

Figure 9.5 IP address formats.

- An address of all 1s means broadcast the packet over the source network.
- An address with a hostid of all 1s means broadcast the packet over the destination network in the netid part.
- A class A address with a netid of all 1s is used for test purposes within the protocol stack of the source host. It is known, therefore, as the **loopback address.**

To make it easier to communicate IP addresses, the 32 bits are first broken into four bytes. Each byte is then converted into its equivalent decimal form and the total IP address is represented as the four decimal numbers with a dot (period) between each. This is known as the **dotted decimal notation** and some examples are as follows:

00001010 00000000 00000000 00000000 = 10.0.0.0.
                                                            = class A, netid 10

10000000 00000011 00000010 00000011 = 128.3.2.3
                                                            = class B, netid 128.3, hostid 2.3

11000000 00000000 00000001 11111111 = 192.0.1.255
                                                            = class C, all hosts broadcast on
                                                               netid 192.0.1

Example 9.1	Assuming the IP address formats shown in Figure 9.5, derive the range of host addresses for classes A, B, and C. Give your answer in dotted decimal notation and also straight decimal.

Answer:

Class A:
Netid = 1 to 127   Hostid = 0.0.0 to 255.255.255
       = 126 networks   = 16 777 214 hosts

Class B:
Netid = 128.0 to 191.255   Hostid = 0.0 to 255.255
       = 16 382 networks   = 65 534 hosts

Class C:
Netid = 192.0.0 to 223.255.255   Hostid = 0 to 255
       = 2 097 152 networks   = 254 hosts

Note that we have not used hostids of all 0s or all 1s.

Class D addresses are reserved for multicasting. As we explained in Section 8.2, in a LAN a frame can be sent to an individual, broadcast, or group address. The group address is used by a station to send a copy of the frame to all stations that are members of the same multicast group (and hence have the same multicast address). In the case of LANs, the group address is a MAC address and the class D IP address format is provided to enable this mode of working to be extended over the complete Internet.

As we can see, unlike the three unicast address classes, the 28-bit multicast group address has no further structure. As we shall expand upon in Section 9.6.9, multicast group addresses are assigned by the **Internet assigned numbers authority** (*IANA*). Although most of these are assigned dynamically (for conferences and so on), some are reserved to identify specific groups of hosts and/or routers. These are known as **permanent multicast group addresses**. Examples are 224.0.0.1 which means all hosts (and routers) on the same broadcast network, and 224.0.0.2 which means all routers on the same site network.

9.4.1 Subnets

Although the basic structure shown in Figure 9.5 is adequate for most addressing purposes, the introduction of multiple LANs at each site can mean unacceptably high overheads in terms of routing. As we described in Section 8.5, MAC bridges are used to interconnect LAN segments of the same type. This solution is attractive for routing purposes since the combined LAN then behaves like a single network. When interconnecting dissimilar LAN types, as we explained in Section 8.8.4, the differences in frame format and, more importantly, frame length, mean that routers are normally used since the fragmentation and reassembly of packets/frames is a function of the network layer rather than the MAC sublayer. However, the use of routers means that, with the basic address formats, each LAN must have its own netid. In the case of large sites, there may be a significant number of such LANs.

This means that with the basic addressing scheme, all the routers relating to a site need to take part in the overall Internet routing function. As we shall expand upon in Section 9.5, the efficiency of any routing scheme is strongly influenced by the number of routing nodes that make up the Internet. The concept of **subnets** has been introduced to decouple the routers – and hence routing – associated with a single site from the overall routing function in the global internetwork. Essentially, instead of each LAN associated with a site having its own netid, only the site is allocated a netid. Each LAN is then known as a **subnet** and the identity of each (LAN) subnet then forms part of the hostid field. This refined address format is shown in Figure 9.6(a).

The same address classes and associated structure are used, but the netid now relates to a complete site rather than to a single subnet. Hence, since only a single gateway/router attached to a site performs internetwide routing, the netid is considered as the **Internet part.** For a single netid with a

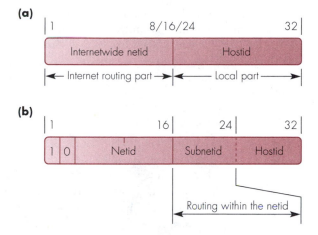

Figure 9.6 Subnet addressing: (a) address structure; (b) example.

number of associated subnets, the hostid part consists of two subfields: a **subnetid part** and a **local hostid part**. Because these have only local significance, they are known collectively as the **local part**. Also, to discriminate between the routers in the global internetwork and those in a local site network, the latter are known as **subnet routers.**

Because of the possibly wide range of subnets associated with different site networks, no attempt has been made to define rigid subaddress boundaries for the local address part. Instead, an **address mask** is used to define the subaddress boundary for a particular network (and hence netid). The address mask is kept by the site gateway and all the subnet routers at the site. It consists of binary 1s in those bit positions that contain a network address – including the netid and subnetid – and binary 0s in positions that contain the hostid. Hence an address mask of

$$11111111 \quad 11111111 \quad 11111111 \quad 00000000$$

means that the first three bytes (octets) contain a network/subnet identifier and the fourth byte contains the host identifier.

For example, if the mask relates to a class B address – a zero bit in the second bit position – this is readily interpreted as: the first two bytes are the internetwide netid, the next byte the subnetid, and the last byte the hostid on the subnet. Such an address is shown in Figure 9.6(b).

Normally, dotted decimal is used to define address masks and hence the above mask is written:

$$255.255.255.0$$

Byte boundaries are normally chosen to simplify address decoding. So with this mask, and assuming the netid was, say, 128.10, then all the hosts attached to this network would have this same netid. In this way, the presence of a possibly large number of subnets and associated (subnet) routers is transparent to all the other Internet gateways and routers for routing purposes.

Example 9.2

The administrator of a campus LAN is assigned a single class B IP address of 150.10.0.0. Assuming that the LAN comprises 100 subnets, each of which is connected to an FDDI backbone network using a subnet router, define a suitable address mask for the site if the maximum number of hosts connected to each subnet is 70.

Answer:

A class B IP address means that both the netid part and the local part are each 16 bits. Hence the simplest way of meeting this requirement is to divide the local part into two: 8 bits for the subnetid and 8 bits for the hostid.

This will allow for up to 254 subnets and 254 hosts per subnet ignoring all 1s and all 0s.

The address mask, therefore, is 255.255.255

9.5 ARP and RARP

As we outlined in Section 9.1, the address resolution protocol (ARP) and the reverse ARP (RARP) are used by the IP in hosts that are attached to a broadcast LAN. The ARP is used to determine the MAC address of another host or gateway that is attached to the same LAN given the IP address of the host gateway. It is defined in **RFC 826**. The RARP performs the reverse function and is defined in **RFC 903**. We explain the operation of each separately.

9.5.1 ARP

Associated with each host are two addresses: its IP address and its MAC address which, since it is assigned to the MAC integrated circuit when it is manufactured, is known also as the host's hardware (or physical) address. Normally, both addresses are stored in the configuration file of the host on the hard disk. In order to describe the operation of the ARP, we shall use the LAN topology shown in Figure 9.7.

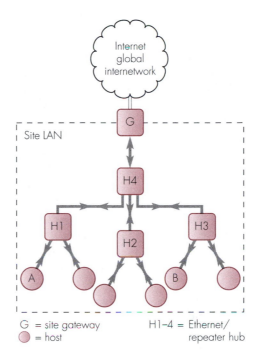

Figure 9.7 Example topology for describing the operation of the ARP.

As we can see, this comprises three Ethernet hubs (H1, H2, and H3) that are interconnected by means of a fourth hub (H4). There is also a connection between H4 and the site gateway (G). We assume that all the hubs are simple repeater hubs and that all hosts have just been switched on and hence have sent no frames. Associated with each ARP is a routing table known as the **ARP cache.** This contains a list of the IP/MAC address-pairs of those hosts with which host A has recently communicated and, when the host is first switched on, it contains no entries. First we shall explain the steps taken by the ARP in host A to send a datagram to another host on the same LAN – host B – and then to a host on a different LAN via the gateway.

On receipt of the first datagram from the IP in host A, the ARP in A reads the destination IP address of B contained in the datagram header and determines it is not in its cache. Hence it broadcasts an **ARP request message** in a broadcast frame over the LAN and waits for a reply. The request message contains both its own IP/MAC address-pair and the (target) IP address of the destination, host B. Being a broadcast frame this is received by the ARP in all hosts attached to the LAN.

The ARP in host B recognizes its own IP address in the request message and proceeds to process it. It first checks to see whether the address-pair of the source is within its own cache and, if not, enters them. This is done since it is highly probable that the destination host will require the MAC address of the source when the higher-layer protocol responds to the message contained within the datagram payload. The ARP in host B then responds by returning an **ARP reply** message (containing its own MAC address) to the ARP in host A using the latter's MAC address contained in the request message. On receipt of the reply message, the ARP in host A first makes an entry of the requested IP/MAC address-pair in its own cache and then passes the waiting datagram to either the LLC sublayer (if one is present) or (if not) to the MAC sublayer together with the MAC address of host B which indicates where it should be sent. At B the datagram is passed directly to the IP for processing.

Being on the same broadcast network as all the site hosts, the LAN port of the gateway receives a copy of all broadcast frames containing ARP request and reply messages. On receipt of each message, the ARP first checks to see if it has the IP/MAC address-pair(s) contained in the message in its cache and, if not, adds them to the cache. In this way, the site gateway learns the address-pair of all the hosts that are attached to the site LAN.

To send a datagram from, say, host A to a host on a different LAN – and hence netid – the ARP in A broadcasts the request message as before. In this case, however, on receipt of the message, the gateway determines that the netid part of the destination IP address relates to a different network and responds by returning a reply message containing its own address-pair. Hence A makes an entry of this in its cache and proceeds to forward the datagram to the gateway as if it was the destination host. The gateway then forwards the datagram/packet over the Internet using one of the global internetwork routing protocols we shall describe later in Section 9.6. The ARP in the gateway is known as a **proxy ARP** since it is acting as an agent for the ARP in the destination host.

When the gateway receives the response packet from the destination host, it reads the destination IP address from the header – host A – and obtains from its cache the MAC address of A. It then transfers the packet to the IP in A using the services provided by the MAC sublayer. A similar procedure is followed for bridged LANs and for router-based LANs except that with the latter, the ARP in the subnet router that is connected to the same subnet as the source host acts as the proxy ARP. Also, in order to allow for hosts to change their network point of attachments, entries in the ARP cache timeout after a predefined time interval.

9.5.2 RARP

As we indicated at the start of the last section, normally the IP/MAC address-pair of a host is stored in the configuration file of the host on its hard disk. With diskless hosts, clearly this is not possible and hence the only address that is known is the MAC address of the MAC chipset. In such cases, therefore, the alternative reverse address resolution protocol (RARP) is used.

The server associated with a set of diskless hosts has a copy of the IP/MAC address-pair of all the hosts it serves in a configuration file. When a diskless host first comes into service, it broadcasts a **RARP request** message containing the MAC address of the host onto its local LAN segment. Being a broadcast, the server receives this and, on determining it is a RARP message, the MAC/LLC sublayer passes the message to the RARP. The latter first uses the MAC address within it to obtain the related IP address from the configuration file and then proceeds to create a **RARP reply** message containing the IP address of the host and also its own address-pair. The server then sends the reply message back to the host and, once its own address-pair is known, the ARP in the diskless host can proceed as before.

9.5.3 ARP/RARP message formats and transmission

As we show in Figure 9.8(a), the format of the ARP and RARP request and reply messages are the same both having a fixed length of 28 bytes. Note that the term "hardware address" is used to refer to a MAC address and "target" the recipient of a request.

The *hardware type* field specifies the type of hardware (MAC) address contained within the message, for example 0001 (hex) in the case of an Ethernet. The ARP and RARP can be used with other network protocols (as well as the IP) and the *protocol type* indicates the type of network address being resolved; for example, 0800 (hex) is used for IP addresses. The *HLEN* and *PLEN* fields specify the size in bytes of the hardware (MAC) and protocol (IP) address lengths respectively, for example 06 (hex) for an Ethernet and 04 (hex) for the IP. The *operation* field indicates whether the message (resolution operation) is an ARP request (0001) or reply (0002) or a RARP request (0003) or reply (0004).

The next four fields specify the hardware (MAC)/IP address-pair of the sender (source) and the target (destination). For example, in an ARP request message just the address-pair of the sender is used while in the reply message all four addresses are used.

As we indicated in the introduction, both the ARP and RARP are integral parts of IP inasmuch as, once the MAC address relating to an IP address is present in the ARP cache, the IP can use this to initiate the transmission of a datagram to its intended recipient directly. Hence, as we can deduce from Figure 9.2, on receipt of a frame, the receiving MAC/LLC sublayer must be able to determine to which protocol the frame contents should be sent: IP, ARP, or RARP. To achieve this, when each of the protocols passes a message/datagram to the LLC/MAC sublayer for transmission, in addition to the MAC address of the intended recipient, it specifies the name of the (peer) protocol in the destination (IP/ARP/RARP) to which the message/datagram should be passed.

As we show in Figure 9.8(b), this is specified in a two-byte *type* field which immediately precedes the message/datagram in the user data field of the MAC frame. As we explained in Section 8.8.3, normally, the LLC sublayer is not used with the original Ethernet MAC standard and hence the *type* field

(a)

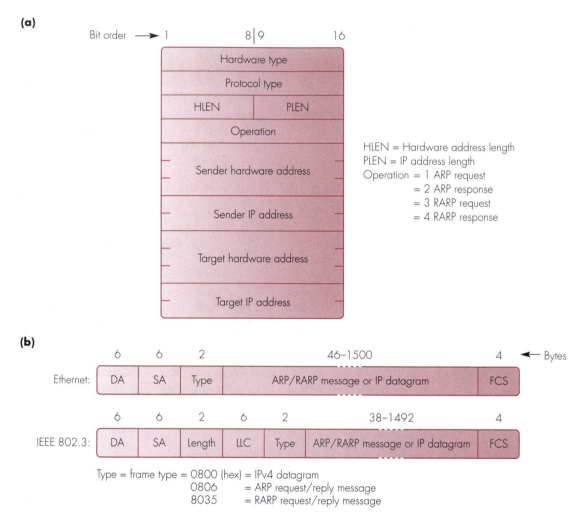

(b)

Figure 9.8 **ARP and RARP message formats and transmission: (a) ARP and RARP message formats; (b) MAC frame format with Ethernet and IEEE802.3.**

immediately follows the MAC *source address* (*SA*). With the more recent IEEE 802.3 MAC standard, however, the LLC sublayer is present and hence the *type* field immediately follows the 6 bytes required for the LLC protocol. However, the maximum frame length associated with the 802.3 standard (1500 bytes) means that the length indicator value in the header is always different from the three *type* field values. Hence the receiving MAC sublayer can readily determine which of the two standards is being used and, therefore, where the *type* field is located. With a token ring LAN, since there is only one standard, this problem does not arise.

Example 9.3

Determine the amount of padding required in a MAC frame when transmitting an ARP/RARP message over (i) an Ethernet LAN and (ii) an IEEE 802.3 LAN.

Answer:

As we explained in Section 9.5.3, each ARP/RARP message comprises 28 bytes. Also, as we explained in Section 8.3, the minimum frame size associated with the CSMA/CD MAC method is 512 bits (64 bytes) including the FCS.

(i) With an Ethernet LAN, the header plus FCS requires 18 bytes and hence the minimum size of the user data field is (64 − 18) = 46 bytes. Thus the number of pad bytes required = (46 − 28) = 18 bytes.

(ii) With an IEEE 802.3 LAN, the header plus FCS requires 26 bytes and hence the minimum size of the user data field is (64 − 26) = 38 bytes. Thus the number of pad bytes required = (38 − 28) = 10 bytes.

9.6 Routing algorithms

The Internet comprises many thousands of access networks that are geographically distributed around the world. As a result, the global internetwork used to interconnect the gateways associated with these (access) networks is not a single network as such but rather a collection of different types of network that have evolved over the lifetime of the Internet. The general architecture of the Internet is shown in Figure 9.9.

As we can see, the various networks making up the Internet global internetwork we showed earlier in Figure 9.1 are in a hierarchical structure. At the highest level, each continent has its own **continental backbone network.** This comprises a geographically distributed set of very high throughput routers which are interconnected by very high bit rate lines leased from one or more network providers. The continental backbones are then interconnected together by means of a **core backbone network** consisting of a small number of very high throughput (intercontinental) routers and leased lines.

At the second level, attached to all of the other routers in each continental backbone are a number of regional and national networks and, in some instances, large internetworks. In general, these also consist of a geographically distributed set of high throughput routers interconnected by high bit rate leased lines. Because of the historical evolution of the Internet, however, in addition, there are a number of legacy networks that operate using a different protocol stack from TCP/IP.

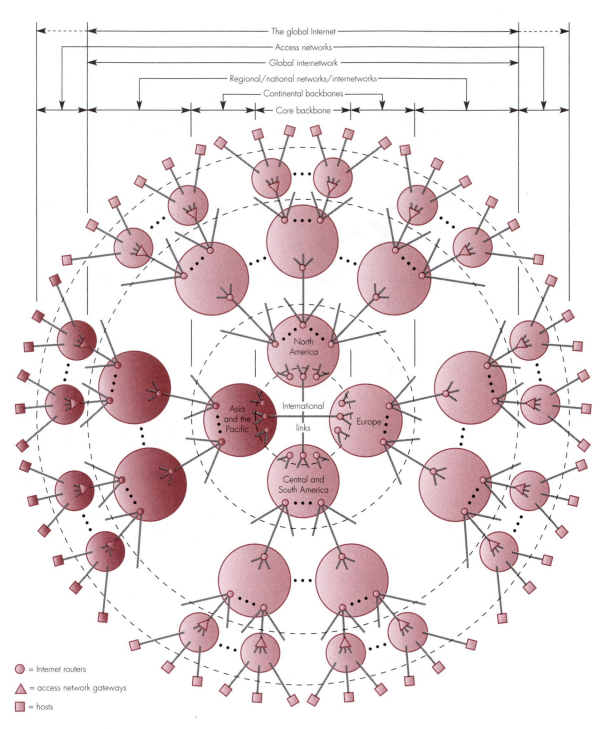

Figure 9.9 General architecture of the global Internet.

The various types of access networks – site/campus LANs, ISP networks, enterprise networks – are then attached to one of the regional or national networks/internetworks by means of either an **IP access network gateway** or, if the access network uses a different protocol stack from TCP/IP, a **multiprotocol gateway.**

All routing within the total global internetwork is carried out by the IP in each router using the netid part of the destination IP address in each datagram header. In practice, as we shall see in the following subsections, there are only a small number of different routing algorithms used and, in order to explain their principle of operation, we shall use the simple internetwork topology shown in Figure 9.10.

As we can see, each of the routers in the interconnection network has a number of access networks attached to it by means of (access) gateways. We assume that each access network is a site/campus LAN with a single netid and that the ARP in each host is used to carry out routing within the access network. Hence, as we explained in Section 9.5.1, the ARP in each gateway acts as an agent (proxy ARP) on behalf of all hosts at the site/campus to relay packets to and from the interconnection network.

The interconnection network itself comprises four routers (R1 – R4) that are interconnected by, say, leased lines. For description purposes, each line has a pair of numbers associated with it. The first we shall use as a line identifier and the second is what is referred to as the **cost** of the line. For example, the cost could be based on the line bit rate and, normally, the higher the line

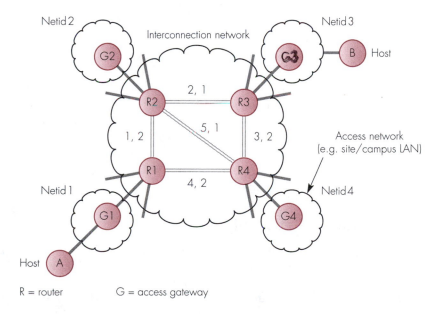

Figure 9.10 Example internetwork topology.

bit rate the lower the cost value. As we shall see, the cost value associated with each line is used during the routing of datagrams/packets and hence is also known as a **routing metric.** The cost of a route/path through the intercon-nection network is determined by summing together the cost value associated with each line that makes up the path. This is known as the **path cost** and, when different paths between two routers are available, the path with the least path cost value is known as the **shortest path.** Other metrics used in rela-tion to the computation of the shortest paths are based on the physical length – and hence propagation delay – of each line, the number of lines (**hops**) in the route (**hop count**), and the mean queuing delay within each router asso-ciated with a line.

Let us assume that host A on netid 1 wants to send a datagram to host B on netid 3. As we saw in Section 9.5.1, on determining that the destination netid in the datagram header is for a different netid from its own, gateway G1 forwards the datagram to router R1 over the connecting line/link. On receipt of the datagram, R1 proceeds to forward it first to R3 over the inter-connection network and then to G3. At this point, the IP in G3 knows how to route the datagram to host B using the hostid part of the destination IP address and the related MAC address of B in its ARP cache. What we do not know, is how the datagram is routed across the interconnection network.

There are three unanswered questions involved:

(1) How does R1 know from the netid contained within the destination IP address that the destination router is R3?

(2) How does R1 know the shortest path route to be followed through the interconnection network to R3?

(3) How does R3 know how to relay the datagram to G3 instead of one of the other gateways that is attached to it?

In relation to the last point, we can accept that a simple protocol can be used to enable each gateway to inform the router to which it is attached, the netid of the access network. The first two points, however, are both parts of the routing algorithm associated with the interconnection network. There are a number of different algorithms that can be used and we shall describe a selection of them in the following subsections. Note that when discussing routing algorithms, the more general term "packet" is used.

9.6.1 Static routing

With this type of routing, the outgoing line to be used to reach all netids is loaded into the routing table of each router when it is first brought into ser-vice. As an example, we show the routing table for each of the four routers in the example internet in Figure 9.11(b). To avoid unnecessary repetition, we assume only one gateway/netid is attached to each router.

(a)

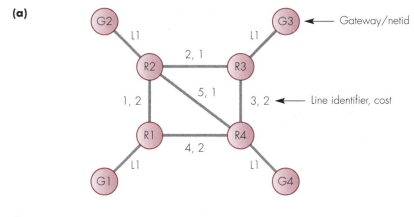

(b)

R1:

Netid	Line
1	L1
2	1
3	1
4	4

R2:

Netid	Line
1	1
2	L1
3	2
4	5

R3:

Netid	Line
1	2
2	2
3	L1
4	3, 2

R4:

Netid	Line
1	4
2	5
3	3, 5
4	L1

Figure 9.11 Static routing: (a) internet topology; (b) routing table entries.

To route a packet from a host attached to, say, netid 1 to another that is attached to netid 3, on receipt of the packet, R1 consults its routing table and determines it should forward the packet on line 1. Similarly, on receipt of the packet, R2 determines it should be forwarded on line 2. Finally, R3 forwards the packet to G3 and from there it is forwarded by G3 to the host specified in the hostid part of the IP address.

As we show in the routing tables for routers R3 and R4, two alternative lines are given for routing packets between these two routers. As we can deduce from the cost values, both routes have the same path cost of 2, one using only line 3 and the other going via R2 and lines 2 and 5. Clearly, however, if a second routing metric of, say, distance was used, then the second path would be longer and hence only a single path would be present. For this reason, more than one metric is sometimes used and the choice of path is then based on the information contained within the related set of routing tables.

We can also make a second observation from this set of routing tables; that is, to go from R1 to R3, the shortest path is via R2 using lines 1 and 2. Also, when we look at the routing table for R2, the shortest path from R2 to R3 is also line 2. More generally, if the shortest path between two routers, A and C, is via an intermediate router B, then the shortest path from B to C is along the same path. This is known as the **optimality principle** and it follows from this that each router along the shortest path need only know the identity of its immediate neighbor along the path. The routing operation is known, therefore, as **next-hop routing** or **hop-by-hop routing**.

The disadvantage of static routing is that all the routing table entries may need to be changed whenever a line is upgraded or a new line is added. Also, should a line or router develop a fault, when the fault is reported, the routing tables in all affected routers need to be changed. For these reasons, static routing is inappropriate for a large, continuously-changing network like the Internet.

9.6.2 Flooding

To explain the operation of the flooding algorithm, we return to Figure 9.10 and again assume we are sending a datagram from host A to host B. The steps followed are summarized in Figure 9.12.

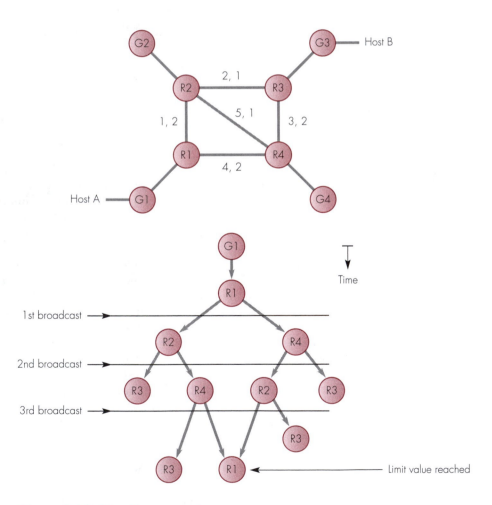

Figure 9.12 Flooding example.

On receipt of the packet from G1, R1 sends a copy of it over both lines 1 and 4. Similarly, on receipt of their copy of the packet, routers R2 and R4 determine from the netid within it that the packet is not for one of their own networks and hence proceed to forward a copy of the packet onto lines 2 and 5 (R2) and lines 5 and 3 (R4). However, since line 2 has a higher bit rate – lower cost value – than line 3, the copy of the packet from R2 will arrive at R3 first and, on determining it is addressed to one of its own netids, R3 forwards the packet to G3. Additional copies of the packet will then be received by R3 but, remembering that each copy will have the same value in the *identifier* field, these can be detected as duplicates and discarded by R3.

In order to limit the number of copies of the packet that are produced, a limit is set on the number of times each copy of the packet is forwarded. In the example, it is assumed that a limit value of 3 has been placed in the *time-to-live* field of the packet header by R1. Prior to forwarding copies of the packet, the limit value is decremented by 1 by the recipient router and only if this is above zero are further copies forwarded.

As we can deduce from the figure, the flooding algorithm ensures that the first copy of the packet flows along the shortest path and hence is received in the shortest time. Also, should a line or router fail, providing an alternative path is available, a copy of each packet should always be received. Flooding, therefore, is an example of an **adaptive** – also known as **dynamic** – routing algorithm. Nevertheless, as we can see from this simple example, even with a limit of three hops, the packet is transmitted 10 times. This compares with just two transmissions using the shortest path. Hence the very heavy bandwidth overheads associated with flooding means that it is inappropriate for use with the large networks that make up the Internet.

9.6.3 Distance vector routing

The distance vector algorithm is a distributed algorithm that enables each router to build up a routing table (the vector) that contains the path cost (the distance) to reach all the netids in the internetwork.

Initially, each router knows only the identity of, firstly, the netids of the networks that are attached to it – through gateways – and their related local line numbers, and secondly, the identity of the lines – and their cost – that form direct links to other routers. Normally, this information is either entered by network management or by the exchange of configuration messages with the other routers when each router is first brought into service. The information is held in a table known as a *connectivity* or *adjacency* table and the contents of the four tables for our example internetwork, together with the contents of the initial routing table for each router, are shown in Figure 9.13(a).

In order for each router to build up its complete routing table – containing the minimum distance (shortest path) to reach all netids – at predefined time intervals, each router first adds the known cost of the lines that connect

(a)

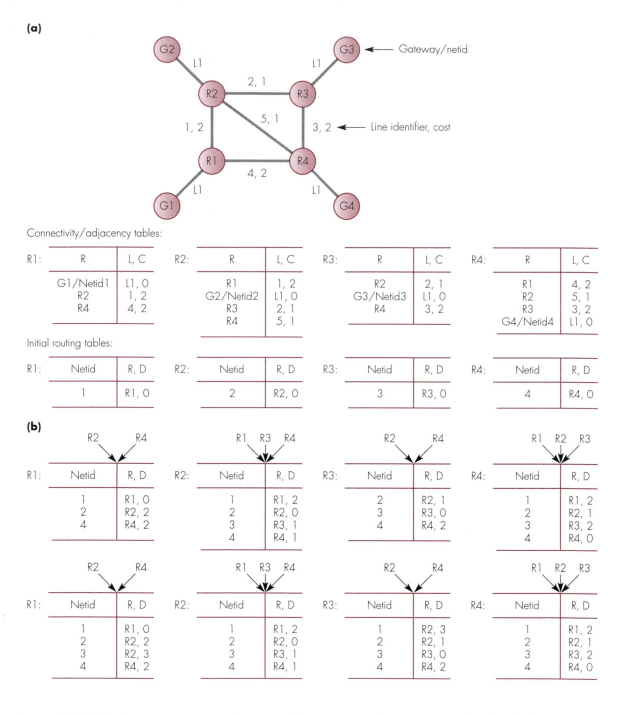

Figure 9.13 Distance vector algorithm: (a) internet topology and initial tables; (b) derivation of final routing tables.

the router to its neighbors to the current distance values in its own routing table and forwards a copy of the related updated table to each of its neighbors. Then, based on the information received, if a reported distance is less than a current entry, each router proceeds to update its own routing table with the reported distance. The same procedure then repeats with the updated table contents. This procedure repeats for a defined number of iterations after which, each router has determined the path with the minimum distance to be followed to reach all netids.

As an example, the build-up of the final routing table for each of the four routers in our example internetwork is shown in Figure 9.13(b). To avoid repetition, we assume that only a single gateway/netid is attached to each router and, as we can see, for this simple internet the contents of each routing table are complete after just two routing table updates.

In the case of R1, this receives the updated contents of the routing tables held by R2 and R4. Hence after R1 receives the first set of updated tables from them, it determines that the shortest path to reach netid 2 has a distance of 2 via R2 and, to reach netid 4, the distance is 2 via R4. At the same time, R2 and R4 have themselves received update information from their own neighbors and, as a result, on receipt of the second set of updated tables from them, R1 determines that the shortest path to reach netid 3 has a distance of 3 via R2. Note that with the distance vector algorithm an entry is updated only if a new distance value is less than the current value. Also, that routes with equal path cost values are discarded.

The final routing table of each router contains the next-hop router and the corresponding distance (path cost) value to reach all of the netids in the internetwork. Hence to route a packet, the netid is first obtained from the destination IP address in the packet header and the identity of the next-hop router read from the routing table. The corresponding line number on which the packet is forwarded is then obtained from the connectivity table.

To ensure that each table entry reflects the current active topology of the internet, each entry has an associated timer and, if an entry is not confirmed within a defined time, then it is timed-out. This means that each router transmits the contents of its complete routing table at regular intervals which, typically, is every 30 seconds. Again, for a small internet this is not a problem but for a large internet like the Internet, the bandwidth and processing overheads associated with the distance vector algorithm can become very high. Also, since entries are updated in the order in which they are received and paths of equal distance/cost are discarded, routers may have dissimilar routes to the same destination. As a result, packets addressed to certain destinations may loop rather than going directly to the desired router/gateway. Nevertheless, the **routing information protocol (RIP)** which uses the distance vector routing algorithm is still widely used in many of the individual networks that make up the Internet.

9.6.4 Link-state shortest-path-first routing

As the name implies, this type of routing is based on two algorithms: link-state (LS) and shortest-path-first (SPF). The link-state algorithm is used to enable each router to determine the current (active) topology of the internet and the cost associated with each line/link. Then, once the topology is known, each router runs (independently) the shortest-path-first algorithm to determine the shortest path from itself to all the other routers in the internet.

Link-state algorithm

As with the distance vector algorithm, initially, each router knows only its own connectivity/adjacency information and, as an example, the table entries for our example internet are repeated in Figure 9.14(a). The link-state algorithm is then run and the build-up of the internet topology by R1 is shown in Figure 9.14(b).

Initially, based on the information R1 has in its own connectivity table, the (incomplete) topology is as shown in (i). At regular intervals, each router broadcasts a **link-state message**, containing the router's identity and its associated connectivity information, to each of its immediate neighbors. Hence in the example, we assume that R2 is the first to send its own connectivity information to R1 and this enables R1 to expand its knowledge of the topology to that shown in (ii). This is followed by the connectivity information of R4 which enables R1 to expand its knowledge of the topology to that shown in (iii). Concurrently with this happening, the same procedure will have been carried out by all of the other routers. Hence in our example internet, R2 and R4 will have received the connectivity information of R3. After this has been received, therefore, R2 and R4 relay this information on to R1 in a second set of link-state messages and this enables R1 to complete the picture of the active topology (iv). Also, since each router has carried out the same procedure, each will have derived the current active topology and, in addition, determined the identity of the router to which each netid is attached. At this point, each router runs the shortest-path-first algorithm to determine the shortest path from itself to all the other routers. In practice, there are a number of algorithms that can be used to find the shortest path but we shall restrict our discussion to the Dijkstra algorithm.

Dijkstra shortest-path-first algorithm

We shall explain the Dijkstra algorithm in relation to our example internet topology. This is shown in Figure 9.15(a) together with the cost of the lines that link the routers together. The sequence of steps followed by R1 to derive the shortest paths to reach the other three routers is shown in Figure 9.15(b).

Shown in parentheses alongside each of the other routers is the aggregate cost from that router back to the source via the router indicated. Hence an entry of (4,R4) means that the cost of the path back to R1 is 4 via R4. Initially, only the path cost of those routers that are directly connected to R1 are known (R2 and R4) and those not directly connected (R3) are marked

(a)

Connectivity/adjacency tables:

R1:

R	L, C
G1/Netid1	L1, 0
R2	1, 2
R4	4, 2

R2:

R	L, C
R1	1, 2
G2/Netid2	L1, 0
R3	2, 1
R4	5, 1

R3:

R	L, C
R2	2, 1
G3/Netid3	L1, 0
R4	3, 2

R4:

R	L, C
R1	4, 2
R2	5, 1
R3	3, 2
G4/Netid4	L1, 0

(b)

Topology build-up by R1:
(i) Initial:

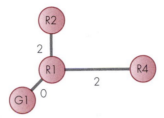

(ii) After connectivity information from R2:

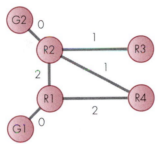

(iii) After connectivity information from R4:

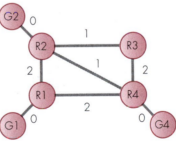

(iv) After connectivity information from R3 via R2:

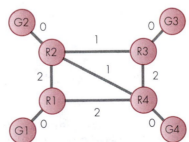

G/Netid	R
G1/1	R1
G2/2	R2
G3/3	R3
G4/4	R4

Figure 9.14 Link state algorithm: (a) initial connectivity/adjacency tables; (b) derivation of active topology and netid location.

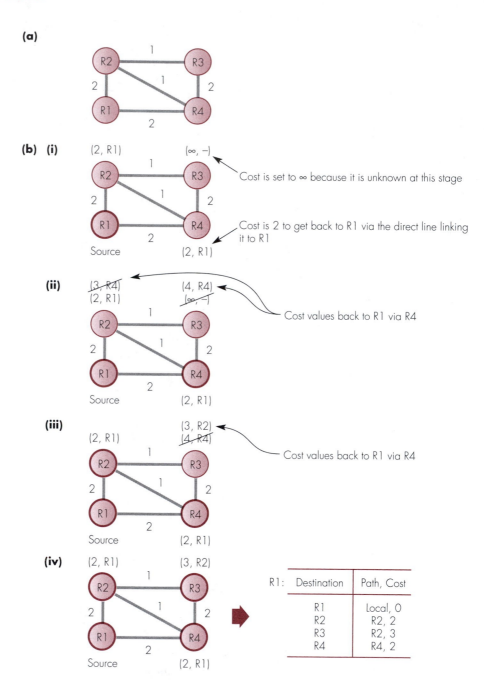

Figure 9.15 Dijkstra algorithm: (a) initial topology; (b) derivation of shortest paths from R1 to each other router.

with an infinite path cost value. Also, until a cost value is known to be the minimum cost, it is said to be **tentative** and only when the cost value is confirmed as the minimum value is it said to be **permanent**. The router is then shown in bold.

Initially, since R1 is the source it is shown in bold and the path costs back to R1 from the two directly connected routers (R2 and R4) are shown equal to the respective line costs (i). Hence R2, for example, has an entry of (2,R1) indicating the cost is 2 to get back to R1 via the direct line linking it to R1. Also, since R3 is not connected directly to R1, it is shown with a path cost of infinity.

Once this has been done, the next step (ii) is to choose the router with the minimum path cost value from all the remaining routers that are still tentative. Hence in our example, the choice is between R2 and R4 – since both are tentative and have a path cost value of 2 – and, arbitrarily, we have chosen R4. This is now marked permanent and the new set of aggregate path cost values via R4 are computed. For example, the cost of the path from R2 to R1 via R4 is 3 (1 from R2 to R4 plus 2 from R4 to R1) but, since this is greater than the current cost of 2, this is ignored. In the case of R3, however, the cost of 4 via R4 is less than the current value of infinity and hence (4,R4) replaces the current entry.

The router with the minimum path cost value is again chosen from those that remain tentative and, since R2 has a path cost of 2, this is marked permanent and the new path costs to R1 via R2 are computed (iii). As we can see, the path cost from R3 to R1 via R2 is only 3 and hence an entry of (3,R2) replaces the current entry of (4,R4). Finally (iv), R3 is made permanent as it is the only remaining router that is still tentative and, now that the minimum path costs from each of the other routers back to R1 are known, the routing table for R1 is complete.

In Figure 9.16 we show the same procedure applied first with R2 as the source – part (a) – then with R3 – part (b) – and finally with R4 – part (c). From these derivations we can make some observations about the algorithm:

■ The derived shortest path routes adhere to the optimality principle.

■ If the computed path costs associated with two or more tentative routers are the same, then an arbitrary selection can be made as to which is made permanent.

■ If the computed aggregate path cost from a (tentative) router to the source via a different router is the same as that via another router, then both can be retained. The choice of route is then arbitrary and load sharing becomes possible.

Datagram routing procedures

The routing of a datagram involves a combination of both link-state tables – one containing the location of all netids and the other the connectivity information – and the derived set of shortest-path routing tables. These are used in slightly different ways depending on the choice of routing method,

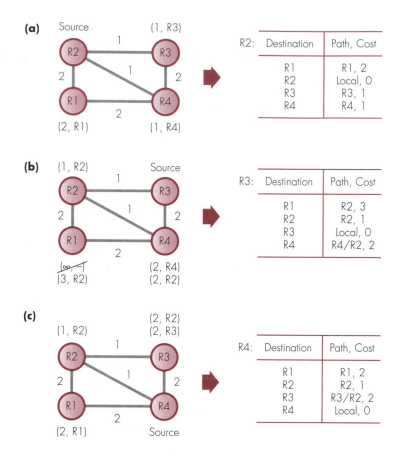

(a)

R2:

Destination	Path, Cost
R1	R1, 2
R2	Local, 0
R3	R3, 1
R4	R4, 1

(b)

R3:

Destination	Path, Cost
R1	R2, 3
R2	R2, 1
R3	Local, 0
R4	R4/R2, 2

(c)

R4:

Destination	Path, Cost
R1	R1, 2
R2	R2, 1
R3	R3/R2, 2
R4	Local, 0

Figure 9.16 Shortest path derivations: (a) by R2; (b) by R3; (c) by R4.

hop-by-hop routing or source routing. We shall explain the procedure followed with each method using the example of a host attached to netid 1 sending a datagram/packet to a host attached to netid 3.

The procedure followed with hop-by-hop routing is summarized in Figure 9.17(a). Using this method, each router computes only its own routing table contents and uses this together with the contents of its own connectivity table. On receipt of the packet from gateway G1, router R1 obtains the netid from the destination IP address in the packet header – netid 3 – and uses its copy of the link-state table to determine that this is reached via router R3. It then determines from the contents of its routing table that the next-hop router on the shortest path to R3 is R2 and hence proceeds to forward the packet to R2 over the line indicated in its connectivity table, line 1.

The same procedure is repeated by router R2 – using its own link-state, routing, and connectivity tables – to forward the packet to R3 over line 2. Finally, on receipt of the packet, R3 determines from its own tables that the packet is addressed to netid 3 and that this is attached to one of its local lines,

(a)

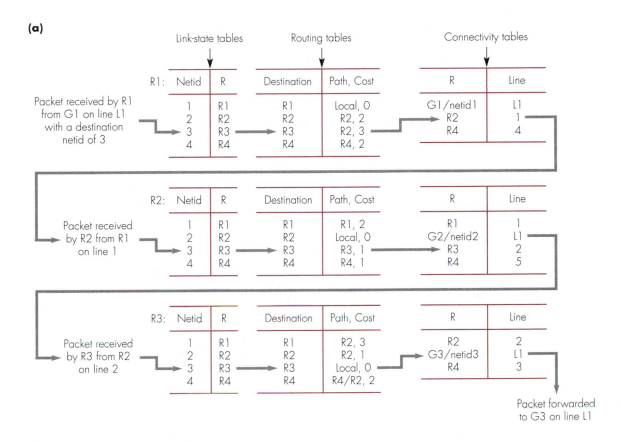

Figure 9.17 LS-SPF routing examples: (a) hop-by-hop routing; (b) source routing.

(b)

1. Datagram received by R1 from G1 on line L1
2. R1 uses its set of routing tables to determine the least path cost is via routers R2, R3, and writes this list into an options field in the datagram header.
3. R1 uses its own connectivity table to forward the packet to the first router in the list, R2, using line 1.

4. On receipt of the packet, R2 reads the second router from the list, R3, and uses its own connectivity table to forward the packet on line 2.

5. On receipt of the packet, R3 determines it is for one of its local gateways and uses its own connectivity table to forward the packet to G3 on line L1.

L1. The packet is then forwarded to the attached gateway and from there to the destination host.

The procedure followed with source routing is summarized in Figure 9.17(b). Using this method, once all the routers have built up a picture of the current active topology using the link-state algorithm, they each compute the complete set of four routing tables. Then, on receipt of a packet from one of its attached gateways – G1 in the example – the source router – R1 – uses the set of tables to determine the list of routers that form the shortest path to the intended destination – R2 and R3. The list is then inserted into an *options* field of the datagram header by R1 and the packet forwarded to the first router in the path, R2, using the corresponding line number obtained from R1's own connectivity table, line 1.

On receipt of the packet, R2 reads from the *options* field the identity of the next router along the path, R3, and uses its own connectivity table to determine the line the packet should be forwarded on, line 2. On receipt of the packet, R3 determines it is intended for one of its local gateways and uses its own connectivity table to determine the packet should be forwarded to gateway G3 on line L1.

Additional comments

Although in the various examples, internet-wide identifiers have been used to identify each of the lines in the example internet topology, this has been done to simplify the related descriptions. In practice, as we can deduce from the description of the LS-SPF algorithm the line identifiers associated with each router have only local significance and, since these are part of the router's configuration information, normally, a different set of line identifiers is used by each router.

In our discussion of the link-state algorithm, we assumed that the transmission of the link-state messages was reliable and that none was lost as a result of transmission errors. Clearly, should a link-state message be corrupted, then the routing tables in each router may be inconsistent and, amongst other things, cause packets to loop. To overcome this, each link-state message, in addition to the identity of the router that created the message and its associated connectivity information, also contains a sequence number and a timeout value. As we have mentioned, link-state information is distributed by each router relaying a copy of the messages it receives from each of its neighbors on to its other neighbors. Hence to avoid messages being relayed unnecessarily, when each new message it created – at defined time intervals – it is assigned a sequence number equal to the previous number plus one. Each router then keeps a record of the sequence number contained within the last message it received from each of the other routers and only if a new message is received – that is, one with a higher sequence number – is a copy forwarded to its other neighbors. In addition, the associated timeout value in each message is decremented by each router and, should this reach zero, the received message is discarded.

Although in the simple example we used to describe the LS-SPF algorithm only a single routing metric (cost value) was used, multiple metrics can be used. In such cases, therefore, there may be a different shortest path between each pair of routers for each metric. Although this leads to additional computation overheads, the choice of path can then be made dependent on the type of information contained within the datagram being routed. For example, for real-time information such as digitized speech, the choice of path may be based on minimum delay rather than bit rate.

As we can deduce from the description of the distance vector algorithm in Section 9.6.3, for large internets, the amount of routing information passed between routers is substantial and, in the limit, involves each router transferring the contents of its complete routing table at regular intervals. In contrast, the link-state shortest-path-first algorithm involves only the transfer of the link-state information of each router. Hence it is far more efficient in terms of the amount of bandwidth that is utilized for routing updates. It is for this reason, that the LS-SPF algorithm is now the preferred algorithm. The protocol based on this is known as the open shortest path first (OSPF) routing protocol and, as we showed earlier in Figure 9.2, this forms an integral part of the IP.

9.6.5 Hierarchical routing

As we showed earlier in Figure 9.9 and explained in the accompanying text, the Internet is made up of a large number of separately managed networks/internetworks that are interconnected together by means of a global backbone network. Each separate network/internetwork is treated as an **autonomous system** (**AS**) – with its own internal routing algorithm and management authority – and is assigned a number to identify it within the context of the total Internet. The general architecture is shown in Figure 9.18(a) together with some (very much simplified) autonomous system topologies.

To discriminate between the routers used within the various types of network, the following terminology is used:

- **subnet router:** this is a router that operates entirely within a single network when subnetting is being used;
- **access gateway:** this is used to connect an access network to an interior gateway;
- **interior gateway:** this is a router that is used to interconnect the networks within an autonomous system (typically a regional or national network);
- **exterior gateway:** this is a router that is used to connect an autonomous system to the core backbone network.

The various routing protocols associated with the Internet are identified in Figure 9.18(b). The routing protocol used by the interior gateways within a single autonomous system is known as an **interior gateway protocol** (**IGP**) and that used by the exterior gateways within the backbone network an **exterior gateway protocol** (**EGP**). Since the Internet consists of an interconnected

(a)

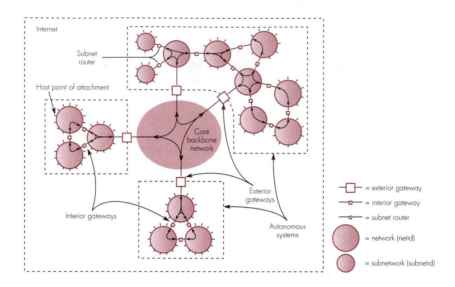

(b)

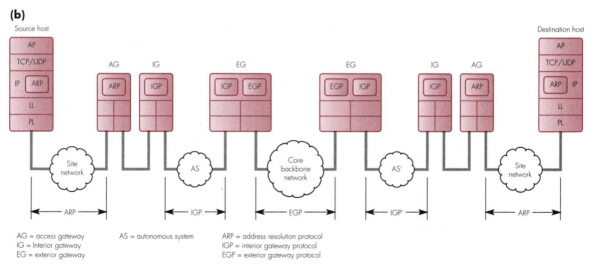

AG = access gateway   AS = autonomous system   ARP = address resolution protocol
IG = Interior gateway   IGP = interior gateway protocol
EG = exterior gateway   EGP = exterior gateway protocol

Figure 9.18 Hierarchical routing over the Internet: (a) generalized architecture and terminology; (b) associated routing protocol terminology.

set of networks and internetworks, many of which have evolved over a relatively long period of time, each autonomous system may have a different IGP. Examples are the RIP and the OSPF the principles of which we described in the previous two sections. The EGP, however, as it must be, is an Internet-wide standard.

To reflect the different types of routing protocols involved, the total routing information is organized hierarchically:

- Hosts maintain sufficient routing information to enable them to forward packets directly to other hosts on the same network, a subnet router (if subnetting is being used), and to an access gateway.
- Subnet routers maintain sufficient routing information to enable them to forward packets to other subnet routers (belonging to the same network) or to the network access gateway.
- Interior gateways maintain sufficient routing information to forward packets to their own access gateways and to other interior and exterior gateways within the same autonomous system.
- Exterior gateways maintain sufficient routing information to forward packets to an interior gateway (if the packet is for the autonomous system to which it is attached) or to another exterior gateway if it is not.

An example protocol used by hosts to route packets to other hosts (and an access gateway) that are attached to the same network is the ARP we described earlier in Section 9.5. Subnet routers are used when a network is divided up into subnets to interconnect the various subnets together. Hence they operate in a similar way to interior gateways – and use similar routing protocols – except that all routing within the network is carried out using the subnet address within the hostid part of the destination IP address rather than the netid part. As we indicated earlier, the interior gateway routing protocol can vary from one autonomous system to another. Example protocols are the RIP (based on the distance vector algorithm which we described in Section 9.6.3) and the OSPF (based on the link-state shortest-path-first (LS-SPF) algorithm we described in Section 9.6.4). In this section, we shall describe the standard exterior gateway protocol known as the **border gateway protocol** (**BGP**).

Border gateway protocol

The management authority associated with each autonomous system nominates one or more gateways to function as exterior gateways for that system. Within the autonomous system, these communicate with the other interior gateways using the interior gateway protocol for that system. Each exterior gateway, through its local routing table, knows about the netids within that system and their distances from that gateway. The contents of the routing table are built up in the same way as the interior gateways of the autonomous system to which it is attached.

When each exterior gateway is first initialized, it is given the unique identity of the autonomous system to which it is attached and the contents of a connectivity table. This is known as the **reachability table** and enables the gateway to communicate with all the other exterior gateways to which it has a direct link. The BGP in each exterior gateway then makes contact with the

BGP in other selected exterior gateways to exchange routing information with them. This routing information consists of the list of netids within the corresponding autonomous system together with their distances and routes from the reporting exterior gateway. This information is used by a sending gateway to select the best exterior gateway for forwarding datagrams to a particular netid and hence autonomous system.

The three main functions associated with the BGP are as follows:

- neighbor acquisition and termination,
- neighbor reachability,
- routing update.

Each function operates using a request-response message exchange. The messages associated with each function are shown in Table 9.1

Since each autonomous system is managed and run by a different authority, before any routing information is exchanged, two exterior gateways attached to different systems must first agree to exchange such information. This is the role of the **neighbor acquisition and termination** procedure. When two gateways agree to such an exchange, they are said to have become **neighbors.** When a gateway first wants to exchange routing information, it sends an

Table 9.1 BGP message types that are exchanged by the BGP in exterior gateways and their meaning

Function	BGP message	Meaning
Neighbor acquisition and termination	Acquisition request	Requests a gateway to become a neighbor
	Acquisition confirm	Gateway agrees to become a neighbor
	Acquisition refuse	Gateway refuses
	Cease request	Requests termination of a neighbor relationship
	Cease confirm	Confirms breakup of relationship
Neighbor reachability	Hello	Requests neighbor to confirm a previously established relationship
	I-heard-you	Confirms relationship
Routing update	Poll request	Requests network reachability update
	Routing update	Network reachability information
Error response	Error	Response to any incorrect request message

acquisition request message to the BGP in the appropriate gateway which then returns either an *acquisition confirm* message or, if it does not want to accept the request, an *acquisition refuse* message which includes a reason code.

Once a neighbor relationship has been established between two gateways – and hence autonomous systems – they periodically confirm their relationship. This is done either by exchanging specific messages – *hello* and *I-heard-you* – or by embedding confirmation into the header of normal routing information messages.

The actual exchange of routing information is carried out by one of the gateways, which sends a *poll request* message to the other gateway asking it for the list of networks (netids) that are reachable via that gateway and their distances from it. The response is a *routing update* message which contains the requested information. Finally, if any request message is incorrect, an *error message* is returned as a response with an appropriate reason code.

As with the other IP protocols, all the messages (PDUs) associated with the BGP are carried in the user data field of an IP datagram. All BGP messages have the same fixed header, the format of which is shown in Figure 9.19.

The *version* field defines the version number of the BGP. The *type* and *code* fields collectively define the type of message while the *status* field contains message-dependent status information. The *checksum*, which is used as a safeguard against the processing of erroneous messages, is the same as that used with IP. The *autonomous system number* is the assigned number of the autonomous system to which the sending gateway is attached; the *sequence number* is used to synchronize responses to their corresponding request message.

Neighbor reachability messages contain only a header with a *type* field of 5, a code of 0 = hello, and a 1 = I-heard-you.

Neighbor acquisition messages have a *type* field of 3; the code number defines the specific message type. The *hello interval* specifies the frequency with which hello messages should be sent; the *poll interval* performs the same function for poll messages.

A poll message has a *type* field of 2. The *code* field is used to piggyback the neighbor reachability information: a code of 0 = hello and a code of 1 = I-heard-you. The *source network IP address* in both the poll and the routing update response messages indicates the network linking the two exterior gateways. This allows the core network itself to consist of multiple networks with an associated routing protocol.

The *routing update* message contains the list of networks (netids) that are reachable via each gateway within the autonomous system arranged in distance order from the responding exterior gateway. As indicated, this enables the requesting gateway to select the best exterior gateway through which to send a packet for forwarding within an autonomous system. Note that to conserve space, each netid address is sent in three bytes (24 bits) only with the most significant 8-bit hostid field missing. The latter is redundant for all IP address class types.

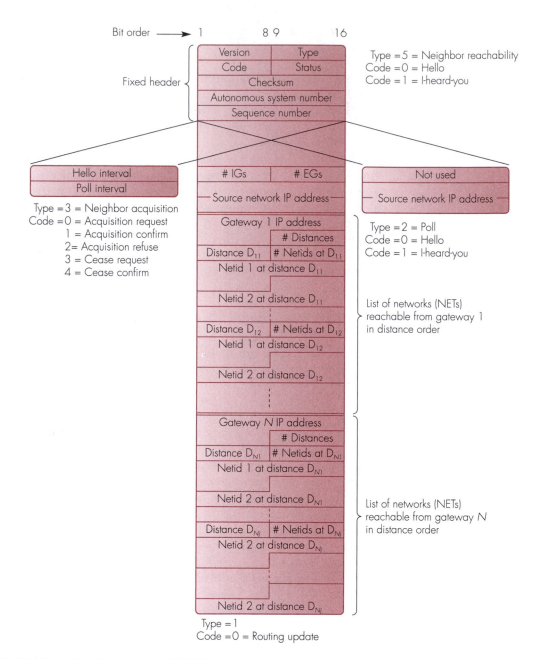

Figure 9.19 Border gateway protocol (BGP) message formats.

9.6.6 Classless inter-domain routing

As we explained earlier in Section 9.4, each IP address is 32 bits in length and is made up of a netid part and a hostid part. The allocation of netids is centrally managed by the Internet Network Information Center and, in order to utilize network addresses efficiently, the number of bits used for the netid part varies. As we showed earlier in Figure 9.5, the number of bits is determined by the address class:

    Class A: netid = 7 bits, hostid = 24 bits

    Class B: netid = 14 bits, hostid = 16 bits

    Class C: netid = 21 bits, hostid = 8 bits

In this way, the manager of a network with many attached hosts can be allocated a class A address, one with a small number of hosts a class C address, and the rest a class B address.

In practice, however, when requesting an IP address, most network managers opted for a class B address since they considered a class C address with just 256 hostids too small and a class A address with 2^{24} hostids too large. As a result, even though there were plenty of netids available with class C addresses, a shortage of class B addresses was predicted. To resolve this problem, an alternative type of routing (which essentially bypasses the fixed divisions associated with each class) known as **classless inter-domain routing** (**CIDR**) was introduced. It is defined in **RFC 1519**.

As we saw in Example 9.1, there are over 2 million class C addresses and hence the primary aim of CIDR was to exploit their usage in a more efficient way. To do this, with CIDR, instead of using the fixed netid/hostid boundary associated with class C addresses, the boundary is made variable and dependent on the number of attached hosts specified by the network manager making a request. For example, if the manager of a new network to be connected to the Internet estimates that the number of hosts may grow to, say, 1000, then a contiguous block of 1024 (2^{10}) class C addresses is allocated.

The alternative CIDR method was introduced relatively recently (post-1996) and, by that time, the general Internet architecture had grown to that we showed earlier in Figure 9.9. Hence in order to reduce the amount of routing information exchanged by exterior gateways, it was decided to abandon the fixed netid/hostid boundary and instead introduce a hierarchical structure that reflected this architecture. Remembering that all class C addresses start with 110, the range of addresses available (in dotted decimal form) is from:

    192.0.0.0 through to 223.255.255.255

Clearly, some of these addresses had already been allocated. Hence the allocations to the networks in the different continents are as follows:

Europe:	194.0.0.0 through to 195.255.255.255
North America:	198.0.0.0 through to 199.255.255.255
Central and South America:	200.0.0.0 through to 201.255.255.255
Asia and the Pacific:	202.0.0.0 through to 203.255.255.255

The remainder of the addresses are held in reserve.

As we can deduce from these allocations, the first byte in the destination IP address indicates the continental backbone to which it should be sent. Hence the routing of packets across the global backbone network with addresses that are in this format is relatively straightforward. For example, any netid that contains 194 or 195 (in dotted decimal) as its first (dotted) decimal number indicates the packet should be sent to the European backbone. However, the absence of a fixed division point in the remaining 24 bits means that each router in the backbone must be informed of the related netid/hostid boundary before it can route the datagram any further.

The approach adopted is similar to that we described earlier in Section 9.4.1 relating to subnetting. As we saw, with subnetting the hostid field is itself divided into a subnetid part and a hostid part with no fixed boundary between them. Instead, the division point is indicated by means of an address mask which contains a binary 1 in all those bit positions that contain the sub-netid (and netid) fields. In a similar way, an address mask is used to indicate the boundary between the netid and hostid parts of the new class C addresses. Each exterior gateway then contains a copy of the address mask of each of the networks within the autonomous systems that are attached to it together with the base address – the netid – of the corresponding network.

Example 9.4

A network attached to the Central and South American backbone has been allocated a block of 1024 contiguous class C addresses from 200.30.0.0 through to 200.30.3.255. Assuming the CIDR addressing scheme, represent these addresses in binary form and hence derive the address mask to be used in dotted decimal form and netid of this network.

Answer:

Address 200.30.0.0	= 11001000	00011110	00000000	00000000
Address 200.30.3.255	= 11001000	00011110	00000011	11111111
Hence address mask	= 11111111	11111111	11111100	00000000
	= 255	. 255	. 252	. 0

and netid = 200.30.0.0

In this way, an exterior gateway, on receiving a packet, reads the destination IP address from the packet header and then performs the logical AND operation on this and the list of address masks that it contains. On detecting a match – that is, the resulting netid is the same as that stored with the corresponding mask – the exterior gateway uses the netid and the related interior gateway protocol to route the packet to the appropriate interior gateway. The packet is then passed on to the related access network gateway by this interior gateway.

As we can deduce from this, each interior gateway in the related autonomous system must also contain a copy of the address masks of the networks within that system. Also, each access gateway has a copy of its own address mask and, by using this, it first extracts the hostid from the destination IP address and then uses this to route the packet to that host.

Finally, as we can see from Example 9.4, it is possible for a number of hosts associated with a network which has been allocated a large block of addresses to produce a match with a mask relating to a network with a smaller block of addresses. However, since all network masks are tested, this will be in addition to the match relating to the mask with the smaller block of addresses. Should this happen, then the mask with the smaller block of addresses – and hence larger number of 1s in its address mask – is chosen as the most probable match.

Example 9.5

Two networks that are attached to the Central and South American backbone have been allocated the following block of class C addresses:

Network 1: Addresses = 200.64.16.0 through to 200.64.31.255
            Mask = 255.192.16.0

Network 2: Addresses = 200.64.17.0 through to 200.64.17.255
            Mask = 255.255.255.0

Assuming the CIDR addressing scheme, determine the address of a host attached to network 1 that will produce a match with the mask of network 2.

Answer:

Network 1   Netid = 11001000   01000000   0001/xxxx   xxxxxxxx

Network 2   Netid = 11001000   01000000   00010001/   xxxxxxxx

Hence

Network 1   Hostid = 11001000   01000000   0001/0001   xxxxxxxx

9.6.7 Tunneling

In the previous sections we have assumed that all networks within the global internetwork operate in a connectionless mode using the IP and its associated routing protocols. In practice, however, this is not always the case. As we showed earlier in Figure 9.9 and explained in the accompanying text, the Internet is made up of many separately managed networks and internetworks which, in some instances, use a different operational mode and/or protocol from the IP.

For example, consider a small enterprise consisting of two sites, both of which have LANs that operate using the TCP/IP stack, but only one of the sites has an access gateway connected to the Internet. Also, for cost reasons, instead of using a leased line to connect the two site LANs together, a public (or private) data network is used that operates in a connection-oriented mode and with a different protocol from the IP. Clearly, it is not possible to transfer each IP datagram directly over the public data network and instead a technique known as **tunneling** is used. Figure 9.20 illustrates this approach.

As we can see, in order to link the two sites together, a device known as a **multiprotocol router** is connected to each site LAN. As the name implies, a multi-protocol router operates using two different protocol stacks: the IP protocol stack on the site side and the protocol stack associated with the non-IP network on the other. The IP in each host simply treats the multiprotocol

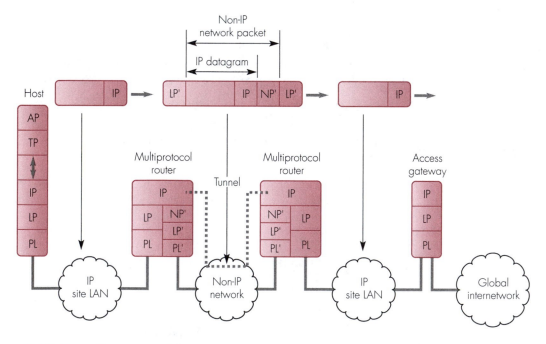

Figure 9.20 Tunneling example.

router as the site Internet access gateway. To send and receive packets to and from a host – a server for example – that is connected to the Internet, the IP simply sends the packet to the multiprotocol router using, for example, the ARP.

Typically, the IP in the source router is given the (non-IP) network address of the multiprotocol router at the remote site by network management. On receipt of the packet, the IP in the source router, on determining that the netid in the destination IP address is not for this site, looks up the non-IP network address of the remote router and passes this, together with the datagram, to the network layer protocol associated with the non-IP network. The latter treats the datagram as user data and proceeds to transfer the datagram to the peer network layer in the remote router using the protocol stack of the non-IP network with the datagram encapsulated in a data packet relating to the network layer protocol.

On receipt of the data packet by the peer network layer protocol in the remote router, the user data – the datagram – contained within it is passed to the IP. The IP first determines from the destination IP address that the required host is not attached to the site LAN and hence proceeds to send the packet to the IP in the Internet access gateway using, for example, the ARP. A similar procedure is followed in the reverse direction to transfer the packets containing the related reply message. Thus, the presence of the non-IP network is transparent to the IP in each host and the access gateway.

In addition to using tunneling to transfer an IP packet over a non-IP network, the same technique is used to send an IP packet over an IP network. As we shall expand upon in Section 9.6.11, tunneling is used by an IP router to relay a packet that contains a multicast destination address to a different router that can handle multicast packets. Normally, the IP address of their nearest multicast router is known by all the other routers and, on receipt of a packet with a multicast address, the source router encapsulates the packet within a new packet with the IP address of the multicast router as the destination IP address.

9.6.8 Broadcast routing

As we explained in the last chapter, LANs such as Ethernet and token ring operate by a station/host broadcasting each frame over the LAN segment to which it is attached. The frame is then received by all the other stations that are attached to the same segment and, by examining the destination (MAC) address in the frame header, the network interface software within each host can decide whether to pass the frame contents on to the IP layer for further processing or to discard the frame. A frame is accepted if the destination MAC address is the same as its own individual address, or is a broadcast address, or is equal to one of the group addresses of which the station is a member. For a bridged LAN, this mode of working is extended to cover the total LAN by each bridge relaying all frames that contain either a broadcast or a multicast address on to all the other LAN segments to which the bridge is attached. In this section we explain how broadcasting is achieved at the IP layer and, in the next section, how multicasting is achieved.

As we identified in Section 9.4, there are a number of different types of IP broadcast address:

■ **limited broadcast**: this is used to send a copy of a packet to the IP in all the hosts that are attached to the same LAN segment or bridged LAN. To achieve this, the destination IP address is set to 255.255.255.255.255. Neither subnet routers nor access gateways forward such packets;

■ **subnet-directed broadcast**: this is used to send a copy of a packet to the IP in all the hosts that are attached to the subnet specified in the destination IP address. To achieve this, the subnet mask associated with the subnet must be known and this is then used to determine the hostid part and set all these bits to 1. Such packets are forwarded by subnet routers but only if the destination netid is different from the source netid are they forwarded by access gateways, interior gateways, and, if necessary, exterior gateways;

■ **net-directed broadcast**: this is used to send a copy of a packet to the IP in all the hosts that are attached to the network specified in the netid part of the destination IP address. Such packets are forwarded by subnet routers but only if the destination netid is different from the source netid are they forwarded by access gateways, interior gateways, and, if necessary, exterior gateways.

Thus, a packet with a net-directed broadcast address whose destination netid is different from the source netid may need to be forwarded across the global internetwork. Since the destination netid is known, however, then the datagram can be routed by interior – and if necessary exterior – gateways in the same way as a packet with a unicast address. This also applies to a packet with a subnet-directed broadcast address whose destination netid is different from the source netid. Also, since with a subnet-directed broadcast address all the subnet routers in both the source and destination networks have a copy of the subnet mask, then they too can use the unicast routing algorithm associated with the network to route the packet to the subnet router specified in the IP address. The latter then broadcasts the packet over this subnet. With a net-directed broadcast, however, this is not possible and the unanswered question is how the packet is broadcast to all the subnets belonging to the network specified in the netid part of the address.

One solution is to use flooding but, as we concluded at the end of Section 9.6.2, this has very high bandwidth overheads associated with it. Two alternative approaches are employed, the choice determined by the routing algorithm that is used to route unicast packets over the network. For description purposes we shall use the example of a large site/campus network that comprises a large number of subnets all interconnected by subnet routers.

The aim of both algorithms is then for the arriving packet with a net-directed broadcast address to be broadcast over all the subnets using a minimum amount of bandwidth.

Reverse path forwarding

This algorithm is used primarily with networks that use the distance vector (DV) algorithm to route unicast packets. To explain the operation of the algorithm we use the network topology shown in Figure 9.21(a). We assume that subnet router 1 (SR1) also acts as the (single) access gateway for the network and that all subnets (SNs) are broadcast LANs.

Using the DV algorithm we explained in Section 9.6.3, in addition to each subnet router deriving the shortest paths to each subnet, they can also derive the shortest paths to reach each of the other subnet routers. To see how this is done, the initial and final routing tables built up by each subnet router (based on a routing metric of hop count) are shown in Figure 9.21(b).

Once the routing tables have been created, the reverse path forwarding algorithm used to route (broadcast) packets works as follows. On receipt of a packet/datagram, the IP in each subnet router (SR) consults its routing table and only forwards a copy of it – onto each of the ports of the SR except the port the packet arrived on – if the packet arrived from an SR that is on the shortest path from SR1 to the SR that is processing the packet. If it is not, then the packet is discarded. Based on this simple rule, the path followed by each copy of an incoming packet is shown in Figure 9.21(c).

As we can see, on receipt of a packet, SR1 broadcasts a copy of it out onto subnets SN1 and SN3. Hence a copy of the packet is received by the IP in SR2 and SR4 respectively. On receiving the packet, the IP in SR2 first consults its routing table and determines from the (first) entry in the table that SN1 (from which the packet was received) is on the shortest path back to SR1. Similarly, when the IP in SR4 consults its routing table it also determines that SN3 (from which the packet was received) is also on the shortest path back to SR1. Hence both SR2 and SR4 are shown in bold in the figure and each proceeds to broadcast a copy of the packet, SR2 onto SN2 and SN4, and SR4 onto SN7.

After the second set of broadcasts, on receipt of its copy of the packet, the IP in SR3 determines from its routing table that SN2 is on the shortest path back to SR1. Similarly for the copy SR5 receives from SR2 via SN4. Hence both SR3 and SR5 are shown in bold and proceed to broadcast a copy of the packet, SR3 onto SN5 and SN6, and SR5 onto SN5, SN7, and SN8. However, in the case of the packet received by SR5 from SR4 via SN7, SR5 determines that SN7 is not on the shortest path back to SR1. Hence SR5 along this path is not shown in bold and the arriving packet is discarded.

The same procedure is repeated by SR5 and SR6 after the third set of broadcasts have been received but this time only SR6 determines from its routing table that SN6 is on the shortest path back to SR1 and proceeds to broadcast a copy of the packet onto SN8. The copies of the packet received

(a)

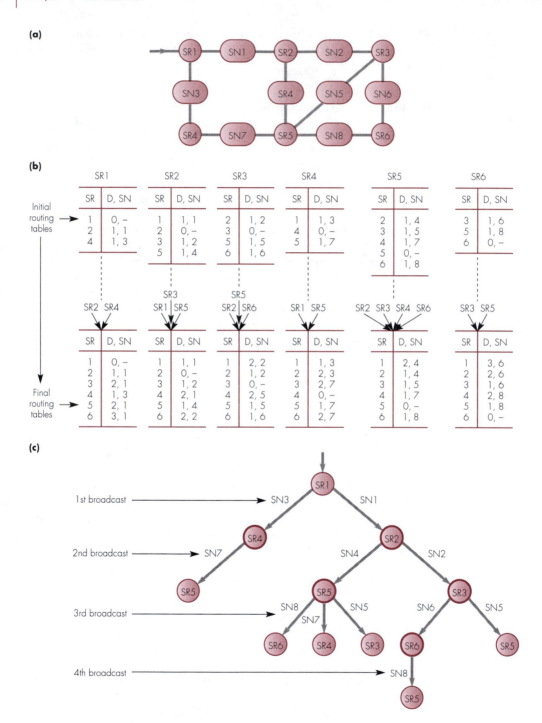

(b)

(c)

Figure 9.21 Reverse path forwarding: (a) network topology; (b) distance vector routing tables using a hop-count metric; (c) broadcast sequence.

from SR5 by SR3, SR4, and SR6 are all discarded as the related subnets – SN5, SN7, and SN8 – are not on the shortest paths back to SR1. Also the packet received by SR5 from SR6 after the fourth broadcast.

As we can deduce from this example, a copy of the packet is broadcast over all the eight subnets that make up the network and only SN7 and SN8 receive two copies. However, since both copies of the packet have the same value in the identifier field of the packet header, the second copy can be detected by each of the hosts on these subnets as a duplicate and is discarded. Note also that the same set of routing tables can be used to perform the same algorithm if a second (or different) SR acts as an additional (or alternative) access gateway. Also, if the broadcast is over the source network.

Spanning tree broadcast

With networks that use a routing algorithm based on the link-state algorithm, an alternative way of routing broadcast packets/datagrams is for each router to use the link-state information to establish a spanning tree active topology with the access gateway/router as the root node.

As we saw in Section 9.6.4, the information gathered as part of the link-state algorithm is used by each router to derive the current active topology of the internetwork. In a similar way, therefore, with networks that consist of multiple subnets interconnected by subnet routers, each subnet router builds up knowledge of the current active topology of the network and then uses this to compute the shortest path to reach all the subnetids in the network.

Hence with the spanning tree broadcast algorithm, in addition to each subnet router computing the shortest paths, they all derive the (same) spanning tree topology from the current active topology using, for example, the algorithm we described in Section 8.5.1. As we saw, a spanning tree topology is established in order to avoid frames looping within a bridged LAN. This is done by defining the ports associated with each bridge as either root ports or designated ports. All ports that are either root or designated ports are then set into the forwarding state and all the other ports are set into the non-forwarding (blocked) state.

Using the same approach, we can derive a spanning tree by setting selected subnet router ports into the forwarding and blocked state. For example, using the network topology we showed in Figure 9.21(a) and the algorithm we described in Section 8.5.1, assuming each subnet router knows the root SR, each will derive the spanning tree shown in Figure 9.22(b). The resulting broadcast sequence is therefore as shown in Figure 9.22(c).

We can make a number of observations from this example:

- For consistency, the port numbers associated with each subnet router are determined by the (known) identifier of the attached subnet.
- Each SR has a root port (RP) associated with it which is the port with the shortest path back to the root. The path costs in the example are based on hop count and, in the event of a tie, the port with the smallest port number is chosen.

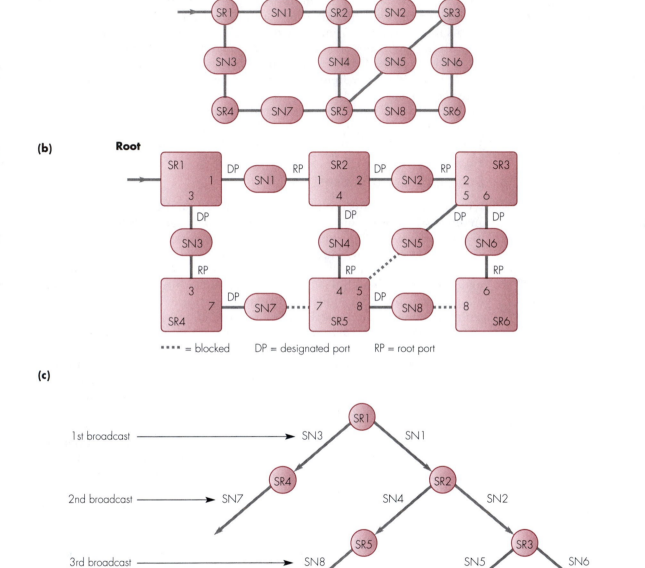

(a)

(b)

Root

•••• = blocked   DP = designated port   RP = root port

(c)

1st broadcast ⟶

2nd broadcast ⟶

3rd broadcast ⟶

Figure 9.22 Spanning tree broadcast: (a) network topology; (b) spanning tree derived by each subnet router; (c) broadcast sequence.

■ For each subnet, there is a designated port (DP) which is the router port on the shortest path from the root to the subnet. In the event of a tie, the SR with the smallest identifier is chosen.

■ All router ports that are not root or designated ports (DP) are set into the blocked state.

■ Only a single copy of each received packet/datagram is broadcast over each subnet.

■ The same spanning tree can be used to broadcast packets if a second (or different) SR acts as an additional (or alternative) access gateway and if the broadcast is over the source network.

9.6.9 Multicast routing

As we explained in Chapter 1, applications such as audio- and videoconferencing require a copy of the information generated by each host participating in a conference to be sent to all the other hosts that belong to the same conference. The term **multicasting** is used to describe the diffusion of a copy of the packets/datagrams generated by each host to all the other hosts and the term **multicast group** is used to identify the hosts that are members of the same conference. Clearly, there can be many conferences in progress concurrently, each involving a different group of hosts. It is to support applications of this type that class D multicast addresses were defined. As we showed in Figure 9.4 and explained in the accompanying text, a single class D address is used to identify all the hosts that are members of the same multicast group. Also, since 28 bits are available, many different multicast groups can be in place concurrently.

A number of multicast addresses are reserved to identify specific groups. For example, all the hosts (and subnet routers) that are attached to a site broadcast network are members of the group with the reserved multicast address of 224.0.0.1. Hence the IP in all hosts that can support multicasting will have this address permanently in their **multicast address table** (**MAT**) and, should a packet be received with this address, the datagram contents will be passed to (and acted upon) by a related application process. Similarly, all the subnet routers belonging to the same network are members of the multicast address 224.0.0.2.

As we showed in Figure 5.4, with networks that do not support broadcasting such as PSTNs and ISDNs, the diffusion operation is achieved by using a central (conference) server known as a multipoint control unit (MCU). Also, in packet-switching networks that support broadcasting such as LANs, as we showed in Figure 5.6, the H.323 standard uses a similar approach with a networked device known as a gatekeeper performing the multipoint control function of an MCU. Using this approach, the IP and MAC address-pair of the MCU is known by the IP in all the hosts that are participating in a conference and, once the IP in the MCU has obtained the IP/MAC address-pair of all the participating hosts, the IP in the MCU can carry out the diffusion operation using only the individual (unicast) IP address of each participant.

This approach is acceptable providing the number of participating hosts is relatively small and the composition of the conference is static. However, for applications such as a conference or meeting which is being transmitted over a LAN or the Internet, a relatively large number of participants – and hence hosts – may be involved. Moreover, hosts may wish to join and/or leave the conference/meeting whilst it is in progress. It is to meet this type of application that multicasting using IP multicast addresses is used.

With this mode of working, the organizer of the conference/meeting first obtains an IP multicast address for it from the Internet assigned numbers authority (IANA). The allocated address is then made known to all the registered participants together with the conference/meeting start time and its likely duration. Each participating host can then request to join the conference at any time during the time the conference/meeting is in progress. To do this, two operating scenarios are used which depend on whether the participating hosts are all attached to the same LAN/subnet or, as is more usual, are attached to many different networks that are geographically distributed around the Internet. We shall discuss each separately.

Multicasting over a LAN

The IANA has been allocated a block of Ethernet MAC addresses for applications that involve multicasting. As we described in Section 8.3, Ethernet MAC addresses are 48 bits in length and the reserved block of addresses in dotted decimal are from

0.0.94.0.0.0 through to 0.0.94.255.255.255

Half of these addresses are used for multicasting. Hence, remembering that all centrally administered Ethernet group (multicast) addresses must start with 10 binary, the block of Ethernet addresses used for centrally administered multicasting applications are from

128.0.94.0.0.0 through to 128.0.94.127.255.255

Thus for a particular conference/meeting, a 3-byte address in the range

0.0.0 through to 127.255.255

is allocated by the IANA. In the case of an Ethernet LAN, this forms the least significant 24 bits of the 48-bit destination MAC address – starting with the three bytes 128.0.94 – and, in the case of the Internet, the least significant 24 bits of the destination IP multicast address. As we explained earlier, class D IP addresses are 28 bits in length – the first four bits being 1110 – and hence, as we show in Figure 9.23(a), the four remaining bits are all set to 0.

So to join a conference/meeting that is being broadcast over the same LAN, once the multicast address is known, the application process running in

(a)

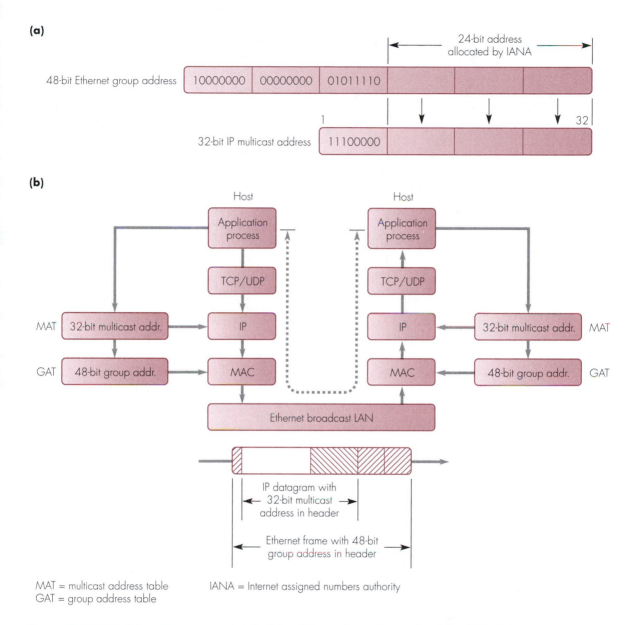

48-bit Ethernet group address

| 10000000 | 00000000 | 01011110 | | | |

24-bit address
allocated by IANA

1   32

32-bit IP multicast address

| 11100000 | | | |

(b)

Host   Host

MAT = multicast address table   IANA = Internet assigned numbers authority
GAT = group address table

Figure 9.23 Multicasting over a LAN: (a) address allocation principle; (b) address usage.

the host that is managing the information associated with the conference/meeting simply loads the allocated IP multicast address into its MAT and the related 48-bit Ethernet group address derived from this into its **group address table (GAT)**. Each datagram relating to the conference/meeting then has the allocated multicast address in the destination IP address field of the datagram header. Each packet is then broadcast over the LAN in an Ethernet frame containing the derived 48-bit group address in the destination MAC address field of the frame header.

On receipt of a frame, the MAC sublayer in each host that is a member of the same multicast group, first checks to see whether the destination MAC address in the frame header is present in its group address table and, if it is, it passes the frame contents – the datagram – on to the IP layer. The latter first determines that the destination IP address is a multicast address and also that it is present in its multicast address table. It therefore passes the information contained within the datagram on to the related application process via the TCP or UDP. This procedure is shown in Figure 9.23(b).

Multicasting over the Internet

When the hosts that are part of a multicast group are attached to different networks/subnetworks geographically distributed around the Internet, then intermediate subnet routers and/or interior/exterior gateways may be involved. Thus, since an IP multicast address has no structure – and hence no netid – associated with it, a different type of routing from that used to route unicast packets must be used.

The sequence of steps followed to route a packet with a multicast address is as follows:

- A router that can route packets containing a (destination) IP multicast address is known as a **multicast router** (**mrouter**).
- Normally, in the case of a network that comprises multiple subnets interconnected by subnet routers, a single subnet router also acts as the mrouter for that network.
- Each mrouter learns the set of multicast group addresses of which all the hosts attached to the networks which the mrouter serves are currently members.
- The information gathered by each mrouter is passed on to each of the other mrouters so that each knows the complete list of group addresses that each mrouter has an interest in.
- On receipt of a packet with a destination IP multicast address, each mrouter uses an appropriate routing algorithm to pass the packet only to those mrouters that are attached to a network which has an attached host that is a member of the multicast group indicated in the destination IP address field.

As with broadcast routing, two different algorithms are used, the choice determined by the routing algorithm that is used to route unicast packets. The aim of both algorithms is to minimize the amount of transmission bandwidth required to deliver each multicast packet to those multicast routers that have an interest in the packet. To explain the two algorithms, we shall use the internetwork topology shown in Figure 9.24(a). The letters by each multicast router (MR) – A, B, and C – indicate the multicast address(es) that each has an interest in and, since all MRs exchange this information, they each have a copy of the multicast address table shown in Figure 9.24(a).

DVMRP

When distance vector routing is being used, an additional set of routing tables (to those used to route unicast packets) based on MR-to-MR distances are derived and, for the six MRs, these are given in Figure 9.24(b). They are based on a routing metric of hop count and have been derived using the same procedure we described earlier in Section 9.6.3. Together with the contents of the MAT in each MR, they are used to route all packets that have a destination multicast address.

(a)

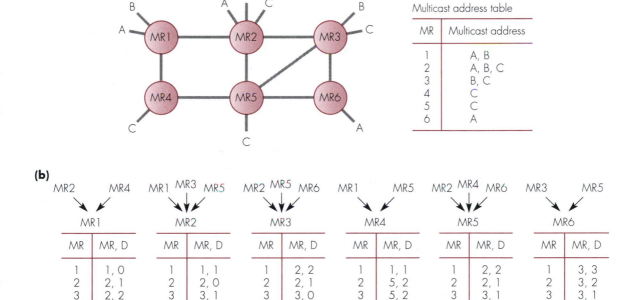

(b)

MR = multicast router   D = distance in hops

Figure 9.24 Distance vector multicast routing: (a) example topology and multicast address table; (b) unicast routing tables of MR1–6.

The protocol is known as the **distance vector multicast routing protocol** (**DVMRP**). To explain how it works, assume a packet with a multicast address of A is received by the IP in MR1 from one of its attached networks. The sequence is as follows:

■ The IP first consults its MAT and finds that a copy of the packet should be sent to MR2 and MR6. It then proceeds to consult its routing table (RT) and finds that the shortest path to MR6 is also via MR2 and hence sends just a single copy of the packet to MR2.

■ On receipt of the packet, MR2 consults its MAT and sees that a copy of the packet should be sent out onto its own network and also to MR1 and MR6. On consulting its RT, however, it finds that the shortest path to MR1 is on the line/port the packet was received and hence it only sends a copy of the packet to MR6. The RT indicates that the shortest path to MR6 is via MR3 and hence it forwards a copy of the packet to MR3.

■ On receipt of the packet, MR3 determines from its MAT that MR1, MR2, and MR6 should be sent a copy of the packet. On consulting its RT it finds that the shortest path to both MR1 and MR2 is via MR2. Hence, since this is the line/port the packet arrived on, it only sends a copy of the packet to MR6.

■ On receipt of the packet, MR6 determines from its MAT that a copy of the packet should be sent out on its own network and also to MR1 and MR2. However, since the shortest path to both MR1 and MR2 is via the line/port the packet arrived on, it only sends a copy out on its local network.

MOSPF

When link-state routing is being used, since each MR knows the current active topology of the internetwork, as we explained in Section 9.6.8, each computes a spanning tree for the internetwork using the algorithm we described in Section 8.5.1. For example, for the internetwork shown in Figure 9.25(a), the spanning tree computed by each MR is shown in Figure 9.25(b). The numbers shown by each line are used as global line identifiers and as port numbers in the derivation of the spanning tree.

At any point in time, each MR knows from its MAT the multicast addresses that each has an interest in. For each address – A, B, and C in the example – each MR proceeds to produce a pruned spanning tree by removing selected links. For the internetwork shown in Figure 9.25(a), the pruned spanning trees produced by each MR for each of the three multicast addresses are as shown in Figure 9.25(b).

For each address, these are produced by starting at the tip of each branch of the basic spanning tree and pruning each line that does not form a path back to the root for this address. Packets are then only forwarded on those lines that make up the resulting pruned spanning tree. The protocol is known as the **multicast open shortest path first** (**MOSPF**) routing protocol

(a)

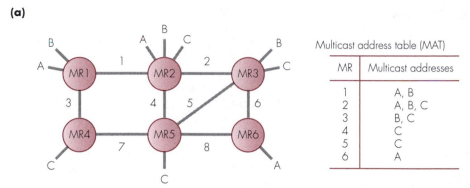

Multicast address table (MAT)

MR	Multicast addresses
1	A, B
2	A, B, C
3	B, C
4	C
5	C
6	A

Note: 1–8 are global line identifiers. These are also used as port numbers in the derivation of the spanning tree

(b)

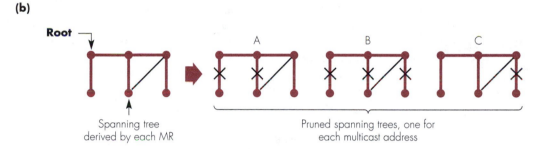

Spanning tree derived by each MR

Pruned spanning trees, one for each multicast address

Figure 9.25 Spanning-tree multicast routing: (a) example topology and multicast address table; (b) set of spanning trees for each multicast address.

and, to explain how it works, assume that a packet with a (multicast) address of A is received from a network attached to MR1. The steps followed by each MR are as follows:

- On detecting the (multicast) address in the packet header is A, MR1 uses the pruned spanning tree for A to determine that a copy of the packet should be sent to MR2.

- On receipt of the packet, MR2 first determines from its MAT that a copy of the packet should be sent out onto its own network. It then uses its own copy of the pruned spanning tree for A to determine that a copy of the packet should also be sent to MR3.

- On receipt of the packet, MR3 first determines from its MAT that it has no interest in the packet. It then uses its own copy of the pruned spanning tree for A to determine that a copy of the packet should be sent to MR6.

- On receipt of the packet, MR6 first determines from its MAT that a copy of the packet should be sent out onto its own network. It then uses its own copy of the pruned spanning tree for A to determine that it is at the end of a branch of the tree and hence discards the packet.

9.6.10 IGMP

The two routing algorithms we described in the last section – the DVMRP and MOSPF – both assumed that each multicast router has stored in its multicast address table the complete list of multicast addresses that are currently in use and also the multicast addresses that each multicast router has an interest in. As we explained, the contents of the MAT are obtained by, first, each multicast router learning the set of multicast addresses of which all the hosts attached to the networks/subnets which the mrouter serves are currently members and second, this information is passed on to all the other mrouters. Clearly, the second step can be carried out using a broadcast procedure similar to that used in the distance vector algorithm to distribute network-wide routing information. Hence the unanswered question is how an mrouter learns the multicast addresses associated with its own attached networks/subnets. In practice, this is the role of the Internet group management protocol (IGMP) which we identified earlier in Figure 9.2. The IGMP is an integral part of the IP layer in all hosts and routers that support multicasting. It is defined in **RFC 1112.**

As we explained at the start of the last section, an application process (AP) within a host can join and leave a currently active multicast group at any time. To do this, the AP must know the 24-bit group address that has been allocated to this group by the IANA. As we showed in Figure 9.23, the AP uses this to derive both the IP multicast address of the group and the corresponding Ethernet group address. It then writes these into the MAT and the corresponding GAT respectively. In the case of a multicast session involving a group of APs in hosts that are all attached to the same LAN, this is all that is needed. In the case of a multicast session over the Internet, however, it is necessary for the host to inform its local mrouter the multicast address of the session that it wishes to join. The sequence of steps followed to do this are shown in Figure 9.26.

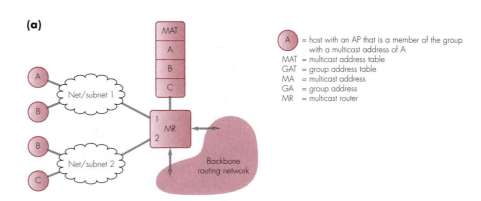

Figure 9.26 IGMP summary: (a) example network topology; (b) IGMP message transfer sequence to join and leave a multicast session; (c) IGMP message format.

(b)

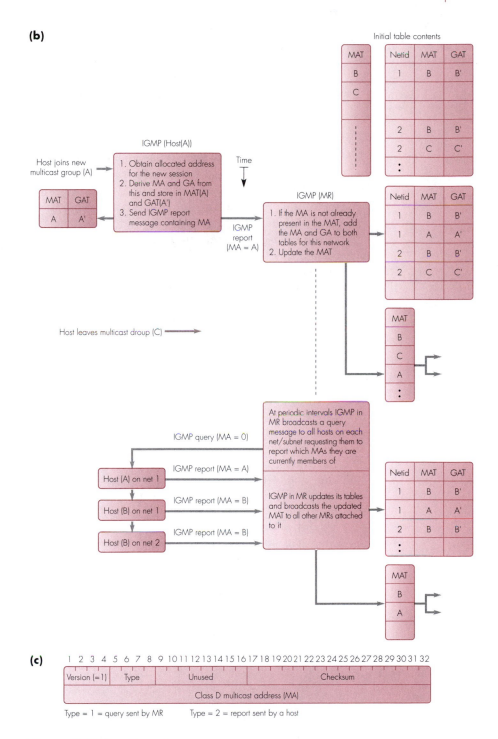

Figure 9.26 Continued

In this example, an AP running in a host that is attached to net/subnet 1 wishes to take part in a multicast session that has a derived multicast address of A. We assume that three other APs/hosts attached to the same multicast router are already members of two existing multicast groups, two with a multicast address of B and one with an address of C. In the case of B, one is attached to net/subnet 1 and the other to net/subnet 2 and, in the case of C, this is attached to net/subnet 2. Hence the contents of the initial tables are as shown in Figure 9.26(b).

First the IGMP in host (A) sends out a message – known as a *report* – to the IGMP in the attached mrouter (MR) containing the multicast address (MA) of the group it wishes to join (A). In addition to the MAT that is used for routing over the backbone network, a separate MAT and GAT are maintained by the MR for both net/subnet 1 and net/subnet 2. Hence on receipt of the report message, the IGMP first writes the MA into the MAT and the related Ethernet group address into the GAT of net/subnet 1. Also, since A is not already present in the backbone routing MAT, this is added to it and the new contents forwarded to each of the attached MRs.

Hosts do not need to inform an MR when it leaves a multicast group. At regular intervals, the IGMP in each MR broadcasts a *query* message to all hosts on each net/subnet requesting them to report of which MAs they are currently members. On receipt of a query, the IGMP in each host responds by returning a separate report message for each MA of which the host is currently a member. In the example shown in Figure 9.26, we assume the host that was a member of MA C has now left the group and hence a report message for C is not returned. Hence the IGMP in the MR removes the entries for C from its tables and proceeds to forward the updated table contents to each of the attached MRs.

The format of the two types of IGMP message – query and report – is the same and is shown in Figure 9.26(c). The *version* field is equal to 1 and the *type* field is either 0 for a report message (sent by a host) or 1 for a query message (sent by a MR). The *checksum* applies to the complete message and is computed using the same 1s complement procedure used with the header of an IP datagram. The *group address* is a 32-bit class D multicast address. In a query message it is set to all 0s and in a report it is set to the multicast group address being reported. Both are transmitted over the attached net/subnet in an IP packet with a *protocol* value of 2 and a *time-to-live* value of 1. In the case of a query, the *destination IP address* is the all-hosts broadcast address of 224.0.0.1 and the *source IP address* is the IP address of the MR. In the case of a report, the two addresses are the group MA being reported and the host IP address respectively.

9.6.11 M-bone

As we explained in Section 9.6.9 when we discussed the two multicast routing algorithms, currently, only a subset of the routers that make up the Internet global internetwork are capable of routing IP packets which have a multicast destination address. These are known as multicast routers (mrouters) and the network formed by the interconnected set of mrouters, the **multicast backbone** (**M-bone**) **network**. The two routing algorithms we described in Section 9.6.9 are then used to route multicast packets between the mrouters that make up the M-bone.

In practice, therefore, because only a subset of the routers in the global internetwork can route multicast packets, there may be other routers that do not support multicasting present in the physical path that links two mrouters together. Hence many of the transmission paths that link the mrouters that form the M-bone are logical links that are implemented using IP tunneling. As we explained in Section 9.6.7, with tunneling, in order to send an IP datagram containing a multicast group address over the logical link that links two mrouters together, the datagram is carried in the user data field of a second IP datagram. This has the (known) IP unicast address of the intended destination mrouter in the destination IP address field of the second datagram. In this way, the packet is routed over the global internetwork in the same way as a unicast packet using either the distance vector or the link-state shortest-path-first algorithm. Then, on arrival at the destination mrouter, the latter extracts the multicast datagram contained within the packet and proceeds to route it using one of the two related multicast routing algorithms we described in Section 9.6.9.

As we can deduce from this, in order to implement the M-Bone, each mrouter has the IP (unicast) address of the adjacent mrouters that are (logically) connected to it stored in their connectivity/adjacency table. Normally, this information is entered by the management authority responsible for the network in which the mrouter is located. In this way, the possible presence of other (unicast) routers between two mrouters is transparent to the two mrouters which simply route (multicast) packets as if there is a physical transmission line linking them together.

9.7 ICMP

The Internet control message protocol (ICMP) forms an integral part of all IP implementations. It is used by hosts, routers and gateways for a variety of functions, and especially by network management. The main functions associated with the ICMP are as follows:

- error reporting,
- reachability testing,
- congestion control,
- route-change notification,
- performance measuring,
- subnet addressing.

The message types associated with each of these functions are shown in Table 9.2. Each is transmitted in a standard IP datagram.

Since the IP is a best-effort (unacknowledged) protocol, packets may be discarded while they are in transit across the Internet. Of course, transmission errors are one cause, but packets can be discarded by a host, router, or gateway for a variety of reasons. In the absence of any error reporting functions, a host does not know whether the repeated failure to send a packet to a given destination is the result of a poor transmission line (or other fault within a network) or simply the destination host being switched off. The various messages associated with the **error reporting** function are used for this purpose.

Table 9.2 ICMP message types and their use

Function	ICMP message(s)	Use
Error reporting	Destination unreachable	A datagram has been discarded due to the reason specified in the message
	Time exceeded	Time-to-live parameter in a datagram expired and hence discarded
	Parameter error	A parameter in the header of a datagram is unrecognizable
Reachability testing	Echo request/reply	Checks the reachability of a specified host or gateway
Congestion control	Source quench	Requests a host to reduce the rate at which datagrams are sent
Route exchange	Redirect	Used by a gateway to inform a host attached to one of its networks to use an alternative gateway on the same network for forwarding datagrams to a specific destination
Performance measuring	Time-stamp request/reply	Determines the transit delay between two hosts
Subnet addressing	Address mask request/reply	Used by a host to determine the address mask associated with a subnet

ICMP = Internet control message protocol

If a packet is corrupted by transmission errors, it is simply discarded. If a packet is discarded for any other reason, the ICMP in the host, router, or gateway that discards the packet generates a *destination unreachable* error report message and returns it to the ICMP in the source host with a reason code. Reasons include the following:

■ destination network unreachable,

■ destination host unreachable,

■ parameter problem,

■ specified protocol not present at destination,

■ fragmentation needed but don't fragment (DF) flag set in datagram header,

■ communication with the destination network not allowed for administrative reasons,

■ communication with the destination host not allowed for administrative reasons.

Although in most cases error reports are received as a result of some type of failure condition arising, in some instances an error report is used to gain some knowledge of the operational characteristics of the path/route followed by a packet. In general, the transfer of a message over the global internetwork is much quicker if no fragmentation is involved. Most networks (and subnetworks) support a maximum transmission unit (MTU) equal to or greater than 576 bytes. Hence one way of ensuring no fragmentation takes place is for the source IP to adopt this as the maximum size of all datagrams (including the IP header). In most cases, however, the actual MTU of the path will be greater than this and hence this would result in more packets being used to send each message than is necessary.

An alternative is for the source IP to use a procedure known as **path MTU discovery** to determine the MTU of a path/route prior to sending any datagrams relating to a session/call. Essentially, the first message received from the transport layer protocol relating to a new call/session is sent in a single datagram with the *don't fragment* bit set. Normally, if a router along the path followed by the packet cannot forward the packet over an attached link without fragmenting it, the router will return an ICMP error report with *fragmentation needed* as a reason code and an indication of the size of MTU that is possible. The source IP then adopts the latter as its own MTU to send all the remaining messages relating to the call/session.

Other error report messages include *time exceeded*, which indicates that the time-to-live parameter in a discarded packet has expired, and *parameter error*, which indicates that a parameter in the header of the discarded packet was not recognized.

If a network manager receives reports from a user that a specified destination is not responding, the reason must be determined using the *reachability testing* function which is implemented in a program called **ping**. Typically, on receipt of such a report, the network manager initiates the sending of an *echo request* message to the suspect host to determine whether it is switched on and responding to requests. On receipt of an echo request message, the ICMP in the destination simply changes this to an *echo reply* message which it returns to the source. A similar test can be performed on selected routers and gateways if necessary.

If a packet is discarded because no free memory buffers are available as a result of a temporary overload condition, a *source quench* message is returned to the ICMP in the source host. Such messages can be generated either by a host or by a router or gateway. They request the source host to reduce the rate at which it sends packets. When a host receives such a message, it reduces the sending rate by an agreed amount. A new source quench message is generated each time a packet is discarded so that the source host incrementally reduces the sending rate. Such messages help to alleviate congestion within the global internetwork. Congestion is discussed further in Section 9.8.

When a network has multiple gateways attached to it, a gateway may receive datagrams from a host even though it determines from its routing table that they would be better sent via a different gateway attached to the same network. To inform the source host of this, the ICMP in the gateway returns a *redirect* message to the ICMP in the source indicating which is the better gateway to the specified destination. The ICMP in the source then makes an entry in its routing table for this destination.

An important operational parameter for an internet is the mean transit delay of packets/datagrams. This is a measure of the time a datagram takes to traverse the internet from a specified source to a specified destination. To ascertain this time, a host or a network manager can send a *time-stamp request* message to a specific destination. Each message contains the following three time-related parameters (known as *time-stamps*):

- the time the datagram was sent by the source,
- the time the datagram was received by the destination,
- the time the datagram was returned by the destination.

On receipt of a time-stamp request message, the ICMP in the destination simply fills in the appropriate time-stamp fields and returns the message to the source. On receipt of the reply, the source can quantify the current round-trip delay to that destination and from this determine the packet transit delay.

Finally, when subnet addressing is being used, the *address mask request* and corresponding reply messages are used by a host to ascertain the address mask associated with a local subnet. This is needed by a host to determine, for example, whether a specified destination is attached to the same subnet. The address mask is held by the local router associated with the subnet. The ICMP in a host can obtain the address mask by sending a request message and reading the mask from the reply.

9.7.1 ICMP message formats and transmission

The format of an ICMP message is shown in Figure 9.27. The first three fields are the same for all messages. The *type* field indicates the ICMP message type and these are related to the functions we listed earlier. For example, a *type* field of 0 relates to the error reporting function, 3 reachability testing, 4 congestion control, and so on. The *code* field then gives additional information such as the reason why a destination is unreachable. For example, 6 indicates the destination network is unknown and 7 the destination host is unknown. The *checksum* covers the entire ICMP message and uses the same algorithm as that used for the checksum present in the IP header. The number and meaning of the following 32-bit words then depend on the *type* and *code* fields in the header.

As we showed in Figure 9.3 and explained in the accompanying text, the *protocol* field in each datagram header is used to route the payload in a datagram to the appropriate protocol – ICMP, IGMP, OSPF, TCP, or UDP. In the case of reply messages, normally, these are for use by the local IP. When unsolicited error reports are received, in most cases, they are passed to an application-level process and result in an appropriate error message being output on the host screen.

9.8 QoS support

Congestion arises within a network when the demand for a network resource exceeds the level that is provided. For example, if a burst of packets arrive at a router (within the global internetwork) on a number of different input lines that all require the same output line, then the output line will become

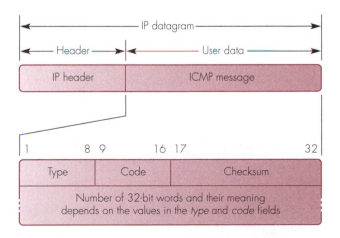

Figure 9.27 ICMP message format and transmission.

congested if the rate of arrival of packets is greater than the rate they can be output. To allow for this possibility, each output line has a first-in first-out (FIFO) queue associated with it which is used to hold a defined number of packets that are awaiting output on that line. Hence, providing the burst is of a relatively short duration and the number of packets to be queued is less than the number of packet buffers available, the congestion will be transient and the only effect should be a small increase in the end-to-end transfer delay experienced by each packet using that line. In the event of a longer burst, however, then all the packet buffers may become full and, as a result, some packets will have to be discarded.

Similarly, at a network-wide level, since the Internet is a best-effort connectionless network, the global internetwork will become congested if, over a sustained period, the aggregate rate at which packets are entering the internetwork exceeds its total capacity in terms of transmission bandwidth and packet buffers. As we saw in Section 1.5.5, associated with each call is a defined set of parameters which form what is called the minimum quality of service (QoS) requirements for the call. For example, with a packet-switched network like the Internet, these include a defined minimum mean packet throughput rate and a maximum end-to-end packet transfer delay. Hence, if as a result of congestion these requirements are not met, then the quality of the call may no longer be acceptable to the user. This is the case with applications involving real-time media streams, for example, such as Internet telephony.

As we can conclude from the above, two levels of congestion control are required, one that operates at the global internetwork level and the other that operates at the router level. The aim of the first is to limit the aggregate rate at which packets are entering the global internetwork to below its maximum rate, and the aim of the second is to maximize the flow of packets through each router. In the following subsections we discuss aspects of two of the schemes that are used to perform these functions.

9.8.1 Integrated services

Most early applications of the Internet were text based and hence relatively insensitive to delay and jitter. Examples include FTP and email, both of which can tolerate the added delays incurred by the use of a host-to-host retransmission control mechanism to overcome the effect of lost packets resulting from the best-effort service provided by IP. Other text-based applications, however, cannot tolerate the delay caused by retransmissions but nevertheless require minimal packet losses. Examples of this type of application are those relating to network control.

More recently, a number of interpersonal applications involving packetized speech and video were introduced. These require the packets that are generated at the source to be transferred over the Internet and played out at the destination in real time. This means that the retransmission of lost pack-

ets is not possible and that the packet flow is particularly sensitive to lost packets and jitter. Such applications also require a guaranteed minimum
bandwidth. To meet this more varied set of QoS requirements, two schemes
have been researched and standardized, one called integrated services
(IntServ) and the other differentiated services (DiffServ). In this section we
describe aspects of the IntServ scheme while aspects of DiffServ are described
in Section 9.8.2.

In both schemes, the packets relating to the different types of call/ses-
sion are each allocated a different value in the precedence bits of the *type of
service* field of the IP packet header. This is used by the routers within the
Internet to differentiate between the packet flows relating to the different
types of call. The IntServ solution defines three different classes of service:

- guaranteed: in this class, a specified maximum delay and jitter and an
  assured level of bandwidth are guaranteed. It is intended for applications
  involving the playout of real-time streams;

- controlled load (also known as predictive): in this class, no firm
  guarantees are provided but the flow obtains a constant level of service
  equivalent to that obtained with the best-effort service at light loads.
  Examples of applications in this class are those involving real-time
  streams that have the capability of adjusting the amount of real-time data
  that is generated to the level that is offered;

- best-effort: this is intended for text-based applications.

To cater for the three different types of packet flows, within each router,
three separate output queues are used for each line, one for each class. In
addition, appropriate control mechanisms are used to ensure the QoS
requirements of each class are met. We shall first discuss a number of these as
these are used in both the IntServ and the DiffServ schemes.

Token bucket filter

This is used with each of the packet flows in both the guaranteed and predictive service classes. A portion of the bandwidth of the outgoing line and an
amount of buffer/queue space is reserved for the packet flow relating to each
call. A control mechanism called the token bucket filter is used to enforce
these allocations so that the guaranteed QoS requirements in terms of bandwidth, delay, and jitter are met.

Associated with each flow is a container called a *bucket* into which tokens
are entered at a rate determined by the bandwidth requirement of the flow.
The size of the bucket is the same as the maximum amount of buffer/queue
space the flow may consume. A packet relating to a flow can only be transferred
to the output queue if there are sufficient tokens currently in the bucket. The
number of tokens required is determined by the packet length and, if sufficient tokens are currently in the bucket, the packet is queued and the
corresponding number of tokens taken from the bucket. As we can deduce

from this, therefore, providing the arrival rate of packets is less than or equal to the rate of entry of tokens into the bucket, then both the agreed bandwidth and delay/jitter will be met. If the arrival rate of packets exceeds the allocated bandwidth, normally these are relegated to the best-effort queue.

Weighted fair queuing

Since the packet rate – and hence bandwidth – associated with each flow may be different, when the packets relating to each flow are queued for transmission, in order to ensure the guaranteed delay bounds are met, it is necessary to ensure that the packets relating to each flow are not delayed by the packets of other flows. Hence a queue management scheme is also required to schedule the order that queued packets are transmitted. The **weighted fair queuing (WFQ)** scheme performs this function.

In order to ensure the delay bounds for each flow are met, the order of transmission of packets from the queue is changed each time a new packet arrives for queuing. When a packet arrives at an incoming line of the router it is given a time-stamp. This is determined from the arrival time of the packet and its scheduled departure time, the latter computed from the bandwidth associated with the flow and the packet length. The time-stamp of the packet is then compared with the time-stamps of the packets that are currently queued and the packet with the smallest time-stamp is transmitted first. In this way the delay bounds of each flow are met.

Random early detection

The requirements of the queue management scheme used with the best-effort queue are different from those of the other two queues. As we indicated earlier, normally, a router simply discards/drops a packet if the required output queue is already full. However, as we shall describe later in Section 12.3.2, with TCP, each time a packet relating to a call/session is lost, the TCP in the source host detects this and halves its current rate of entry of new packets for the call. Since this is done by all the hosts that lose a packet, the utilization of the link bandwidth falls dramatically. This is also detected by the affected TCPs which then quickly ramp-up the rate of entry of new packets. This, in turn, often results in full queues and dropped packets occurring again with the effect that the utilization of the available transmission bandwidth is poor. To stop this occurring, the **random early detection (RED)** queue management scheme is often used.

With RED, when a packet arrives for an output queue and the queue is full, instead of discarding the packet, a packet that is already in the queue is randomly selected for discarding. This has the affect that a reduced number of different applications are affected and hence the bandwidth utilization of the link is much improved.

To implement the scheme, two thresholds relating to the queue are defined: a minimum threshold (MinTH) and a maximum threshold (MaxTH). Also, the average length (AvrLEN) of the queue is continuously monitored and used as a measure of the current level of traffic using the line. The action taken by the scheduler is determined by the current AvrLEN relative to the two thresholds as follows:

AvrLEN < MinTH: the new packet is entered into the queue;

AvrLEN < MaxTH: the new packet is dropped;

MaxTH < AvrLEN < MinTH: a randomly-selected packet from the queue is dropped and the new packet is queued.

As we can deduce from the last condition, the probability of packets that are already in the queue being dropped increases as the AvrLEN increases. This has been found to give high levels of bandwidth utilization during periods of congestion.

Resource reservation protocol

With the IntServ scheme, in order to ensure the aggregate bandwidth of real-time traffic flows does not exceed that which is allocated for both the guaranteed and controlled-load traffic, the resources required for each flow (in terms of transmission bandwidth and buffer capacity) are reserved in advance of each packet flow starting. The protocol used to do this is called the **resource reservation protocol (RSVP)**.

Because many of the new real-time applications involve multiple participants, RSVP is used to reserve resources in each router along either a unicast or a multicast path. The actual routing of the packets associated with both types of call, however, are not part of RSVP and these are carried out in the normal way using one of the routing algorithms we described earlier in Section 9.6. A selection of the messages associated with RSVP are shown in Figure 9.28(a).

Each traffic flow is identified uniquely by the combined source and destination addresses in the IP header and the port number in the UDP header. To perform a reservation, the AP in the host that wishes to set up the call sends a *path* message in a UDP datagram with either the unicast or multicast address of the other host(s) in the destination address field of the IP header and the port number in the UDP datagram header. The purpose of the *path* message is firstly, to enable each router along the path/route followed by the packet to create an entry in a table known as the **path-state table** and secondly, to gather information about the resources that are currently available in each router along the path. The entry in the path-state table includes the flow identifier, a specification of the required parameters associated with the call – known as the traffic specification or Tspec – and the (IP) address of the router from which it received the *path* message.

On receipt of the *path* message, the AP (identified by the port number) in the destination host(s) uses the resource levels reported by each router to determine which type of call – guaranteed, controlled-load, or neither – the

(a)

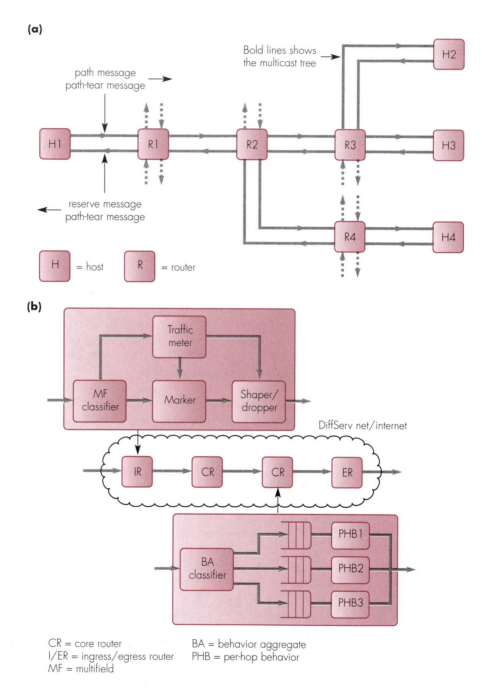

path message
path-tear message

Bold lines shows
the multicast tree

reserve message
path-tear message

H1   R1   R2   R3   H3   H2   R4   H4

H = host   R = router

(b)

Traffic
meter

MF
classifier   Marker   Shaper/
dropper

DiffServ net/internet

IR   CR   CR   ER

BA
classifier   PHB1   PHB2   PHB3

CR = core router   BA = behavior aggregate
I/ER = ingress/egress router   PHB = per-hop behavior
MF = multifield

**Figure 9.28 QoS support mechanisms: (a) RSVP principles;
(b) DiffServ architecture.**

path can support. Assuming the call can be accepted, the AP in each destination host then returns a *reserve* message (containing the Tspec for the call) to the router from which it received the *path* message. If the router still has the necessary resources, it reserves these for the flow (the resources may be different in each direction), makes an entry in the path-state table of the address of the router which sent it the message, and then sends the (*reserve*) message to the next router along the path. If the resources are not available, then a *path-tear* message is returned along the forward and return paths in order to release any resources that have been reserved and delete the entry in the path-state table. This procedure is repeated by each router along the path back to the source which, on receipt of the *reserve* message, proceeds with the call.

The path associated with each call/session may change during the lifetime of a call; for example, due to a router going down. To allow for this occurring, associated with each entry in the path-state table kept by each router is a timer called the *cleanup timer* and, should this expire, the entry is deleted. The timer is restarted each time a *path* message relating to the call is received. At periodic intervals – less than the cleanup timeout period – the source host sends a new *path* message which is acted upon by each router in the same way as the first *path* message. Hence should the new path not include a particular router, its cleanup timer will expire and the related path-state information be deleted. This mode of operation is known therefore as *soft-state* since it may change during a call.

Finally, on completion of the call/session, the AP that set up the call sends out a *path-tear* message which results in the entry in the path-table held by each router along the path(s) being deleted. The RFCs associated with RSVP and the other IntServ procedures are in **RFC 2205–2216**.

The major disadvantage of RSVP is that state information is retained by each router for each call/flow. Although this may be acceptable in a company intranet, for example, in a backbone router of the Internet the tables used for this purpose can be very large. Hence with the very high bit rates that are used, the heavy overheads per call can be unacceptably high. It is for this reason that the alternative DiffServ scheme was developed.

9.8.2 Differentiated services

Using the DiffServ approach, individual flows are not identified and instead the individual flows in each service class are aggregated together. Flows are then treated on a per-class basis rather than a per-flow basis. The general architecture used with a DiffServ network is shown in Figure 9.28(b).

The incoming packet flows relating to individual calls – referred to as microflows – are classified by the router/gateway at the edge of the DiffServ-compliant net/internet into one of the defined service/traffic classes by examining selected fields in the various headers in the packet. Within the DiffServ network the *type of service* (*TOS*) field in the IP packet header is replaced by a new field called the *differentiated services* (*DS*) *field*. As we saw earlier in Section 9.2, this is an 8-bit field although currently only six bits are used for the DS field. The six bits form what is called the (**DS**) **packet codepoint** (**DSCP**) which is used to enable each router to determine the traffic class to which the packet data relates and the output queue into which the packet should be put. The queue management/scheduling procedure relating to each queue is called a **per-hop behavior** (**PHB**) and, since this applies to an aggregated set of packet flows, a PHB is said to be applied to a **behavior aggregate** (**BA**).

Within the DiffServ network, a defined level of resources in terms of the buffer space within each router and the bandwidth of each output line is allocated to each traffic class using, for example, a token bucket filter. As each packet arrives at the ingress router it is first classified as belonging to a particular traffic class. In some instances, however, as we shall see later, the actual classification is also a function of how well the microflow (to which the packet relates) is conforming to the agreed traffic profile for the flow. This is determined by the **traffic meter module** and, based on the level of conformance, the traffic meter informs the **marker module** whether the packet should be marked with a low, medium, or high drop precedence. In addition, the traffic meter also informs the **shaper/dropper** module of this and the latter decides whether the packet should be dropped or allowed into the network.

Normally, real-time microflows with hard QoS guarantees are placed in the highest-priority traffic class. Typically, the traffic meter for this type of stream is a token bucket filter with a defined rate and bucket depth. Hence if an arriving packet relating to a flow in this class is deemed to be out-of-profile, the traffic meter informs the shaper/dropper module of this. The latter then either drops the packet or relegates it to the best-effort class by setting all six DSCP bits to zero.

Once within the network, as each packet arrives at a core router, the **BA classifier** first determines to which traffic class the packet belongs and hence to which output queue the packet should be transferred. Each queue is then serviced using an appropriate PHB. Currently, two PHBs have been defined: **expedited forwarding** (**EF**) and **assured forwarding** (**AF**). The EF PHB is similar to the guaranteed service class associated with IntServ and hence has the highest priority. The PHB used with this is based on a queue scheduling procedure such as weighted fair queuing.

The AF PHB has four ordered traffic classes associated with it each of which has three drop procedure levels: low, medium, and high. Should congestion arise, this is used together with the traffic class to determine which packet(s) should be dropped. The PHB used in this case, therefore, is based on a queue scheduling procedure such as random early discard. The RFCs associated with DiffServ are in **RFC 2474–5**.

9.9 The PPP link layer protocol

As we showed in Figure 9.1 and explained in the accompanying text, access networks are connected to the Internet global internetwork by gateways. Also, as we showed in Figure 9.9, access gateways are connected to interior gateways which, in turn, are interconnected together using high bit rate synchronous transmission lines leased from a network provider. Typically, the leased lines are either from the PDH – DS1/3 or E1/3 for example – or from the SDH/SONET hierarchy – STS-3/STM-1 for example. Hence, since the various types of gateway (router) operate at the IP (network) layer, as we showed in Figure 9.1, a link layer protocol is required to transfer the IP packets/datagrams over the different types of leased line.

In addition, many of the access networks provided by ISPs require a link layer protocol to transfer the information entered by a person at home (using a PC for example) to the ISP network gateway. In many instances, the information is transferred over a switched connection through a PSTN using modems. Normally, the modem at home is connected to the serial port of the PC and, as we explained in Section 6.4, character-oriented asynchronous transmission is usually used. In order to avoid the proliferation of many different protocols, the IETF has defined a standard link layer protocol to meet these requirements. This is known as the **point-to-point protocol** (**PPP**) and is defined in **RFC 1661/2** and **3**.

To give the PPP the necessary flexibility, it has a number of features that enable it to be used in these and other applications. For example, it can operate in either the connection-oriented (reliable) or connectionless (best-effort) mode and with a variety of different types of network layer protocol. The latter feature is necessary, for example, if the access network uses the IPX network protocol rather than the IP. The PPP is based on the HDLC protocol we described in Section 6.8 and the format of all frames is shown in Figure 9.29.

Although the HDLC protocol is bit-oriented, in the PPP all frames are made up of an integral number of bytes/octets encapsulated by the opening and closing flag byte of 01111110. To achieve data transparency with the different types of synchronous transmission lines, zero bit insertion and deletion is used, the operation of which we described in Section 6.5.3.

In the case of asynchronous transmission lines, all characters are made equal to 8 bits and a form of character/byte stuffing is used, the principle of which we described in Section 6.4.3. In this application, however, in addition to flag bytes, a number of different characters/bytes are transmitted transparently. These include all the 32 control characters in the ASCII character set we identified in Figure 2.6(a). The list of bytes/characters and their codes is given in Figure 9.29(b).

As we can see, the escape byte/character used is 01111101 – 7D (hex) – and, whenever this is inserted, the sixth bit of the following byte/character is complemented. This rule is also used to transfer a byte/character that is equal to the escape byte.

(a)

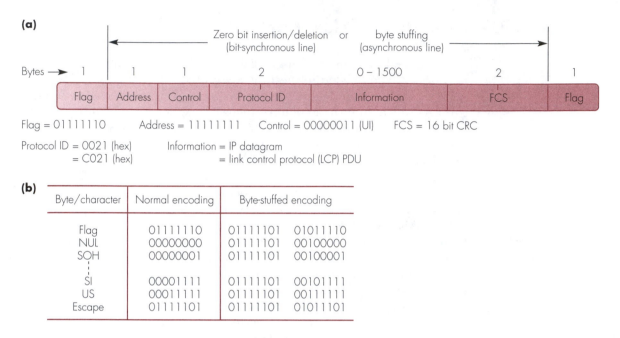

(b)

Byte/character	Normal encoding	Byte-stuffed encoding	
Flag	01111110	01111101	01011110
NUL	00000000	01111101	00100000
SOH	00000001	01111101	00100001
⋮			
SI	00001111	01111101	00101111
US	00011111	01111101	00111111
Escape	01111101	01111101	01011101

Figure 9.29 The point-to-point protocol (PPP): (a) frame format; (b) byte stuffing principle.

Since the PPP is intended for use over point-to-point lines, the *address* field has no role to play. Hence it is always set to all binary 1s. Also, since in most applications all information is transferred over the line in the connectionless mode, as we explained in Section 6.8, the default value in the *control* field is 03 (hex) which is the code used to indicate an unnumbered information (UI) frame.

The default length of the *protocol ID* field is two bytes. It is used to indicate the type of packet – and hence network layer protocol – that is present in the *information* field. For example, a value of 0021 (hex) is used to indicate an IP packet/datagram is present. In addition, since the PPP can be used in a variety of applications, a single request-response protocol known as the **link control protocol** (**LCP**) has been defined to allow the operational mode and associated parameters for the line/link to be negotiated. Associated with the LCP are a number of messages – protocol data units (PDUs) – and, when one is present in the information field, the value in the *protocol ID* field is C021 (hex). For example, when transferring only IP datagrams over a line, an LCP *request* message can be sent to propose the use of a reduced frame header with no address or control fields and just a single byte for the protocol field. The other side then responds by returning either an *accept* message or a *reject* message in which case the default values must be used.

The default maximum size of the information field is 1500 bytes although a different maximum size can be negotiated using LCP request-response messages. The *FCS* field is used to detect the presence of transmission errors in the frame and, as we explained in Section 6.8, it is based on a CRC. The FCS has a default length of 16 bits but a length of 32 bits can be negotiated using the LCP.

9.10 IPv6

Until the mid-1990s the Internet was used primarily by universities, government agencies, research establishments, and some sectors of industry. Since that time, however, it has gone through unprecedented growth owing to a large extent to the rapid rise in interest in the use of the World Wide Web. As a result, most schools, colleges, and many homes now have PCs with connections to the Internet. These are now being used, in addition to Web access, to exploit the range of other applications that are supported by the Internet. Moreover, this growth is predicted to increase even faster as new applications emerge: for example, the widespread use of hybrid mobile phones/computers with Internet interfaces, television set-top boxes with integral Web browsers, plus a potentially vast number of consumer products – such as meters, household appliances, office equipment, and so on – many of which may have an Internet interface.

Although the introduction of CIDR has extended considerably the usable address space of IPv4, the IETF has already defined and is using a new version of IP which has a number of features that have been introduced to meet the predicted growth levels. This is known as **IP version 6** (**IPv6**) or sometimes **IP next generation** (**IPng**). It is defined in **RFCs 1883–7** and a number of supporting RFCs. In addition to providing a large increase in the number of IP addresses, the IETF has taken the opportunity to correct some of the deficiencies associated with IPv4 and to provide a number of other features. The main new features of IPv6 are:

- a much increased address space from 32 bits to 128 bits;
- hierarchical addresses to reduce the size of the routing tables associated with the routers in the core backbone network;
- a simplified header to enable routers and gateways to process and route packets faster;
- the introduction of improved security and data integrity features including authentication and encryption;
- an autoconfiguration facility that enables a host to obtain an IP address via the network without human intervention;
- harder quality-of-service guarantees by means of the preferential treatment by routers of the packets associated with interactive and multimedia applications relative to those relating to traditional applications such as email and file transfers;

■ support for mobile computing by the use of autoconfiguration to obtain an IP address dynamically via the network for the duration of a call/session.

Although many of the above features require some radical changes to IPv4 – for example a different address structure and datagram/packet format – in terms of the protocols that are used within the expanded global internetwork, these operate in much the same way as the current IPv4 protocols. For example, the LS-SPF (OSPF) routing algorithm we described in Section 9.6.4 is used as the standard interior gateway protocol (IGP) for IPv6 except, of course, that 128-bit addresses are used in the link-state and routing tables. There is also an updated version of the RIP – based on the distance vector routing algorithm we described in Section 9.6.3 – called **RIPng**. Similarly, at the backbone level, the border gateway protocol (BGP) we described in Section 9.6.5 (including the CIDR we described in Section 9.6.6) is used but with extensions to allow reachability information based on IPv6 hierarchical addresses to be exchanged. Hence in the remainder of this section we limit our discussion to a selection of the new features that are used.

9.10.1 Datagram format

In relation to the IPv4 datagram/packet header, a number of fields have been dropped and others have been made optional. The result is a basic/main header of 40 bytes, the contents and format of which are shown in Figure 9.30(a). The use of each field is as follows:

Version

This is set to 6 to enable routers to discriminate IPv6 packets from IPv4 packets. It is envisaged that both will need to coexist for many years.

Traffic class

This field plays a similar role to the *ToS* byte in the IPv4 header. It allows the source IP to allocate a different priority to packets relating to, say, multimedia applications involving real-time streams from those relating to traditional applications. It contains a 4-bit priority field and hence 16 priorities are possible, the higher the priority value the higher the packet priority. Values in the range 0–7 are for packets relating to applications for which best-effort delivery is acceptable; for example network news (1) and FTP(4). Both these applications are less sensitive to delay and delay variation (jitter) than applications involving real-time media but FTP is more sensitive to packet loss than network news. Values in the range 8–15 are for packets containing real-time streams such as audio and video. Typically, such streams/packets are more sensitive to delay and jitter than the packets in the first category and hence should be transmitted before them during periods of congestion. Also, within the second category, packets containing compressed video are more sensitive to packet loss than packets containing just audio and hence are given a higher priority.

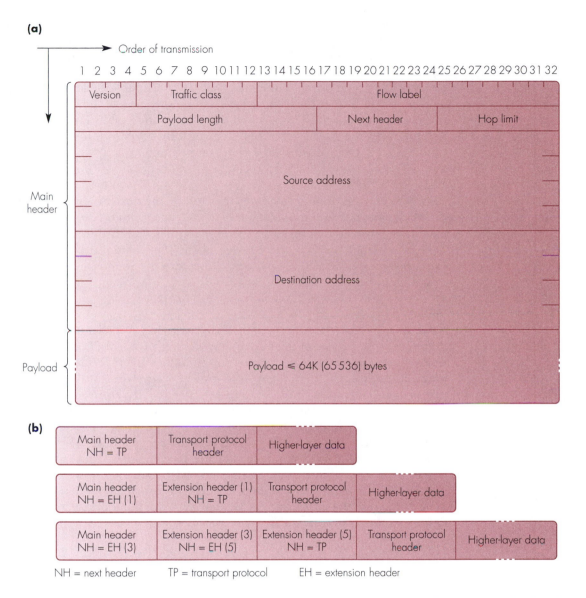

Figure 9.30 IPv6: (a) main header fields and format; (b) position and order of extension headers.

Flow label

This is a new field and is closely linked to the *traffic class* field. It is set to zero in best-effort packets and, in packets in the second category, it is used to enable a router to identify the individual packets relating to the same call/session. As we saw earlier in Section 9.8.1, one approach to handling packets containing real-time streams is to reserve resources – for example transmission bandwidth – for such calls in advance of sending the packets relating to the call. During the reservation procedure, the call is allocated a *flow label* by the source. Also, each router along the reserved path keeps a record of this, together with the source and destination IP addresses, in a table. Routers then use the combined *flow label* and source IP address present in each packet header to relate the packet to a specific call/flow. The related routing information is then retrieved from the routing table and this is used, together with the *traffic class* value, to ensure the QoS requirements of the call/flow are met during the forwarding procedure.

Payload length

This indicates the number of bytes that follow the basic 40-byte header in the datagram. The minimum length of a basic datagram is 536 bytes and the maximum length is 64K bytes. The *payload length* is slightly different from the *total length* field used in the header of an IPv4 datagram since, as we explained in Section 9.2, the *total length* includes the number of bytes in the datagram header.

Next header

As we show in Figure 9.30(b), a basic IPv6 datagram comprises a main header followed by the header of the peer transport layer protocol (TCP/UDP) and, where appropriate, the data relating to the higher layers. With a basic datagram, therefore, the *next header* field indicates the type of transport layer protocol (header) that follows the basic header. If required, however, a number of what are called **extension headers** can be inserted between the main header and the transport protocol header. Currently, there are six types of extension header defined and, when present, each extension header starts with a new *next header* field which indicates the type of header that follows. The *next header* field in the last extension header always indicates the type of transport protocol header that follows. Thus, the *next header* field in either the main header or the last extension header plays the same role as the *protocol* field in an IPv4 datagram header.

Hop limit

This is similar to the *time-to-live* parameter in an IPv4 header except the value is a hop count instead of a time. In practice, as we explained in Section 9.2, most IPv4 routers also use this field as a hop count so the change in the field's name simply reflects this. The initial value in the *hop limit* field is set by the source and is decremented by 1 each time the packet/datagram is forwarded. The packet is discarded if the value is decremented to zero.

Source address and destination address

As we indicated earlier, these are 128-bit addresses that are used to identify the source of the datagram and the intended recipient. In most cases this will be the destination host but, as we shall explain later, it might be the next router along a path if source routing is being used. Unlike IPv4 addresses, an IPv6 address is assigned to the (physical) interface, not to the host or router. Hence in the case of routers (which have multiple interfaces) these are identified using any of the assigned interface addresses.

9.10.2 Address structure

As we showed in Figure 9.9, the various networks and internetworks that make up the global Internet are interconnected in a hierarchical way with the access networks at the lowest level in the hierarchy and the global backbone network at the highest level. However, the lack of structure in the netid part of IPv4 addresses means that the number of entries in the routing tables held by each gateway/router increases with increasing height in the hierarchy. At the lowest level, most access gateways associated with a single site LAN have a single netid while at the highest level, most backbone routers/gateways have a routing table containing many thousands of netids.

In contrast, the addresses associated with telephone networks are hierarchical with, for example, a country, region, and exchange code preceding the local number. This has a significant impact on the size of the routing tables held by the switches since, at a particular level, all calls with the same preceding code are routed in the same way. This is known as **address aggregation**.

As we explained earlier in Section 9.6.6, classless inter-domain routing is a way of introducing a similar structure with IPv4 addresses and reduces considerably the size of the routing tables held by the routers/gateways in the global backbone. From the outset, therefore, IPv6 addresses are hierarchical. Unlike telephone numbers, however, the hierarchy is not constrained just to a geographical breakdown. The large address space available means that a number of alternative formats can be used. For example, to help interworking with existing IPv4 hosts and routers, there is a format that allows IPv4 addresses to be embedded into an IPv6 address. Also, since the majority of access networks are now Internet service provider (ISP) networks, there is a format that allows large blocks of addresses to be allocated to individual providers. The particular format being used is determined by the first set of bits in the address. This is known as the **prefix format** (**PF**) and a list of the prefixes that have been assigned – together with their usage – is given in Figure 9.31(a).

Unicast addresses

As we can see, addresses starting with a prefix of 0000 0000 are used to carry existing IPv4 addresses. There are two types, the formats of which are shown in Figure 9.31(b). As we shall expand upon in Section 9.11, a common requirement during the transition from IPv4 to IPv6 is to tunnel the IPv6 packets being generated by the two communicating IPv6 hosts – often written **V6 hosts** – over an existing IPv4 network/internetwork. Hence to simplify the routing of the IPv4 packet – containing the IPv6 packet within it – the IPv6

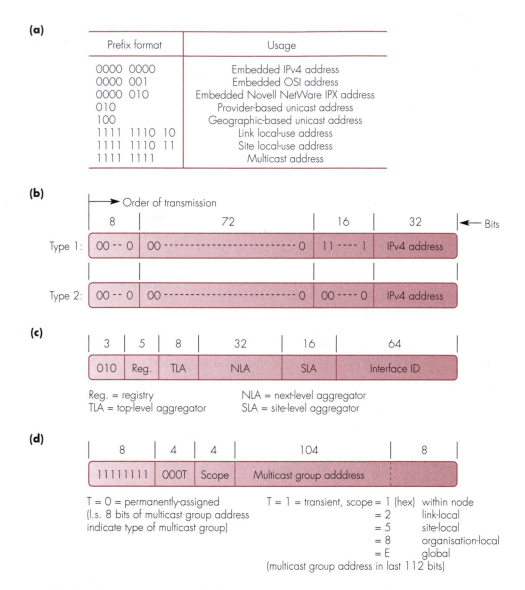

Figure 9.31 IPv6 addresses: (a) prefix formats and their use; (b) IPv4 address types; (c) provider-based unicast address format; (d) multicast address format.

address contains the IPv4 address of the destination gateway embedded within it. The second type is to enable a V4 host to communicate with a V6 host. The IPv4 address of the V4 host is then preceded by 96 zeros. In addition, two addresses in this category are reserved for other uses. An address comprising all zeros indicates there is no address present. As we shall expand upon in Section 9.10.4, an example of its use is for the source address in a packet relating to the autoconfiguration procedure. An address with a single binary 1 in the least significant bit position is reserved for the loopback address used during the test procedure of a host protocol stack.

The OSI and NetWare address prefixes have been defined to enable a host connected to one of these networks to communicate directly with a V6 host. The most widely used is the provider-based prefix as this format reflects the current structure of the Internet. A typical format of this type of address is shown in Figure 9.31(c). As we saw in Figure 9.9, the core backbone of the Internet consists of a number of very high bandwidth lines that interconnect the various continental backbones together. The routers that perform this function are owned by companies known as **top-level aggregators** (**TLAs**). Each TLA is allocated a large block of addresses by what is called a **registry**, the identity of which is in the field immediately following the 010 prefix. Examples include the North American registry, the European registry, the Asia and Pacific registry, and so on.

From their allocation, the TLAs allocate blocks of addresses to large Internet service providers and global enterprises. These are known as **next-level aggregators** (**NLAs**) and, in the context of Figure 9.9, operate at the continental backbone and national and regional levels. The various NLAs allocate both single addresses to individual subscribers and blocks of addresses to large business customers. The latter are known as **site-level aggregators** (**SLAs**) and include ISPs that operate at the regional and national levels. The 64-bit **interface ID** is divided locally into a fixed subnetid part and a hostid part. Typically, the latter is the 48-bit MAC address of the host and hence 16 bits are available for subnetting.

As we can deduce from Figure 9.31(c), the use of hierarchical addresses means that each router in the hierarchy can quickly determine whether a packet should be routed to a higher-level router or to another router at the same level simply by examining the appropriate prefix. Also, the routers at each level can route packets directly using the related prefix. The same over-all description applies to the processing of geographic-based addresses.

As their names imply, the two types of **local-use addresses** are for local use only and have no meaning in the context of the global Internet. As we shall expand upon in Section 9.10.4, *link local-use addresses* are used in the autoconfiguration procedure followed by hosts to obtain an IPv6 address from a local router. The router only replies to the host on the same link the request was received and hence this type of packet is not forwarded beyond the router.

The *site local-use addresses* are used, for example, by organizations that are not currently connected to the Internet but wish to utilize the technology associated with it. Normally, the 64-bit interface ID part is subdivided and used for routing purposes within the organization. In this way, should the organization wish to be connected to the Internet at a later date, it is only necessary to change the site local-use prefix with the allocated subscriber prefix.

Multicast addresses

The format of an IPv6 multicast address is shown in Figure 9.31(d). As we can see, following the multicast prefix are two additional fields which have been introduced to limit the geographic scope of the related multicast operation. The first is known as the *flags* field and is used to indicate whether the multicast is a permanently-assigned (reserved) address (0000) or a temporary (transient) address (0001). In the case of a permanently-assigned address, the least significant 8 bits of the *multicast group address* field identify the type of the multicast operation, while for a transient address, the full 112 bits identify the multicast group address.

In both cases, the 4-bit *scope* field defines the geographic scope of the multicast packet. The various alternatives are identified in the figure and mrouters use this field to determine whether the (multicast) packet should be forwarded further or discarded.

Anycast addresses

In addition to unicast and multicast addresses, a new address type known as an **anycast group address** has been defined. These are allocated from the unicast address space and are indistinguishable from a unicast address. With an anycast address, however, a group of hosts or routers can all have the same (anycast) address. A common requirement in a number of applications is for a host or router to send a packet to any one of a group of hosts or routers, all of which provide the same service. For example, a group of servers distributed around a network may all contain the same database. Hence in order to avoid all clients needing to know the unique address of its nearest server, all the servers can be members of the same anycast group and hence have the same address. In this way, when a client makes a request, it uses the assigned anycast address of the group and the request will automatically be received by its nearest server. Similarly, if a single network/internetwork has a number of gateway routers associated with it, they can all be allocated the same anycast address. As a result, the shortest-path routes from all other networks/internetworks will automatically use the gateway nearest to them.

In order to perform the routing function, although an anycast address has the same format as a unicast address, when an anycast address is assigned to a group of hosts or routers, it is necessary for each host/router to be explicitly informed – by network management for example – that it is a member of an anycast group. In addition, each is informed of the common part of the address prefixes which collectively identify the topological region in which all the hosts/routers reside. Within this region, all the routers then maintain a separate entry for each member of the group in its routing table.

Address representation

A different form of representation of IPv6 addresses has been defined. Instead of each 8-bit group being represented as a decimal number (with a dot/period between them), groups of 16 bits are used. Each 16-bit group is then represented in its hexadecimal form with a colon between each group. An example of an IPv6 address is:

FEDC:BA98:7654:3210:0000:0000:0000:0089

In addition, a number of abbreviations have been defined:

■ One or more consecutive groups of all zeros can be replaced by a pair of colons.

■ Leading zeros in a group can be omitted.

Hence the preceding address can also be written as:

FEDC:BA98:7654:3210:89

Also, for the two IPv4 embedded address types, the actual IPv4 address can remain in its dotted decimal form. Hence assuming a dotted decimal address of 15.10.0.6, the two embedded forms are:

:: 150.10.0.6   (IPv4 host address)
:: FFFF:150.10.0.6   (IPv4 tunnel address)

Example 9.6

Derive the hexadecimal form of representation of the following link-local multicast addresses:

(i)   a permanently-assigned multicast group address of 67,

(ii) a transient multicast group address of 317.

Answer:

The formats of the two types of multicast addresses were shown in Figure 9.31(d). Hence:

The most-significant 16 bits are FF02 = permanently-assigned, link-local
and FF12 = transient, link-local

(i)   A permanently-assigned multicast group address of 67 = 0043 (hex)
        Hence IPv6 address = FF02 :: 67

(ii) A transient multicast group address of 317 = 013D (hex)
        Hence IPv6 address = FF12 :: 13D

9.10.3 Extension headers

As we have just indicated, if required, a number of extension headers can be added to the main header to convey additional information, either to the routers visited along the path followed or to the destination host. The six types of extension header currently defined are:

- **hop-by-hop options**: information for the routers visited along a path;
- **routing**: list of routers relating to source routing information;
- **fragment**: information to enable the destination to reassemble a fragmented message:
- **authentication**: information to enable the destination to verify the identity of the source;
- **encapsulating security payload**: information to enable the destination to decrypt the payload contents;
- **destination options**: optional information for use by the destination.

The two options headers can contain a variable number of option fields, each possibly of a variable length. For these, each option field is encoded using a **type-length-value** (**TLV**) format. The *type* and *length* are both single bytes and indicate the option type and its length (in bytes) respectively. The *value* is then found in the following number of bytes indicated by the *length*. The option type identifiers have been chosen so that the most significant two bits specify the action that must be taken if the type is not recognized. These are:

00 ignore this option and continue processing the other option fields in the header;

01 discard the complete packet;

10 discard the packet and return an ICMP error report to the source indicating a parameter problem and the option type not recognized;

11 same as for 10 except the ICMP report is only returned if the destination address is not a multicast address.

Note also that since the type of extension header is indicated in the preceding *next header* field, the related decoder that has been written to decode the contents of the header is invoked automatically as each header is processed. Some examples of each header type now follow.

Hop-by-hop options

This type of header contains information that must be examined by all the gateways and routers the packet visits along its route. The *next header* value for this is 0 and, if this header is present, it must follow the main header. Hence the *next header* field in the main header is set to 0. An example of its use is for a host to send a datagram that contains a payload of more than 64K bytes.

This is particularly useful, for example, when a host is transferring many very large files over a path that supports a maximum transmission unit (MTU) significantly greater than 64K bytes. Datagrams that contain this header are known as **jumbograms** and the format of the header is shown in Figure 9.32(a).

As we can see, this type of header is of fixed length and comprises two 32-bit words (8 bytes). The *header extension length* field indicates the length of the header in multiples of 8 bytes, excluding the first 8 bytes. Hence in this case the field is 0. This option contains only one option field, the *jumbo payload length*. As we indicated earlier, this is encoded in the TLV format. The *type* for this option is 194 (11000010) and the *length* is 4 (bytes). The *value* in the *jumbo payload length* is the length of the packet in bytes, excluding the main header but including the 8 bytes in the extension header. This makes the *payload length* in the main header redundant and hence this is set to zero.

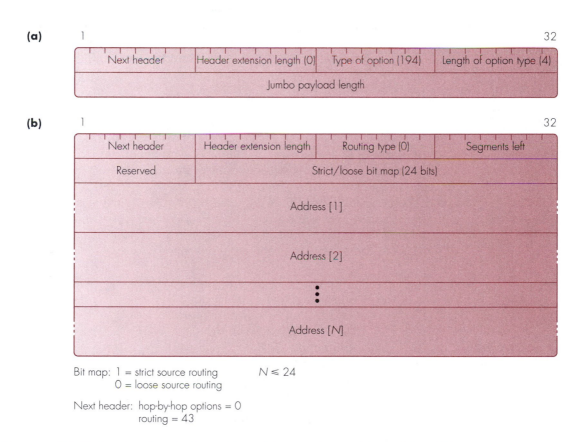

Figure 9.32 Extension header formats: (a) hop-by-hop options; (b) routing.

Routing

This plays a similar role to the (strict) *source routing* and *loose source routing* optional headers used in IPv4 datagrams. The *next header* value for this type of header is 43. Currently only one type of routing header has been defined, the format of which is shown in Figure 9.32(b).

The *header extension length* is the length of the header in multiples of 8 bytes, excluding the first 8 bytes. Hence, as we can deduce from the figure, this is equal to two times the number of (16-byte) addresses present in the header. This must be an even number less than or equal to 46. The *segments left* field is an index to the list of addresses that are present. It is initialized to 0 and is then incremented by the next router in the list as it is visited. The maximum therefore is 23.

The second 4-byte word contains a *reserved* byte followed by a 24-bit field called the *strict/loose bit map*. This contains one bit for each potential address present starting at the leftmost bit. If the related bit is a 1, then the address must be that of a directly-attached (neighbor) router – that is, strict source routing. If the bit is a 0, then the address is that of a router with possibly several other routers in between – loose source routing. The latter is used, for example, when tunneling is required to forward the datagram. In the case of

Example 9.7	A datagram is to be sent from a source host with an IPv6 address of A to a destination host with an IPv6 address of B via a path comprising three IPv6 routers. Assuming the addresses of the three routers are R1, R2, and R3 and strict source routing is to be used, (i) state what the contents of the initial values in the various fields in the extension header will be and (ii) list the contents of the source and destination address fields in the main header and the *segments left* field in the extension header as the datagram travels along the defined path.

Answer:

(i) Extension header initial contents:

Next header = Transport layer protocol
Header extension length = $2 \times 3 = 6$
Routing type = 0
Segments left = 0
Strict/loose bit map = 11100000 00000000 00000000
List of addresses = R1, R2, R3 (each of 16 bytes)

(ii) Contents of main header fields:

At source   SA = A   DA = R1   Segments left = 0
At R1   SA = A   DA = R2   Segments left = 1
At R2   SA = A   DA = R3   Segments left = 2

strict source routing, at each router the destination address in the main header is changed to that obtained from the list of addresses before the index is incremented. In the case of loose source routing, the destination address will be that of an attached neighbor which is on the shortest-path route to the specified address.

Fragment

This header is present if the original message submitted by the transport layer protocol exceeds the MTU of the path/route to be used. The *next header* value for a *fragment* extension header is 44. The fragmentation and reassembly procedures are similar to those used with IPv4 but, in the case of IPv6, the fragmentation procedure is carried out only in the source host and not by the routers/gateways along the path followed by the packet(s). As we saw in Figure 9.30(a), there is no don't fragment (D) bit in the IPv6 main header since, in order to speed up the processing/routing of packets, IPv6 routers do not support fragmentation. Hence, as we explained in Section 9.7, either the minimum MTU size of 576 bytes must be used or the *path MTU discovery* procedure is used to determine if the actual MTU size is greater than this. In either case, if the submitted message (including the transport protocol header) exceeds the chosen MTU (minus the 40 bytes for the IPv6 main header), then the message must be sent in multiple packets, each with a main header and a *fragment* extension header. The various fields and the format of each *fragment* extension header are shown in Figure 9.33(a). An example is shown in Figure 9.33(b).

Each packet contains a main header – plus, if required, a *hop-by-hop options* header and a *routing* header – followed by a *fragment* extension header and the fragment of the message being transmitted. Thus the maximum size of the payload (and hence message fragment) in each packet will be the MTU size being used minus the number of 8-byte fields required for the main header and any extension headers that are present. The *payload length* field in the main header of the first packet indicates the total number of bytes in the message being transmitted – including the IP header – plus the number of bytes that are required for the other extension headers that are being used. The *payload length* in the main header of the remaining packets indicates the number of bytes in the packet following the main header.

The various fields in each *fragment* header have similar functions to those used with IPv4. The *fragment offset* indicates the position of the first byte of the fragment contained within the packet relative to the start of the complete message being transmitted. Its value is in units of 8-bytes. The *M-bit* is the *more fragments bit*; it is a 1 if more fragments follow and a 0 if the packet contains the last fragment. Similarly, the value in the *identification* field is used by the destination host, together with the source address, to relate the data fragments contained within each packet to the same original message. Normally, the source uses a 32-bit counter (that is incremented by 1 for each new message transmitted) to keep track of the next value to use.

(a)

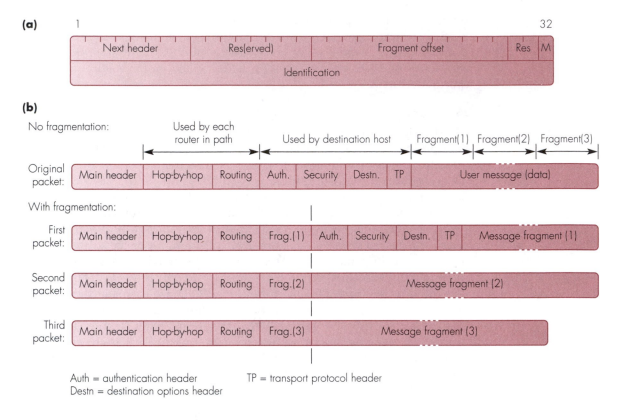

(b)

Auth = authentication header   TP = transport protocol header
Destn = destination options header

Figure 9.33 IPv6 fragmentation: (a) fragment header fields and format; (b) example.

Authentication and encapsulating security payload

As we shall expand upon in Section 13.4, authentication and the related subject of encryption are both mechanisms that are used to enhance the security of a message during its transfer across a network. In the case of authentication, this enables the recipient of a message to validate that the message was indeed sent by the source address present in the packet/datagram header and not by an impostor. Encryption is concerned with ensuring that the contents of a message can only be read by – and hence have meaning to – the intended recipient. The *authentication* and *encapsulating* security payload (ESP) extension headers are present when both these features are being used at the network layer.

When using IPv6 authentication, prior to any information (packets) being exchanged, the two communicating hosts first use a secure algorithm to exchange secret keys. An example is the MD5 algorithm we describe later in Section 13.5. Then, for each direction of flow, the appropriate key is used to compute a checksum on the contents of the entire datagram/packet. The computed checksum is then carried in the authentication header of the packet. The same computation is repeated at the destination host and only if the computed checksum is the same as that carried in the authentication header is it acknowledged that the packet originated from the source host address indicated in the main header and also that the packet contents have not been modified during the packets transfer over the network. We discuss the subject of authentication further in Section 13.6.

The encryption algorithm used with the ESP is also based on the use of an agreed secret key. An example is the DES algorithm we describe later in Section 13.4.3. The agreed key is used to encrypt either the transport protocol header and payload parts of each packet or, in some instances, the entire packet including the main header and any extension headers present. In the case of the latter, the encrypted packet is then carried in a second packet containing a completely different main and, if necessary, extension headers. The first is known as **transport mode encryption** and the second **tunnel mode encryption**. Figure 9.34(a) illustrates the principle of operation of both modes.

As we can deduce from the figure, the overheads associated with the tunnel mode are significantly higher than those of the transport mode. The extra

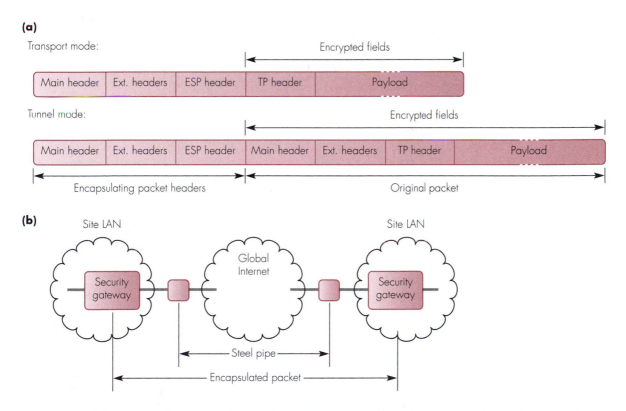

Figure 9.34 Encapsulating security payload: (a) transport and tunnel modes; (b) example application of tunnel mode.

security obtained with the tunnel mode is that the information in the main and extension headers of the original packet cannot be interpreted by a person passively monitoring the transmissions on a line. An example use of this mode is in multisite enterprise networks that use the (public) Internet to transfer packets from one site to another. The general scheme is shown in Figure 9.34(b).

As we showed earlier in Figure 5.16(a) and explained in the accompanying text, associated with each site is a security gateway through which all packet transfers to and from the site take place. Hence to ensure the header information (especially the routing header) of packets is not visible during the transfer of the packet across the Internet, the total packet is encrypted and inserted into a second packet by the IP in the security gateway with the IPv6 address of the two communicating gateways in the source and destination address fields of the main header. The path through the Internet connecting the two gateways is referred to as a **steel pipe**.

Destination options

These are used to convey information that is examined only by the destination host. As we indicated earlier, one of the ways of encoding options is to use the type-length-value format. Hence in order to ensure a header that uses this format comprises a multiple of 8 bytes, two *destination options* have been defined. These are known as Pad1 and Pad*N*, the first to insert one byte of padding and the second two or more bytes of padding. Currently these are the only two options defined.

9.10.4 Autoconfiguration

As we described earlier in Section 9.1, the allocation of the IP addresses for a new network involves a central authority to allocate a new netid – the Internet Network Information Center (InterNIC) – and a local network administrator to manage the allocation of hostids to each attached host/end system. Thus, the allocation, installation, and administration of IPv4 addresses can entail considerable effort and expenditure. To alleviate this, IPv6 supports an autoconfiguration facility that enables a host to obtain an IP address dynamically via the network and, in the case of mobile hosts, use it just for the duration of the call/session.

Two types of autoconfiguration are supported. The first involves the host communicating with a local (site) router using a simple (stateless) request-response protocol. The second involves the host communicating with a site (or enterprise) address server using an application protocol known as the **dynamic host configuration protocol** (**DHCP**). The first is suitable for small networks that operate in the broadcast mode (such as an Ethernet LAN) and the second for larger networks in which the allocation of IP addresses needs to be managed.

With the first method, a simple protocol known as **neighbor discovery** (**ND**) is used. As we show in Figure 9.35, this involves the host broadcasting a *router solicitation* packet/message on the subnet/network and the router responding with a *router advertisement* message. Both messages are ICMPv6

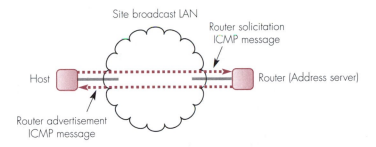

Figure 9.35 Neighbor discovery protocol messages.

messages and hence are carried in an IPv6 packet. The latter is then broadcast over the LAN in a standard frame.

The main header of the IPv6 packet containing the router solicitation message has an IPv6 source address created by the host. This is made up of the (standard) link-local address prefix and the 48-bit MAC address of the host's LAN interface. As we indicated earlier, with IPv6 a number of permanent multicast group addresses have been defined including an all-routers group address. Hence the destination address in the packet main header is set to this and, since the packet is broadcast over the LAN, it is received by the ICMP in all the routers that are attached to the LAN.

A single router is selected to process this type of ICMP message and this responds to a router solicitation message with a route advertisement message containing the Internet-wide address prefix for the subnet/network. On receipt of this, the ICMP in the host proceeds to create its own IPv6 address by adding its 48-bit MAC address to the prefix. As we can deduce from this, in relation to IPv4, this is equivalent to the router providing the netid of the site and the host using its own MAC address as the hostid. Also, the same procedure can be used by mobile hosts.

With the second method, the host requests an IPv6 address from the site address server using the DHCP. The **DHCP address server** first validates the request and then allocates an address from the managed list of addresses the server contains. Alternatively if a site does not have its own address server – for example if the site LAN is part of a larger enterprise network — then a designated router acts as a **DHCP relay agent** to forward the request to the DHCP address server.

9.11 IPv6/IPv4 interoperability

The widespread deployment of IPv4 equipment means that the introduction of IPv6 is being carried out in an incremental way. Hence a substantial amount of the ongoing standardization effort associated with IPv6 is concerned with the interoperability of the newer IPv6 equipment with existing

IPv4 equipment. Normally, when a new network/internetwork is created, it is based on the IPv6 protocol and, in the context of the existing (IPv4) Internet, it is referred to as an **IPv6 island**. It is necessary to provide a means of interworking between the two types of network at both the address level and the protocol level. In this section, we identify a number of situations where interoperability is required and describe a selection of the techniques that are used to achieve this.

9.11.1 Dual protocols

Dual stacks are already widely used in networks that use dissimilar protocol stacks; for example a site server that supports IPX on one port and IP on a second port. In a similar way, dual protocols can be used to support both IPv4 and IPv6 concurrently. An example is shown in Figure 9.36.

In this example, the site has a mix of hosts, some that use IPv4 and others IPv6. In order to be able to respond to requests originating from both types of host, the server machine has both an IPv4 and an IPv6 protocol at the network layer. The value in the version field of the datagram header is then used by the link layer protocol to pass a datagram to the appropriate IP. In this way the upper layer protocols are unaware of the type of IP being used at the network layer.

9.11.2 Dual stacks and tunneling

A common requirement is to interconnect two IPv6 islands (networks/internetworks) through an intermediate IPv4 network/internetwork. To achieve

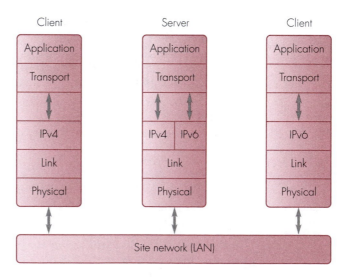

Figure 9.36 IPv6/IPv4 interoperability using dual (IPv6/IPv4) protocols.

this, the gateway/router that connects each IPv6 island to the IPv4 network must have dual stacks, one that supports IPv6 and the other IPv4. The IPv6 packets are then transferred over the IPv4 network using tunneling. The general approach is illustrated in Figure 9.37(a) and the protocols involved in Figure 9.37(b).

As we showed earlier in Figure 9.20 and explained in the accompanying text, tunneling is used to transfer a packet relating to one type of network layer protocol across a network that uses a different type of network layer protocol. Hence in the example shown in Figure 9.37, each IPv6 packet is transferred from one (IPv6/IPv4) edge gateway to the other edge gateway

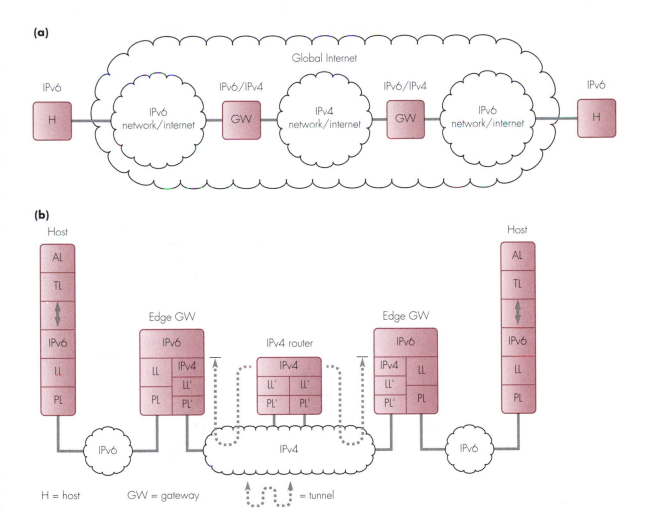

(a)

(b)

Figure 9.37 IPv6/IPv4 interoperability using dual stacks and tunneling: (a) schematic; (b) protocols.

within an IPv4 packet. As we show in the figure, in order to do this, the two edge gateways contain dual stacks each of which has a related IPv6/IPv4 address associated with it. Normally, entered by network management, the routing table entry for the remote destination IPv6 host is the IPv4 address of the remote edge gateway.

The IPv6 in each gateway, on determining from its routing table that an (IPv6) packet should be forwarded to a remote IPv6 network via an IPv4 tunnel, passes the packet to the IPv4 protocol together with the IPv4 address of the remote gateway. The IPv4 protocol first encapsulates the IPv6 packet in an IPv4 datagram/packet with the IPv4 address of the remote gateway in the destination address field. It then uses this address to obtain the (IPv4) address of the next-hop router from its own (IPv4) routing table and proceeds to forward the packet over the IPv4 network/internetwork. On receipt of the packet, the IPv4 in the remote gateway, on detecting from its own routing table that it is a tunneled packet, strips off the IPv4 header and passes the payload – containing the original IPv6 packet – to the IPv6 layer. The latter then forwards the packet to the destination host identified in the packet header in the normal way.

9.11.3 Translators

A third type of interoperability requirement is for a host attached to an IPv6 network – and hence having an IPv6 address and using the IPv6 protocol – to communicate with a host that is attached to an IPv4 network – hence having an IPv4 address and using the IPv4 protocol. In this case, both the addresses and the packet formats are different and so a translation operation must be carried out by any intermediate routers/gateways. As we show in Figure 9.38, the translations can be performed either at the network layer – part (a) – or the application layer – part (b).

Using the first approach, on receipt of an IPv6/IPv4 packet, this is converted into a semantically equivalent IPv4 /IPv6 packet. This involves a **network address translator** (**NAT**) and a **protocol translator** (**PT**). The intermediate gateway is then known as a **NAT-PT gateway**. As we explained earlier in Section 9.10.2, an IPv4 address can be embedded in an IPv6 address. Hence to send a datagram/packet from a host with an IPv6 address to a host with an IPv4 address, the NAT in the gateway can readily obtain the destination IPv4 address from the destination address in the main header of the IPv6 packet. The issue is what the source address in the IPv4 packet header should be.

A proposed solution is for the NAT to be allocated a block of hostids for the destination IPv4 network. These, together with the netid of the destination network, then form a block of unique IPv4 addresses. For each new call/session, the NAT allocates an unused IPv4 address from this block for the duration of the call/session. It then makes an entry in a table containing the IPv6 address of the V6 host and its equivalent (temporary) IPv4 address.

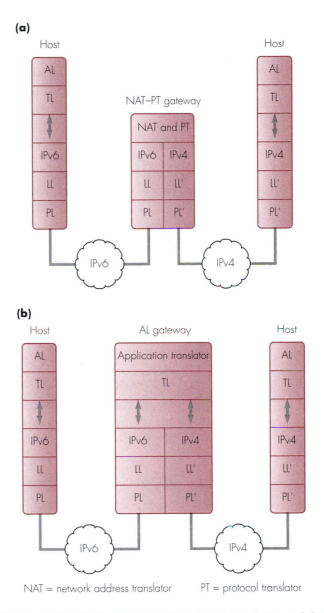

Figure 9.38 IPv6/IPv4 interoperability using translators: (a) network level; (b) application level.

The NAT translates between one address and the other as the packet is relayed. A timeout is applied to the use of such addresses and, if no packets are received within the timeout interval, the address is transferred back to the free address pool.

The protocol translation operation is concerned with translating the remaining fields in the packet header and, in the case of ICMP messages, converting ICMPv4 messages into and from ICMPv6 messages. As we indicated in Section 9.10.1, most of the fields in the IPv6 main header have the same meaning as those in the IPv4 header and hence their translation is relatively straightforward. In general, however, there is no attempt to translate the fields in the options part. Similarly, since ICMPv6 messages have different *type* fields, the main translation performed is limited to changing this field. For example, the two ICMPv4 query messages have *type* values of 8 and 0 and the corresponding ICMPv6 messages are 128 and 129.

The use of a NAT-PT gateway works providing the packet payload does not contain any network addresses. Although this is the case for most application protocols, a small number do. The FTP application protocol, for example, often has IP addresses embedded within its protocol messages. In such cases, therefore, the translation operation must be carried out at the application layer. The associated gateway is then known as an **application level gateway** (**ALG**). This requires a separate translation program for each application protocol. Normally, therefore, most translations are performed at the network layer – using a NAT and a PT – and only the translations relating to application protocols such as FTP are carried out in the application layer.

Summary

Figure 9.39 opposite summarizes the various topics discussed in this chapter.

Exercises

Section 9.1

9.1 With the aid of the network schematic shown in Figure 9.1, explain briefly the role of the following network components and protocols:
  (i) access network gateway,
  (ii) routing gateway,
  (iii) internet protocol (IP),
  (iv) datagram/packet.

9.2 With the aid of the protocol stack shown in Figure 9.2, explain briefly the meaning of the term "adjunct protocol" and how the IP in the destination host determines to which transport protocol – TCP/UDP – the contents/payload of a received IP datagram should be passed.

Section 9.2

9.3 In relation to the IP datagram/packet format shown in Figure 9.3, explain the role of the following header fields:
  (i) IHL,
  (ii) TOS,
  (iii) Total length and Identification,
  (iv) flag bits,
  (v) Fragment offset,
  (vi) Time-to-live,
  (vii) Protocol,
  (viii) Header checksum,
  (ix) Options.

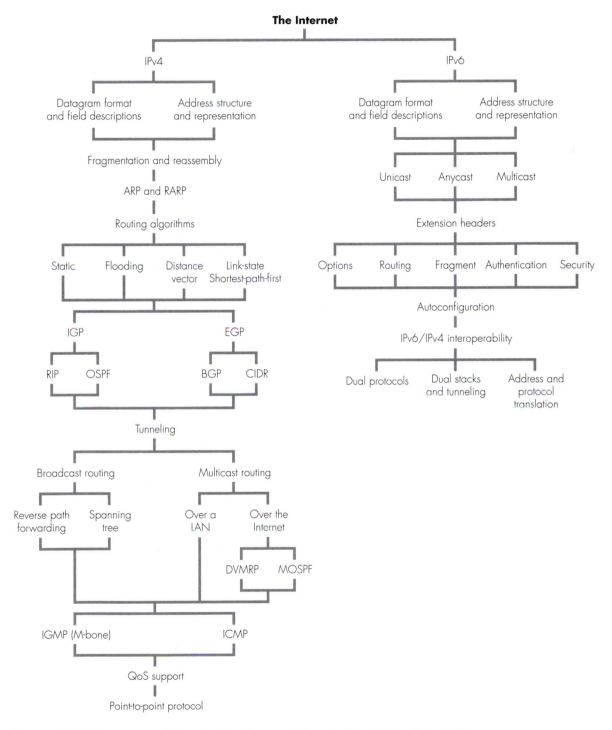

Figure 9.39 Summary of the topics discussed in relation to the Internet.

Section 9.3

9.4 Assume a message block of 7000 bytes is to be transferred from one host to another as shown in the example in Figure 9.4. In this instance, however, assume the token ring LAN has an MTU of 3000 bytes. Compute the header fields in each IP packet shown in the figure as it flows
   (i)   over the token ring LAN,
   (ii) over the Ethernet LAN.

9.5 State why fragmentation is avoided whenever possible and the steps followed within each host IP to achieve this.

Section 9.4

9.6 Explain the meaning of the term "IP address class" and why these classes were created. Hence, with the aid of the three (unicast) address classes identified in Figure 9.5, identify a particular application for each class.

9.7 State the meaning of the following addresses:
   (i)   an address with a netid of all 0s
   (ii)   an address with a netid of all 1s
   (iii) an address with a hostid of all 0s
   (iv)   an address of all 1s.

9.8 Explain the meaning of the term "dotted decimal". Hence derive the netid and hostid for the following IP addresses expressed in dotted decimal notation:
   (i)   13.0.0.15,
   (ii)   132.128.0.148,
   (iii) 220.0.0.0,
   (iv)   128.0.0.0,
   (v)   224.0.0.1.

9.9 With the aid of an example, explain why subnetting was introduced. Hence state the meaning of a subnet router and an address mask.

9.10 A site with a netid of 127.0 uses 20 subnet routers. Suggest a suitable address mask for the site which allows for a degree of expansion in the future. Give an example of a host IP address at this site.

Section 9.5

9.11 Define the terms "IP address", "MAC address", and "hardware/physical address". Also explain the terms "address-pair" and "ARP cache".

9.12 In relation to the simple network topology shown in Figure 9.7, explain why:
   (i)   on receipt of an ARP request message, each host retains a copy of the IP/MAC address-pair of the source host in its ARP cache
   (ii)   on receipt of an ARP reply message, the ARP in the source host makes an entry of the IP/MAC address-pair in its own cache
   (iii) the LAN port of the gateway keeps a copy of the IP/MAC address-pair from each ARP request and reply message that it receives.

9.13 Explain the role of a proxy ARP. Hence explain how an IP packet sent by a host at one site is routed to a host at a different site. Also explain how the reply packet is returned to the host that sent the first packet.

9.14 Explain how the reverse ARP is used to enable a diskless host to determine its own IP address from its local server.

9.15 With the aid of the two frame formats shown in Figure 9.8, explain:
   (i)   how the MAC sublayer in the receiver determines whether a received frame is in the Ethernet format or IEEE802.3
   (ii)   the number of pad bytes required with each frame type.

Section 9.6

9.16 With the aid of the global Internet architecture shown in Figure 9.9, explain the meaning/use of the following:
   (i)   continental backbone network,
   (ii)   core backbone network,
   (iii) regional/national network,
   (iv)   access network gateway,
   (v)   multiprotocol gateway.

9.17 State the meaning of the following terms relating to the routing of packets over the Internet:
(i) line cost,
(ii) path cost,
(iii) hopcount,
(iv) routing metric,
(v) shortest path.

9.18 With the aid of the routing table entries shown in Figure 9.11, explain the meaning of the terms:
(i) static routing tables,
(ii) next-hop routing,
(iii) optionality principle,
(iv) alternative paths.

9.19 With the aid of the broadcast diagram shown in Figure 9.12, explain:
(i) why the broadcast following the route via R2 is assumed to arrive first
(ii) how duplicate copies of a packet are determined by R3
(iii) how the number of copies of the packet produced is limited
(iv) why flooding is an example of an adaptive/dynamic routing algorithm.

9.20 In relation to the distance vector algorithm, with the aid of the example shown in Figure 9.13, explain:
(i) the meaning of the term "connictivity/adjacency table" and how the table's contents are obtained
(ii) how the final routing table entries for R3 are built up
(iii) how a packet from a host attached to netid3 is routed to a host attached to netid1
(iv) the limitations of the algorithm including how looping may arise.

9.21 Assuming the connectivity/adjacency tables given in Figure 9.14(a), show how the overall network topology is built up by router R3 using the link state algorithm. Hence derive the contents of netid location table for R3.

9.22 Assuming the initial network topology shown in Figure 9.15(a), use the Dijkstra algorithm to derive the shortest paths from R3 to each other router. State the meaning of the terms "tentative" and "permanent" relating to the algorithm and the implications of alternative paths/routers.

9.23 Using the set of link state, routing, and connectivity tables for R1, R2, and R3, explain how a packet received by R3 from G3 with a destination netid of 1 is routed using hop-by-hop routing.

9.24 Explain how a packet received by R3 from G3 with a destination netid of 1 is routed using source routing. Include how the routing tables you use are derived.

9.25 In relation to the link-state algorithm, explain why each link-state message contains a sequence number and a timeout value. How are these used?

9.26 With the aid of the generalized Internet architecture shown in Figure 9.18, state a suitable routing algorithm for use
(i) within a single bridged LAN,
(ii) within a single site comprising multiple different LANs interconnected by subnet routers,
(iii) within a single autonomous system such as a regional/national network,
(iv) within the core network of the Internet.

9.27 In relation to the BGP, with the aid of the message types shown in Table 9.1, explain how the following functions are performed:
(i) neighbor acquisition and termination,
(ii) neighbor reachability,
(iii) routing update.

9.28 State the reason why classless inter-domain routing (CIDR) was introduced.

9.29 Derive the range of class C addresses that are available. Hence, using the list of continental addresses given in section 9.6.6, explain how the routing of packets across the global backbone network is carried out.

9.30 State why the lack of a fixed division point within class C addresses with CIDR means a router/gateway is unable to route a packet. Hence explain how this is overcome.

9.31 An example of how when using CIDR a host attached to one network can produce a match with the mask of a second network was illustrated in Example 9.5. How would this be overcome in practice?

9.32 Explain the term "tunneling" and when it is used. Hence with the aid of the schematic diagram shown in Figure 9.20, explain how the host on the lift of the diagram sends an IP datagram/packet to a host attached to the Internet. Include in your explanation the role of the two multiprotocol routers.

State an application of tunneling IP packets over an IP network.

9.33 What are the aims of both the reverse path forwarding algorithm and the spanning tree broadcast algorithm?

9.34 Use the final routing tables and broadcast sequence relating to the reverse path forwarding algorithm shown in Figure 9.21 to explain why only the (broadcast) packet received by SR6 from SR3 is broadcast at the fourth stage. What is the number of duplicate broadcasts that occur?

9.35 Assuming the network topology shown in Figure 9.22(a) and that SR3 is access gateway, determine the spanning tree derived by each subnet router. Use this to derive the broadcast sequence.

9.36 In relation to multicasting over a LAN, describe how IANA controls the allocation of multicast addresses. Also explain how the 48-bit MAC address and 28-bit IP address of a host are derived from the allocated address. Hence with the aid of the schematic diagram shown in Figure 9.23(b), describe how a host joins a multicast session that is taking place over the LAN. Include the role of the multicast address table and group address table held by each member of the group.

9.37 What is the meaning of the term "multicast router"? Outline the sequence of steps that are followed to route an IP packet with a multicast address over the Internet.

9.38 Assume the same topology, multicast address table contents, routing table contents, and routing table entries as shown in Figure 9.24. Assuming the DVMRP, explain how a packet arriving from one of its local networks with a multicast address of C is routed by MR3 to all the other MRs that have an interest in this packet.

9.39 Repeat Exercise 9.37 but this time using the MOSPF routing protocol and the spanning tree shown in Figure 9.25(b).

9.40 What is the role of the IGMP protocol?

With the aid of the example shown in Figure 9.26, explain how a host that is attached to a local network/subnet of an MR joins a multicast session. Include in your explanation the table entries retained by both the host and the MR and how multicast packets relating to the session are then routed to the host.

9.41 With the aid of the example shown in Figure 9.26, explain the procedure followed when a host that is attached to a local network/subnet of an MR leaves a multicast session.

9.42 The multicast backbone (m-bone) network shown in Figures 9.24 and 9.25 comprised a set of multicast routers interconnected by single links. In practice, these are logical links since each may comprise multiple interconnected routers that do not take part in multicast routing. Explain how a multicast packet is sent from one mrouter to another using IP tunneling.

Section 9.7

9.43 Explain briefly the role of the ICMP protocol and the different procedures associated with it. Hence explain how the path MTU discovery procedure is used to determine the MTU of a path/route prior to sending any datagrams.

Section 9.8

9.44 Discuss the reasons why improved levels of QoS support are now being used within the Internet.

9.45 Describe the role and principle of operation of the following control mechanisms used within Internet routers:
(i) token bucket filter,
(ii) weighted fair queuing,
(iii) random early detection.

9.46 Define the three different classes of service used with the Intserv scheme. With the aid of the network topology shown in Figure 9.28 (a) describe the operation of the resource reservation protocol (RSVP). Include in your description the meaning/role of the following:
(i) path, reserve, and path-tear messages
(ii) path-state table,
(iii) cleanup timer,
(iv) soft-state.

9.47 Define the usage of the type of service (ToS) field in each packet header with the DiffServ scheme including the meaning of the term "DS packet codepoint".

9.48 With the aid of the general architecture shown in Figure 9.28(b), describe the operation of the DiffServ scheme. Include in your description the meaning/role of the following components of an ingress router;
(i) behavior aggregate,
(ii) traffic meter module,
(iii) MF classifier,
(iv) marker module,
(v) shaper/dropper.

Also explain the meaning/role of the following components of a core router:
(i) BA classifier,
(ii) per-hop behavior,
(iii) expedited forwarding,
(iv) assured forwarding.

Section 9.9

9.49 Identify a selection of the applications of the point-to-point protocol (PPP) within the Internet. With the aid of the PPP frame format shown in Figure 9.29, explain the meaning/use of the following fields:
(i) opening and closing flags with zero bit insertion,
(ii) the byte stuffing rules used with asynchronous transmission lines.

9.50 State the role of the protocol ID field in the header of a PPP frame. Hence describe in outline the features supported by the link control protocol (LCP) associated with PPP.

Section 9.10

9.51 Discuss the reasons behind the definition of IP version 6, IPv6/IPng, including the main new features associated with it.

9.52 With the aid of the frame format shown in Figure 9.30(a), explain the role of the following fields in the IPv6 packet header:
(i) traffic class,
(ii) flow label,
(iii) payload length (and how this differs from the total length in an IPv4 packet header),
(iv) next header,
(v) hop limit,
(vi) source and destination addresses.

9.53 In relation to to IPv6 addresses, with the aid of the prefix formats shown in Figures 9.31(a) and (b), explain the meaning/use of:
(i) address aggregation,

(ii)   prefix formats,
(iii) embedded IPv4 addresses.

9.54 With the aid of the frame format shown in Figure 9.31(c), explain the meaning/use of the following IPv6 fields:
(i)   registry,
(ii)   top-level aggregators,
(iii) next-level agrregators
(iv)   site-level aggregators
(v)   interface ID.

Comment on the implications of adopting a hierarchical address structure.

9.55 With the aid of examples, explain the use of a link local-use address and a site local-use address.

9.56 Explain the format and use of
(i)   a multicast address,
(ii)   an anycast address.

9.57 With the aid of examples, show how an IPv6 address can be represented:
(i)   in hexadecimal form,
(ii)   with leading zeros removed,
(iii) when it   contains an IPv4 embedded address.

9.58 Explain the role of the extension headers that may be present in an IPv6 packet. List the six types of extension header and state their use. Also, with the aid of examples, state the position and order of the extension headers in relation to the main header.

9.59 The fields in an options extension header are encoded using a type-length-value format. Use the hop-by-hop options header as an example to explain this format.

9.60 In relation to the routing extension header, explain
(i)   the difference between strict and loose source routing, and the associated bit map,
(ii)   the use of the segments left field.

9.61 In relation to the packet formats shown in Figure 9.33, explain:
(i)   the meaning and use of the identification field and the M-bits in each extension header,
(ii)   why the hop-by-hop and routing headers are present in each fragment packet.

9.62 In relation to the encapsulating security payload header, with the aid of diagrams, explain:
(i)   the difference between transport mode and tunnel mode encryption,
(ii)   the meaning and use of the term "steel pipe".

9.63 State the aim of the autoconfiguration procedure used with IPv6 and the application domain of
(i)   the neighbor discovery (ND) protocol and
(ii)   the dynamic host configuration protocol (DHCP).

9.64 With the aid of Figure 9.35, explain the operation of the ND protocol. Include the role of the router solicitation and router advertisement messages and how a host creates its own IP address.

9.65 Explain how an IPv6 address is obtained
(i)   using a DHCP address server,
(ii)   a DHCP relay agent.

Section 9.11

9.66 With the aid of Figure 9.36, explain how a LAN server can respond to requests from both an IPv4 and an IPv6 client using dual protocols.

9.67 With the aid of Figure 9.37, explain how two hosts, each of which is attached to a different IPv6 network, communicate with each other if the two IPv6 networks are interconnected using an IPv4 network. Include the addresses that are used in each message transfer.

9.68 State the meaning of the terms "network address translation" (NAT) and "protocol translation" (PT). Hence, with the aid of the schematic diagram shown in Figure 9.38(a), explain the role and operation of a NAT-PT gateway. Include what the source address in each IPv6 packet should be.

9.69 Identify when the use of a NAT-PT gateway is not practical. Hence, with the aid of schematic diagram shown in Figure 9.38(b), explain the role of an application level gateway.

10

Broadband ATM networks

10.1 Introduction

As we explained in Section 1.3.5, broadband ISDN (B-ISDN) was designed from the outset to support multimedia communication applications involving text, high-resolution images, speech, audio, and video, either singly or a number integrated together in some way. At the time of the design (and standardization) of B-ISDN, the prevailing compression algorithms associated with the different media types were such that the anticipated peak channel bandwidth per call would be well in excess of the 2 Mbps offered by a (narrowband) ISDN.

Since each call may involve different types of media, the transmission and switching system chosen for the network is independent of both the bit rate and whether the source information is in the form of blocks or a variable rate bitstream. The chosen method involves the source information associated with each call being first converted into small fixed-sized packets known as **cells**. And since the rate of generation of the source information varies, so the rate of entry of cells into (and through) the network may also vary. Hence instead of allocating a fixed portion of transmission bandwidth per call, the cell streams relating to different calls are multiplexed together on a statistical basis. The switching units then operate using a form of packet switching called **cell switching**.

The adoption of a small fixed-sized cell means that cell switches can operate at a much higher rate than variable-length packet switches, so cell switching is also known as **fast packet switching**. Also, because the cells relating to different calls have varying time intervals between them during both transmission and switching, this mode of operation is known as the **asynchronous transfer mode** (**ATM**) and networks that operate in this way (broadband) ATM networks.

Having adopted a small cell size and a packet-switching mode of operation, the next decision to be made was whether the network should operate in a connection-oriented (CO) or a connectionless (CL) mode. As we showed in Figure 1.22 and explained in the accompanying text, in a CL mode network, each packet requires the full networkwide address of both the source and destination end systems in its header. The adoption of a small cell size, however, meant that the header may then be disproportionately large compared with the actual cell contents. So in order to keep the header small, the CO mode of operation was chosen. In a packet-switched network, this involves a path/route through the network being established prior to the transfer of any information packets and, on completion of the call, the path being closed down. The resulting path is called a virtual circuit and, in order for each packet-switching exchange to relate incoming packets to a specific virtual circuit, a unique identifier is assigned to the call on each line making up the virtual circuit as this is set up. The identifier used on each line is called the virtual circuit identifier (VCI) and, by assigning a new VCI on each line, only sufficient identifiers are required to identify the packets relating to the different calls on each line rather than the different calls in the total network. This same mode of operation is used in ATM networks.

The final decision was the size of the payload of a cell. Small cells have advantages for constant bit rate traffic since only a short delay is experienced as successive bytes relating to the same call are assembled and disassembled into and from cells at the network interface. Conversely, since each cell must contain additional routing information, small cells have the disadvantage that the overheads associated with each cell (in terms of transmission and switching) are higher. A compromise was reached by the various international standards bodies and a cell size of 53 bytes/octets was chosen. This comprises a 48-byte payload (information) field with a 5-byte header for the VCI and other fields. No error control is performed on cells within the network and hence no sequence numbers are required for retransmission purposes. However, the header does contain error check bits to detect the presence of transmission errors in the various header fields.

Because of the predicted high bit rates per call, an optical fiber access network was to be used to connect subscriber premises to the core network. As we indicated earlier, however, the rapid advances that have taken place in compression mean that the bit rate required for each call is significantly less than originally thought. As a result, existing access networks such as those associated with an ISDN and a PSTN can now support a range of multimedia communication applications. Hence the introduction of a B-ISDN access network has been postponed by most telecom providers. Nevertheless, the asynchronous transfer mode of working has been adopted for a number of other networks in which high bandwidth is required. As we showed in Figure 1.5, examples include ATM LANs and MANs, the latter providing a switched high-speed LAN interconnection facility. Also, as the bit rate of the transmission lines used in the Internet backbone network has increased – owing to the increasing number of multimedia applications – the cell-switching mode has been incorporated into the design of some of the high-speed routers used in the core backbone. In this chapter, we present further details of the operation of cell-switching networks in Sections 10.2 to 10.4 and the operation of ATM LANs in Section 10.5. We then describe the operation of ATM MANs in Section 10.6 and show how they are being used as the basis of broadband wide area networks in Section 10.7.

10.2 Cell format and switching principles

As we have explained, prior to any information cells being sent, a virtual circuit is first established. In an ATM network, the virtual circuit identifier used on each link is known as the **protocol connection identifier** (**PCI**). The principle of the routing scheme used is shown in Figure 10.1(a).

Associated with each incoming link/port is a routing table that contains, for each incoming PCI, the corresponding outgoing link/port and the new PCI to be used. The routing of cells in both directions along a route is thus very fast as it involves a simple look-up operation. As a result, cells from each link can be switched independently and at very high rates. This allows parallel switch architectures to be used and high-speed transmission lines in the gigabit range, each operating at its maximum rate.

In practice, the PCI is made up of two subfields: a **virtual path identifier** (**VPI**) and a **virtual channel identifier** (**VCI**). Routing can be performed using either one or a combination of the two. Two examples are shown in Figure 10.1. In part (b), switching is performed on virtual paths and the VCIs within each virtual path remain unchanged. In part (c) switching is performed on the virtual channels within each virtual path independently and the virtual paths simply terminate at each switch port.

An example of the use of virtual path switching is when multiple calls originating at the same network entry point are all intended for the same destination exit point. Each individual call is assigned a separate VCI and the calls are multiplexed together at the source interface onto a single virtual path. The multiplexed set of calls are then switched using the VPI field only and hence all follow the same path through the network. In this way, the set

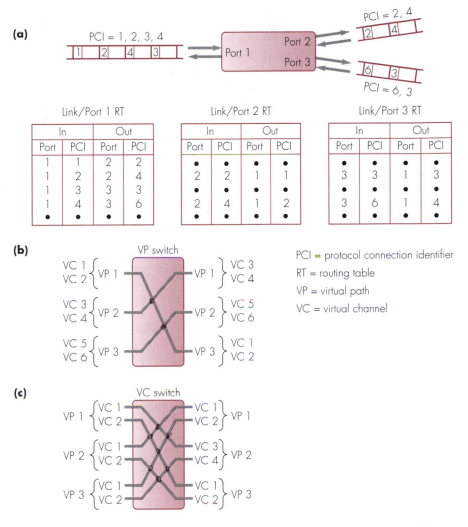

Figure 10.1 Cell switching principles: (a) routing schematic; (b) VP routing; (c) VC routing.

of VCIs remain unchanged and are used at the destination to identify (demultiplex) the individual calls.

An example of the use of virtual channel switching is when each call at the network entry point is intended for a different destination. In this case, each call is again assigned a different VCI but switching is also performed using the VCI field. The VPI field then has local significance to each link only and is used, for example, to allow calls to be multiplexed together for transmission purposes.

The format of each cell is shown in Figure 10.2 and, as we can see, the header is made up of six fields. Their functions are as follows:

■ **generic flow control (GFC):** this is present only in cells transferred over the user–network interface (UNI) and is included to enable a local switch to regulate – flow control – the entry of cells by a user into the network. Within the network, cells transferred over the interexchange links – known as the network–network interface (NNI) – do not contain this field and the four bits are part of the VPI field;

■ **virtual path identifier (VPI):** this is 8 bits at the UNI and, as just indicated, 12 bits at the NNI. As described previously, it is used for identification/routing purposes within the network;

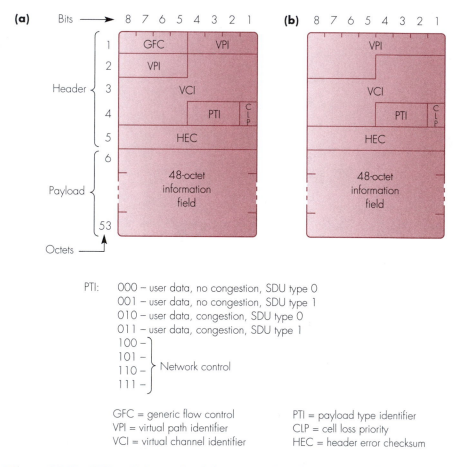

PTI: 000 – user data, no congestion, SDU type 0
 001 – user data, no congestion, SDU type 1
 010 – user data, congestion, SDU type 0
 011 – user data, congestion, SDU type 1
 100 –
 101 –
 110 – } Network control
 111 –

GFC = generic flow control   PTI = payload type identifier
VPI = virtual path identifier   CLP = cell loss priority
VCI = virtual channel identifier   HEC = header error checksum

Figure 10.2 ATM cell formats: (a) user–network segment; (b) within network, network–network interface.

- **virtual channel identifier (VCI):** a 16-bit field used for identification/routing purposes within the network;

- **payload type indicator (PTI):** indicates the type of information carried in the cell; the different types are shown in Figure 10.2. All cells containing user data have a zero in the most significant bit. The next bit indicates whether the cell has experienced excessive delay/congestion or not, and the third bit the service data unit (SDU) type – 0 or 1. We shall discuss its use in Section 10.4.1 in relation to the AAL5 service. The four remaining cell types are used for network control purposes;

- **cell loss priority (CLP):** within the network, the statistical multiplexing of cells on each link may occasionally result in cells having to be discarded during heavy load conditions. This field has been included to enable the user to specify a preference as to which cells should be discarded; CLP = 0 high priority, CLP = 1 low priority and hence discard first;

- **header error checksum (HEC):** generated by the physical layer and is an 8-bit CRC on the first 4-bytes of the header.

10.3 Switch architectures

The general structure of an ATM switch is shown in Figure 10.3(a). Each input link is terminated by an **input controller** (**IC**) which performs the routing of cells arriving at each link (port) to their required output link. This involves a simple look-up and mapping operation of the VPI/VCI in the header of the incoming cell into the corresponding output VPI/VCI. Normally, the output port number obtained from the routing table is used to determine the path to be followed through the switching fabric to the required output controller.

Because there is no reservation of slots on the output links, cells may arrive simultaneously at two (or more) input ports that require the same output port/link. This is handled in one of two ways: either the input controllers contain a set of cell buffers that hold the additional cell(s) or the buffering is provided in the **output controllers**. In both cases the buffers are organized in the form of a FIFO queue to ensure the cells from each input controller are output in the same order as they arrived. The output controllers simply forward received cells at the appropriate link bit (and hence cell) rate.

The main role of the **control processor** is to download routing information into the routing tables in each input controller. Normally, the routing information is received through the network either from a network management station or, if switched VCs are being used, from a signaling control point processor. In both cases, semipermanent VCs are used to relay the cell containing the routing information. Hence on arrival at the switch, the related cells are routed through the switching fabric directly from the input controller that receives the cells to the control processor. In addition, the

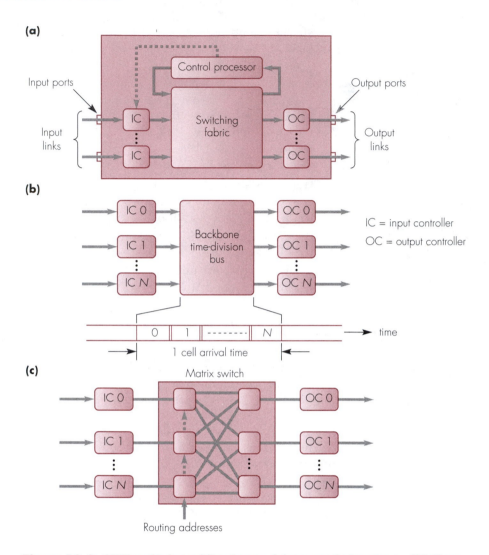

(a)

Input ports

Output ports

Control processor

Input links

IC

Switching fabric

OC

Output links

IC

OC

(b)

IC 0

Backbone time-division bus

OC 0

IC = input controller
OC = output controller

IC 1

OC 1

IC N

OC N

0 | 1 | -------- | N

time

1 cell arrival time

(c)

Matrix switch

IC 0

OC 0

IC 1

OC 1

IC N

OC N

Routing addresses

Figure 10.3 ATM switch architectures: (a) general structure; (b) time-division bus schematic; (c) fully-connected matrix switch.

control processor may generate network management messages itself – fault reports, performance statistics, and so on – and these are also routed through the switch fabric to the required output controller for onward transmission to the network management location again using a semipermanent VC.

A number of alternative switch fabrics are used in ATM switches. They can be classified as either time division or space division. Normally, all the input controllers are synchronized so that each set of incoming cells from all controllers is presented to the switch fabric in synchronism. The switch fabric also operates synchronously which means that the cells from each input controller are transferred to their required output controller in a single cell time.

A schematic diagram of a **time-division switch** is shown in Figure 10.3(b). In such switches we use a time-division backplane bus that is capable of transferring N cells – where N is the number of input ports – in a single cell arrival time. Each input controller is assigned its own cell (slot) time to transfer a cell over the backplane bus. The input controller appends the required output port number to the head of the cell and this is used by the set of output controllers to determine which output controller should read and buffer the cell. If more than one cell is received by an output controller in a single cell arrival time then these are queued in the controller. Also, for one-to-many communications (multicast), more than one output controller may be specified to receive the cell. Typically, this type of switch fabric is used in switch designs which have a relatively small number of ports, the number being limited by the speed of operation of the backplane bus and also the output controllers; for example, a 2.5 Gbps bus can support 16×155 Mbps or 4×622 Mbps duplex links/ports.

In a **space-division switch** the switch fabric comprises a matrix of interconnected **switching elements** that collectively provide a number of alternative paths through the switch. An example is shown in Figure 10.3(c). This is known as a **fully-connected switch matrix** since a path is provided from all input ports/controllers to all output ports/controllers. In the example shown, each input switching element is capable of passing a copy of each received cell to any of the output switching elements. The latter then receive the cells offered and pass them on to the output controller(s) for transmission. Although queuing is necessary in the input or output controllers, normally the aim is to avoid additional queuing within the switching fabric itself. To avoid internal queuing with this type of switch the cell transfer operation must be performed N times faster than the cell arrival rate, where N is the number of input ports. First the cell from the first input switching element is transferred, then the cell from the second element, and so on. Providing this can be done, no additional buffering is required within the switching matrix and the switch is said to be internally **non-blocking**.

We can deduce from Figure 10.3(c) that in a fully-connected switch the number of interconnection paths required through the switch – and hence output/input circuits associated with each switching element – grows as a function of N^2 and the speed of operation of the output switching element by N. In practice, this limits the maximum size of such switches. Hence most practical matrix switch designs use multiple switching stages, each made up of a number of smaller switching elements interconnected in a regular matrix. This also simplifies considerably the implementation of the switch fabric in integrated circuit form.

A switching fabric that comprises multiple switching stages is the **delta switch matrix**, an example of which is shown in Figure 10.4. As we can see, these switches are made up from an interconnected set of identical switching

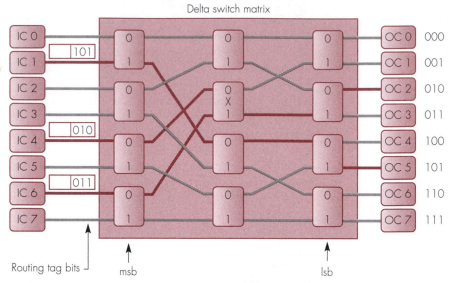

Delta switch matrix

X = blocking, cell with tag 011 assumed dropped

Figure 10.4 Delta switch matrix example.

elements. In this example, a 2×2 switching element is used although larger sizes are also used. In general, the number of switching elements per stage, X, is determined from the expression $X = M/N$ where M is the total number of input lines and N is the number of inputs per switching element. Also, the number of stages required, Y, is determined from the expression $N^Y = M$. In the example, $N = 2$ and $M = 8$ and hence three stages are required each comprising four switching elements.

The internal interconnections between switching elements are such that there is a path through the switch from any input to any output. Associated with each switching element is a routing control bit called the **routing tag**. If the tag bit is a binary 0, then a cell arriving on either input is routed to the upper output, while if the tag is a binary 1, then it is routed to the lower output. As we can deduce from Figure 10.4, the same set of three routing tag bits will route a cell through the matrix from any input port to the same output port. Such networks are said to be **self-routing**.

With this type of switch, to route cells through the switch matrix each input controller simply reads the new PCI and output port number – the routing tag – from its routing table, writes the PCI into the cell header, and then appends the routing tag to the head of the cell. The switching element at each stage along the path through the matrix then uses its own bit from the routing tag – most significant bit first – to perform its routing operation. In this way, routing is very fast and each cell arrives at its intended destination port regardless of the switch port on which it arrived.

The disadvantage of this type of switching fabric is **blocking**. Three example paths through the switch are shown as bold lines in Figure 10.4. As we can see, although the cell addressed to port 5 (101) has an unimpeded path through the matrix, those addressed to ports 2 (010) and 3 (011) both arrive at the second switching element simultaneously. Both require the same output line and blocking is said to occur.

There are a number of ways of overcoming blocking. One approach is for the switching element to discard one of the two cells. It is assumed that this approach is used in the example and that the cell with a tag of 011 is dropped. In support of this, note that not all ports will enter a cell into the matrix during each cell arrival time since only in the heaviest load conditions do cells arrive contiguously at all inputs. This means that under normal loads, several ports will receive idle/empty cells which do not need routing and hence in practice the probability of blocking is small. Nevertheless, in general, discarding cells in this way can lead to an unacceptably high cell loss rate in large switches.

A second approach is to perform the switching operation several times faster than the cell arrival rate, for example by allowing each cell into the matrix after the preceding cell leaves the first stage switching element. There is a limit to the speed of operation of the switching elements and their interconnecting links and hence for larger switching fabrics this becomes impractical on its own. A third approach is to introduce buffering into each switching element but this has the disadvantage of introducing additional delay to the switching operation. In practice, a combination of all three approaches is used in practical switch designs.

An example of a switching fabric that avoids internal blocking is shown in Figure 10.5. It is known as the **Batcher–Banyan switch**. With a delta switch, blocking occurs when either different inputs all require a path through the switch to the same output or, the paths through the switch between different input and output ports involve a common output line from a switching element. In the Batcher–Banyan switch, blocking is avoided firstly, by ensuring that no two cells entering the switching matrix require the same output port and secondly, within the switching matrix itself, by ensuring that there are no common interconnecting links within the paths through the switch.

To satisfy the first condition, the buffering of cells is performed in the input controllers instead of the output controllers. Then, if two (or more) cells arrive simultaneously at different input ports that require the same output port, just one cell is selected for transfer across the switching fabric and the other is queued in the input controller until the next cell transfer time. To satisfy the second condition, as Figure 10.5 shows, the (Banyan) switching matrix is preceded by a (**Batcher**) **sorting matrix** and the two are interconnected using what is called a **shuffle exchange**. The combined effect is that all cells arriving at the switching matrix are ordered such that they each follow a unique path through the switching matrix. Hence, providing independent routing paths are available within each switching element, the

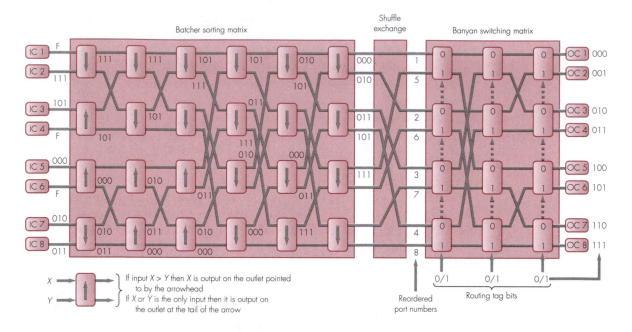

Figure 10.5 Batcher–Banyan switch matrix.

cells from all input ports can be switched simultaneously. The size of a Batcher sorting network grows by $N (\log N^2)$ and can be considerable for large switches.

Another approach used in practical switch designs to reduce the blocking probability is a switching fabric that has multiple paths between each pair of input and output ports. For example, with the simple delta switch, this can be achieved by replicating the total switch matrix an appropriate number of times. Each input controller uses a different matrix to transfer each cell. Alternatively, the basic Banyan switching matrix can be extended by adding extra switching stages. In both cases, the number of additional stages can be selected so that the blocking – and hence cell loss – probability is at an acceptable level.

Another issue which has an impact on switch design is multicasting. Recall from Section 9.6.9 that this requires all the cells from each workstation in a (multicast) group to be sent to all the other workstations in the group. In practice, the most efficient way of achieving this is to use the switches to route copies of cells to multiple destinations. Although this can be done readily with both the time-division and fully-connected switch designs, with matrix switches, because of their self-routing property, additional switching stages are needed if multicasting is to be supported. Further details relating to both these issues can be found in the bibliography for this chapter.

10.4 Protocol architecture

As we show in Figure 10.6, the ATM protocol architecture supports three separate application functions (planes). These are the control (C) plane, the user (U) plane and the management (M) plane. The protocols associated with the **C-plane** are concerned with signaling; that is, the setting up and clearing of on-demand VCs. Typically, these are set up and cleared using a signaling protocol set in the station communicating with a similar protocol set in the network **signaling control point**. The protocols in the **U-plane** depend on the application and, in general, communicate on a user-to-user (peer) basis with a similar protocol set in the destination station. The protocols in the **M-plane** are concerned with the management of the station; examples include reporting any error conditions that may arise during normal operation to the network management station and receiving notifications of the

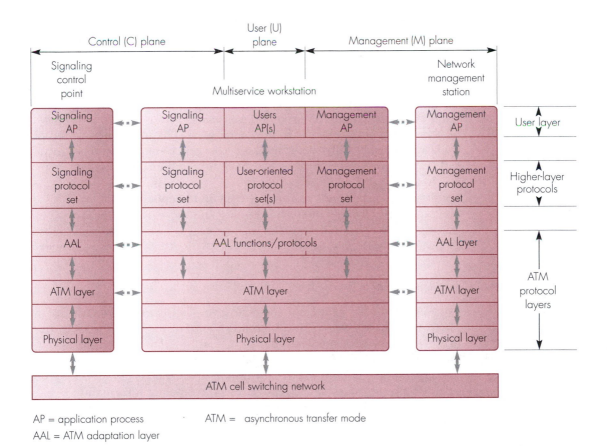

AP = application process   ATM = asynchronous transfer mode
AAL = ATM adaptation layer

Figure 10.6 ATM protocol architecture.

virtual path/channel identifiers that have been allocated for permanent VCs (PVCs). These three application functions then use the services provided by the three lower ATM protocol layers for the transfer of the associated messages over the cell-based ATM switching network.

The ATM network supports a range of different services. The use of cell switching and transmission within the network is transparent to the upper application protocols which view the ATM network simply as a flexible facility for the transfer of information relating to any media type. To achieve this transparency, the highest of the three ATM layers is known as the **ATM adaptation layer** (**AAL**). As the name implies, it performs an adaptation (convergence) function between the service provided to the user layer above – for example the transfer of a data frame between two legacy LANs – and the cell-based service provided by the underlying ATM layer.

To support the various information sources, the AAL layer provides a range of alternative service types known as **service classes**. Associated with each service class is a different adaptation function/protocol which converts the source information into streams of 48-octet segments. It passes these to the **ATM layer** for transfer across the network. The ATM layer is concerned with adding the correct cell header information to each segment and multiplexing the cells relating to different connections into a single stream of cells for transmission over the network. It is also concerned with the demultiplexing of received cell streams and relaying their contents to the appropriate AAL protocol at the destination.

The **physical layer** can take on a number of different forms and depends on the type of transmission circuits being used. The upper part of the physical layer is known as the **transmission-convergence sublayer** and is concerned with such functions as the generation of the header check sequence in the cell header and the delineation of the cell boundaries. The lower part takes on different forms and is known as the **medium-dependent sublayer**. It is concerned with such functions as line coding and bit/clock synchronization. We shall discuss the operation of the AAL and ATM layer in more detail in the following two subsections.

10.4.1 ATM adaptation layer

The AAL provides a range of alternative service types/classes for the transport of the byte streams/message units generated by the various higher protocol layers associated with the U-, C-, and M-planes. It converts the submitted information into streams of 48-octet segments and transports these in the payload field of multiple ATM cells. Similarly, on receipt of the stream of cells relating to the same call, it converts the 48-octet information field contained within each cell into the required form for delivery to the particular higher protocol layer.

The service types are classified according to three criteria: the existence of a time relationship between the source and destination users (for example voice), the bit rate associated with the transfer (constant or variable), and the connection mode (connection-oriented or connectionless). Currently, five service types have been defined. They are referred to as AAL 1–5 and their interrelationship, based on these criteria, is illustrated in Figure 10.7(a).

Both AAL 1 (Class A) and AAL 2 (Class B) are connection-oriented and there exists a timing relationship between the source and destination users. The difference between the two is that AAL 1 provides a **constant bit rate (CBR) service** while AAL 2 provides a **variable bit rate (VBR) service**. An example use of AAL 1 is for the transfer of the constant bit rate byte stream associated with a voice call, for example, 1 byte per 125 μs. AAL 1 is also known as **circuit (switched) emulation**. An example use of AAL 2 is for the transmission of the variable bit rate stream associated with compressed video. Although video produces frames at a constant rate, a video codec will produce frames containing a variable amount of compressed data.

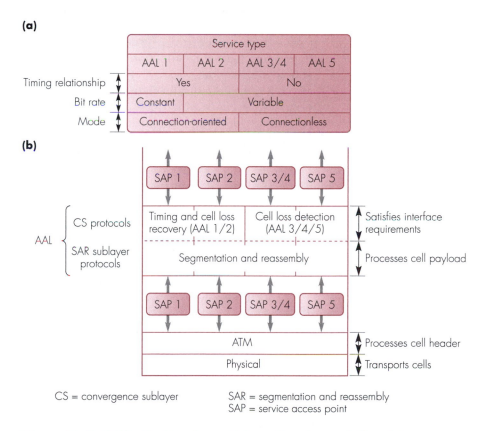

Figure 10.7 ATM adaption layer: (a) service class relationship; (b) sublayer protocols and their functions.

There is no timing relationship between source and destination with either AAL 3/4 (Class C/D) or AAL 5. Initially, AAL 3 was defined to provide a connection-oriented, VBR data service. Later, this service type was dropped and it is now merged with AAL 4. Both AAL 3/4 and AAL 5 provide a similar connectionless VBR service. An example use is for the transfer of data frames between two legacy LANs – through a remote bridge or router for example – or for the transfer of frames containing multimedia information between a workstation and a server. It is also used for the transfer of the message units associated with the signaling and management protocol sets in such work-stations. In all of these cases, as we shall see in Section 10.5.1, although the service offered is connectionless, the resulting cell streams produced by the AAL layer are transferred over previously established PVCs, for example, to the signaling control point or network management station.

In order to implement this range of services, the AAL comprises two sub-layers as we show in Figure 10.7(b). The **convergence sublayer** (**CS**) performs a convergence function between the service offered at the layer interface and that provided by the underlying ATM layer. The **segmentation and reassembly** (**SAR**) sublayer performs the necessary segmentation of the source informa-tion ready for transfer in the 48-octet payload field of a cell and also, the corresponding reassembly function at the destination prior to the delivery of the source information.

Since the submitted information differs for each service type, there is a different convergence function – and hence CS protocol – associated with each service type. Associated with each protocol is a **service access point** (**SAP**) which is used to direct all information submitted for transfer – the ser-vice data unit (SDU) – to the appropriate CS protocol. Similarly, there are four different types of SAR protocol, each with its own PDU structure. As we shall now see, each utilizes the 48-octet information field in each cell in a different way.

AAL 1

For this type of service the CS protocol endeavors to maintain a constant bit rate stream between the source and destination SAPs. The bit rate can range from a few kilobits per second – for example, for a single compressed voice call – to tens of megabits per second – for example, for a compressed video. However, the agreed rate must be maintained, even when occasional cell losses or cell transfer time variations occur. Cell losses are overcome in an agreed way, for example, by inserting dummy bits/bytes into the delivered stream. Cell transfer delay variations are compensated for by buffering seg-ments at the destination: the output of the bits/bytes relating to a call is started only after a predefined number of segments have been received, this number being determined by the user bit rate. Typical figures are two seg-ments at kilobit rates and 100 segments at megabit rates. The use of buffering at the destination also provides a crude way of overcoming any small varia-tions between the input rate at the source interface and the output rate at the destination; for example, if each is based on a separate clock.

The format of each PDU associated with the SAR protocol is shown in Figure 10.8(a). To detect segment losses, the first octet contains a 4-bit *sequence number* (*SN*) and an associated 4-bit *SN protection* (*SNP*) field which is used to protect the sequence number against single bit errors. The sequence number is itself made up of a 3-bit *sequence count* field – for the detection of lost cells – and a single *convergence sublayer indication bit*. The latter can be used for the transfer of timing and/or other information relating to the payload field. The sequence number protection field comprises a 3-bit CRC, generated by the polynomial $x^3 + x + 1$, and an even parity bit. The latter is used to detect errors in the CRC.

AAL 2

With this type of service, although there is a timing relationship between the source and destination SAPs – determined by the frame rate, for example, for compressed video – the amount of information associated with each compressed frame may vary from one frame to the next. The CS protocol at the source receives bursts of information at the frame rate with each burst containing a variable amount of information. Hence the peer CS protocol at the destination must endeavor to output the received information in this same way even when occasional cell losses or cell transfer time variations occur. With AAL 2, the time variations are overcome using similar techniques to those described for AAL 1.

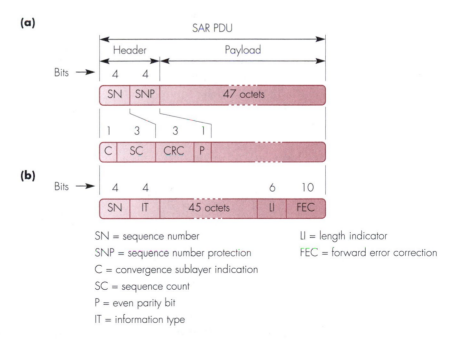

Figure 10.8 SAR protocol data unit types: (a) AAL 1; (b) AAL 2.

The format of each PDU associated with the corresponding SAR protocol is shown in Figure 10.8(b). As with AAL 1, the sequence number is present to detect (and recover from) lost cells and to carry timing information. The *information type* (*IT*) field indicates either the position of the segment in relation to a submitted message unit – for example, a compressed frame – or whether the segment contains timing or other information. The three segment types relating to positional information are beginning of message (BOM), continuation of message (COM), and end of message (EOM). Also, because of the variable size of submitted message units, the last (EOM) segment may not be full and hence the length indicator (LI) at the tail indicates the number of useful bytes in the segment. Finally, the forward error correction (FEC) field enables bit errors to be detected and a selection corrected.

AAL 3/4

AAL 3 was defined initially to provide a connection-oriented data transfer service. Later, this type of service was dropped and combined with AAL 4. AAL 3/4 provides a connectionless data transfer service for the transfer of variable length frames up to 65 535 bytes in length. Error detection and other fields are added to each frame prior to its transfer and the resulting frame is padded so that it is an integral multiple of 32 bits.

The operation of AAL 3/4 is best described by considering the format of the PDUs associated with both the CS and SAR protocols. The format of the additional fields added by the CS protocol to each submitted user SDU – at the corresponding SAP – is shown in Figure 10.9(a). The figure also shows how the resulting CS PDU is segmented by the SAR protocol into multiple 48-octet SAR-PDUs.

The header and trailer fields added to the submitted SDU by the CS protocol at the source are used by the peer CS protocol at the destination to detect any missing or malformed SDUs. The *PDU-type* field is a legacy of the earlier AAL 3 which required multiple types of PDU. It is set to zero with AAL 3/4. The *begin-end* (*BE*) *tag* is a modulo-256 sequence number and is repeated in the trailer for added resilience. It enables SDUs to be delivered at the user interface in the same sequence as they were submitted although, again, this facility is not normally used with a connectionless service. The *buffer allocation* (*BA*) field is inserted in the header by the source to help the CS protocol at the destination allocate an appropriate amount of (buffer) memory for the complete SDU. At the trailer, the *pad* field is used to make the total number of octets in the complete CS-PDU an integral multiple of 4 octets. Similarly, the *alignment* (*AL*) field is a single (dummy) octet to make the trailer 4 octets also. Collectively this leads to easier memory management at the destination. The *length* field indicates the total length of the complete PDU and this is used by the receiving protocol to detect any malformed SDUs.

On receipt of each CS-PDU, the SAR protocol segments this into multiple 48 octet segments – SAR-PDUs – as shown in Figure 10.9(a). In the header, the *segment type* (*ST*) indicates whether the segment is the first, continuation, last, or only segment resulting from the segmentation of the CS-PDU. The

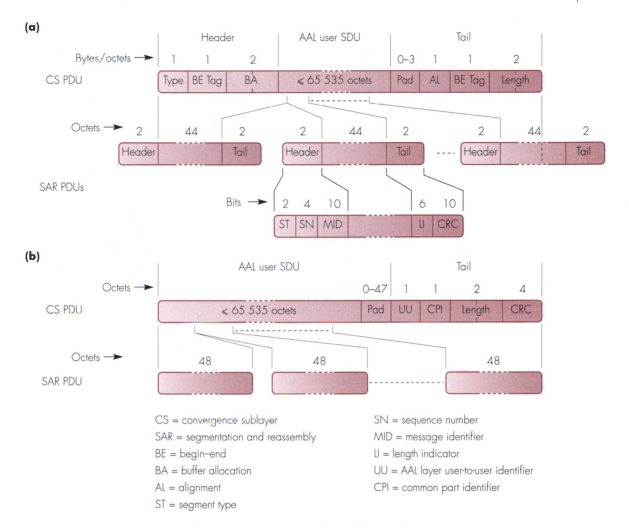

Figure 10.9 CS and SAR PDU formats: (a) AAL3/4; (b) AAL 5.

sequence number (*SN*) is used to detect missing segments. In practice, a device like a network server may have a number of frames – and hence CS-PDUs – being received concurrently from multiple sources. Hence for the receiving SAR protocol to relate each incoming segment to the correct PDU, the source SAR protocol adds the same *message identifier* (*MID*) field to the head of each segment relating to the same CS-PDU. At the tail, the *length indicator* (*LI*) indicates the number of useful octets in the segment since the CS-PDU is not necessarily an integral number of 44 octet segments. Clearly, this field has meaning either in the last segment relating to a multisegment CS-PDU or, if it is the only segment. The *CRC* is used to detect possible transmission errors introduced during the transfer of segments.

AAL 5

Because of the origin of AAL 3/4, the CS-PDU contains a number of fields in the header which were included primarily to support a connection-oriented service. The MID field at the head of each SAR-PDU – which is present to enable the destination to relate segments to a specific frame – performs a similar function to the protocol connection identifier – VPI/VCI – present in the header of each ATM cell. As a result, the alternative AAL 5 service class was defined. This provides a similar service to AAL 3/4 but with a reduced number of control fields in both the CS and SAR PDUs. It is known as the **simple and efficient adaptation layer** (**SEAL**). As with AAL 3/4, its operation is best described by considering the format of the PDUs associated with both the CS and SAR protocols. These are shown in Figure 10.9(b).

As we can see, with AAL 5 there is no header associated with the constructed CS-PDU. Also, the pad field in the trailer is longer (0–47 octets) so that the length of each CS-PDU can be an integral number of complete 48-octet segments. This has the advantage that the fields at the trailer of the CS-PDU are always the last 8 octets of the last segment, which leads to faster processing at the destination. The AAL *user-to-user identifier* (*UU*) enables the two correspondent user layers to relate the AAL SDU to a particular SAP. The use of the *CPI* field has yet to be defined. It is included to support future functions and currently to make the tail an even number of octets. The *length* field indicates the number of octets in the user data field and is an integer value in the range 0 to 65 535. The *CRC* field detects the presence of any transmission errors in the reassembled CS-PDU. If errors are detected, then the user layer above is informed when the SDU contained within the PDU is delivered. In this way, it is left to the user layer to decide what action to take: in some instances this will be to discard the SDU – for example, if it contains normal data – while in others, it will be to accept it and take appropriate recovery steps – for example, if the SDU contents relate to a video or voice portion of a multimedia document.

As we can see, there is no head or tail associated with the SAR PDU. Each comprises the full 48 octets and the SAR protocol is said to be null. The lack of a MID field at the head of each segment means that the segments relating to the same CS-PDU are identified using the field in the header of the ATM cell that is used to transport the segment. With AAL 5, the SDU type bit in user data cells – also known as **ATM-layer user-to-user** (**AUU**) **cells** – is used to indicate whether the cell contents form the beginning or continuation of the CS-PDU (binary 0) or the end (binary 1). Although this means the operation of the AAL layer is now linked with that of the ATM layer, it is done to improve the efficiency of the segmentation process. AAL 5 is also used as the AAL layer in the C-plane for the segmentation and reassembly of messages associated with the signaling protocol. It is then known as the **signaling AAL** or **SAAL**.

10.4.2 ATM layer

The ATM layer performs all the functions relating to the routing and multiplexing of cells over VCs, which may be semipermanent or set up on demand. Its main function is to assign a header to the segment streams generated by the AAL relating to a particular call. Similarly, on receipt of cell streams, its function is to remove the header from each cell and pass the cell contents – segments – to the appropriate AAL layer protocol.

To perform these functions, the ATM layer maintains a table that contains a list of VCIs. Normally, in ATM LANs for example, all switching is carried out using VPIs only and the VCI field in the cell header is then used to multiplex/demultiplex the cells relating to specific calls/transactions which are transported over the same path. In the case of semipermanent VCs, the VPIs are downloaded by network management – via the network management protocol stack – and in the case of on-demand VCs, the VPIs are obtained using the appropriate signaling protocol set. In both cases the cell streams relating to the management/signaling protocol messages are transferred over permanently assigned VCs.

In a public network, the ATM layer offers various service classes each of which has been specified to meet a particular type of application requirement. These are:

- **constant bit rate (CBR):** this supports isochronous traffic such as uncompressed speech, audio, and video;

- **variable bit rate/real time (VBR/RT):** this supports variable bit rate traffic with real-time requirements. An example is the transmission in real time of a compressed video. There is a declared mean and peak rate and, if the peak rate is exceeded, cells are tagged at the network interface to indicate they can be dropped if necessary;

- **variable bit rate/non-real time (VBR/NRT):** this supports variable bit rate traffic but with no real-time requirements. An example is the transfer of a file containing compressed video from a server to a client workstation;

- **available bit rate (ABR):** this supports bursty traffic with a known minimum, mean, and peak rate. The network guarantees the mean rate but provides the additional rate according to competing demands on the available transmission capacity. If the network is unable to provide the additional rate, however, it informs the user to reduce the input rate;

- **unspecified bit rate (UBR):** this service does not provide any guarantees nor is the user informed if the network is unable to transfer the submitted information. The service offered, therefore, is similar to that provided by a best-effort network such as a LAN or the Internet.

Associated with each service class is a network quality of service (QoS) guarantee which forms the basis of a contract between the network provider and the network user. Essentially, the provider agrees to meet the bandwidth, delay, and delay variation (jitter) requirements of the cell stream associated with a user application providing the cell stream conforms to an agreed set of parameters. A range of QoS parameters have been defined and, for each contract, a set of parameter values is negotiated which the network provider agrees to meet or exceed. Collectively, the parameters form what is called the **traffic descriptor** of the call and, to meet the requirements of the various types of call, a different set of parameters may be defined for the cell stream flowing in each direction of a connection.

The parameters relating to the user include:

- **peak cell rate (PCR):** the maximum rate the source will enter cells;
- **sustained cell rate (SCR):** the average rate the source will enter cells;
- **minimum cell rate (MCR):** the minimum cell rate that is acceptable by the source;
- **cell delay variation tolerance (CDVT):** the maximum level of variation in intercell times.

The parameters relating to the network include:

- **cell loss ratio (CLR):** the maximum ratio of cells that will not be delivered owing to transmission errors or excessive delays within the network;
- **cell transfer delay (CTD):** the average transfer delay of cells across the network;
- **cell delay variation (CDV):** the average variation in cell transfer delay.

In order to enforce the contract, for each cell entered into the network and subsequently delivered, the network determines whether the parameters for this call/VC conform to the agreed contract. The algorithm used is known as the **generic cell rate algorithm** (**GCRA**) and the principles on which it is based are shown in Figure 10.10.

As we can see, four examples of cell inter-arrival times are given:

(i) Cell 2 arrives according to the agreed PCR and hence is accepted.

(ii) Cell 2 arrives early but within the agreed CDVT. Hence providing the new SCR is not violated, the cell is accepted. Note, however, that the expected time of arrival of cell 3 is $t_o + 2T$.

(iii) Cell 2 arrives later than the agreed PCR but, since a source can enter cells at a lower rate than the agreed PCR, it also is accepted. Note that the expected time of arrival of cell 3 is the time cell 2 arrived plus T.

(iv) Cell 2 arrives earlier than the agreed CDVT and hence violates the contract. Normally, the network will either set the cell loss priority (CLP) bit in the cell header or discard the cell depending on the current loading of the network.

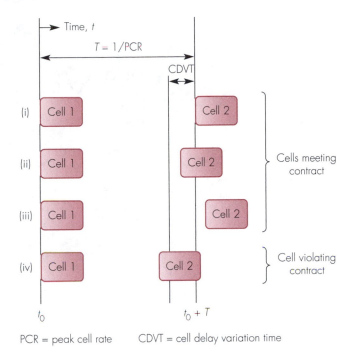

PCR = peak cell rate   CDVT = cell delay variation time

Figure 10.10 Principle of operation of generic cell rate algorithm.

10.5 ATM LANs *dead*

ATM LANs have been designed to meet the high bandwidth demands of multi-media applications and hence are an alternative to the LANs based on fast Ethernet which we described in Section 8.7. A typical site LAN is shown in Figure 10.11.

As we explained earlier in Section 10.3, an ATM switch has a defined number of ports and its function is to provide a high bit rate switched communications path between ports. The cost of a switch is a function of the number of ports that it supports. If all the stations are connected directly to the switch then as the deployment of multimedia PCs/workstations increases, switches with a very large number of ports are required. However, not all stations require network services at the same time. To minimize the number of ports, groups of stations – for example, in a building – are connected to the switch through a **remote concentrator unit** (**RCU**). There is no switching function in the RCU and its role is simply to multiplex/demultiplex the cell streams from/to those stations that are involved in a network transaction onto/from the link connecting the concentrator to a switch port. In this way, providing the interconnecting link has sufficient capacity to support the

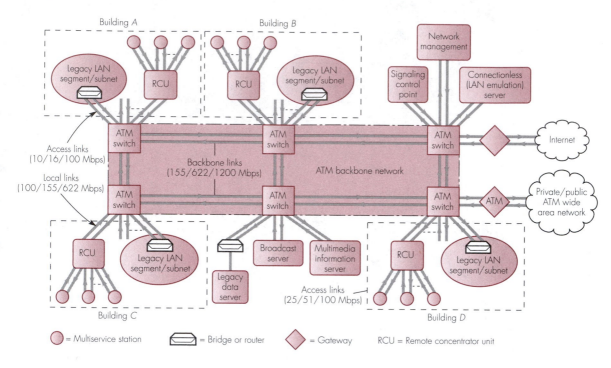

Figure 10.11 ATM LAN schematic.

anticipated number of concurrent transactions, the number of switch ports required is reduced considerably.

Prior to sending any information relating to a call, a communications path through the network is first established. All the cells relating to the call are constrained to follow this same path and are delivered in the same order as they were submitted. Recall that the conversion of all information into streams of fixed-sized cells has the advantage that the cells relating to the different types of call can be switched in a uniform way and independent of the type of media which they contain. In addition, the use of cells has advantages in terms of the utilization of transmission bandwidth.

The applications supported by a multimedia PC/workstation include telephony, videophony, conventional data networking, and access to a range of related servers. These include, in addition to those present with existing data networks – electronic mail, printing services, and so on – a broadcast server, a database server supporting multimedia Web pages, and so on. For example, the **broadcast server** – which performs the same functions as an MCU – enables a user at a multimedia workstation to set up on demand a videoconferencing session between three or more similar workstations by sending the integrated media streams output from all the workstations involved directly to the server in real time. The server relays the appropriate media streams to the other workstations as the conference proceeds.

Similarly, the server holding multimedia Web pages enables a user at a workstation to access a particular page and then interactively browse through it.

In practice, ATM LANs are being introduced in an incremental way and currently a majority of LAN installations are still of the Ethernet type. Within the context of ATM LANs, these are often referred to as **legacy LANs**. The major bottleneck associated with such networks is access to servers, since these require significant bandwidth to support multiple concurrent transactions. Hence in addition to providing direct access to the newer multimedia servers, the backbone switches also provide connections both to the existing data-only LANs in each building – for example through bridges – and to the servers associated with them. Typically, these are all interconnected by a set of point-to-point virtual connections (VCs). In the context of high-speed LANs, the interconnected set of backbone switches can be viewed as providing the same function as a high-speed backbone subnetwork.

All communications across the ATM network are carried out over previously established VCs. These can be set up either on demand by a user or semipermanently by network management. With **on-demand connections**, the user device, before sending any information cells, sends a request for a **switched virtual connection** (**SVC**) to be set up between itself and the required destination. This can be done either in a distributed way involving all the switches in the connection or using a central control unit known as the **signaling control point** (**SCP**). This is responsible for the overall management of both the transmission bandwidth and the setting up and clearing of switched connections through the network. On receipt of the request – known as a **signaling message** – the SCP first determines the availability of both the required destination and the transmission bandwidth appropriate to the call across the network. All the end-user stations are connected to the SCP – normally a powerful workstation – by a separate VC and, assuming the required destination and network resources are available, the SCP sets up routing information in the switch network to link the two user stations (VCs) involved in the call. It then informs the originator of the call that it can commence sending information cells. All the signaling messages associated with the setting up and clearing of calls/connections are transferred across the network to and from the SCP in the form of cells over a separate set of VCs that are permanently set up for this function. The latter are known as **signaling virtual channel connections** (**SVCCs**).

To access networked servers such as electronic mail and multimedia information servers, because the ATM network is connection-oriented, before any frames can be transferred, a VC must be in place between each workstation and the set of servers. In practice, the number of servers may be large and this requirement can be met by setting up **permanent VCs** (**PVCs**) between all user stations and servers and a central data forwarding point known as the **connectionless server** (**CLS**) or, because it provides a similar service to that provided by a legacy (broadcast) LAN, the **LAN emulation server** (**LES**). We shall discuss the operation of this and the SCP in more detail in the next section.

The permanent virtual connections associated with the various services are all set up under the overall control of the network management station. A reserved VC is permanently in place between the **network management station** and the control processor in each RCU and backbone ATM switch. Also between all multimedia stations and servers and their network point of attachments. These are used by the network manager to set up the VCs associated with the various services. The network manager uses these connections to download routing information for entry into the routing tables held by these devices.

As with existing data-only networks, users of multimedia stations, as well as needing to communicate with other users at the same site, also want to communicate with users connected to an ATM LAN at a different site. Hence an ATM LAN has a gateway to the Internet and also to newer private/public wide area ATM networks. To meet these needs, new generations of private networks based on the ATM are being introduced. Also, a number of telecom providers are introducing a new generation of public network based on the same technology. As we shall see in Sections 10.6 and 10.7, these consist of ATM MANs which, in turn, are interconnected together to form an ATM wide area network.

Example 10.1

NO pencil
— 681

A segment of an ATM network is shown in Figure 10.12(a). The numbers alongside each RCU/switch are the port identifiers. Assume that semipermanent VCs are to be set up by network management between stations A, B, C and D, firstly, to the SCP for on-demand calls – for both signaling and information transfer – and secondly, to the CLS/LES for the cell streams relating to connectionless calls. Also, assume that a separate VC is required to connect the server to the CLS/LES. Derive typical routing table entries for RCU 1 and RCU 2 and SW 1 and SW 2 to provide these connections assuming VP-only switching is used within the network switches and, within the RCUs, the VPI/VCI field is used to identify specific calls/stations.

Answer:

A suitable set of routing table entries is given in Figure 10.12(b). Note the following points when interpreting the entries:

- The SCP, CLS, and server are all connected to their switches by separate transmission lines.

- For on-demand calls, two separate VCs are shown: one between each workstation and the SCP for the signaling messages associated with a call – the signaling channel (SC) – and the other for the cell streams associated with the call – the call channel (CC). Since the latter are to be semipermanent, they are shown set up between each workstation and SW 2. Alternatively, they could be set up on demand by the SCP between each pair of workstations involved in a call.

- For connectionless traffic, a separate VC is required between each workstation and the CLS and also between the CLS and the server.

- The SCP, CLS, and server all use the combined VPI/VCI in the cell header to identify the cells relating to specific calls/server transactions.

10.1 Continued

- On the station side of each RCU, the VCI field identifies the port number – and hence station – within each virtual path. Also, in this example, only three virtual paths are required per RCU rather than per station. This allows the approach to be scaled to large installations.
- Within the network, all switching is carried out using VPIs only.
- To set up an on-demand call, the SCP creates entries in the routing table of SW 2 to link the port/VCI of the calling party to that of the called party.
- For connectionless traffic, when relaying the cell streams received from each station to the server, the CLS assigns a new VPI/VCI. Also, in order to relay the cell streams in the reverse direction, it maintains a table that maps the incoming VPI/VCI from the stations to those used for communicating with the server.
- When responding to a request, the server uses the same VPI/VCI values for the cells making up the response as were used in the request.

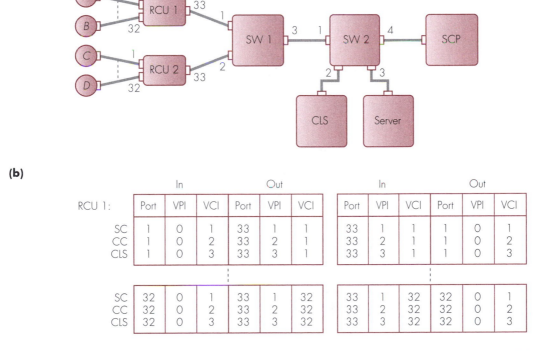

Figure 10.12 ATM LAN routing example: (a) network segment; (b) example routing table entries.

(b cont.)

RCU 2:

	In Port	VPI	VCI	Out Port	VPI	VCI	In Port	VPI	VCI	Out Port	VPI	VCI
SC	1	0	1	33	1	1	33	1	1	1	0	1
CC	1	0	2	33	2	1	33	2	1	1	0	2
CLS	1	0	3	33	3	1	33	3	1	1	0	3
	⋮						⋮					
SC	32	0	1	33	1	32	33	1	32	32	0	1
CC	32	0	2	33	2	32	33	2	32	32	0	2
CLS	32	0	3	33	3	32	33	3	32	32	0	3

SW 1:

	In Port	VPI	VCI	Out Port	VPI	VCI	In Port	VPI	VCI	Out Port	VPI	VCI
SC	1	1	X	3	1	X	3	1	X	1	1	X
CC	1	2	X	3	2	X	3	2	X	1	2	X
CLS	1	3	X	3	3	X	3	3	X	1	3	X
SC	2	1	X	3	4	X	3	1	X	2	4	X
CC	2	2	X	3	5	X	3	2	X	2	5	X
CLS	2	3	X	3	6	X	3	3	X	2	6	X

X = 1–32

SW 2:

	In Port	VPI	VCI	Out Port	VPI	VCI	In Port	VPI	VCI	Out Port	VPI	VCI
SC	1	1	X	4	1	X	4	1	X	1	1	X
CC	1	2	X	1	Y	X	1	Y	X	1	2	X
CLS	1	3	X	2	3	X	2	3	X	1	3	X
SC	1	4	X	4	4	X	4	4	X	1	4	X
CC	1	5	X	1	Y	X	1	Y	X	1	5	X
CLS	1	6	X	2	6	X	2	6	X	1	6	X
CLS'	2	10	Z	3	10	Z	3	10	Z	2	10	Z

X = 1–32
Y = 2/5
Z = 1–64

CLS:

In VPI	VCI	Out VPI	VCI	In VPI	VCI	Out VPI	VCI
3	X	10	Y	10	Y	3	X
6	X	10	Y	10	Y	6	X

X = 1–32
Y = 2/5

SCP: Calls in progress

Signaling channel VPI	VCI	Call channels In Port	VPI	VCI	Out Port	VPI	VCI	Call type details
1	X	1	2	X	1	Y	X	–
4	X	1	5	X	1	Y	X	–

SC = signaling channel   CC = call channel
CLS = workstation/CLS channel   CLS' = CLS/server channel

Figure 10.12 Continued

10.5.1 Call processing

As we saw in Figure 10.11 and its associated text, there are two types of traffic associated with an ATM LAN: that relating to the message flows exchanged between the distributed community of ATM-enabled stations and their associated servers, and that relating to the message flows exchanged between the bridges/routers that form the interface with the various legacy LAN segments/subnets and their associated servers. Also, in the case of multimedia stations, there are two types of call: one connection-oriented and the other connectionless. The first relates to network services such as telephony and videophony, while the second relates to more conventional data services similar to those used with legacy LANs. We shall consider the three types separately.

Connection-oriented calls

Services such as telephony and videophony require a separate VC to be set up between any pair of workstations for the duration of the call. The standards relating to this type of service are based on those used to set up calls in an ISDN since, in principle, the operation of setting up and clearing calls is the same as that used to perform the same function within an ISDN. All the (signaling) messages relating to the setting up and clearing of calls are carried over a separate channel – called the **signaling virtual channel connection** (**SVCC**) – which is independent of that used for carrying the message flows associated with the call. When the network is first configured or a new outlet added, a semipermanent VC is set up by network management between each network outlet and the central signaling control point. This is analogous to installing a physical wire connection between each telephone outlet and a local (telephone) PBX.

When an SVCC is set up by network management, an entry is also made in the routing table of the SCP. This consists of the ATM network address of the workstation together with the allocated routing address; that is, the VPI/VCI addresses used in the headers of cells that are received/output by the SCP from/to this workstation. The network address of each station is analogous to that of a telephone outlet and hence is a hierarchical address that uniquely identifies the station in the context of the total network. These have a standard format and, in ATM LANs, are 20-byte addresses.

To initiate the setting up of a call, the user of the station follows a dialog which involves specifying the address of the required recipient of the call and also the call type – telephony, videophone, and so on. This, in turn, results in the exchange of signaling messages using the signaling protocol set in the station and a similar protocol set in the SCP computer. The protocol architecture to support this was shown earlier in Figure 10.6 and the signaling protocol set is defined in **Recommendation Q.2931**. This is based on the ISDN signaling protocol set to ascertain whether the user is prepared to receive a call. If the response is positive, this is communicated back to the SCP which proceeds to set up a (duplex) VC across the network by adding entries into each switch routing table that links the port/VPI/VCI of the calling station with that of the called station. The SCP then informs the calling station that a VC has been set up and the call commences. In a similar way, either user can invoke the closing down of the connection at any time by initiating the sending of appropriate disconnection messages over the separate signaling channel.

To set up a call involving multiple stations – for example, for a teleconferencing or videoconferencing session – all the stations must be fully interconnected. For small numbers of stations this can be done by the SCP directly using a similar procedure to that used for a two-party call. Since in some instances the number of stations involved may be large, an alternative approach is to route all the information flows relating to such calls via a central routing point called the broadcast server.

Using this approach, to set up a conferencing session, the initiator of the session communicates with the SCP as before – using the signaling channel – but this time indicates a conferencing call – and its type – and the addresses of the stations involved. The SCP, in turn, communicates with the user of each of these stations – using their signaling channels and associated protocol set – to ascertain their availability and willingness to participate in a conferencing session. On receipt of their responses, the SCP initiates the setting up of a switched VC between each station that returns a positive response and the broadcast server. It then informs, firstly, the broadcast server of the type of call and the set of switched VCs involved, and secondly, the users of the stations that the session can commence. The session then proceeds with the broadcast server relaying the information flows received from each station out to all the other stations. These play out the received information under the control of the user of the station, for example, by using a separate window for each member of a videoconferencing session.

Connectionless calls

As we mentioned earlier, ATM-enabled stations are often introduced in an incremental way as existing frame-based LAN segments are replaced by cell-based (ATM) segments. A major issue when considering connectionless working is interworking, not only between ATM (cell-based) stations, but also between such stations and stations that are connected to legacy-LAN segments.

As we explained in Chapter 8, most large legacy LANs consists of a number of LAN segments of the same type interconnected by bridges. Alternatively, if the segments are of different types, as we saw in Chapter 9, they are interconnected by subnet routers. Recall that when using bridges all routing is carried out at the MAC sublayer. When using routers, however, routing is carried out at the IP/IPX layer. Both the MAC and IP layers provide a best-effort connectionless service for the transfer of preconfigured frames or datagrams, respectively. To support interworking between a station with a cell interface and a station connected to a legacy LAN, two alternatives must be supported: one for use with a bridged LAN and the other for use with a router-based LAN. With the first, the interface between the ATM LAN and the legacy LAN is a bridge and with the second the interface is a subnet router. Two different protocol architectures are used, each of which provides seamless interworking in the appropriate environment. We shall consider each separately.

LAN emulation

The method used when bridges form the interface to the legacy LAN has been developed by a group of companies that are all involved in the manufacture of LAN networking equipment. This group is called the **ATM Forum**. The various networking components used with this method are shown in Figure 10.13(a).

The aim of the various networking components is to emulate the broadcast mode of operation of a legacy LAN over a connection-oriented ATM LAN. The term used to describe this method is known as **LAN emulation (LE)**. The three components used are an **LE configuration server (LECS)**, an **LE server (LES)**, and a **broadcast and unknown-address server (BUS)**. Although each is shown as a separate entity in Figure 10.13, for a small LAN, they may all be implemented in a single computer. In this case, the message/frames relating to each component are identified by the type of virtual channel connection (VCC) on which they arrive.

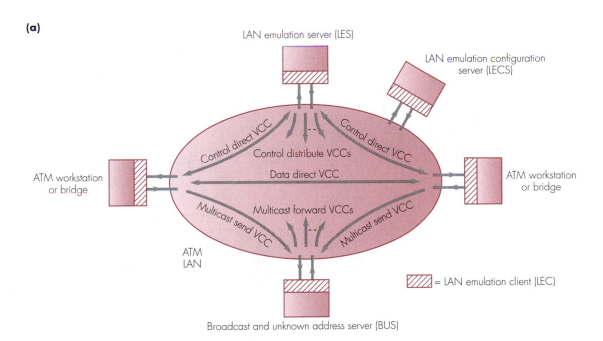

(a)

Figure 10.13 LAN emulation: (a) terminology and networking components; (b) unicast protocol architecture; (c) multicast protocol architecture.

(b)

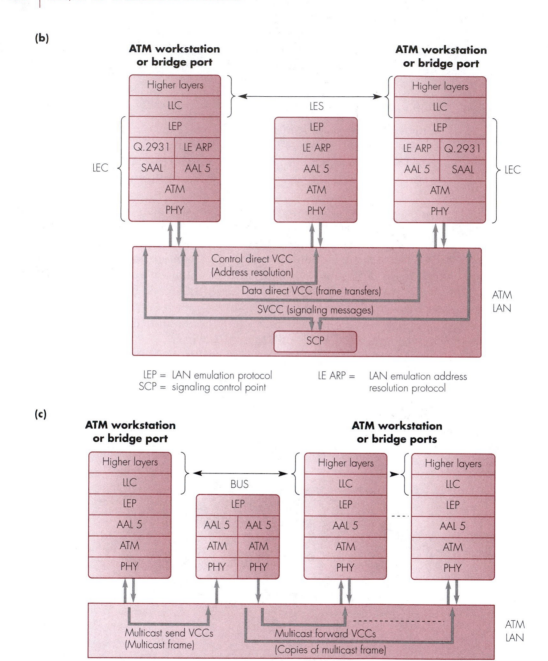

LEP = LAN emulation protocol
SCP = signaling control point

LE ARP = LAN emulation address
resolution protocol

(c)

Figure 10.13 Continued

In a large installation there may be multiple emulated LANs each of which has its own LES and BUS. The LECS is used by all stations that are connected to the total ATM LAN to determine the ATM addresses of the LES and BUS. There is a reserved VCC to connect all stations to the LECS for this purpose. The LES provides an address resolution service to convert from 48-bit MAC addresses into 20-byte ATM addresses. The BUS is responsible, firstly, for supporting multicasting/broadcasting, and secondly, for relaying frames to stations whose MAC address is unknown by the LES.

All stations connected to the ATM LAN – ATM-enabled stations, bridges, and so on – have an **LE client** (**LEC**) subsystem associated with them. This comprises hardware and software that provides a similar service to the MAC chipset (and associated software) in a station that is connected to a legacy LAN. When a station is powered up, it goes through an initialization procedure at the end of which it has initialized certain operational parameters and its own set of addresses – as described below, a station has more than one address. As we can see in Figure 10.13(a), a separate pair of VCCs is used to connect each LEC to the LECS, the LES, and the BUS. Once initialized, the LEC first obtains the pair of VCCs of the LES and BUS from the LECS and then proceeds to register itself with both the LES and BUS. At the end of the initialization phase, both the LES and BUS have the set of addresses of all active stations that are connected to the ATM LAN. In the case of a bridge, the LEC can either register the MAC addresses of all stations that are connected to its legacy LAN port or, more usually, just the address of the port through which it is connected to the ATM LAN. In the first case the bridge operates in the **nonproxy mode** and in the second, the **proxy mode**.

We can see in Figure 10.13(b) that the protocol stack within each LEC contains a **LAN emulation protocol** (**LEP**) layer – immediately below the LLC sublayer – which communicates with a similar layer in the LES. In order to make the underlying network transparent to the LLC sublayer, the service provided by the LEP layer is a connectionless service similar to that offered by the MAC sublayer. The two user service primitives are LE_UNITDATA.request and LE_UNITDATA.indication.

To emulate a broadcast LAN, both primitives have a source and destination MAC address as parameters. This means that each workstation and bridge connected to the ATM LAN, in addition to a 20-byte ATM address, has a 48-bit MAC address associated with it. It also has a 2-byte **LEC identifier** (**LECID**) which is used to identify uniquely the ATM workstation or bridge port among those currently attached to the LES. We shall look at the function of the LECID later.

The VCC that (logically) connects an LEC to the LES is called the **control direct VCC**. On receipt of an LE service request primitive, the LEP in the source LEC reads the source and destination MAC addresses and passes these to the **LE address resolution protocol** (**LE ARP**). The latter forms an address resolution request message – containing the two MAC addresses and the ATM address of the LEC – and sends this to the LE ARP in the LES over the control direct VCC. Assuming the LE ARP in the LES knows the ATM address of the destination LEC, it returns this in a reply message to the requesting LE ARP – the latter initiates the setting up of a **data direct VCC** between itself and the LE ARP in the destination LEC. This is done using either the SCP and the signaling protocol set described earlier for connection-oriented calls or, with some ATM switch architectures, directly by the two LE ARPs involved. The connection is cleared by the LE ARP when no further frames are received for the same destination LEC within a defined timeout interval.

If the LE ARP in the LES does not have the ATM address of the destination LEC – for example, if the destination MAC address relates to a station connected to the legacy LAN port of a bridge – the LES sends a copy of the LE ARP request message to all registered LECs using the set of **control distribute VCCs**. The LE ARP which has knowledge of the destination MAC address then replies with the corresponding ATM address – or its own ATM address if it is a bridge – using the control direct VCC. Once the source LE ARP has obtained the ATM address of the destination, it sets up a data direct VCC as before.

The flow of data frames, each of which has the source and destination MAC addresses at its head, can then start. Since bridges are involved, these can be either Ethernet, 802.3 or 802.5 frames with the frame type defined in the header of the frame. No FCS field is required since, in an ATM LAN, this is performed by the AAL 5 sublayer. Because of the use of the intermediate address resolution phase, the LE connectionless service is said to be provided *indirectly*.

The foregoing relates to unicasting, that is, there is a single destination station for each submitted MAC frame. To implement multicasting, a copy of the created MAC frame must be forwarded to all stations that belong to the same multicast group. Clearly, using the method just described, a multiplicity of switched VCs would be required between each member of the group and all other members. To avoid this requirement, the BUS is used and the associated protocol architecture is as shown in Figure 10.13(c).

An additional pair of VCCs is used between the LEC in each station and the LEC in the BUS. In the station-to-BUS direction, the VCC is known as the **multicast send VCC** and in the reverse direction, the **multicast forward VCC**. On receipt of a service primitive with a multicast destination address, the LEP creates a frame as before but with its own 2-byte LECID at the head. It sends this directly to the LEP in the BUS over the multicast send VCC. On receipt of the frame, the LEP broadcasts a copy of the frame to all stations using the set of multicast forward VCCs. The LEP in each station first determines from the LECID at the head of the frame whether it originated the frame. If it did, then the LEP simply discards the frame. This is known as **echo suppression**. If the LECID does not match that of the station, the receiving LEP determines from the multicast address at the head of the frame whether this station is part of the multicast group. If it is, the frame is passed up to the LLC layer, if not, the frame is discarded.

The unknown address service associated with the BUS enables an LEP to send a limited number of frames to their intended destination during the period a data direct VCC is being set up. The procedure followed is the same as that for a multicast frame and, since multiple copies of each frame are sent – each over a separate multicast forward VCC – a limit is set on the number of such frames the LEP can send. Any further frames received must then be retained – cached – until the data direct VCC is in place.

Classical IP over ATM

The method used when subnet routers form the interface to the legacy LAN has been developed by the Internet Engineering Task Force (IETF). The basic method is known as **classical IP over ATM** (**IPOA**).

Recall from Chapter 9 that, using the IP, before a station/host can exchange datagrams with another station, it must first know the IP/MAC address-pair of its local subnet router. Also, the local subnet router must know the address-pair of all the stations that are connected to the LAN segments to which it is attached. These are acquired using the ARP protocol and exploiting the broadcast nature of legacy LANs. Once these have been acquired, all datagrams/packets are exchanged between two stations via the router and it is this that relays the packets to their intended destination using the MAC address corresponding to the IP destination address in the datagram header.

To emulate the same operation with a non-broadcast ATM LAN, a permanent VCC is set up between all stations and router ports that are connected to the ATM LAN and a central node known as the connectionless server (CLS). The CLS provides a dual function of address resolution and a datagram/packet relaying service. Since with this method all packets are relayed directly by the CLS, the connectionless service is said to be provided *directly*. The protocol architecture used with a CLS is shown in Figure 10.14.

The ARP in each station/router port first registers its own address-pair – IP and ATM addresses – with the ARP in the CLP using the corresponding permanent VCC. In a similar way, the ARP in the CLS can acquire the address-pair of a station or router port that is connected to it by a VCC. In this way, the ARP in the CLS builds up a routing table containing the address-pair of all stations and router ports that are connected to it. Whenever a station IP has a datagram to send, it simply sends the datagram to the IP layer in the CLS over the VCC that connects the station to the CLS. On receipt of the datagram, the IP in the CLS first reads the destination IP address from the head of the datagram and uses this to obtain the corresponding ATM address from its routing table. The IP then forwards the datagram/packet to the destination over the corresponding VCC.

Multicasting with a CLS is carried out in a similar way to that described with an LES except with a CLS a separate broadcast server is not required. Instead, on receipt of a datagram with a multicast address, the IP layer in the

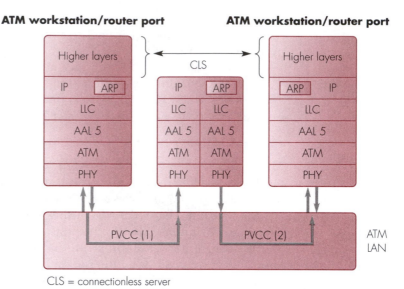

CLS = connectionless server

Figure 10.14 Protocol architecture to support classical IP over an ATM LAN.

CLS simply sends a copy of the datagram to all other stations using their corresponding VCC. Each recipient IP then determines from the multicast address at the head of the datagram whether it is a member of the multicast group. If it is, the datagram is passed to the higher protocol layers, if not, the datagram is discarded.

When a CLS is being used, there are two alternative relaying modes. With the first, the complete datagram is reassembled by the AAL before it is processed by the IP layer. Clearly, this introduces delays and requires significant buffer storage for its implementation. In order to reduce these overheads, we may use a second mode of working known as **streaming** or **pipelining**. In practice, the destination address required for routing is carried in the first ATM segment/cell and hence in this mode, the first (beginning of message) segment is passed directly to the IP layer for processing as soon as it is received by the AAL protocol. The new VC is then determined and this and the remaining segments making up the datagram are relayed directly without reassembly. The AAL with this method is AAL 3/4 since the MID field in the header of each cell is required for identification purposes during the reassembly process.

10.6 ATM MANs

Metropolitan area networks (**MANs**) have been installed by a number of network providers to meet the demand from customers for a switched high-speed LAN interconnection facility. Prior to the introduction of MANs, the only way of interconnecting a set of LANs that belong to different enterprises was by means of high bit rate leased lines. The disadvantage of this approach is the large number of leased lines that are required and, for each additional site, a new set of lines must be put in place. Initially, the LANs were all distributed around a large town or city but later the service was extended to cover multiple towns and cities.

All MANs operate using the asynchronous transfer mode and hence one approach to implementing a MAN is to use a set of interconnected ATM switches similar to the ATM backbone network we showed earlier in Figure 10.11. An alternative (and often less costly) solution is to use a high bit rate shared transmission medium. This is the approach taken in **distributed queue dual bus** (**DQDB**) MANs and, since this has been adopted by a number of providers, we shall limit our discussion of MANs to DQDB.

DQDB is an international standard that is defined in **IEEE 802.6**. The standard relates to a single subnetwork in the context of a larger network; typically, the larger network comprises a number of interconnected DQDB subnetworks. Each subnetwork is made up of **dual contradirectional buses** – that is, two unidirectional buses running in opposite directions – to which a distributed community of **access nodes** – also known as **customer network interface units** – are attached. The buses may be in an **open bus topology** or a **looped bus topology**, in which case the two ends are separate but physically colocated. As we shall see later, this can be used to provide better fault tolerance. Three example applications are shown in Figure 10.15: part (a) shows a single subnetwork MAN; part (b) a typical split-site private network; and part (c) a large wide area public network comprising multiple interconnected MANs.

As part (a) shows, a single DQDB MAN subnetwork can cover an area in excess of 30 miles (50 km). In this example, the access nodes may be located at the telephony switching offices in that area. The use of 34/45/140/155 Mbps circuits provides **seamless interconnection** for many LANs distributed around the city; that is, two users at different sites communicating with one another will be unaware of the fact that an intermediate network is involved.

Part (b) illustrates the use of two DQDB subnetworks in a private network application. In this instance, all the networking equipment located at both sites are privately owned and run and the high bit rate circuit interconnecting both sites leased from a public carrier. One site is assumed to have a looped bus topology and the other an open bus. This example also shows how a DQDB network can be used for the interconnection of two private telephone exchanges (PBXs) which requires a constant bit rate channel.

Part (c) illustrates how several multisubnetwork MANs can be interconnected together to form a larger network that spans several cities. As we can

(a)

(b)

(c)

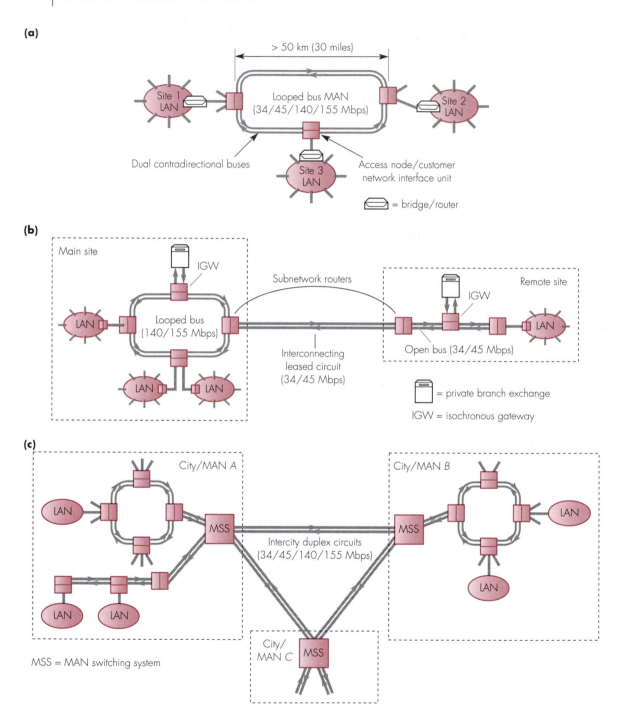

Figure 10.15 DQDB/MAN network architectures: (a) single-site MAN; (b) dual-site private network; (c) wide area multiple MAN network.

see, in this case each DQDB subnetwork in a city is connected to a **MAN switching system** (**MSS**). The MSS, on receipt of each LAN frame, either relays it directly to the required subnetwork – if it is connected to it – or it forwards the frame to the required MSS over the appropriate intercity duplex circuit. Such a network provides a **switched multimegabit data service** (**SMDS**) similar in principle to that provided by a frame relay network.

Normally, a LAN is connected to its nearest access node by either a remote bridge or a router. All frames are transported across each DQDB subnetwork in the form of fixed-sized units known as segments. At the interface to each subnetwork, the frames are first fragmented into segments and then reassembled back into their original form at the destination. Because the format of LAN frames differs from one type of LAN to another, prior to the transfer of a frame, a standard header and trailer are added to it. With public networks, the header contains two new source and destination addresses which are the networkwide addresses of the corresponding customer access/interface units. As we shall see in Section 10.6.7, these are hierarchical addresses which identify the MSS, the subnetwork, and the customer access unit. All segments are transferred over each subnetwork using both buses which, because these pass data in opposite directions, ensures that a copy of each segment transmitted is received by all nodes on the subnetwork. Between subnetworks, routing is carried out on reassembled frames using the networkwide destination address at the head of each frame.

10.6.1 Subnetwork architectures

A schematic diagram of an open dual-bus subnetwork is shown in Figure 10.16(a). At the head of each bus is a **slot generator** which generates a contiguous stream of **slots** each capable of transferring a standard 53-octet cell. Access nodes are attached to both buses through read and write connections, with the read operation performed ahead of the write operation. The physical layer in each access node reads the contents of each slot without modifying its contents, and only if new data is to be sent by an access node does it overwrite the existing contents. We can conclude, therefore, that an access node only copies (reads) data from a bus, it does not remove it. Also, it only changes the contents of a slot when it is permitted to do so by the access protocol. Hence failure of the access unit within a node does not have any effect on the contents of the slots that pass by on the two buses providing the failure does not cause the node continuously to write.

A looped bus architecture is shown in Figure 10.16(b) and, as we can see, in this configuration both slot generators are colocated. Alternatively, the same slot generator can be used for both buses. In both cases, the two buses are still independent and are not connected together as in a ring network. Also, in addition to generating slots, the **head of bus** is responsible for passing management information to the access nodes. Typically, management information is generated by a separate network management station and

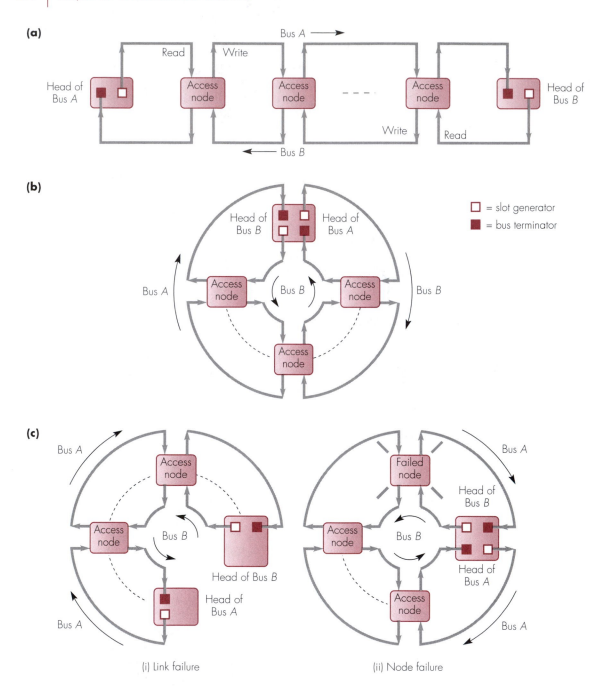

Figure 10.16 DQDB architectures: (a) open bus; (b) looped bus; (c) example reconfigured looped bus networks.

relates to either the allocation of isochronous bandwidth or the operational integrity of the subnetwork.

With a looped bus topology reconfiguration can be supported in the event of a link or a node failure by replicating the head of bus functions so that more than one node can assume the role of head of bus. Two examples of reconfigured loops are shown in Figure 10.16(c); the first illustrates the reconfigured loop after a link failure and the second the reconfigured loop after the failure of an access node. The reconfiguration operation is carried out under the control of a remote network management station.

10.6.2 Protocol architecture

Figure 10.17(a) identifies the components of the protocol architecture defined in IEEE 802.6. As with the other IEEE 802 standards, this defines the operation of the MAC sublayer – known as the DQDB layer in the standard – and the physical layer.

In addition to the normal connectionless (best-effort) data service provided for the interconnection of the frame-based LAN types, the DQDB MAC sublayer provides two additional services: a connection-oriented (reliable) data service and an isochronous service. Typically, the latter is used for the interconnection of two private (telephone) branch exchanges. For such applications, the multiplexed voice samples within the duplex link connecting the exchanges to their access nodes must be transferred across the bus at the same rate as the access link, hence the term "isochronous".

MAC sublayer

As Figure 10.17(a) shows, the MAC sublayer comprises four main functions: convergence, bus arbitration, common, and layer management. As we indicated earlier, all information is transferred across the dual buses in the form of fixed-sized segments. The convergence functions are required to convert all incoming source information into segments before its transfer and back into its original form before its delivery. For example, the MAC convergence function fragments the data frames submitted by a bridge or router into multiple segments ready for their transfer and, on receipt, reassembles them back into frames prior to their delivery.

There are two alternative control modes for gaining access to the slots on the two buses: **queued arbitrated** (**QA**) and **prearbitrated** (**PA**). When isochronous services are supported, in order to provide a constant bit rate service, the required number of slots are preallocated and marked by the head-of-bus node. The prearbitrated function in each node providing the service is responsible for identifying the reserved slots relating to it – from an identifier at the head of each slot – and then either initiating the transmission of the isochronous data within these or receiving the data contained within them. All the remaining bus slots are used for the transfer of LAN information frames. Access to these slots is controlled by a distributed queuing algorithm in the queued arbitrated function block.

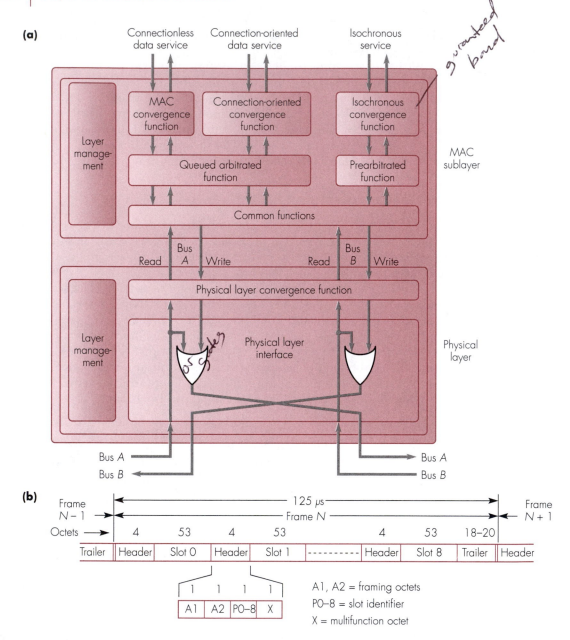

Figure 10.17 DQDB protocol architecture: (a) layer functions; (b) example physical layer convergence function.

We can see from Figure 10.17(a) that the common function block forms the interface between the physical layer and the two bus arbitration function blocks. The physical layer interface takes the form of single octet transfers – read and write – to and from both buses. The main role of the common function block is to relay octets between the physical layer and the appropriate bus arbitration function. This involves detecting the start and end of each slot and examining selected octets within the slot/cell header according to its defined format. We shall consider this in more detail in Section 10.6.6. In addition, since more than one node can act as the head of bus (to enhance reliability) the nodes which can perform this function take part in the reconfiguration operation of the bus/loop when faults are detected. Also, when selected as the head of bus, the node generates contiguous streams of slots. Both these operations form part of the common functions.

Physical layer

The physical layer provides a standard interface to the MAC sublayer. However, as Figure 10.15 showed, the physical layer can be implemented using a range of different transmission media. For example, with public networks this can be 34, 45, 140, or 155 Mbps. As we saw in Sections 7.2.3 and 7.2.4, such circuits utilize different framing formats and so a **physical layer conversion function** – which establishes a contiguous sequence of slots over the selected physical transmission medium – must be provided. An example of how this is achieved is shown in Figure 10.17(b).

The example relates to the use of a 34.368 Mbps E3 digital circuit. As the numbering indicates, this is at the third level in the PHD multiplexing hierarchy and is used to transmit four 8.448 Mbps streams. As we showed in Figure 7.17, a number of bits/octets are used for framing and other purposes and hence a lower bit rate is available for the transmission of DQDB slots. When using such circuits for each bus, the head of bus establishes the frame structure shown in Figure 10.17(b) using the available transmission bandwidth. This has a duration of 125 µs which ensures that the frame can be used to support various constant bit rate voice services as well as data transfer. As we can see, preceding each 53-octet slot is a 4-octet header. The first two octets of the header enable the physical layer convergence function in each node to synchronize to the start of each new frame. The third octet identifies the slots within each frame. The fourth octet is used for a number of functions including the transfer of management information from the head of bus to the two layer management entities in the attached nodes. The physical layer convergence function reads and interprets the octets in the header field but only passes the 53-octet cell in each slot to the MAC sublayer. Because of the fixed 125 µs interval, each frame does not contain an exact multiple of 57 octets. The unused octets in this field arise due to the plesiochronous (nearly synchronous) mode of operation of such circuits as described in Section 7.2.4. With higher bit rate circuits, the 125 µs interval is maintained and hence each frame contains proportionately more (DQDB) slots.

Finally, as with all the protocol layers, the layer management entities associated with the physical layer and MAC sublayer are provided for a remote management entity to control and monitor the operation of both these layers. For the MAC sublayer this involves receiving and acting upon information relating to the slots, for example, the list of identifiers that are carried at the head of each prearbitrated slot and the message identifiers that are at the head of queued arbitrated slots, the use of which we shall describe in Section 10.6.6. It also involves the setting of operational parameters such as timers and the activation of the configuration control procedure. All information relating to such operations is carried in the header that precedes each slot.

10.6.3 Queued arbitrated access protocol

Access to the slots that are available for the transfer of asynchronous data is based on a distributed queuing algorithm. This is known as **queued-packet distributed-switch** (**QPSX**) and the principles of the method are shown in Figure 10.18.

When interpreting the figure, it should be remembered that for an access control unit (ACU) to broadcast a segment/cell to all other ACUs, it must send a copy of the segment on both buses. Also, each bus operates independently and the QPSX algorithm ensures each ACU gains access to both buses in a fair way.

As part (a) shows, each slot contains two bits at its head that are used in the distributed queuing algorithm: the **busy** or **B-bit** and the **request** or **R-bit**. Also, as part(b) shows, access to the slots on each bus is controlled by a separate **request counter**. To ensure access to empty slots on each bus is fair, requests for slots on one bus are made using the R-bit in slots on the other bus. Then, for each counter, whenever a slot passes with the R-bit set, the contents of the corresponding counter are incremented by one. Similarly, whenever an empty slot is repeated at the interface of the opposite bus, the counter is decremented by one. At any point in time, therefore, the request counter for the corresponding bus contains the number of outstanding requests for slots on that bus from the access nodes that are downstream of the access node. Note that since there can be a different number of ACUs on each side of the access mode, each bus operates independently of the other.

Figure 10.18(c) shows that, to transmit a cell (containing a segment of data) on bus A, the sending access node transfers the current contents of the request counter for bus A to a second counter known as the **countdown counter**. The node then resets the contents of the request counter to zero and sets the R-bit in the first slot received on the opposite bus with the R-bit reset. This has the effect of placing the segment into the distributed queue for bus A. The same procedure is followed concurrently with the set of counters associated with bus B to place a copy of the segment in the distributed queue for bus B.

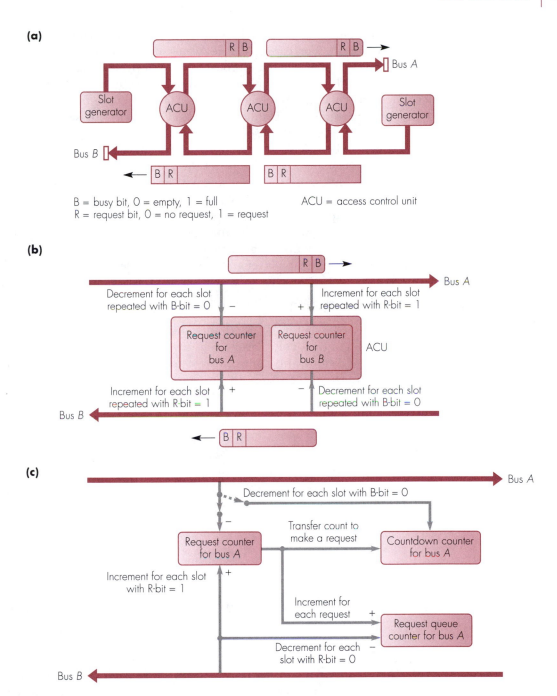

Figure 10.18 DQDB access control principles: (a) request/busy bits; (b) request counters; (c) queuing mechanism.

While a segment is queued for a bus, any slots that are repeated with their R-bit set cause the corresponding request counter to be incremented as before. However, slots which are repeated at the opposite bus interface with their B-bit reset (zero), cause only the countdown counter for that bus to be decremented. The queued segment is then transmitted on the bus when the corresponding countdown counter is zero and an empty slot is received.

In practice, since both buses operate independently, it is possible for a string of slots to be received on the opposite bus all with their R-bits set. This means that it may not be possible to set the R-bit in a slot – in response to a new request – until more than one segment has been queued and transmitted on the opposite bus. To allow for this, a third counter known as the (local) **request-queue counter** keeps a record of outstanding requests. Whenever a new request is made, the counter is incremented and, all the time the counter contents are greater than zero, whenever a slot is received with its R-bit reset, the R-bit is set and the counter is decremented.

10.6.4 Bandwidth balancing

Following the introduction of the draft standard of DQDB, detailed performance analyses of the queued-arbitrated protocol demonstrated that, under heavy load conditions, the nodes nearest to the head of each bus start to obtain preferential access to both buses relative to the nodes nearer the

---

Example 10.2

Derive a flowchart showing the steps taken by the queued arbitrated function to effect the transmission of a set of queued segments produced by the MAC convergence function on a single bus of a dual-bus DQDB subnetwork.

Answer:

A flowchart showing the steps to control the transmission of segments on bus A is given in Figure 10.19. Consider the following points when interpreting the figure:

■ On receipt of a full slot on either bus, the queued arbitrated function simply passes the contents of the slot payload directly to the MAC convergence function. This function determines whether the segment is intended for this node.

■ Only a single segment can be queued for transmission by the queued arbitrated function at one time. Hence only after this function has transmitted a segment does it return to the output queue of the MAC convergence function to determine whether another segment is awaiting transmission.

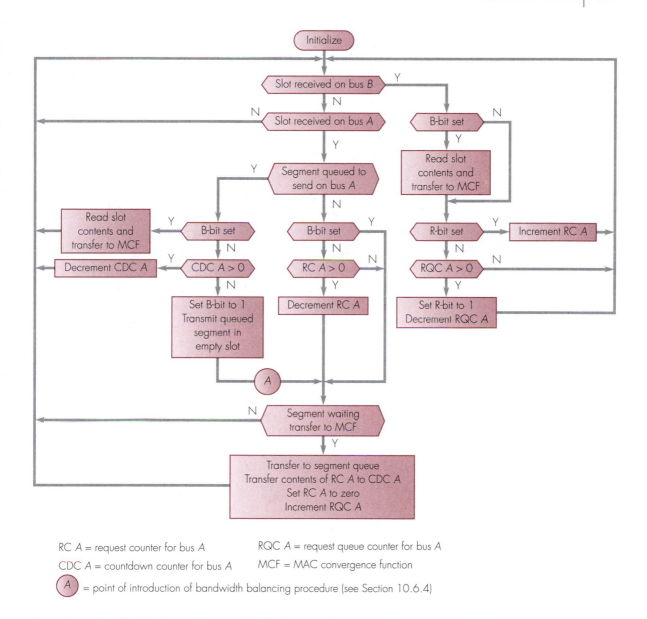

RC A = request counter for bus A   RQC A = request queue counter for bus A

CDC A = countdown counter for bus A   MCF = MAC convergence function

(A) = point of introduction of bandwidth balancing procedure (see Section 10.6.4)

Figure 10.19 Flowchart of the algorithm used to control the transmission and reception of segments on busA of a dual bus DQDB subnetwork.

centre of the bus. We can best understand the reason for the unfairness by remembering that the node at the head of each bus has first call on the use of the request bit in the slots that pass on one of the buses. Also, although the same node is the last to make requests on the other bus, the related empty slots pass this node first. Under heavy load conditions when the demand for slots starts to exceed supply, this has the effect shown in graphical form in Figure 10.20(a). The access delay variation relates to a heavily loaded subnetwork and is the same for both buses. As we can see, the unfairness increases as the network size increases and/or the bit rate increases.

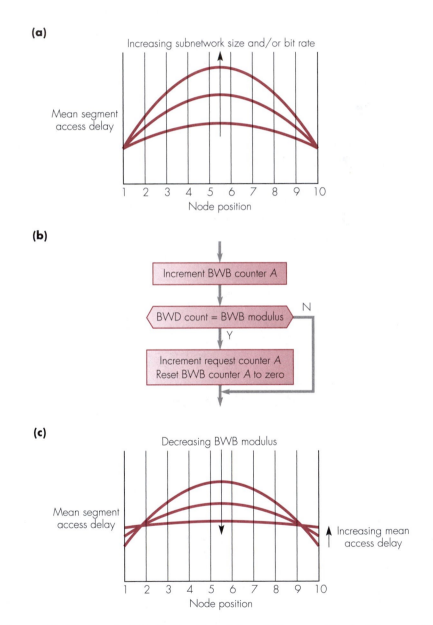

Figure 10.20 Bandwidth balancing: (a) unfairness effect; (b) remedial actions; (c) effect on mean access delay.

To overcome this effect, a modification to the basic access control algorithm known as the **bandwidth balancing mechanism** was introduced. To implement the scheme, a fourth counter called the **bandwidth balancing (BWB) counter** is introduced for each bus. Whenever a segment is transmitted on a bus, the BWB counter for that bus is incremented. Then, whenever the counter reaches a preset limit, the node allows an additional free slot to pass by on this bus by incrementing the corresponding request counter. The BWB counter is then reset to zero and the process repeats. The preset limit is called the **bandwidth balancing modulus**. This operation means that each node, after transmitting a block of segments equal to the BWB modulus, must allow an additional slot to pass by on the related bus. This can be used by the first node lower down the bus which has a queued segment to transmit and a zero countdown counter. The additional processing steps required are shown in Figure 10.20(b) and these are introduced at point A in the flowchart shown in Figure 10.19.

The bandwidth balancing mechanism obtains the necessary effect by reducing the utilization of each bus; the smaller the BWB modulus, the larger the bandwidth loss. This is shown in graphical form in Figure 10.20(c), which illustrates the impact of reducing the modulus for a single network type – size and bit rate. As we can see, as the modulus decreases, the unfairness decreases but at the expense of an increase in the mean access delay. In practice, a compromise is made and a value of 8 is normally used. In the worst case, this results in a loss of utilization of $1/(8+1)$ or 11.1%.

10.6.5 Prioritized distributed queuing

Although not always implemented, the basic queued arbitrated access control scheme just described can be extended to support the transmission of prioritized cells/segments. There can be three priority classes and each has a separate set of counters – request counter, countdown counter, and request-queue counter – for each bus. The three priority classes are 0, 1, and 2, with 2 having the highest priority. Cells/segments relating to data-only frames are always allocated class 0, and class 2 is reserved for the transfer of cells relating to network management messages. Class 1 is intended for the transfer of cells containing information that is sensitive to delay or delay variation. Note that bandwidth balancing is not used in this mode.

An example application that may use class 1 cells is for the transfer of compressed video information. As we saw in Section 4.3.1, although the information is generated at a constant rate – determined by the video frame refresh rate – the amount of information associated with each compressed frame varies and depends on the level of movement that has taken place relative to the previous frame. We can deduce that if the isochronous service is used then the (preallocated) bandwidth needs to be that required to transfer a completely new frame at the refresh rate. However, by using the queued arbitrated access method, the amount of information transferred can vary from one frame to the next. By assigning a higher priority to such segments, the priority control method endeavors to ensure that these are transferred before slots containing other types of LAN traffic.

The general arrangement for controlling access to bus *A* is shown in Figure 10.21. For clarity only the request and countdown counters are shown. A similar arrangement is used for access to bus *B*. As we can see, there is a separate R-bit for each priority class at the head of each slot/cell. These are shown as R0, R1, and R2, where R2 is the highest priority. Assume initially there are no segments waiting transmission on bus *A* from this node – part (a). The operation is as follows:

- When an empty slot (B = 0) is repeated at the interface with bus *A*, the access control unit for this bus decrements all three request counters by one.

- When a slot is repeated at the interface with bus *B* – with a priority of 1 for example – the access unit for bus *B* increments only request counters 1 and 0 – RC 1 and RC 0 – and leaves the higher priority counter – RC 2 – unchanged. This means that lower-priority requests do not delay the transmission of higher-priority segments.

Now assume that a segment becomes ready to transmit on bus *A* of priority 1 – part (b). The steps are as follows:

- The current contents of RC 1 are transferred to CDC 1 (and RC 1 is reset to zero) when a slot is repeated at the interface to bus *B* with the corresponding request bit reset to zero.

- When an empty slot is repeated at the interface with bus *A*, request counters RC 0 and RC 2 and countdown counter CDC 1 are decremented.

- If a slot with an R-bit of, say, priority 2 passes, then request counters RC 0 and 2 and countdown counter CDC 1 are incremented.

- The segment is transmitted when CDC 1 becomes zero and an empty slot is received.

Hence incrementing the lower priority countdown counter when a request for a higher priority slot is received, effectively delays the transmission of the lower-priority segment. This means that segments with a higher priority are always transmitted ahead of lower-priority segments.

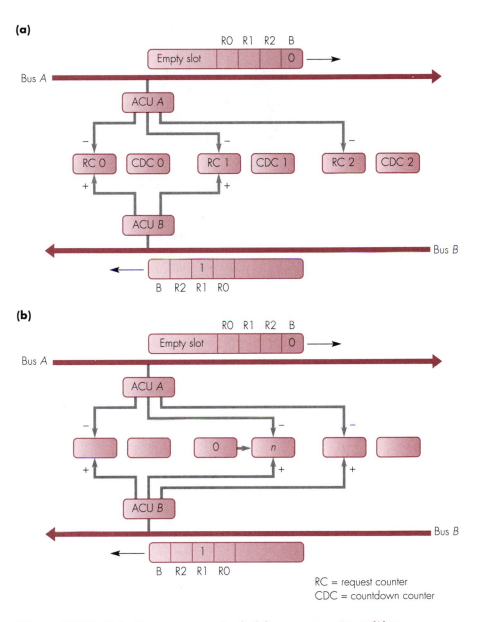

(a)

(b)

RC = request counter
CDC = countdown counter

**Figure 10.21 Priority access control: (a) no segments waiting;
(b) segments queued at priority 1.**

10.6.6 Slot and segment formats

As we saw in Section 10.6.2, the 53-octet slot/cell on each bus comprises a 5-octet header and a 48-octet payload (contents) field. The structure of the header is shown in Figure 10.22(a) and, as we can see, is similar to that used with an ATM network.

The *access control* field contains, in addition to the busy bit and three request bits, a *slot type* bit which indicates whether the slot is to be used for queued arbitrated or prearbitrated (isochronous) data. For slots containing either connection-oriented or isochronous data, the 20-bit *virtual channel identifier* (*VCI*) identifies the logical connection to which the cell contents relate. For LAN (also known as connectionless) data, the VCI is set to all 1s. The *payload type* indicates the type of data being carried. It is 00 for all user data – both queued arbitrated and prearbitrated – and the other bit combinations are used for management information. The *priority* has a default value of 00 and, for the moment, no other values have been defined. Finally, the *header check sequence* is an 8-bit CRC for error detection purposes.

To transfer connectionless data across the subnetwork – for example, a MAC frame between two remote bridges – the submitted frame is first divided

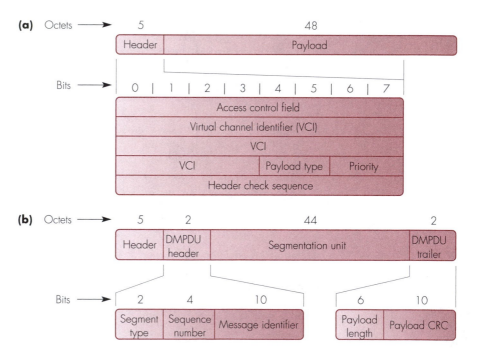

Figure 10.22 Slot and segment formats: (a) slot header; (b) connectionless data segment format.

(segmented) into multiple segments by the MAC convergence protocol in the source access control unit. On receipt, the same protocol at the destination reassembles the received segments back into the original frame. For connection-oriented and isochronous data, the VCI in the cell header is used by the destination to identify those cells which are intended for it. However, for connectionless data, an additional 2-octet header at the start of the 48-octet payload field is used instead. In addition, as Figure 10.22(b) shows, a 2-octet trailer is added at the end of the payload field.

Since segments containing connectionless data are part of a larger (MAC) data frame, they are called **derived MAC protocol data units** (**DMPDUs**). The segments relating to a frame – referred to as a message in the standard – are transferred in one of four segment types:

- **single segment message** (**SSM**): if the frame/message can be carried in a single segment;
- **beginning of message** (**BOM**): indicates this is the first segment of a multiple segment frame/message;
- **continuation of message** (**COM**): indicates the contents are between the start and end of a multiple segment frame/message;
- **end of message** (**EOM**): indicates the last segment.

The *sequence number* and *message identifier* are used together to enable the destination to reassemble the segments relating to a multiple segment message back into its original form.

The *sequence number* is used to detect any missing segments. It is set to zero in the first segment (BOM) and increments for each successive continuation segment (COM) and last segment (EOM). If a missing segment is detected, the remaining segments of the frame/message are discarded.

All segments relating to the same frame are allocated the same *message identifier* (*MID*) by the source access unit. This enables the remaining access units on the bus to identify the segments that relate to the same frame. To ensure these are unique, each access unit is allocated a separate block of identifiers when it is initialized. Clearly, a message identifier is not required in single segment messages and hence it is set to zero.

The trailer comprises two fields: the *payload length* and the *payload CRC*. As we shall see in Section 10.6.7, all submitted frames are padded out to be a multiple of 4 octets. This means that a segment may contain from 4 to 44 octets in multiples of 4 octets. Clearly, not all submitted frames will comprise multiples of 44 octets and hence the payload length indicates the actual number of octets in a single segment message or end of message segment. The payload CRC is a 10-bit CRC and is used to detect transmission errors in the entire 48-octet segment.

10.6.7 SMDS

In a public network the connectionless data service offered by the MAC convergence function is known as the switched multimegabit data service (SMDS) or the **connectionless broadband data service** (**CBDS**) by the ITU-T. In such networks, the various sublayer functions/protocols shown in Figure 10.17 are known as the **SMDS interface protocols** (**SIP**): the MAC convergence protocol is known as SIP level 3; the queued arbitrated protocol SIP level 2; and the physical convergence protocol SIP level 1. A typical interconnection schematic and associated internetworking protocol architecture are shown in Figure 10.23. In part(a) the two LANs are interconnected through MAC bridges while in part (b) IP routers are used.

Recall from Chapter 8 that the different types of LAN utilize different header formats, address types, and maximum frame sizes. To accommodate all types of MAC frame, the size of the **SMDS service data unit** can be up to 9188 octets. Also, because of the different addressing formats, prior to segmenting a submitted frame (SDU), the level 3 SIP first encapsulates the frame between a standard header and trailer. In addition, in order to simplify the buffering operation at the destinations, if necessary, it adds additional padding octets at the tail of the submitted frame so that its length is a multiple of 4-octets. The resulting message unit – referred to as a packet – is known as an initial MAC PDU (IMPDU) – or SIP level 3 PDU – and its format is shown in Figure 10.24(a).

Thus the SMDS network provides a connectionless service that is transparent to the customer's internetworking method. To achieve this, on receipt of a frame the access gateway – known as an SMDS edge gateway – simply broadcasts the frame over its local DQDB subnetwork using the queued-arbitrated access control protocol. In this way, a copy of all submitted frames is received by all the other gateways – access nodes – attached to the same DQDB subnetwork and, through them, by all the other bridges/routers. A decision is made by the latter whether to forward the frame on its LAN or simply discard it.

As we can see, the header comprises two or possibly three fields. The common header contains an 8-bit sequence number – known as the *begin-end tag* and used to enable the level 3 SIP to detect missing frames – and a specification of the amount of buffer memory required to store the complete IMPDU. The MAC convergence protocol (MCP) header contains a number of subfields relating to the protocol. These include the addresses of the source and destination gateways which, in a public network, are 60-bit E.164 addresses as defined for use with an ISDN. However, to cater for other address types these are both 64-bit address fields with the most significant 4 bits identifying the address types used in the remaining 60 bits – for example, 16/48-bit MAC addresses. Other subfields include the number of PAD octets present and an indication of whether a CRC is present or not. The header extension has been included to allow additional subfields to be added in the future.

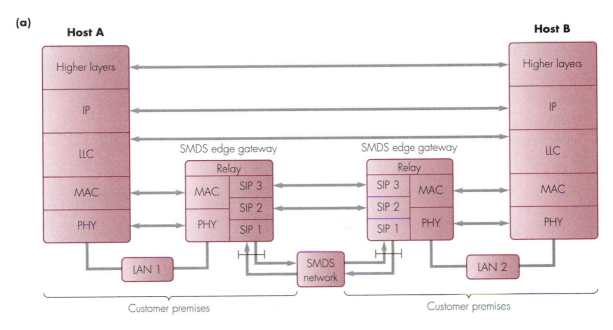

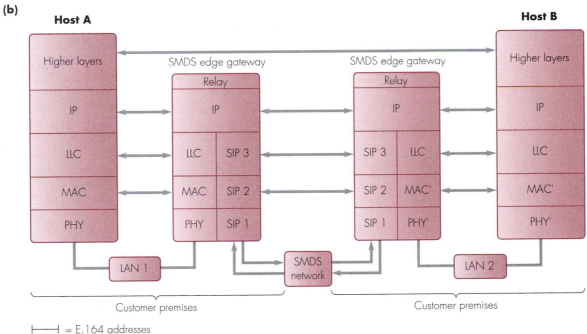

Figure 10.23 SMDS internetworking protocol architectures: (a) bridges; (b) routers.

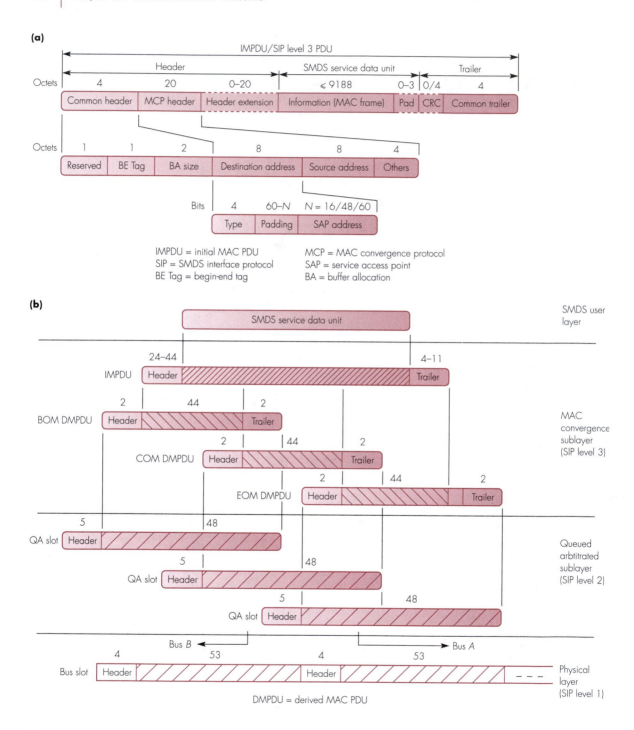

Figure 10.24 Frame transmission overheads: (a) initial MAC PDU format; (b) frame segmentation.

The trailer may include an optional 32-bit CRC which is used for error detection on the complete IMPDU. The common trailer contains the same information as the common header. Hence if the maximum header extension and CRC fields are present and the information field is the maximum 9188 octets, there is an integral number of 210 segments after segmentation.

The steps taken to transfer a submitted MAC frame across the SMDS network, together with the overheads associated with each sublayer function, are summarized in Figure 10.24(b). The submitted SMDS service data unit is first encapsulated by the MAC convergence protocol to form an IMPDU. It then segments this into a number of DMPDUs, each with the corresponding header and trailer. The resulting 48-octet segments are passed to the queued arbitrated function which adds the appropriate 5-octet header to them. Finally these are passed to the common function which initiates their transmission via the physical layer convergence sublayer. We can best quantify the overheads associated with each of these functions using an example.

Example 10.3

A 510-octet MAC frame is to be transferred across an SMDS/DQDB subnetwork. Stating clearly any assumptions you make, derive the number of queued arbitrated slots that are required to carry out the transfer and hence the total number of overhead octets involved.

Answer:

With reference to Figure 10.24(b):

■ MAC convergence protocol:
  – adds 2 octets to make the frame 512 octets which is an integral multiple of 4 octets;
  – assuming a header extension and CRC are not used, a 24-octet header and a 4-octet trailer are added to create a (512 + 24 + 4) 540-octet IMPDU;
  – total overheads = 2 + 24 + 4 = 30 octets;
  – after segmentation, the IMPDU requires 13 DMPDUs: 12 containing a full complement of 44 octets and one with 12 octets;
  – total overheads are 4 for each of the 13 DMPDUs (= 52) plus 32 for the part-full EOM DMPDU.

■ Queued arbitrated (QA) sublayer:
  – a further 5 octets are added to each 48-octet DMPDU to create 13 QA slots;
  – total overheads = 5 × 13 = 65 octets.

▶

10.3 Continued

- Physical layer:
  - a further 4-octet header is added to each QA slot;
  - total overheads = $4 \times 13 = 52$ octets.
- In summary:
  - QA slots required = 13;
  - total overheads = $30 + 52 + 32 + 65 + 52 = 231$ octets.

10.7 Wide area ATM networks

As we showed earlier in Figure 10.15(c), a number of network providers have created wide area ATM networks by interconnecting multiple MAN subnetworks together. As we indicated, each MAN subnetwork can be implemented using either DQDB or conventional ATM switches. Each MAN subnetwork is connected to a MAN switching system (MSS) and these in turn are interconnected by means of high bit rate lines. For the MSSs to perform their routing/switching function, the E.164 addresses in the header of each IMPDU are networkwide addresses which identify the MSS and subnetwork to which each access gateway is attached. In addition, group addressing is supported and, when the access node receives an IMPDU with a preassigned group address in its destination address field, a copy of the IMPDU is sent to all members of the group.

The interconnected LANs in the two protocol architectures we showed in Figure 10.23 were assumed to be frame-based LANs. However, a similar approach can be used to interconnect ATM LANs. Figure 10.25(a) shows typical arrangement, together with the associated protocol architecture. In this example we assume the connectionless service associated with the ATM LAN is provided at the IP layer. Hence, as we showed in Figure 10.14 and described in the accompanying text, a connectionless server (CLS) is used. However a similar approach is used when the connectionless service is being provided at the MAC sublayer with a LAN emulation server (LES).

As we can see in Figure 10.25(a), an ATM gateway is located at each customer site, one port of which is connected to the site ATM LAN and the other port to an ATM MAN. Typically, there are a number of gateways (sites) connected to the MAN in a particular area and this provides a local gathering and distribution function. As before, an MSS is connected to each MAN and the MSSs are interconnected together to form a wide area switched network. The service provided is the SMDS/CBDS and the ATM LAN gateway is the SMDS edge gateway.

(a)

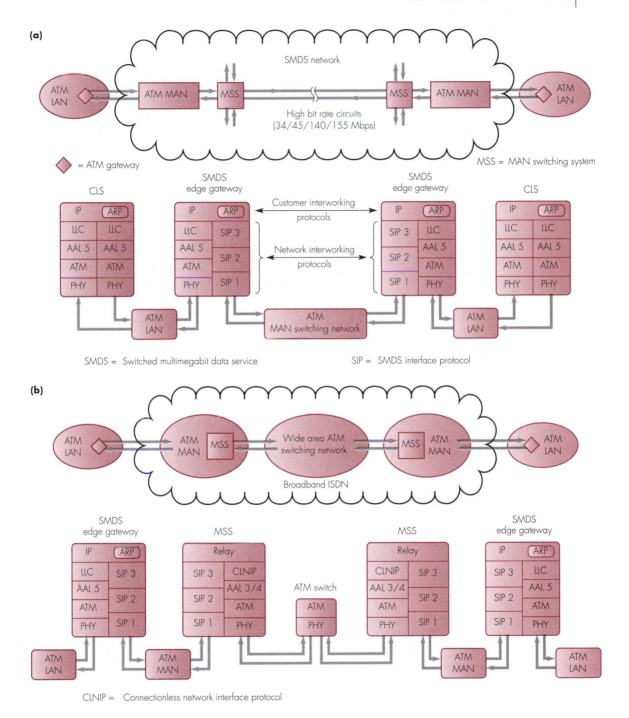

Figure 10.25 Connectionless working over wide area ATM networks: (a) ATM MAN switching network; (b) broadband ISDN.

On receipt of an IP datagram/packet with a destination address that indicates a different site network (netid), the CLS within the ATM LAN relays the packet to the ATM LAN port of the SMDS edge gateway. The packet – or MAC frame if LAN emulation is being used – is first encapsulated into a standardized frame format by the SIP level 3 protocol and then relayed across the SMDS network to the appropriate destination gateway. From there it is relayed first to the site CLS and from there to the destination station.

In some networks, the MSSs are interconnected by an ATM switching network rather than point-to-point high bit rate lines. This type of network, together with the protocol architecture associated with it, is shown in Figure 10.25(b). As we can see, this is similar to part (a) except in this case an intermediate ATM switching network is present. The **connectionless network interface protocol (CLNIP)** provides a similar service to the SIP level 3 protocol and the format of each CLNIP PDU is similar to that given earlier in Figure 10.24(a). The main difference is that there is no common header or trailer with the CLNIP PDU since this is provided by the AAL in an ATM network.

Summary

A summary of the topics discussed in this chapter is given in Figure 10.26.

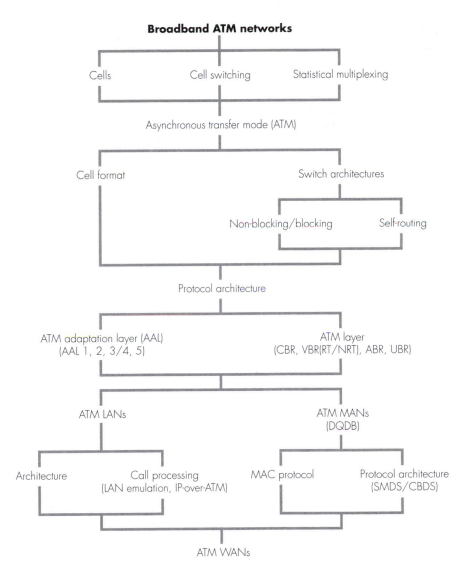

Figure 10.26 Broadband ATM networks, chapter summary.

Exercises

Section 10.1

10.1 Explain the origin/meaning of the following terms relating to B-ISDN networks:
(i) fixed-size cells,
(ii) statistical multiplexing,
(iii) cell switching,
(iv) asynchronous transfer mode.

10.2 Discuss the reasoning behind the choice of a connection-oriented mode of operation for B-ISDN networks and a 53-byte cell size.

10.3 Explain why the development of B-ISDN has been postponed. Identify those networks and networking equipment of that use ATM.

Section 10.2

10.4 With the aid of the cell switching schematic shown in Figure 10.1, explain
(i) how the header of each cell can be relatively short,
(ii) how cells are routed through an ATM switch,
(iii) the difference between VP routing and VC routing. Give an example of each routing type.

10.5 With the aid of the ATM format shown in Figure 10.2, explain the use of
(i) the payload type field,
(ii) the cell loss priority bit,
(iii) the header checksum.

Section 10.3

10.6 With the aid of the switch architecture shown in Figure 10.3(a), explain the principle of operation of an ATM switch. Include in your explanation the role of the input and output controllers, the switching matrix and the switch control processor. Also explain why cell buffers are required in the input and output controllers.

10.7 With the aid of the diagrams shown in Figure 10.3(b) and (c), explain the principle of operation of the following ATM switch matrix types:
(i) time division bus,
(ii) fully-connected.

Assuming they are to operate in a nonblocking mode, estimate the maximum number of I/O ports associated with each matrix type and what determines this.

10.8 Explain why large fabrics consist of multiple switching stages each made up of a number of smaller switching elements interconnected in a regular matrix.

10.9 In the context of a multistage delta switching matrix comprising a number of switching elements, if M is the number of input ports and N is the number of inputs per switching element, derive expressions for the number of switching elements per stage, X, and the number of stages, Y.

10.10 With the aid of the 8-port delta switching matrix shown in Figure 10.4, explain how a cell is routed through the matrix and how blocking can occur.

10.11 An example of a switching matrix that avoids blocking is the Batcher–Banyan switch matrix shown in Figure 10.5. Explain the principle of operation of such switches and how blocking is avoided.

10.12 Using the Batcher–Banyan switch matrix shown in Figure 10.5, identify the paths through the matrix followed by the following set of cells. Assume they arrive simultaneously at the eight input ports and the routing tags given start at port 1:

111, 100, 011, 000, 101, 001, 110, 010

Assume now that the routing tag of the call arriving at port 4 is 111 instead of 000. Determine the effect of this and how it is overcome in practice.

Section 10.4

10.13 With the aid of the protocol architecture shown in Figure 10.6, explain
    (i)   the role of the signaling control point and the network management stations,
    (ii) the meaning of the C, U, and M planes,
    (iii) the role of the AAL and ATM layer protocols.

10.14 With the aid of the diagram shown in Figure10.7, state the application domain of each of the four AAL service classes. Also explain the role of the CS and SAR sublayers in implementing these services. Include the use of the service access point.

10.15 With the aid of the two SAR PDU types shown in Figure 10.8, explain the use of the following fields:
    (i)   SN,
    (ii) SNP,
    (iii) IT.

10.16 Explain the difference between the AAL3/4 and AAL5 layers and why the latter was developed. Hence, using the PDU formats of the CS and SAR sublayers shown in Figure 10.9, derive the number of protocol overhead octets/bytes required to send an AAL service data unit of 1024 bytes using
    (i)   AAL3/4,
    (ii) AAL5.

10.17 Explain the role of the ATM layer including the meaning of the following service classes:
    (i)   CBR,
    (ii) VBR/RT,
    (iii) VBR/NRT,
    (iv) ABR,
    (v) UBR.

10.18 Explain the meaning of the terms "traffic descriptor" as applied to a call and the use of the following parameters associated with it:
    (i)   PCR,
    (ii) SCR,
    (iii) MCR,
    (iv) CDVT,
    (v) CLR,
    (vi) CTD,
    (vii) CDV.

10.19 In order to ensure the agreed operational parameters for a call are being adhered to, the network uses the generic cell rate algorithm. With the aid of the four example cell inter-arrival times shown in Figure 10.10, explain the principle of operation of the algorithm.

Section 10.5

10.20 In relation to the schematic diagram shown in Figure 10.11 of an ATM LAN explain the role of the following:
    (i)   an RCU,
    (ii) the broadcast server,
    (iii) the signaling control point and how stations communicate with it,
    (iv) the LAN emulation server.

10.21 With the aid of the connectionless protocol architecture shown in Figure 10.14, outline the steps followed to enable:
    (i)   a cell-based client to access a cell-based server
    (ii) a PC/workstation attached to a legacy LAN to access a server that is attached to a different legacy LAN (of the same type) both of which are connected to the ATM backbone by bridges
    (iii) a PC/workstation that is attached to a legacy LAN to access a server that is attached directly to the ATM backbone. Assume the legacy LAN is connected to the ATM backbone by a router.

Section 10.6

10.22 With the aid of the three DQDB MAN architectures shown in figure 10.15, explain the meaning/use of
    (i)   dual contradirectional buses,
    (ii) access node/customer network interface unit,
    (iii) open bus and dual bus topologies,
    (iv) isochronous gateway,
    (v) MAN switching system,
    (vii) SMDS.

10.23 With the aid of the DQDB architecture shown in Figure 10.16(a) and (b), state the differences between an open bus and a loop bus architecture. Explain the principle of operation of each type.

10.24 With the aid of the DQDB architecture shown in Figure 10.16(c). describe how a looped bus architecture can continue working in the presence of
(i)   a communications link failure and
(ii) a node failure.

10.25 With the aid of the DQDB protocol architecture shown in Figure 10.17, explain the meaning/use of
(i)   queued arbitrated and MAC convergence functions,
(ii) prearbitrated and isochronous conversion function,
(iii) common functions,
(iv) physical layer convergence function.

10.26 With the of a diagrams in Figure 10.18 and the flowchart in Figure 10.19, explain the principle of operation of the queued-packet distributed-switch (QPSX) access control method. Include the meaning/use of:
(i)   the busy and request bits in the header of each slot,
(ii) the request and countdown counters,
(iii) the request-queue counter.

10.27 With the aid of Figure 10.20(a), explain why bandwidth balancing is necessary with the QPSX access control method. Hence explain how the remedial actions shown in Figure 10.20(b) overcome the unfairness arising with the basic scheme.

10.28 With the aid of the access control schematic shown in Figure 10.21, explain the principle of operation of the distributed priority queuing mechanism used with multimedia applications. Include the role of the various counters and the effect on their contents of the request and busy bits when
(i)   no segments are queued for transmission, and
(ii) a segment is queued at a specified priority level.

10.29 Define the meaning of the terms "DQDB slot" and "DQDB segment". Hence with the aid of the formats shown in Figure 10.22, explain the role of the slot and segment headers.

10.30 Assuming a frame of data is to be transferred over a DQDB subnetwork and the frame requires multiple slots, with the aid of the segment format shown in Figure 10.22(b), explain the function of each field in the DMPDU header and trailer. Describe also the steps followed by the receiver when reassembling the frame.

10.31 Define the service offered by an SMDS network. Hence with the aid of the alternative protocol architectures shown in Figure 10.23, explain the function of the SIP level 3 and SIP level 2 protocols when the SMDS edge gateway is
(i)   a bridge and
(ii) a router.

10.32 Define the format of the source and destination addresses used in the header of an initial MAC PDU and why the size of an SMDS service data unit can be up to octets/bytes.

10.33 A 100-byte MAC frame is to be transferred access a DQDB SMDS network. Using the transmission overheads identified in Figure 10.24, derive:
(i)   the number of queued arbitrated slots that are required to carry out the transfer of the frame,
(ii) the total number of overhead bytes. State any assumptions you make.

Section 10.7

10.34 With the aid of the ATM MAN switching network and associated protocol architecture shown in Figure 10.25(a), explain
(i)   the role of the MAN switching system including the addressing mechanism associated with it,
(ii) how an IP datagram/packet is routed across the total network.

10.35 Identify and explain the differences when an ATM switch is used within the SMDS network. Include the role of the CLNIP protocol in the MSS.

Entertainment networks and high-speed modems

11.1 Introduction

As we saw in Section 1.4.3, entertainment applications include movie/video-on-demand, near video-on-demand, broadcast television, and interactive television. Also, as we saw in Section 4.3.4, the bit rate requirements for the (compressed) audio and video associated with these applications are determined by the bandwidth of the transmission channel to be used. Typical bit rates are:

VCR-quality video with sound:	1.5 Mbps (MPEG-1)
Broadcast-quality video with sound:	4/6/8 Mbps (MPEG-2, Main)
Studio-quality television with sound:	9/15/18 Mbps (MPEG-2, Main)
High-definition television with sound:	60/80 Mbps (MPEG-2, High)

Normally, the user interaction channel need only be a low bit rate channel of hundreds of kilobits per second. Currently, only VCR and broadcast quality video are used and hence the communications requirement to provide these services is an asymmetric channel consisting of a high bit rate (1.5/4/6/8 Mbps) channel from the service provider to the subscriber and a low bit rate return channel for interaction purposes.

In terms of the networks that are used, as we saw in Figure 1.16, interactions with a video server – for movie/video-on-demand – can be through either a cable network or the access network of a PSTN or ISDN. Alternatively, near video-on-demand can be obtained through either a cable network or a satellite/terrestrial broadcast network. Each can also provide interactive television with, in the case of satellite and terrestrial broadcast networks, the user interaction channel provided through a separate network such as a PSTN.

With a PSTN, the modems we described in Section 7.2.2 provide only a relatively low bit rate switched channel of up to 56 kbps. In addition to these, however, as we saw in Figure 1.1(c), high-speed modems are available which provide a non-switched asymmetric channel that can support applications such as VCR or broadcast quality video-on-demand and high-speed access to the Internet. In the case of cable networks, in addition to the modems used to support broadcast television, high-speed (cable) modems are also available that provide high-speed access to the Internet and other packet-based services. In this chapter we describe the principle of operation of the different types of broadcast television networks and how interactive services are provided with these networks. We also describe selected aspects of the technology associated with the high-speed modems used in cable and PSTN access networks for Internet access.

11.2 Cable TV networks

Essentially, a basic cable TV network is a television distribution facility. A set of TV programs is received from satellite and/or terrestrial broadcasts and the cable network is then used to distribute this set of programs to subscriber premises. Early cable television networks – of which there are still many in existence – are based entirely on coaxial cable. These were designed to distribute broadcast television (and radio) programs that are received at a central site to customer premises geographically distributed around an area such as a town or city. Such networks are known as **community antenna television (CATV) networks** and the basic elements of this type of network are shown in Figure 11.1.

A shared-medium, tree-and-branch architecture is used with, at the root, the various antennas and associated equipment located in a unit called the **cable headend (HE)**. Each branch of the tree is implemented using a single coaxial cable. With this type of network, the electrical signals associated with each television (and radio) program are analog. Hence in order to transmit multiple TV programs concurrently, modulated transmission is used with

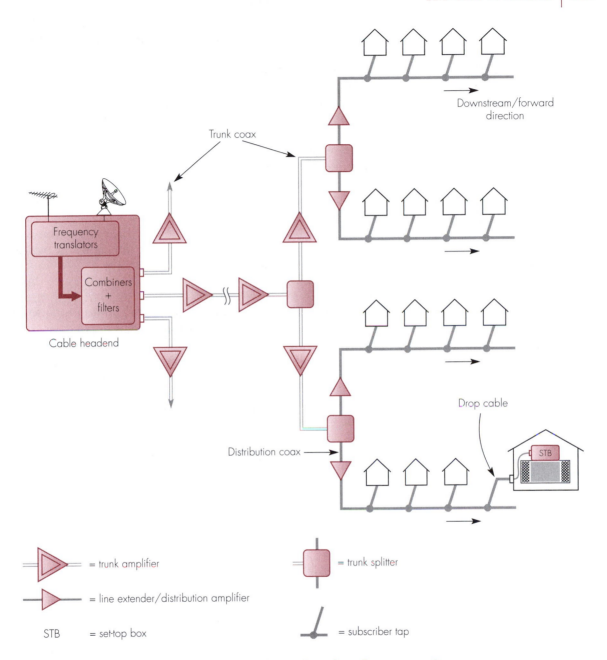

Downstream/forward direction

Trunk coax

Frequency translators

Combiners + filters

Cable headend

Drop cable

STB

Distribution coax

= trunk amplifier

= trunk splitter

= line extender/distribution amplifier

STB = set-top box

= subscriber tap

Figure 11.1 Early analog CATV distribution network and components.

each program/channel allocated a fixed portion of the cable bandwidth. The electrical signals of the complete set of TV programs are then multiplexed together onto the cable for distribution to all the network termination points. This technique is known as **frequency division multiplexing (fdm)**.

At each branch node in the cable distribution network, a **trunk splitter** is used to ensure the same set of signals propagate on each branch. Each home passed has a **subscriber tap** attached to the cable which forms the connection point to the distribution cable. A separate **drop cable** is used to connect the tap to the subscriber network termination unit located in the customer premises. The distance from the cable headend to the remotest customer/subscriber premises can be up to tens of miles/kilometers. So to compensate for signal attenuation, a large number of **trunk** and **distribution amplifiers** are required to ensure that the signal received at each subscriber termination is of an acceptable quality with a defined minimum signal-to-noise ratio.

As we saw in Section 2.6.1, a broadcast analog TV signal comprises the video signal and the sound/audio signal. The video signal is made up of the luminance and two chrominance signals and collectively these are transmitted using a separate (single-frequency) carrier for each signal. A typical broadcast analog TV signal is shown in Figure 11.2(a).

The bandwidth used for each TV program/channel in the cable systems of different countries varies. Nevertheless, the same principles apply. Each channel is allocated an appropriate amount of the cable bandwidth – 6 MHz in North America and 8 MHz in Europe – which ensures the signals relating to the two neighboring channels are cleanly separated (by filters) and do not interfere. Associated with each channel is a separate (radio frequency) carrier signal which is separated by 6/8 MHz from the carrier signals of its neighbors. The analog signal of the TV program allocated to that channel is then used to amplitude-modulate the channel carrier signal. The resulting signal is first filtered – to limit the signal bandwidth to 6/8 MHz – and then combined with the signals of all the other channels. The combined signal is then transmitted onto the distribution cable at the cable headend and hence is received by the set-top box of each subscriber. As the subscriber selects a particular program, so the related channel frequency band – and hence carrier signal – is selected. The corresponding carrier signal is then used to demodulate the received signal to obtain the original analog TV signal for that channel.

As we show in Figure 11.2(b), when modulated transmission is used, the bandwidth of a coaxial cable is in the order of 5 MHz through to 900 MHz. In practice, however, the number of channels supported – and hence bandwidth used – is significantly less than this. As we indicated earlier, because of the relatively large area covered by each trunk cable, there may be up to 20 or 30 trunk amplifiers used in each cable run. Each amplifier causes a level of deterioration of the signal as it also amplifies any noise signals introduced by crosstalk and other (external) transmissions. Normally, therefore, the bandwidth used in early cable systems is limited to 88/110 MHz at the low end through to 300, 450, or 550 MHz at the upper end, the actual upper frequency determined by the size of – and hence number of amplifiers used in – the distribution network.

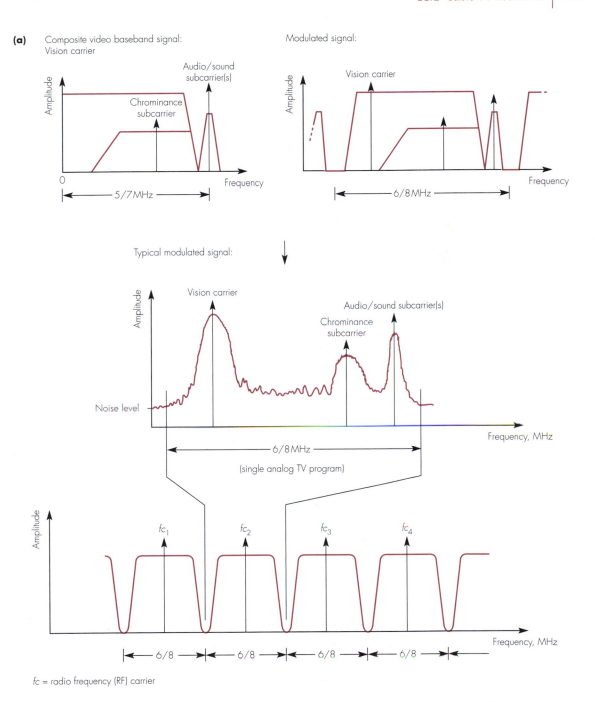

Figure 11.2 Analog CATV principles: (a) analog TV bandwidth requirements; (b) distribution cable bandwidth utilization.

(b)

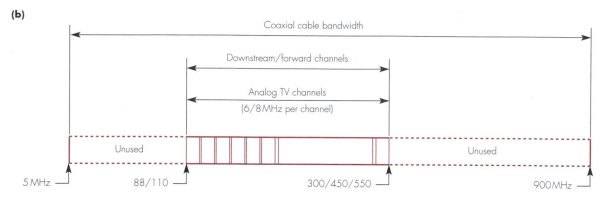

Note: Normally, the band of frequencies from 88 – 110 MHz are used for radio broadcasts.

Figure 11.2 Continued

11.2.1 HFC networks

The advent of digital television and the increasing demand for interactive multimedia services – for interactive TV and high-speed access to the Internet for example – has resulted in many operators of cable networks upgrading their networks to support these newer applications. As we indicated in the previous section, even though there is plenty of unused bandwidth in the existing coaxial cable networks, the amount of usable bandwidth is limited by the number of amplifiers required. This is especially the case in the trunk network and hence in the upgraded networks, the main trunk (coaxial) cables have been replaced with optical fiber cables. The resulting network is called **a hybrid fiber coax (HFC) network** and is illustrated in Figure 11.3(a).

As we can see, optical fiber is used in the main trunk network and coaxial cable is limited to the local distribution network. The retention of coaxial cable in this part of the network is done for cost reasons. The number of lines in the distribution network is much larger than the number in the trunk network and hence the cost of upgrading the distribution network to fiber is considerably higher. The fiber used in the trunk network comprises multiple (fiber) trunk cables each terminated in a unit known as a **fiber node (FN)**. Each performs the optical-to-electrical conversion and serves a number of separate coaxial distribution cables. Each distribution cable provides cable services to between 125 and 500 homes distributed over an area of approximately 3 miles/5 kilometers. Typically, therefore, a single FN serves between 500 and 2000 homes and the total network may comprise many FNs.

The use of fiber cable in the trunk network means that the signal attenuation is much reduced so removing the necessity of having a large number of amplifiers in each trunk line. As a result, a much wider portion of the available bandwidth of the coaxial distribution network can be used. A typical utilization is shown in Figure 11.3(b).

(a)

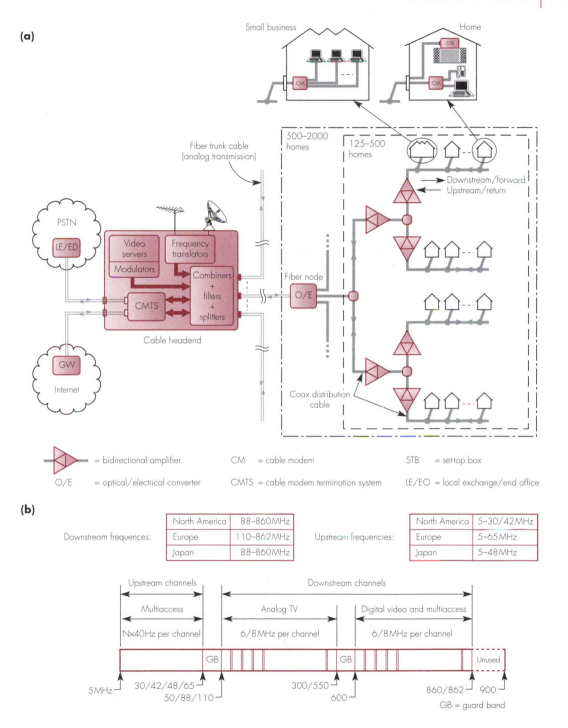

◁ = bidirectional amplifier	CM	= cable modem		STB	= set-top box
O/E = optical/electrical converter	CMTS	= cable modem termination system		LE/EO	= local exchange/end office

(b)

Downstream frequences:	North America	88–860 MHz
	Europe	110–862 MHz
	Japan	88–860 MHz

Upstream frequencies:	North America	5–30/42 MHz
	Europe	5–65 MHz
	Japan	5–48 MHz

Upstream channels — Downstream channels

Multiaccess — Analog TV — Digital video and multiaccess

Nx40Hz per channel — 6/8 MHz per channel — 6/8 MHz per channel

GB — GB — Unused

5 MHz
30/42/48/65
50/88/110
300/550
600
860/862 — 900

GB = guard band

Figure 11.3 Hybrid fiber coax network principles: (a) distribution network and components; (b) cable bandwidth utilization.

As we can see, the bandwidth utilization of the earlier all-coax networks has been extended both at the low and high ends of the available frequency spectrum. To enable existing analog broadcast services to continue to be provided unchanged, the bandwidth from 50/88/100 MHz through to 550 MHz is reserved for such services. Either side of this band is a **guard band** (**GB**) of 50 MHz at the upper end and 8/10 MHz at the lower end. This is necessary to ensure that the new services are cleanly separated – by means of filters – from the existing services. The additional frequency band in the **downstream/forward direction** from 600 MHz to 860/862 MHz is used for the newer digital services. These include digital TV, video-on-demand and near video-on-demand, and the forward path of a range of two-way communication channels for high-speed Internet access, dedicated high bit rate digital circuits – for LAN interconnection for example – and, in some instances, packet-based telephony.

Although the newer services are all digital, modulated (analog) transmission must be used over the cable distribution network in order to be compatible with the existing analog TV transmissions. All transmissions over the coaxial cable distribution network, therefore, are in an analog form and analog transmission is also used over the fiber cable. Hence, since the signals associated with the newer services are all digital, modems similar to those used with a PSTN are needed to convert the source digital bitstream into (and from) an analog signal for transmission over the distribution network. Because the frequencies used are in the radio frequency spectrum, they are known as **RF modems** and even though radio frequencies are involved, they use a similar modulation scheme to that used in higher bit rate PSTN modems. As we saw earlier in Figure 7.6(c) (and explained in the accompanying text), a multilevel modulation scheme known as QAM is used. In the case of RF modems, however, 64 or even 256 different amplitude and phase combinations are used. These produce usable bit rates in the order of:

> 64-QAM: 6 MHz band = 27 Mbps,   8 MHz band = 38 Mbps
> 256-QAM: 6 MHz band = 36 Mbps,   8 MHz band = 50 Mbps

As we can deduce from these values, each additional 6/8 MHz band in the downstream direction can be used to transmit either multiple MPEG-2 (6 Mbps) digital TV programs – or proportionately more MPEG-1 (1.5 Mbps) video programs – or one or more high bit rate data channels. The specific use of the channels is determined by the services to be supported and hence is decided by the cable operator. However, if two-way services are to be supported – interactive TV, video-on-demand, Internet access, and so on – then a related channel in the **upstream/return direction** is required from the subscriber to the cable headend. As we show in Figure 11.3(b), this is achieved by using the lower band of frequencies from 5 MHz through to 30/42/48/65 MHz, the specific upper frequency being determined by the current usage of the cable.

In order to obtain an upstream/return channel, the existing amplifiers in the distribution network are changed to **dual/bidirectional amplifiers**, one to amplify the signals in the downstream frequency bands and the other to amplify the signals in the upstream band. In the case of the fiber trunk network, dual-fiber cable is used, one fiber for the transmission of the downstream signals and the other for the upstream signals. In addition, new subscriber network termination units are required containing **bandsplitting filters** to separate the upstream from the downstream channels.

In some HFC networks, a portion of the upstream bandwidth is already used for the transmission of TV signals (from, say, a camera at a local event to the cable headend for distribution) and hence not all of the bandwidth is available for the newer digital services. Also, in the coaxial cable part of the network, the lower band of frequencies can be of relatively poor quality owing to the ingress of noise from external transmissions and crosstalk from the signals in the various downstream channels. So in order to obtain reliable operation, a more robust modulation scheme is used. This is either QPSK or 16-QAM. Normally, the return channels are not restricted to 6/8 MHz bands and typical bands and example bit rates are:

160 kHz:	320 kbps	1.28 MHz –	2.56 Mbps
320 kHz:	640 kbps	2.56 MHz –	5.12 Mbps
640 kHz:	1.28 Mbps	5.12 MHz –	10.24 Mbps

To support applications such as LAN interconnection and telephony, the forward and return channels are of the same bit rate. Hence symmetric bidirectional communication channels are required. For the various interactive applications, however, the bit rate of the interaction (upstream) channel need only be a fraction of that of the downstream channel. With entertainment applications such as video-on-demand, for example, the traffic in the upstream channel consists mainly of the commands entered by the user at the remote control. Similarly, with Internet access, short commands are used to initiate searching and information retrieval. Hence asymmetry ratios from 10:1 to as high as 100:1 are common.

In some interactive TV applications, the interaction channel is via a PSTN and hence a channel in the upstream direction is required for this. In the case of Internet access, a single high bit rate channel in the downstream direction is used with a lower bit rate channel in the upstream direction for interaction purposes. Each PC/network computer/workstation in all the homes/businesses attached to the cable shares the use of each of these channels in a similar way to the stations attached to a LAN. The channels are known as **multiaccess channels** and we describe aspects of their operation in the next section.

Multiaccess channel operation

As we have indicated, in a cable network all transmissions are either to or from the cable headend rather than between two attached stations as is the case in a LAN. For high-speed Internet access, each pair of channels – one in the downstream direction and the other in the upstream direction – provides a two-way communications path between a station – also referred to as a **customer premises equipment** (**CPE**) – in a home or business and a server attached to the Internet. As we showed in Figure 11.3(a), each station is attached to the cable through a **cable modem** (**CM**). This performs the modulation of the bits in a packet sent by a station for transmission in the upstream channel and the demodulation of the bits in a packet received from the downstream channel. In addition, some CMs support packet-based (IP) telephony. Typically therefore, as we explained in Section 5.3.2, the telephony interface within the CM is based on the H.323 standard. This is concerned with the creation and exchange of call setup and clearing – signaling – messages/packets and the packetization/depacketization of voice samples.

At the cable headend is a unit called a **cable modem termination system** (**CMTS**). This is used to control the transmissions to all the CMs attached to the distribution network and to relay packets to and from the related network – the Internet or a PSTN. Figure 11.4 shows the essential components of a CMTS.

As we shall explain below, in addition to (IP) packets relating to Internet access and telephony, the CMTS uses IP packets to communicate with each CM in order to configure and manage the CM. Typically, therefore, as we see in the figure, a Fast-Ethernet switch is used to relay incoming/outgoing packets to their related interface. This is either a local server (for configuration and management), an access gateway (for Internet access), or an H.323 gateway (for access to a PSTN).

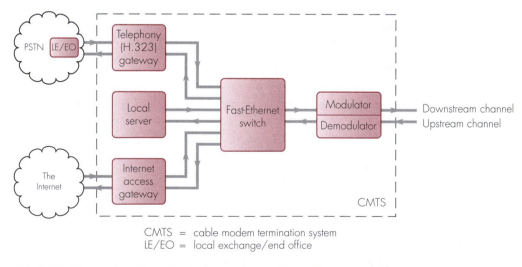

CMTS = cable modem termination system
LE/EO = local exchange/end office

Figure 11.4 Cable modem termination system schematic.

In the downstream direction, each packet is simply broadcast over the assigned downstream channel and hence is received by all the attached CMs. In the upstream direction, however, since the attached CMs must compete for the use of the upstream channel, a suitable medium access control (MAC) protocol must be used to ensure each CM gains access to the channel in a fair way. In a cable network, since a CM cannot receive the transmissions made by a CM that is nearer to the CMTS than itself, MAC protocols such as CSMA/CD and control token cannot be used. So instead, access to the upstream channel is controlled by the CMTS. In practice, there are a number of different schemes that can be used. In the remaining part of this section we describe the principle of operation of just one of these – the **data-over-cable service interface specification** (**DOCSIS**), which is very similar to the **IEEE 802.14** standard.

Protocol stack

A schematic diagram showing the protocol stack associated with the CMTS and CM that is used for Internet access is given in Figure 11.5.

Each CM has an integral repeater hub – for example, 10BaseT – within it, and all the stations – there can be more than one at a site – are attached to the hub by, for example, individual twisted-pair drop cables. Hence each CM has its own 48-bit MAC address – which is used for identification purposes by the CMTS during the configuration and management phase – and an additional set of MAC addresses, one for each station attached to the hub. Normally, the latter are acquired by the hub when each station becomes active.

The aim is to make the presence of the cable network – and hence CM and CMTS – transparent to the IP layer in a station that is communicating with a remote server attached to the Internet. To achieve this, forwarding of IP packets through the CM is carried out at the MAC sublayer and hence the CM acts as a bridge. In the case of the CMTS, although bridging can optionally be used, normally, the forwarding operation is performed at the IP layer with the CMTS acting as an Internet access gateway for all the stations – through their related CMs – that are attached to the cable network. Hence, as we explained in Section 9.5.1, the ARP in the IP layer of the CMTS acts as a proxy ARP for all the attached stations. The IP layer must also support the ICMP (see Section 9.7) and IGMP (see Section 9.6.10) protocols. In addition, as we show in the figure, each CM attached to the cable network has additional higher-level protocols above the MAC sublayer. These enable each CM to be configured at start up once the basic MAC-level transmission structure has been established – DHCP and TFTP – and to be remotely managed – SNMP. We described the operation of DHCP earlier in Section 9.10.4 and we describe a selection of the Internet application protocols including TFTP and SNMP in Chapter 14.

Configuration and management

All CMs are diskless and hence need to be configured at start up. This is carried out in two phases. First, since the only address a CM knows at start up is

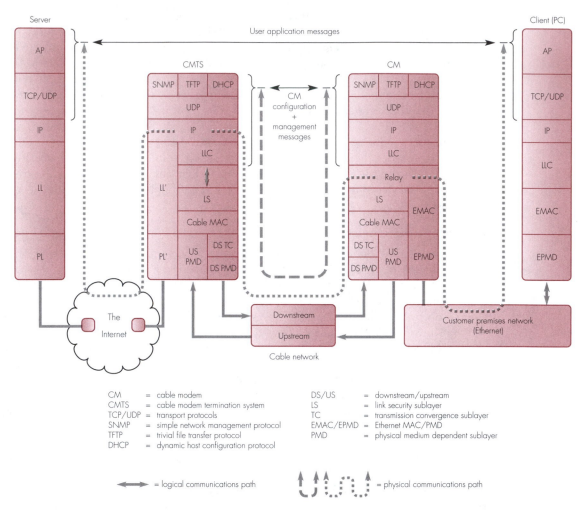

Figure 11.5 CMTS/CM protocol stacks.

its MAC (hardware) address, the **dynamic host configuration protocol (DHCP)** – see Section 9.10.4 – in the CM requests the DHCP in the CMTS to send it the IP address of itself and the CMTS. Also, the name of the servers that supply the time-of-day and hold the modem configuration information. On receipt of this information, the CM proceeds to obtain the time-of-day (ToD) from the ToD server and, using the **trivial file transfer protocol (TFTP)** – see Section 14.5 – the configuration information.

The configuration information includes the public encryption key of the CM and the QoS parameters of the packet flows the CM can support. Examples include best-effort flows associated with Internet access and the constant bit rate flows associated with telephony. We expand upon the subject of encryption later in Section 13.4. Essentially, however, the public key of the CM is used by the CMTS to send the private/secret key that is to be used by the **link security** (**LS**) sublayer of the CM to encrypt/decrypt the payload of each link layer frame sent/received from the cable. Once it has done this, the CM sends a request message to the CMTS to formally register and obtain permission to start to relay frames. The CMTS responds by assigning a unique **service identifier** (**SID**) to the CM and also one or more **service flow identifiers** (**SFID**), one for each type of packet flow the CM can support. The CM can then start to relay frames to/from the stations attached to its **customer premises network** (**CPN**) interface.

As we shall expand upon in Section 14.7, the simple network management protocol (SNMP) is used to enable a management process in the CMTS – or another remote system – to read and change a set of operational parameters that are maintained by the CM. It is also used for a process in the CM to report fault conditions should they arise. Normally, the process in the CMTS displays this information on a computer screen and, should a fault be reported, the network manager can readily determine the location of the CM and the fault that is present.

Cable MAC

As we indicated earlier, all transmissions on the upstream channel – that is, from each CM to the CMTS – are controlled by the cable MAC in the CMTS. Hence when a CM wishes to transmit a frame – containing an IP packet in its payload – the cable MAC in the CM first sends a *Request* (*REQ*) message to the cable MAC in the CMTS which indicates the amount of bandwidth that is required to transmit the frame. On receipt of the REQ message, the CMTS responds by returning a *Grant* message which indicates the amount of bandwidth that has been allocated to the CM.

All transmissions on the upstream channel are scheduled to occur in fixed time intervals of 4 ms. Hence, during a transmission interval, the CMTS may receive a number of requests for a portion of the bandwidth in the next transmission interval. A bandwidth allocation algorithm is used to ensure that requests are granted in a fair way. For example, if the waiting frame contains speech samples then it may be allocated a portion of the bandwidth ahead of, say, a frame containing best-effort data traffic. Once this has been carried out, the CMTS divides the subsequent transmission interval into a number of variable-length (time) intervals each with the SID of the requesting CM that can use it. This information is then broadcast on the related downstream channel during the current transmission interval in what is called an *upstream bandwidth allocation MAP* management message.

For each requesting CM, the corresponding entry in the allocation MAP message gives the duration of time it can transmit. If the time duration for a CM has been set to zero, this indicates the request is still pending and the CM must wait for the next transmission interval. Also, since a CM can have only a single outstanding request (per SID) at a time, this blocks the CM from making a new request.

Because of the relatively wide area of coverage of HFC networks, as we saw in Section 6.2.8, the signal propagation delay over the cable can be relatively large. Hence the precise time each requesting CM receives the allocation MAP varies and depends on the physical distance the CM is from the cable headend. To ensure each CM times its frame transmission with those from all of the other requesting CMs, firstly, all CMs must be in time synchronism with the master clock in the CMTS and secondly, in order for the transmitted frames to arrive at the CMTS in their expected time intervals, each CM must know the round-trip propagation delay time between itself and the CMTS. The procedure used to enable a CM to determine this is known as **ranging** and both time synchronization and ranging must be carried out during the initialization phase of the CM prior to the transmission of any frames containing IP packets.

Time synchronization

To ensure all CMs have a common time reference, the CMTS maintains a 32-bit binary counter that is clocked using its master clock of 10.24 MHz. The CMTS then broadcasts a *SYNC management message* that contains the current state of this counter on the downstream channel at periodic (10 ms) intervals. The counter value in the SYNC message is known as the *SYNC time-stamp* and is used by each CM to synchronize its own time reference to this value. The general principle is shown in Figure 11.6.

The upstream channel bitstream is divided in *time* into a stream of numbered **minislots**. The duration of each minislot is a power-of-two multiple of 6.25 microseconds such that the number of bytes per minislot is equal to 16. For example, assuming a bandwidth of 640 kHz is being used for the upstream channel, as we indicated earlier, a typical bit rate is 1280 kbps. Hence each 6.25 μs interval contains $1280 \times 10^3 \times 6.25 \times 10^{-6} = 8$ bits. Therefore the time duration of a minislot, T, is 6.25×16 μs and hence the power-of-two multiple, M, is 4.

All frame transmissions in each transmission interval – including frames containing request and timing messages – start at a defined (numbered) minislot and the bandwidth allocation MAP uses units of minislots. The CMTS uses a second 32-bit counter to number each minislot. This is clocked at 6.25 μs intervals which is equal to a clocking rate of 160 KHz. Hence, since this is 1/64th of the CMTS master clock of 10.24 MHz, there is always a fixed relationship between the contents of the minislot counter and the broadcast SYNC time-stamp: the least significant 0 to $(25 - M)$ bits of the minislot counter are the same as the most significant $(6 + M)$ to 31 bits of the SYNC time-stamp.

Ranging

Once a CM is in time synchronism, it invokes the ranging procedure to determine its **round-trip correction (RTC) time**; that is, how much earlier the CM should start transmitting a frame relative to a given minislot number in the

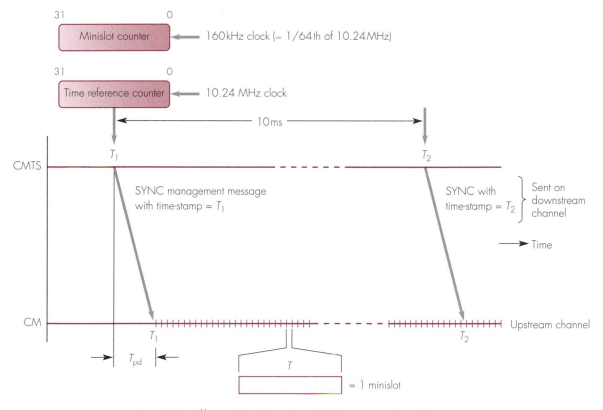

- $T = 6.25 \times 2^M \mu s$ such that 1 minislot = 16 bytes at the channel bit rate
- Minislot N begins at time-stamp reference $N \times T \times 64$
- T_{pd} = propagation delay CMTS to CM

Figure 11.6 Cable MAC time synchronization principles.

bandwidth allocation MAP. As we indicated earlier, this ensures that the transmissions from all the CMs in a transmission interval arrive at the CMTS as if all the CMs were colocated with the CMTS. The principle behind the ranging procedure is shown in the time sequence diagram in Figure 11.7.

At periodic (typically 2 ms) intervals, the CMTS includes in the bandwidth allocation MAP it is transmitting, a reserved time interval – transmission opportunity – known as an *initial maintenance* (*IM*) *region*. This is present to enable a new CM to carry out the ranging procedure. Once the CM is in time synchronism, it searches each MAP it receives from the downstream channel for an IM region and, when it finds one, it immediately transmits a *Ranging Request* (*RNG-REQ*) message with its own (physical layer) fixed delay within it. The duration of this region is such that it can compensate for the worst-case round-trip propagation delay between a CM and the CMTS.

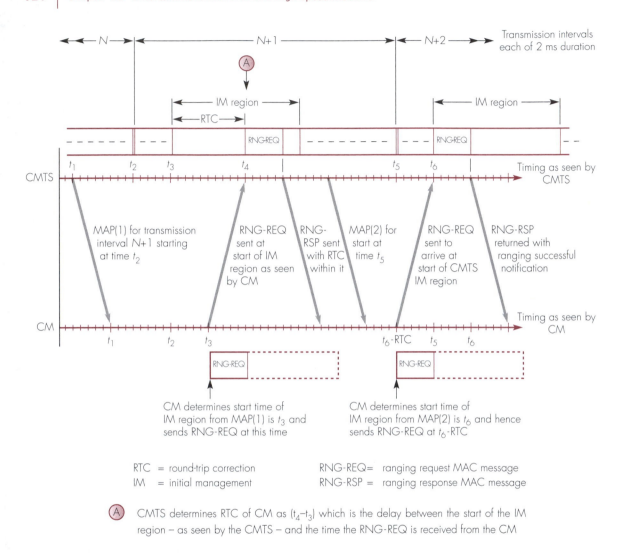

RTC = round-trip correction
IM = initial management

RNG-REQ = ranging request MAC message
RNG-RSP = ranging response MAC message

(A) CMTS determines RTC of CM as (t_4-t_3) which is the delay between the start of the IM region – as seen by the CMTS – and the time the RNG-REQ is received from the CM

Figure 11.7 Cable MAC ranging procedure principles.

On receipt of the RNG-REQ message, since the CMTS knows the time offset from the start of the current transmission interval to the start of the IM region, the CMTS can estimate the round-trip propagation delay from the CM to the CMTS and back again by the time delay the RNG-REQ message is received relative to the start of the IM region. The CMTS responds by returning a *Ranging Response (RNG-RSP)* message in the downstream channel that contains the initial computed timing offset – including the CM fixed delay – to be used by the CM. On receipt of this, the CM first proceeds to locate another IM region in the next MAP it receives. It then sends a second

RNG-REQ message to the CMTS but this time earlier than the start of the IM region – as seen by the CMTS – by a time equal to the initial RTC that it received in the RNG-RSP message. If this arrives at the CMTS at the start of the IM region, then the estimated RTC is correct and the CMTS returns a second RNG-RSP message containing a *Ranging Successful* notification within it. Alternatively, if the arrival of the second RNG-REQ is still later than the start of the IM region, a further REQ/RSP message interchange takes place using a revised RTC time that is indicated in the second RNG-RSP message. This procedure continues until the precise RTC is known and the CM receives a successful notification.

Once a notification success has been received, the CM can then proceed to send frames containing IP packets using the request/grant cycle outlined earlier. First the CM carries out the configuration operation we described in the previous section and this concludes with the CM being registered and allocated a service identifier (SID). It is at this point that the CM can start to relay frames – containing IP packets – to and from the stations that are attached to the hub ports of the CM.

Frame transmission

As we indicated earlier, all transmissions over the upstream channel are controlled by the CMTS using the bandwidth allocation MAP. Prior to sending a frame (containing an IP packet), the CM sends a bandwidth Request (REQ) message to the CMTS indicating the number of minislots required to transmit the frame. The CMTS then responds by including in the next allocation MAP it broadcasts on the downstream channel, a Grant message containing the SID of the CM and the number of minislots within the next transmission interval the CM can use.

Since the Request message must also be sent to the CMTS over the upstream channel, each bandwidth allocation MAP includes a reserved region – similar to the IM region used to send a Ranging Request message – to enable a CM to send a Request message during the current transmission interval. This is called the *REQ region* and, since there may be a number of CMs waiting to send a Request message, a contention resolution procedure must be used to enable each competing CM to share the use of the request region in an equitable way.

Each REQ region can support the transmission of multiple Request messages. Also, as we shall expand upon later, each Request message is 6 bytes long and includes the SID of the CM making the request and the number of minislots requested. The contention algorithm is based on a truncated binary exponential backoff algorithm similar to that used with Ethernet. In the header of each bandwidth allocation MAP is a pair of fields relating to the algorithm, one called the *data backoff start* (*DBS*) and the other the *data backoff end* (*DBE*). Each is a power-of-two value and, in the case of the DBS, a value of 2, for example, indicates a backoff value in the range 0–3, a value of 3, 0–7 and so on. The range is known as the **backoff window** and must always be less than the value derived from the DBE. The latter is known, therefore, as the **maximum backoff window**.

When a CM wishes to make a request, on receipt of the next MAP, it first reads the DBS value from the MAP and proceeds to compute a random number within the derived backoff window. This indicates the number of request opportunities (6-byte slots) from the start of the REQ region the CM must defer – and hence not use – before transmitting its own Request message. For example, if the computed random number from the current backoff window is 3 and the REQ region can support 6 requests, then the CM must defer from using the first 3 request opportunities/slots before transmitting its own request. Alternatively, if the computed random number is 8, the CM must defer from using all 6 request slots and wait for the next REQ region. On determining this from the MAP, the CM must then defer from using a further 2 slots before sending its request.

Once a CM has sent a request, it must then wait for a data *Grant* message in a subsequent MAP containing the SID of the CM and the number of minislots allocated. Providing this is received, then the Request message was received successfully by the CMTS and no collision occurred. If a Grant is not received, then the CM must try again. It first doubles its current backoff window and, providing the size of the new window is less than the maximum backoff window, the CM proceeds to compute a new random number within the limits of the new window. A maximum retry limit of 16 is used and, if this or the maximum backoff window is reached, the CM discards the frame.

This mode of operation is known as the **reservation access mode** and an example transmission sequence illustrating this is given in Figure 11.8. In this example it is assumed that the REQ region contains 4 request slots, the random number generated from the initial backoff window is 2, and the Request message is successfully received by the CMTS. Note that each transmission made by the CM is sent earlier than its allocated time by the round-trip correction time computed during the ranging procedure.

Frame formats

All cable MAC frames have a standard 6-byte header the format of which is shown in Figure 11.9(a). The *frame control* (*FC*) field identifies the type of MAC header and consists of three subfields. The *FC-TYPE* indicates whether the MAC frame contains a user data frame – containing an IP packet – or a cable MAC frame. For the latter, the *FC-PARM* identifies the type of MAC frame; for example, a Request message/frame or a MAC management frame such as a time synchronization frame. The *EHDR-ON* is a single bit and is set to 1 if an extension header is present. We shall give an example of the use of extension headers in the next subsection.

The *MAC-PARM* field in a REQ frame indicates the number of minislots requested or, if an extension header is present, it indicates the number of bytes in the extension header. The *LEN/SID* is either the sum of the number of bytes in the extension header (if present) and the number of bytes following the HCS field or, in a REQ frame, the SID of the requesting

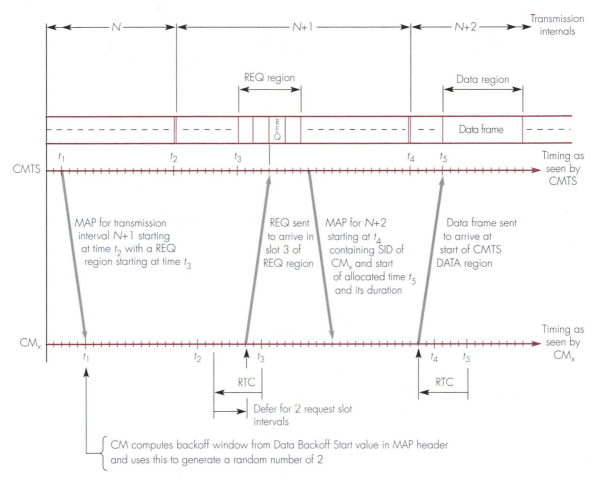

RTC = round-trip correction

Figure 11.8 Cable MAC reservation access mode of transmission.

CM. The *HCS* is a 16-bit CRC that is used to detect transmission errors in the MAC header. It is used to ensure the integrity of the header fields and, in the contention mode, whether a collision has occurred.

Two example MAC frame types are shown in Figure 11.9(b). The first is the format of a MAC frame containing a user data frame. As we saw in Figure 8.3, for an Ethernet/IEEE 802.3 LAN the length of a frame – including a 4-byte FCS – can be from 64 to 1518 bytes and the *LEN* field in the MAC header indicates the number of bytes in the actual frame being transferred. The second example is the format of a REQ frame and, since this consists of the header only, the *SID* indicates the 14-bit SID of the CM making the request. The *MAC-PARM* contains the number of minislots that are being requested.

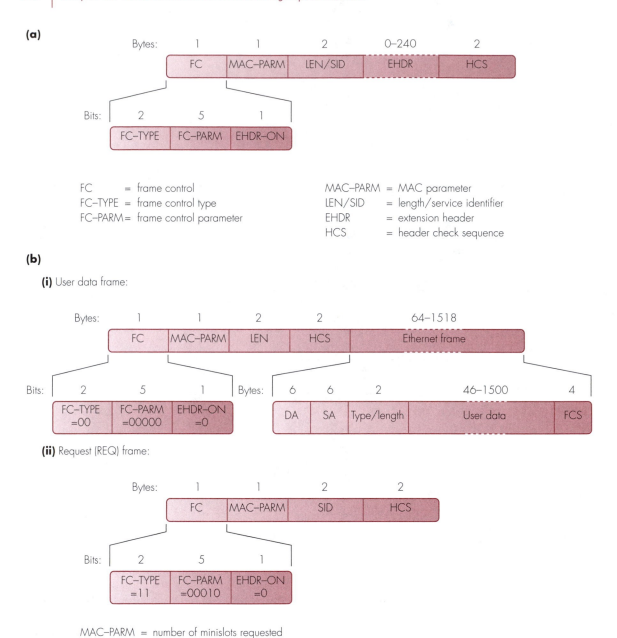

Figure 11.9 Cable MAC frame formats: (a) header field definitions; (b) two example frame types.

Fragmentation

During periods of heavy traffic on the upstream channel, a grant message may specify a smaller number of minislots than have been requested by the CM to transfer the user data frame. When this happens, the MAC layer within the CM automatically fragments/splits the user data frame into a number of smaller fragments for transmission over the cable. At the CMTS, the peer MAC layer then reassembles the fragments to form the initial frame before forwarding this to the Internet gateway.

In order for the cable MAC in the CMTS to determine that a received MAC frame contains a fragment of a larger frame, an extension header is used. The format of each fragment header is shown in Figure 11.10(a) and an example is given in Figure 11.10(b).

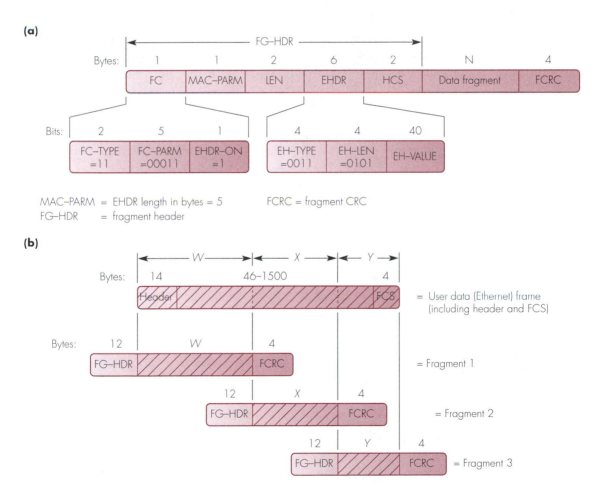

Figure 11.10 User data frame fragmentation principles: (a) fragment header format; (b) example fragmentation overheads.

In general, the EHDR field may contain multiple variable-length fields each of which is defined in a type-length-value (TLV) format. In the case of a fragment EHDR, however, only a single fixed-length field is present. The 4-bit *EH-TYPE* is set to 3 which indicates the MAC frame contains a data fragment. The 4-bit *EH-LEN* is set to 5 and the following 5-byte (40-bit) *EH-VALUE* field then contains a number of fixed-length subfields. These include the 14-bit SID of the CM carrying out the fragmentation, a 1-bit *first fragment* and a 1-bit *last fragment* – each of which is set to 1 for the first and last fragment respectively – and a 4-bit *fragment sequence number*. This is initialized to zero and is incremented by one for each fragment that is sent. Collectively these fields enable the peer cable MAC in the CMTS to reassemble the fragments into the initial user data frame. The 4-byte FCRC is a 32-bit CRC of the fragment. Note that the initial user data frame to be fragmented includes the various (Ethernet) header fields and the original FCS.

In the example shown in Figure 11.10(b), it is assumed that the initial user data frame has to be sent in three cable MAC frames. As we can see, the overheads associated with each of these frames is 16 bytes and hence it is assumed that the first grant message contains sufficient minislots to send $W +$ 16 bytes, the second $X +$ 16 bytes and the third $Y +$ 16 bytes.

Piggyback requests

Also present in the extension header (EHDR) field of each fragment is an 8-bit *REQ* (request) subfield. This plays the same role as the Request message we described earlier. The difference is that there is no contention involved in sending the subsequent request message(s) for the additional minislots that are required to send the remainder of the user data (Ethernet) frame.

When the cable MAC in the CM prepares the first fragment of a larger frame, it computes the number of minislots required to send the remainder of the frame including the 16 bytes of overhead. It then includes this value in the REQ subfield of the frame. This type of request is known as a **piggyback request** since it is being sent in the same frame as the current fragment of data being transferred. As we can deduce from this, this procedure leads to a shorter wait time relative to sending a separate request message. Again, if the number of minislots allocated in the grant message contained in the subsequent bandwidth allocation MAP is less than the number requested, then a further level of fragmentation must be carried out using the same procedure as before. This is repeated until the complete user data frame has been transferred.

Request/data regions

During periods when the upstream channel is lightly loaded, the CMTS may include in each bandwidth allocation MAP it transmits a *Request/Data region*. This is similar to a REQ region except that in addition to Request messages, a CM can also attempt to send a short user data frame. As with a REQ region, this is a contention region and hence the data frame may be corrupted by a simultaneous transmission of a request or data frame from another CM. In order for the CM to know whether a collision has occurred, if the data frame is received without errors, the CMTS returns a *Data Acknowledge* message (containing the SID of the CM) in the next MAP it transmits. In order for the cable MAC in the CM to know the maximum time to wait for an acknowledgment, the CMTS includes in each MAP it transmits an ACK field which indicates the start time of the transmission region that any acknowledgment messages in the MAP relate. If this is later than the time the data message was sent, then a collision is assumed and the CM must try again.

QoS support

The reservation access mode described in the preceding subsections is intended for the transfer of user data frames containing IP packets relating to the best-effort service. Hence all the packets have the same priority value in the type-of-service (ToS) field in the packet header. An additional feature is also included in the cable MAC, however, to enable frames containing packets which have a high priority to be transmitted before frames containing a lower priority packet.

As we saw in Section 1.5.6, the relative priority of a packet is determined by the service class associated with the application/call. There are a number of different service classes each determined by a set of QoS parameters. These may include, for example, a defined worst-case end-to-end delay, jitter, and throughput requirement. In the context of the cable MAC, each service class has a related **service flow** and, for each service flow, the CMTS endeavors to schedule transmissions so that the agreed QoS parameters associated with each service class are met. As we can deduce from this, there are a number of different service flows each of which maps to a related packet priority. Hence packets containing a particular priority value are transmitted according to the rules associated with the related service flow.

Each service flow is characterized by a separate **service flow identifier** and, for applications involving duplex flows – such as telephony – a separate service flow is set up in both the CMTS-to-CM and CM-to-CMTS directions. Also, for applications requiring asymmetric communication channels – that is, the class of service associated with the information flow is different for each direction – the service flow in each direction can be different.

In order to ensure that the agreed QoS parameters associated with each service flow are met, in the upstream direction, a number of additional transmission opportunities are provided by the CMTS for these flows on receipt of the related request from a CM. These include:

■ **unsolicited grant**: these are intended for use for service flows involving packets containing real-time information. The CMTS, on receiving the appropriate request message from a CM, reserves in the allocation MAP specific fixed-sized transmission opportunities that are repeated at periodic intervals. The frequency and duration of the intervals is determined by the type of service flow. The CMTS stops generating intervals when it detects they are not being used;

- **real-time polling**: these also involve the CMTS reserving periodic transmission opportunities and are intended for real-time traffic flows such as voice-over-IP (Internet telephony). The CMTS periodically polls/invites each CM with an active service flow to make a bandwidth request at intervals of about 1 ms. The related transmission opportunities cease when the CM fails to respond to a poll.

- **unsolicited grant with activity detection**: the packetization process associated with voice-over-IP sometimes exploits the silence periods between talk spurts by ceasing to send packets during these periods. This service is intended for use with this type of application. All the time packets associated with this flow are being transmitted by a CM, the CMTS continues to provide periodic transmission opportunities for it. Immediately the CMTS detects these are not being used, however, it stops providing them. Then, when the CM detects the flow of packets resumes – and hence the service flow becomes active – it sends a request message to the CMTS asking for the unsolicited periodic transmission opportunities to be resumed. Normally, the CMTS, after it stops providing transmission opportunities, provides a specific request opportunity for this CM/SID at similar periodic intervals;

- **non-real-time polling**: this service is intended for use with non-real-time applications that involve the transfer of large volumes of data; for example large file transfers. With the basic reservation access mode, during periods of heavy loading such transfers may take unacceptably long times to complete. Hence by using non-real-time polling, the CMTS periodically polls/invites CMs to make a bandwidth request at intervals of about 12 s. Such requests always receive some reserved transmission opportunities even during periods of heavy traffic when contention requests are receiving minimal transmission opportunities.

DS TC sublayer

The MAC frames exchanged between the CMTS and a CM have the same basic structure in both the downstream and the upstream channels. In the downstream direction, however, in order to utilize similar receiving hardware to that used for a digital TV channel, the channel bitstream is divided by the transmission control (TC) sublayer into a stream of 188-byte packets. As we showed earlier in Figure 5.20 and explained in the accompanying text, this is the packet format used by the transport multiplexer to transmit multiple digital TV programs over a single high bit rate channel. Each packet is made up of a 4-byte header and a 184-byte payload. The first byte of the header is for synchronization purposes and enables all the receivers to determine the start of each new packet. A second 13-bit field in the header (known as the *payload identifier (PID)*) is then used to identify the type of contents in the payload and, if this is data relating to Internet access, it is set to 1FFE (hex). Hence if the total channel bandwidth is being used for Internet access, all packets will contain this value in the packet identifier field. Alternatively, if the channel is being used to transmit both Internet data and digital TV programs, then only those packets containing Internet data will have this PID.

The 184-byte payload field of each packet is used to transfer the cable MAC frames. However, since a packet may contain either multiple short frames or a portion of a long frame, in order to use the available bandwidth efficiently, it is necessary for each receiver to be able to determine the start and end of each frame. Also, since there may be unused bits/bandwidth between successive frames, a means of detecting when these are present is required.

To determine the start of a frame within a packet, the first byte following the 4-byte packet header is used as a *pointer* (offset) to the first byte of a new frame should one start within the current packet. If a new frame does not start within a packet, however, and the packet contains, say, a portion of a packet that straddles multiple packets, then the first byte is not used as a pointer. For each CM to determine if a pointer byte/field is present, a single bit in the 4-byte packet header called the *payload unit start indicator* (*PUSI*) bit is set to 1. Idle periods between frames are indicated by the presence of one or more *stuff-bytes* which have the reserved bit pattern of FF (hex). The *frame control* (*FC*) field at the head of each frame cannot be equal to this. Hence, since the length of each frame can be determined from the fields in the (MAC) frame header, each CM can readily determine the start and end of each frame. Three examples are given in Figure 11.11.

The first assumes the start of the frame immediately follows the pointer byte and just a single frame is present in the packet. The second assumes multiple short frames are packed into a single packet and the third, a single long frame spans multiple packets.

DS/US PMD sublayers

A schematic diagram showing typical packet flows in both the downstream and upstream channels is given in Figure 11.12.

In the downstream direction, the signal is continuous and is the allocated carrier for the channel modulated by the bitstream using either 64 or 256-QAM. As we explained in the previous subsection, the bitstream is divided into a contiguous stream of 188-byte MPEG-2 transport packets each with a 4/5-byte header.

In the upstream direction, the signal is the allocated carrier modulated by the bitstream using either QPSK or 16-QAM. The bitstream in this direction, however, is made up of variable-length bursts of bits/frames each sent by a different CM. Hence in order for the PMD sublayer in the CMTS to be able to receive reliably each frame, a *guard-band* between each frame comprising several symbols at the start and end of each frame is present. Also, in order for the receiving electronics to achieve clock/symbol synchronization and determine the start of each frame, a *preamble* sequence of up to 1024 bits precedes each frame starting at the allocated minislot boundary. This is sent as either 512 (QPSX) or 256 (16-QAM) symbols and terminates with a defined symbol pattern. This is followed by the bits in the (MAC) frame and, since the

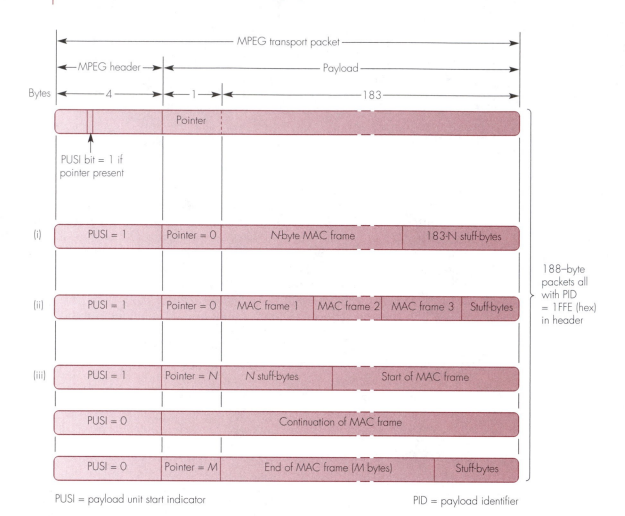

PUSI = payload unit start indicator

PID = payload identifier

Figure 11.11 Downstream transmission convergence sublayer: examples showing the packing of MAC frames into 188-byte MPEG transport packets.

length of a frame can be determined from the fields in the frame header, no end-of-frame sequence is required.

In addition, as we show in the figure, a forward error control (FEC) scheme is optionally used with both the downstream and upstream channels in order to reduce the probability of the received bitstream containing transmission/bit errors. We discuss the principles of such schemes in Appendix B. The scheme used is based on an (n, k, t) Reed–Solomon (RS) code where k is the number of bytes in the original block of data, n the number of bytes in the block after coding, and t the number of bytes in a block that the code will correct. Normally, in order to exploit the use of the same hardware as is used for digital TV, the block size used in both channels, k, is 188 bytes. This has 16 bytes

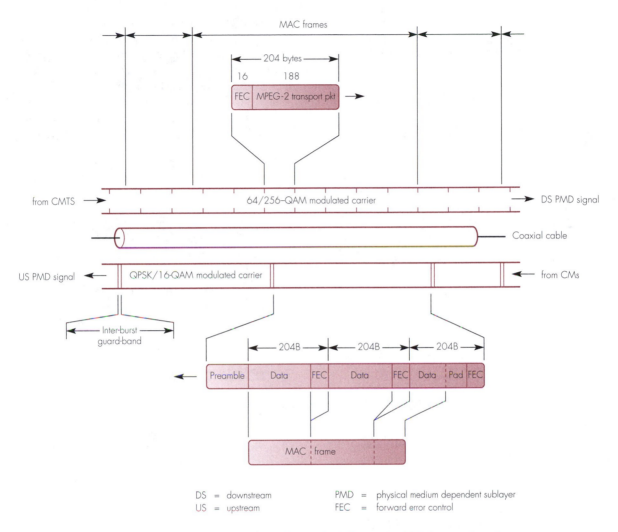

Figure 11.12 DS/US PMD sublayer: example packet flows and their overheads.

of FEC and hence $n = 188 + 16 = 204$ bytes. This code has a minimum *Hamming distance, d,* of 17 bytes and hence will correct up to 8 bytes in each block. This code is written as an RS (204, 188, $t = 8$) code and, in practice, is a shortened version of the RS (255, 239, $t = 8$) code. The FEC bytes are computed by adding 51 zero bytes before the 188 bytes prior to computing the FEC.

Cable intranets

The network architecture we showed earlier in Figure 11.3 is an example of a typical regional HFC cable network. The CMTS in the cable headend provides a single point of access to the Internet and the cable operator acts as an Internet service provider (ISP) for its CM subscribers. Many cable operators, however, have multiple regional networks. Hence, in terms of Internet access, these operators have many thousands of subscribers. In such cases, instead of providing multiple single access points to the Internet, the cable operator creates its own intranet with all the regional headends linked together using high bit rate digital circuits. The general scheme is shown in Figure 11.13.

As we can see, each regional network is similar to a site LAN in a large enterprise intranet. As we saw in Figure 11.4, in the CMTS is a fast-Ethernet switch and, connected to this, are a number of additional local servers that

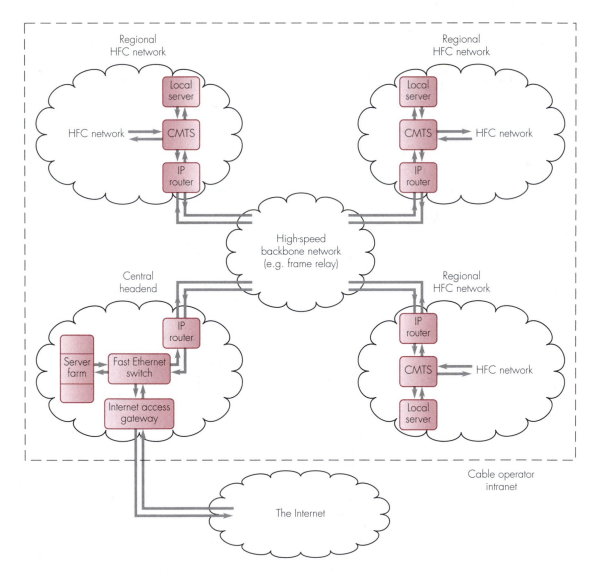

Figure 11.13 Cable operator intranet principles.

provide various services on behalf of its local community of subscribers. For example, an email server, some local Web servers, and one or more cache servers that are used to retain copies of popular Web pages.

When part of an intranet, however, also connected to the switch is a router that forms the interface with other sites. In this way, all communications between subscribers that are connected to the different regional networks of the operator are via the intranet and hence are carried out at high speed. Also, a single high-speed backbone connection with the public Internet can be used so increasing the speed of access to external servers.

MMDS and LMDS

In areas with low subscriber densities or where laying cable is difficult, an alternative to coaxial cable is to use terrestrial microwave broadcast transmissions. As we show in Figure 11.14(a) and (b), two alternatives are available, one called the **multichannel multipoint distribution system** (**MMDS**) and the other the **local multipoint distribution system** (**LMDS**). Both use ommidirectional transmitters and, within their area of coverage, provide a similar range of services to those provided with a coaxial cable distribution network. The main difference between the two systems is the area of coverage of the transmissions and the number of channels supported. The main features of both systems are summarized in Figure 11.14(c).

As we can see, a typical MMDS operates in the 2.15–2.7 GHz frequency band. Normally, it has a relatively wide area of coverage with a direct connection between the transmitter and the cable headend. Multiple 6/8 MHz downstream channels are supported which are used for either analog TV broadcasts or, with suitable modems, digital broadcasts. The latter include digital TV and, together with the upstream (return) channel, interactive services including access to the Internet.

An LMDS operates in a higher frequency band as it is intended for local distribution with an area of coverage of up to 5 km from the transmitter. Normally, the transmitter has a direct connection to a fiber node in an HFC network. Hence an LMDS effectively replaces the coaxial cable part of an HFC network. A similar bandwidth to coax is supported and hence a similar range of services to an HFC network.

11.3 Satellite television networks

Satellite networks have been used for many years to deliver broadcast television direct to the home. Initially, the signals relating to all the TV programs were analog but these have now been complemented with digital TV. Also, as with cable networks, in addition to broadcast television, various interactive data services are now supported. In this section we discuss the operation of, firstly, a direct-to-home broadcast TV system, secondly, the principles behind digital TV over satellite and thirdly, how interactive services are provided.

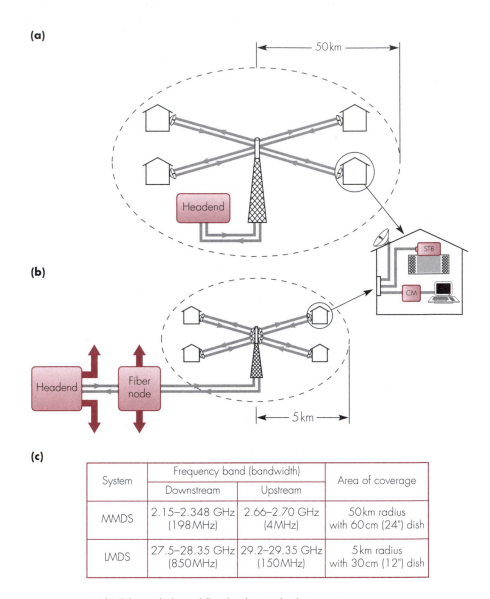

(c)

System	Frequency band (bandwidth)		Area of coverage
	Downstream	Upstream	
MMDS	2.15–2.348 GHz (198 MHz)	2.66–2.70 GHz (4 MHz)	50 km radius with 60 cm (24") dish
LMDS	27.5–28.35 GHz (850 MHz)	29.2–29.35 GHz (150 MHz)	5 km radius with 30 cm (12") dish

M/LMDS = multichannel/local multipoint distribution system

Figure 11.14 M/LMDS principles: (a) MMDS schematic; (b) LMDS schematic; (c) typical operating parameters.

11.3.1 Broadcast television principles

The basic requirement of an entertainment satellite network is to broadcast a set of TV programs from a program source to the set-top boxes of a large number of subscribers who are physically distributed over a wide geographical area. Figure 11.15(a) shows how this is achieved.

The orbital period of a satellite varies according to its distance above the earth's surface. Satellites used for TV broadcasting, however, are **geosynchronous**

(a)

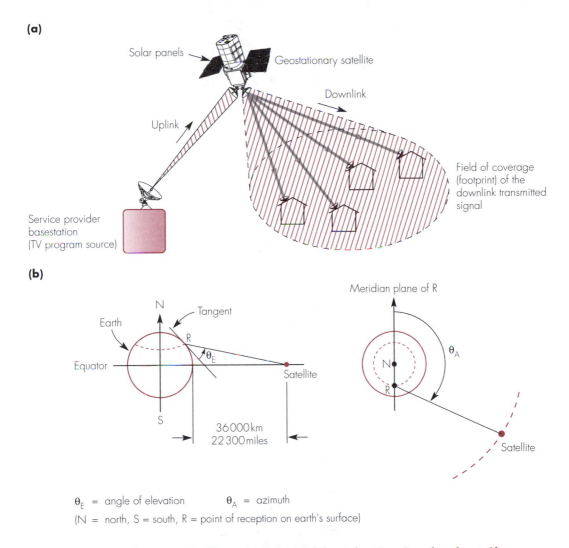

(b)

θ_E = angle of elevation θ_A = azimuth

(N = north, S = south, R = point of reception on earth's surface)

Figure 11.15 Geostationary satellite principles: (a) broadcast network schematic; (b) positioning details.

which means that the satellite orbits the earth once every 24 hours – slightly less than this in practice – in time synchronism with the rotation of the earth. To achieve this, the orbit must be circular and, since the earth rotates around its polar axis, the satellite's orbit must be around the earth's polar axis. A circular orbit is then obtained if the orbit is in the equatorial plane and at an (average) altitude above the equator of approximately 36 000 km/22 300 miles. At this height, the effect of the centrifugal force due to the rotation of the satellite is negated by the terrestrial attraction of the satellite by the earth. Also, from a point on the earth's surface, the satellite appears stationary and hence is known as a **geostationary earth orbit** (**GEO**) – or simply geostationary – satellite.

GEO satellite positioning

The satellite is first launched to an altitude of 36 000 km/22 300 miles above the equator and on-board motors are then used to ensure the orbit is circular and in its assigned position relative to a point on the earth's surface. The on-board motors are also used at periodic intervals during the satellite's operational lifetime to effect small corrections which maintain the satellite's position to within 0.2° of its assigned position. In general, therefore, the useful lifetime of a satellite is determined by the quantity of propellant used to perform these maneuvers. The main power source for the on-board electronic equipment comes from large solar panels but this has to be complemented by batteries to overcome the loss of power from the panels during periods when the satellite is eclipsed by the earth.

Since the latitude of a satellite is 0°, the position of a satellite is defined by its longitude relative to the Greenwich meridian. As we show in Figure 11.15(b), the position relative to a point on the earth is defined by the elevation and azimuth of the satellite. The **elevation** is the angle between the line from the satellite to the point of reception, R, and the tangent to the earth's surface at R. The **azimuth** is the angle between the N–S plane passing through R and the line from the satellite to R measured relative to the north pole.

Frequency allocations

As we saw in Figure 11.2, the bandwidth of an analog TV signal – including guard bands – is either 6 or 8 MHz. As we show in Figure 11.16, with the earliest satellites used for commercial analog television broadcasts, the signal of each TV program is frequency modulated onto a separate carrier which results in a basic channel bandwidth of 36 MHz. A satellite supports multiple channels and these are combined to form the signal that is transmitted from the basestation to the satellite using frequency division multiplexing. Typically, 24 channels are used with a guard band of 4 MHz between adjacent channels.

In order to avoid the signal received from the basestation on the uplink interfering with the signal transmitted by the satellite on the downlink, a separate frequency band is used for transmissions in the uplink and downlink directions. This means that each channel is allocated a separate carrier signal in both the uplink and downlink directions with the same fixed spacing between channels.

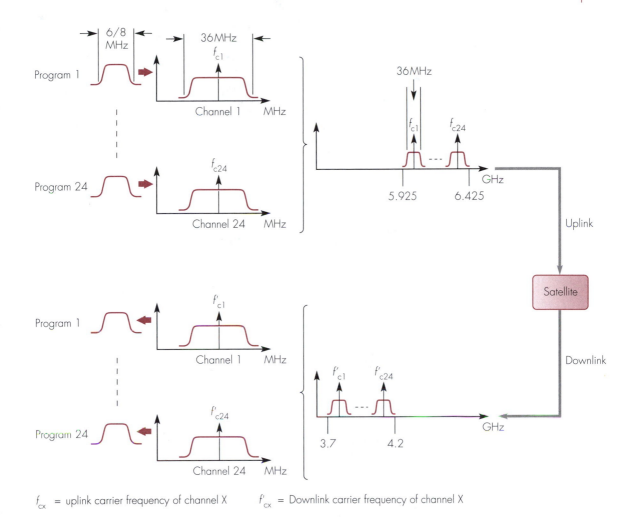

Figure 11.16 Frequency bands used with early satellite systems.

Antenna designs

Owing to the large distance travelled, the signal received from the transmitter is extremely weak. Hence it is essential to receive as much of the transmitted signal as possible. This is achieved by using a parabolic dish made of a reflecting material. Like light, microwaves travel in straight lines and are reflected by metallic surfaces. Hence as we show in part (i) of Figure 11.17(a), the incident waves received from the transmitter are all focussed at the focal point of the dish. Moreover, since the distance travelled by all the waves is the same, they all arrive at the focal point in-phase and their energy, therefore, is additive.

Located at the focal point of the dish is a unit known as a **low-noise block converter (LNB/C)**. This consists of a low-noise amplifier and a frequency

(a)

(i) prime focus antenna:

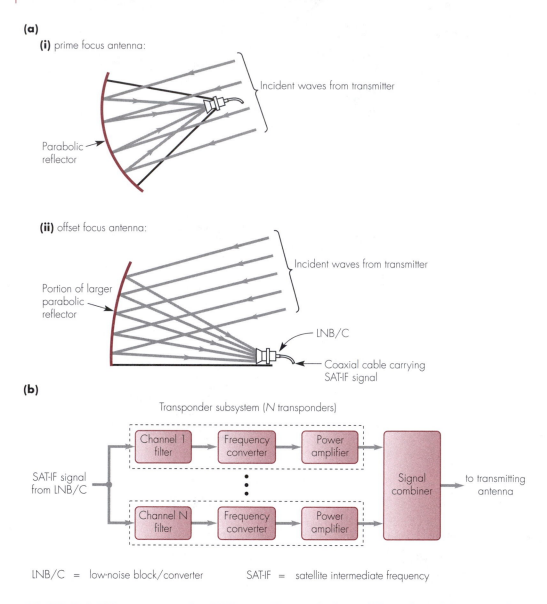

(ii) offset focus antenna:

(b)

LNB/C = low-noise block/converter   SAT-IF = satellite intermediate frequency

Figure 11.17 Satellite components: (a) two antenna designs; (b) on-board transponder subsystem.

downconverter. As we saw in Figure 11.16, the frequency of the uplink signal with early satellite systems is in the range 5.925 through to 6.425 GHz. Since this exceeds the bandwidth of a coaxial cable, prior to passing the received signal to the on-board electronics for frequency conversion, the received signal is first amplified in the LNB/C and then downconverted into a lower frequency band. This is called the **satellite intermediate frequency** (**SAT-IF**) and, with early systems, is 950 MHz. It is this signal that is then passed to the on-board electronics by means of a coaxial cable.

The antenna design shown in part (i) of Figure 11.17(a) is called a **prime focus antenna** since the LNB/C is located in the center of the dish at its focal point. The disadvantage of this design is the LNB/C inhibits the direct waves in the center of the dish from being collected. Clearly this reduces the efficiency of the antenna and, for small dishes, the fall in efficiency can be significant. To overcome this effect, the reflector used with more modern antennas is a portion of a larger parabolic mirror. This type of design is known as an **offset focus antenna** and its principle of operation is shown in part (ii) of Figure 11.17(a). As we can see, with this design the LNB/C is attached to the bottom of the dish and hence out of the way of the incoming waves. This has the effect of increasing significantly the antenna's efficiency.

Transponder subsystem

The signal output by the LNB/C is passed to an electronic module within the satellite. This is known as the transponder subsystem and its composition is shown in Figure 11.17(b).

Microwave power amplifiers are only linear over a limited frequency band which dictates that each channel signal is amplified separately prior to its transmission. As we can see in the figure, the individual modulated channel signals are first separated out using filters. Each is then frequency-shifted to its allocated (downlink) frequency band and then amplified. The resulting signals are then combined to form the downlink signal that is broadcast over a defined area known as the satellite's field of coverage or **footprint**. An antenna – satellite dish – on each subscriber premises is then used to receive the broadcast signal.

The signal received by the antenna is first down-shifted in the LNB/C and then passed to the set-top box over a coaxial cable. Electronic circuitry within the STB demodulates the received signal by first filtering out each channel signal. The corresponding carrier signal for each channel is then used to recover the signal of the related TV program that has been selected by the subscriber.

As we saw in Section 6.2.5, satellites use frequencies in the microwave frequency band since these propagate through free space in straight lines and can be focussed into a beam of a defined width. In the uplink direction a narrow beam width is used to ensure the maximum amount of energy in the signal transmitted by the basestation is received by the satellite's receiving antenna. Conversely, a wide beam width is used in the downlink direction to ensure the signal is received by all the antennas within the satellite's footprint. The size of the dish required to receive the signal broadcast by the satellite is determined by the output power of the satellite's transmitter – which is influenced by the number of transponders – and its area of coverage.

Most early systems use a single satellite and, in many instances, cover a wide geographical area with the effect that dishes of between 1 and 4 meters are required. With later systems, however, multiple satellites are used to cover a similar area and hence dishes as small as 45 cm (15 inches) are common. With such dishes, interference-free reception can be obtained if the satellites have orbital positions with a spacing of in the order of 10°.

For most early commercial analog television broadcasts, the frequency bands used are within what is called the **C-band** of the microwave frequency range. As we saw in Figure 11.16, with this band the frequency range of the uplink channels is from 5.925 to 6.425 GHz and that of the downlink channels from 3.7 to 4.2 GHz. Typical channel bandwidths of 40 MHz – including a guard-band – are used. With microwaves, however, it is possible to use the same frequency band twice using both horizontally polarized and vertically polarized transmissions. Hence the total 500 MHz of available bandwidth can support up to 24 active channels and hence transponders.

Normally, in order to improve reliability, most transponder subsystems contain a number of spare transponders (and other units) to replace any that may become defective. A *command and telemetry subsystem* is then used to send commands to the satellite to switch spare units into service should this be necessary. Typically, a satellite has to be replaced after 10 to 12 years of service.

11.3.2 Digital television

Since all satellite transmissions are within an allocated frequency band (within the microwave frequency spectrum), modulated transmission must also be used for the transmission of a digital TV program. As with cable TV, therefore, the bitstream containing the multiplexed set of (digital) TV programs is passed through a (microwave) modem to convert it into an analog signal within the allocated frequency band. However, in order to obtain the same bit error rate probability as that obtained with a cable distribution network, a more robust modulation scheme must be used. Hence instead of 64 or 256-QAM with 6/8 bits per symbol (signal element), the modulation scheme used is QPSK (4-QAM) which, as we saw in Figure 7.6(b), has just 2 bits per symbol.

For most digital TV transmissions, the frequency band used is in what is called the **Ku band** which covers the frequency range from 10.7 through to 14.5 GHz. In the downlink direction, the lowest part of the band from 10.7 through to 11.7 GHz is used mainly for newer analog TV transmissions. For digital TV, example downlink bands are 12.2 through to 12.7 GHz for the North American **digital broadcast satellites** (**DBS**) and 11.7 through to 12.5 GHz for the European **digital video broadcasting-satellites** (**DVB-S**). The DBS system uses three orbital positions with 9° spacing, each allowing full coverage to be obtained. Each position is used by a separate service provider which then uses a number of satellites – normally three – to obtain interference-free reception with small dishes. Typically, the allocated bandwidth is used to provide 32 channels of 24 MHz each supporting a symbol rate of 20 Mbaud. Hence, with QPSK, this gives a typical channel bit rate of 40 Mbps.

The DVB-S system uses two orbital positions with 6.2° spacing, each of which allows full coverage to be obtained. Each position is used by a separate satellite operator which uses two satellites to obtain interference-free reception with small dishes. With this system, the typical allocated bandwidth is used to provide 40 channels of 33 MHz, each supporting a symbol rate of 27.5 Mbaud which, with QPSK, gives a bit rate of 55 Mbps.

Channel interface

A schematic diagram showing the individual blocks associated with each channel interface is given in Figure 11.18(a). Most satellite digital TV transmissions now use the standard, MPEG-2 transport stream multiplex. As we saw in Figure 5.20, the (multiplexed) bitstreams of multiple TV programs are multiplexed together into a single bitstream that is made up of a contiguous stream of 188-byte packets, each comprising a 4-byte header and a 184-byte payload. As we indicated earlier, satellite channels are more susceptible to transmission (bit) errors than cable networks. Hence in addition to using a more robust modulation scheme, a more rigorous forward error control scheme is applied to each 188-byte packet. This involves the addition of check bytes derived using a Reed–Solomon code – as optionally used with cable networks – byte interleaving, and convolutional encoding of the resulting bitstream.

The RS check bytes are added primarily to detect burst errors and the same coding scheme as is optionally used in cable networks is used. As we saw in Section 11.2.1, this is an RS (204, 188) code and the 16 check bytes that are appended to each 188-byte packet enable up to 8 bytes in error in each 204-byte block to be identified and corrected.

As we explain in Appendix B, very long error bursts in a block – that is, greater than 8 bytes – can be broken down into smaller bursts by using a technique known as **interleaving**. Essentially, this involves rearranging the order of transmission of the bytes in each 204-byte block so that an error burst longer than 8 bytes will affect no more than 8 sequential bytes in the original 204-byte block. The principle is shown in Figure 11.18(b).

Prior to transmission each 204-byte block output by the RS coder is fragmented into twelve 17-byte subblocks. The transmitted byte sequence is then the first byte from each of the 12 subblocks, followed by the second byte in each subblock, and so on. The reverse operation is then performed at the receiver to reorder the bytes into their original sequence. In this way, should an error burst of, say, 12 bytes occur within a block during its transmission, this will affect only every seventeenth byte in the original 204-byte block and hence be detected and corrected by the RS decoder.

In addition to burst errors, satellite transmissions are susceptible to randomly distributed single bit errors. To minimize the effect of such errors, the bitstream output by the byte interleaver is passed through a **convolutional encoder**, the principles of which are also described in Appendix B. A typical encoder used with digital TV broadcasts is shown in Figure 11.18(c).

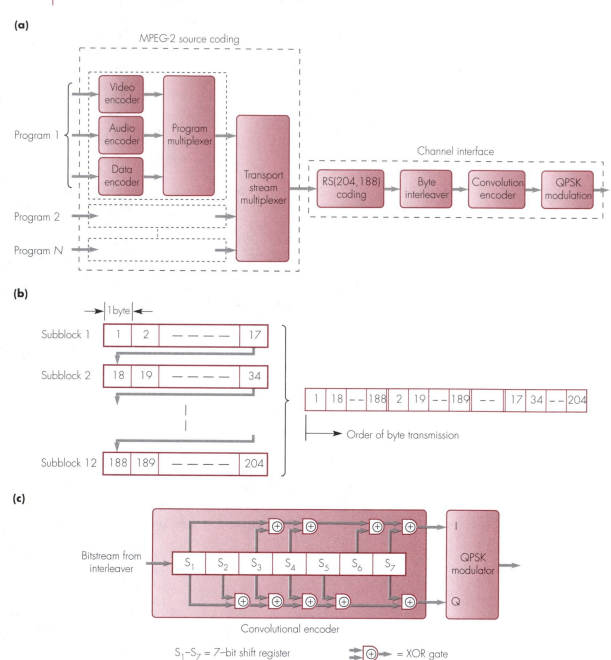

Figure 11.18 Satellite digital television channel interface: (a) schematic; (b) interleaver principle; (c) convolutional encoder.

Essentially, the bitstream output by the byte interleaver is passed through a 7-bit shift register and, for each new bit entering the shift register, two separate XOR operations are performed on the new contents of the register. The pair of bits produced by the two XOR operations are then the two bits that are transmitted for this input bit; that is, for each input bit two bits are transmitted. As we explain in Appendix B, for each type of encoder there is only a limited number of possible pairs of output bits for each new input bit. These are known by the convolutional decoder in the receiver and, for each pair of bits it receives, the decoder computes the *Hamming distance* – see Section 6.6.1 – between the pair of bits it has received and all the known possible pairs. This procedure is repeated for each new pair of bits the decoder receives and, after a predefined number of pairs, the decoder selects the sequence with the smallest Hamming distance as being the most likely sequence of (pairs of) bits that were transmitted. It then replaces each pair of bits in this sequence with the corresponding bitstream that would have produced this sequence.

Since two bits are output for every bit input into the encoder, it is known as a **rate 1/2** convolutional encoder. Hence for every 204-byte block output by the interleaver, 408 bytes are transmitted. It is also possible to operate such encoders at a higher rate by deleting selected bits from the bitstream produced by the encoder. The technique used is called **puncturing** and example rates are 2/3 – 3 output bits for every 2 input bits – 3/4, 5/6, and 7/8. This has the effect, however, of reducing the error correction properties of the code and hence the rate used is a compromise between the level of error correction required and the amount of transmission overheads that are acceptable.

Example 11.1

A digital satellite channel interface uses the MPEG-2 transport stream multiplex, an RS (204, 188) block code, a rate 3/4 convolutional encoder, and QPSK modulation. Determine the number of overhead bits associated with the interface and hence the useful bit rate that is obtained with a channel that operates at (i) 20 Mbaud and (ii) 27.5 Mbuad.

Answer:

MPEG-2 transport stream multiplex comprises a stream of 188-byte packets each of which has a 4-byte header.

With an RS (204, 188) code, for each 188-byte block the RS encoder adds 16 error check bytes.

With a rate 3/4 convolutional encoder, for each 204-byte block the encoder adds 68 bytes of overhead.

Hence total overhead per 184-byte block = 4 + 16 + 68 = 88 bytes.

▶

11.1 Continued

With QPSK, each symbol = 2 bits and hence raw bit rates are

(i) 40 Mbps and (ii) 55 Mbps.

Hence useful bit rate with a raw bit rate of:

(i) 40 Mbps = $40 \times 184/272 = 27.1$ Mbps

(ii) 55 Mbps = $55 \times 184/272 = 37.2$ Mbps

The usage of each channel is determined by the service provider. Examples are multiple 4 Mbps channels for digital TV broadcasts or multiple 1.5 Mbps channels for near video-on-demand.

11.3.3 Interactive services

As we saw in Figure 1.16(b) and the accompanying text, in addition to the transmission of direct-to-home analog and digital television broadcasts, satellite networks are also used to support a range of interactive services. As we saw in the figure, the satellite network is used to provide a high bit rate channel from the service provider to the set-top box of each subscriber. As we have just seen, a single satellite channel can be used to broadcast data at rates of up to 6/8 Mbps if a single TV channel is used or up to 27/37 Mbps with a full transponder channel. Hence applications that involve the transmission of the same data to all of the subscribers concurrently can readily be supported. In some instances only local interaction with the STB is required whilst in others a facility is needed to enable the subscriber to interact with the remote information source. Typically, this is a remote server computer attached to the Internet. Hence the most popular way of providing an interaction channel is through either a PSTN (with modems) or an ISDN.

There are many applications that can exploit this type of facility and, for description purposes, they can be divided into a number of categories determined by the level of interactivity involved:

■ **local interaction**: as we saw in Figure 11.18(a), each MPEG-2 program multiplexer, in addition to the audio and video associated with the (TV) program, also supports an optional data channel. This is used for a variety of purposes. For example, to transmit information about the players in a football game that is being broadcast. Typically, as this is received, it is stored in the STB and the subscriber can then locally interact with the STB to have selected information displayed on the TV screen while the game is being played.

In other applications of this type, the data is not associated with a particular TV program but is from, say, a server that is located at the basestation of the service provider and has a direct connection to the

Internet. Examples of this are electronic newspapers and magazines. Typically, therefore, the data that is broadcast occupies a separate TV channel. This again is stored in the STB and subsequently can be accessed interactively by the subscriber and displayed on the TV screen. Normally, such channels are controlled by **conditional access**, that is, the broadcast bitstream has been scrambled (randomized) and requires a key to be unscrambled. Another example in this category is **pay-per-view**. The local interactions in these cases involve the subscriber inserting a *smart card* into a slot in the STB;

- **anonymous response to broadcasts**: with this category, a low bit rate interaction channel is involved which, typically, is a PSTN. Examples are when a subscriber votes in a talent contest that is being broadcast or responds to an opinion poll. The subscriber simply calls one of a given set of telephone numbers and the call is logged;

- **purchase requests**: typically, this is in response to a product or service that is being offered via a TV broadcast. For such services the subscriber must interact with a remote location in order to enter credit card details and address information, for example. Normally, this is through a PSTN or ISDN and a call center.

11.4 Terrestrial television networks

Prior to the introduction of small-dish direct-to-home satellite broadcasts in the early 1990s, most homes received broadcast television by means of either cable TV networks or terrestrial networks; that is, both the transmitting and receiving antennas are at ground – or nearly ground – level. So although a significant percentage of homes now receive broadcast TV by means of cable and satellite networks, terrestrial networks are still widely used.

11.4.1 Broadcast television principles

Most terrestrial TV transmissions are in the very high frequency (VHF) and the ultra-high frequency (UHF) bands of the electromagnetic frequency spectrum from 47 through to 860 MHz. As we indicated in Section 6.2.5, above 100 MHz electromagnetic waves travel in straight lines. They also suffer more attenuation than lower-frequency radio waves and, since both the transmitter and receiver are at ground level, large buildings, hills, mountains, and so on between the transmitter and a receiver all impair the transmitted signal and hence give rise to poor reception. Thus to cover a wide geographical area requires a significant number of transmitters distributed around the total reception area. A typical arrangement is shown in Figure 11.19(a).

The signal from the program source to the distributed set of transmitters can be sent by microwave links or land lines, typically optical fiber. In some countries, each transmitter operates in a different frequency band from its

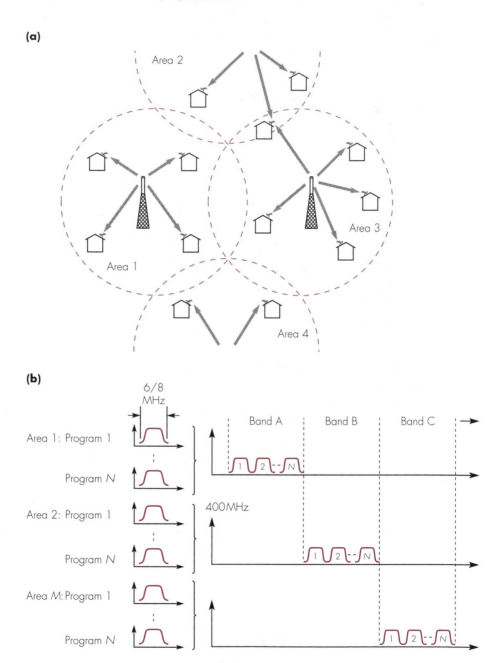

Figure 11.19 Terrestrial television principles: (a) broadcast network schematic; (b) example frequency usage.

neighbors and the network is then known as a **multiple-frequency network (MFN)**. In other countries, all transmitters operate using the same frequency band and hence the network is called a **single-frequency network (SFN)**. An example usage of the frequency band in an MFN is shown in Figure 11.19(b) and, as we saw earlier in Figure 6.6, with an MFN it is possible to reuse the frequency bands using a cell structure.

11.4.2 Digital television

The MPEG-2 source coding and channel interface blocks used for digital TV broadcasts over terrestrial networks are similar to those used with satellite networks which we showed in Figure 11.18(a). The main difference is the type of modulation scheme that is used. In order to obtain a wide field of coverage, terrestrial broadcasts are omnidirectional and, as a result, the receiving antenna may receive multiple copies of the same signal from a variety of paths. Although most power is in the direct path (line-of-sight) signal, microwaves are reflected from buildings. Also, various atmospheric conditions can cause the broadcast signal to be refracted back to earth. These waves take a slightly longer time to reach the receiving antenna than the direct wave and lead to an effect known as **multipath**.

All electromagnetic waves travel through free space at the speed of light, about $(3 \times 10^8 \text{ ms}^{-1})$. The wavelength of a signal is defined as the distance travelled by the wave in the time duration of a single cycle of the signal. That is,

Wavelength, $\lambda = c/f$ meters

where f is the frequency of the signal. Hence a signal of 500 MHz has a wavelength of:

$$\lambda = 3 \times 10^8 / 500 \times 10^6 = 0.6 \text{ meters}$$

Thus, the reflected and refracted waves received by the antenna may have significant phase differences from the direct wave. This is known as **multipath dispersion** or **delay spread** and causes the signals relating to a previous bit/symbol to interfere with the signals relating to the next bit/symbol. This is known as **intersymbol interference (ISI)** and, the higher the transmitted bit rate – and hence the shorter each bit cell period – the larger the level of ISI. It is for this reason that a modulation technique called **coded orthogonal frequency division multiplexing (COFDM)** is used for the transmission of the high bit rates associated with digital television.

COFDM principles

The main components of a COFDM modulator are shown in Figure 11.20(a) and the principle of operation of the scheme is shown in Figure 11.20(b).

Using COFDM, instead of just a single carrier signal, multiple orthogonal (equally-spaced) carriers are used, each of which is independently modulated

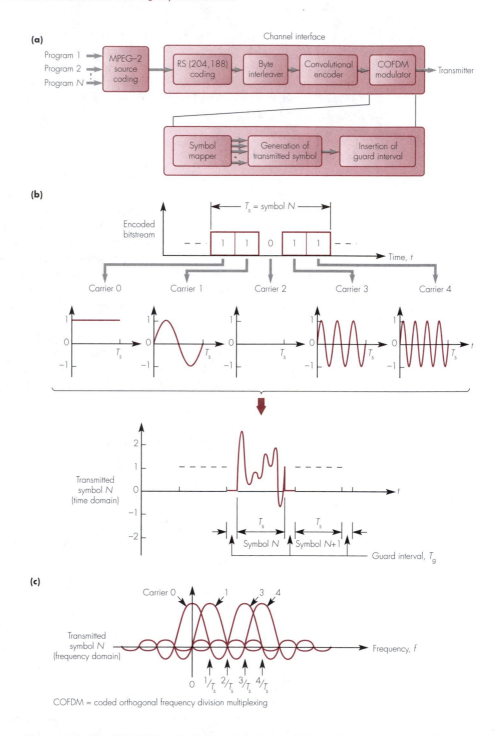

Figure 11.20 COFDM principles: (a) channel interface components; (b) symbol generation (time domain); (c) frequency domain symbol.

by one or more bits from the encoded bitstream to be transmitted. In the simple example shown in Figure 11.20(b), five carriers are used each of which is modulated by a single bit from the transmitted bitstream using on–off keying. The first carrier is a DC level, while the remaining four carriers are all sinusoidal signals of frequencies f_s, $2f_s$, $3f_s$ and $4f_s$ respectively. The period T_s is called the symbol period and, since on–off keying is being used, is equal to the time to transmit 5 bits from the encoded bitstream being transmitted. Alternatively, if N carriers were used each modulated using, say, QPSK, then T_s would be the time to transmit $2 \times N$ bits from the encoded bitstream. During each symbol period, the five modulated signals are added together to form the signal/symbol that is transmitted.

At the receiver, before starting to process each received symbol, the receiver waits a short time interval known as the **guard interval** to ensure that all delayed versions of the direct-path signals that make up the symbol have been received. In this way, instead of the delayed signals interfering with the direct-path symbol, since the same signals make up the symbol, they simply increase the power in the received symbol before it is processed. The processing involves determining which of the five carrier signals are present in the symbol and, based on this (and knowledge of the modulation method that has been used) the receiver can determine the original bitstream that was transmitted. As we show in Figure 11.20(c), by using a set of carriers that are orthogonal, there is a fixed spacing of $1/T_s$ between adjacent carriers which simplifies the processing that is required to determine which of the carriers are present in each received symbol.

In practice, the generation of each symbol is carried out digitally using a mathematical technique called the **inverse discrete Fourier transform (IDFT)**. The digital symbol output by the IDFT is converted into an analog symbol using a digital-to-analog converter prior to transmission. Similarly, the received symbol is first converted into a digital form – using an analog-to-digital converter (ADC) – before the symbol is processed using the DFT to determine the carriers that are present.

Although adding a guard interval avoids intersymbol interference, it also influences the maximum encoded bit rate that can be supported; the longer the guard interval, T_g, the lower the maximum bit rate. Typically, therefore, T_g is limited to a maximum value of $T_s/4$. Hence, in a terrestrial broadcast application, the number of carriers used can be several thousand. For example, with multiple-frequency networks a typical T_g of 50 µs is required to avoid intersymbol interference and hence a typical T_s would be 200 µs. This gives a carrier spacing – and hence fundamental frequency F_s (= $1/Ts$) – of 5 kHz. Hence in a broadcast channel that has a usable bandwidth of, say, 7 MHz, the carriers would be spaced at:

$$0, 5, 10, 15 \ldots 6995, 7000 \, \text{kHz}$$

intervals. This means 1401 carriers would be used. In the case of single-frequency networks, however, a typical guard interval of 200 µs is required. This means a typical T_s of 800 µs, an f_s of 1.25 kHz and hence 5601 carriers.

Example 11.2

The two standards relating to digital terrestrial broadcasting are known as the **2K/8K specifications for digital video broadcasting – terrestrial** (**DVB-T**). For multiple-frequency networks, a guard interval of 56 μs is specified and for single-frequency networks 214 μs. Assuming a usable channel bandwidth of 7.607 MHz, derive (i) T_s, (ii) f_s, and (iii) the number of carriers for both network types.

Answer:

$$T_s = 4 \times T_g \qquad f_s = 1/T_s \qquad N \le (7610/f_s) + 1$$

MFN: (i) $T_s = 4 \times 56 = 224\,\mu s$

(ii) $f_s = 1/T_s = 4.464\,kHz$

(iii) $N = (7607/4.464) + 1 = 1704 + 1 = 1705$ carriers

SFN: (i) $T_s = 4 \times 224 = 896\,\mu s$

(ii) $f_s = 1/T_s = 1.116\,kHz$

(iii) $N = (7607/1.116) + 1 = 6816 + 1 = 6817$ carriers

As we saw earlier, both the IDFT and DFT are performed digitally and hence the processing is carried out in powers of 2. The nearest power of 2 value to 1705 is 2048 (2K) and to 6817 is 8192 (8K) which is the origin of the terms used.

Receiver synchronization

Clearly, it is necessary for the receiver to detect reliably the start of each new symbol that is received; that is, for the receiver to obtain and maintain symbol synchronization. In order to do this, with both network types, the stream of symbols is divided into 68-symbol blocks. Each block of symbols is called a *frame* and the common frame format used is shown in Figure 11.21.

As we can see, along each row are the individual frequency carriers in each symbol. Hence in a 2K system this contains 1705 carriers and in an 8K system 6817 carriers. Although in the simple example we saw in Figure 11.20(b) on–off keying was used, in practical systems each carrier is separately modulated using either QPSK (4-QAM), 16-QAM, or 64-QAM. Since each carrier can transmit 2, 4, or 6 bits per signal transition/element, ignoring the loss of transmission capacity caused by the guard interval, each carrier in an MFN can transmit $4.464 \times 2/4/6$ kbps of data and, in an SFN, $1.116 \times 2/4/6$ kbps of data.

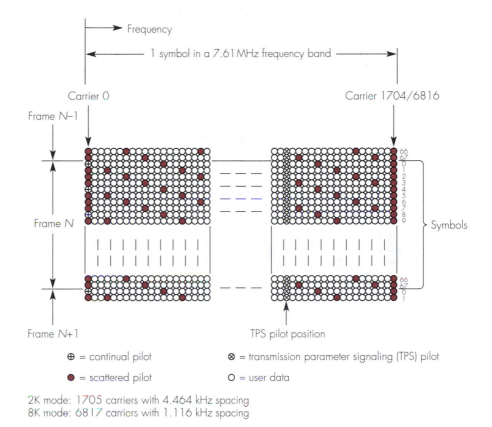

Figure 11.21 DVB-T 2K/8K frame format.

As we show in the figure, the bitstream relating to specific carrier positions in each of the 68 symbols of a frame carries one of two defined bit sequences called **pilots**: one the *continual pilot* and the other the *scattered pilot*. The receiver achieves and maintains symbol synchronization by searching for these two pilot sequences in the known carrier positions. In addition, once in synchronization, the bitstream of the eighteenth carrier from the end of each symbol is used to form a subframe that contains operational parameters to enable the receiver to interpret correctly the received symbol stream. These carriers are called *TPS pilots* and the contents of each subframe include the length of the guard interval, the type of modulation of the other carriers that are being used, and the rate of the convolutional coder.

The bit rate that is available with each 6/8 MHz broadcast channel is determined by the modulation method that is used for each carrier. With the 2K specification and 16-QAM for example, after removing the pilots and allowing for the loss of transmission capacity caused by the guard interval, a typical channel bit rate is 24 Mbps. As we saw earlier in Example 11.1, the overheads associated with the other blocks in the channel interface – the RS (204, 188) coder and a rate 3/4 convolutional coder – reduce this figure to about 16 Mbps ($24 \times 184/272$). This can be used to carry, say, four 4 Mbps digital TV programs in each 8 MHz broadcast channel.

11.4.3 Interactive services

The interactive services available with terrestrial broadcast networks are similar to those we identified in relation to satellite networks. In general, however, the amount of transmission bandwidth/number of channels available with terrestrial networks is much less than with satellite networks. Hence the range of services available is only a subset of those listed in Section 11.3.3.

11.5 High-speed PSTN access technologies

As we saw in Figure 1.1(c), the access network of a PSTN, in addition to supporting the plain old telephone service (POTS) for which it was designed, now supports a number of additional services. For example, a range of low bit rate data applications such as fax are supported by means of low bit rate – less than 56 kbps – modems. Also, as we saw in Section 7.2.3, twisted-pair lines in the PSTN access network are used as the access lines for an ISDN. Bit rates of between 144 kbps (basic rate) and 1.544/2.048 Mbps (primary rate) over several miles/kilometers are obtained using baseband transmission. The access line is then known as a digital subscriber line (DSL). In the case of a basic rate line, this is called an **ISDN DSL** (**IDSL**) and, in the case of a primary rate line, a **high-speed DSL** (**HDSL**). An IDSL uses a single pair and an HDSL two pairs. In addition there is a simpler version of HDSL which operates over a single pair. This is known as **single-pair DSL** (**SDSL**) and bit rates of up to 1.544/2.048 Mbps are supported depending on line length.

Both the basic rate and the primary rate lines of an ISDN are symmetric; that is, they operate with an equal bit rate in both directions. However, as we saw earlier in Section 11.2.1, with most interactive applications the information flow is asymmetric and involves a low bit rate channel from the subscriber for interaction purposes and a high bit rate channel in the downstream direction for the return of the requested information. Asymmetric ratios of from 10:1 to in excess of 100:1 are common. In order to exploit this, many cable operating companies have introduced cable modems that support various applications of this type.

In addition, many **telecommunication operating companies** (**telcos**) have introduced additional types of DSL technologies to meet these same requirements over the twisted-pair lines used in most PSTN access networks. Unlike the various DSL technologies associated with an ISDN, these have been designed to enable the signals associated with the existing telephony services to coexist with those associated with the newer high-speed interactive services on the same twisted-pair line. Two types are used: the first known as **asymmetric DSL** (**ADSL**) and the second **very-high-speed DSL** (**VDSL**). In the case of ADSL, the high-speed asymmetric channel is designed to coexist with the existing analog telephony service. In the case of VDSL, the high-speed channel, in addition to operating at a higher bit rate than that of an ADSL, can operate in either an asymmetric or symmetric mode and is designed to coexist with either analog telephony or basic-rate ISDN services. In this section we discuss both these technologies.

11.5.1 ADSL

The standard relating to ADSL was produced by the ANSI in 1995 and is defined in **T1.413**. It was defined originally to meet the requirements of broadcast-quality video-on-demand (VOD). Hence the standard allows for a bit rate of up to 8 Mbps in the downstream direction – that is, from the local exchange/end office (LE/EO) to the customer premises – and up to 1 Mbps in the upstream direction. In practice, however, high-speed access to the Internet proved to be more popular than VOD. As a result, since the bit rate and QOS requirements associated with Internet applications are less than those of VOD, a variant of the original ADSL standard known as **ADSL-Lite** (or sometimes **G-Lite**) has been defined. This has been developed within the ITU and is defined in standard **G.992.2**. It provides a downstream bit rate of up to 1.5 Mbps and an upstream bit rate of up to 384 kbps. As with ADSL, the actual bit rates achievable depend on the length and quality of the line. Nevertheless, the lower bit rates associated with ADSL-Lite means that it can be used over longer distances and with poorer-quality lines than ADSL. In addition, as we shall see, ADSL-Lite can be used with a passive network termination at the customer premises rather than the active termination that is required with ADSL.

Access network architectures

As we saw in Section 7.2.1, in the earliest PSTN access networks the transmission lines used were made up entirely of interconnected sections of unshielded cable containing multiple twisted-pair wires. Over a period of time, however, sections of these cables have been replaced with optical fiber cable. The architecture of a typical PSTN access network is as shown in Figure 11.22.

As we can see, the amount of twisted-pair cable used varies from zero with **fiber-to-the-home** (**FTTH**) or **fiber-to-the-building** (**FTTB**), short (less than 300 yards/meters) drop cables with **fiber-to-the-kerb/curb** (**FTTK/C**), one or two cable sections with **fiber-to-the-cabinet** (**FTTCab**), and all twisted-pair for direct-to-building cable runs of up to 2.5 miles (4km). Hence, since the objective of ADSL is to provide high-speed interactive services over the twisted-pair portion of the access line, ADSL is designed on the assumption that the maximum length of twisted-pair cable is less than 2.5 miles (4km).

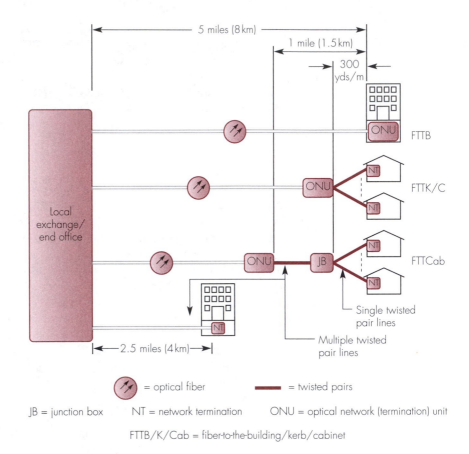

Figure 11.22 Typical modern access network architecture.

Connection alternatives

As we saw in Section 2.5.1, the lower frequency band up to 4 kHz of the bandwidth available with a (single) twisted-pair line is used for analog telephony (POTS). So in order for the two ADSL/ADSL-Lite signals to coexist with the POTS signal on the same line, modulated transmission must be used to take the signals away from the lower frequency band. In the case of ADSL, the two signals are transmitted in the frequency band from 25 kHz through to 1.1 MHz and, for ADSL-Lite, the upper frequency is limited to 500 kHz. The components that are used to deliver both services over the same access line are shown in Figure 11.23. The arrangement shown in part (a) relates to a typical ADSL installation and that in part (b) an ADSL-Lite installation. In both cases it is assumed that the access line is all twisted-pair and this terminates in the LE/EO. With the various fiber access alternatives, the same line termination arrangement is located in the **optical network (termination) unit (ONU)**.

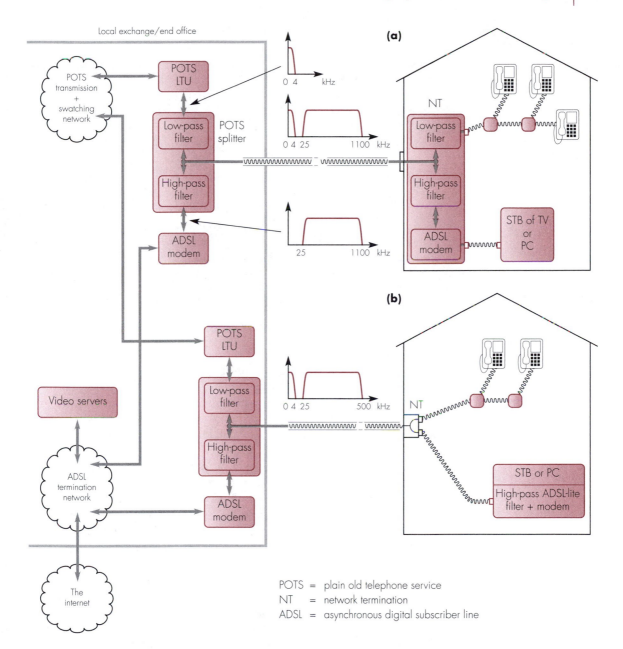

Figure 11.23 Connection alternatives: (a) ADSL with active NT; (b) ADSL-Lite with passive NT.

As we can see in part (a), with an ADSL installation the network termination (NT) at each customer premises is the same as that used in the LE/EO. This comprises an electrical circuit known as a **POTS splitter** and its role is to separate out the POTS and ADSL signals. This is done by means of two filters, a low-pass filter from 0–4 kHz that passes only the POTS signal and a high-pass filter from 25 kHz–1.1 MHz that passes only the forward and return ADSL signals. As we can see, having separated out the POTS signal, the existing customer wiring and connection sockets can be used to connect telephones to the NT. In the case of the ADSL signals, normally the ADSL modem is located within the NT and new wiring is used to connect the customer equipment to the NT. This can be a PC or the TV set-top box depending on the service that is being provided. Alternatively, the ADSL modem can be located within the customer equipment and the latter is then connected directly to the output of the high-pass filter.

As we can see in part (b), with an ADSL-Lite installation the existing (passive) NT and twisted-pair wiring is used. The telephone handsets are attached directly to this as they are responsive only to the low-frequency speech signal. The equipment using the ADSL-Lite line – typically a PC for Internet access – can also be attached to this same wiring. Integrated within the equipment (PC), however, is a high-pass filter and the ADSL-Lite modem. The advantage of this approach is the much simplified NT as it avoids the use of a POTS splitter and filters. Also, the existing wiring and sockets can be used to provide access to both services. To use the fast-access Internet service, the customer simply purchases and installs the line-termination board containing the high-pass filter and ADSL-Lite modem into the PC and informs the telco that they wish to use the fast-access Internet service. The telco then connects the customer line to the newer NT equipment at the LE/EO to provide this service without the need to install any new wiring or visit the customer premises.

The disadvantage of this approach is that, in some instances, since the ADSL-Lite signal is carried over the whole in-house wiring, some interference can be experienced with the basic telephony service when the high bit rate service is being used concurrently. The main cause of the interference arises from the higher-frequency components in the ADSL-Lite signal being down-converted by some telephony handsets into speech-frequency signals and hence heard. This is one of the reasons why the upper frequency used with ADSL-Lite is limited to 500 kHz. In addition, if the existing in-house wiring is poor, then interference may also arise owing to external effects such as radio broadcasts. So in instances where interference is obtained, it is often necessary to install a low-pass filter into the sockets to which telephones are connected.

Modulation method

In the ANSI T1.413 standard, the modulation method used with ADSL modems is called **discrete multitone** (**DMT**). In practice this operates in the same way as COFDM. As we saw earlier in Section 11.4.2, with COFDM the bitstream to be transmitted is divided into fixed-length blocks. The bits in each block are then transmitted using multiple carriers each of which is separately modulated by one or more bits from the block. With this application, the number of carriers is either 256 or 512. However, as we show in Figure 11.24(a), those carriers that lie in the lower part of the frequency spectrum that are reserved for telephony are not used. Also, because with twisted-pair wire the level of attenuation associated with each carrier increases as a function of frequency, a non-linear allocation of bits per carrier is used. Typically, the lower-frequency carriers are modulated using multiple bits per carrier – for example 8-QAM – and the higher-frequency carriers use progressively fewer bits down to 1 bit (PSK), the number of bits per carrier being chosen so that optimum use is made of each carrier.

In addition, because of the relatively high levels of noise present on the lines – caused by the various telephony functions such as ringing, radio frequency signals from other lines, and lightning effects – in order to improve the raw bit error rate (BER) probability of each line, a forward error correction (FEC) scheme similar to that used with satellite and (and terrestrial) broadcast channels is used. As we saw earlier in Section 11.3.2, this involves the bitstream to be transmitted being segmented into 188-byte blocks each of which has 16 FEC bytes appended to it. Byte interleaving is then used to overcome longer noise bursts, the principles of which we showed in Figure 11.18(a) and (b).

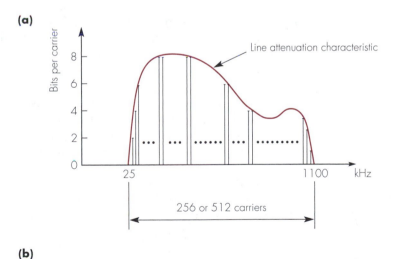

(a)

(b)

| Upstream: | frequency band = 25–200 kHz, bit rate = 32–384/1000 kbps |
| Downstream: | frequency band = 250–1100 kHz, bit rate = 640–1500/8000 kbps |

Figure 11.24 Example DMT frequency usage: (a) bits per carrier allocation, (b) duplex frequency usage.

Duplex transmission

The ADSL baseband signal comprises a duplex bitstream of up to 8 Mbps in the downstream direction and up to 1 Mbps in the return direction. In the case of ADSL-Lite the bit rates are up to 1.5 Mbps downstream and up to 384 kbps upstream. In both cases, however, since a single twisted-pair line is used, a scheme must be employed to enable both bitstreams to be transmitted over the line simultaneously. In the case of both ADSL variants this is achieved using a technique known as **frequency division duplex** (**FDD**). With this the bitstream in each direction is transmitted concurrently using a different portion of the allocated bandwidth and hence set of carriers. An example set of frequencies is given in Figure 11.24(b).

11.5.2 VDSL

Very-high-speed digital subscriber line (VDSL) is the most recent technology for providing high bit rates over existing unshielded twisted-pair access lines. It is intended for use over the twisted-pair section of fiber-to-the-kerb/curb installations with the VDSL modem located in the same cabinet as the ONU. As we saw in Figure 11.22, the maximum length of the twisted-pair section is set at 300 yards/meters and hence higher bit rates than those with ADSL can be achieved. Bit rates can be up to 20 Mbps in each direction when used in a symmetric configuration or up to 52 Mbps in an asymmetric configuration with a return path of up to 1.5 Mbps.

The technical details of VDSL are currently being decided but the modulation scheme is likely to be DMT. As we saw earlier, it is intended that the higher bit rate service should share the use of the access line with both POTS and basic rate ISDN. Hence the amount of bandwidth available for the higher bit rate service is less than that of an equivalent ADSL configuration.

The duplexing method is likely to be based on **time-division duplexing** (**TDD**). Using TDD, instead of both the downstream and upstream signals being transmitted simultaneously by allocating each signal its own portion of the line bandwidth – as is the case with FDD – alternate time intervals are allocated for each direction of transmission. This approach means that the duration of each time interval can be varied to meet the particular configuration required. Also, since the whole of the usable frequency spectrum is used in both directions, filters are not required. As with ADSL, an active network termination is used in the customer premises.

Summary

In this chapter we have studied the principle of operation of the different types of broadcast television networks – cable, satellite, and terrestrial – and how digital TV and interactive services are provided with each of these networks. We have also looked at selected aspects of the technology associated with the high-speed modems that are used with the access networks of a PSTN to deliver high-speed Internet access and other services such as video-on-demand. The topics relating to the different types of broadcast television networks are summarized in Figure 11.25(a) and those relating to high-speed PSTN modems in Figure 11.25(b).

In the case of the different types of broadcast TV networks, first we considered the principle of operation of each network type and then proceeded to study how digital TV is supported and how interactive services are provided. As we saw, with cable networks interactive services are provided using cable modems while with satellite and terrestrial broadcast networks they utilize a separate return channel from, say, a PSTN or an ISDN. We then considered the principles behind the different types of digital subscriber line (DSL) technologies that are used in the high-speed PSTN modems to obtain high bit rates over the unshielded twisted-pair (UTP) lines in the access network. As we saw, these include asymmetric DSL (ADSL), ADSL-Lite, and very-high-speed DSL (VDSL).

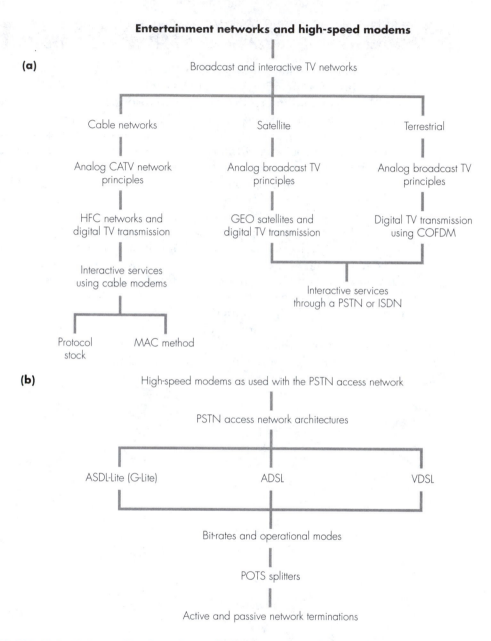

Figure 11.25 Entertainment networks and high-speed modems: (a) broadcast and interactive TV networks; (b) high-speed modems for use with the PSTN access network.

Exercises

Section 11.1

11.1 List the bit rate requirements for the (compressed) audio and video associated with the following entertainment applications:
  (i)   movie/video-on-demand,
  (ii) interactive television.
  State the reason why a return channel is needed with these applications and hence the bit rate of this.

11.2 State the minimum bit rate requirements of a high-speed modem that provides an asymmetric channel over PSTN access lines to support
  (i)   VCR-quality and
  (ii) broadcast quality movie/video-on-demand.
  Give another application for this type of channel.

Section 11.2

11.3 With the aid of the schematic diagram of a CATV distribution network shown in Figure 11.1, explain the meaning/use of the following:
  (i)   cable headend,
  (ii)   trunk and distribution coax,
  (iii) trunk and distribution amplifiers,
  (iv)   trunk splitter,
  (v)   subscriber tap.

11.4 With the aid of the frequency usage diagrams shown in Figure 11.2, state for both an NTSC system and a PAL system,
  (i)   the bandwidth required for the baseband composite video signal with sound,
  (ii)   the bandwidth required for the modulated video and audio signals,
  (iii) the meaning and use of frequency division multiplexing,
  (iv)   the role of the frequency translators, filters, and combiner in the cable headend,
  (v)   how a subscriber selects a particular TV program,
  (vi)   the range of frequencies of the coaxial cable bandwidth that are used.

11.5 In relation to the hybrid fiber coax network shown in Figure 11.3, explain the meaning/use of the following:
  (i)   a fiber node and the number of homes each serves,
  (ii)   bidirectional distribution amplifiers,
  (iii) the utilization of the cable bandwidth in the downstream and upstream directions including the use of guard-bands and bandsplitting filters.

11.6 Explain the role of an RF modem including the modulation schemes used and the bandwidth available with a single 6/8 MHz band. State the additional applications (to broadcast TV) that these channels are used for.

11.7 In relation to the utilization of the upstream channel bandwidth in an HFC network, explain why the available cable bandwidth is divided into smaller subbands than those used for the downstream channels. Why are more robust modulation schemes used? Give some examples of typical bands and their bit rates.

11.8 In relation to the multiaccess channels available with an HFC cable distribution network use Figures 11.3 and 11.4 to explain the role of the following:
  (i)   cable modem,
  (ii)   cable modem termination system including the role of the Fast-Ethernet switch.

11.9 In relation to the protocol stack used in a CM and the CMTS shown in Figure 11.5, state:
  (i)   why a CM has an integral (Ethernet) repeater hub within it,
  (ii)   the role of the cable MAC layer,
  (iii) the role of the SNMP, TFTP, and DHCP protocols.

11.10 With the aid of the protocol stack shown in Figure 11.5, describe the role of the following protocols during the configuration and management phases of a CM:
  (i)   the DHCP and the information obtained,
  (ii)   the TFTP and the information obtained,
  (iii) the SNMP.

11.11 In relation to the utilization of the (shared) upstream channel bandwidth, explain in outline how the cable MAC in a CM obtains bandwidth to send a frame. Include in your explanation the role of:
(i) the request and grant messages,
(ii) the service identifier of the CM,
(iii) the bandwidth allocation MAP,
(iv) time synchronization and ranging.

11.12 With the aid of the timing diagram shown in Figure 11.6, explain the principle of operation of the cable MAC time synchronization procedure. Include the meaning/use of:
(i) the SYNC management message,
(ii) SYNC time-stamp,
(iii) minislot and the power-of-two multiple associated with it,
(iv) the relationship between the minislot counter and the SYNC time-stamp.

11.13 In relation to the timing diagram relating to the cable MAC ranging procedure shown in Figure 11.7, explain:
(i) how the CM side determines when to send the first RNG-REQ message and the contents of the message,
(ii) how the CMTS side computes the RTC of the CM from the received message and informs the CM side of this,
(iii) how the returned RTC value is confirmed.

11.14 With the aid of the timing diagram relating to the cable MAC reservation access mode procedure shown in Figure 11.8, explain how the procedure works. Include in your explanation:
(i) the need for a contention resolution procedure,
(ii) the use of the DBS and DBE fields in the bandwidth allocation MAP and the meaning of the term "backoff window",
(iii) an example computation performed by the CM,
(iv) how a collision is detected by the CM and the actions it takes.

11.15 With the aid of Figure 11.9, state the meaning and role of the various header fields shown in the figure.

11.16 With the aid of the fragment header frame format and example shown in Figure 11.10, explain the fragmentation procedure carried out by a CM to transmit a user data frame that requires more minislots than have been granted. Include in your explanation the use of the EH-TYPE, EH-LEN, and EH-VALUE fields in each fragment header.

11.17 State the role of the following additional procedures relating to the cable MAC protocol:
(i) piggyback requests,
(ii) request/data regions,
(iii) QoS support including the use of unsolicited grant, real-time polling, unsolicited grant with activity detection, and non-real-time polling.

11.18 With the aid of the packet formats shown in Figure 11.11, describe the operation of the downstream transmission convergence (DSTC) sublayer. Include in your description the meaning/use of
(i) the MPEG transport packet format,
(ii) the use of the payload identifier (PID) and PUSI bit in the packet header,
(iii) how the DSTC in the CM determines the length of a MAC frame,
(iv) stuff-bytes.

11.19 With the aid of the two schematic packet flows shown in Figure 11.12, describe the principle of operation of the downstream and upstream transmission convergence sublayers. In relation to the upstream direction, include the meaning/use of
(i) a guard-band,
(ii) a preamble sequence,
(iii) the forward error control field.

11.20 With the aid of the network topology shown in Figure 11.13, explain the motivation for cable operating companies linking their regional HFC networks together to form an intranet. Describe the principle of operation of a cable intranet.

11.21 State the application domains of a multi-channel (M) and a local (L) multipoint distribution system (MDS). Hence, with the aid of the schematic diagrams shown in Figure 11.14, explain the principle of operation and operating frequencies of both systems.

Section 11.3

11.22 With the aid of the network schematic shown in Figure 11.15(a), explain the principle of operation of a geostationary satellite broadcast TV network. Include the meaning of the terms:
(i)   geosynchronous,
(ii) geostationary earth orbit (GEO).

11.23 In relation to a satellite's position, use the diagrams shown in Figure 11.15(b) to explain the meaning of
(i)   angle of elevation,
(ii) azimuth.

11.24 With the aid of the frequency bands shown in Figure 11.16 relating to early analog TV transmissions, state:
(i)   the bandwidth of each modulated TV channel,
(ii) the guard-band between adjacent channels,
(iii) why different frequency bands are used for the uplink and downlink.

11.25 Describe the principle of operation of a satellite dish including the role of the low-noise block/converter (LNB/C). With the aid of Figure 11.17(a), state the difference and advantages of an offset-focus antenna compared with a prime-focus antenna.

11.26 With the aid of the block schematic diagram shown in Figure 11.17(b), state the meaning/use of the following:
(i)   satellite intermediate frequency,
(ii)   transponder subsystem,
(iii) channel filter,
(iv)   frequency converter,
(v)   power amplifier,
(vi)   signal combiner,
(vii) command and telemetry subsystem.

11.27 With the aid of the block schematic diagrams of the (baseband) satellite digital channel interface shown in Figure 11.18, explain the role of:
(i)   the RS coding block,
(ii) the byte interleaver,
(iii) the convolutional encoder including the meaning of puncturing,
(iv) QPSK modulation.

11.28 State the following for the downlink of the DBS and DVB-S digital TV transmissions:
(i)   the allocated bandwidth,
(ii) the number of channels and the bandwidth per channel,
(iii) the symbol rate and raw bit rate of a channel,
(iv) the useful bit rate per channel,
(v)   typical applications of this.

11.29 Explain briefly the following forms of interactivity with satellite broadcast transmission. State an application in each case:
(i)   local interaction,
(ii) anonymous response,
(iii purchase request.

Section 11.4

11.30 With the aid of the diagrams relating to terrestrial TV broadcast transmissions shown in Figure 11.19, discriminate between a multi-frequency network and a single-frequency network.

11.31 Explain the meaning of the following terms relating to the broadcast channel of a terrestrial broadcast TV network:
(i)   multipath,
(ii) wavelength,
(iii) multipath dispersion/delay spread,
(iv) intersymbol interference.

11.32 With the aid of the diagrams shown in Figure 11.20, explain the principle of operation of COFDM transmission. Include the role of:
(i)   the symbol mapper,
(ii) the generation of each transmitted symbol,
(iii) the guard interval.

11.33 With the aid of the diagrams relating to COFDM in Figures 11.20 and 11.21, explain the implications of:
(i) using orthogonal carriers on the spacing between adjacent carriers,
(ii) adding a guard interval between symbols,
(iii) the relationship between the guard interval and the symbol period.

11.34 Assuming a guard interval of 50 µs and a usable channel bandwidth of 7 MHz, derive the number of carriers that would be used.

11.35 Define the origin of 2K and 8K in the 2K/8K specifications for digital video broadcasting-terrestrial (DVB-T).

11.36 With the aid of the 2K/8K frame formats shown in Figure 11.21, explain the meaning/use of the following relating to receiver synchronization:
(i) a frame,
(ii) continual pilots,
(iii) scattered pilots,
(iv) TPS pilots.

11.37 With reasons, estimate the usable bit rate that is available with an 8 MHz broadcast channel assuming the 2K specification, and 16-QAM modulation per carrier. Allow for loss of bit rate caused by the guard interval and the channel interface overheads quantified in Example 11.1. State the number of digital TV programs the channel will support.

Section 11.5

11.38 State the meaning, bit rate, and use of the following PSTN high-speed access technologies:
(i) IDSL,
(ii) HDSL,
(iii) SDSL,
(iv) ADSL-Lite,
(v) ADSL,
(vi) VDSL.

11.39 With the aid of the schematic diagram of a typical modern access network architecture shown in Figure 11.22, state the length of twisted-pair cable with each of the following:
(i) FTTH,
(ii) FTTK/C,
(iii) FTTCab,
(iv) direct-to-building.

Hence state the maximum length of twisted pair cable that can be used with ADSL.

11.40 With the aid of the access network architecture shown in Figure 11.23(a), describe how the POTS and high-speed interactive services are provided with an ADSL installation. Include in your description the role of the low-pass and high-pass filters in the POTS splitter and the ADSL modem.

11.41 With the aid of the access network architecture shown in Figure 11.23(b), describe how the POTS and high-speed interactive services are provided with an ADSL-Lite installation. Include in your description the advantages of using a passive network termination (NT) and one of the potential drawbacks of this.

11.42 In relation to the discrete multitone (DMT) modulation method used with ADSL modems, state:
(i) the number of carriers per symbol that are used,
(ii) the reason why multilevel modulation is not used with all carriers,
(iii) how duplex transmission is obtained.

11.43 State the following for a VDSL installation:
(i) the type of access network and the location of the VDSL modem,
(ii) typical bit rates,
(iii) how duplex transmission is obtained.

Transport protocols

12.1 Introduction

As we saw earlier in Section 5.2, although the range of multimedia applications (and different types of network used to support them) are many and varied, the protocol suites associated with the different application/network combinations have a common structure. As we saw in Section 1.5.3, the different types of network operate in a variety of modes – circuit-switched or packet-switched, connection-oriented or connectionless – and hence each type of network has a different set of protocols for interfacing to it. Above the network-layer protocol, however, all protocol suites comprise one or more application protocols and a number of what are called application-support protocols.

For example, in order to mask the application protocols from the services provided by the different types of network protocols, all protocol suites have one or more transport protocols. These provide the application protocols with a network-independent information interchange service and, in the case of the TCP/IP suite, they are the **transmission control protocol** (**TCP**) and the **user datagram protocol** (**UDP**). TCP provides a connection-oriented (reliable) service and UDP a connectionless (best-effort) service. Normally, both protocols are present in the suite and the choice of protocol used is determined by the requirements of the application. In addition, as we saw in

Figure 5.6, when the application involves the transfer of streams of audio and/or video in real time, the timing information required by the receiver to synchronize the incoming streams is provided by the **real-time transport protocol** (**RTP**) and its associated **real-time transport control protocol** (**RTCP**). In this chapter we describe the operation of these four protocols and the services they provide to application protocols.

12.2 TCP/IP protocol suite

Before describing the various protocols, it will be helpful to illustrate the position of each protocol relative to the others in the TCP/IP suite. This is shown in Figure 12.1. Normally, the IP protocols and network-dependent protocols below them are all part of the operating system kernel with the various application protocols implemented as separate programs/processes. The two transport protocols, TCP and UDP, are then implemented to run either within the operating system kernel, as separate programs/processes, or in a library package linked to the application program.

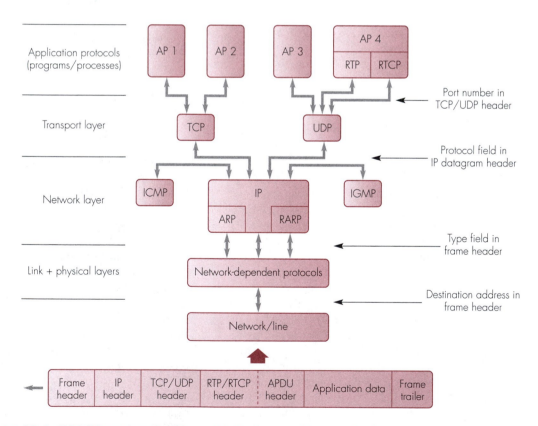

Figure 12.1 TCP/IP protocol suite and interlayer address selectors.

With most networked applications, the client–server paradigm is used. The client application protocol/program runs in one computer – typically a PC or workstation – and this communicates with a similar (peer) application program that runs (normally continuously) in a remote server computer. Examples of applications of this type are file transfers and the messages associated with electronic mail, both of which require a reliable service; that is, the transferred information should be free of transmission errors and the messages delivered in the same sequence that they were submitted. Hence applications of this type use the reliable service provided by TCP.

Thus the role of TCP is to convert the best-effort service provided by IP into a reliable service. For other applications, a simple best-effort service is acceptable and hence they use UDP as the transport protocol. Examples of applications of this type are interpersonal applications that involve the transfer of streams of (compressed) audio and/or video in real time. Clearly, since new information is being received and output continuously, it is inappropriate to request blocks that are received with errors to be retransmitted. Also, it is for applications of this type that RTP and RTCP are used. Other applications that use UDP are application protocols such as HTTP and SNMP, both of which involve a single request-response message exchange.

As we saw in Figure 9.1 and its accompanying text, all message blocks – protocol data units (PDUs) – relating to the protocols that use the services of the IP layer are transferred in an IP datagram. Hence, as we can deduce from Figure 12.1, since there are a number of protocols that use the services of IP – TCP, UDP, ICMP, and IGMP – it is necessary for IP to have some means of identifying the protocol to which the contents of the datagram relate. As we saw in Section 9.2, this is the role of the *protocol* field in each IP datagram header. Similarly, since a number of different application protocols may use the services of both TCP and UDP, it is also necessary for both these protocols to have a field in their respective PDU header that identifies the application protocol to which the PDU contents relate. As we shall see, this is the role of the source and destination *port numbers* that are present in the header of the PDUs of both protocols. In addition, since a server application receives requests from multiple clients, in order for the server to send the responses to the correct clients, both the source port number and the source IP address from the IP datagram header are sent to the application protocol with the TCP/UDP contents.

In general, within the client host, the port number of the source application protocol has only local significance and a new port number is allocated for each new transfer request. Normally, therefore, client port numbers are called **ephemeral ports** as they are short-lived. The port numbers of the peer application protocol in the server application protocols are fixed and are known as **well-known port numbers**. Their allocation is managed by IANA and they are in the range 1 through 1023. For example, the well-known port number of the server-side of the file transfer (application) protocol (FTP) is 21. Normally, ephemeral port numbers are allocated in the range 1024 through to 5000.

As we can see in Figure 12.2, all the protocols in both the application and transport layers communicate directly with a similar peer protocol in the remote host computer (end system). The protocols in both these layers are said, therefore, to communicate on an end-to-end basis. In contrast, the IP protocols present in each of the two communicating hosts are network-interface protocols. These, together with the IP in each intermediate gateway/router involved, carry out the transfer of the datagram across the internetwork. The IP protocol in each host is said to have local significance and the routing of each datagram is carried out on a hop-by-hop basis.

12.3 TCP

The transmission control protocol (TCP) provides two communicating peer application protocols – normally one in a client computer and the other in a server computer – with a two-way, reliable data interchange service. Although the APDUs associated with an application protocol have a defined structure, this is transparent to the two communicating peer TCP protocol entities which treat all the data submitted by each local application entity as a stream of bytes. The stream of bytes flowing in each direction is then transferred (over the underlying network/internet) from one TCP entity to the other in a reliable way; that is, to a high probability, each byte in the stream flowing in

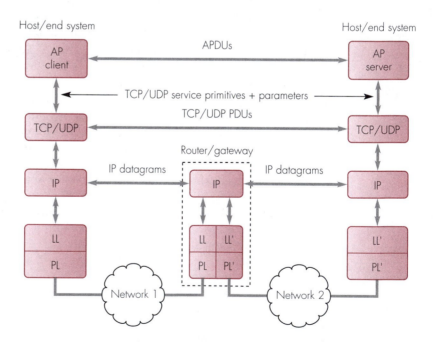

Figure 12.2 TCP/IP protocol suite interlayer communications.

each direction is free of transmission errors, with no lost or duplicate bytes, and the bytes are delivered in the same sequence as they were submitted. The service provided by TCP is known, therefore, as a **reliable stream service**.

As we explained in Section 9.2, the service provided by IP is an unreliable best-effort service. Hence in order to provide a reliable service, as we saw in Section 6.7, before any data is transferred between the two TCP entities, a logical connection is first established between them in order for the sequence numbers in each TCP entity – that are required for error correction and flow control purposes – to be initialized. Also, once all data has been transferred in both directions, the logical connection is closed.

During the actual data transfer phase, in order for the receiving TCP to detect the presence of transmission errors, each TCP entity divides the submitted stream of bytes into blocks known as **segments**. For interactive applications involving a user at a terminal, a segment may contain just a single byte while for large file transfers, a segment may contain many bytes. There is an agreed **maximum segment size** (**MSS**) used with a connection that is established by the two peer TCP entities during the setting up of the connection. This is such that an acceptable proportion of segments are received by the destination free of transmission errors. The default MSS is 536 bytes although larger sizes can be agreed. Normally, the size chosen is such that no fragmentation is necessary during the transfer of a segment over the network/internet and hence is determined by the path MTU. The TCP protocol then includes a retransmission procedure in order to obtain error-free copies of those segments that are received with transmission errors.

In addition, the TCP protocol includes a flow control procedure to ensure no data is lost when the TCP entity in a fast host – a large server for example – is sending data to the TCP in a slower host such as a PC. It also includes a congestion control procedure which endeavors to control the rate of entry of segments into the network/internet to the rate at which segments are leaving.

In the following subsections we discuss firstly the user services provided by TCP, then selected aspects of the operation of the TCP protocol, and finally the formal specification of the protocol. Collectively these are defined in **RFCs 793**, **1122**, and **1323**.

12.3.1 User services

The most widely used set of user service primitives associated with TCP are the **socket primitives** used with Berkeley Unix. Hence, although there are a number of alternative primitives, in order to describe the principles involved, we shall restrict our discussion to these. They are operating system calls and collectively form what is called an **application program interface** (**API**) to the underlying TCP/IP protocol stack. A typical list of primitives is given in Table 12.1 and their use is shown in diagrammatic form in Figure 12.3.

Table 12.1 List of socket primitives associated with TCP and their parameters.

Primitive	Parameters
socket ( )	service type, protocol, address format, return value = socketdescriptor or error code
bind ( )	socket descriptor, socket address (= host IP address + port number), return value = success or error code
listen ( )	socket descriptor, maximum queue length, return value = success or error code
accept ( )	socket descriptor, socket address, return value = success or error code
connect ( )	socket descriptor, local port number, destination port number, destination IP address, precedence, optional data (for example a user name and a password), return value = success or error code
send ( )	socket descriptor, pointer to message buffer containing the data to send, data length (in bytes), push flag, urgent flag, return value = success or error code
receive ( )	socket descriptor, pointer to a message buffer into which the data should be put, length of the buffer, return value = success or end of file (EOF) or error code
close ( )	socket descriptor, return value = success or error code
shutdown ( )	socket descriptor, return value = success or error code

Each of the two peer user application protocols/processes (APs) first creates a communications channel between itself and its local TCP entity. This is called a **socket** or **endpoint** and, in the case of the server AP, involves the AP issuing a sequence of primitive (also known as system of function) calls each with a defined set of parameters associated with it: *socket( )*, *bind( )*, *listen( )*, *accept( )*. Each call has a return value(s) or an error code associated with it.

The parameters associated with the *socket( )* primitive include the service required (reliable stream service), the protocol (TCP), and the address format (Internet). Once a socket has been created – and send/receive memory buffers allocated – a **socket descriptor** is returned to the AP which it then uses with each of the subsequent primitive calls. The AP then issues a

(a)

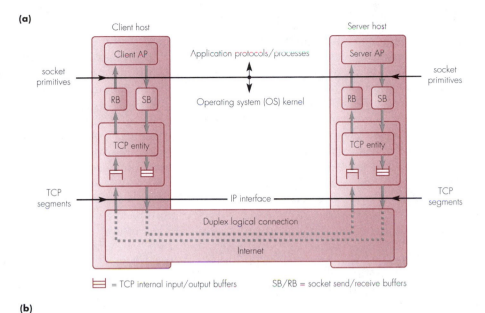

(b)

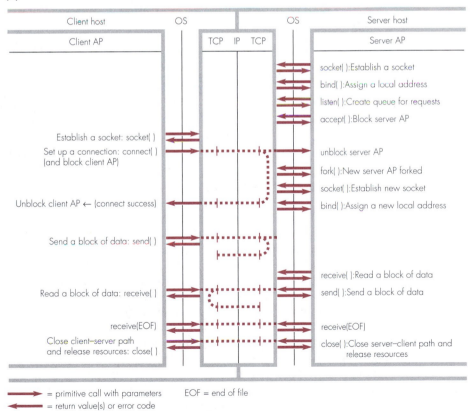

Figure 12.3 TCP socket primitives: (a) socket interface; (b) primitives and their use.

bind( ) primitive which, in addition to the socket descriptor, has an address parameter associated with it. This is the address the AP wishes to be assigned to the newly created socket and is called the **socket address**. This comprises the Internet-wide IP address of the host and, in the case of the server AP, the 16-bit well-known port number associated with this type of application protocol (FTP and so on).

The *listen( )* primitive call results in the local TCP entity creating a queue (whose maximum length is given as a parameter) to hold incoming connection requests for the server AP. The *accept( )* primitive is then used to put the AP in the blocked state waiting for an incoming connection request to be received from a client TCP entity. Collectively, this sequence of four primitives forms what is called a **passive-open**.

In the case of a client AP, since it can only set up a single TCP connection at a time and the socket address has only local significance, it simply issues a *socket( )* primitive to create a new socket with the same parameters as those used by the server (AP). This is then followed by a *connect( )* primitive which, in addition to the locally allocated socket descriptor, has parameters that contain the IP address of the remote (server) host, the well-known port number of the required server AP, the local port number that has been assigned to this socket by the client AP, a precedence value, and an optional item of data such as a user name and a password.

The local port number, together with the host IP address, forms the address to be assigned to this socket. The precedence parameter is a collection of parameters that enable the IP protocol to specify the contents of the *type of service* field in the header of the IP datagram that is used to transfer the segments associated with the connection over the Internet. We identified the contents of this field in Figure 9.3 when we discussed the operation of the IP protocol. Note that the IP address of the remote (server) host and the precedence parameters are used by the IP protocol and not TCP. They are examples of what are called **pass-through parameters**; that is, a parameter that is passed down from one protocol layer to another without modification.

Once the *connect( )* call has been made, this results in the calling AP being put into the blocked state while the local TCP entity initiates the setting up of a logical connection between itself and the TCP entity in the server. Collectively, these two primitives form what is called an **active-open**.

The TCP entity in a client host may support multiple concurrent connections involving different user APs. Similarly, the TCP entity in a server may support multiple connections involving different clients. Hence in order for the two TCP entities to relate each received segment to the correct connection, when each new connection is established, both TCP entities create a **connection record** for it. This is a data structure that contains a *connection identifier* (comprising the pair of socket addresses associated with the connection), the agreed *MSS* for the connection, the *initial sequence number* (associated with the acknowledgment procedure) to be used in each direction, the *precedence value*, and the *size of the window* associated with the TCP flow control procedure. Also, a number of fields associated with the operation of the protocol entity including *state variables* and the current state of the protocol entity.

At the server side, when a new connection request (PDU) is received, the server AP is unblocked and proceeds to create a new instance of the server AP to service this connection. Typically, this is carried out using the Unix *fork primitive*. A new socket between the new AP and the local TCP entity is then created and this is used to process the remaining primitives associated with this connection. The parent server AP then either returns to the blocked state waiting for a new connection request to arrive or, if one is already waiting in the server queue, proceeds to process the new request. Once a new instance of the server AP has been created and linked to its local TCP entity by a socket, both the client and server APs can then initiate the transfer of blocks of data in each direction using the *send( )* and *receive( )* primitives.

Associated with each socket is a *send buffer* and a *receive buffer*. The send buffer is used by the AP to transfer a block of data to its local TCP entity for sending over the connection. Similarly, the receive buffer is used by the TCP entity to assemble data received from the connection ready for reading by its local AP. The *send( )* primitive is used by an AP to transfer a block of data of a defined size to the send buffer associated with the socket ready for reading by its local TCP entity. The parameters include: the local socket descriptor, a pointer to the memory buffer containing the block of data, and also the length (in bytes) of the block of data. With TCP there is no correlation between the size of the data block(s) submitted (by an AP to its local TCP entity for sending) and the size of the TCP segments that are used to transfer the data over the logical connection. As we saw in Section 12.2, normally the latter is determined by the path MTU and, in many instances, this is much smaller than the size of the data blocks submitted by an AP.

With some applications, however, each submitted data block may be less than the path MTU. For example, in an interactive application involving a user at a keyboard interacting with a remote AP, the input data may comprise just a few bytes/characters. So in order to avoid the local TCP entity waiting for more data to fill an MTU, the user AP can request that a submitted block of data is sent immediately. This is done by setting a parameter associated with the *send( )* primitive called the *push flag*. A second parameter called the *urgent flag* can also be set by a user AP. This again is used with interactive applications to enable, for example, a user AP to abort a remote computation that it has previously started. The (urgent) data – string of characters – associated with the abort command are submitted by the source AP with the urgent flag set. The local TCP entity then ceases waiting for any further data to be submitted and sends what is outstanding, together with the urgent data, immediately. On receipt of this, the remote TCP entity proceeds to interrupt the peer user AP which then reads the urgent data and acts upon it.

Finally, when a client AP has completed the transfer of all data blocks associated with the connection, it initiates the release of its side of the connection by issuing a *close( )* – or sometimes a *shutdown( )* – primitive. When the server AP is informed of this (by the local TCP entity), assuming it also has finished sending data, it responds by issuing a *close( )* primitive to release the other side of the connection. Both TCP entities then delete their connection records and also the server AP that was forked to service the connection. As we shall expand upon later, the *shutdown( )* primitive is used when only half of the connection is to be closed.

12.3.2 Protocol operation

As we can see from the above, the TCP protocol involves three distinct operations: setting up a logical connection between two previously-created sockets, transferring blocks of data reliably over this connection, and closing down the logical connection. In practice, each phase involves the exchange of one or more TCP segments (PDUs) and, since all segments have a common structure, before describing the three phases we first describe the usage of the fields present in each segment header.

Segment format

All segments start with a common 20-byte header. In the case of acknowledgment and flow control segments, this is all that is present. In the case of connection-related segments, an options field may be present and a data field is present when data is being transferred over a connection. The fields making up the header are shown in Figure 12.4(a).

The 16-bit *source port* and *destination port* fields are used to identify the source and destination APs at each end of a connection. Also, together with the 32-bit source and destination IP addresses of the related hosts, they form the 48-bit socket address and the 96-bit connection identifier. Normally, the port number in a client host is assigned by the client AP while the port number in a server is a well-known port.

The *sequence number* performs the same function as the send sequence number in the HDLC protocol and the *acknowledgment number* the same function as the receive sequence number. Also, as with HDLC, a logical connection involves two separate flows, one in each direction. Hence the *sequence number* in a segment relates to the flow of bytes being transmitted by a TCP entity and the *acknowledgment number* relates to the flow of bytes in the reverse direction. However, with the TCP, although data is submitted for transfer in blocks, the flow of data in each direction is treated simply as a stream of bytes for error and flow control purposes. Hence the *sequence* and *acknowledgment numbers* are both 32-bits in length and relate to the position of a byte in the total session stream rather than to the position of a message block in the sequence. The *sequence number* indicates the position of the first byte in the *data* field of the segment relative to the start of the byte stream, while the *acknowledgment number* indicates the byte in the stream flowing in the reverse direction that the TCP entity expects to receive next.

The presence of an *options* field in the segment header means that the header can be of variable length. The *header length* field indicates the number of 32-bit words in the header. The 6-bit *reserved* field, as its name implies, is reserved for possible future use.

All segments have the same header format and the validity of selected fields in the segment header is indicated by the setting of individual bits in

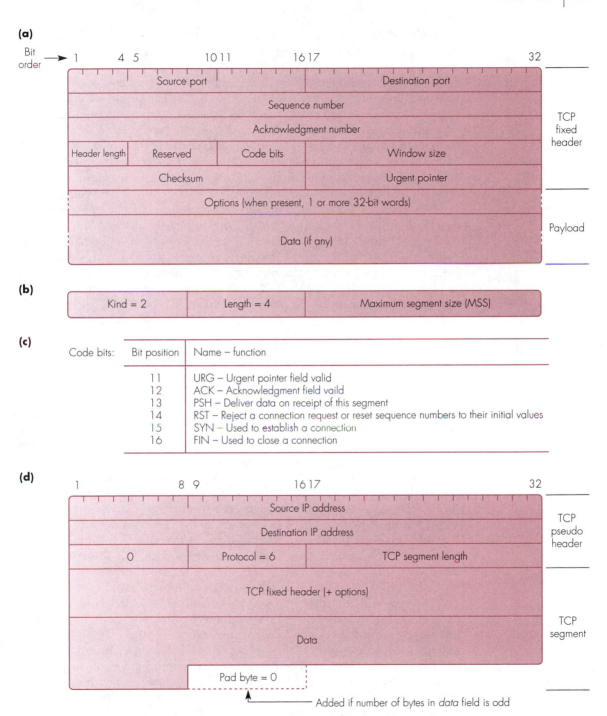

Figure 12.4 TCP segment format: (a) header fields; (b) MSS option format; (c) code bit definitions; (d) pseudo header fields.

the 6-bit *code* field; if a bit is set (a binary 1), the corresponding field is valid. Note that multiple bits can be set in a single segment. The bits have the meaning shown in Figure 12.4(c).

The *window size* field relates to a sliding window flow control scheme the principles of which we considered in Section 6.7.4. The number in the window size indicates the number of data bytes (relative to the byte being acknowledged in the *acknowledgment* field) that the receiver is prepared to accept. It is determined by the amount of unused space in the receive buffer the remote TCP entity is using for this connection. The maximum size of the receive buffer – and hence the maximum size of the window – can be different in each direction and has a default value which, typically, is 4096, 8192, or 16 384 bytes.

As we saw in Section 9.2, the checksum field in the header of each IP datagram applies only to the fields in the IP header and not the datagram contents. Hence the *checksum* field in the TCP segment header covers the complete segment; that is, header plus contents. In addition, since only a simple checksum is used to derive the checksum value in the IP header, in order to add an additional level of checking, some selected fields from the IP header are also included in the computation of the TCP checksum. The fields used form what is called the (TCP) **pseudo header** and these are identified in Figure 12.4(d).

As we can see, these are the source and destination IP addresses and the protocol value (= 6 for TCP) from the IP header, plus the total byte count of the TCP segment (header plus contents). The computation of the checksum uses the same algorithm as that used by IP. As we saw in Section 9.2, this is computed by treating the complete datagram as being made up of a string of 16-bit words which are then added together using 1s complement arithmetic. Since the number of bytes in the original TCP segment *data* field may be odd, in order to ensure the same checksum is computed by both TCP entities, a **pad byte** of zero is added to the data field whenever the number of bytes in the original *data* field is odd. As we can deduce from this, the byte count of the TCP segment must always be an even integer.

When the URG (urgent) flag is set in the *code* field, the *urgent pointer* field is valid. This indicates the number of bytes in the *data* field that follow the current *sequence number*. This is known as **urgent data** – or sometimes **expedited data** – and, as we mentioned earlier, it should be delivered by the receiving TCP entity immediately it is received.

The *options* field provides the means of adding extra functionality to that covered by the various fields in the segment header. For example, it is used during the connection establishment phase to agree the maximum amount of data in a segment each TCP entity is prepared to accept. During this phase, each indicates its own preferred maximum size and hence can be different for each direction of flow. As we indicated earlier, this is called the maximum segment size (MSS) and excludes the fixed 20-byte segment header. If one of the TCP entities does not specify a preferred maximum size then a default value of 536 bytes is chosen. The TCP entity in all hosts connected to the Internet must accept a segment of up to 556 bytes – 536 plus a 20-byte header – and all IPs must accept a datagram of 576 bytes – 556 bytes plus a further

20-byte (IP) header. Hence the default MSS of 536 bytes ensures the datagram (with the TCP segment in its payload) will be transferred over the Internet without fragmentation. The format of the MSS option is shown in Figure 12.4(b). Also, although not shown, if this is the last or only option present in the header, then a single byte of zero is added to indicate this is the end of the option list.

Connection establishment

On receipt of a *connect( )* primitive (system call) from a client AP, the local TCP entity attempts to set up a logical connection with the TCP entity in the server whose IP address (and port number) are specified in the parameters associated with the primitive. This is achieved using a three-way exchange of segments. Collectively, this is known as a **three-way handshake** procedure and the segments exchanged for a successful *connect( )* call are shown in Figure 12.5(a).

As we indicated in the previous section, the flow of data bytes in each direction of a connection is controlled independently. The TCP entity at each end of a connection starts in the CLOSED state and chooses its own *initial sequence number* (*ISN*). These are both non-zero and change from one connection to another. This ensures that any segments relating to a connection that get delayed during their transfer over the internet – and hence arrive at the client/server after the connection has been closed – do not interfere with the segments relating to the next connection. Normally, each TCP entity maintains a separate 32-bit counter that is incremented at intervals of either 4 or 8 microseconds. Then, when a new ISN is required, the current contents of the counter are used.

- To establish a connection, the TCP at the client first reads the ISN to be used (from the counter) and makes an entry of this in the *ISN* and *send sequence variable* fields of the connection record used for this connection. It then sends a segment to the TCP in the server with the SYN code bit on, the ACK bit off, and the chosen ISN (X) in the sequence (number) field. Note that since no window or MSS option fields are present, then the receiving TCP assumes the default values. The TCP entity then transfers to the SYN_SENT state.

- On receipt of the SYN, if the required server AP – as determined by the destination port and IP address – is not already in the LISTEN state, the server TCP declines the connection request by returning a segment with the RST code bit on. The client TCP entity then aborts the connection establishment procedure and returns an error message with a reason code to the client AP. Alternatively, if the server AP is in the LISTEN state, the server TCP makes an entry of the ISN (to be used in the client–server direction and contained within the received segment) in its own connection record – in both the *ISN* and *receive sequence variable* fields – together with the ISN it proposes to use in the return direction. It then proceeds to create a new segment with the SYN bit on and the chosen ISN(Y) in the sequence field. In addition, it sets the ACK bit on

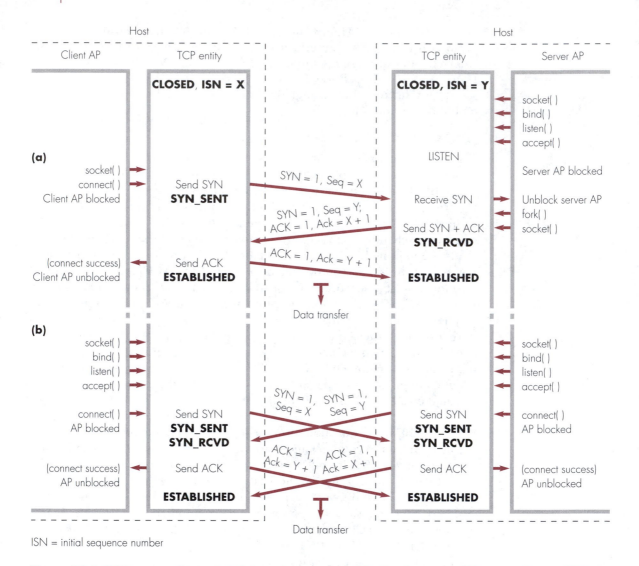

ISN = initial sequence number

Figure 12.5 TCP connection establishment examples: (a) client–server; (b) connection collision.

and returns a value of X+1 in the acknowledgment field to acknowledge receipt of the client's SYN. It then sends the segment to the client and enters the SYN_RCVD state.

■ On receipt of the segment, the client TCP makes an entry of the ISN to be used in the server–client direction in its connection record – in both the *ISN* and *receive sequence variable* fields – and increments the send sequence variable in the record by 1 to indicate the SYN has been acknowledged. It then acknowledges receipt of the SYN by returning a segment with the ACK bit on and a value of Y+1 in the acknowledgment field. The TCP entity then enters the (connection) ESTABLISHED state.

■ On receipt of the ACK, the server TCP increments the send sequence variable in its own connection record by 1 and enters the ESTABLISHED state. As we can deduce from this, the acknowledgment of each SYN segment is equivalent to a single data byte being transferred in each direction. At this point, both sides are in the ESTABLISHED state and ready to exchange data segments.

Although in a client–server application the client always initiates the setting up of a connection, in applications not based on the client–server model the two APs may try to establish a connection at the same time. This is called a **simultaneous open** and the sequence of segments exchanged in this case are as shown in Figure 12.5(b).

As we can see, the segments exchanged are similar to those in the client–server case and, since both ISNs are different, each side simply returns a segment acknowledging the appropriate sequence number. However, since the connection identifier is the same in both cases, only a single connection is established.

Data transfer

The error control procedure associated with the TCP protocol is similar to that used with the HDLC protocol we described earlier in Section 6.8. The main difference is that the sequence and acknowledgment numbers used with TCP relate to individual bytes in the total byte stream whereas with HDLC the corresponding send and receive sequence numbers relate to individual blocks of data. Also, because of the much larger round-trip time of an internet (compared with a single link), with TCP the window size associated with the flow control procedure is not derived from the sequence numbers. Instead, a new window size value is included in each segment a TCP entity sends to inform the other TCP entity of the maximum number of bytes it is willing to receive from it. This is known also as a **window size advertisement.**

In addition, because the TCP protocol may be operating (on an end-to-end basis) over a number of interconnected networks rather than a single line, it includes a congestion control procedure. This endeavors to regulate the rate at which the sending TCP entity sends data segments into the internet to the rate segments are leaving the internet. We shall discuss the main features of the different procedures that are used by means of examples.

Small segments In order to explain the features of the protocol that relate to the exchange of small segments – that is, all the segments contain less than the MSS – we shall consider a typical data exchange relating to a networked interactive application. An example application protocol of this type is Telnet. Typically, this involves a user at the client side typing a command and the server AP in a remote host responding to it. An example set of segments is shown in Figure 12.6(a).

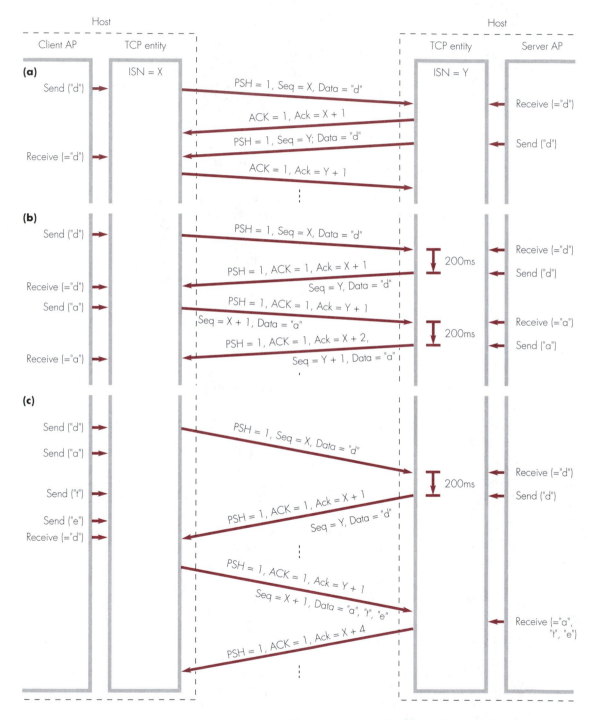

Figure 12.6 Small segment data transfers: (a) immediate acknowledgments; (b) delayed acknowledgments; (c) Nagle algorithm.

With interactive applications involving a user at a keyboard, each character typed is sent directly by the client AP to the server side. The server AP then reads the character from the receive buffer and immediately echoes the character back to the client side by writing it into the send buffer. On receipt of the character, the client AP displays it on the host screen. Hence each typed character is sent directly in a separate segment with the PSH flag on. Similarly, the echoed character is also sent in a separate segment with the PSH flag on. In addition to these two segments, however, each TCP entity returns a segment with the ACK bit on to acknowledge receipt of the segment containing the typed/echoed character. This means that for each character that is typed, four segments are sent, each with a 20-byte header and a further 20-byte IP header.

In practice, in order to reduce the number of segments that are sent, a receiving TCP entity does not return an ACK segment immediately it receives an (error-free) data segment. Instead, it waits for up to 200 ms to see if any data is placed in the send buffer by the local AP. If it is, then the acknowledgment is piggybacked in the segment that is used to send the data. This procedure is called **delayed acknowledgements** and, as we can see in Figure 12.6(b), with interactive applications it can reduce significantly the number of segments that are required.

Although this mode of working is acceptable when communicating over a single network such as a LAN, when communicating over an internet which has a long round-trip time (RTT), the delays involved in waiting for each echoed character can be annoying to the user. Hence a variation of the basic delayed acknowledgment procedure is often used. This is called the **Nagle algorithm** and is defined in **RFC 896**. When the algorithm is enabled, each TCP entity can have only a single small segment waiting to be acknowledged at a time. As a result, in interactive applications, when the client TCP entity is waiting for the ACK for this segment to be received, a number of characters may have been typed by the user. Hence when the ACK arrives, all the waiting characters in the send buffer are transmitted in a single segment. A sequence diagram showing this is given in Figure 12.6(c).

In these examples, the window size has not been shown since, in general, when small segments are being exchanged it has no effect on the flow of the segments. Also, the Nagle algorithm is not always enabled. For example, when the interactions involve a mouse, each segment may contain a collection of mouse movement data and, when echoed, the movement of the cursor can appear erratic. An example application of this type is X-Windows.

Error control As we saw in Figure 12.4(a), each TCP segment contains only a single acknowledgment number. Hence should a segment not arrive at the destination host, the receiving TCP can only return an acknowledgment indicating the next in-sequence byte that it expects. Also, since the packets relating to a message are being transmitted over an internet, when the path followed has alternative routes, packets may arrive at the destination host out of sequence. Hence the receiving TCP simply holds each out-of-sequence segment that it receives in temporary storage and returns an ACK indicating the next in-sequence byte – and hence segment – that it expects. Normally, the out-of-sequence segment arrives within a short time interval at which point the receiving TCP returns an ACK that acknowledges all the segments now received including those held in temporary storage.

At the sending side, the TCP receives an ACK indicating a segment has been lost but, within a short time interval, it receives an ACK for a segment that it transmitted later (so acknowledging receipt of all bytes up to and including the last byte in the later segment). Hence, since this is a relatively frequent occurrence, the sending TCP does not initiate a retransmission immediately it receives an out-of-sequence ACK. Instead, it only retransmits a segment if it receives three duplicate ACKs for the same segment – that is, three consecutive segments with the same acknowledgment number in their header – since it is then confident that the segment has been lost rather than simply received out of sequence.

In addition, to allow for the possibility that the sending TCP has no further segments ready for transmission, when a loss is detected it starts a *retransmission timer* for each new segment it transmits. A segment is then retransmitted if the TCP does not receive an acknowledgment for it before the timeout interval expires. An example illustrating the two possibilities is shown in Figure 12.7. In the example we assume:

- there is only a unidirectional flow of data segments;
- the sending AP writes a block of data – a message – comprising 3072 bytes into the send buffer using a *send( )* primitive;
- the MSS being used for the connection is 512 bytes and hence 6 segments are required to send the block of data;
- the size of the receive buffer is 8192 bytes and hence the sending TCP can send the complete set of segments without waiting for an acknowledgment;
- an ACK segment is returned on receipt of each error-free data segment;
- segments 2 and 6 are both lost – owing to transmission errors for example – as is the final ACK segment.

To follow the transmission sequence shown in the figure we should note the following:

- The sending TCP has a send sequence variable, V(S), in its connection record which is the value it places in the sequence number field of the next new segment it sends. Also a *retransmission list* to hold segments waiting to be acknowledged. Similarly, the receiving TCP has a receive sequence variable, V(R), in its connection record (which is the sequence number it expects to receive next) and a *receive list* to hold segments that are received out of sequence.

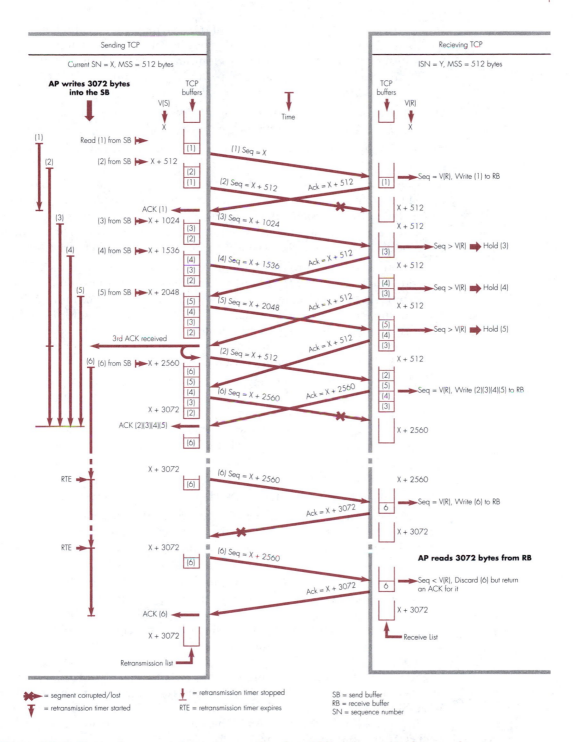

Figure 12.7 Example segment sequence showing TCP error control procedure.

- Segment (1) is received error-free and, since its sequence number (Seq = X) is equal to V(R), the 512 bytes of data it contains are transferred directly into the receive buffer (ready for reading by the destination AP), V(R) is incremented to X + 512, and an ACK (with Ack = X + 512) is returned to the sending side.

- On receipt of the ACK, the sending TCP stops the retransmission timer for (1) and, in the meantime, segment (2) has been sent.

- Since segment (2) is corrupted, no ACK for it is returned and hence its timer continues running.

- The sending TCP continues to send segments (3), (4), and (5) all of which are received error-free. However, since they are out of sequence – segment (2) is missing – the receiving TCP retains them in its receive list and returns an ACK with Ack = X + 512 in each segment for each of them to indicate to the sending TCP that segment (2) is missing.

- On receipt of the third ACK with an ACK = X + 512, the sending TCP retransmits segment (2) without waiting for the retransmission timer to expire. As we indicated earlier, this is done since if three or more ACKs with the same acknowledgment number are received one after the other, it is assumed that the segment indicated has been lost rather than received out of sequence. Because the retransmission occurs before the timer expires, this procedure is called **fast retransmit**.

- This time segment (2) is received error-free and, as a result, the receiving TCP is able to transfer the contents of segments (2), (3), (4), and (5) to the receive buffer – ready for reading by the AP – and returns an ACK with Ack = X + 2560 to indicate to the sending TCP that all bytes up to and including byte 2560 have been received and their timers can be stopped.

- In the meantime, segment (6) has been transmitted but is corrupted. Hence, since no other segments are waiting to be sent, its timer continues running until it expires when the segment is retransmitted.

- This time the segment is received error-free and so its contents are passed to the receive buffer directly and an ACK for it is returned. Also, it is assumed that at this point the receiving AP reads the accumulated 3072 bytes from the receive buffer using a *receive( )* primitive.

- The ACK for segment (6) is corrupted and hence the timer for the segment expires again and the segment is retransmitted. However, since the sequence number is less than the current V(R), the receiving TCP assumes it is a duplicate. Hence it discards it but returns an ACK to stop the sending TCP from sending another copy.

As we can see from this example, a key parameter in the efficiency of the error control procedure is the choice of the **retransmission timeout (RTO) interval**. With a single data link the choice of an RTO is straightforward since the worst-case round-trip time – the time interval between sending a packet/frame and receiving an ACK for it – can be readily determined. The

RTO is then set at a value slightly greater than this. With an internet, however, the RTT of a TCP connection can vary considerably over relatively short intervals as the traffic levels within routers build up and subside. Hence choosing an RTO when the internet is lightly loaded can lead to a significant number of unnecessary retransmissions, while choosing it during heavy load conditions can lead to unnecessary long delays each time a segment is corrupted/lost. The choice of RTO, therefore, must be dynamic and vary not only from one connection to another but also during a connection.

The initial approach used to derive the RTO for a connection was based on an **exponential backoff** algorithm. With this an initial RTO of 1.5 seconds is used. Should this prove to be too short – that is, each segment requires multiple retransmission attempts – the RTO is doubled to 3 seconds. This doubling process then continues until no retransmissions occur. To allow for network problems, a maximum RTO of 2 minutes is used at which point a segment with the RST flag bit on is sent to abort the connection/session.

Although very simple to implement, a problem with this method is that when an ACK is received, it is not clear whether this is for the last retransmission attempt or an earlier attempt. This is known as the **retransmission ambiguity problem** and was identified by Karn. Because of this, a second approach was proposed by Jacobson and is defined in **RFC 793**. With this method, the RTO is computed from actual RTT measurements. The RTO is then updated as each new RTT measurement is made. In this way, the RTO for each connection is continuously being updated as each new estimate of the RTT is determined.

As we indicated earlier, when each data segment is sent, a separate retransmission timer is started. A connection starts with a relatively large RTO. Then, each time an ACK segment is received before the timer expires, the actual RTT is determined by subtracting the initial start time of the timer from the time when the ACK was received. The current estimate of the RTT is then updated using the formula

$$\text{RTT} = \alpha\,\text{RTT} + (1-\alpha)\,M$$

where M is the measured RTT and α is a smoothing factor which determines by how much each new M influences the computation of the new RTT relative to the current value. The recommended value for α is 0.9. The new RTO is then set at twice the updated RTT to allow for a degree of variance in the RTT.

Although this method performed better than the original method, a refinement of it was later introduced. This was done because by using a fixed multiple of each updated RTT ($\times 2$) to compute the new RTO, it was found that it did not handle well the wide variations that occurred in the RTT. Hence in order to obtain a better estimate, Jacobson proposed that each new RTO should be based not just on the mean of the measured RTT but also on the variance. In the proposed algorithm, the mean deviation of the RTT measurements, D, is used as an estimate of the variance. It is computed using the formula:

$$D = \alpha\,D + (1-\alpha)|\text{RTT} - M|$$

where α is a smoothing factor and $|RTT - M|$ is the modulus of the difference between the current estimate of the RTT and the new measured RTT (M). This is also computed for each new RTT measurement and the new estimate of the RTO is then derived using the formula:

$$RTO = RTT + 4D$$

As we indicated earlier, to overcome the retransmission ambiguity problem, the RTT is not measured/updated for the ACKs relating to retransmitted segments.

Note also that although in the above example an ACK is returned on receipt of each data segment, this is not always the case. Indeed, in most implementations, providing there is a steady flow of data segments, the receiving TCP only returns an ACK for every other segment it receives correctly. On sending each ACK, a timer – called the **delayed ACK timer** – is started and, should a second segment not be received before it expires, then an ACK for the first segment is sent. Note, however, that when a single ACK is sent for every other segment, since the V(R) is incremented on receipt of each segment, then the acknowledgment number within the (ACK) segment acknowledges the receipt of all the bytes in both segments.

Flow control As we indicated earlier, the value in the *window size* field of each segment relates to a sliding window flow control scheme and indicates the number of bytes (relative to the byte being acknowledged in the *acknowledgment* field) that the receiving TCP is able to accept. This is determined by the amount of free space that is present in the receive buffer being used by the receiving TCP for the connection. Recall also that the maximum size of the window is determined by the size of the receive buffer. Hence when the sending TCP is running in a fast host – a large server for example – and the receiving TCP in a slow host, the sending TCP can send segments faster than, firstly, the receiving TCP can process them and, secondly, the receiving AP can read them from the receive buffer after they have been processed. The window flow control scheme, therefore, is present to ensure that there is always the required amount of free space in the receive buffer at the destination before the source sends the data. An example showing the sequence of segments that are exchanged to implement the scheme is given in Figure 12.8. In the example, we assume:

- there is only a unidirectional flow of data segments;
- the size of both the send and the receive buffers at the sending side are 4096 bytes and those at the receiving side 2048 bytes. Hence the maximum size of the window for the direction of flow shown is 2048 bytes;
- associated with each direction of flow the sending side maintains a *send window variable*, W_S, and the receiving side a *receive window variable*, W_R;

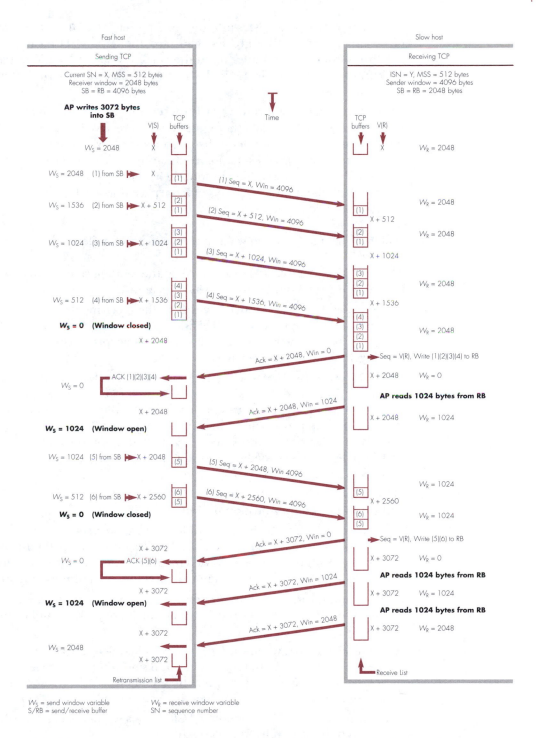

Figure 12.8 Example segment sequence showing TCP flow control procedure.

- the source AP can write bytes into the send buffer up to the current value of W_S and, providing W_S is greater than zero, the sending TCP can read data bytes from its send buffer up to the current value of W_S and initiate their transmission. Flow is stopped when $W_S = 0$ and the window is then said to be closed;

- at the destination, the receiving TCP, on receipt of error-free data segments, transfers the data they contain to the receive buffer and increments W_R by the number of bytes transferred. W_R is then decremented when the destination AP reads bytes from the receive buffer and, after each read operation, the receiving TCP returns a segment with the number of bytes of free space now available in the window size field of the segment.

The following should be noted when interpreting the sequence:

- The flow of segments starts with the AP at the sending side writing 3072 bytes into the send buffer using a *send( )* primitive.

- Since the sending host is much faster than the receiving host, the sending TCP is able to send a full window of 2048 bytes (in four 512-byte segments) before the receiving TCP is able to start processing them. The sending TCP must then stop as W_S is now zero.

- When the receiving TCP is scheduled to run, it finds four segments in its receive list and, since the first segment – segment (1) – has a sequence number equal to V(R), it transfers its contents to the receive buffer. It then proceeds to process and transfer the contents of segments (2), (3), and (4) in the same way and, after it has done this, it returns a single ACK segment to acknowledge receipt of these four segments but with a window size field of zero.

- On receipt of the ACK, the sending TCP deletes segments (1), (2), (3), and (4) from its retransmission list but leaves $W_S = 0$.

- When the receiving AP is next scheduled to run, we assume it reads just 1024 bytes from the receive buffer. On detecting this, the TCP returns a second ACK with the same acknowledgment number but with a window size of 1024. The second ACK is known, therefore, as a **window update**.

- At this point, since its sending window is now open, the sending TCP proceeds to send segments (5) and (6) at which point W_S again becomes zero.

- At the receiving side, when the TCP is next scheduled to run it finds segments (5) and (6) in the receive list and, since their sequence numbers are in sequence, it transfers their contents to the receive buffer. It then returns a single ACK for them but with a window size of zero.

- On receipt of the ACK, the sending TCP deletes segments (5) and (6) from its retransmission list but leaves $W_S = 0$.

- At some point later, the receiving AP is scheduled to run and we assume it again reads 1024 bytes from the receive buffer. Hence when the TCP next runs it returns a window update of 1024.

- Finally, after the receiving AP reads the last 1024 bytes from the RB, the TCP – some time later – returns a window update of 2048. After this has been received, both sides are back to their initial state.

We should note that there are a number of different implementations of TCP and hence the sequence shown in Figure 12.8 is only an example. For example, the receiving TCP may return two ACKs – one for segments (1) and (2) and the other for segments (3) and (4) – rather than a single ACK. In this case there would be a different distribution of segments between the TCP buffers and the receive buffer. Nevertheless, providing the size of the TCP buffers in the receiver is the same as the receive buffer, then the window procedure ensures there is sufficient buffer storage to hold all received segments. A schematic diagram summarizing the operation of the sliding window procedure is given in Figure 12.9.

Congestion control A segment may be discarded during its transfer across an internet either because transmission errors are detected in the packet containing the segment or because a router or gateway along the path being

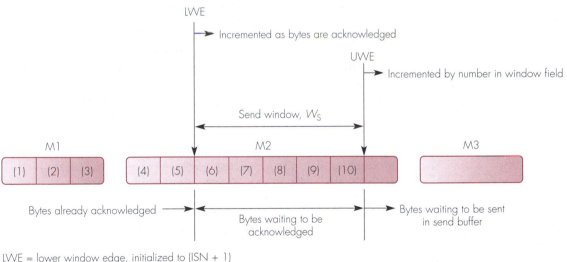

LWE = lower window edge, initialized to (ISN + 1)
UWE = upper window edge, initialized to (ISN + 1) + advertized window
W_S = (UWE − LWE), flow stopped when W_S = 0
M1, 2, 3 = sending AP messages
(1), (2) etc. = segments sent by TCP entity
Note: that TCP chooses the size of segments it sends

Figure 12.9 TCP sliding window.

followed becomes congested; that is, during periods of heavy traffic it temporary runs out of buffer storage for packets in the output queue associated with a line. However, the extensive use of optical fiber in the transmission network means that the number of lost packets due to transmission errors is relatively small. Hence the main reason for lost packets is congestion within the internet.

To understand the reason for congestion, it should be remembered that the path followed through an internet may involve a variety of different transmission lines some of which are faster – have a higher bit rate – than others. In general, therefore, the overall speed of transmission of segments over the path being followed is determined by the bit rate of the slowest line. Also, congestion can arise at the sending side of this line as the segments relating to multiple concurrent connections arrive at a faster rate than the line can transmit them. Clearly, if this situation continues for even a relatively short time interval, the number of packets in the affected router output queue builds up until the queue becomes full and packets have to be dropped. This also affects the ACKs within the lost segments and, as we have just seen, this can have a significant effect on the overall time that is taken to transmit a message.

In order to reduce the likelihood of lost packets occurring, the TCP in each host has a congestion control/avoidance procedure which, for each connection, uses the rate of arrival of the ACKs relating to a connection to regulate the rate of entry of data segments – and hence IP packets – into the internet. This is in addition to the window flow control procedure which, as we have just seen, is concerned with controlling the rate of transmission of segments to the current capacity of the receive buffer in the destination host. Hence in addition to a send window variable, W_S, associated with the flow control procedure, each TCP also has a **congestion window** variable, W_C, associated with the congestion control/avoidance procedure. Both are maintained for each connection and the transmission of a segment relating to a connection can only take place if both windows are in the open state.

As we can see from the above, under lightly-loaded network conditions the flow of segments is controlled primarily by W_S and, under heavily-loaded conditions, it is controlled primarily by W_C. However, when the flow of segments relating to a connection first starts, because no ACKs have been received, the sending TCP does not know the current loading of the internet. So to stop it from sending a large block of segments – up to the agreed window size – the initial size of the congestion window, W_C, is set to a single segment which, because W_C has a dimension of bytes, is equal to the agreed MSS for the connection.

As we show in Figure 12.10, the sending TCP starts the data transfer phase of a connection by sending a single segment of up to the MSS. It then starts the retransmission timer for the segment and waits for the ACK to be received. If the timer expires, the segment is simply retransmitted. If the ACK is received before the timer expires, W_C is increased to two segments, each equal to the MSS. The sending TCP is then able to send two segments and,

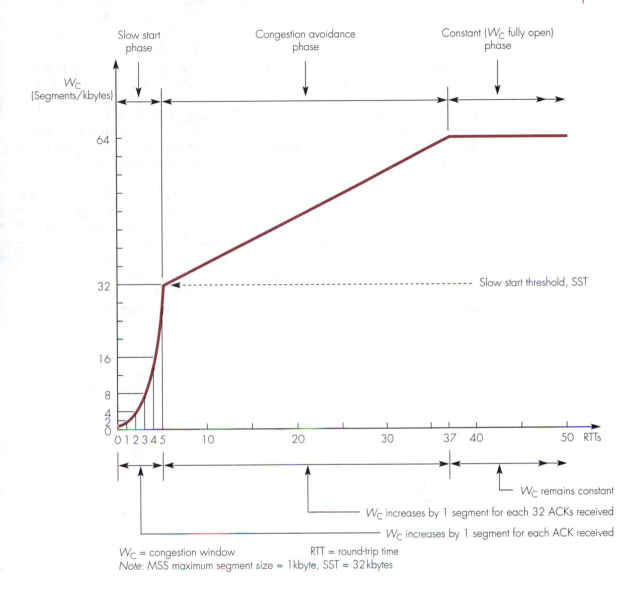

Figure 12.10 TCP congestion control window procedure.

for each of the ACKs it receives for these segments, W_C is increased by one segment (MSS). Hence, the sending TCP can now send four segments and, as we can see, W_C increases exponentially. Even though W_C increases rapidly, this phase is called **slow start** since it builds up from a single segment. It continues until a timeout for a lost segment occurs, or a duplicate ACK is received, or an upper threshold is reached. This is called the **slow start threshold (SST)** and, for each new connection, it is set to 64 kbytes. In the example, however, it is assumed to be initialized to 32 kbytes which, because the MSS is 1 kbyte, is equal to 32 segments. Assuming the SST is reached, this is taken as an indication that the path is not congested. Hence the connection enters a second phase during which, instead of W_C increasing by 1 segment (MSS) for each ACK it receives, it increases by $1/W_C$ segments for each ACK received. Hence, as we can see, W_C now increases by 1 segment for each set of W_C ACKs that are received. This is called the **congestion avoidance** phase and, during this phase, the increase in W_C is additive. It continues until a second threshold is reached and, in the example, this is set at 64 kbytes. On reaching this, W_C remains constant at this value.

The profile shown in Figure 12.10 is typical of a lightly-loaded internet in which none of the lines making up the path through the internet is congested. Providing W_C remains greater than the maximum flow control window, the flow of segments relating to the connection is controlled primarily by W_S. During these conditions all segments are transferred with a relatively constant transfer delay and delay variation. As the number of connections using the internet increases, however, so the traffic level increases up to the point at which packet (and hence segment) losses start to occur and, when this happens, the TCP controlling each connection starts to adjust its congestion window in a way that reflects the level of congestion.

The steps taken depend on whether a lost packet is followed by duplicate ACKs being received or the retransmission timer for the segment expiring. In the case of the former, as we saw earlier in Figure 12.7, the receipt of duplicate ACKs is indicative that segments are still being received by the destination host. Hence the level of congestion is assumed to be light and, on receipt of the third duplicate ACK relating to the missing segment – fast retransmit – the current W_C value is halved and the congestion avoidance procedure is invoked starting at this value. This is called **fast recovery** and an example is shown in Figure 12.11(a).

In this example it is assumed that the first packet loss occurs when W_C is at its maximum value of 64 segments which, with an MSS of 1 Kbyte, is equal to 64 kbyte. Hence on receipt of the third duplicate ACK, the lost segment is retransmitted and W_C is immediately reset to 32 segments/kbytes. The W_C is then incremented back up using the congestion avoidance procedure. However, when it reaches 34 segments, a second segment is lost. It is assumed that this also is detected by the receipt of duplicate ACKs and hence W_C is reset to 17 segments before the congestion avoidance procedure is restarted.

In the case of a lost segment being detected by the retransmission timer expiring, it is assumed that the congestion has reached a level at which no packets/segments relating to the connection are now getting through. As we show in the example in Figure 12.11(b), when a retransmission timeout (RTO) occurs, irrespective of the current W_C, it is immediately reset to 1 segment and the slow start procedure is restarted. Thus, when the level of congestion reaches the point at which RTOs start to occur, the flow of segments is controlled primarily by W_C.

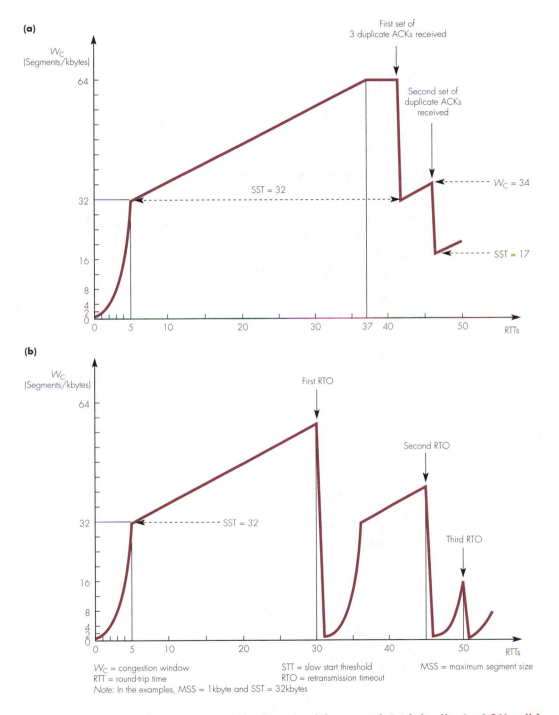

Figure 12.11 TCP congestion window adjustments: (a) on receipt of duplicate ACKs; (b) on expiry of a retransmission timer.

Connection termination

As we indicated earlier, each TCP connection is duplex and hence data can be transferred in both directions simultaneously. To support this, each TCP entity maintains separate send and receive sequence and window variables and a separate state variable for each direction of flow. When a connection is terminated, each direction of flow is closed separately. In practice, there are a number of ways this is carried out and four examples are given in Figure 12.12.

In most cases, the TCP entity at each end of a connection goes through a different sequence of states. In order to discriminate between the two ends, the AP which issues the first *close( )* – and hence the TCP which sends the first FIN segment – performs what is called an **active close** procedure and the other side, a **passive close**. As we can see in the first example – part (a) – each procedure involves a slightly different sequence:

■ In all the examples, both the forward and return paths of the TCP connection are currently in the ESTABLISHED (EST) – data transfer – state.

■ The connection termination is started by one of the APs – normally the client – issuing a *close( )* primitive. The TCP entity at this side then goes through the active close procedure and the TCP at the other side the passive close.

■ On receipt of the *close( )* primitive, the active TCP entity sends a FIN segment – that is, a segment with the FIN bit on – with a sequence number equal to the current V(S), X. It then enters the FIN_WAIT1 state to indicate it is waiting for an ACK for the first FIN.

■ On receipt of the FIN, the passive TCP first returns an ACK indicating correct receipt of the FIN and, when its local AP does the next *receive( )*, an end-of-file (EOF) is returned to indicate that no more data will be coming from the other side for this connection. It then enters the CLOSE_WAIT state to indicate it is waiting for a *close( )* from its local AP. Note that the ack number in the ACK is equal to X + 1 since a FIN consumes a byte of the byte stream.

■ On receipt of the ACK, the TCP performing the active close simply enters the FIN_WAIT2 state to indicate it is now waiting for a FIN from the passive side.

■ At some time later the AP in the passive side issues a *close( )* primitive and, as a result, the local TCP sends a FIN to indicate the closure of the connection in the reverse direction. It then enters the LAST_ACK state to indicate it is now waiting for the last ACK.

■ On receipt of the FIN at the active side, the TCP first returns an ACK for the segment. It then starts a timer called the **2MSL timer** and enters the TIMED_WAIT state. When configuring each TCP entity a parameter called the **maximum segment lifetime** (**MSL**) is entered. This is the

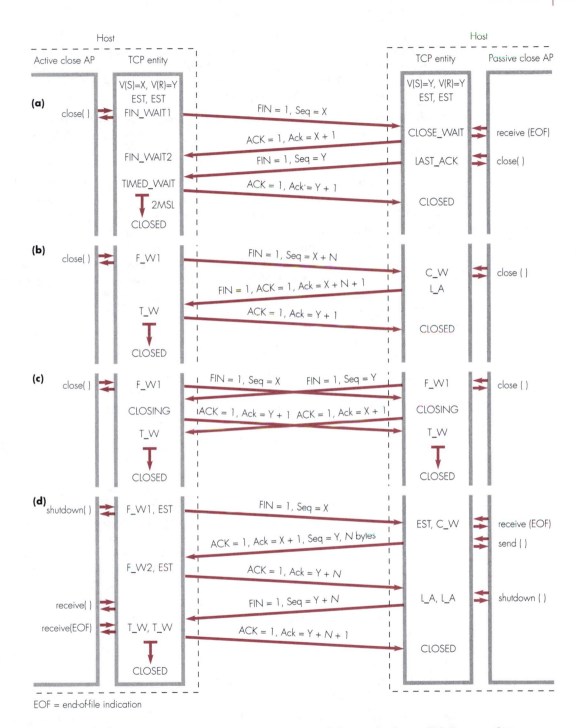

EOF = end-of-file indication

Figure 12.12 Connection close examples: (a) normal (4-way) close; (b) 3-way close; (c) simultaneous close; (d) half-close.

maximum time duration a segment can exist in the internet before being discarded. In practice, therefore, it is related to the time-to-live value used in each IP packet header. Typical values for the MSL are between 30 seconds and 2 minutes. This means that should the ACK for the second FIN be lost, the active TCP is still able to receive the retransmitted FIN.

■ Finally, on receipt of the ACK, the TCP at the passive side deletes the connection record relating to this connection and, when the 2MSL timer expires, the TCP at the active side does the same.

The segment sequence shown in Figure 12.12(b) is similar to that in the first example except that at the passive side data is still waiting to be acknowledged when the *close( )* is received. Hence the passive TCP piggybacks the ACK for the data in the same segment that carries the FIN in the reverse direction. This occurs when the *close( )* is received before the FIN arrives and, as we can see, this reduces the standard closure to a 3-way segment exchange rather than a 4-way exchange. Note that with this, however, data may be lost at the passive side if both sides of the connection are closed on receipt of the *close( )* primitive.

The segment sequence shown in Figure 12.12(c) illustrates what happens when the AP in both hosts issue a *close( )* simultaneously. As we can see, in this case the TCP at both sides carries out the active close sequence. Here, however, the intermediate state CLOSING is entered on receipt of the FIN from the opposite side. Then, as before, on receipt of the related ACK segment, both sides enter the TIMED_WAIT state to wait for the 2MSL timer to expire before closing down.

When an AP initiates the termination of a connection with a *close( )* primitive, this indicates to its local TCP that it has now completed sending the data/messages relating to the session and expects the remote AP to do the same. As a result, both TCPs proceed to close the (duplex) connection using one of the segment exchanges shown in the first three examples. With some applications, however, although the AP in the active side has completed sending data, it still expects to receive further data from the correspondent AP. Clearly, since both directions of a TCP connection are managed separately, this is possible. Hence to enable its local TCP to discriminate between this and a normal close, the AP issues a *shutdown( )* call. The local TCP initiates the closure of its side of the connection but leaves the other side in the ESTABLISHED state. This is known as a **half-close** and an example showing a typical segment sequence is shown in Figure 12.12(d). The following points should be noted:

■ In the figure, we show the state of both the forward and return paths of the connection at both sides and, as before, initially these are both in the ESTABLISHED (EST) state.

■ On receipt of the *shutdown( )* call, the local TCP leaves the return path in the EST state but proceeds to close the forward path. Hence it sends a FIN segment and enters the FIN_WAIT1 state.

- On receipt of this, an EOF is returned to the correspondent AP in response to the next *receive( )* to indicate that it will not receive any further data. It then changes the state of this side of the connection to the CLOSE_WAIT state. The AP then receives some data to send in the return direction and, since this path is still open, it sends the data and, in the same segment, piggybacks the acknowledgment of the FIN segment.

- On receipt of this, the other TCP returns an ACK for the data and, in response to the ACK for the FIN it sent, changes the state of this side of the connection to the FIN_WAIT2 state. Also, at some time later the AP reads the data using a *receive( )* call.

- After the ACK for the data is received, a *shutdown( )* is received from the AP. This results in a FIN segment being sent for the return path and the state of both paths being set into the LAST_ACK state.

- On receipt of the FIN, an EOF is returned to the local AP in response to the next *receive( )* to inform it that no further data will be coming. An ACK for the FIN is then returned and the state of both sides of the connection changed to the TIMED_WAIT state.

- On receipt of the ACK, the TCP deletes the connection record relating to this connection and, when the 2MSL timer expires, the TCP at the other side does the same.

The sequences shown in all four examples relate to what is called an **orderly release** since both FINs are sent either with or after all outstanding data relating to the session has been sent. In some instances, however, a connection is closed abruptly by the TCP at one side sending a segment with the RST bit on. This results in both sides of the connection being closed immediately and hence any data currently being held by either TCP will be lost. This is called an **abortive release** and an example of its use is when the sequence numbers relating to the connection become unsynchronized.

12.3.3 Additional features

The various examples we used in the data transfer section were chosen to explain the main procedures relating to this part of the TCP protocol. In addition, however, there are a number of details relating to these procedures that the examples did not show. In this section we identify a number of these.

Persist timer

In the example shown in Figure 12.8, it was assumed that the duplicate ACK containing the window update – Ack = X + 2048, Win = 1024 – was received by the sending TCP error free. In practice, of course, the packet containing this segment may have been corrupted or lost. If this had occurred, since the TCP entity at the receiving side has initiated the reopening of the window, it is now waiting to receive further segments. However, because the ACK is not received, the send window of the sending TCP is still zero and so it continues to assume that it cannot send any more segments. Although the data within segments is acknowledged, acknowledgments are not. Hence if the window update was not received, deadlock would occur with each side waiting for the other. Figure 12.13 shows how this can be avoided.

As we can see, the example relates directly to the sequence we showed earlier in Figure 12.8. Whenever the sending TCP sets its send window, W_S, to

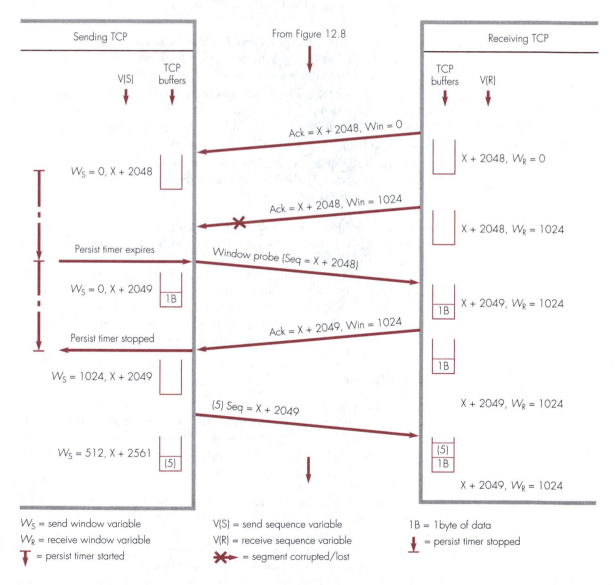

Figure 12.13 Persist timer: application and operation.

zero, it starts a timer. This is known as the **persist timer**, and if a segment containing a window update is not received before the timer expires, the sending TCP sends what is called a **window probe** segment. Even though the send window is zero, a TCP can always send a single byte of data. Hence the probe segment contains the first byte of the remaining data and, as we can see, if the ACK for this has a nonzero window value, then the flow of data segments can be resumed. Alternatively, should the value still be zero, then the timer is restarted and the procedure repeats. This is repeated at 60 s intervals until either a nonzero window value is received or the connection is terminated.

Keepalive timer

Once a connection between two TCP entities has been set up, it remains in place until the connection is terminated by the two communicating APs. As we saw in the previous section, this involves the two APs initiating the closure of their side of the connection. In most client–server applications, however, if the client host is simply switched off (instead of going through the normal log off procedure) then the connection from the server to the client will remain in place even though the client host is no longer responding. To overcome this, although not part of the TCP specification, many TCP implementations in servers include a timer known as the **keepalive timer**. The way this is used is shown in the example in Figure 12.14.

A separate timer is kept by the server TCP for all the connections – of which there can be many – that are currently in place. The default value of the keepalive timer is two hours and, should no data segments be exchanged over a connection during this time interval, the TCP in the server sends a probe segment to the client and sets the timer this time to 75 s. The probe segment has no data and has a *sequence number* of one less than the current $V(S)$ of the server–client side of the connection. If the client host is still switched on – and the TCP connection is still in place – the client TCP simply returns an ACK for this with its current $V(R)$ within it and, on receipt of this, the server TCP restarts the keepalive timer to 2 hours. If the client TCP does not respond, then the timer expires and the TCP in the server sends a second probe with the timer again set to 75 s. This procedure is repeated and, if no reply is received after 10 consecutive probes, the client is assumed to be switched off (or unreachable) and the server terminates the connection.

Silly window syndrome

The combined IP and TCP packet/segment headers are at least 40 bytes. Hence the larger the number of bytes in the data field of each segment, the smaller are the overheads associated with each transfer and the higher is the mean end-to-end data transfer rate. In the flow control example shown earlier in Figure 12.8, it was assumed that the AP at the receiving side read large (1024-byte) blocks of data from the receive buffer which, in turn, enabled the sending TCP to operate efficiently by always sending segments containing large amounts of data. In some interactive applications, however, a condition

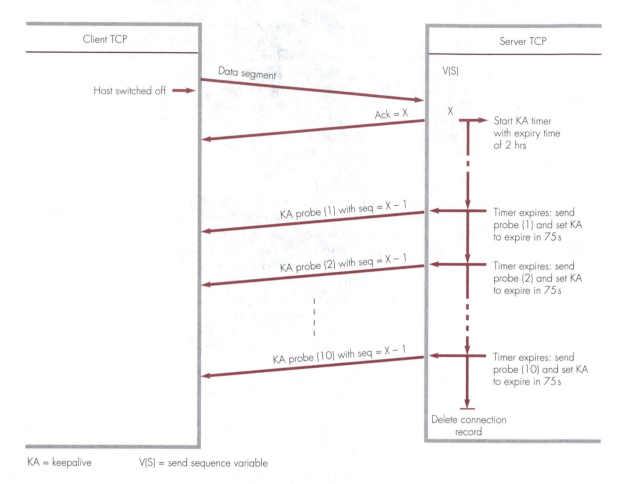

KA = keepalive   V(S) = send sequence variable

Figure 12.14 Keepalive timer: application and operation.

can arise which results in a very small number of bytes being sent in each segment. It is known as the **silly window syndrome** (**SWS**) and can arise either at the receiving side or the sending side.

To avoid this occurring, an added feature defined by Clark is incorporated into the basic flow control procedure we discussed earlier. At the receiving side this forbids a receiving TCP entity from advertising a small window and, at the sending side, it forbids a sending TCP entity from sending segments containing small amounts of data. Note that both features are complementary to the Nagle algorithm we discussed earlier and, in many instances, both operate together.

To illustrate how the problem can arise at the receiver, assume that in an interactive application a server AP initiates the transfer of a large character file to a client AP but the latter proceeds to read it (from the receive buffer of the receiving TCP) a single character at a time. On receipt of the first block of characters/bytes sent by the TCP in the server – up to the current maximum window size – the receiving TCP in the client would first return an ACK for the complete block but with a window value of zero. Then, assuming the procedure we showed in the earlier example in Figure 12.8, each time the client AP reads a character from the TCP receive buffer, the client TCP will return a window update to inform the TCP at the server side that it can now send a further character/byte. This it duly does and, on its receipt, the client TCP returns an ACK for it but again with a window value of zero. Similarly, when the next character is read by the AP, the client TCP returns a second window update of 1 byte/character and the procedure repeats until the complete file has been transferred in this way.

To avoid this happening, a receiving TCP is prevented from sending a window update until there is sufficient space in its buffer either for a segment equal to the maximum segment size in use or, one half of the maximum buffer capacity – and hence window capacity – whichever is the smaller. An example showing this is given in Figure 12.15. Part (a) illustrates the problem and part (b) shows how the solution attributed to Clark avoids the problem occurring.

In the example it is assumed that the window size in use is 1024 bytes and the MSS is also 1024 bytes. Hence, as we can deduce from part (a), after the first 1024-byte block has been transferred, without the Clark extension, each of the remaining 1024 bytes is transferred in a separate segment. Moreover, each of these may require an ACK and a window update segment. With the Clark extension, however, as we can see from part (b), after the first 1024 bytes have been transferred the remaining bytes are transferred in just two 512-byte segments; the choice of 512 being half of the buffer capacity.

As we indicated earlier, the same problem can arise at the sending side. For example, in an interactive application in which a user enters a string of characters at a keyboard, the sending AP may write each character into the send buffer as it is entered. In the absence of the Clark extension, the sending TCP may then proceed to send each character in a single segment. With the Clark extension, however, the sending TCP is made to wait until it has accumulated a sufficient number of bytes/characters to fill a segment equal to either the MSS in use with the connection or, one half of the buffer capacity of the receiving TCP. The latter is determined from the maximum window update value the sending TCP has received from the receiving TCP.

Window scale option

During our discussion of the HDLC protocol in Section 6.8, we saw that for transmission links which have a large bandwidth/delay product, the sizes of the send and receive sequence number fields in the frame header are extended in order to allow a larger window size to be used. As we saw in Example 6.8, this improves the utilization of the available link bandwidth. This can also be a requirement with TCP when the transmission path

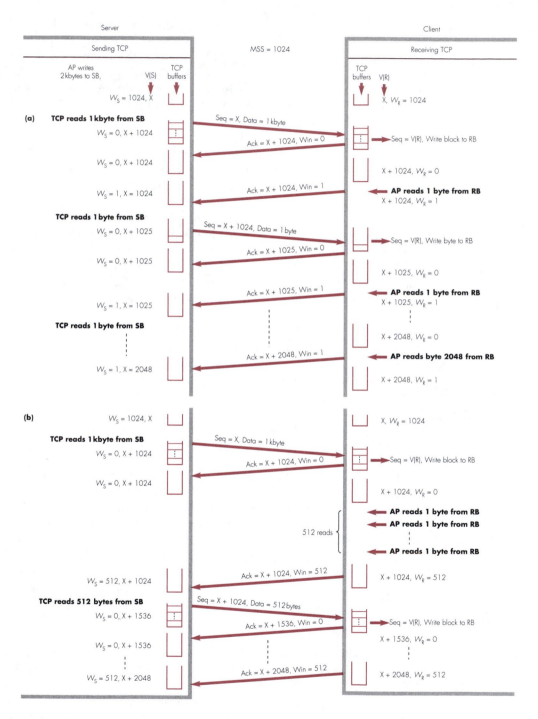

Figure 12.15 Silly window syndrome example: (a) the problem; (b) Clark's solution.

followed through the Internet covers a large distance – and hence has a large signal propagation delay – and a high mean bit rate.

As we saw in Figure 12.4, the *window size* field in the segment header is 16 bits which allows a maximum window size of 65 535 bytes. However, when the path involves intercontinental lines, for example, a typical propagation delay is 40 ms. Also, since optical fiber is now widely used, mean bit rates in excess of 155 Mbps are common. This means that, in order to fully utilize the available transmission capacity, a window size in excess of 775 000 bytes is required. Hence even though a single connection may only use a portion of the available bit rate, it can be seen that, for connections which span large distances, a larger maximum window size is required.

In order to achieve this without changing the format of the segment header, an option has been defined that enables a scaling factor to be applied to the value specified in the *window size* field. This is called the **window scale option** and is defined in **RFC 1323**. The format of this option is shown in Figure 12.16.

Normally, the option is included in the SYN segment when a connection is being established and, since the actual window size is determined by the size of the receive buffer, a different scaling factor can be agreed for use in each direction. Also, since the option is only 3 bytes in length, it is always preceded by a single byte containing a value of 1. This is known as a **no operation (NOP) option** and they are used as pad bytes so that all options are multiples of 4 bytes.

The scaling factor is defined in the *shift count* field of the option. As we can see, this is a 1-byte field and the count value can be between 0 – no scaling in use – and 14. Although the *window size* field in each segment header is only 16 bits, the send and receive window variables kept by each TCP entity are both 32-bit values. The actual window value is then computed by first writing the 16-bit value from the *window size* field into the corresponding window variable and then shifting this left – and hence multiplying it by 2 – by the number in the *shift count* field. A shift count of 1, therefore, means that the

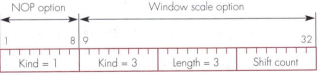

NOP = no operation option: used to pad the window scale option to 4 bytes. The value in the *shift count* field is the power of 2 multiples of the value in the *window size* field. The maximum count value is 14.
Shift count = 0 , no scaling: maximum window = 65 535 (bytes)
Shift count = 1 , multiply by 2^1:   maximum window = 131 070
Shift count = 14, multiply by 2^{14}: maximum window = 1 073 725 440

Figure 12.16 Window scale option format.

maximum window size can be up to $65\,535 \times 2^1 = 131\,070$ bytes and a shift count of 14, a maximum size of $65\,535 \times 2^{14} = 1\,073\,725\,440$ bytes. As we indicated earlier, however, the maximum window size that can be used in each direction is determined by the size of the corresponding receive buffer. Normally, therefore, the shift count to be used for each direction is chosen by the TCP entity since it knows the amount of memory that has been allocated for the receive buffer.

Time-stamp option

During our discussion of the error control procedure, it was assumed that the measurement procedure used to estimate the worst-case round-trip time (RTT) – used by a TCP to compute the retransmission timeout (RTO) interval – is carried out for every data segment that is sent. Although this is the case in some implementations, in others a measurement update occurs only for one segment per window. In general, this is sufficient for transfers involving a small window size – and hence small number of segments per window – but, with a large window, the use of a single segment per window can lead to a poor estimate of the RTT. As we indicated, this can result in many unnecessary retransmissions. Hence to obtain a more accurate estimate of the RTT, the **time-stamp option** is used with these implementations when a large window size is detected. The option is defined in **RFC 1323** and allows the sending TCP to obtain an estimate of the RTT with each ACK it receives.

The option is requested by the TCP that performs an active open, by including the time-stamp option in the SYN segment. The request is then accepted if the receiving TCP includes a time-stamp option in the SYN segment that it returns. Once accepted, both TCPs can then include a time-stamp option in every data segment that they send. The format of the option is shown in Figure 12.17(a) and, as we can see, since it is 10 bytes long, the option is preceded by two NOP option bytes.

The TCP at each side of a connection keeps a 32-bit *timeout timer* which it uses to estimate the RTT for its own direction of transmission. The timer at each side is independent – not synchronized – and is incremented at intervals of between 1 ms and 1 s, a typical interval being 500 ms. For every data segment it sends, the sending TCP reads the current time from the timer and writes this into the *time-stamp value* field. Then, when the TCP returns an ACK for a segment, it writes the same time-stamp value in the *time-stamp echo reply* field. Hence on receipt of each ACK segment, the sending TCP can estimate the RTT for its direction of the connection by computing the difference between the current time in its timer and the time-stamp value contained in the option field of the ACK.

This procedure will work providing the receiving TCP returns an ACK for each data segment it receives. In many implementations, however, as we showed earlier in Figure 12.8, an ACK may be returned only after multiple data segments have been received. Indeed, following the widespread introduction of optical fiber, most TCP implementations now return an ACK for

(a)

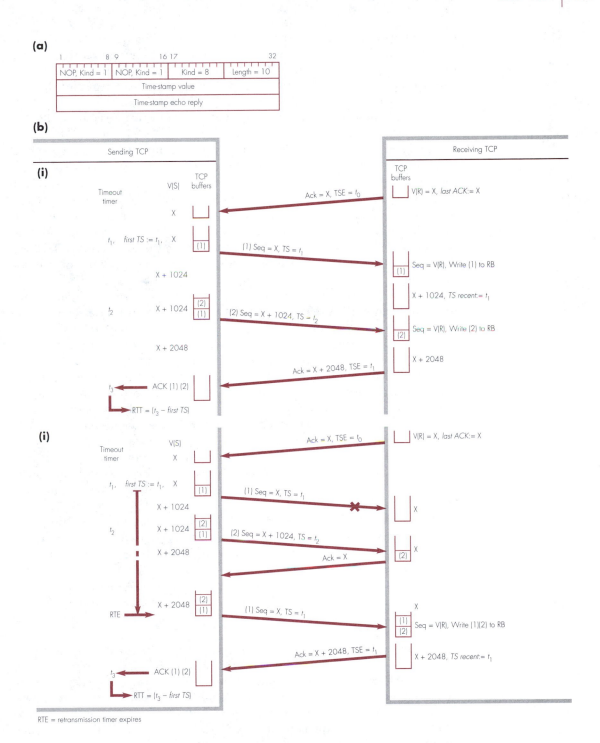

Figure 12.17 Time-stamp option: (a) option format; (b) two examples.

every other data segment received. In such cases, the question arises as to which of the time-stamps – one from each of the data segments that it has received – does the receiving TCP return in the *echo reply* field of the ACK. The answer is the time-stamp from the first in-sequence segment that the receiving TCP received after it returned the last ACK.

To implement this, the receiving TCP maintains two variables in its connection record: *lastACK* and *TSrecent*. Each time the receiving TCP returns an ACK, it keeps a record of the $V(R)$ which it sent in the ACK in *lastACK*. Then, when the first data segment arrives after it has returned the ACK, if the sequence number in the segment header equals that stored in *lastACK*, it keeps a record of the time-stamp value it contains in *TSrecent*. As each subsequent data segment arrives, the TCP simply processes it in the normal way and, when it returns an ACK, includes the current value in *TSrecent* in the *echo reply* field of the option. Thus, the RTT computed by the sending TCP will reflect that the receiving TCP is only returning an ACK on receipt of multiple data segments.

If the sequence number in a segment is not that expected – that is, the sequence number is greater than $V(R)$ – this indicates that a segment has been lost. In this case, the receiving TCP simply returns an ACK and proceeds to wait for the missing segment to be received. Then when it arrives, the time-stamp from this is echoed, not the time-stamp from the out-of-sequence segment. To allow for the possibility of the first segment in a new sequence being corrupted or lost, the sending TCP keeps a record of the time it first sent the segment in a variable called *firstTS*. Should the segment need retransmitting, the value in *firstTS* is used as the *time-stamp value*. In this way, the corrupted RTT also includes the time to retransmit the segment. Although this is an overestimate of the RTT, it is considered to be better than an underestimate, as would have been the case if the later time had been used. Two examples of sequences that show the two alternatives are shown in Figure 12.17(b).

In the first example, it is assumed that no lost segments occur and an ACK is returned on receipt of every other data segment. The time the first segment is sent, t_1, is stored in *firstTS* and, at the receiving side, since it is the segment expected, *TSrecent* becomes equal to the time-stamp value from the segment, t_1. Then, when the ACK is returned after the second segment is received, the value in the *time-stamp echo* field is set to t_1. The RTT is then computed as the difference between the time when the ACK was received and the value in *firstTS*, t_1.

In the second example, it is assumed that the first data segment in the new sequence is corrupted/lost but the second is received error free. In this case, *TSrecent* is not updated until the second copy of the retransmitted first segment is received. However, since this has the same *time-stamp value* as the corrupted first segment, the *time-stamp echo* is the same as before. Hence, as we can see, the computed RTT includes the time taken to retransmit the first segment.

SACK-permitted option

As we indicated earlier, for connections that involve paths through the Internet which span large distances, the propagation delay – also referred to as latency – of the path can be several tens of milliseconds. Hence in addition to influencing the choice of window size, it also has an impact on the efficiency of the error control scheme. As we showed in the example in Figure 12.7, to allow for segments being received out of sequence, a segment is retransmitted only after three duplicate ACKs have been received. Clearly, with connections that have a large RTT associated with them, the delays involved each time a packet/segment is lost or corrupted can be large. In order to reduce this delay, the alternative selective repeat/acknowledgment error control scheme can be used. This is defined in **RFC 2018** and is requested by including the **SACK-permitted option** in the SYN segment header. It is then accepted if the receiving TCP includes the same option in the SYN segment that it returns.

We explained the principle of operation of the selective repeat error control scheme in Section 6.7.3 and gave two example frame sequences showing how the protocol overcomes both a corrupted I-frame and a corrupted ACK-frame. A similar protocol is used with TCP SACK except in this, the SACK segment returned by a receiving TCP contains a list of the data segments that are missing in a specified window of data. In this way, all the missing segments are retransmitted in a single RTT.

Protection against wrapped sequence numbers

When very large amounts of data are being transferred between two hosts using a high bit rate LAN, for example, to speed up the transfer, the window scale option is often used with the maximum shift count of 14. An example is performing a backup of the contents of a disk over a LAN where, since this may involve many gigabytes, it is possible for the sequence numbers to wrap around during the backup. This means that a segment that is lost during one pass through the sequence numbers may be retransmitted and received during a later pass through the numbers so ruining the integrity of the transfer.

To overcome this possibility, the **PAWS** – protection against wrapped sequence numbers – algorithm is often used. This involves the time-stamp option being selected and both sides using the current 32-bit time-stamp as an extension to the 32-bit sequence number. Effectively, this produces 64-bit sequence numbers which overcomes the problem.

12.3.4 Protocol specification

To finish our discussion of TCP we shall illustrate how the segment sequences shown in the various examples, coupled with the socket primitives shown in Table 12.1, relate directly to the formal specification of the TCP protocol entity. Recall from Section 6.7.7 that protocol specifications are carried out in a number of ways. One of the most widely used methods is to use a combination of a state transition diagram and an extended event–state table. A state transition diagram illustrates the various sequences in a pictorial form and hence the various examples relate directly to this. The extended event–state table method, however, is better for implementing a protocol since, as we saw in the example in Section 6.7.7, program code can be derived directly from this. To avoid too much detail, we shall consider only the specification of the connection establishment and termination phases of a basic client TCP and the related server TCP since, as we saw in Figure 6.33, the data transfer phase contains many state variables and predicates.

Using the methodology we established in Section 6.7.7, the various incoming events, protocol states, outgoing events, and specific (internal) actions for both the client and server are shown in parts (a) and (b) of Table 12.2 respectively. As we can see, these relate directly to the segment sequence shown in Figure 12.5(a) – connection establishment – and Figure 12.12(a) – connection termination. The specification of both the client TCP and the server TCP protocols in both state transition diagram and extended event–state diagram forms are then shown in parts (a) and (b) of Figure 12.18 respectively.

Table 12.2 Abbreviated names used in the specification of the TCP protocol: (a) client TCP; (b) server TCP.

(a) Incoming events

Name	Interface	Meaning
connect ( )	AP_user	Initiate the setting up of a connection
SYN+ACK	IP_provider	SYN+ACK received from server (TCP)
DATA	IP_provider	Block of data received from server
close( )	AP_user	Initiate the closure of a connection
ACK	IP_provider	ACK received from server
2MSL	Timer	2MSL timer expires
FIN	IP_provider	FIN received from server
RST	IP_provider	Abort connection

States

Name	Meaning
CLOSED	No connection in place
SYN_SENT	SYN sent to server (TCP)
ESTABLISHED	SYN received from server, connection now in place
FIN_WAIT1	FIN sent to server
FIN_WAIT2	ACK to FIN received from server
TIMED_WAIT	FIN received from server

Table 12.2 continued

Outgoing events		
Name	**Interface**	**Meaning**
SendSYN	IP provider	Send SYN to server (TCP)
SendACK	IP provider	Send ACK to server
SendDATA	IP provider	Send block of data to server
SendFIN	IP provider	Send FIN to server

Specific actions	
[1] Block client AP	[3] Write EOF to receive buffer (RB)
[2] Unblock client AP	[4] Start 2MSL timer

(b) Incoming events

Name	Interface	Meaning
listen ( )	AP_user	Create queue for connection requests
accept ( )	AP_user	Block server AP
SYN	IP_provider	SYN received from client
RST	IP_provider	RST received from client
ACK	IP_provider	ACK received from client
DATA	IP_provider	DATA received from client
FIN	IP_provider	FIN received from client
RST	IP_provider	Abort connection

States	
Name	**Meaning**
CLOSED	No connection in place
LISTEN	Server AP blocked, TCP waiting for a SYN
SYN_RCVD	SYN received from a client AP
ESTABLISHED	ACK for own SYN received, connection now in place
CLOSE_WAIT	FIN received from client TCP
LAST_ACK	FIN sent and waiting for an ACK

▶

Table 12.2 Continued

Outgoing events		
Name	**Interface**	**Meaning**
SendSYN+ACK	IP_provider	Send SYN+ACK to client (TCP)
SendDATA	IP_provider	Send block of data to client
SendFIN	IP_provider	Send FIN to client
SendACK	IP_provider	Send ACK to client

Specific actions	
[1] Create queue for connection requests	[3] Unblock server AP
[2] Block server AP	[4] Write EOF to receive buffer (RB)

It should be stressed that the specifications are only simplified versions of the real specifications. For instance, they do not include the actions taken in the event of simultaneous connection requests or simultaneous closes occurring. Also, when in the ESTABLISHED state, many predicates – for example to check whether sequence numbers are valid and within the current window – and state variables are used when determining the required action and new state. Again, a good insight into the latter can be obtained from the example sequences associated with the data transfer phase.

12.4 UDP

Recall that with TCP there is no correlation between the size of the messages/blocks of data submitted by a user AP and the amount of data in each TCP segment that is used to transfer the messages. Typically, as we saw in Section 12.2, the latter is determined by the path MTU to avoid fragmentation of each segment occurring.

In contrast, with UDP each message/block of data that is submitted by a user AP is transferred directly in a single IP datagram. On receipt of the message, the source UDP simply adds a short header to it to form what is called a **UDP datagram**. This is then submitted to the IP layer for transfer over the internet using, if necessary, fragmentation. At the destination, the IP first determines from the *protocol* field in the datagram header that the destination protocol is UDP, and then passes the contents of the (IP) datagram to the UDP.

The latter first determines the intended user AP from a field in the UDP datagram header and then passes the contents of the (UDP) datagram to the

(a)

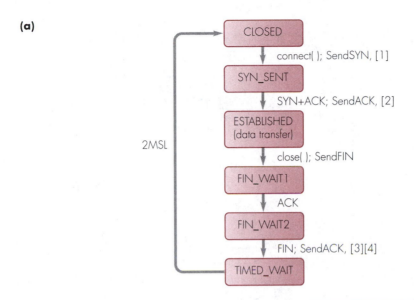

Incoming event / Present state	connect( )	SYN+ACK	close( )	ACK	FIN	2MSL
CLOSED	1	0	0	0	0	0
SYN_SENT	0	2	0	0	0	0
ESTABLISHED	0	0	3	0	0	0
FIN_WAIT1	0	0	0	4	0	0
FIN_WAIT2	0	0	0	0	5	0
TIMED_WAIT	0	0	0	0	0	6

0 = SendRST, CLOSED   1 = SendSYN, [1], SYN_SENT
2 = SendACK, [2], ESTABLISHED   3 = SendFIN, FIN_WAIT1
4 = FIN_WAIT2   5 = SendACK, [3][4], TIMED_WAIT
6 = CLOSED

Figure 12.18 TCP protocol specifications: (a) client; (b) server.

peer user AP for processing. There are no error or flow control procedures involved and hence no connection set up is required. The service offered by UDP to a user AP, therefore, is simply an extension of the service provided by IP. Hence in addition to two-party calls, multicast group calls can be supported. Nevertheless, the set of service primitives and the protocol are both simpler than those of TCP. As with TCP, we shall discuss the services and the protocol separately.

(b)

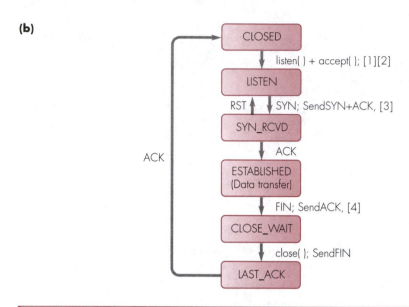

Present state	Incoming event listen( ) + accept( )	SYN	RST	ACK	FIN	close( )
CLOSED	1	0	0	0	0	0
LISTEN	0	2	0	0	0	0
SYN_RCVD	0	0	3	4	0	0
ESTABLISHED	0	0	0	0	5	0
CLOSE_WAIT	0	0	0	0	0	6
LAST_ACK	0	0	0	7	0	0

0 = SendRST, CLOSED
2 = SendSYN+ACK, [3], SYN_RCVD
4 = ESTABLISHED
6 = SendFIN, LAST_ACK

1 = [1][2], LISTEN
3 = LISTEN
5 = SendACK, [4], CLOSE_WAIT
7 = CLOSED

Figure 12.18 Continued.

12.4.1 User services

As with TCP, the most widely used set of user service primitives associated with UDP are the Berkeley Unix socket primitives. With most applications that use UDP, the two user APs either exchange messages on a request-response basis or simply initiate the transfer of blocks of data as these are generated. A typical list of service primitives – system/function calls – is given in Table 12.3 and their use is shown in diagrammatic form in Figure 12.19.

Table 12.3   List of socket primitives associated with UDP and their parameters

Primitive	Parameters
socket( )	service type, protocol, address format, return value = socket descriptor or error code
bind( )	socket descriptor, socket address (= host IP address + port number) return value = success or error code
sendto( )	socket descriptor, local port number, destination port number, destination IP address, precedence, pointer to message buffer containing the data to send, data length (in bytes), return value = success or error code
receive( )	socket descriptor, pointer to message buffer into which the data should be put, length of the buffer, return value = success/error code or end-of-file (EOF)
shutdown( )	socket descriptor, return value = success or error code

As we can see in Figure 12.19(b), prior to exchanging any messages, each of the user APs involved in the call must first establish a socket between itself and its local UDP. The parameters associated with the *socket( )* primitive include the service required (datagram service), the protocol (UDP), and the address format (Internet). Once a socket has been created – and send/receive memory buffers allocated – a socket descriptor is returned to the AP which it then uses with each of the subsequent primitive calls. If this is the only AP that is running in the host, the AP can now start to send and receive messages. If not – for example a server is involved – the AP then issues a *bind( )* primitive which, in addition to the socket descriptor, has an address parameter. This comprises the IP address of the host plus the 16-bit port number the AP wishes to be assigned to the socket. In the case of a server AP, for example, this will be the related well-known port number. When a *bind( )* is not used, the port number will be an ephemeral port number and assigned locally.

Once a socket has been created, the user AP can start to send and receive messages. However, since no connection is involved – and hence no connection record has been created – in addition to the message, the AP must specify the IP address of the destination host – or the IP multicast address in the case of multiple destinations – and the port number of the destination socket/AP. Also, if required, it must specify a precedence value to be sent in the *type of service* field of the IP datagram header. Hence, as we can see in Table 12.3, the *sendto( )* primitive includes each of these fields in its set of parameters. Finally, when all the data transfers associated with the call/session have been carried out, the socket is released by issuing a *shutdown( )* call.

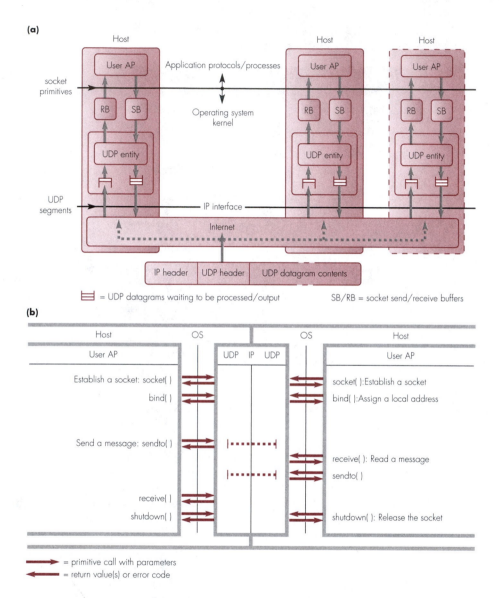

(a)

socket
primitives

UDP
segments

= UDP datagrams waiting to be processed/output   SB/RB = socket send/receive buffers

(b)

= primitive call with parameters
= return value(s) or error code

Figure 12.19 UDP socket primitives: (a) socket interface; (b) primitives and their use.

12.4.2 Protocol operation

The format of each UDP datagram is shown in Figure 12.20(a). The *source port* is the port number of the sending application protocol/socket and the *destination port* is that of the peer (receiving) application protocol(s). Both are 16-bit integers. The value in the *length* field is the number of bytes in the complete (UDP) datagram and includes the 8-byte header and the contents

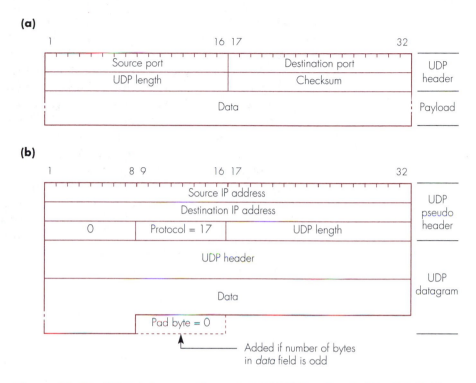

Figure 12.20 UDP datagram format: (a) UDP header fields; (b) fields used in pseudo header for computation of checksum.

of the *data* field. The *checksum* covers the complete datagram, header plus contents. In addition, as with TCP, since only a simple checksum is used to compute the checksum value in the IP header, in order to add an additional level of checking, some selected fields from the IP header are also included in the computation of the UDP checksum. The fields used form what is called the **UDP pseudo header**. These are identified in Figure 12.20(b) and, as we can see, they are the source and destination IP addresses and the protocol value (=17 for UDP) from the IP header, plus the value from the length field in the UDP header.

The computation of the UDP checksum uses the same algorithm as that used by IP. As we saw in Section 9.2, this is computed by treating the complete datagram as being made up of a string of 16-bit words which are added together using 1s complement arithmetic. Using 1s complement number representation, a value of zero is represented as either all 1s or all 0s. With UDP, however, if the computed 1s complement sum is all 0s, then the checksum is sent as all 1s. This is done because the use of a checksum with UDP is optional and, if the value in the checksum field is all 0s, this indicates the sender has not sent a checksum.

Since the number of bytes in the original UDP data field – and hence submitted application protocol data unit – may be odd, in order to ensure the same checksum is computed by both UDPs, a pad byte of zero is added to the data field whenever the number of bytes in the original data field is odd. Thus the value in the length field must always be an even integer. Also, since the UDP datagram is carried in a single IP datagram, as we saw in Section 9.3, in order to avoid fragmentation, the size of each submitted application protocol data unit must be limited to that dictated by the MTU of the path followed through the Internet by the IP datagram. For example, assuming a path MTU of 1500 bytes, allowing for the 8 bytes in the UDP header and 20 bytes in the IP header, the maximum submitted application PDU should be limited to 1472 bytes if fragmentation is to be avoided.

Finally, although the maximum theoretical size of a UDP datagram – as determined by the maximum size of an IP datagram which is 65535 (64K – 1) bytes – is 65507 (65535 – 20 – 8) bytes, the maximum value supported by most implementations is 8192 bytes or less.

12.5 RTP and RTCP

As we showed in Figure 12.1 and explained in the accompanying text, when an application involves the transfer of a real-time stream of audio and/or video over a packet network – for example the speech relating to an Internet phone call – the timing information that is required by the receiver to output the received packet stream at the required rate is provided by the real-time transport protocol (RTP). In addition, for applications that involve both audio and video streams – for example the audio and video associated with a videophone call – the real-time transport control protocol (RTCP) is used to synchronize the two media streams prior to carrying out the decoding operation. We showed a schematic diagram illustrating the use of both these protocols in Figure 5.6 and in this section we describe their main features.

12.5.1 RTP

As we showed in Figure 5.6, normally, the audio and/or video associated with an application are digitized separately using a particular codec. In addition, when the bitstreams are to be transported over a packet network like an internet, each of the bitstreams must be sent in the form of a stream of packets using, for example, the UDP protocol. Similarly, at the receiver, the bitstream must be reconstructed from the stream of received packets. During their transfer over an internet, however, some packets may be lost and/or delayed by varying amounts. Also, since the packets may follow different paths through the internet, they may arrive at the destination in a different order. Hence before the reconstructed bitstream can be passed to the decoder, any missing packets must be detected and compensated for. Similarly, any delay variations in the packet arrival times must be allowed for. These are the functions performed by RTP and a schematic diagram illustrating its use is shown in Figure 12.21(a).

The packet format used with RTP is shown in Figure 12.21(b). The *version* (*V*) field indicates the version of RTP that is being used, *P* is a pad bit and *X* an extension flag to allow extensions to the basic header to be defined and added in the future.

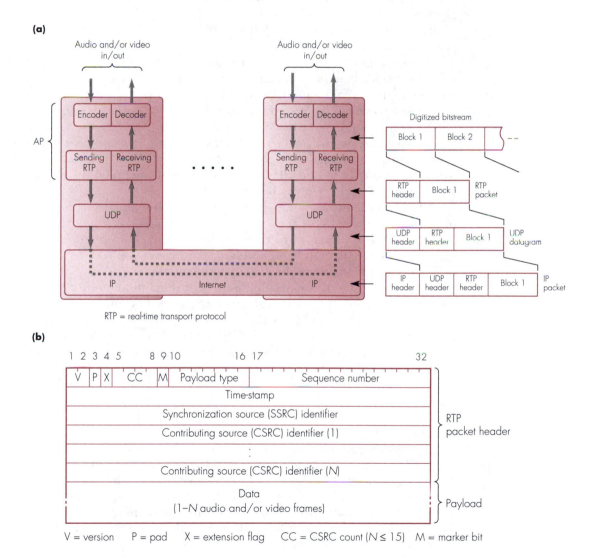

Figure 12.21 Real-time transport protocol: (a) usage; (b) packet format.

In a multicast call/session, each of the participants that contributes to the session – rather than passively listening – is called a **contributing source** (**CSRC**) and is uniquely identified by means of a 32-bit identifier which, typically, is the IP address of the source. During a multicast session the packet stream from multiple sources may be multiplexed together for transmission purposes by a device known as a **mixer**. Hence the resulting RTP packet may contain blocks/frames of digitized information from multiple sources and, to enable the receiver to relate each block/frame to the appropriate participant, the CSRC identifier for each block/frame is included in the header of the new packet. The number of CSRC identifiers present in the packet is given in the *CSRC count* (*CC*) field. Since this is a 4-bit field, up to 15 contributing sources – and hence CSRC identifiers – can be present in the RTP packet header.

As we saw in Chapter 4, the bitstream produced by the different types of audio and video codecs is made up of a sequence of blocks or frames each with a unique start and end delimiter. Associated with the *marker*(*M*) bit is a profile which enables the receiver to interpret the packet data on the correct block/frame boundaries. Also, since there is a range of different audio and video codecs, the *payload type* field indicates the type of encoder that has been used to encode the data in the packet. Moreover, since each packet contains this field, the type of encoder being used can be changed during a call should the QoS of the network being used change.

Each packet contains a *sequence number* which is used to detect lost or out-of-sequence packets. In the case of a lost packet being detected, normally, the contents of the last correctly received packet are used in its place. The effect of out-of-sequence packets being received is overcome by buffering a number of packets before playout of the data they contain starts.

The value in the *time-stamp* field indicates the time reference when the packet was created. It is used to determine the current mean transmission delay time and the level of jitter that is being experienced. This information, together with the number of lost packets, forms the current QoS of the path through the network/internet. As we shall see, periodically this information is returned to the sending RTP by the related real-time transport control protocol. Then, should the QoS change, the sending RTP may modify the resolution of the compression algorithm that is being used. Also, as we saw in Figure 1.22, the level of jitter is used to determine the size of the playout buffer that is required.

The *synchronization source* (*SSRC*) *identifier* identifies the source device that has produced the packet contents. In a videoconferencing call, for example, the data generated by each contributing source may be from multiple different devices – a number of microphones, cameras, computers, and so on – and the SSRC indicates from which device the source information has come. The receiving RTP then uses the SSRC to relay the reconstructed bitstream to the related output device interface.

As we can deduce from Figure 12.21(a), on receipt of each IP packet, the various fields in the UDP datagram header are used within the destination host to deliver the RTP packet to the receiving RTP entity. The various fields in the RTP packet header then enable the receiving RTP to reconstruct the bitstream for each device decoder associated with the session.

12.5.2 RTCP

As we can conclude from the previous section, RTP is concerned with the transfer of the individual streams of digitized data associated with a multimedia call/session. The real-time transport control protocol (RTCP) then adds additional system-level functionality to its related RTP such as the means for a receiving RTP to integrate and synchronize the individual packet streams together and for a sending RTP to be informed of the currently-prevailing network QoS. Hence as we showed in Figure 5.6, the RTCP operates alongside of RTP and shares information with it. However, as we saw in Figure 5.8, each RTCP has a different (UDP) port number associated with it so that it can operate independently of RTP.

The RTCP in all of the systems involved in a call/session, periodically exchange messages with one another. Each message is sent in a RTCP packet to the same network address – but with the RTCP port number – as the RTP to which the message relates. The general scheme is shown in Figure 12.22 and the messages that are exchanged relate to:

■ *integrated media synchronization*: in applications that involve separate audio and video streams that need to be integrated together, as we showed in Figure 5.18, a common system time clock is used for synchronization

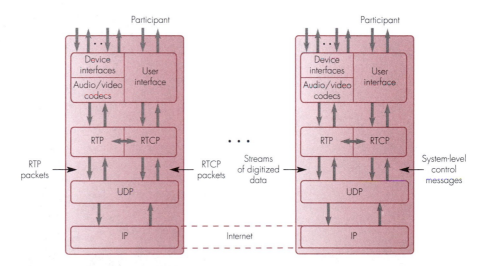

Figure 12.22 Real-time transport control protocol (RTCP) usage.

purposes. Normally, the system that initiates the call/conference provides this function – or sometimes a separate reference time server – and the RTCP in all of the other systems then exchange messages with the RTCP in this system so that they are utilizing the same system time clock;

- *QoS reports*: as we indicated earlier, the number of lost packets, the level of jitter, and the mean transmission delay are continuously computed by each RTP for the packet streams they receive from all of the other contributing sources. The adjoining RTCP then sends a message containing the related information to the RTCP in each of these systems at periodic intervals. The RTCP in each of these systems then performs any system-level functions that may need to be performed; for example, changing the resolution of the compression algorithm or the size of the playout buffer;

- *participation reports*: these are used during a conference call, for example, to enable a participant to indicate to the other participants that it is leaving the call. Again, this is done by means of the RTCP in the participant's system. The participant enters an appropriate message and this is then sent via RTCP to the RTCP in each of the other systems. Typically, a related message is then output on the screen of each of the other systems;

- *participation details*: information such as the name, email address, phone number, and so on of each participant is sent to all of the other participants in a RTCP message. In this way, each of the participants knows the identity and contact information of all of the other participants.

Summary

In this chapter we have described four protocols that are used widely with packet networks to support applications. Both TCP and UDP are transport layer protocols while RTP and RTCP, despite their name, both form an integral part of an application layer protocol/process. A summary of the main features of each protocol is given in Figure 12.23.

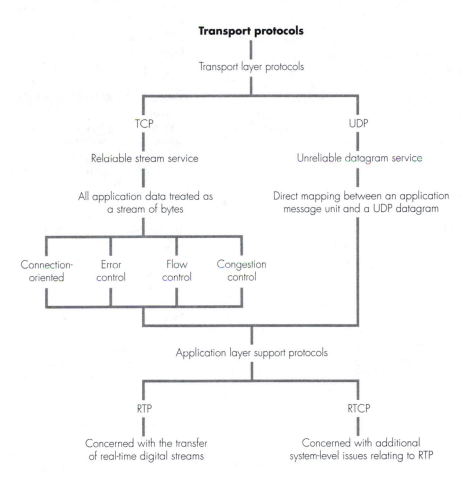

Figure 12.23 Transport protocols chapter summary.

Exercises

Section 12.2

12.1 By means of a diagram, show the position of the TCP, UDP, RTP, and RTCP, protocols in relation to the various network layer and application protocols in the TCP/IP protocol suite. Include in your diagram a received message that contains the headers relating to the various protocols and indicate the interlayer address selectors that are used to route the application data in the received message to the intended application protocol/process.

12.2 In relation to the port numbers that are present in the TCP and UDP protocol headers, explain the meaning of the terms "ephemeral" and "well-known port numbers".

12.3 With the aid of a diagram showing how two application protocols/processes communicate with each other using the TCP/IP protocol suite, explain the meaning of the terms:
(i) end-to-end communication,
(ii) TCP/UDP service primitives,
(iii) network-interface protocol,
(iv) hop-by-hop transfer.

Section 12.3

12.4 Explain the meaning of the term "reliable stream service" in relation to the operation of TCP and why a logical connection between the two communicating TCP entities must be established to provide this service.

12.5 In relation to the data transfer phase of TCP, explain the meaning of the terms:
(i) segment,
(ii) maximum segment size (MSS),
(iii) path MTU.

12.6 State why both flow control and congestion control procedures are required with TCP.

Section 12.3.1

12.7 With the aid of a diagram, explain the meaning of the following terms relating to TCP:

(i) socket interface,
(ii) socket primitives,
(iii) application program interface (API),
(iv) TCP (protocol) entity.

12.8 List the set of four socket primitives that are issued by a server AP to carry out a passive-open; that is, to establish a socket between itself and its local TCP entity. Explain the use of each primitive and the meaning of the terms "socket descriptor" and "socket address".

12.9 By means of a diagram, show the set of socket primitives that are issued by a client AP to carry out an active open and those that are issued by the server in response to these. Describe the effect of each primitive at both the client and server sides and, in relation to the *connect( )* primitive, the parameters that are associated with it.

12.10 Explain the meaning and use of the following relating to a socket:
(i) socket descriptor,
(ii) socket address,
(iii) pass-through parameter.

12.11 State why the TCP entity in both a client and a server needs to create and maintain a connection record for each new (TCP) connection. List the main fields that are present in a connection record and describe their use.

12.12 Associated with a socket is a send buffer and a receive buffer. Explain the use of each and how they relate to the segments that are sent/received by the two TCP entities. Include in your explanation how an AP can force the transmission of a small block of data.

Section 12.3.2

12.13 Use the TCP segment format given in Figure 12.4(a) to explain the use of the following:
(i) source and destination port numbers,
(ii) sequence and acknowledgment numbers,

(iii) code bits,
(iv) window size,
(v) urgent pointer,
(vi) options and the header length.

12.14 Describe the role of the checksum field in a TCP segment header. Include in your description why additional header fields are added to those in the TCP header and why pad bytes are used.

12.15 With the aid of a time sequence diagram, explain how a logical connection between two TCP entities is established using a three-way handshake procedure. Include in your diagram the socket primitives at both the client and server side that trigger the sending of each segment. Also, explain how the initial sequence number in each direction is selected.

12.16 Identify and explain briefly the essential procedures that are followed by two correspondent TCP entities during the data transfer phase.

12.17 With the aid of a time sequence diagram, show how the individual characters entered by a user at a keyboard are transferred over a TCP connection using immediate acknowledgments. Hence quantify the overheads associated with this mode of operation.

12.18 Use a time sequence diagram to show how the overheads identified in Exercise 12.17 are reduced using
(i) delayed acknowledgments, and
(ii) the Nagle algorithm.

Explain the reason why the Nagle algorithm is the preferred mode of working with interactive applications over the Internet.

12.19 Explain why additional buffers to the send and receive buffers associated with the socket are required within the TCP entity at each side of a connection.

12.20 Explain why the sending TCP entity only retransmits a segment if it receives three duplicate acknowledgments for the segment.

Include in your explanation the role of the retransmission timer used by the sending TCP entity and the meaning of the term "fast retransmit".

12.21 The following questions relate to the time sequence diagram shown in Figure 12.7.
(i) Assuming no segments had been corrupted/lost, deduce how many Data and ACK segments would have been sent.
(ii) Assuming segment (2) had not been corrupted/lost, deduce the segments that would have been sent by both TCP entities.
(iii) Explain why the second copy of segment (2) is discarded but an ACK is returned.
(iv) Assuming the MSS for the (TCP) connection was 1024 bytes and one (data) segment was corrupted, deduce how many data and ACK segments would be sent.

12.22 State the meaning of the term "retransmission timeout (RTO) interval" in relation to to TCP connection and why it is necessary to determine this dynamically for each new connection.

12.23 Explain the operation of the exponential backoff algorithm that is used to derive the RTO for a TCP connection. Also explain the retransmission ambiguity problem that can arise with this.

12.24 Explain the early Jacobson algorithm that was used to derive the RTO for a TCP connection. Describe the refinement that was later made to it.

12.25 Explain the meaning of the term "delayed ACK timer" in relation to TCP and why this is required.

12.26 State the relationship between the value in the *window size* field and the value in the *acknowledgment* field in the header of a TCP segment. How is the value in the *window size* field determined?

12.27 The following relate to the time sequence diagram shown in Figure 12.8.
  (i) Why does the Win(dow) field in segments sent by the sending TCP remain the same?
  (ii) Why does the V(R) in the receiving TCP stay at X until after the first four segments have been received?
  (iii) Why does the second ACK returned by the receiving TCP contain a Win = 1024 instead of Win = 2048?
  (iv) Why is the second ACK called a window update?

12.28 With the aid of a diagram, explain the meaning of the following terms relating to the TCP window flow control procedure. Include in your diagram a sequence of messages being sent each of which requires multiple segments to send:
  (i) lower window edge,
  (ii) upper window edge,
  (iii) sliding window.

12.29 What is the main reason for lost packets in the Internet? Hence explain how each host endeavors to minimize this effect. Include in your explanation the meaning of the term "congestion window".

12.30 Explain in a qualitative way the relationship between the send window, W_S, and the congestion window, W_C, that are maintained by the TCP entity in a host for each (TCP) connection. Include in your explanation why W_c is initialized to 1 segment.

12.31 In relation to the graph shown in Figure 12.10, explain the meaning of the following terms:
  (i) slow start phase, including why this is shown to increase exponentially
  (ii) slow start threshold and the congestion avoidance phase, including why this is shown to increase linearly
  (iii) constant phase.

12.32 The graph shown in Figure 12.10 relates to a lightly-loaded internet. During these condi-

tions, what effect does the congestion window, W_C, have on the send window, W_S?

12.33 Explain in a qualitative way why the adjustments to the W_c for a connection depend on whether a lost packet is detected as a result of duplicate ACKs being received or the retransmission timer expiring.

12.34 With the aid of a graph showing the variation of W_c as a function of the connection RTT, show and explain how W_c is affected by:
  (i) a set of 3 duplicate ACKs being received for a segment
  (ii) the retransmission timer for a segment expiring.

12.35 Use the time sequence diagrams shown in Figure 12.12(a) and (d) to explain the sequence of segments that are exchanged with:
  (i) a normal connection close,
  (ii) a half close.

  Include in your explanations why two FIN_WAIT states and a final TIMED_WAIT state are required.

12.36 Explain the role of the persist timer. Hence with the aid of the time sequence diagram shown in Figure 12.13, explain how the effect of a corrupted ACK containing a window update is overcome.

12.37 Explain the role of the keepalive timer. Hence with the aid of the time sequence diagram shown in Figure 12.14, explain how the effect of a client host being switched off is overcome.

12.38 Explain how the phenomenon called the silly window syndrome can arise and the steps that are taken at the client and server sides to avoid this happening. Using the two time sequence diagrams shown in Figure 12.15, explain how the Clark extension prevents this from occurring.

12.39 By means of an example, show how for transmission paths that have a large bandwidth/delay product a window size field of 16 bits may be insufficient. Hence by means of an example, describe how the window scale option used in the TCP segment header can overcome this problem.

12.40 The computation of the RTO for a connection using the method in Exercise 12.24 required the RTT to be computed for every data segment. Explain how, with a large window size, this can lead to a poor estimate of the RTT.

Hence, with the aid of the time sequence diagram shown in Figure 12.17, explain how the number of updates can be reduced by using a time-stamp option field. Include in your explanation the use of the *time-stamp value* and *time-stop echo reply* fields and how the receiving TCP overcomes the fact that not all segments are acknowledged.

12.41 Explain the principles behind:
(i) the SACK-permitted option
(ii) how protection against wrapped sequence numbers can be overcome by using the time-stamp option.

12.42 Use the time sequence diagrams associated with the connection established (Figure 12.5) and connection close (Figure 12.12) procedures to follow the state transitions that occur at the client and server sides shown in Figure 12.18(a) and (b) respectively.

Section 12.4

12.43 What are the main differences between UDP and TCP?

12.44 By means of a diagram, show the socket interface associated with UDP in relation to a user AP. Include in your diagram the send and receive buffers associated with the socket and the input and output buffers associated with the UDP entity.

12.45 Show on a diagram a typical sequence of socket primitives that are issued at both the sending and the receiving sides to:
(i) establish a socket connection,
(ii) exchange a single UDP datagram,
(iii) release the socket connection.
Identify the main parameters associated with each primitive.

12.46 In relation to the UDP datagram format shown in Figure 12.20(b), explain how the checksum is corrupted.

State why the maximum size of UDP datagram is often less than the theoretical maximum.

Section 12.5

12.47 Describe the use of the RTP protocol and, by means of a diagram, show its position in relation to the TCP/IP protocol stack.

12.48 In relation to the RTP packet format shown in Figure 12.21(b), explain the meaning and use of the following fields:
(i) CC and CSRC,
(ii) M and payload type,
(iii) sequence number,
(iv) time-stamp,
(v) SSRC.

12.49 Describe the use of the RTCP protocol and, by means of a diagram, show its position in relation to the TCP/IP protocol stack.

12.50 Identify and give a brief explanation of the four main functions performed by RTCP.

13

Application support functions

13.1 Introduction

Having described the various protocols that are used to transfer information across a network/internet we are now in a position to describe a selection of the standard protocols associated with various applications. Before we do this, however, it will be helpful if we first build up an understanding of some of the support functions that are used with many of these application protocols.

For example, if you were asked to write an application program to process a set of fault reports that have been gathered from the various items of computer-based equipment that make up a network – switching exchanges, bridges, gateways, routers, and so on – then you would, of course, want to use a suitable high-level programming language. Each report would then be declared in the form of, say, a (record) structure with the various fields in each record declared as being of suitable types. However, although the data types used may be the same as those used by the programmer who created the software within each item of equipment, the actual representation of each field after compilation may be quite different in each equipment. For example, in one computer an integer type may be represented by a 16-bit value while in another it may be represented by 32 bits.

Even if the two computers both use 16 bits to represent an integer type, the position of the sign bit or the order of the two bytes that make up each integer may still be different. Similarly, the character types used in different computers also differ. For example, EBCDIC may be used in one and ASCII/IA5 in another. The representation of the different data types are thus said to be in an **abstract syntax** form.

The effect of this is that when we pass a block of data – for example, holding a set of records – from one computer to another, we cannot simply transfer the block of data from one computer memory to that of the other since the program in the receiving computer may interpret the data incorrectly such as on the wrong byte boundaries. Consequently, when we transfer data between computers, we must ensure that the syntax of the data is known by the receiving machine and, if this is different from its local syntax, convert the data into this syntax prior to processing.

One approach to this problem is to define a **data dictionary** for the complete (distributed) application which contains an application-wide definition of the representation of all the data types used in the application. If this representation is different from the local representation used by a machine, we must convert all data received into its local syntax prior to processing and convert it back into the standard form if it is to be sent to another machine. The form used in the data dictionary is known as the **concrete** or **transfer** syntax for the application.

This is a common requirement in many distributed applications, especially when computers and other items of equipment from different manufacturers are involved. Hence to meet this requirement, an international standard has been defined for representing information that is to be transferred between (possibly dissimilar) computers and other items of computer/microprocessor based equipment. This is called **abstract syntax notation one** (**ASN.1**) and is defined in **IS 8824**. As we shall see, this comprises both an abstract syntax for defining the data types associated with a distributed application and also a transfer syntax for representing each data value during its transfer over the network.

A second requirement that relates to many distributed applications is network security. Increasingly, people are using networks like the Internet for banking, home shopping, and many other applications that involve the transfer of sensitive information such as credit card details over the network. As the knowledge of computer networking and their protocols has become more widespread, so the threat of intercepting and decoding the data within messages during its transfer across the network has increased. To combat these threats, a number of security techniques have been developed which, when combined together, provide a high level of confidence that any information that is received from the network has come from the stated source and has not been read or changed during its transfer over the network. In this chapter, we shall present an overview of both these topics and, in the following two chapters, some examples of applications that use them.

13.2 ASN.1

ASN.1 is concerned with the representation (syntax) of the data in the messages associated with a distributed/networked application during its transfer between two application processes (APs). The aim is to ensure that the messages exchanged between the two APs have a common meaning – known as **shared semantics** – to both processes. The approach adopted is shown in Figure 13.1.

With any distributed application all APs involved must know the syntax of the messages associated with the application. For example, if the application involves customer accounts, the APs in all systems that process them must be written to interpret each field in an account in the same way. However, as we indicated earlier, the representation of data types associated with a high-level programming language may differ from one computer to another. To ensure that data is interpreted in the same way, before any data is transferred between two processes it must be converted from its local (abstract) syntax into an application-wide transfer syntax. Similarly, before any received data is processed, it must be converted into the local syntax if this is different from the transfer syntax.

Two questions arise from this: firstly, what abstract syntax should be used, and secondly, what representation should be adopted for the transfer syntax. One solution to the first question is to assume that all programming is done in the same high-level programming language and then to declare all data types relating to the application using this language. However, different programmers may prefer to use different languages. Also, the question of the transfer syntax is still unanswered.

As the representation of data in a distributed application is a common requirement, ISO (in cooperation with ITU-T) has defined ASN.1 as a general abstract syntax that is suitable for the definition of data types associated with most distributed applications. An example application that uses ASN.1 is

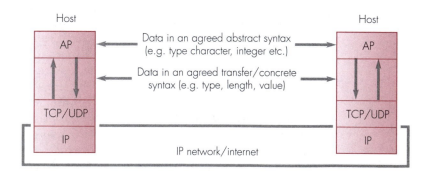

Figure 13.1 ASN.1: abstract and transfer/concrete syntax relationship.

the simple network management protocol which we describe in Section 14.7 of the next chapter. As the name implies, the data types associated with ASN.1 are abstract types. Hence, in addition to the abstract syntax definition, an associated transfer syntax has also been defined.

As an aid to the use of ASN.1, a number of companies now sell **ASN.1 compilers** for a range of programming languages. There is an ASN.1 compiler for Pascal and another for C. The general approach for using such compilers is shown in Figure 13.2.

Firstly, the data types associated with an application are defined using ASN.1. For example, if two APs are to be written, one in Pascal and the other in C, the ASN.1 type definitions are first processed by each compiler. Their output is the equivalent data type definitions in the appropriate language together with a set of **encoding** and **decoding procedures/functions** for each data type. The data type definitions are linked and used with the corresponding application software, while the encoding and decoding procedures/functions are used as library procedures/functions: each encoding procedure/function is used to encode the related value into its corresponding transfer syntax ready for transferring to the destination AP and each decoding procedure/function is used to decode a received value from its transfer syntax into its local syntax prior to processing.

As we shall see, the output of each encoding procedure/function is in the form of a byte – normally referred to as an octet – string comprising an identifier, the length (in bytes) of the encoded value, and the encoded value. The identifier is then used to determine the type of decoding procedure/function that should be carried out on the value.

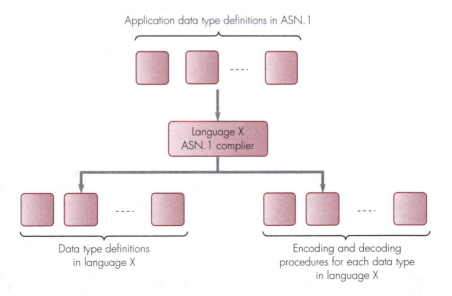

Figure 13.2 ASN.1 compiler function.

13.2.1 Type definitions

The type definitions used with ASN.1 are defined in IS 8824. They are similar to those used with most high-level programming languages for defining the data types associated with the variables used in a program: as each variable is declared, the data type associated with it is also defined. Then, when a value is assigned to the variable, its syntax is of the defined type.

ASN.1 supports a number of type identifiers, which may be members of the following four classes:

■ UNIVERSAL: the generalized types such as integer;

■ CONTEXT-SPECIFIC: these are related to the specific context in which they are used;

■ APPLICATION: these are common to a complete application;

■ PRIVATE: these are user definable but must begin with an upper-case letter.

The data types associated with the UNIVERSAL class may be either primitive (simple) or constructed (structured). A primitive type is either a basic data type that cannot be decomposed – for example, a BOOLEAN or an INTEGER – or, in selected cases, a string of one or more basic data elements all of the same type – for example, a string of one or more bits, octets, or IA5/graphical characters. The keywords used with ASN.1 are always in upper-case letters and the primitive types available include:

UNIVERSAL (primitive): BOOLEAN
INTEGER
BITSTRING
OCTETSTRING
REAL
ENUMERATED
IA5String/DisplayString
NULL
ANY

The names of variables and constants may consist of upper and lower-case letters, digits, and hyphens but must begin with a lower-case letter. Some examples of simple types are shown in Figure 13.3(a).

As with a program listing, we may insert comments at any point in a line; the comments start with a pair of adjacent hyphens and end either with another pair of hyphens or the end of a line. The assignment symbol is ::= and the individual bit assignments associated with a BITSTRING type are given in braces with the bit position in parentheses. A similar procedure is used for the ENUMERATED type to identify the possible values of the vari-

(a)

```
        married ::= BOOLEAN -- true or false
yrsWithCompany ::= INTEGER
   accessRights ::= BITSTRING{read(0), write(1)}
    PDUContents ::= OCTETSTRING
           name ::= IA5String
             pi ::= REAL -- mantissa, base, exponent
        workDay ::= ENUMERATED{monday(0), tuesday(1) ... friday(4)}
```

(b)

```
personnelRecord ::= SEQUENCE{
                       empNumber INTEGER,
                       name IA5String,
                       yrsWithCompany INTEGER
                       married BOOLEAN}
```

```
c.f. personnelRecord =  record
                           empNumber = integer;
                           name = array [1..20] of char;
                           yrsWithCompany = integer;
                           married = boolean
                        end;
```

(c)

```
personnelRecord ::= SEQUENCE{
                       empNumber [APPLICATION1] INTEGER,
                       name [1] IA5String,
                       yrsWithCompany [2] INTEGER,
                       married [3] BOOLEAN}
```

(d)

```
personnelRecord ::= SEQUENCE{
                       empNumber [APPLICATION1] INTEGER,
                       name [1] IMPLICIT IA5String,
                       yrsWithCompany [2] IMPLICIT INTEGER,
                       married [3] IMPLICIT BOOLEAN}
```

Figure 13.3 Some example ASN.1 type definitions: (a) simple types; (b) constructed type; (c) tagging; (d) implicit typing.

able. INTEGER types are signed whole numbers of, in theory, unlimited magnitude while REAL types are represented in the form {m, B, e} where m = mantissa, B = base, and e = exponent, that is $m \times B^e$.

A NULL type relates to a single variable and is commonly used when a component variable associated with a constructed type has no type assignment. Similarly, the ANY type indicates that the type of the variable is defined elsewhere.

A constructed type is defined by reference to one or more other types, which may be primitive or constructed. The constructed types used with ASN.1 include the following:

■ UNIVERSAL (constructed) SEQUENCE: a fixed (bounded), ordered list of types, some of which may be declared optional, that is, the associated typed value may be omitted by the entity constructing the sequence;

- SEQUENCEOF: a fixed or unbounded, ordered list of elements, all of the same type;

- SET: a fixed, unordered list of types, some of which may be declared optional;

- SETOF: a fixed or unbounded, unordered list of elements, all of the same type;

- CHOICE: a fixed, unordered list of types, selected from a previously specified set of types.

An example of a constructed type is shown in Figure 13.3(b), together with the equivalent type definition in Pascal for comparison purposes.

To allow the individual elements within a structured type to be referenced, ASN.1 supports the concept of **tagging**. This involves assigning a **tag** or **identifier** to each element and is analogous to the index used with the array type found in most high-level languages.

The tag may be declared to be one of the following:

- CONTEXT-SPECIFIC: the tag has meaning only within the scope of the present structured type;

- APPLICATION: the tag has meaning in the context of the complete application (collection of types);

- PRIVATE: the tag has meaning only to the user.

An example of the use of tags in relation to the type definition used in Figure 13.3(b) is given in part (c). In the example, we assume that *empNumber* is used in other type definitions and hence is given a unique application-wide tag. The other three variables need be referenced only within the context of this sequence type.

Another facility supported in ASN.1 is to declare a variable to be of an **implied type**, using the keyword IMPLICIT which is written immediately after the variable name and, if present, the tag number.

Normally, the type of a variable is explicitly defined, but if a variable has been declared to be of an IMPLICIT type, then the type of the variable can be implied by, say, its order in relation to other variables. It is used mainly with tagged types since the type of the variable can then be implied from the tag number. An example is shown in Figure 13.3(d), where the types of the last three variables can be implied – rather than explicitly defined – from their tag number. The benefit of this will become more apparent when we discuss the encoding and decoding rules associated with ASN.1 in the next section.

To illustrate the use of some of the other features and types associated with ASN.1, let us consider the use of ASN.1 for the definitions of the protocol data units (PDUs) associated with a protocol. The PDU type definitions discussed so far are all defined in the form of an ordered bit string with the number of bits required for each field and the order of bits in the string defined unambiguously. This ensures that the fields in each PDU are interpreted in the same way in all systems.

To minimize the length of each PDU, many of the fields have only a few bits associated with them. With this type of definition, it is not easy to use a high-level programming language to implement the protocol since isolating each field in a received octet string – and subsequent encoding – can involve complex bit manipulations.

To overcome this problem, the PDU definitions of all of the protocols defined by ISO are now defined using ASN.1. By passing each PDU definition through an appropriate ASN.1 compiler, the type definitions of all the fields in each PDU are automatically produced in a suitable high-level language compatible form. The protocol can be written in the selected language using these type definitions. Again, however, since the fields are now in an abstract syntax, the corresponding encoding and decoding procedures produced by the ASN.1 compiler must be used to convert each field into/from its transfer syntax when transferring PDUs between two peer protocol entities.

An example of the use of ASN.1 for the definition of a PDU is shown in Figure 13.4. This relates to an ISO application protocol called **file transfer access and management** (**FTAM**) which is sometimes used instead of FTP.

The complete set of PDUs relating to a particular protocol entity is defined as a **module**. The name of a module is known as the **module definition**. In the example of Figure 13.4, this is *ISO8571-FTAM DEFINITIONS*. It is followed by the assignment symbol (::=); the module body is then defined between the BEGIN and END keywords.

Following BEGIN, the CHOICE type indicates that the PDUs used with FTAM belong to one of three types: *InitializePDU, FilePDU*, or *BulkdataPDU*. A further *CHOICE* type indicates that there are six different types of PDU associated with the *InitializePDU* type: *FINITIALIZErequest, FINITIALIZE response*, and so on. Note that these are tagged so that they can be distinguished from one another. Also, since the tags are followed by *IMPLICIT*, the type of PDU can be implied from the tag field, that is, no further definition is needed, such as a PDU type. Note that since the *FINITIALIZErequest* PDU is always the first PDU received in relation to FTAM, it is assigned an application-specific tag number of 1. The remaining PDU types then have a context-specific tag; note that the word CONTEXT is not needed as these types will have meaning in the context of FTAM. The definition of each PDU is then given and, in Figure 13.4, the *FINITIALIZErequest* PDU is defined.

The *SEQUENCE* structured type is used in this definition to indicate that the PDU consists of a number of typed data elements, which may be primitive or constructed. Although with the *SEQUENCE* type the list of variable types is in a set order, normally the individual elements are (context-specifically) tagged since, as we shall see in the next section, this can lead to a more efficient encoded version of the PDU. The first element, *protocolId*, is of type *INTEGER* and is set to zero, which indicates it is FTAM (*iso FTAM*).

```
ISO8571-FTAM DEFINITIONS ::=

BEGIN

PDU ::= CHOICE {
                    InitializePDU,
                    FilePDU,
                    BulkdataPDU
                    }
InitializePDU ::= CHOICE    {
                            [APPLICATION 1]     IMPLICIT FINITIALIZErequest,
                            [1]                 IMPLICIT FINITIALIZEresponse,
                            [2]                 IMPLICIT FTERMINATErequest,
                            [3]                 IMPLICIT FTERMINATEresponse,
                            [4]                 IMPLICIT FUABORTrequest,
                            [5]                 IMPLICIT FPABORTresponse

                            }

FINITIALIZErequest          ::= SEQUENCE {
                            protocolId [0] INTEGER { isoFTAM (0) },
                            versionNumber [1] IMPLICIT
                                        SEQUENCE { major INTEGER,
                                                    minor INTEGER},
                                        -- initially { major 0, minor 0}
                            serviceType [2] INTEGER { reliable (0),
                                                user correctable (1)}
                            serviceClass [3] INTEGER { transfer (0),
                                                access (1),
                                                management (2)}
                            functionalUnits [4] BITSTRING { read (0),
                                                        write (1),
                                                        fileAccess (2),
                                                        limitedFileManagement (3),
                                                        enhancedFileManagement (4),
                                                        grouping (5),
                                                        recovery (6),
                                                        restartDataTransfer (7) }
                            attributeGroups [5] BITSTRING {storage (0),
                                                    security (1) }
                            rollbackAvailability [6] BOOLEAN DEFAULT FALSE,
                            presentationContextName [7] IMPLICIT ISO646String {"ISO8822"},
                            identifyOfInitiator [8] ISO646String OPTIONAL,
                            currentAccount [9] ISO646String OPTIONAL,
                            filestorePassword [10] OCTETSTRING OPTIONAL,
                            checkpointWindow [11] INTEGER OPTIONAL }

FINITIALIZEresponse ::= SEQUENCE {
                                :
END
```

Figure 13.4 ASN.1 PDU definition example.

The second element, *versionNumber*, is defined as a *SEQUENCE* of two *INTEGER* types – *major* and *minor*. As before, the use of the word *IMPLICIT* means that the type (*SEQUENCE*) can be implied from the preceding tag field and need not be encoded. A comment field is used to indicate the initial setting of the two variables. The next two elements are both of type *INTEGER*; the possible values of each are shown in the braces.

The next element, *functionalUnits*, is of type *BITSTRING*; the eight bits in the string are set to 1 or 0 depending on whether the particular unit is (1) or is not (0) required. Finally, some of the later elements in the sequence are declared *OPTIONAL*, which means that they may or may not be present in an encoded PDU. Since the individual elements in the PDU have been tagged, the receiver of the PDU can determine if the element is present or not. The keyword *DEFAULT* has a similar meaning except that if the element is not present in a PDU, it is assigned the default value.

Finally, there is a primitive type that has been defined to enable an object definition to be unique within a wider context than its current definition. For example, as we shall expand upon in Section 14.7.1, within the context of network management, the various managed objects associated with a network – a bridge, a router, a protocol, and so on – are each assigned an OBJECT IDENTIFIER that is unique within the context of all the different network types – PSTN/ISDN/Internet/and so on.

Within any one of these networks there is a host of multinational vendors that supply equipment and software to be used within that network. Also, many vendors supply equipment that is used in a number of these networks. In order to ensure that the management information produced by a particular piece of equipment or software relates to a specific network type, the various international standards bodies have defined an **object naming tree** so that the set of object identifiers associated with each of these network types are unique within a global context.

13.2.2 Transfer syntax

As we indicated earlier, all the ASN.1 data types associated with an application have an abstract syntax. This means that their values may be represented in different ways within the various computers/items of equipment involved in the application. Hence as we saw in Figure 13.1, before each value associated with the various data types used within an application is transferred from one AP to another, it is first encoded into a standard transfer – also called concrete – syntax. Similarly, on receipt of each encoded value, the destination AP first decodes each value into its local (abstract) syntax before it is processed. In this section we describe the principles behind both the encoding and decoding operations.

Encoding

The standard representation for a value of each type is a data element comprising the following three fields:

- *identifier*, which defines the ASN.1 type;
- *length*, which defines the number of octets in the contents field;
- *contents*, which defines the contents (which may be other data elements for a structured type).

Each field comprises one or more bytes/octets. The structure of the identifier octet is shown in Figure 13.5 and example encodings of different typed values are given in Figure 13.6. To help readability, the content of each octet is represented as two hexadecimal digits and the final encoded value (always in the form of a string of octets) is given at the end of each example. If the number

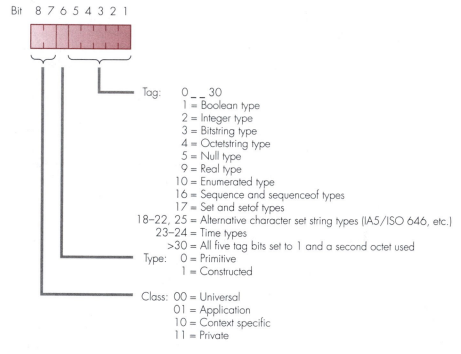

Bit 8 7 6 5 4 3 2 1

Tag: 0 _ _ 30
       1 = Boolean type
       2 = Integer type
       3 = Bitstring type
       4 = Octetstring type
       5 = Null type
       9 = Real type
       10 = Enumerated type
       16 = Sequence and sequenceof types
       17 = Set and setof types
       18–22, 25 = Alternative character set string types (IA5/ISO 646, etc.)
       23–24 = Time types
       >30 = All five tag bits set to 1 and a second octet used
Type: 0 = Primitive
       1 = Constructed

Class: 00 = Universal
        01 = Application
        10 = Context specific
        11 = Private

Note: The null type is used to indicate the absence of an element in a sequence.

The two time types are used to specify time in a standardized way as a string of IA5/ISO 646 characters. For example:
YY MM DD hh mm ss
00 09 30 20 45 58   = current time

Figure 13.5 ASN.1 encoding: identifier bit definitions.

of octets in the contents field exceeds 127, the most significant bit of the first length octet is set to 1 and the length is defined in two (or more) octets.

In Figure 13.6(a), the identifier 01 (Hex) indicates that the class is UNIVERSAL (bits 8 and 7 = 00), it is a primitive type (bit 6 = 0), and the tag (bits 1 through 5) is 1, thus indicating it is Universal 1 and hence BOOLEAN. The length is 01 (Hex) indicating that the content is a single octet. TRUE is encoded as FF (Hex) and FALSE as 00 (Hex).

(a) BOOLEAN – UNIVERSAL 1

e.g., *Employed* ::= *BOOLEAN*
– – assume true

Identifier = 01 (Hex)   – – Universal 1
Length   = 01
Contents = FF

i.e., 01 01 FF

INTEGER – UNIVERSAL 2

e.g., *RetxCount* ::= *INTEGER*
– – assume = 29 (decimal)

Identifier = 02   – – Universal 2
Length   = 01
Contents = 1D   – – 29 decimal

i.e., 02 01 1D

BITSTRING – UNIVERSAL 3

e.g., *FunctionalUnits* ::= *BITSTRING* {*read* (0), *write* (1), *fileAccess* (2)}
– – assume read only is required

Identifier = 03
Length   = 01
Contents = 80   – – read only = 1000 0000

i.e., 03 01 80

UTCTime – UNIVERSAL 23

e.g., *UTCTime* ::= [*UNIVERSAL 23*] *IMPLICIT ISO646String*
– – assume 2.58 p.m. on 5th November 1999 = 99 11 05 14 58

Identifier = 17 (Hex)   – – Universal 23
Length   = 0A
Contents = 38 39 31 31 30 35 31 34 35 38

i.e., 17 0A 38 39 31 31 30 35 31 34 35 38

Figure 13.6 ASN.1 encoding examples: (a) primitive types; (b) constructed type; (c) use of implicit tag.

(b) SEQUENCE/SEQUENCEOF – UNIVERSAL 16

e.g., *File ::= SEQUENCE {userName IA5String, contents OCTETSTRING}*
– – assume userName = "FRED" and contents = 0F   27   E4   Hex

```
Identifier = 30 (Hex)                                – – Constructed, Universal 16
Length     = 0B                                      – – Decimal 11
Contents = Identifier = 16                           – – Universal 22
             Length   = 04
             Contents = 46  52  45  44
             Identifier = 04                         – – Universal 4
             Length   = 03
             Contents = 0F  27  E4
```

i.e., 30 0B 16 04 46 52 45 44 04 03 0F 27 E4

(c) Tagging/IMPLICIT

e.g., *UserName ::= SET {surname [0] IMPLICIT ISO646String, password [1] ISO646String }*
– – assume surname = "BULL" and password = "KING"

```
Identifier = 31                                      – – Constructed, Universal 17
Length     = 0E                                      – – Decimal 14
Contents = Identifier = 80                           – – Context-specific 0 = surname
             Length   = 04
             Contents = 42  55  4C  4C
             Identifier = A1                         – – Context-specific 1 = password
             Length   = 06
             Contents = Identifier = 16              – – Universal 22
                          Length   = 04
                          Contents = 4B 49 4E 47
```

i.e., 31 0E 80 04 42 55 4C 4C A1 06 16 04 4B 49 4E 47

Figure 13.6 Continued

Integer values are encoded in 2s-complement form with the most significant bit used as the sign bit. Thus, a single octet can be used to represent a value in the range −128 to +127. More octets must be used for larger values. Note, however, that only sufficient octets are used to represent the actual value, irrespective of the number of bits used in the original form, that is, even if the value 29 shown in Figure 13.6(a) is represented as a 16-bit or 32-bit integer locally, only a single octet is used to represent it in its encoded form. Similarly, if the type is BITSTRING, the individual bits are assigned starting at the most significant bit with any unused bits set to zero.

Two examples showing the encoding of constructed types are given in Figure 13.6(b) and (c). With a variable of type SEQUENCE (or SEQUENCEOF), the identifier is 30 (= 0011 0000 binary). This indicates that the class is UNIVERSAL (bits 8 and 7 = 00), it is a constructed type (bit 6 = 1), and the tag equals 16 (bit 5 = 1 and bits 4 through 1 = 0). Similarly, the identifier with a SET (or SETOF) type is 31, indicating it is UNIVERSAL, constructed with tag 17.

Note also that in Figure 13.6(c), the two fields in the type *UserName* have been tagged as context-specific – [0] and [1]. The two identifiers associated with these fields are 80 (= 1000 0000 binary) and A1 (= 1010 0001 binary), respectively. The first indicates that the class is context-specific (bits 8 and 7 = 10), it is a simple type (bit 6 = 0), and the tag is 0. However, the second is context-specific, constructed, and the tag is 1. This is because the first context-specific tag has been declared IMPLICIT, in which case the type field can be implied from the tag. However, with the second, the type field must also be defined so two additional octets are required. Note that in all cases the resulting octet string is transmitted in the order left to right.

In order to illustrate a more complete definition, an example PDU encoding is given in Figure 13.7. The PDU selected is *FINITIALIZErequest*, which we defined earlier in its ASN.1 form in Figure 13.4. The actual values associated with the PDU are defined in Figure 13.7(a) while Figure 13.7(b) shows how the selected values are encoded. Typically, the various fields in the PDU are abstract data types associated with a data structure in a program. However, after encoding, the PDU consists of a precisely defined string of octets which, for readability, are shown in hexadecimal form. The complete octet string is then transferred to the correspondent (peer) FTAM protocol entity where it is decoded back into its (local) abstract form.

Decoding

On receipt of the encoded string, the correspondent AP performs an associated decoding operation. For example, assuming that the received octet string relates to the PDU shown in Figure 13.7, the leading octet in the string is first used to determine the type of PDU received – Application-specific

(a) *FINITIALIZErequest* = {   protocolId = 0,
                                    versionNumber {major = 0, minor = 0}
                                    serviceType = 1,
                                    serviceClass = 1,
                                    functionalUnits {read = 0, write = 1, fileAccess = 2,
                                              limitedFileManagement = 3
                                              enhancedFileManagement = 4,
                                              grouping = 5, recovery = 6,
                                              restartDataTransfer = 7}
                                    attributeGroups {storage = 0, security = 1}
                                    rollbackAvailability = T,
                                    PresentationContextName = "ISO8822"}

Figure 13.7 Example PDU encoding: (a) PDU fields and their contents; (b) encoded form.

(b) Identifier = 61   – – Application-specific 1 = *FINITIALIZErequest*

    Length   = 31   – – decimal 49

    Contents = Identifier = A0   – – Context-specific 0 = *protocolId*

               Length   = 03

               Contents = Identifier = 02   – – Universal 2 – *INTEGER*

                         Length   = 01

                         Contents = 00   – – *isoFTAM*

               Identifier = A1   – – Context-specific 1 = *versionNumber*

               Length   = 06

               Contents = Identifier = 02   – – Universal 2

                         Length   = 01

                         Contents = 00   – – *major*

               Identifier = 02   – – Universal 2

                Length   = 01

                Contents = 00   – – *minor*

               Identifier = A2

               Length   = 03

               Contents = Identifier =02

                         Length   = 01

                         Contents = 01   – – *serviceType* = user correctable

               Identifier = A3

               Length   = 03

               Contents = Identifier = 02

                         Length   = 01

                         Contents = 01   – – *serviceClass* = access

               Identifier = A4   – – Context-specific 4 = *functionalUnits*

               Length   = 03

               Contents = Identifier = 03   – – Universal 3 = *BITSTRING*

                         Length   = 01

                         Contents = E0   – – *read, write, fileAccess* = 1110 000

               Identifier = A5   – – Context-specific 5 = *attributeGroups*

               Length   = 03

               Contents = Identifier = 03

                         Length   = 01

                         Contents = 40   – – *security* 0100 000

               Identifier = A6   – – Context-specific 6 = *rollbackAvailability*

               Length   = 03

               Contents = Identifier = 01   – – Universal 1 = *BOOLEAN*

                         Length   = 01

                         Contents = FF   – – *true*

               Identifier = A7   – – Context-specific 7 = *PresentationContextName*

               Length   = 07

               Contents = 49   53   4F   38   38   32   32   – – "ISO8822"

Concrete syntax of the above PDU is thus:

```
61   2F   A0   03   02   01   00   A1   06   02   01   00   02   01   00   A2
03   02   01   01   A3   03   02   01   01   A4   03   03   01   E0   A5   03
03   01   40   A6   03   01   01   FF   A7   07   49   53   32   38   38   32
32
```

Figure 13.7 Continued

1 = *FINITIALIZErequest*. Clearly, since each PDU has a unique structure, we must have a separate decoding procedure for each PDU type. Hence, on determining the type of PDU received, the corresponding decoding procedure is invoked. Once this has been done, the various fields (data elements) making up the PDU will be in their local (abstract) syntax form and processing of the PDU can start. Thus in the example, the various context-specific tags are used to determine the field within the PDU and the appropriate decoded value – now in its local syntax – is then assigned to this.

13.3 Security

As we indicated in the introduction, increasingly people are using networks such as the Internet for on-line banking, shopping, and many other applications. The generic term used is **electronic commerce** or **e-commerce** and this often involves the transfer of sensitive information such as credit card details over the network. Hence to support this type of networked transaction, a number of security techniques have been developed which, when combined together, provide a high level of confidence that any information relating to the transaction that is received from the network:

- has not been altered in any way – **integrity**;
- has not been intercepted and read by anyone – **privacy/secrecy**;
- has come from an authorized sender – **authentication**;
- has proof that the stated sender initiated the transaction – **nonrepudiation**.

Below we shall describe a number of the techniques that are used to carry out these four functions. As we shall see, secrecy and integrity are achieved by means of **data encryption** while authentication and nonrepudiation require the exchange of a set of (encrypted) messages between the two communicating parties. We shall give some examples of applications that use these techniques later in Chapters 14 and 15.

13.4 Data encryption

As the knowledge of computer networking and protocols has become more widespread, so the threat of intercepting and decoding message data during its transfer across a network has increased. For example, the end systems (stations/hosts) associated with most applications are now attached to a LAN. The application may involve a single LAN or, in an internetworking environment, the Internet. However, with most LANs, transmissions on the shared transmission medium can readily be intercepted by any system if an intruder sets the appropriate MAC chipset into the promiscuous mode and records all transmissions on the medium. Then, with a knowledge of the LAN protocols being used, the intruder can identify and remove the protocol control information at the head of each message, leaving the message contents. The message contents, including passwords and other sensitive information, can then be interpreted.

This is known as **listening** or **eavesdropping** and its effects are all too obvious. In addition and perhaps more sinister, an intruder can use a recorded message sequence to generate a new sequence. This is known as **masquerading** and again the effects are all too apparent. Therefore, encryption should be applied to all data transfers that involve a network. In the context of the TCP/IP reference model, the most appropriate layer to perform such operations is the application layer. This section provides an introduction to the subject of data encryption.

13.4.1 Terminology

Data encryption (or **data encipherment**) involves the sending party – for example, the application protocol entity – in processing all data prior to transmission so that if it is accidentally or deliberately intercepted while it is being transferred it will be incomprehensible to the intercepting party. Of course, the data must be readily interpreted – **deycrypted** or **deciphered** – by the intended recipient. Consequently, most encryption methods involve the use of an **encryption key** which is hopefully known only by the two correspondents. The key features in both the encryption and the decryption processing. Prior to encryption, message data is normally referred to as **plaintext** and after encryption as **ciphertext**. The general scheme is illustrated in Figure 13.8.

When deciding on a particular encryption algorithm we must always assume that a transmitted message can be intercepted and recorded, and that the intruder knows the context in which the messages are being used, that is,

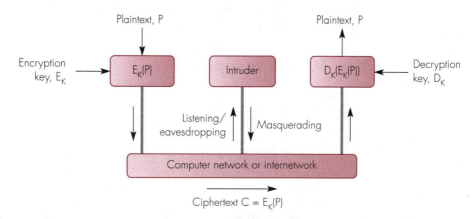

Figure 13.8 Data encryption terminology.

the type of information being exchanged. The aim is to choose an encryption method such that an intruder, even with access to a powerful computer, cannot decipher the recorded ciphertext in a realistic time period. There are two widely used algorithms but before we discuss them, let us consider some of the more fundamental techniques on which they are based.

13.4.2 Basic techniques

The simplest encryption technique involves **substituting** the plaintext alphabet (codeword) with a new alphabet known as the **ciphertext alphabet**. For example, a ciphertext alphabet can be defined which is the plaintext alphabet simply shifted by n places where n is the key. Hence, if the key is 3, the resulting alphabet is as follows:

        Plaintext alphabet: a b c d e f g . . .
        Ciphertext alphabet: d e f g h i j . . .

The ciphertext is obtained by substituting each character in the plaintext message by the equivalent letter in the ciphertext alphabet.

A more powerful variation is to define a ciphertext alphabet that is a random mix of the plaintext alphabet. For example:

        Plaintext alphabet   a b c d e f g . . .
        Ciphertext alphabet: n z q a i y m . . .

The key is determined by the number of letters in the alphabet, for example, 26 if just lower-case alphabetic characters are to be transmitted or 128 if, say, the ASCII alphabet is being used. There are therefore $26! = 4 \times 10^{26}$ possible keys with the first alphabet or many times this with the larger alphabet. Notice that in general, the larger the key the more time it takes to break the code.

Although this may seem to be a powerful technique, there are a number of shortcuts that can be used to break such codes. The intruder is likely to know the context in which the message data is being used and hence the type of data involved. For example, if the messages involve textual information, then the statistical properties of text can be exploited: the frequency of occurrence of individual letters (e, t, o, a, and so on), are all well documented. By performing statistical analyses on the letters in the ciphertext such codes can be broken relatively quickly.

Substitution involves replacing each character with a different character, so the order of the characters in the plaintext is preserved in the ciphertext. An alternative approach is to reorder (**transpose**) the characters in the plaintext. For example, if a key of 4 is used, the complete message can first be divided into a set of 4-character groups. The message is then transmitted starting with all the first characters in each group, then the second, and so on. As an example, assuming a plaintext message of "this is a lovely day", the ciphertext is derived as follows:

1	2	3	4	←	key
t	h	i	s		
–	i	s	–		
a	–	l	o		
v	e	l	y		
–	d	a	y		

Ciphertext = t–av–hi–edisllas–oyy

Clearly, more sophisticated transpositions can be performed but, in general, when used alone transposition ciphers suffer from the same shortcomings as substitution ciphers. Most practical encryption algorithms tend to use a combination of the two techniques and are known as **product ciphers**.

Product ciphers

These use a combination of substitutions and transpositions. Also, instead of substituting/transposing the characters in a message, the order of individual bits in each character (codeword) is substituted/transposed. The three alternative transposition (also known as **permutation**) operations are shown in Figure 13.9(a). Each is normally referred to as a **P-box**.

The first involves transposing each 8-bit input into an 8-bit output by cross-coupling each input line to a different output line as defined by the key. This is known as a **straight permutation**. The second has a larger number of output bits than input bits; they are derived by reordering the input bits and passing selected input bits to more than one output. This is known as an **expanded permutation**.

The third has fewer output bits than inputs; it is formed by transposing only selected input bits. This is known as a **compressed** or **choice permutation**.

To perform a straight substitution of 8 bits requires a new set (and hence key) of 2^8 (=256) 8-bit bytes to be defined. This means the key for a single substitution is 2048 bits. To reduce this, a substitution is formed by encapsulating a P-box between a decoder and a corresponding encoder, as shown in Figure 13.9(b). The resulting unit is known as an **S-box**. The example performs a 2-bit substitution operation using the key associated with the P-box. An 8-bit substitution will require four such units.

Product ciphers are formed from multiple combinations of these two basic units, as shown in Figure 13.10. In general, the larger the number of stages the more powerful the cipher. A practical example of product ciphers is the **data encryption standard (DES)** defined by the US National Bureau of Standards. This is now widely used. Consequently, various integrated circuits are available to perform the encryption operation in hardware thereby speeding up the encryption and decryption operations.

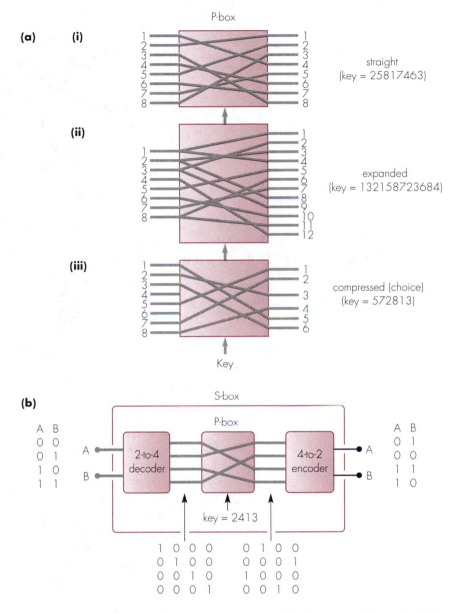

Figure 13.9 Product cipher components: (a) P-box examples; (b) S-box example.

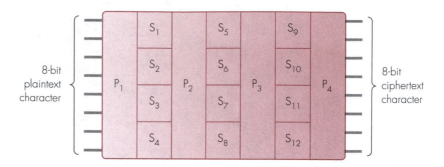

Figure 13.10 Example of a product cipher.

13.4.3 The data encryption standard

The DES algorithm is a **block cipher**, which means that it works on fixed-sized blocks of data. Thus, a complete message is first split (segmented) into blocks of plaintext, each comprising 64 bits. A (hopefully) unique 56-bit key is used to encrypt each block of plaintext into a 64-bit block of ciphertext, which is subsequently transmitted through the network. The receiver uses the same key to perform the inverse (decrpytion) operation on each 64-bit data block it receives, thereby reassembling the blocks into complete messages.

The larger the number of bits used for the key, the more likely it is that the key will be unique. Also, the larger the key, the more difficult it is for someone to decipher it. The use of a 56-bit key in the DES means that there are in the order of 1017 possible keys from which to choose. Consequently, DES is regarded as providing sufficient security for most commercial applications.

A diagram of the DES algorithm is shown in Figure 13.11(a). The 56-bit key selected by the two correspondents is first used to derive 16 different sub-keys, each of 48 bits, which are used in the subsequent substitution operations. The algorithm comprises 19 distinct steps. The first step is a simple transposition of the 64-bit block of plaintext using a fixed transposition rule. The resulting 64 bits of transposed text then go through 16 identical iterations of substitution processing, except that at each iteration a different subkey is used in the substitution operation. The most significant 32 bits of the 64-bit output of the last iteration are then exchanged with the least significant 32 bits. Finally, the inverse of the transposition that was performed in step 1 is carried out to produce the 64-bit block of ciphertext to be transmitted. The DES algorithm is designed so that the received block is deciphered by the receiver using the same steps as for encryption, but in the reverse order.

The 16 subkeys used at each substitution step are produced as follows. Firstly, a fixed transposition is performed on the 56-bit key. The resulting transposed key is then split into two separate 28-bit halves. Next, these two

(a)

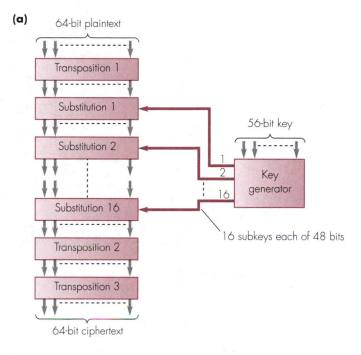

(b)

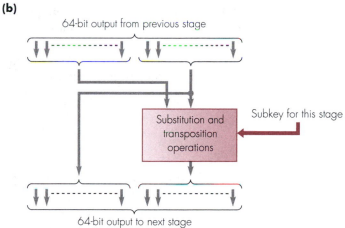

Figure 13.11 DES algorithm principles: (a) overall schematic; (b) substitution schematic; (c) substitution operation.

halves are rotated left independently and the combined 56 bits are then transposed once again using a compression operation to produce a subkey of 48 bits. The other subkeys are produced in a similar way except that the number of rotations performed is determined by the number of the subkey.

(c)

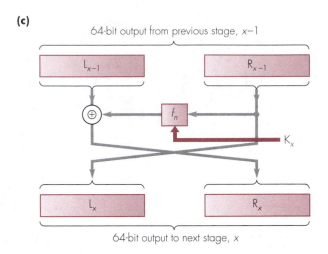

Figure 13.11 Continued.

The processing performed at each of the 16 intermediate substitution steps in the encryption process is relatively complex as it is this that ensures the effectiveness of the DES algorithm. This processing is outlined in Figure 13.11(b). The 64-bit output from the previous iteration is first split into two 32-bit halves. The left 32-bit output is simply the right 32-bit input. However, the right 32-bit output is a function of both the left and right inputs and the subkey for this stage. The principle is shown in Figure 13.11(c).

As we can deduce from the figure, in the forward (encryption) direction:

$$L_x = R_{x-1}$$

and

$$R_x = L_{x-1} \oplus f_n (R_{x-1}, K_x)$$

where f_n is a bitwise function called the **Feistel cipher**. First, since the subkey for the stage, K_x, is 48 bits, R_{x-1} is expanded into a 48-bit value using a P-box – similar to that shown in part (ii) of Figure 13.9(a) – with a fixed key. This is then exclusive-ORed with K_x and the 48-bit output is then converted back again into a 32-bit value. This is done by first dividing the 48-bit value into eight 6-bit groups and then passing each group through an S-box – similar to that shown in Figure 13.9(b) – each with a different key. In this case, however, the internal P-box performs a compression operation by transposing the 64-bit output from the 6-to-64 decoder into 16 bits. The resulting 16 bits are then passed to a 16-to-4 bit encoder to produce a 4-bit value. The 4-bit output from each of the eight S-boxes is then combined to form a 32-bit value which is passed through a second (straight) P-box to produce the output of the function block (f_n).

As we indicated earlier, the DES algorithm is designed so that the received block is deciphered by the receiver using the same steps as for encryption, but in the reverse order. As we can deduce from Figure 13.11(a), since transposition 1 is the inverse of transposition 3 and transposition 2 is a simple swap operation, by passing the received input through the stack in the reverse direction the output at the top will be the original plaintext. This is only true of course, if passing the 64-bit block through each substitution operation in the reverse direction also produces the inverse of that produced in the forward direction.

To illustrate that the Feisel cipher has this property, as we can deduce from Figure 13.11(c), in the reverse (decryption) direction:

$$R_{x-1} = L_x$$

and

$$L_{x-1} = R_x \oplus f_n(L_x, K_x)$$

Hence, since $L_x = R_{x-1}$, the output of the Feisel cipher – and hence each substitution operation – is invertible.

For example, if we work with two 4-bit groups and assume f_n is a simple exclusive OR operation with a key, K_x, of 1011, then if:

$$L_{x-1} = 1001 \quad \text{and} \quad R_{x-1} = 0110$$

in the forward (encryption) direction:

$$L_x = 0110 \quad \text{and} \quad R_x = 0100$$

And in the reverse (decryption) direction:

$$R_{x-1} = 0110 \quad \text{and} \quad L_{x-1} = 1001$$

which, as we can see, are the same as the two original inputs.

Triple DES

Although DES is still widely used, the use of a 56-bit key means that, with increasingly powerful computers, the time taken to exhaustively try each of the possible keys is reducing steadily. To counter this, a variant called **triple DES** has been developed. The principle of the scheme is shown in Figure 13.12.

As we can see, the scheme involves the use of two keys and three executions of the DES algorithm. Key K_1 is used with the first (DES) block, K_2 with the second block, and K_1 again with the third block. The use of two keys gives an effective key length of 112 bits and, because of this, the scheme is now widely used in many financial applications.

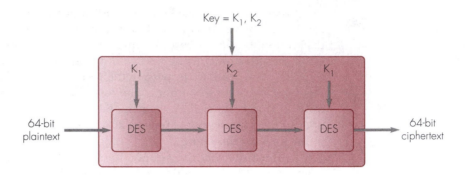

Figure 13.12 Triple DES schematic.

Chaining

The basic mode of working of DES is known as **electronic code book** (**ECB**) since each block of ciphertext is independent of any other block. Thus each 64-bit block of ciphertext has a unique matching block of plaintext, which is analogous to entries in a code book. The ECB mode of working is shown in Figure 13.13(a).

As we can deduce from Figure 13.11, the ECB mode of operation of DES has good secrecy properties and gives good protection against errors or changes that may occur in a single block of enciphered text. It does not, however, protect against errors arising in a stream of blocks. Since each block is treated separately in the ECB mode, the insertion of a correctly enciphered block into a transmitted stream of blocks is not detected by the receiver; it simply deciphers the inserted block and treats it as a valid block. Consequently, the stream of enciphered blocks may be intercepted and altered by someone who knows the key without the recipient being aware that any modifications have occurred. Also, if the order of the blocks is changed in some way then this will not be detected. The ECB mode, therefore, has poor integrity properties. Hence to obtain integrity as well as secrecy, an alternative mode of operation of DES based on a technique called **chaining** is often used. It is called the **chain block cipher** (**CBC**) mode and is shown in Figure 13.13(b).

As we can see, although the chaining mode uses the same block encryption method as previously described, each 64-bit block of plaintext is first exclusive-ORed with the enciphered output of the previous block before it is enciphered. The first 64-bit block of plaintext is exclusive-ORed with a 64-bit random number called the **initial vector**, which is sent prior to the cipher text. Then, after the first block has been encoded/decoded using this, subsequent blocks are encoded/decoded in the chained sequence shown in the figure. Thus, since the output of each block is a function both of the block contents and the output of the previous block, any alternations to the trans-

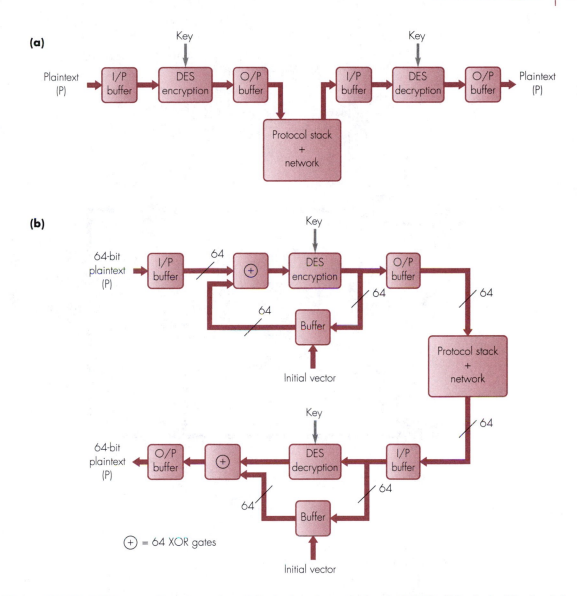

Figure 13.13 DES operational modes: (a) electronic code book (ECB); (b) chain block cipher (CBC); (c) cipher feedback mode (CFM).

(c)

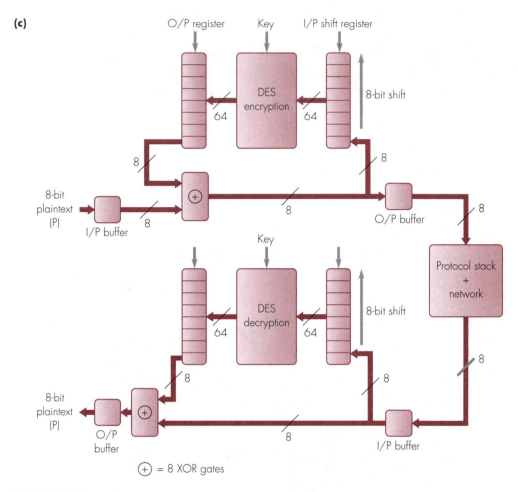

Figure 13.13 Continued.

mitted sequence can be detected by the receiver so giving a high level of integrity. Also, identical blocks of plaintext yield different blocks of ciphertext which makes the breaking of the code much more difficult. For these reasons, this is the mode of operation normally used for digital communication applications.

Since the basic CBC mode operates with 64-bit blocks, all messages must be multiples of 64 bits. Otherwise padding bits must be added. However, as we have seen in earlier chapters, the contents of all messages consist of strings of octets, so the basic unit of all messages is 8 bits rather than 64. An alternative mode of DES known as the **cipher feedback mode** (**CFM**) has also been defined which operates on 8-bit boundaries. A schematic of the scheme is shown in Figure 13.13(c).

With this mode, a new DES encryption operation is performed after every 8 bits of input rather than 64 with the CBC mode. A new 8-bit output is also produced which is the least significant 8 bits of the DES output, exclusive-ORed with the 8 input bits. Then, after each 8-bit output has been loaded into the output buffer, the 64-bit contents of the input shift register are shifted by 8 places. The 8 most significant bits are thus lost and the new 8-bit input is loaded into the least significant 8 bits of the input shift register. The DES operation is performed on these new 64 bits and the resulting 64-bit output is loaded into the output register. The least significant 8 bits of the latter are then exclusive-ORed with the 8 input bits and the process repeats.

CFM is particularly useful when the encryption operation is being performed at the interface with the serial transmission line. This mode of operation is used with the DES integrated circuits; each new 8-bit output is loaded directly into the serial interface circuit.

13.4.4 IDEA

The **international data encryption algorithm** (**IDEA**) is another block cipher method that is similar in principle to DES since it also operates on 64-bit blocks of plaintext. It can also be used, therefore, in the various chaining modes we described in the last section. To obtain added resilience, however, it uses a 128-bit key and more sophisticated processing during each phase of the encryption operation. Also, it has been designed so that it can be implemented equally well in both hardware and software and, in particular, with 16-bit microcomputers. A schematic diagram of the encryption operation is shown in Figure 13.14(a).

As we can see, each 64-bit block of plaintext passes through a series of eight bit-manipulation iterations followed by a final transposition. At each of the eight iterations, each of the 64 output bits is a function of all 64 input bits. The various processing operations that are carried out to achieve this are shown in Figure 13.14(b).

The 128-bit key is first used to generate 52 subkeys each of 16 bits. As we can see in the figure, six subkeys are used at each iteration and the remaining four subkeys are used in the final transposition stage. Decryption uses the same algorithm but with a modified set of keys.

Each 64-bit input is first divided into four 16-bit words each of which goes through a series of multiplication, addition, and exclusive-OR operations. All the lines shown in the figure are 16 bits and all the multiplication operations involve first the 32-bit product of the two 16-bit inputs being computed and then dividing this by $2^{16} + 1$. The output is then the 16-bit remainder. In the case of the addition operations, the two 16-bit inputs are added together and any carry that is generated is ignored.

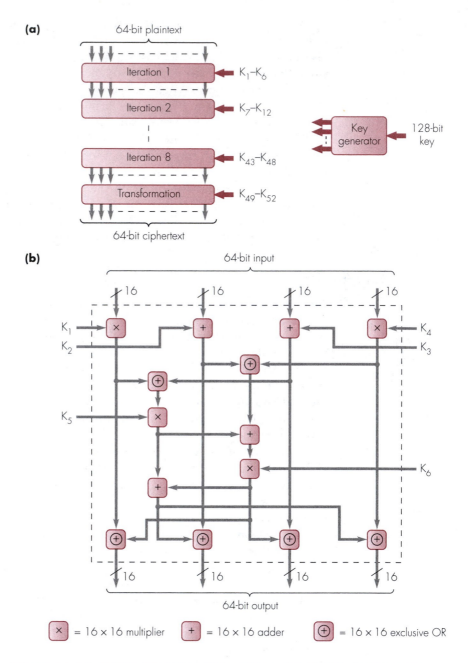

Figure 13.14 IDEA: (a) encryption schematic; (b) single iteration detail.

13.4.5 The RSA algorithm

Both DES and IDEA rely, of course, on the same key being used for both encryption and decryption. An obvious disadvantage is that some form of key notification must be used before any encrypted data is transferred between two correspondents. This is perfectly acceptable as long as the key does not change very often, but in fact it is common practice to change the key on a daily, if not more frequent, basis. Clearly, the new key cannot reliably be sent via the network, so an alternative means, such as a courier, must be used. The distribution of keys is a major problem with private key encryption systems. An alternative method, based on a public rather than a private key, is sometimes used to overcome this problem. The best known public key method is the **RSA algorithm**, named after its three inventors: Rivest, Shamir, and Adelman.

The fundamental difference between a private key system and a public key system is that the latter uses a different key to decrypt the ciphertext from the key that was used to encrypt it. A public key system uses a pair of keys: one for the sender and the other for the recipient.

Although this may not seem to help, the inventors of the RSA algorithm used number theory to develop a method of generating a pair of numbers – the keys – in such a way that a message encrypted using the first number of the pair can be decrypted only by the second number. Furthermore, the second number cannot be derived from the first. This second property means that the first number of the pair can be made available to anyone who wishes to send an encrypted message to the holder of the second number since only that person can decrypt the resulting ciphertext message. The first number of the pair is known as the **public key** and the second the private or **secret key**. The principle of the method is shown in Figure 13.15.

As indicated, the derivation of the two keys is based on number theory and is therefore outside the scope of this book. However, the basic algorithm used to compute the two keys is simple and is summarized here together with a much simplified example.

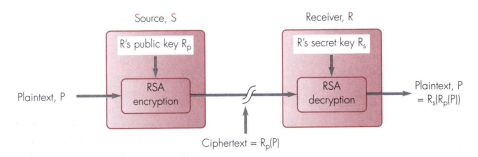

Figure 13.15 RSA schematic.

To create the public key K_p: *Example:*

- select two large positive prime numbers P and Q $P = 7$, $Q = 17$
- compute $X = (P - 1) \times (Q - 1)$ $X = 96$
- choose an integer E which is prime relative to X, i.e., not a prime factor of X or a multiple of it, and which satisfies the condition indicated below for the computation of K_s $E = 5$
- compute $N = P \times Q$ $N = 119$
- K_p is then N concatenated with E $K_p = 119, 5$

To create the secret key K_s:

- compute D such that MOD $(D \times E, X) = 1$ $D \times 5/96 = 1$, $D = 77$
- K_s is then N concatenated with D $K_s = 119, 77$

To compute the ciphertext C of plaintext P:

- treat P as a numerical value $P = 19$
- $C = $ MOD (P^E, N) $C = $ MOD $(19^5, 119)$ $C = 66$

To compute the plaintext P of ciphertext C:

- $P = $ MOD (C^D, N) $P = $ MOD $(66^{77}, 119)$
     $P = 19$

The choice of E and D in this example is best seen by considering the factors of 96. These are 1, 2, 3, 4, 6, 8, 12, 16, 24, 32, 48. The list of numbers which are prime relative to 96 are thus 5, 7, 9, 10, 11, and so on. If we try the first of these, $E = 5$, then there is also a number $D = 77$ which satisfies the condition MOD $(D \times E, X) = 1$ and hence these are chosen.

We can deduce from this example that the crucial numbers associated with the algorithm are the two prime numbers P and Q, which must always be kept secret. The aim is to choose a sufficiently large N so that it is impossible to factorize it in a realistic time. Some example (computer) factorizing times are:

$N = 100$ digits ≈ 1 week

$N = 150$ digits ≈ 1000 years

$N > 200$ digits ≈ 1 million years

The RSA algorithm requires considerable computation time to compute the exponentiation for both the encryption and decryption operations. However, there is a simple way of avoiding the exponentiation operation by performing instead the following algorithm which uses only repeated multiplication and division operations:

C : = 1

begin for i = 1 to E *do*

C : = MOD (C × P, N)

end

Decryption is performed in the same way by replacing E with D and P with C in the above expression; this yields the plaintext P. For example, to compute $C = MOD(19^5, 119)$:

Step 1: C = MOD (1 × 19, 119) = 19

    2: C = MOD (19 × 19, 119) = 4

    3: C = MOD (4 × 19, 119) = 76

    4: C = MOD (76 × 19, 119) = 16

    5: C = MOD (16 × 19, 119) = 66

Note also that the value of *N* determines the maximum message that can be encoded. In the example this is 119 and is numerically equivalent to a single ASCII-encoded character. Therefore, a message comprising a string of ASCII characters would have to be encoded one character at a time.

Although a public key system offers an alternative to a private key system to overcome the threat of eavesdropping, if the public key is readily available it can be used by a masquerader to send a forged message. The question then arises as to how the recipient of a correctly ciphered message can be sure that it was sent by a legitimate source. As we indicated earlier, this relates to authentication and nonrepudiation and there are a number of solutions to this problem.

13.5 Nonrepudiation

Public key systems like RSA are particularly useful for nonrepudiation; that is, proving that a person sent an electronic document. With a paper document, normally a person adds his or her signature at the end of the document – sometimes with the name and signature of a witness – and, should it be necessary, this is then used to verify that the person whose signature is on the document sent it.

One solution is to exploit the dual property of public key systems, namely that not only is a receiver able to decipher all messages it receives (which have been encrypted with its own public key) using its own private key, but any receiver can also decipher a message encrypted with the sender's private key, using the sender's public key.

Figure 13.16(a) shows how this property may be exploited to achieve nonrepudiation. Encryption and decryption operations are performed at two levels. The inner level of encryption and decryption is as already described. However, at

(a)

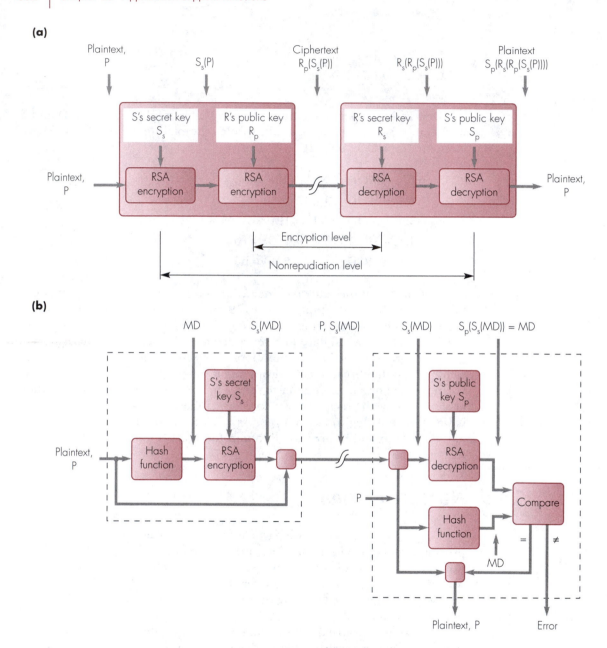

Figure 13.16 Nonrepudiation using RSA: (a) on complete message; (b) on message digest.

the outer level, the sender uses its own private key to encrypt the original (plaintext) message. If the receiver can decrypt this message using that sender's public key, this is proof that the sender did in fact initiate the sending of the message. The scheme is said therefore to produce a **digital signature**.

Although this is an elegant solution, it has a number of limitations. Firstly, the processing overheads associated with the RSA algorithm are high. As we saw with the earlier (much simplified) example, even with a small message (value), the numbers involved can be very large. Therefore a complete message must be divided into a number of smaller units, the size of which is a function of the computer being used. Hence, even though integrated circuits are available to help with these computations, the total message throughput with RSA is still relatively low. Secondly, the method requires two levels of encryption even though it may not be necessary to encrypt the actual message, that is, although only nonrepudiation is required, the actual message contents must still be encrypted.

One solution is to compute a much shorter version of the message based on the message contents, similar in principle to the computation of a CRC. The shorter version is called the **message digest** (**MD**) and the computation function that is used to compute it the hash function. The principle of the scheme is shown in Figure 13.16(b).

The MD is first computed using the chosen hash function. This is then encrypted using the sender's private key. The encrypted MD is then sent together with the plaintext message. At the receiver, the encrypted MD is decrypted using the sender's public key. The MD of the received plaintext message is also computed and, if this is the same as the decrypted MD, this is taken as proof that no one has tampered with the message and the sender whose public key was used to decrypt the MD did in fact send the message.

There are two widely used schemes that use this approach. One is called **MD5**, which was designed by Rivest, and the other the **secure hash algorithm** (**SHA**) which is a US government scheme. Both schemes operate on 512-bit blocks of plaintext. In the case of MD5 the computed MD is 128 bits long and for SHA, 160 bits long. As we shall see in the following chapters, MD5 is widely used with Internet applications and, because of its origin, SHA is used in government applications.

13.6 Authentication

In general, authentication is required when a client wishes to access some information or service from a networked server. Before the client is allowed access to the server, he or she must first prove to the server that they are a registered user. Once authenticated the user is then allowed access. The authentication process can be carried out using either a public key or a private key scheme. We shall give an example of each approach.

13.6.1 Using a public key system

The general principle of a scheme that is based on a public key system is shown in Figure 13.17. The scheme assumes that all potential users know the public key of the server, Sp. The client first creates a message containing the

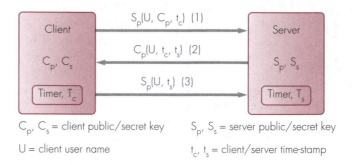

Figure 13.17 User authentication using a public key scheme.

client's user name, U, the client's public key, C_p, and a time-stamp, t_c. The latter indicates when the message was created and a record of this is kept by the client. The message is then encrypted using S_p and sent to the server (1).

The server first decrypts the message using its own secret key, S_s, and then proceeds to validate that there is such a registered user from the user name, U. Assuming this is the case, it then proceeds to create a response message comprising the client's user name, U, and time-stamp, t_c, plus a second time-stamp indicating when the response was created by the server, t_s. The server keeps a record of this and encrypts the message using the client's public key, C_p. It then sends the encrypted message to the client (2).

On receipt of the response, the client first decrypts the message using its own secret key, C_s, and, on determining that the t_c within it is the same as it sent, assumes that it has been authenticated by the server. It then proceeds to acknowledge this by creating a second message containing the client's user name, U, and the server's time-stamp, t_s. This again is encrypted using the server's public key, S_p, and sent to the server (3). The server decrypts this using its own secret key, S_s, and, on determining the t_s within it is the same as it sent, prepares to accept service requests from the client.

Note that in both cases, if the time the message was received exceeds the time-stamp value in the related response message by more than a defined time interval, then the message is discarded and access remains blocked. Also, should the transaction require the subsequent messages to be encrypted, then the key to be used would be returned by the server in message (2).

13.6.2 Using a private key system

An example of a method that is based on a private key system is **Kerberos**. This is widely used in many practical systems and, as we shall see, the method requires a trusted third party to act as a **key distribution server**.

The basic security control mechanism employed in Kerberos is a set of encrypted **tickets** – also known as control or permission tokens – which are used to control access to the various servers that make up the system. These include a range of application servers – file servers, electronic mail servers, and so on – and the system server that issues the tickets is known as the **ticket granting server**. All messages that are exchanged between a user and the ticket granting server and between a user and an application server, are encrypted using private keys which form part of the corresponding ticket. In addition, each message/ticket has a **nonce** associated with it. This comprises two date-and-time values the first of which specifies when the nonce was first generated. A nonce is used both to verify the origin of a message and to limit the validity of a ticket to a defined lifetime. This is determined by the second date-and-time value in the nonce. This feature means an eavesdropper has only a limited time to decrypt an intercepted ticket.

The key distribution server is a networked system with which all users and application servers must be registered. It comprises two servers: an **authentication server** and a ticket granting server. The authentication server provides, firstly, management services to allow all users, together with their related passwords, to be registered. It also provides the names and secret keys of all Kerberos servers, including the ticket granting server and all application servers. This information is retained in an **authentication database**. It then provides additional runtime services to enable a user to be authenticated as a registered user of the system before being allowed to access any of the Kerberos servers. A schematic diagram summarizing the various interactions between a user and the two types of server is given in Figure 13.18(a).

Running within each client workstation is a process called the **user agent** and it is through this that all interactions between a user and the various Kerberos servers take place. Before a user (agent) can access an application server, it must first obtain from the ticket granting server an **authentication ticket** and a **session key**; the first verifies that the user has been authenticated as a registered user and the second is used to encrypt all the subsequent dialog units that are exchanged in this session between the user agent and the application server. Note that in practice more than one application server can be involved in a single session. Also, both keys have a limited lifetime associated with them to guard against a user, whose registration has expired for example, from reusing a ticket.

At the start of a session, the user is prompted by the user agent (UA) for his/her user name (1). Before the UA can communicate with the ticket granting server (TGS), the user must first be authenticated as a registered user and a (permission) ticket obtained to access the TGS. Both these functions are performed by the authentication server (AS). On receipt of the user name, the UA creates a message containing the names of the user and the TGS and a nonce. The UA keeps a record of the nonce used and sends the message to the AS (2).

All subsequent messages associated with the session are encrypted using various keys. These are defined in Figure 13.18(b) together with the components that make up the two tickets; the first granting permission for the UA to communicate with the TGS and the second for the UA to communicate with the application server. The contents of the messages exchanged during a successful session are listed in Figure 13.18(c).

On receipt of the initial UA request message, the AS first validates the user is registered and, if positive, proceeds to create a response message. The

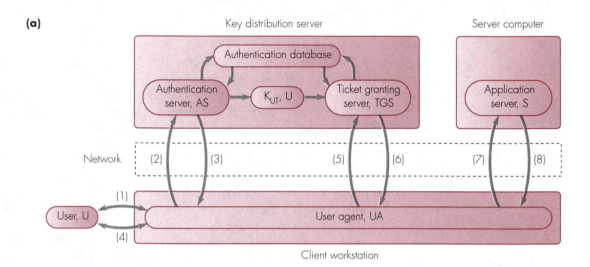

(b) K_U = The private key of the user – the user password
K_T = The private key of the TGS
K_S = The private key of the application server
K_{UT} = A session key to encrypt UA $\leftrightarrow$ TGS dialog units
K_{US} = A session key to encrypt UA $\rightarrow$ S dialog units

TGS ticket, $T_{UT} = K_T (U, T, t_1, t_2, K_{UT})$
Application server ticket, $T_{US} = K_S (U, S, t_1, t_2, K_{US})$
t_1, t_2 = start, end of ticket lifetime

(c)

	Direction	Message
(1)	U $\leftrightarrow$ UA	User name, U
(2)	UA $\rightarrow$ AS	(U, T, n_1)
(3)	AS $\rightarrow$ UA	$K_U (K_{UT}, n_1)$; T_{UT}
(4)	U $\leftrightarrow$ UA	User password, K_U
(5)	UA $\rightarrow$ TGS	$K_{UT} (U, t)$; T_{UT}, S, n_2
(6)	TGS $\rightarrow$ UA	$K_{UT} (K_{US}, n_2)$; T_{US}
(7)	UA $\rightarrow$ S	$K_{US} (U, t)$; T_{US}, n_3
(8)	S $\rightarrow$ UA	$K_{US} (n_3)$

$K_{UT}/K_{US} (U, t)$ are both authenticators and t is a time-stamp

Figure 13.18 User authentication using Kerberos: (a) terminology and message exchange; (b) key and ticket definitions; (c) message contents.

latter comprises two parts. The first part consists of a newly generated session key, K_{UT} – to be used to encrypt the subsequent UA/TGS dialog units – together with the nonce, n_1, contained in the initial UA request message. A record is kept of K_{UT} and this part of the response message is then encrypted using the user's password, K_U – obtained from the authentication database – as a key. The second part comprises the permission ticket for the UA to access the TGS, T_{UT} – encrypted using the private key of the TGS, K_T. The two-part message is then returned to the UA (3).

At this point the UA prompts the user to enter his/her password, K_U (4). The latter is then used to obtain, firstly, the nonce, n_1 – which verifies the message relates to its earlier request – and secondly, the key K_{UT}. Clearly, a user impersonating as the registered user would not be able to decrypt this message and hence would be foiled at this stage. The UA then proceeds to use the retrieved key, K_{UT}, to create what is referred to as an **authenticator**. This is a token which verifies the user has been authenticated and comprises the user name, U, and a time-stamp, t, both encrypted using K_{UT}. To this is added the encrypted permission ticket, T_{UT}, the name of the required application server, S, and a second nonce, n_2. The complete message is then sent to the TGS (5).

The authenticator is decrypted by the TGS using the retained key K_{UT} and, since this was granted for the same user, U, it is accepted by the TGS as proof that the user has permission to be granted a session key to communicate with an application server. In response, the TGS generates a new session key, K_{US}, to be used by UA to encrypt the dialog units exchanged with the named server, S. Note that if multiple servers were to be accessed during the session, then multiple keys are issued at this stage, one for use with each server. The TGS then creates a message, the first part comprising K_{US} and the nonce n_2 – encrypted using K_{UT} – and the second comprising an encrypted permission ticket for the UA to access B, T_{US}. The complete message is then sent to the UA (6).

On receipt of this, the UA uses K_{UT} to decrypt the first part of the message to obtain K_{US} and the nonce n_2. The latter is used to confirm the message relates to its own earlier request message to the TGS, and K_{US} is used to create an authenticator, which verifies the user has been granted permission to access the named server. The authenticator is then combined with the permission ticket granted by the TGS, T_{US}, and a third nonce n_3. The resulting message is then sent by the UA to server S (7).

As Figure 13.18(b) shows, the permission ticket, T_{US}, is encrypted using the private key of S, K_S. Hence, on receipt of the message, S proceeds to use its own private key to decrypt T_{US} and obtain the name of the user, U, and the allocated session key, K_{US}. It uses the latter to decrypt the authenticator and confirm that U has been authenticated as a registered user and granted permission to access S. The server responds by returning the nonce, n_3, encrypted using K_{US} (8). This concludes the authentication procedure and the exchange of data messages between UA and S can now commence. If required, the data messages are encrypted using K_{US}.

13.7 Public key certification authorities

In the examples in previous sections that used the RSA public key scheme it was assumed that the public key was obtained in some way; for example by sending it in an email message prior to the transfer or making it available in a Web page. However, sending a public key in this way without any supporting proof of identify has potential drawbacks. The example shown in Figure 13.19 illustrates one of these.

In this example it is assumed that the person sending the message wants to discredit the person whose name is on the message. To do this, he or she sends a message that will achieve this in such a way that the recipient thinks the message has been sent by the person whose name is on it. To avoid this type of misuse of public key systems, in most applications the public key is obtained from a recognized **certification authority** (**CA**).

When a person registers with a recognized CA, after careful checks, an electronic **certificate** is created by the CA. This contains, in addition to the public key of the owner of the certificate, other information about the owner. The IETF have defined the complete list of contents of a certificate in **RFC 1422** and this is now used widely by a number of CAs. The fields present include:

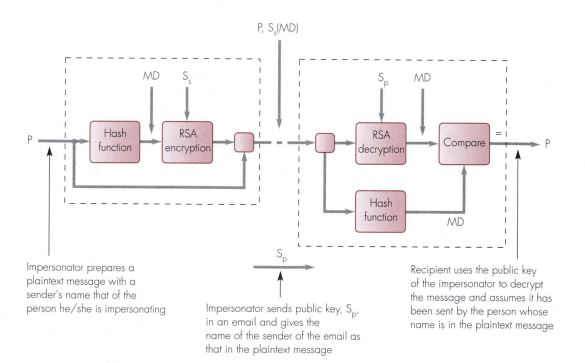

Figure 13.19 A possible threat when using a public key system.

- issuer name: the identify (called the **distinguished name**) of the CA in a syntax defined in RFC 1779;
- serial number: the unique identifier of the certificate;
- subject name: the identity of the owner of the certificate, for example, an email address, a URL of a Web server, or an IP address of, say, a router;
- public key: the owner's public key and the key algorithm, for example RSA;
- validity period: start and end date of the validity of the certificate;
- signature: the algorithm used by the CA to encrypt the certificate contents, for example RSA.

Once a certificate has been created, the public key it contains can only be accessed through the CA. Typically, the CA is on a list of recognized CAs. The list is located at a well-known Web site and, for each CA on the list, its location and its public key are given. Then, when a public key is required from the CA, the subject's name is submitted and, in response, the CA returns the related certificate. The recipient proceeds to decrypt the contents of the certificate using the public key of the CA. It then reads the public key from the certificate and, before using it, validates that the name of the person on the certificate is that whose key is required.

Summary

In this chapter we have discussed two topics that are used widely in a range of distributed/networked applications. The first is concerned with ensuring that the shared information relating to a distributed application has the same meaning in all the computers/items of equipment that process the information. To achieve this, an international standard called ASN.1 has been defined. As we show in Figure 13.20, this comprises a standard abstract syntax that is used to define the data types associated with the shared information and also a set of encoding and decoding procedures that are used to convert the value associated with each data type into and from a standard transfer syntax.

The second topic relates to network security. This is concerned with four interrelated issues: secrecy, integrity, authentication, and nonrepudiation. We described the principle of operation of both the data encryption standard (DES) and the RSA algorithm. The first is useful for providing both secrecy and integrity and the second authentication and nonrepudiation. We also described the Kerberos system which is a widely used system for authentication.

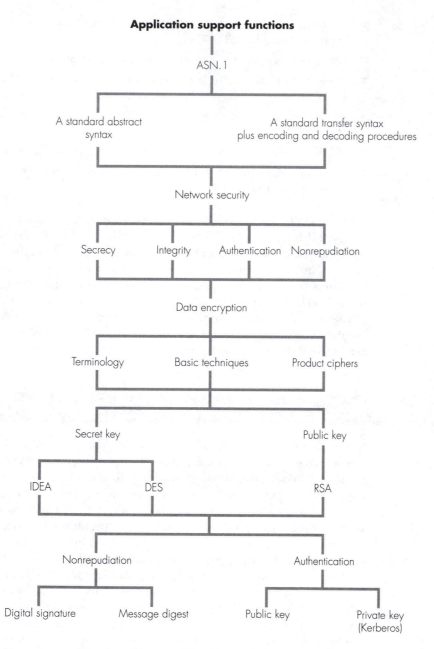

Figure 13.20 Summary of topics discussed in Chapter 13.

Exercises

Section 13.1

13.1 Explain the meaning of the following terms relating to a distributed application involving multiple different computers:
(i) data dictionary,
(ii) abstract syntax,
(iii) transfer/concrete syntax,
(iv) shared semantics.

Section 13.2

13.2 Explain the role of ASN.1 in relation to a distributed application and, with the aid of a diagram, describe the functions performed by an ASN.1 compiler.

13.3 Give an example variable name and ASN.1 type definition for each of the following primitive data types:
(i) boolean,
(ii) integer,
(iii) bitstring,
(iv) character string.

13.4 Give an example variable name and ASN.1 type definition for a sequence constructed type which includes the set of variables you listed in Exercise 13.3.

13.5 Explain the meaning of the terms "tag", "context-specific", and "application-specific". Hence modify the sequence type definition you used in Exercise 13.4 to include three context-specific tags and an application-specific tag.

13.6 Explain the meaning and use of the terms "implicit" and "explicit" in relation to a tag. Hence modify the sequence type definition you used in Exercise 13.5 to include a number of implicit type definitions.

13.7 Outline the role that ASN.1 can play in relation to the definition of the messages/PDUs relating to a protocol.
State an advantage and a disadvantage of using ASN.1 as an alternative to defining a message/PDU in the form of a number of fixed-length fields.

13.8 With the basic encoding rules associated with ASN.1, the transfer syntax used to transfer the value of a variable consists of an identifier, length, and contents field. Explain the use of each of these fields and, in the case of the identifier, the use of the class, type, and tag subfields.

13.9 Use example value assignments for each of the variables you defined in Exercise 13.3 to illustrate how each data type is encoded.

13.10 Assuming the same value assignments you used in Exercise 13.9, encode the two sequence-type variables you defined in Exercises 13.5 and 13.6.
Hence identify the benefits of using an implicit tag.

13.11 As an example, use the second of the encoded octet/byte strings you derived in Exercise 13.10 to explain how the decoding procedure in a correspondent application process determines the value to be assigned to each variable.

Section 13.3

13.12 Explain the meaning of the following terms relating to a secure transaction:
(i) integrity,
(ii) privacy/secrecy,
(iii) authentication,
(iv) nonrepudiation.

Section 13.4

13.13 With the aid of a diagram, explain the meaning of the following terms relating to data encryption:
(i) plaintext and ciphertext,
(ii) encryption key and decryption key,
(iii) eavesdropping and masquerading.

13.14 The following encrypted phrase has been produced using a simple substitution for the ciphertext alphabet. Assuming the phrase relates to communications, derive the ciphertext alphabet and hence the plaintext of the phrase:

ciphertext = frpsxwhu qhwzrunlgj

13.15 The following encrypted phrase has been produced using a simple transposition for the ciphertext alphabet. Derive the key that has been used and hence the plaintext of the phrase:

ciphertext = dcniaoiotmcnnamas ut

13.16 By means of a diagram, show the difference between a straight, expanded, and compressed or choice permutation/transposition. Use for example purposes a P-box with 8 input bits. State the key used in each case.

13.17 Assuming an S-box with 8 input bits, derive the size of the key that is required to perform a straight substitution operation.

With the aid of a diagram, show how the size of the key can be reduced by encapsulating a P-box between a binary decoder and a corresponding encoder. Use for example purposes an S-box with 2-input bits and 2-output bits.

Define a key for the P-box and hence list the four outputs for the four possible combinations of the two input bits.

13.18 A product cipher uses a combination of transpositions and substitutions. Design an encryption unit based on a product cipher that operates on 8 input bits. The unit is to be composed of a straight P-box followed by a block of 4 S-boxes of the type used in Exercise 13.17 and a second straight P-box. Define a suitable key for each stage. Hence for a selected 8-bit input, derive the 8-bit encrypted output from the unit.

13.19 With the aid of a diagram, outline the structure of the product cipher used with the DES algorithm. Show the steps that are carried out for each substitution operation within the product cipher assuming the bitwise function used in each substitution is the Feistel cipher.

13.20 State the three transposition operations that are carried out in the DES product cipher algorithm. Hence use a simple example to show that the output of the set of three transpositions is reversible.

Use a simple example to show how each substitution operation is reversible also. What are the implications of this?

13.21 With the aid of a diagram, describe the operation of the triple DES scheme. Hence explain why it is now being used in place of DES in some applications.

13.22 With the aid of schematic logic diagrams, describe the following operational modes of DES: electronic code book (ECB), chain block cipher (CBC), cipher feedback mode (CFM).

Quantify the number of encryption operations that are used to encrypt a 2048-byte file using
(i) CBC and
(ii) CFM.
Hence identify the main use of CFM.

13.23 With the aid of a schematic diagram, describe the operation of the IDEA scheme. Include in your description the size of the key used and the number and size of the subkeys associated with each encryption stage.

13.24 Each encryption stage in the IDEA scheme involves multiple addition and multiplication operations on pairs of 16-bit operands. Explain how the 16-bit product and 16-bit sum are derived.

13.25 With the aid of an example, explain the principle of operation of the RSA algorithm including how the public and private keys are derived. Use for example purposes the two prime numbers 3 and 11. State the maximum numeric value that can be encrypted with your choice of keys.

13.26 By means of an example, show how the exponentiation operations associated with the encryption and decryption stages of the RSA algorithm can be avoided. Hence assuming only messages composed of the 26 uppercase characters are to be sent, encrypt the string of characters AFKP using the public and private keys you derived in Exercise 13.25. Remember the limitation imposed by the choice of prime numbers.

Section 13.5

13.27 With the aid of a diagram, show how nonrepudiation can be obtained using the RSA algorithm:
(i)   on the complete message,
(ii) on a digest of the message.

Clearly identify on your diagram the keys used and the encrypted/decrypted values at each stage.

Section 13.6

13.28 With the aid of a diagram, explain how user authentication can be carried out using a public key scheme. Include in your diagram

the contents of each message and the key used to encrypt the message.

13.29 Explain the meaning and use of the following terms in relation to the authentication procedure associated with Kerberos:
(i)   tickets,
(ii)   ticket granting server,
(iii) nonce,
(iv)   authentication server,
(v)   authentication database,
(vi)   authenticator.

13.30 With the aid of a diagram, identify a possible security threat that can occur with a public key system when the public key is made readily available. Describe how a certification authority can be used to overcome this threat. Include in your description a list of the fields that are present in the certificate and their use.

14

Internet applications

14.1 Introduction

As we showed in Figure 12.1 and explained in the accompanying text, in the TCP/IP protocol suite, given the IP address and port number of a destination application protocol/process (AP), the services provided by TCP or UDP enable two (or more) peer APs to communicate with each other in a transparent way. That is, it does not matter whether the correspondent AP(s) is(are) running in the same computer, another computer on the same network, or another computer attached to a network on the other side of the world. Also, since neither TCP nor UDP examines the content of the information being transferred, this can be a control message (PDU) associated with the application protocol, a file of characters from a selected character set, or a string of bytes output by a particular audio or video codec. Hence application protocols are concerned only with, firstly, ensuring the PDUs associated with the protocol are in the defined format and are exchanged in the specified sequence and secondly, the information/data being transferred is in an agreed transfer syntax so that it has the same meaning to each of the applications.

In this chapter, we discuss both the role and operation of a selection of the application protocols associated with the Internet. These are the simple (electronic) mail transfer protocol (SMTP) and the related multipurpose Internet mail extensions (MIME) protocol, the file transfer protocol (FTP) and a simpler version of this (Trivial FTP), and Internet telephony. In addition, we describe two protocols which, in many instances, a user of the Internet is unaware of. The first is invoked every time we use the Internet and is called the Domain Name System (DNS). The second is concerned with the management of the various networking devices that make up the Internet and is called the **simple network management protocol** (**SNMP**). Because of its role, we shall describe the DNS protocol first.

14.2 Domain name system

As we saw in Figure 12.1 and its accompanying text, an application protocol/process (AP) communicates with a correspondent AP using the latter's IP address and port number. The IP address of the destination AP is first used to route a message – contained within one or more datagrams – across the Internet to the required host and the port number is then used within the host protocol stack to route the received message to the required destination AP. As we saw, however, in the TCP/IP protocol suite the port number of a server AP is allocated a well-known port number which is known by all the client APs that communicate with it. Hence in order to communicate with a remote AP, the source AP need only know the IP address of the host in which the AP is running. Nevertheless, even if this is represented in dotted decimal, it can require up to 12 decimal digits to be remembered, with many more for an IPv6 address. To avoid users from having to cope with such numbers, a directory service similar to that used with a PSTN is used. This is called the **Domain Name System** (**DNS**) and it enables each host computer attached to the Internet to be allocated a **symbolic name** in addition to an IP address.

There are many millions of hosts attached to the Internet each of which has a unique IP address assigned to it. Each host, therefore, must also have a unique name assigned to it and hence an efficient naming scheme is a major part of the DNS. In addition, given a symbolic name, this must be mapped into the related IP address before any communication can take place. This procedure is called name-to-address mapping and is part of the DNS. As we indicated in the introduction, this must be done every time a network application is run and hence it is essential that the procedure is carried out in an efficient way. We shall limit our discussion of the DNS to these two components. They are defined in **RFCs 1034** and **1035**.

14.2.1 Name structure and administration

All the data in the DNS constitutes what is called the **domain name space** and its contents are indexed by a name. The structure of the name space is important since it strongly influences the efficiency of both the administration of the name space and the subsequent address resolution operation. Basically there are two approaches. One is to adopt a **flat structure** and the other a **hierarchical structure**. Although a flat structure uses the overall name space more efficiently, the resulting DNS must be administered centrally. Also, since in a large network like the Internet multiple copies of the DNS are required to speed up the name-to-address mapping operation, using a flat structure would mean that all copies of the DNS would need to be updated each time a change occurred. For these reasons, the domain name space uses a hierarchical naming structure.

In terms of the administration of the name space, the advantages of using a hierarchical structure can best be seen by considering the structure and assignment of subscriber numbers in the telephone system. At the highest level there is a country code, followed by an area code within that country, and so on. The assignment of numbers can be administered in a distributed rather than a centralized way. The assignment of country codes is administered at an international level, the assignment of area codes within each country at a national level, and so on, down to the point where the assignment of numbers within a local area can be administered within that area. This can be done knowing that as long as each higher-level number is unique within the corresponding level in the address hierarchy, the combined number will be unique within the total address space.

The adoption of a hierarchical structure also means that it is possible to partition the DNS in such a way that most name-to-address mapping operations – and other services – can be carried out locally. For example, if names are assigned according to the geographical location of hosts, then the name space can be partitioned in a similar way. Since most network transactions, and hence requests, are between hosts situated in the same local area – for example, between a community of workstations and a local server or email system – then the majority of service requests can be resolved locally and relatively few referred to another site.

As we show in Figure 14.1, the overall structure of the domain name space is represented in the form of an inverted tree with the single root at the top. The root is called the **root domain** and the top-level branch nodes in the tree, domain nodes or simply **domains**. Each domain has further branches associated with it until, at the lowest level of the tree, is a single host that is attached to the Internet. The names of the top-level domains reflect the historical development of the Internet. Initially, when the Internet spanned just the United States with a small number of international organizations linked to it, at the top level was a set of what are called **generic domains** each of which identified a particular organization to which the owner of the host belonged. These are:

com: this identifies hosts that belong to a commercial organization,

edu: an educational establishment,

gov: the US federal government,

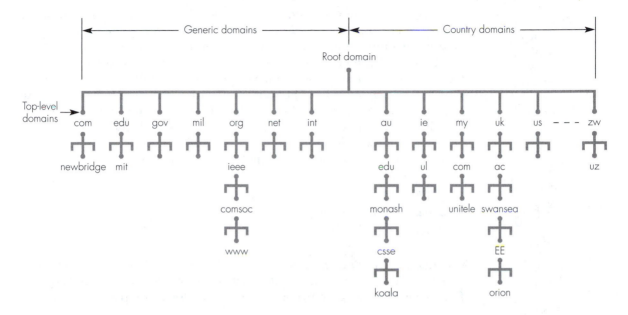

Figure 14.1 The structure of the domain name system together with some examples.

mil: the US armed forces,

org: a non-profit organization,

net: a network provider,

int: an international organization.

Later, as the Internet expanded its area of coverage, so a set of **country domains** were introduced. There is now a separate country domain for each country and these are defined in **ISO 3166**. For this reason, most hosts in the United States are identified by means of a generic domain and those outside of the US by their country domain. However, this is not always the case. Most large multinational companies, for example, often use the *com* generic domain. Also, since each domain is responsible for allocating the names of the (sub)domains that are linked to it, then some countries use different names from those used in the generic domain. For example, in the UK and a number of other countries, the domain name for *edu* is *ac* – academic community – and that for *com, co*. Note also that all names are case-insensitive and hence can be written in either upper-case or lower-case and still have the same meaning.

As we indicated earlier, the allocation of names is managed by the authority responsible for the domain where the name is to appear. For example, if a host located within the electrical engineering department of a new university is to be attached to the Internet, then, assuming the country is outside of the

US, first the university is assigned a name within the edu/ac domain of the country by the appropriate national authority, then the name of the department by an authority acting at a university level, and finally the name of the host by an authority within the department. The name of the host is then derived by listing the various domain names – each called a *label* – starting with the host name back to the root. These are listed from left-to-right with each label separated by a period (.) which is pronounced "dot". In this way, providing each label is unique within its own domain, then the resulting name is unique within the context of the total domain name space of the Internet. Note that the root has a null label and hence some examples are:

> *newbridge.com.*
>
> *orion.EE.swansea. ac.uk.*
>
> *unitele.com.my.*

Note that since each name ends in a period, they are all examples of **absolute domain names** which are also called **fully qualified domain names** (**FQDN**). If the name does not end in a period, it is said to be incomplete or relative.

14.2.2 DNS resource records

Each domain name in the DNS name space may have information associated with it. This is stored in one or more **resource records**, each of which is indexed by the related domain name. A host name, for example, has a resource record that contains the IP address of the host. In practice there are a number of different types of record each of which has the standard format shown in Figure 14.2(a).

The *domain name* is the name of the domain to which the record relates. It consists of the string of labels that make up the domain name and is in the format shown in Figure 14.2(b). Each label is preceded by a 1-byte count that indicates the number of characters/bytes in the label. A label can be up to 63 characters long and the full domain name must be less than 256 characters. The final byte is always 0 which indicates the root.

The *type* field indicates the record type and a selection of these are listed in Figure 14.2(c). A type-A record, for example contains an IPv4 address which is stored in its 32-bit binary form. A type-NS record contains the name of the name server for this domain and is stored in the same format as the domain name. A type-PTR record contains an IP address stored in its dotted decimal form. A type-HINFO record contains the type of host and its operating system both of which are stored as an ASCII string. An MX-record contains the name of a host – an email gateway, for example, as we showed in Figure 5.12 – that is prepared to accept email for forwarding on a non-Internet (IP) site. There is also a type-AAAA record which contains an IPv6 address stored in its hexadecimal form. We shall discuss the use of some of these records in the next section.

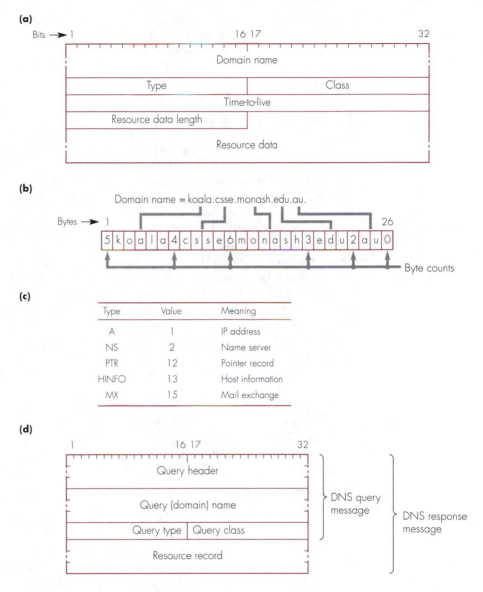

Figure 14.2 DNS resource records and queries: (a) resource record format; (b) domain name format; (c) a selection of resource record types; (d) query and response message formats.

For Internet records the *class* field is always 1 and has the mnemonic IN. The *time-to-live* field indicates the time in seconds the information contained within the record is valid. As we shall see, this is required when the IP address contained in the record has been cached. A typical value is 172 800 which is the number of seconds in 2 days.

The *resource data length* field specifies the length of the *resource data* field. As we have just indicated, the format of the latter differs for different record types and hence the number in the length field relates to the type of data present. For example, if it is an IPv4 address then the length field is 4 to indicate 4 bytes.

14.2.3 DNS query messages

The DNS database is queried using a similar list of (query) types to those used to describe the list of different resource record types. Hence there is a name-to-address resolution query – type A – and so on. A standard format is used to represent each query and this is shown in Figure 14.2(d).

The *query name field* holds the domain name – and hence resource record – to which the query relates. So for a name-to-address resolution query, for example, this contains the domain name of the host and this has the same format that we showed in Figure 14.2(b).

To initiate a query of the DNS – also called a *question* – a **DNS query message** is formed by adding a standard 12-byte header to the particular query. The **DNS response message** is then made up of the query message with one or more resource records – also called *answers* – appended to it. The 12-byte header contains a 16-bit *identification* field and a 16-bit *flags* field. The value in the identification field is assigned by the client that sent the query. It is then returned unchanged by the server in the response message and is used by the client to relate the response to a given query.

The flags field consists of a number of subfields. For example, a 1-bit field is used to indicate whether the message is a query (=0) or a response (=1). There is also a 4-bit field to indicate the type of search involved. As we shall see, this can be standard, recursive, iterative, or inverse.

14.2.4 Name servers

As we indicated earlier, the adoption of a hierarchical structure also facilitates the partitioning of the total DNS database so that most service requests – name-to-address mappings for example – can be carried out locally. To do this, the total domain name space is partitioned into a number of **zones** each of which embraces a unique portion of the total name space. Each zone is then administered by a separate authority which is also responsible for providing one or more **name servers** for the zone. Depending on its position in the hierarchy, a name server may have authority over a single zone or, if it is higher up in the hierarchy, multiple zones.

Associated with each zone is a *primary (name) server* and possibly one or more *secondary (name) servers*. The allocation of names and addresses within the zone is carried out through the primary server and it keeps this information – and hence its portion of the total database – in a block of resource records on hard disk. The resource records within its database are said therefore to be **authoritative records**. The records held in a secondary server are held in volatile storage and are cached versions of those held in a primary server. As we shall see, caching occurs when a primary or secondary server, on finding it does not have the resource record relating to a request, refers the request to a higher-level server. Then, on receipt of the requested IP address, the server that initiated the request retains a copy of this in its cache for a limited time period. The time is stored in the time-to-live field of the accessed resource record and, as we indicated earlier, typically, it is set to 2 days.

Some examples of (fictitious) zones are shown in Figure 14.3. As we can see, the top-level zones in the hierarchy have authority over multiple zones. The zone boundaries in the lower levels are intended to reflect the level of administrative overheads – and hence query requests – associated with the zone.

14.2.5 Service requests

All the information that is stored in each primary name server is accessible to both its secondary servers and also to any other primary server. Because of the excessive overheads that would be involved, however, each primary name server does not know how to contact – that is, does not have the IP address of – every other primary name server. Instead, each primary server knows only how to contact a set of top-level *root name servers*. There are only a small number of these and their IP addresses are stored in the configuration file of each primary server. In turn, each root server holds the name and IP address of each of the second-level servers in the hierarchy and, on receipt of a request from a primary server, the root server returns the name and IP address of the second-level server that should be used. The primary then proceeds to query this server and so on down the hierarchy until a resource record containing the required IP address is obtained. This procedure is

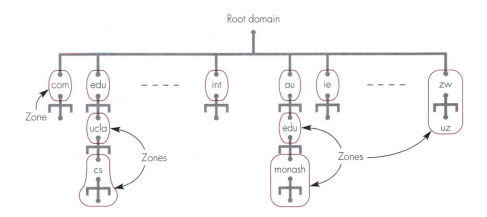

Figure 14.3 Some examples of DNS zones.

called a **recursive name resolution**. Alternatively, in order to reduce the amount of processing done by each name server, an iterative approach can be used. Before we describe each of these approaches, however, we shall describe first how a simple name resolution is carried out using a name server that is local to the host making the request.

Local name resolution

As we show in Figure 14.4, an AP running in a host that is attached to the Internet obtains the IP address of a named host through a piece of software called a **resolver**. Normally, this is a library procedure that is linked to the AP when the AP is first written. The resolver is given the IP address of the local name server – either a primary or a secondary server – that it should use to carry out name-to-address resolutions. Note that the (well-known) port number of a name server is 53.

As we shall see later, as part of all applications – file transfers, email transfers, and so on – the source (client) AP is given the name of the host in which the required destination (server) AP is running. Then, prior to initiating the networked application/transaction, the source AP invokes the resolver to obtain the IP address of the given destination host name (1). In the figure it is assumed that the resolver first sends a type-A query to its local name server requesting the IP address of the (destination) host specified in the query name field (2).

In this example it is assumed that the local name server has the resource record containing the IP address and hence this is returned in a type-A

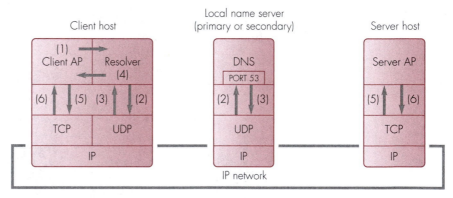

(1)   = resolver invoked by client AP with the name of the server host
(2)   = resolver sends a type-A query containing the name of the server host to its local DNS
(3)   = local DNS returns a type-A resource record containing the IP addresss of the server
(4)   = resolver returns IP address of the server to the client AP
(5)/(6) = client and server APs carry out networked application/transaction

Figure 14.4 Example showing the sequence of messages exchanged for a local name resolution.

resource record (3). This is passed first to the resolver in the source – using UDP – and the resolver then returns the IP address contained within the record to the linked source AP (4). Once the source (client) AP has the IP address of the destination (server) AP, the two can start to carry out the networked application using TCP (5)/(6).

Recursive name resolution

When a local name server does not have a resource record relating to a given destination host name, it carries out a search for it. A schematic diagram showing the procedure followed using the recursive search method is given in Figure 14.5.

As we indicated earlier, all primary name servers have the IP addresses of the set of top-level root name servers. Hence as we can see, the local name server first sends a *recursive query* message containing the name of the required host – for example the *newbridge.com*. gateway – to one of the *root* name servers (1). From the name in the query message, the root server determines that the *com* name server should be queried and hence it returns the IP address of this in the reply – called an answer – message (2). On receipt of this, the local server sends a second query message to the *com* name server

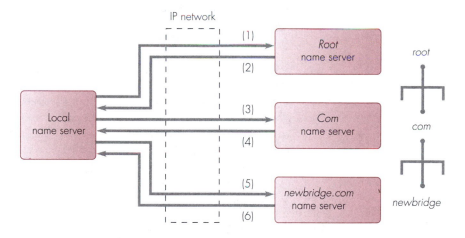

(1) = local name server sends a recursive query message containing name of the destination
      host – for example, the *newbridge.com*. gateway – to the *root* name server
(2) = the *root* server returns the IP address of the *com* server
(3) = local server sends a recursive query to *com* name server
(4) = the *com* server returns the IP address of the *newbridge.com* server
(5) = local server sends a recursive query to *newbridge.com* server
(6) = the *newbridge.com* server sends IP address of *newbridge.com*. gateway (host)

Figure 14.5 Example showing the sequence of messages exchanged for a recursive name resolution.

using the returned IP address (3). In response, the *com* name server determines from the name in the query that the *newbridge.com* name server should be queried and hence it returns the IP address of this in the reply (4).

On receipt of this, the local server sends a third query message to the *newbridge.com* server (5) and, in the example, it is assumed that this has the requested resource record. Hence it returns this – containing the IP address of the destination host – to the local name server (6). The latter then relays the answer to the resolver in the source host and this, in turn, returns the IP address in the answer message to the source AP. The related client–server application can then start.

Note that in this example it was assumed that the local server was a primary server. If it was a secondary server, however, then this would send the first query to its (known) primary server and it is this that would initiate the sequence shown. Also, in order to reduce the number of queries that take place, each name server retains all resource records it receives – each containing an IP address – in a cache. In many instances, therefore, the answer to a query from a resolver is available in the cache so avoiding any external queries being sent out.

Iterative name resolution

In order to avoid always going to a root server – and hence to the top of the name tree – to initiate the search for an unknown resource record, with the iterative search method the local server starts its search for the requested record from the server that is nearest to it. Figure 14.6 illustrates the procedure.

To support the iterative method, instead of each primary name server having the IP addresses of the set of top-level root servers, it has the name and IP address of the next higher-level server to it in the naming hierarchy. Then, when a resolver sends a query – this time called an *iterative query* message – to its local server, if the local server does not have the requested resource record, instead of sending a query to a root server, it sends an (iterative) query to the next higher-level name server in the hierarchy – the *com* server in the example. If this has the record, it responds directly. If it hasn't, then it parses the name and returns a response containing the IP address of the server that it thinks might have (or is nearest to) the requested record. The local server then sends an (iterative) query to this server and so on until it receives a response message containing the requested record/IP address. As we can deduce from the figure, the search only proceeds up the tree to the level that is necessary to obtain the requested record thereby reducing the load on the top-level root servers.

Pointer queries

Although most queries of the DNS database relate to name-to-address translations, there are also queries that require an address-to-name translation. These are called *pointer queries* and, normally, they are from a system program that carries out a diagnostic operation, for example. They are also used by email servers and file servers to validate users.

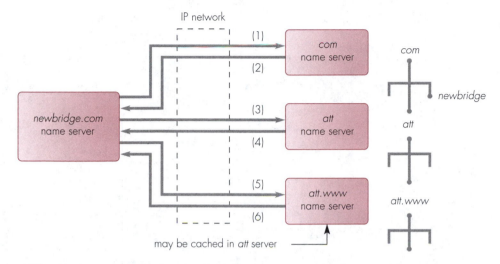

(1) = local name server sends an iterative query message containing the name of the destination host – *att.www* – to the next higher-level server – *com*
(2) = the *com* server replies with the IP address of the *att* server
(3) = local server sends an iterative query to the *att* server
(4) = the *att* server returns the IP address of the *att.www* server
(5) = local server sends an iterative query to the *att.www* server
(6) = the *att.www* server returns the IP address of the requested Web host

Figure 14.6 Example showing the sequence of messages exchanged for an iterative name resolution.

To support this type of query, the resolver, given the IP address of a host, must initiate a search of the DNS and return the host name. As we indicated earlier, however, the search key of the DNS is a domain name. This means that with the database structure we showed in Figure 14.3, this type of query would require a complete search of the database starting with the set of top-level domain names. Clearly this is impractical and hence to support pointer queries an additional branch in the DNS name space to those shown in Figure 14.1 is present. This is shown in Figure 14.7.

As we can see, it starts with the top-level domain name *arpa*, followed by the second-level name *in-addr*. This is then followed by the four bytes (in dotted-decimal) that make up the IP address of each host whose name is in the DNS name space starting with the address-type byte. This order is used since the netid part of the address is assigned by *arpa.in-addr* and the hostid part by the authority that has been allocated the netid. Hence to be consistent with the other types of query message, the domain name in the pointer-type query message for the IP address 132.113.56.25 is:

25.56.113.132.in-addr.arpa

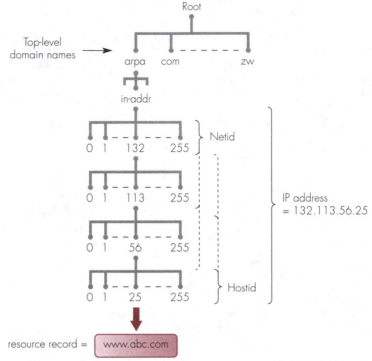

resource record = www.abc.com

IP address specified in domain name of query message as 25.56.113.132. in-addr.arpa. Host name in reply message assumed to be www.abc.com.

Figure 14.7 Pointer query principles.

that is, it starts with the last byte of the IP address first. The search of this portion of the database then yields a resource record as before but this time it contains the domain name of the host that has the given IP address. Hence in the example shown in the figure, this is assumed to be *www.abc.com*. Because of the reverse order of the labels in the domain name, a pointer query is also known as an **inverse query**.

14.3 Electronic mail

From a user perspective, electronic mail (email) – apart from Web surfing which we describe in the next chapter – is probably the most popular application on the Internet. We identified the standards relating to email over the Internet in Section 5.3.3 and, as we showed in Figure 5.10, an email system comprises two main components: an email client and an email server. Normally, an email client is a desktop PC or workstation which runs a program called the user agent (UA). This provides the user interface to the email system and provides facilities to create, send, and receive (email) messages. To do this, the UA maintains an IN and an OUT mailbox and a list of selections to enable the user to create, send, read, and reply to a message, as well as selections to manipulate the individual messages in the two mailboxes, such as forward and delete.

The email server is a server computer that maintains an IN mailbox for all the users/clients that are registered with it. In addition, the server has software called the UA server to interact with the UA software in each client and also software to manage the transfer of mail messages over the Internet. The software associated with the latter function is called the **message transfer agent** (**MTA**) and is concerned with the sending and receiving of mail messages to/from other email servers that are also connected directly to the Internet.

The protocol stack that is used to support email over the Internet was shown earlier in Figure 5.11. Normally, the protocol stack associated with the access network – the internet service provider (ISP) network and the site/campus LAN shown in the figure – is either the PPP protocol we described in Section 9.9 – used with an ISP network – or, with a PC network, a protocol stack such as Novell NetWare. A number of different vendors then provide proprietary software to carry out the various interaction functions between the user and the UA client. In addition, there are a number of protocols that can be used to control the transfer of messages over the access network. For example, the **POP3 protocol** – post office protocol 3 – is often used to fetch messages from the user's IN mailbox in the server to the IN mailbox maintained by the UA. Essentially, POP3 defines the format of the various control messages that are exchanged between the UA client and UA server to carry out a transfer and also the sequence of the messages that are exchanged. POP3 is specified in **RFC 1939**.

The application protocol that is used to control the transfer of messages between two MTAs over the Internet is called the **simple mail transfer protocol** (**SMTP**). It is specified in **RFC 821**. In this section we first describe the structure of mail messages and the use of the various fields in each message header. We then present an overview of how a typical message transfer is carried out and finally, the operation of SMTP.

14.3.1 Structure of email messages

When we send a letter using a postal service, we first write our own name and address at the head of the letter followed by the message we wish to send. Typically, this comprises the name and address of the intended recipient followed by the actual letter/message content. We then insert the letter into an envelope and write the name and address of the intended recipient on the front of the envelope. Also, to allow for the possibility of the recipient having changed address, we often write our own name and address on, say, the back of the envelope. We then deposit the envelope into a mailbox provided by the postal service. The latter then uses the name and address on the front of the envelope to forward and deliver it to the address of the intended recipient. Alternatively, if this is not possible, it uses the address on the back of the envelope to return it to the sender. The recipient knows who sent the letter by the name and address at the head of the letter.

Thus there are two distinct procedures involved in sending a letter: the first involving the sender of the letter and concerned with the preparation of the letter itself and the second with the transfer of the addressed envelope to the intended recipient by the postal service. We note also that the structure and content of the letter itself has only meaning to the sender and recipient of the letter.

In a similar way, the sending of electronic mail involves two separate procedures. The first is concerned with the entry of various fields – including the sender's and recipient's name/address at the head of the message – and the actual message content via the UA; the second with the encapsulation of the message into an (electronic) envelope containing the sender's and recipient's address and with the transfer of the envelope over the network by the message transfer system. In the case of electronic mail, however, since the writing of the addresses on the envelope is performed by the mail system itself, it is necessary for the addresses at the head of the message to have a standard structure so that they can be extracted and used directly by the message transfer system. The terminology associated with the structure of an email message showing these two parts is shown in Figure 14.8(a).

As we can see, during its transfer across the network an email message is composed of an *envelope* and the *message*. The envelope contains the email address of the sender of the message (*MAIL FROM*) and its intended recipient (*RCPT TO*). In the case of the Internet, all email addresses are of the form *user-name@mailserver-name* where *mailserver-name* is the DNS name of the mail server and *user-name* is selected by the user and confirmed by the local mail manager at subscription/registration time. The manager also creates an IN mailbox for the user on the mail server at the same time.

The format of an email address is defined in RFC 821 and, as we shall see, the recipient mailserver-name is used by the message transfer system to route the message over the Internet to the intended recipient mail server and the user-name is then used by the MTA to determine the IN mailbox into which the mail should be deposited. Like a DNS name, the user-name is case insensitive and the two names are separated by the @ symbol.

The message itself is composed of a *header* and a *body*, the latter containing the actual message that has been entered by the user via the UA. As we show in Figure 14.8(b), the header comprises a number of fields some of which are optional. Also, since there are many different vendors of UA software, the optional fields that are used by the UA in the sender and those used by the recipient UA may differ. However, all of the header fields have a standard format which is defined in RFC 822. Each field comprises a single line of ASCII text starting with the (standardized) field name. This is terminated by

(a)

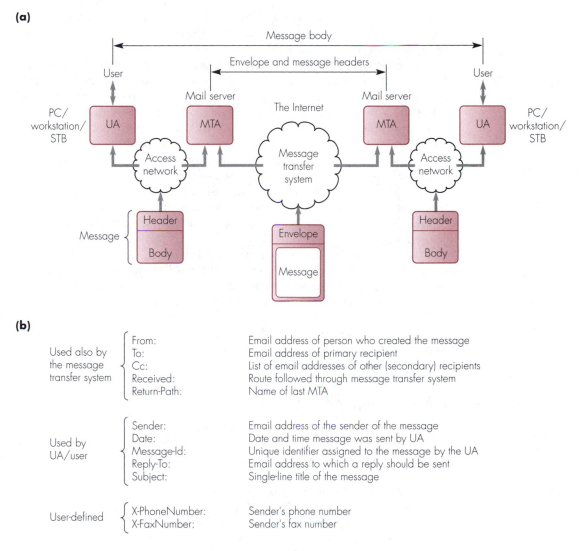

(b)

Used also by the message transfer system	From: To: Cc: Received: Return-Path:	Email address of person who created the message Email address of primary recipient List of email addresses of other (secondary) recipients Route followed through message transfer system Name of last MTA
Used by UA/user	Sender: Date: Message-Id: Reply-To: Subject:	Email address of the sender of the message Date and time message was sent by UA Unique identifier assigned to the message by the UA Email address to which a reply should be sent Single-line title of the message
User-defined	X-PhoneNumber: X-FaxNumber:	Sender's phone number Sender's fax number

Figure 14.8 Email message structure: (a) terminology and usage; (b) selection of the fields in the message header and their use.

a colon and is followed by the field value. A single blank line is then used to separate the header from the message body.

As we can see, some fields are also used by the message transfer system and others by the UA/user. It is also possible for a user to add one or more private header fields. Some examples of fields in each category are shown in the figure together with their usage. Most are self explanatory. Note, however, that *From:* and *Sender:* may be different. For example, the person who created – and is sending – the message (*From:*) may be the secretary of the person who is identified in the *Sender:* field. Also, if the reply to the message should be sent to a third party, then the email address of the person who is to receive the reply is in the *Reply-To:* field.

Note also that even though the *Received:* and *Return-Path:* fields are in the header of the message – rather than the envelope – they are used primarily by a network manager during fault diagnosis to determine the path that is followed by a message through the message transfer system. To initiate this procedure, the source MTA enters its own name together with the message identifier and the date and time the message was sent in a *Received:* field. A new *Received:* field containing the same information is then added to this by each MTA along the path that the message takes. In the case of the *Return-Path:* field, this contains only the name of the last MTA. In practice, however, this field is often not used and, if present, contains only the email address of the sender. Note that user-defined fields must always start with the character sequence *X-.*

In RFC 822, the transfer syntax used for all the header fields is the US version of the ASCII code we showed earlier in Figure 2.6(a) with the addition that each 7-bit character is first converted into an 8-bit byte by adding a 0 bit in the most-significant bit position. Also, the codeword used to represent an *end-of-line* is the 2-byte combination of a carriage return (CR) and a line feed (LF) and, because of this, the codeword for a CR is the 2-byte combination of a CR and a NUL. This modified version of the ASCII codeword set is called **network virtual terminal (NVT) ASCII**.

14.3.2 Message content

With the RFC 822 standard the content part of a message – the body – can only be lines of ASCII text with the maximum length of each line set at 1000 characters. The sending UA then converts each character into NVT ASCII as the transfer syntax with each character converted into its 8-bit form. This ensures that there can be no combinations of codewords in the content field that can be misinterpreted by an MTA as a protocol message.

The RCF 822 standard was first introduced in 1983 and is still used widely for sending text messages. As the use and coverage of the Internet widened, however, so the demand for alternative message types increased, for example, to allow messages to contain binary data and other media types such as audio and video. Also messages containing different languages and alphabets. As a result, an extension to the RFC 822 standard was introduced. This is known as **Multipurpose Internet Mail Extensions (MIME)**. It was first specified in **RFC 1341** and later updated in **RFCs 2045/8**.

The aim of MIME was to enable users to send alternative media types in messages but still use the same message transfer system. The solution was to add a number of extra header fields to the existing fields which collectively enable the user to define alternative media types in the message body. It also provided a way of converting the alternative media types that are supported into strings of ASCII characters which can then be transferred using NVT ASCII.

MIME headers

The additional MIME header fields and their meaning are listed in part (a) of Table 14.1. The first field following the standard header fields is the *MIME-Version:* which, when present, informs the recipient UA that an alternative message content to ASCII text is present in the message body. It also includes the version number of MIME that is being used. If the field is not present, the

Table 14.1 MIME: (a) additional header fields; (b) alternative content types.

(a) Header	Meaning
MIME-Version:	Defines the version of MIME that is being used
Content-Description:	Short textual description of the message content
Content-Id:	Unique identifier assigned by the UA
Content-Type:	Defines the type of information in the body
Content-Transfer-Encoding:	The transfer syntax being used
Content-Length	The number of bytes in the message body

(b) Type	Subtype	Content description
Text	Plain	Unformatted ASCII
	Richtext	Formatted text based on HTML
Image	GIF	Digitized image in GIF
	JPEG	Digitized image in JPEG
Audio	Basic	Digitized audio
Video	MPEG	Digitized video clip or movie
Application	Octet-stream	A string of bytes
	Postscript	A printable document in PostScript
Message	Rfc822	Another MIME message
	Partial	Part of a longer message
	External-body	Pointer to where message body can be accessed
Multipart	Mixed	Each part contains a different content and/or type
	Alternative	Each part contains the same content but with subtype of a different type
	Parallel	The parts should be output simultaneously
	Digest	Multiple messages

recipient UA assumes the content is NVT ASCII. When it is present, the following four fields then expand upon the type of content that is there and the transfer syntax that is being used.

The *Content-Description:* field is present to allow a user to enter a short textual string in ASCII to describe to the recipient user what the contents are all about. It is similar, therefore, to the *subject:* field in the standard header. One or other is often used to decide whether the message/mail is worth reading. Similarly, the *Content-Id:* field performs a similar function to the *Message-Id:* field in the standard header.

The *Content-Type:* field defines the type of information in the message body. The different types are defined in RFC 1521 and a selection of them are listed in part (b) of the table. As we can see, each type comprises two parts: a specification of the type of information – text, image, and so on – followed by a subtype. The type of information in the message body is then defined by a combination of the type and its subtype, each separated by a slash. Some examples are:

> *Content-Type:Text/Richtext*
>
> *Content-Type:Image/JPEG*

Some contain one or more additional parameters. The format used is as follows:

> *Content-Type:Text/Plaintext; charset=US-ASCII*
>
> *Content-Type:Multipart/Alternative;boundary="NextType"*

Clearly, for each type/subtype combination a standard format must be used so that the recipient UA can interpret (and output) the information in a compatible way with how it has been encoded by the sending UA. Hence associated with each combination is a defined (abstract) syntax. For example, the Text/Plaintext combination implies the contents are ASCII text while for the Text/Richtext combination a markup language similar to HTML is used, an example of which we showed earlier in Figure 2.8. Similarly, digitized images, audio, and video are all represented in their compressed form. As we saw in Chapters 3 and 4, there is a range of standard compression algorithms available with each of these media types. In the case of images, for example, the two alternative subtypes supported are GIF – Section 3.4.1 – and JPEG – Section 3.4.5. The subtype selected for audio is a form of PCM – Section 4.2.1 – and that for video a version of MPEG – Section 4.3.4. In the case of a movie (video with sound), the MPEG subtype is used with the audio and video integrated together using the format we described in Section 5.5.1.

The *Application:* type is used when the body contents require processing by the recipient UA before they have meaning on the user's display. For example, an *Octet-stream* subtype is simply a string of bytes representing, say, a compiled program. Typically, therefore, on receipt of this type of information the UA would prompt the user for a file name into which the data should be written. Similarly, for the *Postscript* subtype unless the UA contains a PostScript interpreter to display the contents on the screen.

The *Message:* type is used when the contents relate to another MIME message. For example, if the contents contain another RFC 822 message, then the **Rfc822** subtype is used, possibly to forward a message. Similarly, the *Partial* subtype is used when the contents contain a fragment of a (larger) message. Typically, additional parameters are then added by the sending UA to enable the recipient UA to reassemble the complete message. This feature is used, for example, to send a long document or audio/video sequence. The *External-body* subtype is used when the message content is not present in the message and instead an address pointer to where the actual message can be accessed from; for example, the DNS name of a file server and the file name. This feature is often used to send an unsolicited message such as a long document. Typically, the UA is programmed to ask the user whether he or she wishes to access the document or not. Some examples of parameters with the different message subtypes are:

Content-Type:Message/Partial;id="file-name@host-name";number=1;total=20

Content-Type:Message/External-Body;access-type="mail-server";server="server-name"

The *Multipart:* type is used to indicate that the message body consists of multiple parts/attachments. Each part is clearly separated using a defined delimiter in a parameter. With the *Mixed* subtype each part can contain a different content and/or type. With the *Alternative* subtype each part contains the same content but with a different subtype associated with it; for example, the same message in text or audio or in a number of different languages/alphabets. Normally, the alternative parts are listed in the preferred order the user/sending UA would like them to be output. The *Parallel* subtype indicates to the recipient UA that the different parts should be output together; for example a piece of audio with a digitized image. Finally the *Digest* subtype is used to indicate that the message body contains multiple other messages; for example to send out a set of draft documents that the sender may have received from a number of different members of a working group.

An example of a simple multimedia mail showing a number of the features we have just considered is shown in Figure 14.9. The message is simply ***Happy birthday Irene*** and this is sent in three different formats. The first is in the form of an audio message which would necessitate the recipient's PC/workstation having a sound card with associated software. Also, the recipient UA must have software to interpret the contents of the accessed audio file and output this to the sound card. If this is not available, normally the UA is programmed to move to the next option and, if the UA cannot interpret richtext, then the message will be output in plaintext. As we can see from this, what we have described in this section relates only to the (abstract) syntax of the messages that are used by a UA to send a multimedia mail to another UA. What the user sees/hears depends on how the UA has been programmed.

Transfer encoding

The next-to-last field in the MIME header we showed earlier in Table 14.1 is the *Content-Transfer-Encoding:* field and an example of its use was shown in

From: xyz@abc.com
To: abc@xyz.com
Subject: Happy birthday Irene
MIME-Version: 1.0
Content-Type: Multiport/Alternative; boundary = "TryAgain";

– – TryAgain

Content-Type: Message/External-body;
        name = "Irene.audio";
        directory = "Irene";
        access-type = "anon-ftp";
        site = "myserver.abc.com";
Content-Type: Audio/Basic;   *(Message in audio accessed remotely)*
Content-Transfer-Encoding: Base64

– – TryAgain

Content-Type: Text/Richtext;
<B> ✶✶✶Happy birthday Irene✶✶✶ </B> *(Message in richtext)*

– – TryAgain

Content-Type: Text/Plain;
        ✶✶✶Happy birthday Irene✶✶✶ *(Message in plaintext)*

– – TryAgain

Figure 14.9 MIME: example type and subtype declarations.

Figure 14.9. As the name implies, it is concerned with the format of the message content during its transfer over the Internet. Since all the extension fields in the extension header are in 7-bit ASCII, they are encoded in 8-bit NVT ASCII. Recall also that with an RFC 822 message, the UA uses the same transfer syntax to send lines of 7-bit ASCII over the Internet in order to ensure there can be no combinations of codewords in the content field that can be misinterpreted by an MTA as an SMTP protocol message. With the additional media types associated with MIME, however, the message content may be in an 8-bit form with a binary 1 in the eighth bit – a string of 8-bit speech samples for example. As we indicated earlier, the aim of MIME is to use the same message transfer system which means that the message body should be encoded in NVT ASCII. Hence once the message contents have been input, the UA first converts all non-ASCII data first into lines of (7-bit) ASCII characters and then into lines of NVT ASCII. Collectively this is referred to as transfer encoding.

Two alternative transfer encodings are defined in RFC 1521 for use with an RFC 821-conformant message transfer system (MTA):

■ quoted-printable: this is used to send messages that are composed of characters from an alternative character set that is mostly ASCII but has a small number of special characters which have their eighth bit set to 1. Examples are all the Latin character sets;

■ base64: this is used to send blocks of binary data and also messages composed of strings of characters from a character set that uses 8-bit codewords such as EBCDIC.

When the MIME header field contains *Content-Transfer-Encoding: Quoted-printable* the UA converts the codewords of those characters which have their eighth bit set into a string of three characters. The first is the = character and this is followed by the two characters that represent the (8-bit) character in hexadecimal. For example, if the codeword for a special character was 1 110 1001, then the hexadecimal representation of the character is E9 (hex). Hence this would be converted into the three-character sequence =E9.

When the MIME header field contains *Content-Transfer-Encoding:Base64* the message content, instead of being treated as a string of 8-bit bytes, is treated as a string of 24-bit values. Each value is then divided into four 6-bit subvalues, each of which is then represented by an ASCII character. The 64 ASCII characters used to represent each of the possible 6-bit values are listed in Table 14.2. In the event that the contents of a message do not contain a multiple of three bytes, then one or two = characters are used as padding.

Table 14.2 Base64 encoding table.

6-bit value (Hex)	ASCII char	6-bit value (Hex)	ASCII char	6-bit value (Hex)	ASCII char	6-bit value (Hex)	ASCII char
00	A	10	Q	20	g	30	w
01	B	11	R	21	h	31	x
02	C	12	S	22	i	32	y
03	D	13	T	23	j	33	z
04	E	14	U	24	k	34	0
05	F	15	V	25	l	35	1
06	G	16	W	26	m	36	2
07	H	17	X	27	n	37	3
08	I	18	Y	28	o	38	4
09	J	19	Z	29	p	39	5
0A	K	1A	a	2A	q	3A	6
0B	L	1B	b	2B	r	3B	7
0C	M	1C	c	2C	s	3C	8
0D	N	1D	d	2D	t	3D	9
0E	O	1E	e	2E	u	3E	+
0F	P	1F	f	2F	v	3F	/

Example 14.1

A binary file containing audio data contains the following string of four 8-bit samples:

      10010101   11011100   00111011   01011000

Assuming Base64 encoding,

(i) using the codewords for ASCII characters given earlier in Figure 2.6(a), derive the contents of the file in NVT ASCII;

(ii) show how the original contents are derived from the received NVT ASCII string.

Answer:

(i) Input first converted into two 24-bit values using two = characters as padding:

      Value 1 = 10010101   11011100   00111011
      Value 2 = 01011000   00111101(=)   00111101(=)

Each 24-bit value is converted into four 6-bit values:

      Value 1 = 10 0101   01 1101   11 0000   11 1011

              2   5   1   D   3   0   3   B
      Value 2 = 01 0110   00 0011   11 0100   11 1101
              1   6   0   3   3   4   3   D

Using Table 14.2:

      Value 1 represented as the four ASCII characters: *ldw*7
      Value 2 represented as the four ASCII characters: *WD*09

Hence from codewords in Figure 2.6(a), contents in NVT ASCII are:

      Value 1 = 0 110 1100   0 110 0100   0 111 0111   0 011 0111
      Value 2 = 0 101 0111   0 100 0100   0 011 0000   0 011 1001

(ii) Received bytestream first converted back into the equivalent ASCII string using codewords in Figure 2.6(a):

      Value 1 = *ldw*7
      Value 2 = *WD*09

The equivalent four 6-bit subvalues then obtained from Table 14.2:

      Value 1 = 2   5   1   D   3   0   3   B
            = 10 0101   01 1101   11 0000   11 1011
      Value 2 = 1   6   0   3   3   4   3   D
            = 01 0110   00 0011   11 0100   11 1101

14.1 Continued

These are then combined and converted into two 24-bit values:

Value 1 = 10010101	11011100	00111011
Value 2 = 01011000	00111101	00111101

Last two 8-bit values of the last (second) 24-bit value are the NVT ASCII of the = character and hence are discarded.

File contents restored as:

10010101　11011100　00111011　01011000

Encryption

As with all Internet applications, it is relatively straightforward to read messages during their transmission over the access networks and the Internet itself. It is now becoming common practice with many companies, for example, to monitor the email that is being sent and received by their employees. Increasingly, therefore, people and organizations are applying encryption methods to the mail messages that they send.

When two people are communicating using ASCII text and wish to foil a casual eavesdropper from reading their mail, a simple approach to obtaining privacy is to encode the message body using Base64 before it is entered. This can be done very easily by interpreting the stream of ASCII characters that make up the message as a bitstream. Then, by applying Base64 to the bitstream, the resulting transmitted (NVT) ASCII character string is meaningless to the casual eavesdropper.

For example, using the table of ASCII codewords in Figure 2.6(a), the character string *I LOVE* in 7-bit ASCII is:

1001001(I)　0100000(SP)　1001100(L)　1001111(O)　1010110(V)
1000101(E)

Hence, when this bitstream is interpreted as a string of 6-bit groups, it yields:

10 0100　10 1000　00 1001　10 0100　11 1110　10 1101　00 0101

In hexadecimal these are equivalent to:

24　　28　　09　　24　　3E　　2D　　05

or, using the Base64 encoding in Table 14.2, the ASCII character string:

k　　o　　J　　k　　+　　t　　F

which, of course, is less interesting should it be observed.

Clearly it is a trivial task to break this code and for applications that demand a high level of security, a number of more sophisticated encryption schemes are now used. Since it uses a number of the encryption methods we discussed in the last chapter, we shall limit our discussion to a widely used scheme devised by Zimmermann called **pretty good privacy** (**PGP**). As we shall see, PGP does not only provide a high level of privacy, but also authentication, integrity, and nonrepudiation. The various steps followed to encrypt a message are shown in Figure 14.10. Normally the header fields are repeated in the message body which is then encrypted.

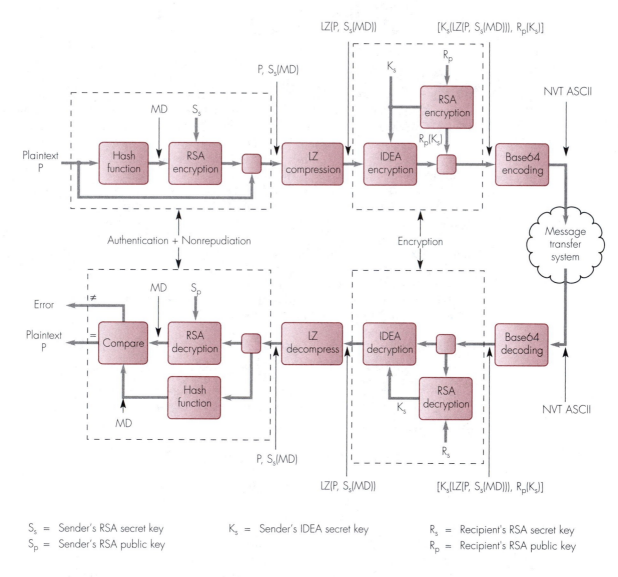

S_s = Sender's RSA secret key K_s = Sender's IDEA secret key R_s = Recipient's RSA secret key
S_p = Sender's RSA public key R_p = Recipient's RSA public key

Figure 14.10 Email privacy: PGP encryption and decryption.

As we can see, the overall process involves a combination of MD5 (Section 13.5), RSA (Section 13.4.5), IDEA (Section 13.4.4) and Base64. It also uses the Lempel–Ziv (LZ) compression algorithm we discussed in Section 3.3.4.

The first block is concerned with authentication and nonrepudiation. It uses the same scheme that we showed in Figure 13.6. This produces the plaintext, P, and a 128-bit message digest (MD). The MD is then encrypted using the sender's RSA secret key, Ss. At the recipient side, the MD is again computed using the same hash function and, if this is the same as the decrypted MD that was sent with the message, this is taken as proof that the message was indeed sent by the sender in the *From:* field of the message header. This is then taken as authenticating the sender and, should it be necessary, nonrepudiation.

The output of the authentication and nonrepudiation block – P, S_s (MD) – is compressed using the LZ algorithm and the output of this is passed to the encryption block. This is based on IDEA and uses a 128-bit secret key, K_s, to encrypt the LZ compressed block. K_s is also encrypted using the recipient's RSA public key, R_p, to produce $R_p(K_s)$. This, together with the output of the IDEA compression block, forms the binary output. Finally, this is Base64 encoded to yield an ASCII string which is then transmitted in the form of an NVT ASCII string.

The processing at the receiver is the inverse of that carried out at the sending side. First the sender's IDEA secret key, K_s, is obtained by using the recipient's RSA secret key, R_s, to decrypt $R_p(K_s)$. K_s is then used to decrypt the LZ compressed block. After being decompressed, the resulting output is passed to the authentication and nonrepudiation block.

It should be noted that, because of the high processing overheads associated with RSA, the two RSA stages operate only on small block sizes, the first the 128-bit MD and the second the 128-bit secret key used by IDEA. Also the message contents are encrypted using IDEA which, as we saw in Section 13.4.4, is very fast.

14.3.3 Message transfer

The main components that make up the message transfer system are shown in Figure 14.11(a). Once a user has created a mail message and clicked on the SEND button, the UA first formats the message into NVT ASCII and then sends it to the UA server in its local mail server using the protocol stack of the access network. On receipt of the message, the UA server deposits the message into the message queue ready for sending by the MTA over the Internet.

The client MTA checks the contents of the message queue at regular intervals and, when it detects a message has been placed in the queue, it proceeds to format and send the message. The MTA first reads the email addresses from the *From:* and *To:* fields of the message header and writes them into the *MAIL FROM:* and *RCPT TO:* fields in the envelope header. It then examines the *Cc:* field in the message header and, if other recipients are listed, it proceeds to create further copies of the message each with a different *RCPT TO:* value in the envelope header.

(a)

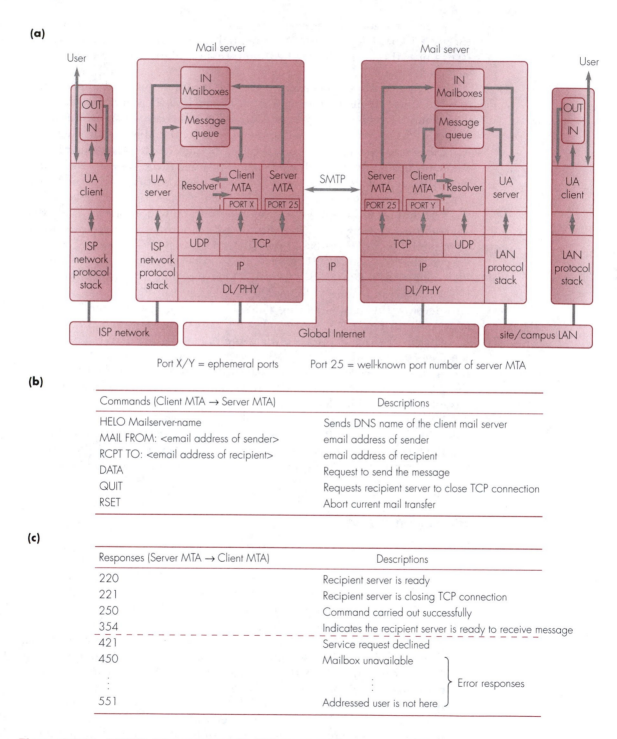

Port X/Y = ephemeral ports   Port 25 = well-known port number of server MTA

(b)

Commands (Client MTA → Server MTA)	Descriptions
HELO Mailserver-name	Sends DNS name of the client mail server
MAIL FROM: <email address of sender>	email address of sender
RCPT TO: <email address of recipient>	email address of recipient
DATA	Request to send the message
QUIT	Requests recipient server to close TCP connection
RSET	Abort current mail transfer

(c)

Responses (Server MTA → Client MTA)	Descriptions
220	Recipient server is ready
221	Recipient server is closing TCP connection
250	Command carried out successfully
354	Indicates the recipient server is ready to receive message
421	Service request declined
450	Mailbox unavailable
⋮	⋮ } Error responses
551	Addressed user is not here

Figure 14.11 SMTP: (a) components; (b) command messages; (c) response messages.

As we saw earlier, all email addresses are in the form *user-name@mailserver-name* where *mailserver-name* is the DNS name of the mail server. Hence before the client MTA can send any of the formatted messages over the Internet, it must first obtain the IP address of each of the recipient mail servers. As we saw in Section 14.2.5, this is done using the resolver procedure that is linked to all Internet APs. Once the set of IP addresses have been obtained, the client MTA is ready to initiate the transfer of each message. The protocol that is used to control the transfer of a message from one MTA to another is the simple mail transfer protocol (SMTP). The various control messages that are used by SMTP and the sequence in which they are exchanged are defined in RFC 821. All the control messages are encoded in NVT ASCII.

Each message is transferred over a previously established TCP connection. Hence to send each message, the client MTA first initiates the establishment of a logical connection between itself and the MTA server in the recipient mail server using the latter's IP address and port 25 which is the well-known port number for SMTP. The server MTA accepts the incoming (TCP) connection request and, once this is in place, proceeds to exchange SMTP control messages (PDUs) with the client MTA to transfer the message. The control messages that are sent by the MTA client are called *commands* and a selection of these are shown in Figure 14.11(b). As we can see, most are composed of four uppercase characters. The MTA server responds to each command with a three-digit numeric reply code with (optionally) a readable string. A selection of the reply codes are given in Figure 14.11(c).

A typical exchange sequence of SMTP control messages to send a mail message is shown in Figure 14.12. To avoid confusion, the TCP segments that are used to transfer the messages are not shown. As we can see, once the server has received the acknowledgment indicating a TCP connection is now in place, the server MTA returns a 220 response indicating it is ready to start the message transfer sequence. This starts with the MTA client sending a HELO command and the MTA server returning a 250 response indicating it is prepared to accept mail from the sending server. The client MTA then sends the sender's email address and, if this is accepted, it sends the intended recipient's email address. In the example, this is accepted by a 250 response. If this was not acceptable, typically the MTA server would return either a 450 (mailbox unavailable) or a 551 (addressed user is not here).

Assuming both addresses are valid, the client proceeds to send a DATA command to determine if the server MTA is now ready to receive the message itself. If it is, the server returns a 350 response and, on receipt of this, the transfer of the message takes place. The message consists of multiple lines, each of up to 1000 characters, with a single "." character on the last line. All characters are encoded in NVT ASCII. Note also that the number of TCP segments used to transfer the message is determined entirely by the two TCP entities. On receipt of the (reassembled) message, the server MTA transfers the message to the IN mailbox of the recipient user and returns a 250 response to the client MTA. The latter then sends a QUIT command to request the MTA server closes the TCP connection.

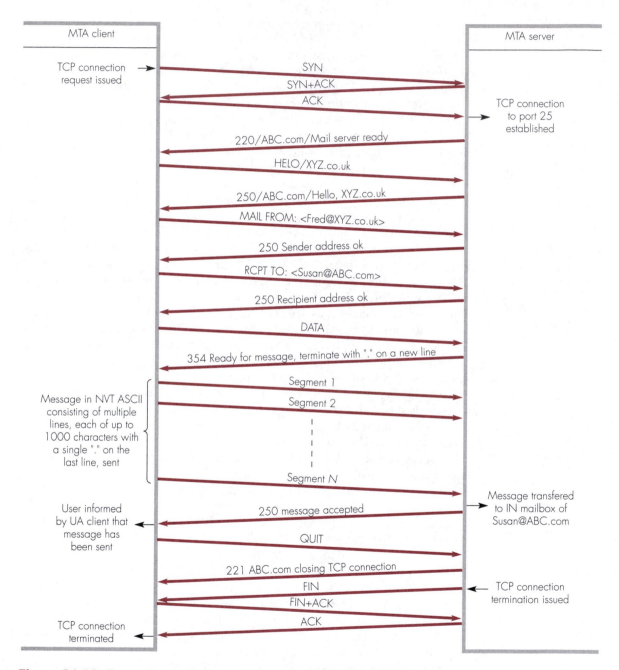

Figure 14.12 Example email message transfer from Fred@XYZ.co.uk to Susan@ABC.com using SMTP.

The UA client in each user terminal periodically sends an enquiry to its local UA server to determine whether any new mail has arrived. Hence when the UA server next receives an enquiry from the UA client in the recipient's terminal, it transfers the received message to the UA client. The latter then places the message in the user's IN mailbox and, typically, outputs a message indicating a new (mail) message has arrived.

At the sending side, once the MTA client receives the final 250 response indicating the message has been transferred successfully, it informs the UA server. The latter then informs the UA client in the sending terminal and this, in turn, informs the user that the message has been sent.

14.4 FTP

The transfer of the contents of a file held on the file system of one computer to a file on another computer is a common requirement in many distributed/networked applications. In some applications the two computers involved may both be large servers each running a different operating system with a different file system and character set. In another application, one of the computers may be a server and the other an item of equipment such as a cable modem or a set-top box which does not have a hard disk. Hence in this case all the data that is transferred must have been formatted specifically for running in the cable modem or set-top box. Clearly, therefore, the file transfer protocol associated with the second type of application can be much simpler than the first. Hence to meet the different requirements of these two types of application, there are two Internet application protocols associated with file transfer. The first is called the **file transfer protocol** (**FTP**) and the second the **trivial file transfer protocol** (**TFTP**). In this section we give an overview of the operation of FTP and we describe the operation of TFTP in the next section.

14.4.1 Overview

FTP is a widely used Internet application protocol that has been designed to enable a user at a terminal to initiate the transfer of the contents of a named file from one computer to another using the TCP/IP protocol suite. The two computers may use different operating systems with different file systems and, possibly, different character sets. It also supports the transfer of a number of different file types such as character and binary. It is specified in **RFC 959**. We describe first how the file contents are represented and then the operation of the protocol itself. We conclude with some examples.

14.4.2 File content representation

Although FTP has been designed to enable files stored in many different types of computer to be transferred, to gain an understanding of FTP's operation without including too much detail, we shall limit our description to file transfers involving just two different file types, ASCII and binary, and files containing a stream of bytes with no internal structure. As with the contents of email messages, for a file containing 7-bit ASCII characters the file contents are first converted into NVT ASCII by the sending side before they are transferred. They are then converted back again into 7-bit ASCII at the recipient side for storage. With a binary file, the end of the file is signaled by the sending side initiating the closure of the TCP connection.

14.4.3 FTP operation

A schematic diagram showing the essential components involved in a file transfer using FTP is shown in Figure 14.13. The computer initiating the transfer request is called the client and the computer responding to the request the server.

As we can see, each FTP entity consists of two parts: a control part and a data transfer part. The control part is concerned with the exchange of control messages – commands and their replies – relating to the file to be transferred, and the data transfer part with the actual transfer of the file contents.

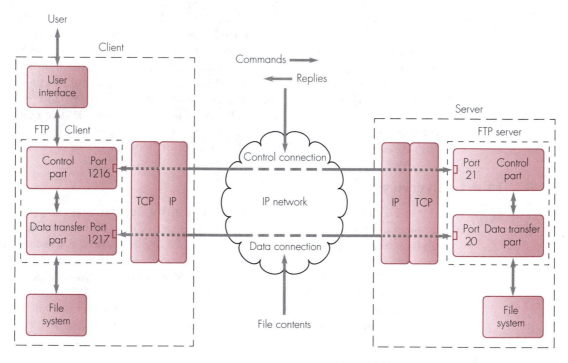

Ports 1216/1217 = ephemeral ports

Port 21 = well-known port of control connection
Port 20 = well-known port of data connection

Figure 14.13 FTP components and terminology.

The user interacts with his or her local FTP through an appropriate (user) interface. The user interface software then converts each command that is selected/entered by the user into a standard format that is understood by the FTP control part. There is also a standard format used for each FTP command and response message exchanged by the control part in the two computers.

On receipt of the first command from the user, the (FTP) control part in the client initiates the establishment of a TCP connection between itself and the control part in the server. This is called the **control connection** and it remains in place until the related file transfer has been carried out. The port number at the client side is an ephemeral port – shown as 1216 in Figure 14.13 – and that at the server side port 21 which is the well-known port number for the FTP control connection. The reply message to a command is returned by the control part in the server over the control connection.

A second TCP connection called the **data connection** is used for the transfer of the contents of a specified file. Once the control part in the client has sent and received the replies to all the command messages it has sent relating to the file transfer, it sends a further command informing the server side of the ephemeral port number that should be used for its side of the data connection. The control part in the client then issues a passive open and waits for a TCP connection request (SYN) segment from the server side. On receipt of the port number, the control part in the server proceeds to establish the TCP data connection using port 20 – the well-known port number for the FTP data connection – as the source port and the received ephemeral port as the destination port. Once this is in place, the contents of the specified file are transferred over this connection. Note that this can be in either direction depending on the command and after the transfer has taken place, the data connection is then closed by the side that sends the data. Finally, the control connection is closed by the client.

14.4.4 Command and reply message format

A selection of some of the more common command messages that are sent across the control connection (from the control part in the client to the control part in the server) are listed in part (a) of Table 14.3 and the structure of the reply messages that are returned in the opposite direction in part (b). All the command and reply messages are made up of ASCII characters. They are encoded for transmission into 8-bit NVT ASCII with each command/reply terminated by a CR/LF pair of characters.

As we can see, all the commands are in upper-case and many have parameters – referred to as arguments – associated with them. Most of the commands are self explanatory. In the case of the *PORT* command, however, the six parameters associated with it (n1–n6) are all decimal numbers. The four decimal numbers n1–n4 form the IP address of the client host in dotted decimal. The two numbers n5–n6 then specify the ephemeral port number

Table 14.3 FTP client–server communication: (a) example commands; (b) structure of the replies.

(a) Command	Description
USER username	User name on the (FTP) server
PASS password	User's password on the server
SYST	Type of operating system requested
TYPE type	File type to be transferred: A (ASCII), I (Image/Binary)
PORT n1, n2, n3, n4, n5, n6	Client IP address (n1–n4) and port number (n5, n6)
RETR filename.type	Retrieve (get) a file
STOR filename.type	Store (put) a file
LIST filelist	List files or directories
QUIT	Log off from server

(b) Reply	Description
1yz	Positive reply, wait for another reply before sending a new command
2yz	Positive reply, a new command can be sent
3yz	Positive reply, another command is awaited
4yz	Negative reply, try again
5yz	Negative reply, do not retry
x0z	Syntax
x1z	Information
x2z	Control or data connection
x3z	Authentication
x4z	Unspecified
x5z	File status

for the data connection on the client side. Each port number is 16 bits long and n5 is the decimal equivalent of the most significant 8 bits and n6 the least significant 8 bits. Hence the two parameters n5 and n6 for port 1217 would be 4, 193; that is, $4 \times 256 + 193$.

Each of the reply messages comprises a 3-digit code followed by an optional text message. The first digit indicates the type of reply, positive (successful) or negative. The second digit expands on this by indicating to what the reply relates (control or data connection, data, and so on) and the third digit gives additional information relating to error messages. A selection of some of the more common reply messages, together with a typical text message, are as follows:

220   FTP server ready
331   Password required for <username>
230   User <username> logged in
215   Server OS Name Type: Version
200   File type acknowledged
200   PORT command successful
150   Opening ASCII/Binary mode data connection for <file name>
226   File transfer complete
221   Goodbye
425   Data connection cannot be opened
500   Unrecognized command
501   Invalid arguments
530   User access denied

14.4.5   Example

In order to illustrate the use of some of the listed commands and their replies we shall show some example message exchanges.

There are three types of file transfer supported over the data connection:

- the transfer of the contents of a named file from the client file system to the server system;
- a similar transfer in the server–client direction;
- the transfer of the listings of the files (or the directories in a file) held by the server and saved in a named file on the client.

A typical exchange of commands and replies to carry out (successfully) the transfer of a named file and file type from the server file system to the client system is shown in Figure 14.14. The following additional comments should be noted when interpreting the exchange sequence:

- The client FTP control part has a resolver procedure linked to it and, when the DNS name of the server is passed to it by the user interface, it uses the resolver to obtain the IP address of the server.
- If the user had issued a put<filename.type>, then the client (control part) would send a STOR<filename.type> command. Also, since the file transfer is in the client–server direction, if the TYPE is I, then the client would initiate the closure of the data connection.

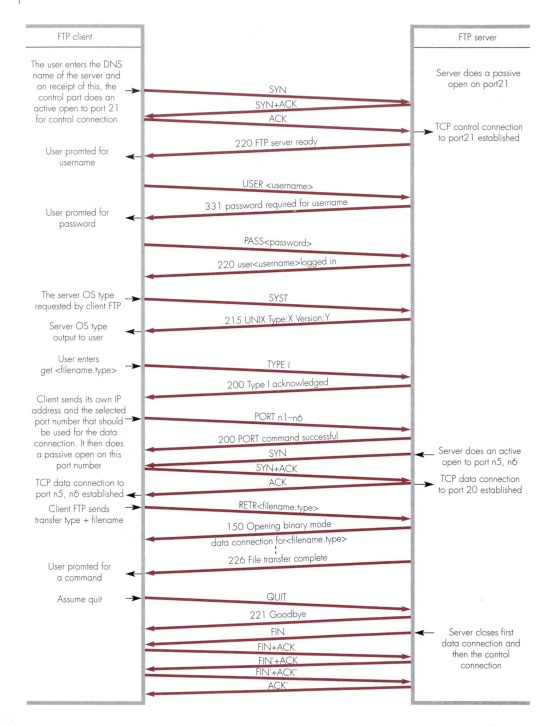

Figure 14.14 Example of command–reply message exchange sequence to get a file from the FTP server.

14.4.6 Anonymous FTP

The example shown in Figure 14.14 assumed that the (client) user had a username/password on the named server. This is not always the case since FTP is also used to access information from a server that allows unknown users to log in to it. To access information from this type of server, the user must know the DNS name of the server but, when prompted for a username, he or she enters *anonymous* and, for the password, his or her email address. Normally, in response, the server replies with something like

> 230 Visitor login ok, access granted

at which point the same procedure shown in the example in Figure 14.14 follows.

In some instances, however, before granting the user access, the server carries out a rudimentary check that the client host has a valid domain name. Although the IP address of the client host has not been formally sent at this point – this does not occur until the PORT command is sent – it is present in the (IP) source address field of each of the IP datagrams that have been used to set up the (TCP) control connection and to send the username and password. Hence before granting access, the control part in the server uses its own resolver to check that the IP address of the host is in the DNS database. As we saw earlier in the latter part of Section 14.2.5, this involves the control part issuing a pointer query to the resolver with the host IP address in the query name. If a valid domain name is returned, then access is granted as before. If a negative response is received then access to the server is blocked and, typically, the server sends a reply of

> 530 User access denied, unknown IP address

14.5 TFTP

As we mentioned at the start of Section 14.4, TFTP is used mainly in applications in which one of the two communicating hosts does not have a hard disk. Typically, TFTP is then used to download – normally referred to as bootstrapping – the application code that is to be run on the diskless host. We showed an application of TFTP earlier in Figure 11.5 and, as we explained in the accompanying text, it is used to download the application code for cable modems from the cable modem termination system (CMTS). As we showed in the figure, TFTP uses UDP as the transport protocol since this is less complicated than TCP and hence requires less memory. The specification of TFTP is given in **RFC 1350**.

14.5.1 Protocol

There are just five message types (PDUs) associated with the TFTP protocol and their format is shown in Figure 14.15. The first field in each message is called the *opcode* and indicates the message type. The different types are shown in the figure.

As with FTP the host/item of equipment that initiates a transfer is called the client and the host that responds to the request the server. Each transfer starts with the client making a request to the server either for a named file – read request – or to receive a named file – write request. Hence in an application such as downloading code, the diskless host is the client and the first message that is sent is a *read request (RRQ)*. The *filename* field in the message is used to specify the name of the file on the server to be transferred/downloaded. The filename is an NVT ASCII string that is terminated by a byte of zero. This is followed by the *mode* field which is also an NVT ASCII string indicating whether the file contents are lines of ASCII text – *netascii* – or a string of 8-bit bytes – *octet*. In both cases the string is terminated by a byte of zero.

The contents of the requested file are transferred by the server in one or more *DATA* messages. Since UDP is a best-effort protocol, normally an error control protocol is used to transfer the complete file contents. The protocol supported is based on the stop-and-wait (idle RQ) error control scheme. It is a variant of the protocol we showed earlier in Figure 6.23, the difference being that there are no NAK messages and hence the retransmission of a lost DATA message is triggered by the timer for the message expiring. An example message exchange illustrating the main features of the protocol is shown in Figure 14.16.

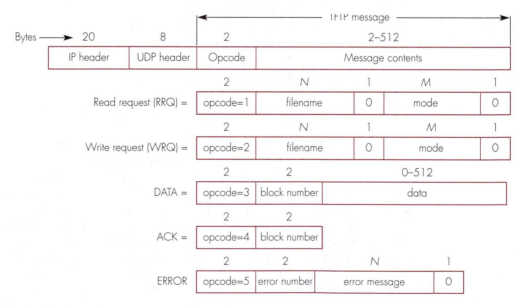

Figure 14.15 TFTP PDU message formats.

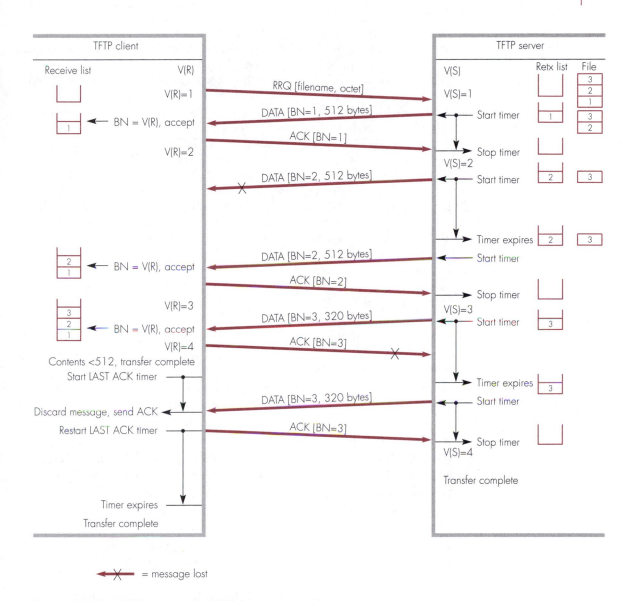

Figure 14.16 TFTP example PDU message exchange.

Recall that with the idle RQ protocol, the total message – the file contents – are first divided into multiple blocks the size of each block
determined by the characteristics of the underlying data link/transport service. With the TFTP protocol the maximum size of each block – the *data* field
in each DATA message – is 512 bytes. The end of a message/file transfer is
then indicated when a DATA message is received containing less than 512
bytes in it, that is, a data field containing from 0–511 bytes.

As with idle RQ, to detect duplicates, each DATA message contains a sequence number – called the *block number* (*BN*) in TFTP – in the message header and, on receipt of each error-free DATA message, an *ACK* message is returned containing the same BN within it as that contained in the DATA message. To implement the scheme, the server side maintains a send sequence variable, V(S), which contains the BN that is to be allocated to the next DATA message to be transmitted, and the client side maintains a receive sequence variable, V(R), which indicates the BN in the next in-sequence DATA message it expects to receive. Both are initialized to 1.

The transfer starts with the client sending a RRQ message containing the filename and file type. In response, the server proceeds to send the contents of the filename. In the example file transfer shown in Figure 14.16 the file contents are assumed to require three DATA messages shown as 1, 2, and 3. The following should be noted when interpreting the sequence shown:

- The first DATA message (BN = 1) is assumed to be received and acknowledged correctly and hence both V(S) and V(R) are now incremented to 2.

- The second DATA message (BN = 2) is corrupted and hence is not received. This can be due, for example, to the IP datagram containing the DATA message being discarded during its transfer or the checksum in the UDP header failing in the client.

- At the server side, the absence of an ACK for BN2 means that the retransmission timer expires and another attempt is made to send it.

- This time it is assumed to be received correctly and both V(S) and V(R) are now incremented to 3.

- When the last DATA message is sent (BN = 3), this is received free of errors and hence V(R) is incremented to 4 and an ACK is returned with BN = 3.

- During its transfer, the ACK is corrupted/lost and hence the retransmission timer in the server expires. The server retransmits another copy of BN3 which is assumed to be received error free.

- The client determines from the BN that the message is a duplicate – BN = 3 instead of 4 – and hence discards it but returns an ACK to stop the server from sending another copy.

- The client determines that the file has now been received by the fact that the contents of BN3 are less than 512 bytes.

- The LAST ACK timer is used to allow for the possibility of the last ACK being lost.

- Should the number of attempts to send a block exceed a defined limit, then an error message is sent and the transfer aborted.

In the case of a write request, the client sends a WRQ message with the filename and mode in it and, if the server is prepared to accept the file, it returns an ACK message with a BN = 0. The client side then proceeds to send the file contents using the same procedure as for a read request.

A number of error messages are also provided. The particular error message is indicated by the value in the *error number* field. The contents in the *error message* field then contain an additional text message in NVT ASCII that is terminated by a byte of zero. In addition, even though there is no authentication procedure associated with TFTP, in most implementations the server only allows the client to read or write from/to a specific file name or names.

14.6 Internet telephony

Unlike email which uses the services provided by the message transfer system as an intermediary between the two (or more) communicating participants, Internet telephony requires a communications path that supports real-time communications between the two or more participants involved in the call/session. Also, although the early IETF standards relating to Internet telephony were concerned with providing a basic two-party telephony service between two IP hosts, the more recent standards provide a more versatile facility supporting multiparty calls/sessions involving audio, video, and data integrated together in a dynamic way. The number of participants involved can vary as the session proceeds. Also, the location of each participant is not necessarily at a fixed IP address. For example, at one point in time a participant may be using a workstation attached to an enterprise network while at another time using a PC at home or, possibly, a fixed or mobile phone.

Thus the main requirement associated with Internet telephony is a set of signaling protocols that support, in addition to call/session establishment, features for dynamic user location and the negotiation of a suitable set of capabilities that are supported by all the user devices involved. In this section we describe the main features of three of the protocols that have been defined by the IETF to provide these services. These are the **session initiation protocol** (**SIP**), the **session description protocol** (**SDP**), and the **gateway location protocol** (**GLP**).

14.6.1 SIP

SIP provides services for user location, call/session establishment, and call participation management. It is a simple request-response – also known as transaction – protocol and is defined in **RFC 2543**. The user of a host device that wants to set up a call sends a request message – also known as a command or method – to the user of the called host device which responds by returning a suitable response message. Both the request and response are made through an application program/process called the **user agent** (**UA**) which maps the request and its response into the standard message format used by SIP.

Each UA comprises two parts, a **UA client** (**UAC**), which enables the user to send request messages – to initiate the setting up of a call/session for example – and a **UA server** (**UAS**) which generates the response message determined by the user's response. A schematic diagram showing a typical stack associated with Internet telephony is shown in Figure 14.17(a) and a list of the request and response messages used by SIP – together with their usage – is shown in part (b).

(a)

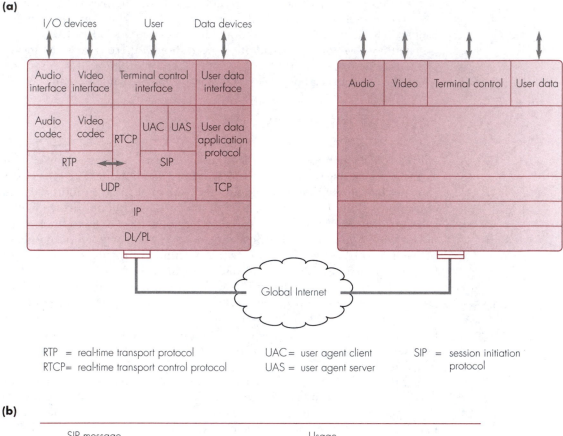

Figure 14.17 Internet telephony: (a) example host device protocol stack; (b) SIP request/response signaling message types.

(b)

SIP message	Usage
INVITE	Invites a user to join a call/session
ACK	Used to acknowledge receipt of an INVITE response messge
REGISTER	Used to inform a SIP redirect server of the current location of a user
OPTIONS	Used to request the capabilities of a host device
CANCEL	Terminates a search for a user
BYE	Inform the other user(s) that the user is learning a call/session

Each request and response message comprises a header and a body. The header contains a set of fields a number of which are similar to those used with email. For example, a selection of the header fields associated with the INVITE request/response message include:

To:	The SIP address of the called participant
From:	The SIP address of the caller
Subject:	A brief title of the call
Call-ID:	Unique call identifier assigned by the caller
Require:	List of capabilities the host device can support
Content-Type:	Type of information in the message body
Content-Length:	Length of body contents

Each SIP name/address is similar to an email name/address with the addition that it has a prefix of *sip*. Hence two example SIP name/addresses might be *sip:tom.C@university.edu* and *sip:karen.S@company.com*.

The type of call/session being set up is determined by the contents of the message body which describes the individual media streams to be used in the call. These are defined using the companion SDP protocol which we describe in the next section.

As we have just seen, a SIP name/address is similar to an email name/address. Hence before a SIP message can be sent over the Internet it is necessary first to obtain the IP address of the intended recipient host. As we indicated earlier, a user may be contactable at a number of alternative locations. Hence when a user registers to use the Internet telephony service, the user provides a number of alternative SIP addresses where it can be located. For example, karen.S may be contactable at either *sip:karen.S@company.com* or *sip:karen.S@organization.org*. This list of names is then sent to a server called the *redirect server* at each of the sites involved – for example, *company.com* and *organization.org* – using a REGISTER message with the list of alternative addresses in the *Contact:* header field.

To explain how a call/session is set up we shall use two examples. In the first, we assume the called user is currently at the given SIP address. Figure 14.18(a) shows the protocols and network components that are used to set up the call. To simplify the description, assume that the SIP name/address of the calling user is *sip:tom.C@university.edu* and that of the called user is *sip:karen.S@company.com*.

Associated with each access network – enterprise network, campus, and so on – is a second server called a *proxy server* to which all SIP INVITE messages are sent. In the figure we show these as PS-A and PS-B. Each host knows the IP address of its local proxy server. Also, the proxy server knows the SIP name and address of each user that is currently logged in at the site and the IP address of the user's host device. Typically, the latter is determined using ARP.

On receipt of an INVITE request message from the calling host, PS-A first reads the SIP name/address from the *To:* field in the message header and proceeds to obtain the IP address of the proxy server for *company.com* (PS-B) using the domain name service (DNS). On receipt of this, the SIP in PS-A sends the INVITE request message to PS-B. The latter first reads the SIP name/address from the *To:* field in the message header and determines from

(a)

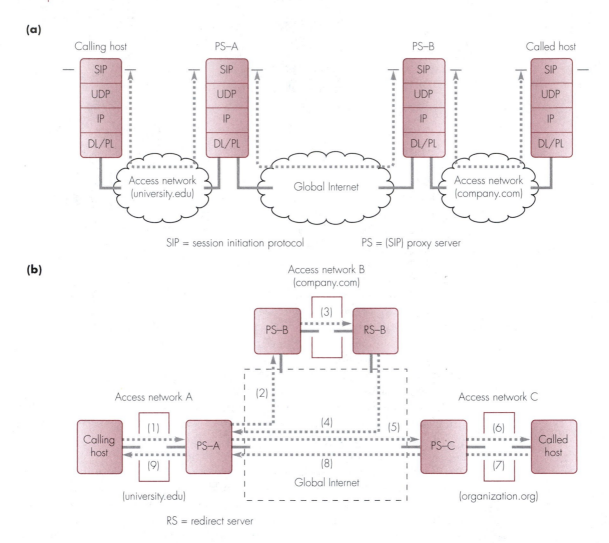

SIP = session initiation protocol   PS = (SIP) proxy server

(b)

RS = redirect server

Figure 14.18 SIP message routing examples: (a) direct using proxy servers; (b) indirect using a redirect server.

this firstly, that *karen.S* is currently logged in at this location and secondly, the local IP address of the called host. It then uses the IP address to send the INVITE request to the called host. Assuming the latter is able to accept the call, an INVITE response message is returned over the same path. On receipt of this, the SIP in the calling host returns an ACK message and it is at this point that the two users/hosts can start to exchange the information relating to the call.

In the second example we assume that the called user *sip:karen.S* is currently located at *organization.org* not *company.com*. Hence this time, on receipt of the INVITE request from PS-A, PS-B determines that *karen.S* is not currently logged in at this location and hence forwards the request to the redirect server for the site, RS-B. As we indicated earlier, the latter has the list of alternative SIP addresses for this user and determines from this that *karen.S* can also be located at *organization.org*. The SIP in RS-B returns this information in a *Contact:* header field in the INVITE response message. On receipt of this, PS-A proceeds as before but this time by first obtaining the IP address of the SIP proxy server at *organization.org* using the DNS. A summary of the message sequence involved is shown in Figure 14.18(b).

14.6.2 SDP

As we indicated earlier, the role of the session description protocol (SDP) is to describe the different media streams that are to be involved in a call/session and also additional information relating to the call. This is described in each SIP message body in a textual format and includes:

- media streams: a multimedia call/session may involve a number of different media streams including speech, audio, video, and more general data. The proposed list of media types and their format are contained in the message body. Each SIP INVITE request message contains a list of the media types and the compression formats that are acceptable to the calling user (host device) and the INVITE response message contains a possibly modified version of this that collectively indicates what is acceptable to the called user;

- stream addresses: for each media stream, the destination address and UDP port number for sending and/or receiving each stream is indicated;

- start and stop times: these are used with broadcast sessions and enable a user to join a session during the time the broadcast is being carried out.

14.6.3 GLP

The two examples we considered in Section 14.6.1 assumed that the two host devices – or more if multicast addresses are used – were both attached directly to the Internet. In some instances, however, one of the host devices may be attached to a different network such as a PSTN or ISDN. Such cases require a device called a gateway to convert the different signaling messages – a **signaling gateway** (**SGW**) – and the different media formats – a **media gateway** (**MGW**).

In practice, both the PSTN/ISDN and the Internet are global networks/ internetworks. Hence when the called user is attached to a PSTN/ISDN, because of the potentially higher bandwidth associated with the Internet, it is preferable to utilize the Internet for as much of the connection path as possible. To do this requires, firstly, a gateway associated with each PSTN/ISDN access network and secondly, when a call is made, to utilize the gateway that is closest to the called – or calling – user. As we saw earlier in Figure 9.9, the

Internet is composed of an interconnected set of networks/internetworks. Typically, therefore, each Internet regional/national network has a number of gateways associated with it. Also, each of these networks has one or more **location servers (LS)**. This general architecture is shown in Figure 14.19.

As we can deduce from the figure, when the called user device is attached to a segment/subnet of a PSTN/ISDN, the SIP INVITE message must be sent to the (signaling) gateway that is nearest to the segment/subnet to which the called terminal equipment is attached. The main issue, therefore, is, given a conventional telephone number, how is the INVITE message routed to the gateway that is nearest to the subscriber with this number? This is the role of the location servers and their operation is as follows.

Each gateway knows the regional/national code of the segment of the PSTN/ISDN to which it is attached. Typically this is entered by network management. In addition, on the Internet side, each gateway has an IP address and it also knows the IP address of the LS(s) that is (are) attached to the same (Internet) regional/national network. Each gateway then uses the IP address of each of its local LSs to inform them of the regional/national code of the segment of the PSTN/ISDN to which it is attached. In this way, each LS

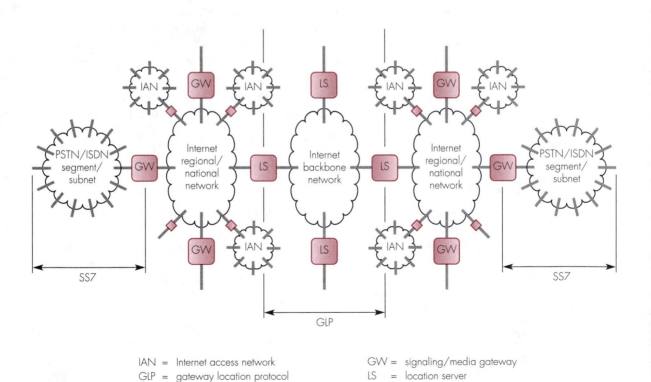

IAN = Internet access network
GLP = gateway location protocol
SS7 = signaling system number 7

GW = signaling/media gateway
LS = location server

Figure 14.19 Interworking between Internet hosts and PSTN/ISDN terminal equipment.

learns the regional/national codes of the segments of the PSTN/ISDN to which all of its gateways are attached and, from this, the IP address of the gateway that should be used for each of these codes.

Each LS then exchanges this information with each of the other LSs using the gateway location protocol (GLP). In this way each LS builds up a database of the IP address of the LS that should be used to reach all of the gateways in other regional/national networks and also the PSTN/ISDN codes associated with each of these gateways. Thus the gateway local protocol which carries out this function is very similar to the interdomain routing protocol BGP – the border gateway protocol – which we described earlier in Section 9.6.5. Indeed, GLP is based on BGP and hence we shall not expand upon it here.

14.7 SNMP

The simple network management protocol (SNMP) is concerned not with providing Internet-wide application services to users – SMTP, FTP, and so on – but rather with the management of all the networking equipment and protocols that make up the Internet. As we saw in earlier chapters, the Internet is composed of a range of different items of networking equipment. These include LAN bridges, subnet routers, access gateways, interior gateways/routers, exterior gateways, communication links/subsystems, and so on, all of which need to be functioning correctly.

Clearly, in any networking environment, if a fault develops and service is interrupted, users will expect the fault to be corrected and normal service to be resumed with a minimum of delay. This is often referred to as **fault management**. Similarly, if the performance of the network – for example, its response time or throughput – starts to deteriorate as a result of, say, increased levels of traffic in selected parts of the network, users will expect these to be identified and additional equipment/transmission capacity to be introduced to alleviate the problem. This is an example of **performance management**. In addition, most of the protocols associated with the TCP/IP suite have associated operational parameters, such as the time-to-live parameter associated with the IP protocol and the retransmission timer associated with TCP. As a network expands, such parameters may need to be changed while the network is still operational. This type of operation is known as **layer management**. Others include **name management**, **security management**, and **accounting management**.

Associated with each managed element – a protocol, bridge, gateway, and so on – is a defined set of management-related information. This includes variables – also known as **managed objects** – that can be either read or written to by the network manager via the network. It also includes, when appropriate, a set of **fault reports** that are sent by a managed element when a related fault occurs. In the case of IP, for example, a read variable may relate to, say, the number of IP datagrams/packets discarded when the time-to-live parameter expires, while a write variable may be the actual time-to-live timeout value. Similarly, in the case of an exterior gateway, if a neighbor gateway ceases to respond to hello messages, in addition to modifying its routing table to reflect the loss of the link, the gateway may create and send a fault report – via the network – to alert the management system of the problem. If the management system receives a number of such reports from other neighbors, it can conclude that the gateway is probably faulty and not just a communications line failure.

SNMP is an application protocol so a standard communication platform must be used to enable associated messages – PDUs – to be transferred concurrently with the messages relating to user services. To achieve this, normally SNMP uses the same TCP/IP protocols as the user application protocols. The general scheme is shown in Figure 14.20.

The role of the SNMP is to allow the **manager process** in the manager station to exchange management-related messages with the management processes – each referred to as a **management agent** – running in the various managed elements: hosts, gateways, and so on. The management process in

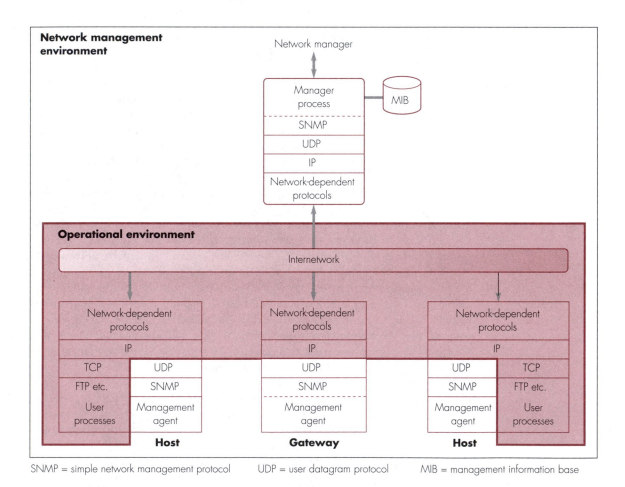

Figure 14.20 Network management schematic and terminology.

these elements is written to perform the defined management functions asso-ciated with that element. Examples include responding to requests for specified variables (counts), receiving updated operational variables, and generating and sending fault reports.

Management information associated with a network/internet is kept at the network manager station (host) associated with that network/internet in a **management information base** (**MIB**). A network manager is provided with a range of services to interrogate the information in the MIB, to initiate the entry and collection of additional information, and to initiate network config-uration changes. Clearly, the manager station is the nerve center of the complete network, so strict security and authentication mechanisms are imple-mented. Normally, there are various levels of authority depending on the operation to be performed. In large internetworks like the Internet, multiple manager stations are used, each responsible for a particular part of the Internet. Examples include each campus/enterprise access network, each regional/national network, the global backbone network and its gateways, and so on. We shall describe first the structure of the management information associated with the Internet and then the operation of the SNMP protocol.

14.7.1 Structure of management information

The management agent software in each networking element maintains a defined set of variables – managed objects – which are accessible by the net-work manager process using SNMP. In some instances, a variable can only be read (read-only) and in others it can also be written to (read-write). The MIB contains a similar set of variables/objects each of which reflects the current value/state of the same variable in the managed element.

Clearly, in a large network/internet, the managed equipment may come from a variety of different vendors, each with its own preferred processor/ micro-processor. Hence, since all the management information relating to each item of equipment is to be processed by a single management process – often running in a computer that has a different processor from that used in the managed equip-ment – it is essential to ensure that the management information relating to each item of equipment has the same meaning in both the equipment and the man-ager station. As we explained in section 13.2, one way of achieving this is to define the data types of each of the managed objects associated with each item of equipment using ASN.1. Then, to ensure that the value(s) associated with each managed object is interpreted in the same way in both the equipment and the manager station, before each value is transferred over the network it is first con-verted into the related standard transfer syntax using the basic encoding rules associated with ASN.1. This is now the standard approach used with most net-work management systems including that associated with the Internet.

The current version of the MIB for the Internet is **MIB-II** and is defined in **RFC 1213**. The data types of all the variables (managed objects) in the MIB are a subset of the ASN.1 types we described in Section 13.2.1. These are listed in Figure 14.21(a). In addition, a number of subtypes are used and a selection of these, together with a description of their use, is given in Figure 14.21(b).

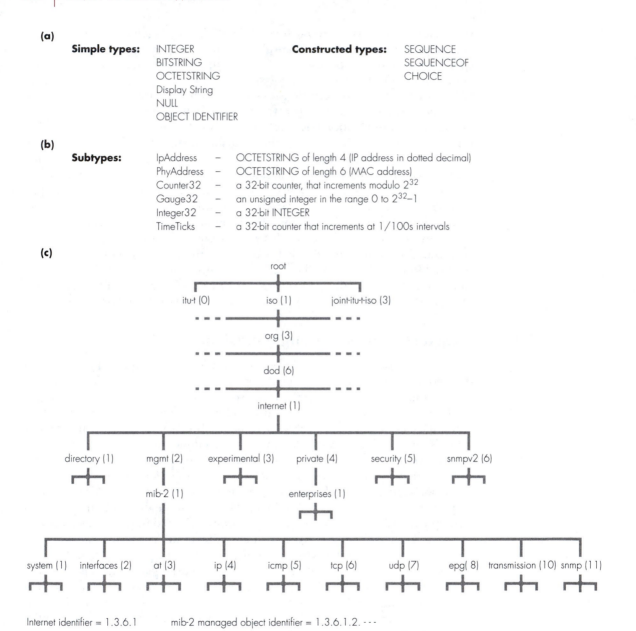

(a)

Simple types:	INTEGER	Constructed types:	SEQUENCE
	BITSTRING		SEQUENCEOF
	OCTETSTRING		CHOICE
	Display String		
	NULL		
	OBJECT IDENTIFIER		

(b)

Subtypes:
- IpAddress – OCTETSTRING of length 4 (IP address in dotted decimal)
- PhyAddress – OCTETSTRING of length 6 (MAC address)
- Counter32 – a 32-bit counter, that increments modulo 2^{32}
- Gauge32 – an unsigned integer in the range 0 to $2^{32}-1$
- Integer32 – a 32-bit INTEGER
- TimeTicks – a 32-bit counter that increments at 1/100s intervals

(c)

Internet identifier = 1.3.6.1   mib-2 managed object identifier = 1.3.6.1.2. - - -

Note: at group not used in MIB-II and there is no group (9)

Figure 14.21 Structure of management information: (a) ASN.1 types used; (b) subtypes; (c) portion of ASN.1 object naming tree relating to the Internet.

As we explained at the end of Section 13.2.1, the OBJECT IDENTIFIER data type is used to identify a managed object within the context of an internationally defined object naming tree. The portion of this tree that relates to the Internet MIB is shown in Figure 14.21(c).

As we can see, each branch node in the tree is identified by means of a label and a number. A specific node is then identified by listing either the label – together with its number – or simply the number of each branch node starting at the root. In this way, all the managed objects within the total Internet MIB can be uniquely identified and all start with

iso(1) org(3) dod(6) internet(1) mgmt(2) mib-2(1) ...

or, more usually,

1.3.6.1.2.1 ...

Note that the address translation (at) group – arp and rarp – is not present in MIB-II as this is now part of the ip group. Note also that there is no group (9) and that path 1.3.6.1.4.1 is defined for vendor-specific MIBs. This is necessary to ensure that there is no ambiguity when equipment from a number of different vendors is being used.

Each item of equipment that is to be managed, and the various managed objects associated with it, are defined using the object name tree shown in Figure 14.21(c) as a template. The system(1) group contains a number of variables that include the name (textual description) of the equipment, the vendor's identity, the hardware and software it contains, the domain name of the equipment, and its location on the Internet. All the management information that is subsequently obtained from this location relates to the given named item of equipment in the object name tree.

Each managed object can be defined either as an individual entity or, more usually, as a member of a larger group of related objects. Also related groups of objects can be defined in the form of a module. For example, a group may contain all the managed objects (variables) associated with a particular protocol such as IP while a module may contain the complete set of managed object groups associated with a particular item of equipment.

Each managed object definition is in the form of a macro with a minimum of four defined parameters associated with it. An example of an object/variable definition relating to the eighteenth variable in the IP group is as follows:

IpFragFails OBJECT TYPE
SYNTAX Gauge32   -- a count value up to $2^{32}-1$
MAX-ACCESS read-only   -- the manager station can only read this object
STATUS current   -- the object is currently supported
DESCRIPTION "Number of IP datagrams described because don't fragment flag set"
::={ip18}

As we can see, the object/variable name precedes the reserved word OBJECT TYPE. The meaning of the four required parameters associated with each object definition are:

■ SYNTAX: this defines the data type of the object;

■ MAX-ACCESS: defines whether the variable is read-only or read-write (as viewed from the manager station);

■ STATUS: indicates whether the variable is current or obsolete;

■ DESCRIPTION: an ASCII string describing what the object is used for. When the macro is invoked, the final ::= sign places the variable into the object name tree of the device.

When a number of groups are collectively defined in a module, the module is defined using a macro that starts with MODULE-IDENTITY. Its parameters include the name and address of the implementer of the module and its revision history. This is followed by an OBJECT-IDENTITY macro, which identifies where the module is located in the object name tree, and a list of OBJECT TYPE macros.

Each managed object in the MIB is uniquely identified and some examples relating to the *ip* group are shown in Figure 14.22. As we can see, an object can be either a simple variable with a single value – for example *ipForwarding(1)* – or a table containing a set of variables – for example *ipAddrTable(21)*. The object identifier of a simple variable in the MIB is the name/identifier of the variable/object with .0 appended to it. For example, the simple variable *ipForwarding* – which indicates whether the system is forwarding IP datagrams (=1) or not (2) – is accessed using either *ipForwarding.0* or, more specifically, as 1.3.6.1.2.1.4.1.0 since this is the form used by the

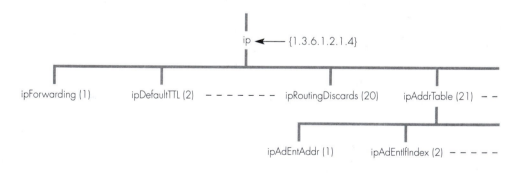

ipDefaultTTL identifier = 1.3.6.1.2.1.4.2.0
ipAdEntAddr identifier = 1.3.6.1.2.1.4.21.1

Figure 14.22 Example MIB objects in the ip group.

SNMP protocol to transfer the value over the Internet. In the case of a table of values, normally the index used is the name/identifier of the table and this is then followed by a string of get-next value commands until the complete table of values has been obtained. For example, assuming the table *ipAddrTable(21)* – which contains the list of addresses (IP address, subnet mask) and other information – this would be accessed using first *ipAddrTable* – 1.3.6.1.2.1.4.21.

14.7.2 Protocol

As we can deduce from the previous section, the management of an item of equipment – host, router, and so on – involves the manager process reading the current value of a defined set of variables (managed objects) that are being maintained by the agent process in the equipment and also with transferring a value to the agent for writing into a given variable. It also involves receiving fault reports from the agent in the equipment should these occur. To perform these functions, there is a set of request-response messages supported by the SNMP and also a separate command – known as a trap – message for fault reporting. The list of message/PDU types used in SNMPv1 are defined in RFC 1157. They are summarized in Figure 14.23(a).

Each SNMP message is transferred over the Internet as a separate entity using UDP. The UDP well-known port number of the SNMP in the agent for the three request messages is port 161 and that in the manager station for trap messages port 162. As we can deduce from this, the use of UDP as the transport protocol means that there is no guarantee that a message is delivered. Hence when this is deemed to be necessary, a timer is often used and, if a response is not received within a defined time interval, the request is resent.

The role of each of the five messages that are used is as follows:

- *Get-request*: this is used by the manager to get the current value(s) of one or more named variables from an agent. The agent then returns the value(s) using a *Get-response* message. The name/identity of each variable is in its numeric form and each value in the response message is encoded using the basic encoding rules of ASN.1 As we saw in Section 13.2.2, each returned value is in the form of a variable-length byte/octet string comprising a type, length, and value field. In the case of the *Get-request* message, the type of each value field(s) is set to Null;

- *Get-next-request*: this is used by the manager to get the next variable that is located in the MIB name tree immediately following each variable in the list of names in the message. These are then returned in a *Get-response* message. This type of message is used primarily to obtain the consecutive values relating to a table variable;

- *Set-request*: this is used by the manager to write a given set of values into the corresponding named variables;

(a)

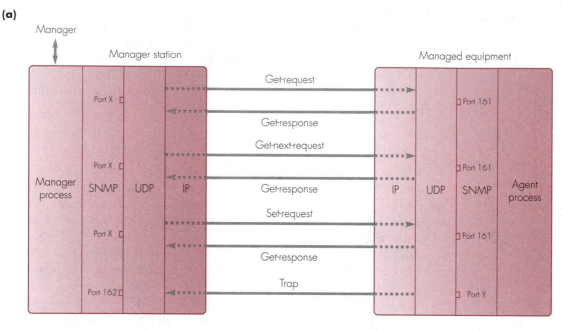

Port X/Y = ephemeral ports

(b)

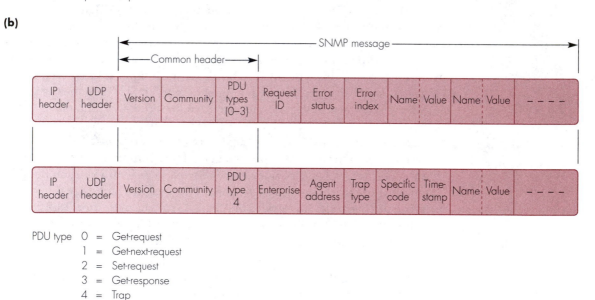

PDU type 0 = Get-request
          1 = Get-next-request
          2 = Set-request
          3 = Get-response
          4 = Trap

Figure 14.23 SNMPv1 messages/PDUs: (a) types and their sequence; (b) formats.

■ *Trap*: this is used by the agent in the equipment identified in the *enterprise* field to notify the manager of the occurrence of a previously defined event. The event type is specified by the value in the *trap type* field together with the value in the specific code field. The time of occurrence of the event is specified in the *time-stamp* field and, where appropriate, a number of related variable values may be returned.

The *community* field in the common header contains a character string that is a password in cleartext exchanged by the manager and agent. Typical examples are public and secret. The *request ID* field in PDU types 0–3 is used to enable the manager to relate a response to a specific request message. It is selected by the manager and is returned in the related response message. Finally, the *error status* is an integer value that is returned by an agent in a *Get-response* message. For example, a value of 0 indicates no errors, a value of 1 indicates the response is too big to fit into a single SNMP message and a value of 2 there is a nonexistent variable in the list. The latter is then identified by the value in the *error index* field.

SNMPv2

SNMP is continuously evolving and there is now a second version defined in **RFC 1441**. This is directed primarily at internets in which multiple manager stations are involved. The main additions in SNMPv2 are:

■ A new message type called *Get-bulk-request*. This has been added to enable the retrieval process of the contents of large tables to be carried out more efficiently.

■ A new message type called *Inform-request*. This has been added to enable a manager process in one manager station to send information to a manager process in another manager station.

■ An additional MIB for handling the variables associated with manager-to-manager communication.

■ The encryption of the password contained in the *community* field.

Summary

In this chapter we have studied the essential features of a selection of the most widely used application protocols of the Internet. These were the application protocols associated with electronic mail (SMTP and MIME), file transfers (FTP and TFTP), and Internet telephony (SIP, SDP, and GLP). In addition, we discussed two system-level application protocols that are essential for the correct functioning of the Internet (DNS and SNMP). The various topics that we have studied relating to these protocols are summarized in Figure 14.24.

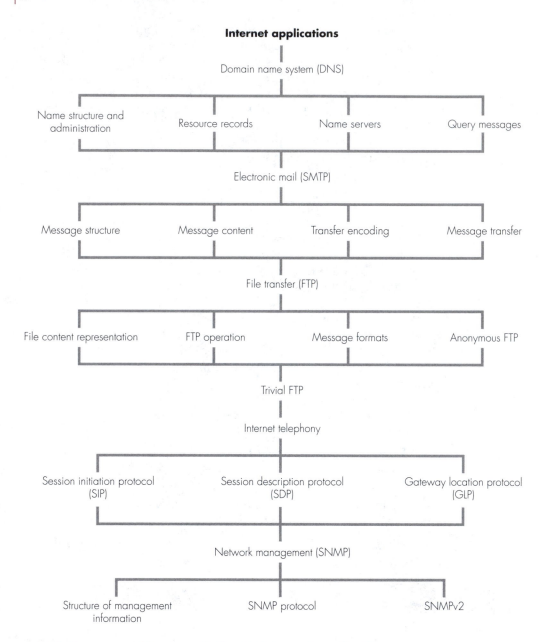

Figure 14.24 Summary of topics relating to Internet applications.

Exercises

Section 14.2

14.1 Explain why a domain name system (DNS) is required with the Internet and describe its main functional parts.

14.2 In relation to the DNS, explain why a hierarchical naming structure is used instead of a flat structure.

14.3 Show the structure adopted for the DNS in the form of a diagram. Include in your diagram:
  (i) the root domain,
  (ii) a selection of generic domains,
  (iii) a selection of country domains,
  (iv) some examples of fully qualified domain names.

14.4 Each domain name in the DNS name space/database has a resource record associated with it. With the aid of diagrams, explain:
  (i) the format of a resource record,
  (ii) the format used for a domain name,
  (iii) a selection of the resource record types,
  (iv) the use of the time-to-live field.

14.5 Show in outline the format of a DNS query and response message.
  Hence give an example of a query relating to a type-A name-to-address resolution query. State the use of the identification and flag fields used in the query header.

14.6 Explain the meaning of the following terms relating to the administration of DNS name servers:
  (i) zones,
  (ii) primary name server,
  (iii) secondary name server,
  (iv) authoritative (resource) records.

14.7 With the aid of a diagram, show the sequence of query/response messages that are exchanged to carry out a local name-to-address resolution. Include in your diagram a client host, a local name server, and a server host. Also include the resolver and the set of higher-level protocols that are used in each.

14.8 With the aid of a diagram, show the sequence of query/response messages that are exchanged to carry out a recursive name-to-address resolution. Include in your diagram a root name server, a top-level name server, and a lower-level name server.

14.9 With the aid of a diagram, show the sequence of query/response messages that are exchanged to carry out an iterative name-to-address resolution. Include in your diagram a top-level name server and a lower-level name server.

14.10 Explain the meaning of the term "pointer query" and why pointer queries cannot be resolved using the database structure shown in Figure 14.1. Hence with the aid of a diagram, show the extension to this structure that is used with pointer queries. Give an example showing how an IP address in a query message is resolved into a host name.

Section 14.3

14.11 With the aid of a diagram, explain the function/meaning of the following terms relating to email over the Internet. Include in your diagram two communicating hosts and two related mail servers. Also include the structure of the messages during their transfer over the access networks and the Internet:
  (i) user agent,
  (ii) message transfer agent,
  (iii) POP3,
  (iv) message transfer system,
  (v) SNMP.

14.12 List a selection of the fields that are present in a message header and the envelope header of an email message. Identify the use of each field in relation to the diagram you used in Exercise 14.11.
  Show how user-defined fields are added to the header and give an example of their use.

14.13 Explain the transfer syntax that is used for both the contents of a text-only email message and all the header fields. Include in your description how each field is delimited and how the end of the message header is indicated.

14.14 List a selection of the additional header fields that are used with MIME. Explain the use of each field and how the recipient UA determines the type of contents that are present in the message body and their transfer syntax.

14.15 By means of an example, show how a short message can be sent in both richtext and plaintext. Include the MIME headers that are required and how each form of the message is separated. Is the order of the two message types important?

14.16 Explain the transfer encoding scheme that is used to transfer messages comprising strings of 8-bit bytes. Include in your explanation the use of Base64 and how this relates to NVT ASCII.

14.17 A binary file containing a string of 8-bit audio samples is to be sent in an external file attached to an email message. Assuming the first three bytes in the file are:

　　10010101　　11011100　　00111011

use the Base64 table in Table 14.2 and the list of ASCII codewords in Figure 2.6(a) to show how these three bytes are converted and sent in NVT ASCII. Also how the recipient UA determines the original three bytes from the received NVT ASCII string.

14.18 A number of companies have been invited to prepare and submit a tender for a contract using email. To provide a high level of privacy and to authenticate each tender and ensure nonrepudiation, each company has been asked to encrypt their tender using PGP. By means of a block schematic diagram, assuming no compression is to be used, show the various steps that are followed to carry out:

(i) the authentication and nonrepudiation steps and
(ii) the encryption and decryption of the tender contents.

14.19 With the aid of a diagram, explain the function of the various components that make up the application process in a mail server to transfer an email message over the Internet. Include in your diagram the protocol stack that is used in two peer mail servers and also how the UA in each server interacts with the UA in each of the client hosts.

14.20 Using the list of SNMP command and response messages given in Figure 14.11, show a typical message interchange between an MTA client and an MTA server to transfer an email message over the Internet.

Section 14.4

14.21 With the aid of a diagram, describe the role of the control and data transfer parts of the AP in both a client and a server to transfer the contents of a file over a CTP/IP network using the file transfer protocol (FTP). Include in your description how the FTP in the client and the server are involved in the establishment and closing down of a TCP connection.

14.22 With the aid of a time sequence diagram, use the list of FTP command and reply messages given in Table 14.3 to show a typical exchange of messages to carry out the transfer of a named file from the file system on a server to the file system on a client. Explain how the port numbers in both the client and server sides are determined.

14.23 Outline the steps that are taken by a user to log in to a remote server using anonymous FTP. Explain how the server side performs a check on the user before granting the user access.

Section 14.5

14.24 Explain how trivial FTP (TFTP) is different from FTP. Give an example of the use of each protocol.

14.25 List the five message types associated with TFTP. Hence show an example message exchange that illustrates the main features of the protocol. Include in your example how the sending side detects a lost/corrupted data message and a lost/corrupted acknowledgment message. Also include the use of a LAST ACK timer.

Section 14.6

14.26 Outline the different types of call/session associated with Internet telephony. Hence identify the main requirements of the set of signaling protocols that are associated with it. Namely, the session initiation protocol (SIP), the session description protocol (SDP), and the gateway location protocol (GLP).

14.27 By means of a diagram, identify the protocol stack that is present in each host device that wishes to take part in an Internet telephony call/session. Describe briefly the role of each protocol.

14.28 In relation to the SIP, explain briefly the usage of the following (SIP) message types: INVITE, ACK, REGISTER, OPTIONS, CANCEL, and BYE.

14.29 List a selection of the header fields associated with a SIP INVITE message and state their use. Give an example of a SIP address.

14.30 Outline how a user informs the system that he or she can be contacted at a number of different locations using a SIP REGISTER message.

14.31 With the aid of a diagram, explain how a call/session is set up using SIP between a user and a called user who is currently located at their primary SIP address. Include in your diagram the proxy server at each of the sites involved and the protocol stack that is used in both hosts and proxy servers. Explain clearly the role that is carried out by the proxy servers.

14.32 With the aid of a diagram, explain how the sequence followed in Exercise 14.31 is different when the called user is currently located at a secondary address. Explain clearly the

role carried out by the redirect server in setting up the call/session.

14.33 Assuming the session description protocol is being used, explain the use of the following fields that may be present in the body part of a SIP INVITE message:
(i) media streams,
(ii) stream address,
(iii) start and stop times.

14.34 With the aid of a diagram, explain how interworking between a host that is attached to an IP network and a terminal equipment – a telephone for example – that is attached to a PSTN/ISDN is carried out. Include in your diagram a signaling/media gateway and a location server. Hence explain the role of the gateway location protocol (GLP) in relation to the interworking procedure.

Section 14.7

14.35 Describe the role of the simple network management protocol (SNMP) in relation to the Internet. Include in your description the role of fault, performance, and layer management and the meaning of the term "managed object".

14.36 By means of a diagram, show the protocol stack associated with a host and a router that enables them to be managed from a remote management station attached to the Internet. Include in your diagram a management agent and a manager process and explain how the two interact.

14.37 Explain the role of the management information base (MIB). Also explain why ASN.1 is used to define the structure of all the management information that it contains.

14.38 All managed objects within the Internet are identified within the context of an internationally defined object naming tree. By means of a diagram, show the structure of this tree down to a level that includes the various managed objects in a particular item of equipment. Give an example of the identifier of one of the managed objects in the tree.

14.39 Using the object naming tree you derived as part of Exercise 14.37 as a template, explain how a specific managed object within a particular item of equipment is (uniquely) identified.

14.40 By means of an example, show how a managed object/variable relating to the IP protocol is defined. Include in your definition an OBJECT TYPE, SYNTAX, STATUS, and DESCRIPTION parameter. State the role of each parameter and how the variable is placed in the object name tree of the device in the MIB.

14.41 By means of examples, show how each managed object/variable in the MIB is identified uniquely. Use for example purposes a variable with a single value and also one comprising a table of values.

14.42 With the aid of a diagram, list the five message/PDU types associated with SNMPv1. Include in your diagram the protocol stack and the well-known port numbers that are used.

Explain briefly the role of each of the five message types and how a lost message can be detected.

14.43 With the aid of the SNMP message/PDU formats defined in Figure 14.23(b), explain how a manager process obtains the current value of a named variable – managed object – from the agent process in a specified item of (managed) equipment. Include in your explanation the use of the Community, RequestID, Error Status, and Error Index fields in the SNMP messages/PDUs.

14.44 Outline the extensions to SNMPv1 that are present in SNMPv2. Hence explain how the security features of SNMPv1 have been enhanced.

The World Wide Web

15.1 Introduction

The World Wide Web – normally abbreviated to "the Web" or sometimes "the Net" – is a vast collection of electronic documents each composed of a linked set of pages that are written in HTML. The documents are stored in files on many thousands of computers that are distributed around the global Internet. The concepts behind the Web were conceived in 1989 by Tim Berners-Lee when he was working at the European Particle Physics Laboratory, CERN. An agreement was signed in 1994 between CERN and the Massachusetts Institute of Technology, MIT to set up a consortium whose aim was to further develop the Web and to standardize the protocols associated with it. The National Center for Supercomputing Applications (NCSA) also made a major contribution to the current widespread use of the Web with the development of MOSAIC which was the first interactive Web browser based on a graphical user interface. Since that time, many related developments have taken place and, in terms of volume, the Web is now the largest source of data transferred over the Internet.

We presented an overview of the operation of the Web and the essential protocols and standards associated with it in Section 5.4. In this chapter we expand upon these descriptions as we discuss the following:

- **URLs and HTTP**: a URL comprises the name of the file and the location of the server on the Internet where the file is stored while HTTP is the protocol used by a browser program to communicate with a server program over the Internet;

- **HTML**: this is used to define how the contents of each Web page are displayed on the screen of the user's machine – a PC, workstation, or set-top box – and to set up the hyperlinks with other pages;

- **forms and CGI script**: these are used in e-commerce applications. Fill-in forms are integrated into a Web page and displayed on the screen of the browser machine to get input from the user and a CGI script is then used at the server to process this information;

- **helper applications and plug-ins**: these are used to process and output multimedia information such as audio and/or video that is incorporated into an HTML page;

- **Java applets**: these are separate programs that are called from an HTML page and downloaded from a Web server. They are then run on the browser machine. Typically, they are used for code that may change or to introduce interactivity to a Web page such as for games playing;

- **JavaScript**: this is also used to add interactivity to a Web page but in this case the code is not a separate program but is included in the page's HTML code;

- **security** in e-commerce applications;

- **the operation of the Web** including the role of search engines and portals.

In relation to HTML and Java/JavaScript, since there are now many books on each of these topics, the aim here is to give sufficient detail for you to build up a working knowledge of them. Further details can then be found in the bibliography for this chapter.

15.2 URLs and HTTP

The Web is made up of a vast collection of documents/pages which are stored in files located on many thousands of (server) computers distributed around the global Internet. As we saw in Section 2.3.3, using HTML it is possible to create on a server an electronic document in the form of a number of pages with defined linkages between them. A user then gains access to a specific page using a client program called a browser which runs on a multimedia PC/workstation/set-top box that has access to the Internet.

Associated with each access request is the uniform resource locator (URL) of the requested file/page. This comprises the domain name of the server computer on which the file/page is stored and the file name. To obtain a page the browser communicates with a peer application process in the named Web server computer using the HyperText transfer protocol (HTTP). The contents of the named file are then transferred to the browser and displayed on the screen according to the HTML markup descriptions the page contains. A schematic diagram showing this overall mode of operation is given in Figure 15.1. In this section we describe first the structure of URLs and then the operation of HTTP. We defer how a URL is embedded into an HTML page until section 15.3 when we describe HTML in more detail.

15.2.1 URLs

The standard format of the URL of an HTML page consists of:

■ the application protocol to be used to obtain the page,
■ the domain name of the server computer,
■ the pathname of the file,
■ the file name.

Thus an example URL referring to an HTML page on the Web is:

http://www.mpeg.org/mpeg-4/index.html

where *http* is the protocol used to obtain the Web page, *www.mpeg.org* is the domain name of the server, */mpeg-4* is the path name, and *index.html* is the file name.

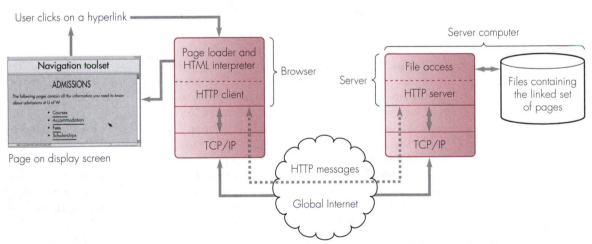

Note: Hyperlinks contain a URL which includes the domain name of the server computer and the name of the file containing the HTML code of the selected page

Figure 15.1 Basic principles and terminology associated with the World Wide Web.

The main services offered by a browser were identified earlier in the book in Figure 2.9. Normally, a browsing session starts by a user entering the URL of the home page associated with a particular document in the *location* field provided by the browser. If the URL of the page is not known then it can be obtained either from the user's own local Web/Net directory – which is built up from previously given or previously used URLs – or by using the search facility supported by the browser. We shall expand upon this feature later in Section 15.7. Once a URL has been entered, the browser proceeds to access the (home) page from the server named in the URL using the specified protocol and the given file name.

Note that when we access most home pages it is not necessary to specify the full URL since the server will look for the file named *index.html* if one is not specified. For example, the home page associated with the above URL could be specified as:

> *http://www.mpeg.org*

Note also that a final forward slash is used to indicate the URL relates to a directory rather than a file name. For example:

> *http://www.mpeg.org/mpeg-4/*

In addition to obtaining a page/file using HTTP, most browsers allow a user to obtain a file using a range of other application protocols. In general, these are standard Internet application protocols that predate the Web. For example, as we saw in Section 14.4, FTP is the standard Internet application protocol used to transfer a file. As a result, many servers still use FTP for all file transfers. Hence to obtain the contents of a file from such a server it is possible to specify *ftp:* as the protocol in a URL instead of *http:*. An example of a typical URL is then of the form:

> *ftp://yourcompany.com/pub/*

Typically, this file will contain the list of publications/files – note that *pub/* indicates a directory – that are available from the file server *yourcompany.com*. Normally, as we saw in Section 14.4.6, a user logs on to most public domain FTP servers using *anonymous* for the user name and his or her email address for the password. Hence these are entered when requested by the browser. The browser then obtains the file using the FTP protocol and displays the contents on the browser screen.

A protocol name of *file:* is used to indicate the file is located on the same computer as the browser; that is, your own computer. This is a useful facility when developing a Web page since it allows you to view the contents of the page before you make it available on the Web. An example URL is:

> *file://hypertext/html/mypage.htm*

Note that since some older versions of DOS allow only three characters in a file name extension, the final *l* of *html* is sometimes missing.

The *news:* protocol relates to an Internet application protocol defined in **RFC 977** called the **network news transfer protocol** (**NNTP**). It is used to transfer the text-only messages associated with **UseNet** which is also called **NetNews**. This consists of a world-wide collection of **newsgroups** each of which is a discussion forum on a specific topic. Two examples are COMP – which has topics relating to computers, computer science, and the computer industry – and SCI which has topics relating to the physical sciences and engineering. A person interested in a particular topic can subscribe to be a member of the related newsgroup. A subscriber can then post (send) an article to all the other members of the same newsgroup and receive the articles that are written by all the other members of the same group.

To do this, a user agent similar to that used with SMTP is used. This is called a **news reader** and the protocol that is used to transfer the messages associated with UseNet is NNTP. Some examples of the request/command messages associated with NNTP are:

- LIST: this is used to obtain a list of all the current newsgroups and their articles;
- GROUP *grp*: this is used to obtain a list of the articles associated with the newsgroup *grp*;
- ARTICLE *id*: this is used to obtain article *id*;
- POST *id*: this is used to send article *id* to the members of a specified newsgroup.

The *news:* protocol enables a member to both read a news article and to post an article from within a Web page. An example of a URL relating to a newsgroup involved in the preparation of HTML documents is:

news:comp.infosystems.www.authoring.html

Note that in this case the two forward slashes following the colon are not required. When this URL is entered, typically, the news reader part of the browser responds by first obtaining the list of articles on this topic using the GROUP command and the NNTP protocol. It then displays the articles on the screen in the form of a scrollable list. The user can then click on a specific article in the list and the browser/news reader will obtain the article contents using the ARTICLE command and display this on the screen. Normally, each article has the email address of the author, his or her affiliation, and the date the article was posted. A similar procedure is followed to post an article using the POST command. Normally, the user is prompted by the news reader for, say, the name of the (local) file containing the article. The file contents are then sent using NNTP.

The *gopher:* protocol relates to an Internet application protocol called **Gopher**. The Gopher system is similar in principle to the Web inasmuch as it is a global delivery and retrieval system of documents. In Gopher, however, all items of information are text only. When a user logs on to a Gopher server a hierarchical menu of files and directories is presented each of which may have links to the menus on other servers. A user can then access the contents of a file or directory by clicking on it. The *gopher:* protocol enables the user of the browser to do this within a Web page.

The *mailto:* protocol is provided to enable a user to send an email from within a Web page. Typically, this facility is initiated by the user entering a URL with *mailto:* in the protocol part. This is followed by the email address of the intended recipient. Normally, the (email) user agent part of the browser responds by displaying a **form** containing the other (email) header fields at the top (to be filled in) and space for the actual message. A facility is then provided to initiate the sending of the mail which, typically, is sent either SMTP or, if the email server supports it, HTTP. An example URL is:

mailto:yourname@youruniversity.edu

Note that the two forward slashes following the colon are not required with this protocol.

Universal resource identifiers (URIs)

A limitation of a URL is that it specifies a single host name. In many instances, however, a Web site may have so many access requests/hits for a particular document/page that copies of the document must be placed on multiple hosts. Also, to reduce the level of Internet traffic, each of these hosts may be geographically distributed around the Internet. To enable this to be implemented, an alternative page identifier called a URI can be specified with some browsers. Essentially, this is a generic URL since, typically, it contains only the file name. The remaining parts of the URL are determined by the context in which the URI is given and these are filled in by the browser itself. We shall given an example of this in the next section when we discuss cache servers.

15.2.2 HTTP

HTTP is the standard application protocol – also known as a method – that is used to obtain a Web page and also other items of information relating to a page such as an image or a segment of audio or video. The earlier version of HTTP is defined in **RFC 1945** and a later version (1.1) in **RFC 2068**. It is a simple request-response protocol: the browser side sends a request message and the server side returns a response message. Figure 15.2(a) shows the protocol stack associated with Web browsing, and a selection of the *commands/methods* associated with request messages, together with their use, are shown in part (b) of the figure.

In general, these are self explanatory. Note, however, that the GET method is used also to, say, obtain an image or segment of audio – shown as a

(a)

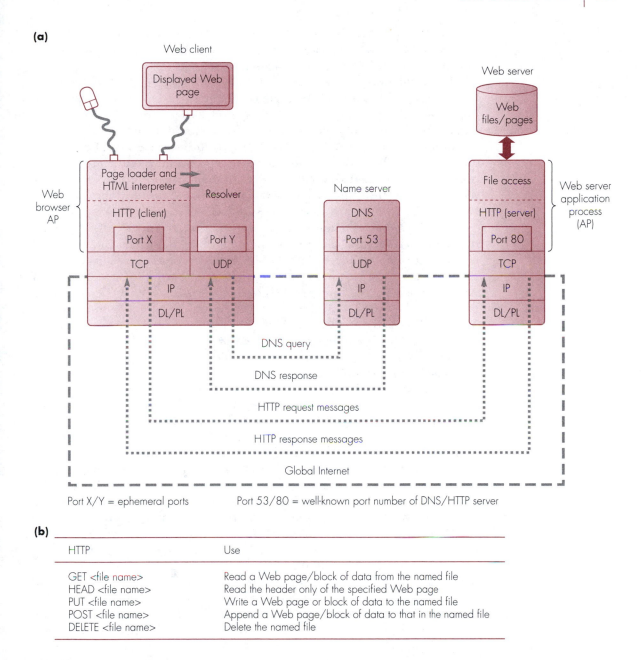

Port X/Y = ephemeral ports   Port 53/80 = well-known port number of DNS/HTTP server

(b)

HTTP	Use
GET <file name>	Read a Web page/block of data from the named file
HEAD <file name>	Read the header only of the specified Web page
PUT <file name>	Write a Web page or block of data to the named file
POST <file name>	Append a Web page/block of data to that in the named file
DELETE <file name>	Delete the named file

Figure 15.2 HTTP principles: (a) protocol stack; (b) a selection of the requests/methods supported.

block of data – from a named file. We shall expand upon this in later sections. Also, as we shall see in Section 15.3.6, the POST method is used to send the information entered by a user in e-commerce applications.

The well-known port number of HTTP is port 80. The Web server application process (AP) at each Web site continuously listens to this port for an incoming TCP connection request (SYN) from a Web browser. Note that in a Unix machine the AP is referred to as a **daemon** and the HTTP in these machines is sometimes called **HTTPD**. When a browser has an HTTP request message to send, it initiates the establishment of a new TCP connection to port 80 on the named server in the URL. It then initiates the sending of the request message over the established connection and, with earlier versions of HTTP, after the related response message has been received correctly by the browser, the server initiates the release of the connection. The TCP connection associated with this mode of operation is called **nonpersistent**.

As we can deduce from our earlier discussion of TCP in Section 12.3.2, the use of a new TCP connection for each request/response message transfer has a number of disadvantages. First, when accessing a Web page that contains multiple entities within it – an image for example – a time delay is incurred for each entity that is transferred while a new TCP connection is established. This is a function of the network round-trip time (RTT) which can be significant. Second, each new transfer starts with the slow start procedure and hence for a large entity, this can lead to additional delays.

To reduce the effect of these delays, when multiple entities are specified within a page – and hence to be transferred – many browsers set up a number of TCP connections so that each entity can be transferred concurrently. Typically, a browser may establish up to five or even 10 concurrent connections. However, although this can reduce the overall time delay associated with a Web access, the use of multiple connections leads to added overheads at both the client and server sides since both must maintain state information for each of the connections. This can be particularly significant for a popular/busy server which may get many hundreds of concurrent requests.

Hence with later versions of HTTP – version 1.1 onwards – unless informed differently, the server side leaves the initial TCP connection in place for the duration of the Web session. The TCP connection is then called **persistent** and, once in place, the browser may send multiple requests without waiting for a response to be received. Typically, the end of a session is determined by a timer expiring when no further transfers over the connection take place. Note, however, that the different versions of HTTP can interwork with each other.

Message formats

All HTTP request and response messages are NVT ASCII strings similar to those used with SMTP. With the earlier versions of HTTP – up to HTTP version 0.9 – what are called *simple request/response messages* are used. This means there is no type information associated with the request message which comprises only the method – GET, HEAD, and so on – followed by the related file name in the form of an ASCII string. The response message is in the form of a block of ASCII characters with no headers and no MIME extensions. An example of a simple HTTP request message is:

GET/mpeg-4/index.html

which is sent over the previously established TCP connection to the related server AP.

With the later versions of HTTP – version 1.0 onwards – MIME extensions are supported using what are called *full request/response messages*. To discriminate a full request from a simple request, a field containing the HTTP version number is added to the request line. This is followed by the text associated with a number of other RFC 822 headers, each of which is on a separate line. These were given earlier in Table 14.1 and include:

- general headers: these do not relate to the entity to be transferred and an example is the MIME version number;
- request headers: these are used to specify such things as the sender's name/ email address and the media types and encodings that the browser supports;
- entity headers: these relate to the entity to be transferred and include the content type and, when sending an entity, the content length.

The end of the header is indicated by a blank line. Then, if the request contains a message body, this is followed by the entity being transferred such as a block of HTML text – a script – relating to a page.

The header fields associated with a full response message start with the HTTP version number followed by the response status code. Some examples are:

200   accepted

304   not modified: the requested page has not been modified

400   bad request

404   not found: requested page does not exist on this server.

This is followed by the name and location of the server and, if the response contains an entity in the message body, a *Content-Type:* and a *Content-Length:* field. Also, if the contents relate to a binary file, a *Content-Transfer-Encoding:Base64* header field.

An example showing a selection of the header fields associated with a full request/response message interchange is shown in Figure 15.3. The example relates to the transfer of the HTML page with the URL of:

http://www.mpeg.org/mpeg-4/index.html

Hence prior to sending the GET message, a TCP connection to the server *www.mpeg.org* will have been established.

(a) Example request message relating to a URL of

http://www.mpeg.org/mpeg-4/index.html

GET/mpeg-4/index.HTML HTTP/1.1
Connection:close
User-agent: Browser name/version number
Accept: text/html, image/gif, image/jpeg

(b) Example response message relating to this request:

HTTP/1.1 200 Accepted
Server: Aname
Location: www.mpeg.org
Subject: MPEG home page
Last-Modified: Day/month/year/time
Content-Type: text/html
Content-Length: 7684

Entity body comprising a string
of 7684 NVT ASCII characters

Figure 15.3 An example of a full request/response message relating to HTTP: (a) request message; (b) response message.

The meanings of the various fields in the request message shown in part (a) of the figure are as follows. The *Connection: close* header line indicates to the server that the browser does not need a persistent connection. The *User-agent:* line contains the name of the browser and its version number. Often the server contains a number of versions of a page and this enables the server to send the version that is best suited to the browser. The *Accept:* line indicates the entity types that the browser is able to accept which, as we can see, is determined by the compression software/hardware it supports.

The meanings of the various header fields in the response message shown in part (b) are mainly self explanatory. In the example, the body contains an entity comprising a string of NVT ASCII characters representing the HTML text of a Web page. Alternatively, if the *Content-Type:* was, say, *image/jpeg* then a *Content-Type-Encoding: Base64* header field would be present. For a more complete list of the MIME headers you should refer back to Table 14.1 and Figure 14.9 and their accompanying text.

Conditional GET

As we saw earlier in Figure 5.16(b), in many instances a browser does not communicate directly with the required server but rather through an intermediate system called a proxy server. In the figure it was assumed that the browsers at a site supported only the HTTP protocol and that the proxy server was used to access the contents of files using different protocols such as FTP and NNTP. As we can deduce from our discussion of URLs, this will avoid each of the browsers having the code of each of these protocols. In addition, however, a proxy server normally caches the Web pages and other entities that it obtains – on behalf of the browsers that it serves – on hard disk. Then, when a browser makes a request for a page/entity that the proxy server has cached, the proxy server can return this directly without going back to the server holding the original source. The latter is called the **origin server** and, when it performs this function, the proxy server is also known as a (Web) **cache server**.

Although caching reduces the response time for subsequent requests for a cached page/entity, there is a possibility that the cached entity may be out of date as a result of the original being modified/updated subsequent to the cache server receiving it. Hence because caching is widely used, an additional request message called a **conditional GET** is used by the cache server to ensure the response messages that are returned to the browsers contain up-to-date information.

A conditional GET request message is one which includes a header line of *If-Modified-Since:* and its use is illustrated in Figure 15.4. To avoid duplication, the header fields that have already been discussed are left out of the messages shown. The following should be noted when interpreting the message sequence.

- It is assumed that the browsers in all the client machines attached to the access network – site/campus LAN, ISP network, and so on – have been configured to send all request messages to the proxy/cache server.

- The sequence starts with a browser requesting an HTML page from the proxy server using a GET request message (1).

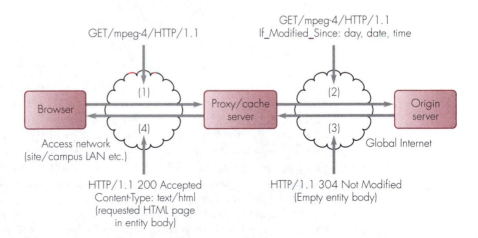

Figure 15.4 Proxy/cache server operation with conditional GET.

- The proxy server has a cached copy of the page and, associated with it, the day/date/time when the page was cached. This is obtained from the *Last-Modified:* header field in the response message returned by the origin server to an earlier request.

- Before returning the cached page to the browser, the proxy server sends a conditional GET request message to the origin server – defined in the page URL – with the date and time the current copy of the page it holds was last modified in the *If-Modified-Since:* header field (2).

- On receipt of this, the origin server checks to see if the requested page has been modified since the date in the *If-Modified-Since:* field.

- In the figure it is assumed that the contents have not been changed and hence the origin server returns a simple response message with a status code of *304 Not modified* in the header and an empty entity body (3).

- On receipt of this, the proxy server returns a copy of the cached page to the browser (4).

In the event that the requested page/entity had been changed, then a copy of the new page/entity would be returned by the origin server. A copy of the new page would then be cached by the proxy server – together with the date and time from the *Last-Modified:* field – before it is forwarded to the browser. Thus the savings obtained with a cache server come from the absence of an entity body in the response message from the origin server. Clearly for large pages/entities this can be considerable. In addition, further savings can be obtained by also having a higher-level cache server associated with, for example, each regional/national network. The proxy server associated with each access network is then configured to send all request messages to a specified higher-level cache server. In general, the higher the level this is in the Internet hierarchy the more requests it will receive and, as a result, the more cached pages/entities it holds.

15.3 HTML

The Hyper Text Markup Language, HTML, is the standard language used to write Web pages. As we saw in Section 2.3.3, HTML is the markup language that is used to describe how the contents of a document/page are to be displayed on the screen of the computer by the browser. Moreover, since the markup commands relate to a complete page, the browser automatically displays the page contents within the bounds allocated for the page; that is, irrespective of whether this is a small window on a low resolution screen or a large window on a high-resolution screen.

The markup/format commands are known as directives in HTML and the majority are specified using a pair of **tags**. In addition to the various types of directive associated with a string of text – which specify how the string is to be presented on the display – there are tags to enable a hyperlink to be specified as well as tags to specify an image or a segment of audio or video within a page and how these are to be displayed/output. There are also fill-in forms and other features. In this section we describe how each of these features is specified in HTML. It should be stressed, however, that HTML is continuously being revised and what follows should be considered only as an introduction to the subject.

15.3.1 Text format directives

The HTML text associated with a Web page is written in the **ISO 8859-1** Latin-1 character set which, for the English alphabet, is the same as the ASCII character set. However, for someone creating Web pages in a Latin alphabet, when using an ASCII keyboard, escape sequences must be used. For example, the Latin character *è* is represented by the ASCII string *&egrave* and *é* by *&eacute.*

The HTML text can be entered using either a word processor with facilities for creating and editing an HTML document/page or directly using the facilities provided by a Web browser. Typically, the complete string of characters consists of a number of substrings each of which may be displayed in a different format when the substring is output on the display by the HTML parser/interpreter part of the browser. In order for the interpreter to do this, each substring is sandwiched between a pair of tags that specify the format directive to be used. For example, if the substring

this is easy

is to be displayed in boldface, then this is written as

<B> *this is easy* </B>

As we can see, the opening tag comprises the format directive (B) between the pair of characters < and > and the closing tag is the same directive between </ and >. Note that the directive itself is case insensitive but normally upper-case is used to make the directives easier to identify. This format is used for a majority of the tags and a selection are listed in Table 15.1.

An example of an HTML script that includes some of these tags is shown in Figure 15.5(b). The example relates to the simple Web page we showed earlier in Figure 2.9 excluding at this stage the university crest. Typically, since this is the home page of the UoW, its URL would be:

hhtp:www.UoW.edu

The start of a page is indicated in the script by a <HTML> tag and the end of the page by a </HTML> tag. The <HTML> tag is followed by the page

Table 15.1 A selection of the HTML text format directive/tags.

Opening tag	Closing tag	Use
<HTML>	</HTML>	Specify the start and end of the complete document/page
<HEAD>	</HEAD>	Specify the start and end of the page header
<TITLE>	</TITLE>	Specify the title of the page. It is not displayed as part of the page
<BODY>	</BODY>	Specify the start and end of the contents of the displayed page
<Hn>	</Hn>	Specify the start and end of a level n heading
<B>	</B>	Display the related text in boldface
<I>	</I>	Display the related text in italics
<UL>	</UL>	Specify the start and end of an unordered/bulleted list
<OL>	</OL>	Specify the start and the end of an ordered/numbered list
<LI>		Specifies the start of a listed item
 		Specifies the start of a new line
<P>		Specifies the start of a new paragraph
<A HREF = "URL">	</A>	Specify an anchor/link to another page
<A HREF = "#NAME">	</A>	Specify an anchor/link to another point in the same page
<! -- >	- ->	Start and end of comments

header which is entered between the <HEAD> and </HEAD> tags. Primarily, the header contains the title of the page which is written between the <TITLE> and </TITLE> tags. Note that the title is not output as part of the displayed page. In some instances, however, it is output by the browser in a field at the top or bottom of the display. The displayed page contents are then entered between the <BODY> and </BODY> tags.

In the example, there is only one heading and this is written between the <H1> and </H1> tags. If there were some subheadings, they would each be defined in the place they are to be displayed using the format:

<H2> Subheading name </H2>

Note, however, that it is the browser that decides the relative size of each heading/subheading on the display screen. Normally, they are in decreasing size with the first-level heading <H1> displayed in the largest font size and,

(a)

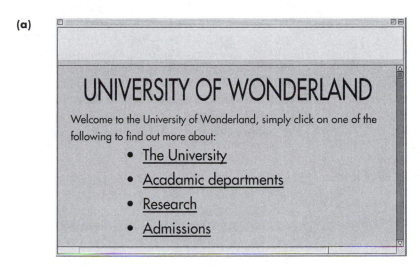

(b)
```
<HTML>
<HEAD>
<TITLE> U of W Prospectus </TITLE>
</HEAD>
<BODY
<H1> UNIVERSITY OF WONDERLAND </H1>
<BR> Welcome to the University of Wonderland, simply click on one of the
following to find out more about:
<UL><LI><A HREF = "university"> The University </A>
     <LI><A HREF = "academic"> Academic departments </A>
     <LI><A HREF = "research"> Research </A>
     <LI><A HREF = "admissions"> Admissions </A>
</UL>
</BODY>
</HTML>
```

Figure 15.5 HTML text format directives: (a) example Web page; (b) the HTML script for the page.

typically, in boldface with one or more blank lines above and below it. Each level of subheading is then displayed in a decreasing size.

The <BR> is used to ensure that the welcome message starts on a new line. This is followed by an unordered (bulleted) list of items. These are listed between the <UL> and </UL> tags with each item starting with a single <LI> tag. The default for the start of the items in a first-level list is a solid bullet. In the example, each bulleted item is a hyperlink to a different page and hence starts with the <A HREF = "URL"> tag where A stands for **anchor**. This is followed by the textual name of the hyperlink – for example, The University – that is to appear on the display screen. Also, since this is a hyperlink name, the HTML interpreter displays it highlighted using, for example, an underline – as shown – or, if colored text is being used, a different color. Then, when this is clicked on, the interpreter uses the URL to fetch the related file. The end of a hyperlink is indicated by the </A> tag.

Note that since the prospectus consists of a linked set of pages, all of which are stored at the same site/server, once the full URL of the home page has been given, any links in the remaining linked set of pages can each use a **relative URL**. This means that the file names used in these URLs are assumed to have the same protocol/method and site/server domain name as that of the home page; that is, in the example, the browser assumes that each is preceded by:

http:www.UoW.edu/

For this reason, therefore, the URL of the home page is said to be an **absolute URL**. Hence as we can deduce from this example, by using relative URLs in all the remaining linked set of pages, it is then straightforward to relocate them by changing only the (absolute) URL of the home page.

In this example, the page containing the top-level index is relatively short and so fits into the display window. Also, it was assumed that further details relating to each of the listed headings were on a different page and accessed by an external link. However, if the index were larger and could not be displayed in a single window, then the user would have to scroll the page to find the remainder of the index. Alternatively, if the page/index is particularly long, it is sometimes preferable to have internal links within the page.

For example, if the second-level subheadings relating to each first-level heading shown in the example in Figure 2.9 were all on the same page, then the link associated with each first-level heading would be an internal link. These are specified using the format:

<A HREF "#University">The University</A>

The words *The University* would then be displayed highlighted and, if the user clicks on this, the parser would jump to the point in the current page where the words *The University* next occur and start to display from this point in the page. The related subheadings could then be either internal links if further subheadings are defined or, if not, external links to the pages where the actual descriptions are located.

15.3.2 Lists

The example shown in Figure 15.5(b) contained a single unordered list. In addition, an ordered (numbered) list can be used as well as nested lists of different types. An example of an HTML script that illustrates these features is shown in Figure 15.6(b) and the resulting displayed page is shown in part (a).

As we can see, the listed items appear in the HTML script in the order they are to be displayed. The format directives associated with each item then enable the HTML interpreter in the browser to determine the position of

(a)

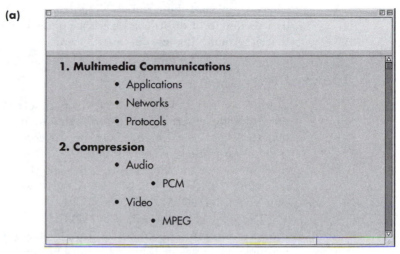

(b)
```
<HTML>
<HEAD><TITLE> Lists </TITLE></HEAD>
<BODY>
<OL><LI> Multimedia Communications
        <UL><LI> Applications
                <LI> Networks
                <LI> Protocols
        </UL>
        <LI> Compression
        <UL><LI> Audio
                <UL><LI>PCM</UL>
                <LI>Video
                <UL><LI>MPEG</UL>
</OL>
</BODY></HTML>
```

Figure 15.6 Lists in HTML: (a) example of displayed page; (b) HTML script for this page.

each item in relation to the others. Note that the default for an ordered list is a numeric value but it is also possible to define a number of alternatives. This is done by adding the required type to the opening tag:

   <OL TYPE=X>

where X is the type of numbering. For example, X = i selects lowercase roman numerals (i, ii, and so on). It is also possible for a user to define the number he or she wants by using

   <OL><LI VALUE=Y>

where Y indicates the number. Note that the default for the start of the items in a second-level unordered list is a hollow bullet and that it is the browser that determines the level of indentation.

15.3.3 Color

Color is used in a number of ways by browsers to enhance a displayed page. For example, hyperlinks are often highlighted in the color blue and, when a hyperlink has been selected, normally the color changes from blue to purple. In addition to these colors, however, most browsers allow the user to specify their own color for the background color (BGCOLOR), the text (TEXT), a hyperlink (LINK), and a visited link (VLINK) as part of the <BODY> tag at the head of the HTML script.

The way a color is defined in HTML is determined by the number of bits used to represent each color on the display of the machine the browser is running. As we saw in Table 2.1, this can range from 8 bits through to 24 bits. Normally, each 8 bits is represented by two hexacimal digits and hence each alternative color to be used is specified using either two (8 bits), four (16 bits), or six (24 bits) hexadecimal digits. For example, if 24 bits are used for each color, normally, the three sets of 8 bits represent the strength of each of the three primary colors (red, green, and blue) the color contains. The format used to represent the color is then:

#RRGGBB

where RR are the two hexadecimal digits that represent the strength of the color red, GG the color green, and BB the color blue. Hence the three primary colors are represented as:

#FF0000 = red, #00FF00 = green, #0000FF = blue

Some other examples are:

#FFFFFF = white, #FCE503 = yellow, #F1A60A = orange, #000000 = black

Hence if, for example, the background color is to be blue, the text is to be yellow, a hyperlink orange, and a visited hyperlink green, these would be specified as:

<BODY BGCOLOR = "#0000FF" TEXT = "#FCE503" LINK = "#F1A60A"
VLINK = "#00FF00">

Note, however, that most browsers use a color look-up table (CLUT) which displays only a defined set of 256 colors. Also, a number of these are reserved for the browser's own use. Hence although in theory a vast range of colors can be defined, in practice most browsers will simply approximate most of them to the nearest color-match in the usable colors in their CLUT. Typically, the usable colors that are available consist of any combination of the hexadecimal pairs:

00 33 66 99 CC FF

Hence when defining colors, if these hexadecimal pairs are used then the colors will be displayed in their unmodified form.

15.3.4 Images and lines

Images can be used both as an alternative to a white background for a page and for displaying a specific object within the page itself. Although the image can be in any format, most browsers support only GIF and JPEG images; that is, they only have the software to decompress an image held in either a *gif* or *jpeg* file. Horizontal lines in various forms can also be displayed on a page. We shall outline each feature separately.

Background images

In order to specify an alternative background image for a page, the file containing the image – for example *bgimage.gif* – is specified as part of the <BODY> tag using the format:

<BODY BACKGROUND = "*bgimage.gif*">

For example, most Web browsers have a file called *clouds.gif* which is often accessed and used as an alternative background. When the parser encounters this, the interpreter first obtains the contents of the file and, after this has been decompressed, displays this on the screen as the background. The page contents are then superimposed on it.

Images

An image that is displayed from within a page is specified at the point in the HTML script – that is, relative to the other markup directives in the script – where the image is to be displayed using the tag

<IMG SRC = "*file name*">

where *file name* is the name of the file containing the image on the current page server. For example, assuming the file name containing the logo/crest of the UoW shown on the Web page in Figure 2.9 is *crest.jpeg*, this could be displayed on the page by replacing the first line in the body of the HTML script shown earlier in Figure 15.5(b) with

<IMG SRC = "crest.jpeg"> <H1> UNIVERSITY OF WONDERLAND</H1>

Note, however, that some later versions of HTML may use the tag <OBJECT> to include an image where <OBJECT> applies not only to images but also to a number of other data items/objects. We shall expand on this later in Section 15.5.1.

Using the above method it is the browser that ultimately decides on the size and the position of the image. Hence it is possible that the heading will be displayed below the logo/crest with the above script. In addition, however, a number of optional attributes – also called parameters – can be defined with the IMG tag to inform the browser of the required position and other attributes. These include the ALT and the ALIGN attributes. The ALT attribute is used to specify a text string that should be displayed if the browser is not able to display an image. For example,

<IMG SRC = "crest.jpeg" ALT"UoW crest">

could be used to display the words *UoW crest* instead of the actual crest/logo if, for example, the user has disabled images or the related decompression software is not supported.

The ALIGN attribute is used to align an image with respect to either the display window or to some displayed text. In the first case, the related image can be displayed aligned to the LEFT window edge, which is the default, in the CENTER of the page, or aligned with the RIGHT edge. An example showing a segment of an HTML script to align an image in the center of the page is shown in Figure 15.7(a).

An image can also be aligned with respect to some given text. In this case the text following an IMG tag can start at various specified points relative to the image. For example, the text can start on the first line at the TOP of the image, the MIDDLE, or the BOTTOM. A segment of HTML script showing how the text starts at the middle of the image is shown in Figure 15.7(b).

Normally, before displaying any text that comes after a specified image, the browser waits until it receives the complete image to determine the amount of display space the image needs. For a large image this can delay the display of the complete page. To overcome this (and speed up the display process) the size of the image can be included with the image specification. Also, the size of the margin that should be left around the image. With this information the browser is able to reserve the requisite amount of display space and, while the image is being transferred and displayed, output any remaining text. The format used to do this is:

<IMG WIDTH = "x" HEIGHT = "y" HSPACE = "a" VSPACE = "b"
SRC = "image.gif ">

where x, y, a, and b are all specified in screen pixels. Note, however, that by specifying the dimensions in pixels the size of the displayed image will depend on the pixel resolution of the display. An image can also be used as a hyperlink by including the image specification within the hyperlink tags:

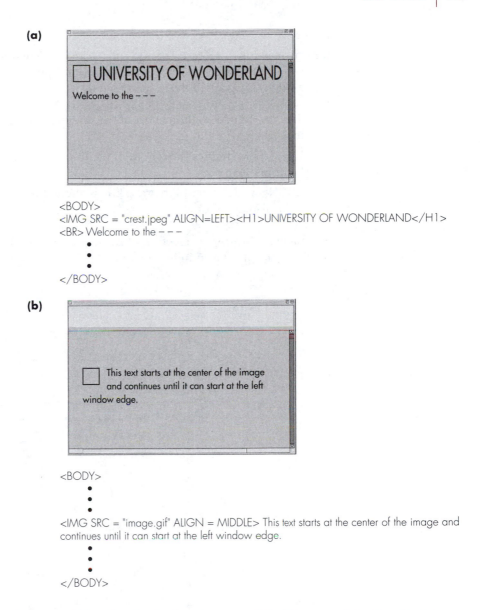

(a)

```
<BODY>
<IMG SRC = "crest.jpeg" ALIGN=LEFT><H1>UNIVERSITY OF WONDERLAND</H1>
<BR> Welcome to the – – –
        •
        •
        •
</BODY>
```

(b)

```
<BODY>
        •
        •
        •
<IMG SRC = "image.gif" ALIGN = MIDDLE> This text starts at the center of the image and
continues until it can start at the left window edge.
        •
        •
        •
</BODY>
```

Figure 15.7 Aligning in-line images: (a) with respect to the display screen; (b) with respect to subsequent text.

```
<A HREF = "http://www.UoW.edu/images"><IMG
SRC = "image.gif "></A>
```

The displayed image *image.gif* will then be displayed highlighted and the user can click on any part of this to activate the hyperlink.

Lines

A horizontal line – referred to as a rule – can be displayed from within a page using the <HR> tag. The thickness, length, and position of the line/rule can be varied by using attributes. These include:

- SIZE = s: defines the thickness of the line as a multiple of the default thickness;
- WIDTH = w: defines the length of the line as a percentage of the width of the display window;
- ALIGN = y: defines whether the line is aligned to the left, center, or right of the display window.

An example showing a selection of displayed lines and the related fragment of HTML script is given in Figure 15.8.

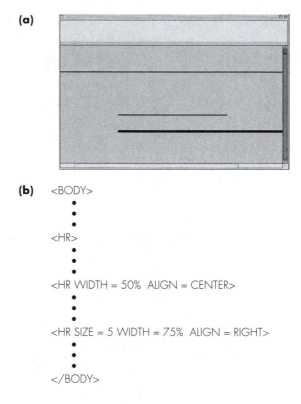

(b) <BODY>

    •
    •
    •

<HR>

    •
    •
    •

<HR WIDTH = 50% ALIGN = CENTER>

    •
    •
    •

<HR SIZE = 5 WIDTH = 75% ALIGN = RIGHT>

    •
    •
    •

</BODY>

Figure 15.8 Horizontal lines: (a) a selection of displayed lines; (b) associated fragments of HTML.

15.3.5 Tables

Tables can be used in Web pages not only to display a particular set of data in tabular form but also to control the overall layout of a page. A table consists of one or more rows and one or more columns. The intersection of each row and column is called a **cell** and a cell can contain a string of text, a number, an image, a hyperlink or, if required, another table. Each column can have a heading and, if required, a heading can span multiple columns. A selection of the tags that can be used to create a table are shown in Figure 15.9(a), an example of a displayed table in part (b) of the figure, and the HTML script relating to this in part (c).

As we can see, both the headings and the contents of each cell are defined a row at a time starting at the left column using the <TH> and <TD> tags respectively. Note that, normally, the column headings are displayed in boldface by the browser and that the <CAPTION> tag is defined within the pair of <TABLE> tags. Also, as we can deduce from this example, an unboxed table can be used to control the layout of a page by dividing the page into regions/cells.

(a)

Opening tag	Closing tag	Use
<TABLE>	</TABLE>	Start and end of an unboxed table
<TABLE BORDER>	</TABLE>	Start and end of a boxed table
<TR>	</TR>	Start and end of a row
<TH>	</TH>	Start and end of a heading
<TD>	</TD>	Start and end of a cell content
<CAPTION>	</CAPTION>	Start and end of a table caption

(b)

NETWORK	CO/CLS	CBR/VBR
PSTN/ISDN	co	cbr
LAN	cls	vbr
ATM	co	vbr
Internet	cls	vbr

Network operating modes

(c)
```
<HTML><HEAD><TITLE> Example table</TITLE></HEAD>
<BODY>
<TABLE BORDER  ALIGN = CENTER>
<TR><TH>NETWORK</TH><TH>CO/CLS</TH><TH>CBR/VBR</TH></TR>
<TR><TD>PSTN/ISDN</TD><TD> co </TD><TD> cbr </TD></TR>
<TR><TD>LAN</TD><TD> cls </TD><TD vbr </TD></TR>
<TR><TD>ATM</TD><TD> co </TD><TD vbr </TD></TR>
<TR><TD> Internet </TD><TD> cls </TD><TD> vbr </TD></TR>
<CAPTION> Network operating modes </CAPTION>
</TABLE>
</BODY></HTML>
```

Figure 15.9 HTML tables: (a) selection of tags; (b) an example of a displayed table; (c) HTML script for the table.

The position of the table on the display and the size of each cell is determined by the browser based on the maximum length of either the heading or the contents of each cell in a column and the number of rows. The contents of each heading and cell are then centered within the cell. Alternatively, the ALIGN attribute can be used with the <TABLE>, <TH>, and <TD> tags to align the table/heading/cell contents either to the left edge of the display/cell, the right edge, or the center. Two examples showing the format used are:

<TABLE BORDER ALIGN = CENTER>
<TH ALIGN = LEFT>

In addition, a user can define the size of the table themselves by specifying either the number of pixels to be used or as a percentage of the actual table size relative to the size of the display window. The format used is:

<TABLE BORDER WIDTH = 50% LENGTH = 50%>

Also, the size of individual cells can be defined by adding attributes to the <TH> and <TD> tags. Some examples are:

<TH ROWSPAN = 2> <!- -> the depth of the heading should be 2 rows - ->
<TD COLSPAN = 3> <!- -> the cell should span 3 columns - ->

15.3.6 Forms and CGI scripts

The previous subsections have been concerned with how a selection of the HTML directives/tags associated with text, images, and tables can be used to specify the contents of a Web page, and how the page is displayed on the screen of a client machine by the browser. However, as we saw in Section 5.4.2, in applications relating to e-commerce, for example, in addition to the server returning the contents of a file/page that have been requested by a browser, it is also a requirement for the server to receive and process information that has been input by the user. For example, payment card details and other information relating to the purchase of a ticket or product. As we saw, this is entered by means of a fill-in form and, typically, the entered information is then sent back to the server where it is processed by a piece of software called a common gateway interface (CGI) script. In this section we expand upon both these topics.

Forms

A form provides the means for the browser to get input from a user. A form is declared within an HTML page between the <FORM> and </FORM> tags. In addition, the <FORM> tag has two mandatory attributes, ACTION and METHOD. The ACTION attribute specifies the URL of the server where the data entered by the user should be sent and includes the path name and the name of the file containing the CGI script that will process the data. The METHOD attribute specifies how the entered data should be sent. When using HTTP it is always set to POST which means that the data will be sent using a POST request message over a previously established TCP connection between the browser and the named server. An example showing the format used is:

```
<FORM ACTION = "http://company.com/cgi-bin/orderform1"
METHOD = POST>
```

A form can contain a number of alternative ways for obtaining input from a user. These include fill-in boxes for textual input and check-boxes or pull-down menus for making selections. Then, when the user has completed filling in the form, the user can either initiate the sending of the entered information to the named server (if all is well) or, if not, reset the form to its initial state and start again.

When creating a form – normally within a page – to obtain input from a user, the <INPUT> tag is used. There is a range of attributes associated with the tag which determine how the information is to be obtained. A selection of these are as follows:

- <INPUT TYPE = TEXT NAME = "aname" Size = "n" >: this is used to create a fill-in box of length n characters. The entered text is given an identifier of the value in NAME, that is, *aname*;
- <TEXTAREA NAME = "aname" ROWS = "m" COLS = "n"> </TEXTAREA>: this is similar to the previous type except that the fill-in box comprises m rows each of length n characters. Normally, the box has a scroll bar for more than 2 rows;
- <INPUT TYPE = PASSWORD NAME = "aname" SIZE = "n">: this is similar to TEXT except that the entered password is displayed on the screen of the browser as a string of * characters, one per entered character;
- <INPUT TYPE = CHECKBOX NAME = "aname" VALUE = "avalue">: this is used to select a single option from a list of options of which the user can select more than one. All the options in the list have the same NAME ("aname") but each option has a unique VALUE;
- <INPUT TYPE = RADIO NAME = "aname" VALUE = "avalue">: this is the same as CHECKBOX except that the user can select only one from the list;
- <INPUT TYPE = SUBMIT VALUE = "aname">: this is used to create a submit button with the name given in the VALUE attribute displayed on the face of the button. When selected, this causes the browser to send the set of data entered by the user to the server;
- <INPUT TYPE = RESET VALUE = "aname">: this is used to create a reset button with the name given in the VALUE attribute displayed on the face

of the button. When selected, this causes the browser to reset the form to its initial state;

■ <INPUT TYPE = BUTTON VALUE = "aname">: this is used to create additional buttons each of which can have a script associated with it that is invoked when the button is activated.

An example of a displayed form that has been created using a selection of the above is shown in Figure 15.10(a) and the HTML script associated with this is given in part (b). Note that if no TYPE is specified it is assumed that the INPUT is plain text.

Once the user activates the SUBMIT button – given the label *Submit request* in the example – this causes the browser to send the set of data entered by the user to the CGI script/program in the server named in the URL of the ACTION attribute. The data is sent in a POST request message containing the name of each variable followed by an = character and the value entered by the user. Note, however, that only those variables that have an entered value are sent. Each variable name and its associated value is separated by an **&** character and any spaces in the entered value are replaced by a **+** character. For example, assuming the displayed form shown in Figure 15.10(a), an entered set of data might comprise the block of characters:

> name=FirstName+Surname&address=AStreet+ATown+ACountry &phoneno=888-99999&ProdType=modems&ProdType=hubs& PurchDate=now

with no spaces between the characters. Hence assuming the URL shown in part (b), the HTTP in the browser first establishes a TCP connection to port 80 – the HTTP well-known port – in server *www.NetCo.com*. The block of characters is then sent over this connection using a POST request message with a file name of */cgi-bin/literature* and

> Content-Type: *text/html*
> Content-Length: *115*

in the message header. This is followed by a blank line and the block of 115 characters in the message body.

Normally, on receipt of a POST request message with a directory name of *cgi-bin* the HTTP in the server invokes the CGI script/program in the named file and passes the contents of the request message to it for processing. The CGI script, after processing the contents of the POST message, may then return in the POST response message that it returns to the HTTP in the browser, a message such as that shown at the bottom of the display in the figure or, if some information is missing, a request to fill in the form again. Alternatively, it might return a Web page containing descriptions of the selected products.

(a)

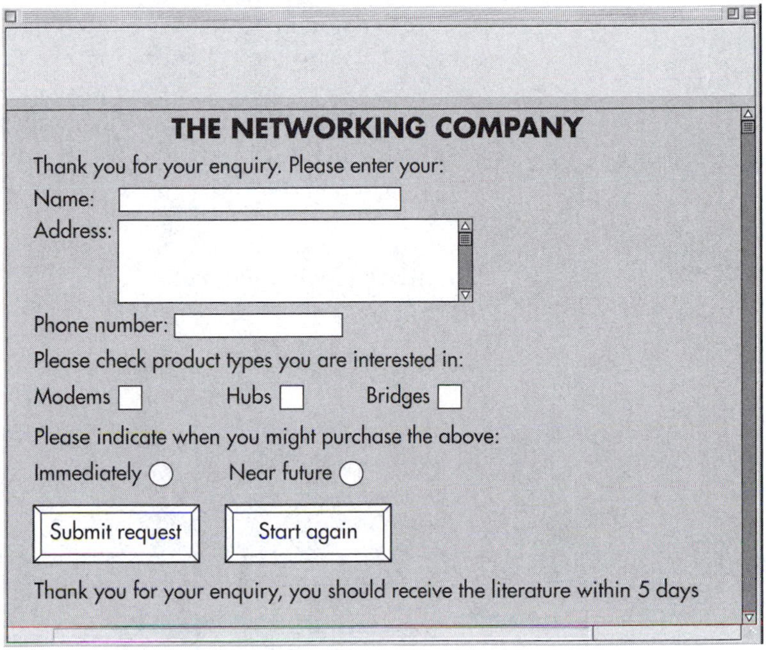

(b)
```
<HTML><HEAD><TITLE> Literature Request </TITLE></HEAD>
<BODY>
<H1> THE NETWORKING COMPANY </H1>
<FORM ACTION = "http://www.NetCo.com/cgi-bin/literature" METHOD = POST>
Thank you for your enquiry. Please enter your: <P>
Name: <INPUT NAME = "name" SIZE = 30> <P>
Address: <TEXTAREA NAME = "address" ROWS = 3 COLS = 40> </TEXTAREA>
Phone number: <INPUT NAME = "phoneno" SIZE = 20><P>
Please check product types you are interested in: <P>
Modems <INPUT TYPE = CHECKBOX NAME = "ProdType" VALUE = "modems">
Hubs <INPUT TYPE = CHECKBOX NAME = "ProdType" VALUE = "hubs">
Bridges <INPUT TYPE = CHECKBOX NAME = "ProdType" VALUE = "bridges"><P>
Please indicate when you might purchase the above: <P>
Immediately <INPUT TYPE = RADIO NAME = "PurchDate" VALUE = "now">
Near future <INPUT TYPE = RADIO NAME = "PurchDate" VALUE = "later"><P>
<INPUT TYPE = SUBMIT VALUE = "Submit Request">
<INPUT TYPE = RESET VALUE = "Start Again"><P>
</FORM></BODY></HTML>
```

Figure 15.10 HTML forms: (a) an example of a displayed form; (b) HTML script for the form.

An alternative way of selecting an item from a list of options is in the form of a pull-down menu. A menu is created by defining each option between the <SELECT> and </SELECT> tags. Associated with the opening <SELECT> tag is a NAME attribute which is assigned the name of the list of options. Also, if more than one option can be selected, a MULTIPLE attribute. An example showing how the two list of options in the example in

Figure 15.10 could be displayed in the form of pull-down menus is shown in Figure 15.11(a) and the HTML script for this is given in part (b).

As we can see, since more than one option can be selected from the first menu, the MULTIPLE attribute is included. We can also see that the SELECTED attribute is used with one of the <OPTION> tags to show a default selection at start-up. The option selected with *PurchDate* is then sent in the form (say):

&PurchDate = Immediately

(a)

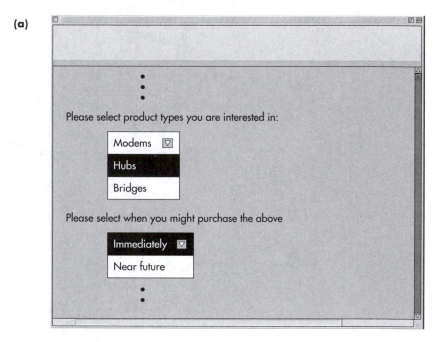

(b)
•
•
•
Please select product types you are interested in: <P>
<SELECT NAME = "ProdType" MULTIPLE>
<OPTION> "Modems"
<OPTION SELECTED> "Hubs"
<OPTION> "Bridges"
</SELECT><P>
Please select when you might purchase the above:
<SELECT NAME = "PurchDate">
<OPTION SELECTED> "Immediately"
<OPTION> "Nearfuture"
</SELECT><P>
•
•
•

Figure 15.11 HTML pull-down menus: (a) two examples; (b) HTML script.

15.3.7 Web mail

In addition to a user communicating with an email server – to send and receive mail messages – using an (email) user agent and, say, the POP3 protocol, it is also possible for a user to communicate with an (HTTP-enabled) email server using a Web browser and HTTP. In this case, the browser performs the user agent functions and all message transfers between the browser machine and the user's email server are carried out using HTTP rather than POP3.

As we saw in Section 14.3, a protocol like POP3 is used to transfer messages to/from the user agent and the user's email server over a point-to-point link. Using a browser and HTTP, however, has the advantage that, since any browser can be used to access a (registered) user's email server, the browser can be located anywhere around the world. The disadvantage is that accessing and sending mail in this way can be relatively slow. As we saw in the last section, since information – an entered email message in HTML for example – must be returned by the browser to the server, then all interactions with the email server must be through the intermediary of a form and an associated CGI script. In general, therefore, if a conventional email user agent can be used, this is the preferred choice when the user is working at his or her home or place of work. A Web browser is used when the user is away from home. In both cases, however, all message transfers between the email servers involved are carried out using SMTP.

15.3.8 Frames

Frames are used to enable the user to display and interact with more than one page on the display window of the browser at the same time. This is achieved by dividing the display window into multiple self-contained areas. Each area is called a **frame** and a separate page can be displayed in each frame. The user is able to interact with the page displayed in one frame while the pages in each of the other frames remain unchanged on the screen.

To divide the display window into multiple frames the start and end tags <FRAMESET> and </FRAMESET> are used. Associated with the <FRAME-SET> tag are two attributes: COLS, which is used to divide the display vertically, and ROWS which is used to divide the display horizontally. For example, to divide the display vertically into two frames of equal size the following definition is used:

<FRAMESET COLS = "50%,50%">

It is then possible to subdivide one or both of these frames using the ROWS attribute. For example, the left frame can be divided by following the previous definition with:

<FRAMESET ROWS = "70%,30%">

Once the display has been divided into the required number of frames (each of a defined size), the URL (or local file name) of the page to be displayed in each frame is defined using the SRC attribute in a <FRAME> tag. The HTML script of the page to be displayed in each frame is defined independently in the standard format (using all of the previously described features) and is stored in the related URL or local file name. Two example structures are shown in Figure 15.12(a) and the HTML script associated with each structure in part (b). Note that the <FRAMESET> tag effectively replaces the <BODY> tag when frames are being used.

In these two examples, any images and/or hyperlinks in the displayed pages are accessed by the browser in the standard way and displayed in the frame displaying the related page. In addition, it is possible for a hyperlink in a page displayed in one frame to be used to access and display a page in one of the other frames. To do this it is necessary to give a name to the frame that is to be used to display the page when the frame is defined; for example, left, right, and so on. This is done using the NAME attribute with the <FRAME> tag. The same name is then added to the URL (or local file name) of the page that is to be displayed in this frame using the TARGET attribute. An example illustrating this feature is shown in Figure 15.13(a) with the HTML script in part (b) of the figure.

The example relates to that shown earlier in Figure 15.5 and the modifications that are necessary to the HTML script shown in Figure 15.5(b) to display the home page in the left frame and the selected pages from this in

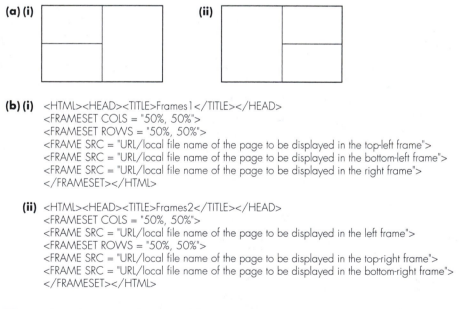

(a) (i)   **(ii)**

(b) (i) <HTML><HEAD><TITLE>Frames 1</TITLE></HEAD>
<FRAMESET COLS = "50%, 50%">
<FRAMESET ROWS = "50%, 50%">
<FRAME SRC = "URL/local file name of the page to be displayed in the top-left frame">
<FRAME SRC = "URL/local file name of the page to be displayed in the bottom-left frame">
<FRAME SRC = "URL/local file name of the page to be displayed in the right frame">
</FRAMESET></HTML>

(ii) <HTML><HEAD><TITLE>Frames2</TITLE></HEAD>
<FRAMESET COLS = "50%, 50%">
<FRAME SRC = "URL/local file name of the page to be displayed in the left frame">
<FRAMESET ROWS = "50%, 50%">
<FRAME SRC = "URL/local file name of the page to be displayed in the top-right frame">
<FRAME SRC = "URL/local file name of the page to be displayed in the bottom-right frame">
</FRAMESET></HTML>

Figure 15.12 HTML frames: (a) two example frame divisions; (b) order of the related HTML scripts.

(a)

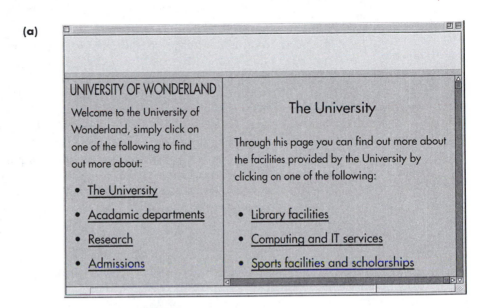

(b)
```
<HTML><HEAD><TITLE> Frames2 </TITLE></HEAD>
<FRAMESET COLS = "35%, 65%">
<FRAME SRC = "http://www.UoW.edu">
<FRAME SRC = "university" NAME = "right">
</FRAMESET></HTML>
```

(c)
```
        •
        •
        •
<UL><LI><A HREF = "university" TARGET = "right"> The University </A>
        •
        •
        •
    <LI><A HREF = "admissions" TARGET = "right"> Admissions </A>
        •
        •
        •
```

Figure 15.13 Nested frames: (a) example display composed of two vertical frames; (b) HTML script for the display; (c) modifications to the HTML script shown earlier in Figure 15.5(b).

the right frame are given in Figure 15.13(c). As we can see, for the frame on the right we have given it an initial URL of *The University* and a NAME = "*right*". Also, in order for the browser to know to display all the subsequently accessed pages in the right frame, each URL has an added attribute of TARGET = "*right*".

In addition to dividing the display window into multiple fixed-sized frames, it is also possible to display a second page in another frame that is defined in the HTML script of the currently displayed page. The second frame is called an **in-line frame** as it is created by inserting an <IFRAME> tag in the place in the current page where the frame is to be created. The <IFRAME> tag has a number of attributes which include SRC to specify the URL (or local file name) of the page to be displayed in the second frame, WIDTH and HEIGHT to define the size of the second frame, and FRAMEBORDER to indicate whether the frame should have a border (=1) or not (=0). An example is shown in Figure 15.14(a) and the HTML script for this in part (b).

As we can see, in this example the in-line frame is used to display the contents of a second paper that is referenced in the first paper. In this way, if the reader of the first paper is not familiar with the referenced paper then he or she can read it through the in-line frame.

(a)

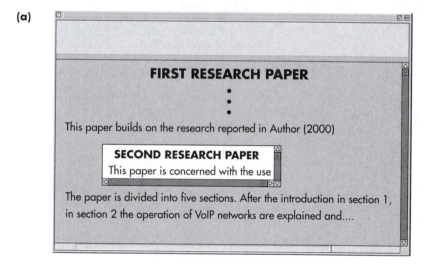

(b)
```
<HTML><HEAD><TITLE> In-line frames </TITLE></HEAD>
<BODY>
<H1> FIRST RESEARCH PAPER </H1><P>
    •
    •
    •
This paper builds on the research reported in Author (2000) <P>
<IFRAME SRC = " URL of page Author (2000)" WIDTH = "600" HEIGHT = "200"
    FRAMEBORDER = "1"></IFRAME><P>
The paper is divided into five sections. After the introduction in section 1, in section 2 the
operation of VoIP networks are explained and...
    •
    •
    •
```

Figure 15.14 In-line frames: (a) a segment of a displayed page containing an in-line frame; (b) a segment of the HTML script to produce this.

15.4 Audio and video

With Web pages comprising text and/or images, the contents of the file containing the page are downloaded from the server to the client machine. The browser then displays the page contents on the screen and, in the case of a large file/page, the user can use the scrolling facilities to view the whole page.

In the case of audio and video, however, the volume of information to be transferred increases linearly with time and hence is determined by the duration of the audio/video clip. As we saw in Chapter 4, typical bit rates for compressed audio – for example MPEG layer 3 (**MP3**) – are 128 kbps for two-channel stereo and 1.5 Mbps for MPEG-1 video with sound. Hence even a short audio/video clip can require a significant time to download. For example, a 5 minute audio clip/track compressed using MP3 produces $5 \times 60 \times 128 \times 10^3$ bits or 38.4 Mbits. Even with a relatively high access rate of, say, 1 Mbps this requires 38.4 s to download which, for this type of application, may not be acceptable. For video, of course, the delay would be an order of magnitude larger.

Hence when a user requests a file containing (compressed) audio and/or video, except for relatively short files containing spoken messages and short audio and/or video clips, the contents of the file must be played out as they are being received. As we saw in Section 1.5.1, this mode of working is called **streaming**. Also, as we saw in Section 1.5.6, to overcome variations in the time between each received packet in the stream – jitter – normally a **playout buffer** is used. This operates using a first-in first-out (FIFO) discipline and typically, holds several seconds of audio and/or video. The received compressed bitstream is then passed through the buffer and output from the buffer does not start until the buffer is, say, half full.

Each of these functions is in addition, of course, to the decompression of the audio and/or video bitstream. To perform these various functions the browser uses a range of helper applications. Normally, these are referred to as **media players** as they form the interface between the incoming compressed media bitstream and the related sound and/or video output card(s). In the case of audio, the appropriate audio media player – MP3 for example – decompresses the audio bitstream taken from the playout buffer and passes it to the sound card. The latter first converts the decompressed bitstream(s) back into an analog signal(s) and, after amplification, the signal(s) is/are output to the speakers. For video, the browser first creates a window in the Web page from where the request was initiated and then passes the coordinates of the window to the selected video media player. The latter first initializes the video card with the assigned coordinates and, as it decompresses the video bitstream taken from the playout buffer, it passes it to the video card for rendering on the browser screen.

In addition, as we saw in Section 1.4.3, with entertainment applications such as audio/video-on-demand, the user requires control of the playout process using features such as pause and rewind. Hence with this type of application it is necessary for the media player to pass the control commands to the server. To do this, the media player is divided into two parts: the first that performs the preceding playout functions – playout buffering and decompression – and the second that manages the portion of the browser display window that has been assigned for the various control buttons. This displays and monitors the buttons on the screen and, when a button is selected, it first adapts the playout process – for example stops output if the pause button is activated – and then passes an appropriate command to a remote server. A protocol has been defined to perform this function called the **real-time streaming protocol** (**RTSP**). The server then implements the command by, for example, stopping further output from the file.

Although it has been implied that the server is a conventional Web server, in most entertainment applications involving streaming, in order to meet the very high playout rates that are required when a large number of browsers are accessing the server simultaneously, special servers called **streaming servers** have to be used. In this section we shall expand upon several of these issues.

15.4.1 Streaming using a Web server

Before describing how an audio and/or video file is accessed using a streaming server, it will be helpful first to review how such files are accessed using a conventional Web server. Figure 15.15 shows the protocols that are used.

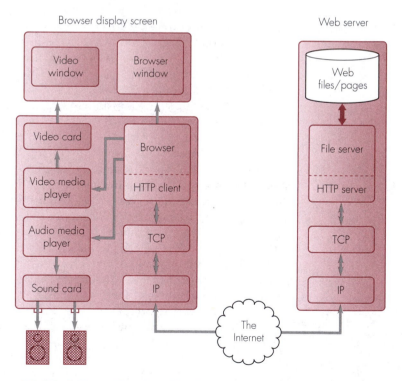

Figure 15.15 Schematic of audio/video streaming with a conventional server.

Using this structure, when the user clicks on a hyperlink in a page for an audio or video file, the browser follows the same procedure as for a text/image file. Hence the HTTP in the browser first establishes a TCP connection with the HTTP in the server named in the hyperlink. It then sends a request for the contents of the file named in the hyperlink using a GET request message. The server responds by returning the contents of the file in a GET response message. On receipt of this, the browser determines from the *Content-Type* field at the head of the message – for example *Content-Type = Audio/MP3* – that the accessed file contains audio that has been compressed using MP3. Hence the browser proceeds to invoke the MP3 media player and, at the same time, passes the contents of the compressed file to it. The media player then proceeds to decompress the contents of the file and outputs the resulting byte stream to the sound card.

As we can deduce from this, the disadvantage of this approach is that since the browser must first receive the contents of the file in its entirety, an unacceptably long delay is introduced if the contents are of any significant size. Hence for larger files, an alternative approach is used which enables the file to be sent directly to the media player rather than through the browser. A schematic diagram showing how this is achieved is shown in Figure 15.16.

Using this approach, when an audio and/or video vile is created, a second file is also created. The second file contains the URL of the first/original file – containing the compressed audio/video – and also a specification of the content type that is in the file. The second file is called the **meta file** of the original file or, because of its function, a **presentation description file**.

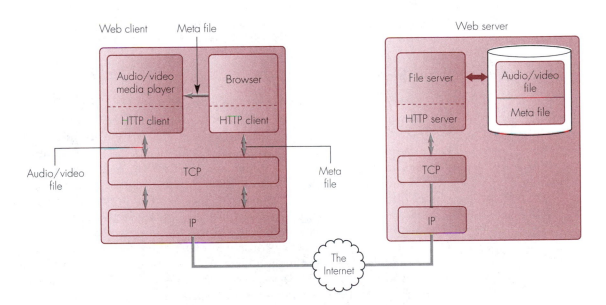

Figure 15.16 Audio/video streaming with a conventional server and a meta file.

This also has a URL associated with it and, when the creator of a page wishes to include a hyperlink to an audio/video file in the page, he or she uses the URL of the meta file rather than that of the original file.

Thus when a user clicks on the hyperlink, the GET response message contains the contents of the meta file. The browser first accesses the *Content-Type:* field from it and then uses this to invoke the related media player as before but this time it simply passes the presentation description in the meta file to the media player. The media player, on determining that this is a meta file, reads the URL of the original file and then proceeds to obtain the contents of the original file in the normal way using HTTP/TCP. On receipt of the file contents, the media player simply streams the received compressed contents into the playout buffer. After a predefined delay to allow the playout buffer to partially fill, it starts to read the stream from the buffer and, after decompression, outputs the resulting byte stream to the sound/video card.

As we can see from the above, this approach removes the delays that are introduced when the file contents are accessed through the browser and hence it is widely used when the audio/video is stored on a conventional Web server. The limiting factor with this approach is that since the audio/video file is accessed in the same way as a text or image file using HTTP and TCP, as we saw in Section 12.3, TCP will transfer the file contents in segments and, if it detects a segment is missing, the TCP at the server side will retransmit it. In general, for files containing real-time information such as audio and/or video, the delays introduced by the TCP retransmission process mean that large playout buffers are required in the media player to mask the effect of a missing segment from the user. Because of this, the preferred transport protocol for audio and/or video files is UDP rather than TCP. This means that HTTP cannot be used and so a different file server from the Web server must be used to hold the audio and/or video files. This is called the streaming server.

15.4.2 Streaming servers and RTSP

As we indicated earlier in this section, the main demand for streaming servers is in entertainment applications such as audio-on-demand and movie/video-on-demand. Typically these are provided by either a TV or a multimedia PC/workstation via a set-top box that is connected to either a cable modem or a high-speed modem. With such applications, as we saw in Section 1.4.3, in order to meet the very high playout rates that are required when a large number of concurrent users are involved, special-purpose streaming servers are used. Also, as we indicated at the end of the last section, in order to overcome the delays introduced by the retransmission procedure associated with TCP, the preferred transport protocol is UDP. Hence when accessing an audio/video file from a streaming server, normally UDP is used with the real time transport protocol (RTP) to transfer the integrated audio and video. A typical set-up for movie/video-on-demand is shown in Figure 15.17. A similar set-up is used for audio-on-demand except no video is involved.

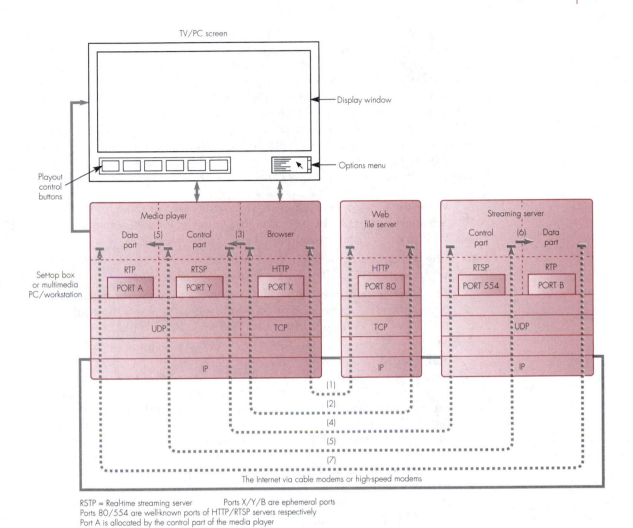

Figure 15.17 Protocols associated with audio/video streaming.

As we can see, the set-up is similar to that shown in Figure 15.16 except the streaming server is separate from the Web server. Also, at the browser side, the media player is divided into two parts: a data part and a control part both of which interact with peer parts in the streaming server. The data part is concerned with the transfer of the integrated audio and video packet streams – see Section 5.5.1 – from the server to the client, the buffering of the incoming packet stream in the playout buffer, the demultiplexing and decompression of the audio and video components, and the output of synchronized audio and video to the respective media cards. The control part manages the playout process according to the commands entered by the user via the set of on-screen control buttons.

Typically, the screen of the TV/PC is divided by the browser into three windows. The first is for use by the browser itself to display a menu of audios (CDs) and movies/videos, the second for use by the control part of the media player to display the set of control buttons, and the third for use by the data part of the media player to display the video output. Also, as with streaming using a conventional Web server, associated with each file containing the integrated audio/video packet stream is a meta file containing the URL of the file and a description of such things as the compression algorithms used and the presentation format.

The sequence of steps that occur when the user selects a movie/video from the menu are identified as (1) through (7) in Figure 15.17. These are:

1   When the user clicks on a movie/video, the browser sends an HTTP GET request message for the related meta file to the Web server named in the URL of the selected hyperlink.

2   The Web server responds by returning the contents of the meta file to the browser in a (HTTP) GET response message.

3   The browser determines from the *Content-Type:* field in the meta file the media player – helper application – to invoke and passes the contents of the meta file to the control part of the selected media player.

4   The control part reads the URL of the file(s) containing the integrated audio/video packet stream and requests the control part in the streaming server (named in the URL) for permission to start a new session by sending an *RTSP SETUP* request message. Associated with this are a number of parameters including the name of the file containing the movie/video, the RTSP session number, the required operational mode (PLAY, although RECORD is supported also), the RTP port number to use, and authorization information. In response, if these are acceptable, the control part in the server returns an RTSP accept response message which includes a unique session identifier allocated by the server for use with subsequent messages relating to the session.

5   When the user clicks on the *play* button, the control part of the media player sends a *RTSP PLAY* request message – which includes the allocated session identifier – to the control part in the streaming server. The latter knows from the identifier that access permission has been granted and returns an acknowledgment to this effect to the control part in the media player. On receipt of this, the latter prepares the data part to receive the incoming integrated audio/video packet stream.

6   At the streaming side, after a short delay to allow the client side to prepare to receive the packet stream, the control part initiates the access and transmission of the packet stream using the allocated port number of RTP – port A – in the header of each UDP datagram.

7   The stream of packets containing the integrated audio and video are first passed into the playout buffer of the data part of the media player and, after a preset time delay, the packets are read from the buffer. Each packet in the stream is first identified – audio or video – and then decompressed using the previously agreed algorithm.

Once the play button has been selected and the movie/video started, the user may wish to activate further control buttons such as pause, visual fast forward, rewind, stop, and quit. In order to relay the appropriate command to the streaming server, RTSP has a corresponding set of control messages. A selection of these are shown in the example in Figure 15.18(a) and the format of some of the messages in part (b).

Note that in order for the streaming server to send the integrated stream of audio/video packets to the data part of the media player, the port number that has been allocated by the control part to RTP – port A – is included in the SETUP request message. The data part of the streaming server inserts this in the destination port field of each UDP datagram header. Note also that the session identifier – allocated by the control part in the streaming server – is returned in the response message to the SETUP request and that this is used subsequently in all further request messages relating to this session. Normally, the RTSP TEARDOWN request message is sent by the control part of the media server when the user activates the quit/end button.

15.5 Java and JavaScript

A short introduction to both Java and JavaScript was presented earlier in Section 5.4.4 and, as we saw, they are used primarily to add some form of action and interactivity to a Web page in a more flexible way than helper applications and plug-ins. Essentially, with Java, a program written in the Java programming language is first compiled into what is called an *applet*. Each applet is held in a file on a Web server and can be called from within an HTML page. When called, the applet is downloaded from the file (in the server named in the URL) in a similar way to downloading the contents of an image file. When the browser receives the applet code, however, it passes it directly to an integral piece of software called a *Java interpreter* which proceeds to execute the applet code. A simple example that shows how action can be added to a Web page is an applet which obtains an audio file and plays this out as background music while the page is displayed. Alternatively, a moving object/image could be displayed in a small window. A more complex example that shows how interactivity can be introduced is an applet which obtains and displays a digitized map on the browser screen and, given a pair of coordinates – for example entered by the user in a frame in a separate window – calculates and displays the best route between the two coordinates. Games playing within a Web page is implemented in a similar way.

Similar functionality can be obtained using JavaScript except, like HTML, this is a scripting language and the action/interactivity is obtained by embedding individual scripts written in JavaScript into an HTML page when it is written. Each script is entered into the HTML script of a page between a pair of tags and, when the start tag is encountered, the HTML interpreter invokes the JavaScript interpreter to execute the script.

(a)

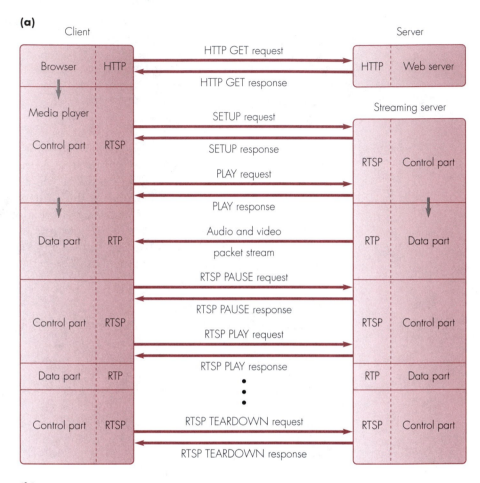

(b)

Assume URL of movie/video meta file = http://www.movie server.com/movies/amovie.mfile
URL of movie/video file = rtsp://movieserver.com/movies/amovie.mpeg

SETUP Request: SETUP/movies/amovie.mpeg RTSP/1.0
Accept: audio/MP3, video/MPEG1
Transport: RTP/UDP, port = A, Mode = PLAY
SETUP Response: RTSP/1.0 200 Accepted
Server: Movie player
Location: movieserver.com
Session: 1234
PLAY Request: PLAY/movies/amovie.mpeg RTSP/1.0
Session 1234
PLAY Response: RTSP/1.0 200 Accepted

**Figure 15.18 Real-time streaming protocol (RTSP): (a) example
message exchange sequence; (b) a selection of message formats.**

Both Java and JavaScript have many similar features to those provided by the C and C++ programming languages. Hence a complete description of them is outside of the scope of this book. In this section, therefore, we restrict our discussion to how an applet/script written in these languages is incorporated into an HTML page.

15.5.1 Java

Java applets provide a browser with similar functionality to helper applications and plug-ins. In the case of the latter, however, they are an integral part of the browser whereas a Java applet is downloaded from a Web server when it is required. The advantage of this is that the applet code can be changed at any time without modifying the browser code. Then, when the old version of the applet is replaced with the new version, this is downloaded automatically the next time the applet is called. For example, if the applet implements a compression algorithm and a new one is developed, the existing applet can be replaced by a new applet without changing the page contents or the browser.

In order for the downloaded code of an applet – the file of which has the type **class** – to run on a range of different computers/machines, when an applet is written it is compiled into a machine-independent code called **bytecode** and it is this version of the applet that is stored in the file on the Web server. Essentially, the bytecode of an applet is an intermediate code between the high-level Java programming language code and the machine-code version of the applet produced for running directly on a specific target machine. To run the bytecode version of an applet, a browser that supports applets has an integral piece of software – or sometimes a helper application – called a **bytecode interpreter**. This parses the bytecode to identify the individual commands – called **methods** – that it contains and then executes each of these using a related procedure/function written in the machine code of the target machine. Hence when an applet is called from within a Web page, the downloaded bytecode is simply passed by the browser to the bytecode interpreter for execution.

Applet tags

In versions of HTML before HTML 4.0, the inclusion of a Java applet in an HTML page is carried out using the <APPLET> tag. For example, assuming the URL of the current Web page is:

http://www.UoW.edu/java-apps/"

to include the applet stored in the file *bgsound.class* on the same server as the current Web page, the script

<APPLET CODE = "*bgsound.class*"></APPLET>

is used. When the HTML interpreter in the browser encounters the <APPLET> tag in the HTML code, it proceeds to obtain the contents of the file – the bytecode – from *bgsound.class* and passes it to the bytecode inter-preter. The latter proceeds to interpret the bytecode of the applet which, typically, accesses a specific file of compressed audio, decompresses it and then outputs the resulting byte stream to the sound card to play the back-ground music.

As we can deduce from this, there is no separation between the applet bytecode and the data on which it operates. Also, there is no type definition associated with the data. So to obtain more flexibility, in HTML 4.0 and later versions, the <APPLET> tag is replaced with the more general <OBJECT> tag. Using this, in addition to Java applets, a number of other types of object can be included within an HTML page. These include an image (file), an audio and/or video (file) or, if required, another Web page (file). To achieve this added flexibility, the <OBJECT> tag has a number of attributes associated with it. These include:

- CODEBASE: this is the URL of the file server and the pathname of where the objects – for example the applet and any data it operates on – are located;
- CLASSID: this specifies the name of the file containing the agent – for example the applet bytecode – that will render the data. Normally, the file name of an applet is prefaced by the new URL type *java*;
- DATA: this specifies the name of the file containing the object/data on which the agent specified in CLASSID operates;
- CODETYPE: this specifies the type of the object/data defined in DATA in MIME format;
- ALIGN, HEIGHT, WIDTH, ALT: these have the same meaning as those we defined earlier in Section 15.3.4 relating to images.

An example declaration showing the use of some of these attributes – using the same URL as before – is as follows:

```
<OBJECT CODEBASE = "http://www.UoW.edu/java-apps/"
        CLASSID = "java:bgaudio.class"
        DATA = "bgaudio.data"
        CODETYPE = "audio/MP3"> </OBJECT>
```

In this example when the HTML interpreter in the browser encounters the <OBJECT> tag, it requests the Java applet stored in the file specified in CLASSID to be downloaded by the server specified in CODEBASE (which also includes the pathname of the file). The name of the file specified in DATA and the datatype – audio/MP3 – specified in CODETYPE are then passed to the bytecode interpreter together with the bytecode of the applet. In the case of an image or video object, the HEIGHT and WIDTH attributes would be used to specify the size of the window that should be used to display the image/video.

Java basics

Java is an object-oriented language which means that almost everything is defined in the form of an **object**. Normally, like a procedure or function in a programming language like Pascal or C, an object contains one or more variables encapsulated within it. Also, associated with each object are one or more operations called **methods** and it is these that are invoked to manipulate the variables within the object. This concept is referred to as **encapsulation**.

Multiple instances of an object can be created – either statically or dynamically during the execution of a program/applet – each of which is said to be an instance of the same object *class*. A typical Java applet comprises many objects – and hence methods – each of which is an instance of a particular object class. Also, in addition to writing your own object class definitions from scratch, like all programming languages, there is a large library of standard object classes that can be included with your own. These are grouped into what are called **packages** and two examples are:

- Java.io: all input and output such as reading a file, outputting a byte stream, and so on is done using the methods associated with the object classes in this package;
- Java.applet: this contains object classes and methods for getting a Web page from a given URL, displaying a Web page, decompressing and playing out the contents of an audio and/or video file, and so on.

There is also a range of Java development kits available that can be used to create applets. A good source of information for this is at

http://www.javasoft.com/

15.5.2 JavaScript

As we indicated earlier, despite its name, JavaScript is a completely different language from Java. It is a scripting language and the script is embedded within an HTML Web page between the <SCRIPT> and </SCRIPT> tags. Providing the browser is able to interpret JavaScript code, when it detects the <SCRIPT> tag it proceeds to interpret the code up to the </SCRIPT> tag as JavaScript rather than HTML.

Unlike HTML, JavaScript has many high-level programming language features similar to those available with C and C++. For example, a variable can be of type boolean, numeric, or string. Also, arithmetic, logical, and bitwise operators are supported as are for( ) and while( ) control loops. Functions are also supported.

Objects

JavaScript is object-oriented. Each object has one or more methods associated with it that allow the object to be manipulated in some way. For example, the current displayed Web page – referred to as a document in JavaScript – is an example of a library/predefined object class and one or more expressions (such as a text string) can be displayed in the page window using

document.write (text string/expression(s))

Here the object name is *document* and the method is *write* – *writeln* can also be used. Additional methods are also provided to determine such things as:

- the URL of the document: *document.URL*,
- the title of the document: *document.title*.

A simple example that shows how a JavaScript is embedded into an HTML page and how the above two methods can be used is shown in Figure 15.19.

(a)

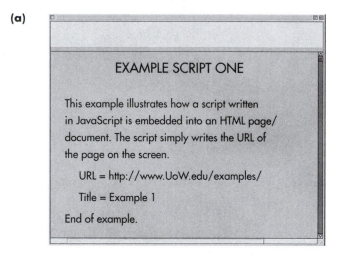

EXAMPLE SCRIPT ONE

This example illustrates how a script written in JavaScript is embedded into an HTML page/ document. The script simply writes the URL of the page on the screen.

URL = http://www.UoW.edu/examples/

Title = Example 1

End of example.

(b)
```
<HTML><TITLE> Example 1 </TITLE>
<BODY>
<H1> EXAMPLE SCRIPT ONE </H1>
This example illustrates how a script written in JavaScript is embedded
into an HTML page/document. The script simply writes the URL of the page
on the screen: <P>
<SCRIPT LANGUAGE = "JavaScript">
document.write ("URL =", document.URL) <P>
document.write ("Title =", document.title) </SCRIPT>
<P> End of example.
</BODY></HTML>
```

Figure 15.19 JavaScript principles: (a) an example of a displayed page/document containing a JavaScript embedded into it; (b) the script for the page.

Another widely used predefined object class that is used to obtain interactivity is *window* and again several methods are provided with this. For example, to create a new window – as a dialog box for example – the *open* method is used. An example statement is:

"MyWindow"= window.open (width = "200", height = "200", scrollbars = "Yes")

This would open a new window called *MyWindow* of a defined size (in pixels) and with scrollbars. Some text could then be included in the script and this would be displayed within the window. The same window can later be closed using the *close* method. The statement in this case would be:

Mywindow.close

Other widely used methods associated with the window object class are:

- *window.confirm ("message")*: this is used to display a confirmatory dialog box with the specified message within it and an OK and Cancel button;
- *window.prompt ("message")*: this is used to display a prompt dialog box with the specified message within it and an input field;
- *window.alert ("message")*: this is used to display a box with the specified message within it.

Some other predefined object classes are array, boolean, date, and math. For example, the math object class includes methods to return a value for pi and to carry out the sin and cos functions. An example segment of script showing their use is:

avariable = math.PI*math.cos (math.PI/6)

Alternatively, when the script contains several occurrences of methods from the same object class the *with* statement can be used:

with (math)
{avariable = PI*cos (PI/6)}   //comment: note the use of curly braces

A new instance of an object class can be created within a script using the *new* operator and the keyword *this* is used to refer to the current object in which the keyword appears.

Forms and event handling

We introduced the <FORM> and <INPUT> tags earlier in Section 15.3.6. As we saw, these provide the means for the browser to get input from a user which, typically, is sent to a CGI script in a remote server for processing. In addition, a form can be declared without the ACTION and METHOD attributes and the input processed locally by the browser using a JavaScript script. Also, in order to enhance this capability, JavaScript allows a number of what are called **event handlers** to be specified. Then, when a specific event occurs – for example the user clicks on an entry in a displayed table of values – a related block of JavaScript code is invoked which, for example, might be to perform a computation on the value that has been clicked on. Two examples of event handlers that are supported are:

- onBlur: a Blur event occurs when an option from a list on a form is selected or some text is entered in a text field;
- onClick: the Click event occurs when an option on a form is clicked. The option can be selected using either a button, check-box, radio, reset, submit, or link.

An example showing a segment of script that illustrates the use of an event handler is given in Figure 15.20. In this example the user is prompted for his or her user name and password and, when each is entered, the related onBlur event handler is invoked to check its validity. As we can see, each is checked using a different function and, if either fails, an appropriate message is output in an alert window.

15.6 Security

When carrying out a transaction over the Web relating to an e-commerce application, since in many instances this involves sending details of a user's payment card, the security of such transfers is vitally important. For example, an eavesdropper with knowledge of Internet protocols could readily intercept the information entered on the order form and, having got the name and other details about the card, proceed to use these to carry out purchases of their own. A second potential pitfall is that the Web site from where the purchase is being made may not in reality have anything for sale and, prior to the agreed delivery date, abscond with the money that it has collected. In addition, in electronic banking (e-banking) and other financial applications, a client may masquerade as another person. Any security scheme, therefore, must be able to counter each of these threats.

15.6.1 SSL

An example of a widely used scheme is the **secure socket layer** (**SSL**) protocol. As the name implies, SSL operates at the socket interface which, as we saw earlier in Section 12.3.1, is between the transport layer (TCP) and the application layer in the TCP/IP reference model. Essentially, SSL carries out the authentication of the server by the client – and the authentication of the

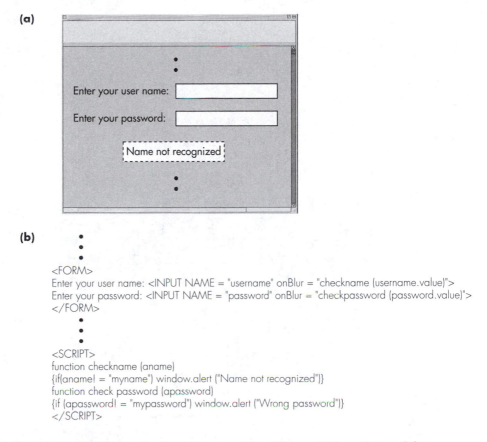

(a)

Enter your user name:

Enter your password:

Name not recognized

(b)

```
<FORM>
Enter your user name: <INPUT NAME = "username" onBlur = "checkname (username.value)">
Enter your password: <INPUT NAME = "password" onBlur = "checkpassword (password.value)">
</FORM>
          •
          •
          •
<SCRIPT>
function checkname (aname)
{if(aname! = "myname") window.alert ("Name not recognized")}
function check password (apassword)
{if (apassword! = "mypassword") window.alert ("Wrong password")}
</SCRIPT>
```

Figure 15.20 Example showing event handling within a form: (a) a portion of the display; (b) the script associated with it.

client by the server if required – by using a recognized certification authority – see Section 13.6 – and the establishment of a symmetric encryption algorithm and key for the session. It then uses the key – called a **session key** – to encrypt/decrypt all of the messages that are transferred as part of the transaction. The location of the SSL protocol in the stack is shown in Figure 15.21(a) and a summary of the steps that are followed to establish a secure socket connection are listed in part (b) of the figure.

As we can see, the HTML interpreter part of the browser has two pathways/sockets available to it, an insecure socket connection and a secure socket connection. When a user clicks on a link to an SSL-enabled server, the protocol/method part of the URL is *https:* rather than *http:* . On detecting this, the HTML interpreter invokes the SSL protocol code which proceeds to carry out the steps shown in Figure 15.21(b).

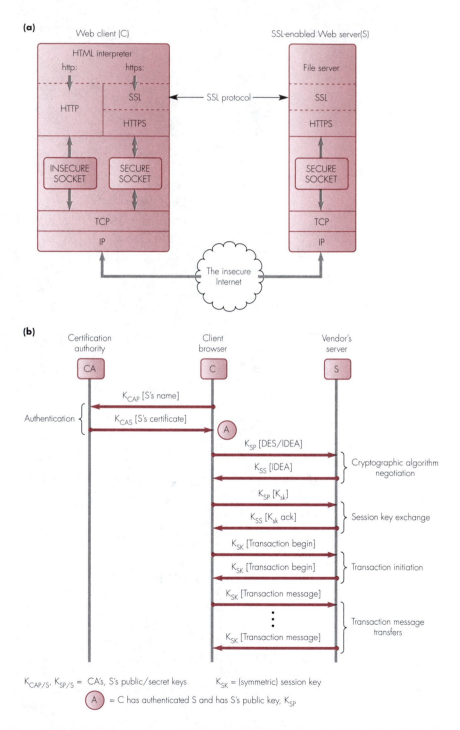

Figure 15.21 The secure socket layer (SSL) protocol: (a) protocol stack; (b) outline of the authentication and transaction initiation phases.

As we can deduce from the list of steps, the establishment of a secure socket connection is carried out by the exchange of an ordered set of HTTP request/response messages which collectively form the SSL protocol. When interpreting the steps shown in the figure, the following should be noted:

■ **Authentication using a CA**:
  - C authenticates S by first checking that the CA named in S's Web page is on the list of recognized CAs. If so, C reads the public key of the CA from the list and then requests S's certificate from the CA by sending it S's name in a request message. The CA then sends the certificate in a response message.
  - On receipt of the certificate, C decrypts it using CA's public key and checks that the name on the certificate is that of S. If so, C assumes S is authentic and reads the public key of S from the certificate.

■ **Cryptographic algorithm negotiation**:
  - Once S has been authenticated, C proceeds to negotiate with S a suitable (symmetric) cryptographic algorithm for the transaction.
  - To do this, C sends its preferences – DES or IDEA for example – together with proposed operational parameters in a request message to S. S responds with its choice of one of these in the response message.

■ **Session key exchange**:
  - C generates a random (symmetric) key for the transaction and encrypts it using S's public key. C then sends the encrypted key in a message to S.
  - On receipt of the message, S decrypts the message using its own private key and returns a response message to C acknowledging that it, too, now has the session key.

■ **Transaction initiation**:
  - C sends an encrypted message to S informing S that it is now ready to start the transaction and that all future messages will be encrypted.
  - On receipt of this, S returns an encrypted response message that it, too, is now ready to start the transaction.

■ **Transaction information transfer**:
  - Once a secure socket connection has been established, each message relating to the transaction that is sent/received over the socket is encrypted/decrypted using the agreed symmetric session key.

When using SSL in banking and other financial applications, normally, when a client starts a new session, it is the SSL in the server that authenticates the client before entering into a transaction.

15.6.2 SET

A potential loophole with SSL is that although the scheme allows the client to authenticate that the server is a recognized server, because the server's bank is not involved in the authentication process, the server's certificate does not guarantee that it is authorized to enter into transactions that involve payment cards. Similarly, the client's certificate does not guarantee that the client is using his or her own card. To counter these loopholes, the major card companies have introduced a scheme that has been designed specifically for card transactions over the Web/Internet. The scheme is called **secure electronic transactions** (**SET**).

In the SET scheme, in addition to the client (the purchaser) and server (the vendor), the client and vendor's banks are also involved also in carrying out a transaction. The purchaser, vendor, and vendor's bank all have certificates and, in the case of the purchaser and vendor, the certification authority is their respective bank. The purchaser's certificate, in addition to the purchaser's public key, also contains the name of the purchaser's bank. This enables, firstly, the purchaser to verify that the vendor is allowed to enter into payment card transactions and secondly, that the purchaser is using a legitimate card.

In practice, the SET scheme is relatively complex. However, an outline of the sequence of steps followed to carry out a card purchase electronically is shown in Figure 15.22. The following should be noted when interpreting the sequence shown:

- Three items of software are involved:
  - the *browser wallet*: this runs in the client and contains details of all the payment cards the vendor currently holds;
  - the *vendor server*: this is the Web server and, in addition to responding to requests for product information, it manages the (electronic) purchase of items from the vendor's catalog;
  - the *acquirer gateway*: this is located in the vendor's bank computer and manages the payment phase of a purchase;
- For each new purchase, the vendor allocates a unique transaction identifier (TI) and this is included in all subsequent messages.
- During the order and purchase phases, the order information sent to the vendor contains only the card name and it is the purchase information that is sent to the vendor's bank that contains the actual card number.
- The payment request is carried out using existing inter-bank fund transfer procedures.

Further information about SET can be found in the bibliography for this chapter.

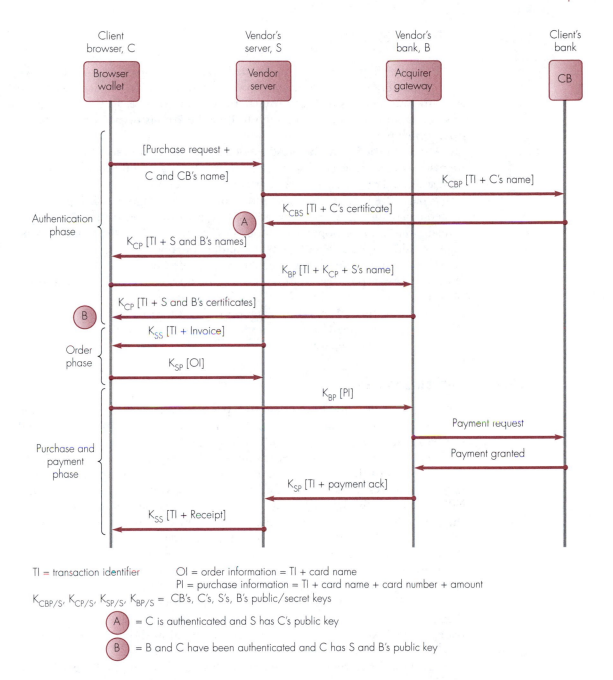

Figure 15.22 Outline of the operation of secure electronic transactions (SET).

15.7 Web operation

So far in this chapter we have described a range of topics relating to how a Web page is created and transferred over the Internet. In the last section we saw how transactions over the Internet are made secure. In this section we describe a number of issues relating to how the Web is organized and its key operational parts.

The first issue is how the presence of a server with a new set of pages/documents becomes known to users of the Web. There are a number of ways this can be done. For example, as we saw earlier in Section 15.2.1, the URL of the home page (together with a description of what the page is offering) can be posted to a related newsgroup within UseNet using the *news:* protocol/method. Alternatively, a more popular method is to use what is called a **search engine** together with a special browser called a **spider** (or **robot**).

The volume of information on the Web is already vast and is increasing continuously. In practice, however, only a small subset of this information is of interest to a particular user. The second issue, therefore, is how a user gains access to this subset of information without having to search the entire Web. This is done using an intermediary called a **portal**. We shall describe each of these issues separately.

15.7.1 Search engines

Before we can describe how a new Web page is made available over the Web we must first build up an understanding of how the search process is carried out by a search engine to find and retrieve a Web page. As we saw in Section 15.2, each Web page/document is accessed using the page's URL which, since it contains the unique domain name of the server computer on which the page/file is stored, is unique within the entire Web/Internet. Hence providing we know the URL of a page, a browser can readily obtain and display the page contents. To help with this, all browsers allow the user to keep a list of URLs in a table and provide facilities for the user to select, add, and delete entries. Nevertheless, in many instances, when searching for information on the Web, the user does not have a URL but rather he or she is interested in, say, any pages relating to a specific topic/subject. As a result, a directory is required. This is analogous to a telephone directory since, for each entry, a Web directory contains some information that describes the contents of the page plus its URL. A key issue is what this information should be and how it is used to find a specific URL.

A second issue relates to the size of the directory. As we have said, the number of Web pages is already vast and is increasing continuously. It would be totally infeasible to have a single large directory since the time required to carry out each search operation would be endless. This also applies to the telephone directory system of course and, to make searching the latter faster, the directory is fragmented into many separate sections. Typically, this is based on geographic location and, at a local level, the directory is divided into business and residential subscribers. When the telephone number of a customer is required, in addition to the customer's name, the location of the customer and whether it is a business or private residence is requested. In this way the search for the given name is restricted to a small subsection of the total directory.

The same approach is followed for the Web directory except the partitioning of the directory is not as straightforward. As we indicated earlier, with the Web the search information/index is based on a given topic/subject which is much less precise than a given name and location. For example, since each page has a title field, in principle, this could be used as the search index for the page. In practice, this cannot be done since in many instances a title is not given and, when one is given, it often bears no relation to the actual page contents. Instead, therefore, for each page, an additional block of information – normally in the form of a string of **keywords** – that describes the contents of the page is defined and it is these that are used as search indexes.

In practice, the choice of keywords to go with each URL varies widely and, as a result, there are a large number of different search engines in existence. In general, however, most allow a user to add the URL of the home page of a new set of pages to their current set of directories. Normally, this is done by first accessing the home page of the company that manages the search engine and, through this, a fill-in form is obtained. This is then filled in by the user and, when it is submitted, the page is added to the related directory. Alternatively, there are commercial organizations which, when a new URL is submitted, will add this to a number of search engines for you.

Spiders and robots

There are two different ways to obtain the search indexes for each page. One involves the person who submits the page providing a set of keywords in the same fill-in form that is submitted/posted to the owner of the search engine. These are then used to determine into which directory the URL should be inserted. In the second method, only the URL is submitted and it is the company which manages the search engine that obtains the keywords. It does this by using a special browser called a spider – also called a robot or simply **bot** – which, when given the submitted URL, accesses and then searches the contents of the page for specific keywords. It then uses these to enter the URL into the most appropriate directory(ies). The spider then follows all the links from the submitted home page and derives a set of keywords for each of these pages too. In addition, to make people aware that a new set of pages is now available, most search engine companies allow the URL of the home page (together with an associated set of keywords) to be posted to their **What's New** site. Normally, the page is then kept in the What's New directory for a set period of time.

Since in the second method it is the spider/robot that determines the set of keywords to be used, these may not be an optimum set as seen by the writer of the page. Hence when a spider is used, it is possible to direct the spider by including in the page header a list of the keywords that the writer feels should be used. The given list of keywords is called the **meta information** for the page and is included in the page header between the <HEAD> and </HEAD> tags. The list of keywords is given within the <META> tag using the following arguments:

- NAME = "keywords": to allow for other types of meta information, this informs the HTML interpreter that what follows is a list of keywords;
- LANG = "language": the language used for the keywords, for example en-US, es (Spanish), fr (French);
- CONTENT = "list of keywords": the list of keywords with a space between each.

An example format is:

```
<META NAME     = "keywords"
      LANG     = "en-US"
      CONTENT = "vacations holidays walking beach activity hotels
                 scubadiving - - -">
```

15.7.2 Portals

As we indicated earlier, there are many different search engine companies/sites available which, given a set of keywords, will carry out a search through their directories and return details of a list of up to, say, 10 Web sites that give the best matches with a given set of keywords. Typically, the returned details for each site are in the form:

Match: "80%"
Title: "The name of the Web site"
URL: "The URL of the home page"
Summary: "A summary of what this site has to offer"
More: "Click on this link to initiate a search for more pages like this one"

and are listed according to their match field.

To help you find the best search engine sites, most browsers have a button on the display which, when clicked, returns a list of a number of sites together with some information about what each has to offer. In addition, many Internet service providers (ISPs) provide a facility to help a user find the best search engine site(s) for a given set of keywords. This is referred to as the ISP's portal since it acts as a gateway to the vast collection of Web sites/pages that are now available.

Essentially, the portal has knowledge of a large collection of search engine sites and their directories. Given a set of keywords, the portal will select the site that it thinks has the best directory relating to the query. In addition, some portals will interact with the user through a form to obtain a more focussed set of requirements before returning the URL of what it thinks is the best site. Some ISPs also allow a user to create his or her own personalized portal. Then, by simply clicking on the portal page, the user is able to access his or her own preferred sources of information relating to, say, news, sport, weather, entertainment, and so on.

Summary

In this chapter we have described selected aspects of the operation of the World Wide Web. The list of topics is summarized in Figure 15.23. They can be grouped under the following headings:

- how a Web page is written in HTML and accessed over the Internet;
- how audio and video are incorporated into a Web page and accessed in real time using either a Web server or a streaming server. Also, how the user can control the way the audio and/or video is played out using the real-time streaming protocol (RTSP);
- an introduction to Java and JavaScript and the features each provides;
- security in e-commerce applications using the secure socket layer (SSL) and secure electronic transactions (SET) protocols;
- an introduction to the operation of the Web including the role of search engines and portals.

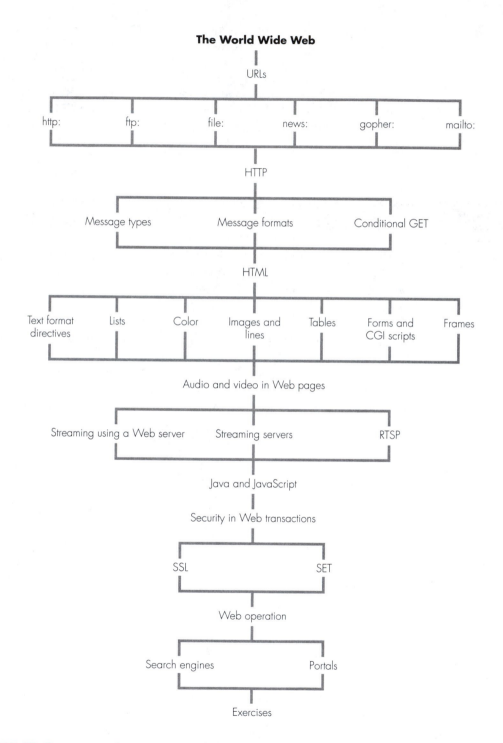

Figure 15.23 Summary of the topics discussed relating to the Web.

Exercises

Section 15.2

15.1 With the aid of a diagram, in a few sentences, explain each of the following terms relating to the Web: a browser, a server, HTTP, HTML, hyperlinks, URLs.

15.2 Assuming the URL of a Web page is:

http://www.UoW.edu/prospectus/index.html

identify the application protocol/method that is used to access the page, the domain name of the server, the pathname of the file, and the file name.

15.3 Assuming the URL

ftp://www.mpeg.org/mpeg-4/

determine the directory and file name of the page.

15.4 Assuming a user clicks on the URL

ftp://www.mpeg.org/mpeg-4

explain what type of information is returned.

15.5 Give an example of a URL that uses the *file:* method and explain one of its uses.

15.6 Outline the operation of UseNet including the role of newsgroups, a news reader, and NNTP. Hence explain how the home page of a new set of linked pages could be announced from within a Web page to a related newsgroup over UseNet.

15.7 Outline the steps that are followed by the browser to enable a user to send an email message from within a Web page.

15.8 Explain the meaning of the term "URI" and how it differs from a URL.

15.9 With the aid of a diagram, show the protocol stack that is used in a Web client and Web server to obtain a page/block of data using the HTTP application protocol/method. Include in your diagram a DNS name server and explain its role in relation to obtaining the page.

15.10 Describe how it is possible to obtain satisfactory performance with a simple request/response application protocol for transferring a page over the Web.

15.11 List the advantages and disadvantages of using the following types of TCP connections for a Web session:
(i) nonpersistent connections,
(ii) multiple concurrent nonpersistent connections,
(iii) persistent connections.

15.12 In relation to HTTP, state the difference between a simple request message and a full request message. How does HTTP discriminate between the two message types?

15.13 Using the example HTTP request/response messages shown in Figure 15.3:
(i) state the implications of the presence of the *HTTP/1.1* and *Connect:close* fields in the request message
(ii) if the response message related to, say, a JPEG image rather than an HTML page, give a typical set of content-related fields.

15.14 Explain the role of a cache server and how its use can speed up the time to obtain a Web page. Clearly indicate where the savings arise and how they can be reduced further by using a hierarchy of cache servers.

15.15 State how a conditional GET request message differs from a GET request. Hence, with the aid of a diagram, illustrate the message sequence that is followed when a browser obtains the contents of a named file from a named (origin) server via a proxy/cache server. Assume the contents of the file have been modified since the date given in the conditional GET request message.

Section 15.3

15.16 With the aid of an example, explain the terms "absolute URL" and "relative URL" including the relationship between the two.

15.17 In relation to the HTML script shown in Figure 15.5, assume the contents of the page accessed through the link *The University* are as shown in the right frame of 15.13(a). Assuming frames are not being used, write the HTML script for the portion of the page that is displayed.

15.18 In relation to the HTML script shown in Figure 15.5, show the changes to the script if the complete prospectus was on a single page rather than a linked set of pages. State the advantages and disadvantages of doing this.

15.19 Assuming the index for this book is to be on a single Web page, write the fragment of HTML script for the first five entries in the list of contents for this chapter using the <OL> tag.

15.20 In order to enhance your Web page, you decide to introduce color into it. Show how you could direct the HTML interpreter in a browser to make the background color yellow, the text in the page orange, each link red, and a visited link blue.

15.21 In relation to the two displayed images shown in Figure 15.7, produce a segment of HTML script:
(i) to display the UoW crest/logo in the center of the page with the first-level heading starting below it – part (a),
(ii) to start the text at the top edge of the text – part (b)
(iii) to make the image shown in part (b) a hyperlink.

15.22 Give the additions to the HTML script shown in Figure 15.5 to produce a bold line that divides the heading from the remaining text.

15.23 Assume the table shown in Figure 15.9(b) is to be changed so that there are four columns CO, CLS, CBR, and VBR with a + character in those column positions where the related feature is true. For example, for the LAN row, the CLS and VBR columns would each have a + character and the other two columns would be left blank. Produce the HTML script for the table.

15.24 Give the changes to the HTML script shown in Figure 15.9(c) to align the contents of the cells in the NETWORK column to the left edge of the cell.

15.25 Give the outline of an HTML script to produce a table that comprises 3 columns and 3 rows with the second and third cells of the first column combined and the second and third cells of the second row combined. Assume the 3 cells in the first row are for headings and the contents of all cells are to be left blank.

15.26 (i) State the purpose of a fill-in form and an associated CGI script.
(ii) Use an example FORM declaration to explain the use of the ACTION and METHOD attributes.
(iii) List some of the alternative ways input can be obtained from a user.

15.27 Use the <INPUT> tag with appropriate attributes to create the following form. Include in your HTML script an example URL for the ACTION attribute.

ICE CREAM ORDER FORM
Name:
Address:

Phone number:
Please check flavors:
Vanilla ☐   Chocolate ☐   Strawberry ☐
Please indicate how many boxes you require:
One ☐   Two ☐   Three ☐
Payment card Type: MC ☐   Visa ☐
Number: Expiry date:
Submit order   Reset order

15.28 List a typical set of responses for the various fields in the form shown in Exercise 15.27. Explain how these are sent to a CGI script/program in the server given in your example URL.

15.29 Show how the choice of flavors in your HTML script for Exercise 15.27 could be presented using a pull-down menu.

15.30 Assume you want to create an album for your digitized photographs on your own computer which can be viewed through the browser. Write a segment of an HTML script for a page template that divides the display window into four quarters using frames. Include in your script the URL of the image/photograph you want to display in each frame.

15.31 Explain the meaning and use of an in-line frame. Write a segment of an HTML script that shows how a second frame can be used to display the contents of a page that is referenced in the current page.

Section 15.4

15.32 When downloading a Web page comprising audio and/or video, by means of examples, explain why streaming and a playout buffer are used. Hence list and explain the functions performed by a media player.

15.33 With the aid of a diagram, explain how a file containing a short video clip – comprising audio and video – is streamed from a Web server and played out by a browser that has both an audio and a video media player. Include in your diagram the protocols that are used to transfer the media.

15.34 With the aid of a diagram, explain how the playout process used in the last exercise can be improved by using a meta file. Include in your diagram the protocols that are used to transfer the meta file and the media streams.
   Identify the limitations associated with this approach.

15.35 With the aid of a diagram, explain how a movie/video is accessed from a streaming server and played out by a browser. Include in your diagram the protocols that are used at both the server side and the client side including, in the case of the various application protocols, their port numbers and use. Include in your explanation the sequence of steps that occur when the user first selects a movie/video.

15.36 List a typical set of control buttons associated with the playout of a movie/video on the screen of a TV/PC. Hence use a diagram to illustrate the application protocol and control/data parts of the media player that is involved when the user carries out the following sequence:
   (i)   initiates the showing of a movie/video
   (ii)   activates the play button
   (iii) activates the pause button
   (iv)   activates the quit button.

Section 15.5

15.37 Both Java and JavaScript can be used to add action and interactivity to a Web page. Explain briefly how this is done in each case.

15.38 In relation to the Java programming language, explain the meaning of the following terms:
   (i)   an applet,
   (ii)   bytecode,
   (iii) bytecode interpreter.

15.39 Give an example segment of HTML script that uses the <APPLET> tag. Explain the actions that are followed by the HTML parser and bytecode interpreter when the tag is encountered in the script. Include in your description an example URL for the page and the name of the file associated with the <APPLET> tag.

15.40 In HTML 4.0 and later versions, the <OBJECT> tag is used in preference to the <APPLET> tag. Explain why this change has come about. Give an example declaration of a Java applet using the <OBJECT> tag and an associated set of attributes. Clearly identify the role performed by each attribute.

15.41 Explain the meaning of the following terms relating to the Java programming language:
   (i)   an object,
   (ii)   a method,
   (iii) encapsulation,

(iv)   object class,

(v)   package.

Give two examples of a Java library package and explain their function.

15.42   Like Java, JavaScript is object-oriented. Show how the *document* object class and the associated *.write*, *.URL* and *.title* methods can be used in a JavaScript that is embedded in an HTML page.

15.43   By means of examples, explain the meaning of the term "event handler" in the context of the JavaScript programming language. Hence explain how an event handler can be used in conjunction with a form to perform a specific action when the event occurs. Use as an example a form that takes as input the name and password entered by a user and performs checks on these.

Section 15.6

15.44   Give three examples of security threats that illustrate the need for additional security measures in e-commerce and e-banking applications.

15.45   In relation to the secure socket layer (SSL) scheme, with the aid of a diagram, explain the function of the various protocols that are used to carry out a secure transaction. Include in your description how the HTML interpreter differentiates between a secure and an insecure transaction.

15.46   To carry out a secure transaction using the SSL scheme, the following five steps are required:
(i)   authentication using a certification authority
(ii)   cryptographic algorithm negotiation
(iii) session key exchange

(iv)   transaction initiation

(v)   transaction information transfer.

With the aid of a diagram and selected keys, illustrate how each of the above steps is carried out.

15.47   Identify a potential security loophole with the SSL scheme and state how the secure electronic transactions (SET) scheme overcomes this.

15.48   Identify the four main players that are involved in the SET scheme and give a brief description of the role of the software associated with each of them.

15.49   Assuming public key cryptography throughout, use a diagram to show how:
(i)   the client authenticates the vendor and vice versa
(ii)   the client sends an order to the vendor
(iii) the client carries out the purchase and payment operations.

Section 15.7

15.50   Outline the role of a search engine. Identify the two main issues that influence its design and explain why keywords are used.

15.51   Explain the role of a spider/robot in relation to a search engine and how this can be influenced by the writer of a page by providing meta information. By means of an example, show how the latter is included in a Web page using the <META> tag and the NAME, LANG, and CONTENT attributes.

15.52   By means of an example, explain the structure of the information that is returned from a search operation. Also explain the role of a portal in carrying out a search.

appendix a CRC implementation

Although the requirement to perform multiple (modulo-2) divisions to compute a CRC may appear to be relatively complicated, in practice it can be done quite readily in either hardware or software. To illustrate this, a hardware implementation of the scheme used in Figure 6.22 is given in Figure A.1(a).

In this example, since we are to generate four FCS digits, we need only a 4-bit shift register to represent bits x^3, x^2, x^1, and x^0 in the generator polynomial. We often refer to these as the active bits of the generator. With this generator polynomial, digits x^3 and x^0 are binary 1 while digits x^2 and x^1 are binary 0. The new states of shift register elements x^1 and x^2 simply take on the states of x^0 and x^1 directly; the new states of elements x^0 and x^3 are determined by the state of the feedback path exclusive ORed with the preceding digit.

The circuit operates as follows. The FCS shift register is cleared and the first 8-bit byte in the frame is parallel-loaded into the PISO transmit shift register. This is then shifted out to the transmission line, most significant bit first, at a rate determined by the transmitter clock TxC. In time synchronism with this, the same bitstream is exclusive-ORed with x^3 and passed via the feedback path to the selected inputs of the FCS shift register. As each subsequent 8-bit byte is loaded into the transmit shift register and bit-serially transmitted to line, the procedure repeats. Finally, after the last byte in the frame has been output, the transmit shift register is loaded with zeros and the feedback control signal changes from 1 to 0 so that the current contents of the FCS shift register – the computed remainder – follow the frame contents onto the transmission line.

In Figure A.1(a) the contents of the transmit and FCS shift registers assume just a single-byte frame ($N = 1$), and hence correspond to the earlier example in Figure 6.22. In the figure the contents of both the transmit and FCS shift registers are shown after each shift (transmit clock) pulse. The transmitted bitstream is as shown in the hashed boxes.

The corresponding receiver hardware is similar to that used at the transmitter, as shown in Figure A.1(b). The received data (RxD) is sampled (shifted) into the SIPO receive shift register in the centre (or later with Manchester encoding) of the bit cell. Also, as before, in time synchronization with this the bitstream is exclusive-ORed with x^3 and fed into the FCS shift register. As each 8-bit byte is received, it is read by the controlling device. Again, the contents shown are for a frame comprising just a single byte of data.

(a)

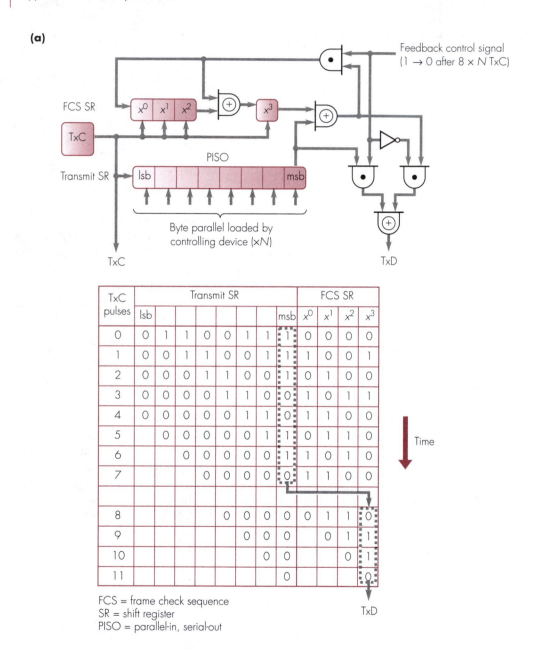

Figure A.1 CRC hardware implementation schematic: (a) CRC generation; (b) CRC checking.

(b)

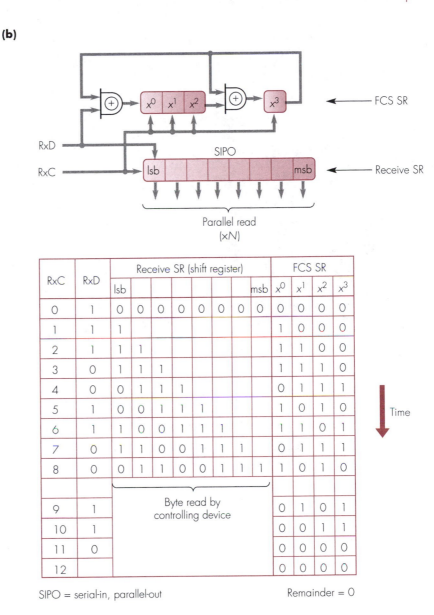

| RxC | RxD | Receive SR (shift register) | | | | | | | | | FCS SR | | | |
		lsb							msb	x^0	x^1	x^2	x^3
0	1	0	0	0	0	0	0	0	0	0	0	0	0
1	1	1								1	0	0	0
2	1	1	1							1	1	0	0
3	0	1	1	1						1	1	1	0
4	0	0	1	1	1					0	1	1	1
5	1	0	0	1	1	1				1	0	1	0
6	1	1	0	0	1	1	1			1	1	0	1
7	0	1	1	0	0	1	1	1		0	1	1	1
8	0	0	1	1	0	0	1	1	1	1	0	1	0
9	1	Byte read by controlling device								0	1	0	1
10	1									0	0	1	1
11	0									0	0	0	0
12										0	0	0	0

SIPO = serial-in, parallel-out   Remainder = 0

Figure A.1 Continued.

The hardware in Figure A.1 is normally incorporated into the transmission control circuits associated with bit-oriented transmission. In some instances, however, a CRC is used in preference to a block sum check with character-oriented transmission. In such cases, the CRC must normally be generated in software by the controlling device rather than in hardware. This is relatively straightforward as we can see from the pseudocode in Figure A.2.

{Assume a preformatted frame to be transmitted (including a zero byte at its tail) or a received frame is stored in a byte array buff[1.. count]. Also that the 8 active bits of a 9-bit divisor are stored in the most-significant 8 bits of a 16-bit integer CRCDIV. The following function will compute and return the 8-bit CRC}

```
function  CRC : byte;
var       i, j : integer;
          data : integer

begin     data := buff[1] shl 8;
          for j := 2 to count do
              begin
                  data := data + buff [j];
                  for i := 1 to 8 do
                      if ((data and $8000) = $8000) then
                      begin  data := data shl1;
                             data := data xor CRCDIV; end
                      else   data := data shl 1;
              end;

          CRC := data shr 8;
end;
```

Figure A.2 Pseudocode for the computation and checking of an 8-bit CRC.

The code assumes an 8-bit generator polynomial (divisor) and that the preformatted frame – STX, ETX, and so on – is stored in an array. The same code can be used for CRC generation and checking; for generation the array will contain a byte/character comprising all zeros at its tail.

appendix b Forward error control

B.1 Introduction

With an automatic repeat request (ARQ) error control scheme, additional check digits are appended to each transmitted message (frame) to enable the receiver to detect when an error is present in a received message, assuming certain types of error. If an error is detected, additional control procedures are used to request another copy of the message. With forward error control (FEC), sufficient additional check digits are added to each transmitted message to enable the receiver not only to detect the presence of one or more errors in a received message but also to locate the position of the error(s). Furthermore, since the message is in a binary form, correction is achieved simply by inverting the bit(s) that have been identified as erroneous.

In practice, the number of additional check digits required for error correction is much larger than that needed for just error detection. In most applications involving terrestrial (land-based) links, ARQ methods similar to those described in Chapter 6 are more efficient than FEC methods, and hence are the most frequently used. Such methods rely on a return path for acknowledgment purposes. However, in most entertainments applications, a return path is simply not available or, even if one was available, the round-trip delay associated with it may be very long compared with the data transmission rate of the link. For example, with many satellite links the propagation delay may be such that several hundred megabits may be transmitted by the sending station before an acknowledgment could be received in the reverse direction. In such applications, FEC methods are used. The aim of this appendix is to give an introduction to the techniques most widely used with FEC methods.

B.2 Block codes

An example of a block code is the Hamming single-bit code. In practice, this FEC method is of limited use for digital transmission. Nevertheless, we shall look at it briefly to introduce the subject of block codes and some of the terms associated with coding theory. Clearly, a comprehensive description of the subject of coding theory is beyond the scope of this book and hence the aim here is simply to give a brief introduction. If you have an interest in coding theory and would like to gain a more extensive coverage, consult some of the references given in the bibliography at the end of the book.

Recall that the term used in coding theory to describe the combined message unit, comprising the useful data bits and the additional check bits, is **codeword**. The minimum number of bit positions in which two valid codewords differ is known as the **Hamming distance** of the code. For example, consider a coding scheme that has seven data bits and a single parity bit per codeword. Assuming even parity is being used, consecutive codewords in this scheme are as follows:

```
0000000  0
0000001  1
0000010  1
0000011  0
```

We can see from this list that such a scheme has a Hamming distance of 2, as each valid codeword differs in at least two bit positions. This means that it does not detect 2-bit errors since the resulting (corrupted) bit pattern will be a different but valid codeword. However, it does detect all single-bit errors since, if a single bit in a codeword is corrupted, an invalid codeword will result.

In general, the error-detecting and error-correcting properties of a coding scheme are both related to its Hamming distance. It can be shown that to detect n errors, we must use a coding scheme with a Hamming distance of $n + 1$, while to correct for n errors, we must use a code with a Hamming distance of $2n + 1$.

The simplest error-correcting coding scheme is the Hamming single-bit code. Such a code detects not only when a single-bit error is present in a received codeword but also the position of the error. The corrected codeword is derived by inverting the identified erroneous bit. This type of code is known as a block code, since the original message to be transmitted is treated as a single block (frame) during the encoding and subsequent decoding processes. In general, with a block code, each block of k source digits is encoded to produce an n-digit block (n greater than k) of output digits. The encoder is said to produce an (n, k) code. The ratio k/n is known as the **code rate** or **code efficiency** while the difference $1 - k/n$ is known as the **redundancy**.

To illustrate this, consider a Hamming code to detect and correct for single-bit errors assuming each codeword contains a 7-bit data field – an ASCII character, for example. Such a coding scheme requires four check bits since, with this scheme, the check bits occupy all bit positions that are powers of 2. This code is known as an (11, 7) block code with a rate of 7/11 and a redundancy of $1 - 7/11$. For example, the bit positions of the value 1001101 are as follows:

```
11 10 9 8 7 6 5 4 3 2 1
 1  0 0 x 1 1 0 x 1 x x
```

The four bit positions marked 'x' are used for the check bits, which are derived as follows. The 4-bit binary numbers corresponding to those bit positions with a binary 1 are added together using modulo-2 arithmetic and the four check bits are the following 4-bit sum:

$$11 = 1\ 0\ 1\ 1$$
$$7 = 0\ 1\ 1\ 1$$
$$6 = 0\ 1\ 1\ 0$$
$$3 = 0\ 0\ 1\ 1$$
$$= \overline{1\ 0\ 0\ 1}$$

The transmitted codeword is thus:

$$11\ 10\ 9\ 8\ 7\ 6\ 5\ 4\ 3\ 2\ 1$$
$$1\quad 0\ 0\ \textit{1}\ 1\ 1\ 0\ 0\ \textit{1}\ 0\ \textit{1}$$

Similarly, at the receiver, the 4-bit binary numbers corresponding to those bit positions with a binary 1, including the check bits, are again added together. If no errors have occurred, the modulo-2 sum is zero:

$$11 = 1\ 0\ 1\ 1$$
$$8 = 1\ 0\ 0\ 0$$
$$7 = 0\ 1\ 1\ 1$$
$$6 = 0\ 1\ 1\ 0$$
$$3 = 0\ 0\ 1\ 1$$
$$1 = 0\ 0\ 0\ 1$$
$$= \overline{0\ 0\ 0\ 0}$$

Now consider a single-bit error: say bit 11 is corrupted from 1 to 0. The new modulo-2 sum is now:

$$8 = 1\ 0\ 0\ 0$$
$$7 = 0\ 1\ 1\ 1$$
$$6 = 0\ 1\ 1\ 0$$
$$3 = 0\ 0\ 1\ 1$$
$$1 = 0\ 0\ 0\ 1$$
$$= \overline{1\ 0\ 1\ 1}$$

Firstly, the sum is nonzero, which indicates an error, and secondly, the modulo-2 sum, equivalent to decimal 11, indicates that bit 11 is the erroneous bit. The latter is inverted to obtain the corrected codeword and hence data bits.

It can also be shown that if two bit errors occur, the modulo-2 sum is nonzero, thus indicating an error, but the positions of the errors cannot be determined from the sum. The Hamming single-bit code can correct for single-bit errors and detect two-bit errors but other multiple-bit errors cannot be detected.

As we saw in Chapter 6, the main types of error in many data communication networks are error bursts rather than, say, isolated single or double-bit errors. Hence, although the Hamming coding scheme in its basic form appears to be inappropriate for use with such networks, a simple technique called interleaving is often used to extend the application of such a scheme.

Consider, for example, a requirement to transmit a block of data, comprising a string of, say, eight ASCII characters, over a simplex channel that has a high probability of an error burst of, say, seven bits. The controlling device first converts each ASCII character into its 11-bit codeword form to give a block of eight 11-bit codewords. Then, instead of transmitting each codeword separately, the controlling device transmits the contents of the block of codewords a column at a time. Thus the eight, say, most significant bits are transmitted first, then the eight next most significant bits and so on, finishing with the eight least significant bits. The controlling device at the receiver then performs the reverse operation, reassembling the transmitted block in memory, prior to performing the detection and, if necessary, correction operation on each codeword.

The effect of this approach is that if an error burst of up to seven bits does occur, it affects only a single bit in each codeword rather than a string of bits in one or two codewords. This means that, assuming just a single error burst in the 88 bits transmitted, the receiver can determine a correct copy of the transmitted block of characters.

Although the approach just outlined provides a way of extending the usefulness of this type of encoding scheme, Hamming codes are used mainly in applications that have isolated single-bit errors; an example is in error-correcting semiconductor memory systems. As we showed in Figure 11.18, the preferred method of achieving FEC in most digital communication systems is based on a combination of a Reed–Solomon block code and a convolutional coder. We shall now briefly describe the operation of convolutional coders.

B.3 Convolutional codes

Block codes are *memoryless* codes as each output codeword depends only on the current k-bit message block being encoded. In contrast, with a convolutional code, the continuous stream of source bits is operated upon to produce a continuous stream of output (encoded) bits. Because of the nature of the encoding process, the sequence of source bits is said to be convolved (by applying a specific binary operation on them) to produce the output bit sequence. Also, each bit in the output sequence is dependent not only on the current bit being encoded but also on the previous sequence of source bits, thus implying some form of memory. In practice, as we shall see, this takes the form of a shift register of a finite length, known as the **constraint length**, and the convolution (binary) operation is performed using one or more modulo-2 adders (exclusive-OR gates).

Encoding

An example of a convolutional encoder is shown in Figure B.1(a). With this encoder, the three-bit shift register provides the memory and the two modulo-2 adders the convolution operation. For each bit in the input sequence, two bits are output, one from each of the two modulo-2 adders. The encoder shown is thus known as a rate $1/2 (k/n)$ convolutional encoder with a constraint length of 3.

Because of the memory associated with a convolutional encoder, we must have a convenient means of determining the specific output bit sequence generated for a given input sequence. Three techniques can be used, each based on a form of diagrammatic representation: a tree diagram, a state diagram, and a trellis diagram. In practice, the last is the most frequently used method because it is the most useful for demonstrating the decoding operation. However, before we can draw this, we must determine the outputs for each possible input sequence using either the tree or state diagram.

As an example, Figure B.1(b) shows the **tree diagram** for the encoder in Figure B.1(a). The branching points in the tree are known as nodes and the tree shows the two possible branches at each node; the upper of the two branches corresponds to a 0 input bit and the lower branch to a 1 bit. The pair of output bits corresponding to the two possible branches at each node are shown on the outside of each branch line.

As we can see, with a tree diagram the number of branches in the tree doubles for each new input bit. However, the tree is repetitive after the second branch level since, after this level, there are only four unique branch nodes. These are known as *states* and are shown as *A, B, C,* and *D* in the figure.

As we can see, from any one of these nodes the same pair of output bits and new node state occurs, irrespective of the position of the node in the tree. For example, from any node *C* the same pair of branch alternatives occur: 10 output and new state *A* for a 0 input, or 01 output and new state *B* for a 1 input.

Once we have identified the states for the encoder using the tree diagram, we can draw the **trellis diagram**. As an example, the trellis diagram for the same encoder is shown in Figure B.2(b). As we can see, after the second branch level, the repetitive nature of the tree diagram is exploited by representing all the possible encoder outputs in a more reduced form.

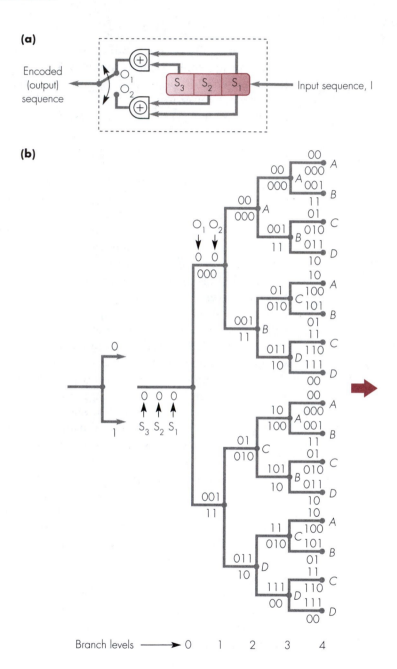

Figure B.1 Convolutional coder principles: (a) example encoder circuit; (b) tree diagram representaton of the encoder.

(a) Encoded (output) sequence

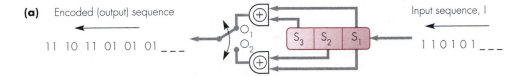

Input sequence, I

11 10 11 01 01 01 _ _ _   110101 _ _ _

Input sequence I	Shift register contents S_1 S_2 S_3			Output sequence O_1 O_2	
1	1	0	0	1	1
1	1	1	0	1	0
0	0	1	1	1	1
1	1	0	1	0	1
0	0	1	0	0	1
1	1	0	1	0	1
¦	¦		¦	¦	

(b)

Branch nodes

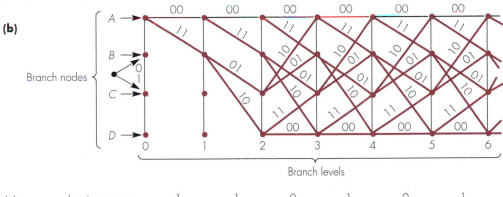

Branch levels

(c)

Input sequence: 1   1   0   1   0   1
Encoded sequence: 11   10   11   01   01   01

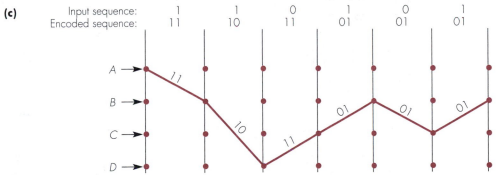

Figure B.2 Convolutional encoder output derivation: (a) circuit; (b) trellis diagram; (c) example output.

The trellis diagram shows the outputs that result from this encoder for all possible input bit sequences. Then, for a specific input sequence, a single path through the trellis – and hence sequence of output bits – results. As an example, Figure B.2(c) shows the path through the trellis, and hence the output sequence, corresponding to the input sequence 110101... .

Initially, we assume that the shift register is cleared, that is, it is set to all 0s. After the first bit in the input sequence has been shifted (entered) into the shift register, its contents are 001. The outputs from the two modulo-2 adders are 0 + 1 = 1 (adder 1) and 0 + 1 = 1 (adder 2). Thus, the first two output bits are 11 and these are output before the next input bit is entered into the shift register. Since the input bit was a 1, the lower branch path on the trellis diagram is followed and the output is 11, as derived.

After the second input bit has been entered, the shift register contains 011. The two adder outputs are 0 + 1 = 1 (adder 1) and 1 + 1 = 0 (adder 2). Thus, the two output bits are 10 and again these are output before the next input bit is processed. Again, since the input bit was a 1, the lower branch on the trellis diagram is followed and the output is 10, as derived. Continuing, the third input bit makes the shift register contents 110 and hence the two output bits are 11; 1 + 0 = 1 (adder 1) and 1 + 0 = 1 (adder 2). Also, since the input bit was a 0, the upper branch path on the trellis diagram is followed. This process then continues.

Decoding

The aim of the decoder is to determine the *most likely* output sequence, given a received bitstream (which may have errors) and a knowledge of the encoder used at the source. The decoding procedure is equivalent to comparing the received sequence with all the possible sequences that may be obtained with the respective encoder and then selecting the sequence that is closest to the received sequence. Recall that the Hamming distance between two codewords is the number of bits that differ between them. Therefore, when selecting the sequence that is closest to the received sequence, the Hamming distance between the received sequence and each of the possible sequences is computed, and the one with the least distance is selected. Clearly, in the limit this necessitates comparing the complete received sequence with all the possible sequences, and hence paths through the trellis. This is impractical in most cases and hence we must compromise.

Essentially, a running count is maintained of the distance between the actual received sequence and each possible sequence but, at each node in the trellis, only a single path is retained. There are always two paths merging at each node and the path selected is the one with the minimum Hamming distance, the other is simply terminated. The retained paths are known as **survivor paths** and the final path selected is the one with a continuous path through the trellis with a minimum aggregate Hamming distance. This procedure is known as the **Viterbi algorithm**. The decoder, which aims to find the most likely path corresponding to the received sequence, is known as a **maximum-likelihood decoder**. Example B.1 describes the Viterbi algorithm.

Example B.1

Assume that a message sequence of 1001110... is to be sent using the encoder shown in Figure B.1(a). From the trellis diagram for this encoder, we can deduce that this will yield a transmitted (output) sequence of:

> 11 01 10 11 10 00 11 ...

Now assume a burst error occurs so that two bits of this encoded sequence are corrupted during transmission. The received sequence is as follows:

> 11 01 00 11 11 00 11 ...
>   ↑   ↑

Use the Viterbi algorithm to determine from this the most likely transmitted sequence.

Answer.

The various steps associated with the encoding and decoding procedures are shown in Figure B.3. Part (a) shows the path through the trellis corresponding to the original output from the encoder and part (b) shows how the survivor paths are chosen. The number shown by each path merging at a node in Figure B.3(b) is the accumulated Hamming distance between the path followed to get to that node and the actual received sequence.

If the path chosen is that starting at the root node (branch level 0), the received sequence is 11 and the Hamming distances for the two paths are 2 for path 00 and 0 for path 11. These two distance values are added to the paths emanating from these nodes. Thus, at branch level 1, the received sequence is 01 and the two paths from node *A* have Hamming distances of 1 for path 00 and 1 for path 11. The accumulated distances are thus 2 + 1 = 3 for each path. Similarly, the two paths emanating from node *B* have Hamming distances of 0 for path 01 and 2 for path 10, and hence the accumulated distances are 0 + 0 = 0 and 0 + 2 = 2, respectively. A similar procedure is repeated at branch level 2.

At branch level 3 and onwards, however, the selection process starts. Thus, the two paths merging at node *A* (at branch level 3) have accumulated distances of 3 and 1, of which the latter is selected to be the survivor path for this node – this is shown as a bold line on the trellis diagram. A similar selection process is followed at nodes *B*, *C*, and *D*. At node *C*, however, we can see that the two merging paths both have the same accumulated distance of 4. In such cases, the upper path is selected. Also, after the selection process, all subsequent distances are calculated relative to the accumulated distance associated with the selected path.

▶

B.1 Continued

It now remains to select the most likely path and hence the output sequence. Although the decoding procedure continues, by inspection of the portion of the trellis shown, we can see that:

- only four paths have a continuous path through the trellis;
- the distance corresponding to the path *ABCABDDC* is the minimum.

Thus, this is the path that is selected, the corresponding output sequence being 11 01 10 11 10 00 11..., which corresponds to the original encoded (and hence transmitted) sequence.

Finally, note that no FEC method can identify all errors. In general, codes like the convolutional code are used primarily to reduce the error probability (bit error rate) of a link to a more acceptable level. A typical reduction with a rate $1/2$ convolutional coder is between 10^2 and 10^3. Hence when used with a Reed–Solomon (block) coder, the number of residual bit errors after the block decoding process is reduced to a level that is acceptable for most entertainment applications involving audio and video streams.

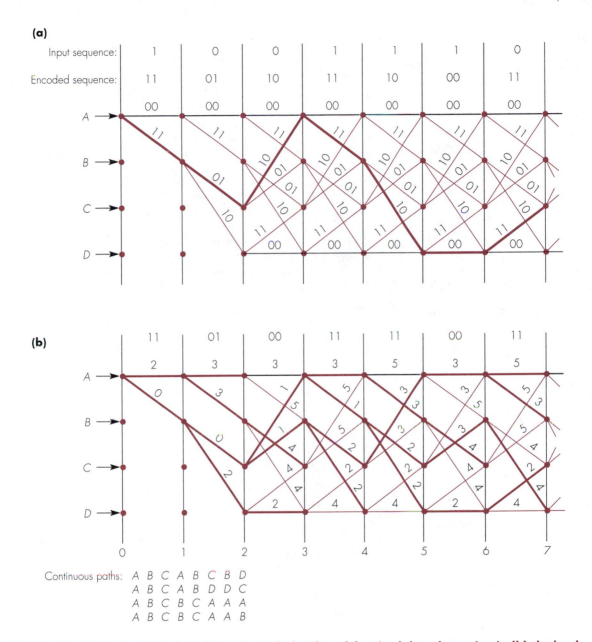

Figure B.3 Convolutional decoder output derivation: (a) actual decoder output; (b) derived survivor paths.

bibliography and further reading

In order to keep abreast of developments in the communications and networking fields, you should try to read on a regular basis the journals and magazines published in these fields by the major institutions. The most widely read journals that contain a range of technical papers in the area of communications and networks are: *IEEE Transactions on Communications, IEEE Journal on Selected Areas in Communications, IEE Proceedings on Communications, Communications of the ACM*, and *Computer Networks and ISDN*. In addition, the IEEE publish four magazines: *IEEE Network, IEEE Communications, IEEE Multimedia,* and *IEEE Internet Computing* all of which contain articles relating to state-of-the-art developments in their related fields.

The listing of titles within this Bibliography reflects the order in which the related topic is discussed in the text.

Chapter 1

Bell T.E. (1996). Communications. *IEEE Spectrum,* January
Decina M. and Trecordi V. (1999). Voice over IP and e-commerce. *IEEE Communications,* September
Comerford R. and Perry T.S. (1996). Wired for interactivity. *IEEE Spectrum,* April
IEEE (1998). *IEEE Network: Special Issue on Transmission and Distribution of Digital Video,* November
Riezenman M.J. (2000). Communications. *IEEE Spectrum,* January
Landon K.C. and Landon J.P. (1998). *Information Systems and the Internet.* Dryden Press
Comerford R. (2000). The Internet. *IEEE Spectrum,* January
Kwok T. (1995). A vision for residential broadband services. *IEEE Network,* September
Berners-Lee T. et al. (1994). The World Wide Web. *Communications of the ACM,* August

Chapter 2

Bellamy J. (1991). *Digital Telephony* 2nd edn. Wiley
Alber A.F. (1985). *Videotex/Teletext, Principles and Practices.* McGraw-Hill
Fisher S. (1995). *Multimedia Authoring.* Academic Press
Musciano C. and Kennedy B. (1996). *HTML, The Definitive Guide.* O'Reilly and Associates
Petersen D.(1992). *Audio, Video and Data Telecommunications.* McGraw-Hill
Nielsen J. (1995). *Multimedia and Hypertext.* AP Professional

Chapter 3

Hill R. (1986). *A First Course in Coding Theory.* Oxford: Clarendon Press
Shannon C. (1948). A mathematical theory of communication. *Bell System Tech. Journal*
Storer J.A. (1988). *Data Compression: methods and theory.* Computer Science Press
Vitter J.S. (1987). Design and analysis of dynamic Huffman codes. *Journal of the ACM,* October

Welch T.A. (1984). A technique for high performance data compression. *IEEE Computer*, June

Witten I.H. (1987). Arithmetic coding for data compression. *Comm. ACM,* June

ISO (1994). *Digital Compression and Coding of Continuous Tone Still Images (JPEG).* (ISO 10918-1)

Wallace G.K. (1991). The JPEG still picture compression standard. *Comm. ACM,* September

Clarke R.J. (1995). *Digital compression of still images and video.* Academic Press

Chapter 4

Bellamy J. (1991). *Digital telephony* 2nd edn. Wiley

Cox R.V. and Kroon P. (1996). Low bit rate speech coders for multimedia communication. *IEEE Communications,* December

Ambikairajah E. et al. (1997). Auditory masking and MPEG-1 audio compression. *IEE Electronic and Communication Engineering,* August

Jayant N. et al. (1993). Signal compression based on models of human perception. *Proc. IEEE,* October

Pan D. (1995). A tutorial on MPEG audio compression. IEEE *Multimedia,* June

Sikora T. (1997). MPEG digital video coding standards. *IEEE Signal Processing,* September

Bhaskaran V. and Konstantinides K. (1995). *Image and video compression standards, algorithms and architectures.* Academic Press

Tudor P.N. (1995). MPEG-2 video compression. *IEE Electronic and Communication Engineering,* December

Ghanbari M. (1999) Video Coding: an introduction to standard codecs. *IEE Telecommunications,* Series 42

ITU-T(1990). *Video Codec for Audio Visual Services at $p \times 64$ kbps.* Recommendation H.261

Rijkse K. (1996). H.263: Video coding for low bit rate communication. *IEEE Communications,* December

Chen C.T. and Wong A.(1993). A self-governing rate buffer control strategy for pseudoconstant bit rate video coding. *IEEE Trans. on Communications,* January

Redmill D.W. (1998). Error-resilient image and video coding. *IEE Electronics and Communication Engineering,* August

Benoit H. (1997). *Digital Television: MPEG-1, MPEG-2 and DVB,* Arnold

Koenen R. (1999). MPEG-4: Multimedia for our time. *IEEE Spectrum,* February

Schafer R. (1998). MPEG-4: A multimedia compression standard for interactive applications. *IEEE Electronics and Communication Engineering,* December

IEEE (1998). *IEE Trans. on Circuits and Systems: Special Issue on Segmentation for Video,* September

Pancha P. and El Zarki M. (1994). MPEG coding for variable bit rate transmission. *IEEE Communications,* May

Solari S.J. (1997). *Digital Video and Audio Compression.* McGraw-Hill

IEEE (1998). *IEEE Communications: Special Issue on Wireless Video,* June

Chapter 5

ITU-T (1995). *Narrowband ISDN Video Telephone Systems and Terminal Equipment.* (Recommendation H.320)

ITU-T (1995). *Terminal for Low Bit Rate Multimedia Communications.* (Recommendation H.324)

Lindbergh D. (1996). The H.324 multimedia communication standard. *IEEE Communications*, December

ITU-T (1995). *Adaptation of H.320 Terminals to B-ISDN Environments.* (Recommendation H.321)

ITU-T (1996). *Broadband Audio-visual Communications Systems and Terminals.* (Recommendation H.310)

ITU-T (1995). *Visual Telephone Systems and Terminals for LANs with Guaranteed QoS.* (Recommendation H.322)

ITU-T (1996). *Visual Telephone Systems and Terminals for LANs with Non-guaranteed QoS.* (Recommendation H.325)

Thom G.A. (1996). H.323: The multimedia communication standard for LANs. *IEEE Communications*, December

ITU-T (1996). *Media Stream Packetization and Synchronization (for H.323).* (Recommendation H.225)

ITU-T (1988). *PCM of Voice Frequencies.* (Recommendation G.711)

ITU-T (1988). *7 kHz Audio Coding within 64 kbps.* (Recommendation G.722)

ITU-T (1995). *Dual-rate Speech Codec at 6.4 and 5.3 kbps.* (Recommendation G.723.1)

ITU-T (1992). *Speech Coding at 16 kbps.* (Recommendation G.728)

ITU-T (1995). *Speech Codec for Multimedia Communications at 8/13 kbps.* (Recommendation G.729)

ITU-T (1993). *Video Codec for Audio-visual Communications at $p \times 64$ kbps.* (Recommendation H.261)

ITU-T (1995). *Video Codec for Low Bit Rate Channels less than 64 kbps.* (Recommendation H.263)

ITU-T (1994). *Transmission Protocols for Multimedia Data.* (Recommendation T.120)

ITU-T standards are available at *http://www.itu.ch*

Postel J. (1981). *The Internet Protocol (IP)*, September (RFC 791)

Postel J. (1981). *The Transmission Control Protocol (TCP)*, September (RFC 793)

Postel J. (1982). *The Simple Mail Transfer Protocol (SMTP)*, August (RFC 821)

Crocker D.H.(1982). *Standard Format for Internet Text Messages*, August (RFC 822)

Mockapetris P.V. (1987). *Domain Names: Concepts and Facilities*, November (RFC 1034)

Myers J. and Rose M. (1996). *Post Office Protocol, Version 3 (POP3)*, May (RFC 1939)

Freed N. et al. (1996). *Multipurpose Internet Mail Extensions (MIME)*, November (RFC 2045/6/7/8)

Berners-Lee T. et al. (1996). *The Hypertext Transfer Protocol. HTTP/1.0*, May (RFC 1945)

Postel J. and Reynolds J. (1985). *The File Transfer Protocol (FTP)*, October (RFC 959)

Kantor B. and Lapsley P. (1986). *The Network News Transfer Protocol (NNTP)*, February (RFC 977)

RFC standards information is available at *http://info.internet.isi.edu/in-notes/rfc/files/rfc xyz.txt*

ISO/IEC (1991). *MPEG-1: Coding of Moving Pictures and Associated Audio for Digital Storage Media at up to 1.5 Mbps.* (ISO/IEC Recommendation 11172)

ISO/IEC (1994). *MPEG-2: Coding of Moving Pictures and Associated Audio Information.* (ISO/IEC Recommendation 13818-2)

Chapter 6

Halsall F. (1996). *Data Communications, Computer Networks and Open Systems.* Addison-Wesley

Spragins J.D. et al. (1991). *Telecommunications Protocols and Design.* Addison-Wesley

Black U.D. (1993). *Data Link Protocols.* Prentice Hall

Marano K. et al. (1990) Echo cancellation and applications. *IEEE Communications.* January

Pearson J.E. (1992). *Basic Communication Theory.* Prentice Hall

Sklar B. (1988). *Digital Communications: fundamentals and applications.* Prentice Hall

Fletcher J. (1982). An arithmetic checksum for serial transmissions. *IEEE Trans. on Communications,* January

Ramabadroan T. (1988). A tutorial on CRC computations. *IEEE Micro,* August

Choi T.Y. (1985). Formal techniques for the specification of protocols. *IEEE Communications,* January

Conrad J. (1980). Character-oriented data link control protocols. *IEEE Trans. on Communications,* April

Danthine A.A.S. (1970). Protocol representation with finite-state models. *IEEE Trans. on Communication,* April.

Pouzin L. and Zimmerman H. (1978). A tutorial on protocols. *Proc. IEEE,* November

Carlson D.E (1980). Bit-oriented data link control procedures. *IEEE Trans. on Communications,* April

IEEE (1985). *Logical Link Control (LLC).* (IEEE Standard 802.2)

Chapter 7

Bellamy J.(1991). *Digital Telephony* 2nd edn. Wiley

Flood J.E. (1995). *Telecommunications Switching, Traffic and Networks.* Prentice Hall

Ericsson (1987). *Telecommunications: telephone networks 1 and 2.* Chartwell-Bratt

Nortel (1992). *Synchronous Transmission Systems.* Northern Telecom Europe

Omidyar C.G. and Alridge A. (1993). Introduction to SDH/SONET. *IEEE Communications,* September

Fergusson S.P. (1994). Implications of SONET and SDH. *IEE Electronic and Communication Engineering,* June

Flood J. and Cochraine P. (1991). *Transmission Systems.* Peter Peregrinus

Bissell C.C. and Chapman D.A. (1992). *Digital Signals Transmission.* Cambridge University Press

Freeman R.L.(1989). *Telecommunication System Engineering* 2nd edn. Wiley

Stallings W. (1989). *ISDN: an introduction.* Macmillan

Held G. (1994). *The Complete Modern Reference* 2nd edn. Wiley

EIA (1987). *Standard Interface between a DTE and DCE for Serial Data Interchange.* (EIA-232D)

Lechleider J.W. (1989). Line codes for digital subscriber lines. *IEEE Communications,* September

Doyle J.S. and McMahon C.S. (1988). The intelligent network concept. *IEEE Trans. on Communications,* December

Chapter 8

Metcalf R.M. and Boggs D.R. (1976). Ethernet: distributed packet switching for local computer networks. *Comm. ACM,* July

IEEE (1985). *802.3 CSMA/CD Access Method and Physical Layer Specifications*

Bux W. et al. (1983). Architecture and design of a reliable token-ring network. *IEEE Journal on Selected Areas in Communications*, November

IEEE (1985). *802.5 Token Ring Access Method and Physical Layer Specifications*

Stuck B.W. (1983). Calculating the maximum throughput rate of LANs. *IEEE Computer*, May

Backes F. (1988). Transparent bridges for interconnection of IEEE 802 LANs. *IEEE Network*, January

Bederman S. (1986). Source routing. *Data Communications*, February

Dixon R. and Pitt D. (1988). Addressing, bridging and source routing. *IEEE Network*, January

Perlman R. (1992). *Interconnections: bridges and routers.* Addison-Wesley

IEEE (1988). *802.1D MAC Bridges*

Hart J. (1988). Extending the IEEE 802.1 bridge standard to remote bridges. *IEEE Network*, January

IEEE (1985). *802.5 (Appendix D) Multiring Networks – Source Routing*

Ross F.E. (1986). FDDI – A tutorial. *IEEE Communications*, May

Ross F.E. (1989). An overview of FDDI. *IEEE Journal on Selected Areas of Communications*, September

Jain R. (1994). *FDDI Handbook: high-speed networking using fiber and other media.* Addison-Wesley

Molle M. and Watson G. (1996). 100Base T and IEEE 802.12 packet switching. *IEEE Communications*, August

Ozveren C. (1994). Reliable and efficient hop-by-hop flow control. *Sigcomm 94*

IEEE (1995). *802.3 u MAC and Physical Layer Parameters for 100Base T*

Cisco (1998). *Designing Switched LAN Internetworks.* Cisco Systems Inc.

Cisco (1999). *LAN Switches.* Cisco Systems Inc.

Molle M. (1997). Frame bursting: a technique for scaling CSMA/CD to gigabit speeds. *IEEE Network*, July

Frazier H. and Johnson H. (1999). Gigabit Ethernet: from 100 to 1000 Mbps. *IEEE Internet Computing*, January

Haddock S. (1996). *Carrier Extension Issues.* IEEE 802.3 Study Group Meeting, Netherlands, July

IEEE (1985). *Logical Link Control (LLC) Protocol*, (Standard 802.2)

Duc N. and Chew E. (1985). ISDN protocol architecture. *IEEE Communications*, March

Bush J. (1989). Frame relay promises WAN bandwidth on demand. *Data Communications*, July

Lai W. (1989). Frame relaying service: an overview. *IEEE InfoCom 89*

Smith P. (1993). *Frame Relay.* Addison-Wesley

Chapter 9

Comer D.E. (1995). *Internetworking with TCP/IP* 3rd edn. Prentice Hall

Postel J. (1980). *The Internet Protocol*, September (RFC 791)

Stevens W.R. (1994). *TCP/IP Illustrated* Vol.1. Addison-Wesley

Huitema C. (1995). *Routing in the Internet.* Prentice Hall

Sahasrabuddhe L.H. and Mukherjee B. (2000). Multicast routing: a tutorial. *IEEE Network*, January

Mills D. (1984). *The EGP Formal Specification*, April (RFC 904)

Braden R.T. et al. (1988). *Computing the Checksum for the IP Protocols*, September (RFC 1071)

Plummer D.C. (1982). *An Ethernet Address Resolution Protocol.* November (RFC 826)

Finlayson R. et al. (1984). *A Reverse Address Resolution Protocol*, June (RFC 903)

Hendrick C.L. (1988). *Routing Information Protocol*, June (RFC 1058)

Waitzman D. et al. (1988). *Distance Vector Multicast Routing Protocol*, November (RFC 1075)

Deering S. (1991). *ICMP Router Discovery Messages*, September (RFC 1256)

Moy J. (1991). *OSPF Version 2*, July (RFC 1247)

Moy J. (1994). *Multicast Extensions to OSPF*, March (RFC 1584)

Simpson W. (1994). *The Point-to-Point Protocol (PPP)*, July (RFC 1661)

Simpson W. (1994). *PPP in HDLC-like Framing*, July (RFC 1662)

Metz C. (1999). A pointed look at the PPP. *IEEE Internet Computing*, July

Xiao X. and Ni L.M. (1999). Internet QoS: a big picture. *IEEE Network*, March

Metz C. (1999). RSVP: general purpose signaling for IP. *IEEE Internet Computing*, May

Braden R. (1997). *RSVP Version 1 Functional Specification*, September (RFC 2205)

Blake S. et al. (1998). *An Architecture for Differentiated Services*, December (RFC 2475)

Bernet Y. (2000). The complementary roles of RSVP and differentiated services in the full-service QoS network. *IEEE Communications*, February

Wang B. and Hou J.C (2000). Multicast-routing and its QoS extension. *IEEE Network*, January

Armitage G. (2000). MPLS: The magic behind the myths, *IEEE Communications*, January

Newman P. et al. (1997). IP switching and gigabit routers. *IEEE Communications*, January

Deering S. and Hinden R. (1995) *IPv6 Specification*, December (RFC 1883)

Hinden R. and Deering S. (1995). *IPv6 Addressing Architecture*, December (RFC 1884)

Floyd S. and Jacobson V. (1993). Random early detection gateways for congestion avoidance. *IEEE Trans. on Networking*, August

Gilligan R. and Nordmark E. (1996). *Transition: Mechanisms for IPv6 Hosts and Routers*, April (RFC 1993)

Huitema C. (1997). *IPv6: The New Internet Protocol*. Prentice Hall

Chapter 10

LeBoudec J.L. (1992). The asynchronous transfer mode: a tutorial. *Computer Networks and ISDN*

ATM Forum (1994). *ATM User/Network Interface Specification*, July

Lee B.G. et al. (1996). *Broadband Telecommunications Technology* 2nd edn. Artech House

Cuthbert L.G. (1993). *ATM: the broadband telecommunications solution*. IEE London

Stallings W. (1992). *ISDN and Broadband ISDN* 2nd edn. Macmillan

Händel R. et al. (1994). *ATM Networks: concepts, protocols, applications*. Addison-Wesley

Heinanen J. (1993). *Multiprotocol Encapsulation over ATM Adaption Layer 5*. (RFC 1483)

ITU-T (1993). *B-ISDN Adaptation Layer (AAL) Specification*. (Recommendation I.363)

ITU-T (1993). *Support of Broadband Connectionless Data Service on B-ISDN*. (Recommendation I.364)

Rao S.K. and Hatamian M. (1995). The ATM physical layer. *Complete Comms. Review*, April

Karak N. (1995). Data communications in ATM networks. *IEEE Network*, May

Lanbach M. (1994). Classical IP and ARP over ATM. (RFC 1577)

McDysan D.E. and Spohn D.L.(1995). *ATM Theory and Application*. McGraw-Hill

Newman P. (1994). ATM local area networks. *IEEE Communications*, March

Partridge C. (1994). *Gigabit Networking*. Addison-Wesley

Chao H.J. et al. (1994). IP on ATM local area networks. *IEEE Communications*, August

Truong H.L. et al. (1995). LAN emulation on an ATM network. *IEEE Communications*, May

Finn N. and Mason T. (1996). ATM LAN emulation. *IEEE Communications*, June

Dixit S. and Elby S. (1996). Frame relay and ATM interworking. *IEEE Communications*, June

Akyildig I.F. and Bernhardt (1997). ATM LANs: a survey of requirements, architectures, and standards. *IEEE Communications*, July

Griffiths J.M. (1996). ATM: customer needs in the transition to B-ISDN. *IEE Electronic and Communication Engineering*, October

White P.P. (1998). ATM switching and IP routing integration. *IEEE Communications*, April

Luetchford J.C. et al (1998). Applications of ATM in global networks. *IEEE Communications*, August

Sadiku M.N.O. and Arvind A.S. (1994). Bibliography on DQDB. *Computer Comms. Review*, January

Guarene U. et al (1998). IP and ATM integration perspective. *IEEE Communications*, January

Gerla M. et al. (1993). Internetting LANs and MANs to B-ISDN for connectionless traffic support. *IEEE JSAC*, October

IEEE (1996) *IEEE Communications Special Issue: An introduction to flow and congestion control in ATM networks*, November

Chapter 11

IEEE (1997). *IEEE Network: Special Issue on Broadband Services over Residential Networks*, January

Bisdikian C. et al. (1996). Residential broadband data services over HFC networks. *IEEE Communications*, November

Pugh W. and Boyer G. (1995). Broadband access: comparing alternatives, *IEEE Communications*, August

Armbruster H. (1997). Information infrastructures and multimedia communications. *IEEE Communications*, September

Khasnabish B. (1997). Broadband to the home: architectures and access methods. *IEEE Network*, January

Lin Y-D. (1998). The IEEE 802.14 MAC protocol. *IEEE Communications Surveys*, October

Cable Television Laboratories Inc. (1999). *Data-over-cable Service Interface Specification: Radio Frequency Interface Specification*. http://www.cablemodem.com

Kiniry J.R. and Metz C. (1998). Cable modems: cable TV delivers the Internet. *IEEE Internet Computing*, May

Droms R. (1997). *Dynamic Host Configuration Protocol (DHCP)*, March (RFC 2131)

Paff A. (1995). Hybrid fiber/coax in the public telecommunications infrastructure. *IEEE Communications*, April

Benoit H. (1999). *Satellite Television: techniques of analogue and digital television*. Arnold

Arcidiacono A. (1997). Multimedia services and data broadcasting via satellite. *IEE Electronic and Communication Engineering Journal*, February

Drury G.M. (1997). DVB channel coding standards for broadcasting compressed video services. *IEE Electronic and Communication Engineering Journal*, February

Reimers U. (1997). DVB-T: the COFDM-based system for terrestrial broadcast television. *IEE Electronic and Communication Engineering Journal*, February

Yasuda H. and Ryan H.J.F. (1998). DAVIC and interactive multimedia services. *IEEE Communications*, September

Czajkowski I.K. (1999). High-speed copper access: a tutorial overview. *IEE Electronic and Communication Engineering Journal*, June

Maxwell K. (1996). ADSL: interim technology for the next 40 years. *IEEE Communications*, October

Saltzberg B.R. (1998). Comparison of single-carrier and multitone digital modulation for ADSL applications. *IEEE Communications*, November

Cioffi J.M. et al. (1999). Very-high-speed digital subscriber lines. *IEEE Communications*, April

IEEE (1999). *IEEE Communications Special issue on Broadband Access Copper Technologies*, May

Sweeney P. (1991). *Error Control Coding: an introduction*, Prentice Hall

Chapter 12

Socolofsky T. and Kale C. (1991). *A TCP/IP Tutorial*, January (RFC 1180)

Stevens W.R. (1994). *TCP/IP Illustrated* Vol.1. Addison-Wesley

Comer D.E. (1995). *Internetworking with TCP/IP* Vol.1, 3rd edn. Prentice Hall

Black U.D. (1995) *TCP/IP and Related Protocols*. McGraw-Hill

Stevens W.R. (1990). *UNIX Network Programming*. Prentice Hall

Postel J.B. (1981). *The Transmission Control Protocol (TCP)*, September (RFC 793)

Nagle J. (1984). *Congestion Control in TCP/IP Internetworks*, January (RFC 896)

Mogul J.C. (1993). IP network performance. In *Internet System Handbook*. Addison-Wesley

Karn P. and Partridge C. (1987). Improving RTT estimates in reliable transport protocols. *Computer Comms. Review*, August

Jacobson V. (1988). Congestion avoidance and control. *Computer Comms. Review*, August

Jacobson V. (1990b). Modified TCP congestion avoidance algorithm, *end2end mailing list*, April

Clark D.D. (1982). *Windows and Acknowledgement Strategy*, July (RFC 813)

Mogel J.C. and Deering S.E. (1990). *Path MTU Discovery*, April (RFC 1191)

Braden R.T. (1992a) *TIME-WAIT Association Hazards in TCP*, May (RFC 1337)

Jacobson V., Braden S. and Borman D. (1992). TCP Extensions for High Performance, May (RFC 1323)

Stevens W. (1997). *TCP Slow Start, Congestion Avoidance, Fast Retransmit and Fast Recovery Algorithms*, January (RFC 2001)

Mathis M. et al. (1996). *TCP Selective Acknowledgement Options*, October (RFC 2018)

Allman M., Paxson V. and Stevens W. (1999). *TCP Congestion Control*, April (RFC 2581)

Postel J.B. (1980). *The User Datagram Protocol (UDP)*, August (RFC 768)

Partridge C. and Pink S. (1993). A faster UDP. *IEEE Trans. on Networking*, August

Schultzrinne H. et al. (1989). *RTP A Transport Protocol for Real-time Applications* – also includes specification of RTCP. (RFC 1889)

Brackmo L. and Peterson L. (1995). TCP Vegas: end-to-end congestion avoidance on a global Internet. *IEEE Journal on Selected Areas in Communications*, October

Chapter 13

Hoschka P. (1997). *ASN.1 homepage*, http://www-sop.inria.fr/rodeo/personnel/hoschka/asn1.html

ISO (1988). *ASN.1 and its Encoding Rules* (IS 8824/5)

Tanteprasut D. et al. (1997). ASN.1 Protocol specification for use with arbitrary encoding schemes. *IEEE Trans. on Networking*, August

Denning D. (1997). *Internet Besieged: countering cyberspace scofflaws*. Addison-Wesley

Diffie W. and Landau S. (1998). *Privacy On The Line: the politics of wire-tapping and encryption*. MIT Press

Kahn D. (1967). *The Code Breakers: the story of secret writing*. Macmillan

Netscape (1998). *Introduction to Public-Key Cryptography*. Netscape Communications Corp.

Kaufman C. et al. (1995). *Networking Security: private communication in a public world*. Prectice Hall

Kessler G.C. (1998). *An Overview of Cryptography*, Hill Associates, available on-line at http://www.hill.com/library/staffpubs/crypto.html

NIST (1993). Data Encryption Standard (DES). *National Institute of Standards and Technology, Processing Standards Publication 46-2*

NIST (1999b). Triple DES standard. *Draft Federal Information Processing Standard (FIPS) 46–3*

Kummert H. (1998). *The PPP Triple-DES Encryption Protocol*, September (RFC 2420)

Lai X. and Massey J. (1990). A proposal for a new block encryption standard. Advances in cryptology. *Proceedings of Eurocrypt 90*. Springer-Verlag

Rivest R.L., Shamir A. and Adelman L. (1978). On a method for obtaining digital signatures and public key cryptosystems. *Comm. ACM*, February

Kaliski B. and Staddon J. (1998). *PKCS#1-RSA Cryptography Specifications Version 2*. (RFC 2437)

Rivest R.L.(1992). *The MD5 Message-digest Algorithm*, April (RFC 1321)

Neuman B.C. and TS'O T. (1994). Kerberos: an authentication service for computer networks. *IEEE Communications*, September

Kohl J. and Neuman B.C. (1993). *The Kerberos Network Authentication Service*, V5, September (RFC 1510)

Maughan D. et al. (1998). *Internet Security Association and Key Management Protocol (ISAKMP), November* (RFC 2408)

IEEE (1997). *IEEE Network: Special Issue on Network and Internet Security*, May

IEEE (1999). *IEEE Network: Special Issue on Networking Security*, November

ITU-T (1993). *Directory: Authentication Framework*, November (Recommendation X.509)

Kent S. (1993). *Certificate-based Key Management*, February (RFC 1422)

Netscape (1999). *Netscape Certificate Server FAQ*. Netscape Communications Corporation

Chapter 14

Mockapetris P.V. (1983). *Domain Names: Implementation Specification*, November (RFC 833)

Mockapetris P.V. (1987). *Domain Names: Concepts and Facilities*, November(RFC 1034)

Mockapetris P.V. (1987). *Domain Names: Implementation and Specification*, November (RFC 1035)

IANA (1999). Internet Assigned Number Authorities, http://www.iana.org/

Albitz P. and Liu C. (1993). *DNS and BIND*. O'Reilly and Associates

Reynolds J. and Postel J. (1994). *Assigned Numbers*, October (RFC 1700)

Kille S. (1995). *A String Representation of Distinguished Names*, March (RFC 1779)

Vixie P. et al. (1997). *Dynamic Updates in the DNS*, April (RFC 2136)

Postel J.B. (1982). *Simple Mail Transfer Protocol (SMTP)*, August (RFC 821)

Crocker D.H. (1982). *Standard Format for Internet Text Messages.* August (RFC 822)

Myers J. and Rose M. (1996). *Post Office Protocol, Version 3 (POP3),* May (RFC 1939)

Freed N. and Borenstein N. (1996). *Multipurpose Internet Mail Extensions,* November (RFC 2045/8)

Zimmerman P.R. (1995). *The Official PGP User Guide.* MIT Press

Zimmerman P.R. (1995). *PGP: Source Code and Internals.* MIT Press

Rivest R.L. (1992). *The MD5 Message-digest Algorithm,* April (RFC 1321)

Postel J. and Reynolds J. (1985). *The File Transfer Protocol (FTP),* October (RFC 959)

IEEE (1999). *IEEE Network: Special Issue on Internet Telephony,* May

Kostas T.J. et al. (1998). Real-time voice over packet-switched networks. *IEEE Network,* January

Morgan S. (1998). The Internet and the local telephone network: conflicts and opportunities. *IEEE Communications,* January

Dalgic I. et al. (1999). True number portability and advanced call screening in a SIP-based IP telephony system. *IEEE Internet Computing,* July

Asatani K. (1998). *Standardization on multimedia communications: computer-telephony-integration related issues. IEEE Communications,* July

Stallings W. (1993). *SNMP, SNMPv2, and CMIP.* Addison-Wesley

McCloghrie K. and Rose M.T. (1991). *MIB-IL for Network Management of TCP/IP Internets,* March (RFC 1213)

IEEE (1997). *IEEE Communications: Special Issue on Network Management,* October

IEEE (1999). *IEEE Network: Special Issue on Networking Security,* November

Chapter 15

Berners-Lee T. et al. (1994). The World-Wide Web. *Comm. ACM,* August

Vetter R.J. et al. (1994). Mosaic and the World-Wide Web. *IEEE Computer,* October

World Wide Web Consortium home page: http://www.w3.org

Khare R. (1999). Anatomy of a URL. *IEEE Internet Computing,* September

Berners-Lee T. et al.(1996). *Hypertext Transfer Protocol, HTTP/1.0,* May (RFC 1945)

Fielding R. et al. (1997). *Hypertext Transfer Protocol, HTTP 1.1,* January (RFC 2068)

Cheswick W.R. and Bellovin S.M.(1994): *Firewalls and Internet Security.* Addison-Wesley

Baentsch M. et al. (1997). Web caching: the application-level view of the Internet. *IEEE Communications,* June

Luotoren A. and Altis K. (1994). World Wide Web Proxies. *Computer Networks and ISDN,* November

Berghel H.L. (1996). The client side of the Web. *Comm. ACM,* January

Kwan T.T. et al. (1995). NCSA's WWW server: design and performance. *IEEE Computer,* November

Meyers P. (1998). *The HTML Web Classroom.* Prentice Hall

Bryan M. (1997). *SGML and HTML Explained.* Addison-Wesley

Rule J. (1999). *Dynamic HTML.* Addison-Wesley

Castro E. (1997). *Perl and CGI for the World Wide Web.* Addison-Wesley

Pancha P. and El Zarki M. (1994). MPEG coding for variable bit rate video transmission. *IEEE Communications,* May

Schulzrinne H. et al. (1998). *Real Time Streaming Protocol (RTSP),* April (RFC 2326)

Real Networks. *RTSP Resource Center.* http://www.real.com/devzone/library/fireprot/rtsp/

Campione M. and Walrath K. (1996). *The Java Language Tutorial.* Addison-Wesley

Arnold K. and Gosling J. (1996). *The Java Programming Language.* Addison-Wesley

Van der Linden P. (1996). *Just Java.* Prentice Hall

Sun Microsystems. *Java Tutorial*. http://java.sun.com/nav/read/tutorial/index.html

Netscape. *Java Script*. http://home.netscape.com/eng/mozilla/2.0/handbook/javascript/

Dierks T. and Allen C. (1998). *The TLS Protocol*, January (RFC 2246)

MasterCard (1999). *SET Secure Electronic Transaction*. http://www.mastercard.com/shoponline/set/

Merkow M. et al. (1998). *Building SET Applications for Secure Transactions*. Wiley

IEEE (1999). *IEEE Communications: Special Issue on Electronic Commerce*, September

IEEE (1997). *IEEE Internet Computing: Special Issue on Electronic Commerce*, November

IEEE (1997). *IEEE Spectrum: Special Issue on Technology and the Electronic Economy*, February.

IEEE (1997). *IEEE Network: Special Issue on Network and Internet Security*, May

index

acronyms

continued from inside front cover

MAT	Multicast address table
M-BONE	Multicast (Internet) backbone
MCU	Multipoint control unit
MD	Message digest
MDS	Multipoint distribution system
MFN	Multifrequency network
MGW	Media gateway
MIB	Management information base
MIDI	Music instrument digital interface
MII	Media-independent interface
MIME	Multipurpose Internet mail extension
MIT	Management information tree
MMDS	Multichannel MDS
MMR	Modified–modified read
MO	Managed object
MOD	Movie on demand
MOSPF	Multicast OSPF
MPEG	Motion pictures expert group
MP3	MPEG layer 3 (audio)
MRP	Multicast routing protocol
MS	Message store
MSC	Mobil switching center
MSL	Maximum segment lifetime
MSS	MAN switching system
MTA	Message transfer agent
MUX	Multiplexer
NAK	Negative acknowledgment
NBS	National Bureau of Standards
NEXT	Near end crosstalk
NMOD	Near movie-on-demand
NMS	Network management system
NNTP	Network news transfer protocol
NOP	No operation
NPA	Network point of attachment
NRM	(Unbalanced) normal response mode
NRZ	Non-return to zero
NRZI	Non-return to zero inverted
NSAP	Network service access point
NSDU	Network service data unit
NT	Network termination
NTE	Network termination equipment
NTSC	National Television Standards Committee
NVT	Network virtual terminal
ONU	Optical network (termination) unit
OSI	Open systems interconnection
OSPF	Open shortest path first
PAL	Phase alternation line
PAWS	Protection against wrapped sequence (numbers)
PBX	Private branch exchange
PC	Personal computer

PCI	Protocol connection identifier
PCM	Pulse-code modulation
PDH	Plesiochronous digital hierarchy
PDU	Protocol data unit
PEL	Picture element
PGP	Pretty good privacy
PHB	Per-hop behavior
PISO	Parallel in, serial out
PIXEL	Picture element
PL	Physical layer
PMD	Physical medium dependent
POP	Post Office Protocol
POTS	Plain old telephone service
PPP	Point-to-point protocol
PRI	Primary rate interface
PSE	Packet switching exchange
PSK	Phase-shift keying
PSTN	Public switched telephone network
PTE	Path termination equipment
PTT	Post, telephone, and telecommunications (authority)
PVC	Permanent virtual connection
QA	Queued arbitrated
QAM	Quadrature applitude modulation
QCIF	Quarter CIF
QoS	Quality of service
QPDS	Queued packet distributed switch
RAM	Random access meomory
RARP	Reverse ARP
RCU	Remote concentrator unit
RDN	Relative distinguished name
READ	Relative element address designate
RED	Random early detection
RF	Radio frequency
RGB	Red, green, blue
RI	Ring indication
RIP	Routing information protocol
ROM	Read only memory
RP	Root port
RPC	Root path cost
RSA	Rivest, Shamir, Adelman
RSU	Remote switching unit
RSVP	Resource reservation protocol
RTC	Round-trip correction
RTCP	Real-time transport control protocol
RTD	Round-trip delay
RTO	Retransmission timeout
RTP	Real-time transport protocol
RTS	Request to send
RTT	Round-trip time
RTSP	Real-time streaming protocol